THEOLOGY
OF THE
OLD
TESTAMENT

FORTRESS PRESS BOOKS
BY WALTER BRUEGGEMANN

The Land: Place as Gift, Promise, and Challenge
in the Biblical Faith (1977)

The Prophetic Imagination (1978)

The Creative Word: Canon as a Model
for Biblical Education (1982)

David's Truth in Israel's Imagination and Memory (1985)

Hopeful Imagination: Prophetic Voices in Exile (1986)

Israel's Praise: Doxology against Idolatry and Ideology (1988)

Finally Comes the Poet: Daring Speech for Proclamation (1989)

Interpretation and Obedience:
From Faithful Reading to Faithful Living (1991)

Old Testament Theology:
Essays on Structure, Theme, and Text (1992)

Texts under Negotiation:
The Bible and Postmodern Imagination (1993)

A Social Reading of the Old Testament:
Prophetic Approaches to Israel's Communal Life (1994)

The Psalms and the Life of Faith (1995)

The Threat of Life:
Sermons on Pain, Power, and Weakness (1996)

THEOLOGY
OF THE
OLD
TESTAMENT

Testimony, Dispute, Advocacy

WALTER
BRUEGGEMANN

Fortress Press
Minneapolis

THEOLOGY OF THE OLD TESTAMENT
Testimony, Dispute, Advocacy

Library of Congress Cataloging-in-Publication Data
Brueggemann, Walter.
    Theology of the Old Testament : testimony, dispute, advocacy /
Walter Brueggemann.
      p. cm.
    Includes bibliographical references and indexes.
    ISBN 0-8006-3087-4 (alk. paper)
    1. Bible. O.T. – Theology. I. Title.
BS1192.5.B79 1997
221.6'01 – dc21   97-21888
                                    CIP

Manufactured in the U.S.A.   AF 1-3087

01   00   99   98   3   4   5   6   7   8   9

For Mary

Summary of Contents

Part IV
ISRAEL'S EMBODIED TESTIMONY

Part V
PROSPECTS FOR THEOLOGICAL INTERPRETATION

Contents

Part II
ISRAEL'S COUNTERTESTIMONY

Part III
ISRAEL'S UNSOLICITED TESTIMONY

Part IV
ISRAEL'S EMBODIED TESTIMONY

Preface

O LD TESTAMENT THEOLOGY has been dominated in the twentieth century by the magisterial work of Walther Eichrodt and even more by the powerful model of Gerhard von Rad. Any subsequent work in the field, such as the present effort, is enormously indebted to these bench-mark contributions and proceeds not only in their shadow but also with continuing appeal to their influence. It is neither possible nor desirable to begin *de novo;* subsequent work is inescapably an effort at revision and subversion, not departing too far or too quickly from these governing versions of the discipline.

It is equally clear, however, that one cannot, at the end of the twentieth century, simply reiterate and replicate those heretofore governing models of theological exposition. Since Eichrodt's publication in the 1930s and von Rad's in the 1950s, much has changed both in interpretive work and in interpretive context. That change, moreover, requires and permits an effort at a fresh and venturesome alternative interpretation. Thus, for example, Old Testament theological interpretation at mid-century was able to appeal to and rely on the "assured results" of the critical consensus of scholarship. It is fair to say that much of the old critical consensus from which theological exposition confidently moved at mid-century is now unsettled, if not in disarray. A fresh theological exposition must work its way cautiously and provisionally in the midst of that enormous unsettlement. It is my judgment, however, that the unsettlement is not primarily a problem but is itself an important datum to be taken into account in fresh, venturesome efforts at Old Testament theology. It belongs to the nature of Old Testament theological interpretation that we are not permitted to be so sure as we once thought we were about such critical matters. This unsettlement is in part a result of our so-called postmodern epistemological situation. Underneath that reality, however, the unsettlement is a reflection of the nature of the Old Testament text itself and, speaking theologically, of the unsettled Character who stands at the center of the text. Thus the unsettlement is not simply a cultural or epistemological one, but in the end it is a theological one. That awareness, now so poignantly available to us, provides a context for interpretation at the end of the twentieth century that is very different from the context in which Eichrodt and von Rad determined the governing models of work through the twentieth century.

The practical manifestation of this unsettlement that must be honored but not resolved is a multilayered pluralism that is newly insistent in the discipline of Old Testament studies. That pluralism may be recognized as (a) *a pluralism of faith affirmations* and articulations of Yahweh in the text itself, a pluralism that von Rad had begun to see in his break with unilateral developmentalism and which Rainer Albertz has more fully explicated; (b) *a pluralism of methods* that has displaced the long-standing hegemony of historical critical approaches; and (c) *a pluralism of interpretive communities,* each of which is now to be seen as richly contextual in its epistemological practices and in its socioeconomic, political interests, a contextualism that now acknowledges that even so-called objective historical criticism in fact is situated in specific epistemological practices and specific socioeconomic, political interests. There is no going back, in any of these levels, to older assured hegemony—no going back to a singular coherent faith articulation in the text (much as canonical approaches might insist on it), no going back to agreed-on critical methods that can maintain hegemony, and no going back to a dominant interpretive community that imagines itself to be immune to contextual-ideological shaping and interest.

In the face of such a new interpretive situation, it is evident that matters must be conducted differently from the dominant models available to us from Eichrodt and von Rad. Early on, I concluded that it is impossible to fashion a coherent statement concerning theological substance or themes in the Old Testament unless the themes or substance be framed so broadly and inclusively as to be useless. Alternatively I have proposed that the coherence required for an Old Testament theology, in a way that hopefully avoids premature reductionism, must focus not on substantive or thematic matters but on the *processes, procedures, and interactionist potential* of the community present to the text. It is for that reason that I have focused on the metaphor and imagery of courtroom trial in order to regard the theological substance of the Old Testament as a series of claims asserted for Yahweh, the God of Israel. All of these claims share a general commonality but also evidence considerable variation, competition, and conflict. Thus I propose, in an interpretive context that attends to pluralism in every dimension of the interpretive process, that such interaction constitutes the practice of revelation and embodies the claims of truth in this text. This focus on the processive, interactionist modes of assertion and counterassertion not only allows for a *plurality of voices* that together constitute and construe the theological substance of Old Testament theology. It also allows for profound conflict and disputation through which Israel arrives at its truth-claims. These truth-claims, arrived at through incessant engagement and held along the way and at the end with vigor and courage, bespeak radical practical risk for the interpreting community.

This concern for the processive, interactionist modes of adjudication led me to the three terms of my subtitle (first suggested to me by Norman Gottwald):

• *Testimony:* The character and mode of theological claim in the Old Testament may be regarded as testimony—as assertion that awaits assent, is open to review, and must make its way amid counterassertions. The beginning point for reflection on the God of Israel is in the utterance of Israel, an utterance that is continually reassessed concerning its validity and persuasiveness. This means that such discourse does not appeal in the first instant either to history in any positivistic sense nor to any classical claims of ontology. Everything moves from utterance judged variously to be valid and persuasive.

• *Dispute:* As in any lawcourt wherein a serious case is under consideration, competing, conflicting offers of truth are put forth. Indeed, in the absence of competing and conflicting versions of truth, the court case is pro forma. But where truth is at issue and at risk, testimony is given by many witnesses, witnesses are vigorously cross-examined, and out of such disputatious adjudication comes a verdict, an affirmed rendering of reality and an accepted version of truth.

• *Advocacy:* The role of testimony is to advocate a rendering of truth and a version of reality that are urged over against other renderings and versions. The witnesses for Yahweh in the Old Testament advocate a truth and a reality in which Yahweh stands as the leading and preeminent Character. Within Israel's advocacy of a Yahweh-dominated truth and a Yahweh-governed reality, subordinated disputes occur even among Israelite witnesses. But taken all together, these witnesses, different as they are, advocate a Yahweh-version of reality that is strongly in conflict with other versions of reality and other renderings of truth that have been shaped without reference to Yahweh and that determinedly propose a reality and truth that is Yahweh-free.

I believe that this process of testimony-dispute-advocacy faithfully reflects both the process of theological utterance (and thought) in the Old Testament, and issues in the truth-claims and the shapes of reality that are given in the Old Testament. Thus this process eventuates in substantive claims but in ways that I believe are congruent with the reality of pluralism (a) in the text, (b) in the methods of interpretation, and (c) in interpretive communities. This process of testimony-dispute-advocacy is, in my judgment, a match for the unsettling settlements that mark Israel's faith as truth-claim.

The completion of this book calls for a rather extravagant expression of gratitude to many who have made a difference in my long-term reflection of which this study is an outcome. This project has been made possible by the generous support of a Luce Theological Fellowship of the Association of Theological Schools and by a generous sabbatical leave from Columbia Theological Seminary.

Beyond that, first I express my gratitude to several generations of students at Eden Theological Seminary and Columbia Theological Seminary who have watched and waited responsively as I have found my way to these present formulations. These students, moreover, are seconded in their responsive presence to me by a host of other students—including pastors—with whom I have studied in a variety of ad hoc appointments.

Second, I express three long-term and enduring debts concerning the work I have been able to do here. M. Douglas Meeks has, over time, taught me most about thinking theologically with energy and courage. Gail R. O'Day (seconding my teacher James Muilenburg) has taught me most about close reading of the text and the cruciality of rhetoric for biblical faith. Gerald P. Jenkins has stayed with me through some thinness to help me locate the freedom required to take the risks of this study. My own work has moved in directions that are my own, beyond these impetuses, but not beyond my lingering gratitude.

Third, as in much of my writing, I mention two "usual suspects" on whom I gratefully rely. I am, as usual, grateful to Marshall Johnson of Fortress Press for his willingness to take on this publication and to see it through with care, and to his skilled and faithful colleagues at Fortress to whom my debts are considerable. It is almost impossible to express adequately my appreciation for the ways in which my secretary, Tempie Alexander, makes my work possible. In general she attends to endless details in a way that keeps my work ordered and gives me freedom to focus on my proper tasks. More specifically she has worked patiently—over and over—on drafts of this manuscript, paying more attention than I to some details, even to learning how to mark the occasional Hebrew word properly.

Fourth, work on this particular study has been greatly supported and corrected by two readers who have given careful attention both to my argument and to my articulation of it. Tod Linafelt has been involved in every stage of the manuscript, aiding me greatly in editing, organizing, and in thinking through my presentation. Patrick D. Miller has given me wise and judicious counsel and much encouragement, being supportive of my work as he characteristically is, but also helping me to render, correct, and clarify important points. This manuscript is stronger because of the work of Linafelt and Miller. I am, moreover, grateful to Tim Simpson, who has generously prepared the indices.

Finally, I am glad to dedicate this book to Mary Miller Brueggemann in thanks and affection. Mary has stood with me and by me and for me through the long, inchoate work of gestation and through the demands of shaping, writing, and editing. She shares with me the costs and joys of the faith here explicated, and I am grateful.

Abbreviations

AB	Anchor Bible
ABD	D. N. Freedman (ed.), *Anchor Bible Dictionary*
AnBib	Analecta biblica
BA	*Biblical Archaeologist*
BASOR	*Bulletin of the American Schools of Oriental Research*
BDB	F. Brown, S. R. Driver, and C. A. Briggs, *Hebrew and English Lexicon of the Old Testament*
BETL	Bibliotheca ephemeridum theologicarum lovaniensium
BHT	Beiträge zur historischen Theologie
Bib	*Biblica*
BJRL	*Bulletin of the John Rylands University Library of Manchester*
BJS	Brown Judaic Studies
BTB	*Biblical Theology Bulletin*
BWANT	Beiträge zur Wissenschaft vom Alten und Neuen Testament
BZAW	Beihefte zur *ZAW*
CBQ	*Catholic Biblical Quarterly*
CBQMS	Catholic Biblical Quarterly—Monograph Series
ConBOT	Coniectanea biblica, Old Testament
EvT	*Evangelische Theologie*
FRLANT	Forschungen zur Religion und Literatur des Alten und Neuen Testaments
HAR	*Hebrew Annual Review*
HBT	*Horizons in Biblical Theology*
HSM	Harvard Semitic Monographs
HSS	Harvard Semitic Studies
HTR	*Harvard Theological Review*

IB	*Interpreter's Bible*
IDB	G. A. Buttrick (ed.), *Interpreter's Dictionary of the Bible*
IDBSup	Supplementary volume to *IDB*
Int	*Interpretation*
IRT	Issues in Religion and Theology
JAAR	*Journal of the American Academy of Religion*
JAOS	*Journal of the American Oriental Society*
JBL	*Journal of Biblical Literature*
JNES	*Journal of Near Eastern Studies*
JR	*Journal of Religion*
JSOT	*Journal for the Study of the Old Testament*
JSOTSup	Journal for the Study of the Old Testament—Supplement Series
JTS	*Journal of Theological Studies*
KD	*Kerygma und Dogma*
LCC	Library of Christian Classics
NFT	New Frontiers in Theology
NKZ	*Neue kirchliche Zeitschrift*
OBT	Overtures to Biblical Theology
OTL	Old Testament Library
SBLDS	SBL Dissertation Series
SBLSS	SBL Semeia Studies
SBT	Studies in Biblical Theology
SJLA	Studies in Judaism in Late Antiquity
SJT	*Scottish Journal of Theology*
ST	*Studia theologica*
StABH	Studies in American Biblical Hermeneutics
ThB	Theologische Bucherei
ThStud	Theologische Studien
TLZ	*Theologische Literaturzeitung*
TS	*Theological Studies*

TToday	*Theology Today*
USQR	*Union Seminary Quarterly Review*
VT	*Vetus Testamentum*
VTSup	Vetus Testamentum, Supplements
WBC	Word Biblical Commentary
WMANT	Wissenschaftliche Monographien zum Alten und Neuen Testament
WW	*Word and World*
ZAW	*Zeitschrift für die alttestamentliche Wissenschaft*
ZTK	*Zeitschrift für Theologie und Kirche*

ONE

Retrospect 1:
From the Beginning to the End
of a Generative Period

E NTRY INTO THE STUDY of Old Testament theology, like the study of any discipline, begins with the awareness of the governing questions of the discipline.[1] No intelligible study begins *de novo* but must be situated in past and present ongoing conversations. Old Testament study receives its shaping, governing questions from two sources. First, the discipline has a long history in the church and in the academy, and the gains and scars of that history continue to linger and exercise strong influence on current discussions. Second, the discipline continues to be practiced by contemporary scholars who in varying ways and degrees are attentive and responsive to new questions that arise out of contemporary contexts, problems, and possibilities. Advances in the discipline can be made only by taking into serious and critical account both that long history of shaping questions and new questions arising out of contemporary contexts. The identification of these questions is indeed a perilous matter, in some measure a subjective articulation. I shall nonetheless begin with an attempt to identify in turn both sets of inquiries with which we must be concerned.

Beginnings in the Reformation

It is not obvious at what point a consideration of the history of scholarship in Old Testament theology should begin.[2] For our purposes, we may begin with

---

1. I am not unaware of the problematic nature of the phrase *Old Testament*. I use the term with diffidence, but use it nonetheless, because I write and exposit as a Christian interpreter. At the same time it will be clear in what follows that I am acutely aware of and concerned about the destructiveness implicit in every form of supersessionism. In the current unsettled state of the discussion, it seems wise to avoid clumsy neologisms. I do so with appropriate and gladly acknowledged uneasiness. On the issue, see Roger Brooks and John J. Collins, eds., *Hebrew Bible or Old Testament? Studying the Bible in Judaism and Christianity* (Notre Dame, Ind.: University of Notre Dame Press, 1990).

2. A variety of important discussions of the history of the discipline exists. Among the more helpful for my understanding have been Hans Frei, *The Eclipse of Biblical Narrative: A Study of Eighteenth and Nineteenth Century Hermeneutics* (New Haven: Yale University Press, 1974); John H. Hayes and Frederick C. Prussner, *Old Testament Theology: Its History and Development* (London: SCM Press,

the sixteenth-century Protestant Reformation. That beginning point may be taken as legitimate for several reasons. First, Old Testament theology, in its modern intention, has been until recently almost exclusively an enterprise of Protestant Christianity—until very recently, of German Protestant Christianity. Second, the Reformation itself may be understood as an effort to emancipate the evangelical reality of the Bible from the reductive insistences of church interpretation, and that text, more or less emancipated from church interpretation, has become the subject and problematic of Old Testament Theology.[3] The extent or desirability of such emancipation continues to be a matter of important dispute. Third, in the wake of the sixteenth-century Reformation, though not simply as its consequence, a seismic change occurred in the epistemological content of the European intellect in which the present discipline was shaped. That change featured a departure from the long-regnant medieval Christian epistemological domination to what we will subsequently characterize as "modern" epistemology. For all of these reasons, we may take the sixteenth-century Reformation as our beginning point.

The Reformation proceeded as a response to the "gospel truth of the Bible," without primary or defining reference to the dogmatic assumptions and controls of established church interpretation. The key insight of Martin Luther concerning the graciousness of God apart from the church's administration of a sacramental system and from the church's expectation of a religio-moral quid pro quo in relation to the sacraments is well known.[4] Luther was first of all a biblical interpreter. His great and revolutionary insight, though in the service of and informed by his personal theological struggle, arose in his attentive and scholarly study of Scripture. *Luther asserted that the "evangelical substance" of biblical faith is not and cannot be contained in the habituated, accustomed, and reductionist reading of church theology that made God simply an integral part of a church-administered system of salvation.* While Luther's theological accent and its political ramifications are widely recognized, for our purposes it is important to notice the interpretive-hermeneutical pivot point that was crucial for Luther: namely, that the Bible is a voice of revelation not to be confused with, encumbered by, or contained in any human categories of interpretation that make the voice more coherent, domesticated, or palatable. Such a recognition of the liberated, liberating reality of revelation, odd and unencumbered as it is, had as its match Luther's defiant and energizing courage to identify this peculiar faith-generating and faith-driven affirmation. This was, for all of the work of God's

---

1985); Emil G. Kraeling, *The Old Testament since the Reformation* (London: Lutterworth Press, 1955); Hans-Joachim Kraus, *Geschichte der historisch-kritischen Erforschung des Alten Testaments* (Neukirchen-Vluyn: Neukirchener Verlag, 1969); H. Graf Reventlow, *The Authority of the Bible and the Rise of the Modern World* (London: SCM Press, 1984); and John Rogerson, *Old Testament Criticism in the Nineteenth Century* (London: SPCK Press, 1984).

3. Historical surveys of Old Testament theology, for good reason, regularly begin with the Reformation. See, for example, Frei, *The Eclipse of Biblical Narrative;* Hayes and Prussner, *Old Testament Theology,* 8–15; and Reventlow, *The Authority of the Bible,* 9–87.

4. Luther's principle of *sola scriptura* cannot be taken by itself, but belongs with his affirmation of *sola gratia* and *sola Christi.* It is instructive that Kraus, *Geschichte der historisch-kritischen Erforschung,* 6–24, begins his survey of historical-critical study with *sola scriptura.*

Spirit, a theological act of interpretation and imagination. Luther's intellectual, interpretive courage set the work of biblical theology in a wholly new direction.

The political force of the Reformation (insofar as Reformation might enact a political and cultural revolution) is complicated and cannot be reduced to a single cause or explanation. It is possible, nonetheless, to assert that for all of the political interests and interpretive vagaries that came to be associated with the Reformation, its chief advocates shared Luther's primary passion that Scripture have its own voice, to be heard in its own liberated radicality. This "voice of the Bible" speaks its truth and makes its claim in its own categories, categories that are recurringly odd and unaccommodating. The substance of that truth is God, the Creator of heaven and earth, the God known decisively and uniquely in Jesus of Nazareth. The Bible bears primal witness to and discloses this God, without any intellectual, epistemological accommodation to any other categories, including those of the (Roman) Catholic Church whose children those Reformers were. The Bible is to be understood "as Scripture" in the community that gathers in response to the claim that here God is decisively disclosed.[5] Thus the Bible is a revelation, and Scripture study is an attempt to receive, understand, and explicate this revelation—hopefully to receive, understand, and explicate this revelation in all its oddity, without reductionism, domestication, or encumbrance.[6]

For purposes that will become apparent, it is important to note that the *Institutes* of John Calvin, the most formidable and influential codification of Reformation reading of the Bible, was not offered as a systematic theology designed to counter or compete with older medieval systems.[7] It was rather offered as a guide for the reading of Scripture evangelically. That is, Calvin did not write so that the faithful would read "away from the Bible" into a coherent system (as the *Institutes* have often been taken), but so that the faithful would read "into the Bible" and into its evangelical claim, which Calvin shows to be pertinent to and definitional for every aspect of life, both personal and public.

The practical effect of the Reformation, as far as the Bible is concerned, is to let the Bible have its own voice, without regard for or indebtedness to any estab-

---

5. In contemporary discussion, it is Brevard S. Childs, above all, who has insisted on and helped recover the canonical, theological understanding of the Bible as Scripture. See Childs, *Introduction to the Old Testament as Scripture* (Philadelphia: Fortress Press, 1979) 69–83 and passim.

6. Having said that the Bible is taken as revelation, it is nonetheless important and difficult to specify what is referenced by the term *revelation*. The term may refer to the inscrutable disclosure of the mystery of God, but it easily slides over into a scholastic assumption that revelation is a settled package of propositions. The difficulty is that to understand revelation as the inscrutable disclosure of the mystery of God does not mean that revelation is content-less. But to harden that substance into an administrable package is to disregard the character of the text that portrays God with remarkable, intentional artistic elusiveness. On the extraordinary and inscrutable character and quality of occasions of evaluation (which then become "texts of redescription"), see Paul Ricoeur, "The Bible and the Imagination," *Figuring the Sacred: Religion, Narrative, and Imagination* (ed. Mark I. Wallace; Minneapolis: Fortress Press, 1995) 144–49.

7. Thus John Calvin, *Institutes of the Christian Religion* (LCC 20; Philadelphia: Westminster, 1960) 7, can say in his preface: "I can at least promise that it can be a key to open a way for all children of God into a good and right understanding of Holy Scripture." Calvin offers to provide "some guidance and direction to know what he ought to look for in scripture."

lished category of church interpretation. In this sense, the Reformation was indeed an act of interpretive emancipation. Luther and those who came after him in the Reformation perforce established categories of and criteria for reading that are not negotiable. They insisted with great passion, however, that their evangelical modes of Bible reading were not imposed but in fact arose from the substance of the biblical text itself. As we shall see, this practice of devising categories of interpretation that appear to be given is an ongoing issue in Old Testament theology.

Post-Reformation Biblical Interpretation

The post-Reformation period of biblical interpretation may be summarized in two facets. First, the Reformation evoked in Roman Catholicism what has come to be termed the Counter-Reformation. The Council of Trent resisted the Reformation effort to free biblical interpretation from the interpretive authority of the church (the very interpretive authority that the Reformers regarded as a decisive cause of distorted reading). The Tridentine formulation of authority is that Christian truth is rooted in two sources, Scripture and tradition.[8] "Tradition" means the accumulated substance of church teaching, thus providing that the Bible will be heard and understood in the categories of Catholic church faith, the very categories that Luther understood to be the means whereby the evangelical claim of the text had been silenced, denied, or distorted.

When the polemics of Trent are understood in context, it is evident that Trent was correct in its formulation; though in that polemical situation, Reformation Christianity could not accept the claim as practiced in the Roman Catholic Church. *It is nonetheless the case that Scripture cannot be understood apart from the ongoing role of communal tradition.*[9] Not even the principal Reformers thought that Scripture could be held apart from an ongoing interpretive community with already declared interpretive assumptions. In the midst of the sixteenth-century polemics, however, such a common acknowledgment would have been unthinkable. Rapprochement on this crucial point is only now an available option in ecumenical conversation.

Second, in the context of the sixteenth-century Reformation and in the presence of Tridentine polemics on both sides, it is usual to speak of the hardening

---

8. In contrast to the problems of the traditions of the Reformation, the Roman Catholic struggle has been to relate the Bible to the magisterial interpretive authority of the church. In commenting on the Council of Trent (vis-à-vis E. Lessing), Karl Barth, *Church Dogmatics* 1/1, *The Doctrine of the Word of God* (Edinburgh: T. & T. Clark, 1936) 118, comments: "They agree in their result, in the relative independence which they give the present church compared with the canon of Holy Scripture, i.e., in the relative devaluation of the said canon." Among key markers in the Roman Catholic emancipation of scriptural authority is the encyclical *Divino Afflante Spiritu*, which followed *Providentissimus Deus*.

9. Clearly there is no such thing as presuppositionless exegesis. The presuppositions that govern exegesis, either hidden or acknowledged, arise from the community in which and for which the interpretation is done. Thus in practice the authority of Scripture is intimately linked to the claims of the interpretive community, a reality not easily accepted in Protestantism. This awareness is not far removed from the Tridentine formula of "Scripture and tradition," if tradition is understood as the lens of interpretation. Such a lens is present in the traditions of the Reformation, for such a lens is undiminished by the slogan of *sola scriptura*.

of Protestant biblical interpretation. Such interpretation, in the generations after the breakthrough of the Reformation itself, moved away from and toned down the radical emancipatory notion of the Bible voiced by Luther and his cohorts. While later generations of Reformation interpreters continued to reiterate the slogans of the early Reformation concerning *sola scriptura,* that is, Scripture apart from the interpreting authority of the church, in fact those slogans, in both Lutheran and Calvinist versions, were readily situated in hardened systems of orthodoxy that rivaled Trent's closed formulation in their certitude and lack of porousness. In the work of such theologians as Martin Chemnitz, Matthias Flacius, and Francis Turretin, the Bible came to be located in Protestant systems of faith that kept the form of Reformation radicality, but that froze the substance of interpretation in a way that seriously jeopardized and compromised the "freedom of the gospel."[10]

The ongoing community of interpreters, on the whole, found the Bible's "oddness" excessive, and did what it could to counter and reduce the oddness. Thus it is unwise for our purposes to claim too much for a Reformation understanding of the Bible, unless at the same time we recognize that the oddness of the Bible (more or less) on its own terms was a greater challenge than the ongoing institutional church could tolerate. This rather hasty "settlement" of Reformation questions, in both Roman Catholic and Protestant responses, raises for us a principal problem of Old Testament theology: the difficult relation between the Bible and church theology; in other words, between text and reading community.[11] It is clear that the large notion of "Rule of Faith," a term used both for the Bible itself and for the church's confessional rules of interpretation, intends to hold together Bible and church interpretation, or perhaps even to cover over the tension that belongs to our work of scholarship in Old Testament theology.[12] It is equally clear, however, that no amount of careful formulation can completely conceal the deep problematic of the Bible's relation to church faith. The Reformation itself, especially in Luther's work, was a remarkable moment of emancipation—one might call it an epistemological spree—but it could not be sustained. Matters were quickly compromised, perhaps inevitably so in order to make the Bible institutionally palatable and useful.

Thus emerged a struggle for the control of interpretation among (a) the *orthodox,* who sought to enlist the Bible in a defense of Reformation doctrine; (b) the *rationalists,* who adhered to newer modes of autonomous learning that eventu-

---

10. See Kraeling, *The Old Testament since the Reformation,* 38. The great problem at issue for a Protestant theologian is how to escape the logic of the Roman Catholic claim that the church is the proximate source of the canonical authority of Scripture.

11. By "reading community" I refer to the church. The term *church* permits a theological insistence, whereas the generic term *reading community* acknowledges that the church is not per se a privileged reading community with reference to the Bible but, like every other reading community, is not neutral or innocent and so reads with some interest at stake. See Stephen E. Fowl and L. Gregory Jones, *Reading in Communion: Scripture and Ethics in Christian Life* (Grand Rapids: Eerdmans, 1991).

12. See the discussion of "the Rule of Faith" by Brevard S. Childs, *Biblical Theology of the Old and New Testaments* (Minneapolis: Fortress Press, 1992) 55–79. Childs has been unable to escape the problem that "the Rule of Faith" is claimed to be operative in the canonical process yet is not the work of the reading community.

ated in Deism;[13] and (c) the *pietists*, who resisted both hardened orthodoxy and autonomous rationalism.[14] If these interpretive struggles are taken seriously and understood as efforts that, while perhaps misguided, were by the lights of their practitioners acts of good faith, we can see that exceedingly important and difficult issues were under discussion and in dispute. It is clear, in short, that the approaches of orthodoxy, rationalism, and pietism put very different questions to the Bible out of very different concerns from very different social locations. Thus it does not surprise us that these interpretive perspectives arrived at very different readings of the text. What may seem to us rather picky issues were in fact very large issues about power and confidence in a world known to be deeply at risk.

It is clear that these parties to the conflicted conversations about interpretation represented and embodied continuing propensities in interpretation. Thus, those we now call rationalists continue their work in "the guild," intending that their "objective" research should not be curbed by fideistic limitation. The "orthodox" continue to be those who come at the text through the categories of church creeds and assumptions. While our main issues will concern the dispute between rationalists and the orthodox, the pietistic tradition continues to operate at a more popular interpretive level, unwilling to be drawn into the subtleties of the other two parties. These old quarrels are yet with us, and the stakes continue to be regarded as high.

As a result of such passionately disputed interpretation, the churches of the Reformation, the first natural habitat of biblical theology, were not hermeneutically prepared for the major challenge of modernity that they promptly faced. The winds of change (perhaps God-driven?) that set in motion the stirrings of the Reformation did not stop there. They continued to move to yet greater challenges to the task of Bible interpretation.

The Critical Enterprise

It is important to keep in focus the fact that Luther's work and the upheaval of religious life in Europe were immediately followed by a second, very different movement that was a harbinger of the coming European Enlightenment. It is not necessary for a student of Old Testament theology to know about the emergence of "modern" thinking in detail, but it is necessary to understand that a profound change of sensibility emerged in the post-Reformation period.[15] Luther died in 1546. René Descartes was born in 1596 and published his major work between 1637 and 1650. John Locke, his English counterpart (after Francis Bacon), was born in 1632, during the lifetime of Descartes, and published his decisive work

---

13. See Reventlow, *The Authority of the Bible*, on the rise and influence of Deism.

14. Hayes and Prussner, *Old Testament Theology*, 36–41, helpfully explore the triadic relationship among Pietism, orthodoxy, and rationalism.

15. See James Kugel, "The Bible in the University," *The Hebrew Bible and Its Interpreters* (ed. William Henry Propp et al.; Winona Lake, Ind.: Eisenbrauns, 1990) 143–65, on the changed sensibility of the contemporary context of biblical interpretation. The "changed sensibility" of which Kugel writes is reminiscent of the change at the beginning of the modern period.

within fifty years of Descartes' work. The relation between the Reformation and the rise of modernity (the latter commonly associated with Descartes and Locke) is indeed complex. It is not necessary for our purposes to consider in detail that many-faceted issue.[16] It is enough for us to recognize that the rise of modernity followed quickly after the emergence of the Reformation and reaped a benefit from some aspects of the Reformation.

The Reformation, with its accent on the emancipation of interpretation from the control of the church hierarchy, may be in some important way a prelude to modernity. In any case, the rise of modernity offered to intellectual Europe, and thus to the church, a notion of truth and a scenario of how truth is to be arrived at, assessed, and transmitted that were different from the conviction and practice of the medieval church. The decision of the Reformation churches to champion and to bear witness to an unfettered, evangelical Bible was promptly taken into the interpretive climate of modernity. The emergent cultural-intellectual climate that came to dominate Europe, moreover, is of decisive importance for understanding the contemporary issues facing Old Testament theology.

For our work it is essential to be familiar in broad outline with the far-reaching challenge posed in the Enlightenment to (a) the epistemological oddness claimed by the Reformation; (b) the defensive claims of post-Tridentine Catholicism; and (c) the reductionist Protestantism of the period after the great Reformers. The urgency and vitality of the Reformation notwithstanding, Trent and the parallel emergence of Protestant Scholasticism had left the Bible, at the eve of modernity, still deeply enmeshed in and dependent on church authority and church interpretation. The power of rationalism, manifested in the capacity to articulate faith in logically coherent formulations, was very much in the air after the time of the primary Reformers. Protestant orthodoxy, in both Lutheranism and Calvinism, produced a hardened scheme of theological reflection that closely followed the contours of the church's dogmatic affirmation. That is, the great evangelical insights of the Reformers hardened into a cognitive scheme that kept the form of evangelical faith but was increasingly remote from the substance and emancipatory power of its urging.

Three Strands in Modernity

The continuing power of the synthesis of the medieval church with its unchallenged appeal to revelation and the defensive maneuvers of orthodoxy were met, already at the outset of the seventeenth century, with the rise of modernity.[17] The complexity of this intellectual and political transformation in Europe precludes any

---

16. Kraus, *Geschichte der historisch-kritischen Erforschung,* 3–4, regards the linkage of the Reformation to the subsequent critical enterprise as a peculiarly pressing problem: "Was ist aus dem reformatorische Bekenntnis *sola scriptura* unter dem Anwachsen der historisches Kritik geworden?"

17. For a brief summary of the problem "modernity" poses in Scripture study, see Walter Brueggemann, *Texts under Negotiation: The Bible and Postmodern Imagination* (Minneapolis: Fortress Press, 1993). I have found especially helpful Stephen Toulmin, *Cosmopolis: The Hidden Agenda of Modernity* (New York: Free Press, 1990); Paul Hazard, *The European Mind, 1680–1715: The Critical Years*

easy reportage, but the emergence of modernity may be identified briefly as having three strands.

First it is impossible to overestimate the importance of the *rise of science*, which is commonly associated with the work of Francis Bacon and his dictum that "knowledge is power."[18] The emergence of scientific thought was driven by the fresh awareness that the human agent was unfettered in the capacity to probe, know, and control. (One spin-off of the rise of science was the exploration of the now-to-be-probed globe and the practice of colonialization, whereby European power became world power.) The emergence of the human agent as knower reached fruition in the work of Galileo and Copernicus, which rendered the old synthesis of knowledge in the authority of the church an epistemological impossibility. Thus the shifts in epistemology driven by scientific perspectives were of enormous importance.[19]

Second, the *philosophical advances* in Europe are commonly identified as having begun with Descartes and his program of rationalism, which culminated in the work of Immanuel Kant and Georg Wilhelm Friedrich Hegel. It was Descartes' achievement to provide an alternative epistemology to that which appealed to the interpretive authority of the church and its claim of revelation. That alternative epistemology focused on the human agent as the unfettered, unencumbered doubter and knower who could by objective reason come to know what is true and reliable. A new epistemological environment was nurtured, one that by design scuttled every appeal to tradition (including that of the church) and the situatedness of knowledge in concrete contexts. Thus the Cartesian program is commonly associated with reason, objectivity, autonomy, and eventually with positivism, which believed that what is knowable can be exhaustively known by human thought.

The rationalism of Descartes was matched in British philosophy by the empiricism of John Locke.[20] Such appeal to lived human experience was very different from the rationalism of the Continent. Locke celebrated the availability of knowledge to the individual knower, if that knower paid attention to the surrounding world. While very different, this empiricism shared with its partner rationalism the passion that genuine knowing must avoid appeal to context and to tradition. The conventional authority of the church as the arbiter of truth was seen as a great impediment to true knowledge, and empiricism held that the Bible as "supernatural revelation" needed to be driven out of the center and assessed in terms of its agreement with the gains of "emancipated knowledge." This autonomous knowledge

---

(New York: Fordham University Press, 1990); and Susan Bordo, *The Flight to Objectivity: Essays in Cartesianism and Culture* (Albany: SUNY Press, 1987).

18. Brian Wren, *What Language Shall I Borrow? God-Talk in Worship: A Male Response to Feminist Theology* (London: SCM Press, 1989), has commented in helpful ways about the impact of Bacon's metaphorical arsenal on modern consciousness.

19. See Arthur Koestler, *The Sleep-Walkers: A History of Man's Changing Vision of the Universe* (New York: Viking, Penguin, 1990); and Richard J. Blackwell, *Galileo, Bellarmine, and the Bible: Including a Translation of Foscarini's Letter on the Motion of the Earth* (Notre Dame, Ind.: University of Notre Dame Press, 1991).

20. See Reventlow, *The Authority of the Bible*, 243–85; and Rogerson, *Old Testament Criticism*.

partook of some of the emancipating impetus of the Reformation but carried it in very different directions.

Along with such scientific and philosophical efforts, Klaus Scholder has recently made an important argument concerning the *political dimensions of Enlightenment epistemology*.[21] Scholder proposes that it was the theological division of Europe between Rome and the Reformation, accomplished in bloody fashion through the Thirty Years' War (fought during the lifetime of Descartes), that brought to an end the universal claim of Christian theology in Europe. Even if one intended to trust the established teaching of the church as the truth, the problem was that there was now more than one established teaching of more than one church. Obviously, these teachings differed, disagreed, and contradicted each other in important ways. In the landscape of theological interpretive Europe, there was no innocent or objective arbiter between such authorized, competing claims. In the climate of the seventeenth century, it is not surprising that *reason* emerged as the trustworthy arbiter; that is, what was reliable was the human capacity to think through and to make a judgment.[22] Thus the appeal to reason was in part a political necessity, given the fact that the church claimants to truth turned out to be advocates and not arbiters as they had been seen heretofore. Reason, as it was understood in an innocent way, became the test by which revelation was to be assessed. It is impossible to overestimate the importance of the emancipation of reason from the revelatory underpinnings that had long been accepted as normative.

Paul Hazard has nicely commented on what happened to the European mind in the thirty-five-year period (1680–1716) when new interpretive modes and assumptions emerged with the rise of empiricism and rationalism. He has traced how in one generation European intellectual life arrived at a new sensibility that no longer accepted the interpretive domination of the church and its appeal to the authority of tradition. For our purposes it is sufficient to recognize, as Hazard has shown, that a "new spirit" came to be dominant, a "new consciousness," against which the old appeal to revelation fought a defensive and increasingly hopeless battle.[23]

Emergence of Historical Criticism

A student of Old Testament theology will not appreciate what is given and demanded in the rise of criticism unless the emergence of historical criticism is seen as a part of this greatly shifting sensibility away from authority and tradition and toward confidence in objective, detached scholarship.[24] The rise of science meant that the Bible came to occupy no privileged position of interpretation. Instead of

---

21. Klaus Scholder, *The Birth of Modern Critical Theology: Origins and Problems of Biblical Criticism in the Seventeenth Century* (Philadelphia: Trinity Press International, 1990).

22. Reventlow, *The Authority of the Bible*, has traced the way in which the liberated capacity of the individual emerged from humanistic study.

23. Hazard, *The European Mind*, 198–236 and passim.

24. Hayes and Prussner, *Old Testament Theology*, 27–34, present a helpful consideration of Spinoza, who recognized the incompatibility of reason and the Bible. What was regarded as reason was in substance a "turn to the subject," as in Immanuel Kant.

the Bible functioning as a court of appeal for settling the great knowledge questions (as it had been in some sense in an earlier mood), the Bible itself became the material that was assessed and measured and, in some cases, found wanting.

The rise of criticism may be understood positively as a derivative aspect of the rise of modernity, and negatively as an effort to wrench the Bible, still much valued and respected, away from the reductionist categories of church interpretation. Church interpretation was viewed, given the "new spirit," as a censoring activity that prevented the Bible being taken on its own terms and being forced to confirm to established categories and claims. The specific cause and details of the rise of historical criticism have been often well rehearsed. For our purposes, what is important is to recognize the new importance of the individual scholar and the scholarly academic guild, apart from the aegis of the church.

As one aspect of the transition from the medieval synthesis to the practice of modernity, biblical interpretation became a test case for the tension between church authority and the authority of the emancipated, scientific scholar. It was recognized in this "new sport" that the texts of the Bible were not absolute givens but emerged in the process of Israel's living, either by oral or written formulation. That is, the biblical texts were generated through human effort, human faith, human passion, and human idiosyncrasy. The central scholarly enterprise from the seventeenth century onward was to try to locate and understand this human enterprise. Thus a scholarly tradition developed, with growing consensus among critical scholars, concerning which texts were older, how they had been transmitted and changed in transmission, and which texts were more reliable, more accurate, and more sophisticated. That is, historical criticism, in the practice of the spirit of the age, began to make differentiations in texts and to sort them out by varying scholarly criteria. The practical effect of this enterprise was to relativize the revelatory claims of the text and to treat it like any other book. The outcome was to make the biblical text subservient, at least methodologically, to the rational claims of the interpretive elite.

When we move into the nineteenth century and especially into the influence of Hegel, we witness the rise of history, which stands in some tension with the older reigning rationalism of the eighteenth and nineteenth centuries and in some ways appeals to a kind of Lockean empiricism.[25] In the nineteenth century "history" became a dominant mode of knowing, so that everything was understood to have a history, a developmental career.

_____

25. The rise of science greatly threatened the theological authority of the church, but it was the rise of history later on that posed more acute problems for Old Testament theology. Rogerson, *Old Testament Criticism*, 17, notes the move from the eighteenth to the nineteenth century and the changed questions that now had to be faced. Specifically, Wilhelm Martin Leberecht De Wette pursued questions of historical consciousness, so that a gap was recognized between Old Testament reportage and "the facts of history." Owen Chadwick, *The Secularization of the European Mind in the Nineteenth Century* (Cambridge: Cambridge University Press, 1975) 163, notes the sharp opposition of "knowledge in the seventeenth century versus knowledge in the nineteenth century."

History as a category of theological interpretation is no innovation of the nineteenth century. As early as the federalist (covenantal) theology of the sixteenth and seventeenth centuries, harking back to the dramatic perspectives of Irenaeus, efforts were made to link biblical text and historical drama under the rubric of salvation history. That is, the sequence of experiences narrated in the text as "real events" were taken to constitute the arena in which the God of the Bible is decisively known and seen to act. It is important to recognize, however, that the time-honored notion of salvation history and what Enlightenment scholarship understood by history are quite distinct matters. This distinction, as we shall see, has haunted and vexed the enterprise of Old Testament theology through the twentieth century. Thus criticism has sought to link text to experience (event) but has so defined experience as to make interpretation exceedingly problematic.

By the end of the eighteenth century and into the nineteenth century, history had acquired a very different dimension and significance from all previous understandings. First, history had taken on a positivistic character, so that events came to be regarded as completely decipherable, to the exclusion of any inscrutable density. This change entailed that events have a simple, discernible, unambiguous meaning from which all mystery can be squeezed out. Second, in the nineteenth century the idea of history as development came to be crucial, so that events came to be seen as progressively arranged in sequence. Events without inscrutable density but with progressive sequencing leave nothing for theology to do. And so history could and did become an autonomous enterprise, without reference to any larger or coded significance.

The accent on evolutionary developmentalism placed interpretive work in profound tension with those who sought in the Bible for the absolute claims of faith. Thus, in broad outline, we may say that in the seventeenth and eighteenth centuries intellectual categories were those of *rational* science, which sought to establish what is "bedrock" true; and in the nineteenth century new issues were posed in terms of *historical* development, which moved away from a settled reality to a developing reality. What was left as a matrix for theological interpretation was the tension between eighteenth-century *absolutism* and nineteenth-century *developmentalism*, a tension that continued into the battle over modernism in the early twentieth century.[26] This tension still operates in the church today under the unhappy labels of so-called liberals (developmentalists) and conservatives (absolutists). *It is of great importance for a student of Old Testament theology to notice that in every period of the discipline, the questions, methods, and possibilities in which study is cast arise from the sociointellectual climate in which the work must be done.*

---

26. See Hayes and Prussner, *Old Testament Theology*, 13, on the problem of absolutism. Jack B. Rogers and Donald K. McKim, *The Authority and Interpretation of the Bible: An Historical Approach* (San Francisco: Harper and Row, 1979), suggest specifically how this problematic impinged on U.S. theological practice. See a conservative critique of Rogers and McKim by John D. Woodbridge, *Biblical Authority: A Critique of the Rogers/McKim Proposal* (Grand Rapids: Zondervan, 1982).

Thus, given the emergence of Baconian *science*, of Cartesian *rationalism*, of Lockean *empiricism*, and eventually of Hegelian *history*, it was likely not possible for the study of Scripture to resist being cast as it was in any particular circumstance. This is not because scholars in that milieu were required to think in these terms, nor that they willfully decided to do so; it is simply that these were the categories available to scholars as children of the moment and citizens of a real sociointellectual world. Therefore, in my judgment, there is no point in accusing scholarship of betrayal or lamenting what has happened. Scholarship of a theological kind, if it is to matter at all, must take up the issues given in its time and place. Thus with the new spirit of the age in the seventeenth and eighteenth centuries, the temptations to "scientific" modes of criticism were powerful, and in the nineteenth century the commitment to "historical" modes of analysis were inescapable. As we gain perspective on the ways in which cultural climate and context shape scholarship and interpretation, it is important for us to recognize that we, no less than our predecessors, are children of our time and place and must deal with the issues as we find them shaped. In what follows, we shall see that interpretation at the end of the twentieth century, in ways very different from the ways of the seventeenth, eighteenth, and nineteenth centuries, must live and work in an interpretive context that focuses on pluralism and adjudication between competing rhetorical and ideological claims. No scholarly interpreter can refuse to take account of the shapings given in context, though it is equally clear that each scholarly interpreter has some maneuverability in determining how to take up the questions and the shapings in which they are presented.

Thus the rise of criticism that eventuated in the Wellhausian synthesis is a product of the rise of modernity.[27] In the aftermath of Hegel, it became clear that everything had a history, for this was the period of Charles Darwin and the growing, albeit disputed, claim that the human race has had a long history from the simple to the complex.[28] (Our own fashionable version of this conviction about developmentalism is the idea that everything—from faith to sex to happy marriage to great wealth—happens in stages, with so many steps from here to there.) Thus also in the study of the Bible, we must reckon with the concept of development. Everything has a historical development: the Bible, Israel, and even God. The Wellhausian synthesis that has governed Old Testament scholarship reflects the spirit of the age. In that synthesis, it was possible for scholars to agree upon early (JE), middle (D), and late (P) documents, which in turn reflected Israel's

---

27. It is impossible to overstate the importance of Julius Wellhausen for our study, both for what he did and for what he came to represent. On the enduring importance of his work, see *Julius Wellhausen and His Prolegomena to the History of Israel* (ed. Douglas A. Knight; *Semeia* 25 [1983]).

28. Thus Charles Darwin's *On the Origin of Species*. On the milieu in which Darwin worked and on his awareness of the danger of his insight, see Adrian Desmond and James Moore, *Darwin* (London: Michael Joseph, 1991). It is now a consensus position that Wellhausen was not directly influenced by Hegel. Nonetheless, it is clear that a sense of historical dynamic, in general seen to be progressive and evolutionary, constituted the epistemological grid for Wellhausen's time and place.

religion: early-primitive, ethical monotheism, and "degenerate legalism."[29] The development reflects the history of documents, the history of Israel, the history of Israel's religion, and the history of Israel's God (understood as the history of Israel's *understanding* of God).[30] While nineteenth-century developmentalism is very different from eighteenth-century rationalism and empiricism, it is in continuity with them in practicing *an epistemology of the human knower as an unencumbered objective interpreter who was understood to be a nonpartisan, uninvolved reader of the data.* One is persistently struck by the "innocence" of interpreters who refuse to take up the rhetorical density of the text.[31]

Thus the long sweep of the modern period is reflected in the dominance of historical criticism. For our purposes, it is important to notice especially two reference points. First, a famous lecture by J. P. Gabler in 1787, in an attempt to distinguish theological interpretation of the Old Testament apart from the dogmatic program of the church, identified the task of Old Testament interpretation as historical.[32] Scholars understood themselves as historians who were engaged in a reconstructive enterprise. Second, the consequence of this self-understanding meant that any "normative" sense of the biblical text in theological and ethical matters that appealed to the interpretive authority of the church was rejected. The approach championed by Gabler, which reflected the spirit of the age with its unfettered, emancipated objective knowledge, did indeed seek to establish what was normative. It did so, however, not on the basis of established church authority and interpretation, but by an appeal to emancipated reason that could produce "universal" norms. Old Testament study then became a study of different context-situated texts (and genres of literature); instances of religious practice and political organization; contextualized social movements and encounters, exchanges with, borrowings from, and resistances to environmental influences. All such work was undertaken, however, in an attempt to reach universal norms that eschewed any of the particularities

---

29. The conclusion that late Judaism was "degenerate" was, of course, a pejorative Christian judgment. Wellhausen connected his "history of the documents" with a developmental theory of Israel's religion.

30. That this is "an understanding of God" and not "God" is important. This sort of criticism made a required distinction between affirmation and reality, presumably because it was not possible, in an enlightened context, to take the witness of the text as "realistic." Enlightenment epistemology is in principle a distancing project.

31. The Enlightenment in principle resisted any notion of the density of the text. It is Friedrich Nietzsche, Fyodor Dostoyevsky, and Sigmund Freud—"masters of suspicion" who reject the positivistic claims of the Enlightenment—who attend to the density of the text. Thus historical criticism of a remarkably thin kind (as reflected in many commentaries) is indeed a determined practice of Enlightenment epistemology.

32. Gabler's address is rendered in English in an abridged form by John H. Sandys-Wunsch and Laurence Eldredge, "J. P. Gabler and the Distinction between Biblical and Dogmatic Theology: Translation, Commentary, and Discussion of His Originality," *SJT* 33 (1980) 133–58. See most recently the comprehensive review of Gabler's work by Rolf P. Knierim, "On Gabler," *The Task of Old Testament Theology: Substance, Method, and Cases* (Grand Rapids: Eerdmans, 1995) 495–556. On the work of Gabler, see especially the critical judgment of Ben C. Ollenburger, "Biblical Theology: Situating the Discipline," *Understanding the Word: Essays in Honor of Bernhard W. Anderson* (ed. James T. Butler et al.; JSOTSup 37; Sheffield: JSOT Press, 1985) 37–62. Notice that the first comments of Hayes and Prussner, *Old Testament Theology*, 2–5, concern the pivotal work of Gabler.

of biblical faith that were a hindrance to the claims of reason. Modern scholarship, reflective of Enlightenment epistemology, was to eschew any traditionally normative statement—any notion that a faith claim in the biblical text could possibly continue to be authoritative for a particularistic community of interpretation. As a consequence of this scholarly propensity, for a very long period, that of high, emancipated historical criticism, no major efforts at Old Testament theology sought to articulate the normative claims of biblical faith per se. All such possible claims were firmly subordinated to the larger claims of reason.

The practical effect of this scholarship was that it did indeed leave biblical interpretation free of church authority. In an odd way, critical scholarship continued the effort of Luther and the Reformers in providing space for the text as distinct from church interpretation. The unrecognized outcome, however, is that the Old Testament was largely appropriated in the metahistory of the Enlightenment—a metahistory that eschewed the hiddenness, density, and inscrutability of the text. The *theological result* is that much of what was crucial in the testimony of ancient Israel was explained away. The *literary result* is that much of what was most interesting and compelling about the literature was "resolved" by cutting apart into sources and layers much that the artistry of the Bible intended to locate beyond such facile decoding.

The gains of historical criticism are immense, and no informed reader can proceed without paying attention to those gains.[33] *What has not been noticed is that such scholarship is not as innocent as it imagined itself to be.* Thus the Cartesian program, fully embraced by much of biblical scholarship, was not as innocent, objective, or decontextualized as it supposed itself to be, for this scholarship made easy, common cause with certain modes of power that it left unchallenged.[34] As Hans-Georg Gadamer has argued, the Enlightenment has "a prejudice against prejudice."[35] It cannot tolerate intellectual or theological claims and affirmations that run against its thin objectivism, which is itself an acknowledged intellectual, theological claim. In principle, the metanarrative of modernity, with its vigilance against authority, made Old Testament theology as a normative enterprise impossible. The emancipation of the Bible from dogmatic authority, which received its major impetus in the Reformation, was lost in a practice of reductionist criticism. It is fair to say that, by the end of the nineteenth century, the Old Testament had ceased to be

---

33. Walter Wink, *The Bible in Human Transformation* (Philadelphia: Fortress Press, 1973), has notoriously pronounced historical criticism "bankrupt," and Wink's verdict was an important one, if a bit sensationalist. Here I do not say "bankrupt," but "inadequate." That inadequacy becomes apparent only when the interpreting community is itself situated outside of (or beyond?) the metahistory of the Enlightenment. The interpretive crisis and possibility of the church now is that it is discovering that the Enlightenment is not its natural habitat. Therefore the church is having to relearn its own way of reading. In this regard, I am in complete agreement with Brevard Childs, contrary to his judgment of my work. It will be evident in what follows that I differ markedly from him in how to go about that task.

34. See Jon Sobrino, *The True Church and the Poor* (Maryknoll, N.Y.: Orbis Books, 1984) 7–38, on the two Enlightenments.

35. Hans-Georg Gadamer, *Truth and Method* (London: Sheed and Ward, 1989) 241–45.

a part of Scripture with any authoritative claim for the church. In the academy, it continued to be an object of study in the context of the metahistory of positivism, but it was a study that in principle had to distort or deny the most defining characteristics of the text itself.[36] It was not possible to reread the text in terms of Enlightenment historicism without at the same time distorting everything else crucial in this textual construal of reality, including its theological claims. The very supersessionism that Christian faith seemed to require had become, in the hands of modernist criticism, an *intellectual supersessionism* committed in the name of Enlightenment rationality.

The Recovery of Theological Interpretation

The nineteenth century is conventionally understood as beginning with the Congress of Vienna in 1814, which brought "a grand peace" to Europe in the wake of Napoleon, and as ending in 1914 with the outbreak of the Great War. The period 1814–1914, which featured the high period of historical criticism in Scripture study, was a time of great intellectual ferment in Europe, and of enormous cultural development, along with a political climate that permitted confidence in reason and buoyancy about human autonomy and progress. It fostered the belief that everything human was now possible. While there is not a one-to-one correspondence between this general mood and the Wellhausen consensus, it is plausible that the hypothesis could have arisen only in the context of a widely shared sense of well-being and self-congratulation.

As the development of the scholarly consensus of progressivism in revelation reflected a cultural setting of well-being, so the challenges to the hypothesis that arose in the twentieth century also reflected a specific cultural context. The Great War of 1914–18 with its disastrous culmination in the Treaty of Versailles witnessed powerfully against any naive optimism and against any confidence in the human capacity to construct an adequate world, to say nothing of an adequate hypothesis of progressive developmentalism. The Western situation after 1918 required a fresh recognition of the tenuousness of the human situation and the power of evil in the world. It required, moreover, a theological enterprise that could make theological sense outside of what came to be called liberal progressivism.

---

36. While the church has carelessly tended to practice supersessionism (i.e., the claim that the Old Testament text is superseded by the New Testament), in effect the dominant force of historical criticism has in its own way also practiced a kind of supersessionism. For a thorough and insightful assessment of the theological dimensions of supersessionism, see Kendall Soulen, *The God of Israel and Christian Theology* (Minneapolis: Fortress Press, 1996); on subtle, well-meaning modes of supersessionism, see Stephen R. Haynes, *Jews and the Christian Imagination: Reluctant Witnesses* (New York: Macmillan, 1995). Whereas the church has too often confessed that the Old Testament is superseded in the Christian gospel, historical criticism affirmed in its practice that the Old Testament, in its faith claims, is superseded by Enlightenment rationality and its accompanying autonomous objectivity. For an inventory of the different forms and options in supersessionism, see Gabriel Fackre, "The Place of Israel in Christian Faith," *Gott lieben und seine Gebote halten: Loving God and Keeping His Commandments* (ed. Markus Bockmuehl and Helmut Burkhardt; Giessen, Germany: Brunnen, 1991) 21–38.

Karl Barth

Into that situation erupted, as though a *novum* without antecedent, Karl Barth's 1919 *Epistle to the Romans,* which inaugurated a radically new season of theological discourse that refused the well-established assumptions of self-confident liberalism.[37] As a daring and resourceful pastoral interpreter of Scripture, Barth refused the accommodationist theological assumptions in which he had been schooled and which dominated the theological scene of his day in Germany. He asserted, in his daring interpretation of the Letter to the Romans, that the truth of the gospel is other than the conventional intellectual assumptions of cultural progressivism that dominated culture, academy, and much of the church.

The content of Barth's explosive challenge to the theology of his day had to do with the sovereign grace of God known in Jesus of Nazareth. As Stephen Webb has noted, Barth's rhetoric was a necessary match for his content.[38] Barth refused the acceptable, reasonable discourse of "the cultured despisers of religion" and proceeded in a mode of discourse that was abrasive, abrupt, polemical, and filled with contradictions that went under the name of dialectical. His rhetoric, necessary to what he wanted to assert, was filled with irony, hyperbole, and incongruity, as though his very words of interpretation were designed to enact the scandalous challenge to culture that he undertook in the name of the Christian gospel.

It is difficult to overestimate the cruciality of Barth's daring work for the recovery of theological interpretation of the Old Testament. In the course of the nineteenth century and under the aegis of historical criticism, any notion of normative theological assertion in the Old Testament—that is, any claim for truth—had vanished from interpretation. The Bible was understood almost exclusively as a series of religious developments, each of which was completely contained in its own particular cultural milieu, each of which was tested by a "reasonable universal." Against that powerful intellectual assumption of religion, Barth thundered with theological normativeness.[39] Thus Barth committed an overt act of epistemological subversion in his break with the nineteenth-century valuing of "reasoned universals."

Although a critique of historical criticism, a method of interpretation that had come to dominance in the nineteenth century, was of no central importance to Barth, his work embodied a major challenge and alternative to the widely held confidence in critical methods.[40] Barth saw the theological enterprise, since Descartes

---

37. Karl Barth, *The Epistle to the Romans* (6th ed.; New York: Oxford University Press, 1968). The book is everywhere known in theological conversation as *Der Römerbrief* (Zürich: Theologischer, 1985), as it was first published. See a revised assessment of Barth's program by Bruce L. McCormack, *Karl Barth's Critically Realistic Dialectical Theology: Its Genesis and Development, 1909–1936* (Oxford: Clarendon Press, 1995).

38. Stephen H. Webb, *Re-configuring Theology: The Rhetoric of Karl Barth* (Albany: SUNY Press, 1991).

39. The contrast of "faith" and "religion" is programmatic to Barth. See, for example, *The Word of God and the Word of Man* (London: Hodder and Stoughton, 1928).

40. Barth was fully aware of the claims and practices of historical criticism, but those ways of approaching the text held no interest or benefit for him. See Bruce L. McCormack, "Historical Criticism

and Locke and culminating in Ludwig Feuerbach, as having accommodated itself to autonomous reason—to the notion of objective knowledge as it had been championed in the rise of science.[41] The outcome of such assumptions, as Barth saw clearly, is that all of the oddness of the biblical witness has to be explained away or made to fit with the prevailing modes of what is deemed to be reasonable. As a consequence criticism addressed itself to explaining away what was odd in the text, including what was theologically odd.

The challenge that Barth took up was to find a beginning point for theological assertion that was not, in its very inception, already compromised decisively by objective relativizing. Barth took his revolutionary stand on a christological claim, but that claim was intimately linked to the authority of Scripture. It is a primary assumption of Barth that the Bible, on its own terms and without appeal to "natural reason," is the beginning point of faith. Thus Barth programmatically reached behind Descartes and appealed to Anselm's notion of "faith seeking understanding."[42] That is, faith is not a conclusion that may or may not result from reflection. It is, rather, a nonnegotiable premise and assumption of all right reading of the Bible and all right faith. Barth understood that over against this claim, the premise of Enlightenment autonomy as expressed in historical criticism is also not a conclusion, but a nonnegotiable premise and assumption. In this enormous epistemological maneuver, Barth placed in question the entire enterprise of modern criticism, which sought to conform the text to the canon of modern reason. At its foundation, the epistemological reference point of nineteenth-century criticism is irreconcilable with Barth's beginning point.

It is relatively easy to indict Barth for fideism and theological positivism, and that indictment has been reiterated often. The problem is that there is obviously no legitimate starting point for theological reflection, and one must begin somewhere. The counterindictment is somewhat less obvious and has only more recently been mounted: that *the Cartesian program of autonomous reason, which issued in historical criticism, is also an act of philosophical fideism.*[43] Because such critical thought and method have seemed detached and objective, it has not been so obvious that "objective scholarship" is not neutral but is itself theory-laden, engaged in an ideological practice.[44]

---

and Dogmatic Interest in Karl Barth's Exegesis of the New Testament," *Biblical Hermeneutics in Historical Perspective: Studies in Honor of Karlfried Froehlich on His Sixty-Fifth Birthday* (ed. Mark S. Burrows and Paul Rorem; Grand Rapids: Eerdmans, 1991) 322–38.

41. See Barth's analysis of the emergence of autonomy in nineteenth-century theology, *Protestant Theology in the Nineteenth Century: Its Background and History* (London: SCM Press, 1972). On autonomy as a theme in Barth, see John Macken, *The Autonomy Theme in the "Church Dogmatics": Karl Barth and His Critics* (Cambridge: Cambridge University Press, 1990).

42. Karl Barth, *Anselm: Fides quaerens intellectum: Anselm's Proof for the Existence of God in the Context of His Theological Scheme* (London: SCM Press, 1960).

43. See especially Gadamer, *Truth and Method.* More broadly, the most profound struggle against such positivism is perhaps Max Horkheimer and Theodor W. Adorno, *Dialectic of Enlightenment* (New York: Continuum, 1975).

44. The current methodological debates and tensions in Old Testament scholarship in part consist of an exposé of the theory that drives historical criticism. In current conversations it becomes increas-

Since Barth exposed objective scholarship as theory-laden, it does not follow that his theological premise would be granted any privilege. It does, however, make inescapable the recognition that there is no innocent or neutral scholarship, but that all theological and interpretive scholarship is in one way or another fiduciary.[45] Barth's sustained polemic against religion is that *all such practice of meaning that eventuated in liberalism must be critiqued, not because it is not neutral, but because it flies in the face of the subject it purports to study*—namely, the work and presence of the Holy God who cannot be grasped in such conventional and autonomous categories.

Barth's programmatic importance is difficult to overstate. Negatively, he interrupted the assumptions of modernity that had emptied the biblical text of any serious theological claim. Positively, he asserted that biblical faith has its own distinctive voice. Against Feuerbach, Barth argued that the Bible is not an echo of other (cultural) voices, but needs to be heard in and for itself. Moreover, Barth asserted, the Bible is "about something" (Someone!). That is, the reality of God is asserted first, not as an afterthought after one asserts the "possibility of God" established in modernist categories.[46] Thus Barth created the rhetoric and the space in which normative (that is, "true") statements about biblical faith can be made, not to be adjudicated on the basis of the naturalistic epistemology of autonomy.

In crediting Barth with the re-creation of the possibility of a biblical theology, we should note an important issue that is present for Barth and for those who come after him. Barth's claim for the reality of God is an exercise in daring rhetoric, so that for Barth, reality is deeply grounded in speech. In Barth's mediation of faith, one must contend with the powerful rhetoric of the Bible, which in turn is given to us through the powerful, compelling rhetoric of Barth. Apart from these acts of rhetoric, the "real" of Barth is neither known nor available.[47] The history of recent Christian theology (indeed of all Christian theology, rooted as it is in the categories of Hellenistic philosophy) is to leap toward an ontological claim. Given such an inclination toward ontology, the claim of the "real" and the "substantial" is readily taken to be an ontological reality that exists behind the text and, in the end, apart from the text. That is, systematic theology in its strong appeal to ontology

---

ingly evident that "pure historical criticism" now (even if not in the past) serves socially conservative interpretation. In making this judgment I refer to historical criticism in distinction from rhetorical and sociological criticism, which have been taken up by scholars who, for the most part, are prepared to move outside a long-standing epistemological hegemony. More important, such a move is implicitly and inescapably also a move against a sociopolitical hegemony that both serves and benefits from that epistemology. For a searching critique of the power aspects of conventional criticism, see Daniel Patte, *The Ethics of Biblical Interpretation* (Louisville: Westminster/John Knox Press, 1995).

45. On the fiduciary element in knowledge, see Michael Polanyi, *Personal Knowledge: Toward a Post-critical Philosophy* (Chicago: University of Chicago Press, 1974).

46. Barth, *Church Dogmatics* 1/2, 1–44, turned modernist questions about "the possibility" on their head, and spoke first of the "reality" in light of which talk of possibility is shaped very differently.

47. My own beginning point concerning testimony is resonant with what I understand to be Barth's point. See chap. 3 on testimony as speech that generates the theological substance of Israel's faith. As I note there, my appeal to testimony is deeply informed by Barth.

tends to make a complete break between ontology and rhetoric, so that rhetoric itself in the end is of minimal importance for the theological claims being made.

Such a complete break between ontology and rhetoric may be necessary and inescapable for systematic theology. For biblical theology, however, such a complete break is in my judgment unthinkable. The available "real" and "substantive" of biblical theology are only rhetorically available. Barth, at least at points, knew this, for his rhetoric corresponds to the oddness of his subject. Thus, for Barth the choice is not simply a religious technique or a christological ontology, but the third factor of rhetoric must be taken into serious account. *The God of the Bible is not "somewhere else," but is given only in, with, and under the text itself.* Barth's energetic and provocative program, among other things, seemed to resist an ontological reductionism that tends to eliminate most about the biblical God that is crucial and interesting. This point about rhetoric in Barth is only noted here, but it will be important subsequently in our effort to trace the rhetoric whereby the Old Testament speaks about God.

Because Barth represents a decisive interruption in the course of biblical scholarship, everything in biblical theology after his famous Romans commentary is considered as "post-Barth." Barth himself made a nearly complete epistemological break with the modernity in which he had been schooled, although it can be argued that even Barth could not break so cleanly as he claimed. Be that as it may, those who have come after Barth have for the most part been either unwilling or unable to go all the way with Barth's epistemological break.

Therefore, most scholars who have attempted to work in Old Testament theology since Barth have been double-minded (to cite a usual critical verdict) or bilingual (to give positive credit). The tension that scholars face is between the epistemological assumptions of modernity that issue in historical criticism and that resist normative statements as fiduciary and potentially authoritarian, and the neoevangelical statement of normative theological claims that are perhaps impositions on the biblical materials. Thus the option of doing descriptive-historical or normative-theological work is not simply a choice for the kind of substantive argument to make about the Bible. The choice is an interpretive decision about epistemological assumptions and whether to locate one's interpretive work in the narrative of modernity or in the narrative of faith claims that refuse the skepticism of modernity. In what follows, I will suggest that such a way of putting the problem continued to be powerful for both parties to the controversy but, in a postmodern milieu, it may no longer be the most helpful form of the question.

Old Testament scholarship until recently has refused to choose and has sought to have it both ways. This refusal to choose has constituted the great problem for Old Testament theology. But perhaps this same refusal also has been the reason that Old Testament interpretation has refused theological reductionism. This articulation of the tension and a refusal to choose is not the same as saying that historical criticism is the problem. To be sure, to choose in the direction of historical criticism is a choice toward modernity. But the alternative choice is also not without problem, because it is a choice toward authoritarian reductionism that tends to deaden the claim of the text itself. Thus there is no easy choice about interpretive assumption. Through the present century, an endless adjudication of this issue has taken place. One reason for undertaking a fresh attempt at Old Testament theology is to consider whether we are in a cultural, epistemological circumstance that may permit a rearticulation of the grounds for facing the normative-descriptive issue.

The demise of the nineteenth-century era in the war of 1914–18 and the ensuing rise of National Socialism made an openness to the normative again urgent.[48] It was Barth above all, however, who gave impetus and credibility to the articulation of the normative. Barth's mood and style were not to derive the normative from the landscape, as was the wont of his liberal antecedents. Rather, on the basis of the Word (which he understood variously as Jesus Christ, the scriptural text, and/or the preaching moment), Barth dared to assert the normative claim of the gospel defiantly against the landscape.[49] What is normative is odd and peculiar, distinctive and scandalous, and can never be accommodated to the landscape of cultural ideology. For Barth this profound tension was primally expressed as "faith versus religion," a formulation not far removed from Luther's "faith and reason," nor from "a theology of the cross" vis-à-vis a "theology of glory."[50] Barth's articulation of contrast, conflict, and polemic gave impetus for Old Testament theology in the next period of scholarship, which we now consider.

Albrecht Alt and Martin Noth

The recovery of the articulation of the distinctiveness of Old Testament faith represents an important break from the agenda that had long governed Old Testament study. While there are other important antecedents to the theological contributions of Walther Eichrodt and Gerhard von Rad, we will focus primary attention on the work of Albrecht Alt and his student Martin Noth, with a lesser reference to the influence of William Foxwell Albright. Both Alt and Noth understood themselves primarily as historians and thus as in close continuity with their nineteenth-century scholarly forebears. In focusing on the distinctiveness of Israel in its ancient world, it is clear that their historical work had crucial theological-interpretive consequences, if not theological-interpretive intentionality. Alt and Noth (and in a different way Albright) reversed the usual domain assumptions of Old Testament study. For the long period dominated by historical criticism and its developmentalism, it was assumed that Israel's great theological categories came late in Israel's historical development—in Wellhausen's scheme only with Deuteronomy and the prophets, after the JE materials.

---

48. The movement that came to be called neoorthodoxy is to be understood against the backdrop of the collapse of human confidence that had dominated the nineteenth century and that gave credence to developmentalism, which dominated Old Testament interpretation.

49. See Barth, *Church Dogmatics* 1/1, 98–212, on the word in its variegated dimensions.

50. On this contrast rooted in Luther, see the helpful discussion of Douglas John Hall, *Lighten Our Darkness: Toward an Indigenous Theology of the Cross* (Philadelphia: Westminster Press, 1976).

A consequence of Alt's work was the claim that very early, even from its inception, Mosaic Israel operated with distinct theological assumptions. In Alt's work, we may identify two hypotheses that became crucial for scholarship in the next period. First, in his study of Israelite law, Alt distinguished on form-critical grounds between case law (casuistic law) and apodictic law.[51] Case law, which grew out of specific court rulings, is characteristic of law collections that are older than Israel and known in other cultures. This legal formulation is widely shared in Israel's cultural environment. By contrast, apodictic law voices absolute commands and prohibitions (for example, "thou shalt not . . . ") that are peculiar to Israel, found nowhere else in Near Eastern law collections. This apodictic command, stated so absolutely that no sanction is provided for it, is based on the absolute sovereignty of Yahweh, the God of Israel.[52] Thus the form of the law is taken as evidence of the rigorous, uncompromising monotheism that was already present in Israel and decisive at the Mosaic beginning of Israel. Martin Noth followed Alt's insight with the claim that it is Yahweh's "exclusive sovereignty" that is the bedrock of Israel's self-understanding as a community under the command of Yahweh.[53] From Alt's close form-critical analysis comes a major theological premise that was to be crucial for the emergence of Old Testament theology in the twentieth century.[54]

Second, Alt gave equally close attention to the "religion of the ancestors" in Genesis 12–36.[55] He articulated a sharp contrast between "the God of the fathers" and the other pre-Israelite gods of whom traces are found in the Genesis narratives. The other gods, such as El-Roi (Gen 16:13) and El Elyon (Gen 14:18), are characteristically linked to places and to natural phenomena; that is, they are static and fixed. By contrast, "the God of the fathers" is linked not to places but to persons. And so this God in the Book of Genesis, unlike other gods, goes with the ancestors of Israel in their journey to the land of promise.

There is something ironic in the consequences of Alt's study. A meticulous historian, Alt proceeded by the careful consideration of historical parallels and analogues in other religious claims. But the usable gain of Alt's study was to stress the distinctiveness of the promissory God. The theological construal beyond Alt's historical claim is not that "the God of the fathers" is unlike every other god, but

---

51. Albrecht Alt, "The Origins of Israelite Law," *Essays on Old Testament History and Religion* (Sheffield: JSOT Press, 1989) 79–132.

52. It is conventional among Christian interpreters to vocalize the tetragrammaton (YHWH). I continue that practice, albeit with some uneasiness, being fully aware of the reasons Jews refuse such a practice.

53. Martin Noth, "The Laws in the Pentateuch: Their Assumptions and Meaning," *The Laws in the Pentateuch and Other Essays* (London: SCM Press, 1966) 54 and passim, has seen that the exclusive claim of Yahweh is the core of Israel's legal tradition.

54. See Thomas L. Thompson, *Early History of the Israelite People: From the Written and Archaeological Sources* (Studies in the History of the Ancient Near East 4; Leiden: E. J. Brill, 1992) 27–34 and passim, for an accent on the importance of Alt's conclusions, even though Thompson regards Alt's work as unfortunate and misguided. More generally, see the dismissive broadside against the scholarship represented by Alt, Philip R. Davies, *In Search of "Ancient Israel"* (JSOTSup 148; Sheffield: Sheffield Academic Press, 1992).

55. Albrecht Alt, "The God of the Fathers," *Essays on Old Testament History and Religion,* 1–77.

rather is unlike the other gods present in the ancestral narratives. Thus "the God of the fathers" is a dynamic agent who is mobile and on the move with intentionality. Moreover, it is the promissory utterance and activity of this peculiar God that initiate Israel's historical process.[56] Alt was purportedly doing nothing more than investigating the fragmentary evidence of the history of early Israelite religion. It is clear, nonetheless, that Alt's historical investigation had enormous theological implications, first in the work of Gerhard von Rad, and eventually in the *Theology of Hope* of Jürgen Moltmann.[57] Alt's interpretation of the gods of Genesis 12–36 went far toward establishing the peculiarity of Israel's faith.[58]

These interpretive possibilities fostered by Alt—apodictic law and the God of the fathers—were given plausible institutional placement by his student Noth in the enormously influential study *The Twelve-Tribe System.*[59] Building on later and non-biblical parallels, Noth proposed that early tribal Israel consisted in a rather fluid system of twelve tribes (not always the same twelve), related to a lunar calendar of twelve months, organized around a central shrine or sanctuary. The important and definitional life of the system focused on activities in the shrine, variously presented in the hypothesis as Bethel, Gilgal, Shechem, or Shiloh.

According to this hypothesis, the tribes convened regularly at the shrine for a hearing of the Torah (Deut 31:10-13) and for taking oaths of allegiance that bound the tribes to each other in common loyalty to Yahweh, the God of the federation.[60] Thus the tribes regularly participated in these ceremonies, which ostensibly governed all parts of their life.

Noth's hypothesis, which largely captivated Old Testament scholarship (including U.S. scholarship, which ostensibly resisted some of his assumptions), goes far toward articulating the distinctiveness of Israel. Three themes became crucial for Old Testament scholarship in its concern for the peculiarity of Israel, which was historically based but which required theological articulation.

First, this group of tribes, which met regularly in order to profess a common loyalty, entered into a solemn covenantal agreement.[61] Covenant becomes the dis-

---

56. Gerhard von Rad, "The Form-Critical Problem of the Hexateuch," *The Problem of the Hexateuch and Other Essays* (New York: McGraw-Hill, 1966), saw that the promises to the ancestors formed the driving motif of the Pentateuch. See also David J. A. Clines, *The Theme of the Pentateuch* (JSOTSup 10; Sheffield: JSOT Press, 1978).

57. Jürgen Moltmann, *Theology of Hope: On the Ground and Implications of Christian Eschatology* (1967; Minneapolis: Fortress Press, 1993).

58. Alt, "The God of the Fathers," 62, termed those gods "tutors" (*paidagogei*) making preparation for Yahweh. The relation between the "religion of Genesis" and the Mosaic themes of the Pentateuch is not an obvious one; see Walter Moberly, *The Old Testament of the Old Testament: Patriarchal Narratives and Mosaic Yahwism* (OBT; Minneapolis: Fortress Press, 1992).

59. Martin Noth, *Das System der zwölf Stämme Israels* (BWANT 41; Stuttgart: Kohlhammer, 1930).

60. Frank M. Cross, "The Cultus of the Israelite League," *Canaanite Myth and Hebrew Epic: Essays in the History of the Religion of Israel* (Cambridge: Harvard University Press, 1973) 77–90 and passim, substituted the term *federation* (as well as *league*) for the more problematic term *amphictyony* that Noth had offered.

61. Thus the Alt-Noth hypothesis had argued that covenant was an early and definitive idea in Israel. On a challenge to that hypothesis, see especially Ernest W. Nicholson, *God and His People: Covenant and Theology in the Old Testament* (Oxford: Clarendon Press, 1988).

tinguishing mark of this community, giving its members a peculiar identity in a world of many tribes and nations. Israel, as it was understood, was unlike all other tribes and nations, because none of the others was so bound in allegiance to this God (cf. Deut 4:7-8).

Second, the core substance of this covenantal agreement was in the proclamation of law, whereby this unrivaled sovereign pronounced (through covenant mediators) a sovereign will for the community that was rigorous, demanding, and uncompromising. It may well be that we now have in the text various versions of what was proclaimed. Focus for such material tends to be on the Decalogue (Exod 20:1-17), a second decalogue (Exod 34:10-26), and a stringent recital of curses in Deut 27:15-26. These uncompromising utterances sought to bring every phase of Israel's life, personal and public, civil and cultic, under the peculiar will and purpose of Yahweh.

A third feature of this tribal confederation was apparently holy war. Scholars subsequent to Noth, especially von Rad, have hypothesized that one dimension of the confederation was a military possibility that was legitimated and ordered by cultic activity.[62] The purpose of the military dimension of the community was a mutual defense pact, whereby the member tribes pledged to support each other in times of military danger (cf. Judg 5:13-18). This ideology of war, however, was not simply a political agreement of mutual support. It was also an affirmation that Yahweh, the sovereign of the federation, was a warrior God who actively intervened on behalf of the member tribes as a military agent.[63]

We should note two important features of this theory of war. First, scholars have not been agreed whether this theory of war served only for defensive purposes or if it also applied to offensive campaigns. Because this theory of war is peculiarly appropriate only to the tribes, it seemingly did not pertain in the first instant to the wars of territorial aggrandizement fought by the subsequent monarchy (cf. 2 Sam 8:6, 14). Second, it is of crucial importance to note that this notion of holy war, as understood in this phase of Old Testament scholarship, was not about Israel fighting for Yahweh. It was rather about Yahweh fighting for Israel. Yahweh thus is understood to be an active agent capable of taking an armed initiative, and thus like no other god.

On all three counts—apodictic law, proclamation of law, and holy war—these historians make a comprehensive case for the distinctiveness of Israel, which was in fact a theological distinctiveness rooted in the peculiar character of Yahweh, the putative God of the federation. It is this taproot of Yahweh's distinctiveness that gave impetus to the historical distinctiveness of Israel as a peculiar people among the nations and tribes (cf. 2 Sam 7:22-23).

While this remarkable German scholarship provided the primary categories for Old Testament theology, a comparable development in the United States was, in

---

62. Gerhard von Rad, *Holy War in Ancient Israel* (Grand Rapids: Eerdmans, 1991).
63. See Patrick D. Miller, *The Divine Warrior in Early Israel* (HSM 5; Cambridge: Harvard University Press, 1973).

its own way, equally remarkable, inventive, and influential. The dominant figure in U.S. scholarship was William Foxwell Albright, in many ways the U.S. counterpart to Alt in Germany. Albright, a learned scholar, was the main force in generating and defining biblical archaeology, a peculiarly U.S. enterprise.[64] Albright worked particularly in the Late Bronze and Early Iron periods, and thus was concerned with the formative period of Israel's pre-monarchal life. His work in archaeology tended to "demonstrate" the "historical" reliability of the biblical text. Moreover, in his great book, *From Stone Age to Christianity*, Albright directly denounced the dominant developmental hypothesis that claimed that Israel's great theological self-understanding was late.[65] He insisted that everything important for Israel's faith was already present, *in nuce*, already in Moses.

Albright's work was presented as inductive research. That is, he took the archaeological-historical data as he found them and discovered that in compelling ways the data confirmed the biblical claim of Israel's distinctiveness in the historical process. Recently Burke Long has provided evidence that Albright's inductive archaeology was driven from the beginning by a deep commitment to and trust in the theological insistence of the biblical text itself concerning the cruciality of Yahweh and the distinctiveness of Israel.[66] Such an argument does not greatly detract from Albright's work. Rather it reminds us of what should have been recognized all along: there is no innocent "history"; all "history" carries with it some theological intentionality. This is equally true for those scholars who now expose the ideology operative in the Albrightian synthesis.

The United States enterprise under the aegis of Albright proceeded with great energy in the 1940s, '50s, and '60s. While the Albright school had great conflicts with the German school of Alt and Noth and often seemed opposed to it in principle, *it is clear in retrospect that the distinguishable programs of Alt and Albright performed service in the same enterprise.* Their shared purpose, though not clearly articulated at the time, was to exposit the Old Testament in ways that demonstrated *the singularity of Israel's faith.* This accent is surely a response against the developmentalism that preceded their work. The chosen mode of articulation

---

64. See William Foxwell Albright, *Archaeology and the Religion of Israel* (Baltimore: Johns Hopkins University Press, 1946); Albright, *History, Archaeology, and Christian Humanism* (London: Adam and Charles Black, 1965); and G. Ernest Wright, *Biblical Archaeology* (Philadelphia: Westminster Press, 1957). Albright and especially his student Wright urged that archaeology could greatly illuminate the specificity of the Bible. The interface of Bible and archaeology is not an easy one, and the notion of biblical archaeology is now largely rejected. Among others, William Dever, "The Contribution of Archaeology to the Study of Canaanite and Early Israelite Religion," *Ancient Israelite Religion: Essays in Honor of Frank Moore Cross* (ed. Patrick D. Miller et al.; Philadelphia: Fortress Press, 1987) 209–47, has urged that archaeology must be taken on its own terms as a scientific enterprise with no particular reference to the Bible.

65. William Foxwell Albright, *From Stone Age to Christianity: Monotheism and the Historical Process* (Baltimore: Johns Hopkins University Press, 1946) 11.

66. Burke O. Long, "Mythic Trope in the Autobiography of William Foxwell Albright," *Biblical Archaeology* 56 (1993) 36–45. For a more vitriolic assessment of Noth's work, see Thomas L. Thompson, "Martin Noth and the History of Israel," *The History of Israel's Traditions: The Heritage of Martin Noth* (ed. Steven L. McKenzie and M. Patrick Graham; JSOTSup 182; Sheffield: Sheffield Academic Press, 1994) 81–90.

of this advocacy in both cases was history, perhaps better stated as historical reconstruction. In both cases, however, the historical reconstruction served crucial theological purposes. And at least in the case of Albright, Long has suggested that the theological purpose was not accidental but was intentional and determinative.

Two dimensions of the Albright program merit our attention. First, G. Ernest Wright, one of the earliest of Albright's students, was the most formidable theological interpreter of the Albright group and functioned in ways not unlike von Rad in the Alt school. Wright issued a series of monographs that contended for the distinctiveness of Israel: *The Challenge of Israel's Faith* (1944), *The Old Testament against Its Environment* (1950), and *God Who Acts* (1952).[67] In the first two works, Wright contended directly for the distinctiveness of Israel's faith. In the first of these, Israel's faith is understood as a challenge to Canaanite religion. In the second, the argument hardens so that Israel's faith is contrasted with polytheism in every regard. The importance of Wright's assertion can be appreciated only if we recall the older critical consensus that Israel's monotheism emerged belatedly from an Israelite faith that had been polytheistic. Thus Wright insists that Israel's monotheism was already inchoately present from the Mosaic period.

The second major contribution we may mention from the Albright trajectory of scholarship is George Mendenhall's *Law and Covenant*, published in 1954.[68] This small monograph completely refocused Old Testament scholarship in nothing short of a revolution of categories. Mendenhall proposed that the Mosaic covenant was patterned on international political treaties of the fourteenth century B.C.E., so that the idiom and intent of Moses' covenant at Sinai had nothing in common with Canaanite religion. From its beginning, Israel's covenant was a political theory of justice. Mendenhall thus suggested that the Decalogue constitutes a policy statement for the ordering of Israel's peculiar notion of public power. The absolute power of Yahweh thus deabsolutizes every other claim and pretension to power, and so makes Israel a most peculiar political phenomenon in the world of Canaanite religion.[69]

The achievements of the Alt and Albright schools, to be sure, are a long way from the initiatory work of Barth. It is important, nonetheless, to see that the work of these Old Testament scholars in the two generations after Barth occupied ground that only Barth had made available. That is, they programmatically insisted on *Israel's distinctiveness*. While they are engaged in historical-critical work, that work surely has an eye fixed on theological gains. It is possible to conclude that

---

67. G. Ernest Wright, *The Challenge of Israel's Faith* (Chicago: University of Chicago Press, 1944); *The Old Testament against Its Environment* (SBT 2; London: SCM Press, 1950); and *God Who Acts: Biblical Theology as Recital* (SBT 8; London: SCM Press, 1952).

68. George E. Mendenhall, *Law and Covenant in Israel and the Ancient Near East* (Pittsburgh: Biblical Colloquium, 1954).

69. George E. Mendenhall, "The Conflict between Value Systems and Social Control," *Unity and Diversity: Essays in the History, Literature, and Religion of the Ancient Near East* (ed. Hans Goedicke and J. J. M. Roberts; Baltimore: Johns Hopkins University Press, 1975) 169–80. See also John Bright, *The Kingdom of God in Bible and Church* (London: Lutterworth Press, 1955).

they "cheated" as historians and sponsored interpretive constructs that made certain kinds of theological claims inevitable. Or it is possible to consider their work somewhat more innocent, if we recognize that notions of distinctiveness were in the air, and one proposal gave room for or generated another.

However one may assess the motives of this scholarship, two things are clear. First, the scholarship generated by Alt and Albright completely dominated Old Testament studies for two generations and went far toward challenging the developmental scheme that had gone along with historical criticism. Second, for their time and place, these scholars found an adequate way to hold together critical practice and theological interest. Subsequently, of course, it is possible to wonder about the effectiveness and legitimacy of this enterprise. It should be noted nonetheless that during the period of this dominant scholarship, few scholars of note failed to subscribe to the model and constructs for the history of Israel that Alt and Albright proposed. Eventually serious critical response would be generated . . . but not for a time.

These two scholarly programs in Germany and in the United States effected an important reversal of the nineteenth-century critical consensus. Whereas that consensus had been determinedly evolutionary, this twentieth-century work resisted evolutionary understandings of Israel's history. The older critical consensus found Israel's faith embedded in and arising from its cultural religious environment and continuing to partake of that environment. Now, however, it was proposed that Israel's faith was *de novo,* in its very emergence incompatible with and in opposition to its cultural religious environment. In what appears to be a by-product of such an inversion, we may also notice what is for us a more crucial matter.

The nineteenth-century consensus sought to describe what had appeared historically. It did so without rendering explicit value judgment, though the evolutionary evaluative criteria of nineteenth-century objective rationalism did operate. In this newer research in mid-twentieth century, scholarship was not content to describe what had emerged in the life of Israel, but inclined to regard the emergence of Israel as itself normative. Whereas nineteenth-century scholarship was dominated by university scholars who stood in important tension with church authority or at least owed little to it, the most influential Old Testament interpreters in the twentieth century were admitted and convinced church believers, and they understood their work to be in the service of the church. (Although not as explicitly as Barth, they intended to serve the preaching of the church.)[70]

For purposes of our subsequent reflection, it is important to recognize that these several scholars understood themselves to be historians. That is, they assumed they were investigating "how it was" and "what had happened." In their investigation,

---

70. The theological revolution instigated by Karl Barth, especially in the climate of the rise of National Socialism in Germany, made the theological task urgent. It is fair to say that this impetus at the beginning of the twentieth century lasted as a driving force in Old Testament theology until as late as 1970. This church orientation is clearly true for Albright, Wright, and von Rad. It is less directly so for Noth, and not evident in Alt. Nonetheless, even the work of Alt could be readily mobilized for such an interest.

the biblical text itself was important, *but the Bible was not important on its own terms and for its own sake.* It was important as a comment on or a clue to what was true "on the ground"—that is, logically and empirically. A kind of innocent realism is at work here, in which no suspicious distance is entertained between text and reality. Historical investigation must assume some such correlation between event and textual evidence; in retrospect, however, the correlations here assumed are excessively innocent. That innocence is at least in part a theological innocence, a readiness to trust the biblical text as a reliable witness to historical reality. As we shall see, this uncritical and unexamined practice came to be recognized as increasingly problematic. But for now, the assumptions of Alt and Albright and their heirs provided a fully reconstructed world in which Israel's text could be intelligently faced and Israel's faith could be determinedly understood and practiced.

Thus it is evident, in my judgment, that Barth permitted and authorized a whole new work of Old Testament interpretation that focused on what were taken to be its normative theological claims concerning the sovereignty of Yahweh and the covenant obligations of Israel. This set of interpretive constructs becomes most illuminating when we consider the two major syntheses of Old Testament theology in the twentieth century.

Walther Eichrodt

The first important model of Old Testament theology after the Barthian revolution of 1919 was the work of Walther Eichrodt, published in three volumes in German in 1933 and only belatedly in English (in two volumes) in 1961 and 1967.[71] Eichrodt was a colleague of Barth at Basel, though the extent of their interaction is not known. The publication date of 1933 does not indicate the beginning of Eichrodt's research and writing on the subject. Eichrodt's formative work was either in the context of or in the wake of Barth's initial work, and the publication in German came at the outset of the National Socialist crisis in Germany.

Eichrodt's preface to his initial edition in 1933 is duly modest. He indicates that he is undertaking a very difficult task, and that he can contribute, if only provisionally, to the new work that now must be faced. Two points in the preface are especially noteworthy. First, positively, Eichrodt considers the Old Testament "as a self-contained entity exhibiting, despite ever-changing historical condition, a constant basic tendency and character."[72] That is, Eichrodt acknowledges the historical dynamic and change in the text that has preoccupied the last century of critical scholarship. Against that, however, Eichrodt dares to identify what is "a constant basic tendency and character." Second, negatively, he takes aim against "the values of rationalistic individualism and the structure-patterns of developmental theories"—that is, against the entire descriptive enterprise of historical criticism.[73]

---

71. Walther Eichrodt, *Theology of the Old Testament* (2 vols.; OTL; Philadelphia: Westminster Press, 1961, 1967).

72. Ibid., 1:11.

73. Ibid., 1:12.

Eichrodt self-consciously seeks to articulate what is constant, and therefore norma-tive, against an excessively developmental historical perspective. *Mutatis mutandis*, Eichrodt seeks to do in Old Testament study what Barth undertook in dogmatic theology, against his liberal antecedents.

Eichrodt's program is to explore how all of the variations and developments of Israel's religion can be seen to be in the service of a single conceptual notion, covenant. It is impossible to overestimate what a singular intellectual achievement this project is. In his three volumes, Eichrodt considers the covenant God, the instruments of covenant, and covenant in the life of individual persons.

It is conventional to cite Eichrodt's importance in terms of his attempt to sub-sume all of the Old Testament under one idea. And indeed, he does this. That he works with "one idea" means that his approach is intellectual, cognitive, and conceptual. It is an extraordinary insight to be able to see that this one idea illu-minates and brings into relation a rich variety of themes and images. Subsequently other scholars have also worked with a single concept.[74] For them, as for Eichrodt, the rich diversity of the text presents the risk that the "one idea" must be inevitably reductionist. To the extent that a scholar focuses on one idea, the approach is exces-sively cognitive and must necessarily tilt matters toward thinking, as distinct from the rich emotional, aesthetic, rhetorical, and cultural reality that does not easily accommodate the cognitive.

Eichrodt's greatness, however, is not only that he worked with one idea; it is that his one idea was *covenantal relatedness*. While Eichrodt's articulation of his central notion now seems highly conceptual, he had nonetheless seen and expressed what is most characteristic of Israel's vision of reality: namely, that all of reality—God, Israel, human persons, the world—partakes of a quality of *relatedness*. Eichrodt's entire program is to consider the quality of relatedness from as many angles as possible, with reference to as many subjects as possible.

Four aspects of his argument continue to be generative well beyond his own conceptualization:

(1) Without doubt, Eichrodt's program intends to be polemical. In his initial preface, he weighs against "rationalistic individualism" and "the structure-patterns of developmental theories." In our current parlance, we might say that Eichrodt polemicizes against the categories of modernity that critical study had imposed on the text; these categories feature individualism and autonomy and resist artic-ulations that are dialogical and therefore complex, ambiguous, and unsettled. The fundamental relatedness of all of reality, which is most characteristic of Israel's faith, makes the Old Testament inimical to the categories of modernity. For, as Eichrodt understood, "being" in the Old Testament means "being with": being in the presence of, being committed to, being identified with, being at risk with. With this thematic, Eichrodt shows that all of our conventional attempts to contain the

---

74. E.g., Samuel Terrien, *The Elusive Presence: Toward a New Biblical Theology* (New York: Harper and Row, 1978).

Old Testament either in modern-scientific or in theological-scholastic categories are futile. To be sure, Eichrodt himself was held in check by categories that did not permit him to explore fully his own rich insight about relatedness. But for any who took notice of his work, he has required a complete redescription of more conventional categories of interpretation.

(2) At the outset, Eichrodt asserts that this covenantal relation is "bilateral... two-sided."[75] The implications of this insight are enormous. In his supplemental book, *Man in the Old Testament*, however, Eichrodt could not go far with this notion, for his discussion of "man" revolves around the issues of God's sovereignty and "man's" obedience.[76] The relation is characteristically portrayed as a one-way enterprise from God to humankind, with no significant action in the other direction. Eichrodt's own resistance to the category of "bilateral" indicates how this insight fights against all of our classical, conventional theological presuppositions.

It remained for others long after Eichrodt, and perhaps culminating in Jürgen Moltmann's *The Crucified God*, to see that God's relatedness entails God's risk and vulnerability.[77] As we shall see later, this break with "common theology" represents a defining characteristic of Israel's faith.[78] While Eichrodt did not follow his own inclination in this regard, he did provide the categories for subsequent interpretive work.

(3) Eichrodt's accent on covenant did not happen in a vacuum, but in a world that was coming to see reality in terms of interactionism. It may be a remote connection to mention the emergence of the newer physics in the decades just before Eichrodt. It is clear, however, that in his lifetime reality was being reunderstood scientifically in terms of interactionism that broke down the notion of discrete, distinct elements. Closer to hand, we may note Hans Urs von Balthasar's remarkable awareness that in the period after the end of the war in 1918 the notion of reality as interactionist was alive in the venturesome exploration of a variety of thinkers.[79] Among these, we may mention Emil Brunner's notion of encounter and, more programmatically, Martin Buber's "I-Thou," in which Buber understood that human life is essentially generated in and through the gift of a "thou" that permits and authorizes an "I."[80] Indeed, we may wonder if this interactionism is

---

75. Eichrodt, *Old Testament Theology*, 1:37.

76. Walther Eichrodt, *Man in the Old Testament* (SBT 4; London: SCM Press, 1951).

77. Jürgen Moltmann, *The Crucified God: The Cross of Christ as the Foundation and Criticism of Christian Theology* (1974; Minneapolis: Fortress Press, 1993).

78. See chap. 2, n. 39; also Walter Brueggemann, "A Shape for Old Testament Theology I: Structure Legitimation," *CBQ* 47 (1985) 28–46.

79. Hans Urs von Balthasar, *Theo-Drama: Theological Dramatic Theory* 1: *Prolegomena* (San Francisco: Ignatius Press, 1988) 626–27.

80. Emil Brunner, *Truth as Encounter* (London: SCM Press, 1964), Martin Buber, *I and Thou* (Edinburgh: T. & T. Clark, 1969). See Rivka Horwitz, *Buber's Way to I and Thou: An Historical Analysis of the First Publication of Martin Buber's Lectures, "Religion als Gegenwort"* (Heidelberg: Lambert Schneider, 1978); and Martin Buber, "Dialogue," *Between Man and Man* (trans. Ronald Gregor Smith; London: Kegan Paul, 1947) 1–39.

in some way a characteristically Jewish affirmation, as it is now articulated in the remarkable work of Emmanuel Levinas.[81]

Eichrodt's disciplined, cognitive work does not go as far as an exploration of the radicality of this interactionist notion of the bilateral. As we shall see, the extent and limit of the bilateral constitutes a major issue in Israel's faith. The extreme form of the bilateral is to the recognition that *God is also a party to the interaction and is in some sense dependent on the life and witness of Israel for God's own sovereignty in the world.*[82] Thus, if "bilateral" entails something that is genuinely mutual, restrained as the insight may be, we begin to see the radical possibility of Eichrodt's core insight. The rubric of covenant thus requires a departure from the more conventional philosophical categories of immanence and transcendence and the entire Cartesian temptation to dualism, for covenant is not balancing of transcendence and immanence, but is a complete rejection of a dualism that is too tidy and free of risk.

(4) Finally we come to the second part of Eichrodt's presentation, "God and the world." This volume has not received great attention, but Eichrodt's readiness to relate "cosmology and creation" to covenant suggests that even "the world" is to be understood not as an independent system, but as a creature and partner to God. This is an enormous claim when viewed in the context of Enlightenment thinking about the autonomy of the scientific world. Eichrodt's presentation parallels Barth's rigorous attempt to show that creation and covenant are complementary articulations, external and internal, of the same reality.[83] To subsume creation under the rubric of covenant directly nullifies any attempt to understand the world either autonomously or pantheistically. Even attempts at panentheism pose issues in a very different form from those of covenanting.[84] Thus Eichrodt's capacity to treat creation in this way was an extraordinary insight in his time and place. Moreover, as interest grows in the relation between "the ecological crisis" and biblical faith, this covenantal interpretation of world reality is likely to continue to be important.[85]

---

81. Emmanuel Levinas, *Totality and Infinity: An Essay on Exteriority* (Pittsburgh: Duquesne University Press, 1969). The later work of Levinas makes the Jewish dimension of his thought more explicit, but *Totality and Infinity* provides the decisive categories for his work, in which he presents face-to-faceness as definitive for human existence. Such a way of thinking is intimately connected to Israel's most elemental notions of covenant.

82. The assertion that the relationship of God and Israel is so radically bilateral as to make God a genuine party to the interaction is a step that Christian theology characteristically resists. It is a step, however, that Jewish thought can entertain. Moreover, such a notion seems evident in the text of the Old Testament. It is perhaps the measure of the impingement of covenantal transactionism on divine sovereignty that constitutes the most difficult and most important issue in biblical theology. That question, in Christian categories, emerges in the relationship between the cross and Easter.

83. Karl Barth, *Church Dogmatics* 3/1, *The Doctrine of Creation* (Edinburgh: T. & T. Clark, 1958) 42–329.

84. On panentheism, see the discussion of Jürgen Moltmann, *God in Creation: An Ecological Doctrine of Creation* (London: SCM Press, 1985).

85. On creation, understood in covenantal terms, as the horizon of Old Testament theology, see Walter Brueggemann, "The Loss and Recovery of 'Creation' in Old Testament Theology," *TToday* 53 (1996) 177–90; note especially the references to the work of Hans Heinrich Schmid and Rolf Knierim. See also Patrick D. Miller, "Creation and Covenant," *Biblical Theology: Problems and Perspectives* (ed. Steven J. Kraftchick et al.; Nashville: Abingdon Press, 1995) 155–68.

As Eichrodt seeks to resist rationalistic individualism, he also shows the way in which the normative faith of Israel refuses to regard the world as an autonomous reality, readily subject to human use and abuse. The world, rather, is situated in the context of Yahweh's governance and in the interaction with Yahweh that makes life possible.

It is unfortunate that Eichrodt's work is too easily and too often understood methodologically simply as presenting the Old Testament under "one idea." Covenant is no accidental "one idea." It is not as though covenant is one among many possible themes he might have chosen as an organizing principle. In this theme, it is evident that Eichrodt has broken new ground within the context of historical criticism. Not only his method but also the substance of his exposition broke decisively with rationalistic developmentalism. The relational quality of reality signified in the term *covenant* moves against all naturalistic presuppositions, so that no notion of developmentalism could ever move Israel from "common theology" to the peculiar claims it makes in its faith. It is precisely this *novum* that Eichrodt finds early, late, and pervasive in Israel's faith. And it is this *novum* on which Eichrodt stays fixed in his exposition.

Gerhard von Rad

The second great model for Old Testament theology in this post-Barth context, a model that has exercised much influence in the United States, is the work of Gerhard von Rad.[86] His work appeared in two volumes twenty years after Eichrodt's.[87] More than is the case with Eichrodt, von Rad is greatly indebted to his teacher Albrecht Alt and his cohort Martin Noth and their historical constructs concerning pre-monarchal, tribal Israel.[88] Like Alt and Noth, von Rad regards this period as theologically normative. As we have seen, Alt and Noth hypothesized that premonarchal Israel was organized into a tribal confederation that was constituted by regular worship, the proclamation of Torah commandments, and the periodic reaffirmation of covenant loyalty.

Von Rad, well beyond Alt and Noth, had a remarkable theological sensitivity, whereby he was able to place the sociohistorical constructs of Alt and Noth in the service of theological interpretation. Von Rad's programmatic statement, which his two-volume work subsequently exposited, appeared as early as 1938 as "The Form-Critical Problem of the Hexateuch." Note well that this enormously influential essay, appearing in English only in 1966, came within a decade of the great hy-

---

86. Von Rad, "The Form-Critical Problem of the Hexateuch," 1–78; *Old Testament Theology* (2 vols.; San Francisco: Harper and Row, 1962, 1965).

87. The two volumes have been presented in several German editions. The English edition of 1962, 1965 is based on the second German edition.

88. Eichrodt did his work even as Alt and Noth were articulating their influential historical proposals and reconstructions. Eichrodt, however, was asking a very different kind of question and had no interest in such speculative historical reconstructions.

potheses of Alt and Noth and soon after the publication of Eichrodt's work.[89] It is also important to note that it appeared immediately after the Barmen Declaration of 1934, and surely reflects the church struggle in Germany with reference to the National Socialist regime.

Von Rad's beginning point in his essay of 1938, based on a form-critical analysis, is to propose that the recitals of Deut 26:5-9, 6:20-24, and Josh 24:1-13 constitute Israel's earliest and most characteristic theological articulation.[90] These highly studied recitals, situated in contexts of worship and instruction, narrate Israel's remembered "historical" experience of the decisive ways in which Yahweh, the God of Israel, has intervened and acted in the life of Israel. Thus at the outset, von Rad understands Israel's theology as *a narrative rendering* of what has happened in Israel's past, a narrative that still has decisive, defining power for subsequent generations.

The substance of the credo recital itself, in its earliest formulations, consists in three primary memories. First comes a brief allusion to the ancestors who appear in Genesis 12–36, but the decisive events are the liberation from Egyptian slavery and the entry into the land of promise. Thus Israel's confessional life is situated between "going out" (of Egypt) and "coming in" (to the land of promise). Both events derive from and depend on the sovereign and faithful involvement of Yahweh in the life of Israel.

From this core recital, to which he points as the beginning of Israel's faith, von Rad proposes two developments that bring Israel's faith to its full expression. First, this thin line of recital over time was filled out not only in greater detail, but also with other themes: the "addition" (*Vorbau*) of the creation materials of Genesis 1–11 (in their early parts); the later "development" (*Ausbau*) of the ancestral materials of Genesis 12–50, which in the initial credo had been only a passing reference; and the belated "inclusion" (*Einbau*) of the Sinai material, which had had an independent development. These additional features, when all in place, provided the outline for what subsequently became the Hexateuch (Genesis–Joshua). This enlarged credo provides the "story line" for Israel's faith, stretching from the promise of the land in Gen 12:1-3 to the completed settlement in the land in Josh 21:43-45. Thus Israel's faith moves in a great arc from promise to fulfillment.[91]

Second, the recital itself as stated—for example, in Deut 26:5-9—occurs in an act of worship. That is, the recital is a liturgical act. In the ongoing life of Israel, however, with its advancing secularization, the recital was taken out of the context of worship and became simply an epic recital, whereby Israel asserted its place in

---

89. Lamentably this decisive essay was not published in English until 1966. It had exercised important influence in the United States before its translation, especially in the work of George Ernest Wright.

90. That von Rad regards these recitals as early, at the chronological beginning of a trajectory of traditions, indicates the large extent to which von Rad attempted to continue to work in historical categories.

91. Von Rad, "The Form-Critical Problem of the Hexateuch," 68–74.

the world vis-à-vis the other peoples of the world and its raison d'être and mission in the world.[92]

Von Rad's understanding of Old Testament theology is that it is an ongoing "traditioning" process in which each subsequent generation in Israel retells the narrative recital, but retells it with the incorporation of new materials and with a recasting, so that the ancient recital may be kept pertinent to new circumstance and new crisis.[93] The completed form of the tradition is then the accumulation of many retellings of Israel's core memory. While many new materials and new construals are introduced in the process, the core material is constant.

The essay of 1938 established the categories for von Rad's subsequent theology. Von Rad was drawn to term these stylized recitals as credos, as bottom-line articulations of what is unquestioned and nonnegotiable in Israel's faith. The proximity of von Rad's enterprise to the confessing church in Germany surely suggests that von Rad imagined an Israelite community that was, not unlike the German church, seeking to find standing ground against a formidable theological alternative. In Israel's case, the challenge was of "Canaanite religion"; in the case of the German church, it was the blood-and-soil ideology of the National Socialist regime.[94]

The 1938 essay on the Hexateuch became the substance and the program of the first volume of von Rad's Old Testament theology, which is subtitled "The Theology of Israel's Historical Traditions."[95] This volume is essentially an exposition of the themes of the Hexateuch that are in substance the characteristic "actions" of Yahweh, whereby Yahweh has decisively intervened in the life of Israel. This first volume, through which von Rad has exercised his greatest influence, has made it possible to understand Israel's faith in a narrative mode. Thus the Old Testament is, in the first instant, the *constant retelling* of the canonical tale of Israel's life with Yahweh. Von Rad understands this process of retelling as Israel's central theological activity. Each new generation "attempts to make the divine acts of salvation relevant for every new age and day—this ever new reaching-out to and avowal of God's acts which in the end made the old creedal statements grow into such enormous masses of tradition."[96] Von Rad appreciates and calls attention to the historical dynamic of Israel's faith and the ongoing process whereby the material required new articulation. Many scholars have noted that, in contrast to Eichrodt's work, von Rad's theology lacks a center, and thus one may not say that there is one normative

---

92. Von Rad spoke of the Hexateuch as "an aetiology" for Israel; ibid., 66.

93. On this method, see Douglas A. Knight, *Rediscovering the Traditions of Israel: The Development of the Traditio-historical Research of the Old Testament, with Special Consideration of Scandinavian Contributions* (SBLDS 9; Missoula, Mont.: Scholars Press, 1975).

94. We are now able to see that "Canaanite religion" became, in this phase of scholarship, a foil for the articulation of Israel's distinctiveness. That cipher is still in use, as in current polemics against feminist theology, which in some quarters is regarded as a reembrace of Canaanite religion. It is clear that the contrast between Israelite and Canaanite religion was greatly overstated. It is equally clear that the use of this antithesis by way of continuing analogy is most problematic.

95. Von Rad, *Old Testament Theology* 1: *The Theology of Israel's Historical Traditions*.

96. Ibid., 1:vi.

articulation; rather it is the ongoing process itself that is normative,[97] and each new generation is invited to participate in this ongoing normative, norm-giving process.

In making this genuinely innovative proposal that focuses on the ongoing historical dynamic, von Rad self-consciously takes critical aim at theologies that are organized "under the heading of various doctrines [which] cannot do justice to these creedal statements which... are completely tied up with history, or to this grounding of Israel's faith upon a few divine acts of salvation and the effort to gain an ever new understanding of them...."[98] In this assertion von Rad speaks against Eichrodt's model, which he regards as too much committed to doctrinal, thematic accents to take into account the vitality of the material itself. Thus von Rad stands almost alone among major Old Testament interpreters in refusing an ideational approach, in an attempt to witness to the character of the material itself.

The substance of Old Testament theology, as von Rad presented it in volume 1, consists in a recital of God's "mighty deeds" that had been worked in Israel's past. These mighty acts continued to claim Israel's imagination and to evoke Israel's trust and confidence. Israel trusted that the God who had delivered, led, and given land would continue to act in the same ways in the present and into the future.

Von Rad's "theology of recital" in volume 1 was matched in the United States by the publication in 1952 of *God Who Acts: Biblical Theology as Recital* by G. Ernest Wright.[99] This small monograph presented in clear, much more available form a model of theology similar to von Rad's. Wright refers to von Rad's essays of 1938 and was no doubt influenced by the German scholar.[100] It is not to be imagined, however, that Wright is simply trading upon von Rad, for Wright's earlier work shows a movement in the same direction, independent of von Rad. In any case, as a brilliant teacher, churchman, and interpreter, Wright exercised disproportionate influence in the United States, especially as von Rad's theology did not appear in English until 1962, a full decade after *God Who Acts*.[101]

The substance of Wright's book, closely parallel to that of von Rad, established the recital of "mighty deeds" as the substance of Israel's faith. The work of von Rad and Wright, along with others of like mind, generated in the mid-twentieth century extraordinary energy and excitement in biblical theology in what came to be called by its critics "the biblical theology movement" or, more pejoratively, "the so-called biblical theology movement." This relatively accessible interpretive model, which was not complicated by philosophical matters, produced a formida-

---

97. On the problem of a "center" in Old Testament theology, see H. Graf Reventlow, *Problems of Old Testament Theology in the Twentieth Century* (London: SCM Press, 1985) 125–33. Attention should be paid to Rudolf Smend, *Die Mitte des Alten Testaments* (ThStud 101; Zürich: EVZ-Verlag, 1970); and *Die Bundesformel* (ThStud 68; Zürich: EVZ-Verlag, 1963).

98. Von Rad, *Old Testament Theology*, 1:vi.

99. See n. 67 above.

100. See Wright, *God Who Acts*, 70.

101. The other early and important presentation of von Rad's work in English was by B. Davie Napier, *From Faith to Faith: Essays in Old Testament Literature* (New York: Harper, 1955). I note my enormous debt to and appreciation of Napier's work, for it was this book that decisively drew me to Old Testament study.

ble engagement in the church with the actual substance of the Bible. Von Rad and Wright sought to reiterate the rhetoric of the Bible itself, without appeal to any dogmatic categories.

In retrospect, scholarship is now struck by the relative innocence of the presentation. When one assesses von Rad and Wright critically—that is, according to the categories of modernity—acute problems arise in their proposals. Von Rad insisted on the historicality of the events recited, and Wright was a leader in what came to be called biblical archaeology, which sought to provide historical counterparts to the theological claims of the recital.[102] While the notion that "God acts in history" made an appealing program, the category of history continued to vex this approach. Since the rise of historical criticism, biblical scholarship has been troubled by the seeming incapacity to leap across Gotthold Lessing's "ugly ditch" that separates the historical from the theological.[103] Some have attempted to make the connection by speaking of "secular history" and "salvation history," or by contrasting "historical minimum" and "theological maximum," but the problem persists.[104]

For example, in Exod 15:21, perhaps one of Israel's oldest poems, Miriam and the other women sing, "horse and rider he has thrown into the sea." As a theological articulation, this lyrical statement is clear enough. But what could it mean historically? Does the statement mean that the Israelite women saw Yahweh in the water, pushing Egyptian soldiers off their horses? If not that, what?

As another example, Wright commented on Moses' ability to catch quail in order to provide meat for Israel.[105] Wright proposes that the quail had flown across the sea, were completely exhausted, and so were easily picked up off the ground. If this ingenious proposal (which lacks any textual support) is credited, the wonder of the narrative is explained away; the meat is no longer a gift of Yahweh, as anyone can pick up exhausted quail. Wright's careless explanation satisfied the requirements of secular history, but salvation history evaporates in the process. Or must we finally say that creedal articulations of ancient Israel have a kind of pre-Enlightenment innocence about them, to which modernity has no credible access? In that case biblical interpreters must forgo the very concreteness that von Rad and Wright intended to accent, and we are left with an ideational scheme that has no contact with Israel's concrete, lived reality. Most of this critique of von Rad and Wright, however, was held in abeyance for several decades. While such a criticism now seems inescapable, in the peak years of biblical theology the perspective of recital gave great energy and viability to biblical interpretation.

---

102. Wright's publications at the interface of Bible and archaeology are many. See his summary and synthesis in *Biblical Archaeology*.

103. See Van Harvey, *The Historian and the Believer: The Morality of Historical Knowledge and Christian Belief* (New York: Macmillan, 1966); as well as Leo G. Perdue, *The Collapse of History* (OBT; Minneapolis: Fortress Press, 1994), on the problematic of this approach and on new initiatives in the face of its demise.

104. See von Rad, *Old Testament Theology*, 1:108.

105. Wright, *Biblical Archaeology*, 65.

Whatever else one may say in retrospect, von Rad and Wright took up Barth's demand that Old Testament interpretation should be not only descriptive, but also normative. This theology of recital focused on the peculiar God who worked normative acts, and on this peculiar community that benefited from and bore witness to these claims. No attempt was made to accommodate the recital to the intellectual requirements of historical positivism, and no concession was made to trim the Actor of these events to Enlightenment size. Von Rad insisted on the normativeness of these recitals for the Bible itself, and Wright went further in asserting the enduring authority of these events for the ongoing life of the church in the world. Here we are indeed a long distance from the historical reductionism of nineteenth-century developmentalism!

Von Rad completed his formal theology with a second volume on the prophets of Israel.[106] It is instructive that the subtitle of the volume is "The Theology of Israel's Prophetic Traditions." Von Rad placed at the beginning of the volume the text Isa 43:18-19: "Remember not the former things, nor consider the things of old. Behold, I am doing a new thing." In this second volume, von Rad explores the theme of continuity and discontinuity between Pentateuchal and prophetic traditions, or the tension between the old articulation of which he had made so much, and the fresh rearticulation of the tradition in a new time and circumstance. In this way von Rad shows how the prophetic voice in Israel takes up and utilizes the Hexateuchal tradition and also mounts a critique against the old tradition. As von Rad had shown how the repeated rearticulation of the credo had a profound dynamic, now he shows in a similar fashion that the prophetic dimension of Israel's faith is also dynamic in moving beyond the old tradition, thus witnessing and giving voice to the God of Israel who is always restlessly and vigorously at the front edge of Israel's life.

Von Rad's theology, presented in English in 1962 and 1965, was offered as a full and complete statement of Old Testament faith. It was soon observed that a theology of mighty deeds allowed no room for the wisdom materials of the Old Testament in which God did not "act." Indeed, one way to handle the problem of wisdom was to treat the sapiential materials of the Old Testament as substandard, largely borrowed, and largely utilitarian, so that they hardly qualify as elements of Israelite theology.[107] In his first volume, von Rad had devoted considerable coverage to the sapiential and psalmic materials under the rubric "Israel before Jahweh (Israel's answer)."[108] In fact, the rubric did not fit the material very well, for it is

---

106. Von Rad, *Old Testament Theology* 2: *The Theology of Israel's Prophetic Traditions*.

107. Wisdom continued to vex Old Testament theology throughout most of the twentieth century, for the controlling categories of the discipline made no room for such a perspective. See Perdue, *The Collapse of History*, on the reemergence of wisdom studies in Old Testament theology. The work of Hans Heinrich Schmid cannot be overestimated in this regard. Few scholars today would follow the dismissive strictures of H. D. Preuss against wisdom as a component of Old Testament theology. See Preuss, "Erwägungen zum theologischen Ort alttestamentlicher Weisheitsliteratur," *EvT* 30 (1970) 393–417; and "Das Gottes Bild der alteren Weisheit Israels," VTSup 23 (1972) 117–45.

108. Von Rad, *Old Testament Theology*, 1:355–459.

not obvious that these materials are in any sense a response to the credo tradition. It seems obvious that von Rad so placed the materials as a matter of convenience, in order to include them at all. Even though the materials did not fit his scheme very well, nevertheless in these pages von Rad exhibits his great theological sensitivity and his capacity for reading texts in showing that the wisdom materials are a meditation on the ordered reliability of the world under Yahweh's governance.[109] The exposition is brilliant, even though it does not fit the rubric and is given a subordinate position in von Rad's scheme of things.

One of the remarkable achievements of von Rad's scholarly career was his publication in the last year of his life of another important book, *Wisdom in Israel*.[110] Although it was published as an independent book, it is not inappropriate to regard it as the third volume in his theology. In the book, von Rad further explicates the themes he had adumbrated in the final section of volume 1. It is a mark of his greatness that when it became time in scholarship to move away from and beyond his model in volumes 1 and 2, von Rad himself led the way to new formulations.

In contrast with the sapiential discussion in volume 1, in this final volume the wisdom materials, especially Proverbs and Job, are not subordinated to the historical traditions but are treated on their own terms as legitimate and serious theological materials. As in the discussion of volume 1, this treatment of wisdom materials turns on the problem of the theological-moral order in the world, thus opening a question beyond the historical traditions to include consideration of creation as a datum of theology, and culminating in the crisis of theodicy.[111]

In many ways, von Rad in this latter volume does an about-face on his previous work. By the time this book was published in 1970, scholarly criticism of his credo hypothesis had begun to mount. It is as though von Rad recognized this criticism, as though he acknowledged that a theology of "mighty acts" had run its course. Instead of a defensive rear-guard action on their behalf, he writes a remarkably fresh reflection that anticipates the next phase of scholarship.[112] Thus this book is not subject to the criticisms concerning von Rad's treatment of the historical traditions, but moves in a wholly new direction.

As early as 1936 von Rad had written that creation was not a primary theme in Israel's faith, but had been articulated late and remained marginal.[113] It is likely

---

109. Walther Zimmerli, "The Place and Limit of the Wisdom Framework of the Old Testament Theology," *SJT* 17 (1964) 148, summarized the conclusion toward which scholarship moved: "Wisdom thinks resolutely within the framework of a theology of creation." Zimmerli's dictum anticipates major developments in the field, especially in the work of Hans Heinrich Schmid (cf. n. 114 below).

110. Gerhard von Rad, *Wisdom in Israel* (Nashville: Abingdon Press, 1972).

111. Claus Westermann has articulated "creation as a datum of theology" under the rubric of blessing. He notes that in the ordinary processes of life, the force for life given by God is operative. See Westermann, "Creation and History in the Old Testament," *The Gospel and Human Destiny* (ed. Vilmos Vajta; Minneapolis: Augsburg Publishing House, 1971) 11–38.

112. Since von Rad's book on wisdom, an enormous explosion of literature on the subject has occurred. Among the best summaries is that of Roland E. Murphy, *The Tree of Life: An Exploration of Biblical Wisdom Literature* (Garden City, N.Y.: Doubleday, 1990).

113. Gerhard von Rad, "The Theological Problem of the Old Testament Doctrine of Creation," *The Problem of the Hexateuch*, 131–42.

that von Rad's judgment on this matter was informed by Barth's strictures against "natural theology" as it had been taken up by the National Socialist regime in Germany and by the "German Christians."

In response to that national and church crisis, von Rad, perhaps following Barth, had simply bracketed out a possible emphasis on creation. Von Rad's early essay to this effect was enormously influential and almost single-handedly discouraged a generation of Old Testament scholars from undertaking a sustained study of creation materials. Only quite late, perhaps in the work of Hans Heinrich Schmid, did this matter begin to change.[114]

In his 1970 volume, however, it is as though von Rad recognized that we were in a new moment of theological possibility. Now the old polemic against Canaanite fertility religion, which had so propelled Wright's work, and all the slogans against "natural theology" had disappeared and seemed no longer pertinent. Many scholars joined the chorus, declaring that the recital theology concerning God's mighty acts was spent. None, however, recognized that more directly than von Rad himself. This does not mean that he repudiated his earlier work. Rather, he recognized that in a new circumstance new work needed to be done around new issues. His final book was an extraordinary act of taking up new issues. *Thus it is possible to see a great tension in von Rad's work between historical and sapiential materials, a tension that reflects a foundational detector of Old Testament faith.*

In the Wake of Eichrodt and von Rad

The high period of biblical theology, which was modeled in very different ways by Eichrodt and von Rad, is a matter of great importance for our continuing discussion. *But it is impossible, in my judgment, to take either Eichrodt or von Rad as a model for our own work.* It is more important, I suggest, to notice the way in which these works resonated with their own particular time and place, to recognize the brilliance of the works, and to see that a dimension of their brilliance is their context-specificity. Eichrodt responded to the challenge posed by Barth: to articulate that which is normative, characteristic, and enduring in Israel's faith, against a developmentalism that relativized every theological claim. Von Rad, perhaps more specifically, sought in the credo hypothesis both a substance and a method to find standing ground for faith in a social context that was fundamentally opposed to its confession. It seems clear that von Rad's model for interpretation was a venturesome response to the crisis of the German church in his early years. That response served well the United States church in the middle of the century, when the church sought standing ground amid the great upheavals of war and race. Both Eichrodt

---

114. Hans Heinrich Schmid, *Wesen und Geschichte der Weisheit: Eine Untersuchung zur altorientalischen und israelitischen Weisheitsliteratur* (BZAW 101; Berlin: A. Töpelmann, 1966); *Gerechtigkeit als Weltordnung: Hintergrund und Geschichte des alttestamentlichen Gerechtigkeitsbegriffes* (BHT 40; Tübingen: J. C. B. Mohr [Paul Siebeck], 1968); and "Creation, Righteousness, and Salvation: 'Creation Theology' as the Broad Horizon of Biblical Theology," *Creation in the Old Testament* (ed. Bernhard W. Anderson; Philadelphia: Fortress Press, 1984) 102–17.

and von Rad, as well as Wright, understood biblical faith as a faith over against its environment: either the Israelites in a Canaanite context, believers in a sea of positivistic developmentalism, or confessors amid a challenge of paganism. The drive for the normative was of enormous importance and was served well by these scholarly ventures.

In a retrospective sweep such as this one, it is possible to see that Eichrodt and von Rad were closely allied in this enterprise. It is important to notice their crucial differences in method and substance, but we cannot appreciate the boldness and imagination of their work until we have noticed that they are both responding (as was Barth) to an intellectual situation in which faith had become only a weak echo of cultural assumptions. In very different ways, they both asserted that faith from ancient Israel has its own claim to make. In their shared Christian context, they asserted that faith from ancient Israel, without excessively trimming that faith to Christian conviction, was important to the faithfulness and vitality of the church in their time and place.

In that shared passion, the differences between Eichrodt and von Rad and their two models are of great importance. Eichrodt, as we have seen, seeks to exposit "a *constant* basic tendency and character" to Old Testament theology. That is, he wants to overcome the developmentalism fostered by historical criticism, to locate what persists and defines Israel's faith in every changed historical circumstance. Von Rad, in contrast, seeks to underscore the *dynamic* of Israel's faith that is constantly being articulated in new versions of the ancient creedal formulation. Taking aim at Eichrodt and those who reiterate his model, von Rad asserts a theology open to the radical historicality of faith that cannot be contained in a set of doctrines. Von Rad aims to take the historical dynamic of Israel's faith seriously; this in turn means to take seriously the dynamic of the traditions, the ongoing formulation of faith that is always being reformulated. These different accents between Eichrodt and von Rad are important because they respectively stress the constancy and the dynamic of Israel's faith. When their work is considered in relation to each other, we may make three observations:

(1) In each case, what is affirmed is convincingly stated. Eichrodt has made a powerful case for the constancy of covenant, whereby the Old Testament understands everything in transactional categories. Conversely, von Rad has shown how Israel's several theological statements are "completely tied up with history," so that no single theological affirmation may be taken as ultimate but is sure to be displaced in turn by a subsequent articulation.

(2) At the same time, neither Eichrodt nor von Rad has been able to make an interpretive statement that makes sufficient allowance for what the other stresses. Eichrodt's accent on constancy makes it difficult, even as he seeks to do so, to allow for historical dynamic in Israel's faith; thus Eichrodt is easily indicted for reductionism. Conversely, von Rad's emphasis on historical dynamic means that in the end, one finds in his work many theologies but no single theological formulation. Indeed, von Rad concludes that such a statement is impossible. The

variegated material precludes such a statement without an unbearable cost in terms of reductionism.[115]

Given that the casting of issues since Barth has authorized the pursuit of the normative, a comparison of Eichrodt and von Rad reveals an unsettled issue in Old Testament theology: the interplay of the constant and the historical. Israel's articulation itself would seem to stress the historical, and in this von Rad seems to have the better part. That is what makes the Old Testament text odd for doing theology. But theology for a long time has stressed the constant, which Eichrodt seeks to do, and so this material does not respond well to "doing theology" as it has most often been understood. This is why many scholars have concluded that Old Testament theology is at the outset an impossibility, because the material referred to as Old Testament refuses a casting as theology. (As we shall see, the articulation of Brevard Childs concerning "[historical] *criticism*" and "*canonical* [theology]" is another way of getting at the same issue.)

Thus at the end of this period of scholarship set in motion by Barth, the issue of constancy and dynamic remains unsettled and perhaps must always remain so. *Pushed to its extreme, the tension between the constant and the dynamic may make the term "Old Testament theology" something of an oxymoron.* Our work now will be to see whether we can move in a fresh way concerning what is something of an impasse.

(3) Both Eichrodt and von Rad utilize methods intimately connected with the substance of the exposition. Thus Eichrodt is often cited as organizing his work around one idea. We must note well, however, that Eichrodt's idea of covenant is a *peculiarly characteristic and persuasive one* for Israel, so that Eichrodt must be understood as an expositor of covenant faith, and not of a method of "one idea." In the same way, von Rad is now recognized for his work on historical recital or, in his own words, "ancient creedal formulae." But his intent is not in the recitals per se, but in this *particular recital of a few paradigmatic memories* that give peculiar identity to Israel over the generations. These odd paradigmatic memories speak of a God who actively intrudes into the life of this community.

Thus, with both Eichrodt and von Rad, too much attention must not be given to method as such. For both are theological interpreters, and both wade into the peculiar and problematic substance of the Old Testament with a central concern for what is there. Finally it is the substantive claim of the text, and not method, that must preoccupy us. For Eichrodt, the main point is the God who covenants; for von Rad, it is the God who acts.

In making an assessment of this generative period of study dominated by Eichrodt and von Rad, we may pay attention to the passing assessment that each

---

115. This awareness of the variegated character of the text leads some to conclude that Old Testament theology is an impossibility. Such a judgment wants to resist the reductionism that is thought to be required by the term *theology*. Those who make that judgment are forced to settle for a history of Israelite religion. On the problem of pluralism in Old Testament faith and its implications for the history of that religion, see the excellent study of Rainer Albertz, *A History of Israelite Religion in the Old Testament Period* 1 (London: SCM Press, 1994), and 2: *From the Exile to the Maccabees* (Louisville: Westminster/John Knox, 1994).

makes of the other. Eichrodt's assessment of von Rad's work is explicit and succinct.[116] He identifies three criticisms of von Rad: (a) von Rad has not found a
way to take Israel's actual history seriously; (b) von Rad is able to offer "no self-
contained system of belief"; and (c) von Rad employs an unacceptable typological
approach. The conclusion Eichrodt draws is that von Rad proposes that "the existentialist interpretation of the biblical evidence is the right one."[117] Eichrodt's
own understanding of what constitutes theology—a unified, coherent intellectual
scheme that accounts for a normative claim of faith—may indeed be problematic
in itself, but it constitutes a major criticism often leveled at von Rad. The criticism
enables us to see how problematic von Rad's work is. But we are also enabled to
see what a daring, new thing he was seeking to do.

Although von Rad does not specifically respond to Eichrodt, in his introduction he explicitly mentions Edmond Jacob and Th. C. Vriezen, and Walther
Eichrodt must surely be in purview.[118] While there is no point-by-point response
to Eichrodt, von Rad is endlessly impressed by the pluralism and developmental
dynamic of the text itself, which proceeds as an "unfolding" or a series of "actual-
izations," each of which must be taken seriously and normatively in its own context
of utterance.[119] Von Rad's appeal to Heb 1:1 ("in many and various ways") is an
insistence that Israel's faith is not a series of variations behind which lies a single
coherent constancy; the series of variations is the thing itself.[120]

In the end, there is no resolution of this issue between Eichrodt and von Rad,
and it is this matter of pluralism and coherence that poses the most difficult issue
for the ongoing work of Old Testament theology. Moreover, as we shall see, in
the midst of the current epistemological shifts in which we must do our work, this
issue may provide an important opportunity for rediscovering the claim that the
Old Testament is "doing theology." Obviously, insofar as it is "doing theology," it
is a very different sort of exposition of faith.

It is important to note that while Eichrodt and von Rad together have dominated this generative period of study, Eichrodt came two decades before von Rad.
Eichrodt was perhaps indispensable in establishing a baseline of normativeness after a long season of developmentalism. Perhaps von Rad may rightly be understood
as a response against the (excessive?) closure given to Old Testament theology by
Eichrodt. As a result, the more lively discussion has concerned von Rad and not
Eichrodt, for von Rad's work has more recently occupied the center of the field.

Even as we find problems with von Rad's presentation, clearly there is no
responsible going back to the singular constancy of Eichrodt. The general epistemological climate in which we work and the current needs of the theological
community do not permit such a return. Since the moment when von Rad com-

---

116. Eichrodt, *Old Testament Theology*, 1:512–20.
117. Ibid., 1:515.
118. Von Rad, *Old Testament Theology*, 1:v.
119. Ibid., 1:115.
120. Ibid., 1:110.

pleted his work in 1970, we have been left with a dominant presentation that may appear to some, as to Eichrodt, as disastrously existential, or as faithfully, inescapably reflecting the character of the biblical material itself. It is material that insists on being taken seriously, and it refuses to be reduced or domesticated into a settled coherence. This refusal may not be simply a literary one but a theological one, pertaining to its central Subject. The restless character of the text that refuses excessive closure, which von Rad understood so well, is reflective of the One who is its main Character, who also refuses tameness or systematization. *Thus it is the very God uttered in these texts who lies behind the problems of perspective and method.*

An Ending to a Generative Period

It is now conventional to recognize that the great period of Old Testament theology dominated by Eichrodt, and even more by von Rad, came to an end around 1970. In fact the choice of an "ending" point depends on when and in what way one identifies the transition. I choose 1970, both because of the publication of von Rad's last book, *Wisdom in Israel,* which itself seemed to move "beyond von Rad," and because in the same year Brevard Childs issued his book *Biblical Theology in Crisis* and called attention to a changed situation in Old Testament theology.[121] In 1970 (or thereabouts) there was a widespread acknowledgment that the modes of theological interpretation to which Old Testament study had grown accustomed were no longer adequate.

Critiques of the So-Called Biblical Theology Movement

While the entire work of theological interpretation stretching back to Barth was now in question, it is a mark of von Rad's dominance that most of the rejectionist rhetoric was aimed against von Rad and the enterprise that he had set in motion. The general approach that he represented came to be called the biblical theology movement. The nomenclature is misleading and unfortunate, for it suggests that von Rad set out to lead a movement; he did not. Moreover, the phrase suggests that von Rad's approach was an isolatable phenomenon without past or future; it was not. Von Rad, like every scholar, was seeking to take a next step in scholarly investigation. The fact that his approach came to dominate the field suggests that many thoughtful people found his perspective helpful, and that his approach resonated in important ways with the cultural and epistemological climate in which he worked.

In the period of the demise of von Rad's influence, there has been a propensity to dismiss his work as though it were uninformed, ill-conceived, or facile. This dismissal fails to recognize the great achievement of his work. It is not possible to ignore von Rad, as though his important work had not irreversibly changed the discipline. No doubt von Rad's work, like that of every scholar, belongs to his

---

121. Brevard S. Childs, *Biblical Theology in Crisis* (Philadelphia: Westminster Press, 1970).

time and place.[122] In my judgment, his time and place required standing ground—confessional standing ground—for a community of faith that was under profound assault by a hostile culture and a virulent ideology. The influence of von Rad's work may well be reflective of a faith community that has excessively accommodated itself to culture and its epistemology (so Barth), and that there was widespread resonance with his credo hypothesis as a way to counter the accommodation. *Thus while one can say that von Rad's work has been subsequently found inadequate or lacking in ongoing power, one cannot conclude that it was a failure.* Indeed, von Rad himself might say, congruent with his own method, that his work was one articulation of faith that in the ongoing life of the community requires articulations subsequent to his own.

In any case, the period from 1970 until perhaps 1990 featured two developments in Old Testament study that could not have been anticipated a decade earlier. The first was the rather complete rejection of von Rad's way of doing Old Testament theology and a return to historical-critical work with its characteristic suspension of any theological interpretation that claims to be normative.[123] The principal criticism of von Rad and his "recital of God's mighty deeds" is that neither von Rad nor anyone else has found a way to relate salvation history (the recital of theological, creedal data) to secular history as it could be recovered by secular scholarship. Von Rad had tried to do so by stating the tension between "historical minimums" and "theological maximums," but this formulation only offered a recognition of the problem and the tension, not a solution.[124]

Already in 1961, Langdon Gilkey had identified the problem covered over by language, and since that time a great deal of energy has been devoted to the question of what might be meant by the phrase "act of God."[125] The outcome of this discussion is that "act of God" is either understood in a naive, commonsense way that fails to satisfy critical scrutiny, or it becomes a very large philosophical notion (as in Paul Tillich or Gordon Kaufman) that has no discernible connection to what is recited in the Old Testament. In the end, proponents of von Rad's approach were unable to define in any way convincing to modern criticism what was meant by "act of God."[126] We may note in passing that the problem may not be

---

122. On von Rad in his historical setting, see James M. Crenshaw, *Gerhard von Rad* (Waco, Tex.: Word Books, 1978).

123. I do not suggest that historical-critical work ceased during the time of von Rad's hegemony. But there was in some quarters a sigh of relief that this "Barthian episode" had ended, permitting a singular return to "proper" critical work, with no larger interpretive categories impinging on the enterprise.

124. Von Rad was never able to bridge "the ugly ditch," and so his elegant arguments never effectively held together "history" and "salvation history."

125. The problematic of the notion of "act of God" is noted in a well-established literature. Among the more important discussions is that of Langdon Gilkey, "Cosmology, Ontology, and the Travail of Biblical Language," *JR* 41 (1961) 194–205. Early in current discussions, Gilkey recognized the problematic character of biblical rhetoric and of the rhetoric of the classical interpreters.

126. As a result scholars who proceeded with some "innocence" about "God's mighty deeds in history" were forced to settle for narrative as the privileged form of discourse in Israel's faith. This embrace of narrative was vigorously championed by H. Richard Niebuhr, *The Meaning of Revelation* (New York: Macmillan, 1967). For representative views on narrative theology, see Stanley Hauerwas and L. Gre-

with von Rad but with the textual material itself, which continues to make its bold testimony without regard to modern critical categories and sensibilities. Thus the problem may be intrinsic to Old Testament claims.

This profound epistemological-linguistic problem, which haunted the work of von Rad, was accompanied by a range of historical-critical objections to von Rad's credo hypothesis and the supportive hypothetical constructs of Alt and Noth, Albright and Wright.[127] For our purposes, however, it is sufficient to mention the pivotal critique mounted against the biblical theology movement by Brevard Childs and James Barr, who, though they joined in a critique that proved to be decisive, did so in different ways and for very different reasons.

In his lectures published in 1970, Childs spoke of the crisis in biblical theology.[128] At the end of the book, he proposed as an antidote to the crisis a focus on the canon of Scripture as a clue to the proper way of reading the Old Testament theologically. Since 1970 Childs has published a series of books on this question, culminating in the ambitious and formidable *Biblical Theology of the Old and New Testaments*.[129] Over this period of more than twenty-five years, Childs has offered a variety of perspectives on this issue, and one may conclude that he himself has been in process, always coming to a clearer understanding of what might be meant by "canonical."

Here our only purpose is to mention the critique that Childs makes of the previous so-called movement. It was Childs's crucial judgment that such interpretation of the Old Testament, theological as it intended to be, had cut itself off from its necessary reference points: clues given in the text itself, and guidance given in the community of faith concerning a responsible theological reading—for example, creeds and doctrinal statements. As a result, so-called theological interpretation tended to work autonomously (echoes of Eichrodt's "existential"?), according to

gory Jones, eds., *Why Narrative? Readings in Narrative Theology* (Grand Rapids: Eerdmans, 1989). W. B. Gallie, "The Historical Understanding," *History and Theory* (ed. George H. Nadel; Middletown, Conn.: Wesleyan University Press, 1977) 149–202, has offered a compelling argument for the validity of the epistemology that serves narrative modes of knowledge. In retrospect over this phase of biblical interpretation, the problem was not that the Bible failed to make a compelling presentation of its claims, but that the positivistic categories imposed on the Bible were ill suited for the task. That is, the issue is not the character of the Bible, but the categories of modernity that now are under severe criticism. In any case, my argument in what follows, with reference to testimony, stands in important continuity with narrative modes of certainty.

127. For an early critique of von Rad's credo hypothesis, see J. Philip Hyatt, "Were There an Ancient Historical Credo in Israel and an Independent Sinai Tradition?" *Translating and Understanding the Old Testament: Essays in Honor of Herbert George May* (ed. Harry Thomas Frank and William L. Reed; Nashville: Abingdon Press, 1970) 152–70. More broadly, the historical synthesis on which the theological construction is based is under assault in many ways. See, for example, John van Seters, *Abraham in History and Tradition* (New Haven: Yale University Press, 1975); and the strictures of Thompson and Davies cited in n. 54 above. For a recent response to the "new skepticism," see Iain W. Provan, "Ideologies, Literary and Critical: Reflections on Recent Writing on the History of Israel," *JBL* 114 (1995) 585–606.

128. Childs, *Biblical Theology in Crisis*.

129. Brevard S. Childs, *Introduction to the Old Testament as Scripture* (Philadelphia: Fortress Press, 1979); *Old Testament Theology in a Canonical Context* (Philadelphia: Fortress Press, 1985); and *Biblical Theology of the Old and New Testaments* (Minneapolis: Fortress Press, 1992).

constructs rooted neither in the text itself nor in the theological traditions of the church. Stated another way, *biblical theology was not theological enough,* because it was too much informed by historical-critical judgments that carried with them theological presuppositions alien to the material itself. Childs therefore proposed that rather than theological interpretation being done according to the schema of historical criticism, it must be done according to the "canonical intentionality" of the text.

Not until well after 1970 did Childs give full articulation to his meaning. But it is clear that he intends a cognitive-ideational notion of theology, so that biblical theology yields ideas that can serve an interpreting church that is self-conscious about its doctrinal inheritance. This is a major move away from von Rad's accent on "events" that are to be found in "history" rather than in the cognitive residue that derives from the interpretation of the events. In any case, for Childs, von Rad's entire program was a betrayal of the larger canonical intention of "the final form of the text," an abandonment of too much that responsible Christian theology has valued and must value.

From a quite different direction, James Barr has also critiqued the work of von Rad and biblical theology.[130] In his criticism of von Rad, Barr agreed with Childs, though he vigorously rejected Child's offer of a canonical alternative. Barr's scholarship began with a pioneering and masterful study of semantics and the role semantic theory may play in Scripture interpretation.[131] He conducted a sustained criticism of the irresponsible semantic practices used in much biblical theology. Barr addresses himself to three elements of biblical theology, not all of which pertain directly to von Rad.

First, Barr's early work was a broadside against poor linguistic method, in which Hebrew language was thought to have some peculiar theological force per se and in which certain biblical words were treated as though they had reified power and meaning. It was Barr's great contribution to biblical scholarship to show that it is not a word but a sentence—words in context—that has theological significance. Barr sought to demystify much that had tried to claim special privilege as theological discourse, and he insisted that theological discourse in the Old Testament must be understood as intelligible; that is, it must be taken for what it says, with no hidden advantage or privilege.

Second, Barr addressed von Rad's unsolved issue of history, wherein von Rad (and many others) had been unable to bring together theological claim and recoverable datum. Barr was at the forefront of those who proposed that the Israelite

---

130. James Barr, "Gerhard von Rad's *Theologie des Alten Testaments,*" *Expository Times* 73 (1961-62) 142–46. See the review of the critique of Childs and Barr by Steven J. Kraftchick, "Facing Janus: Reviewing the Biblical Theology Movement," in *Biblical Theology: Problems and Perspectives,* 54–77.

131. James Barr, *The Semantics of Biblical Language* (Oxford: Oxford University Press, 1961), *Biblical Words for Time* (SBT 33; London: SCM Press, 1962). For the significance of Barr's work in this area as it pertains to biblical theology, see Samuel E. Balentine, "James Barr's Quest for Sound and Adequate Biblical Interpretation," *Language, Theology, and the Bible: Essays in Honour of James Barr* (ed. Samuel E. Balentine and John Barton; Oxford: Clarendon Press, 1994) 5–15.

recital of God's deeds is "story" or "history-like," rather than "history."[132] Two decades later, such a judgment may seem commonplace. But it should be recognized that this seemingly innocent word change from "history" to "story" is in fact a major decision to forgo the "happenedness" of biblical recital and to allow for a dimension of fictive imagination in the account in the text. One may continue to ponder the extent of fictive imagination, but to begin with that acknowledgment both permits and requires a very different interpretive enterprise.

Third, the enterprise of von Rad and Wright had focused on God's action. Barr, in his characteristic no-nonsense adjudication of the text, simply observed that *in the text itself God does not so much act as speak,* and therefore theological interpretation can and must focus on the utterance of God.[133] There may be many insoluble aspects to the "utterance of God" in terms of critical-historical questions, but speech is a given of the text and thus the material for theological interpretation.

Childs and Barr together have made a powerful case for the demise of von Rad's program. Together they have shown that von Rad's core idea of recital is enormously problematic, and they have persuaded most practitioners of Old Testament theology that one cannot, in any direct and simple fashion, continue the approach of recital. As we shall see later on, having made this common critique, Barr and Childs have decisively parted company, for they disagree vigorously on the way ahead.

Finally, in terms of understanding the break point in Old Testament theology at the end of the twentieth century, students will profit by paying close attention to *The Collapse of History* by Leo Perdue.[134] While the substance of Perdue's fine book is a consideration of the probes now being made beyond von Rad, the baseline of Perdue's discussion is a recognition that the problematic of twentieth-century Old Testament theology was its inability to come to terms with history as it had been understood in nineteenth-century criticism and as it continued to operate rather uncritically in the twentieth century. We have already seen how, since Gabler in 1787, Old Testament study was generally understood as a historical study.[135] The emergence of history as the primary co-discipline of Scripture study at the end of the eighteenth century signaled the determination of Bible scholars to break free of church interpretation that had long regarded philosophy

---

132. James Barr, "Story and History in Biblical Theology," *JR* 56 (1976) 1–17. On the matter of history, "history-like," and story, see Hans Frei, *The Eclipse of Biblical Narrative;* and David Tracy, *The Analogical Imagination: Christian Theology and the Culture of Pluralism* (New York: Crossroad, 1981) 259–81.

133. James Barr, "The Concept of History and Revelation," *Old and New in Interpretation: A Study of the Two Testaments* (London: SCM Press, 1966) 65–102, has made an important argument that preoccupation with God's acts has led to a neglect of God's speech, which is what we mostly have in the Bible. See another version of the argument, Barr, "Revelation through History in the Old Testament and in Modern Theology," *Int* 17 (1963) 193–205. Barr's attention to speech is an important antecedent to my own focus on the rhetoric of testimony.

134. Leo G. Perdue, *The Collapse of History,* 1–68.

135. See n. 32 above.

as its proper co-discipline.[136] The embrace of history as the proper perspective on biblical texts reflected the spirit of the nineteenth century and was undoubtedly an attempt to be scientific rather than confessional. Therefore the great historical-critical enterprise of the nineteenth century asked primarily historical questions. Indeed, Wellhausen's great culminating "documentary hypothesis" was an attempt to order historical sources in a proper and reliable way so that Israel's history of religion could be reconstructed.[137]

In order to understand the crisis of biblical theology at the end of the twentieth century, we must pause to understand what was entailed in this singular preoccupation with the "historical," as it enthralled Old Testament scholarship. It is best perhaps to recognize Hegel's articulation of "absolute history," which reflected a convinced Eurocentric view of all human reality. That is, history, in any practical reckoning, consisted in European history and reflected the uncritical hegemony of the writers of that history. Two other facets of history are readily noted in the work of Old Testament scholarship in the nineteenth century. First, history was considered as moving in a single, developmental line, again reflective of a hegemonic perspective. Second, in a mood of positivism, it was widely believed that an objective investigation could recover history "as it happened," with no ambiguity. And indeed, there need be no interpretive playfulness about "what it meant."[138]

This investigation proceeded with an enormous sense of confidence vested in the "knower" (described by Descartes) who used the correct methods, so that all of history could be readily available for analysis and dissection. From our perspective, it is not difficult to see that such a view of history is remarkably thin; it allows for none of the density or ambiguity of the actual human process, nor for the ways in which different perspectives will yield different versions of the same "happening." It is clear in retrospect that such a thin positivism cannot engage the density of the biblical text itself. I do not want to overstate this criticism of the approach of positivistic history, but a sample of nineteenth-century scholarship in the Old Testament discloses an innocent confidence in historical reportage and reconstruction that could no longer be entertained at the end of the twentieth century. Moreover, as "facts" were innocently available, so also the "meanings" embodied and enacted in those facts were also innocently available. Thus the "recovery of the past" served, in the nineteenth century, to reinforce the scholarly assumption, most often un-

---

136. The change from philosophy to history as the primary co-discipline of biblical study was enormously important. At the end of the twentieth century, we face both a crisis and an opportunity, as history is now largely displaced as the primary co-discipline of Scripture study in favor of rhetorical and sociological disciplines.

137. Wellhausen's decisive book, now much assessed and much criticized, is *Prolegomena to the History of Ancient Israel* (New York: Meridian Books, 1957). For a full discussion of Wellhausen and his contributions to Old Testament study, see *Julius Wellhausen and His Prolegomena to the History of Israel,* cited in n. 27 above.

138. The insistence that these materials in the Old Testament mean to be taken as history is especially held by John van Seters, *Prologue to History: The Yahwist as Historian in Genesis* (Louisville: Westminster/John Knox Press, 1992); and Baruch Halpern, *The First Historians: The Hebrew Bible and History* (San Francisco: Harper and Row, 1988).

stated, that all of this interesting and recoverable past is preliminary to the more developed, more sophisticated present that culminates in the "advanced" European learning, culture, and criticism.[139]

While the cultural-political grounds for such self-congratulatory history came to an end in the Great War of 1914–18, the epistemological assumptions of such an enterprise continued to be a powerful scholarly residue almost through the twentieth century. Thus history and historical criticism, which sought to recover the recoverable past but which also bootlegged its developmental scheme, continued to be the defining characteristic of twentieth-century scholarship, including Old Testament theology. While Barth had issued a mighty challenge to these presuppositions, he did not disrupt this major propensity of scholarship. Thus Albrecht Alt, though heavily informed by the form-critical advances of Hermann Gunkel, worked primarily as a historian, and his student Martin Noth reconstructed the early history of Israel, greatly influenced by Alt's work.[140] In the United States, Albright was primarily a historian, even though his great book, *From Stone Age to Christianity*, challenged the innocent developmentalism of the nineteenth century.

Thus the surge of new Old Testament scholarship in the twentieth century, which informed the matrix in which Eichrodt and von Rad worked, is largely defined in terms of historical questions, proposals, and reconstructions. As we have seen, von Rad's theology was committed to "God's mighty deeds in history." Every word in the formula (except perhaps "mighty") is problematic, but the most problematic is "history," for in the end von Rad could not take history with defining seriousness and is castigated by Eichrodt for being existentialist. And indeed, Barr had linked von Rad with Rudolf Bultmann, presumably with reference to his existentialist treatment of the historical.[141]

Thus Perdue's "collapse of history" is a conclusion that had already been adumbrated by Childs and Barr, who recognized that an entire way of doing scholarship was now no longer persuasive nor adequate. It is important to note that while Perdue's diagnosis applies most directly to the work of von Rad, in fact it concerns the entire enterprise of Old Testament scholarship as practiced in Euro-American circles of the past two hundred years. The "collapse" signifies not only a recognition that something like salvation history is too innocent, but that the epistemological assumptions of European modernity, with their hegemonic privilege, have now come up short. Our capacity to know, as it had been assumed, is radically called into question. Our assumption of progressive developmentalism is exposed as a

---

139. Such a view represents an unstated arrogance that regards the flowering of European culture and learning as the absolute norm toward which all had been moving. Thus what was offered as objective assessment turned out, in some circles, to be uncritical self-congratulation. It appears to me that the recent "victory of capitalism" is also regarded as the arrival at the culmination of cultural development; see, for example, Francis Fukuyama, *The End of History and the Last Man* (London: Hamish Hamilton, 1992).

140. Martin Noth, *The History of Israel* (2d ed.; London: Adam and Charles Black, 1960) 53–163.

141. See James Barr, "The Old Testament and the New Crisis of Biblical Authority," *Int* 25 (1971) 24–40.

self-serving conviction. Our uncritical notion of a singular, developmental line in cultural history, culminating with Euro-American culture, is now exposed to the challenges of a disordered pluralism, each element of which has its own version of what constitutes reality. While we must now attempt to take a new step in theological interpretation, *it is likely that we have not yet understood with sufficient clarity the epistemological break before which we now stand,* which places in acute jeopardy the long-standing privilege of Euro-American interpreters of Scripture. All of this Perdue has articulated with clarity.

Sociological Approaches

In the period of 1970–90, then, we may recognize that a historical mode of scholarship is at least problematic and inadequate, even if we do not, with Walter Wink, term it bankrupt. Second, we may recognize that in the same twenty-year period, considerable methodological confusion arose. On the one hand, it became increasingly clear that older methods could not continue in their long-standing innocence. On the other hand, it was not at all clear what alternative methods might be able to continue to advance scholarly work in theological interpretation.

It is not especially remarkable that methodological confusion has occurred during a time in which a variety of methods were attempted, some of which were found wanting and readily rejected. What is remarkable is that in such a short time one can begin to see the emergence of new methodologies that bring with them the beginnings of research programs and interpretive trajectories. It is already conventional to suggest two such methodologies that surely will be influential in the next phase of scholarly work, and that stand in varying degrees of continuity with older scholarship. We shall consider these approaches in turn.

First, *sociological analysis* has emerged within the past two decades as a rich possibility.[142] Sociology, itself a discipline only two hundred years old, seeks to understand the forces through which communities and societies order their life through arrangements of power and symbol. Sociological tools per se have been no stranger to Old Testament scholarship, for early in the twentieth century, German scholarship had made important use of the work of Max Weber.[143] It is fair to say, however, that more narrowly understood historical investigation until recently had minimized the importance of sociological analysis.

---

142. See Robert R. Wilson, *Sociological Approaches to the Old Testament* (Philadelphia: Fortress Press, 1984); and Norman K. Gottwald, "Sociological Method in the Study of Ancient Israel," *Encounter with the Text: Form and History in the Hebrew Bible* (ed. Martin J. Buss; Philadelphia: Fortress Press, 1979) 69–81.

143. Max Weber, *Ancient Judaism* (Glencoe: Free Press, 1952). See also the sociologically attentive work of Antonin Causse (*Du groupe ethnique à la communauté religieuse* [Paris, 1937]). It is likely that both Weber and Emile Durkheim operate in the shadows of Old Testament scholarship and will continue to do so. Norman K. Gottwald, *The Tribes of Yahweh: A Sociology of the Religion of Liberated Israel, 1250–1050 B.C.E.* (Maryknoll, N.Y.: Orbis Books, 1979) 591–667, 700–709, has considered the way in which idealistic sociology has been assumed in Old Testament scholarship, and he has urged a materialist reading in its place.

The production of sociological literature in Old Testament study has been almost explosive, paying attention variously to every phase and aspect of Israel's public life. This includes the work of Robert Wilson on the prophets, as well as anthropological investigations by Thomas Overholt and Paul Hanson on the postexilic period, and George Mendenhall on the monarchy.[144] The most formidable and influential work, however, has been that of Norman Gottwald, with which the work of Frank Frick and Marvin Chaney is also associated.[145]

At the beginning of his sociological work, Gottwald challenged the domain assumptions of Old Testament scholarship—assumptions of the discipline that already anticipated and predetermined some outcomes of study and precluded others.[146] Gottwald proposed alternative domain assumptions that radically opened up what is thinkable and possible in the discipline. But it was his great book of 1979, *The Tribes of Yahweh*, that decisively impacted scholarship. In this book, Gottwald took up the thesis of George Mendenhall that the narrative reports of the Book of Joshua do not in fact narrate an invasion of outsiders into the land of Canaan, but rather reflect a violent, internal dispute between overtaxed peasants and privileged, urban elites who lived well off the surplus wealth made possible by peasant taxes. The peasant revolt produced the social movement that came to be known as Israel and the revolution that sought to destroy Canaanite city-states, which were emblems and embodiments of social privilege and oppression.

Already in 1962, Mendenhall had proposed that it was Yahweh, the God of justice, who was the instigator of the revolution that was undertaken under the aegis of Yahweh.[147] In his book, Gottwald decisively broke with Mendenhall in one important regard. By appealing to the categories of Karl Marx concerning base and superstructure, Gottwald argued that it was *the material condition* of the peasants that generated the revolution, and that Yahweh is a belated legitimation of that materially driven revolutionary activity. To be sure, Gottwald's formulation of the nature of early Israel is formally evenhanded, asserting in turn that Yahweh is a "function" of the revolution even as the revolution is a "function" of Yahweh.[148] While Mendenhall has vigorously rejected the use of such sociological categories in interpretation, Gottwald, surely correctly, has insisted that it is not a question of whether one uses sociological categories, but only a question of which sociological model one utilizes. If one does not use materialist sociology of Marxian categories,

---

144. Robert R. Wilson, *Prophecy and Society in Ancient Israel* (Philadelphia: Fortress Press, 1980); Thomas W. Overholt, *Channels of Prophecy: The Social Dynamics of Prophetic Activity* (Minneapolis: Fortress Press, 1989); Paul D. Hanson, *The Dawn of Apocalyptic: The Historical and Sociological Roots of Jewish Apocalyptic* (Philadelphia: Fortress Press, 1975); and George E. Mendenhall, *The Tenth Generation: The Origins of the Biblical Tradition* (Baltimore: Johns Hopkins University Press, 1973).

145. In addition to Gottwald, *The Tribes of Yahweh*, see *Social Scientific Criticism of the Hebrew Bible and Its Social World: The Israelite Monarchy* (ed. Norman K. Gottwald; *Semeia* 37 [1986]), with particular reference to the work of Marvin Chaney and Frank Frick.

146. Norman K. Gottwald, "Domain Assumptions and Societal Models in the Study of Premonarchal Israel," VTSup 28 (1974) 89–100.

147. George E. Mendenhall, "The Hebrew Conquest of Palestine," *BA* 25 (1962) 66–87.

148. Gottwald, *The Tribes of Yahweh*, 608–21.

then one may unwittingly employ the idealistic categories of Weber and Durkheim, which are inherently conservative and protective of the status quo.

Much in Gottwald's book is open to question, in need of revision, and in sharp dispute. Since its publication in 1979, Gottwald has offered other, greatly refined articulations.[149] The primary point from which Gottwald has not retreated, however, is that Israelite faith is not a disembodied set of ideas, as Euro-American theology had assumed in its hegemonic innocence, but that this faith, like every statement of meaning, is deeply enmeshed in and shaped by material reality such as demography, technology, and food supply. This means that the Old Testament contains no innocent, one-dimensional, or disembodied theological statements, but that every theological articulation in the text is, in important ways, intimately and inexorably linked to lived reality.

It is immediately clear that Gottwald has not in principle broken from historical criticism, for no serious scholar can cut himself/herself off from scholarly antecedents. Rather, Gottwald has called into question the innocence of any "ideal" reading of the biblical text that proceeds as if Israel lived in a realm of pure ideas. Gottwald takes for granted and works with the whole apparatus of historical-critical scholarship, including the documentary analysis of the Pentateuch. But he understands every such textual witness as a witness to an actual, material reality that stands in, with, and under every utterance of meaning.

Thus Gottwald and others who share in his perspective have made it irreversibly the case that every textual utterance in the Old Testament needs to be understood as engaged in the realities of power, the securing of power, the maintenance of power, or the legitimating of power. Therefore, every text lives in the vexed reality of vested interest and faces issues of ideology.[150] Gottwald's perspective, along with those who share this interpretive practice, is enormously sophisticated and nuanced. If, however, one comes to the crux of the Marxian program of reading, then everything comes down finally to a class conflict, in which some have access to power and goods while others do not. One does not need to be reductionist about such a matter in order to recognize that, according to this view, every theological and interpretive utterance is somehow situated in this ongoing reality, which is powerfully political and economic in character.[151]

---

149. See his collected papers, Norman K. Gottwald, *The Hebrew Bible in Its Social World and in Ours* (SBLSS; Atlanta: Scholars Press, 1993).

150. The notion of ideology is now an important and pervasive one in Old Testament scholarship, and a student of Old Testament theology cannot afford to neglect its significance. Confusion results because two distinct meanings for the term *ideology* are at the same time operative. On the one hand, Karl Marx understood ideology to be theoretic distortion; on the other hand, Clifford Geertz has taken the term to refer to any sense-making narrative that gives meaning and coherence to social experience. The term is used in Old Testament study without care and consistency. See the helpful reflective comments on ideology by Paul Ricoeur, *Lectures on Ideology and Utopia* (New York: Columbia University Press, 1986).

151. This reality about textual and interpretive matters has been made clear through various liberationist exposés of conventional knowledge which make evident that much that has been taken for granted as objective is in fact a reflection of the interest of the interpretive hegemony.

While Gottwald tends to focus on the interests at play in the text itself, he certainly knows that as issues of power, interest, and ideology are operative in the text, so they are also operative in interpretive work. That is, various readings of the text are also informed and driven by the class location of the reader. What emerges from this awareness about the text and about the reader is the recognition that as there are no innocent texts, so there are no innocent readers. In each case, Old Testament theology must pay attention to the processes of power and powerlessness that are at work in the witness and in the interpretation. Without giving too close attention to the particularities of the Book of Joshua and the peasant revolt hypothesis per se, one can see immediately that *Gottwald has disrupted the assumption of innocence that has prevailed in the older positivistic historical-critical reading. Indeed, we are now able to see that what has passed for objective reading (and still does in some quarters) is often the work of a privileged elite who agreed upon methods of reading that kept the text in the sphere of ideas where it did not come into contact with material advantage and disadvantage.*[152]

Among other things, this exposé of interest calls into question the easily made assumption that critics of the text, of whatever ilk, are innocent and objective, whereas theological interpretation is confessional and fideistic. If Gottwald is correct about the material dimension of text and reading, as I believe he is, then there is no innocent or objective reading. Every reading in important ways is fideistic and confessional, including those readings that reject the theological claim of the text. As it often turns out (and I will treat this more fully in what follows), historical criticism now tends to become the gathering point for those who would prefer to fend off the more revolutionary invitations of the text in an "objective," distancing operation.

We should note that sociological analysis need not by definition be Marxian. Thus, for example, Wilson's consideration of the prophets in a sociological perspective is informed by rich anthropological theory, and Hanson's study of the postexilic traditions appeals to the sociological constructs of Karl Mannheim. But even where the sociological assumptions are not Marxian, such a way of reading requires us to see more or less that the texts do trade in power and in vested interest.

The work of Old Testament theology is not to reiterate sociological insights. Nonetheless, theological readers of the Old Testament do not have and cannot have any textual resources that are above, beyond, or outside the traffic of social conflict. That is, there are no innocent texts above the fray of social intercourse, for all texts are inevitably situated there. Thus, doing theology of the Old Testament requires a certain amount of courage (which is not the same as naiveté), in order to permit texts of partisan power to be at the same time, and without denying their concrete role in power conflicts, statements of meaning that may be received

---

152. Richard Rorty makes the most powerful critical assault on conventional notions of objectivity. See, for example, his *Contingency, Irony, and Solidarity* (Cambridge: Cambridge University Press, 1989); and *Objectivity, Relativism, and Truth: Philosophical Papers* 1 (Cambridge: Cambridge University Press, 1991).

as normative. To be sure, sociological analysis makes great demands on theological interpretation. The way ahead, however, given the emergence of this method, is to see that normative statements are characteristically and inescapably statements wrought in conflict, which serve power interests and which continue to be endlessly in dispute.

Normativeness, we are able to see at the end of the twentieth century, is not something arrived at in quiet innocence. Rather *normativeness is that on which one will stake one's life.*[153] It is precisely in such contexts of risk, I propose, that what we receive as theological data were voiced, heard, valued, and transmitted in the life of this ancient community. Or, stated negatively, normative statements that are not aimed at something dangerous and disputed are not likely to be useful, or interesting, or, in the end, true.

Rhetorical Criticism

The most ready criticism to be made of Gottwald is that he characteristically attends to the power realities in a reconstructed social situation, so that he does not pay attention to the biblical text itself in any sustained way. Like Marx before him, he has little interest in or appreciation for the artistic quality of the text itself. Given that recognition, it is important to turn to the second emerging method in our own time that is an indispensable complement to sociological analysis: *rhetorical criticism.*

Historical criticism, as it has come to be practiced, has been notorious for its lack of interest in the actual expression of the text itself. Indeed, the primary references for historical criticism characteristically are outside the text or, as is often said now, "behind the text" in the historical process. Generations of students of Scripture have tended not to read the text itself, believing that matters of real interest lay behind the text, to which the text only referred or to which it bore remote witness. This inattentiveness to the text is evident in the characteristic way that historical questions have been posed in Scripture study. Conservatives have characteristically been intensely interested in whether something reported in the biblical text "actually happened," and to determine that one had to go behind the texts, perhaps by means of archaeology. Conversely, liberals have been endlessly interested in explanatory, comparative material outside the text. The case was similar in the posing of theological questions. The text was thought only to point to the God who is ontologically situated somewhere else "in reality," but certainly not in the text as such. Thus in both historical investigation and in theological interpretation, reality was assumed to be elsewhere than in the text.

As a consequence the biblical text itself was only incidentally or instrumentally important to the study of what is "real," whether the "real" is understood historically or theologically. This problematic of Scripture study in avoiding the

---

153. This dimension of risk in praxis is what distinguishes the normativeness of the particular in biblical faith. This is a very different kind of normativeness from that of reasoned universals.

text for what is "real" is an old difficulty, though it is not easy to determine from whence the difficulty arose. One may suspect that the issue is as old as Plato versus the Sophists. In any conventional understanding, Plato is always "the good guy" who deals with "reality," whereas the Sophists are charlatans who deal only with words—that is, who devise texts. The bias against rhetoric runs very deep in Western philosophy and Western thought generally, certainly given impetus by Aristotle.[154]

This deep bias, moreover, reappeared in the form of nineteenth-century positivism, which with enormous self-confidence was able to reduce everything to technical data; and belatedly in the twentieth century in the fine art of the memo. In such a world that is able to draw close to "how things really are," the actual craft of expression is of secondary importance or interest and in any case is suspect, for such expressions may be at variance from the "real."

In Scripture study, this same positivism is evident in the great commentaries of the historical critics and in the culminating work of Wellhausen. The commentaries are characteristically occupied with sorting out what is "genuine" in the text and with identifying parallels in other cultures. Such treatment of the text does not at all attend to the statements of the text itself, but is in effect a sustained raid on the text, looking for clues that support historical reconstruction. It is odd that an enterprise as preoccupied with the text as Scripture study is, should in the end have so little genuine interest in the text and in its rhetorical, artistic character.

The road back to rhetoric was initiated by Hermann Gunkel at the turn of the century, with his studies in the Psalms and Genesis.[155] His practice of form criticism assured that scholarly attention would look at the form of the text itself. Gunkel himself had an acute sense of artistry. But subsequent to Gunkel, the work of form criticism tended to become quite rigid in some quarters, until in some of the work on the Form Critical Project, form analysis is reduced to nothing more than an inventory or even an outline of content.[156] On the whole, however, form criticism lost its force as a distinct method because it completely permeated scholarly practice and became an unquestioned perspective on texts.

Form criticism prepared the way for the more recent emergence of rhetorical criticism as a major force in Old Testament studies, one that has become indispensable for the work of Old Testament theology. Rhetorical criticism is a method that insists that *how* what is said is crucial and definitive for *what* is said, so that the theology of the Old Testament does not trade in a set of normative ideas that

---

154. See C. Jan Swearingen, *Rhetoric and Irony: Western Literacy and Western Lies* (Oxford: Oxford University Press, 1991).

155. The singular impact of Hermann Gunkel on Old Testament studies is attested in many handbooks. See, for example, John H. Hayes, ed., *Old Testament Form Criticism* (San Antonio: Trinity University Press, 1974); Klaus Koch, *The Growth of the Biblical Tradition: The Form Critical Method* (New York: Macmillan, 1975); and Gene M. Tucker, *Form Criticism of the Old Testament* (Philadelphia: Fortress Press, 1971).

156. The several volumes in the Form Critical Project are published by Eerdmans. On the enduring significance of Gunkel's work, see Martin J. Buss, "The Study of Forms," *Old Testament Form Criticism,* 1–56; "Understanding Communication," *Encounter with the Text,* 3–44.

may be said in many ways, but in a peculiar utterance that is spoken and/or written in a certain way.

It is now agreed that the primary impetus for rhetorical criticism as an intentional Old Testament enterprise stems from the address of James Muilenburg, "Form Criticism and Beyond," presented in 1968 and published in 1969.[157] This address brings to high visibility Muilenburg's career-long attentiveness to the artistic intentionality of the text itself.[158] Muilenburg almost single-handedly made credible the practice of close reading, whereby one notices the detail of the text, such as word patterns and arrangements, the use of key words in repetition, the careful placement of prepositions and conjunctions, and the reiteration of sounds of certain consonants. It was Muilenburg's insistence that, in order to attend to the communicative intention of text, one must notice each and every detail. Moreover, he held that such detail in the text is characteristically intentional, and that the force of the text cannot be understood apart from noticing such detail. In terms of theological interpretation, because the *what* is linked to the *how*, one cannot generalize or summarize but must pay attention to the detail.

The parallel insistence of Muilenburg and of Gottwald, who was Muilenburg's student, is worth noting. Gottwald has insisted that texts are not statements of detached ideas, but that ideas are characteristically situated in the pressures and requirements of social forces and power. In parallel fashion, Muilenburg insists that biblical texts do not provide free-floating concepts or ideas, but are statements that must be understood in terms of their full rhetorical situation. Thus both Muilenburg with rhetoric and Gottwald with sociology insist that Old Testament substance, either historical or theological, cannot be extracted from the text, but must be taken in its full density, in the text where it is situated.

Since Muilenburg's programmatic proposal in 1969, rhetorical criticism has emerged as a major methodological investment, less in dispute than Gottwald's sociological program. Consideration of the method draws attention to the work of Phyllis Trible, among Muilenburg's most important students and certainly heir to his rhetorical concerns. As practitioner of Muilenburg's methods of close reading, Trible has published two books of essays, *God and the Rhetoric of Sexuality* and *Texts of Terror*.[159] Long before feminism as a hermeneutical force became fashionable Old Testament study, Trible elected to study texts that pertained to women and to feminist imagery. In her first such study, *God and the Rhetoric of Sexuality*, she paid particular attention to metaphor, and thereby began to explore a range of literary tropes that moved outside the one-dimensional perspective of historical criticism. More recently, Trible has published a third book, *Rhetorical Criticism*, in

---

157. James Muilenburg, "Form Criticism and Beyond," *JBL* 88 (1969) 1–18.

158. The most important and characteristic work of James Muilenburg is "Isaiah 40-66," *IB* (Nashville: Abingdon Press, 1956), 5:381–773.

159. Phyllis Trible, *God and the Rhetoric of Sexuality* (OBT; Philadelphia: Fortress Press, 1978); and *Texts of Terror: Literary-Feminist Readings of Biblical Narratives* (OBT; Philadelphia: Fortress Press, 1984).

which she has situated the method in historical perspective and provided a model of practice through a study of the Book of Jonah.[160]

Two matters emerge from her study to which special attention must be paid. First, Trible regularly exhibits the remarkable density of the text, in order to make available the complexity and the fully laden quality of a text in which a great deal, by design, is under way.[161] This density regularly warns us against any easy historicism or any facile theological extraction. Second, Trible characteristically avoids any heavy-duty ideological output from her reading. She is a feminist reader attentive to matters of sexist assumptions and practice in the text, but her attentiveness to such matters is not intrusive nor controlling of her reading. What becomes evident in her work is that if one is patient with the detail of the text, one does not need to impose theological conclusions, for the text will regularly yield at least hints of its own advocacy, even if it does so with reticence and delicacy. Such attention to detail obviously requires that Old Testament theology be done differently than in times past, not first of all by large generalization, but *one text at a time*. Rhetorical criticism enables the reader to stay close to the text itself and does not assume that something more important, either historical or theological, lies behind it. At the same time, it is important to recognize, given the generative character of the text, that much that is theological lies "in front of the text." A theological interpreter should not be so protective of the text as to shrink from that generative extrapolation.

Other practitioners of rhetorical criticism have also shown how such close reading may serve the theological enterprise. David J. A. Clines has considered the literary coherence and intention of the entire Pentateuch.[162] In the course of his discussion he has also indicated the ways in which rhetoric can generate a world in which the hearers of the text can live.[163] Clines attends to the generative power of rhetoric. In so doing, he moves beyond Muilenburg's close reading in the direction of theory, upon which we will comment later. In his early books on Saul and David, David M. Gunn has provided important examples of how a close reading can attend to the intentionality of the text.[164] While Gunn, in these books, has stayed close to the text, he has also thematized his reading around the motifs of "Gift and Grasp."[165] In two books that have attracted much attention, Robert Alter has given great impetus to rhetorical analysis, showing that the artistic patterns

160. Phyllis Trible, *Rhetorical Criticism: Context, Method, and the Book of Jonah* (Guides to Biblical Scholarship; Minneapolis: Fortress Press, 1994).

161. I use the term *density* here in a way not unlike Clifford Geertz's use of "thick" description.

162. David J. A. Clines, *The Theme of the Pentateuch.* On the artistic capability of a text to move beyond historicity, see Gabriel Josipovici, *The Book of God: A Response to the Bible* (New Haven: Yale University Press, 1988).

163. Clines, *The Theme of the Pentateuch,* 102.

164. David M. Gunn, *The Fate of King Saul: An Interpretation of a Biblical Story* (JSOTSup 14; Sheffield: JSOT Press, 1980); and *The Story of King David: Genre and Interpretation* (JSOTSup 6; Sheffield: JSOT Press, 1978).

165. David M. Gunn, "David and the Gift of the Kingdom (2 Sam 2-4, 9-20, 1 Kgs 1-2)," *Semeia* 3 (1975) 14–45.

of rhetoric in the Old Testament, in both prose and poetry, have a subtlety and density to which historical criticism characteristically has not paid sufficient attention.[166] If this density and subtlety are not noticed in critical work, they will surely not be available for later theological interpretation.

Although the work of Paul Ricoeur is theory-laden and hermeneutically self-conscious in a way that Muilenburg's programmatic statement is not, it is not inappropriate to refer here to Ricoeur's influential work.[167] In a series of books, Ricoeur has reflected on the character of the biblical text, particularly with reference to narrative, as an enterprise of generative imagination. Ricoeur has seen that historical-critical perspectives regularly seek to recover (or reconstruct) "the world behind the text," a process that Robert Alter has termed "excavative."[168] The turn in interpretive perspective referred to here has in general recognized that "the world behind the text" is not available. Thus this perspective represents an important challenge to the entire program of historical criticism. The pursuit of "the world behind the text" in historical criticism has exercised a suffocating hegemony over the text in the past century. There is no sure safeguard against newer approaches exercising a like suffocating hegemony. For that reason, the interpreting community, academic and ecclesial, must be endlessly vigilant and self-critical. Moreover, were that world behind the text available, it would not be in any direct way generative for theological interpretation.

Ricoeur has given us phrasing for two alternative ways in which to consider the relation of the text to "world." First, he speaks about "the world *in* the text." This phrase refers to a set of assumptions and interactions that are conducted in the wording of the text itself, without checking to see if these assumptions and interactions are possible in the "real world." Thus, for example, in "the world in the text," it is possible for Elijah to pray the Syrians blind (2 Kgs 6:18), and it is possible for the king of Babylon to be turned into a beast (Dan 4:33), and the characters in the text so experience their reality. In the world in the text, the checks and restraints of the "world out there" are suspended. (We may note that this literary procedure, which gives great freedom to the imagination of an alternative world, is not incongruent with Barth's insistence that the "real" must come before

---

166. Robert Alter, *The Art of Biblical Narrative* (New York: Basic Books, 1981); and *The Art of Biblical Poetry* (New York: Basic Books, 1985). See also Meir Sternberg, *The Poetics of Biblical Narrative: Ideological Literature and the Drama of Reading* (Bloomington: Indiana University Press, 1985).

167. The work of Paul Ricoeur is published in many places under many titles. It is impossible to identify any one text of his as a specific reference point, but a student of Old Testament theology will do well to attend to Ricoeur's work on time, narrative, and imagination. Among his important collections of essays that have been originally published in a variety of places, see *The Conflict of Interpretations: Essays in Hermeneutics* (ed. Don Ihde; Evanston, Ill.: Northwestern University Press, 1974); *The Philosophy of Paul Ricoeur: An Anthology of His Work* (ed. Charles E. Reagan and David Stewart; Boston: Beacon Press, 1978); *From Text to Action: Essays in Hermeneutics 2* (Evanston: Northwestern University Press, 1991); *A Ricoeur Reader: Reflection and Imagination* (ed. Mario J. Valdés; Toronto: University of Toronto Press, 1991); and *Figuring the Sacred: Religion, Narrative, and Imagination* (see n. 6 above). For an orientation to Ricoeur's work, see Mark I. Wallace, "Introduction," *Figuring the Sacred*, 1–32.

168. Robert Alter, *The World of Biblical Literature* (New York: Basic Books, 1992) 133.

the "possible," because if one decides the "possible" first, it will be decided on the terms of the taken-for-granted world of dominant reason.)[169]

Second, Ricoeur speaks of "the world *in front* of the text"—the life-world generated by the text and mediated to the hearers of the text as they receive it. Attentive and consenting readers and hearers are drawn into the assumptions and interactions of the text itself which, if the text is credited, do indeed become possible. This "real-life possibility," generated by the text itself, becomes the practical datum of theological reflection and insists on not being supervised or monitored by the "world behind the text." Thus even with reference to God, the imaginative, generative power of rhetoric offers to the hearer of this text a God not otherwise known or available or even—dare one say—not otherwise "there." Thus the text intends not to describe, but to generate, and attentiveness to the text is the act of permitting the text to have its full, imaginative say and to "follow" the text without any prior restraint.[170]

With reference to the older pursuit of "the world behind the text," two aspects of Ricoeur's suggestion make a decisive difference. Critically, we are able to see that as long as the text is enthralled to the world behind the text, the text cannot be more than reportage of what is there. Thus "the world behind the text" becomes the norm against which the text is tested. Where the text departs from credible reportage, it must be rejected or at least explained away.[171] Positively, "the world in the text" and "the world in front of the text," when no longer in check to "the world behind the text," have the chance to evoke a genuine *novum* in the imaginative act of hearing, so that the text may indeed subvert, offering an alternative version of reality that creates new perspective, new possibility, and new activity well beyond the assumed world behind the text.

The ultimate consequence of this generative sense of rhetoric is the deabsolutizing of "the world behind the text" that historical criticism takes as normative, and that the hegemonic authority of the high critical period has had no intention of challenging. Thus when the imaginative forays of a generative text are measured by the assumed world behind the text, the outcome is that the text is measured by the status quo, which comes to be valued as a given beyond criticism. Ricoeur's programmatic statement suggests that such generative literature as we have in the Bible in the end destabilizes "the given" and lets us entertain the thought that long-honored givens may turn out to be only avidly accepted imaginative construals of reality. It is clear that as theological artistry, the Old Testament invites its

---

169. See n. 46 above.

170. See W. B. Gallie, "The Historical Understanding," 151 and passim, on the term *follow.*

171. One of the most poignant cases for this matter in the biblical text is the narrative in which Elisha "miraculously!" raises an iron ax head out of the swampy water (2 Kgs 6:1-7). The standard test of positivistic interpretation is that the narrative must be rejected unless one is able to affirm that iron floats—i.e., to affirm something that is contrary to scientific reason. Such a test of the narrative misunderstands the narrative density of the text and its power in generating an alternative world, outside the domain of royal administration.

hearers into a very different world, where things happen that are not allowed by hegemonic interpretive powers.[172]

Between Power and Rhetoric

Ricoeur's program of generative imagination goes well beyond anything that Muilenburg articulated in his disciplined approach to the text. It seems clear to me, however, that even without such articulation, Muilenburg understood intuitively, given his great sensitivity to the artistry of the text, that *rhetoric is indeed capable of construing, generating, and evoking alternative reality.*

Thus the moment of "the collapse of history" and the emergence of new methodologies are two sides of the same coin. It can now be recognized that a historical approach on the face of it is thin and one-dimensional. Indeed, the Enlightenment, whose child is historical criticism, intended that everything should be seen, understood, and explained, so that nothing should remain hidden.[173] But when everything is visible, understood, and explained, and reality is brought under control, what interests us and compels us is lost. These two emerging methods, I propose, are attempts to escape an explanatory approach to the biblical text. There are great differences between Gottwald's sociological approach and Muilenburg's rhetorical approach, and certainly Gottwald is much more in an explanatory mode than is Muilenburg. Indeed, Gottwald's approach, in hands other than his own, can lead to a new reductionism in which everything must be explained and justified on the grounds of social history. Nonetheless, these approaches share a commonality accenting the density of the interpretive process. Gottwald insists that texts are to be understood within the density of social interaction and social conflict, bespeaking vested interest and ideological cunning. If that density is neglected, it becomes too easy to take the text as innocent. Muilenburg insists that texts are to be understood within the density of artistic imagination and intentionality, and if this density is neglected, the text is easily taken as exhausted in a surface reading. It is this density, which complicates and jeopardizes the easy reading of the text in our accustomed hegemonic familiarity, that must now occupy us.

If this density is essential for social and rhetorical analysis, it is surely no less so for theological interpretation. It is perhaps a major contribution of theological reflection on the Bible to more "respectable" theological enterprises to witness to the density of the material that precludes excessive certitude. As we are learning that Enlightenment reading of history is now highly doubtful, Enlightened theol-

---

172. Karl Barth, *Word of God, Word of Man,* referred to "the strange new world of the Bible." Barth's capacity to accept the artistic, imaginative dimension of the text permitted his theological assertion to function powerfully and authoritatively outside the conventionally possible. Much interpretation has found that strange new world too strange and has domesticated it into a more familiar, more manageable world, thus robbing the Bible of its threatening, energizing capacity.

173. The "enemies of the Enlightenment"—e.g., Freud, Marx, Nietzsche, Dostoyevsky, Søren Kierkegaard—were precisely those who attended to the hidden and inscrutable in lived reality, who refused a surface understanding of human reality.

ogy in parallel fashion is prone to more certitude than is credible or than is given in the material.

Thus the new situation of Old Testament theology is reflective of a major breakpoint in Western culture. That major breakpoint does not especially concern the Bible, but it does concern the interpretive engine of the dominant modes of Western Christendom. The breakpoint concerns modes of knowledge that have too innocently yielded certitude. In parallel fashion, it concerns modes of power that have too readily granted control. The convergence of innocent certitude and ready control have made the treatment of biblical theology enormously useful for hegemonic purposes. Now that these excessively trusted modes of knowledge and these excessively relied-upon modes of power have been shown to be inadequate, however, our ways of theological interpretation can also be changed. We are only at the beginning of thinking about how to proceed in fresh ways. There can be little doubt, however, that this is the task before us in doing Old Testament theology.

TWO

Retrospect 2:
The Contemporary Situation

I T IS IMPORTANT for a student of Old Testament theology to take into full account the claim that our interpretive work now happens in a new context concerning both power and knowledge. While Walther Eichrodt's and Gerhard von Rad's works are relatively recent, in terms of interpretive work we are now situated a long way from them. We have suggested that Leo Perdue's phrase "the collapse of history" refers not only to changed methods, but also to the cultural assumptions and political supports that made interpretive work of a certain kind tenable through the twentieth century.

The Postmodern Interpretive Situation

As yet no consensus exists about how to characterize the new sociopolitical-interpretive situation, but here I shall use the term *postmodern*. I have no special brief for that term, but take it as a shorthand reference to the end of a cultural period that was dominated by objective positivism that made a thin kind of historical scholarship possible, and that granted interpretive privilege to certain advantaged perspectives.[1] Without lingering over the term itself, I suggest several facets of our new sociopolitical-interpretive situation that operate with reference to doing Old Testament theology.

Pluralistic Context

Interpretation now takes place in a new political situation. In an older political situation that was tightly controlled and largely homogeneous, it was not necessary or perhaps even possible to notice that interpretive work took place in a political situation—but of course it did. Our awareness of that reality has now changed drastically.

The great new fact of interpretation is that we live in a pluralistic context, in which many different interpreters in many different specific contexts representing

---

1. See Walter Brueggemann, *Texts under Negotiation: The Bible and Postmodern Imagination* (Minneapolis: Fortress Press, 1993), chap. 1.

many different interests are at work on textual (theological) interpretation. The old consensus about limits and possibilities of interpretation no longer holds. Thus interpretation is no longer done by a small, tenured elite, but interpretive voices and their very different readings of the texts come from many cultures in all parts of the globe, and from many subcultures even in Western culture.[2] The great interpretive reality is that there is no court of appeal behind these many different readings. There is no court of appeal beyond the text itself, and we are learning in new and startling ways how remarkably supple the text is and how open the varied readings are. The postmodern situation is signified precisely by the disappearance of any common, universal assumption at the outset of reading.

This new situation means, inevitably, that varied interpretations conflict and clash. Paul Ricoeur had already seen this in his programmatic statement, *Conflict of Interpretations*. Alasdair MacIntyre, in *Three Rival Versions of Moral Enquiry* and *Whose Justice? Which Rationality?*[3] has argued that in general, the intellectual landscape is occupied by competing construals and accounts of moral reality in which there is no arbiter. The same applies to Old Testament theology. We now have rival accounts or construals of Old Testament theology, of which the most visible alternatives appear to be canonical, liberationist in its several submodels, and historical-critical, which tends to yield a minimalist or skeptical account of the matter. These rival accounts inevitably conflict, not only in what they conclude, but in what interpretive questions they deem legitimate. The conflict cuts to the core of the matter of interpretation.

Moreover, it is now clear that such rival accounts of the interpretive project, while each is surely held in good faith, are not at all innocent. Each of these rival accounts is in fact the advocacy of a vested interest, which may be highly visible or hidden. One obvious practice of interest is that of feminist interpretation, a subset of liberation reading, which intends at least to expose the patriarchal oppression that is present in the text and in the history of interpretation.[4] Less obvious, but undoubted in my judgment, is the interest at work in what has come to be called canonical perspective, in which outcomes are predictably conservative and in line with the classical consensus of Protestantism.[5] Less obvious but surely operative is

---

2. The opening up of the interpretive conversation is signaled, for example, by the annual international meeting of the Society of Biblical Literature, which intends to give a platform to those who are not given voice in conventional academic procedures, and by the new journal *Biblical Interpretation*, which intends to be genuinely multicultural, thus permitting interpretation outside academic hegemony.

3. Paul Ricoeur, *The Conflict of Interpretations: Essays in Hermeneutics* (ed. Don Ihde; Evanston, Ill.: Northwestern University Press, 1974); Alasdair MacIntyre, *Three Rival Versions of Moral Enquiry: Encyclopedia, Genealogy, and Tradition* (Notre Dame, Ind.: University of Notre Dame Press, 1990); and MacIntyre, *Whose Justice? Which Rationality?* (Notre Dame: University of Notre Dame Press, 1989).

4. See the helpful bibliography by Alice Ogden Bellis, *Helpmates, Harlots, and Heroes: Women's Stories in the Hebrew Bible* (Louisville: Westminster/John Knox, 1994).

5. Thus Brevard S. Childs, *Biblical Theology of the Old and New Testaments* (Minneapolis: Fortress Press, 1992), draws conclusions that are predictably congruent with consensus Calvinism. It is evident that Childs's strictures against a liberation hermeneutic are not innocent. See the review of Childs's work along with that of James Barr and Jon D. Levenson by John J. Collins, "Historical Criticism and the State of Biblical Theology," *Christian Century* (1993) 7434–47.

the interest of historical critics who seem to believe that any theological interpretation that credits the ostensive theological affirmations of the text is fideistic and obscurantist, and who in the practice of skepticism champion a kind of innocent autonomy—that is, the old-line innocence of the Enlightenment. This position in theological interpretation seems to regard any theological interest as inherently authoritarian, so that the old drama between Gottfried Leibniz and Jacques Bossuet is replayed.[6] My only insistence here is that this positivistic position is no more innocent concerning theological interpretation than are the liberationist and the canonical.

There seems to be no way out of this competitive, conflictual situation; there are no "answers in the back of the book" to which all will assent—not critical, not classical, not advocacy. Moreover, it is apparent that every such advocacy—whether an admitted one (liberationist), or one in the service of the creedal tradition (canonical), or one in the service of Enlightenment autonomy (critical)—is readily checked and seemingly countered in the treatment of any text by the citation of a countertext, which can most often be identified, or by the offer of a counterinterpretation.

We now recognize that there is no interest-free interpretation, no interpretation that is not in the service of some interest and in some sense advocacy. Indeed, it is an illusion of the Enlightenment that advocacy-free interpretation can exist. Interpretation as advocacy is an ongoing process of negotiation, adjudication, and correction. This means, most likely, that there can be no right or ultimate interpretation, but only provisional judgments for which the interpreter is prepared to take practical responsibility, and which must always yet again be submitted to the larger conflictual conversation.[7] Therefore any adequate interpretive conclusion is likely to enjoy its adequacy only for a moment. Such an interpretive enterprise is a profound departure from the older, long-established hegemonic work of interpretations in which one could enjoy "assured results." In my judgment, however, faithful interpretation—that is, interpretation congruent with the text being interpreted, requires a willingness to stay engaged in such an adjudicating process and not to retreat to a separated interpretive community.

The warrant for such an interpreting process is that precisely this kind of process is evident in the biblical text itself. Whereas in the older criticism it was commonly thought that Israelite religion could be understood in a singular,

---

6. See Paul Hazard, *The European Mind, 1680–1715* (New York: World Publishing, 1963) 198–236 and passim.

7. David J. A. Clines, *Interested Parties: The Ideology of Writers and Readers of the Hebrew Bible* (JSOTSup 205; Sheffield: Sheffield Academic Press, 1995). In a series of important articles, Clines has moved to a position of radical pluralism in which each interpreter is free to address only his or her own interpreting community and need feel no obligation to or challenge from any interpretation outside a particular community of interpretation. Note well that my own view is quite different from that of Clines. While we do operate primarily in a specific community of interpretation, it is my judgment that the work of any distinctive community of interpretation must be in critical contact with the larger interpretive conversation and with the work of other, very different specific communities of interpretation. That is the only way in which pluralism can resist devolving into a series of sectarian readings.

straight-line development, we now recognize otherwise. Rainer Albertz, in an important advance concerning the history of Israelite religion, shows that Israel's religion, and thus the texts, are incessantly pluralistic.[8] On every religious question the matter is under dispute, and we frequently are able to identify the several voices to the adjudication that are sounded in the text. Albertz, moreover, concludes that the canon itself is a compromise, in which no party to the adjudication is silenced or driven from the field, meaning from the text,[9] and no party completely dominates.

Thus if Albertz is correct, the faith of Israel as given in the Old Testament has no agreed-on consensus point, but the canon itself is an exercise in adjudication. Much that the scholarly community has regarded as editing or redaction is in fact that ongoing work of adjudication, in which any settled point is reached only provisionally and is in turn subject to reconsideration. I shall argue, then, that theological interpretation as ongoing adjudication is faithful to the character of the text itself. This process, moreover, applies not only to this or that subject, but to the very character of Yahweh, the God of Israel. Yahweh, in the life of the text, is pulled this way and that by the adjudicating rhetoric of Israel. And any theological interpretation must take care not to cover over the process by which the God of the Bible is made available to us.

In assessing this new interpretive awareness, Rowan Williams has commented that the several texts, which are not easily harmonized with each other, are in fact "bids" for a truth-statement, each of which must make its way and live in the presence of other serious "bids."[10] To wish for a more settled interpretive process is to wish for something that is not available in the Old Testament, and no amount of historical criticism or canonical interpretation can make it so. Our interpretive work is to attend to the way in which these several bids live in tension with each other and occasionally prevail over each other. Interpretation, in the end, cannot overcome the irascibly pluralistic character of the text.

The Role of Rhetoric

Because the work and life of the Old Testament text is primarily to state competing claims, primary attention must be given to the rhetoric and the rhetorical character of faith in the Old Testament. We have already noticed, in the ancient dispute of Plato with the Sophists, and again in the Enlightenment, the propensity to empty rhetoric of any serious power. Our intellectual inheritance has characteristically preferred "being" to rhetoric, and therefore has assumed that metaphysics is a much more serious matter than is speech. The outcome is that issues of God are foreclosed before disputatious utterance rather than in and through disputatious utterance. But the adjudication that must take place in the midst of pluralism

---

8. Rainer Albertz, *A History of Israelite Religion in the Old Testament Period* 1 (London: SCM Press, 1994); and 2: *From the Exile to the Maccabees* (Louisville: Westminster/John Knox, 1994).

9. Ibid., 2:481 and passim.

10. Rowan Williams, "The Literal Sense of Scripture," *Modern Theology* 7 (1991) 121–34.

places speech at the center of Israel's life of faith and positions metaphysics as a by-product of provisional triumphs of rhetoric.

Thus our current, postmodern situation of interpretation cannot easily appeal to any essentialist tradition in an attempt to articulate the faith of Israel. Rather the interpreter must be an at-risk participant in a rhetorical process in which being is regularly at stake in and through utterance. The issues are exceedingly difficult, but we must at least recognize that what has passed for an essentialist or realist position has in fact been the attempt of hegemonic speech that sought to silence all alternative utterance. In the adjudicating pluralism of the Old Testament, however, any would-be hegemonic speech that claims essentialist privilege is unable to silence other speech, and therefore is unable to establish hegemonic utterances as essence. We are pressed back to the persuasive process of speech. It is my judgment that while the Old Testament can make assumptions about and claims for what is real, it is unable and unwilling to do so by way of silencing countervoices.

Thus it appears to me that in a practical way, speech leads reality in the Old Testament. Speech constitutes reality, and who God turns out to be in Israel depends on the utterance of the Israelites or, derivatively, the utterance of the text.[11] We are so long practiced in hegemonic utterance that such a claim about speech being constitutive of reality is exceedingly difficult for us. I shall argue, nonetheless, that practically and concretely, the very character of God in the Old Testament depends on the courage and imagination of those who speak about God, and who in speaking make available to Israel (and belatedly to the church) not only God, but a specific God of a very odd and unprecedented kind. Brevard Childs writes, in his canonical approach, about "the reality of God" behind the text itself.[12] In terms of Old Testament theology, however, one must ask, What reality? Where behind? It is clear that such an approach as that of Childs derives its judgments from somewhere else, from an essentialist tradition, claims about God not to be entertained in the Old Testament text itself. In doing Old Testament theology, one must be vigilant against importing claims from elsewhere. I do not imagine in what follows that I am sufficiently vigilant, but I agree that the issue is urgent and therefore merits our continuing attention.

In an analysis of classic literature, Richard Lanham has made a compelling and helpful distinction between "the serious man" (*homo seriosus*) and "the rhetorical

---

11. On the notion of speech as constitutive of reality, see Walter Brueggemann, *Israel's Praise: Doxology against Idolatry and Ideology* (Philadelphia: Fortress Press, 1988), chap. 1. I have found the issue of speech/reality among the most problematic for my current study. I do not wish to claim that these textual utterances make no assumptions about being, but I do wish to recognize that such assumptions depend on speech for their establishment as viable, credible claims. While there is assumed reality outside the text (God), that assumed reality depends on utterance for force, authority, and availability in the community. God in the Old Testament is not a mere rhetorical construct, but is endlessly in the process of being rhetorically reconstructed. This is an exceedingly important and dense issue, one I am not able to resolve clearly. I wish only to note that it is an issue that Old Testament theology, perhaps much more than systematic theology, must continue to host as a demanding question.

12. Childs, *Biblical Theology of the Old and New Testaments*, e.g., p. 20.

man" (*homo rhetoricus*).[13] While it may be true that the Platonic tradition and the entire tradition of classical theology have been conducted by "the serious man," I insist that it is characteristic of the Old Testament, and characteristically Jewish, that God is given to us (and exists as God "exists") only by the dangerous practice of rhetoric. Therefore in doing Old Testament theology we must be careful not to import essentialist claims that are not authorized by this particular and peculiar rhetoric. *I shall insist, as consistently as I can, that the God of Old Testament theology as such lives in, with, and under the rhetorical enterprise of this text, and nowhere else and in no other way.* This rhetorical enterprise operates with ontological assumptions, but these assumptions are open to dispute and revision in the ongoing rhetorical enterprise of Israel. As we take up the rhetorical character of Old Testament theology, we may identify several aspects of rhetoric to which attention must be paid.

Narrative framework. Already in the work of Gerhard von Rad and G. Ernest Wright, it is clear that story in the Old Testament has some special privilege as a governing genre.[14] To be sure, much of the Old Testament is not in narrative form. But in other genres such as commandment, song, and oracle, I suggest that the same claims of narrative reality are operative, albeit one step removed from narrative rendering. Thus the great hymns of Israel (Exodus 15; Judges 5; Deuteronomy 33) operate with a narrative framework. The commandments are regularly embedded in the stories of Exodus and sojourn. Prophetic oracles characteristically tell what Yahweh has done and will do. It is likely that in the uttering of Yahweh, even in nonnarrative genre, Israel depended peculiarly on the assumptions of narrative.[15] Israel characteristically employed Yahweh's intervention or Yahweh's utterance in a story of need-intervention-resolution, for which Yahweh's intervention is the decisive factor for Israel's sense of reality, and in which Yahweh's intervention, by act or speech, is decisive for the larger characterization of Yahweh.[16]

Important phenomenological studies suggest that narrative is the privileged genre for being human, and that may be so.[17] Our point here, however, is not a general phenomenological one, but one about Israel's life with Yahweh, the modes of transaction between Yahweh and Israel, and the shape of their shared world. Thus in our closer study of texts, we shall focus first on verbal sentences, suggest-

---

13. Richard A. Lanham, *The Motives of Eloquence: Literary Rhetoric in the Renaissance* (New Haven: Yale University Press, 1976).

14. On the privileged status of narrative, see Amos N. Wilder, "Story and Story-World," *Int* 37 (1983) 353–64; and Stanley Hauerwas and L. Gregory Jones, eds., *Why Narrative? Readings in Narrative Theology* (Grand Rapids: Eerdmans, 1989).

15. In his study of the divine name, Frank M. Cross, *Canaanite Myth and Hebrew Epic: Essays on the History of the Religion of Israel* (Cambridge: Harvard University Press, 1973) 60–75, has proposed a way in which the noun *Yahweh* is derived from the verb *hyh* in a verbal sentence, thus yielding a narrative character.

16. On the thematic of need-intervention-resolution as characteristic of Israel's life with Yahweh, see Patrick D. Miller, *They Cried to the Lord: The Form and Theology of Biblical Prayer* (Minneapolis: Fortress Press, 1994).

17. See Stephen Crites, "The Narrative Quality of Experience," *Why Narrative?* 65–88; and James B. Wiggins, *Religion as Story* (New York: University Press of America, 1986).

ing that such sentences were Israel's first and foremost strategy for making available the character of Yahweh, around which its life is to be understood and lived. That is, the characteristic rhetoric of Israel is not narrative per se, but narrative that features Yahweh as actor and agent. Indeed, the characteristic things to which Israel testified in its life and its world could be said primarily in narrative, because this world has at its center inexplicable transformations that may be replicated in other times and places but that cannot be readily classified as a characteristic type.[18]

Amos Wilder has suggested that stories generate story-worlds, so that the characters in the narrative themselves are permitted and required to respond and live according to the transactions of the narrative.[19] Derivatively, those who hear and trust these narratives are invited as well to live in a world where the same sort of characters are available and the same sorts of transactions are possible. As long as the hegemony of the Enlightenment prevailed, it was necessary to regard Old Testament narratives as enchanted accounts of a wish-world, finally assessed by reality. Where that hegemonic account of reality has been deabsolutized, however, as in the work of Alasdair MacIntyre, it is possible to see that the hegemonic construal of reality is yet one more narrative account, and it must compete with other accounts and make its bid with no special privilege.[20]

Imagination as crucial ingredient. The cruciality of speech in the faith of Israel (and of narrative speech in particular) suggests that imagination is a crucial ingredient in Israel's rendering of reality.[21] A narrative rendering of experience or of proposed futures entails the freedom and daring to plot, shape, construct, and construe around certain sequences and images that are indeed acts of constitutive imagination, not bound to what is flatly, evidently "on the ground." Israel engages in a dense rhetoric that makes available the density of its God who refuses every exhaustible domestication. As the classical, hegemonic tradition has been inclined toward essence and away from rhetoric, so it has also been inclined toward sober descriptiveness and away from imagination. The history of imagination, as it has been variously traced by Richard Kearney, Garrett Green, and David Bryant, indicates that since Aristotle, imagination has been regarded as an inadequate and unreliable mode of knowledge, in contrast to reasonable, logical,

---

18. The data are nicely presented by Robert C. Culley, *Studies in the Structure of Hebrew Narrative*, (Semeia Supplements 3; Missoula, Mont.: Scholars Press, 1976). Culley's work, however, tends to flatten into predictable, recurrent forms, a procedure that overlooks the peculiar "happenedness" of each transformative event given narrative reportage. While there may be recurrent propensities in these narrative accounts, it is important not to be excessively reductionist.

19. Wilder, "Story and Story-World," 361–64.

20. Garrett Green, *Imagining God: Theology and the Religious Imagination* (San Francisco: Harper and Row, 1989), has presented this competitive process as a matter of adjudicating between rival "ases." The importance of Green's work is to acknowledge that there is "no answer in the back of the book," but that formally, every "as" has as much claim as any other, and the competing versions of reality simply must be adjudicated, perhaps through hard-nosed reason, but probably finally through practice—the living out of a particular "as" with all the adherent risks.

21. See Brueggemann, *Texts under Negotiation*, chap. 1. Moreover, as Green makes clear, even readings of reality that are long established and taken for granted as given are in fact acts of imagination.

or empirical discourse.[22] And the classical theological tradition, with its bent toward the philosophical, has been reserved about imagination that moves beyond the logical or the empirical.

The Old Testament, in its theological propensity, refused such monitoring by the reasonable and the logical, or even by the empirical. Old Testament rhetoric characteristically takes great liberty in moving away from, beyond, and in contradiction to "sober reality," which might usually be regarded as a given.[23] What we in our modernity may regard as given may not be so much a function of genuine knowledge as it is a function of hegemonic power. For it is clear that in the ancient world of the Old Testament, the taunters of Yahwism, characteristically the urban power elite, likewise held on to givens that precluded Yahweh in principle—and that without the benefit of Enlightenment epistemology! (Cf. 2 Kgs 18:31-35 for an example of such mocking, and Ps 73:9-12 for an example internal to Israel.)

The imaginative force of Old Testament rhetoric refuses to live with the restraints of either hegemonic power or Enlightenment epistemology. Therefore in its construal of reality, propelled as it is by Yahweh, the Character who continually astonishes the other characters in the narrative, Israel's rhetoric notices and bears witness to what the world judges to be impossible. Indeed, at the center of Israel's imaginative enterprise are Yahweh's "impossibilities" (*pela'*), which regularly transform, reverse, and invert lived reality, either to the delight or to the dismay of the other participants in the narrative.[24]

Without a precise definition of imagination, we may characterize its work as the capacity to generate, evoke, and articulate alternative images of reality, images that counter what hegemonic power and knowledge have declared to be impossible. This counterversion (sub-version) of reality thereby deabsolutizes and destabilizes what "the world" regards as given, and invites the hearers of the text to recharacterize what is given or taken as real.[25]

Such a way of articulating and construing reality is problematic both for realistic history (which believes it can recover "what happened" and which characteristically serves "reasons of state") and for classical theology (with its temptation to excessive certitude and orthodoxy). It is nonetheless the case that in Israel's rhetoric, a Yahwistic version of reality refuses to be monitored or tamed by safer, more controllable, more credible givens.

---

22. Richard Kearney, *The Wake of Imagination: Ideas of Creativity in Western Culture* (London: Hutchinson Education, 1988), Green, *Imagining God;* and David Bryant, *Faith and the Play of Imagination: On the Role of Imagination in Religion* (Macon, Ga.: Mercer University Press, 1989).

23. Reference here might be made to poet Wallace Stevens's marvelous phrase concerning "the supreme fiction."

24. See Walter Brueggemann, "'Impossibility' and Epistemology in the Faith Tradition of Abraham and Sarah (Gen 18:1-15)," *ZAW* 94 (1982) 615–34.

25. Whereas Green, *Imagining God,* suggests that we "see as," Bryant, *Faith and the Play of Imagination* suggests that we "take as." The verb *take* is much more active and suggests that the confessor of any particular *as*, i.e., imaginer or witness, forcibly decides what is there. Green's view is thus much more conservative than is Bryant's, though Bryant does not go as far in a constructivist direction as does Gordon Kaufman, *The Theological Imagination: Constructing the Concept of God* (Philadelphia: Westminster Press, 1981).

Dramatic mode. This way of rendering reality, then, is in a dramatic mode, or as Hans Urs von Balthasar suggests, a theo-drama.[26] A dramatic mode for doing theology suggests that we deal with action that is plotted into scenes in which there is plot development, played by characters in whom development also occurs. The "large plot" of Old Testament faith—perhaps arranged around such overarching themes as promise and fulfillment, or deliverance and covenant, or exile and homecoming, or order and freedom—is a way of relating the material of the Old Testament to systemic theology. In truth, however, Old Testament theology as "large plot" is constituted by many smaller subplots, each of which bears its own weight as a theological datum. The characteristic subplot is centered in an intervention (sometimes a sustenance) that is preceded by a situation and followed by a changed situation. In order to sense the drama, one must see the plotting in its sequence and in its wholeness.

In like manner, the characters, the plot, and the subplots must be recognizable in order to sustain the plot. This means that the characters must have consistency and constancy.[27] It also requires, however, that the characters must change, grow, or develop, in order that successive scenes are not simply a reiteration of the first scene. For our theological interest, it is important to see that in this way of understanding Israel's God, Yahweh is presented as a key character in the drama or in the many subdramas that constitute Israel's theological data. This means that *Yahweh is not subject to the norms of critical inquiry, nor to the expectations and categories of classical theology in its commitment to essence. Yahweh is subject only to the rules of the drama itself, in which hearers of the text are invited to participate at second hand.*

This mode of presentation featuring Yahweh as a character in Israel's many dramas is important because drama is a very different mode for theology as distinct from essentialism and its ontological claim. Here we treat drama as a subset of rhetoric, and it is our purpose to suggest that Yahweh is to be understood in Israel's text as a rhetorical articulation. No doubt this rhetoric is proposed as realistic, is intended to be taken as real, and is indeed so taken characteristically in Israel. But such realism is of an innocent, precritical kind that entertains no dualism; the rhetoric is taken at face value, not at all with the denial of the ontological, but with no felt necessity to claim it.

This means, I suggest, that Israel's dramatic rendering of Yahweh is characteristically intended to be playful, inviting, teasing, rarely hardened into claims that push outside the drama itself. It may well be that Israel's theological articulation takes this form because ancient Israel characteristically commits its rhetorical

---

26. Hans Urs von Balthasar, *Theo-Drama: Theological Dramatic Theory* 1 (San Francisco: Ignatius Press, 1988). See Brueggemann, *Texts under Negotiation*, on dramatic modes of reality in distinction to metaphysical modes. I find this an important and telling distinction, even though the claims of the dramatic seem weak in the face of conventional assumptions about metaphysics. Less directly, notice that Reinhold Niebuhr, *The Self and the Dramas of History* (New York: Charles Scribner's Sons, 1955), has some important things to say about the dramatic dimension of story and of self.

27. See Dale Patrick, *The Rendering of God in the Old Testament* (OBT; Philadelphia: Fortress Press, 1981).

act against an established given. As the text, in any particular utterance, bids for Israel's allegiance, it must do so most often against established givens of some alien overlord, or against established power in its own community.[28] (Here I intentionally overstate, for in some Old Testament texts it is the text itself that is the establishment utterance, and therefore the text is less playful.)

In any case, a dramatic mode of theology requires the belated critic to stay inside the drama—inside the text itself—and to resist any venture outside or behind the text, either to critical possibility or to metaphysical essence. Yahweh is a player in the life of Israel, only as long as Yahweh is "played" in the drama of Israel.

Metaphor. Accent on rhetoric and consideration of narrative, imagination, and drama bring us finally to comment on metaphor as a central element in Israel's articulation of Yahweh. Metaphor, in which a subject is uttered according to properties that do not readily belong to it, provides a way in which something of the oddity of Israel's God can be expressed, an oddity that does not quite permit direct articulation. The use of metaphor again calls our attention to the playful, open quality of Israel's most serious speech and its theological imagination. While the most comprehensive treatment of metaphor available to us is that of Paul Ricoeur, the student may better refer to the study of Sallie McFague, who is much informed by Ricoeur and by the scholarship on metaphor to which Phyllis Trible made an earlier appeal.[29] Two observations of McFague are particularly important in engaging Israel's theological rhetoric.

First, McFague emphasizes that metaphor includes an understanding that the noun *is* the metaphor—for example, "Yahweh *is* a shepherd"—but at the same time, the noun *is not* the metaphor—"Yahweh *is not* a shepherd." Thus speech is kept open, in the awareness that the noun, in our theological case *Yahweh*, resists any articulation that gives excessive closure.[30] Metaphor is yet another case in point indicating that Israel's theological rhetoric is at its best evocative and not descriptive.

Second, McFague concludes that a monotheistic faith must practice metaphor in order not to become idolatrous. Monotheism, which is a propensity of Israel's faith, tends to focus everything on Yahweh.[31] The danger in such a singular claim is that the assertion of Yahweh should be thinly reduced, and obviously Israel's rhetoric concerning Yahweh does not intend this. Thus metaphor becomes a strat-

---

28. I do not wish to overstate the contrast between playful speech and establishment rhetoric. I understand playful speech to leave room for maneuverability and interpretive freedom on the part of the receiver. Authoritarianism—whether a stressed, authoritarian parent, the church's need to be infallible, or the technobabble of the Defense Department with its penchant for passive verbs—cannot allow for such playfulness.

29. Sallie McFague, *Metaphorical Theology: Models of God in Religious Language* (Philadelphia: Fortress Press, 1983). See also Janet Soskice, *Metaphor and Religious Language* (Oxford: Oxford University Press, 1987).

30. On the problematic of theological speech, i.e., God-talk, see Elizabeth Johnson, *She Who Is: The Mystery of God in Feminist Theological Discourse* (New York: Crossroad, 1992).

31. See James A. Sanders, "Adaptable for Life: The Nature and Function of Canon," *From Sacred Story to Sacred Text: Canon as Paradigm* (Philadelphia: Fortress Press, 1987) 9–39.

egy whereby Israel's faith, in its monotheistic tendency, can allow for the richness, diversity, and variegated character of Yahweh.

McFague tends to treat metaphor, including newly proposed ones, in a vacuum. Against such a practice, a reader of the Old Testament must insist that authoritative and generative metaphor must arise from and be embedded within a narrative context. The character so metaphorized cannot be abstracted from the plot in which the character is articulated. Thus Yahweh must be understood, in various metaphorical articulations, always in a narrative that gives context and locus to the metaphor.

In sum, then, our postmodern situation, which refuses to acknowledge a settled essence behind our pluralistic claims, must make a major and intentional investment in the practice of rhetoric, for the shape of reality finally depends on the power of speech. In Israel's theological rhetoric, it is evident that Israel employed a rich strategy in order to find speech to match the continuing Character whom it rendered at the center of its life. If we honor Israel's rhetoric as James Muilenburg has taught us to do, we can see a complexity, oddity, and dangerousness about Yahweh, qualities that could hardly be taken into account by the conventions of positivistic history or by the modes of classical theology. Yahweh, it appears, is always prepared for some new, outrageous self-disclosure, depending on the courage and freedom of Israel's boldest speakers.

Changes in Recent Old Testament Study

Given the political circumstance of pluralism and the rhetorical reality of Israel's speech as beginning reference points for new work in Old Testament theology, we may note some preliminary considerations of the character of the Old Testament in recent study that make a decisive difference in doing Old Testament theology. The items noted here are diverse, but it will be evident that each represents an important awareness that was not available prior to "the collapse of history."

The pluralism we have noticed, following Albertz, tends not to be a matter of "anything goes," as though every question carried a variety of options. Rather, the ongoing work of theological articulation tends to present *conflicting perspectives* on a particular point at issue, and we may offer a provisional summary of those conflicting perspectives.

Iconic and aniconic texts. As one might expect, every social dispute includes voices for change and voices for caution, advocates for transformational activity and adherents to some maintenance of present equilibrium. It is not possible to line up all the texts in the Old Testament in such a simple contrast, but one can notice tendencies and inclinations.[32] Writ most large, these hermeneutical postures found within the text itself may be termed *iconic* and *aniconic*. Patrick Miller has suggested that Israel's aniconic tendency is the distinguishing mark of the Old Tes-

---

32. See Odil H. Steck, "Theological Streams of Tradition," *Tradition and Theology in the Old Testament* (ed. Douglas A. Knight; Philadelphia: Fortress Press, 1977) 183–214.

tament, its point of contrast from its cultural neighbors and its environment, and the mark of its extreme radicality.[33] Thus the Second Commandment (Exod 20:4-6), which prohibits images of God, is taken as a focal interpretive principle for every aspect of Israel's life, concerning not only God, but also the establishment of enduring institutions and safe, reliable theological conclusions. This is what gives Israel its revolutionary character, which generates in Israel an ongoing critical awareness about itself and a restlessness in every social situation and circumstance.

Not all of the Old Testament shares this radicality, however, and perhaps no community enduring through time can sustain such a posture in any purity. Thus the Old Testament text includes a countering inclination toward the iconic. This does not mean actual images of God, but the articulation of symbols, practices, and institutions that have long-term staying power and that compromise the extreme radicality of the aniconic principle. The aniconic may characterize Israel's distinctiveness, yet it is clear that there are interests and voices in the Old Testament that seek to depart from or compromise that revolutionary distinctiveness.

Both of these inclinations, aniconic and iconic, are present in the Old Testament, perhaps reflecting different vested interests, or the requirements of different sociopolitical circumstances, or the needs and sensibilities of different authoritative speakers. Thus, to cite an easy example, the dispute over the establishment of the monarchy in 1 Samuel 7–15 articulates exactly such a conflict in which iconic forces understand monarchy as God's will, and aniconic forces understand monarchy as an act of infidelity to Yahweh.[34] What is interesting is that no clear answer to the crisis is given beforehand. There are, to be sure, practical victories and defeats with which Israel learns to live. But this dispute is ongoing in the life of Israel, indeed in the very character of Yahweh. Students of Old Testament theology will do well to see that Israel's best utterances are shot through with disputes that must always be reconsidered. James Sanders has well understood this at the hermeneutic level, speaking about a hermeneutic tendency that is constitutive and one that is prophetic.[35]

Bipolar schemes: Liberation and consolidation. In an earlier review, I have observed that in the period of Old Testament theology at the tail end of the twentieth century, and before the new accents here being exposited, a variety of attempts have been made to identify and characterize this ongoing and pervasive tension.[36] Indeed, it had become a truism of Old Testament theological interpretation that

---

33. Patrick D. Miller, "Israelite Religion," *The Hebrew Bible and Its Modern Interpreters* (ed. D. A. Knight and G. M. Tucker; Chico, Calif.: Scholars Press, 1985) 211–13. On the sociopolitical aspects of Israel's monotheism, see Ronald S. Hendel, "The Social Origins of the Aniconic Tradition in Early Israel," *CBQ* 50 (1988) 365–82.

34. On the sociopolitical forces at work in the dispute over monarchy, see Norman K. Gottwald, "The Participation of Free Agrarians in the Introduction of Monarchy to Ancient Israel: On the Application of H. A. Landsberger's Framework for the Analysis of Peasant Movements," *Semeia* 37 (1986) 77–106.

35. James A. Sanders, "Hermeneutics," *IDBSup* (Nashville: Abingdon Press, 1976) 402–7.

36. See Walter Brueggemann, "A Convergence in Recent Old Testament Theologies," *JSOT* 18 (1980) 2–18.

such a bipolar scheme is necessary in order to allow for the conflictual, disputatious quality of Old Testament articulation.

This writer has sought to schematize the ongoing bipolar propensity of the Old Testament around the themes of liberation and consolidation.[37] While that schematization is now somewhat dated and has been subject to important criticism, I cite it as a grid to illuminate the fundamental dispute that was inevitable in Israel's faith, a dispute that took many varied forms. To that grid I would now add, especially from the analysis of Fernando Belo, a recognition that Israel's legal traditions contain a trajectory of liberation that is concerned with debt cancellation and a trajectory of consolidation that is characteristically preoccupied with purity.[38] To take one other effort at stating this governing and pervasive dispute, I have also suggested that the more consolidating propensity of the text should be understood as "structure legitimating," and the revolutionary alternative as a practice of "the embrace of pain."[39] One does not want to overdo a schematic tendency, but it is helpful to see that one can detect some constancy in the matters about which Israel conducted its ongoing theological conflict.

Ongoing, unsettled dispute. Every contemporary interpretation of Old Testament theology will have an inclination about how to enter into and resolve the defining dispute that concerns both the public life of Israel and the character of Yahweh. Because the dispute, in a variety of articulations, is text-based, it is possible to find textual support for any generalized conclusion. In any case, such an interpretive judgment is never innocent or disinterested and may be decided variously—on the basis of one's own personal need and inclination, one's particular social setting or circumstance, or one's theological nurture and tradition. On any of these bases, the judgment made will finally not be innocent. It behooves the interpreter, therefore, to have a good bit of self-knowledge in rendering such a verdict, and a good measure of modesty in defending that verdict.

It is no doubt preferable if we recognize that this dispute, which may take many forms, is not settled in the Old Testament itself in any definitive way, and cannot be settled. Attentive and responsible interpretation, in my judgment, is required to continue to attend to that ongoing dispute; the very maintenance of the dispute in candor is the real work of interpretation.

Having said that, two points will be useful for our continuing discussion. First, it is correct, I believe, that most scholarly Old Testament interpreters who pay any attention to such interpretive questions are inclined toward the aniconic-prophetic, revolutionary propensity of the text. For many of us, our first serious exposure to the Old Testament was through some reading or some teacher who opened to us

---

37. Walter Brueggemann, "Trajectories in Old Testament Literature and the Sociology of Ancient Israel," *JBL* 98 (1979) 161–85.

38. Fernando Belo, *A Materialist Reading of the Gospel of Mark* (Maryknoll, N.Y.: Orbis Books, 1981).

39. Walter Brueggemann, "A Shape for Old Testament Theology I: Structure Legitimation," *CBQ* 47 (1985) 28–46, "A Shape for Old Testament Theology II: Embrace of Pain," *CBQ* 47 (1985) 395–415.

the revolutionary claims of the Old Testament. Even when this initial enthusiasm is cooled by critical study, that inclination tends to persist.

Second, the reader should understand that the present writer is unflagging in his empathy toward that revolutionary propensity in the text. This is a long-term interpretive judgment, rooted perhaps in history and personal inclination as well as in more informed critical judgment. For that I make no apology, for I believe it is not possible to maintain a completely evenhanded posture, and one may as well be honest and make one's inclinations known.[40] Having said that, it will be my intention in what follows to be fair-minded and fully appreciative of several bids for truth, iconic as well as aniconic, that are surely present in the text. It is in any case certain that one can no longer speak innocently about a straight-line development of Israel's faith. Every inch of interpretive advantage had to be struggled for. And in the outcome of such a struggle, one is only positioned and readied for the next surfacing of what is roughly the same struggle to occur all over again, sometimes with a different outcome.

Response to the Crisis of Exile

It is now increasingly agreed that *the Old Testament in its final form is a product of and a response to the Babylonian exile.* This premise needs to be stated more precisely. The Torah (Pentateuch) was likely completed in response to the exile, and the sub-sequent formation of the prophetic corpus and the "writings" as bodies of religious literature (canon) is to be understood as a product of Second Temple Judaism. This suggests that by their intention, these materials are not to be understood in their final form diachronically—that is, in terms of their historical development—but more as an intentional and coherent response to a particular circumstance of crisis. The readiness of scholars now to locate this literature in the sixth century B.C.E. or thereafter reflects a major reversal from the dominant twentieth-century incli-nation of both Albrecht Alt and William Foxwell Albright. Primarily through the schools of Alt and Albright, great emphasis had been placed on the theologically formative impact of the earliest (pre-monarchal) Israel. Now scholars are increas-ingly skeptical about that claim and about our capacity to know anything critically about that period.[41] This is yet another measure of the extent to which we are in a new interpretive situation at the end of the twentieth century.

Whatever older materials may have been utilized (and the use of older materi-als can hardly be doubted), the exilic and/or postexilic location of the final form of the text suggests that the Old Testament materials, understood normatively,

---

40. My work is often criticized for being one-sided, as in Ben C. Ollenburger, *Zion, City of the Great King: A Theological Symbol of the Jerusalem Cult* (JSOTSup 41; Sheffield: JSOT Press, 1987) 150–55; and J. Richard Middleton, "Is Creation Inherently Conservative? A Dialogue with Walter Brueggemann," *HTR* 87 (1994) 257–77; See my "Response to J. Richard Middleton," *HTR* 87 (1994) 279–89.

41. See chap. 1, nn. 54 and 127 concerning the work of John van Seters, Thomas L. Thompson, and Philip R. Davies.

are to be taken precisely in an acute crisis of displacement, when old certitudes—sociopolitical as well as theological—had failed. Indeed, the crisis of displacement looms as definitive in the self-understanding of Judaism that emerged in the exile and thereafter. With the failure of long-trusted institutions, the faith community that generated the final form of the text, and that was generated by it, was thrown back in a singular way on the textual-rhetorical possibility for life-space. In acute dislocation when appeal could no longer be made to city, king, or temple, it was to this text that Israel increasingly had to look.

In the generation of this text, there were no obvious lines of certitude, no ready formulations of assurance, no self-evident reliabilities. Therefore it is not surprising that the exile is a moment of enormous literary generativity, when a variety of daring articulations of faith were undertaken.[42] Moreover, this variety comes to characterize the theological articulation of Judaism and the self-understanding of this community of faith. Any attempt, therefore, to schematize the rich and varied responses to this foundational crisis is sure to diminish the richness of this formative, imaginative moment.

Reuse of older materials. It is clear that this literary-theological generativity utilized materials that had been treasured in earlier times. Thus there is important continuity between older materials and the exilic final form. In large part, the reuse of older materials continued to respect the earlier locus of materials, so that one can continue to identify Priestly, prophetic, legal, and sapiential inclinations. At the same time, however, the depth of the exilic crisis and the daring of this generative moment also worked an important discontinuity in the material. As a consequence, the final form of the material has become something new.

This ready capacity to reuse older materials in imaginative ways, which marks the restless activity of the exiles, is important in two ways. First, it reminds us that for all of the material of the text, we must entertain the practice of a double reading. Thus, for example, the material of the wilderness sojourn must be read as it is presented, as the experience of early Israel in its formative period under the leadership of Moses. It may make use of older materials or the portrayal may be largely fictive. In either case, it must be read according to Israel's self-presentation. At the same time, however, we must read it according to the way the materials are reused, so that "wilderness" is regularly reciphered as "exile." Our theological reading of the material must maintain both of these angles; we may not, like the historian, choose between them.

Second, this reuse of older materials (or putatively older materials) is not a one-time practice; it makes visible in Jewish textual practice the *principle of reading as reuse;* thus texts often take on double or multiple readings, which are to be understood in their putative time and place as well as in their reused time and place.

---

42. See Peter R. Ackroyd, *Exile and Restoration: A Study of Hebrew Thought of the Sixth Century B.C.* (OTL; Philadelphia: Westminster Press, 1968); Enno Janssen, *Juda in der Exilzeit; ein Beitrag zur Frage der Entstehung des Judentums* (FRLANT 51; Göttingen: Vandenhoeck and Ruprecht, 1956); and Ralph Klein, *Israel in Exile: A Theological Interpretation* (OBT; Philadelphia: Fortress Press, 1979).

Moreover, it seems to me evident that the later reader may not choose either of these readings to the neglect of the other, but must always be engaged in and attentive to both. I suggest that this principle of reading as reuse, which is definitional for the exilic community, is belatedly taken up by the Christian community in its reuse of older texts in its articulation about Jesus. In the case of Christian reuse of Jewish sources, it is precisely the insistence on double reading that precludes any straightforward supersessionism. Thus exilic or postexilic reuse of older material did not supersede Mosaic preeminence, nor can Christian reuse supersede older Jewish claims.

Counter-reality. Altogether, the many responses to the crisis of the exile that constitute this remarkable corpus bespeak an extraordinary range of faithful imagination. Thus if we consider only the most obvious cases, all in relation to the crisis, the Priestly material ventures Israel's future in terms of cultic presence, the Deuteronomic materials venture that future in terms of an exacting symmetrical obedience, the lyrics of exilic Isaiah are a revisitation of older narratives of deliverance, the poetry of Lamentations grieves an irreversible loss, and the Joban poem presents a magisterial dispute of Israel with God over who is in the right. What strikes one about all of these responses is that these daring formulations had little to go on in terms of available, lived, circumstantial data. Thus a proposal of Priestly presence had no temple to which to appeal. Exilic Isaiah had only an anticipation of international upheaval. And surely the Deuteronomists and the Joban poet had little ground for imagining that somehow Torah-righteousness was a useful subject for reflection among exiles. Thus in all of these various articulations of faith, the formers of this literature were not deterred by how little they had to go on in their own circumstance. In fact, they articulated, as artists always must, against the data at hand.[43] They refused to curb their imagination, buoyantly moving in their imaginative anticipation beyond the data of their circumstance. And so, taken in large, these materials are to be understood as an act of unrestrained grief, which denied nothing, and as a counter-act of defiant hope, which refused to give in to circumstance.[44]

At the outset, then, it is important for a student of Old Testament theology to recognize that *this material is an enterprise of counter-reality.* It refuses given imperial reality and summons its hearers to an alternative reality. It is possible to say that these artistic utterances and daring contrasts are based in old memories, or in present sufferings, or in defiant imagination, or in profound faith, or in all of these. The only thing such candid grief and defiant hope are not rooted in is available cir-

---

43. On the critical, subversive responsibility of literary figures, see André Brink, *Writing in a State of Siege: Essays on Politics and Literature* (New York: Summit Books, 1983), Vaclav Havel, *Open Letters: Selected Prose, 1965–1990* (London: Faber, 1991); Havel, *Living in Truth: Twenty-Two Essays Published on the Occasion of the Award of the Erasmus Prize to Vaclav Havel* (London: Faber, 1989); and Havel, *The Writer and Human Rights* (ed. Toronto Arts Group for Human Rights; Garden City, N.Y.: Doubleday, 1983).

44. See Alan Mintz, *Ḥurban: Responses to Catastrophe in Hebrew Literature* (New York: Columbia University Press, 1984).

cumstance. Whatever theory of inspiration and revelation one may have concerning the text, one can see at work an artistic, determined buoyancy that is relentlessly available in the text. This phenomenon, however it be justified or explained, is what grips us in endless fascination with and regard for this textual corpus.

The actual historical circumstance of exile is far from clear. Some scholars minimize the significance of the historical exile for emerging Judaism, regarding the Babylonian community of Jews as only one competitor for the Jewish future. Daniel Smith, however, has provided a much more formidable scenario of that history.[45] It may be that the picture of the exile dominating the biblical materials and subsequent Judaism is the imaginative, forceful, interpretive act of an elite minority in Babylon who imposed their "Yahweh alone" conviction on Judaism, and who thereby presented themselves as the only true carriers, embodiment, and interpreters of emerging Judaism.

Exile-homecoming model. In any case, the achievement of this literary-theological effort is such that it has established exile as a paradigmatic event for the Jewish community, and therefore homecoming as a profound anticipation for members of this textual community. As a consequence of this interpretive achievement, members of the community who have never been physically or materially displaced must, as children and products of this text, understand and imagine themselves as displaced and as waiting for homecoming.[46]

When exile is taken as definitional and paradigmatic for this text and for its ongoing community, we may extrapolate two important implications. First, in terms of theological models (not to speak of historicity), it is not a far reach of imagination to see that the Jewish model of exile and homecoming received a christological equivalence in terms of crucifixion and resurrection. I do not suggest a Christian displacement of the Jewish claim, nor a supersession. But rather I suggest that in its paradigmatic focus on crucifixion and resurrection, the Christian community seeks roughly to speak about the same experienced and anticipated reality as do Jews. Any Christian theology that seeks to take the Old Testament seriously must ponder well that the core of faith, for Christians as for Jews, is situated in the matrix of exile.

Second, this emergent and definitional model of exile and homecoming is an important point of contact with the larger public discussion of social possibility. I do not have in mind the cosmological homesickness about which the Romantic poets have written. I have in mind, rather, two different and more immediate phenomena. (a) Peter Berger, following Max Weber, long ago recognized that the reduction of human life to technique and bureaucracy produced a "homeless mind,"

---

45. Daniel L. Smith, *The Religion of the Landless: The Social Context of the Babylonian Exile* (Bloomington, Ind.: Meyer-Stone, 1989).

46. Jacob Neusner, *Understanding Seeking Faith: Essays on the Case of Judaism* (Atlanta: Scholars Press, 1986), 1:137–41, has indicated the paradigmatic power of the exile for all Jews. Moreover, Neusner has exhibited the way in which the defining power of the exile permeates and is enacted in small daily acts such as table prayers.

which we are now seeing expressed in terms of profound fearfulness and predictable brutality.[47] To be sure, the "homeless mind" of modernity is not a close equivalent to Jewish displacement. But the parallels are enough to let us entertain the possibility that the homecoming anticipated in these texts is an important contemporary and public line of discourse.

(b) With the worldwide economic and environmental crisis that indicates no soon-to-come abatement and with the frantic response of intensified militarism, the world political economy is actively engaged in the production of exiles, as was the old Babylonian empire.[48] That is to say, the large number of refugees, displaced persons, and (in the local economy) homeless persons is not an accident or an unfortunate aberration in the system. It is rather an inescapable and predictable outcome of a world society that has become increasingly inhospitable in its fearfulness. In such a world situation as the present one, it is of enormous importance to have a theological literature that is candid about exile, that is insistent on homecoming, and that believes relentlessly in dimensions of moral accountability and aspects of holy presence that are inalienably germane to the human situation and the human prospect. The reality of exile and the prospect of homecoming, of course, pertain first of all to the community of this text. What makes this text publicly significant in an enduring way, however, is that the issues that preoccupied this textual community inescapably preoccupy the larger public community with the same kind of relentless urgency.

Intertextuality

The turn away from history to the actual rhetoric of the text has made important the awareness of the *intertextuality* of the text: the readiness of the text to quote the text. The awareness of intertextuality represents an important alternative to our long-standing preoccupation with the historical. Thus a diachronic reading of the text has sought to keep texts related to events, experiences, or circumstances. Intertextuality, by contrast, has seen that *texts are primarily related to other texts,* and that the interaction between texts generates a realm of discourse, dialogue, and imagination that provides a world in which to live. Michael Fishbane has explored in exhaustive detail the ways in which intertextuality works, whereby the corpus of textual materials, its images and its phrasing, are palpably available in the process of new texts, so that old texts continue to recur by reference, by hint, and by nuance.[49]

Those who are outsiders to the text may spot only the most explicit quotations, but those who are situated deeply and imaginatively in the world of the text can

---

47. Peter L. Berger et al., *The Homeless Mind: Modernization and Consciousness* (New York: Random House, 1974).

48. See Philip Wheaton and Duane Shank, *Empire and the Word: Prophetic Parallels between Exilic Experience and Central America's Crisis* (Washington: EPICA Task Force, 1988), on the United States as "Babylon."

49. Michael Fishbane, *Biblical Interpretation in Ancient Israel* (Oxford: Oxford University Press, 1989). Less directly, see Richard B. Hays, *Echoes of Scripture in the Letters of Paul* (New Haven: Yale University Press, 1993).

detect many other allusions. The outcome of this process is that a certain field of imagery, as well as grammar, dialect, and cadence, emerge in which all of reality is uttered and therefore construed and therefore experienced in a certain way. Those who value the texts, moreover, are engaged in an ongoing conversation that is as urgent and as contemporary as the present moment, but it is also a conversation that stretches over the generations and includes the voices of ancestors whom the historians have thought to be long departed. Intertextuality is a process of conversation by which the entire past and memory of the textual community is kept available and present in concrete and detailed ways. While those of us who come late to the text—Christians, for example—can never fully engage the whole text, it is a part of our work and our joy to be increasingly at home in that grammar, dialect, and cadence, as a place of believing and a place of being.

This process gives us a sense that the conversation over time within the community is the most crucial life-giving enterprise. This passion in turn gives some distance to other transactions extraneous to the text, which seek to interrupt, disrupt, or discredit this inner-community conversation. This does not mean that the practitioners of this dialogue are indifferent to or cut off from the outer world. It does means, however, that life consists in the ongoing practice of this textuality, without reference to the outside, or without providing any justification to the outside for how life is uttered and practiced on the inside.

Such an approach to lived reality, however, does not suggest any rigidity or intransigence about this grammar, dialect, or cadence, as though it remains completely unchanging. It is self-evident that through time and over time, the modes and nuances of discourse change in new cultural contexts.[50] But it is equally self-evident that this grammar has remarkable staying power and sustains unapologetically its own character and quality over time and through time. Thus there can be no translation of this grammar, dialect, or cadence into alien modes, as Rudolf Bultmann and Paul Tillich, for example, have proposed. This community of textuality is not embarrassed about the practice of its own speech, for it knows that to give up this practice of its uttered memory is surely to give up its identity and its life in the world.

The practitioners, speakers, and listeners of this intertextual conversation are clearly text-saturated people. To attend to the text ceaselessly in various ways is their true delight. They are not worried about being caught in this odd transaction, nor about missing out on other enterprises in the larger world, for they know that the practice of this treasured and long-established tradition of utterance is the source of their life and their identity in the world. This conversation is itself

---

50. The reality of this change poses an important challenge to the categories of George A. Lindbeck, *The Nature of Doctrine: Religion and Theology in a Postliberal Age* (Philadelphia: Westminster Press, 1984); see William C. Placher, *Unapologetic Theology: A Christian Voice in a Pluralistic Conversation* (Louisville: Westminster/John Knox, 1989); and David J. Bryant, "Christian Identity and Historical Change: Post Liberals and Historicity," *JR* 73 (1993) 31–41. In the same way, this change poses important questions for my attempt herein to identify Israel's characteristic speech practices.

a good. Such utterance, spoken and heard, is an act of being at home in sheer delight and security.

Such practice of utterance, however, is also a way to fend off intrusive alternatives. This community that attends so vigilantly to its characteristic phrasing knows that to host other rhetorics is, in the long run, to give up its identity and its odd way of being in the world. This community of practiced speech, moreover, knows that when it yields its characteristic utterance and seeks a community outside its own idiom, it quickly ends up in oppression and at risk. Thus intertextuality is not simply a literary device nor an interesting aesthetic phenomenon to observe in the midst of the text. It is also one of the principal strategies taken up by this community, whereby the community is able to remain itself in the midst of many temptations and pressures. This texted community lives through time by its intentional, long-established utterance. We who would belatedly enter into that discourse must marvel at the glad saturation in the text undertaken by its members, and must see to our own attentiveness to that same saturation. Thus the practice of intertextuality is in the end a political act—a sustained public insistence about identity, freedom, power, and responsibility, which argues against and refuses alternative insistences about the shape of public reality. Moreover, this political insistence about public shape has at its center the God of Israel as a key political player. Most broadly understood, this rhetoric as politics insists that reality should be known, experienced, and practiced through this and not some other construal. Israel's construal of reality, moreover, turns not on large propositional generalizations, but on the detail of utterance.

The recognition of this urgency of utterance in the text and in its transmission and interpretation clearly requires that Old Testament theology must be done differently than it has been done in a cognitive, ideational mode. Old Testament theology does not aim at an outcome of a system of settled propositions. Rather Old Testament theology, understood in these categories, is an attempt to engage this life-in-rhetoric, which has no logical beginning or end and no rational shape judged by more discursive rhetorics. Therefore, in identifying the characteristic accents and themes, one may begin anywhere and notice a kind of coherence in which all themes are held in relation to all others. In such a discernment, one is not likely to complete a system of theology, but only to observe and participate for a while in the practice of this rhetorical activity, whereby the whole of reality is received and appropriated differently. This means, in the end, that theological interpretation is a modest enterprise that always, inevitably, must leave much unsaid and perhaps even unnoticed.

Jewishness of the Text

The comments that I have made about the disputatious character, the exilic locus, and the intertextual practice of the text point to another marking of the Old Testament text that is now immediately available to us with the "collapse of history": The Old Testament text is *resiliently Jewish*. In some ways, of course, that is a truism, but it is a truism that is too readily neglected. It is not possible to argue that the Jewish community is the only community to conduct a disputatious literature, nor the only community that has exile at its center, nor the only community to practice intertextuality with a passion. But it can be insisted on all these counts that the Jewish community is the model practitioner.

Only two aspects of the Jewishness of the text need concern us. First, this text is of, with, and for a particular historical community that has its own distinct life through time, a life characterized by much abuse and displacement. When the text is seen from a historical perspective, this community is its subject matter. It is possible to move away from that particularity, and in the end, a Christian interpretation must of necessity treat what is concretely Jewish in a paradigmatic or typological way. The particularity of the Jewishness of the text, however, requires that in any use of the text, one must take great care against universalizing the text—particularly, in our present situation, against universalizing the text so that it is read in a generically Western way. Like every classic text, this text is expansive in its claim and wants its prism to be ever-wideningly definitional. In its expansiveness, however, it wants never to compromise or forfeit its particularity concerning this community or its God. Thus expansiveness moves toward universalizing, but never at the cost of particularity.

Second, and more specifically, it is important to recognize the Jewish modes of discourse through which the text proceeds. Here I must issue something of an ill-informed disclaimer. I do not suggest anything like a Jewish spirit or a Jewish genius, nor do I suggest that there is something given as ethnic about Jewish modes of discourse. I refer rather descriptively and practically to ways of speaking that seem to be characteristic of how Jewish discourse is conducted.

On the one hand, the discourse to which I refer is committedly concrete and particular, refusing any ultimate transcendentalism. Partly that concreteness is an insistence on the concreteness of this community of Jews, the scandal of particularity. Partly it is an insistence on here-and-now lived reality as the locus of meaning from which there is no escape or alternative. Thus the rhetoric regularly pertains to the dailiness, immediacy, and availability of lived life.[51] On the other hand, such discourse is characteristically polyvalent, open to a variety of meanings, not insistent on a single interpretation, and on the whole refusing to give closure or clear explanation. It may well be that other communities speak in the same way. I do not absolutize this observation. I intend only to contrast this particularistic, polyvalent mode of discourse with the pervasive Western, Christian propensity to flatten, to refuse ambiguity, to lose density, and to give universalizing closure.[52]

This particularistic and polyvalent propensity shows itself in a variety of ways. First, we may notice that many texts, in and of themselves, are enigmatic, whether

---

51. There is, to be sure, a Jewish mystical tradition (Kabbalah) that is transcendental, but such inclinations are largely postbiblical and extrabiblical.

52. On this point, I am informed by Susan Handelman, *The Slayers of Moses: The Emergence of Rabbinic Interpretation in Modern Literary Theory* (Albany: SUNY Press, 1983).

by design or not. One cannot easily make out what is intended, and a great deal of work is left to the hearer in order to complete the text. It may be that the interpreter will invest in one particular, possible reading of a text, but this leaves open and available much that any one interpreter does not explore. Indeed, as James Kugel has indicated, it was the practice of the great rabbis to attend especially to what was unstated, unclear, or unresolved in the text, and to let that element propel hearing in a new direction.[53] This discourse, moreover, refuses to generalize or to systematize. It characteristically presents one text at a time, and is not at all vexed about juxtaposing texts that explicitly contradict each other. Most often, the editorial process seems to exhibit no great need to overcome such contradictions.[54] At a cognitive or ideational level, the text, taken as a whole, seems to have no sustained interest in sorting matters out or bringing to resolution many of the contradictions that mark both Israel's faith and Yahweh's character. For example, it is characteristically Jewish not to reduce hope to a single Messiah; in the course of Israel's history, there is the potential of many messiahs.[55]

I state all of this diffidently and with lack of precision. The matter becomes clearer, however, and more important when this mode of discourse is contrasted with the methods of classical Western theological discourse, which wants to overcome all ambiguity and give closure in the interest of certitude. I am not sure why the Western Christian tradition has tended to such closure that tilts toward reductionism. It may be because classical Western Christianity has been committed, from early on, to Aristotelian logic that could not countenance the existence of opposites at the same time. Or perhaps such a tendency to closure is powerfully operative since the Constantinian establishment of Christianity, whereby the political purpose of the religion is to provide reliable legitimacy for the claims of power. Obviously, great political power cannot be legitimated in a religious tradition that is fraught with ambiguity. As an alternative, William Placher has suggested that it is the endless openness of Christianity to engagement with culture, an openness Judaism was not obligated to share, that has required Christianity to give closure on many matters as a means of ensuring its survival and identity as a particular community.[56]

These complex issues need not be resolved or even fully exposited here. It is enough for us to notice the ways in which Christian readers of the Old Testament have tended to run roughshod over the relatively playful and open inclination of Old Testament rhetoric in order to serve the less tensive propensities of the Chris-

---

53. James L. Kugel, "Early Interpretation: The Common Background of Later Forms of Biblical Exegesis," *Early Biblical Interpretation* (ed. James L. Kugel and Rowan A. Greer; Philadelphia: Westminster Press, 1986) 9–106.

54. Historical criticism, in its conventional, long-established practice, has been bent on overcoming, resolving, dissolving, or explaining away all such contradictions. One of the primary strategies for such disposal has been source dissection, whereby different parts of tension or contradiction have been assigned to different sources, thus eliminating what may be precisely the point of interest in the text.

55. Thus, for example, see A. Joseph Everson, "The Days of Yahweh," *JBL* 93 (1974) 329–37, on Israel's refusal to reduce hope to any single "day of the Lord."

56. William Placher, personal communication with the author.

tian tradition. Indeed, to read the Old Testament in order to articulate ordered, cognitive constancies in the text is likely to read against the character of the text itself. I do not suggest that the Old Testament does not voice ordered, cognitive constancies, but only that the text, when taken as a whole, treats such constancies as highly provisional. The point of provisionality will be evident in my exposition. It is, moreover, likely that any Christian exposition, including this one, cannot finally resist such a temptation.

Dialectical and Dialogical Quality

Among the general matters to be noted at the outset of our work in the face of "the collapse of history" is this: *the Old Testament in its theological articulation is characteristically dialectical and dialogical, and not transcendentalist.*[57] This is perhaps another articulation of the point concerning Jewish and nonhegemonic readings, for Jewishness is characterized by dialogical-dialectical modes of discourse, whereas Western Christianity has long practiced a flight to the transcendent.[58] Moreover, one cannot say that the Old Testament everywhere and at all times shuns the transcendental. But I shall insist that it characteristically does so.

By this I mean that the God of Israel is characteristically "in the fray" and at risk in the ongoing life of Israel. Conversely the God of Israel is rarely permitted, in the rhetoric of Israel, to be safe and unvexed "above the fray." Even where God is said to be elsewhere, this "elsewhere" is most often in response to Israel's life, either negatively or positively.[59]

The dialogical-dialectical quality of the text that keeps God "in the fray" brings one inevitably to the question of theodicy. Indeed theodicy is the quintessential question of Jewish rhetoric. But Israel's text is not capable of or willing to give a resolution to that question. Israel's text, and therefore Israel and Israel's God, are always in the middle of an exchange, unable to come to ultimate resolution. There may be momentary or provisional resolution, but because both parties are intensely engaged and are so relentlessly verbal, we are always sure that there will be another speech, another challenge, another invitation, another petition, another argument, which will reopen the matter and expend the provisional settlement. Thus Israel's religious rhetoric does not intend to reach resolution or to achieve closure. This rhetoric, rather, is for the very long run, endlessly open-ended, sure to be taken up again for another episode of adjudication, which this time around may have a different—but again provisional—outcome. And because the God of Israel lives so long in Israel's rhetoric, we may say finally that Israel's God also partakes of this provisional way in the world.

---

57. I have no doubt that the work of Mikhail Bakhtin will be crucial for future work in this direction in Old Testament study. See Walter L. Reed, *Dialogues of the Word: The Bible as Literature According to Bakhtin* (New York: Oxford University Press, 1993).

58. John D. Caputo, *Demythologizing Heidegger* (Bloomington: Indiana University Press, 1993) 6–7 and passim, follows Jacques Derrida in using the term *jewgreek* as one who opposes such universalizing.

59. Thus the point of Amos 9:2-4, Ps 139:7-12 is not the pervasive immanence of Yahweh but Yahweh's dangerous inescapability.

This dialectical-dialogical character for theological discourse flies in the face of all of our long-established, conventional theological practices. Our propensity is to reason things through to a settlement, to reach conclusions that then stand as certitudes to which appeal can subsequently be made. Israel's characteristic mode of discourse, however, tends not to claim such destinations for itself, and tends not to grant them to God. There is in Israel's God-talk a remarkable restlessness and openness, as if each new voice in each new circumstance must undertake the entire process anew. Remarkably, the God of Israel, perhaps so characteristically Jewish, is willing to participate yet again in such an exchange that must be inordinately demanding. For Israel and for Israel's God, there is no deeper joy, no more serious requirement, no more inescapable burden, than to be reengaged in the process of exchange that never arrives but is always on the way.

Options Facing the Theological Enterprise

Concerning these preliminary comments, we may finally briefly note some options facing the theological enterprise in the present demanding moment. These options are under adjudication, and because of our new theological situation, we are not yet able to see a way past these disagreements. The most one can do is to be aware of the spectrum of possibility, and to state as clearly as possible where one is situated.

Foundationalism. A term arising in Roman Catholic conversations, foundationalism seeks to carry on theological discourse in a way that has credibility to a larger, nonbelieving public.[60] It consists in a willingness to assume and operate from the epistemological assumptions of conventional intellectual discourse. Such an assumption tends to tone down or silence the more subversive aspects of radical theological claim in the interest of "making sense." In important ways, this perspective continues the work of Friedrich Schleiermacher, which seeks to make faith claims available to "the cultured despisers of religion." The strength of this perspective is that Christian faith has the credibility of being reasonable in public discourse. The problem is whether in making faith reasonable, the scandalous particularity—the peculiar claim that is at its core unreasonable—has been compromised.

Not many Old Testament scholars are drawn to foundationalism, for our proper work is exactly to take up the oddity of this peculiarly Jewish text, which in any case will not be accommodated to the dominant reason of culture. And yet much of what passes for historical criticism is in fact in the service of something like foundationalism. For it is the oddity of the tradition, the inscrutable and the miraculous, that are characteristically smoothed out and explained away in historical

---

60. David Tracy is the most prominent foundationalist theologian in the United States, but the work of Francis Fiorenza should also be noted. See Olaf Tollefsen, *Foundationalism Defended: Essays on Epistemology, Ethics, and Aesthetics* (Manchester, N.H.: Sophia Institute Press, 1994); for helpful comments from a Roman Catholic perspective, see John E. Thiel, *Nonfoundationalism* (Minneapolis: Fortress Press, 1994); and Thiel, *Imagination and Authority: Theological Authorship in the Modern Tradition* (Minneapolis: Fortress Press, 1991).

criticism, with its alliance with modern rationality. What is left, then, as compatible with modern reason is exactly what is least challenging, least interesting, and least important in the theological claim of the Old Testament.

It is not for general and theoretical reasons of foundationalism that historical criticism has become suspect to many Old Testament interpreters. Quite concretely, there is a growing wonderment, shared by this writer, whether the very criticism that set out to make the text available on its own terms has now made the text unavailable on its own terms, as it has become available according to the canon of modernity. One cannot reject the gains and possibilities of modernist criticism out of hand, but one must be attentive to the risks in explaining too much that intends to be inexplicable and by its very character inscrutable.

Canon criticism. In response against exaggerated forms of historical criticism that rearticulated the Old Testament text according to modernist categories, a live option in interpretation is what has come to be called canon criticism. I shall comment in another section on the work of Brevard Childs. Here I note only that Childs in his canonical perspective resists the fragmentation of the text by seeking to read all parts of the text in terms of the whole.[61]

In effect, however, it appears that this approach in the end has generated a reading of the Old Testament text in and through the categories of Christian systematic theology. To the extent this is true, it is a reading that steers clear of the dangers of modernist criticism. But such an approach features its own reductionism, which in turn overrides and distorts the specificity of the text. The gain of a canonical perspective is that without embarrassment it takes up theological themes that modernist foundationalism must eschew. But an accent on such themes, theological as they are, tends to override the specific theological data of the text that refuse to be flatly thematized.

A seriatim **reading.** In an exposé of the universalizing tendencies of Western theology, Friedrich Nietzsche observed that truth "is an army of metaphors."[62] That is, the large claim of truth in conventional idealistic thought is in fact constituted by a collage of particularities, and the particulars are not overcome or eradicated by generalization, either modernist or canonical.

Nietzsche's approach can issue in a kind of nihilism, but it need not. We may refer rather to the suggestive work of David Blumenthal, who proposes to take the several texts of the Old Testament *a seriatim* and read them one at a time without reference to a larger overview.[63] Perhaps it could be said of Blumenthal that he

---

61. Jon D. Levenson, "The Eighth Principle of Judaism and the Literary Simultaneity of Scripture," *The Hebrew Bible, the Old Testament, and Historical Criticism: Jews and Christians in Biblical Studies* (Louisville: Westminster/John Knox, 1993) 62–81, has explicated the "Eighth Principle" of Maimonides to this effect. It is important to note that in this regard Levenson explicitly stands close to Childs.

62. Friedrich Nietzsche, "On Truth and Lie," *The Portable Nietzsche* (ed. Walter Kaufmann; New York: Viking Press, 1954) 46–47.

63. David Blumenthal, *Facing the Abusive God: A Theology of Protest* (Louisville: Westminster/John Knox, 1993).

inevitably bootlegs some overarching assumption, as do we all, even if it is kept hidden. I wonder, however, if such a notion of hidden system perhaps peculiarly applies to Western Christians. It may be that Blumenthal's attempt at an *a seriatim* reading is one that could only be done by a Jew.

As a Western Christian, I am finally unable to practice Blumenthal's one-at-a-time approach.[64] It is emotionally and intellectually impossible for me to do so, for other texts keep crowding into my reading of any particular text, and so I must read a particular text in the presence of other texts. Nonetheless, I can be instructed in important ways by Blumenthal, and reminded of the particularity that belongs to his way of doing Jewish reading. Such a sensitivity, among many other things, requires one to be on the alert, to notice and attend precisely to the particularity of the text that does not "fit the pattern." Thus an *a seriatim* valuing of particular texts stands as a warning both against modernist criticism that may smooth things out, and against a canonical perspective that is bent toward systematic closure.

A postliberal approach. My own effort in what follows is an attempt to be postliberal, or nonfoundational, as this approach is variously articulated by Hans Frei, George Lindbeck, and Stanley Hauerwas.[65] I understand this approach to refer to an attempt to exposit the theological perspectives and claims of the text itself, in all its odd particularity, without any attempt to accommodate to a larger rationality, either of modernity or of classical Christianity.

Thus I intend to pay attention to the internal logic of the texts, and to attend, as best I can, to the peculiar grammar and dialect of this textual tradition. To that extent I am informed by Lindbeck's analysis of the "grammar of faith," though I recognize there is a great difference of reference between my own attention to Old Testament texts and his concern for the history of Christian doctrine.[66] The Old Testament surely has a discernible grammar and dialect that are present everywhere in its articulation.

At the same time, however, I subscribe to the criticism of Lindbeck's argument, insofar as Lindbeck holds that the rules of grammar are constant and unchanging. It is the great contribution of the entire historical-critical enterprise to indicate that Israel's ongoing life of faith is impinged on and impacted in powerful and discernible ways by circumstance and by experience. Thus, for example, one is able to see in exilic Isaiah that a whole new genre of utterance is required in the disputation speeches, because the critique of the gods is now required in place of the older prophetic lawsuits against Israel.[67] And surely the text of Qoheleth witnesses

---

64. See Walter Brueggemann, "Texts That Linger, Not Yet Overcome," *TToday* (forthcoming).

65. Hans Frei, *The Eclipse of Biblical Narrative: A Study of Eighteenth and Nineteenth Century Hermeneutics* (New Haven: Yale University Press, 1974); George Lindbeck, *The Nature of Doctrine: Religion and Theology in a Postliberal Age* (Philadelphia: Westminster Press, 1984); and Stanley Hauerwas, *A Community of Character: Toward a Constructive Social Ethic* (Notre Dame, Ind.: University of Notre Dame Press, 1981).

66. See especially George Lindbeck, "Barth and Textuality," *TToday* 43 (October, 1986) 361–76.

67. On such disputatious speech, see Claus Westermann, "Sprach und Struktur der Prophetie Deuterojesajas," *Forschung am Alten Testament; Gesammelte Studien* (ThB 24; Munich: Kaiser, 1964)

to the impact of Hellenization that puts the text at a considerable distance from the older sapiential materials. One must indeed allow, as David Tracy indicates, for the impact of experience to evoke fresh modes of articulation.[68] Thus while my fundamental sympathies are allied with Lindbeck's suggestions, we know too much about the history of Israelite religion to ignore the changes, transformations, and adjustments that have taken place in Israel's rhetoric. Israel's grammar was indeed impinged on by the vagaries of historical experience, so that the "constancies" of that grammar could remain "constant" only by staying current in the always new and demanding places where Israel was summoned to make its candid, hopeful utterance.

Second listening community. Thus the enterprise of Old Testament theology is put, I believe inescapably, in a situation where exposition is always conducted in the presence of two audiences.[69] In the first instant, exposition is directed at the self-understanding, self-discernment, and authorization of the community that begins in assent to this text. (I include "authorization" because the intention of such exposition, due to its central Character, is never just knowledge, but always obedient activity.)[70] To that extent, the expository task is within the horizon suggested by Lindbeck. This ongoing community must keep relearning its own peculiar grammar and dialect, in order that it may maintain itself through time and have the courage and energy for the obedience inherent in its identity.

At the same time, however, the Old Testament and its resultant Jewish and Christian communities have not characteristically been able to live in isolation, nor have they intended to, nor does their character, vis-à-vis the God who claims governance of the world, permit such isolation. For that reason, the Old Testament is always addressing, belatedly, a second listening community: the larger public that is willing to host many alternative construals of reality.[71] The long history of this text, especially in the West, attests to the endless points of impingement, whereby

---

124–44, a study closely related to Westermann, *Basic Forms of Prophetic Speech* (Atlanta: John Knox, 1967).

68. David Tracy, *The Analogical Imagination: Christian Theology and the Culture of Pluralism* (New York: Crossroad, 1981).

69. Tracy, ibid., 3–46, identifies three constituencies: the church, the academy, and the public. Note well, however, that William C. Placher, *Narratives of a Vulnerable God: Christ, Theology, and Scripture* (Louisville: Westminster/John Knox, 1994), urges that theological interpretation has as its primary constituency the church, whereas the academy and the wider society may only "overhear." Such a way of thinking is a considerable departure from Tracy's model. The tension between the two perspectives is an important one, over which adjudication will continue.

70. See my comments in *Interpretation and Obedience: From Faithful Reading to Faithful Living* (Philadelphia: Fortress Press, 1991) 1–4. In recent hermeneutic conversations, a seductive "self-understanding" and "self-discernment" arises from the tradition of Wilhelm Dilthey, and therefore the accent of Karl Marx on praxis is important for faithful hermeneutics.

71. "The second listening community" agrees with the public as a constituency identified by Tracy. In some ways, the academy is a subset of that second community. It may be that in terms of biblical faith, the public is a second listening community, simply because of the long habits of Christendom. I believe, however, that serious texts that sound the cadences of truth as it is felt in the human process inevitably draw to themselves this second listening community. This is true for the Bible, I suggest, even without the social reinforcement and habit of Christendom. This criticism, often made of Lindbeck, in my judgment has merit but does not defeat Lindbeck's primary intention.

this text has provided the categories, the discernment, the energy, and the impetus for a different shape of life in the world.[72]

To the extent that the Old Testament receives this second hearing that is inevitably Jewish but reaching beyond the limits of Jewishness, exposition is concerned with more than the internal coherence of grammar and dialect. In these texts Israel speaks not only to itself, but to many others beyond its own grammar and dialect. Thus Israel's rhetoric is endlessly an appeal to the nations. The wonder and the mystery of this text, for whatever reason and however it may be understood, is that this text, in the past and in the present, speaks powerfully and compellingly to those outside this community of coherent grammar. In some sense, this second hearing, which can never be far from the purview of the expositor, draws us closer to Tracy's insistence that the claims of the text are not only revelational in a close and direct way, but also classic in the sense that "all sorts and conditions of men" and women continually refer again to what is given in this text.[73]

The inclination of this expositor and, I suggest, the primary inclination of the text itself (though that is an open issue) is toward the primary community that speaks and listens in the cadences of this grammar. But beyond this inclination of expositor and text, the second hearing community is also addressed in powerful and transformative ways by this text. The expositor must attend, as best as he or she is able, to both listening communities. Whereas Israel is the primary addressee in the text, in the end it is the nations who are the beneficiaries, as they are invited into the Torah-based peace and justice that are rooted in Yahweh's governance. Thus in Ps 96:10, for example, the "gospel" is to the "nations."

Polyphonic character. In seeking to address this second listening community, I am helped greatly by Mark Coleridge's article, "Life in the Crypt or Why Bother with Biblical Studies."[74] Coleridge agrees with many critiques, following Jean-François Lyotard, that the claim of any "totalizing metanarrative," including that of the Bible, is long gone in the contemporary world. But Coleridge also notes that secular, academic critics, in their resistance to a kind of deconstructive void that ends in solipsism, are looking again at the Bible, not as an old "totalizing metanarrative" but as a very different sort of master narrative, one almost lost from view by the habits of Christian totalizers.

Thus Coleridge suggests that what is characteristic and peculiar to the Bible is its "polyphonic character":

---

72. See, for example, Michael Walzer, *Exodus and Revolution* (New York: Basic Books, 1986); George Steiner, *Real Presences: Is There Anything in What We Say?* (London: Faber and Faber, 1989); and Northrop Frye, *The Great Code: The Bible and Literature* (London: Routledge and Kegan Paul, 1982).

73. On the classic, see David Tracy, *The Analogical Imagination*, 99–229 and passim. It is my impression that Tracy's notion of classic is a category more important and not so easily dismissed as hard-nosed canonists seek to do. I understand Tracy to mean that the classic has drawing power not because of manipulative management, but because of the inherent, intrinsic power of the text.

74. Mark Coleridge, "Life in the Crypt or Why Bother with Biblical Studies," *Biblical Interpretation* 2 (July 1994) 139–51.

The Bible insists upon a common narrative, but one which includes a diversity of voices; many stories comprise *the* story. God's story is both single and several. It also insists upon a narrative which at times is most disjointed and the connectedness of which is perceived only by way of struggle. The Bible is no easy read.[75]

It is precisely this quality that makes the writing of an Old Testament theology so problematic but also so urgent. Our effort thus is to give availability to this polyphonic character of the text, which is no more bearable by rationalistic historical critics than it is by the fundamentalists against whom Coleridge warns us. Christian interpretation has "totalized" the text, and it is likely that Blumenthal's *seriatim* approach is also no more bearable in the long run. A rendering of the text that is faithful to its polyphonic character is what is now required, centered enough for its first listening community, which trusts its coherent grammar and its reliable cadences; open enough to be compelling for its second listening community, which may be drawn to its truthfulness but is fearful of any authoritarian closure or reductionism. This quality of *many voices as the voice* of the text has let this text persist with such authority, and has enabled its first listening community to persist through time, through many "toils and dangers."

In order to situate our exposition of Old Testament theology in the current scholarly, interpretive conversation, we may pause to consider other current efforts at Old Testament theological interpretation, in the midst of which the present work is to be understood.

Centrist Enterprises

We may identify four current interpreters of Old Testament theology who are representative and who enact the most visible, available options in the field. I term these scholars centrist both because their work in various ways stands in close continuity to what has gone before, and because they are enormously influential scholars at major research institutions, thus representing the best of scholarship in the classical tradition. (It will be noticed, in addition, that they are, as is the writer, tenured white males.)

Brevard Childs

First among these is Brevard S. Childs, senior scholar at Yale Divinity School. Childs has become the most formidable practitioner of biblical theology, and his work is something of a reference point for all subsequent work. Therefore any student of Old Testament theology must take careful account of his work. In 1970 Childs first signaled his concern about the crisis in biblical theology, by which he meant the end of the biblical theology movement centered in the work of Gerhard

---

75. Ibid., 148.

von Rad and G. Ernest Wright.[76] Childs was schooled in the German tradition of scholarship but concluded, as early as 1970, that Old Testament theology which seeks to work within the limits of historical criticism is doomed to failure, for it operates with assumptions that are inimical to the text and the task as such.

Childs's alternative to theological exposition informed by historical criticism is to work at what he terms a canonical perspective. Since 1970 Childs has issued a series of important books in which he has sought to characterize what he means by canonical, though it is clear that his own understanding of the term has evolved over time. In his book of 1970, he proposed to do "canonical" theology by attending to New Testament quotations of the Old Testament. Since that time he has explored many other ways of doing canonical theology, perhaps none as satisfying as that initial enterprise. Among the more important of his books are his commentary on Exodus, in which he argued that canonical exposition means taking into account the reading of the text as it has been done over time by faithful readers in ecclesial communities, Jewish and Christian.[77] Thus "canonical" concerns the "belief-ful" reading of the text by the community of faith. In his most influential book, *Introduction to the Old Testament as Scripture,* Childs suggested that "canonical" means the actual literary shape of each of the books of the Bible, for the literary shape itself is an act of theological intentionality.[78] In his book *Old Testament Theology in a Canonical Context,* Childs exposited a variety of themes and topics, apparently meaning by "canonical" that any particular biblical reference to a theme or topic must be taken in the context of how that theme or topic is treated elsewhere and everywhere in the text, so that each part must be read and understood with reference to the whole.[79]

Through his several discussions, several themes emerge as critical for Childs's work. First, Childs regards historical criticism in principle as a distorting enterprise that casts the Bible in categories alien to its own intention. Childs regards an adequate coming to terms with historical criticism, however, as the primary precondition of doing serious theological work:

> The crucial problem of Biblical Theology remains largely unresolved, namely the challenge of employing the common historical critical tools of our age in the study of the Bible while at the same time doing full justice to the unique theological subject matter of Scripture as the self-revelation of God.[80]

---

76. Brevard S. Childs, *Biblical Theology in Crisis* (Philadelphia: Westminster Press, 1970).

77. Brevard S. Childs, *Exodus: A Commentary* (OTL; Philadelphia: Westminster Press, 1974).

78. Brevard S. Childs, *Introduction to the Old Testament as Scripture* (Philadelphia: Fortress Press, 1970). See also Childs, *The New Testament as Canon* (Philadelphia: Fortress Press, 1984). The latter book has not attracted much attention and is not as important for this discussion as *Introduction to the Old Testament.* Childs's canonical program has received a careful assessment from Paul R. Noble, *The Canonical Approach: A Critical Reconstruction of the Hermeneutics of Brevard S. Childs* (Leiden: E. J. Brill, 1995).

79. Brevard S. Childs, *Old Testament Theology in a Canonical Context* (Philadelphia: Fortress Press, 1985).

80. Brevard S. Childs, "Critical Reflections on James Barr's Understanding of the Literal and the Allegorical," *JSOT* 46 (1990) 8.

Childs's way of coming to terms with historical criticism seems to be to reach behind the modern critical period, back to the Reformation, to consider and replicate its way of interpretation, which is not yet contaminated by modern criticism. Such an enterprise appears to be precritical in its inclination, and we may wonder if such a project can be intellectually credible in the present discussion. To the extent that such work is precritical, as though the critical project had not been enacted, it is not likely to make effective contact with what is our roughly postcritical situation.[81]

Indeed, this brief historical survey has suggested that the vexing problem is adjudication between the interpretive authority of the church and the interpretive authority of the critical, academic community. These interpretive authorities are at times in profound tension and at times in a dialectical relation with each other. It is clear that Childs proposes to solve that problematic simply by moving completely to one side of the tension. Many regard this move as a doubtful one. As we shall see, when one moves to the other extreme and seeks in principle to exclude the claims of the interpreting authority of the church, the outcome is equally unsatisfactory. In the face of Childs's proposal, it seems wise to acknowledge that no easy resolution to this long-standing, long-vexing problem is at hand, and surely resolution will not be achieved by preempting the debate with an old-fashioned claim for either church authority or rationalist criticism.

Another major accent of Childs is to insist at the outset that Old Testament theology is singularly a Christian enterprise. That is, reading the Old Testament is already a confessional responsibility for believing Christians, and Jews who read the Hebrew Bible are in fact reading a different book. The Old Testament, for Christians, as implied in the word "Old," is always to be read in relation to the "New." For Childs the terms *old-new* do not signify supersessionism, but rather the claim that the two bodies of literature must be read together, for that is their very character, and to read them in any other way is to misunderstand from the outset.

In clearing the ground in this way, Childs in principle eliminates the vexing issues of how Jews and Christians can live together and read together in the same book, for their books are not the same. Moreover, Childs would thereby eliminate the rich possibilities for shared reading, even though in his Exodus commentary he pays sporadic attention to Jewish exegesis.

In his most recent book, *Biblical Theology of the Old and New Testaments*, which I assume to be the culmination of his argument, one can see clearly the intention of Childs's singularly Christian accent.[82] Childs begins with the thesis that the Old and New Testaments are "two witnesses to Jesus Christ." One can detect in this book Childs's awareness of a twofold task. In the first part of the book, Childs

---

81. On the postcritical "second naiveté" proposed by Paul Ricoeur, see Mark I. Wallace, *The Second Naiveté: Barth, Ricoeur, and the New Yale Theology* (StABH 6; Macon, Ga.: Mercer University Press, 1990). My impression is that Childs has not found an effective way to move beyond criticism, but instead moves back behind criticism to the Reformers. Much can be learned from such a strategy, but in the end, I believe, that approach fails to make contact with the actual situation in which faithful interpretation must be done.

82. Childs, *Biblical Theology of the Old and New Testaments*, with its frontal christological accent.

does rather standard Old Testament exposition. In the second part, however, he rereads with reference to the New Testament and the Christian gospel. In this mode of biblical theology, the Old Testament almost disappears, because it does not lend itself fully to the task. The Old Testament has much to say about God, but not much to say about Jesus as the Christ.

It is not surprising that Childs's bold enterprise is enormously controversial. His project will lend power and buoyancy to those who are engaged in systematic Christian theology. One can detect, moreover, important continuities with his teacher, Walther Eichrodt, in identifying the cognitive and conceptual constants of the faith that are congenial to the categories of conventional Christian theology. To many others, however, including this writer, Childs's proposal seems difficult and problematic on many counts.

Childs's project strikes this writer as massively reductionist. To limit the reading of the Old Testament text to what is useful for Christian theology—that is, for witness to Jesus Christ—means that much in the text must be disregarded. Even where texts are taken up, the playfulness and ambiguity that we have marked as characteristically Jewish must be disregarded in the interest of a flat conceptualization. It is my impression that to force this text into such categories prepares the way for a programmatic misreading. Childs is surely correct in his warnings against an obsessive commitment to modernist critical categories in which the theological enterprise evaporates; but his positive alternative to this seems, in my reading, to deny the text its own say. And when Childs does the interpretation that he deems canonical, his reading seems one as subjective as those against which he protests.

Earlier, Childs had suggested that it is the shape of the text itself that constitutes the "Rule of Faith" for Christians. Such a statement is congruent with a long-standing Protestant affirmation that Scripture is "the only rule for life and faith." In his recent book, however, Childs makes a major and problematic interpretive move. Now he concludes that the Bible is to be read "according to the Rule of Faith," by which he now apparently means the doctrinal tradition of the church.[83]

Such a maneuver is odd, and in my judgment completely unacceptable, for it means that the text itself is now subject to a set of interpretive categories that come from elsewhere. The odd outcome of such a statement is an unqualified embrace of the Tridentine inclination to subject the text and its possible interpretation to the control of church categories. When we remember that one of the intentions and functions of historical criticism in the modern period was to emancipate the text from church control, it becomes evident that in his rejection of the categories of historical criticism, Childs seems to have opted for a return of the interpretive task to the authority of the church. This in itself may not be so astonishing, until we recall that the Reformation as well as the Enlightenment had sought to liberate the text from church control. Now Childs proposes to resubmit the text exactly to that interpretive authority.

---

83. Ibid., 63–68.

My own perspective, against that of Childs, suggests that such an overtly christological reading of the Old Testament is not credible or responsible. As Paul Van Buren has shown, we do indeed read in the Old Testament about the same God who is known in the New Testament.[84] But the Old Testament is a witness to this God that cannot be closely forced into a witness of the one received by Christians as God's Messiah. Childs has alerted us to exceedingly important issues in doing Old Testament theology, especially vis-à-vis historical criticism. But his positive proposals, in my judgment, pose insurmountable difficulties. Not the least of these is that in a conceptual mode, they do not allow for what I regard as most Jewish in the utterance of the text. In my judgment, an Old Testament theology should make texts and their claims available for Christian theological usage, but with the clear and modest recognition that they are not exclusively available for Christian theological usage, and with an awareness that Christian theology may be allied with and instructed by the ways these same texts are taken up by others.

Jon D. Levenson

A second current interpreter is Jon D. Levenson of Harvard Divinity School. In a series of recent books, Levenson has established himself, along with Michael Fishbane, as among the most serious and imaginative Jewish theological interpreters of the Bible, with whom Christian interpreters can expect to have serious interaction.[85] Early on, Levenson asserted that the primary reason Jews were reluctant to undertake theological reflection at all is that Old Testament theology has been, for a long time but especially in the twentieth century, a distinctly Christian enterprise that was unashamedly supersessionist in its articulation.[86] Surely no Jew could responsibly participate in a conversation that assumed supersessionism as a beginning point. Levenson has cited representative scholars from an earlier period (Robert Denton, as well as Eichrodt and von Rad) who simply assumed (like Childs) that the Old Testament inevitably and indisputably culminates in the New Testament and in the messiahship of Jesus.[87]

For that compelling reason, Levenson, like other Jewish interpreters, has been reticent about engaging in the theological task, especially because Jewish propensity has been consistently against large, intellectual conceptualizations (systematization).[88] Having said all of that, Levenson, happily, has taken up the task of

---

84. Paul Van Buren, *Discerning the Way: A Theology of Jewish-Christian Reality* (New York: Seabury, 1980).

85. Jon D. Levenson, *Sinai and Zion: An Entry into the Jewish Bible* (Minneapolis: Winston Press, 1985); *Creation and the Persistence of Evil: The Jewish Drama of Divine Omnipotence* (San Francisco: Harper and Row, 1988); *The Hebrew Bible, the Old Testament, and Historical Criticism;* and *The Death and Resurrection of the Beloved Son: The Transformation of Child Sacrifice in Judaism and Christianity* (New Haven: Yale University Press, 1993).

86. Levenson, "Why Jews Are Not Interested in Biblical Theology," *The Hebrew Bible, the Old Testament, and Historical Criticism,* 33–61.

87. Ibid., 40–45.

88. An important exception is M. H. Goshen-Gottstein, "Tanakh Theology: The Religion of the Old Testament and the Place of Jewish Biblical Theology," *Ancient Israelite Religion: Essays in Honor of Frank Moore Cross* (ed. Patrick D. Miller, et al.; Philadelphia: Fortress Press, 1987) 617–44.

theological interpretation, making exclusive use of Jewish interpretive traditions and occasionally engaging in polemics against Christian preemption of what is a properly Jewish claim.[89]

For our purposes it is important to focus on Levenson's book *The Hebrew Bible, the Old Testament, and Historical Criticism*. The reason I have cited Levenson immediately after Childs is that, given the decisive departure Childs makes from Jewish concerns and the comparable departure Levenson makes from Christian claims, Levenson and Childs agree on their main points concerning the theological interpretive task. First, Levenson agrees with Childs on the problematic distorting work of historical criticism.[90] As might be expected, his rejection of historical criticism is more pointed and polemical than is Childs's, because historical criticism has been almost completely a Christian enterprise and has bootlegged the Wellhausian consensus that pictured late Judaism as decadent, degenerate, and legalistic, a caricature of Judaism fostered by Christian scholarship that has legitimated profound Christian distortions of Jewish tradition. Second, Levenson agrees with Childs that Jews and Christians do not at all read the same Bible.[91] When Christians read the Old Testament with reference to the New, they are doing something that is impossible with the Hebrew Bible. Third, following the eight interpretive rules of Moses Maimonides, Levenson insists, like Childs, that each particular text must be read in light of the whole, thus yielding something very like Childs's "canonical reading."[92]

The counterpoint of Levenson to Childs is exceedingly important, because it helps us identify the problematic of the odd triangle of interpretation in which we find ourselves concerning Jewish, Christian, and critical perspectives. While Levenson agrees in principle with Childs on the main points, we should notice that the outcome for the two is very different. Levenson's determination to fend off Christian supersessionist reading is a very different matter from Childs's resolve to have a Christian reading that inevitably stands in a long tradition of supersessionism.

In my judgment, Levenson is correct both in his polemical claims against Christian supersessionism and against those forms of historical criticism that have profoundly undermined serious theological reading. Levenson, moreover, is no doubt correct that there has been an (unwitting) collusion between Christian supersessionism and historical criticism with its developmental propensity. Hav-

---

89. Thus, for example, Levenson, *The Death and Resurrection of the Beloved Son*, indicates that the notion of the father giving his beloved son is a pervasive Jewish one. In its christological claims, however, the church has taken over this Jewish image and turned it against Jews in a polemical, exclusivist way.

90. Levenson, "The Hebrew Bible, the Old Testament, and Historical Criticism," *The Hebrew Bible, the Old Testament, and Historical Criticism*, 1–32. Frederick E. Greenspahn, "How Modern Are Modern Biblical Studies," *Minḥah-Le-Naḥum: Biblical and Other Studies Presented to Nahum M. Sarna in Honour of His 70th Birthday* (ed. Marc Brettler and Michael Fishbane; JSOTSup 154; Sheffield: Sheffield Academic Press, 1993) 164–82, however, has suggested that Jews have not always regarded such criticism in such a negative way. Thus the close and negative alliance between criticism and Christian interpretation against which Levenson polemicizes is perhaps an overstatement. The matter needs to be given more careful nuance.

91. Levenson, "The Eighth Principle of Judaism," 71–81.

92. Ibid., 62–71.

ing said all of that, what is important about Levenson's work is not his several polemics, but the way in which his comments on the Jewish tradition of interpretation can instruct Christian reading, both to enhance awareness in the face of our great ignorance of that tradition and to correct our misreadings that are often committed in ignorance. My own anticipation is that if the supersessionism of Christian historical criticism could ever be overcome, the positive benefit of doing self-consciously Christian reading in the presence of Jewish exposition could be enormously enriched. But the process of redress will be long, difficult, and costly for Christians.

Levenson's work is a crucial reminder of the ways in which our Christian expository history has been both ill-informed and destructively self-serving. In the end, Levenson finally must assert that any reading of the text, Christian or critical, that is not Jewish is a misreading. I can understand how Levenson arrived at such a conclusion. And given the history of Christian domination, a Jewish monopoly of the text is not as problematic as a Christian preemption of the text. Nonetheless, a Christian interpreter cannot simply settle for the verdict of Levenson. In the end, Levenson's preemption of the text for Jewish reading is unacceptable, not simply because it does not leave room for Christian interpretation, but because it violates the character of the text itself. In the text, there is a recurring restlessness about a Jewish reading and a push beyond that to a reading as large as the nations and as comprehensive as creation. In my judgment, Levenson's inclination in this regard is a misreading of the text that has consequences as unfortunate, if not as dire, as a Christian preemption. This text simply will not be contained in any such vested reading, which is what makes the text both compelling and subversive. Thus we are left in the midst of this patrimony, with a terrible question to which we do not know the answer. While Levenson agrees formally with Childs, the substance of his claim is a complete rejection of what Childs sets out to do. In any case, Levenson's insistence makes Childs's preemption of the text for Christian reading, in my judgment, an impossibility.

James Barr

James Barr, a senior scholar at Vanderbilt Divinity School, figures as a major reference point in Old Testament theology. Barr was closely allied with Childs in the 1960s and '70s in their common critique of the biblical theology movement.[93] On other than that point, however, Barr and Childs could hardly disagree more.[94] Whereas Childs's bent is to engage in a constructive theological task along

---

93. James Barr's assessment and critique of the biblical theology movement recurs in many of his writings. See, for example, *The Bible in the Modern World* (London: SCM Press, 1973); *Holy Scripture: Canon, Authority, Criticism* (Oxford: Oxford University Press, 1983); and "The Theological Case against Biblical Theology," *Canon, Theology, and Old Testament Interpretation* (ed. Gene M. Tucker et al.; Philadelphia: Fortress Press, 1988) 3–19.

94. See the strictures of Barr against Childs in Barr, *Holy Scripture: Canon, Authority, Criticism;* and see Barr's review of Childs, *JSOT* 16 (1980).

traditional Christian lines, Barr's inclination characteristically is critical, if not iconoclastic.

We may identify two beginning points that provide a basis of Barr's critical perception. First, Barr early established his uncommon authority as a Scripture scholar with *The Semantics of Biblical Language,* in which he brought to the discipline of Old Testament studies a proper understanding of the analysis of speech and the use of words.[95] On that basis Barr was able to show that much of what passed for theology in the biblical theology movement was irresponsible and was based on wrong methods in the interpretation of isolated words. Specifically Barr exposed the false claims that there was something peculiar about Hebrew mentality or about Hebrew language, and that individual Hebrew words could not bear the heavy theological freight that had been assigned to them. This debunking of popular biblical interpretation led Barr to take a lean or reticent stand toward the theological claims of the Old Testament.

Second, over the course of his career, Barr has expended considerable energy combating the inordinate and authoritarian claims of fundamentalism.[96] This accent has meant that Barr is especially alert both to the totalizing propensity of theological interpretation and to the authoritarian way in which such totalizing claims are offered, and he will have none of it. Thus Barr takes a positive view of the historical-critical tradition and understands it as an emancipatory movement, a protest against totalizing authoritarianism. It is clear that Barr does not regard historical criticism as a distorter of the tradition, as does Childs. But conversely, whereas Childs views the congruence of the Old Testament to the dogmatic, systematic claims of Christian theology, Barr regards such an interface as problematic, both because of the readings it requires and because of the authoritarian quality of articulation that seems invariably to accompany those readings.

To this point, Barr has not issued anything like a full Old Testament theology, though he is at work on one. In the meantime, one may reference his more preliminary work, most recently and especially his Gifford lectures.[97] While the Gifford lectures continue to express his polemic against the entire Barthian program, we may anticipate in these lectures how Barr will go about an Old Testament theology. He will clearly avoid any correlation with the dogmatic tradition of Christianity; with equal force he will avoid many of the scholarly constructs that have come to be uncritically accepted in most of the discussion. He will, moreover, take for granted the main claims of the historical-critical enterprise, so long as those claims are modestly related to the texts and stop short of any conceptual reification. The outcome of such a theology is likely to be not a large, systematic account, but a se-

---

95. James Barr, *The Semantics of Biblical Language* (Oxford: Oxford University Press, 1961); and *Biblical Words for Time* (SBT 33; London: SCM Press, 1962).

96. James Barr, *Fundamentalism* (London: SCM Press, 1981); and *Beyond Fundamentalism* (Philadelphia: Westminster Press, 1984).

97. James Barr, *Biblical Faith and Natural Theology: The Gifford Lectures for 1991* (Oxford: Clarendon Press, 1993). See also Barr, *The Garden of Eden and the Hope of Immortality* (Minneapolis: Fortress Press, 1993).

ries of lesser arguments that are not heavily indebted either to the critical tradition or to the Christian theological tradition.

Unlike Childs with his Christian propensity and Levenson with his parallel Jewish claim, Barr, I suspect, will seek to exposit textual claims as much as possible on their own terms. But his community of reading is likely to be the critical guild and not the church. He is an excellent reader of texts, and while his product may not satisfy a desire for larger assertion, his reading will help us to see in the text much that we have not seen, primarily because of our critical or dogmatic presuppositions. His work will be particularly important as a contrast point to approaches that are more totalizing and confessional.

Rolf Rendtorff

A fourth centrist scholar, Rolf Rendtorff, is the distinguished professor emeritus of Heidelberg University, where he was a foremost student, and then colleague, of von Rad. As much as anyone, he may be reckoned to be von Rad's heir in his theological enterprise. He is, moreover, among those German scholars who have become most engaged with recent interpretive conversation in the United States. Like Barr, he has not yet completed his Old Testament theology, thus I comment only on the preliminary papers published under the rubric of *Canon and Theology*.[98]

Rendtorff's work is sympathetic to the canonical categories of Childs, though it seems unlikely that he would go as far as Childs's recent submission of the Old Testament to the church's "Rule of Faith." It is likely that Rendtorff may be understood as something of a mediating figure who attends both to the concerns of historical criticism and the categories of canonical criticism.

What interests us primarily in his work at this point is his openness to be engaged with Jewish counterparts in the interpretive enterprise and therefore to avoid claims that move in a supersessionist direction.[99] Rendtorff's openness on this issue is likely to be understood as a personal and practical one. (I cite this because we may learn from it that what finally appear to be large intellectual judgments may often be propelled at the outset by matters quite personal. Thus I have no doubt that something like this is operative in Childs's retreat from the fragmentation of criticism, surely in Levenson's polemic against Christian supersessionism, and likely in Barr's abhorrence of 1970s totalizing authoritarianism.) In the Heidelberg scene, Rendtorff has had important Jewish counterparts in conversation. In any case, in his German context, Rendtorff had to make a decision about whether and how to take into account the recent brutalizing history of German-Jewish relationships.

We do not know the contours of Rendtorff's coming work. It will surely take into account von Rad's work, and certainly will move beyond it. It will be attentive to the claims of canon, though likely it will not go so far as does Childs. It will

---

98. Rolf Rendtorff, *Canon and Theology* (OBT; Minneapolis: Fortress Press, 1993).
99. Ibid., 31–45.

take into account the fact that Christian reading of these texts must be done in the presence of Jewish readers and Jewish sufferers.

It will be evident from this brief review that current work in Old Testament theology is rich and varied.[100] There is no close consensus on how to proceed. At the same time, there is emerging agreement about the shaping issues and the limit questions to which attention must be paid. It is clear that we have moved beyond the work of Eichrodt and von Rad. It is equally clear, happily, that we have moved beyond the methodological confusion of the 1970s and 1980s.

Efforts at the Margin

The works of Childs, Levenson, Barr, and Rendtorff represent the efforts of established figures in the field. Moreover, all of them are continuing to do what can still be recognized as Old Testament theology as previously understood, so that their work exhibits important continuities with twentieth-century antecedents. This is to be expected of those who belong to establishment scholarship. We give brief attention here, however, to a second way of thinking about the enterprise of Old Testament theology. This approach represents those who are not such centrist, established scholars. Although they also read the text with theological questions, they do work that would not conventionally be regarded as Old Testament theology. Their work perforce proceeds in bits and pieces and tends not to take up large thematic questions nor to provide architectonic, interpretive coherence. This scholarship from the margin is a new and growing phenomenon in Old Testament study (as in every discipline), no doubt witnessing to a new pluralism that was not present two generations ago and, conversely, giving evidence that hegemonic interpretation that was once taken for granted can no longer be assumed or sustained.

Three such interpreters serve as examples of those who operate at the margins of the discipline, and certainly away from hegemonic tendencies.

The Feminist Interpretation of Phyllis Trible

Phyllis Trible of Union Theological Seminary in New York is perhaps the most effective feminist interpreter of the Old Testament. Trible was most recently honored as president of the Society of Biblical Literature, the first woman Old Testament scholar to hold the post. This may in some modest way negate her marginality in the discipline, but not by more than a cubit. Her location as a person and as a scholar continues to be at the margin, where she is able to see and to say what centrists cannot (cf. Luke 10:23-24).[101] A student of James Muilenburg, Trible is

---

100. A number of other scholars are at work in what I have termed the centrist project. These include John Collins, who is attentive to a Jewish interface; Paul Hanson, who works from the gains of historical criticism; and Terence Fretheim, who takes a perspective from process hermeneutics.

101. Trible's marginality is indicated both in general by the dismissive tendency of Brevard Childs concerning a feminist hermeneutic, and in particular by the gratuitous attack on her work by Robert Carroll in *Jeremiah: A Commentary* (OTL; Philadelphia: Westminster Press, 1986). Whether Trible and other feminist interpreters are right or wrong on any particular point is not at issue. What matters

committed to the practice of rhetorical criticism with an unrivaled skill and sensitivity. While she has published other works, attention should be given in this context to her two most important efforts, *God and the Rhetoric of Sexuality* and *Texts of Terror*.[102] The first of these engages in a bit more theoretical discussion than the second, but both books are primarily close readings of particular texts. Trible is as good a reader of texts as anyone in this generation of scholarship.

A great spectrum of people fall into the category of feminist, and Trible has intentionally found her own stance in that spectrum. She is aware of the heavy patriarchal accent in the Old Testament, but nonetheless continues to pay close attention to the text itself as her proper focus of study. Her work evidences no heavy ideological theory, though she persists in studying texts that raise issues about how women are treated by men. Her several investigations into texts concerning Hagar, Miriam, Jezebel, Ruth, and Esther, among others, have called attention both to abusive practices that are expressed in the main line of the text, and also to the subtle play of the rhetoric that signals to readers that the transaction of the text, while surely abusive, is at the same time more dense and complex than a surface reading may indicate.[103]

Trible's superb textual treatments characteristically do not eventuate in any large interpretive conclusion. She is content to exhibit the text in its full subtlety, and then to desist from any larger interpretation. Never, as far as I know, has Trible made any declaration on canonical perspective, historical criticism, or Jewish-Christian interpretation.

Thus one may ask, Is she doing Old Testament theology? Well, no; at least not if the centrist tradition determines what is Old Testament theology. She and her perspective clearly do not belong in such company. She does nothing that hegemonic interpretation might regard as theological. Yet Trible does indeed practice the very polyphonic reading championed by Mark Coleridge, showing us that the utterance of meaning (=theology) of the text is not only dense and subtle, but also determined and insistent. The outcome of Trible's work, as with the work of some other feminist readers, is to make available to us a troubled world of faith where Israel had to live.[104] The world such study exhibits is one in which the God of Israel is frequently drawn into an alliance with male abusers. But it is also a world in which an angel of God is dispatched to care for Hagar, and in which Esther is offered to Israel as a model for how faith is to be portrayed at risk.

---

is that such a considerable scholarly perspective can be so lightly dismissed out of hand, without any serious engagement, thus making unmistakable the marginality of the enterprise.

102. Phyllis Trible, *God and the Rhetoric of Sexuality* (OBT; Philadelphia: Fortress Press, 1978); *Texts of Terror: Literary-Feminist Readings of Biblical Narratives* (OBT; Philadelphia: Fortress Press, 1984).

103. See most recently, Phyllis Trible, "Exegesis for Storytellers and Other Strangers," *JBL* 114 (1995) 3–19.

104. For full bibliographies on feminist biblical studies, see Kathryn Pfisterer Darr, *Far More Precious Than Jewels: Perspectives on Biblical Women* (Louisville: Westminster/John Knox, 1991); and Alice Ogden Bellis, *Helpmates, Harlots, and Heroes: Women's Stories in the Hebrew Bible* (Louisville: Westminster/John Knox, 1994).

George Pixley and Liberation Theology

George Pixley may be cited as a representative scholar in Central American liberation work. Because Central American liberation theology has been preoccupied with making its hermeneutical case prior to concrete exegesis, few scholars have done extensive textual work from that perspective. Pixley is an important exception in this regard, and therefore we review his work briefly, as yet another attempt to do Old Testament theology from the margin.

Pixley's most important book, in this judgment, is his commentary on Exodus.[105] In this commentary, Pixley is highly selective in the texts he chooses to address—some parts of the Book of Exodus are treated sketchily or not at all. We should note that this is a characteristic mark of theology at the margin (as is also evident in the work of Trible). But we should remember that those scholars who write in dissent against the hegemony are not the first to be selective; every commentary on Exodus tends to be selective. These marginated interpreters only make a *different* selection, but to do so is indeed to depart from what has come to be the normative selection; their choice of texts is no doubt not a disinterested one.

Pixley offers his presentation of the Exodus text through a sociological analysis, informed by Marxian categories and much influenced by the work of Norman Gottwald. Thus it requires no great imaginative maneuver to see that the liberation narrative of the Book of Exodus involves a profound socioeconomic, political conflict between the established regime that possesses technology, bureaucracy, and theoretical legitimacy (which is provisionally granted by the narrative) and the slave-peasant community that moves against the established center of power. Pixley has little interest in literary-rhetorical matters; he focuses on the hard realities of social power. The outcome of such a reading is not simply a reflection of an ancient conflict. Pixley's statement is saturated with what James Sanders has termed "dynamic analogy," wherein the ancient conflict in the text is taken as an illumination of current social conflicts.[106] Pixley construes the protesting actions of Moses and his community as a model and legitimation for praxis in contemporary communities of oppression. Pixley makes no attempt to conceal his conviction or intention that the text, and his reading of it, live close to contemporary revolutionary practice.

This reading, now fairly typical in liberationist circles, is a radical departure from consensus reading in the centrist tradition. Indeed, such readings evoke at least wonderment, if not resistance, from the older interpretive hegemony. Pixley's work has evoked a vigorous protest from Jon Levenson, who regards it as a catastrophic misreading of the text.[107] In the end, Levenson's harsh strictures against a liberationist reading appear to be in part a protest against such radicality in the

---

105. George V. Pixley, *Exodus: A Liberation Perspective* (Maryknoll, N.Y.: Orbis Books, 1987).

106. James A. Sanders, "Hermeneutics," *IDBSup* (Nashville: Abingdon Press, 1976) 406.

107. Jon D. Levenson, "Exodus and Liberation," *The Hebrew Bible, the Old Testament, and Historical Criticism*, 127–59. See, in response, Walter Brueggemann, "Pharaoh as Vassal: A Study of a Political Metaphor," *CBQ* 57 (1995) 27–51.

text and in part an expression of his concern against Christian supersessionism, whereby others besides the Israelites become the subject of the liberation narrative. Remarkably, by the end of his polemic, Levenson agrees that the Exodus narrative can be paradigmatic for liberation movements beyond that of the Jews, so long as the concrete and primary Jewishness of this narrative is acknowledged.[108]

Given the reservations of Terence Fretheim about the Exodus narrative as a script for liberation praxis, and the resistance of Levenson, one may ask if Pixley's reading is legitimate. But such a question poses the next question: legitimate by whose norms? *The question of legitimacy assumes a centrist consensus of the hegemony,* either ecclesial or academic. But such *a centrist consensus itself is now exceedingly problematic.* As a result, Old Testament theology must recognize that other readings outside the centrist consensus must be acknowledged as operative and must be taken seriously. It is evident in the work of Pixley, as in the work of Trible, that such marginated readings can see dimensions of the text that established readings of a historical-critical or theological-dogmatic kind have missed. Indeed, a reading like Pixley's is crucial if we are to attend to the polyphonic character of the text.

Black Theology and Itumeleng Mosala

As it is difficult to identify Central American liberationist readers who attend primarily to textual matters, so it is difficult to identify black African or African-American readers who attend in a sustained way to actual interpretive work. For our purposes, Itumeleng Mosala and his daring book on hermeneutics serves as a third example of marginated reading.[109] While this book is an essay in interpretive assumptions, its importance for text work is unmistakable. Mosala's analysis makes it clear that our conventional text work is shot through with racist assumptions. One major result of such assumptions is to keep the text as remote as possible from actual questions of praxis, so that when the oppressed community reads the text through its sighs and groans for freedom and dignity, those sighs and groans must be screened out in the interest of objectivity.

The important gain of Mosala and those who share his work is to show, negatively, that consensus reading is partisan and in the service of the social status quo; and, positively, that a challenging and revolutionary counter-reading is also permitted, evoked, and legitimated by the text. Thus, Mosala proceeds on the premise that the historical and cultural struggles of the disfranchised, in this case black people, constitute the hermeneutical beginning point for interpretation. This struggle, which has economic and political dimensions, is reflected both in the text

---

108. Levenson, "Exodus and Liberation," 159.

109. Itumeleng J. Mosala, *Biblical Hermeneutics and Black Theology in South Africa* (Grand Rapids: Eerdmans, 1989); Mosala and Buti Thlagale, eds., *The Unquestionable Right to Be Free: Essays on Black Theology in South Africa* (Maryknoll, N.Y.: Orbis Books, 1986). See also Cain Hope Felder, ed., *Stony the Road We Trod: African American Biblical Interpretation* (Minneapolis: Fortress Press, 1991); Felder, *Troubling Biblical Water: Race, Class, and Family* (Maryknoll, N.Y.: Orbis Books, 1989); James H. Cone and Gayraud S. Wilmore, eds., *Black Theology: A Documentary History* 1: *1966–1979.* and 2: *1980–1992* (Maryknoll, N.Y.: Orbis Books, 1993).

and in our reading of it. Mosala offers an example of this linkage in his exposition of Micah. Clearly this notion of cultural struggle is not on the horizon of conventional centrist interpretations.[110]

Interface between Conflicting Readings

I know of no way to bring resolution to the growing tension between what I have called centrist and marginated readings of the text, nor is it clear that resolution is desirable. It is not likely that the established community of reading—ecclesial and academic—will be displaced. These communities of reading will continue to dominate our discernment of the text. Nor is it possible to imagine that marginated readings will be silenced, even though the silencing capacity of dominant reading communities—ecclesial and academic—is considerable. The strictures of centrist interpreters against feminist readings is of little importance, and the polemics of Levenson against liberationist readings, so far as their readers are concerned, are simply irrelevant. Our interpretive theological situation is, and will be for the foreseeable future, one of conflict and contention, and no maneuver of self-proclaimed authority will be able to silence the challenge to the hegemony.

In any case, a student of Old Testament theology in our present interpretive context must attend to the centrist voices that represent a long-established consensus in ecclesial and academic communities. Such a student must also attend to the insistent voices of those at the margin who are able to see things in the text that centrist interpretation, either by doctrinal conviction or Enlightenment restraint, is not able to discern. While we do not know how to do it very well, *one of the primary demands of Old Testament theology in our present context is to work precisely at the interface between these readings in conflict.* The conflict between these readings not only concerns interesting methodological questions and incidental interpretive issues, but cuts to the core *theological* claims of the text. That point, where the core theological claims are in dispute, is where Old Testament theology must now work, if it is to be responsible.

Four Insistent Questions

The current work in Old Testament theology, as it has emerged in the last two decades, has put before us urgent issues that must be kept in purview as we seek a fresh course in the discipline. Here I will identify four such issues that, while not addressed directly, pervade the entire discussion.

---

110. Itumeleng Mosala, "The Case of Micah," *Biblical Hermeneutics and Black Theology,* 101–22, 123–53. On Micah, see also Hans Walter Wolff, "Micah the Moreshite—The Prophet and His Background," *Israelite Wisdom: Theological and Literary Essays in Honor of Samuel Terrien* (ed. John G. Gammie et al.; Missoula, Mont.: Scholars Press, 1978) 77–84; and George V. Pixley, "Micah—A Revolutionary," *The Bible and the Politics of Exegesis: Essays in Honor of Norman K. Gottwald on His Sixty-Fifth Birthday* (ed. David Jobling et al.; Cleveland: Pilgrim Press, 1991) 53–60.

Historical Criticism

So much is included under the rubric "historical criticism" that it is difficult to make precise statements about the relationship between historical criticism and Old Testament theology. Nonetheless, it seems evident now that historical criticism, as it came to be shaped in the nineteenth century and continues through the twentieth century, is problematic in and of itself; some scholars, notably Walter Wink, have found it to be inadequate. Wink even terms it "bankrupt."[111] It is clear, moreover, that historical criticism as an interpretive tool used in the service of Old Testament theology must be held under close scrutiny.

I have sought to show that historical criticism emerged in a variety of methods congruent with modernity, as an alternative to ecclesial authority for interpretation. No doubt important gains have been made by these several methods. Even if important gains had not been made, this is our past in Scripture interpretation, a past that was congruent with the spirit of the age. But as that spirit has waned and we face a new sensibility, we are able to see the inadequacy of this approach, even though some, fearful of ecclesial authority, will continue to champion such a perspective. In any case, a student of Old Testament theology must think through carefully the role that historical criticism is to play in theological interpretation.

Historical criticism is reflective of a certain set of epistemological assumptions that go under the general terms *objective, scientific,* and *positivistic,* assumptions that sought to overcome the temptations of fideism. These epistemological assumptions no longer command the field uncritically in any serious intellectual endeavor, and Scripture interpretation cannot naively persist in such a notion of knowledge.[112] Insofar as historical criticism reflects the assumptions and interest of modernity and the Enlightenment's declaration of war on church tradition, historical criticism served to fend off any objectionable supernaturalism in the text and to explain away whatever was considered, by the norms of modernity, to be odd in the text. While such an undertaking was aimed at theological supernaturalism, the propensity to "explain away" extended, characteristically, to literary cunning, so that by explanatory schemes of editing and redaction, what is interesting and dense in the text has often been forfeited.

Moreover, historical criticism, given the spirit of the age, carried with it a theory of development that regarded as preferable and superior what was most like "Enlightened," modern Europe. Thus the hidden agenda of such developmentalism is to trace the way in which biblical religion (and all else) developed toward and culminated in nineteenth-century Europe, in which everything can be explained and nothing is left odd, hidden, dense, or inscrutable. Above all, any witness in

---

111. Walter Wink, *The Bible in Human Transformation: Toward a New Paradigm for Biblical Study* (Philadelphia: Fortress Press, 1973) 1.

112. That positivism is now effectively undermined, especially by the seminal work of Michael Polanyi, *Personal Knowledge: Towards a Post-critical Philosophy* (Chicago: University of Chicago Press, 1974); and by the effective assault on positivistic knowledge by Thomas Kuhn, *The Structure of Scientific Revolutions* (Chicago: University of Chicago Press, 1962).

the text to the mysterious workings of God was either slotted as primitive or explained away.

Such an enterprise, while completely congruent with the spirit of the times, is, on the face of it, incongruent with the text itself. The text is saturated with the odd, the hidden, the dense, and the inscrutable—the things of God. Thus in principle, historical criticism runs the risk that the methods and assumptions to which it is committed may miss the primary intentionality of the text. Having missed that, the commentaries are filled with unhelpful philological comment, endless redactional explanations, and tedious comparisons with other materials. Because the primal Subject of the text has been ruled out in principle, scholars are left to deal with these much less interesting questions.

The upshot of this sustained sort of criticism—at times hypercriticism, because the method could not curb itself but only do more, better—is that scholarship was capable of a great deal of criticism, but characteristically weak and unsure about interpretation. (By interpretation I mean readiness to give full and imaginative expression to the claims of the text itself.) This is evident, for example in the *Interpreter's Bible*, which created a design so that interpretation ("exposition") did not need to be informed by criticism ("exegesis"), and even in the Biblischer Kommentar (and reflected in Hermeneia), in which, at the end, the "goal" is anemic and characteristically thin.[113] Indeed, not all of the dense exegetical work was necessary in order to produce the "goal." Thus it is clear that criticism had become an end in itself, criticism understood now as debunking suspicion and skepticism, and not in the service of interpretation.

One other aspect of the dominance of criticism in our common work bears mentioning: It may be theoretically possible to separate intelligible analysis from the developmental scheme that nineteenth-century criticism brought with it. Many scholars have noted that intelligible analysis and developmentalism are two distinct matters. Nonetheless, we have had almost no sustained, intelligible analysis of the text apart from the developmental scheme (until very recently) because the developmental scheme came to dominate historical criticism. Specifically, this scheme presented Second Temple Judaism as a legalistic, degenerate, and inferior form of religion, failing to recognize Judaism as an ongoing, living tradition of faith that responded to the circumstance in which it found itself. It is not possible to reckon the destructiveness wrought by this judgment in the name of critical scholarship. But there can be little doubt that the developmental scheme is informed by Christian supersessionism, and that it fostered anti-Jewish sentiment, saturated with ignorance about the ongoing vitality of the believing Jewish community.

---

113. *The Interpreter's Bible* is published by Abingdon Press. The format has been retained in the newly launched *New Interpreter's Bible*. Biblischer Kommentar, which expressed the high period of the so-called biblical theology movement insofar as it was evident in Germany, is published by Neukirchener Verlag, and Hermeneia is a project of Fortress Press. A number of recent commentary series have eschewed this unfortunate distinction and seek to focus more directly on theological exposition. The foremost among these is perhaps the Interpretation series of John Knox Press.

It is not my purpose or interest here to dismiss historical criticism out of hand, but only to state its problematic character to which students must be attentive. Some will continue to champion its work, some out of profound conviction, and others out of wounds inflicted by authoritarian ecclesial communities. Such champions are likely to continue to insist that it is impossible to write an Old Testament theology. Indeed, they may be correct. I shall nonetheless attempt the task, because I believe it is urgent to attend in imaginative ways precisely to the odd, hidden, dense, and inscrutable dimensions in the text that historical criticism, in principle, is disinclined to credit.

We do not know the extent to which historical criticism can be a partner for Old Testament theological interpretation, nor the extent to which historical criticism is necessarily congruent with the nineteenth-century spirit of the age. Since we cannot answer those questions, we continue to engage in such criticism, but with some vigilance about its temptation to overreach. Thus we must be closely attentive to Childs's warning about criticism. We must not heed that warning, however, without at the same time noticing our next problem, that of church theology.

Church Theology

Brevard Childs is acutely aware of the problems of historical criticism for doing Old Testament theology. The alternative he offers, however, is to align Old Testament theology completely with the doctrinal claims of the church (Calvinism in his case, but the particular tradition of church theology to which the principle is applied is a matter of indifference in this regard). In his fullest articulation of the matter, Childs is willing to bring Old Testament theology completely under the aegis of church theology, in terms of its core claim about Jesus, and in terms of the thematics under which that claim is developed and construed.

In my judgment, in contrast to that of Childs, the relation of Old Testament theology to church doctrine is proximately as problematic as is the relation to historical criticism.[114] Whereas Childs is resistant to the claims of criticism and is ready to move toward church theology, we may cite James Barr as an interpreter who is fully appreciative of the claims of criticism but is vigilant about the impingement of church theology on Old Testament theology. On this present point, then, we state concerns congruent with those of Barr, as in our previous point our concern was more resonant with the perspective of Childs.

In the medieval church, theological interpretation had established a coherent system of belief, and the Bible was utilized to provide materials and support for those beliefs. In large part, the churches of the Reformation did not depart from that coherent system of belief, though very different nuance and perspective were given to elements of the classic system of faith. In such an approach, the bibli-

---

114. See the important and helpful study of Francis Watson, *Text, Church, and World: Biblical Interpretation in Theological Perspective* (Grand Rapids: Eerdmans, 1994).

cal materials are almost completely subsumed under the thematic organization of church faith.

The rise of modern criticism was aimed against that coherent system of church belief in two ways. First, a fixed system of doctrinal theology has a great propensity toward reductionism about variation and diversity in the text. Conventional systematic theology cannot tolerate the unsettled, polyphonic character of the text. This is evident in terms of any doctrinal claim of the church. Thus, for example, if theology, in its metaphysical propensity, holds to an affirmation of God's omnipotence, an interpreter must disregard texts to the contrary, as Terence Fretheim has exhibited them.[115] If it is claimed that God is morally perfect, the rather devious ways of the God of the Old Testament must either be disregarded or explained away. In truth, some of the most interesting and most poignant aspects of the Old Testament do not conform to or are not easily subsumed under church theology.

Second, historical criticism that attends to the variegated quality of the text chafes under the imposed canonical interpretation of the text. That is, established church authority (the magisterium) decrees the limits of scholarly interpretation, beyond which "obedient" or "credentialed" interpretation may not go, even if research leads elsewhere.[116] In part the challenge to church authority has to do with substantive disagreement; also in part it has to do in principle with the capacity of Bible scholars for unfettered freedom in research and interpretation. Thus Old Testament scholarship has sought to maintain some interpretive freedom, and therefore some interpretive distance from systematic theology and from church authority.

It is important that a student of Old Testament theology not regard this issue as an ancient one that no longer pertains. To be sure, the old church sanctions, including book burning, silencing, excommunications, and charges of heresy, have softened to a large extent, even in Roman Catholicism. But the issue endures as critically informed theological interpreters seek to live in and serve ecclesial communities.[117] The problem often is not so much explicit sanctioning authority as it is the long-established and uncritical reflexes of church communities, who have known only a reductionist Bible for so long that they neither know nor can tolerate what is actually said in the Bible.

---

115. Terence E. Fretheim, *The Suffering of God: An Old Testament Perspective* (OBT; Philadelphia: Fortress Press, 1984).

116. The classic case of such authority exercised by the church is the Roman church's assault on Galileo. Richard J. Blackwell, *Galileo, Bellarmine, and the Bible* (Notre Dame, Ind.: University of Notre Dame Press, 1991), has demonstrated that in Galileo's second trial before church authorities, there was no warrant for the treatment of the astronomer—it was the sheer maintenance of ecclesial power that was operative.

117. The most recent, scandalous cases include the purging of the faculty of Concordia Theological Seminary by the Lutheran Church, Missouri Synod; and the current struggle in the Southern Baptist Convention concerning control of theological seminaries. On the first, see John Tietjen, *Memoirs in Exile: Confessional Hope and Institutional Conflict* (Minneapolis: Fortress Press, 1990); on the latter, see Walter B. Shurden, *The Struggle for the Soul of the SBC: Modern Responses to the Fundamentalist Movement* (Macon, Ga.: Mercer University Press, 1993).

It is the work of a serious theological interpreter of the Bible to pay close and careful attention to what is in the text, regardless of how it coheres with the theological habit of the church. This is particularly true of the churches of the Reformation that stand roughly in the tradition of *sola scriptura*. The truth of the matter, on any careful reading and without any tendentiousness, is that *Old Testament theological articulation does not conform to established church faith,* either in its official declaration or in its more popular propensities. There is much that is wild and untamed about the theological witness of the Old Testament that church theology does not face. It is clear on my reading that the Old Testament is not a witness to Jesus Christ, in any primary or direct sense, as Childs proposes, unless one is prepared to sacrifice more of the text than is credible.

It is my urging that a serious Old Testament student, situated in an ecclesial community, has a responsibility to do careful reading of the Old Testament and to present to the ecclesial community not only those readings that confirm church theology, but also (and perhaps especially) those that clash with, challenge, and undermine seemingly settled church theology. It is my judgment that church theology as commonly practiced is characteristically reductionist concerning the Bible, that it engages in providing settlement and certitude. Such reading may be disturbing and unsettling to "the world," but it provides a coherence for the faithful.

In tension with that propensity to reductionism, I propose that it is the work of biblical theology to counter the reductionism and to bear resilient witness to those texts and their interpretations that do not "fit." Thus the work of biblical theology, vis-à-vis systematic theology, is one of tension that is honest but not quarrelsome. In practice, I suggest that it is the liturgy that is to enact the settled coherence of church faith, and the sermon that provides the "alien" witness of the text, which rubs against the liturgic coherence.[118] There can, in my judgment, be no final resolution of the tension between the systemizing task of theology and the disruptive work of biblical interpretation. It is the ongoing interaction between the two that is the work of interpretation.

Thus I propose that the Old Testament lives with systematic theology with as much uneasiness as it does with historical criticism. Sound theological interpretation, in my judgment, must be informed about and make use of both historical criticism and systematic theology. Neither is an enemy of Old Testament theology, but in quite parallel ways, neither is a permanent partner nor an easy ally of Old Testament theology.

The Jewishness of the Old Testament

A third issue that must be faced in doing Old Testament theology concerns the ways in which Old Testament theology must attend to the Jewish character and claims of the text. In the sixteenth and seventeenth centuries, Christian

---

118. I use the term *alien* in a way congruent with Karl Barth's phrase "the strange new world of the Bible." In much church practice, liberal as well as conservative, what is alien or strange in the Bible has been lost or programmatically repressed.

scholarship and theological interpretation were increasingly cut off from Jewish conversation partners, which before that time had been present in the interpretive enterprise.[119] With the elimination of Jewish conversation partners, Old Testament scholarship predictably had before it two primary options. First, Old Testament interpreters who sought to cohere to Christian doctrine had their reference point in Christian ecclesial communities and felt no obligation to attend to matters Jewish. Second, historical criticism in eighteenth- and nineteenth-century Europe was almost exclusively a gentile, Christian, Protestant operation. And as we have noted, the Wellhausian synthesis was inherently biased against Jewishness in its characterization of Second Temple Judaism.

In the current discussion of the Old Testament, Childs has been willing to return to or continue the Christian ecclesial preoccupation of having interpretation contained within a Christian confession. Because of Childs's capacity to define the discussion, it is fair to say that this elemental separation of Jewish and Christian readings is an influential option in current conversation. It is equally important, however, that many historical-critically minded scholars refuse to follow Childs's inclination, which may be regarded as sectarianism. But that refusal of Childs's position, for many scholars, only concerns the unfettered character of scholarship and a refusal to take confessional positions; it does not concern the question of Jewish and Christian readings vis-à-vis each other. Of major scholars in the field, only Rolf Rendtorff has explicitly sought another way that is more open to Jewish voices in the midst of Christian interpretation.

In what follows, I mean to resist Childs's inclination to distinguish at the outset Christian from Jewish reading. I attempt this present Old Testament theology as a Christian. I have no doubt that some of my interpretive judgments are Christian, some made knowingly and others unwittingly. I am nonetheless resistant to making a claim on the text that is narrowly Christian. While I am fully appreciative of Childs's notion that we read a different book from the Hebrew Bible, and of Levenson's concurrence, too much should not be made of the point. For in many ways Christians and Jews do read the same text, and we should not engage in theological mystifications and reifications as we do our theological reading.

It is my judgment that, theologically, *what Jews and Christians share is much more extensive, much more important, much more definitional than what divides us.*[120] We must seek to sort out those theological commonalities that have been distorted by later interpretive impositions in the church that are no essential part of our faith. (I say "must" for practical reasons—the reality of brutality and abuse that has characterized our recent past.) A distinction must be made between misguided polemical additions in the history of interpretation and genuine Christian insight generated

---

119. On the earlier contact between Jewish and Christian expositors, see Beryl Smalley, *Study of the Bible in the Middle Ages* (Notre Dame, Ind.: University of Notre Dame Press, 1964).

120. The commonalities are especially underscored in the work of Paul Van Buren, *Discerning the Way: A Theology of Jewish-Christian Reality* 1: *Discerning the Way*; 2: *A Christian Theology of the People Israel* (San Francisco: Harper and Row, 1983); and 3: *Christ in Context* (San Francisco: Harper and Row, 1988).

by the text in the midst of experience, so that "Scripture might be fulfilled." In such usage, it is Scripture—that is, the Old Testament—that is fulfilled. This is not to suggest that it is fulfilled *only* in a Christian horizon, but surely there.

As Christians must allow for legitimate Jewish readings, so a common reading requires that Jews allow for readings by Christians that are integral to their lived faith. When Jews and Christians must part company on theological interpretation, we must do so openly and candidly. I find, however, that we reach that point only very late. There is something diabolical, in my judgment, in parting company whenever and wherever it is possible for us to do theological reading together. I do not deny or minimize the profound differences between Christians and Jews, some of which are theologically substantive, some of which are historical accidents, and some of which are demonic political emergents. But acknowledging all of that, we do not escape the papal declaration, "Spiritually we are all Semites."[121] There is, to be sure, something glib and romantic in such an utterance, but there is also something crucially true, and this we must ponder.

Several points pertain to our question. First, a Christian Old Testament interpretation must face the question of supersessionism, a question that is intrinsic in the attempt of a Christian Old Testament. In what follows, I shall assume and insist that the Old Testament (even the Old Testament as a confessional Christian document) does not narrowly or resolutely point to Jesus of Nazareth. Rather it points beyond itself in its promissory dimensions to God's news, which may take more than one form (more forms than we know). It is clear that the "fulfillment in Jesus Christ" is read from the side of the fulfillment rather than from the side of the promise, and therefore the Christian reading to which I am committed allows for those anticipated futures being seen and received in more ways than the person of Jesus. Indeed, the prayer of the coming kingdom in the mouth of Jesus (John 17:11) is not a prayer for the coming of the kingdom of Jesus, but for the coming of God's rule.

Therefore what I regard as a Christian reading of the Old Testament does not need to preempt or foreclose how and in what ways God's future may come. It appears to me that the waiting of Jews (for Messiah) and the waiting of Christians (for the second coming) is a common waiting that stands against a despairing modernity. Beyond that, in my judgment, Christians do not need to crowd the reading of the Old Testament into a confessional corner. To claim more than this is to preempt the polyphonic character of the text, a polyphony that also pertains to God's future. Thus a Christian reading, in my judgment, claims not to foreclose, but to attend to the rich possibilities of the text, which in one construal are Chris-

---

121. It is crucial to note the recent judgment of the papacy that God's covenant with the Jews was never revoked. See Norbert Lohfink, *The Covenant Never Revoked: Reflections on Christian-Jewish Dialogue* (New York: Paulist Press, 1991). While such an acknowledgment might be cause for celebration, we may more likely wonder why it has come so late and after so much barbarism tacitly endorsed by the church.

tian, but which are presented with the awareness that more than one construal is available, given the nature of the material and its claims.

Moreover, the issue of supersessionism is not, in my judgment, simply confined to the question of "Jesus or not." Christian readers must also attend to the character and mode of the concrete text, without regard to its large ideational outcome. The text itself is remarkably open and refuses a simple or firm cognitive closure. That is, the text is available for many readings of particular texts, and seems at many points to delight in a playful ambiguity that precludes certitude.

We may identify, for example, three common rhetorical propensities that characterize the text. First, the text is saturated with *metaphors*, figures of speech that bespeak a kind of ineluctability, and which characteristically seem to take away with one hand what is given with the other. Cynthia Ozick has opined that the Jewish tradition revels in and relishes metaphors that maintain a kind of impressionistic openness.[122] She goes so far as to suggest that the Greek tradition of the Delphic oracle is one of uttered certitude, which cannot host or tolerate the openness of metaphor. Whether her negative statement about the Delphic oracle can be sustained or not, her positive point merits attention.

Second, the Old Testament text is rich with *hyperbole* in which the extremes of life are given to sweeping overstatement. Thus Paul Ricoeur can say of prophetic speech:

> The prophet through whom the word is expressed . . . does not "think" in the Hellenistic sense of the word; he cries out, he threatens, he orders, he groans, he exults. His "oracle" . . . possesses the breadth and the depth of the primordial word that constitutes the dialogical situation at the heart of which sin breaks forth.[123]

There is nothing measured or reasonable about such utterance. And clearly the hymns and laments of Israel are "limit expressions," for Israel's dealings with its God are regularly "limit experiences."[124] When, therefore, Israel proposes to utter its need to God, one hears a torrent of risk, danger, exposure, helplessness, and threat, as though more reasoned speech will fail in its address to God.

Third, the rhetoric of the Old Testament is characteristically *ambiguous and open*, in the sense that the text is "fraught with background."[125] So much is left unsaid, that the reader is left uncertain and is required to make decisions that the text refuses to make for the reader. Thus in 2 Samuel 3, for example, concerning the death of Abner at the hand of Joab, David's complicity in the death is left open, and the reader must make a decision, depending on how accepting or suspicious

---

122. Cynthia Ozick, "Metaphor and Memory," *Metaphor and Memory: Essays* (New York: Knopf, 1989) 265–83. Susan Handelman, *The Slayers of Moses*, points out that while metaphor is a usage of Christian interpreters, the rabbis characteristically employed metonymy.

123. Paul Ricoeur, *The Symbolism of Evil* (Boston: Beacon Press, 1969) 53.

124. Cf. Paul Ricoeur, "Biblical Hermeneutics," *Semeia* 4 (1975) 107–45.

125. The well-known phrase is from Erich Auerbach, "Odysseus' Scar," *Mimesis: The Representation of Reality of Western Literature* (Princeton, N.J.: Princeton University Press, 1953) 12.

the reader may be concerning David. In regard to David's affront against Uriah by the hand of Joab in 2 Samuel 11, Meir Sternberg has nicely explored the teasing quality of the narrative.[126] The narrator presents David so that neither the king nor the reader knows how much Uriah knows about David's conduct. If David knew that Uriah knew about his violation of Uriah's wife, David could proceed on one basis with Uriah. If David knew that Uriah did not know about his affront, David could proceed in another way. But David does not know what Uriah knows, and neither does the reader. David's not knowing is not a lack of historical information, but a rhetorical strategy in which the reader must inevitably participate.

These rhetorical strategies of metaphor, hyperbole, and ambiguity—to which could be added irony, incongruity, and contradiction—are not marginal or incidental to the text. They are the very stuff of the Old Testament. We have no Old Testament text without them, for they form the way this textual community gives voice to its reality, its life, and its life with God.

I am not wont to label such models of rhetoric as Jewish, for there is nothing definitionally Jewish about any of them. All of them together, however, add up to the openness, playfulness, and oddness that seem to embody the Jewishness of the text. Even if they are not Jewish, such characteristic modes of speech contrast sharply with Christian modes of theology that are characteristically settling and closing. Thus without insisting on the Jewishness of such rhetorical strategies, it is in any case important to contrast rhetorical modes of the Old Testament with conventional Christian theology's bent toward the rational, the philosophical, and the ontological. It is not usual, or easy, for a Christian theological reading of the Old Testament to honor or host the openness and unsettled quality of the text. I suspect, in any case, that it is the overriding of this playful, open rhetoric, rather than a christological claim, that constitutes the most elemental and characteristic practice of Christian supersessionism. It is not only a preemption of the substantive claims of the text, but also a preemption of the style and mode of the text that invite a distorted reading.[127]

After considering both the substantive theological claims of Jews and Christians, and the rhetorical style of Jewish texts and Christian interpretation, I raise one other question about the Jewish dimensions of a Christian theology, a question seldom addressed: Must we make allowances in our interpretation in response to the long history of anti-Semitism that has marked the Christian use of the Bible? My answer is a positive one.

There is no doubt that the Old Testament has been used by Christians in a variety of ways to assault Jewish faith and to foster anti-Semitism with its virulent

---

126. Meir Sternberg, *The Poetics of Biblical Narrative: Ideological Literature and the Drama of Reading* (Bloomington: Indiana University Press, 1985) 190–229.

127. Thus in the title of Handelman's *The Slayers of Moses*, I take the term *slayers* with utmost seriousness. It is a Western reading of the text, fully allied with christological claims, that has made the Old Testament text nearly unavailable to the church.

political consequences.[128] There is no doubt that Reformation interpretation was profoundly anti-Jewish.[129] Equally, there is no doubt that nineteenth-century developmentalism championed a form of degenerate Second Temple Judaism, so that Solomon Schechter could conclude, "Higher criticism is a higher form of anti-Semitism."[130] The supersessionist inclination of Christian scholarship simply kept Jewish reality off the screen of perception, so that _silence in the scholarly community, even concerning scholarly questions, amounted to collusion in the systemic violence against Jews._

Because I believe that all of our scholarship is contextual, and because I believe that all of our interpretation is in some sense local praxis, it is my judgment that for this long-standing Christian practice of negation—not, to be sure, all malevolent in intent—compensations must be made. Thus I dare imagine that for those _political_ affronts (with interpretation understood as a political activity), _theological_ reparation must be made. I am not sure what that might mean, but it is clear, even in official Roman Catholicism, that such reparations are being made. In 1980 Pope John Paul II, in the presence of official Jewish representatives, spoke of Jewish faith as "the covenant that has never been revoked by God." The declarations of Vatican II have moved slowly, ever so slowly, in the direction of recognizing that Jews and Christians are co-believers.

Thus I have no doubt that a theological supersessionism which breeds practical anti-Jewishness, which is rooted in the absolutist claims of Christian theology, must be reexamined.[131] The reparation to be made is not merely a political one (as in the Vatican's recognition of the state of Israel), it is a theological one as well. It invites us to the difficult task of recognizing that absolutist claims for the Christian gospel are not only practically destructive but theologically inimical to the gospel itself. The issues are complex and will require the best work of doctrinal theology, with particular reference to the doctrine of the Trinity. It is not necessary that an Old Testament theology should take up this task directly. But the point at issue matters enormously to the mood and sensibility in which a Christian Old Testament theology is construed. While the open future of the Old Testament can and has been taken up by Christian claims, the Old Testament itself does not mandate that outcome to a specifically promised future. Much must therefore be left open, more than in the past.

---

128. See the comprehensive analysis of Steven Katz, _The Holocaust in Historical Context: Ancient and Medieval Cases_ 1 (Oxford: Oxford University Press, 1994).

129. See Heiko Obermann, _The Impact of the Reformation: Essays_ (Grand Rapids: Eerdmans, 1994).

130. Solomon Schechter, "Higher Criticism—Higher Anti-Semitism," _Seminary Addresses and Other Papers_ (Cincinnati: Ark Publishing, 1915) 36–37.

131. On the relationship between absolutism, supersessionism, and anti-Semitism, see Katz, _The Holocaust in Historical Context._ It is his judgment that the key theological work on the part of Christians in producing anti-Semitism was not any directly negative activity, but the reification of "the Jews" into a metaphysical reality or principle of negativity.

Public Possibilities

The intellectual and therefore the economic-political crisis in which we live in Western culture concerns the decentering of the long-established privilege of Euro-American Christendom. That privilege has been social, economic, cultural, and political, as well as intellectual and moral. The loss of a sense of legitimacy about that privilege is evident with the emergence of former colonies claiming their own way in the world, with growing restlessness about the disparity of North and South, and with the relentless rise of Islam as a challenge to Christian domination.[132] The loss of a legitimated privilege creates a situation of revolutionary struggle that will not abate any time soon. Even within the borders of the United States, moreover, the struggle between center and margin grows more acute, indicated by the failure of our social system to deliver basic services, and by the frantic pressure to "secure our borders" in order to keep out those who do not "by right" have access to the well-being we enjoy.

Our interpretive situation is thus one of profound struggle, in which the adjudication of goods, power, and access is deeply contested. I do not suggest that an Old Testament theology should be in the service of such a revolutionary struggle. It cannot, however, be indifferent to that context of interpretation. For that reason, our knowledge of faith can never be separated from power issues that permeate both the text and our reading of it. That is why those whom I have called marginated readers are crucial for our common work, for they refuse an exercise in knowledge that is not also an exercise in power.

I propose that an Old Testament theology at the end of the twentieth century is not simply a religious exercise, nor is it finally only an in-house project for an ecclesial community (though it is surely that). It is at the same time a contribution to the *public discussion* of how matters are to be adjudicated in the midst of a revolutionary struggle. The Old Testament clearly serves, in the first instant, an ecclesial community (or communities), but it is more than an ecclesial document. From the outset it is operative in the world of power, and it concerns the rise and fall of empires and the living and dying of human persons and communities. It bears witness to a holy purpose and a holy will that in hidden and/or public ways are at work in power processes.

The Old Testament insists that there is a moral shape to the public process that curbs the raw exercise of power. It equally insists that there is a hidden cunning in the historical process that is capable of surprise, and that prevents the absolutizing of any program or power. Thus at the edge of an Old Testament theology, we must ask about the ways in which this odd text might make a difference in the large public crisis in which we are all, willy-nilly, involved. It is astonishing to

---

132. As there are interrelated cycles of oppression, so there are emerging spheres of liberation that overlap. Thus the ending of privilege, which permits fresh voices in the world, touches every aspect of the social organization of knowledge and power. One important umbrella term for this revolution is the *overthrow of patriarchal privilege,* but the term needs to be understood in a most comprehensive way.

notice, as the exclusive power of hegemonic reading has waned, how aware we have become in recent decades about the conflictual dimensions of every phase of text and interpretation. Such a growing awareness suggests that issues of the moral dimension of power and the resultant concrete issues of public life are never far from the horizon of an Old Testament theology.

Part I

ISRAEL'S CORE TESTIMONY

THREE

Israel's Practice of Testimony

THE PRIMAL SUBJECT of an Old Testament theology is of course God. But because the Old Testament does not (and never intends to) provide a coherent and comprehensive offer of God, this subject matter is more difficult, complex, and problematic than we might expect. For the most part, the Old Testament text gives us only hints, traces, fragments, and vignettes, with no suggestion of how all these elements might fit together, if indeed they do. What does emerge, in any case, is an awareness that *the elusive but dominating Subject of the Old Testament cannot be comprehended in any preconceived categories.*[1] The God of the Old Testament does not easily conform to the expectations of Christian dogmatic theology, nor to the categories of any Hellenistic perennial philosophy. As a result, most of our categories are unhelpful for the elucidation of this Subject, and we shall have to proceed concretely, a text at a time, a detail at a time. The Character who will emerge from such a patient study at the end will still be elusive and more than a little surprising.

To cite God as the subject of theology, however, is to take only the *theos* of theology. There is also the speech (*logos*) element of theology. Thus our proper subject is *speech about God,* suggesting yet again that our work has to do with rhetoric. The question that will guide our work is, How does ancient Israel, in this text, speak about God? In addition to Israel's speech about God, much in the Old Testament is *spoken by God* to Israel. For our purposes, I do not make a distinction between the two modes of speech, because even where God speaks, the text is *Israel's testimony* that God has spoken so. Perhaps a greater distinction should be made, but in terms of our discussion, both sorts of speech function in the same way as testimony. It is remarkable that the Old Testament does not accent thought or concept or idea, but characteristically *speech.* God is the One about whom Israel speaks. Thus, in the formulation of Gerhard von Rad's credos, the introduction to the formula is "you shall make this response" (Deut 26:5), "then you shall say" (Deut 6:21), "And Joshua said" (Josh 24:1).[2] In Israel's more intimate practice of faith in the Psalms, moreover, the key activity is speech. It is "a joyful noise" (Ps 100:1), "I will sing" (Ps 101:1), "I said in my prosperity" (Ps 30:6), "To you, O Lord, I cried" (Ps 30:8).

---

1. See Samuel Terrien, *The Elusive Presence: Toward a New Biblical Theology* (New York: Harper and Row, 1978).

2. Gerhard von Rad, "The Form-Critical Problem of the Hexateuch," *The Problem of the Hexateuch and Other Essays* (New York: McGraw-Hill, 1966) 1–8.

117

What we have available to us is the speech of this community, which has become text, and which is our proper subject of study.

Note well that in focusing on speech, we tend to bracket out all questions of historicity.[3] We are not asking, "What happened?" but "What is said?" To inquire into the historicity of the text is a legitimate enterprise, but it does not, I suggest, belong to the work of Old Testament theology. In like manner, we bracket out all questions of ontology, which ask about the "really real."[4] It may well be, in the end, that there is no historicity to Israel's faith claim, but that is not a position taken here. And it may well be that there is no "being" behind Israel's faith assertion, but that is not a claim made here. We have, however, few tools for recovering "what happened" and even fewer for recovering "what is," and therefore those issues must be held in abeyance, pending the credibility and persuasiveness of Israel's testimony, on which everything depends.

For this community and its derivative ecclesial communities that purport to stand with and under this text, the speech is the reality to be studied. Therefore while our subject is limited, it is not modest. For in this text, there is ample utterance about God, much of it on the lips of Israel, some of it on the lips of God, and some if it on the lips of God's (and Israel's) adversaries. We shall be asking, *what* is uttered about God? And this will require us to pay attention to *how* Israel

---

3. Clearly Israel's speech about Yahweh is deeply embedded in lived socioeconomic-political realities—the stuff that comprises history. The exilic experience, for example, clearly impinged on what Israel said about Yahweh and, conversely, on how Yahweh addressed Israel. Israel's speech about Yahweh is characteristically situated historically. I intend only to rule out questions of positivistic history that seek to limit Israel's imaginative utterance about Yahweh to recoverable happenings. Stated another way, the history to be reckoned with in this project is *emic*, i.e., as accepted by the Israelite cast of characters, and not *etic*, i.e., the past recoverable by the reckonings of the rationality of modernity. I have attempted to stake out this general perspective in *Abiding Astonishment: Psalms, Modernity, and the Making of History* (Louisville: Westminster/John Knox, 1991). The distinction made by James M. Robinson, "The Historicality of Biblical Language," *The Old Testament and Christian Faith: Essays by Rudolf Bultmann and Others* (ed. Bernhard W. Anderson; London: SCM Press, 1964) 124–58, between "historicity" and "historicality" is likely a useful one for our purposes.

4. This decision to bracket questions of ontology is parallel to the decision about bracketing questions of historicity. I do not deny that those who speak about Yahweh in the Old Testament had made some judgment about the reality and existence of Yahweh. But the ontology of Yahweh that is available on the basis of Israel's testimony in the Old Testament is *after* the testimony, based on finding the testimony credible and persuasive. After testimony, the Old Testament provides a rich statement on ontology.

A student of Old Testament theology must be alert to the problem of conventional thinking about ontology, thinking that is essentially alien to Old Testament testimony. M. Douglas Meeks has called my attention to two discussions that I have found greatly illuminating, which in very different ways make the same point. John D. Zizioulas, *Being as Communion: Studies in Personhood and the Church* (London: Dartman, Longman and Todd, 1985), resists the monistic, closed ontology of the ancient Greeks and insists that the early church fathers broke with Hellenistic ontology in seeing that the personal, communal propensities of God, who acts as a person in freedom, are prior to any substance or being. Jean-Luc Marion, *God without Being, Hors-Texte* (Chicago: University of Chicago Press, 1991), follows Martin Heidegger in liberating God from the question of being, for the question of being is restrictive of God's freedom and of itself ends in idolatry.

Old Testament thought does not align with the categories of either patristic thought or that of Heidegger. What it has in common, and the point on which I insist, is that one must not foreclose Israel's witness to Yahweh by already settled categories of being. Jewish ways of speaking (and thinking) are simply not easily commensurate with our standard Western notions of being, and that difference is enormously important and must be recognized at the outset.

uttered about God, for the "what" of Israel's God-talk is completely linked to the "how" of that speech.[5]

I suggest that the largest rubric under which we can consider Israel's speech about God is that of testimony. Appeal to testimony as a mode of knowledge, and inevitably as a mode of certainty that is accepted as revelatory, requires a wholesale break with all positivistic epistemology in the ancient world or in the contemporary world. In an appeal to testimony, one must begin at a different place and so end up with a different sort of certitude.[6] Here I am much informed by an essay of

---

5. No doubt the "how" and the "what" of biblical testimony are intimately related. One of the problems of much Old Testament theology is that it has been too cognitive and ideational, paying insufficient attention to the ways of Israel's rhetoric. We have the curious situation of rhetorical critics who pay primary attention to the ways of Israel's speech, but who look askance at theological claims; and, conversely, theological interpreters so focused on content that they neglect mode of speech. For a way to relate the two, see Gail R. O'Day, *The Word Disclosed: John's Story and Narrative Preaching* (Philadelphia: Fortress Press, 1987); and *Revelation in the Fourth Gospel: Narrative Mode and Theological Claim* (Philadelphia: Fortress Press, 1986).

6. The most helpful discussion of these issues known to me is C. A. J. Coady, *Testimony: A Philosophical Study* (Oxford: Clarendon Press, 1992). Coady argues for an alternative mode of knowledge and certitude, which for being alternative is no less legitimate. Coady undertakes a serious critique of R. G. Collingwood's dominant positivistic objectivism.

As subpoints of the general rubric of testimony, I note the following:

(a) The appeal to testimony as a ground of certitude has particular and peculiar importance for the thought of Karl Barth. (I am grateful to Mark D. J. Smith for specific references.) See *Church Dogmatics* 1/1 (Edinburgh: T. & T. Clark, 1975) 98–124; *Church Dogmatics* 1/2 (Edinburgh: T. & T. Clark, 1956) 457–740, especially 457–72, 514–26. See also Martin Rumscheidt, *Revelation and Theology: An Analysis of the Barth-Harnack Correspondence of 1923* (Cambridge: Cambridge University Press, 1972) 29–53, especially 45–47. For efforts to understand Barth's peculiar assumptions, see David Kelsey, *The Uses of Scripture in Recent Theology* (Philadelphia: Fortress Press, 1975); David Ford, "Barth's Interpretation of Scripture," *Karl Barth—Studies of His Theological Method* (ed. S. W. Sykes; Oxford: Clarendon Press, 1979); and Ford, *Barth and God's Story* (Frankfurt: Peter Lang, 1981).

(b) Andrew Lincoln has helpfully pointed out that testimony is of crucial importance in the Fourth Gospel. See Andrew T. Lincoln, "Trials, Plots, and the Narrative of the Fourth Gospel," *Journal for the Study of the New Testament* 56 (1994) 3–30; A. A. Trites, *The New Testament Concept of Witness* (Cambridge: Cambridge University Press, 1977) 78–127; and Robert V. Moss, "The Witnessing Church in the New Testament," *Theology and Life* 3 (1960) 262–68. The importance of the linkage to the Fourth Gospel is the recognition that the epistemological claims made for Jesus in the early church also depend on the acceptance of testimony. The elemental case for this is the list of witnesses to the resurrection in 1 Cor 15:3-6.

(c) Much less directly, I mention in this connection the role of the Sophists in ancient Greece, practitioners of the public activity of rhetorical persuasion. The entire story of realist philosophy has tended to silence and discredit the Sophists, for their appeal to rhetoric continually subverted the would-be settled claims of the Platonic realists. From a perspective of rhetorical adjudication, however, it is clear that the realists wanted to shut down ongoing rhetoric, and therefore to foreclose the political process. See Eric A. Havelock, *The Liberal Temper in Greek Politics* (New Haven: Yale University Press, 1957); Brian Vickers, *In Defense of Rhetoric* (Oxford: Clarendon Press, 1988); and Terence Irwin, *Plato's Moral Theory* (Oxford: Oxford University Press, 1977).

(d) The issue of testimony is particularly acute now, with reference to the evidence concerning the fact and the character of the Nazi Holocaust. That is, the primary evidence for the Holocaust is personal testimony, without which this unthinkable barbarity is to be lost. Elie Wiesel, "The Holocaust as Literary Inspiration," *Dimensions of Holocaust* (Evanston, Ill.: Northwestern University Press, 1977) 9, has understood the urgency of testimony in his aphorism: "If the Greeks invented tragedy, the Romans the epistle, and the Renaissance the sonnet, our generation invented a new literature, that of testimony." See also Shoshana Felman and Dori Laub, *Testimony: Crisis of Witnessing in Literature, Psychoanalysis, and History* (New York: Routledge, 1992). Felman and Laub see that testimony is urgent when truth is in crisis, i.e., a crisis of evidence. Acutely so in the twentieth century, perhaps that is the characteristic circumstance of Yahweh's community of testimony.

Paul Ricoeur.[7] Nevertheless, testimony as a metaphor for Israel's utterance about Yahweh is deeply situated in the text itself. Specifically, the disputation speech is a dominant form of witness in Second Isaiah, precisely in the exile when truth is in crisis and evidence is uncertain. Thus I regard testimony not simply as a happy or clever convenience for my exposition, but as an appropriate way to replicate the practice of ancient Israel.[8]

Testimony and Trial Metaphor

The proper setting of testimony is a court of law, in which various and diverse witnesses are called to "tell what happened," to give their version of what is true. In any trial situation the evidence given by witnesses is a mixed matter of memory, reconstruction, imagination, and wish. The court must then determine, with no other data except testimony, which version is reality. It is on the basis of *testimony* that the court reaches what is *real*.

Working with the metaphor of trial, we consider first the peculiar phenomenon of a witness. Here I make general comments, without particular reference to Israel's peculiar witness about Yahweh. The situation of a trial means that there is a reality in question, and there are different, competing accounts of what that reality is (or was). In the trial situation, presumably, some actual event or experience occurred, to which appeal is made and which is under dispute. The witness allegedly had access to that actual event, was there, saw it and experienced it, and so is qualified to give testimony. The actual event, however, is enormously supple and elusive and admits of many retellings, some of which are only shaded differently, but some of which are drastically different.

I do not suggest that all open rhetoric constitutes testimony as I am here using the term with reference to Israel's faith. I suggest, nonetheless, that these several different forms share a conviction that somehow reality is deeply contingent on speech. Therefore Israel's testimony about Yahweh is inherently subversive of all non-Yahwistic shapes of reality.

It is ironic that the same issue between reality as constituted by speech, on the one hand, and reality that resists speech, on the other hand, is a tension now resurfacing around issues of exclusive and inclusive language. In that tension, the subverting power of inclusive speech is here and there silenced by an appeal to metaphysical realism, which seems, on the face of it, to be essentially a long-accepted practice of rhetoric.

7. Paul Ricoeur, *Essays on Biblical Interpretation* (Philadelphia: Fortress Press, 1981) 119–54. Ricoeur's study has been carefully exposited by Jean-Daniel Plüss, *Therapeutic and Prophetic Narratives in Worship* (New York: Peter Lang, 1988), especially chap. 2. On the problems and possibilities of testimony in the pursuit of establishing "truth," see Richard K. Fenn, *Liturgies and Trials: The Secularization of Religious Language* (Oxford: Blackwell, 1982); and *The Death of Herod: An Essay in the Sociology of Religion* (Cambridge: Cambridge University Press, 1992).

8. Second Isaiah surely stands at the center of Israel's effort to utter Yahweh faithfully and effectively, in a most demanding and dangerous situation. Israel gave testimony to "the truth of Yahweh," which intended to subvert and undermine the dominant truth of Babylon's preeminence and Israel's commensurate despair. On this genre and its cruciality for Second Isaiah, see Claus Westermann, "Sprache und Struktur der Prophetie Deuterojesajas," *Forschung am Alten Testament; Gesammelte Studien* (ThB 24; Munich: Christian Kaiser, 1964) 124–44. It will be evident in much of what follows that Second Isaiah occupies a privileged place in my interpretation, a position informed by my study with Prof. James Muilenburg, but already in place for me as early as my B.D. thesis in 1955 under Lionel A. Whiston, Jr.

The court, however, has no access to the "actual event" besides the testimony. It cannot go behind the testimony to the event, but must take the testimony as the "real portrayal." Indeed, it is futile for the court to speculate behind the testimony.

From the perspective of the witness, we may observe three matters. First, the witness is able to choose the version of construal to be uttered. This choice may be made on advice of counsel or under the coaching of an attorney. It may be a calculated utterance, designed to produce a certain outcome, or it may be a happenstance utterance, made with no intentionality, but one by which the witness must subsequently stand. It is important to recognize that the witness had other options and could have spoken differently, could have chosen other words and images to portray reality with another nuance.

Second, when the witness utters testimony, the testimony is a public presentation that shapes, enjoins, or constitutes reality. In this sense, the testimony is *originary:* it causes to be, in the courtroom, what was not until this utterance. In this sense, the utterance leads reality in the courtroom, so that the reality to which testimony is made depends completely on the utterance.

Third, when the court makes a decision and agrees to accept some version of reality based on some testimony, the testimony is accepted as true—that is, it becomes true. In the decision of the court, by the process of the verdict, the testimony is turned into reality. The defendant is pronounced to be acquitted or guilty. In the parlance of the court, the verdict is the establishment of a legal reality.

If we describe this process theologically—or, more specifically, in the practice of the Old Testament—we may say that testimony becomes revelation. That is, the testimony that Israel bears to the character of God is taken by the ecclesial community of the text as a reliable disclosure about the true character of God. Here we touch on the difficulty of the authority of Scripture, which has usually been articulated in the scholastic categories of inspiration and revelation. It is simpler and more helpful, I believe, to recognize that when utterance in the Bible is taken as truthful, human testimony is taken as revelation that discloses the true reality of God.[9]

Thus, much of the Old Testament, the part that von Rad listed under "response," is explicitly human utterance.[10] For example, the familiar utterance of Ps 23:1, "The Lord is my shepherd," is a human utterance, and a metaphor at that. That utterance is taken by the faithful as revelation, as a true and reliable disclosure of who God is. In less direct fashion, historical criticism has seen that all utterance in the Old Testament about God, even utterance placed in the mouth of God, has

---

9. The phrase "taken as" is informed for me by the analysis of David Bryant, *Faith and the Play of Imagination: On the Role of Imagination in Religion* (Macon, Ga.: Mercer University Press, 1989) 115 and passim. Bryant sees that to "take" something as reality is an active process of establishing reality. A lesser verb is "to see as," as exposited by Garrett Green, *Imagining God: Theology and the Religious Imagination* (San Francisco: Harper and Row, 1989) 139–42 and passim.

10. Gerhard von Rad, *Old Testament Theology* (2 vols; San Francisco: Harper and Row, 1962), 2:355–459, treated the Psalms and wisdom under the rubric of "response." The rubric does not fit the material very well, as has often been noted, but the notion employed by von Rad is important.

a human speaker or writer as its source. But that human utterance, as for example in Isa 40:1-11 or Job 38-41, is taken as a true and reliable disclosure. It is by no means clear how this odd transposition from testimony to revelation is accomplished, though we assume it all the time in our theological treatment of the Bible. This means that witnesses, who had other options available, who for whatever reasons chose to utter the matter in just this way, established through their utterance what is "true" about the character of God.

Our purpose in examining this strange transposition from testimony to revelation, from utterance to reality, is to indicate that for Old Testament faith, *the utterance is everything.*[11] The utterance leads to the reality, the reality of God that relies on the reliability of the utterance. Presumably other utterances could have been accepted as true, but these particular utterances are the ones that have been preserved, trusted, treasured, and given to us. The upshot of this process is, first, that Israel's claim of reality is as fragile as an utterance, and we must be exceedingly wary of flights from utterance to some presumed pre-textual reality. Second, this process makes it clear that a student of Old Testament theology must pay close attention to the shape, character, and details of the utterance, for it is in, with, and under the utterance that we have the God of Israel, and nowhere else.

Normative Shape of Israel's Utterance

We may now consider the peculiar and characteristic way in which Israel formulates its testimony about God. Here I suggest what appears to be a normative way in which such utterance is given in Israel, a way that constitutes the primary witness of Israel. We shall have to make important allowances, however, for much in Israel's testimony that does not conform to this way of speech. We must pay attention to Israel's characteristic speech about God. The term *characteristic* is important for my argument.[12] I do not say *earliest* or *most original,* as I do not want to become enmeshed in the difficulties that von Rad had with his insistence on the "early" credos of Israel. Rather, by *characteristic,* I mean the most usual modes of speech, so that one test is the quantity of use. Beyond quantity, I mean by *characteristic* the ways Israel spoke in its most freighted, exalted, or exposed situations. Israel's most characteristic testimony is the speech to which Israel reverted when circumstance required its most habituated speech.[13]

---

11. On the cruciality of utterance, see the general accent on "articulacy" for moral discourse in Charles Taylor, *Sources of the Self: The Making of the Modern Identity* (Cambridge: Harvard University Press, 1989), chap. 4.

12. I use the term *characteristic* to recognize that one cannot say "always" about such speech, because exceptions are inevitable. On the notion of characteristic speech, see Walter Brueggemann, "Crisis-Evoked, Crisis-Resolving Speech," *BTB* 24 (1994) 95–105.

13. Concerning the testimony of Israel, one may speak of Israel's "habits of the lips," as in the phrase, "Say in our heart." The phrase "habits of the lips" plays on the title of Robert Bellah et al., *Habits of the Heart: Individualism and Commitment in American Life* (Berkeley: University of California Press, 1985).

It is important, first of all, to recognize that Israel's utterance about God is characteristically stated in full sentences, and the sentence is the unit of testimony that most reliably is taken as revelation. Here we do well to follow James Barr in his warning against overreliance on isolated words.[14] I insist that God is embedded in Israel's testimony of full sentences and cannot be extracted from such full sentences. Moreover, we may identify the characteristic form of such sentences, even if they can be arranged in a variety of imaginative ways. The full sentence of testimony, which characteristically becomes revelation in Israel, is organized around an active verb that bespeaks an action that is transformative, intrusive, or inverting.[15] Thus special attention may be paid to causative verbs in the *hiph 'il* stem. In what follows, we shall give detailed attention to the regular stock of verbs used by Israel in its testimony. Each of these verbs regularly attests to the claim that the enactment of the verb creates a new situation or a changed circumstance that did not exist prior to its enactment.

Second, Yahweh the God of Israel, who may variously be designated by many titles and metaphors, is characteristically the subject of the active verb.[16] Thus the characteristic claim of Israel's testimony is that Yahweh is an active agent who is the subject of an active verb, and so the testimony is that Yahweh, the God of Israel, has acted in decisive and transformative ways.[17] Remember that we are

---

14. James Barr, *The Semantics of Biblical Language* (Oxford: Oxford University Press, 1961). It is Barr's now well-established urging that words can only be understood in the context of their usage in sentences. In what follows, my consideration of verbs, adjectives, and nouns that speak of Yahweh is an effort to treat Israel's characteristic terms in context.

15. On the privileged function of the verb, see Michel Foucault, *The Order of Things: An Archaeology of the Human Sciences* (trans. A. M. S. Smith; New York: Vintage Books, 1973) 92–96. Foucault observes on p. 93:

The verb is the indispensable condition for all discourse; and wherever it does not exist at least by implication, it is not possible to say that there is a language. All normal presuppositions conceal the invisible presence of the verb.

Foucault also reflects on the verb *to be,* a matter that interests us in terms of nominal sentences. On the cruciality of verbs for Old Testament theology, see Terence E. Fretheim, "The Repentance of God: A Key to Evaluating Old Testament God-Talk," *HBT* 10 (1988) 47–70.

16. My way of approaching the character and identity of Yahweh provisionally precludes other approaches. Thus, for example, I will not deal with the several titles for Yahweh that reflect Israel's history of religion. On these, see Tryggve N. D. Mettinger, *In Search of God: The Meaning and Message of the Everlasting Names* (Philadelphia: Fortress Press, 1988). I am aware of the complex history of the antecedents of Yahweh; see Mark S. Smith, *The Early History of God: Yahweh and Other Deities in Ancient Israel* (San Francisco: Harper and Row, 1990); and Tryggve N. D. Mettinger, *The Dethronement of Sabaoth: Studies in the Shem and Kabod Theologies* (Lund, Sweden: CWK Gleerup, 1982). These antecedents to Yahweh, in my judgment, belong to questions of the history of Israel's religion and do not directly concern Old Testament theology.

17. I have arranged my discussion of Israel's God-talk around the issue of verbs. It is important to recognize that in Israel's God-talk and in God's talk to Israel, an important body of material is expressed in nominal sentences, sentences without verbs. While I will not deal with these extensively or explicitly, what I have said of verbal sentences applies, *mutatis mutandis,* to nominal sentences. That is, Yahweh is, in nominal as in verbal sentences, embedded in full sentences and cannot be extracted from them. In these sentences, however, the consequence for characterizing Yahweh tends to be presence rather than action. It may be that Foucault's general judgment that nominal sentences conceal hidden verbs does not apply directly to Hebrew usage, but I do not doubt that the usages in verbal and nominal sentences are commensurate.

here paying attention to the utterance of testimony given by Israel as witness. This strange grammatical practice serves to give a version of reality that flies in the face of other versions of reality, and most often it wants to defeat the other versions of reality, which it judges to be false. There is, to be sure, a large and vexed literature about "the acts of God," literature that tends to proceed either by recognizing that such utterances make no sense historically, or by reifying the phrase into a philosophical concept.[18] Israel's testimony, however, is not to be understood as a claim subject to historical explication or to philosophical understanding. It is rather

---

Two usages of nominal sentences are particularly important for Israel's witness to Yahweh. First, the enigmatic statement of Exod 3:14, "I will be who I will be," is exceedingly important, even if problematic. Frank M. Cross, "The Religion of Canaan and the God of Israel," *Canaanite Myth and Hebrew Epic: Essays in the History of Israelite Religion* (Cambridge: Harvard University Press, 1973) 60–75, has made a powerful argument that the name of Yahweh, as reflected in Exod 3:14, was originally part of a verbal sentence, in which the verb *to be* is understood as *cause to be*, i.e., *create*, or *pro-create*. Such a way of understanding embeds the nominal sentence in an assumed verbal sentence. In any case, it is plausible that the entire Exodus narrative is an exposition of the name of Exod 3:14, requiring all of its powerful verbs for an adequate exposition.

Second, the salvation oracles of Second Isaiah (41:8-13; 43:5-6; 44:8; cf. Jer 30:10-11) are indeed nominal sentences, characteristically asserting, "Fear not, I am with you." On the form, see Claus Westermann, *Praise and Lament in the Psalms* (Atlanta: John Knox, 1981); Edgar W. Conrad, *Fear Not Warrior: A Study of 'al tira' Pericopes in the Hebrew Scriptures* (Chico, Calif.: Scholars Press, 1985); and Patrick D. Miller, *They Cried to the Lord: The Form and Theology of Biblical Prayer* (Minneapolis: Fortress Press, 1994) 141–73. There is no verb in any of these assurances. Nonetheless, in my judgment, even the nominal assertions bespeak an active, transformative agency, in which some kind of verbal activity is implied or is to be inferred. The problem is in part a grammatical one. But it is also a substantive one, in that Yahweh's very person is itself a transformative force most often expressed in verbs. That is, "God is with" (*Immanuel*), and by "being with," circumstance is changed. That change, in its precise utterance, requires something like the articulation of a verb. Thus I wish to acknowledge the importance of sentences without verbs, but to include them in my general index of statements about the reality of Yahweh in Israel's utterance. On the grammatical issues of nominal sentences, see Francis I. Andersen, *The Hebrew Verbless Clause in the Pentateuch* (JBL Monograph Series 14; Nashville: Abingdon Press, 1970).

It is possible, as Patrick D. Miller reminds me, to distinguish between nominal sentences that state Yahweh's *relationship* to Israel and nominal sentences that attest to Yahweh's *being or character*. This distinction greatly enriches and complicates the matter, but I think it does not finally affect my decision to treat such claims as commensurate with verbal sentences in their "produce."

18. The notion of "God acting" is a long-honored one in Old Testament theology, especially with reference to the work of Gerhard von Rad and G. Ernest Wright. See especially Wright, *God Who Acts: Biblical Theology as Recital* (SBT 8; London: SCM Press, 1952). More recently, the notion has been recognized as having immense problems. The literature is as immense as the problems. The notion of "God's action in history" has been a privileged reference point in Old Testament theology, especially under the influence of von Rad and Wright. But while Old Testament theology had gone a long while with rather innocent reference to such a notion, it had at the same time been deeply problematized by theologians.

The familiar reference point for that problematizing is an early article by Langdon Gilkey, "Cosmology, Ontology, and the Travail of Biblical Language," *JR* 41 (1961) 194–205. The subsequent discussion has largely been conducted by philosophically inclined theologians, with Scripture scholars contributing little. The most helpful discussion known to me is Thomas Tracy, *God, Action, and Embodiment* (Grand Rapids: Eerdmans, 1984). See also William P. Alston, *Divine Nature and Human Language: Essays in Philosophical Theology* (Ithaca, N.Y.: Cornell University Press, 1989); Vincent Brümmer, *Speaking of a Personal God: An Essay on Philosophical Theology* (Cambridge: Cambridge University Press, 1992), especially 108–27; Austin Farrer, *Faith and Speculation: An Essay in Philosophical Theology* (London: Adam and Charles Black, 1967); A. J. Freddoso, ed., *The Existence and Nature of God* (Notre Dame, Ind.: University of Notre Dame Press, 1983); T. V. Morris, *Divine and Human Action: Essays in the Metaphysics of Theism* (Ithaca, N.Y.: Cornell University Press, 1988); Gordon Kaufman, *God the Problem* (Cambridge: Harvard University Press, 1972); and Maurice Wiles, *God's Action in the World: The Bampton Lectures for 1986* (London: SCM Press, 1986).

an utterance that proposes that this particular past be construed according to this utterance. For our large purposes we should note, moreover, that such testimonial utterance in Israel is characteristically quite concrete, and only on the basis of many such concrete evidences does Israel dare to generalize.

The third element of this standard testimony of Israel is that the active verb has a direct object, the one acted on, the one for whom transformation has been wrought.[19] In the first instant, the direct object may be a personal pronoun—me, us—as the witness speaks about his or her own changed circumstance. Or this direct object may be expressed more formally as "Israel," who is regularly the recipient of Yahweh's direct activity.[20] But then, as we shall see, the direct object may vary greatly to include all of creation or even nonhuman parts of it, or the nations who are acted on by God in this rhetoric.

In this complicated grammar, we are close to the core claim of Israel's faith. In this faith, all of reality is comprehended in this simple sentence, organized around the verb. It is the verb that binds Yahweh to the object—variously, individual persons, Israel, creation, or the nations. The two parties, however, are bound in a relation that is profoundly asymmetrical, for Yahweh, as the subject of the verb, is the party who holds the initiative and who characteristically acts on the other party. The object is in the sentence to receive whatever Yahweh chooses to enact.

We notice immediately the manifold oddness of this claim, which constitutes the central fascination of Old Testament theology. First, the sentence governed by the verb promptly refuses any autonomy for the object, for all of the objects (which comprehend everything) are subject to the force of the verb and to the intent of the Subject. Second, God as the subject of the sentence is engaged in activity that binds God to these objects. Israel rarely and only belatedly can speak about God per se, but regularly speaks about God engaged transformatively with and on behalf

---

It is evident that a naive biblical notion of God's action is not plausible in the categories of modernism. Thus one is faced with either abandoning the notion of God's action or trimming it down to irrelevance, which an Old Testament theology can scarcely do, or refusing the categories of modernity that make one susceptible to the charge of fideism. The rich and suggestive discussion now available does not go far beyond these choices. In what follows, I have sought to explicate the rhetoric of ancient Israel in terms of its own claims, without submitting that rhetoric to the critique of modernist epistemological categories. I am aware that such a procedure begs the most difficult questions. I have taken this tack because, in terms of explicating Old Testament faith, any other strategy would end in being immobilized.

19. This subject-object transaction as reflected in the grammar of Israel's characteristic testimonial speech preserves the theological claim of Yahweh as the one who holds initiative and Israel as the one who receives what Yahweh gives. In my discussion of "Countertestimony" (Part 2) and "Unsolicited Testimony" (Part 3), I have indicated that the relationship between Yahweh and Yahweh's partners is not as simple as subject and object. The actual practice of Israel's testimony includes many variegated departures from that simple connection that has dominated scholastic theology. Jürgen Habermas, *Theology and Practice* (trans. John Viertal; Boston: Beacon Press, 1973) 244, comments that Christian theology preserves a distinction "between the subject of history and the subject who acts historically, between the Lord of history and those who are merely subjected to it."

20. In my exposition of Israel as Yahweh's object and partner, I refer to Israel as a theological entity, generated by the testimony of the text as a rhetorical exercise. I do not use the term with any assumptions about historicity for any part of the testimony. Judgments about historicity, in any positivistic sense, emerge only from a study of the history and culture of the ancient Near East. The results of such study bear only indirectly on the testimonial articulations of Israel in the text.

of the object. Third, the linkage of the subject God to the active verbs, while not unfamiliar to us, is intellectually problematic. It appears, according to our conventional horizons, to be an ill match of categories because the verb bespeaks forceful activity, whereas God is classically understood as Being or Substance. But of course Israel's way of utterance is not restrained by our conventional assumptions. Clearly Israel in its utterance is up to something that it is not willing to accommodate to our more commonsense notion of reality. And clearly it is willing to make such an utterance because the Subject so compels Israel that Israel must render a version of reality that is odd, given our more static or controlling ways of speech.

Thus while we recognize this peculiarity and Israel's repeated insistence on it, we must also recognize the fragility of the witness. No doubt other, more credible witnesses to reality were always available, even in the ancient world. The Old Testament is that literature which has in large rendered a verdict accepting this testimony as reliable. While we are paying attention to this testimony and hosting it as revelation, we must be aware that within and outside of Israel, alternative construals of reality were always more readily credible.

Normative Substance of Israel's Utterance

It is now possible to make some suggestion about the substance of the testimony that is characteristically expressed in this full and odd sentence. We may pay attention to the particular kind of sentence that seems most characteristic in Israel's testimony, whereby Israel's speech offers a version of reality that is from the outset in conflict with our versions of reality. Or we may see that Israel, from the outset, articulated a "sub-version" of reality that means to subvert other, more dominant versions.[21]

Testimony as Thanksgiving

I propose as a beginning point that Israel's testimony, in which it offers its version of reality (and therefore of God), is a sentence offered as a *tôdah*. It is a statement of gratitude and thanksgiving, offered in a confessional mode, whereby Israel expresses joy, wonder, and gratitude for a gift given or an action performed, a gift or action that has decisively changed Israel's circumstance.[22] Moreover, the characteristic setting of the utterance of a *tôdah* is speech in a worship setting, wherein a material offering accompanies the speech. The speech and the offer-

---

21. I have taken over the notion of sub-version as an alternative version that means to undermine the accepted version from J. Cheryl Exum, *Fragmented Women: Feminist (Sub)versions of Biblical Narrative* (Philadelphia: Trinity Press International, 1993). The effect of the term used this way is to insist that accepted reality is not a given, but simply one more version of what is there. Moreover, the usage suggests that there is nothing given behind the versions, but that everything about what is "there" depends on the embrace of some version.

22. On the *tôdah* as an important usage in Israel's liturgy and faith, see Harvey H. Guthrie, *Theology as Thanksgiving: From Israel's Psalms to the Church's Eucharist* (New York: Seabury, 1981); and Miller, *They Cried to the Lord*, 179–204.

ing together signify in a concrete way the grateful acknowledgment for the gift or action now narrated.

Several characteristic examples of the *tôdah* can be taken to be the standard context for Israel's most elemental testimony:

> I will give to the Lord the thanks (*tôdah*) due to his righteousness (*ṣdq*),
> and sing praise to the name of the Lord, the Most High. (Ps 7:17)

This utterance comes at the end of a psalm of petition, and so it *anticipates* God's positive response to its desperate plea. The term *tôdah* is parallel to "sing praise" (*zmr*), and therefore it is likely that the anticipated *tôdah* is cultic. Moreover, the substance of Yahweh's characteristic action is Yahweh's *ṣdqh*, which is the way in which Yahweh is present to this needy Israelite. Thus the *tôdah* in anticipation is a glad response to Yahweh's righteousness.

> I will give thanks (*tôdah*) to the Lord with my whole heart;
> I will tell (*spr*) of all your wonderful deeds.
> I will be glad and exult in you;
> I will sing praise (*zmr*) to your name, O Most High. (Ps 9:1-2)

In this articulation of *tôdah*, the verb is matched by four others: *tell, be glad, exult,* and *sing praise* (*zmr*). All of these verbs bespeak utter and ecstatic joy in the presence of the community, joy that is enacted through speech. The body of this psalm then provides an inventory of the ways in which Yahweh has impinged in transformative ways on the life of the speaker.

> With a freewill offering (*ndvh*) I will sacrifice to you;
> I will give thanks (*'dh*) to your name, O Lord, for it is good.
> For he has delivered me from every trouble,
> and my eye has looked in triumph on my enemies. (Ps 54:6-7)

This utterance again comes at the conclusion of a petitionary prayer. In this case, unlike Psalm 7, the well-being given by God is not anticipated, but is *in hand*. Yahweh has delivered (*nṣl*), and the speaker has enjoyed triumph over the adversaries. This usage also makes explicit the cultic setting for the *tôdah* as a vow (*ndv*) that is to be kept, certainly in the presence of the congregation.

> I will come into your house with burnt offerings (*'olôth*);
> I will pay you my vows (*ndr*),
> those that my lips uttered
> and my mouth promised when I was in trouble.
> I will offer to you burnt offerings (*'olôth*) of fatlings,
> with the smoke of the sacrifice (*qṭr*) of rams;
> I will make an offering of bulls and goats.
> Come and hear, all you who fear God,
> and I will tell (*spr*) what he has done for me. (Ps 66:13-16)

This presentation again is liturgic and anticipates the offering of cultic sacrifices (*'ôlôth, ndr, qṭr*). The giving of sacrifices is the completion of a vow that was part of a petition made "in trouble," a trouble that has now been resolved by the reality and activity of Yahweh. In vv. 3-7, the psalmist bears witness to the awesome deeds that Yahweh has wrought, deeds that defeat enemies and that evoke glad acknowledgment and praise in "all the earth." The awesome deeds are only mentioned, with an allusion to the Exodus (v. 6) and to a powerful ordering that prevents damage done by "the rebellious" (v. 7).

A more general usage of the same mode of testimony is offered in Ps 111:1-2:

> Praise the Lord!
> I will give thanks (*'dh*) to the Lord with my whole heart,
> in the company of the upright, in the congregation.
> Great are the works of the Lord,
> studied by all who delight in them.

Again the utterance is "in the congregation" and bears witness to Yahweh's great works (v. 2), which are marked by righteousness, graciousness, and mercy. This psalm, however, lacks the concreteness and detail we have seen in other references, and evidences the process by which Israel's speech begins to generalize, thus moving, as Claus Westermann has termed it, from *declarative* praise to *descriptive* praise.[23]

The reader will note well that I have proposed that *the beginning point for articulating an Old Testament theology is in the liturgical, public acknowledgment of a new reality wrought by Yahweh* in the life of the speaker and in the community of the speaker. One cannot on any grounds demonstrate that this is the "correct" beginning point. I begin here because it seems the most obvious and concrete utterance of what is most characteristic in Israel's testimony of faith. Israel, in voiced utterance, acknowledges in an unrestrained way that something decisive has happened that is taken to be the work of Yahweh. Thus, I propose that the *tôdah* (a public act of thanksgiving) is the context in which the grammar of Israel's faith (that is, the verb of transformation, Yahweh as the active subject, and the direct object who is acted on) is fully uttered.

We may notice, moreover, that testimony in this liturgical context signifies that a certain kind of rhetoric is characteristic for Israel's speech about God. In its liturgical context, the speech is doxological; that is, it is confessional, unrestrained, unembarrassed, and uttered by the fully committed self.[24] It is the language of unrestrained commitment done with one's "whole heart" (Ps 111:1). It is speech that

---

23. Westermann, *Praise and Lament in the Psalms.* See also Frank Crüsemann, *Studien zur Formgeschichte von Hymnus und Danklied* (WMANT 32; Neukirchen-Vluyn: Neukirchener Verlag, 1969).

24. On emancipated doxological practice in Israel, see Walter Brueggemann, *Israel's Praise: Doxology against Idolatry and Ideology* (Philadelphia: Fortress Press, 1988); and "Praise and the Psalms: A Politics of Glad Abandonment," *The Psalms and the Life of Faith* (ed. Patrick D. Miller; Minneapolis: Fortress Press, 1995) 112–32.

offers for verification of its claim nothing more and nothing less than Israel's willingness to accept this utterance as true and reliable, and on which it will stake its life.[25]

Much of the importance of this liturgical procedure is in the utterance. Israel needed to speak its witness out loud, for the *saying* is effective in affirming and enhancing the relationship. The testimony in *tôdah* is also *heard*, to great effect. The testimony is surely heard in the liturgical community itself. But beyond that gathered community, Israel's testimony is also, at a second level, addressed to the nations who are thought to be attending to what Israel is saying and doing in worship.

Thus, for example, the *tôdah* in Psalm 22 culminates with an expectation that the nations will hear and accept the testimony to Yahweh as compelling:

All the ends of the earth shall remember
and turn to the Lord;
and all the families of the nations
shall worship before him. (v. 27)

In Psalm 126 it is the nations who observe and draw the conclusion:

Then it was said among the nations,
"The Lord has done great things for them." (v. 2)

The *tôdah* is presented as an attractive invitation that will win adherence and allegiance to the rule of Yahweh among those outside the liturgical community.

This doxology, moreover, is a *political* utterance in two ways. First, it is a polemic against the adversary in the troubles to which the utterance points. That is, the glad identification with Yahweh, the subject of the strong verbs, intends to put the (defeated) adversary in a position of diminishment with a tone of gloating condescension and scolding. Second, the doxology is polemical in the face of any would-be observer of the *tôdah* who is neutral, who reserves judgment, or who seeks to stand outside this rhetorical claim. The speaker regards any such alternative version of reality, either adversarial or neutral, as ludicrous. Thus the exuberance of the doxological mode of utterance intends to sweep all before it and to establish the reality narrated in these poems of testimony as reliable and true. But we note well that there is no supportive evidence for the utterance. There is nothing to go on except the utterance itself. The speaker anticipates that the whole congregation will subscribe to the utterances that will shape its reality in a specific way.

But we may draw closer to see what the substance of Israel's Yahwistic grammar is, which in the *tôdah* is Israel's characteristic response. These songs of thanksgiving use various terms to comment on Yahweh's "awesome deeds." God is "righteous" (Pss 7:11, 17; 9:4, 8; 111:3), given to "equity" (9:8), attentive to the oppressed (9:9)

---

25. "Staking its life" means that verification is given only in uncompromising praxis.

and the afflicted (9:12), the needy and the poor (9:18), ready to deliver (56:13), mighty (66:7), given to "steadfast love" (66:20), "gracious and merciful" (111:4), "faithful and just" (111:7), and "faithful and upright" (111:8). While these terms may be sorted out with different nuances, it is fair to say that all of this testimony—which is based on what are claimed to be concrete experiences and which issues in *tôdah*—bespeaks Yahweh's powerful reliability for and solidarity with those who speak.

The Righteousness of Yahweh

With somewhat more focus, we may say that Israel's *tôdah* characteristically testifies to Yahweh's righteousness (*ṣdqh*). By righteousness we mean Yahweh's ready capacity to be present in situations of trouble and to intervene powerfully and decisively in the interest of rehabilitation, restoration, and well-being.

In order to consider more carefully the characteristics assigned to Yahweh in Israel's grateful, doxological, polemical utterance, we may consider three texts in which Yahweh's righteousness is spoken of in the plural, "righteousnesses" (*ṣdqôth*). In these texts, Israel begins to gather in a more general way the specific of its own concrete witness. All three uses, scattered through the literature, are uttered in contexts where testimony is a required mode of speech.

The first of these texts is in the song of Deborah, commonly taken to be one of Israel's most formidable and earliest articulations of its faith in Yahweh. The poem is a victory song, celebrating what apparently was a decisive and surprising defeat of Israel's enemies:

> Tell of it, you who ride on white donkeys,
>> you who sit on rich carpets
>> and you who walk by the way.
> To the sound of musicians at the watering places,
>> there they repeat the triumphs (*ṣdqôth*) of the Lord,
>> the triumphs (*ṣdqoth*) of his peasantry in Israel. (Judg 5:10-11)

Israel, in every circumstance, is urged to "repeat" (*prz*) the "triumphs" (*ṣdqôth*= "righteousnesses") of Yahweh. Israel is to do so when riding, when sitting, when walking—all the time. They are to do so at "the watering places," where people gather to exchange news and gossip. Everywhere and always, everyone in Israel is invited to tell and retell Yahweh's triumphs. What is to be told concerns Yahweh's repeated and characteristic interventions that redress the disadvantages Israel regularly faces. In the battle of Judges 5, Israel had no chance against its more powerful, better-armed enemy. But when "new gods were chosen" (v. 8), when Yahweh entered the contest on the side of Israel, everything was altered. Israel triumphed and well-being was established in Israel. The outcome of the battle is unexpected and inexplicable . . . except for Yahweh, to whom Israel bears testimony, everywhere, always, by everyone. What Israel asserts is that Yahweh acts to make things right for Israel.

The second text in which the righteousness of Yahweh is testified to in the plural is 1 Sam 12:7. It is a speech of Samuel, heavily marked with what seems to be Deuteronomic phrasing. Thus its mode is very different from that of the speech in Judges 5. In this text Samuel the judge gives his farewell address, in which he seeks to establish his virtue and effectiveness as Israel's leader. He asserts his innocence by aligning himself with Yahweh and Yahweh's actions, perhaps suggesting that it is Samuel's actions that have made possible the decisive actions of Yahweh, or even that Samuel's career of leadership is one of Yahweh's decisive actions. In his own defense, Samuel asserts:

> Now therefore take your stand, so that I may enter into judgment with you before the Lord, and I will declare to you all the saving deeds (*sdqôth*) of the Lord that he performed for you and for your ancestors.

The speech then follows with an inventory of Israel's remembered past with Yahweh, all the way from the Book of Genesis through the Book of Judges (vv. 8-11), incidentally alluding to Sisera and Barak, the characters in Judges 5 just cited. What interests us, however, is that these remembered events, with which Samuel identifies his own work, are all regarded as *sidqôth* ("saving deeds") whereby Yahweh is said to have acted decisively in the interest of Israel's well-being. Thus Israel's core memory, here given in (self-serving?) testimony, is presented as a series of righteousnesses of Yahweh.

The third reference to "the righteousnesses of Yahweh" is an oracle of prophetic poetry. Yahweh, through the utterance of the prophetic speaker, defends Yahweh's own faithful attentiveness to Israel, and challenges Israel to provide any counterevidence that Yahweh has not been utterly faithful and attentive to Israel:

> O my people, what have I done to you?
> In what have I wearied you? Answer me!
> For I brought you up from the land of Egypt,
> and redeemed you from the house of slavery;
> and I sent before you Moses, Aaron, and Miriam.
> O my people, remember now what King Balak of Moab devised,
> what Balaam son of Beor answered him,
> and what happened from Shittim to Gilgal,
> that you may know the saving acts (*sdqôth*) of the Lord. (Mic 6:3-5)

In this recital of Yahweh's past with Israel, Yahweh alludes to the major transformative points in that past, with particular reference to the Exodus deliverance and to several events reported in the Book of Numbers. This statement specifically includes the Balaam narrative of Numbers 22–24. The general reference "Shittim to Gilgal" alludes to the events from Numbers 25 to the crossing of the Jordan River at Gilgal in Joshua 3–4. What interests us, however, is that all of these memories are now consolidated into the plural term "righteousnesses," all now regarded as acts of transformation wrought by Yahweh on behalf of Israel, all making it possible for Israel to have a chance of well-being in the world. The statement surely implies that without Yahweh's decisive intervention, Israel would have had no chance in the world. Everything depends on these startling, unparalleled events to which the prophetic speaker bears testimony.

These three references (Judg 5:10-11, 1 Sam 12:7, Mic 6:3-5), in very different modes and contexts, provide evidence of a characteristic way in which Israel understood, construed, and spoke about the reality of Yahweh in its life. *It understood that the reference points of life with Yahweh have to do with interventions that made possible what was otherwise not possible.* And Israel's *tôdah* responded in exuberant gratitude to this rendering of its past.

We notice that in the *todôth* of Israel and in the *ṣidqôth* to which the *todôth* bear witness, we have already arrived at certain stylistic constancies in Israel's way of construing reality and utilizing its narrative grammar. We should not miss that in this mode of speech something very odd has come to be taken for granted in Israel's testimony. That is, Yahweh is taken to be an accepted, unquestioned, and indispensably key character in Israel's rendering of reality. Indeed, the utterance suggests no curiosity or awkwardness about this character, no questioning that we might think inevitable, no speculative justification that we might seek to give, but simply, from a rhetorical perspective, a commonplace. Moreover, it is clear that Israel's rhetoric depends on this active agent of a subject to give force to the strong verbs that dominate Israel's speech. Indeed, the reference to Yahweh cannot be removed from the rhetoric without the disintegration of Israel's testimony. Without Yahweh, Israel has nothing to say and no subject about which to speak.

This commitment of Israel's grammar to the subject of Yahweh may be self-evident, but we should not fail to recognize its importance and its oddness. Israel's rhetorical world has as its central and driving power this Thou who is named and palpably present in this world. It is this Thou who characteristically acts in powerless Israel's behalf, who dominates Israel's speech, who is the enactor of life-permitting *ṣidqôth,* and who is the only thinkable subject of Israel's *tôdah.* It is not that ancient Israel, in its narrative testimony, acknowledges divine powers, or recognizes the supernatural, or makes allowances for the holy. It is rather that Yahweh is a known, nameable, and named character who lives Yahweh's own life according to Yahweh's own will and purpose. Therefore Israel must, in giving account of its life, always refer to Yahweh. When Israel moves from descriptive language to address, moreover, Israel must characteristically say "Thou" to this agent who haunts its whole life, known in the present by memories of how Yahweh has been discerned in the past.

Israel's life as a theological enterprise consists in coming to terms with this particular Thou, coming to terms with the nonnegotiable purposes and commands of Yahweh, but also coming to terms with the immense problematic that Yahweh turns out to be: often uttering promise and command, but sometimes silent; often present and visible, but sometimes ashamedly absent; often evident in righteous and faithful ways, but sometimes unreliable and notoriously cunning, all to doubtful effect. The *tôdah* of Israel is a fair beginning point from which to understand Israel's testimony. It is clear, however, that Israel's relentless witness to this Thou could not stay uniformly positive and affirmative, because much in Israel's life with Yahweh did not evoke gratitude and doxology. Nonetheless, Israel could never shake off its resolve to continue its utterance about Yahweh, for in this very utterance Israel knew its own life to be differently characterized in holiness, sometimes savage and sometimes beneficent.

This point about the cruciality of Thou is perhaps too obvious to need explication. I linger here, however, because contemporary interpreters are remote from Israel's availability for the utterance of Thou. Between Israel and us lies the whole enterprise of modernity, beginning in Cartesian doubt and culminating in Kant's "turn to the subject." This turn has meant a turn away from "Thou" to "I," and this focus on "I" dominates the entire modern scene, conservative as well as liberal. Our response to this turn has taken two forms: either we may continue the suspicion of Descartes and so decode the Thou into something less alive, or we may hedge the Thou with speculative excuses until the Thou has been sufficiently tamed to be an object and not a subject. Now, at the end of the twentieth century, we are learning in excruciating ways that this turn in modernity has given less than it promised—indeed, not enough by which to live. We do not know if there is any way to reconnect with this more risky world of Thou. If there is, then it requires, at the outset, a readiness to reentertain this relentlessly odd rhetoric. The cadences of *tôdah* about Yahweh's *ṣidqôth* seem incredibly remote from us. It is our burden in this study to reconsider this rhetoric of Israel, rhetoric which, like any court witness, may have some reality behind it. But for the most part, the reality that is judged to be behind it depends on acceptance of the witness.

In the cases cited as our beginning point, it is important to note that all three citations of Yahweh's *ṣidqôth* are in contexts of witness. In Judg 5:10-11, the witness is at the village well, where some are persuaded of Yahweh's victory and tell others about that wonder. Some at the well may not have known about Yahweh's intentions. Some may have doubted, and so the testimony is intended to persuade. Or perhaps all believed, but the testimony needs constant reiteration in order to sustain revolutionary nerve in that ancient community. In 1 Sam 12:7, apparently the retiring Samuel is under some criticism, and he must clear his name. Indeed, Samuel invites his listeners (presumed to be adversaries) to provide evidence against him, which they are not able to do. Samuel's recital provides a narrative account of the past, which functions as his defense and vindication. In Mic 6:3-5, it is Yahweh in court giving a self-defense, establishing Yahweh's own reliability and fidelity, which must have been questioned. The testimony of Yahweh to Yahweh's own *ṣidqôth* is in a different mood, daring anyone in Israel to provide counterevidence. Of course no one does. Thus in all three cases, the witness to Yahweh's *ṣidqôth* is advocacy, an argument for a certain rendering of reality that defies anyone to offer a different account. In each case, a counter-reading of the past that excludes Yahweh is imaginable, but none is given. We are left to conclude that the positive testimony for Yahweh's *ṣidqôth* wins the day and is established, at least in that time and place of utterance, as reality.

As these incidental testimonies (which may be located more specifically by critical analyses) merged by repeated usage into larger units and eventually into canonical form and authority, it is clear that Israel's testimony is intended to generate an accepted, normative narrative construal of reality in which the members of Israel can live. But we note that living in that world of testimony depends on the persistence and credence of the testimony. It is readily imaginable that other testimonies were always available in Israel, other construals of reality, some of which were powerful and attractive, some of which were no doubt more "commonsense" and more readily championed by the dominant legitimating power. Thus Israel's testimony (as revelation that became canon) always has an edge of advocacy and urgency to it, for its members can, in any given circumstance, fall out of the life-world generated by this rhetoric. We may imagine that some who heard and accepted the testimony did so completely and without reserve. We may imagine as well that some did so only provisionally, never free from alternative offers that sometimes prevailed. There is no reason to imagine that ancient Israel lacked the same range of passions and commitments known in our own contemporary communities concerning the same testimony.

When any member falls out of this narrated life-world into another, moreover, a decisive loss of this Thou occurs—the *ṣidqôth* of this Thou, the hovering possibilities of this Thou, and the full sentences of affirmation that depend on this Thou for viability. Thus the testimony of Israel, in many variegated forms and patterns, is crucial and indispensable for Israel's peculiar existence in the world.[26] We may imagine, moreover, that in every new circumstance the testimony must all be done over again, for this version of reality, rendered with freedom and imagination, always lives in the presence of other versions of reality, which are less odd, less problematic, less demanding, and less laden with possibility.

We are now able to see why Paul Ricoeur's metaphor of trial is such a suggestive perspective from which to begin our exposition of Old Testament theology. The matrix of trial-witness-testimony is one of the few social contexts in which it is clear that reality is dependent on speech. That is, the eyewitness purports to have seen something that happened, and witnesses are characteristically "eyewitnesses."[27] But "what happened" is unavailable, and so everything depends on the witness. Everything depends on the credibility of the witness, but credibility may be heavily influenced by gesture or phrasing or inflection, by any detail, whether intentional or unwitting.

---

26. Ricoeur, *Essays on Biblical Interpretation*, 73–95, has noted that Israel's testimony requires a rich and variegated set of genres in order to assert all that Israel must assert in order to be Israel. In effect Ricoeur accepts all genre in biblical rhetoric as testimony that becomes revelation.

27. On eyewitness as distinct from expert witness, see Richard K. Fenn, *Liturgies and Trials: The Secularization of Religious Language* (New York: Pilgrim Press, 1982).

After the witnesses have been heard (presumably witnesses in dispute), a verdict must be given. A judgment is made about which witnesses are trustworthy. When the verdict is given, reality is decided. And when reality is decided, the court does not look back, does not second-guess. Appeals have to do with evidence, process, and procedure, but appeals are only an elongated form of what happens in the initial trial. From the verdict forward, the court will entertain no rival version of alleged reality. (Of course there may be competing informal versions, as with the Warren Commission in the case of the assassination of President Kennedy.) The process is quite complex but, in the end, what has been *spoken* is decisive for what *is*.

I propose that this imagery of trial indicates the way in which the *logos* of Israel evokes the *theos* of Israel. And in the *theos-logos* process of the Old Testament, everything depends on the rhetoric of Israel, which in the first instant is subject neither to the explanatory doubts of historical criticism nor to the overburdened hedging of supernatural theology that seeks to make the advocacy of testimony more coherently compelling. Thus we have begun by asking the single, simple question: How did Israel in the Old Testament speak about God?[28] Our provisional answer is that Israel's rhetoric is ordered by strong, transformative verbs with Yahweh, the active agent, as subject, acting on a variety of direct objects, whose shape and destiny are completely in the hands of the subject of the verbs.

Negative and Wrong Utterances

Before we take up the details of this pervasive grammar of testimony, we may state two digressions, one negative and one positive. First, negatively: While Israel's testimony about Yahweh characteristically assumes something like willing speech and correct speech, we may observe briefly the negative counterparts of willing and correct speech. First, willing speech is evidenced when Israel is forthcoming and does not hesitate to speak about the God who inhabits this peculiar grammar. The regular alternative to willing speech is reluctant speech or, in an extreme case, the refusal to speak at all. We may place the refusal to speak about Yahweh under the modern rubric of atheism, and we may observe that atheism is scarcely a problem in the ancient world of Israel.[29] Nevertheless, two peculiar cases show that Israel is aware of this potential refusal to speak. In Ps 14:1, Israel asserts,

> Fools say in their hearts, "There is no God."
> They are corrupt, they do abominable deeds;
> there is no one who does good. (cf. Ps 53:1)

Clearly this is not an explicit statement attributable to the fools; it is "in their hearts." The second half of the verse makes clear that the putative utterance of the

---

28. I have proposed above that this rubric includes as well the material in which Yahweh speaks directly to Israel.

29. On the modern problem of atheism and its origin, see Michael J. Buckley, *At the Origins of Modern Atheism* (New Haven: Yale University Press, 1987).

fool is in fact done through deeds that are corrupt and abominable, deeds that "eat up my people" (v. 4) and "confound the plans of the poor" (v. 6). Such foolishness in social relations violates Yahweh's ordering of viable community. Gerhard von Rad terms this "practical atheism."[30] Such a mode of atheism is premised on the practical (not cognitive) assumption that Yahweh does not exist, or in any case is irrelevant.

In Psalm 10, a closely related text, these words are placed in the mouth of the wicked:

"God will not seek it out"...
"There is no God." (v. 4)

"God has forgotten,
he has hidden his face,
he will never see it." (v. 11)

"You will not call us to account"... (v. 13; cf. Isa 47:7, 8, 10)

The denial of God, here as in Psalm 14, is practical and not cognitive. Such a sense of reality without Yahweh, which falls outside the life-world of Israel's testimony, is marginal indeed in the Old Testament. I cite it here only to evidence the extreme alternative that was available to Israel, an alternative that its normative text would scarcely entertain.[31]

The much greater and more pervasive problem in ancient Israel is not a refusal to speak of Yahweh—that is, not a practical readiness to dismiss Yahweh as a factor in life, but the temptation to engage in *wrong* speech about Yahweh, which amounts to idolatry.[32] In that ancient community, as even now, idolatry (wrong speech about God) rather than atheism (refusal to speak about God) is the more compelling and dangerous issue.

To speak wrongly about Yahweh—to bear false witness, to provide an inadequate construal of Yahweh—is to treat Yahweh as though Yahweh were one of the impotent, irrelevant idols that were all around Israel. In terms of the grammar of faith, it is to speak of Yahweh as though Yahweh were not the subject of powerful, transformative verbs. Three prophetic texts reflect the temptation in Israel to compromise the distinctiveness of Yahweh in this way:

30. Gerhard von Rad, *Wisdom in Israel* (Nashville: Abingdon Press, 1972) 65.

31. On the continuing power of "the extreme alternative," see Pablo Richard, ed., *The Idols of Death and the God of Life: A Theology* (Maryknoll, N.Y.: Orbis Books, 1983).

32. This is evident in the general issue of "false prophets," on which see below. More specifically, see Thomas W. Overholt, *The Threat of Falsehood: A Study in the Theology of the Book of Jeremiah* (SBT 16, 2d series; London: SCM Press, 1970), with particular reference to the dispute of Jeremiah 27–28 (cf. also Ezekiel 13). In a different context, the argument between Job and his friends is a dispute about right speech for Yahweh (cf. Job 13:4-12). Whatever the sociopolitical dimension of these conflicts may be, they concern an argument about Yahweh, who must be rightly spoken. In each case, moreover, what the canonical presentation regards as false is an attempt to domesticate Yahweh, or to make Yahweh compatible to social control, i.e., to produce an idol.

They have spoken falsely of the Lord,
and have said, "He will do nothing.
No evil will come upon us,
and we shall not see sword or famine." (Jer 5:12)

. . . those who say in their hearts,
"The Lord will not do good,
Nor will he do harm." (Zeph 1:12)

Yet you say, "How have we wearied him?" By saying, "All who do evil are good in the sight of the Lord, and he delights in them." Or by asking, "Where is the God of justice?" (Mal 2:17)

To these statements we may add a mocking assault on the idols who are so unlike Yahweh:

Tell us what is to come hereafter,
that we may know that you are gods;
do good, or do harm,
that we may be afraid and terrified.
You, indeed, are nothing
and your work is nothing at all;
whoever chooses you is an abomination. (Isa 41:23-24)

Israel's characteristic grammar in speaking of Yahweh, governed by active verbs, regularly insisted that Yahweh is a major player in Israel's life and in the life of the world. Yahweh's characteristic presentation in Israel's rhetoric is that Yahweh acts powerfully, decisively, and transformatively. Yahweh is morally serious and demanding, so that Yahweh is endlessly attentive to distinctions of good and evil, justice and injustice. Indeed, it is palpable power and moral seriousness that distinguish Yahweh from all rival gods, who have no power to act decisively and no capacity for moral distinctions. Thus the critique made of Israel's speech in Jer 5:12 and Zeph 1:12 is that Yahweh is being misconstrued (falsely witnessed to), as though Yahweh were as irrelevant to life as the other gods, as though Yahweh were not a serious player in the life of the world, and as a consequence Israel need not heed Yahweh's moral seriousness. The other gods cannot do good or harm, and if Yahweh is so construed, Yahweh disappears into the landscape of irrelevant, non-Israelite religion. In the end, Israel is rendered mute on the witness stand.

Idolatry—wrong speech about God—in any critical sense may occur late in ancient Israel.[33] But the temptation to soften the rhetoric about Yahweh is pervasive in Israel, from its first utterance of *tôdah*. Therefore the peculiarity of Yahweh is a matter of great importance to the testimony of Israel. We may cite three

---

33. Yehezkel Kaufman, *The Religion of Israel: From Its Beginnings to the Babylonian Exile* (London: George Allen and Unwin, 1961), made idolatry the focal point of his magisterial treatment of Hebrew Scriptures. To do so he had to work outside the critical consensus, so that he did not take idolatry as occurring only late in ancient Israel, but as characteristic and pervasive in all of Israel's life and practice.

cases in which right speech about Yahweh distinguishes the God of Israel from all other gods.

The idols, the competitors to Yahweh, are easy to dismiss because they have no power to act:

> Their idols are silver and gold,
> the work of human hands.
> They have mouths, but do not speak;
> eyes, but do not see.
> They have ears, but do not hear;
> noses, but do not smell.
> They have hands, but do not feel;
> feet, but do not walk;
> they make no sound in their throats. (Ps 115:4-7)

Unlike them, however, Yahweh, so the witness affirms, has power to act:

> Our God is in the heavens;
> he does whatever he pleases. (v. 3)

Yahweh, who made heaven and earth (v. 15), has the power to bless (vv. 12-13) and to multiply (v. 14). Yahweh has the power to cause creation to function in all its fruitfulness—the power to give life.

The same contrast between Yahweh, the God of power, and the other gods is evident in the doxology of Jer 10:1-16. The other gods are objects, not subjects:

> Their idols are like scarecrows in a cucumber field,
> and they cannot speak;
> they have to be carried,
> for they cannot walk.
> Do not be afraid of them,
> for they cannot do evil,
> nor is it in them to do good....
> They are the work of the artisan
> and of the hands of the goldsmith;
> their clothing is blue and purple;
> they are all the product of skilled workers....
> for their images are false,
> and there is no breath in them.
> They are worthless, a work of delusion. (vv. 5, 9, 14-15)

By contrast, Yahweh is an agent of creative power, who makes a decisive difference:

> It is he who made the earth by his power,
> who established the world by his wisdom,
> and by his understanding stretched out the heavens.

When he utters his voice, there is a tumult of waters
    in the heavens,
and he makes the mist rise from the ends of the earth.
He makes lightnings for the rain,
    and he bring out the wind from his storehouses. (vv. 12-13)

It is evident from the outset, in Israel's most characteristic testimony, that right speech about Yahweh concerns Yahweh's power to transform, to create, and to engender.

Finally the contrast is evident in Isa 44:9-20, 44:24−45:7. These lines, expressed in lyrical, surging poetry that contrasts with the preceding, dismissive prose, present Yahweh as agent, subject, and actor, who commands the waters, who commands Jerusalem, who commands Cyrus, who creates *shalôm* and evil, who does all these things! While the texts of Psalm 115, Jer 10:1-16, and Isaiah 44−45 are all judged by critical consensus to be relatively late, they represent no substantive departure from Israel's earlier articulations of Yahweh as the subject of its life-giving verbs. Old Testament theology, I propose, is the elucidation of Israel's *willing* speech concerning Yahweh (contra the refusal to speak, which is practical atheism) and *right* speech (contra timid, distorted speech, which is idolatry).

In all of its seasons, with great freedom and venturesome imagination, Israel sought to speak willingly and rightly about Yahweh. In the doxology of Jer 10:1-16, Yahweh is distinguished from the other, powerless gods as a God who is true (*'mth*) and living (*hyym*) (v. 10), and "not like these" other gods (v. 16). Indeed, after Jer 10:1-5, which castigates and mocks the other gods, the initial assertion concerning Yahweh is a lyrical explosion: "There is none like you, O Lord" (v. 6). Willing speech and right speech about Yahweh characteristically make utterance about Yahweh's incomparability.

Yahweh's Incomparability: Two Formulas

We now turn to the incomparability of Yahweh as a second, this time, positive digression. This theme is a digression only because in the path we will take in sketching out Israel's Yahwistic grammar, the assertion of Yahweh's incomparability comes, rightly, as Israel's summary doxological conclusion. The formulations of incomparability to which we will pay attention are a leap outside the grammar we have suggested as definitional. We will consider this leaping conclusion and then return to our review of the way in which Israel's practice of grammar made this conclusion credible and inescapable. The statement of incomparability is located most often in *concrete situations of testimony*, but its utterance itself is a remarkably *sweeping and generalizing claim*. Thus we place it near the beginning of our study of Israel's rhetoric, but its function in Israel's actual confession makes it the final, sweeping claim on the lips of Israel. Because the statement of incomparability comes early and yet is a most sweeping generalization, we may regard it as the most poignant spine and leitmotif of all of Israel's testimony concerning Yahweh.

Two formulas may be identified whereby Israel asserts Yahweh's incomparability.[34] The first is a question, most often directly addressed to Yahweh: "Who is like you?" (*mî-kamokāh*). The question is usually in a context where it functions as an astonished certitude. Thus it is a rhetorical question that does not require an explicit answer. But clearly the anticipated answer is "No one." No one, no god, is like Yahweh. The detail of Israel's theological testimony means to give the ground for this sweeping conclusion. And while the conclusion may be sweeping, the ground must be specific, to show precisely in what ways, in what concrete experiences, Yahweh is incomparable. In this question-affirmation, the characteristic subjects for which Yahweh is celebrated are "wondrous deeds" (*npl'ôth*) and "great things" (*gdlôth*) (Ps 71:17, 19). These are the astonishing acts of transformation that exhibit Yahweh's enormous, unfettered power (cf. Isa 44:7; Jer 49:19; 50:44; Pss 77:13-14; 89:6-9). In Ps 89:7, Yahweh is explicitly contrasted with the other gods "in the council of the holy ones," because none there can do what Yahweh can do and has done.

Four uses of the formula, examined in greater detail, serve as examples of Israel's most extreme testimonial claim.

Exod 15:11. This poem is commonly thought to be among the most crucial, perhaps earliest, of Israel's theological confessions.[35] In its present location it is a victory song celebrating "The Divine Warrior" who, in a show of enormous power, has overcome the power of Egypt's pharaoh in order to liberate the Hebrew slaves. The main body of the poem concerns Israel's two pivotal affirmations of Exodus (vv. 4-9) and the entry into the land (vv. 13-17). Between these two citations—which narrate Yahweh's power over pharaoh and then over the "chiefs" in Canaan and the Transjordan—the song breaks into lyrical doxology employing the phrase, "Who is like you?" (vv. 11-12). Israel makes this affirmation on the basis of the "events" of vv. 4-9 and vv. 13-17. There is no other god who warrants such doxology, or who possesses the attributes of majesty and awe; none other is capable of such "wonders," which defeat and destroy "them" (that is, the enemies of Israel), and which create a possible new life for Israel.

Thus the poem focuses on Yahweh's power. But we notice in v. 13, as a minor note, that in the tradition of the entry into the land, the poem stresses not only Yahweh's power, but also Yahweh's steadfast love (*ḥsd*). The second characteristic of Yahweh here noted, along with power, is loyal solidarity with the Hebrew slaves, the purpose for which unrivaled power is employed.

Ps 35:10. Here the use of the formula of incomparability is in a very different context, that of an individual complaint. The speaker is in sore straits, pursued by adversaries without cause (vv. 4, 7). The speaker cries out for help; left alone the speaker is helpless. The purpose of the cry is to summon Yahweh into action. In

---

34. See a review of the data by C. J. Labuschagne, *The Incomparability of Yahweh in the Old Testament* (Leiden: E. J. Brill, 1966).

35. See Patrick D. Miller, *The Divine Warrior in Early Israel* (HSM 5; Cambridge: Harvard University Press, 1973) 113–18.

v. 10, where our formula occurs, and in v. 18, the speaker anticipates deliverance and being able to testify about it. But the deliverance has not yet been given, hence the speaker's cry. In this formulation, which is ostensively praise, the speaker in effect bears witness to Yahweh, *reminding* Yahweh that Yahweh is not like other gods and therefore is rightly expected to act differently. That is, the God who is incomparable must act in order to exhibit that incomparability.

While the incomparable power of Yahweh is here assumed and affirmed, it is not the point of this prayer. Rather,

> All my bones shall say,
>   "O Lord, who is like you?
> You deliver the weak
>   from those too strong for them,
>   the weak and needy from those who despoil them." (v. 10)

The emphasis falls on Yahweh's solidarity with the weak and needy, who are themselves powerless and hopeless. The appeal is twice made to Yahweh's righteousness (*ṣdqh*), which issues in *shalôm* for "his servant." We may take *ṣdq*, for now, as a reference to Yahweh's power enacted in solidarity, but here it is Yahweh's solidarity with the speaker and with the social group represented by the speaker. Thus this psalm of complaint makes testimony in a personal, intimate scope, the same testimony about Yahweh that is quite public in Exodus 15.

Ps 113:5. This psalm, anticipated in the song of Hannah (1 Sam 2:1-10) and echoed in the song of Mary (Luke 1:46-55), culminates with specific reference to the "barren woman," but its opening praise is much more sweeping. Thus it combines the large scope of Exodus 15 and the intimate concern of Psalm 35. While the first part of the psalm concerns Yahweh's power as creator, it culminates in vv. 7-9 with concrete acts that express Yahweh's solidarity with the poor, needy, and helpless, who by Yahweh's attentiveness find their circumstance transformed into well-being. Whereas Psalm 35 seems to reflect a specific case, this psalm already generalizes by the use of participles, to make clear that these are the characteristic marks of Yahweh, on which Israel may count in many different circumstances.

Mic 7:18-20. This doxology begins with the question of incomparability spoken in doxological fashion of Yahweh in the third person. By the middle of v. 19, the third-person reference has become direct second-person address. The third-person speech is utilized to testify in general, but the second-person address seems to function as a petition that reminds Yahweh of Yahweh's characteristic propensity that needs to be made visible here and now. Placed as they are in Micah 7, among a people in distress, these concluding verses provide a ground for hope. The hope, rooted in the proclaimed character of Yahweh, is that Yahweh is unlike the other gods, specifically concerning Yahweh's readiness to forgive, to work newness, and to begin again, precisely for the community of Jacob and Abraham (v. 20). What marks Yahweh's incomparability in this text, as we shall see later, is Yahweh's readiness for solidarity, for compassion, faithfulness, and loyalty (*rḥm, 'mth, ḥsd*) (the latter term is rendered as "clemency" in v. 18). In deepest travail, late in its history, as it did in Exodus 15 early in its history, Israel bears witness to this powerful God who is in solidarity, who is the only source of Israel's possible future.

The second formula expressing incomparability concerns the same claims and the same utterance, except now the formula is not a rhetorical question but a declarative sentence: "There is none like Yahweh" (Exod 8:10; cf. Deut 33:26) (*kī-'ēyn kayhwh*), or in variation, "There is none like you" (Ps 86:8, addressed to Yahweh); or "There is none like me" (Exod 9:14, uttered by Yahweh; see also Deut 33:26, 1 Sam 2:2, 2 Sam 7:22). In all the variations, the claim of incomparability is unambiguous. We may cite three examples of this formula.

1 Kgs 8:23. In what is likely a late and highly stylized prayer, reflecting perhaps a temple or dynastic interest, Solomon asserts Yahweh's incomparability. (It is likely as well that in royal-temple contexts, such an assertion has an implicit ideological component, suggesting the incomparability of the political or sacerdotal establishment as well; cf. 2 Sam 7:22-23). Solomon's assertion of Yahweh's incomparability begins with reference to "heaven above or on earth beneath," thus taking in all of creation as witnesses to Yahweh's enormous power. The accent, however, is immediately followed by reference to covenant and steadfast love (*ḥsd*), so that it is solidarity that receives the primary emphasis. Because the later part of the prayer (vv. 46-53) reflects a needful situation, perhaps exile, the emphasis on solidarity is important. Incomparability thus is expressed, as in Mic 7:18-20, as Yahweh's willingness and readiness to forgive, to break the vicious cycles of Israel's life, so that perhaps Israel may begin again.

Jer 10:1-16. We have already considered this text as one that seeks to refute idols, and so to "speak rightly" about Yahweh. In the middle of this contrast between Yahweh and the idols is the assertion of incomparability (v. 6). Whereas the other gods are stupid, false, and powerless (vv. 14-15), Yahweh is living and true (v. 10)—that is, Yahweh has substance, force, and reality. More specifically, Yahweh has power to create and to command all the powers of heaven and earth, which must obey. Thus this doxology is focused fully on Yahweh's unrivaled power. In the conclusion of this poem (v. 16), however, we are surprised to hear that while the accent throughout is on Yahweh's cosmic power, finally this power is linked to Israel, "the tribe of his inheritance." Thus the Old Testament testimony characteristically will not choose between power and solidarity, for it is the combination of the two that marks this One about whom Israel must make its claim.

Ps 86:8. This complaint prayer of an individual seeks to mobilize Yahweh to intervene in a situation of acute distress. The formula itself is uttered in the middle section of the psalm, which is a sweeping assertion of Yahweh's power, which will be acknowledged by all the nations (vv. 8-10). All around this central statement of God's power, a more personal, intimate point is made that concerns Yahweh's solidarity with the speaker. Thus the speaker reminds Yahweh that Yahweh is "good and forgiving, abounding in steadfast love" (*ḥsd*) (v. 5, 13). In v. 15 the psalm quotes one of Israel's most characteristic recitals of God's way with Israel:

But you, O Lord, are a God
   merciful and gracious,
 slow to anger and abounding in
    steadfast love and faithfulness. (cf. Exod 34:6)

The cluster of terms—merciful, gracious, slow to anger, steadfast love, faithfulness—together express Yahweh's resilient, reliable commitment to Israel.

It cannot be claimed that this statement of Yahweh's incomparability is uttered everywhere in the Old Testament. I insist only that it is Israel's most extreme witness about God, and that this affirmation, or something like it, is everywhere assumed in the Old Testament. It is important to remember that we are here considering theological claims. We are not engaged in a comparative study, and a case can be made that much that Israel asserts in fact is not without parallel elsewhere.[36] One can say that the rhetoric of incomparability is made by Israel in innocence and with simple disregard of data to the contrary. Israel did not know or care that other peoples made similar claims for their gods. Or one can say, as I prefer, that the rhetoric of incomparability places the accent not on the claim that there is no other like Yahweh, but that Yahweh really is as said—in extreme form a God of astonishing power and reassuring solidarity. In this case, the formula of incomparability is a strategic one, designed to enforce and underscore Israel's exuberant embrace of this God, without reference to any rival or comparable claim.

These two formulas, as we take them as the extreme cases, provide a guideline for our exposition of Israel's testimony about Yahweh. Our consideration of these two formulas suggests that it is Yahweh's sovereign power and covenantal solidarity that mark the God to whom Israel bears witness. As we shall see, the range of Israel's rhetoric about God is rather limited and predictable. *What is important is the recognition that for Israel, power and solidarity are held together, and that both are crucial for Israel's normative utterance about Yahweh.* Power without solidarity yields nothing that reassures Israel in its need. And solidarity without power yields empty hope. To be sure, Yahweh's power and solidarity are often shown to be in odd tension, and on different occasions one or the other quality becomes more important in Israel's testimony. It is nonetheless the two together, power in the service of solidarity, solidarity as the evidence of sovereignty, that mark this God.

While this pairing appears in many places, Psalm 82 provides a clear example. This poem, likely very old and certainly reflecting an assumption of polytheism, engages in a question about what constitutes "godness." In the world of the politics of the "divine council," one might imagine that the God of gods would be the one

---

36. One way to make this important differentiation is by distinguishing the *etic* and *emic* aspects of study. Cf. this distinction in Norman K. Gottwald, *The Tribes of Yahweh: A Sociology of the Religion of Liberated Israel, 1250–1050 B.C.E.* (Maryknoll, N.Y.: Orbis Books, 1979), nn. 558, 564. Critical scholarship in general is devoted to *etic* aspects of study, i.e., it assesses the claims of the text as an uncommitted outsider. For purposes of understanding the theological claims of the text, however, scholarship must, as much as possible, take a stand within those claims, and thus pay attention to the *emic* aspects of study.

with the most power.[37] We are astonished, however, to hear the decree given, "in the midst of the gods" who are scolded for not having the true marks of godness:

> Give justice to the weak and the orphan;
> maintain the right of the lowly and the destitute.
> Rescue the weak and the needy;
> deliver them from the hand of the wicked. (vv. 3-4)

That is, these would-be gods are condemned to death (v. 7), precisely because they fail to measure up to the godness here given as normative. That godness is constituted by solidarity with the weak and needy, in this case not even specified as the weak and needy of Israel. Thus from the outset, Israel's testimony marks godness by power in the service of compassionate solidarity.

Summary

According to Israel's self-understanding, Israel does not begin with some generic notion of God, to which Yahweh conforms. It begins its utterance, rather, in witness to what it has seen and heard and received from Yahweh. It is Yahweh and only Yahweh who provides the peculiar norms by which "godness" is now understood in Israel. It is clear to Israel, moreover, that beyond Yahweh, there are no serious candidates for the role of God. There are only fraudulent candidates who do not have a capacity for power in solidarity. It is important to accent that something like "God's preferential option for the poor" is deeply rooted in Israel's testimony, so deeply rooted as to be characteristic and definitional for Israel's speech about God.[38] The claim is not a belated, incidental addendum to Israel's ethical reflection, but belongs integrally and inalienably to Israel's core affirmation of the character of Yahweh. The course of Israel's testimony about God attends to the ways in which this God—full of sovereign power and committed in solidarity to the needy, and especially to Israel in need—dominates the narrative of Israel's liturgy and imagination (cf. Deut 10:12-22).

Thus we have attempted to define the grammar of Israel (full sentences, governed by strong verbs, dominated by the subject of the verbs who is an active agent, effecting changes in various direct objects), and we have considered the extreme and most sweeping testimony given to Yahweh, namely incomparability. Our purpose now is to trace in some detail the ways in which Israel's grammar is led ineluctably to its conclusions of incomparability.

---

37. See E. Theodore Mullen, *The Divine Council in Canaanite and Early Hebrew Literature* (HSM 24; Chico, Calif.: Scholars Press, 1980); and Patrick D. Miller, "Cosmology and World Order in the Old Testament: The Divine Council as Cosmic-Political Symbol," *HBT* 9 (December 1987) 53–78.

38. The classic study of this claim is Gustavo Gutiérrez, *A Theology of Liberation: History, Politics, and Salvation* (Maryknoll, N.Y.: Orbis Books, 1988).

FOUR

Testimony in Verbal Sentences

A T THE CORE of Israel's theological grammar are sentences governed by strong verbs of transformation. Such sentences are so familiar to us that we may fail to notice the oddity of their grammar and therefore neglect such a theological beginning point. This focus on sentences signifies that Israel is characteristically concerned with the action of God—the concrete, specific action of God—and not God's character, nature, being, or attributes, except as those are evidenced in concrete actions. This focus on verbs, moreover, commits us in profound ways to a *narrative* portrayal of Yahweh, in which Yahweh is the one who is said to have done these deeds. In what follows, I will consider, as a beginning point, the verbs that stand characteristically at the center of Israel's narrative testimony to Yahweh's action.[1] This is not to claim that such narrative testimony is the only way or even the most important way that Israel witnessed to Yahweh. It does, however, provide us with a basic orientation from which to begin, an orientation that I will critique in subsequent discussion.

Yahweh, the God Who Creates

In its most mature testimony, the witness of the Old Testament asserts of Yahweh,

> ...who created (*bara'*) the heavens and stretched them out,
> who spread out the earth and what comes from it,
> who gives breath to the people upon it
> and spirit to those who walk in it:
> I am the Lord.... (Isa 42:5-6a)

---

1. It will be evident that I am here close to the ways in which Gerhard von Rad, "The Form-Critical Problem of the Hexateuch," *The Problem of the Hexateuch and Other Essays* (New York: McGraw-Hill, 1966) 1–78; and *Old Testament Theology* 1 (San Francisco: Harper and Row, 1962), presented the faith of the Old Testament. A major difference exists, however, between von Rad's presentation and the approach taken here. Von Rad (perhaps inevitably) was trapped in the conventional insistence of scholarship that the claims for God in the Old Testament were rooted in history and in God's actions in history. It should be clear at the outset that my concern is with the rhetoric of the claims as testimony. It is entirely plausible that von Rad's hypothesis of credo and recital can be understood as uttered testimony, but the categories then operative in scholarship precluded such a lean perspective.

Israel's testimony to Yahweh as creator concerns Yahweh's ultimate power to work an utter *novum,* one that on any other terms is impossible. In this testimony, the world is characterized, according to Yahweh's intention and action, as a hospitable, viable place for life, because of Yahweh's will and capacity to evoke and sustain life.

Verbs of Creation

In this doxology, as in many assertions in Isaiah of the exile, the governing verb is *bara',* the most majestic of terms for God's action as Creator, a verb used with no other subject except Yahweh, the God of Israel. It is Yahweh, the God of Israel, who creates the heavens and the earth and all that is, who summons, orders, sustains, and governs all of reality.[2] In this poetic assertion, as in many other uses, the awesome verb *bara'* is supported by parallel verbs that bear roughly the same witness but that lack the singular majesty of *bara'.* In this text the other verbs are "stretch out" (*nth*), "spread out" (*rq'*), "gives" (*ntn*), all in the participial form, indicating Yahweh's continuing action.

Among the more important verbs that are employed alongside *bara'* in the testimony of Israel are the following:

(a) By the word of the Lord the heavens were made (*'sh*),
and all their host by the breath of his mouth....
For he spoke (*'amr*), and it came to be;
he commanded (*swh*), and it stood firm. (Ps 33:6, 9)

Yahweh causes to be by utterance. The imagery is of a powerful sovereign who utters a decree from the throne, issues a fiat, and in the very utterance the thing is done. In this psalm, three words are used, *dbr, 'mr, swh,* all concerning powerful, sovereign, generative speech. Even in the verses we cite, however, we note also the supportive verbs "gather" (*kûn*) and "put" (*ntn*), so that God's speech is not apart from action.

(b) ...who created (*bara'*) the heavens (he is God!),
who formed (*ysr*) the earth and made (*'sh*) it,
(he established [*kûn*] it;
he did not create [*bara'*] it a chaos,
he formed [*ysr*] it to be inhabited!)... (Isa 45:18)

In this text, along with *bara',* the verb *ysr* occurs twice. This verb reflects the imagery of a potter forming clay, thus working an existing material. The term

---

2. It can be insisted on that the generative capacity to bringing to being what was not (cf. Rom 4:17) belongs intrinsically to Yahweh's character, so that where Yahweh is, that generative power is in effect. The ground for such an elemental claim for Yahweh is the judgment that the name YHWH drives from the verb *to be* (*hyh*), which may be taken as a *hiph'il,* causative assertion, i.e., cause to be. That reading of the divine name has been most fully argued by Frank M. Cross, who follows the arguments of Paul Haupt and William Foxwell Albright. On such a reading, it is suggested that it is impossible to host the name Yahweh without being aware of Yahweh's generative capacity and inclination. For a helpful survey of the pertinent themes and issues, see Richard J. Clifford, "The Hebrew Scriptures and the Theology of Creation," *TS* 46 (1985) 507–23.

bespeaks active, material engagement with the stuff of creation, in an artistic endeavor. The term is used most often by Israel in the creation of humankind, or more especially in the creation of Israel. In this text, however, "the earth" in parallel to "the heavens" is the object of the verb. These two verbs, *bara'* and *yṣr*, each used twice, are supported by the verbs *kûn* and *'sh*.

(c) O Lord of hosts, God of Israel, who are enthroned above the cherubim, you are God, you alone, of all the kingdoms of the earth; you have made (*'sh*) heaven and earth (Isa 37:16).

This verb, *'sh*, often used in parallel to *bara'* and *yṣr*, refers to the process of actual manufacture of the product, thus portraying God as a working agent who produces heaven and earth as the outcome of work.

(d) The same field of imagination is operative with the verb *qnh:*

Blessed be Abram by God Most High,
maker (*qnh*) of heaven and earth....
I have sworn to the Lord, God Most High,
maker (*qnh*) of heaven and earth.... (Gen 14:19, 22)

This doxology likely referred to an earlier God (El Elyon) and was taken over for Yahweh. The usage here (as in Deut 32:6) suggests a generative act of begetting, and perhaps thereby establishing ownership and property rights to creation.[3]

(e) Was it not you who cut (*ḥṣb*) Rahab in pieces,
who pierced (*ḥll*) the dragon? (Isa 51:9)

This text reflects an ancient tradition that God, in the act of creation, engages in combat with the dragon of chaos and defeats the threat of chaos.[4] Two reservations about this usage in the Old Testament may be registered. First, the imagery of struggle in combat, as it relates to creation, is subdued and marginal in the Old Testament.[5] In this text, what must have been creation imagery is tilted toward the specificity of Israel's Exodus memory, so that "the sea" and "the waters of the great deep" serve doubly in Israel's rhetoric as the watery, threatening chaos in the arena of creation and as the escape route of the Exodus.[6] In both usages, the God of Israel is confessed to be in ready control, able to administer the waters. We

---

3. On the term *qnh*, see Gale A. Yee, "The Theology of Creation in Proverbs 8:22-31," *Creation in the Biblical Traditions* (ed. Richard J. Clifford and John J. Collins; CBQMS 24; Washington: Catholic Biblical Association of America, 1992) 89 n. 7.

4. On chaos as monster, see John Day, *God's Conflict with the Dragon and the Sea: Echoes of a Canaanite Myth* (Cambridge: Cambridge University Press, 1985); and Mary K. Wakeman, *God's Battle with the Monster* (Leiden: E. J. Brill, 1973).

5. Jon D. Levenson, *Creation and the Persistence of Evil: The Jewish Drama of Divine Omnipotence* (San Francisco: Harper and Row, 1988), has well summarized the data.

6. Frank Moore Cross, *Canaanite Myth and Hebrew Epic* (Cambridge: Harvard University Press, 1973) 112–44, has shown how reference to the waters of chaos and the "historical waters" of the Exodus converge and are identified. Thus it is not possible to make a clean distinction between what is myth and what is history.

also note the parallel verb "pierce" (ḥll), which testifies to the motif of combat (cf. Job 26:13).

(f) You were unmindful of the Rock that bore (yld) you,
    you forgot the God who gave you birth (ḥll). (Deut 32:18)

    Before the mountains were brought forth (yld),
    or ever you had formed (ḥll) the earth and the world,
    from everlasting to everlasting you are God. (Ps 90:2)

These two texts have in parallel the verbs yld and ḥll. In each case, the first verb refers to the paternal role in begetting, and the second refers to the maternal role of birthing. These terms for creating are not common in the Old Testament witness. I cite them because they are pertinent in current discussions concerning adequate metaphors for God, and they exhibit the remarkable range of verbs used in Israel's testimony concerning evidence that Yahweh creates.

(g) By the word of the Lord the heavens were made,
    and all their host by the breath of his mouth. (Ps 33:6)

    Then God said, "Let there be light"; and there was light. (Gen 1:3)

Israel attests that Yahweh creates the world by speech—by royal utterance, a powerful decree that in its very utterance is eagerly and dutifully enacted. This "theology of the word" is exceedingly influential in subsequent theological reflection. It is important to recognize, however, that even this most exalted way of speaking about Yahweh's generative sovereignty is not unique to Israel. Even this mode of creation, given in the testimony of Israel, has important antecedent and parallel in the ancient Egyptian theology of Memphis concerning the god Ptah.[7] Israel uses a variety of terms in this presentation of Yahweh as Creator by speech, all of which bespeak the unquestioned authority of the sovereign to effect a genuine newness in the world, simply by making desire and intention known to the royal court so eager to obey.

This list of verbs is a fair representation of the primary terms Israel used in its testimonies concerning God's agency as one who creates. The list is by no means comprehensive but is sufficient for our purposes. In its ongoing stylized usage, this range of testimony does not require that each term should be taken at its most particular, concrete reference. Nonetheless, these concrete reference points are present in the text and should not be ignored. In this range of terms (to which others might be added), Israel appealed to all of the models of creation that were already present and available in the ancient Near East, including royal fiat, combat struggle, artistic rendering, material productivity, economic purchase, and the process

---

7. See James Pritchard, *Ancient Near Eastern Texts Relating to the Old Testament* (2d ed.; Princeton, N.J.: Princeton University Press, 1955) 5.

of birthing. It is also clear that Israel, with the exception of *bara'*, had no special, privileged category for creation, but made use of terms from many arenas of ordinary daily life.

Israel settled on no single articulation of creation as a proper one, but daringly made use of rich and diverse vocabulary in order to make its normative utterance about God. As we shall see repeatedly, *Old Testament theology, when it pays attention to Israel's venturesome rhetoric, refuses any reductionism to a single or simple articulation;* it offers a witness that is enormously open, inviting, and suggestive, rather than one that yields settlement, closure, or precision.

It was not difficult for Israel to make its testimony concerning Yahweh as "the God who creates." The religious world of the ancient Near East was already permeated with such talk of creation and such conviction about the creation work of the gods. It is plausible to assume that Israel could readily appropriate such speech and conviction.

We must recognize, however, that the great liturgical rhetoric of creation was sponsored by the great royal regimes, which easily co-opted the evocative theological assertions of created order for their specific political accomplishments and interests. Thus creation faith was recruited for royal ideology and propaganda. There is no reason to imagine that the royal establishment in Jerusalem was immune to this temptation (cf. 1 Kgs 8:12-13, Ps 89:3-37). In Psalm 89, the guarantees given by God to the house of David come easily along with the celebration of the goodness and reliability of Yahweh's created order.

Given the easy utilization of creation rhetoric and creation faith, Israel nonetheless faced a demanding task. The demanding element in this testimony is not to claim creation faith as its own; it is to claim creation for the God of Israel, as willed, gifted, and governed by Yahweh and made for glad dependence and fruitful obedience to Yahweh. It is to articulate creation faith in a peculiar way, so that it is congruent with the rest of the normative testimony that Israel would utter about its God. We shall consider in some detail a series of texts that indicate the ways in which Israel's testimony fashioned rhetoric to meet this important theological demand.

The Context of Exile

In the Old Testament, creation faith receives its fullest articulation in Isaiah of the exile.[8] In the context of exile, Israel faced a twofold crisis that invited Israel to despair and to abandonment of its confidence in Yahweh. The concrete ground for the despair is the formidable reality of Babylonian military-political power. Behind that visible authority, however, is the legitimating power of the Babylonian gods who guaranteed the regime and who appear to be stronger than the counterpower of Israel's own God.

---

8. See, for example, Carroll Stuhlmueller, *Creative Redemption in Deutero-Isaiah* (AnBib 43; Rome: Biblical Institute Press, 1970).

In the face of that challenge, Israel's despairing doubt is countered by the witness of faith that asserts that Yahweh is stronger than the Babylonian gods, and therefore that Israel's capacity for liberated action is stronger than the restraining coercion of the Babylonian regime. It is testimony to Yahweh's work as Creator that counters the ostensive power of Babylon.

> I made ('sh) the earth,
> and created (br') humankind upon it;
> It was my hands that stretched out (nth) the heavens,
> and I commanded (swh) all their hosts.
> I have aroused Cyrus in righteousness,
> and I will make all his paths straight;
> He shall build my city
> and set my exiles free,
> not for price or reward,
> says the Lord of hosts. (Isa 45:12-13)

> Have you not known? Have you not heard?
> The Lord is the everlasting God,
> the Creator (br') of the ends of the earth.
> He does not faint or grow weary;
> His understanding is unsearchable.
> He gives power to the faint,
> and strengthens the powerless.
> Even youths will faint and be weary,
> and the young will fall exhausted;
> but those who wait for the Lord
> shall renew their strength,
> they shall mount up with wings like eagles,
> they shall run and not be weary,
> they shall walk and not faint. (Isa 40:28-31)

In these cases, the large claim is made for Yahweh as the subject of the verb: Yahweh created heaven and earth. In each case, however, the large claim moves from cosmic scope to the reality of Israel. Thus in Isa 45:12-13, the rhetoric moves quickly to Cyrus and the freedom of the exiles. In Isa 40:28-31, the large claim is aimed at the faint and powerless in Israel who will be given strength. The rhetorical combat with the other gods is undertaken in a series of disputation speeches, which assert Yahweh's power and in turn assert the weakness and impotence of the Babylonian gods who have neither authority nor power (Isa 40:12-13; 41:1-5, 21-29; 43:8-13). The purpose of this testimony concerning the Creator is to assert (and so to establish) that Yahweh is the only God who has demonstrated power as Creator, and therefore the other gods merit no obedience or deference.

Creation faith is used in the testimony of Israel in order to dismiss the claim of the other gods. This function of testimony is matched by a second purpose: the affirmation of Israel. This God created not only heavens and earth, as the other gods could not; this God created Israel as a special object of Yahweh's attentive faithfulness:[9]

> But now thus says the Lord,
> he who created (*br'*) you, O Jacob,
> he who formed (*yṣr*) you, O Israel:
> do not fear.... (Isa 43:1)

> Do not fear, for I am with you;
> I will bring your offspring from the east,
> and from the west I will gather you;
> I will say to the north, "Give them up,"
> and to the south, "Do not withhold;
> bring my sons from far away
> and my daughters from the end of the earth—
> everyone who is called by my name,
> whom I created (*br'*) for my glory,
> whom I formed (*yṣr*) and made (*'sh*)." (Isa 43:5-7)

> I am the Lord, your Holy One,
> the Creator (*br'*) of Israel, your King. (Isa 43:15)

> Thus says the Lord who made (*'sh*) you:
> who formed (*yṣr*) you in the womb and will help you:
> Do not fear.... (Isa 44:2)

This way of speaking of God's creating activity utilizes the same verbs as cosmic creation. Only now the rhetoric appeals directly to Israel, inviting Israel to confidence in Yahweh, and therefore to derivative confidence in its own capacity to act in freedom, apart from the threat of Babylonian intimidation and coercion.

Creation Faith Mobilized

Two other prophetic texts show ways in which creation faith is mobilized in the service of Israel's larger testimony. We have already seen that Jer 10:1-16 makes a sharp and dramatic contrast between the weak and false gods and the true, living God, Yahweh. Yahweh's incomparability (v. 6) is articulated in royal imagery: "He is the living God and the everlasting King" (v. 10). Moreover, the poem utilizes a

---

9. Rolf Rendtorff, "Die theologische Stellung des Schopfungsglaubens bei Deuterojesaja," *ZTK* 51 (1954) 3–13; and Rainer Albertz, *Persönliche Frömmigkeit und offizielle Religion: Religionsinterner Pluralismus in Israel und Babylon* (Calwer Theologische Monographieren Series A 9; Stuttgart: Calwer Verlag, 1978), have suggested that a distinction can be made between Yahweh's creation of the world and Yahweh's creation of Israel, or of individual human persons. The distinctions should not be drawn too rigorously, but it is clear that Israel spoke differently about these matters in different genres, depending on the need being served.

series of verbs, some participial, to assert Yahweh's powerful activity: who makes ('śh), who establishes (kûn), who stretched out (nṭh), he utters (lqôl), who makes rise ('lh), who makes ('śh), who brings out (yṣ'). This extraordinary inventory of verbs evidences Yahweh's presiding over the processes of world order by a show of power that the other gods cannot rival. We are, by such large claims, hardly prepared for the rhetorical maneuver of v. 16, which turns out to be characteristic of Israel's way of thinking about creation:

> Not like these is the Lord, the portion of Jacob,
> for he is the one who formed (yṣr) all things,
> and Israel is the tribe of his inheritance;
> the Lord of hosts is his name.

Yahweh did indeed form (yṣr) all things, but Yahweh is nonetheless "the portion of Israel," and Israel is "his inheritance." This twofold statement first identifies Yahweh as belonging to Israel, and then Israel as belonging to Yahweh. Yahweh is not named in the doxology until this final verse. In the end, the one who is celebrated as the powerful Creator of all is none other than "the Lord of Hosts." The poem withholds the name until the final utterance, when all is disclosed. The God who is stronger than the idols, who outranks them all in power, is none other than the one whom Israel knows in its own memory.

The citation of the name "Lord of Hosts" in Jer 10:16 points us nicely to a second text, Amos 4:13.[10] This verse is one of three doxologies oddly situated in the Book of Amos (cf. 5:8-9; 9:5-6). In its present location, the doxology comes at the end of Amos 4, which issues a devastating threat to disobedient Israel, who must be punished because it has oppressed the poor and crushed the needy (v. 2). This terrible indictment is followed by a recital of Yahweh's great acts of punishment (curses), which show how Yahweh may disrupt creation itself (famine, drought, blight and mildew, pestilence, and earthquake) against a disobedient people (vv. 6-11). This exposition of Yahweh's righteous will for Israel is now sealed in its severity by the doxology of v. 13. In this doxology, the witness employs a series of participial verbs:

> who forms (yṣr)
> who creates (bara')
> who reveals (ngd)
> who makes ('śh)
> who treads (drk)

The language is sweeping and cosmic in scope. The last line appeals to ancient mythological imagery. In the end, it is the utterance of the old tribal name, "the Lord, the God of hosts," echoing the same phrasing as Jer 10:16, which links the

---

10. On these doxologies with the name of Yahweh, see James L. Crenshaw, *Hymnic Affirmations of Divine Justice: The Doxologies of Amos and Related Texts in the Old Testament* (SBLDS 24; Missoula, Mont.: Scholars Press, 1975).

majesty of Yahweh, the powerful Creator, to the ancient covenantal encounters. *Creation* faith is put into the service of *covenantal* sanctions. The God who can be *trusted* in the face of the Babylonians is the same God who must be *obeyed* in a season of Israel's self-indulgence. All the forces of heaven and earth are at the disposal of the One who enforces Torah requirements.

Liturgical Narrative in Genesis 1–2

The preceding lyrical statements are likely prior to Gen 1:1–2:4a, even though the Genesis text is put first in the Bible and is best known. This text is something of a liturgical narrative, which tells the tale of creation in a highly stylized way. It is conventional to understand this text as a liturgical assertion against the temptations of the Babylonian gods in exile and thus in concert with Isaiah of the exile.

It is well known that the first verse of the Bible is grammatically problematic and perhaps cannot be adjudicated on purely grammatical grounds. My inclination is to accept Gen 1:1 as a temporal, dependent clause, rendered, "When God began to create...," which makes v. 2 the main clause of the opening sentence of the Bible.[11] This way of understanding the grammar of the verse suggests that God is said to be at work on already present reality (chaos), which God orders by speech and enlivens by wind (spirit). Through the remainder of the chapter, God continues by utterance and by act to create a life-world of order, vitality, and fruitfulness that makes life possible and that, in the end, is judged by God to be "very good" (v. 31).

The mood of this rhetoric is to evidence that God is serenely and supremely in charge. There is no struggle here, no anxiety, no risk. If it is correct, as critical consensus holds, that this is an exilic text, then the intent and the effect of this liturgical narrative is to enact by its very utterance a well-ordered, fully reliable, generative world for Israelites who are exiles in Babylon. The world given in these liturgical utterances is a "contrast-world," compared to the world of exile that holds threat, anxiety, and insecurity. On this reading, the chaos already extant in v. 2 represents the reality of exile—life at risk and in disorder. The effect of the liturgy is to create an alternative world of ordered life, made possible by Yahweh's powerful word and will. Exilic Israelites can live in this world and, if they choose, withdraw (emotionally, liturgically, politically, geographically) from the disordered world of Babylon, which in this recital is powerfully delegitimated.

This liturgical narrative portrays the ordering-creating activity of Israel's God culminating in the Sabbath (2:2-3). This Sabbath rest is ordained into the very fabric and structure of created life. But even if Sabbath is thereby given cosmic significance, the observances of the day of rest still remain concretely and precisely a Jewish enactment, whereby Jews in Babylonian exile (and in every other circumstance) visibly and publicly distinguish themselves from a world that is too much

---

11. For an exegetical justification of the traditional rendering, see Walther Eichrodt, "In the Beginning: A Contribution to the Interpretation of the First Word of the Bible," *Creation in the Old Testament* (Philadelphia: Fortress Press, 1984) 65–73.

given to the power of restless anxiety and control. Again, as in Jer 10:6 and Amos 4:13, creation rhetoric is placed in the service of the identity and conduct of a life of knowing, intentional Jewish existence. Israel has no interest in bearing testimony to Yahweh as the one who creates, except as Yahweh can be linked to the practicalities of living faithfully in the world.

Creation Faith in Israel's Larger Testimony

In three texts from Psalms the polemic of Israel's creation testimony is subdued, perhaps reliant on the framing affirmations of the liturgy of Genesis 1. Indeed, the Psalter readily integrates creation testimony into its larger witness to faith.

Psalm 33. This psalm is of interest to us because of its assertion that Yahweh creates by utterance:

> By the word of the Lord the heavens were made,
>   and all their host by the breath of his mouth....
> For he spoke, and it came to be;
>   he commanded, and it stood firm. (vv. 6, 9)

This assertion coheres with what is narrated in Genesis 1. The picture is of a settled sovereign, securely in control, who need only speak to have Yahweh's command carried out.

This assertion, however, is set in the midst of two other important affirmations. First, this serene governance from heaven is over against the recalcitrant nations. Yahweh sees all, and resists the plans of peoples that are counter to Yahweh's own plan (v. 10). Indeed, the capacity of the God who creates leads to the conclusion that kings are not autonomous, no matter their military strength (vv. 16-17). The rhetoric here is not unlike that of Psalm 2, which leads in the end to the certification of the throne of David. Creation faith pertains to political reality. Second, this poem is situated within Israel's covenantal terminology, so that creation faith is embedded in covenantal trust. That is, the word as a means of creation is not simply an enactment of sovereign power; it is an act that has a covenantal quality to it. The creator creates out of a commitment to faithfulness, righteousness, justice, and steadfast love:

> For the word of the Lord is upright,
> and all his work is done in faithfulness.
> He loves righteousness and justice;
>   the earth is full of the steadfast love of the Lord. (vv. 4-5)

The very act of creation thus offers concrete assurance to Israel and to those who embrace the Creator's intention for justice. Thus at the outset, Yahweh is marked by faithfulness, righteousness, justice, and steadfast love (vv. 4-5, 8; cf. v. 18). Moreover, the psalm ends with a series of first-person promises that refer to Israel:

> Our soul waits for the Lord;
>> he is our help and shield.
> Our heart is glad in him,
>> because we trust in his holy name.
> Let your steadfast love, O Lord, be upon us,
>> even as we hope in you. (vv. 20-22)

Creation faith is a ground for active, concrete hope in Israel that concerns daily circumstance, possibility, and responsibility.

Psalm 146. In this psalm, Yahweh, the God of Israel, is contrasted with princes and human agents who cannot help, who lack "breath," and whose plans cannot succeed. Against all such would-be sources of help, Yahweh is championed as the one who can indeed help, and on whom Israel may hope: Yahweh is presented as the one who makes (*'sh*) "heaven and earth, the sea and all that is in them" (v. 6). Israel's characteristic testimony, however, cannot assert creation by itself, for creation affirmations are always linked to more concrete matters. In this case, this large verb "makes" is linked to God's "faith" (*'mth*) and "justice" (*mšpt*), which is then enacted quite concretely:

> ... who executes justice for the oppressed;
> who gives food to the hungry.
> The Lord sets the prisoners free;
> the Lord opens the eyes of the blind.
> The Lord lifts up those who are bowed down;
> the Lord loves the righteous.
> The Lord watches over the strangers;
> He upholds the orphan and the widow.... (vv. 7-9a)

The one who creates is the one who governs in a quite specific way. Thus the Creator has ordered, and continues to order, a world marked by a particular ethic. In this psalm, Israel is not enjoined to obedience, but is reminded that Yahweh's creating work is not raw power but is a work that intends and provides well-being precisely to the oppressed, the hungry, prisoners, the blind, the bowed down, the righteous, strangers, widows, and orphans (cf. Prov 17:5). The world as God's creation has a specific ethical commitment and bias, against the "plans" of the wicked, who attempt to utilize the powers of creation for their own destructive ends (v. 4).

Psalm 104. This extraordinary psalm, likely appropriated from Egyptian sources, is perhaps the fullest rendition of creation faith in the Old Testament. The first part provides a full inventory of the constituents of creation as wrought by God (vv. 1-23). The doxology begins with God's work of ordering the "layers" of creation, the heavens (v. 2), chambers of waters (vv. 3-4), and the foundations of the earth (v. 5). The psalm marvels at the bountiful supply of waters (vv. 8-13) and the myriad of animals that are thereby sustained (vv. 14-23). This inventory moves from the general to the particular, and finally to human persons who rely on bread and wine (v. 14) and who work and rest (v. 23). The psalm bears witness to the reliable, sustaining rhythms of life that are guaranteed by God.

The second half of Psalm 104 reflects on the Yahwistic import of this wondrous network of gifts (vv. 24-35). We may identify four elements of awareness in this meditation on God's work in creation:

(a) God is the secure governor of all creation, including the sea and leviathan, both of which in other contexts might have been untamed and rebellious (vv. 24-26).[12]

(b) The creation that God has formed is a great food chain, which generously supplies all that every creature needs (vv. 27-28). This affirmation is not only about the character of God, but also about the world that results from the generous, beneficent character of Yahweh. Moreover, it is Yahweh's wind/spirit (*rûaḥ*) that, instant by instant, makes life possible (vv. 29-30). The mystery of life is kept for Yahweh's own self, and Yahweh is utterly reliable in giving life. The world may be "there," but the world has no capacity for generativity on its own. Its life depends on closeness to and reliance on the God who breathes life.

(c) These awarenesses of God's goodness and power lead to an outbreak of praise (vv. 31-34). Doxology is the appropriate Israelite (and human) response to the assertion of goodness of creation that is a gift of Yahweh. Creation faith does not, in the first instant, invite to speculation or explanation. It invites wonder, awe, and gratitude that life—Israel's life, human life—is situated in the midst of a reliable generosity that precedes all human effort.

(d) The poem culminates with a brief but somber ethical notice (v. 38). "Sinners, the wicked" are those who refuse to receive life in creation on terms of generous extravagance, no doubt in order to practice a hoarding autonomy in denial that creation is indeed governed and held by its Creator. Creation has within it the sovereign seriousness of God, who will not tolerate the violation of the terms of creation, which are terms of gift, dependence, and extravagance. Thus for those who refuse the doxology-evoking sovereignty of Yahweh, creation ends on an ominous warning.

The Witness of Creation Itself

We have been considering the way in which Israel testifies to the wonders of creation that point to the power and generosity of the Creator. Beyond the exclamatory utterance of Israel, however, we may notice yet another dimension of testimony concerning creation. Creation itself is said to point to—that is, to witness directly to—the Creator. This witness to Yahweh is prior to and more majestic than Israel's own utterance. The key text for this aspect of Israel's faith in the Creator is in Psalm 19: "The heavens are telling the glory of God, and the firmament proclaims his handiwork" (v. 1). The verbs "tell" (*spr*) and "proclaim" (*ngd*) suggest utterance. In other psalms (65:12-13, 96:11-12) creation is understood as

---

12. On this affirmation, see Jon D. Levenson, *Creation and the Persistence of Evil*, 53–65.

responsive and animated, and in Psalm 148 creation is engaged in praise of the Creator:

> Praise him, sun and moon;
> praise him, all you shining stars!
> Praise him, you highest heavens,
> and you waters above the heavens! (vv. 3-4)[13]

These texts move in a direction that has been most polemically termed "natural theology."[14] That is, the experienced world itself gives knowledge of Yahweh. These "witnesses" move behind Israel's own utterance in their testimony to Yahweh. In this purview, all of creation is taken to be lively, responsive (conscious?) creatures, whose work is obedience (fruitfulness) and praise.

We may wonder what testimony these creatures might yield, were that testimony not mediated through Israel's doxological utterance. But Israel in these lyrical poems takes creation seriously in and for itself as reference to Yahweh. This is not simply aesthetic delight, though it may include that. It is a theological witness to the wondrous reality of Yahweh, the same reality known and made available in Israel's own utterance.

Rich Play of Rhetoric

It is not possible to reduce or even to order this torrent of rhetoric into a systematic claim. It is important, first of all, to notice the rich play of many elements of rhetoric, which refuse easy containment. As pointers for a coherent reading of this rich testimony, four observations are in order:

(a) The rhetoric of this testimony is *exuberant and effusive,* in response to the reality of life in a reliable, generous, gift-giving world. The language is doxological and lyrical (oracular in Job 38–41), and even when it has a discipline to its utterance, it refuses to be restrained, but must be cut free to match the subject of extravagance. It is most likely that these utterances are situated in liturgy, so that they are utterances in the construction of a contrast-world. It follows, moreover, that this material does not easily lend itself to the explanatory analysis with which it has often been forced in the interest of a "creation science" or creation vis-à-vis science.

(b) Israel's testimony about Yahweh as Creator is fully embedded in Israel's larger *covenant testimony.* As Israel believes that its own life is covenantally ordered, so Israel believes that creation is covenantally ordered; that is, formed for

---

13. See Terence E. Fretheim, "Creation's Praise of God in the Psalms," *Ex Auditu* 3 (1987) 16–30.

14. See Gerhard von Rad, *Wisdom in Israel* (Nashville: Abingdon Press, 1972) 144–76; John Barton, "Natural Law and Poetic Justice in the Old Testament" *JTS* 30 (1979) 1–14; Barton, "Ethics in Isaiah of Jerusalem," *JTS* 32 (1981) 1–18; Markus Bockmuehl, "Natural Law in Second Temple Judaism," *VT* 45 (1995) 17–44; James Barr, "Mowinckel, the Old Testament, and the Question of Natural Law: The Second Mowinckel Lecture—Oslo, 27 November 1987," *ST* 42 (1988) 21–38; and Claus Westermann, "Karl Barth's Nein: Eine Kontroverse um die Theologia Naturalis," *EvT* 47 (1987) 386–95.

continuing interactions of gift and gratitude, of governance and obedience. This is the reason these testimonies easily move toward Israel's linkage of creation to its own particular life in the world. Thus Israel may, on occasion, suggest that Israel is "the goal of creation."[15] It is more likely, however, that Israel is capable of being a knowing, willing practitioner of creation, capable of gratitude and obedience, with no need to assert itself as the fulfillment of creation.

(c) Israel's articulation of creation faith is marked by God's gift of the power for life, which has a *relentless ethical dimension*. Thus we have seen that creation is marked by justice, righteousness, and steadfastness, and that it is aimed at needy Israel in exile and, more generally, to the stranger, the widow, and the orphan. How could it be otherwise? For the God who is subject of these verbs of creation is also the subject of more particular verbs in Israel's own life. Yahweh's work in creation is never an act of raw, sovereign power, but is an act saturated with covenantal, ethical intentionality. Yahweh characteristically intends not only to have a world, but to have a certain kind of world, one that generously and gladly attends to the goodness and extravagance of life. The power for life finally will not be administered in partisan ways by the "plans of humankind," by kings and nations, but is a power of undifferentiated generosity to which all have access, and to which the needy have privileged access. Those who seek to block this access and to violate this privileged access are, in the end, sure to be crushed by the very power they seek to control.

(d) A student of the theme of creation in the Old Testament must inevitably face the issue of whether the Old Testament claims creation *ex nihilo:* Did God create out of nothing? It is correct, as it is conventional, to say that there is no unambiguous evidence for such a claim before 2 Maccabees, which is very late indeed in the faith of Israel. Other texts, perhaps even Gen 1:1-2, permit but do not require such a reading. The large claims made for Yahweh would admit of such a radical claim of sovereignty, but Israel seems not to have said it so, nor to have conceptualized it so. And if not *ex nihilo,* then we are bound to conclude that Israel understood Yahweh's activity of creation to be one of forming, shaping, governing, ordering, and sustaining a created world out of the "stuff of chaos," which was already there. Unlike some speculative traditions, Israel evidences no interest or curiosity about the origin of the "stuff of creation." It is simply there as a given, which Yahweh then addresses in lordly fashion.

This way of understanding creation may strike some as an inadequate claim that seems to concede something crucial of Yahweh's almighty power. It would appear, however, that such a matter troubled neither Yahweh nor Israel. The more important recognition, it seems to me, is that what may appear to be a theological concession to the stubbornness of "stuff" is in fact a characteristic pastoral strength of Israel's faith. That is, Israel's faith is markedly in the middle of things, responding to what is given concretely "on the ground." And what is given—daily and

---

15. Von Rad, "The Form-Critical Problem of the Hexateuch," 66, concludes that this text, so arranged and placed, "provides the aetiology of all Israelite aetiology."

everywhere, in ancient times and in our own—is vexation, trouble, and destructiveness that appear to be untamed and on the loose. We may say that all such evil is
the result of sin, but Israel resists such a conclusion, if by sin is meant human failure. Evil is simply there, sometimes as a result of human sin, sometimes as a given,
and occasionally blamed on God. Jon Levenson has made a powerful case that there
is on the loose in the world, according to Old Testament texts, *something untamed
and destructive that has still not been brought under the rule of Yahweh.*[16] While it is
promised that Yahweh will prevail over such counterpowers, it is clear that Yahweh has not yet gained such mastery and does not now prevail. Fredrik Lindström
has shown, moreover, how in many psalms such deathliness makes headway in the
midst of Israel only when and where Yahweh is absent, neglectful, or inattentive.[17]

The issue of evil is a difficult one to which we shall return. Suffice it now to
suggest that the pastoral realism of Israel's testimony is enormous. Israel knows
how life is in fact lived. And it dares to assert, in its testimony of a world ordered
by Yahweh, that the threat of life, so palpable among us, is a threat that can and
will be countered by the Creator who continues the work of governance, order,
and sustenance. Creation faith is the summons and invitation to trust the Subject
of these verbs, even in the face of day-to-day, palpable incursions of chaos. The
testimony of Israel pushes toward a verdict that the One embedded in these doxological statements can be trusted in the midst of any chaos, even that of exile and
finally that of death.

Shift in Models of Interpretation

Before leaving our discussion of creation, students of Old Testament theology will
profit by being aware of the enormous shift now taking place in the larger pattern-
ing of Old Testament faith with reference to testimony about a God who creates.
Old Testament theological interpretation in the twentieth century has been dominated by von Rad's statement, "The Theological Problem of the Old Testament
Doctrine of Creation," which he first published in 1936.[18] Again, it is important
to notice that von Rad's essay was published in the midst of the crisis of the rise
of National Socialism in Germany, and surely has behind it Barth's programmatic
contrast between faith and religion. Von Rad notes only that the place of creation
in Old Testament faith is "the subject of much controversy today."[19] In his exposition, von Rad moved immediately to say that, "The most serious attack which the
faith of Israel has had to meet with regard to the conception of nature came from
the Canaanite Baal religion."[20] Thus it is evident, in my judgment, that Barth's con-

---

16. Levenson, *Creation and the Persistence of Evil.*
17. Fredrik Lindström, *Suffering and Sin: Interpretations of Illness in the Individual Complaint Psalms*
(ConBOT 37; Stockholm: Almqvist and Wiksell International, 1994).
18. Gerhard von Rad, "The Theological Problem of the Old Testament Doctrine of Creation,"
The Problem of the Hexateuch, 131–43. For a retrospective assessment of von Rad's influential thesis, see
Walter Brueggemann, "The Loss and Recovery of 'Creation' in Old Testament Theology," *TToday* 53
(1996) 177–90.
19. Von Rad, "The Theological Problem of the Old Testament Doctrine of Creation," 131.
20. Ibid., 132.

trast of faith and religion was programmatically transposed into Israel's faith versus Canaanite fertility religion, a contrast that became influential in the United States through the work of G. Ernest Wright.[21] In this influential way of reasoning, "creation faith" came to be closely linked to fertility religion and its celebration of the natural processes of reproduction. This came to be expressed in the categories of "nature versus history," or "space versus time."[22] Von Rad stated that Israel's faith is "primarily concerned with redemption,"[23] and he concluded that creation faith was (a) lacking in Israel's early credos, and (b) never achieved status in the Old Testament as a full, independent affirmation.

It is difficult to overstate the power of this model of interpretation, which generated a great deal of expository literature. In retrospect we see that such a reading of the Old Testament (perhaps we may say *mis*reading) cut off Israel's faith off from the elemental human processes of birth and death, and eventually served, no doubt unwittingly, a masculine mode of interpretation that accented the virility of God in a most polemical way. In current Old Testament theological conversation (including this discussion), that model is now largely dismissed; as far as I know, it is held in current discussion only by H. D. Preuss.[24]

The shift of models is important, not only for its substantive opening of different categories of interpretation, but also for the instruction it offers concerning the way in which context provides interpretive categories that are always both opening and limiting. No doubt it was the church struggle in Germany in the 1930s that dictated von Rad's governing judgment, with the equation of National Socialism ("Blood and Soil") with Canaanite fertility religion. As that acutely influential context of interpretation has passed, such a model of interpretation has been found to be less and less adequate. It is instructive and striking that von Rad cites, in his 1936 article, the same repertoire of texts cited here and in many like reviews of the theme of creation. But his presentation is governed by another presupposition, and so the different outcomes are not surprising. Thus, it is evident that the categories that permit us to see certain things are also decisive for the outcomes of theological reflection on the text.

We may identify six important scholarly contributions to the shift away from this conflictual model of interpretation.

(a) It is to von Rad's great credit that he moved past this way of thinking later in his life. It is evident already in *Old Testament Theology* 1 that the sharp, polem-

---

21. G. Ernest Wright, *The Old Testament against Its Environment* (SBT 2; London: SCM Press, 1950); and *God Who Acts: Biblical Theology as Recital* (SBT 8; London: SCM Press, 1952).

22. These antitheses have now been criticized by many scholars. An early exposé was by James Barr, *The Semantics of Biblical Language* (Oxford: Oxford University Press, 1961).

23. Von Rad, "The Theological Problem of the Old Testament Doctrine of Creation," 131.

24. Horst Dietrich Preuss, *Theologie des Alten Testaments* 1: *JHWH's erwählendes und verpflichtendes Handeln* (Stuttgart: W. Kohlhammer, 1991) 259–74. The most vigorous and extensive argument for creation on the horizon of Old Testament theology is by Rolf P. Knierim, *The Task of Old Testament Theology* (Grand Rapids: Eerdmans, 1995).

ical rhetoric of 1936 is softened.[25] Especially in his 1970 book, *Wisdom in Israel,* von Rad attends to the texts of the Old Testament that speak of creation as an ordered construction of life with ethical demands that permit ongoing life in the community.[26]

(b) Claus Westermann, a close associate of von Rad, was much influenced by the credo hypothesis of 1938. But Westermann had studied the Book of Genesis extensively. Out of that study he set "a theology of blessing" alongside a "theology of deliverance," which saw God's genuine sustaining work in the daily existence of the human community.[27] That is, God is evident in Israel, not primarily in the great dramatic public events, but in the ongoing processes of life. Presumably Westermann was led in this direction not only by the creation texts, but also by the ancestral narratives of Genesis 12–50, which concentrate on the sustenance of the human community from one generation to the next. When one juxtaposes "blessing" to "deliverance," as Westermann does, one can see dialectically related the themes of sustenance and intrusion, maintenance and transformation. And though Westermann himself would not say so, one can identify "feminine" nurture alongside "masculine" assertiveness. Thus I suggest that it is the neglect of creation themes that has produced some of the current crisis of patriarchalism in biblical interpretation.

(c) A little-noticed book by Walter Harrelson should be mentioned, *From Fertility Cult to Worship.*[28] In this book Harrelson begins with the contrast between fertility religion and Israel's faith that was, in the time of his writing, quite conventional. But he noticed, especially in the Book of Hosea, that fertility functions of reproduction and generativity were assigned to Yahweh and not simply to the Baalim. Moreover, Israel's poets did not flinch from utilizing the language and imagery of the hostile Canaanite alternative, in order to claim that Yahweh is indeed the God of fertility.

(d) Perhaps the most powerful treatment in the recovery of creation as a proper dimension of Israel's faith is Hans Heinrich Schmid's book *Gerechtigkeit als Welt-*

---

25. Von Rad, *Old Testament Theology,* 1:418–59. In that volume, von Rad gave extended attention to the wisdom traditions. This was already an inchoate articulation of a creation theology that departed from the categories of his definitive article of 1936.

26. The shift under way in *Old Testament Theology* 1 was extended even further in *Wisdom in Israel,* wherein von Rad asserts a creation theology that appears to be almost a parallel or alternative to the theology of "mighty deeds" he had earlier championed. Thus it is important to view von Rad's theological work as it emerged over time. It is a misrepresentation of his work to focus on any particular point in his writing as his most characteristic presentation. It is a mark of his greatness that he was willing to experiment beyond what seemed to be his settled judgments.

27. Claus Westermann presented his "theology of blessing" in a variety of discussions. See "Creation and History in the Old Testament," *The Gospel and Human Destiny* (ed. Vilmos Vajta; Minneapolis: Augsburg Publishing House, 1971) 11–38; *Creation* (Philadelphia: Fortress Press, 1971); *Elements of Old Testament Theology* (Atlanta: John Knox, 1982); *What Does the Old Testament Say about God?* (London: SPCK, 1979); and *Blessing in the Bible and in the Life of the Church* (OBT; Philadelphia: Fortress Press, 1978).

28. Walter Harrelson, *From Fertility Cult to Worship* (Garden City, N.Y.: Doubleday, 1969).

ordnung.[29] Schmid has no interest in the old quarrel over fertility religion. Rather he studies the wisdom materials of the Old Testament, especially the Book of Proverbs. The title of his book, which summarizes his argument, indicates that the order of the world, given by the Creator, is one intending and insisting on righteousness—the proper maintenance of all that is necessary for a life of *shalôm.* Thus creation faith, as Schmid presents it, is no longer tainted with polemical categories, but is seen as a proper way of speaking about Yahweh, who orders the world in good, generous, reliable ways toward life.

(e) Most recently, James Barr has joined the ranks in a polemical statement against Karl Barth. Barr has insisted that "natural theology" is much available in the Old Testament and that Barth's categories, wrought in a highly dangerous situation, were misinformed.[30] Whatever one may say about Barth's argument and the derivative position of von Rad in that context, it is now credible to recognize the legitimacy of scholarship that sees creation as the horizon of Israel's faith.

(f) Bernhard Anderson, more than anyone else in the United States, made von Rad's credo hypothesis popular and usable. Anderson's book *Understanding the Old Testament,* built around the credo hypothesis, is the normative textbook for Old Testament study in the United States.[31] It is therefore ironic that Anderson, more than any other scholar in the United States, has focused on the creation traditions of the Old Testament.[32] Anderson was familiar with the polemical side of Israel's faith vis-à-vis Baalism, but he has also seen right along that creation is a proper theme of Old Testament theology. He has paid attention to the ways in which this theological material is pertinent to current discussion of the ecological crisis.[33]

Because the current tendency in Old Testament scholarship is to see creation as the horizon of the Old Testament—and because the earlier models of Israel versus Canaan (fostered by von Rad) and faith versus religion (enunciated by Barth) have faded—we begin our consideration of the verbs of Israel's testimony about Yahweh with creation.[34] To take such a "horizon" as a beginning point yields enormous gains. This large scope for the governance of Yahweh overcomes the ethnocentric

29. Hans Heinrich Schmid, *Gerechtigkeit als Weltordnung: Hintergrund und Geschichte des alttestamentlichen Gerechtigkeitsbegriffs* (BHT 40; Tübingen: J. C. B. Mohr [Paul Siebeck], 1968). See also his earlier book, *Wesen und Geschichte der Weisheit: Eine Untersuchung zur altorientalischen und israelitischen Weisheitsliteratur* (BZAW 101; Berlin: A. Töpelmann, 1966); and his later, enormously influential article, "Creation, Righteousness, and Salvation: 'Creation Theology' as the Broad Horizon of Biblical Theology," *Creation in the Old Testament* (ed. Bernhard W. Anderson; Philadelphia: Fortress Press, 1984) 102–17.

30. James Barr, *Biblical Faith and Natural Theology: The Gifford Lectures for 1991* (Oxford: Clarendon Press, 1993).

31. Bernhard W. Anderson, *Understanding the Old Testament* (New York: Prentice-Hall, 1986).

32. Bernhard W. Anderson, *From Creation to New Creation: Old Testament Perspectives* (OBT; Minneapolis: Fortress Press, 1994), has offered a series of important articles on creation, published in various places throughout his long career. The articles together form an important corpus and reference point for subsequent scholarship.

33. See especially Bernhard Anderson, "Human Dominion over Nature," *From Creation to New Creation,* 111–31.

34. On creation as a proper focus and beginning point for Old Testament theology, see Rolf Knierim, "The Task of Old Testament Theology," *HBT* 6 (1984) 25–57.

and anthropocentric propensities that are more likely to prevail in interpretation that lacks such a horizon. The existence of Israel as a community of faith is thus situated in a much larger context, so that Yahweh's proper sphere of governance is seen to be much more comprehensive than Israel, or any other community that imagines itself to have a privileged status.

This fresh emergence of creation faith in Old Testament theology is especially welcome on two contemporary points. First, creation faith can contribute in important ways to a crucial engagement with the ecological, environmental crisis we now face.[35] Creation faith invites reflection on human responsibility for the well-being of all creation, and engages the costly sanctions that go along with the abuse of creation. Second, creation faith, understood as doxological polemic against human autonomy, can enter the discussion of science and religion in a way that the conflictual model of Old Testament faith could not.[36] Creation faith, with its ethical dimension, can insist that the wonder and mystery of creation invites not Promethean control, but respect, reverence, and care for the world, making the "force of life" finally unavailable for human knowledge, administration, or manipulation. Thus, it is a matter of great importance that creation faith did not lead Israel to self-sufficiency, but to doxological self-abandonment in praise.

We must insist at the same time, however, that creation faith, unless it is seen as pronouncedly Yahwistic (that is, congruent with the remainder of Israel's testimony), is open for ideological use. This may be true politically when the order of creation is equated with a preferred social order, such as by appeal to "natural law." We have ample evidence of the destructiveness of such an equation. The same potential for destruction also applies to the kind of immanentism which imagines that the power for life is inherent in creation and can be harnessed by technological know-how without reference to the ethical character of Yahweh's gift of life. When the "power for life" is separated from the ethical requirements inherent in the order of creation, deathliness takes on great and dangerous power.

Finally, we may observe that Israel's testimony concerning "Yahweh who creates" does not arrive at anything like a doctrine of creation. As we have noted, Yahweh "creates" by word (Gen 1:3ff.), by wisdom (Jer 10:12), and by spirit (Gen 1:12), so that the materials are available for the articulation of a trinitarian doctrine of creation. The Old Testament, however, in its doxological, polemical inclination, leaves matters much more inchoate, and must not be pushed beyond this inchoate quality. Said another way, *Israel's testimony stays at the level of testimony, one utterance*

---

35. It is now conventionally accepted that current ecological concerns are intimately connected to a biblical understanding of creation. While this has become a commonplace of scholarship, it is worth noting that this accent is very recent, only alive as the question has surfaced in the larger scope of society. While the claims for ecology were latent in the material, they were unnoticed in most of scholarship until interpretation was placed in the midst of the particular, demanding emergency of the environment.

36. On the interface of science and religion as it concerns creation, see these representative discussions: Langdon Gilkey, *Nature, Reality, and the Sacred: The Nexus of Science and Religion* (Minneapolis: Fortress Press, 1993); Jürgen Moltmann, *God in Creation: An Ecological Doctrine of Creation* (1985; Minneapolis: Fortress Press, 1994); and Sallie McFague, *Metaphorical Theology: Models of God in Religious Language* (Philadelphia: Fortress Press, 1983).

at a time. The hearer may weave the utterances into a unity, but such an interpretive maneuver inevitably runs beyond Israel's witness. There is nothing here of doctrine or of system, only utterances that insist that this verbal sentence affirms a Subject/Agent whose activity decisively reshapes the life-world in which the witnesses live. Creation faith is the place where this testifying community stands in its resistance to life as technique and in its insistence that the generosity of God will override the scarcity that is the driving ideology of greed, which in turn diminishes creation and makes human life yet more desperate.

Israel meditates on chaos in the midst of its own life. It does not speculate on the source or origin of chaos: chaos is simply there, in the great, inscrutable cosmic threats that Israel could see but not explain. The same threat of chaos is more immediate for Israel in the sociopolitical pressures that rob the weak of a chance for life. Israel knows chaos as well in the intimacy of family barrenness, communal disregard, and personal death. The astonishment of Israel's polemical doxologies is that Israel refused the claims of chaos, refused to cringe in helplessness before the powers that negated life. In its daring testimony, Israel seized on this ineluctable term *create* (and its less exotic synonyms). In the use of such verbs, Israel claims to know the name of the Subject powerful enough to enact the verbs. In these utterances, chaos is decisively driven back. In practice, the testimony provides a place (safe, dry land) in which Israel and the world may be fruitful and multiply.

Yahweh, the God Who Makes Promises

In its oddest testimony, the witness of the Old Testament asserts that Yahweh said to father Abraham:

> By myself I have sworn (*šbʿ*) . . . I will indeed bless you, and I will make your offspring as numerous as the stars of heaven and as the sand that is on the seashore. And your offspring shall possess the gate of their enemies, and by your offspring shall all the nations of the earth gain blessing for themselves, because you have obeyed my voice. (Gen 22:16-18)

Later on, in very different traditions, Israel appealed back to that remarkable assertion of Yahweh:

> . . . so that you may go in and occupy the good land that the Lord swore (*šbʿ*) to your ancestors to give you. . . . (Deut 6:18)

> He brought us out from there in order to bring us in, to give us the land that he promised on oath (*šbʿ*) to our ancestors. (Deut 6:23)

Israel's testimony to Yahweh as a promise-maker presents Yahweh as both powerful and reliable enough to turn life in the world, for Israel and for all peoples, beyond present circumstance to new life-giving possibility. Yahweh's promises keep the world open toward well-being, even in the face of deathly circumstance.

Verbs of Promise

The key verb, on which Israel meditates persistently, is *šb'*, "swear," or as the NRSV renders it in Deut 6:23, "promised on oath." This verb is what makes this testimony about Yahweh so odd, for it concerns utterance that comes from the very lips of Yahweh, whereby Yahweh speaks an obligation to Yahweh's own self ("By myself I have sworn...") about the future of Israel. The testimonial sentence here recalled is not an act, unless such an utterance be regarded as performative, as doing what it asserts.[37]

This utterance, on the lips of Yahweh, is not to be flattened into some "word of God," as though it were a principle or a rational logos. It is, rather, an out-loud speech, an oath uttered in solemn context, whereby Yahweh is formally and solemnly committed to Israel and takes on obligation for Yahweh's own self for time to come. This self-commitment means that Israel's witness to Yahweh, and derivatively its own life in the world, are focused on something as fragile and elusive, as solemn and serious, as a formal oath that Yahweh has promised to enact. Moreover, Israel can identify the time and place of the oath and the hearer to whom the oath was uttered.

The verbs that derive from or supply the substance of *šb'*, the content of the oath, are most characteristically "give" (*ntn*) and "bless" (*brk*). Yahweh swears to give, to hand over freely, and to guarantee. Israel is to be the recipient of a gift that is as sure as Yahweh's oath. Moshe Weinfeld has suggested that this oath on Yahweh's part to give Israel an unconditional gift of land is on the order of a land grant, whereby a king has power to bestow land to a privileged subject.[38] The verbal sentence is thus not an amorphous wish, but a solemn, public decree announcing legal rights and guarantees for time to come.

The second substantive verb, "bless," is not as easy to characterize, but clearly "bless" is not simply a friendly wish. It is rather a bestowal of life-force, related to generativity, birth, and reproduction, which the powerful giver entrusts to the recipient. Thus its use, for example in Gen 22:17, is an act whereby the power-for-life monopolized by Yahweh generously is transmitted to Abraham and to his descendants.

In this sequence of verbs—swear, give, bless—we are indeed in the realm of testimony, for Israel retells what Yahweh has been heard to say in the hearing of Israel. Everything about Israel's life in the world depends on these words having been uttered by Yahweh. Of course, beyond Israel's insistence, we have no evidence that Yahweh has uttered these words. The testimony of the Bible would have

---

37. On performative utterance, see John L. Austin, *How to Do Things with Words* (Cambridge: Harvard University Press, 1975). Currently, Dale Patrick is at work on an Old Testament theology from the perspective of performative speech. His provisional title is "The Rhetoric of Revelation."

38. On the power of the throne to enact such a grant of land, see Moshe Weinfeld, "The Covenant of Grant in the Old Testament and in the Ancient Near East," *JAOS* 90 (1970) 184–203; and more generally Suzanne Booer, *The Promise of the Land as an Oath* (BZAW 205; Berlin: W. de Gruyter, 1992). This royal prerogative is evident in the Old Testament in David's dealings with Mephibosheth and Ziba, in 2 Sam 9:1-13, 16:1-4, and 19:24-30.

us take Israel's word as certification that these promises have indeed been uttered with ensuring power and significance. Beyond such testimony, Israel can provide no warrants for the claim, and certainly historical research cannot touch the issue. Israel can only tell tales that function as vehicles for these awesome, decisive, community-creating, and history-generating utterances.

Ancestral Narratives of Promise

The materials for this extraordinary testimony to Yahweh, as the God who makes solemn oaths, is given in the ancestral narratives of Genesis. Albrecht Alt has paid particular attention to the narrative promises of Genesis and has insisted that this utterance of promise is the distinguishing mark of Yahweh.[39] We may consider briefly several such utterances of Yahweh around which the Genesis narrative is organized.

Claus Westermann has proposed that the promise given in the narrative of Gen 18:1-15 is perhaps the primal utterance of promise by Yahweh, because unlike most of the other Genesis promises in the mouth of Yahweh, this one is integral to its narrative context.[40] Without the promise, there would be no narrative. In this narrative, Yahweh (or "three men") visit Abraham and Sarah in their old age. The visitor(s) becomes recognizable only as the narrative advances. Earlier (Gen 12:1-3; 15:1-6), a son had been promised to Abraham and Sarah, but now they are old, beyond child-bearing years. They have no son, no heir, and no prospect of one. Without a son and heir, there will be, for this family, no future reception of a land of promise. The hopeless circumstance of Abraham and Sarah is made clear in the narrative.

But the visitor(s), in one utterance, radically overrides the circumstance of the old people: "Your wife Sarah shall have a son" (v. 10). The utterance evokes disbelief, humor, astonishment, mockery. The visitor adamantly will not yield to their disbelief. Instead, the visitor utters the supreme challenge to the faith of Abraham and Sarah: "Is anything too wonderful for the Lord?" (v. 14). No answer is given in this narrative.[41] For now, Israel must live with the question. In the subsequent narrative, an answer is given: a son is born to Sarah (Gen 21:1-

---

39. Albrecht Alt, "The God of the Fathers," *Essays on Old Testament History and Religion* (Oxford: Blackwell, 1966) 1–77. Alt's thesis undoubtedly influenced von Rad, "The Form-Critical Problem of the Hexateuch," as von Rad understood the Hexateuch through a scheme of promise and fulfillment. Alt's influence, moreover, extended through von Rad to Jürgen Moltmann, whose *Theology of Hope: On the Ground and the Implications of Christian Eschatology* (1967; Minneapolis: Fortress Press, 1993) is decisively influenced by von Rad's accent on promise.

40. Claus Westermann, *The Promise to the Fathers: Studies on the Patriarchal Narratives* (Philadelphia: Fortress Press, 1980) 11–12, suggests that this narrative is the one in the Abraham-Sarah cycle in which the promise is intrinsic and integral to the narrative. In almost all of the other cases in the Genesis narratives, the promise seems to be added to a narrative that could stand without the promise; in this case, there is no narrative without the oracle of promise. Thus in Gen 18:1-15 we may have the most elemental narrative memory of Israel concerning the promise.

41. On the text, see Walter Brueggemann, " 'Impossibility' and Epistemology in the Faith Tradition of Abraham and Sarah (Gen 18:1-15)," *ZAW* 94 (1982) 615–34.

7). The promise is kept; circumstance is overcome by the reliability of Yahweh. Impossibility is enacted, and the promise made in 12:1-3 and 15:1-6 is kept intact.

The promise to Abraham must be transmitted to his beloved son Isaac, the one who survived God's demand only by a wonder (Gen 22:1-14). Now in 26:3-4, the promise given to Abraham is given over to the next generation:

> . . . I will be with you, and will bless you; for to you and to your descendants I will give all these lands, and I will fulfill the oath that I swore to your father Abraham. I will make your offspring as numerous as the stars of heaven, and will give to your offspring all these lands; and all the nations of the earth shall gain blessing for themselves through your offspring, because Abraham obeyed my voice and kept my charge, my commandments, my statutes, and my laws.

The oath now uttered to Isaac is to "fulfill the oath" already made to Abraham. The utterance persists into the next generation of this family.

Yet again the promise is in jeopardy, as the next mother in Israel, Rebekah, is like Sarah barren (Gen 25:21). Only by God's blessing are the sons Esau and Jacob born. By chicanery Jacob prevails over his brother, for moral quality is not a condition for the promise (27:1-40). Jacob, now in the same line of generativity, receives the promise:

> . . . I am the Lord, the God of Abraham your father and the God of Isaac; the land on which you lie I will give to you and to your offspring; and your offspring shall be like the dust of the earth, and you shall spread abroad to the west and to the east and to the north and to the south; and all the families of the earth shall be blessed in you and in your offspring. Know that I am with you and will keep you wherever you go, and will bring you back to the land; for I will not leave you until I have done what I have promised you. (Gen 28:13-15)

The promise is, with varying phrasing, the same: land, accompaniment ("I will be with you"), and blessing to the nations. The promise is given, "until I have done what I have promised" (*dbr*). Once again, the promise is safely transmitted to the next generation, yet another generation birthed only by the power of Yahweh.

Beyond Jacob, the Genesis narrative does not tell of the promise being given over to Joseph, because Joseph is cast in another genre of literature. To Joseph's sons, Ephraim and Manasseh, a blessing is indeed given (Gen 48:13-14, 20). The narrative surprises us, because in vv. 15-16, sandwiched between reference to the grandsons, "He blessed Joseph." Jacob blessed, bestowed life-force, instructing Joseph to "bless the boys" (v. 16). The blessing here again looks back to the fathers, Abraham and Isaac. It also looks forward to a "multitude" on the earth. As Westermann has shown, the form of the utterance is an oath-promise.[42]

The substance of the utterance, however, is a blessing, the bestowal of life-force, as energy, prosperity, abundance, well-being. Yahweh is a God unlike any other, who has the gift of good life in Yahweh's own power. All of that is in the verb *šb'*. The Book of Genesis understands the urgency of transmitting the solemn oath of Yahweh to the next generation of Israel, for *it is this oath that gives Israel power to survive and prosper in demanding and debilitating circumstance.* This oath is not a general promise that floats in the air. It is concrete and specific. And it must be entrusted to the next generation, concretely and formally, certainly by reutterance, but also by appropriate physical gesture, whereby the next generation is identified with and empowered as the carrier of this circumstance-defying power in the world.

The substance of the oath is carried by two words, *bless* and *give*, verbs over which Yahweh presides with singular sovereignty. The term *bless* bespeaks God's power for life, which concerns intimately the generation of the next wave of children. Thus it is connected to sexual reproduction, which the Bible knows (long before Freud) is linked to the core mystery of life. Alongside that intimacy of generating heirs, the verb *bless,* in these narratives, has in purview a large arena of new life that is to be transmitted, via Israel, to the nations. These repeated utterances indicate a characteristic way in which Israel thinks and speaks. This most intimate act is linked to Israel's reproductive processes, whereby God's power for life is released into the world and made available for all. By this linkage, Israel is given significance and responsibility well beyond itself. And the world of nations is recharacterized as an arena in which God's faithful power for life is being enacted. In these traditions of promise, Israel, by its life and its obedience, is entrusted with the well-being of the nations.[43]

Between the intimacy of reproduction and the expansiveness of the nations, both under the aegis of the verb *bless,* is the second derivative verb, *give.* Yahweh will give, not first of all to named ancestors, nor to the nations, but to the whole people Israel. And what Yahweh has sworn to Israel is land. It is plausible to imagine that this promise was first heard, received, and trusted by the *landless,* for whom the gift of land is the quintessential anticipation of all of life. Thus already in Yahweh's first utterance to Abraham, we notice the oddness of this testimony (Gen 12:1-3). Yahweh, the Creator of heaven and earth, the one who dwells high and lifted up, has as a most characteristic subject of utterance, land.[44] *Holiness is*

---

42. Claus Westermann, "The Way of the Promise through the Old Testament," *The Old Testament and Christian Faith: Essays By Rudolf Bultmann and Others* (ed. Bernhard W. Anderson; London: SCM Press, 1964) 200–224.

43. It is now commonly accepted that Gen 12:1-3 is the pivotal text linking the history of the world (Genesis 1–11) to the history of Israel. It is not necessary to follow von Rad's source analysis (with reference to the Yahwist) in order to make the interpretive point. On the cruciality of the text, see Hans Walter Wolff, "The Kerygma of the Yahwist," *Int* 20 (1966) 131–58; and Patrick D. Miller, "Syntax and Theology in Genesis XII 3a," *VT* 34 (1984) 472–75.

44. On the centrality of land for biblical faith, see W. D. Davies, *The Gospel and the Land: Early Christianity and Jewish Territorial Doctrine* (Berkeley: University of California Press, 1974); and *The*

thereby linked to the concreteness of material existence in the world. Israel understands that full, whole life, life intended by Yahweh, requires land: a safe, fruitful, secure, productive place of one's own.[45] And the drive of this testimony is to insist most concretely on this awareness in every coming generation.

Israel testifies, moreover, not only that land is a sine qua non for its life, but that Yahweh—the instigator of its existence in the world, the governor of its primary verbs—is a giver of land. Never again in the testimony of Israel will the sovereignty of Yahweh be separated from the legitimacy of land. The two are joined by the concreteness and specificity of utterance that has the force of oath. Yahweh, in the testimony of Israel, moves through history, obligated and propelled by this utterance. The function and potential of the oath is an abiding preoccupation of this community of testimony. Israel is certain, for all time to come, that this God does not want this people to live without a secure land. This is a most important point for the self-discernment of Israel. It is also a crucial element in the discernment of Yahweh as a God who is committed to the healthy materiality of human existence.

Fulfillment and Expectation

The family narratives of Genesis 12–50 are the seedbed of Israel's promissory faith, of Israel's oddest testimony, and of Yahweh's emergence as a God who makes promises. It is on the basis of this promissory testimony that two things happen to Israel, who trusts those promises from Yahweh. First, on a few occasions Israel notices, receives, and acknowledges the fulfillment of a promise. Von Rad has noticed that Josh 21:43-45 is the most sweeping of such acknowledgments:[46]

> Thus the Lord gave to Israel all the land that he swore to their ancestors that he would give them. . . . Not one of all the good promises that the Lord had made to the house of Israel had failed; all came to pass.

Yahweh's oath does on occasion come to fruition.

Second, and more characteristically, Israel waits and hopes—in joy, in perplexity, in eager longing, but also in wonderment and near-despair, because most often the promises are *not yet kept*, and Yahweh's oath is held in abeyance. This abeyance marks Israel as a people of hope, waiting in expectation.

Territorial Dimension of Judaism (Berkeley: University of California Press, 1982); Walter Brueggemann, *The Land: Place as Gift, Promise, and Challenge in Biblical Faith* (OBT; Philadelphia: Fortress Press, 1978); and most recently, Norman C. Habel, *The Land Is Mine: Six Biblical Land Ideologies* (OBT; Minneapolis: Fortress Press, 1995).

45. It is not possible to consider the land promises to the ancestors without at least a reference to the ways in which these promises continue their force in relation to the contemporary state of Israel. That continuing force is endlessly problematized concerning contemporary Israel by the awareness that a theological-ideological appeal to the promises stands in profound tension with the *Realpolitik* that is manifestly operative in the state of Israel. Moreover, the theological-ideological claims rooted in these promises run against Palestinian claims that appeal to very different ideological force. See the judicious assessment of the matter from a Christian perspective by W. Eugene March, *Israel and the Politics of Land: A Theological Case Study* (Louisville: Westminster/John Knox, 1994).

46. Von Rad, "The Form-Critical Problem of the Hexateuch," 72–74.

At the same time, two things happen to Yahweh's promises. First, these promises continue to be reiterated through the generations of Israel, so that they echo and resound with assurance through Israel's life and Israel's ongoing testimony. Thus the promises to the ancestors become one basis for the summons made to Moses, in anticipation of the Exodus (Exod 2:24; 3:7, 16; 6:3-8; 33:1). The same promises become a foundation for subsequent demands in the Torah (Deut 1:8; 6:10; 29:13). As older materials are reused, these old land promises become a ground in the exile for hope for the landless and the displaced.[47] It is a source of astonishment that this waiting, hoping community found such ancient utterance to be theologically empowering so many centuries later (Isa 43:8; 51:2; 63:16; Ezek 33:24; and Mic 7:20). It is no wonder that in derivative Christian tradition, this enduring utterance of Yahweh to Israel was termed by Paul "the gospel beforehand," *proeuēggelisato* (Gal 3:8). The oath of Yahweh is taken to be an assurance that Yahweh has the power and the resolve to bring the people of the promise to a better circumstance, no matter what present circumstances may indicate to the contrary (cf. Hebrews 11).

The second development in Yahweh's promises to Israel is that Yahweh keeps making new promises. It is not as though the utterance in the text of Genesis is Yahweh's best, last word on the future of Israel. Through the life of Israel, Yahweh finds new ways in which the future may be anticipated. We may identify three sorts of promises that are generated in and through Israel's later testimony, all derivative from and congruent with the foundational promises of Genesis.

(a) The *promise to David* and to the house of David may have been intentionally anticipated in the Abraham narratives as we have them, or given retrospectively in that tradition. But the primary commitment to the dynasty, which became the taproot of subsequent messianism, is beyond the Book of Genesis. Thus in the mouth of Nathan, the promise is uttered for the coming dynasty:

> But I will not take my steadfast love from him, as I took it from Saul, whom
> I put away from before you. Your house and your kingdom shall be made sure
> forever before me; your throne shall be established forever. (2 Sam 7:15-16)

There is no doubt that this utterance of Yahweh was taken as solemnly and seriously as anything already voiced in the Book of Genesis:

> Once and for all I have sworn by my holiness;
> I will not lie to David.
> His line shall continue forever,

---

47. John van Seters, *Abraham in History and Tradition* (New Haven: Yale University Press, 1975), in the most radical way has urged that these land promises that served the exiles were in fact generated in the exile and do not represent older traditions. While the questions of source and date for these traditions are now in considerable flux, the conclusions of van Seters seem improbable. Nonetheless, the interpretive point I am making does not depend on an insistence that the traditions in some form are older than van Seters will allow. Van Seters's impressive program of publications continues from the assumptions of his earlier work on Genesis.

> and his throne endure before me like the sun.
> It shall be established forever like the moon,
> an enduring witness in the skies. (Ps 89:35-37)

From the moment of this utterance, the Davidic dynasty becomes an enduring theological datum in Israel's life.

(b) Scattered through *the prophetic literature* are a variety of promissory utterances in God's own mouth. Through many different images and figures, these promises anticipate new well-being for Israel in time to come. These include, for example, new well-being rooted in Jerusalem as the city of the Torah (Isa 2:2-4; Mic 4:1-5); a new king as practitioner of justice (Isa 11:1-5), who will assure the rehabilitation of a hostile creation (Isa 11:6-9); a new, restored land of generativity and productivity (Amos 9:11-15); and a restoration of strength and well-being (Hab 3:18-19). From a theological perspective, what is important about these prophetic promises, whatever the specific content and whenever they may be dated, is that they are situated in the presence of prophetic judgments and threats. Thus they are characteristically God's second act, after judgment, in dealing with recalcitrant Israel.[48] This sequence, as in Jer 31:27-30, makes clear that judgment and promise are not an either/or matter for Yahweh. Yahweh, over time, with Israel, will do both.

(c) Most remarkably, *the exile* becomes for Israel an arena in which Yahweh utters new promises. This is a theological datum of special importance. Neither Israel nor the God of Israel would concede anything to the exile. In the face of that most discouraging circumstance, Yahweh issues the most far-reaching promises. In addition to a variety of utterances guaranteeing restoration, rehabilitation, and homecoming for Israel, we should especially notice that in the midst of exile, Yahweh utters a very different kind of promise, bespeaking an intimate connection to and solidarity with Israel that is to be expressed as presence: "I will be your God and you shall be my people" (Jer 11:4; 24:7; 30:22; 31:33; 32:38; Ezek 11:20; 14:11; 36:28; 37:23, 27; cf. Hos 2:23).[49]

It is exceedingly important that the majority of texts with this promise of presence are situated in the exile. The promise indicates that Yahweh is prepared to submit, with Israel, to the circumstance of exile. But more than submit, it is understood in these texts that the very presence of Yahweh with Israel in exile holds the potential to transform exile into a viable place for life. That presence may well be a more elemental promise and a more drastic commitment on Yahweh's part than is intrusive activity.[50] Israel, in its embrace of this promise from Yahweh, was assured

---

48. On the canonical shaping of the sequence of judgment and then promise after judgment, see Ronald E. Clements, "Patterns in the Prophetic Canon," *Canon and Authority: Essays in Old Testament Religion and Theology* (ed. George Coats and Burke O. Long; Philadelphia: Fortress Press, 1977) 42–55.
49. On this formula and its pivotal function in the faith of Israel, see Rudolf Smend, *Die Bundesformel* (ThStud 68; Zürich: EVZ Verlag, 1963).
50. While this repeated and stylized covenantal formula is primarily situated in the exile and issued in the exilic salvation oracles of Second Isaiah, the promise of presence, often issued in a nominal

that not even in its most dire circumstance would it be abandoned or forsaken by Yahweh.

Thus in every season of its life, Israel lived with the uttered promise of Yahweh in its ears. This promise, which defies every logic but which could not be devised by those who reiterated the oath, assures Israel that its life, and eventually all of the historical process, is not a cold, hard enactment of power and brutality. It is, rather, an arena in which a powerful intention for well-being is resolutely at work.

In the end, we see that *the promissory character of Yahweh in the subsequent life of Israel took two distinct forms.* On the one hand, the promise was heard and received in a way we may term *prophetic* and *messianic.* That is, the promises of God are to be enacted in the historical horizon of Israel, in the midst of its public institutions and possibilities. We may term these promises prophetic, because their substance concerns the public, concrete prospect of peace, justice, security, and abundance. Israel's prophetic promises from Yahweh relentlessly insist that the public practices of power will, in the end, conform to the resolve of Yahweh. These promises may also be termed messianic, because they anticipate that the enactment of God's future will be effected through human agents. Although the term *messiah* refers primarily to the line of David, in Isa 45:1 Cyrus the Persian is assigned the same role as that previously held by members of the Davidic family. Thus Israel's discernment and articulation of the promise is that this resolute God will recruit as necessary from the human cast in order to reorder human history. Therefore both those who trust the promises and those who have never heard of the promises are recruited for this large resolve of Yahweh.

On the other hand, at the edge of the Old Testament, promises of Yahweh also take an *apocalyptic* form, so that the newness Yahweh intends does not emerge within present public processes or through effective human agency.[51] Rather by the sovereign incursion of Yahweh, whose newness is not extrapolated from the present, something utterly new will be given. Scholars speak of proto-apocalyptic promises, as in Isa 65:17-25, and the more properly apocalyptic rhetoric of Zechariah 9–14, and the Book of Daniel, which culminates in the most extreme anticipation of the resurrection of the dead in Isa 26:19 and Dan 12:2.

No doubt these two sorts of promises, expressed in very different rhetoric, operate in very different genre and in very different social contexts. Yet, from a theological perspective, too much of a distinction should not be made between them. It is likely that more intransigent historical circumstance requires or evokes a

---

sentence, is quite old in Israel. See for example Exod 3:11-12 with the verb *hyh:* "I will be with you." This use of the verb provides the context for the name Yahweh in Exod 3:14, which we have, following Cross, understood as derived from the verb *hyh.* This promise of presence in vv. 11-12, moreover, is what makes possible the daunting task of confronting pharaoh. The same promise of presence is given in the term *Emmanuel* (Isa 7:14; 8:8; cf. Matt 1:23, which belongs to the same promissory trajectory).

51. Much of recent discussion has been in response to the thesis of Paul D. Hanson, *The Dawn of Apocalyptic: The Historical and Sociological Roots of Jewish Apocalyptic Eschatology* (Philadelphia: Fortress Press, 1974). While Hanson's thesis is much in dispute, his study has nonetheless determined the shape of much of the discussion.

more dramatic utterance of promise. But all of the promises—prophetic-messianic and apocalyptic, within history and beyond history—issue from the same God, anticipate the same outcome, and appeal to the same community. All of these promises of Yahweh, of every sort, on every subject, intend that Israel should not surrender its life or its destiny to the present circumstance, especially when that present circumstance is deathly and appears insurmountable.

Thus this odd testimony of Israel puts forth a theological claim that is profoundly subversive of the present. Israel has known, ever since the barrenness of Sarah, that there is a deep incongruity between the *intention* of Yahweh and the *circumstance* of lived experience. Israel, in the face of that incongruity, did not have many alternatives. It could accept the circumstance of its life as the true state of reality—thus, for example, Sarah is barren and then the promise is voided within one generation. The alternative, Israel's chosen one in most seasons, is to rely on Yahweh's oath as a resolve to override circumstance, so that it is the oath and not the circumstance that tells the truth about reality. In this theological intentionality, Israel embraces this uttered testimony as the true version of its life.

This testimony would have been odd and daring in the ancient world, because lived circumstance has a certain credibility on the face of it. Thus this testimony is accepted publicly only by the boldest. One may indeed conclude that this testimony is even more odd and more daring in our contemporary world. In our current theological work, we recognize that the epistemological assumptions of our world tilt our inclination toward visible circumstance. Indeed, the epistemology of modernity has, as much as possible, banished promise from our world. It has become evident, however, that *when promise is banished and circumstance governs, we are most likely left with nothing but despair,* whether the despair of the self-sufficient or of the disempowered. And despair is no basis for a viable social community. Thus our recovery of these texts brings a wonderment about whether such old utterance is a credible antidote to our ready embrace of despair. Such utterance may strike us as remote from our circumstance. But then, it has always struck Israel as remote from circumstance. In the end, our consideration of these promissory statements is as it always was for Israel: a massive assurance grounded in the flimsy evidence of the witnesses.

Yahweh, the God Who Delivers

In its most revolutionary testimony, the witness of the Old Testament asserts that Yahweh said,

> I am the Lord, and I will free (*yṣ'*) you from the burdens of the Egyptians and deliver (*nṣl*) you from slavery to them.
> I will redeem (*g'l*) you with an outstretched arm and with mighty acts of judgment. (Exod 6:6)

Israel's testimony to Yahweh as deliverer enunciates Yahweh's resolved capacity to intervene decisively against every oppressive, alienating circumstance and force that precludes a life of well-being. Yahweh is more than a match for the powers of oppression, whether sociopolitical or cosmic.

Verbs of Deliverance

This remarkable assertion of Yahweh's intention for Israel already contains three of the decisive "Exodus verbs," of which Yahweh is prepared to be the subject.

(a) *yṣ'* "Yahweh brings out":

> ... the Lord brought you out from there by strength of hand.... (Exod 13:3; cf. Exod 12:41; 14:8; Deut 16:3, 6)

This verb speaks about a geographical exit. Whatever we may judge to be true about the historicity of the Exodus from Egypt, Israel's testimony is uncompromisingly about a geographical departure. Israel's story is the flight "from there to here." At times, the verb is a simple *qal* grammatical form, "you went out." With reference to Yahweh, however, the verb is in the causative *hiph'il* form, so that Yahweh is the agent who sanctions, propels, and enacts the departure of Israel. This verb is matched by *'lh*, "to go up," which may also be in the *qal* or *hiph'il*.[52]

(b) *nṣl* "Yahweh delivers":

> ... I have come down to deliver them from the Egyptians.... (Exod 3:8; cf. 5:23, 6:6, 18:9)

This verb references an abrupt physical act of grasping or seizing—often, as here, grasping or seizing in order to pull out of danger. It is the same verb used by David, who was "snatched" from the danger of the paw of a lion (1 Sam 17:37), and by Amos, referring to Israel being "snatched" by God like a brand from the fire (Amos 4:11). The latter perhaps refers to the Exodus narrative, where Israel is "snatched" out of the danger of Egyptian slavery in a forceful, physical gesture by Yahweh.

(c) *g'l* "Yahweh redeems":

> I will redeem you with an outstretched arm and with mighty acts of judgment. (Exod 6:6; cf. Exod 15:13; as completed action, Ps 106:10)

The verb *g'l* bespeaks a transformative action that is as radical as that of *yṣ'*, but the ambience of the term is quite different. This term appears, in the first instance, to refer to economic action within a family in order to maintain family property (Lev 25:25ff.), or retributive terms to avenge in order to maintain family honor (Deut 19:6, 12). The image of the verb suggests something like family solidarity, in which

---

52. On the function and usage of the several verbs, see J. N. Wijngaards, *The Dramatization of Salvific History in the Deuteronomic Schools* (Oudtestamentische Studien 16; Leiden: E. J. Brill, 1969); and *The Formulas of the Deuteronomic Creed* (Tilburg: A. Reijnen, 1963).

Yahweh acts as a kinsperson for the maintenance and well-being of the family. It is clear that without this intervention on the part of Yahweh, these "kinfolk" of Yahweh would have disappeared in the empire and been dishonored for having been abandoned by their potential redeemer.

Each of these three verbs arises from a different context and range of images, but all agree on their main claim. The verbs witness to a decisive, intrusive act of transformation, whereby Yahweh has interrupted the life of Israel, with its "burdens of Egypt" and its "slavery to them."

To these verbs we may add three others (often synonyms) that recur often and decisively in the tradition of Exodus testimony:

(d) *yš'* "Yahweh delivers":

> Thus the Lord saved (*yš'*) Israel that day from the Egyptians.... (Exod 14:30; cf. Ps 106:8; and as a noun, Exod 14:13, 15:2)

The term is one of power, perhaps bespeaking political action, but more likely a forceful military action. The verb in this most characteristic sentence tells of Yahweh's forceful activity, which ended a situation of fear, suffering, and helplessness and created the possibility of an alternative life that is received by Israel with joy. The action of the verb is agonistic, in which Yahweh must struggle against counter-powers that want to prevent the well-being of Israel. This transformation wrought by Yahweh, so the testimony claims, happened in real-life history, and it accomplished for Israel what Israel was powerless to do for itself. In this utterance, Israel passionately moves across the "ugly ditch" between history and theology, and knows the name of the One who refuses either category of history or theology. Yahweh, as the Subject of this verb, is the One to whom Israel relentlessly testifies.

(e) *pdh* "Yahweh redeems":

> ...every firstborn of my sons I redeem. (Exod 13:15; cf. Deut 7:8; 15:15; 24:18; Ps 78:42)

This verb reflects an economic transaction whereby one is freed from a situation of hardship or risk—for example, slavery—when someone pays a cash equivalent. Thus the one who pays performs an act of great generosity, which is done freely and without obligation. In Exod 13:15 the language refers to the custom that the firstborn is to be given as a sacrifice unless redeemed; that is, unless payment is made that is thought to be equivalent to the son. Jon Levenson, reviewing the textual evidence for this practice, has concluded that while it was not a required rite in ancient Israel, it did exist.[53] The Exodus narrative thus takes up the practice, under the imagery that Yahweh's "firstborn" is to be bought out of slavery or redeemed

---

53. Jon D. Levenson, *The Death and Resurrection of the Beloved Son: The Transformation of Child Sacrifice in Judaism and Christianity* (New Haven: Yale University Press, 1993).

(Exod 4:22). Conversely the firstborn of pharaoh cannot be redeemed, but must be destroyed (Exod 11:5, 12:12).[54]

(f) '*lh* "Yahweh brings up" (*hiph'il*):

> . . . I have come down to deliver them from the Egyptians, and to bring them up ('*lh*) out of that land. . . . (Exod 3:8)

> I declare that I will bring you up out of the misery of Egypt. . . . (Exod 3:17)

This term has meanings close to that of *yṣ'* (cf. Exod 17:3; 32:4, 8; 33:1; Num 14:13; Judg 6:13; 1 Sam 8:8; 10:18; Jer 11:7; in Judg 6:8 the two terms are used in parallelism). The verb '*lh* of which Yahweh is subject has a geographical connotation: to move from a lower place to a higher. The fact that one "goes up" from slavery to freedom, from the land of Egypt to the land of promise, permits the term to have a suggestion beyond its root geographical intentions. In the liberation from Egypt, Yahweh elevates or exalts Israel—changes its circumstance for the better. In Ps 71:20 the same verb is used metaphorically for a personal rescue and transformation by Yahweh.

The verbs used in Israel's testimony concerning Yahweh's Exodus activity are rich and varied and may be given a variety of nuances appropriate to the semantic fields from which the terms arise. While the verbs arise from very different spheres of life, it is not necessary, for our purposes, that the initial nuance of each verb should be retained. Perhaps by the time they arrive in the settled form of the testimony, the verbs are now all more or less synonymous. What is important for our purposes is that *Yahweh is the subject of all of these verbs*. This cluster of verbs becomes a poignant and elemental way in which Yahweh is characterized in the testimony of Israel. This is why the Old Testament, in its theological formulation, can never shake free of reference to a concrete event, because it is in the sphere of lived, public reality that Yahweh is said to be known and visible. At the core of Israel's God-talk is the persistent claim that Israel knows no God except the One who in an ancient, remembered time acted in a way that made the life of Israel as a people a genuine historical possibility.

Israel never wearied of reciting these verbal sentences, characterizing Yahweh by using powerful verbs in these sentences. It is what Israel sang about in its psalms that gave density to its present (Ps 78:12-13; 105:26-36; 106:7-9; 136:10-15). It is, moreover, what Israel told its children in its most self-conscious instruction (Exod 12:26-27; 13:8-9, 14-15; Deut 6:21-23).

---

54. On the notion of ransom as a substitution, see also the usage in Isa 43:3-5. Peter Stuhlmacher, "Vicariously Giving His Life for Many, Mark 10:45 (Matt. 20:28)," *Reconciliation, Law, and Righteousness: Essays in Biblical Theology* (Philadelphia: Fortress Press, 1986) 16–29, has persuasively argued that the text of Isa 43:3 is the source of Jesus' statement in Mark 10:45, clearly a pivotal theological utterance.

Retelling through Exodus Memory

When Israel began telling of its subsequent history, about what happened in other times and places and circumstances, Israel characteristically retold *all* of its experience through the powerful, definitional lens of the Exodus memory. That is, Yahweh did not enact these powerful, transformative, liberating verbs only once at the outset of Israel's life in the world. Rather Yahweh repeatedly, characteristically, and reliably enacted like transformations in like circumstances throughout Israel's normative memory. While the ancestral material of Genesis is of a very different sort, at least in Gen 15:7 the narrative manages to make the departure (*yṣʾ*) from Ur of the Chaldeans sound like an anticipation of the Exodus. When Israel came into the land of promise under the leadership of Joshua, Israel quite self-consciously presented the crossing of the Jordan River as a belated version of the crossing of the Red Sea:

> "...Israel crossed over the Jordan here on dry ground." For the Lord your God dried up the waters of the Jordan for you until you crossed over, as the Lord your God did to the Red Sea, which he dried up for us until we crossed over.... (Josh 4:22-23)

In the crisis with the Philistines, there is no doubt that the narrative rendition has the Exodus deliverance in purview (1 Sam 4:1–7:1). Even the Philistines are mindful of the God of the Exodus:

> ...the Philistines were afraid; for they said, "Gods have come into the camp." They also said, "Woe to us! For nothing like this has happened before. Woe to us! Who can deliver us from the power of these mighty gods? These are the gods who struck the Egyptians with every sort of plague in the wilderness." (1 Sam 4:7-8)

> Why should you harden your hearts as the Egyptians and Pharaoh hardened their hearts? After he had made fools of them, did they not let the people go, and they departed? (1 Sam 6:6)

In the end, the retelling of this episode is shaped as an entry by Yahweh into the oppressive situation governed by the Philistine gods, and as a powerful, inexplicable emancipation for Israel. Unmistakably, the gods of the Philistines are no more a match for the God of these powerful verbs than were the gods of Egypt (cf. Exod 12:12).

Later when the Old Testament arrives at a larger awareness concerning the other nations, the power and authority of this verb-centered recital persists. Thus in the Isaiah texts of the exile, as Bernhard Anderson has shown, the capacity of Israel to depart the controlling hegemony of Babylon depends on this same God to commit like "actions," which make a departure possible.[55] In what may be the most extreme

---

55. On the cruciality of the memory of the Exodus in the poetry of Second Isaiah, see Bernhard W. Anderson, "Exodus Typology in Second Isaiah," *Israel's Prophetic Heritage: Essays in Honor of James*

case, when the prophet Amos wishes to counter the self-congratulatory faith of Israel as God's special people, he appeals to the Exodus memory. In the time of the prophet, the community of Israel apparently celebrated its special privilege in identifying with Yahweh, the God who had enacted their deliverance from Egypt. Amos does not contradict this claim made by Israel, but in a terse utterance he deabsolutizes the claim:

> Are you not like the Ethiopians to me,
> O people of Israel? says the Lord.
> Did I not bring Israel up from the land of Egypt,
> and the Philistines from Caphtor
> and the Arameans from Kir? (Amos 9:7)

The Exodus memory is left intact for Israel's affirmation, but the exclusiveness between Israel as an Exodus people and Yahweh as an Exodus God is broken. For now it is asserted that the God who brought up (*'lh*) Israel from Egypt does many other like deeds as well. This same God has wrought exoduses for the Philistines and for the Arameans, Israel's most persistent enemies. Yahweh is characteristically a God who enacts exoduses, and who does so in many places, perhaps everywhere. Wherever people are in oppressive situations and are helpless to extricate themselves, there this God might be engaged. This statement by the poet Amos skillfully retains Israel's testimony for Yahweh, but denies Israel an exclusive claim on Yahweh.

Thus the Exodus grammar of Yahweh saturates the imagination of Israel. The Exodus recital, either as a simple declarative sentence enacting Israel's primal theological grammar or as a fuller narrative, becomes paradigmatic for Israel's testimony about Yahweh. It becomes, moreover, an interpretive lens to guide, inform, and discipline Israel's utterances about many aspects of its life. As the paradigmatic function of the utterance is unmistakable, it is equally unmistakable that the entire field of grammar never departs from the concrete, specific reference point rooted in Israel's memory.[56]

This foray into Exodus verbs may advance the project of an Old Testament theology in two ways. First, it provides us with defining material. Israel's God, in all parts of this material, is said to be filled with sovereign power to override all settled structures of power in the world and in tune enough with slavery, helplessness, and suffering to respond to the social needs of the powerless. Second, this review suggests a way to understand the theological processes of the Old Testament itself.

Muilenburg (ed. Bernhard W. Anderson and Walter Harrelson; London: SCM Press, 1962) 177–95; and "Exodus and Covenant in Second Isaiah and Prophetic Tradition," *Magnalia Dei, the Mighty Acts of God* (ed. Frank Moore Cross et al.; Garden City, N.Y.: Doubleday, 1976) 339–60.

56. The memory of the Exodus came to function paradigmatically for many other events in the Old and New Testaments, and recent Old Testament scholarship has made much of that usage. Just now, however, Old Testament scholarship is not much engaged in typology, but prefers to see the enduring and pervasive influence of the Exodus memory through intertextuality. The approaches of typology and intertextuality are not mutually exclusive, but it is useful to recognize the current inclinations of scholarship.

What we have most often in this material are decisive claims uttered, so to speak, "on the run," when Israel is at risk or when Israel remembers being at risk. To be sure, Israel offers more reflective statements concerning the character of Yahweh (as in Exod 34:6-7). My urging, however, is that these statements are of another order and likely derive from these verbal affirmations that I take to be more elemental.[57]

As the work of Yahweh in this testimony is agonistic—variously against the Egyptians, the Philistines, the Babylonians—so also the Exodus utterance itself is agonistic. It means to defeat and refute either despair about situations that appear to be beyond change, or arrogance that assumes situations need not be changed. *Yahweh, as the subject of these transformative verbs, is characteristically said to be a restless agent of social newness.* Neither Israel's despair nor arrogance (nor the arrogance or despair of anyone or anything else) will stop the utterance of this God, an utterance that regularly places Israel in a new situation of jeopardy and/or possibility.

In the New Testament, we can see how this same Exodus grammar continues its effective claim. Thus, for example, Matthew must begin his account of the Gospel with an exodus from Egypt, quoting from Hos 11:1 (Matt 2:13-15). Luke, in his narrative of the transfiguration of Jesus, explicitly uses the term *exodus* (Luke 9:31). But the cruciality of the Exodus tradition for the articulation of the Christian gospel is not to be found primarily in such explicit references. It is found, rather, in the larger affirmation that Jesus acts transformatively in solidarity with the bound and bonded, the weak and marginated (Luke 7:22). Thus it is possible to see that the narratives of Jesus' powerful transformative acts (miracles) are in effect enactments of exodus, whereby a gift of power decisively transforms the circumstance of the subject. Indeed, the general and pervasive appeal to this particular narrative rendering of reality is the ground whereby Christian faith is a religion of salvation. The very name Jesus, from the verb *yš'*, concerns the capacity of Jesus to "save" his subjects from the powers of destruction.[58]

While the narrative account of Jesus stays close to episodic accounts of human transformation, the theology of Paul escalates the rhetoric, so that the particular disabilities of individual persons are made to be general and cosmic. As a consequence, the enemy whom Jesus must defeat for the sake of liberation is finally not poverty, leprosy, or blindness—it is Satan, sin, and death. This theologizing, however, is parallel to the way in which the concrete circumstance of Israel in bondage to slavery requires a defeat of the Egyptian gods (Exod 12:12). Thus there is no contrast between the larger rhetoric of religious combat and the local tales of concrete transformation, for it is the cosmic powers of evil arraigned

---

57. Thus, for example, see pp. 215–18 and 269–70 of this volume on Exod 34:6-7.
58. On the agonistic dimension of the New Testament gospel as it makes use of the image of Yahweh versus pharaoh, see the trilogy of Walter Wink, *Engaging the Powers: Discernment and Resistance in a World of Domination* (Minneapolis: Fortress Press, 1992); *Naming the Powers: The Language of Power in the New Testament* (Philadelphia: Fortress Press, 1984); and *Unmasking the Powers: The Invisible Forces That Determine Human Existence* (Minneapolis: Fortress Press, 1986); see also Ched Myers, *Binding the Strong Man: A Political Reading of Mark's Story of Jesus* (Maryknoll, N.Y.: Orbis Books, 1988).

against Yahweh that are evidenced in specific circumstance. The Old Testament witnesses, like the derivative Christian accounts, move back and forth between the local and the cosmic.

Another issue concerning the ways in which the Christian account of rescue in Jesus is informed by the Exodus tradition is more important. There is no doubt that the Old Testament witness concerns real socioeconomic and political circumstances, from which Yahweh is said to liberate Israel. There is also no doubt that the rhetoric of the New Testament permits a "spiritualizing" of Exodus language, so that the liberation of the gospel is more readily understood as liberation from sin, in contrast with concrete socioeconomic-political bondage. It is not necessary here to reiterate the arguments concerning the genuine material forms of rescue presented in the New Testament. It is important to recognize, however, that already in the Old Testament, the witnesses to Yahweh understood that real, concrete, material bondage is authorized and enacted by "the powers of death" that actively resist the intention of Yahweh. Thus we must not argue, in my judgment, that deliverance is material rather than spiritual, or that salvation is spiritual rather than material. Rather, either side of such dualism distorts true human bondage and misreads Israel's text, which well understood the larger, mythic component of human bondage. The issue for the Bible, in both Testaments, is not one of either/or but of both/and. It will not do to be reductionist in a materialist direction. Conversely, it is simply wrong to refuse the material dimension of slavery and freedom in a safer spiritualizing theology, to which much Christian interpretation is tempted.[59]

The world of bondage, so well known by Israel, persists in our time. The power of deathliness, which resists the liberating intention of Yahweh, continues powerfully, perhaps in more clever form than in ancient times. In the face of that enduring threat, Israel's testimony continues to be recited in hope and courage. This testimony is about the resolve of Yahweh and the work of Yahweh's recruited human agents. It is possible, as Israel does, to speak about Yahweh's direct activity in the interest of liberation. It is equally possible for Israel to say that Moses must go to meet pharaoh (Exod 3:10), so that the Exodus is in some sense a human work, done by human agents who see themselves as legitimated by Yahweh, who never meets pharaoh one-on-one.

This most radical of all of Israel's testimony about Yahweh verifies that the God of Israel is a relentless opponent of human oppression, even when oppression is undertaken and sponsored by what appear to be legitimated powers. Thus Yahweh functions in Israel's testimony as a delegitimator of failed social institutions and as a legitimator of revolutionary human agents. Michael Walzer has traced the ways in which this testimony from ancient Israel has functioned pervasively in human

---

59. To be more precise, it is not even correct to speak of "both/and," which is a concession to our modern, pervasive Cartesian dualism. Patrick D. Miller, "Luke 4:16-21," *Int* 29 (1975) 417–21, has paid careful attention to the term *forgiveness* (*aphesis*), in order to demonstrate that the use of the term in the "inaugural proclamation" of Jesus refuses any tilt toward the spiritual or material, or any split, but pertains to every aspect of life. Such a usage is characteristic of Israel's affirmation of Yahweh's liberating activity.

history and particularly in the West, which has lived under the aegis of this text.[60] He has shown how this text has generated continuing and repeated revolutionary activity. Walzer explores the ways in which this revolutionary legitimacy has functioned in both violent and nonviolent ways, some directly linked to the theological claims of the witness, and some less directly appealing only to its political dimension. This testimony has moved against every absolutizing power that denies full humanness to others in the political process.

In our belated military-technological enterprise in the United States, it remains to be seen whether this witness has continuing power in the face of ruthless oppression. The twentieth century has witnessed sufficient brutality to wonder whether this narrative witness can still have authority; and yet the extraordinary cases of Yasser Arafat, Vaclav Havel, Martin Luther King, Jr., Nelson Mandela, and Lech Walesa give one pause. The alternative to such testimony, it would appear, is a reduction of power processes to simple, harsh technological containment, so that the historical process of emancipation is shut down.[61] Israel, of course, would never countenance that alternative, which is why it insists on the continuing witness to these verbs.

As this tradition stands as a witness and authorization against oppression, it is also a powerful alternative to repression. This tradition is relentlessly public in its orientation, and it resists any psychologizing. Nonetheless, where individual persons find themselves in bondage in more intimate ways, there is no doubt that this same witness to the God who claims these verbs is a powerful force for *personal* emancipation. As the power of death may take many forms, so also Yahweh's power of life is said to be operative in every dimension of life where issues of liberated existence are at stake.

Yahweh, the God Who Commands

In its most pervasive testimony, the witness of the Old Testament asserts: "Observe what I command (*ṣwh*) you today" (Exod 34:11). Commandment dominates Israel's witness about Yahweh. Yahweh is a sovereign ruler whose will for the world is known and insisted upon. Israel as the addressee of command exists and prospers as it responds in obedience to these commands.

Verbs of Command

Yahweh is a God who commands (*ṣwh*). The foremost mode by which Yahweh communicates to Israel is by commandment (*miṣwāh*), and Israel's crucial mode of engagement with Yahweh is by obedience (*šmʿ*).[62] In a few scattered, likely late

---

60. Michael Walzer, *Exodus and Revolution* (New York: Basic Books, 1986).

61. Still a basic treatment of the issue from a particular perspective is Jacques Ellul, *The Technological Society* (London: Jonathan Cape, 1965).

62. On obedience as definitional for faith in God and knowledge of God, see from a Christian perspective, John Calvin, *Institutes of the Christian Religion* (LCC 20; Philadelphia: Westminster Press,

references, verbs such as "say" (*'mr*) (Pss 106:34, 107:25) and "speak" (*dbr*) (Num 27:23) are used as parallels for "command" (*ṣwh*). But this one verb dominates the utterance of this commanding God toward this people.

There is nothing difficult in properly understanding this claim of Yahweh. The commandment is understood as an utterance of a lordly sovereign who has a legitimate right to command, who expects rightly to be obeyed, and who has the power to match legitimacy in order to enforce the commands. Israel, conversely, is the community that understands itself as bound in this relationship of obedience, sometimes accepting its role in glad compliance, sometimes acting in resistance and recalcitrance to Yahweh's command. Yahweh's linkage to this verb is elemental for the Old Testament and is *perhaps Yahweh's defining and characteristic marking.* Yahweh's command dominates the Sinai tradition (Exod 19:1–Num 10:10) and the Book of Deuteronomy (chapters 12–25), so that a large portion of Israel's core literature (the Torah) is given over to the commandments of Yahweh. Israel's preoccupation with these commands is ongoing and intense, in every season of its life.[63]

In Israel's core story (or credo), Israel is at the outset under the command of pharaoh. Pharaoh commanded Israel: "Go and get straw yourselves, wherever you can find it; but your work will not be lessened in the least" (Exod 5:10-11). The command of pharaoh, infused by his fierce powers of state, was burdensome and finally unbearable. The Exodus narrative, which creates the context for the encounter at Sinai, is the tale of Yahweh wresting Israel from enslavement to the commands of pharaoh and bringing Israel under the command of Yahweh. Thus it is the exchange of one command for another.[64] When Israel came under this alternative command of Yahweh at the outset, Israel willingly obeyed (Exod 19:8).

The Exodus was not a contextless emancipation. Rather, it was an exchange of overlords. Thus the new overlord can say:

> For they are my servants, whom I brought out of the land of Egypt; they shall not be sold as slaves are sold. (Lev 25:42)

Israel is a "slave" (or "servant," *'ebed*) to Yahweh and shall not be a slave to anyone else. Israel's life is fully under the governance of Yahweh, whom Israel is bound to obey, because Yahweh is the new "owner" of Israel.

As Exodus is not a contextless emancipation, so the commands of Yahweh at Sinai do not replicate absolute Egyptian power; Yahweh, moreover, is not a sovereign like pharaoh. That is, the new "command society" of Sinai is one of dig-

---

1960), 1:72; and from a Jewish perspective, Abraham Heschel, *Who Is Man?* (Stanford, Calif.: Stanford University Press, 1965) 97–98 and passim.

63. On the commandments as decisive for the life and faith of Israel, see Eckart Otto, *Theologische Ethik des Alten Testaments* (Stuttgart: W. Kohlhammer, 1994).

64. See Walter Brueggemann, "Pharaoh as Vassal: A Study of a Political Metaphor," *CBQ* 57 (1995) 27–51.

nity, freedom, and well-being. It is important not to stress the command structure of Sinai without appreciating the emancipatory impulse of Yahweh. Conversely, it is impossible to appreciate the emancipatory impulse of Yahweh, operative in the Exodus narrative, without paying close attention to the command structure of Sinai.

Yahweh's Primal Command

The meeting at Sinai, which will come to occupy a large portion of Israel's core literature, is presented as the occasion whereby the terms of the new bondage to the new overlord are made explicit. At the outset, it is decreed that obedience to the voice of Yahweh and to the covenant are the nonnegotiable conditions of this relationship (Exod 19:5) to which Israel assents (Exod 19:8). The intensity of this claim is evident in the use of the absolute infinitive for the verb "obey," *šm'*. As the text stands, Israel assents to the commands of Yahweh, even before the commands have been uttered. That is, Israel signs a blank check of obedience.

The primal command of Yahweh, presented here as the First Commandment (Exod 20:1) but everywhere traded upon in the Sinai tradition, is the exclusive claim of loyalty from Israel to Yahweh.[65] This is not a claim of monotheism, as though there were no other gods. Indeed, the command precisely assumes a world of polytheism, in which there were other possible objects of loyalty. Other gods exist, some of whom may be attractive and may bid powerfully for the loyalty of Israel, but all other loyalties are precluded by Yahweh. Israel's work of obedience is to bring every aspect of its life under the direct rule of Yahweh.

As the drama of Israel—the drama of command—is presented, we may notice two formal features in the arrangement of Exodus 20, where the fundamental rule of Yahweh is enunciated. First, Exod 20:1-17 is presented as the direct utterance of Yahweh (20:1) and is preceded and followed by dramatic theophany (Exod 9:16-25; 20:18). Thus the theophanic narratives frame the ten commands and bracket them as the peculiar speech of Yahweh. No one but Yahweh issues these ten commands. Second, immediately after Exod 20:18, the people move to make Moses their authorized mediator, so that a human agent is authorized to speak, transmit, and interpret Yahweh's commands for Israel. By this twofold arrangement, Israel has at the same time asserted the ultimacy of God's command and provided a practical, available device for ongoing instruction and discipline. Both of these are necessary for the dynamic of the relationship between this God and this people, who are bound together by command.

The ten commands thus are situated so as to be the bedrock of Yahweh's intention for Israel, from which all other command in Israel is understood to be

---

65. Martin Luther, in his catechism, has provided the classic comment on the First Commandment. See also Edmund LaCherbonnier, *Hardness of Heart: A Contemporary Interpretation of the Doctrine of Sin* (London: Victor Gollancz, 1956), for a consideration of sin in a faith that insists on exclusive loyalty; and Martin Noth, "The Laws in the Pentateuch: Their Assumptions and Meaning," *The Laws in the Pentateuch and Other Essays* (London: Oliver and Boyd, 1966) 51 and passim, in his stress on exclusiveness as the hallmark of the commands of Yahweh.

derivative. A number of valuable expositions of the Ten Commandments exist, to which students will profitably attend.[66] Here we may make several observations about the ten commands that base Israel's life in obligation.

The commandments are introduced in the very utterance of Yahweh, as situated in the memory of the Exodus. *The God who commands is the God who delivers.*[67] Such a linkage suggests that the governance now to be enacted in and by Israel is not to replicate the governance of pharaoh, but is to establish a social rule contrasted with that of pharaoh. Stated another way, reference to the Exodus suggests that the theological intention of the Ten Commandments is to institutionalize the Exodus: to establish perspectives, procedures, policies, and institutions that will generate Exodus-like social relationships. The reason the commands are so urgent and insistent is that they are Yahweh's (and therefore Israel's) strategy for fending off a return to pre-Exodus conditions of exploitation and brutality within the community. Thus this linkage to the Exodus suggests that the commandments are policies to create a society that practices Yahweh's justice instead of pharaoh's injustice, and to establish neighborly well-being instead of coercion, fear, and exploitation. The Exodus, so Israel asserts, is not a one-time rescue; it is the liturgic memory that continues to propel the tradition of command in Israel and the ways in which Israelites will relate to Yahweh and to each other.

If one asks of the Ten Commandments what "policies" are indispensable for the institutionalization of the Exodus in order to preclude a return to pre-Exodus exploitation, one may consider each of the ten in response.[68] For our purposes, it will be sufficient to indicate *three lines of interpretation* that comprehend the ten commands.

First, the possibility of a viable alternative to Egyptian slavery requires *a Holy God who, as a critical principle, deabsolutizes every other claimant to ultimate power.* Thus the first three commands (Exod 20:2-7) assert the oddity of Yahweh, who has no utilitarian value and who cannot be recruited or used for any social or human agenda. The God who commands Israel is an end to be honored and obeyed, and not a means to be used and exploited. If it is correct, as Patrick D. Miller suggests, that an imageless quality is Yahweh's distinctive characteristic, then we may see in the prohibition of images an assertion of the unfettered character of Yahweh, who

---

66. Walter Harrelson, *The Ten Commandments and Human Rights* (OBT; Philadelphia: Fortress Press, 1980); and Brevard S. Childs, *Old Testament Theology in a Canonical Context* (Philadelphia: Fortress Press, 1985) 63–83.

67. On the interplay of *command* and *deliver* (*Aufgabe/Gabe*), see Emil Fackenheim, *God's Presence in History: Jewish Affirmations and Philosophical Reflections* (New York: New York University Press, 1970) 8–19, on the rubric of "Saving and Commanding Presence."

68. George M. Mendenhall, *Law and Covenant in Israel and in the Ancient Near East* (Pittsburgh: Biblical Colloquium, 1954), has made a distinction between "policy" and "technique," and has shown how the Ten Commandments function as policy for Israel. On the political aspects of Israel's faith, see Henning Graf Reventlow et al., eds., *Politics and Theopolitics in the Bible and Postbiblical Literature* (JSOTSup 171; Sheffield: Sheffield Academic Press, 1994).

will not be captured, contained, assigned, or managed by anyone or anything, for any purpose.[69]

Second, the commandments concerning human social relationships (Exod 20:12-17) seek to make human community possible by *setting limits to the acquisitive capacity of members of the community*—the capacity to seize and confiscate by power or by cunning what is necessary to the life of the neighbor. The commands require that the legitimacy (entitlement?) of other members of the community sets a limit on the autonomous capacity of any member of the community to take what another must have in order to live. It is not necessary to explicate each of these commandments to see that the commands lay down fundamental limitations that require each person to conduct himself/herself as a responsible member of the community. This set of limitations has in purview both the protection of persons and the protection of property. We may imagine that the protection of property is to be understood in the first instant not as a rule of property, but as a defense of the weak against the rapacious capacity of the strong.

Third, special attention may be paid to the fourth command on Sabbath (Exod 20:8-11), where *we find at the core of creation the invitation to rest*. Alternatively, the Sabbath commandment in its Deuteronomic version (Deut 5:12-15) is rooted in the Exodus memory and concerns rest for slaves. The juxtaposition of *creation* (Exod 20:8-11) and *rest for slaves* (Deut 5:12-15) nicely articulates Israel's characteristic way of linking cosmic and concrete social realities. In commenting on the Deuteronomic version of this command, Patrick Miller has proposed that the commandment, at least in the tradition of Deuteronomy, occupied the central position in the Decalogue, and looks both backward and forward.[70] It looks backward to the rule of Yahweh and imagines that Yahweh on the seventh day was either spent and needed rest—thus vulnerable—or was serenely situated in creation and able to be at ease. Either way, the conduct of Yahweh on the seventh day is in sharp contrast to the world of pharaoh, in which there is no rest but only feverish productivity. The command on Sabbath also looks forward: to a human community, an Israelite community peaceably engaged in neighbor-respecting life that is not madly engaged in production and consumption, but one that knows a limit to such activity and so has at the center of its life an enactment of peaceableness that bespeaks the settled rule of Yahweh. Moreover, as Sabbath became increasingly a distinguishing mark of Jews in the world, this commandment provides a way in which Jewishness can be visibly enacted, in order to exhibit the claim that Jewishness is indeed an alternative way of being in the world; alternative to the exploitative ways of the world that begin in self-serving idolatry and end in destructive covetousness.

---

69. See Patrick D. Miller, "Israelite Religion," *The Hebrew Bible and Its Modern Interpreters* (ed. Douglas A. Knight and Gene M. Tucker; Philadelphia: Fortress Press, 1985) 211–12; and Walter Brueggemann, "A Shape for Old Testament Theology II: Embrace of Pain," *CBQ* 47 (1985) 395–415.

70. Patrick D. Miller, "The Human Sabbath: A Study in Deuteronomic Theology," *Princeton Theological Seminary Bulletin* 6 (1985) 81–97.

The Ten Commandments are a crucial line of defense against the destructive nihilism in the world. Nihilism, the conviction that there are no reliable values, may be expressed in high-powered rhetoric. The true appearance of nihilism, however, is not in some philosophical argument, but in the brickyard of pharaoh where human life is completely exploitable, a deep, deathly disorder that is located not far from the ovens at Auschwitz. The God who commands knows very well what the exploitative commands of pharaoh will yield, and knows as well an alternative set of commands that authorize another way in the world. And to these alternative commands, Israel assents (Exod 24:3, 7).

Moses' Interpretation

Thus far we have considered only the utterance that the tradition has in the mouth of Yahweh, the one sandwiched between the theophanic notices in Exodus 19 and 20. It remains for us now to consider the derivative, interpretive, instrumental work of Moses concerning the vitality and pertinence of the command of Yahweh. In Exod 20:19-21, Moses is accepted by Israel as the true voice of the command of Yahweh. It is plausible, as we understand the history of command in ancient Israel, that many interpretive voices over time did their part in the formation of the final form of the Torah. For our theological purposes, however, it is Moses alone who enacts interpretation of the command of Yahweh. *Moses is regarded as the single, unrivaled voice of interpretation.*

Concentric circles of command. As we seek to understand this mass of command material in Israel's testimony, we may approach the extensive work of Moses in two ways. First, in a rough sort of way we may see this large material of command in concentric circles, concerning at its center the most intimate and local (perhaps early) issues of community life and then moving expansively in other directions. The purpose of such a scenario of interpretation is to suggest that Israel's interpretive work brings all of life, every detail of it—public and personal, cultic and economic—under the aegis of the God of the Exodus. Especially notable as an example of this enterprise is Exod 21:1–23:19, which appears to be early material concerned with interactions in a small, agrarian community, addressing matters as mundane as loose livestock (22:5) and as urgent as the physical abuse of a slave (21:20-21).[71] Other attempts to expand the scope of Yahweh's rule come in the set of commands in Exod 34:11-26.

Following the concentric circles outward, the Book of Deuteronomy plays a peculiar and crucial role in the articulation of Yahweh's command. Deuteronomy, with the legal corpus of chapters 12–25 at its center, is not integrally related to the Sinai tradition as such. Indeed, we are told that this utterance of Moses occurred at a later time and in a different place (Deut 1:1-5; 5:3). The horizon of Deuteronomy is not the desert severity of Sinai, but the risks, threats, dangers, and potential of life in the new land. On the plains of Moab, Moses not only reiterates the

---

71. On the covenant code see Dale Patrick, *Old Testament Law* (London: SCM Press, 1986) 63–96.

commands of Sinai (Deut 5:6-21), but he "expounds" them (1:5) so that they may be pertinent to the new time and place of Israel (5:3). The law proclamation of the Book of Deuteronomy helps Israel to make the transition from a seminomadic to an agrarian peasant economy. As such, the substance of the book has intrinsic interest. In this proclamation, Moses insists that Yahweh's intention for an alternative community pertains as directly to an agrarian society as it did to a pre-land venue. Thus the interpretation represented by Deuteronomy must take up all manner of new social issues, such as kingship, cities of refuge, the charging of interest, runaway slaves—issues that were not on the horizon of the Sinai proclamation.

Along with this intrinsic interest in the material of Deuteronomy as such, the book's proclamation has another important point for us. The Book of Deuteronomy is so named from the Greek rendering of Deut 17:18, which speaks of a "copy" (*deuteros*) of the Torah. A "second" can be a *copy*, but it can also be, as it appears to be here, a second *version* of the commands. That is, the Book of Deuteronomy is the primary exemplar in the Bible of the dynamic of the Torah, whereby the Torah insists on regular, authoritative restatement in order to keep the command of Yahweh current to the time, place, and circumstance in which the people of the command live.[72] Moses surely believes that there is no circumstance in which Yahweh does not will something concrete. But all of that is not known ahead of time. It is known only in the moment of new utterance "today" when given by the authorized interpreter.

Social justice and purity: Two trajectories. The second way in which we may understand the Mosaic articulation of Yahweh's command in the Old Testament is by twin trajectories that are in tension with each other.[73] The entire substance of command is attributed to Moses and serves the core affirmation of Yahweh's exclusive claim to governance over Israel. But very different expositions of that core claim can be given, and were given in Israel over time.

One trajectory is aimed at the practice of *social justice* and is found primarily, though not exclusively, in the Book of Deuteronomy. Deuteronomy most consistently contrasts the recommended modes of Israelite obedience with the ways of the Canaanites.[74] At the center of this tradition of command is the sabbatic principle, which we have seen to be rooted in the Decalogue (Exod 20:8-11; Deut 5:12-15). The sabbatic principle holds that on a regular basis, the rhythms of a life of faith require a cessation of all activity as an act of acknowledging the rule

---

72. See Walter Brueggemann, *Finally Comes the Poet: Daring Speech for Proclamation* (Minneapolis: Fortress Press, 1989) 79–110; and "The Commandments and Liberated, Liberating Bonding," *Interpretation and Obedience: From Faithful Reading to Faithful Living* (Minneapolis: Fortress Press, 1991) 145–58, for the suggestion that the Decalogue in ancient Israel is "completely non-negotiable, endlessly negotiated."

73. On this tension, see Fernando Belo, *A Materialist Reading of the Gospel of Mark* (Maryknoll, N.Y.: Orbis Books, 1981) 1–86.

74. The term *Canaanite* in the tradition of Deuteronomy is clearly an ideological term referring to all practices that resist or subvert covenant. Against such "Canaanite" ways, the tradition of Deuteronomy champions covenantal justice.

of Yahweh and handing one's life back to Yahweh in gratitude.[75] A comparison of the Sabbath command in Exod 20:8-11 and Deut 5:12-15 indicates that the command may be variously rooted in creation or in exodus, both elements of Israel's narrative testimony.

In the command tradition of Deuteronomy, Deut 15:1-11 may be proposed as the central and signature affirmation of Yahweh's rule.[76] The basic command (15:1) perhaps reflects an older command in Exod 21:2-11 concerning a remission of debts granted every seventh year. The seventh-year provision allows that members of the community in bondage for nonpayment of debts can be held in lieu of payment for only six years, no matter how large the debt or what the circumstance may be. Thus the cause of bondage is indebtedness, and the end of bondage consists in debt cancellation. The intention of the command is that maintenance of viable community and protection of the dignity of each of its members are more important to this community of obedience than is the flat reality of an economic transaction. The economic transaction is submitted to the viability of the social fabric.[77] In effect, Israel refuses the permanent underclass that long-term indebtedness is sure to produce.

The exposition of the command, in addressing modes of implementation, makes a strong appeal that the creditor should be generous with the debtor; five infinitive absolutes are used to mark the force and urgency of this social requirement (vv. 7-11). It is required, moreover, that when the debtor is released from debt, he will be given ample economic wherewithal so that he has both economic viability and dignity as he reenters the life of the community as a freed person. In the end, the exposition of this command departs from the detail of the act itself and makes a more general statement about care for the poor and needy neighbor (v. 11). This command is a radical proposal for the economic administration of an alternative community. This is indeed an Exodus ethic, for Israel could well remember that it was an exaggerated debt that first led to bondage in Egypt (Gen 47:13-21), and it was an exaggerated debt that produced Israel's helpless state of suffering (cf. Exod 2:23-24).

To be sure, not all of the commands in Deuteronomy are so committed to this radical vision of social possibility. But provisions are made for runaway slaves (23:15-16), for refusal to charge interest to Israelites (23:19-20), for protection

---

75. See Matitiahu Tsevat, "The Basic Meaning of the Biblical Sabbath," *The Meaning of the Book of Job and Other Biblical Studies: Essays on the Literature and Religion of the Hebrew Bible* (New York: KTAV, 1980) 39–52.

76. On this text, see Jeffries Hamilton, *Social Justice: The Case of Deuteronomy 15* (SBLDS 15; Atlanta: Scholars Press, 1992). Patrick Miller has paid particular attention to the sabbatic principle. More generally, see Moshe Weinfeld, *Social Justice in Ancient Israel and in the Ancient Near East* (Minneapolis: Fortress Press, 1995).

77. See Michael Polanyi, *The Great Transformation: The Political and Economic Origins of Our Time* (Boston: Beacon Press, 1957), on the ways in which the economy was understood as a part of the social fabric and the ways in which the economy was wrenched out of the social fabric, to take on a life of its own. More broadly, see also M. Douglas Meeks, *God the Economist: The Doctrine of God and Political Economy* (Minneapolis: Fortress Press, 1989).

against kidnapping (24:7), against seizure of a poor person's property as equity for a loan (24:10-13), for prompt payment of wages to the poor (24:14-15), for care of the socially marginated (24:17-18, 21-22), and for the maintenance of the dignity of an offender (25:1-3). It is clear that *this tradition of command intends that social power must be in the service of justice:*

> You must not distort justice; you must not show partiality; and you must not accept bribes, for a bribe blinds the eyes of the wise and subverts the cause of those who are in the right. Justice, and only justice, you shall pursue, so that you may live and occupy the land that the Lord your God is giving you. (Deut 16:19-20)

The justice that is proposed and for which concrete implementation is provided, moreover, is a social practice in which the maintenance, dignity, security, and well-being of every member of the community are guarded in concrete ways. This trajectory of Yahweh's command, in the mouth of Moses, offers a revolutionary notion of the ways in which economics must be practiced, whereby the community has active responsibility for the well-being of each of its members.

The sabbatic principle comes to its most complete articulation in Leviticus 25. In that speech, two practices are urged upon Israel as the will of Yahweh. First, the land itself shall be subject to the sabbatic principle (vv. 1-7)—the land shall have periodic rest from cultivation. This may be a wise principle of agriculture, so that the land is not exhausted from overuse. In the total witness of Israel, however, this practice of Jubilee for the land is to be understood as an acknowledgment of creation, as respect for creation, and as awareness that the land belongs to Yahweh and not to Israel. This remarkable chapter enunciates the practice of the Jubilee year, a celebration of the fiftieth year (after seven sevens), in which there will be a return to one's property and one's family—a homecoming—and in which family land that has been forfeited in the normal transactions of business is returned.[78] This is a remarkable provision, for it relativizes all economic transactions for the sake of rootage in the community. It is also a wise and cunning provision, for it recognizes the limitations of the practice (vv. 29-33) and the capacity for exploitation and opportunity to take advantage that are present in the provision itself (vv. 13-17).

Through all of the provisions for land and for family, at the core stands the repeated claim of the governance of Yahweh (v. 17). Yahweh is the God who enacted the Exodus (vv. 38, 42, 55) and who now proposes social practices designed to perpetuate the Exodus community. It is difficult to imagine a more radical social possibility than the sabbatic principle, particularly as it leads to the Jubilee year. The intention of the command is that Israel's regular, daily transactions should

---

78. On the theological pertinence of the Jubilee as an ethical reference point, see John Howard Yoder, *The Politics of Jesus: Vicit Agnus Noster* (Grand Rapids: Eerdmans, 1975) 64–77; Marie Augusta Neal, *A Socio-theology of Letting Go: The Role of a First World Church Facing Third World Peoples* (New York: Paulist Press, 1977) 5–7; and Sharon Ringe, *Jesus, Liberation, and the Jubilee Year: Images for Ethics and Christology* (OBT; Philadelphia: Fortress Press, 1985).

be shot through with the radicality of Yahwism, for the God who commands, commands precisely certain acts and policies that pertain to the lived reality and practice of social power.

Because the provision is so radical, it is not surprising that the question often arises, "There is no evidence, is there, that Israel ever in fact implemented this command?" I am asked this question more often than a like question of any other command in the Bible. Moreover, the question is usually asked negatively, as if the inquirer hopes to receive assurance that even Israel did not practice this radical act—perhaps hopes for practical reassurance against Israel's radical social vision and Yahweh's radical requirement. We do not know if Israel "practiced" this radical vision, just as we do not know if Israel did much else about which this text testifies. Jeremiah 34 and Nehemiah 5 contain evidence that this visionary law was on the horizon of Israel. And it is likely that the poetic scenario of Isa 61:2, which refers to "the year of the Lord's favor," is an allusion to the year of Jubilee. *Whether it was "practiced" or not, however, there the provision sits in the text,* the culminating assertion of the God of Sinai (who is the God of the Exodus), who intends a very different regimen of social wealth and social power. Indeed, the function and character of the political economy are shaped very differently in this horizon. The relative importance of wealth and social fabric is, from our conventional vantage point, precisely inverted. That is, the social fabric has the political economy as its instrument, unlike our practice, where the social fabric receives the leftovers of the political economy.

The second trajectory of command, also derivative from the exclusive claim of Yahweh, is that of *purity.* Moses is also linked to this tradition of command, though Gerhard von Rad has noticed that in this cluster of texts, we are given direct address of Yahweh to Moses rather than the address of Moses to Israel.[79] This material is found largely in the Priestly tradition of the Pentateuch, especially but not exclusively in Leviticus; articulations of it occur in Deuteronomy as well. The God who commands at Sinai is a God of order, who wills that all of life should be lived, according to this tradition, in an orderly way. It is plausible that the tradition of debt cancellation that we have just considered reflects the theological needs and sensibilities of the economically disadvantaged. In complementary fashion, it is plausible that this tradition of purity in the Book of Leviticus reflects the theological sensibilities and needs of those who experience life as profoundly disordered, and who have no doubt (and so testify) that Yahweh has provided concrete disciplines whereby the life-threatening disorder may be overcome.

If we imagine that this tradition of command is Yahweh's response to such disorder, we may suggest that the disorder experienced as life-threatening can take many forms. It may be viewed as the surging of chaos on the grand scale of cosmos, to which the liturgy of creation is an antidote of order. It may be a social experience of disorder, which in Israel may refer especially to the loss of the Jerusalem temple

---

79. Gerhard von Rad, *Studies in Deuteronomy* (SBT 9; London: SCM Press, 1953) 25–36.

and king and the profound displacement of exile. Or it may be experienced more immediately as a moral disintegration in which life is deeply marked by behavior that is felt to be contaminating, thereby placing everything in jeopardy. In actual experience it is not possible or necessary to distinguish between these dimensions of the problem. The disorder may be present in a host of ways, all of which are of a piece, and all of which are massively threatening.[80]

In such an arena of disorder, which may indeed be large and deep and ominous, it is not surprising that one should look to Yahweh, the Creator of heaven and earth, to counter the chaos with a powerful ordering and continual reordering of creation. More specifically, it is plausible that the ordering activity of Yahweh, in the face of such a threat, should be activated in public worship, where life may be experienced in order, symmetry, coherence, and propriety. *The enactment of such worship serves as a powerful counter-act to the threat of disorder.* Thus much of the "command of order" is given as an instrument to the priests, so that the priests can wisely and rightly order worship space, time, and activity, whereby worship becomes an environment for a God-given order available nowhere else. We may imagine that the depth, intensity, and specificity of order authorized in the text are commensurate to experienced disorder, even to a degree that we might regard as punctilious. It is crucial that the authorized enactment of order should fully match—or perhaps overmatch—the concrete threat of disorder.

Thus the priestly installation, given by Yahweh to Moses at great length, prescribes the proper course of sacrifices and offerings, for it is important that one should come properly to the presence of the Guarantor of order (Leviticus 1–7). The authorization and empowerment of these priests, now held accountable for a right ordering of life, is to be carefully done in an act of ordination, so that the action of the priests may be trusted as reliable and valid (Leviticus 8–10). Like provision is made for the right ordering of food (Leviticus 11), the purification of women after childbirth (Leviticus 12), and the management of bodily discharges (Leviticus 15). There is an element of practical hygiene in all of this (cf. Leviticus 13–14), as disease in such a social context is understood as a religious phenomenon that can only be managed in religious ways.[81]

The threats of disorder are not primarily understood to be moral. Rather, the power of disorder is palpable, material, physical, and can be managed only by careful and powerful attention. The power of disorder that is reflected in these texts and contained by the command of Yahweh is difficult for us to grasp in our scientific milieu. I suggest two analogues for our own time. First, the palpable threat of contamination is not unlike the danger posed by nuclear waste products that cannot

---

80. On the creation liturgy of Gen 1:1–2:4a and the Priestly tradition more generally as responses to the chaotic reality of exile, see Robert B. Coote, *In the Beginning: Creation and the Priestly History* (Minneapolis: Fortress Press, 1991).

81. See Baruch A. Levine, "Magic, Purity, and Biblical Monotheism," *In the Presence of the Lord: A Study of Cult and Some Cultic Terms in Ancient Israel* (SJLA 5; Leiden: E. J. Brill, 1974) 77–91; and Mary Douglas, *Purity and Danger: An Analysis of the Concepts of Pollution and Taboo* (Boston: Ark Paperbacks, 1984) 41–57.

be willed away but must be managed, and that persist as threat for all foreseeable future. Second, the management of toxic waste products such as mercury requires careful, legal supervision, for the threat cannot be wholly detoxified, even by our technological finesse. In a similar matter, impurity in this ancient world must have been a profound threat to sensitivity as well an actual physical threat. The remarkable thing about this trajectory of command is that the God of Sinai graciously attends to this enterprise and sanctions procedures, practices, and agents by which an ordered, reliable, livable life is maintained and guaranteed. It will not do for us to regard this tradition of purity as primitive and therefore obsolete, for the issues are still with us, even when they gather around different sorts of threats.

The focus of this tradition of holiness, which we may find rooted in the first three commands of the Decalogue, is that those zones of life that are inhabited by Yahweh in an intense way must be kept pure and uncontaminated.[82] Thus this material is instructional and has a status not unlike canon law to protect such zones of holiness and, in a more general way, to prevent the disordering power of impurity from disrupting the life of Israel. The great threat to holiness that can jeopardize the presence of Yahweh in the community of Israel is to create a disorder by mixing things in ways that confuse and distort.[83] The antidote to such confusion is to sort out and make distinctions, so that nothing is wrongly mixed that will disturb the order that belongs to the holiness of the Creator. The distinctions that make for order may concern quite ordinary matters (cf. Deut 22:9-11), or they may concern such freighted issues as the danger of a corpse (cf. Hag 2:11-13). In any case, it is the work of priestly instruction to maintain orderly distinctions. And when this practice of making distinctions is neglected, trouble comes upon the community:

> Its priests have done violence to my teaching and have profaned my holy things; they have made no distinction between the holy and the common, neither have they taught the difference between the unclean and the clean, and they have disregarded my sabbaths, so that I am profaned among them. (Ezek 22:26)

Perhaps inevitably, order is not maintained, impurity enters into the life of the community, so that processes need to be initiated in order to overcome the threat to the community. Profaned elements of the community must be sanctified, made holy, so that they are congruent with the Holy God, for "You shall be holy as I am holy." This tradition of command aims at reestablishing holiness when the community is in jeopardy. This tradition of "making holy" when "being holy" has failed

---

82. The notion of holiness in the Priestly traditions is regarded as almost physical in its force and in its threat. See Philip P. Janzen, *Graded Holiness: A Key to the Priestly Conception of the World* (JSOTSup 106; Sheffield: JSOT Press, 1992); and John G. Gammie, *Holiness in Israel* (OBT; Minneapolis: Fortress Press, 1989) 9–70.

83. This general approach to holiness in the cultic traditions of Israel is especially rooted in the anthropological studies of Douglas, *Purity and Danger*, 41–57; and *In the Wilderness: The Doctrine of Defilement in the Book of Numbers* (JSOTSup 158; Sheffield: JSOT Press, 1993).

culminates in the provision for the Day of Atonement (*yôm kippur*) in Leviticus 16, which seems to live at the edge of the biblical text.

It is clear that the process of making holy is a priestly activity authorized by Yahweh, that it must be done with care and punctiliousness, and that it aims at covering the impurity that endangers the community. The problem addressed in the prescribed ritual activity is "the uncleannesses (*ṭm'*) of the people of Israel" (v. 19):

> For on this day atonement (*kapper*) shall be made for you, to cleanse you (*ṭhr*); from all your sins you shall be clean (*ṭhr*) before the Lord. (v. 30)

It is unfortunate that the nature of *kippur* has been conventionally translated as "atonement" and then popularly understood by Christians as "at-one-ment," for such a translation suggests a relational concern, as though the ritual restores a relationship. The rhetoric of the ritual, however, suggests not restored *relationship*, but *containment of a material threat* in the form of uncleanness. When the material threat is banished, Yahweh can again take up presence in the holy place. This is a metaphor that moves very differently from any romantic notion of relationship.[84]

Both the Deuteronomic emphasis on *justice* and the Priestly accent on *holiness* have moved some considerable interpretive distance from the core commands of Sinai. Precisely such interpretive dynamic marks the command tradition of Sinai, for Yahweh is endlessly at work in new ways of reasserting, reclaiming, and extending sovereignty. It is equally clear that these trajectories of command serve very different sensibilities and live in profound tension with each other. The tradition of justice concerns the political-economic life of the community and urges drastic transformative and rehabilitative activity. The tradition of holiness focuses on the cultic life of the community and seeks a restoration of a lost holiness, whereby the presence of God can again be counted on and enjoyed. No doubt these trajectories reflect needs at different times and in different circumstances in the life of Israel and respond to different sensibilities on the part of Israel's authorized interpretive agents. Both trajectories belong crucially to the horizon of command for the God of Israel. The justice command witnesses to Yahweh's preferential option for the ordering of a neighborly community. The holiness commands evidence the claim that God's preoccupation is with God's own life, which must remain protected from all profanation. One tradition looks toward the neighbor; the other looks toward the well-being of Yahweh.

The maintenance of the tension between these two interpretive trajectories, I suggest, is crucial in Israel's testimony that God is *"for us,"* but that God is also jealously *for God's own self* and takes with dreadful seriousness every threat of profanation to God's own life (cf. Ezek 36:22-23). In subsequent reflection, a conventional Christian interpretation of the Old Testament is likely to favor the justice

---

84. Thus the work of reconciliation and rehabilitation is not simply a matter of loving inclination, but it is a matter of the careful management of those powerful elements of distortion that jeopardize the relationship. For this reason forgiveness must be a carefully observed sacramental process, and not simply a decree.

tradition at the expense of the holiness tradition. There is a very old assumption among Christians that the ethical commands of the Old Testament continue to pertain to Christians, while the cultic commands can be left behind. Fernando Belo has made a powerful case that, at least in the Gospel of Mark, Jesus champions the tradition of justice, and his scorned opponents are advocates of the holiness tradition.[85] Evidence exists to support such an argument, and my own sympathies tend to correspond with this conclusion.

Before making such a judgment, however, we must ponder three reasons for resisting the diminishment of the holiness commands that stand at the core of Israel's testimony about the God who commands. First, at least in Hebrews 7–10, it is clear that the Christian community continued to value the holiness commands, for the rhetoric of these chapters finds the imagery of sacrifice and atonement crucial for a full articulation of the significance, authority, and identity of Jesus. This imagery, moreover, is operative in much Christian piety that cherishes speech and imagery about blood atonement. Even in Paul's witness to the saving work of Jesus, the use of the term *ilasterion* or "means of expiation" (Rom 3:25) suggests that Pauline Christianity continued to rely on the imagery and significance of the holiness tradition in order to articulate the radicalness of its claim for Jesus.

Second, ample evidence shows that the tradition of justice commands, by themselves, can move in the direction of a purely political program. That is, the commands of justice, taken by themselves, easily become separated from the theological, Yahwistic matrix in which they are given to Israel. It is credible that it is the tradition of holiness that keeps the life of obedience from becoming a self-propelled human crusade in the world. Taken together, the two trajectories reflect the internal disciplines of identity that balance the external disciplines of transformative activity.[86] If the commands of holiness are taken by themselves and separated from the commands of justice, a like distortion happens in the opposite direction. Then the community of obedience may become an insulated operation, excessively preoccupied with the quality of its own life. (See Isaiah 56 for a critique of such a temptation.)

Third, it is evident that the current and freighted dispute in the U.S. church concerning homosexual persons, especially their ordination, indicates the continuing felt cruciality of the tradition of holiness, even after we imagine we have moved beyond such "primitiveness." It is my impression that the question of equal rights and privileges for homosexuals (in civil society as in the church) is a question that may be adjudicated on the grounds of justice. It is equally my impression, however, that the enormous hostility to homosexual persons (and to proposals of justice for them) does not concern issues of justice and injustice, but rather concerns the more

---

85. Belo, *A Materialist Reading of the Gospel of Mark.*

86. Richard L. Rubenstein, *After Auschwitz: Radical Theology and Contemporary Judaism* (Indianapolis: Bobbs-Merrill, 1966) 103, rightly concludes: "The customary dichotomy between the sacrificial and the moral types of religion cannot withstand examination."

elemental issues of purity—cleanness and uncleanness.[87] This more elemental concern is evidenced in the widespread notion that homosexuals must be disqualified from access to wherever society has its important stakes and that physical contact with them is contaminating.

The urge for order, the manifest experience of disorder, and the resilient reality of Yahweh's holiness suggest that the core alienation and vexations of human life cannot finally be managed in terms of morality. Something unmanageable, inscrutable, and mysterious about these alienations and vexations suggests the abiding importance of Israelite texts about sacrifice as "the mechanism of holiness."

I do not suggest the direct and simple utilization of such texts and their practices, for they are exceedingly problematic. I do, however, suggest that what the "sacrificial system" seeks to do is not outgrown through enlightenment and sophistication. After human efforts at righting wrongs and making reparations have been done as fully as possible, an unsettled "residue of ache" remains that requires another kind of action, action in a priestly domain.[88]

The sacrificial system of ancient Israel attests both to the generous availability of Yahweh to Israel and the ominous, unapproachable holiness of Yahweh. The sacrificial system mediates between availability and holiness. That arrangement of sacrifices has two recurring intentions, one that celebrates a good relation with Yahweh and one that redeems and rehabilitates a skewed relationship with Yahweh. Concerning the latter, Richard Rubenstein observes that sacrifice is "the drama of man's hatred of God and his ultimate submission to him."[89] Here it is my point only to insist that under the general rubric of holiness, the sacrificial system in the text is of theological significance and that this attestation on Israel's part has contemporary pertinence in the practice of faith that must push behind moral resolution to the enigmatic, where Yahweh's holiness is faced in all of its ominous, generous, enigmatic reality.

I do not suggest that the contemporary issue should be adjudicated in those terms or categories. But I do believe that the practice of holiness provides the categories whereby we may understand pastorally what is being sensed and felt in the massive hostility to homosexuals and their rights, and may help us see how a useful, responsible response to homophobia is to be made. The sensibilities of holiness and justice are not commensurate, and therefore an advocacy of justice does not meet the alarm experienced in what is felt to be uncleanness. It is my judgment that the adrenaline mobilized around this issue concerns much larger issues

---

87. Two influential studies have established that purity issues are more elemental than justice issues. Erik H. Erikson, *Identity and the Life Cycle* (New York: Norton, 1980) 67–87, has made clear that in personality development, shame precedes guilt. Paul Ricoeur, *The Symbolism of Evil* (Boston: Beacon Press, 1969), moreover, has shown that defilement is a much more elemental religious problem than is a moral dimension of obedience and disobedience. It is my judgment that the controversy over homosexuality in the church is propelled by a sense of shame and defilement, and therefore responses to the issue that move from concerns of morality do not touch the more serious aspects of the controversy. This is especially problematic for Protestantism that lacks sacramental density.

88. See Brueggemann, *Finally Comes the Poet.*

89. Rubenstein, *After Auschwitz,* 92.

of disorder than simply issues of sexuality, as most of the old reliabilities in our social world are now in jeopardy. As a consequence, large measures of social disorder, completely unrelated to the issue of homosexuality, are displaced and heaped upon this particular issue where uncleanness is felt to be operative. I cite this example to indicate that the issues evoked in these two very different testimonies to Yahweh's command are not at all old-fashioned. They are mandates and felt needs for transformative justice and for consolidating order that are seen to be linked to Yahweh's exclusive claim for loyalty. The way in which these issues surface in our society are surely parallel to the ways in which they surfaced in this community of intentional interpretation of Yahweh's command. This full range of Yahweh's commanding voice, including the large expanse of ongoing interpretation, must be engaged as the community of the text practices obedience.

Undoubtedly the tension between the felt threat of disorder (as currently expressed in the church around issues of homosexuality) and the voiced urgings of justice (as concerns full rights and dignity for homosexuals) will continue to be a disputed, vexed issue. My own judgment is that, following Fernando Belo in Christian extrapolations from the Old Testament, the justice trajectory has decisively and irreversibly defeated the purity trajectory. Thus the purity trajectory of the text may help us understand pastorally the anxiety produced by perceived and experienced disorder, but it provides no warrant for exclusionary ethical decisions in the face of the gospel.

Taken as a whole, the initial commands of Sinai, the concentric circles of command that apply to many zones of life, and the fuller trajectories of interpretation are to be understood as testimony to Yahweh's lordly, commanding capacity. The full and comprehensive testimony to Yahweh's command concerning justice and holiness asserts that Yahweh is a commanding sovereign who can enact sanctions against the disobedient. These sanctions, moreover, give moral reliability to the world over which Yahweh presides. The sanctions of covenant curse, punishment for those who violate oaths of obedience, may be enacted in a variety of ways, though Deuteronomy 28 and Leviticus 26 suggest a rather stock inventory of penalties and punishments. Israel envisioned a precise symmetry of act and outcome, so that those who obeyed received all the blessings of life—well-being, prosperity, fruitfulness, security, and land—and those who disobeyed received a negation of life, whether by extermination, exile, barrenness, or natural disaster (cf. Deut 30:15-20). The commands, together with the sanctions, constituted the life-world in which Israel proposed to live. That life-world offered its adherents enormous blessing and was known to be morally reliable. The violator of that life-world as willed by Yahweh was commensurately to receive all the deathliness that came with a denial of the governance of Yahweh.

Command beyond Sinai: Three Aspects of Larger Witness

Of all the elements of testimony in ancient Israel concerning Yahweh, and the verbs of which Yahweh was willing to be the subject, the phrasing, "what I command you today" permeates Israel's witness to Yahweh and consequently Israel's own self-understanding. In looking beyond Sinai, we may mention three aspects of that larger witness that are informed and shaped by this tradition of command.

First, the prophetic literature, understood canonically, is focused on a series of penalties and judgments that follow from disobedience.[90] Only twice can we identify in the prophets direct appeal to the Decalogue:

> Hear the word of the Lord,
> O people of Israel;
> for the Lord has an indictment
> against the inhabitants of the land.
> There is no faithfulness or loyalty,
> and no knowledge of God in the land.
> Swearing, lying, and murder,
> and stealing and adultery break out;
> bloodshed follows bloodshed. (Hos 4:1-2)

> Will you steal, murder, commit adultery, swear falsely,
> make offerings to Baal, and go after other gods
> that you have not known...? (Jer 7:9)

Everywhere in the prophetic literature that addresses Israel's life in the monarchy, the prophets articulate the jeopardy in which Israel lives because of its disregard of Yahweh's commands. Widely recognized and best known are those prophetic warnings voiced because Israel has violated Yahweh's core command for the practice of justice (Amos 5:7, 24; 6:12; Hos 6:6; 10:12; 12:6; Isa 5:7; Jer 4:2; 22:15-16). The prophets, for all their great variation, can now be understood as taking up the tradition of Mosaic command when Israel has failed in its work of obedience. While the prophetic materials focus extensively on the tradition of justice, we can also identify, at least in Ezekiel, a concern that trouble is coming upon Israel precisely because the priestly requirements for holiness have been violated and Jerusalem has been profaned.

Second, attention has recently been given to "Torah piety" in the Psalter.[91] It has long been recognized that Psalms 1, 19, and 119 are songs or poems that celebrate the cruciality of the Torah for the life of Israel and that find in obedience to the Torah the quintessential joy of faith. More recently, it has been shown that these particular Psalms are situated, in the final form of the text, at strategic places or seams in the Psalter and are intended to guide the reading of the entire Psalter.[92] Thus many psalms that likely originated in many contexts and for many purposes are now canonically subsumed under the Torah and are to be understood as practices of faith that flow from and eventuate in Torah obedience. Thus the piety

---

90. See Claus Westermann, *Basic Forms of Prophetic Speech* (Atlanta: John Knox, 1967).

91. See James L. Mays, "The Place of the Torah-Psalms in the Psalter," *JBL* 106 (1987) 3–12.

92. See especially Gerald H. Wilson, *The Editing of the Hebrew Psalter* (Chico, Calif.: Scholars Press, 1985).

of Israel, as the final form of the Psalter proposes it, is a glad obedience to the commands of Yahweh, enacted in full confidence that such obedience produces a life of joy, well-being, and blessing. Psalm 1 is reckoned, on this reading, to be an interpretive clue for the whole collection.[93]

Third, Gerhard von Rad has focused on Nehemiah 8, often taken as the pivotal event that generated and ordered Second Temple Judaism.[94] In this, he follows the rabbinic traditions that regarded Ezra as the second founder (after Moses) of Judaism. In the reported event of Nehemiah 8, the postexilic community is reconstituted by a reading and interpretation of the Torah. We cannot be sure how much of the larger text of the Pentateuch, or what sections, constituted the Torah that was read. Yet in the context of the reform instituted by Ezra and Nehemiah, the refounding of Judaism was clearly aimed at and constituted by obedience to the commands of Yahweh. It is this act that most characterizes Judaism in the world, and therefore the testimony of Israel is pervasive in its claim that Yahweh is most and best known as the One who commands.

Theological Reflections on Commandment and Covenant

This exposition of the commandments is sufficient for our characterization of the verbal testimony, "Yahweh who commands." But in Old Testament theology, in my judgment, one has an obligation to reflect on the theological significance of the commandment and on the characterization of Yahweh as the One who commands. It is an obligation for Old Testament theology that is evoked and made acute by the long temptation of Christianity to antinomianism, whereby law is considered extraneous to faith, an antinomianism that has fed the Western, Christian stereotype of Jews as legalist. It is an obligation, moreover, that is evoked by the moral autonomy championed in the ideology of modernity that has brought Western society to a sorry state of affairs, and in which Christianity has massively conspired. Christianity and modernity make common cause in this respect against Judaism.[95]

Clearly the law constituted a major preoccupation of early Christianity and a source of major conflict between Judaism in the first century and the Christian movement as it separated from Judaism and entered the larger Hellenistic world. Those issues, both concerning Jesus as the fulfillment of the law (Matt 5:17-20) and concerning Paul in his struggles for the freedom of the gospel, are profoundly complex and need not concern us here. It will suffice for our purposes to recognize that commandment is always, in Israel's faith, in the context of covenant, so that the commands of Yahweh are through and through covenantal commands. That is, the commands belong to, make possible, and function for a relationship of trust, fidelity, and submissiveness that is generous, but in which the two parties are not

---

93. See Walter Brueggemann, "Bounded by Obedience and Praise: The Psalms as Canon," *The Psalms and the Life of Faith* (Minneapolis: Fortress Press, 1995) 189–213; and Patrick D. Miller, *Interpreting the Psalms* (Philadelphia: Fortress Press, 1986) 81–86.

94. Von Rad, *Studies in Deuteronomy*, 13–14.

95. This is fundamental to the strictures of Jon D. Levenson, *The Hebrew Bible, the Old Testament, and Historical Criticism* (Louisville: Westminster/John Knox, 1993) 1–32, 82–126.

commensurate. It is unthinkable to Israel that the One who creates heaven and earth, who promises land to the ancestors, and who liberates a slave community to be a treasured possession should have no overriding intention related to and propelled by such transformative acts. It is precisely in the disclosure of commands at Sinai that Israel (and the nations) learn the purpose of all that has gone before. What Israel learns that is completely nonnegotiable in Yahweh's sovereignty is that Yahweh intends justice for the neighbor in the world (so Deuteronomy) and holiness in the presence of God (so the Priestly tradition).

To subsume command to the context of covenant with Yahweh means that questions of unconditionality and conditionality, an issue that has much preoccupied scholars, are questions that evaporate. A great deal of energy has been given to this issue.[96] It has been suggested often (by this writer among others) that the ancestral traditions of Genesis witness to an unconditional relation with Yahweh and the Mosaic traditions to a conditional covenant. Surely these several traditions are given very different nuances on this question. In the end, however, and taken as a theological datum, the command of Yahweh is relational and cannot be factored out as conditional or unconditional. Rather, like any thinkable relationship rooted in profound fidelity, this covenant relation is characteristically conditional and unconditional at the same time. Israel does not worry about that logical contradiction in the nature of its relation to Yahweh; thus this relationship is unconditional, because Yahweh is utterly committed to Israel. Yet the relationship is conditional, because Yahweh has large intentions that pertain, above all, to Israel. Different texts in different circumstances bear witness to the different nuances of that relationship. It is, in my judgment, a profound disservice of Christian and modern thought to tear command out of the context of covenant, and thus to distort by setting at odds law and gospel, or as Ernst Kutsch put it, "obligation" and "relationship."[97]

It well may be that in Paul's context, his opponents had come to treat the commands of Yahweh as positive law and therefore Paul goes behind command to covenant. Attention should be paid to the arguments of Krister Stendahl and E. P. Sanders, who claim that the Western tradition of Augustine and Luther has betrayed and distorted Paul.[98] I suggest that we are at a moment when Christians must rethink this question, and we may expect to be instructed by a Jewish sense of obedience, which is not informed by resistance to command, but is shaped by glad trust and gratitude. The Western tradition of Christian theology, especially in its Lutheran propensity, stands in some continuity with the autonomy of modernity as articulated by René Descartes and John Locke. Indeed, the entire project of

---

96. See David Noel Freedman, "Divine Commitment and Human Obligation," *Int* 18 (1964) 419–31.

97. Ernst Kutsch, "Gesetz und Gnade: Probleme des alttestamentliche Bundesbegriffs," *ZAW* 79 (1967) 18–35.

98. Krister Stendahl, "The Apostle Paul and the Introspective Conscience of the West," *Paul among Jews and Gentiles and Other Essays* (London: SCM Press, 1977) 78–96; and E. P. Sanders, *Paul and Palestinian Judaism: A Comparison of Patterns of Religion* (Philadelphia: Fortress Press, 1977).

modernity, expressed in Kant's autonomy and culminating in Freud's theory of re-pression, concerns emancipation from authority that impedes full maturation. Such a program, informed as it is by Western theology, surely misconstrues the com-manding authority of Yahweh, which is not coercive but generative, not repressive but emancipatory.

A student of Old Testament theology must think seriously about how this af-firmative tradition of obligation, rooted in the God who commands, is now to be appropriated in a Christian tradition tempted to antinomianism, and in a mod-ern tradition tempted by an illusion of autonomous freedom.[99] Two perspectives on the issue of obedience to command may be useful; both are faithful to Israel's testimony in recovering the tradition of command.

First, the obedience to which Israel is summoned in this testimony is "Exodus obedience." The God of Israel intends that the emancipatory power of the Exodus tradition should be a constant practice of Israel, permeating its public and insti-tutional life. Thus the commands, rightly understood, are not restraints as much as they are empowerments. Those who obey are able to participate in the ongoing revolution of turning the world to its true shape as God's creation.

Second, in its Torah piety, Israel understood Yahweh as the true subject of its desire (cf. Pss 27:4, 73:25), so that Israel wanted nothing so much as communion with Yahweh. This communion, which may have a mystic dimensions, is, however, rooted in obedience that is inescapably the first element of communion. Therefore Torah obedience corresponds to Israel's true desire. This most intrinsic of all desire can be misdirected and distorted, but it cannot finally be satisfied in any prac-tice except that of obedience to Yahweh.[100] Yahweh is indeed the ultimate joy of human desiring. Both notions of (a) participation in a revolution and (b) embrace of intrinsic desire are chances whereby the caricature of command as legalism may be overcome. It is distorting to imagine command outside of covenant; it is equally distorting to imagine covenant that has at its center anything other than command.

It is not excessively alarmist to say that our present acquisitive society, in its crisis of greed and brutality, is a society that tries to live outside of command. Such a way of life recognizes no limit, until finally such brutality arrives at the nihilism of Auschwitz. The truth of the testimony, "Yahweh who commands," is that *unfettered, autonomous freedom is in fact not available.* Life is fundamentally relational, and the One who instigates and stands as the source of life's relatedness is the God who commands. There is no doubt, according to this witness, that the practice of command sometimes becomes ideological and self-serving, as for example in the instance of Job's friends or with some of Jesus' opponents. Such distortion of the tradition of command has never been an excuse or invitation for

---

99. See Walter Brueggemann, "Duty as Delight and Desire," *Journal for Preachers* 18 (1994) 2–14.

100. Margaret R. Miles, *Desire and Delight: A New Reading of Augustine's Confessions* (New York: Crossroad, 1992), has shown how desire lies at the center of Augustine's notion of faith and obedience and at the core of his literary intention.

escape from the God who commands, for without such command creation reverts to chaos.[101]

Finally, we may notice the extraordinary linkage made in the prophetic appeal to the Decalogue:

> There is no faithfulness or loyalty,
> and no knowledge of God in the land.
> Swearing, lying, and murder,
> and stealing and adultery break out;
> bloodshed follows bloodshed.
> Therefore the land mourns,
> and all who live in it languish;
> together with the wild animals
> and the birds of the air,
> even the fish of the sea are perishing. (Hos 4:1-3)

The indictment offered by the prophet reflects the Decalogue and its prohibitions: swearing, lying, murder, stealing, adultery. The outcome of such disobedience is the failure of creation, at the cost of life to the wild animals, birds, and fish. *The claim of this testimony is that the viability of creation depends on keeping the commands.* When the commands are disregarded, creation disintegrates and reverts to chaos. The commands of Yahweh are not social conveniences or conventional rules. They are, according to this testimony, the insistences whereby life in the world is made possible. Sinai articulates what Yahweh has intended for the well-being of the earth.

Yahweh, the God Who Leads

In perhaps its most intimate testimony, the witness of the Old Testament asserts:

> Remember the long way that the Lord your God has led (*hlk*) you these forty years in the wilderness, in order to humble you, testing (*nsh*) you to know what was in your heart, whether or not you would keep his commandments. He humbled you by letting you hunger, then by feeding (*'kl*) you with manna, with which neither you nor your ancestors were acquainted.... (Deut 8:2-3)

Israel's testimony concerning Yahweh who leads concerns Yahweh's availability to Israel in every circumstance, Yahweh's readiness to enter into situations of risk, vulnerability, and exile, in order to be in dangerous and transformative solidarity with Yahweh's at-risk people.

---

101. Terence E. Fretheim, *Exodus* (Interpretation; Louisville: Westminster/John Knox, 1991), has deftly reinterpreted the Exodus narrative (and especially the plague cycle) with reference to the categories of creation and chaos. In such a reading, pharaoh is a chaotic disrupter of the order of creation, and not simply the oppressor of Israel.

Verbs of Leading, Testing, Feeding

The larger, louder testimony of Israel is that Yahweh "*brought us out* of Egypt and *brought us into* the land." These two assertions provide the spine of Yahweh's story line, as Israel tells it. A closer reading of the tale must deal with the period between the verb of exit and the verb of entrance. This in-between material is less assertive and smaller in quantity, but for that no less important.

The sojourn tradition has a journey motif that ostensibly holds the material together in a unity. The materials, however, strike one as more random and ad hoc than the greater traditions we have already considered. Such an occasion in the story line permits Israel to reflect on its life of vulnerability, when it is exposed to threats of death and at risk without sure resources, on the way in faith but without visible support systems. The story itself seems to require a telling different from the other verbal sentences we have considered. Here the memory is not so public and not so fully on display; there is no public reference point like pharaoh, and nothing so dramatic as Sinai occurs. Therefore the texture of what must be said of Yahweh is perhaps more intimate, though we must take care not to romanticize this aspect of the testimony of Israel.

Israel's theological reflection and testimony on this in-between moment in its life focuses on the contradiction to which Israel was subjected. The sojourn exposure was at the same time an occasion for risk and desperation, and for peculiar sustenance and care. This twofold horizon, which does not permit easy resolution, generates a two-sided testimony concerning Yahweh. On the one hand, Yahweh tests (*nsh*) Israel (Deut 8:2, 16; Exod 15:25; 16:4) in order to find out if Israel is serious in its loyalty to Yahweh. Thus the sojourn experience is a trial in a judicial sense, in order to measure Israel's allegiance to Yahweh. This verb attests to Yahweh's concern for Yahweh's own sovereignty. Yahweh will brook no rival, no anemic or cowardly practice of faith. Presumably, Israel would fail the test if it set up alternative loyalties that, in the imagination of Israel, would provide better provision in the wilderness, or if it abandoned Yahweh's leadership and resubmitted to the authority of pharaoh (Num 14:4). The use of the governing term "lead" is intensified by the additional verb "to humble you" (*'nh*)—to reduce Israel to drastic need and unambiguous dependence. This verb witnesses to the disputatious way in which Yahweh relates to Israel, the ominous tendency of Yahweh to deal with Israel for Yahweh's own sake, and the extreme measures to which Yahweh will go for the sake of Yahweh's own reputation, without reference to Israel's need (as in Genesis 22). Not that the entire motif of testing belies any claim of Yahweh's omniscience. Yahweh must test to find out what Yahweh does not yet know.

Yahweh's propensity to test is balanced (or, better stated, overcome) by the generous ministrations of Yahweh to Israel. Two principal motifs here attest to Yahweh's generous attentiveness, willingness, and capacity to overturn deathly circumstances for Israel, including the circumstance created by Yahweh's own readiness to test. Yahweh feeds Israel, and turns out to be a source of adequate food in a context where none seemed available. In addition to the witness of Deuteronomy 8, attention should be given to the narrative of Exodus 16, which is the paradigmatic event of Yahweh feeding Israel. In this narrative, the focus is especially on bread, which Yahweh wondrously supplies. The act of feeding is narrated as "a mighty deed." In many other contexts, the way in which God feeds is to be reckoned as an act of blessing, that is, as a gift from the natural produce of the fruitful earth (cf. Josh 5:12; Pss 104:27-28; 145:15-16). Here, however, the action of Yahweh is of quite another kind, having a dimension of wonder attached to it that makes it an action on a par with the deliverance from Egypt.

The verb "eat" is intensified in both Exodus 16:8 and Deut 8:10 by the verb *śb'*, "to be satisfied or satiated." The two verbs together, "eat and be satisfied," affirm Yahweh's extravagant generosity, which gives abundantly beyond Israel's need, and Israel's complete delight in Yahweh's abundance. Yahweh is the God who performs in situations of hazardous scarcity in order to generate abundance.

The second positive verb is "lead," here expressed as *hlk,* but elsewhere also as *nhl* (Exod 15:13) and *nḥh* (Exod 13:17, 21; Pss 77:20; 78:14, 52-53). This cluster of verbs bespeaks Yahweh's inordinate fidelity to Israel, in being with Israel in circumstances of high risk, willing to submit to the very circumstance of risk, and to assure Israel's safety and well-being. The leadership of Yahweh, characterized quite concretely, is to accompany Israel in danger, both to provide safe passage and to fend off threats. The wilderness, the place without life supports, cannot be safely traversed by Israel on its own resources. It is, one may imagine, almost inevitable that in telling this tale, Israel will employ pastoral-shepherd imagery for Yahweh.

This tradition witnesses to Yahweh's accompanying fidelity and to Yahweh's power to override circumstances of death for the sake of Israel. The motifs of testing and of feeding/leading/providing are kept in tension. In the end, however, it is the positive testimony that comes to prevail in the memory and witness of Israel.

We have termed this testimony one of intimacy (which may not be quite the correct term), because the evidence given points to incidental moments of care, and because the memories yield rather remarkable resources for Israel's life of faith. These verbs and their narrative usage witness to a time in the life of Israel when Israel is completely dependent and Yahweh is unexpectedly and attentively gracious, ministering to Israel's most elemental survival needs. This dimension of Israel's witness is situated in the midst of the most dominant narratives of the Pentateuch. But the same emphases show up in the very different practice of piety in the testimony of the Psalms.

The familiar Psalm 23, a statement of profound confidence in Yahweh, takes up both the aspects of leading and feeding, as well as accompaniment:

> ... he leads (*nhl*) me beside still waters; ...
> He leads (*nḥh*) me in right paths....
> you are with me;
> your rod and your staff—

they comfort (*nḥm*) me.
You prepare ('*rk*) a table before me
in the presence of my enemies.... (Ps 23:2-5)

These specific verbs whereby Yahweh ministers to Israel serve the more sweeping affirmation, "You are with me."

In something of a derivative usage, psalms of trust often petition Yahweh to lead (*nḥh*) the speaker in a way of fidelity and well-being (Pss 5:8; 27:11; 31:3; 61:2; 139:24; 143:10). And in Ps 26:2, the petitioner states his innocence with verbs of testing: "Prove me, O Lord, and try me; Test my heart and mind."

The imagery of leading and feeding shades in a pastoral direction, the actions being those of a shepherd tending sheep. The imagery bespeaks tenderness, gentleness, and attentiveness. The same utterances, however, also suggest that the God who feeds and leads has *maternal* qualities, and in these verbs does what a mother does. Thus, most spectacularly in Num 11:11-14, Moses' protest suggests that Yahweh has conceived (*hrh*) and birthed (*yld*) this people and is now responsible for it and obligated to feed it.

The other theme that might be related to this imagery is the term "comfort" (*nḥm*). The verb is used in Ps 23:4, "your rod and your staff—they comfort me." In this usage, the theme of feeding immediately follows the shepherd imagery. That same rhetoric is subsequently utilized in the Isaiah traditions, bespeaking Yahweh's attentiveness to Israel in exile. Thus in Isa 40:11 the pastoral image recurs, and in Isa 66:12-13 the motif of comfort is linked to maternal imagery. The verbs are used in the Pentateuch in situations where Yahweh overrides high risk. They are also used more pastorally and more intimately in other contexts. In both sorts of contexts, however, the characteristic actions of Yahweh in feeding and leading transform situations of threat and distress into livable circumstance, wherein Israel surprisingly experiences joy and well-being.

A Creation Theology of Blessing

While these verbs of Yahweh witness to actions of Yahweh that might be regarded as "mighty deeds of rescue," in fact in Israel's rhetoric these verbs and the actions they describe shade over into a creation theology of blessing. That is, the giver of abundant life generates a world of blessing where none seemed possible. And while the gifts of life are indeed miraculous, they are not exceptional, but bear witness to Yahweh's capacity to bring life and fruitfulness out of circumstances of chaos and conditions of barrenness.

Thus writ very large, *what Yahweh does in the wilderness traditions is what Yahweh does cosmically in creation.* For in creation, God is dealing with a formlessness incapable of generating life. But Yahweh transforms that situation into one of productivity, well-being, and fruitfulness. In both the historical account of Israel and in the cosmic account given as hymn, Yahweh transforms scenes of hopelessness into occasions of life, possibility, and joy.

The motif of God's "presence with," in transformative ways, is taken up in the narratives of Jesus, so that Jesus is perceived to be doing what Yahweh characteristically does. The story of manna, whereby Yahweh feeds Israel and transforms a desert situation into a place of life, is generative of the feeding narratives enacted by Jesus. In Mark 6:30-44, for example, the narrative, on the face of it, is about a wondrous feeding. The narrative, however, is more dense than a simple account of feeding. The narrative deliberately utilizes the characteristic eucharistic verbs "took," "blessed," "broke," "gave" (v. 41). The larger portrayal of Jesus is expressed in v. 34: "As he went ashore, he saw a great crowd; and he had compassion for them, because they were like sheep without a shepherd...." They had no shepherd to lead, to feed, to comfort them—no one to do what Yahweh characteristically does to transform a context of threat into one of well-being. And Jesus had compassion on them and was attentive to their need.

Harvey Guthrie has shown the ways in which the Israelite songs and rites of thanksgiving eventuated, in a Christian rendering, into the practice of the Eucharist, the quintessential act of thanksgiving.[102] It is not necessary to force these verbs of leading and feeding in that particular interpretive direction. But reference to the Christian Eucharist indicates what is in any case present, pervasively but inchoately, in the testimony of the verbs. The God of Israel is peculiarly present in wilderness circumstance in transformative ways. The narrative testimony of Israel responds to such acts and gifts with wonder and gratitude. In turn, these narrative testimonies evoke and authorize other petitions for like action from God in new circumstances of threat.

An Overview of Verbal Testimony

In our brief review of Israel's verbal testimony about Yahweh, we have traversed the main points of what have been identified, most recently by Martin Noth and Gerhard von Rad, as "the Pentateuchal themes."[103] That is, we have considered what is surely the dominant story line of Israel's most treasured and most characteristic testimony concerning Yahweh. We have seen that what Israel does, when it bears witness to the character of Yahweh, is to retell sentences governed by powerful, transformative verbs, in which Yahweh is the primary actor.

We may observe several points about these characteristic forms of testimony:

Choosing from Rich Resources

The quantity and diversity of the material are nearly overwhelming, and it is impossible to take it all into account. At the most, we are able to cite characteristic and representative utterances of Israel, which reflect Israel's primary propensity as a

---

102. Harvey H. Guthrie, *Theology as Thanksgiving: From Israel's Psalms to the Church's Eucharist* (New York: Seabury, 1987).

103. Martin Noth, *A History of Pentateuchal Traditions* (Englewood Cliffs, N.J.: Prentice-Hall, 1972); von Rad, "The Form-Critical Problem of the Hexateuch," and *Old Testament Theology* 1.

witness, and the characteristic markings of Yahweh, as Yahweh lives in and through the testimony of Israel. On any particular theme or verb that we have mentioned, there are rich resources still to be explored.

Finished Coherence Is Impossible

It is not possible to formulate this rich array of verbal narrative witnesses with anything like a coherent, systematic account. We can, as is often done, articulate a dominant story line. When one examines the texts, however, they are too specific and in many cases too odd to be made coherent. Israel does not offer a finished portrayal of Yahweh. Israel only provides the materials out of which a coherent account of Yahweh, *in any particular setting,* might be presented. Israel offers odd, incidental, concrete, episodic case studies, whereby material is given from which the listener may do constructive work. But for each such formulation proposed by a listener to the witnesses, we recognize that other listeners with the same material may arrive at a significantly different general portrayal of Yahweh. All such formulations may be credible but, because of the nature of the material, it will not do to imagine that any such portrayal is the right one or the master one. The nature of the material precludes such a claim.

No Going behind the Witnesses

This testimony is relentlessly narratival in its utterance, and therefore the narrative articulations are the originary form and way of Yahweh in Israel. That is to say, one cannot go behind the narratival (liturgical?) accounts, but will have to take the word of the witnesses. The witnesses sometimes claim to be eyewitnesses, but often no such claim is made. Even where it is not made, however, the authority of the witness is grounded in nothing more and nothing less than the willingness of the text community to credit, believe, trust, and take seriously this testimony.

In principle, the hearer of this text who listens for its theological cadences refuses to go behind these witnesses. This means that theological interpretation does not go behind the witness with questions of history, wondering "what happened." What happened, so our "verdict" is, is what these witnesses said happened. In complementary fashion, this means that theological interpretation does not go behind this witness with questions of ontology, wondering "what is real." What is real, so our "verdict" is, is what these witnesses say is real. Nothing more historical or ontological is available. But this mode of "knowing" finds such a claim to be adequate.

Incomparability

In all of this variegated, rather disordered picture, this jumble of testimonies, we arrive at the conclusion already considered above, the conclusion that is Israel's characteristic theological intention: Yahweh is incomparable! There is none like Yahweh! No rival is or claims to be the subject of these active, transformative verbs. Indeed, we can imagine Israel, called to the dock to bear witness, almost defiant in giving testimony so sure, so confident, daring any rival witness to bring forth any evidence that there is another enactor of such verbs (cf. Isa 41:21-29). And if not defiant, then we may imagine the witnesses have a kind of quiet confidence, a trust mostly talked about only in the community itself, that the world is the arena wherein Yahweh's verbs are enacted; that the world, circumstances to the contrary notwithstanding, is responsive to and necessarily conforms to the actions of this irresistible Character. We may, moreover, imagine witnesses inculcating their young into these characteristic utterances, thus placing at the center of the imagination of their children this odd and nonnegotiable version of what happened, of what is real.

This imagined courtroom may contain other witnesses giving other testimony, other accounts of reality. But Israel is adamant, and will give its testimony that intends to counter every other testimony. Thus:

(a) *The God who creates* (*br'*, *'sh*, *qnh*, *dbr*, *yṣr*) is the one who can transform any circumstance of chaos into an ordered context where fruitfulness, blessing, prosperity, and well-being are obtainable. The verbs of creation refuse to accept as a given any situation of death and disorder:

> For thus says the Lord,
> who created the heavens
> (he is God!),
> who formed the earth and made it
> (he established it;
> he did not create it a chaos,
> he formed it to be inhabited!):
> I am the Lord, and there is no other.
> I did not speak in secret,
> in a land of darkness;
> I did not say to the offspring of Jacob,
> "Seek me in chaos."
> I the Lord speak the truth,
> I declare what is right. (Isa 45:18-19)

(b) *The God who promises* (*šb'*, *dbr*) is the one who can move decisively against every situation of barrenness and transform it into a circumstance of well-being, joy, and possibility. The verbs of promise refuse to accept as given any situation of despair, whether in the barrenness of ancient families or in the exhaustion of technological societies that believe there are no gifts to be given. The Subject of these verbs is at work, making all things new:

> He raises the poor from the dust,
> and lifts the needy from the ash heap,
> to make them sit with princes,
> with the princes of his people.

He gives the barren woman a home;
making her the joyous mother of children.
Praise the Lord! (Ps 113:7-9).

(c) *The God who delivers* (*yṣ'*, *pdh*, *yš'*, *'lh*, *g'l*) is the God who can disrupt any circumstance of social bondage and exploitation, overthrow ruthless orderings of public life, and authorize new circumstances of dancing freedom, dignity, and justice. The verbs of deliverance refuse to accept as a given any circumstance of oppression:

The spirit of the Lord God is upon me,
because the Lord has anointed me,
he has sent me to bring good news to the oppressed,
to bind up the brokenhearted,
to proclaim liberty to the captives,
and release to the prisoners;
to proclaim the year of the Lord's favor,
and the day of vengeance of our God.... (Isa 61:1-2)

(d) *The God who commands* (*ṣwh*) is one who can bring any circumstance under a sovereign decree, insisting on holiness and justice, and thereby creating a livable order. In that order, righteousness is guaranteed and community is made possible. The verbs of command refuse to accept any situation of autonomy wherein might makes right and wherein each opposes all, the outcome of which is greedy brutality. Israel bears witness that the commands of Yahweh are not a burden or a coercion, but are a guarantee of a livable, viable life:

Do not take the word of truth
utterly out of my mouth,
for my hope is in your ordinances.
I will keep your law continually,
forever and ever.
I shall walk at liberty,
for I have sought your precepts.
I will also speak of your decrees before kings,
and not be put to shame;
I find my delight in your commandments,
because I love them.
I revere your commandments, which I love,
and I will meditate on your statutes. (Ps 119:43-48)

(e) *The God who guides* (*nhl*, *nḥh*), *feeds* (*'kl*), *and tests* (*nsh*) is the God who can transform any circumstance of deathly abandonment and threat into a place of discipline, nourishment, and life. The verbs of attentive nurture refuse to accept circumstances of wretchedness that bring death, and effect the possibility of a good life in the most unlikely of situations:

The wilderness and the dry land shall be glad,
   the desert shall rejoice and blossom;
like the crocus it shall blossom abundantly,
   and rejoice with joy and singing.
The glory of Lebanon shall be given to it,
   the majesty of Carmel and Sharon.
They shall see the glory of the Lord,
   the majesty of our God....
Then the eyes of the blind shall be opened,
   and the ears of the deaf unstopped;
then the lame shall leap like a deer,
   and the tongue of the speechless sing for joy.
For waters shall break forth in the wilderness,
   and streams in the desert;
the burning sand shall become a pool,
   and the thirsty ground spring of water;
the haunt of jackals shall become a swamp,
   the grass shall become reeds and rushes. (Isa 35:1-2, 5-7)

Incomparable indeed! In that ancient world of utterance, Israel generated, one verb at a time, one sentence at a time, one narrative at a time, this alterative Agent. And this Agent of an alternative life in the world gave to Israel (and to the world):

- instead of deathly chaos, ordered life;

- instead of despair, possibility for a future;

- instead of oppression, dancing freedom;

- instead of absolutizing autonomy, obedience in viable community;

- instead of wretched abandonment, nourishment and care.

One can indeed thematize Israel's great and characteristic utterances about Yahweh—but not for long. Then one must return to listening to the tales and songs and poems and liturgies, in which the Subject lives.

Unresolved Openness of the Pentateuch

The great themes of the main story line of Israel, as told in the Pentateuch, do not come to fruition in the horizon of the Pentateuch. The fact that Israel's core text ends in Deuteronomy 34, with Moses seeing the land of promise but not entering, has been much recognized by scholars. This shape of the literature requires some interpretive adjudication. The most influential resolution of the problem has been that of Gerhard von Rad, who overcame this problem by simply disregarding the limit of the Pentateuch. He spoke of Hexateuch, six books, including the Book of Joshua. In that way, von Rad found a fulfillment of the promise of the land, and the promise of the Pentateuch generally, in the conquest of Joshua:

> Thus the Lord gave to Israel all the land that he swore to their ancestors that he would give them; and having taken possession of it, they settled there.... Not one of all the good promises that the Lord had made to the house of Israel had failed; all came to pass. (Josh 21:43-45)

Such a resolution of the Pentateuch has had enormous influence in theological interpretation. But it is also widely recognized as problematic in its violation of the literary limit of the Pentateuch and the shape of the authority of Moses.

A second resolution of the unkept promise of the Pentateuch is to locate some traces of the land reception in older Pentateuchal sources in the Book of Numbers, suggesting that prior to the completed formulation of the canon of the Pentateuch, Israel had traditions whereby the core recital of Exod 3:7 had its tale of completion.[104]

In recent scholarship, however, it is more compelling to take the termination of the Pentateuch, short of fulfillment in the land, not as a theological problem but as an important theological datum.[105] We have already remarked that Old Testament faith, as we now have it, is understood as a product of and pastoral response to the crisis of Israel's exile in the sixth century B.C.E. The closure of the Pentateuch in Deuteronomy 34, short of the land, is perhaps a memory of a moment in ancient Israel, allegedly in the time of Moses and Joshua. But given our suggestion of a double reading, it is plausible to suggest that the community waiting at the brink of the land of promise in Joshua 1, just outside the Pentateuch, is not an ancient community of Moses; it is sixth-century Israel, waiting in anticipation for an entry (reentry) into a land from which they had been displaced by the geopolitics of a Babylonian world.

Thus the unresolved openness of the Pentateuch is not an oversight or a theological mishap: it is a statement of candor ("You are not yet returned home") and of hope ("You will be returned home"), to a community profoundly displaced and living somewhere between despair and hope. Thus the structure of the Pentateuch and the recognition that promises have not yet been kept by Yahweh, and the affirmation that they will yet be kept, constitute an appropriate posture for a believing community that cherishes the God of these verbs, yet looks its own circumstance full in the face. The wonder of this faith is that the circumstance faced did not discredit the testimony of the verbal sentence; nor does the testimony lead to denial about the circumstance. Rather *the literature is put together in order to exhibit and to explore the tension between verbal testimony and circumstance,* with the clear "canonical" insistence that the testimony will prevail over every circumstance.

---

104. The older source analysis assumed that there are J (i.e., early) elements of tradition concerning the land in the Book of Numbers. Currently, however, such source analysis is in disarray and one cannot readily make such an assumption, given the inclination of a number of scholars—for example, John van Seters.

105. This point has been made with great subtlety by James A. Sanders, *Torah and Canon* (Philadelphia: Fortress Press, 1972) 9–53.

Beyond that sixth-century community that generated this articulation of its crisis of life and faith, the open-ended, unresolved, and promissory shape of the Pentateuch may be regarded as broadly paradigmatic for the ongoing life of the communities propelled by this text. In this way, the theological witness of the Pentateuch bears resilient witness to the characteristic situation of Jews as a displaced community. The text, moreover, is left open to all sorts of displaced human communities, for the Pentateuch, in the end, is a promise of a homecoming and a home, to be given by the God of all promise who will not finally settle for wilderness, exile, or displacement. Thus there is in the Pentateuch a tremendous push toward the future that is under the aegis of the God of these verbs. That impetus for the future is given in a way that is profoundly theological: the shape of the literature is a match to the God to whom it bears witness.

Intended Fulfillment

The entire sequence of verbs (and thus themes) of creation, promise, deliverance, command, and nourishment, is a recital in waiting. Our last question of the verbal recital is this: What fulfillment does the Pentateuch intend? We may suggest four ways of thinking in response to this question:

(a) The first, obvious, and unarguable aim of the Pentateuch is the land of promise: the known, identifiable turf of the land bridge of the Fertile Crescent. The Bible is in and of and for and to that land. This reality precludes any spiritualizing away from the material intention in the text. It also precludes any notion of land that lacks this particularity. In Isa 36:17, the Assyrian emissary to Hezekiah makes the ill-informed proposal that his Jerusalem community should be taken away to live in "a land like your own land, a land of grain and wine, a land of bread and vineyards." What the Assyrians do not know is that there is no land "like" this one. It is not tradable or negotiable. Thus the Pentateuch is the taproot of what has come in modern times to be Zionism, an insistence that the Jewishness of reality is linked to this land.

(b) On occasion it is possible to be more precise. There are suggestions that the goal of the promise of the Pentateuch is the city of Jerusalem and its temple. Thus it is plausible that in the ancient poem of Exod 15:1-18, the reference to "your abode, the sanctuary" (v. 17) specifically means the Jerusalem temple. And if the whole sweep of normative literature is understood, as David Noel Freedman suggests, as a unity from Genesis through 2 Kings, then 1 Kings 8 and the dedication of the temple stands at the center of the literature and is the interpretive pivot of the whole.[106] Moreover, Joseph Blenkinsopp has argued that in the Priestly tradition, the parallelism of creation, tabernacle, and land suggests that the "place of

---

106. Thus, for example, David Noel Freedman, *The Unity of the Hebrew Bible* (Ann Arbor: University of Michigan Press, 1991). See also Danna Nolan Fewell and David Gunn, *Gender, Power, and Promise: The Subject of the Bible's First Story* (Nashville: Abingdon Press, 1993).

presence," in the purview of the priests, is the goal of all of Israel's promises.[107] This reading of the future would conclude that *worship* is the very form of Israel's future life. Israel will be at home when it is fully, freely, safely at home in worship.[108]

(c) Closely related to the Jerusalem-Zion tradition, but distinct from it, is the move of the text toward the Davidic dynasty. Thus it is possible that the Abraham stories, wherein the promise is most surely lodged, represent a self-conscious anticipation of the Davidic dynasty, wherein the land promises come to fulfillment. This would suggest, as in older scholarship, that a tenth-century B.C.E. form of the Pentateuchal story line is deliberately shaped to move the entire material toward the legitimacy of the monarchy. Such a casting, however, is only a particular political form of the more general anticipation of the land.

(d) Without escaping the concreteness of the claims of land-temple-monarchy, it is possible to suggest that the promises of the Pentateuch, as Moses arrives at Mount Pisgah, are not to be understood as specifically as any of these possible readings may suggest. Rather the promise is open, and what is hoped for in the testimony of Israel is *shalôm*, well-being in whatever configuration Yahweh may yet give it. Such a view of the promise runs the risk of escaping the concreteness of Jewishness and becoming generically human. We must note, however, that there are serious trusters in these promises who are not Zionist—not committed to the concreteness of land and its institutions—who only say, "Next year Freedom." I conclude this comment with some diffidence, as I do not want to detract from the evident concreteness of the promise.

In both Jewish and Christian perspective, the promise has tended to be taken with great interpretive freedom and imagination, so that what is hoped for is what is needed in any immediate circumstance of the hoping community. Perhaps writ most large, what is promised and hoped for in this core testimony to Israel is "the rule of God" over the whole of creation.[109] The political metaphor for that, "kingdom of God," is a useful referent, except that it opens itself to ideological particularity. What is abundantly clear is that this conclusion of the core verbal testimony of Israel at Mount Pisgah is not a "history of failure."[110] It is testimony about an Agent who has begun what is not yet finished. In the end, this narrative testimony leaves Israel waiting but full of hope. It is characteristic of Old Testament faith that a recital of verbs already enacted creates ground for verbs yet to be enacted, of the same sort, but perhaps carried out very differently in time to come.

---

107. Joseph Blenkinsopp, *Prophecy and Canon: A Contribution to the Study of Jewish Origins* (Notre Dame, Ind.: University of Notre Dame Press, 1977) 54–79.

108. On worship in Jerusalem as Israel's "safe place," see Ben C. Ollenburger, *Zion, City of the Great King: A Theological Symbol of the Jerusalem Cult* (JSOTSup 41; Sheffield: JSOT Press, 1987).

109. See Martin Buber, *The Kingship of God* (3d ed.; London: George Allen and Unwin, 1967).

110. This unfortunate articulation of "a history of failure" is from Rudolf Bultmann, "The Significance of the Old Testament for the Christian Faith," *The Old Testament and Christian Faith* (ed. Bernhard W. Anderson; London: SCM Press, 1964) 8–35.

FIVE

Adjectives: Yahweh with Characteristic Markings

THE VERBAL SENTENCES by which Israel bears testimony to Yahweh focus on finite verbs referring to specific, nameable actions. A variation on this practice is the move toward participial verbs in what Claus Westermann terms "descriptive" sentences, which report what Yahweh characteristically does.[1] These statements are derivative from declarative sentences. The God to whom the Old Testament bears witness is known primarily and characteristically through these concrete statements of the way in which the circumstance of Israel was changed by Yahweh's direct enactment of transformative verbs.

Israel, however, does not always stay within the rhetoric of specificity. Nor can theological interpretation stay within the rhetoric of specificity if it is to consider all of Israel's testimony concerning Yahweh. Thus I now consider one important rhetorical maneuver by which Israel transforms its testimony about Yahweh from specificity to a larger, more general claim. Our subject is adjectives, the terms Israel characteristically employs in order to speak about the character of Yahweh as it is discerned in Israel as an outcome of a variety of concrete verbal sentences.

Generalizing Adjectives from Specific Verbal Sentences

We may observe the generalizing strategy of Psalm 136, which Gerhard von Rad identified as a later recital of Israel's core credo.[2] This psalm begins with a three-fold doxological summons to *tôdah* (thanksgiving), issuing in what may be a thesis sentence for the entire psalm: "... who alone does great wonders, for his steadfast love endures forever" (v. 4). The subject of the psalm is Yahweh's "great wonders" (*npl'ôth gdlôth*), which the psalm then recites. The "great wonders" include the wonders of creation (vv. 5-9), the deliverance from Egypt (vv. 10-15), the wilderness sojourn (v. 16), and the entry into the promised land (vv. 17-22). The psalm

---

1. On the distinction between declarative and descriptive hymns of praise, see Claus Westermann, *Praise and Lament in the Psalms* (Atlanta: John Knox, 1981).
2. Gerhard von Rad, "The Form-Critical Problem of the Hexateuch," *The Problem of the Hexateuch and Other Essays* (New York: McGraw-Hill, 1966) 8–13.

213

culminates with a threefold general conclusion (vv. 23-25) in which Yahweh remembers, rescues, and gives food. A final summons of thanks (v. 26) reiterates the summons of vv. 1-3. The body of the recital features a rich variety of verbs, all of which bespeak Yahweh's transformative engagement with creation and then with Israel.

What interests us now, however, is that the second half of each verse has the constant refrain throughout the psalm, "for his steadfast love (_ḥsd_) endures forever." I suggest that the movement made repeatedly in this psalm, from concrete assertion to a general refrain about Yahweh's fidelity, is an exemplar of Israel's rhetorical maneuver to generalizing adjectives from specific verbal sentences. The concrete verbal action of the first line of the verses might permit a liturgical response in the second line—something like "Yahweh acted in _ḥesed._" But that is not what Israel says in this psalm. Rather, Israel asserts, in any particular verse of the psalm, that the concrete verbal action of Yahweh cited permits the larger sweeping affirmation, "Yahweh's fidelity endures forever." This is not to claim that the one act is the means whereby Yahweh's fidelity lasts for all time. Rather the act is one element among many and is taken as characteristic of many others. The culminating effect of the claim is the assertion of enduring fidelity. That is, out of all of their verbal sentences of testimony, Israel draws the larger testimony that what is evident in specific acts of Yahweh is generally the case concerning Yahweh.

These specific actions that live on the lips of Israel permit the larger witness that Yahweh is indeed everywhere and always reliable, as Yahweh is shown to be in these concrete bits of evidence. We may question whether Israel's relatively few verbal sentences about Yahweh in this psalm, and the relatively few verbal sentences that Israel can cite in all of its text, in fact warrant such a large, general conclusion as Israel characteristically claims in its testimony. But that is how the theological witness of Israel emerges and works, and in principle that is how the evidence of character witnesses accumulates and proceeds.[3] One cites a few examples of concrete experience for which one can personally vouch, and then generalizes on the basis of them to insist that the one for whom testimony is given is in general, consistently and reliably, the same as these few specific instances indicate.

The two-way interaction between concrete verbal sentences and larger adjectival generalization is important for understanding Israel's testimony concerning Yahweh. On the one hand, the specific verbal sentences receive and insist on generalization. On the other hand, the generalization must always be linked to and informed by the specificity of concrete verbal sentences. An outsider may wonder if the adjectival generalization is a non sequitur from the verbal sentence. But the witnesses themselves, and their community, have complete confidence that the adjectival generalization follows necessarily and legitimately from the testimony of a few concrete verbal utterances.

---

3. It occurs to me that this is the way in which letters of reference and commendation proceed: a few specific details are cited, from which sweeping generalizations are extrapolated. The power of the generalization depends on the poignancy of the specifics, not on the quantity of the details.

The question, in taking up adjectival generalizations, is this: To what theological generalization does the cumulative verbal testimony of Israel about Yahweh add up? As with the verbal sentences, for the doing of Old Testament theology there is no clear "first usage" of adjectives that is clearly normative. We may, however, identify recurrent and stylized uses of adjectives that are evidently characteristic for Israel's testimony about Yahweh.[4] That is, the way in which Israel speaks about Yahweh shows a consistent propensity in its adjectival generalizations.

Exodus 34:6-7: A Credo of Adjectives

The text from which many scholars begin such an investigation is the statement concerning Yahweh in Exod 34:6-7:[5]

The Lord, the Lord,
a God merciful and gracious,
slow to anger,
and abounding in steadfast love and faithfulness,
keeping steadfast love for the thousandth generation,
forgiving iniquity and transgression and sin,
yet by no means clearing the guilty,
but visiting the iniquity of the parents
upon the children
and the children's children,
to the third and the fourth generation.

We may begin with this text, both because it occurs in such a poignant context, on which the entire future of Israel seems to pivot, and because the statement itself appears to be a rich convergence of Israel's preferred adjectives for Yahweh. In context, this self-declaration of Yahweh comes at a crucial moment in Israel's life with Yahweh.[6] The crisis in which Moses and Israel find themselves has been evoked by the ill-conceived golden calf made by Aaron, to which Yahweh responds in destructive rage (Exod 32:10). In 32:11-14 and 33:12-16, Moses intercedes with Yahweh on behalf of Israel, parrying with Yahweh. Moses insists that Yahweh must go with Israel into the wilderness if there is to be any Israel. In response Yahweh assures Moses that Yahweh is marked by profound and free graciousness, and will act graciously according to Yahweh's own free inclination. In an escalation of the bargaining with Yahweh, Moses asks to see Yahweh's glory (33:18). Yahweh refuses the request, but offers to show Moses "my back" (Exod 33:23).

---

4. On "characteristic" use, see Walter Brueggemann, "Crisis-Evoked, Crisis-Resolving Speech," *BTB* 24 (1994) 95–105.

5. See Michael Fishbane, *Biblical Interpretation in Ancient Israel* (Oxford: Clarendon Press, 1985) 341–50.

6. It is not clear from the text whether the speaker is Moses or Yahweh. It has become conventional in recent translations to regard Yahweh as the speaker, so that the assertion is Yahweh's self-disclosure. On the context, see Walter Moberly, *At the Mountain of God: Story and Theology in Exodus 32–34* (JSOTSup 22; Sheffield: JSOT Press, 1983).

In a characteristic non sequitur, as Yahweh "passed before him" (Exod 34:6), nothing is said about Moses seeing Yahweh, either front or back. Instead, 34:6-7 makes an announcement about the character of Yahweh, out of which comes Yahweh's resolve to continue the life of Israel by means of a new covenant arrangement (34:10). Thus vv. 6-7 are a self-disclosure on the part of Yahweh, which provides the grounds for the continued life of Israel, after the unparalleled affront to Yahweh in the golden calf.

Our interest focuses on vv. 6-7 and what is said about Yahweh therein. Scholars believe this is an exceedingly important, stylized, quite self-conscious characterization of Yahweh, a formulation so studied that it may be reckoned to be something of a classic, normative statement to which Israel regularly returned, meriting the label "credo."[7] If that is true, as seems plausible, it is a credo of adjectives about the character of Yahweh, very different in texture from the credo of verbs on which von Rad has focused our attention. It is possible that this is an alternative way of doing theology in ancient Israel, for it is clear that Israel had repeated recourse to this recital, as indeed it did to the recital of verbs. In light of what I have said about specific verbal sentences and generalizing adjectives, however, I suggest that the "credo of adjectives" is not an alternative way of doing theology; rather it is a way of doing theology that depends on and gathers together the claims of the verbal recitals that are much more concrete. The statement of Exod 34:6-7 features a variety of adjectives. For each of these adjectives, *I suggest that Israel must have available for itself a rich variety of verbal sentences that support and give credence to the adjectival claims.*

Positive Adjectives

The adjectives used here to characterize Yahweh, to which Israel makes repeated and recurring reference, are of two kinds. First, in Exod 34:6-7a, the part of this tradition that will most concern us, the adjectives are positive. Yahweh is characterized by a cluster of terms that are evident in and through many verbal sentences. Thus Yahweh is *merciful* (*rḥm*). In order to make this statement, Israel must have, I propose, many verbal sentences that narrate times and events in which Yahweh is seen to be concretely merciful. The most influential treatment of this term is by Phyllis Trible, who has shown that this usage as pertains to Yahweh is intimately connected to the word "womb," which shares the same root, *rḥm*.[8] Thus a God who is compassionate has a quality something like mother love. Yahweh is *gracious* (*ḥnn*). The term is used most often to suggest that Yahweh acts gratuitously, without need for compensation or hope of benefit, but freely and generously. Yahweh is *slow to anger* (*'rk 'ppym*). The actual Hebrew idiom translates as "has long nostrils." The usage perhaps indicates that Yahweh's long nose permits divine rage and anger to cool off before they threaten Israel. Such a notion might be reinforced

---

7. On this text, see Phyllis Trible, *God and the Rhetoric of Sexuality* (OBT; Philadelphia: Fortress Press, 1978) 1–30.

8. Ibid., 31–71.

by Yahweh's propensity to "burn hot" against Israel (32:10, 11; cf. v. 19). Yahweh has *steadfast love* (*ḥsd*). The studies of Nelson Glueck, Katherine Sakenfeld, and Gordon Clark show that the term is related to tenacious fidelity in a relationship, readiness and resolve to continue to be loyal to those to whom one is bound.[9] Yahweh "abounds in faithfulness" (*'emeth*). The term bespeaks complete trustworthiness and reliability, which then becomes the term *true/truth*. The words *ḥsd* and *'emeth* become a characteristic and much-used word pair in the Old Testament, together marking Yahweh as utterly reliable and trustworthy (see John 1:14).

In this recital of the character of Yahweh, the only term used more than once is *ḥsd*, suggesting that this term receives special accent. This accumulation of positive adjectives concerning Yahweh culminates in the surprising and rarely used word "forgive" (*ns'*). This final positive statement uses Israel's full vocabulary for sin, "iniquity, transgression, and sin" (*'wn, pš', ḥṭ'*), suggesting that Yahweh will keep safe from destruction those with whom Yahweh is bound in covenant.[10]

It is possible to do close lexical work on each of these terms, and to discern in each a peculiar rhetorical nuance. For our purposes, such closer investigation is not required, though one can always learn from such an enterprise. What concerns us is the cumulative effect of all of these terms together, which bespeak Yahweh's intense solidarity with and commitment to those to whom Yahweh is bound. The generalizing adjectives assert, on the basis of verbal sentences of testimony such as Psalm 136, that Yahweh's life with Israel is marked by a fundamental, inalienable loyalty. Israel's life, at this pivotal point of risk in Exodus 34, is now guaranteed by the assertion on the very lips of Yahweh that Yahweh abides for Israel in complete fidelity, even among those who enact "iniquity, transgression, and sin."

Given the substance of this remarkable characterization of Yahweh, we are more than a little surprised by the ominous second half of the stylized statement in v. 7b. The second half of v. 7 is introduced by a conjunction that must be rendered as an adversative "but" (NRSV, "yet"). This negative statement is introduced by a negative infinitive absolute, "he will really not acquit" (*nqh*), but will "visit (*pqd*; in the participle) iniquity." This second half of the sentence surprises, because it indicates that Yahweh takes affront (as in the case of Aaron in Exodus 32) very seriously, so seriously as to affect the relationship for as many as four generations. It interests us especially that it is "iniquity" that is visited on subsequent generations, the very same iniquity that is *pardoned* in v. 7a, along with transgression and sin. This second half of the sequence surprises, and at the same time it alerts Israel to the reality that Yahweh's full character is not subsumed under Yahweh's commitment

---

9. Nelson Glueck, *Hesed in the Bible* (New York: KTAV, 1968); Katherine Sakenfeld, *Faithfulness in Action: Loyalty in Biblical Perspective* (OBT; Philadelphia; Fortress Press, 1985); *The Meaning of Hesed in the Hebrew Bible: A New Enquiry* (HSM 17; Missoula, Mont.: Scholars Press, 1978); and Gordon R. Clark, *The Word "Hesed" in the Hebrew Bible* (JSOT Sup 157; Sheffield: JSOT Press, 1993).

10. On this vocabulary, see Rolf Knierim, *Die Hauptbegriffe für Sünde im Alten Testament* (Gütersloh: Gütersloher Verlaghaus Gerd Mohn, 1965).

to Israel in solidarity.[11] There is something in Yahweh's sovereign rule—Yahweh's own self-seriousness—that is not compromised or conceded, even in the practice of solidarity.

Other adjectives are added over time to this standard characterization of Yahweh, but this collage of words represents something of a constant in Israel's testimony. We may say that this convergence of terms is a rather full characterization of the One to whom Israel owes its allegiance and on whom it trusts for its life. The utterance of the second half of this formula may indicate how demanding the allegiance due Yahweh is, and it makes clear how risky the trust is that Israel vests in Yahweh. Neither the allegiance owed to Yahweh nor the trust placed in Yahweh is easy or one-dimensional.

Representative Uses of the Adjectival Formula

This more-or-less set formula of adjectives concerning Yahweh is taken up in many different contexts in Israel's subsequent testimony. That is, when Israel spoke about Yahweh, this formulation recurred in many different settings and circumstances. It will not surprise us that the full recital is used with great rhetorical and imaginative freedom; occasionally parts of it are accented or omitted, as they are either particularly poignant or irrelevant to the situation of utterance. Here we mention some of the fairly representative uses of this formula.

Hymns of Praise

Israel uses the positive recital of Yahweh (34:6-7a) in its hymns of praise when it wants to speak about Yahweh in the third person, as the One whom Israel knows to be utterly reliable and who makes life possible for Israel. In the hymn of Psalm 145, the doxology of Israel takes up the rhetoric of Exod 34:6:

> The Lord is gracious and merciful,
> slow to anger and abounding in steadfast love.
> The Lord is good to all,
> and his compassion is over all that he has made. (Ps 145:8)

This verse includes many of the terms from Exod 34:6. Verse 9 uses somewhat different rhetoric, but the term *compassion* (*rḥm*) is employed, though now the scope of Yahweh's compassion is all of creation. In this lyrical doxology, the fidelity of Yahweh that characterizes Yahweh's relation to Israel is now available for all of creation. This usage bespeaks Yahweh's goodness and generosity, and it makes an unqualified affirmation of exuberant trust.

---

11. James Crenshaw, "Who Knows What YHWH Will Do? The Character of God in the Book of Joel," *Fortunate the Eyes That See: Essays in Honor of David Noel Freedman* (ed. Astrid B. Beck et al.; Grand Rapids: Eerdmans, 1995) 185–96, has seen the profound ambiguity expressed here concerning Yahweh.

Prayers of Complaint

Israel uses the positive recital concerning Yahweh in its prayers of complaint when it wants to address Yahweh directly in the second person as the One who is expected to be gracious and faithful. Thus in Psalm 86, the speaker is under threat and appeals to Yahweh for rescue. The usage of the standard adjectives here functions as a motivational clause, seeking to move Yahweh to act:

> For you, O Lord, are good and forgiving,
> abounding in steadfast love to all who call on you....
> But you, O Lord, are a God
> merciful and gracious,
> slow to anger and abounding in steadfast love and faithfulness....
>   (Ps 86:5, 15)

The formula is used here to *remind Yahweh of who Yahweh is,* and who Yahweh declared God's own self to be. The purpose of the prayer is to motivate Yahweh to be Yahweh's true self, and so to overcome the present situation of danger by a powerful show of solidarity. The prayer proceeds as if the disclosure of Exod 34:6-7a were an agreed-upon baseline that is mutually accepted by Yahweh and Israel, but from which Yahweh has departed and to which Yahweh now needs urgently to return. The speaker does not doubt that Yahweh is "merciful and gracious." That is who Yahweh really is. But Yahweh has become, it would appear, careless or neglectful or indifferent, and must be returned to Yahweh's true self. Clearly the tone and intent of the same formula are very different when it is used as a motivation in a complaint rather than in a doxology of praise. In one case the utterance is about Yahweh but is addressed to a third party who is invited to join in praise of Yahweh. In the other it is urgently addressed to Yahweh in an imperative tone.

A Daring Appeal

In addition to hymns and complaints, we may refer to one other rather singular usage. In Numbers 14, Yahweh is completely provoked by Israel, who endlessly complains about its treatment by Yahweh. Yahweh's patience with Israel is exhausted. In weariness, Yahweh confides in Moses that Yahweh would like simply to destroy Israel and to start over with only Moses (v. 12). Moses seeks to talk Yahweh out of this declared destructive intention. Moses employs two strategies in seeking to persuade Yahweh not to act in rage. First, Moses appeals to Yahweh's pride, shaming Yahweh in the eyes of the Egyptians and in the eyes of the inhabitants of the land (vv. 13-16). Second, Moses makes an alternative suggestion to Yahweh, proposing that instead of destroying recalcitrant Israel, Yahweh forgive (vv. 17-19). The basis of this daring appeal is a direct and complete quotation of Exod 34:6-7, which Moses now quotes as a prayer, concerning Yahweh's self-commitment to Israel made at Sinai, which Yahweh proposes to disregard.

Not unlike Psalm 86, Moses proposes that Yahweh should act according to Yahweh's self-commitment, so that this model prayer consists in praying Yahweh's own self-characterization back to Yahweh. Yahweh's response to Moses in v. 20 indicates that Yahweh has been persuaded by being urged back to this baseline of the relationship. It is equally evident in v. 21, however, that Yahweh takes into full account the second half of Exod 34:6-7; for Yahweh, against the prayer of Moses, will indeed destroy the disobedient in Israel. Thus Moses dutifully appeals to the older formulation, but Yahweh also remembers that textual formulation and appeals to the part of it that Moses chose not to accent. Both Moses and Yahweh show great agility in their use of the formula.

Positive and Negatives Sides of the Confession

Israel's doxologies and complaints appeal primarily to the first, positive part of Exod 34:6-7. This is understandable, because the doxologies intend to celebrate Yahweh's positive character and the complaints seek to mobilize Yahweh's positive character; neither celebration nor mobilization is served by the threat of Exod 34:7b. Yet Moses in Num 14:18 is cognizant of the second, negative part of the confession. That negative part is kept in purview as needed. Thus, in the harsh verbal attacks on Israel's enemy, Assyria, the poet can utilize the whole of the confession: "The lord is slow to anger but great in power, and the Lord will by no means clear the guilty" (Nah 1:3). The very God who is "slow to anger" is the one who is "great in power." The latter phrase is not mentioned explicitly in Exod 34:7. But the one "great in power" is mobilized here to be "jealous and avenging" against Israel's enemy, who is also "Yahweh's adversary" (v. 2). The God of steadfast love is no wimp, but will act in the service of God's own sovereignty, which in this case is to the enormous benefit of Israel.

It is the positive side of the recital that dominates Israel's theological utterance. Most often, this affirmation of Yahweh is to Israel's great benefit. The usage of the formula in the tale of Jonah, however, shows that on occasion, Yahweh's characteristic "steadfast love and faithfulness" can become problematic for Israel. In the story of Jonah, which is perhaps a parody on Israel's excessive religious rigidity, Jonah is perturbed that hated Nineveh should be forgiven by Yahweh when it repents. Indeed, Jonah would settle for the statement of Nah 1:2-3 in response to Nineveh's wickedness.

In the narrative of Jonah, however, Israel must struggle with Yahweh's readiness to enact the first, positive side of the recital, even toward Nineveh, which in turn precludes the second, negative side that is preferred by Nahum. Given that (for Jonah) unhappy eventuality, this displaced voice of Israel expostulates Yahweh:

> O Lord! Is not this what I said while I was still in my own country? That is why I fled to Tarshish at the beginning; for I knew that you are a gracious God and merciful, slow to anger, and abounding in steadfast love, and ready to relent from punishing. (Jonah 4:2)

God is indeed steadfast and gracious. And Jonah wishes Yahweh were otherwise— like the second part of the recital of Exod 34:6-7.

Yahweh's self-disclosure in Exod 34:6-7 evokes in Israel, variously, profound trust but also confrontive resistance. The profound trust in Yahweh who is so disclosed is found in the hymns, one of which we have cited, and in the assault of Nah 1:2-3. But sometimes Yahweh does not enact this disclosure in effective ways (as in the complaints), and sometimes Yahweh does enact this self-disclosure, but to Israel's felt detriment (as in Jonah). The upshot is that Israel not only treasures this characterization of Yahweh and relies heavily on it, but also argues with Yahweh about it. The argument is often that Yahweh is not fully who Yahweh is said to be. Occasionally the argument is that Yahweh is as said, but Israel wishes it were not so. Either way, the character of Yahweh is a reference in Israel to be counted on and/or to be contended against.

Preferred Accents in Characteristic Recital

It is important for us to recognize that this classic recital in Exod 34:6-7 is not claimed *by Israel,* in its text, to be focal and normative. That claim, which I make here along with a number of other scholars, is *based on characteristic usage.* This is how Israel found it recurringly valid to speak about Yahweh. This recital in itself does not say everything that is to be said—in adjectives—about Yahweh. Conversely, it is not necessary that all of this should be everywhere said about Yahweh. It is, however, the characteristic way in which Israel spoke its witness about Yahweh; though often, as we shall see, it preferred certain accents in the recital.

Two examples show how Israel picked "the best part" of the recital to be used in characteristic fashion in a pastoral-theological crisis. In Lamentations 3, a poem concerning the dread-filled loss of Jerusalem and its temple, Israel is bereft, defeated, and hopeless:

> . . . so I say, "Gone is my glory,
> and all that I had hoped for from the Lord." (Lam 3:18)

Then, in a remarkable reversal, the poet asserts:

> But this I call to mind,
> and therefore I have hope:
> The steadfast love of the Lord never ceases,
> his mercies never come to an end;
> they are new every morning;
> great is your faithfulness.
> "The Lord is my portion," says my soul,
> "therefore I will hope in him." (vv. 21-24)

It is astonishing that the poem moves from hopelessness in v. 18 to hope "in him" in v. 24. The move from hopelessness to hope, in a circumstance of utter defeat, comes in the remembering of Yahweh (v. 21).

We are not told why Israel remembered. This act of remembering is characteristically what Israel does. Its life is pervaded by this resilient rhetoric. And what

Israel remembers in its moment of despair is centered in three great adjectives of Yahweh derived from the recital of Exod 34:6-7: steadfast, merciful, faithful. Presumably in Israel, each of these adjectives is a code supported by a host of concrete verbal connections. In any case, Israel can recall enough about Yahweh's characteristic fidelity so that Israel's confidence in Yahweh overrides the moment of despair. Theologically, it is evident that Israel could not have responded in faith in the midst of such a crisis, had it not available a stylized rhetoric about the God of fidelity.

In similar fashion, sometime after Lamentations 3, Isaiah in the exile continues to deal with the devastating loss of Jerusalem. In the verses before the reference in Isa 54:7-8, the poet twice appeals to Yahweh's compassion as a basis for life beyond abandonment.[12] Then in vv. 9-10 the poet likens the devastation of exile to Noah's flood. Just as the flood ended with Yahweh's promise of protective fidelity (Gen 9:7-18), so now Yahweh promises, at the end of the exile, to be faithful:

> This is like the days of Noah to me:
> Just as I swore that the waters of Noah
> would never again go over the earth,
> so I have sworn that I will not be angry with you
> and will not rebuke you.
> For the mountains may depart
> and the hills be removed,
> but my steadfast love shall not depart from you,
> and my covenant of peace shall not be removed,
> says the Lord, who has compassion on you. (Isa 54:9-10)

The climactic promise made to Israel in the midst of the chaos revolves precisely around Yahweh's steadfast love and compassion, which issue in a "covenant of peace." The notion of *shalôm* is new vocabulary in this trajectory, but it is completely congruent with what we have seen in prior usage, for it is God's fidelity that has a consequence of well-being.

In Lam 3:18-24 and Isa 54:9-10, the ongoing life of Israel, as Israel presents it in testimony, focuses on the core claims of the old recital made to Moses, identifying the adjectives that most poignantly affirm what matters most about Yahweh in Yahweh's propensity toward Israel.

In two other texts the core claims of the old recital are seen to be known and available, but are supplemented by other terms that also belong to Israel's core witness about Yahweh.

In Hos 2:2-23, the poet deals with the collapse of northern Israel, a crisis as profound for the north as the loss of Jerusalem subsequently was for Judah. The terrible loss suffered by the north at the hands of the Assyrians is treated by the

---

12. On this text, see Walter Brueggemann, "A Shattered Transcendence? Exile and Restoration," *Biblical Theology: Problems and Perspectives* (ed. Steven J. Kraftchick et al.; Nashville: Abingdon Press, 1995) 169–82.

poet under the rubric of divorce. The military-political destruction is understood by the poet as evidence of a violated covenant relation that evokes the rage of the husband Yahweh. Yahweh's divorce (abandonment) of Yahweh's wife Israel was, so the poet asserts, due to Israel's fickleness as a spouse. Even before we take up the standard vocabulary that it is our purpose to study, we note the daring rearticulation of experienced reality by the use of metaphor of marriage and divorce. In this usage the metaphor is made even more radical, for now the poet moves beyond divorce to contemplate remarriage, a move unthinkable in the old law of Moses (cf. Deut 24:1-4; Jer 3:1).

What is most remarkable is that in the middle of the poem (v. 14) the imagery is sharply reversed.[13] The husband Yahweh, who has been angry with wife Israel, does an about-face, woos her and renews the relationship. This rehabilitated relationship culminates in a restored marriage, expressed precisely as a wedding vow:

> And I will take you for my wife forever; I will take you for my wife in righteousness and in justice, in steadfast love, and in mercy. I will take you for my wife in faithfulness; and you shall know the Lord. (Hos 2:19-20)

This vow on the part of husband-Yahweh to wife-Israel completely overcomes the negativity of vv. 2-13. For our purposes, it is important that the vow includes three terms we have found in Exod 34:6-7: *steadfast love, mercy,* and *faithfulness*. To these are added two other words, *righteousness* (*ṣdq*) and *justice* (*mšpṭ*), which are not used in Exod 34:6-7 but become a recurring word pair in the prophetic tradition, witnessing in yet another way to the shape of Yahweh's fidelity toward Israel. This word pair has a different nuance from the three terms used from Exod 34:6-7, suggesting much more of expectation and requirement. All five terms together function now to bespeak the character of the faithful husband Yahweh, who will override Israel's fickleness and, in the process, override the old prohibition of Mosaic command against remarriage. That prohibition now must yield to Yahweh's newly disclosed propensity to love Israel in spite of Israel's conduct. The five terms that characterize Yahweh's new way of relating to Israel culminate in the verb *know* (*yd'*), which anticipates an acknowledgment on the part of Israel of an enduring commitment and relation of responsibility.

A somewhat enigmatic text, Ps 85:10-13, employs the vocabulary of the trajectory we are investigating:

---

13. See David J. A. Clines, "Hosea 2: Structure and Interpretation," *Studia Biblica 1978* (JSOTSup 11; Sheffield: JSOT Press, 1979) 83–103. For a critical assessment of the sexual ideology of the text, see Renita Weems, "Gomer: Victim of Violence or Victim of Metaphor," *Interpretation for Liberation* (ed. Katie Geneva Cannon; *Semeia* 47 [1989] 87–104. It is conventional to view the structure of this entire poem as an assertion of Yahweh's generous compassion toward a fickle partner, and no doubt that is the intention of the poem. In recent times we have become aware, however, that the patriarchal assumptions of the poem give Yahweh (the husband) full freedom to act without restraint in the relationship, and portray Israel (the wife) as unfaithful. Indeed, the term conventionally rendered "allure" can also be rendered "rape," permitting Yahweh's forcible action. Obviously such imagery is profoundly problematic if it is taken as a model for sexual roles in human transactions. In my judgment, we must read this poem in its positive intent, but without any naiveté about its ideological undercurrent.

> Steadfast love and faithfulness will meet;
> righteousness and peace will kiss each other.
> Faithfulness will spring up from the ground,
> and righteousness will look down from the sky. . . .
> Righteousness will go before him,
> and will make a path for his steps.

Of the old, now familiar, vocabulary, the terms here reused are *steadfast love, faithfulness,* and *righteousness. Faithfulness* is used twice, and *righteousness* three times. In addition, the term *shalôm* is included, as in Isa 54:10. The cluster of terms here witnesses to the full harmonization of heaven and earth in a peaceable, fruitful enterprise under the benevolent generosity of Yahweh.

Thus in two texts, Lam 3:18-24 and Isa 54:9-10, we find a focus on what seem to be the most crucial and preferred terms of the stylized confession. In two other texts, Hos 2:19-20 and Ps 85:10-13, we find those core terms, with a supplement of others that are surely appropriate cognates. While the collage of terms employed for Yahweh is somewhat fluid, at the core of Israel's utterances we find a constancy of terminology, while away from the core the edges are more open to the nonuse of these terms or to the inclusion of other terms that cohere with the model uses.

Four Provisional Conclusions

From this review of generalizing adjectives by which Israel makes a larger testimony to its God beyond concrete verbal sentences, we may draw four provisional conclusions.

Generalizing Adjectives

First, the adjectival terms are generalizing, permitting Israel to say that Yahweh's *ḥesed* "endures forever." This is a tremendously generalizing assertion, and presumably Israel would incline to generalize in the same way about each of the terms we have considered. Methodologically, however, I will insist that in the awareness of Israel, these generalizing adjectives must regularly have in purview concrete occasions to which reference can be made to substantiate the claim. A flight from the concrete is unlikely in Israel's faith, and we shall misconstrue Israel's testimony about Yahweh if we imagine any such floating generalization. Thus, for example, in the brief hymn of Psalm 117, Israel summons or invites all nations and peoples to join in praise of Yahweh. The reason given for such praise is: "For great is his steadfast love toward us, and the faithfulness of the Lord endures forever" (v. 2).[14] This doxological formula takes up two of the terms used in Exod 34:6-7, but here they are uttered as almost empty ciphers. The only specificity expressed is steadfast love "toward us," that is, toward Israel. The recital as such includes nothing attractive

---

14. On the dynamic relationship between summons and reason, see Walter Brueggemann, *Israel's Praise: Doxology against Idolatry and Ideology* (Philadelphia: Fortress Press, 1988).

or compelling that would motivate the nations or peoples to join Israel in doxology to Yahweh. We must imagine then that Israel was prepared—always prepared—to give concrete substance to the coded adjectives *ḥesed* and *'emeth*. The concrete substance would be, characteristically, verbal testimonies to experienced transformations. Thus the adjectives do not themselves articulate the concretenesses. Their persuasive power depends on having at hand the concretenesses that are pervasively available to Israel. Psalm 136 is a powerful example of this characteristic move of boldly moving from the concrete to the verbal.

Relational Adjectives

Second, the adjectival terms in which Israel bears witness to Yahweh are characteristically relational. That is, they articulate the ways in which Yahweh relates to "us," to Israel, to whomever is Yahweh's partner in a particular testimonial utterance.[15] The terms used by Israel to speak about Yahweh characteristically assume an "other" who is on the receiving end of Yahweh's transformative action and character, toward whom Yahweh is faithful and steadfast or on whom Yahweh visits iniquity. Specifically named as partners and recipients are those "for the thousandth generation," or "children and children's children to the third and fourth generations." Yahweh is known and said to be a God "in relation." To be sure, the relation may take many forms, positive and negative, and both options are worked out in extremis in Israel's narrative life.

What is most crucial about this relatedness is that Israel's stock testimony is unconcerned to use a vocabulary that speaks about Yahweh's own person per se. Israel has little vocabulary for that and little interest in exploring it. Such modest terminology as Israel has for Yahweh's self might revolve around "Yahweh is holy," but this sort of language is not normally used, and most often it occurs only in specialized priestly manuals. More important, Israel's characteristic adjectival vocabulary about Yahweh is completely lacking in terms that have dominated classical theology, such as *omnipotent, omniscient, omnipresent*. This sharp contrast suggests that classical theology, insofar as it is dominated by such interpretive categories and such concerns, is engaged in issues that are not crucial for Israel's testimony about Yahweh and are in fact quite remote from Israel's primary utterance.

Israel, lacking much of a philosophical inclination, is practically oriented and concerned with what Yahweh does "for us," and so is "for us." Or it may be that in its practical modes of testimony, Israel discerned early on that the God who is the primal Character in this speech simply cannot be accommodated to such philosophical categories. That is, perhaps Israel understood, even or especially in the presence of more philosophically inclined neighbors, that Yahweh, as known in its text, simply does not qualify as omnipotent, omniscient, or omnipresent, and so

---

15. Jon D. Levenson, "Exodus and Liberation," *The Hebrew Bible, the Old Testament, and Historical Criticism* (Louisville: Westminster/John Knox, 1993) 127–59, strongly insists that Yahweh's relatedness is characteristically and uncompromisingly to Israel and only, in this first instant, to Israel.

Israel does not seek to locate Yahweh in such speech that is fundamentally incongruent with who Yahweh is. The Old Testament, in its discernment of Yahweh, is relentlessly committed to the recognition that all of reality, including the reality of Yahweh, is relational, relative to the life and destiny of Israel. And the God of Israel has no propensity to be otherwise than related to Israel.

Focus on Fidelity

Third, given the range of the recital of adjectives concerning Yahweh in the stylized testimony of Israel, the primary propensity of Israel is to focus on Yahweh's fidelity, expressed particularly in the terms *merciful, gracious, abounding in stead-fast love,* and *faithfulness.* These terms, *rḥm, ḥnn, ḥsd, 'mth,* saturate Israel's speech about Yahweh and Israel's imagination. This is not to say that other terms, including those of forgiving and visiting, are not used. But Israel's most elemental and most recurring practice is to speak about Yahweh's reliability and trustworthiness.

This confessional inclination can hardly be overvalued. Israel, like every living community, knew all about fickleness and unreliability. Moreover, Israel lived in a religious world that was saturated with gods, and with religious talk about gods, who were fickle and petty and who functioned in terms of bribery and flattery. At the center of Israel's liturgical life and derivative ethical reflection, we find the belief that at the core of life is a Presence (not a principle), an Actor and Agent, who is marked decisively by fidelity and trustworthiness.[16] In this affirmation we are near the center of Israel's testimony about Yahweh, and we are near what it is about the Old Testament that is continually compelling and urgent, even in our own time. Yahweh is a different kind of "other," Israel affirmed, certainly different from any other agent or actor known in their life.

We notice, moreover, that in this recurring vocabulary, *Israel says almost nothing about the power of Yahweh.* It may well be assumed that Yahweh is powerful enough to effect Yahweh's purpose, and no comment is needed. In any case, one does not easily identify in the Old Testament a fixed, recognizable, recurring terminology for power, as we have done here concerning fidelity. We have seen in Nah 1:3 that the phrase "great in power" (*gdl-kḥ*) intrudes into our confessional language. But it strikes us immediately as an intrusion, and we would not mistake it for a standard element in the confession. Perhaps Israel assumed the power of Yahweh and found fidelity both the more important and more problematic category, and so dwelt at length upon it. Consequently, it may be that the statement Israel regularly made about Yahweh's fidelity was a more wondrous statement than anything that might be said about power. It seems to be the assumption of the psalms of complaint, for example, that Yahweh is amply powerful. The problem is typically not the power of Yahweh; it is rather Israel's capacity to mobilize that power in faithful ways, so that appeal is regularly made to promises of fidelity.

---

16. See Jack Miles, *God: A Biography* (New York: A. Knopf, 1995). Miles takes Yahweh as character and as agent with utmost and relentless seriousness.

Statements of Warning

Fourth, the primary accent on fidelity in this characteristic statement about Yahweh in adjectives should not blind us to the second part of the statement of Exod 34:6-7—namely, that Yahweh will surely not acquit the guilty, but will visit sins on the community. To be sure, this statement is not precisely symmetrical to the statements of vv. 6-7a, and this negative statement of warning is not expressed in the same way in adjectives. Nonetheless, it is offered, ostensibly from the very lips of Yahweh, as part of this seemingly decisive self-disclosure of Yahweh, which completes the adjectival statement of vv. 6-7a.

This statement lives in profound tension with the first half of the statement. It may be suggested that this statement also expresses Yahweh's fidelity—that Yahweh will keep faithfully to the sanctions announced with the commandments—but that is certainly not what is characteristically intended in the great terms *rḥm, ḥnn, ḥsd, 'mth*. It may also be suggested that this later statement is subordinate to the positive affirmation, because the "visitation" is to no more than the fourth generation, whereas the positive inclination of Yahweh is to "a thousandth generation." Given these possible interpretations, I suggest that this negative statement of warning is more properly a parallel to the positive affirmation, because the same "iniquity" (*'wn*) that is here "visited" is "forgiven" in v. 7a. While some interpretive maneuverability is possible in relating the two statements to each other, in the end I suggest that these two characterizations of Yahweh are in profound tension with each other, and that finally they contradict each other. Moreover, if we take these statements as serious theological disclosures, then the tension or contradiction here voiced is present in the very life and character of Yahweh.

The tension or contradiction is that Yahweh is *for Israel* (or more generally "for us," *pro nobis*) in fidelity, and at the same time Yahweh is intensely and fiercely *for Yahweh's own self*. These two inclinations of Yahweh are not fully harmonized here, and perhaps never are anywhere in the Old Testament. This reading of the statements entails the conclusion that there is a profound, unresolved ambiguity in Yahweh's life. As a consequence, in any moment of Yahweh's life with Israel, Yahweh has available more than one alternative response to Israel, and Israel is never fully, finally certain of Yahweh's inclination toward it. Thus, quite specifically, in the aftermath of Exodus 32 and Aaron's affront against Yahweh, Moses does not know in Exod 34:8-9 how Yahweh will next deal with Israel. Indeed, Moses (and Israel) cannot know, until Yahweh's next utterance in v. 10, which is a response out of massive fidelity and graciousness.

The adjectives reflect the verbal sentences that provide the data for Israel's larger testimony. Yahweh's actions, as given us in Israel's verbs, are not all of a piece. Along with love and care, there are holiness, wrath, and rage, and so this adjectival generalization is congruent with the data of the verbal sentences. Israel knows that there is a dimension of the unsettled in Yahweh, making a relationship with Yahweh endlessly demanding and restless. This second half of the adjectival testimony asserts Yahweh's freedom, so that Yahweh's fidelity does not become Yahweh's domestication. But this freedom of Yahweh is freedom of a certain dangerous kind, which means that the relationship, as crucial to Yahweh as to Israel, is deeply at risk. Moses understands this in his urgent prayer of Exod 34:8-9.

These qualities of Yahweh's life in adjectival witness—specific, relational, faithful, contradictory—yield a God who is self-giving, harshly demanding, and endlessly restless, as the reference point for Israel's life. It is no wonder that Israel's ultimate testimony to Yahweh concerns Yahweh's incomparability:

- There is no one like Yahweh, whose concrete disclosure permits a generalizing in this particular way.

- There is no one like Yahweh, whose whole existence and life are committed in a relation to Israel.

- There is no one like Yahweh, a God marked by tenacious fidelity toward and solidarity with Yahweh's subject people.

- There is no one like Yahweh, who while endlessly faithful, hosts in Yahweh's own life a profound contradiction that leaves open a harshness toward the beloved partner community.

Yahweh's incomparability is not in any one of these affirmations, but in the odd collage of all of them together. Thus one cannot generalize beyond Yahweh—one cannot speak generically about this God. Israel can only testify to the peculiar convergences that signify Yahweh, but that also, derivatively, mark Israel's own life. It is clear that the way in which this Subject is present in the life of Israel introduces into Israel's existence categories of discernment and self-understanding that are profoundly reassuring and endlessly demanding. It is no wonder that Israel's primary rhetorical responsibility is to try to bring Yahweh to adequate speech, for on the adequacy of that speech turns the viability of Israel's peculiar life in the world.

SIX

Nouns: Yahweh as Constant

C ONVENTIONAL THEOLOGY uses nouns to speak of God. Israel's testimony employs nouns to speak of Yahweh. Nouns, among other things, are naming devices that identify the constancy, substance, and graspability of characters who play roles in one's explanatory narrative. By using nouns to name and characterize Yahweh in this explanatory narrative of testimony, Israel assigns to (or recognizes in) Yahweh elements of constancy and substance that make Yahweh in some ways knowable and available to Israel.[1]

Elizabeth Johnson has recently shown how difficult theological language is, and she gives particular attention to patriarchal languages.[2] I suggest that for Israel's testimony, nouns for Yahweh are peculiarly problematic, for they affirm a kind of substantive constancy about Yahweh that is only grudgingly affirmed in Israel's verbal testimony. Yet, problematic as they are, nouns are indispensable for Israel's theological discourse. Israel, in its testimony in nouns, might have anticipated and agreed with Karl Barth's verdict:

> As ministers we ought to speak of God. We are human, however, and so cannot speak of God. We ought therefore to recognize both our obligation and our inability and by that very recognition give God the glory. This is our perplexity.[3]

In chapter 4 I suggested that Israel's primary discourse about Yahweh is organized in sentences built around verbs. This focus on verbs makes clear that it is, first of all, the action of Yahweh that Israel noticed and valued and to which it wanted to bear witness. Consistently the substantive character of Yahweh is informed by the verbal activity assigned to Yahweh in a series of particular instances. Building from that judgment about the cruciality of verbs and immediate concrete action given in verbs as the way in which Israel first of all testifies to Yahweh, chapter 5 considered Israel's generalizing adjectives as a way in which Israel gathered a collage of concrete verbs in order to make a larger, more enduring statement

---

1. On this dimension of the dramatic portrayal of Yahweh, see Dale Patrick, *The Rendering of God in the Old Testament* (OBT; Philadelphia: Fortress Press, 1981).

2. Elizabeth Johnson, *She Who Is: The Mystery of God in Feminist Theological Discourse* (New York: Crossroad, 1992).

3. Karl Barth, *The Word of God and the Word of Man* (New York: Harper and Brothers, Harper Torch Books, 1957) 186.

about Yahweh. Thus if Yahweh acts graciously in certain events (see, for example, Psalm 136), Israel eventually is prepared on the basis of such concrete evidences to use an adjective: "Yahweh is gracious." In such a statement, Israel suggests that Yahweh is enduringly gracious, even between the times and events to which the verbal sentences bear testimony. These larger adjectival claims, which give staying power to Yahweh's character, depend on constant feeding and replenishing by verbal testimony that is intensely concrete.

In Israel's testimony about Yahweh, nouns stand in relation to adjectives as adjectives stand in relation to verbs, so that nouns are an even bolder, larger, and more generalizing testimony to Yahweh. Thus if Israel can say about many occasions that Yahweh "saves," and then moves to an adjective, saying, "Yahweh is saving" (with a participle), Israel can eventually use a noun: "Yahweh is savior." The substance of the nominal claim is informed by reference to many adjectival claims, which in turn are informed and given concrete reference by many verbal sentences of testimony.[4] *Thus I propose that in speaking about Yahweh, Israel regularly moves from the particular to the general, from the verb to the adjective to the noun.* In order to maintain the generalizing nouns, Israel must regularly be prepared to return to the more particular adjectival claims, and behind that to the most particular verbal sentences of testimony.[5]

The Testimony of Metaphors

If nouns for Yahweh arise out of adjectives, which in turn arise out of verbs, then the noun characterizations of Yahweh are not as firm and stable as they first appear to be and as they are often taken to be in classical theological traditions that trade in "substances." In fact, I suggest that nouns are used as a gathering of adjectives for Yahweh, so that nouns are much less settled and substantive than our use of them might suggest. The matter is now widely expressed thus: Nouns used for Yahweh in the Old Testament are metaphors, and there is no one-to-one match between the metaphor and that to which it refers. In fact, the noun as metaphor always stands in a tenuous and proximate relation to the One to whom it bears witness. The following points bear upon nouns as metaphors in Israel's theological testimony.

1. Metaphors are nouns that function in Israel in order to give access to the Subject of verbs, who is endlessly elusive.[6] The metaphor will be misunderstood

---

4. The relationship among verbs, adjectives, and nouns that I propose is not unlike "declarative" and "descriptive" hymns, as proposed by Claus Westermann (see chap. 5, n. 1).

5. In *Israel's Praise: Doxology against Idolatry and Ideology* (Philadelphia: Fortress Press, 1988), I have suggested that our characteristic propensity is to "read up" from reason to summons, i.e., to move from the particular to the general, so as to expand the claim of the hymn. Critical reflection requires, conversely, that we "read back down," from summons to reason, i.e., from the general claim to its specific grounding in lived experience.

6. On metaphor as a means to express what is elusive, see the magisterial study of Paul Ricoeur, *The Rule of Metaphor: Multi-disciplinary Studies of the Creation of Meaning in Language* (London: Routledge and Kegan Paul, 1978).

and misused if it is not recognized that the One named by the metaphor is not contained or comprehended by the noun. Yet nominal speech usage in Israel does give access to Yahweh, so that Israel can indeed respond toward the One testified to as judge, king, or father.

2. Metaphors, as Sallie McFague has shown, are nouns used to characterize the Subject, God.[7] But because the metaphor does not fully match the elusive Subject, the Subject both "is" and "is not" made available in the utterance of the noun. Thus when Israel testifies, "Yahweh is my shepherd," the noun *shepherd* gives Israel certain specific access to Yahweh. At the same time, Yahweh is *not* a shepherd. This is not because *shepherd* is a poor or inadequate metaphor, but because speech about the elusive Yahweh, in its very character, allows for this reservation. Failure to take seriously the "is not" quality of the noun is a failure to recognize that the noun is metaphor and cannot draw closer to the Subject than through the practice of metaphor.

3. Metaphor, as McFague suggests, is a guard against idolatry in a testimony that tends toward monotheism. It is likely correct, as James Sanders proposes, that Israel never fully arrives at monotheism.[8] To the extent that its faith is *on the way* to monotheism, Israel in its testimony risks being too sure about God and is tempted to give closure to a Subject who is characteristically elusive. As the move to monotheism tends toward closure, the practice of metaphor works against closure, in order to maintain a witness that honors the tentativeness, openness, and elusiveness of the testifying process. Monotheism, unprotected by metaphor, moves toward idolatry; for without the elusiveness of nouns, the God of monotheism may come to be fully known and thus completely exhausted in utterance. But of course Yahweh is neither fully known nor completely exhausted in Israel's testimony, because Yahweh is hidden, free, surprising, and elusive, and refuses to be caught in any verbal formulation. Thus, metaphor precludes the reification of any noun label for Yahweh, as though the label were the thing itself—that is, were God.

4. Along with reification, the other temptation to theological closure is reductionism, the temptation to reduce metaphors about Yahweh to a few or a single one. Such reductionism, as in finding the "right" noun for Yahweh, in the end is another form of reification. Against such reductionism, the testimony of Israel practices a determined pluralism in its nouns for Yahweh. As Brian Wren has urged "many names" for God because no single name is adequate,[9] so the Old Testament employs many metaphors for Yahweh because no single metaphor can say

---

7. Sallie McFague, *Metaphorical Theology: Models of God in Religious Language* (Philadelphia: Fortress Press, 1983), explores the conventional stock of metaphors for God, but tilts the topic in a fresh direction. On the specificity and range of biblical metaphors for God, see Robert J. Banks, *God the Worker: Journeys into the Mind, Heart, and Imagination of God* (New York: Judson Press, 1994).

8. James A. Sanders, "Adaptable for Life," *From Sacred Text to Sacred Story: Canon as Paradigm* (Philadelphia: Fortress Press, 1987) 9–39. See Walter Brueggemann, "'Exodus' in the Plural (Amos 9:7)" (forthcoming), for a suggestion of a counter-pluralizing tendency in Amos 9:7.

9. Brian Wren, *What Language Shall I Borrow? God-Talk in Worship: A Male Response to Feminist Theology* (New York: Crossroad, 1990). More specifically, see his hymn, "Many Names," ibid., 143–70.

all that Israel needs to say about their God. The full gamut of nouns for Yahweh contains not only a rich variety, but also a panorama of possibilities, many of which contradict each other. The witnesses in Israel, moreover, do not undertake to harmonize or make all the metaphors fit together. Rather, the rich range of metaphors often stand in tension with each other, so that one metaphor may say what is left unsaid by another, so that one may correct another, or so that one may deabsolutize another.

Second Isaiah provides one example of testimony in which nouns for Yahweh are set side by side, with no attempt to harmonize, but perhaps with the precise intention of asserting an incongruity:

> See, the Lord God comes with might,
> and his arm rules for him;
> his reward is with him,
> and his recompense before him.
> He will feed his flock like a shepherd;
> he will gather the lambs in his arms,
> and carry them in his bosom,
> and gently lead the mother sheep. (Isa 40:10-11)

In the opening lines Yahweh is portrayed as a mighty warrior, as a returning, conquering military hero. But this is followed immediately by a portrayal of Yahweh as something like a nursemaid, who gently carries the lambs and leads the mother sheep. Surely the metaphor of *shepherd* for Yahweh is matched by the metaphor of *flock* with reference to Israel. Taken together, these images characterize Yahweh as an agent both of fierce power and of inordinate gentleness and tenderness.[10] In our theological discourse, we are characteristically tempted to pick one of these in preference to the other, to let our preferred one crowd out the other, and to absolutize the preferred one. The witness of Israel, by the rich diversity of nouns, makes such a reductionism in any direction impossible. Thus, one may say that Yahweh is something of a warrior and something of a shepherd, but not finally shepherd and not fully warrior, something of each but not fully either.

Israel's flattest language for Yahweh, the language of nouns, is exercised in ways that militate against the normal, substantive claim of nouns. That is, what Israel intends to claim or point to in such speech is not the same as the function performed by substantive nouns in normal Western discourse. The images and metaphors used to speak about Yahweh will be regularly misunderstood and distorted into idolatry unless it is endlessly remembered that the claim of the noun is always held loosely, in light of the metaphorical character of the noun and the elusive quality of the Subject. Such nouns serve Israel in the moment of utterance and in the durable testimony of the utterance, but such nouns cannot be absolutized or torn away from

---

10. See the powerful juxtaposition of images voiced in the remarkable statement of Deut 1:30-31.

the concrete utterance of testimony in which they are embedded. Such absolutizing runs counter both to the mode of Israel's speech and to the Subject of its witness.[11]

The nouns for Yahweh in the testimony of Israel may not be extracted from the larger utterance of narrative testimony that is Yahweh's proper habitat. This articulation of the matter suggests that nouns for Yahweh are important for a full exploration of Israel's testimony, but that nouns participate in the elusive quality of the Character to which they testify. The nouns should be valued in their full freight and poignancy, but they belong to their occasion of utterance and to the environment in which the utterance is placed. This means, then, that Yahweh is always open to new nouns and new utterances that may correct, protest against, or destabilize other nouns. It is striking that in the exilic utterance of Isaiah, Jeremiah, and Ezekiel, some of the most suggestive metaphors for Yahweh are freshly employed, utterances of testimony that invite new verdicts about who and how Yahweh is.[12]

Our work now is to explore the rich variety of metaphorical nouns for Yahweh in Israel's testimony, nouns that bear witness to Yahweh's elusive constancy, but do so in ways that guard Israel's monotheistic tendency against the temptations of reification and reductionism that end in idolatry. We may divide our consideration of nouns for Yahweh into two groups: (1) those that seem to be dominant in Israel's testimony, and (2) those that are more marginal, but that function as a cautionary subversion of the dominant nouns.

Metaphors of Governance

The metaphors that appear to dominate Israel's speech about Yahweh may be termed images of governance, wherein Israel witnesses to Yahweh's capacity to govern and order in ways that assert sovereign authority and that assure a coherent ordering of life in the world. G. Ernest Wright and Patrick D. Miller have in different ways dealt with this cluster of images, in which we may include judge, king, warrior, and father.[13] Each of these images pertains to the use of power. Indeed, it is possible, as has often been recognized, that these metaphors are open to a "macho" understanding of the character of Yahweh, for they are often associated with masculinity and virility.[14] There is no doubt that these images for Yahweh, on the lips of Israel, have been taken to authorize masculine control that has often been

---

11. Eberhard Jüngel, "Metaphorical Truth," *Theological Essays* (Edinburgh: T. & T. Clark, 1989) 58–71, proposes that all theological language is "through and through" metaphorical. See Roland D. Zimany, *Vehicle for God: The Metaphorical Theology of Eberhard Jüngel* (Macon, Ga.: Mercer University Press, 1994), for a review of Jüngel's helpful exposition.

12. My observation here takes up much of the same material as does Gerhard von Rad, *Old Testament Theology* 2 (San Francisco: Harper and Row, 1965). My intention, however, is very different from that of von Rad, who approached the textual material with questions different from those I am urging.

13. G. Ernest Wright, *Theology and the Old Testament* (New York: Harper and Row, 1969); Patrick D. Miller, "The Sovereignty of God," *The Hermeneutical Quest: Essays in Honor of James Luther Mays on His Sixty-Fifth Birthday* (ed. Donald G. Miller; Princeton Theological Monographs 4; Allison Park, Pa.: Pickwick Publications, 1986) 129–44.

14. In Christian interpretation, the metaphors are kept drastically open in christological assignation by the central, defining reality of the cross.

heavy-handed, exploitative, and brutalizing. Without denying that these renderings of Yahweh have had destructive sociopolitical spin-offs, it is equally important to recognize that these articulations of Yahweh were theologically urgent in a community that was characteristically marginated, a community that appeals to this pro-Israel power as a counter and antidote to hostile and brutalizing powers (divine and human). That is, Yahweh's power, mediated in these metaphors, functions as a counterpower to deabsolutize injurious power. Having said that, however, it is equally important to recognize that these metaphors as mediations of power cannot be flatly reduced to one-dimensionality. These metaphors remain more open and elusive than that, and in Israel's imagination assert more than and other than sheer power.[15]

Yahweh as Judge

This rendering of Yahweh is predominant in the life and speech of Israel.[16] It is evident that the metaphor *judge* presents Yahweh as committed to a rule of just law, as one who can be counted on to intervene on behalf of those who are treated unjustly or against what is regarded as inequitable treatment according to Israel's radical notions of justice, which stand against the exploitative "realism" of much self-serving, self-aggrandizing justice. Thus Yahweh is said to be a "lover of justice" (Ps 99:4, Isa 61:8), one who cares about justice, who is committed to this practice, and who can be trusted to act in societal affairs on behalf of covenantal justice.

The role of Yahweh as judge is one on which Israel counts heavily, for it is often affirmed that the law which informs the judgment of Yahweh is a law of well-being for all, which Yahweh enforces. This equity of Yahweh does not simply mete out "just deserts"; it includes active intervention (reparations?) for those who are weak and powerless. Thus it is affirmed in Israel's great doxology:

> The world is firmly established;
> it shall never be moved.
> He will judge the peoples with equity....
> for he is coming to judge the earth.
> He will judge the world with righteousness,
> and the peoples with his truth. (Ps 96:10, 13)

This action of this judge will set the world right. This activity of the judge is given positive content in litigation against other would-be gods who do not practice the justice of Yahweh:

> How long will you judge unjustly
> and show partiality to the wicked?
> Give justice to the weak and the orphan;

---

15. G. Ernest Wright, *The Challenge of Israel's Faith* (Chicago: University of Chicago Press, 1944) 66, speaks of the "virile" aspects of the biblical God.

16. On this theme, see Richard Nelson Boyce, *The Cry to God in the Old Testament* (SBLDS 103; Atlanta: Scholars Press, 1988).

maintain the right of the lowly and the destitute.
Rescue the weak and the needy;
deliver them from the hand of the wicked. (Ps 82:2-4)

Thus Israel affirms that Yahweh's role as judge is a source of solace and reassurance that exploitative social situations will be righted. This content of Yahweh's role as judge becomes a ground for appeal, even for individual persons who plead their cause before "the judge of all the earth":

Let the assembly of the peoples be
gathered around you,
and over it take your seat on high.
The Lord judges the peoples;
judge me, O Lord, according to my righteousness
and according to the integrity that is in me....
God is a righteous judge,
and a God who has indignation every day. (Ps 7:7-8, 11)

He judges the world with righteousness;
he judges the peoples with equity....
For the needy shall not always be forgotten,
nor the hope of the poor perish forever. (Ps 9:8, 18)

The ground for intimate, personal appeal is also the ground for Israel's belief that large social forces that practice exploitation will be called to account by this judge:

As for you, my flock, thus says the Lord God: I shall judge between sheep and sheep, between rams and goats: Is it not enough for you to feed on the good pasture, but you must tread down with your feet the rest of your pasture? When you drink of clear water, must you foul the rest with your feet? And must my sheep eat what you have trodden with your feet, and drink what you have fouled with your feet? Therefore, thus says the Lord God to them: I myself will judge between the fat sheep and the lean sheep. Because you pushed with flank and shoulder, and butted at all the weak animals with your horns until you scattered them far and wide, I will save my flock, and they shall no longer be ravaged; and I will judge between sheep and sheep. (Ezek 34:17-22)

To be sure, Yahweh's judgeship has a severe side. The rhetoric of Israel suggests that sometimes Yahweh is deeply affronted by injustice and will strike back at those who affront Yahweh's passionate commitment to justice. Moreover, this testimony of Israel concerning Yahweh contains an element of danger, for Yahweh's response appears to be on occasion disproportionate to the affront. In such a context as Genesis 18–19, Abraham must firmly call Yahweh back to Yahweh's proper function:

Far be it from you to do such a thing, to slay the righteous with the wicked, so that the righteous fare as the wicked! Far be that from you! Shall not the Judge (*špṭ*) of all the earth do what is just? (*mšpṭ*) (Gen 18:25)

This point should not be overly stressed. Nonetheless, the recognition that the righteous may be destroyed with the wicked indicates Israel's awareness of potential disproportion in the severity of Yahweh as judge.

On the whole, however, Yahweh's fierceness as a judge is not found to be capricious. It is, rather, the implementation of law and sanction to which Yahweh is known to be committed. Thus George Mendenhall has shown that Yahweh's "vengeance" is not wild and capricious, but is in fact the exercise of a rule of order to which Yahweh from the outset is committed.[17] This constant of Yahweh as a judge who upholds "right law" against offenders is the ground on which much of Israel's rhetoric is cast in juridical language. In its confidence in Yahweh, Israel attests to the reliable justice of Yahweh. At the same time, it is not inattentive to severity in lived reality that cannot be contained in any credible, explanatory moral calculus. Israel's confidence in Yahweh as judge is evident in Psalm 82, where true "godness," the claim of Yahweh, is intimately linked to Yahweh's attentiveness to the weak and destitute (vv. 3-4). Indeed it is to this judge that Israel makes appeal when every other chance of justice has failed (cf. v. 8).

Thus in the prophets of Israel, Yahweh the judge often brings charges against Israel and implements appropriate judicial sentences:[18]

Hear the word of the Lord,
O people of Israel;
for the Lord has an indictment against the inhabitants
of the land.
There is no faithfulness or loyalty,
and no knowledge of God in the land.
Swearing, lying, and murder,
and stealing and adultery break out;
bloodshed follows bloodshed.
Therefore the land mourns,
and all who live in it languish;
together with the wild animals
and the birds of the air,
even the fish of the sea are perishing. (Hos 4:1-3).

Yahweh's sphere of judicial administration, however, is not limited to Israel, who has signed on with the law of Sinai. It extends as well to other nations, all

---

17. George E. Mendenhall, "The Vengeance of Yahweh," *The Tenth Generation: The Origins of the Biblical Tradition* (Baltimore: Johns Hopkins University Press, 1973) 69–104.

18. See Claus Westermann, *Basic Forms of Prophetic Speech* (Atlanta: John Knox, 1967).

of whom in the end are subject to the justice of Yahweh.[19] Thus in large scope, Yahweh judges:

> At the set time that I appoint
> I will judge with equity. . . .
> but it is God who executes judgment,
> putting down one and lifting up another. . . .
> All the horns of the wicked I will cut off,
> but the horns of the righteous shall be exalted. (Ps 75:2, 7, 10)

> Rise up, O judge of the earth;
> give to the proud what they deserve!
> O Lord, how long shall the wicked,
> how long shall the wicked exult? . . .
> They crush your people, O Lord,
> and afflict your heritage.
> They kill the widow and the stranger,
> they murder the orphan. . . .
> Can wicked rulers be allied with you,
> those who contrive mischief by statute? (Ps 94:2-3, 5-6, 20)

In the end, the "oracles against the nations" (Amos 1–2; Isaiah 13–23; Jeremiah 46–51; Ezekiel 25–32) are evidence that Yahweh exercises judicial control over the affairs of the nations and metes out judgment according to Yahweh's own passionate justice. For example, in the oracles of Amos 1:3–2:8, the conduct of other peoples is taken into the lawsuit form of prophetic speech. Thus these other peoples, who have never been to Sinai, are subject to the judgment of Yahweh. For example, Yahweh punishes the Ammonites for savaging Gilead women (Amos 1:13).

There is indeed a potential for severity and fierceness in Israel's rhetoric about Yahweh as judge. This judge takes seriously the rule of law. This severity and fierceness, which on occasion seem to break out in arbitrariness, are the foundation of Israel's affirmation that the world has moral coherence to it, on which even the weak can count. That moral coherence has credibility, moreover, because the judge is willing and able to effect sanctions against violators.

It is important to remember that the claim for Yahweh as judge is metaphorical. As a result, Israel does not have a fully articulated case for what law it is by which the judge proceeds, but only an inchoate notion of justice based on law that arises

---

19. For a survey of the oracles against the nations, see Norman K. Gottwald, *All the Kingdoms of the Earth: Israelite Prophecy and International Relations in the Ancient Near East* (New York: Harper and Row, 1964). More recently, see the fine treatment by Paul R. Raabe, "Why Prophetic Oracles Against the Nations?" *Fortunate the Eyes That See* (ed. Astrid B. Beck et al.; Grand Rapids: Eerdmans, 1995) 236–57. On the ground for the judgment made against the nations, see Graham Davies, "The Destiny of the Nations in the Book of Isaiah," *The Book of Isaiah* (ed. J. Vermeylen; Leuven University Press, 1989) 93–120; G. R. Homberg, "Reasons for Judgment in the Oracles against the Nations in the Prophet Isaiah," *VT* 31 (1981) 145–59.

in the very utterances about the judge. Thus the metaphor of judge does not have its locus in a theory of law. It lives, rather, in a world of desperate, practical appeal of those who have no other ground of appeal or hope and in a world of righteous rage among those who are appalled at exploitative brutality that must be called to accountability. Thus the metaphor arises in the very practice of faith and life. Israel does no more, in the end, than to provide the materials out of which a more coherent theory of law may be formulated.

Yahweh as King

This image for Yahweh is closely related to that of judge. The source and age of this rhetoric for Yahweh have been the subject of a long scholarly debate.[20] There is no doubt that the phrase "Yahweh is king" is informed by and linked to political models that were available to Israel in the ancient world. And there is no doubt that Israel took up these models for theological testimony in ways that could be congruent with what else Israel had to say about Yahweh. As with the metaphor of judge, the metaphor of king is a way of witnessing to Yahweh's work in ordering creation as a viable, reliable place for life and well-being. And, as with the metaphor of judge, this rhetoric for Yahweh is open for exploitative ideological use, as the rhetoric for Yahweh was available for use by the Jerusalem dynasty that easily claimed Yahweh's functions as its own. Nonetheless, it is important to recognize that Israel's rhetoric is permeated with "Yahweh as king" and that Israel's preferred mode of theological discourse is political. Israel's speech about Yahweh is never far removed from issues of power, which are freighted with great temptation and with endless ambiguity.

George Mendenhall's influential model for the Mosaic covenant has made a powerful case that Yahweh is to be understood as a suzerain in a newly established rule of reliable law.[21] This establishment of Yahweh's new rule of law is the beginning point for Israel's utterance about Yahweh as king. Mendenhall had been anticipated in this notion by Martin Buber's notion of theopolitics at Sinai, wherein Israel comes under the governance and will of this king as a "contrast-society" to every other governance.[22] Thus in Psalm 29, Yahweh has seemingly won a contest over other gods, and so rightly takes the throne above the flood from which a decree of *shalôm* is given:

> The Lord sits enthroned over the flood;
> The Lord sits enthroned as king forever.

---

20. Much turns on a critical judgment about the relationship of the enthronement language for Yahweh in the Psalms and in Second Isaiah. Hermann Gunkel and Hans-Joachim Kraus hold that the Isaiah materials are earlier and so the usage is relatively late. If, however, one follows Sigmund Mowinckel and treats the Psalms as the earlier material, then the usage of Yahweh as king may be very early in the liturgy and faith of Israel.

21. George E. Mendenhall, *Law and Covenant in Israel and the Ancient Near East* (Pittsburgh: Biblical Colloquium, 1954).

22. Martin Buber, *The Kingship of God* (trans. Richard Schiemann; New York: Harper and Row, 1967).

May the Lord give strength to his people!
May the Lord bless his people with peace! (Ps 29:10-11)

In the parallel of Psalm 96, the news given to the nations is the claim that Yahweh has just arrived at governance, whether in a liturgical recognition by the other gods, or by a massive defeat of the other gods: "Say among the nations, 'The Lord is King!'" (Ps 96:10).[23] This declaration of new governance, moreover, is marked by righteousness, equity, and truth (vv. 10, 13), and it is a cause for great joy and exultation among all creatures (vv. 11-12).

The rule of Yahweh—as king in Israel and king over all of creation, over all other gods and over all the nations—has two functions in the rhetoric of Israel. First, the kingship of Yahweh functions as a critical principle to deabsolutize or even to delegitimate all other governances that imagine they are unfettered and absolute. This deabsolutizing and delegitimating are evident at the beginning of Israel's testimony in the Exodus narrative, wherein Yahweh delegitimates the rule of pharaoh. That narrative culminates in a glad acknowledgment of Yahweh's kingship: "The Lord will reign forever and ever" (Exod 15:18).

At the other end of the Old Testament, Nebuchadnezzar is taken up as a cipher for all pretentious worldly power and is dramatically shown to be completely dependent on Yahweh. For Yahweh not only rules from the heavens, but also determines who will rule proximately in the earth with Yahweh's authorization. The climactic delegitimating of Nebuchadnezzar in Daniel 4 makes a claim for Yahweh that is almost a liturgical response:

How great are his signs,
How great his wonders!
His kingdom is an everlasting kingdom,
and his sovereignty is from generation to generation. (v. 3)

...the Most High is sovereign over the kingdom of mortals;
he gives it to whom he will
and sets over it the lowliest of human beings. (v. 17)

...until you have learned that the Most High has sovereignty
over the kingdom of mortals, and gives it to whom he will. (v. 25,
    repeated in v. 32).

All the inhabitants of the earth are accounted as nothing,
and he does what he wills with the host of heaven
and the inhabitants of the earth.
There is no one who can stay his hand
or say to him, "What are you doing?" (v. 35)

---

23. It is possible, as Mowinckel has urged, to render the phrase as "Yahweh has just become king," i.e., in this moment of liturgic enactment. For the hypothesis of Mowinckel that provides a context for this alternative rendering, see the critical review of Ben C. Ollenburger, *Zion, City of the Great King: A Theological Symbol of the Jerusalem Cult* (JSOTSup 41; Sheffield: JSOT Press, 1987) 24–33.

> ... for all his works are truth,
> and his ways are justice;
> and he is able to bring low
> those who walk in pride. (v. 37)

Yahweh is indeed sovereign. Any other ruler is derivative from and dependent on Yahweh, which means that Nebuchadnezzar can make no claim for himself. This extraordinary claim for Yahweh contains *the seed of revolutionary civil disobedience,* for any rule not congruent with the rule of Yahweh is in the end illegitimate.[24]

Yahweh as king thus operates as a formidable critical principle. But the claim of Yahweh as king also has positive content that draws closer to Israel's own lived experience. In a pivotal affirmation in the tradition of Deuteronomy, Israel asserts in doxological fashion:

> Although heaven and the heaven of heavens belong to the Lord your God, the earth with all that is in it ... For the Lord your God is God of gods and Lord of lords, the great God, mighty and awesome.... (Deut 10:14, 17)

In the end, that awesome rule of Yahweh comes down to concrete generosity and restorative compassion for those in need.

Concerning Israel:

> ... yet the Lord set his heart in love on your ancestors alone and chose you, their descendants after them, out of all the peoples, as it is today. (Deut 10:15)

Concerning the needy:

> ... who executes justice for the orphan and the widow, and who loves the strangers, providing them food and clothing. (Deut 10:18)

The kingship of Yahweh is concerned with concrete rehabilitative practice toward those who are in need. In the hymn of Psalm 145, Israel's praise of Yahweh begins in recognition of Yahweh's kingship:

> I will extol you, my God and King,
> and bless your name forever and ever. (v. 1)

The substance of that rule is said to be attentive, generous care:

> The Lord upholds all who are falling,
> and raises up all who are bowed down.
> The eyes of all look to you,
> and you give them their food in due season.

---

24. On the enduring importance of this model for political conduct, see W. Sibley Towner, "Were the English Puritans 'The Saints of the Most High'? Issues in the Pre-critical Interpretation of Daniel 7," *Int* 37 (1983) 46–63. John Calvin, *Institutes of the Christian Religion* (LCC 21; London: SCM Press, 1960), 2:1521, concludes his theological exposition with an appeal to Acts 5:29, a warrant for civil disobedience rooted in the sovereignty of God.

> You open your hand,
> satisfying the desire of every living thing.
> The Lord is just in all his ways,
> and kind in all his doings. (vv. 14-17)

In Isa 43:15, the "Creator of Israel, your King" is the one who will be actively engaged for the liberation of the exiles from Babylon by a show of enormous power.

As Israel can celebrate the king in doxological hymn, so Israel also addresses the king in petition in its psalms of complaint. It is this king, the one who rules in rehabilitative compassion and who delegitimates exploitative power, to whom Israel has recourse in its most intimate appeals for help:[25]

> Listen to the sound of my cry,
> my King and my God,
> for to you I pray. (Ps 5:2)

> The Lord is king forever and ever;
> the nations shall perish from his land.
> O Lord, you will hear the desire of the meek;
> you will strengthen their heart,
> you will incline your ear
> to do justice for the orphan and the oppressed,
> so that those from earth may strike terror no more. (Ps 10:16-18)

The king is indeed the judge. As king, however, Yahweh the judge is active and powerful in intervention, in order to bring the world to healthy function, to restore the possibility of well-being among the nations by crushing the exploiters, and to attend to the needy who have no other advocate except this king.

Yahweh as Warrior

This metaphor for Yahweh is intimately linked to those of judge and king.[26] Yahweh as warrior is the one who, as a judge committed to a rule of law, acts to stabilize, maintain, or implement that rule, over which the king will preside. As in the case of judge and king, the notion of Yahweh as warrior serves as a critical principle, in order to assert that Yahweh will fight against and defeat all the illicit claimants to public power. This metaphor, like the other two, moreover, functions as a point of reference and as a court of appeal for those who are without help or hope from any other source.

---

25. On intimate dimensions of personal piety in ancient Israel, see Rainer Albertz, *A History of Israelite Religion in the Old Testament Period*, 1: *From the Beginnings to the End of Monarchy* and 2: *From the Exile to the Maccabees* (OTL; Louisville: Westminster/John Knox, 1994).

26. See Patrick D. Miller, *The Divine Warrior in Early Israel* (HSM 5; Cambridge: Harvard University Press, 1973); and the basic study of Gerhard von Rad, *Holy War in Ancient Israel* (Grand Rapids: Eerdmans, 1991). Attention should be paid to Ben C. Ollenburger's critical introduction to the English edition of von Rad's work, pp. 1–33.

Patrick Miller has demonstrated that Exod 15:1-18, among the most crucial of Israel's testimonial utterances, is the lead case for "God the warrior."[27] Indeed, Yahweh is said to be "a man of war" (v. 3; RSV), one who acts in fierce and violent ways on behalf of Israel. Thus Yahweh's defeat of pharaoh (vv. 4-10) and subsequent defeat of the kings of Transjordan and Canaan (vv. 13-16) are indeed acts of mighty power. The work of Yahweh who engages in violent battle is first of all to create a future for Israel outside every sphere of oppression, and then to secure for Israel room for life—that is, the land promised in Genesis.

This same rhetoric about Yahweh as warrior is taken up again in Isaiah of the exile, as Israel testifies to the defeat of Babylon and emancipation from imperial exile. Thus,

> See, the Lord God comes with might,
> and his arm rules for him;
> his reward is with him,
> and his recompense before him. (Isa 40:10)

> The Lord has bared his holy arm
> before the eyes of all the nations;
> and all the ends of the earth shall see
> the salvation of our God. (Isa 52:10)

These two pivotal victories, in Egypt and in Babylon, which transform the destiny of Israel, have as their doxological counterpart the liturgy of entrance in Psalm 24:

> Who is the King of glory?
> The Lord, strong and mighty,
> the Lord, mighty in battle....
> The Lord of hosts,
> he is the King of glory. (vv. 8, 10)

Here the images of king and warrior converge. The last lines of the poem utter the ancient title for Yahweh, "Yahweh of hosts," referring to Yahweh's military legions.

The role of Yahweh as warrior is a partisan one. Yahweh is engaged in violent, enforcing, liberating activity on behalf of Israel:

> He clogged their chariot wheels so that they turned with difficulty. The Egyptians said, "Let us flee from the Israelites, for the Lord is fighting for them against Egypt."...Thus the Lord saved Israel that day from the Egyptians; and Israel saw the Egyptians dead on the seashore. (Exod 14:25, 30)

---

27. See Miller, *The Divine Warrior*, 113–17.

The Lord your God, who goes before you, is the one who will fight for you, just as he did for you in Egypt before your very eyes.... Do not fear them, for it is the Lord your God who fights for you. (Deut 1:30; 3:22)

This rhetoric, which apparently emerges in the midst of Israel's testimony about the founding events of Exodus and the promised land, is also a ground of appeal in the more personal prayers of Israel. The individual worshiper can also petition Yahweh the warrior to act:

Rise up, O Lord, in your anger;
lift yourself up against the fury of my enemies.... (Ps 7:6)

Break the arm of the wicked and evildoers;
seek out their wickedness until you find none. (Ps 10:15)

Thus Israel characteristically imagines that Yahweh is allied with it in the great, momentous, and risky emergencies of its life. Yahweh is a warrior *in the service of Israel*. In the tradition of Jeremiah, however, it is recognized that Yahweh the warrior, who is the righteous king and the judge of justice, is not blindly and unconditionally committed to Israel. In an extreme case, this judge and king is affronted by Israel, and so Yahweh as warrior is mobilized against Israel:

I myself will fight against you with outstretched hand and mighty arm, in anger, in fury, and in great wrath. (Jer 21:5)[28]

In this text, the tradition inverts the characterization of Yahweh the warrior to make Yahweh *the enemy of Israel* (cf. Lam 2:5). Yahweh now threatens the existence of Israel, who has violated the rule of Yahweh, in the same way that Yahweh the warrior had on other occasions jeopardized the existence of Egypt and Babylon.

This metaphor for Yahweh coheres with those of judge and king. All three images witness to the attractive possibility of order in the world, an order of justice established and maintained by Yahweh. The image of Yahweh as warrior, however, goes well beyond judge and king, both in its assurance and in its problematic. Its assurance is greater than that of the other images because Yahweh as warrior is one who actively and vigorously intervenes with decisive power. The warrior is not simply a king who issues decrees or a judge who renders verdicts. This is an agent forcibly engaged.

To the same extent that this is a poignant, palpable assurance, the image of Yahweh as warrior is also problematic because it puts violence into the middle of Israel's speech about God, and it evidences that Israel celebrates God-sponsored, God-enacted violence. A theological interpretation of the Old Testament must face this problematic, which is intrinsic to Israel's God-talk.[29] I suggest that without seeking to explain away or to apologize for this dimension of Israel's theological

---

28. On holy war against Israel, see William L. Moran, "The End of the Unholy War and the Anti-Exodus," *Bib* 44 (1963) 333–42.

29. On such violence with a Yahwistic dimension, see Walter Brueggemann, *Revelation and Violence: A Study in Contextualization* (Milwaukee: Marquette University Press, 1986).

rhetoric, it is important to give nuance to what Israel testifies. Three points seem in order.

First, Israel lives (as do we) in a threatening world of many competing powers, all of which struggle for control. Thus the violence undertaken by Yahweh as warrior is not characteristically a blind or unbridled violence. It is rather an act of force that aims to defend and give life to the powerless against demonic power that aims to give life to none.

Second, the violence is sociologically differentiated and requires a class reading. This rhetoric of violence is characteristically on the lips of those who otherwise have no effective weapons.[30] The utterance of testimony is not in itself an equivalent to actual physical violence, but it is an act of public imagination whereby reference to Yahweh as warrior helps imagine the force field of social power as more complicated than it is without this utterance. Moreover, this rhetoric of violence, characteristically, is on the side of the reestablishment of justice and the redress of abuse.

Third, while the image of Yahweh as warrior presents the material and seeming justification for "macho" violence in the world, such *human* violence is not text-sponsored or text-based. To be sure, the image of Yahweh as warrior lives at the edge of such violence. But to step over that edge, as has often been done in the service of ideological reading, goes well beyond the text. It is likely that the violence assigned to Yahweh is to be understood as counterviolence, which functions primarily as a critical principle in order to undermine and destabilize other violence.[31] There is, to be sure, nothing innocent about Israel's rhetoric of violence, and consequently there is nothing innocent about Yahweh. But then, neither Israel nor Yahweh pretends for one moment to live in a world of innocence. Israel looks power straight in the face, power that enhances and power that crushes, power that kills and enlivens, and out of its cherished verbal sentences, utters the best nouns it can muster.

Yahweh as Father

This metaphor for Yahweh is not nearly as pervasive as the three we have already considered.[32] We treat it here, along with the dominant ones, first because this image partakes of many of the qualities of judge-king-warrior; second, because

---

30. The rhetorical violence offered in these texts is to be understood as a "weapon of the weak," for those who have no other weapons. On such a notion, see James C. Scott, *Weapons of the Weak* (New Haven: Yale University Press, 1987).

31. On violence, counterviolence, and resistance to violence, see Dom Helder Camara, *Spiral of Violence* (London: Sheed & Ward, 1975); Robert M. Brown, *Religion and Violence* (Louisville: Westminster/John Knox, 1987); and Walter Wink, *Engaging the Powers: Discernment and Resistance in a World of Domination* (Minneapolis: Fortress Press, 1992).

32. An important feminist literature on the subject now exists. For older presentations of the data prior to feminist awareness, see G. Ernest Wright, "The Terminology of Old Testament Religion and Its Significance," *JNES* 1 (1942) 404–14; and "How Did Early Israel Differ from Its Neighbors?" *BA* 6 (1943) 1–20. I noted the problematic of this language in Walter Brueggemann, "Israel's Social Criticism and Yahweh's Sexuality," *A Social Reading of the Old Testament: Prophetic Approaches to Israel's Communal Life* (Minneapolis: Fortress Press, 1994) 149–73.

this metaphor has become dominant (and problematic) in Christian theology. This metaphor for Yahweh is used with reference to Yahweh's commitment and care for Israel and to Israel's sense that it belongs to and is accountable to Yahweh. It is debatable whether this imagery bespeaks a biological begetting or whether it is an appeal to a set of well-defined social relationships. In either case, the metaphor bespeaks a peculiar intimacy that characterizes Israel's life with Yahweh.

In Deut 32:6, a very old poem, the role of Yahweh as father of Israel is taken as fundamental and orienting for Israel's identity in the world: "Is not he your father, who created you, who made you and established you?" The following verses speak of Yahweh's peculiar valuing of Israel (vv. 7-9) and Yahweh's peculiar attentiveness to Israel in need (vv. 10-14). In these verses the nurture of the sojourn tradition is cited as evidence of Yahweh's fatherliness. Conversely, in vv. 15-18, Israel is reprimanded for not responding in gratitude to the goodness of the father. In v. 6 three verbs are used as the ways in which Yahweh "fathered" Israel: *acquire* (*qnh*), *create* ('*sh*), and *establish* (*kûn*). This is the characteristic language of creation, and does not as such indicate any biological act. Yet in v. 18, remarkably, the verb for *beget* (*yld*) is used, and is matched with *birth* (*ḥll*), thus alluding to "mothering" as well as "fathering," both terms suggesting a biological process.

This early, orienting reference is matched near the end of the Old Testament period: "Have we not all one father? Has not one God created us?" (Mal 2:10). In this text, the verb is *create* (*br*'), but the point is the shared inheritance and commonality of all Jews, as distinct from other peoples.

The imagery of father is used in a peculiar way in the Exodus narrative, identifying Israel as Yahweh's firstborn—that is, one of special privilege and value (Exod 4:22). It is likely that this language is used in order to match and escalate the threat to the "firstborn of Pharaoh" (Exod 11:5; 12:29). The reference in Exod 4:22 likely lies behind the usage in Hos 11:1: "When Israel was a child, I loved him, and out of Egypt I called my son." This text suggests patient, attentive nurturing by the father, Yahweh, of the small child, Israel. This usage suggests a hint of tenderness, gentleness, and compassion.

These two texts, Exod 4:22 and especially Hos 11:1-3, provide a way for us to see that this image for Yahweh concerns a kind of intimacy that is open to pathos, which will appear later in Israel's testimony about Yahweh. Three other texts in particular indicate that Yahweh as father is a source of enormous appeal for Israel in need, and that Israel as a child/son is a source of consternation for the father, Yahweh. In Jer 3:19-20, Yahweh speaks wistfully as a disappointed father who had high expectations for his son:

> I thought how I would set you among my children,
> and give you a pleasant land,
> the most beautiful heritage of all the nations.
> And I thought you would call me, My Father,
> and would not turn from following me.

> Instead, as a faithless wife leaves her husband,
> so you have been faithless to me, O house of Israel,
> says the Lord. (Jer 3:19-20)

The relationship has failed. It is worth noting that here (and perhaps in Jer 31:20, though there the rhetoric is not explicitly of father) as in Hos 11:8-9, Yahweh as father continues to yearn for, seek, and hope for Israel, even after the child has been recalcitrant and insolent and is seemingly rejected.

This openness toward pathos is especially expressed in Ps 103:9-14:

> He will not always accuse,
> nor will he keep his anger forever.
> He does not deal with us according to our sins,
> nor repay us according to our iniquities.
> For as the heavens are high above the earth,
> so great is his steadfast love
> toward those who fear him;
> as far as the east is from the west,
> so far he removes our transgressions from us.
> As a father has compassion for his children,
> so the Lord has compassion for those who fear him.
> For he knows how we were made;
> he remembers that we are dust.

In this text Israel, burdened with guilt, must reckon with how seriously Yahweh takes Israel's sin. This psalm, however, witnesses to the limit of Yahweh's rage and the capacity of Yahweh to move beyond anger in compassion and forgiveness. The ground for Yahweh's capacity to forgive, moreover, is that Yahweh is "as a father." The "father" is here characterized by compassion (*rḥm*); moreover, the unit ends with reference to creation. Yahweh the father of compassion remembers "how we were made" (*yṣr*)—how fragile and dependent the human creature is.[33]

This inclination of Yahweh as a father to have compassion becomes the basis for the petition in Isa 63:15–64:12. In this text Israel, or some part of Israel, is in extremity and without resource. In such a circumstance Israel appeals to Yahweh:

> For you are our father,
> though Abraham does not know us
> and Israel does not acknowledge us:
> you, O Lord, are our father;
> our Redeemer from of old is your name. (Isa 63:16)

---

33. On the theological trajectory out of the notion of "how we were formed," see Walter Brueggemann, "Remember, You Are Dust," *Journal for Preachers* 14 (Lent 1991) 3–10.

> Yet, O Lord, you are our Father;
> we are the clay, and you are our potter;
> we are all the work of your hand. (Isa 64:8)

The language of Isa 63:15 concerns Yahweh's yearning and compassion, and the phrase "from of old" in v. 16 echoes Deuteronomy 32. In Isa 64:8 the fatherliness of Yahweh is linked (as in Ps 103:14) to creation through the verb *form* (*yṣr*), so that Israel is the product of Yahweh's attentive, artistic work. While this poem appeals to Yahweh as a compassionate father, for the extent of the poem the father is silent and absent.

Nonetheless, this image for Yahweh provides a way in which Israel can speak about Yahweh's profound commitment to Israel, a commitment on which Israel can count for special, positive attention. The same imagery, though not directly tied to a father metaphor, is evident in Pss 22:10 and 27:10. Israel on occasion found that the image of father was readily accommodated to the image of judge-king-warrior (cf. Isa 40:9-11; Deut 1:30-31). It is evident that the father, while tender and generous, is not romantic about the relationship but is capable of regret and fierceness. In Jer 3:19 and 31:15 and Hos 11:1-9, the metaphor of father is employed in order to exhibit the tension between fierceness and compassion in the inclination of Yahweh. In these texts, as in Psalm 103, Yahweh's compassion prevails.

Provisional Portrayal in Substantive Nouns

From these images (admittedly from the first three more than the fourth), a provisional portrayal of Yahweh in substantive nouns emerges. These nouns are devices whereby Israel's testimony gives staying power to Yahweh's more important adjectives, which in turn have arisen from verbal sentences. These nouns begin to generalize and schematize who it is that lives at the center of Israel's theological rhetoric. Of the God embedded in these metaphors, we may say the following.

Yahweh's mercy and love. These metaphors bear witness to a God who is "merciful and gracious, slow to anger, abounding in steadfast love." This God is capable of kind, gracious, restorative, rehabilitative, sustaining, liberating actions, with particular reference to Israel, but not exclusively toward Israel.

As judge, Yahweh enacts governance for the sake of strangers, widows, and orphans, implementing a kind of justice that gives well-being to those who cannot work for justice for themselves.

As king, Yahweh enacts a governance, a public ordering of reality that makes life possible. The rhetoric of kingship lies at the core of the gospel proclamation, both in Ps 96:10 in its liturgical expansiveness, and in the "historical" concreteness of Isa 52:7. The rule of Yahweh ("Yahweh has become king") creates joy in Israel, the opportunity for return home from exile, and exultation among all the creatures who, by the new rule of the king, are protected from the threat of chaos.

As warrior, Yahweh intervenes with ferocious power on behalf of Israel in Egypt, defeating Israel's oppressors and initiating a new possibility for life.

As father, Yahweh makes Israel's life possible and attends in compassion to needy, despairing Israel, as in Psalm 103. Yahweh in fatherliness enacts steadfast love for those who have forfeited their claim on Yahweh.

Israel utilizes all of these terms in order to bear witness to the powerful and loyal ways in which Yahweh makes life possible in a context of profound threat and endless jeopardy.

Yahweh's awesome power. The God given us in these nouns, however, is not maudlin or romantic. This is a God of awesome power, who will enact that power and order life for Israel and for the world only on Yahweh's own terms. Thus any gentleness and tenderness are matched by the God who will "by no means clear the guilty."

As judge, Yahweh does indeed, in the rhetoric of Israel, enact justice, but it is a justice that is demanding, fierce, and uncompromising. Thus the "judge of all the earth" (Gen 18:25) does justice by destroying Sodom. The same judging dimension of Yahweh's life is evident in the prophets, in Yahweh's severity toward Israel, and especially toward Jerusalem, which has violated the justice proposed for all the earth.

As king, Yahweh is "God of gods and Lord of lords, the great God, mighty and awesome" (Deut 10:17). A primal function of this king who is to be revered above all kings is to deabsolutize and delegitimate other kings, who do not govern according to Yahweh's intention. Thus in the Exodus, Yahweh the king (cf. Exod 15:18) dethrones royal pharaoh. And in Isaiah of the exile, Yahweh dethrones Nebuchadnezzar (cf. Jeremiah 50–51). In Dan 4:27 as in Isa 47:6, Nebuchadnezzar is sharply reminded that Yahweh's governance is about mercy. And those who govern without mercy cannot endure in power.

As warrior, Yahweh intervenes powerfully on behalf of Israel, fighting for Israel when Israel cannot fight for itself. The warrior, however, can turn against Israel and become the enemy of Israel or of Jerusalem. In the tradition of Jeremiah, for example, Yahweh fights as vigorously against Jerusalem as Yahweh ever had done on behalf of Israel.

As father, Yahweh is filled with compassion and concern for firstborn Israel. It may well be that the negative potential in this image is not as powerful as in the others we have reviewed. It is clear, nonetheless, that in Hos 11:4-7 the father is capable of entertaining the thought of complete rejection and abandonment of the child. This is a minor note, but it is at least hinted at in the text.

Shifting Nuances

In this collage of images, Yahweh is said to have capabilities both positive and negative, so that Yahweh in these several roles is capable of affirmative action, but also of severity. The delicate balance in any particular textual witness may be given one of many available nuances that position the judge-king-warrior-father in many different ways.

Severity in the service of sovereignty. The severity of Yahweh as judge-king-warrior-father is not an undisciplined or arbitrary response to Yahweh's partner. In all of these images, Yahweh is known in Israel as an utterly reliable God, a father who cares, a judge who seeks justice, a king who provides order, a warrior who defends and protects. In all of these aspects, Israel bears witness to a good and generous Agent who makes life possible. The severity of Yahweh is an intentional severity that is understood as a function of the fundamental ordering of reality for which Yahweh is responsible and about which Yahweh cares intensely.[34] Thus the actions of Yahweh that have a destructive dimension are sanctions and enforcements of an ordered regime that will brook no threat or fundamental challenge. In this sense the severity is rational, and as George Mendenhall has urged, even harsh vengeance is coherent to the maintenance of order that must be sustained if life is to be viable.

Contradiction within the character of Yahweh. If we push underneath this rationalizing justification for Yahweh's severity, however, we are bound to say that each of these metaphors contains an unresolved tension. This tension may be understood as a contradiction within the very character of Yahweh. Thus, it is not known ahead of time if this judge-king-warrior-father will be merciful and gracious, or if this Yahweh will "by no means clear the guilty." One can take these two inclinations of Yahweh as rationally coherent if one accepts a rule of law; but such a rule of law allows no place for the slippage of pardon, which also belongs to Yahweh in these roles. One may argue that on the whole, Yahweh in these roles is to be understood as a reliable God, for whom these several actions of mercy and severity are coherent. At the edge of many of these texts, however, is a severity that seems to belong to Yahweh's unfettered sovereignty rather than to a reasoned response of governance. That unfettered sovereignty provides ample justification for the assertion of Dan 4:35: "There is no one who can stay his hand or say to him, 'What are you doing?'"

An ominous dimension. Old Testament theology must reckon with an ominous dimension to Yahweh that falls outside any rule of law, outside vengeance as legitimate sanction. It must recognize an untamed quality in Yahweh that on occasion runs beyond reason at a destructive rate. Such a dimension in the character of Yahweh does not lend itself easily to a reasoned theology, but Israel's witness to Yahweh admits of rhetorical outcomes that need not be reasoned or coherent. Israel's testimony thus on occasion utters Yahweh in extremis. I suggest that while Yahweh on balance is a coherent agent, this coherent agent is portrayed, in Israel's testimony, with something like the ominous, brooding music of the film *The Godfather.* One has the sense that a violent potential is always present where Yahweh is. Most of the time that violence can be accepted and justified in terms of the justice through which Israel comes to understand Yahweh. And yet, an undomesticated

---

34. G. Ernest Wright, "The Nations in Hebrew Prophecy," *Encounter* 26 (1965) 225–37, has proposed that Yahweh's judging actions are to be understood as actions that maintain and enact Yahweh's legitimate "imperium" over the nations.

quality of Yahweh allows a play of violence, on occasion, that cannot be contained in any sense of justice. That potential violence can break out at any time, because Yahweh is not finally accountable to any other agent, not even to Yahweh's partner Israel to whom fidelity has been pledged. This is indeed the God who is gracious and merciful. But in this testimony, the danger intrinsic to the character of Yahweh is never fully or finally banished. In utilizing these various noun-metaphors, Israel finds a way to bear witness to this One known in sentences of verbal testimony and in generalizing adjectives as the One who operates in an awesome range of immense freedom and costly fidelity.

Metaphors of Sustenance

A second set of noun-metaphors is utilized in Israel's testimony about Yahweh. These metaphors are not so central to Israel's speech, but are important for the full portrayal of Yahweh. What I have termed the metaphors of governance, taken in large sweep, concern the capacity of Yahweh to maintain a viable order in which life is possible for Israel and for all of creation. That order requires heavy sanctions for its maintenance. Now I set alongside the metaphors of governance what I term metaphors of sustenance, which are not as stern or rigorous, but which represent Yahweh as one who nurtures, evokes, values, and enhances life. These images for Yahweh are much softer and, I believe, live in some tension with the metaphors of governance. The latter have a harshness to them because they actively work for order in the midst of an endangered and recalcitrant world that is under threat and at risk. The metaphors of sustenance, I suggest, count on the order made possible by the judge-king-warrior-father and operate within the safe space made possible by Yahweh's ordering activity. While other metaphors might be included in this subset, I will mention five.

Yahweh as Artist

The Old Testament is characteristically preoccupied with ethical concern, so that aesthetic dimensions of Yahweh's character receive less attention, both in the text and in interpretations.[35] Nonetheless, both the temple traditions and the wisdom traditions of the Old Testament are alert to aesthetic dimensions of reality and to Yahweh's availability and skill as an artist.[36] More specifically, Yahweh as artist is portrayed as a potter, who with skill, sensitivity, and delicacy forms the human person (Gen 2:7-8), forms the animals and birds (Gen 2:19) and the earth (Isa 45:18; Ps 95:5), and forms Israel (Isa 43:1, 7, 21; 44:2, 21, 24; 45:9, 11). Not a great deal is made of the aesthetic dimension of this metaphor, because the accent is on

---

35. As much as anyone, Samuel Terrien has understood this imbalance and has sought to redress it. In addition to his programmatic book, *The Elusive Presence: Toward a New Biblical Theology* (New York: Harper and Row, 1978), see *Till the Heart Sings: A Biblical Theology of Manhood and Womanhood* (Philadelphia: Fortress Press, 1985).

36. In *The Elusive Presence,* Terrien takes up both the temple and wisdom traditions and notes their aesthetic dimension.

Yahweh's great power and on the obligation of the "clay" to be obediently formed according to the intention of Yahweh the potter. Nonetheless, the image is aesthetic, and the verb *form* (*yṣr*) may signify a certain satisfaction or delight on the part of Yahweh, who is able to imagine a formed object that has never yet existed, and then implements this from imagination to reality. (Though it does not use the verb *form*, the delighted exclamation of Gen 1:31, "It was very good," is likely an aesthetic judgment.)[37] Yahweh the artist is able to enact in a most imaginative way a form of life never before extant.

More specifically, the "forming" action of Yahweh, while usually a verb, issues into a noun-metaphor: Yahweh as potter (Isa 29:16; 45:9-10; 64:7-8; Jer 18:1-11; 19:1-13). In these uses, however, as we might come to expect from the metaphors of governance, the metaphor of artistry also has a more demanding, ominous dimension. In what may be an early usage, the poet accuses Israel (the clay) of distorting and confusing its relationship with the potter by a refusal to be responsive to the potter's will:

> You turn things upside down!
> Shall the potter be regarded as the clay?
> Shall the thing made say of its maker,
> "He did not make me";
> or the thing formed say of the one who formed it,
> "He has no understanding?" (Isa 29:16)

This same negativity is expressed, in the same image, toward Israel's recalcitrance:

> Woe to you who strive with your Maker,
> earthen vessel with the potter!
> Does the clay say to the one who fashions it,
> "What are you making"?
> or "Your work has no handles"? (Isa 45:9)

Because the clay refuses to submit to the will of the potter, the potter is free and ready to smash the pot and to begin again:

> The vessel he was making of clay was spoiled in the potter's hand, and he reworked it into another vessel, as seemed good to him. (Jer 18:4)[38]

> So I will break this people and this city, as one breaks a potter's vessel, so that it can never be mended. (Jer 19:11)

Thus a metaphor that holds potential for delight and affirmation is transposed into a threat in the juridical cast of Israel's larger rendition of reality. A startling, important exception to this negative development of the metaphor occurs in the pathos-filled petition of Isa 64:8-9:

---

37. Claus Westermann, *Genesis 1–11: A Commentary* (London: SPCK, 1984) 167, renders this as, "It is very good (beautiful)" (German: *sehr gut [schön]*).
38. The Hebrew idiom for "rework" is "returned and made."

Yet, O Lord, you are our Father;
we are the clay, and you are our potter;
we are all the work of your hand.
Do not be exceedingly angry, O Lord,
and do not remember iniquity forever.
Now consider, we are all your people.

In this prayer, it is not denied that Israel the clay has been recalcitrant to the will of
the potter. Nonetheless, in the end, this clay does belong to the potter; this people
does belong to this God; this child does belong to this Father. So, with what seems
to be a clear linkage to Ps 103:14, the clay seeks forgiveness—seeks to have Yahweh
the potter, who is justified in anger, move beyond anger in response to the needy
pot. Thus the image moves characteristically from affirmation to negation. In the
end, however, Israel bids one last time that Yahweh will act as the potter did at the
outset, to make wholeness possible again. (The image is utilized in Rom 9:21 to
bespeak God's overriding authority over human beings, who are the clay.)

Yahweh as Healer

Although not a major image for Yahweh, the doctor image occurs in Israel's speech
at pivotal places, witnessing to Yahweh's capacity to restore, rehabilitate, and re-
pair all that has been damaged or hurt. A large claim is made for Yahweh, an
affirmation that all that happens for good or for ill is in Yahweh's capacity:

See now that I, even I, am he;
there is no god beside me.
I kill and I make alive;
I wound and I heal;
and no one can deliver from my hand. (Deut 32:39)

Come, let us return to the Lord;
for it is he who has torn, and he will heal us;
he has struck down, and he will bind us up. (Hos 6:1)

In these uses, Yahweh's healing work is matched to Yahweh's destructive, punishing
work, so that Yahweh can heal what Yahweh has damaged. The claim that Yahweh
has a healing capacity, however, is not limited to restoration of what Yahweh has
damaged. Yahweh's healing capacity pertains to whatever damage has been done,
by whatever agent.

Perhaps the most pivotal use of the imagery is at the conclusion of the Exodus
narrative:

If you will listen carefully to the voice of the Lord your God, and do what
is right in his sight, and give heed to his commandment and keep all his
statutes, I will not bring upon you any of the diseases that I brought upon
the Egyptians; for I am the Lord who heals you. (Exod 15:26)

The concluding claim of the Exodus story is that Yahweh is Israel's "doctor," and that the Exodus is an act of healing and rehabilitation from Egyptian bondage, which is a killing ailment. The naming of Yahweh as healer here is preceded by a strong insistence on obedience. That is, Israel must "do what the doctor orders."[39] Yahweh's healing is an alternative to the "diseases of Egypt" (cf. Deut 28:60). It may be possible to identify biological ailments in the empire to which this phrase refers, but it is equally compelling to identify the sociological pathologies of the empire from which Israel is rescued. Either way, Yahweh's rescuing act is a restoration from a situation of terminal suffering.

Thus the metaphor of healing has a public dimension, in which Yahweh can restore the well-being of a wounded city or people (cf. Ps 60:2; Hos 14:4; Jer 30:17; 2 Chron 7:14, 30:20; Isa 57:18-19). It is important that the same term applied to Yahweh's public agenda is also the rhetoric Israel utilizes in intimate personal need, in which Yahweh is the one who can restore damaged or distorted life. Reference to Yahweh as healer is made both in petition by those in need (Pss 6:2, 41:4) and in thanksgiving by those who have been restored in their personal existence (Pss 30:2, 107:17-22). The image bears witness to the capacity and willingness to have life made right by Yahweh in every zone of existence. To this capacity and willingness on Yahweh's part, Israel bears witness in metaphor.

Four aspects of this powerful image, however, suggest that Israel's use of this metaphor is not that simple and straightforward.

Pathos and healing. First, the healing that Yahweh does (or may do) is not always an act of pure power as it seems to be in Exod 15:26. In the prophet Jeremiah, as Abraham Heschel has seen, the healing work of Yahweh is freighted with anguish, pathos, and problematic.[40] Thus in Jer 3:22, Yahweh promises to "heal your faithlessness," but the promise is made on the condition of an appeal for return. Moreover, it is preceded in vv. 19-20 by Yahweh's terrible hurt about a son who betrays like a fickle spouse. And in Jer 8:22, Yahweh asks the haunting question:

Is there no balm in Gilead?
Is there no physician there?
Why then has the health of my poor people not been restored?

The familiar rendering of the first of these questions in an African American spiritual is not a question but an affirmation: "There is a balm. . . ." But here, in Israel's testimony, the statement is a question, with the anticipated answer being no—there is no balm, no physician, no healing, no rehabilitation, no hope. And in Jer 9:1-3, Yahweh/Jeremiah dissolves in tears of love and anguish. This same utterance of pathos in relation to healing is evident in Jer 30:12-17, which begins in terminal illness (v. 12) and ends with restoration and health (v. 17).[41] But the way to heal-

---

39. The demand is stated with an infinitive absolute, thus with enormous force.
40. Abraham Heschel, *The Prophets* (New York: Harper and Row, 1962) 103–39 and passim.
41. On this text, see Walter Brueggemann, "The 'Uncared For' Now Cared For (Jer 30:12-17): A Methodological Consideration," *JBL* 104 (1985) 419–28.

ing is not an easy one for Yahweh; Yahweh goes through loss, anguish, rage, and humiliation. The healing costs the healer a great deal.

Truth-telling. Second, healing begins in and requires truth-telling (cf. Pss 32:3-5; 38:3-8). Where there is mendacity (denial), healing cannot happen. While such deception and denial are available for individual persons in stress, as the psalms recognize, Jeremiah bears witness to the same falsehood that precludes public, communal healing: "They have treated the wound of my people carelessly, saying, 'Peace, peace,' when there is no peace" (Jer 6:14; cf. 8:11). When the community, through its leaders, denies its communal pathologies, healing is impossible and death comes.[42]

Limits to healing. Third, Yahweh is portrayed as the healer par excellence, endlessly gracious and attentive, but there are limits to Yahweh's performance as doctor. In Jeremiah 51 the poetry utilizes motifs and themes from the earlier parts of the Book of Jeremiah, including the motif of healing. Healing is intended even for awesome, hated Babylon:

> Suddenly Babylon has fallen and is shattered;
> wail for her!
> Bring balm for her wound;
> perhaps she may be healed. (51:8)

But healing for the awesome empire is not possible. The metaphor for healing is crowded out by the juridical issues unresolved between Yahweh and Babylon:

> We tried to heal Babylon, but she could not be healed.
> Forsake her, and let each of us go to our own country;
> for her judgment has reached up to heaven
> and has been lifted up even to the skies.
> The Lord has brought forth our vindication;
> come, let us declare in Zion
> the work of the Lord our God. (Jer 51:9-10)

This usage of the metaphor is instructive for the way in which one metaphor may be overcome or superseded by another, in this case to the profound detriment of Babylon.

Human agents of healing. Fourth, although Yahweh is the healer par excellence, it is important to recognize that the healing intended by Yahweh may be enacted by human agents. In what has become an important text for Christian extrapolation, the great healing in the exile is wrought by the enigmatic "servant":

> But he was wounded for our transgressions,
> crushed for our iniquities;

---

42. The application of medical imagery to public crisis is not unfamiliar in the contemporary world. A well-known example is White House counsel John Dean's warning to President Richard Nixon that there was a "cancer" in his administration.

upon him was the punishment that made us whole,
and by his bruises we are healed. (Isa 53:5)

This entire chapter of Isaiah, though much cited, is enormously problematic. I do not cite it here to make any christological extrapolation, but only to notice that the role assigned to Yahweh in the metaphor of healing has an openness for other usage. This text, part of the long dispute between Jews and Christians, in any case stresses a human agent of healing. It is an appropriate text to which to relate the current and urgent theme of *Tiqqun Olam.* It is indeed human work to "mend (heal) the world."[43] It is not inappropriate to suggest that the way in which healing is anticipated in this statement—through the wound of the healer—is already a mode of healing decisively embraced by Yahweh.

In the New Testament extrapolation of this metaphor, we may notice two claims. First, Jesus is portrayed characteristically as a healer, as though the tradition has deliberately assigned to him the work of Yahweh (cf. Mark 1:34; Luke 7:22, 9:11). At the extreme edge of the New Testament, moreover, the poetry envisions the healing of the nations:

On either side of the river is the tree of life with its twelve kinds of fruit, producing its fruit each month; and the leaves of the tree are for the healing of the nations. (Rev 22:2)

The claim here for healing is even more sweeping than is usually made in the Old Testament, but the vision is in continuity with the work attributed to Yahweh in the Old Testament. Yahweh has the will and capacity to rehabilitate persons, nations, and all of creation that are distorted. The healing is wrought through Yahweh's pathos and depends on truth-telling about "the diseases of Egypt."

Yahweh as Gardener-Vinedresser

Another metaphor for Yahweh is the gardener who plants a garden or vineyard. The garden may be linked to acts of creation (Gen 2:8) and certainly connotes fruitfulness and the full function of creation (Num 24:6). But most often, the work of the gardener is to "plant Israel," to give to Israel a safe, fruitful life in the land. The imagery is already used in Exod 15:17, in anticipation of Israel's reception of the land of promise:

You brought them in and planted them on the mountain
of your possession,
the place, O Lord, that you made your abode,
the sanctuary, O Lord, that your hands have established.

In this usage, the reference may be to the land in general or more precisely to Jerusalem and to the temple site.

---

43. So Emil Fackenheim, *To Mend the World: Foundations of Post-Holocaust Thought* (New York: Schocken Books, 1989).

The imagery occurs elsewhere, most often in the prophets, in their reflection on land loss and the regiving of the land after exile. We may cite two texts that concern land loss. The best known and perhaps fullest articulation of the metaphor is in the song of the vineyard in Isa 5:1-7. We are told at the end of the poem the intention of the imagery:

> For the vineyard of the Lord of hosts
> is the house of Israel,
> and the people of Judah
> are his pleasant planting;
> he expected justice, but saw bloodshed;
> righteousness, but heard a cry! (v. 7)[44]

The drama of the imagery is in two parts. First, Yahweh has been generous and attentive in caring for the vineyard that is Israel/Judah:

> He dug it and cleared it of stones,
> and planted it with choice vines;
> he built a watchtower in the midst of it,
> and hewed out a wine vat in it;
> he expected it to yield grapes.... (5:2)

The intent of Yahweh was to create a garden that produced good grapes. Failing that (v. 7b), Yahweh the vinekeeper will destroy the vineyard:

> I will remove its hedge,
> and it shall be devoured;
> I will break down its wall,
> and it shall be trampled down.
> I will make it a waste;
> it shall not be pruned or hoed,
> and it shall be overgrown with briers and thorns;
> I will also command the clouds
> that they rain no rain upon it. (vv. 5-6)

Thus the positive image of Yahweh as gardener and vinedresser eventuates in a harsh negative assertion of judgment.

In the same way, in Jer 2:21 Yahweh planted Israel "a choice vine, from the purest stock." But again, the generous vinedresser is disappointed, for the vineyard is degenerate. In Hos 9:10 the image is used in the same way, though less fully developed. The vine (or fig tree) was valued at first, but was indeed a failure. In context, the negative side of the imagery is used for land loss in exile.

In the case of this figure, however, the metaphor makes a comeback, so to speak, to be used positively. Thus in Amos 9:15:

---

44. The wordplay in v. 7, *mišpaṭ/mispaḥ, ṣedaqah/ṣeʿaqah*, is important, even if it cannot be readily reproduced in English translation.

I will plant them upon their land,
and they shall never again be plucked up
out of the land that I have given them,
says the Lord your God.

This poetic assurance surely refers to some recovery of land after displacement, whenever it is dated. In Jeremiah the theme of planting (and building) becomes a leitmotif for hope (Jer 24:6, 31:28, 42:10),[45] as it does in several late Isaiah texts:

Your people shall all be righteous;
they shall possess the land forever.
They are the shoot that I planted,
the work of my hands,
so that I might be glorified. (Isa 60:21)

They will be called oaks of righteousness,
the planting of the Lord, to display his glory. (Isa 61:3)

Like the other nouns we have reviewed, this metaphor is enormously supple, able to express both the destructive potential of Yahweh against a recalcitrant object of love, and the remarkable generosity of Yahweh, which becomes the source of hope for rehabilitation in time of displacement. In the midst of destructive potential and remarkable generosity, we note that the gardener-vinedresser has firm, clear, nonnegotiable expectations for the vine. The vineyard must be productive, yielding in obedience the fruit intended by the planter.

The imagery is utilized in the New Testament in a similar way. In an important usage, however, the New Testament goes beyond the Old Testament in a christological maneuver. In a statement fully congruent with Old Testament rhetoric, John the Baptist warns of plants that do not bear good fruit (Matt 3:8-10). Even in the imagery in John 15:1-6, which is characteristically understood as a statement of God's solidarity with God's people, the negative dimension is unambiguous:

Whoever does not abide in me is thrown away like a branch and withers; such branches are gathered, thrown into the fire, and burned. (John 15:6)

It is likely that the poem of Isa 5:1-7 is the paradigmatic use of the metaphor in the Old Testament. In like manner, the parable of Matt 21:33-41 is the most extended and complex usage of the imagery in the New Testament. Here, as in Isa 5:1-7, an image that is potentially positive toward Israel and a witness to Yahweh's attentive generosity is utilized as an assertion of judgment:

He will put those wretches to a miserable death, and lease the vineyard to other tenants who will give him the produce at the harvest time. (Matt 21:41)

---

45. For the Jeremiah tradition, the verb *plant* must be seen amid the cluster of verbs in 1:10; see Robert Carroll, *From Chaos to Covenant: Uses of Prophecy in the Book of Jeremiah* (London: SCM Press, 1981) 55–58.

Thus, again, a metaphor of sustenance is made to serve the demanding aspects of Yahweh's governance.

Yahweh as Mother

We have already seen that Yahweh as Father of Israel intervenes for the sake of the firstborn (cf. Exod 4:22; and less directly Jer 31:9; Isa 43:6) and is capable of a fierceness that considers rejection (Hos 11:4-7). But we have also seen that Yahweh is impinged upon by the need of the child Israel, is moved to compassion, and is capable of "motherly" acts toward Israel. That is, Yahweh as parent runs the emotional-relational gamut from harshness to tenderness. It is not necessary to label the positive acts of Yahweh as motherly, for the metaphor of father should be open enough to include such positive dimensions of Yahweh.

As a parallel theme, we notice that few texts portray Yahweh as mother, but some texts do show that this image of Yahweh was available to Israel.[46] We have already noticed, in another context, that in Deut 32:18 the verbs *yld* and *ḥll* seem to suggest both the begetting of a father and the bearing of a mother. And in Num 11:12, Moses places responsibility on Yahweh for having conceived (*hrh*) and given birth (*yld*) to Israel. In Deut 32:18 the accent is on Israel's obligation to obey Yahweh. In Num 11:12 the emphasis is on Yahweh's obligation to care for Israel by providing food.

The most important texts for our consideration of Yahweh as mother are in the later tradition of Isaiah. There Yahweh is said to have "carried (Israel) from the womb" (Isa 46:3; cf. 63:9). Yahweh is also portrayed as the mother who comforts Israel in Jerusalem:

> As a mother comforts her child,
> so I will comfort you;
> you shall be comforted in Jerusalem. (Isa 66:13; cf. vv. 11-12)

The motif of comfort is prominent in the later Isaiah text. In light of this particular usage, the term is drawn into Yahweh's motherly functions as the one who will feed, care for, sustain, and remember Israel in its time of exilic displacement and postexilic distress. Thus the image is one of enormous reassurance.

In what may be the most illuminating text, the metaphor of mother is utilized to respond to and counter Israel's sense of abandonment by Yahweh. Israel complains: "The Lord has forsaken me, my Lord has forgotten me" (Isa 49:14; cf. Lam 5:20).

Yahweh responds decisively:

> Can a woman forget her nursing child,
> or show no compassion for the child of her womb?
> Even these may forget,
> yet I will not forget you.

---

46. One of the earliest reflections on this motif is by P. A. H. de Boer, *Fatherhood and Motherhood in Israelite and Judean Piety* (Leiden: E. J. Brill, 1974).

> See, I have inscribed you on
> the palms of my hands.... (Isa 49:15-16)[47]

Perhaps the image of Yahweh as mother does not include any dimension that is not already available with the image of Yahweh as father. On the whole, the metaphor of mother is positive and reassuring. To be sure, there is an extreme suggestion that Yahweh as mother may be neglectful (Num 11:12). And in Isa 49:15 it is recognized that a mother may forget, but there the image is used only to assert that Yahweh remembers even when mothers may forget. Thus even this image is not completely unambiguous, but its primary force is positive. That positive note is qualified in Israel's rhetoric only in extremis.

In Isa 63:7 Yahweh is said to have acted "according to his mercy" (*rḥm*), and in both 46:3 and 49:15 the same term *mercy* (*rḥm*) is rendered *womb*. This recurrent term *rḥm* is a primary term for compassion, often motherly compassion. This convergence of uses has led Phyllis Trible to suggest that compassion is Yahweh's motherly inclination toward Israel, for the depth and intensity of mother love is the kind Yahweh shows toward Israel, a kind of compassion showed by no other.[48]

I do not suggest that this metaphor for Yahweh is radically different from the others we have considered. Two observations, however, give special significance to this metaphor. First, as mentioned above, this image of Yahweh seems unmitigatedly positive. It does not shade over into harsh governance, as do even the images of potter, gardener, and doctor. Second, this image for Yahweh is insistently maternal: the sustaining, feeding, nurturing, caring functions of Yahweh are voiced in this noun of testimony. For appropriating what it is to which Israel witnesses in this image, it is likely unhelpful to merge or coalesce the terms *maternal* and *feminine*. It is pointedly the *mothering* of Israel that is here affirmed. As such, the witness to Yahweh as mother, even though it occurs infrequently in Israel's testimony, stands as a reference point against all those metaphors for Yahweh that have at their edge potential violence and abuse.

Yahweh as Shepherd

This pastoral image for Yahweh is not unrelated to other metaphors for governance, for a long tradition reckons human kings as shepherds of the flock—that is, the community (cf. Isa 44:28; Ezek 37:24). The image evokes a wise, caring, attentive agent who watches over, guards, feeds, and protects a flock that is vulnerable, exposed, dependent, and in need of such help.

---

47. I am indebted to my student Linda Chenowith for having long ago helped me to see that the imagery of Yahweh as a nursing mother in this passage indicates that Yahweh remembers the child, because the mother feels the need to nurse as much as does the child. Thus the metaphor of nursing mother bespeaks something about the physical condition and need of the mother and not simply unconditional love. See Mayer I. Gruber, "The Motherhood of God in Second Isaiah," *Revue Biblique* 90 (1983) 351-59.

48. Phyllis Trible, *God and the Rhetoric of Sexuality* (OBT; Philadelphia: Fortress Press, 1978) 31-71.

The most important usages of the image of Yahweh as shepherd appear in the exile. The exile is said to be a time when the flock was "scattered"; that term is used regularly to refer to the exile. The work of the shepherd Yahweh is to gather the sheep in safety, often when they are exposed to serious danger. The imagery of the gathering shepherd is a powerful one:

> He will feed his flock like a shepherd;
> He will gather the lambs in his arms,
> and carry them in his bosom,
> and gently lead the mother sheep. (Isa 40:11)

> He who scattered Israel will gather him,
> and will keep him as a shepherd a flock. (Jer 31:10)

The fullest exposition of the theme is in Ezekiel 34. In that narrative, commenting on Israel's past and future, the shepherd-kings of the Davidic dynasty are indicted for being irresponsible shepherds, who by their neglect caused the exile (vv. 3-6; Jer 23:1; 50:6). Yahweh's response to the crisis of the flock in exile is twofold. Major attention is given to the rescue of the flock, which royal neglect has placed in great jeopardy. Yahweh will act as a proper and responsible shepherd in order to recover the flock:

> I will bring them out from the peoples and gather them from the countries, and will bring them into their own land; and I will feed them on the mountains of Israel, by the watercourses, and in all the inhabited part of the land. I will feed them with good pasture, and the mountain heights of Israel shall be their pasture; there they shall lie down in good grazing land, and they shall feed on rich pasture on the mountains of Israel. I myself will be the shepherd of my sheep, and I will make them lie down, says the Lord God. I will seek the lost, and I will bring back the strayed, and I will bind up the injured, and I will strengthen the weak, but the fat and the strong I will destroy. I will feed them with justice. (Ezek 34:13-16)

Yahweh will not only restore the flock. Yahweh will also attend in harshness to the "fat sheep" who abuse and exploit, who deny food to the "lean sheep," and who trample the pasture (vv. 7-19).

In this assertion, the positive image of shepherd turns harsh and negative; the shepherd looks harshly on exploitative sheep, and distinguishes between strong, abusive sheep, and vulnerable, weak sheep. Thus the good shepherd attends especially to the most vulnerable sheep—in this case, needy exiles.

On the basis of this imagery, Israel appeals to Yahweh, "shepherd of Israel," for help: "Give ear, O Shepherd of Israel, you who lead Joseph like a flock!" (Ps 80:1). On the basis of the same imagery, moreover, the most familiar Psalm 23 can be seen, not as an isolated poem, but as a full statement of a recurrent metaphor for Yahweh. In Psalm 23 Yahweh the shepherd is the subject of a series of life-giving verbs: lead, restore, be with, prepare, anoint. Yahweh does everything that must be done so that the trusting sheep may live; Yahweh provides what they cannot secure for themselves.

In the use of this metaphor, Israel also provides texts that speak not only about the shepherd, but also about the sheep. Thus Israel, as the flock of Yahweh, lives in glad trust of the shepherd:

> For he is our God,
> and we are the people of his pasture,
> and the sheep of his hand. (Ps 95:7)

> Know that the Lord is God.
> It is he that made us, and we are his;
> we are his people, and the sheep of his pasture. (Ps 100:3; cf. Ps 79:13)

These psalms echo the confidence of Psalm 23. But Israel's honest testimony also recognizes the jeopardy of the flock. Sometimes the trouble is the fault of Yahweh, who has been inattentive and neglectful (Pss 44:11, 22; 74:1); but sometimes the sheep have gone astray (Isa 53:6). Thus the imagery holds potential for a rich variety of reflections and affirmations concerning Israel's proper relation to Yahweh, Yahweh's inclination toward Israel, and the right ordering of the communal life of Israel.

This imagery functions in dramatic ways in the New Testament. Jesus is the good shepherd who "calls his own sheep by name and leads them out" (John 10:3). Jesus comes upon a great crowd who were "like sheep without a shepherd," for whom he has compassion (Mark 6:34). And clearly the parable in Luke 15:3-7 is freighted enough to make a statement about Jesus, surely enough to witness to the Shepherd whom Israel has long confessed and long trusted.

Overview of Noun Testimony

These two sorts of metaphor-nouns for Yahweh, which I have cataloged as metaphors of governance and metaphors of sustenance, suggest the rich variety of images and metaphors that enabled Israel to give effective testimony about the character of Yahweh. The metaphors we have mentioned are among the most important for Israel's testimony, but they are by no means exhaustive; many others might be cited as well. These might include images of Yahweh as wind, rock, refuge, shield, a priest who cleanses, a kinsman who protects.[49] Indeed, Israel appears to be capable of finding reference points in every dimension of its daily life that can be taken as ways to bear witness to Yahweh, ensuring that Yahweh as a character will be continually and closely linked to the dailiness of Israel's life.

---

49. In Ps 104:29-30, one might suggest that Yahweh is presented as a reliable "artificial lung"!

Multiplicity of Nouns

Some metaphors for Yahweh are more decisive for the testimony of Israel than others; it is likely that metaphors for governance are more crucial in Israel's testimony than are images of sustenance. But what should occupy us at the end of this reflection—rather than settling for one set of metaphors over the other—is the sheer multiplicity and polyvocality of the nouns that are necessary in order to speak Yahweh fully and faithfully.

(a) There are *multiple images;* Israel resists any reductionism in its speech about Yahweh.

(b) These images are *fluid and porous.* They do not all fit conveniently or smoothly together, and Israel did not seem bothered about the awkwardness created by the richness.

(c) The porous, contradictory, incongruous character of the several nouns for Yahweh is fully honored as the testimony of Israel *resists homogenization.* The texts explore, exploit, and probe images and metaphors, permitting imaginative awareness to arise to the full and "float" in the life of Israel, with no concern to discipline, domesticate, or explain. It is precisely this process that prevents nouns for Yahweh from being reified into idols.

(d) Israel seems to engage in the articulation of *fresh images* particularly in times of crisis and need. Times of distress (Paul Ricoeur's "limit experiences") seem to evoke new, fresh, and daring images (Ricoeur's "limit expressions").[50] Perhaps the most obvious case in point is the way in which the later Isaiah tradition, perhaps anticipated by Hosea, probes familial images for Yahweh. More broadly, it is the exile that prompts Israel to generate or radicalize metaphors, especially those of sustenance. Thus, for example, the healer recognizes Israel's incurable illness (Jer 30:12), but will heal (30:17). The shepherd who rejects all other shepherds (Ezek 34:1-10) will intervene and do the work of a shepherd (34:11-16). The mother of Israel will go beyond all conventional mothering propensities (Isa 49:14-15). The gardener will authorize a new planting of myrtle and cypress (Isa 55:13). It may be that in exile, Israel found the established metaphors of governance, taken by themselves, inadequate for all that was now available to them of Yahweh. It is clear that in exile, a probe of Yahweh's capacity for pathos was required in order to find ground for hope. The emergence of new metaphors for Yahweh in exile especially serves that probing of pathos.

(e) This process of probing images, of voicing new ones, of letting them live together in incongruity, suggests that *the work of voicing Yahweh in nouns is never finished.* Israel is apparently capable, always, of risking yet another utterance of Yahweh, which is given in, with, and under some contemporary aspect of its daily existence.

---

50. Paul Ricoeur, "Biblical Hermeneutics," *Semeia* 4 (1975) 107-45.

Thematization through Nouns

Finally, four observations complete our discussion of the thematization of Yahweh through noun-metaphors.

Use and reuse. In his study of the metaphor of father, Paul Ricoeur has found in the Old Testament a usage of the image, a silence, and then a reusage.[51] (In this he agrees with the data as mobilized by G. Ernest Wright.)[52] Ricoeur's judgment is that in this process, Israel broke an old metaphor that contained unusable dimensions of content, held the metaphor in abeyance for a time, and then reused it, assigning to it claims more congruent with Israel's intentions and passions. No doubt Ricoeur's scheme is too clean and simple, and we may wonder if the metaphor is ever as profoundly broken of its old use as he suggests.

Ricoeur's observation is nonetheless instructive. Israel, in its appropriation of nouns for Yahweh, never simply takes over and uses available nouns, but always reuses them, so that they participate in the density of Israel's rhetoric and Israel's imaginative construal of its life in relation to Yahweh. Thus the nouns for Yahweh never mean simply and thinly what the nouns themselves mean. Rather the nouns, in the repeated utterance of Israel, take on freight that is appropriated from Israel's rich deposit of verbs and adjectives. The nouns for Yahweh are endlessly reviewed and transformed in Israel's ongoing utterance. No noun for Yahweh can be taken at face value; each must be attended to in its rich, contextual density.

Rich reservoir of images. Robert Jay Lifton has spent his professional life studying the impact of massive public violence on the human psyche.[53] He has investigated the impact of Hiroshima, Auschwitz, and Vietnam, to name only his most dramatic case studies. Early on in his study of policy-legitimated violence, Lifton observed that such systemic violence is bearable only because societies (and governments) arrive at "psychic numbness," a capacity not to notice, not to know, not to feel, not to experience, not to care. Psychic numbness is possible, says Lifton, because of a "gap of symbols," meaning that a community lacks adequate symbols to mediate and communicate the horror and brutality of its own life. Thus where symbolic life in a community is thin, lean, or one-dimensional, violence can be implemented, accepted, and denied with numbed indifference. I find Lifton's interpretation of twentieth-century barbarism and brutality altogether persuasive. Where there are no adequate symbols, acts of violence can be undertaken without due notice.

I cite Lifton because I want to suggest that Israel, in its generativity about noun-metaphors for Yahweh, suffered no symbol gap or deficiency. It had a rich stock of available images through which to utter and experience its life with Yahweh, and it

---

51. Paul Ricoeur, *The Conflict of Interpretations: Essays in Hermeneutics* (Evanston, Ill.: Northwestern University Press, 1974) 468–97.

52. See Wright, "The Terminology of Old Testament Religion and Its Significance," and "How Did Early Israel Differ from Its Neighbors?" See n. 32 above.

53. Robert Jay Lifton, *The Nazi Doctors: Medical Killing and the Psychology of Genocide* (New York: Basic Books, 1986); *Home from the War: Learning from Vietnam Veterans* (New York: Basic Books, 1985); *Death in Life: The Survivors of Hiroshima* (New York: Random House, 1967).

continued to generate more such images. As a consequence, Israel had access to its experience and was able to engage the extremities of its life in serious, imaginative ways. The dense range of images protected Israel both from denial and from despair. This reservoir of viable images and figures gave Israel access to the profound suffering and negativity of its life. Israel needed to deny nothing. It also kept that profound suffering and negativity on the horizon of Yahweh. Israel did not need to end in despair. It is my urging, then, that Old Testament theology must seek to attend to the full range of noun-metaphors for Yahweh, and to resist reductionism, reification, or homogenization of its images.

Technical reason and technological communication want to reduce the wild world of image and metaphor for purposes of control. But we must reckon as well with the parallel inclination of frightened theology to domesticate Israel's range of noun-metaphors for Yahweh. Specifically, a theology as the practice of closure will certainly want the metaphors of governance to drive out or veto metaphors of sustenance, for the latter do not easily conform to measured, administered order. To assure that this does not happen, we must continue to attend to those metaphors that may seem more marginal.

Critique of patriarchal images. A special case in point, in light of the categories of Ricoeur and Lifton, concerns issues now being raised by the feminist critique of patriarchal imagery. An Old Testament theology is not the place in which to deal extensively with this issue, but in my judgment the issue cannot be avoided or settled preemptively. The feminist critique of patriarchal ideology, both in the text and in interpretation, is a matter of great importance and urgency.

It is an unavoidable observation that the great preponderance of noun-metaphors for Yahweh are patriarchal, especially the metaphors of governance. This patriarchal casting of Israel's testimony about Yahweh is undeniable. It is not clear to what extent this casting was simply a given of that ancient world, and to what extent it was done intentionally and polemically in order to oppose and resist Canaanite fertility religion. This particular intention is often assigned to Deuteronomic tradition and to the "Yahweh alone" party.[54] But if this posture of faith is indeed assigned to certain traditions in the text, the important issue still remains: to what extent is this a unitary ideology in Israel, and to what extent is this one voice in the mix of a pluralistic faith?[55] This issue of opposing and resisting Canaanite fertility religion was of paramount importance in the work of G. Ernest Wright and the entire casting of Old Testament theology "against its environment." It seems clear, as I have already suggested, that this posture was profoundly shaped by the crisis of the German church in the face of National

---

54. It is now a commonplace among Old Testament scholars that Yahwism was quite variegated and that it was especially the Deuteronomic tradition which imposed a certain exclusivist view of faith. That insistence on exclusivism becomes the proper subject of Old Testament theology, as distinct from a history of Israelite religion. To be sure, that assertion of exclusivism was not completely successful, for traces of pluralism in faith still persist in the text.

55. On such persistent pluralism, see Albertz, *A History of Israelite Religion in the Old Testament Period.*

Socialism, when Old Testament theology received its dominant twentieth-century casting. Another major issue also remains: To what extent is patriarchalism as polemic present *in the text,* and to what extent have the evident elements of it been hardened and underscored by an ongoing polemical *interpretation?* This interpretive propensity is evident in translations and in the imposition of interpretive constructs and categories on the material.

We have seen that Israel had no single fixed set of symbols and metaphors, but that the metaphorical process in Israel was an open-ended, ongoing one, through which new noun-metaphors for Yahweh were always being generated. No doubt some belatedly generated noun-metaphors for Yahweh performed a critical function vis-à-vis older, established practices of speech. This dynamic process, especially evident in the great prophets of the exile, raises the question of the extent to which that ongoing interpretive enterprise gives warrant for its continuation in contemporary interpretive work.[56] This ongoing process is evident in the interplay of continuity and discontinuity whereby the New Testament takes up, expands, and critiques the metaphorical offer of the Old Testament. Moreover, the same dynamics are surely at work in the great ecumenical formulations of the Catholic tradition that practiced both continuity and discontinuity with the biblical imagery in its trinitarian and christological formulations. The same is abundantly evident in the bold work of the Reformers in the sixteenth century, particularly Luther, who was an engine for new metaphors.

It is evident that no adjudication of this issue of patriarchalism is ever disinterested or innocent. Those who urge the elaboration and accent of feminist imagery do so as part of an enterprise of liberation, which is not at all disinterested.[57] In like manner, I submit, those who resist such ventures in the interest of staying with traditional formulations and interpretations do so in part in order to maintain advantage and privilege, even if this agenda is unintended or undertaken unwittingly. Given the reality that all such interpretive enterprises are "interested," this poses the question of whether those habitually excluded from the long-established patriarchal enterprise are entitled to "reparations"—that is, some intentionally granted advantage in the current process of interpreting the patriarchal tradition. Obviously such a concession is difficult. It is my judgment, however, that the very character of the political rhetoric in much of the text itself bespeaks an openness to such

---

56. Reference should be made, for example, to the work of Sallie McFague, *Models of God: Theology for an Ecological Nuclear Age* (London: SCM Press, 1987); and Gordon D. Kaufman, *The Theological Imagination: Constructing the Concept of God* (Philadelphia: Westminster Press, 1981); and *In the Face of Mystery: A Constructive Theology* (Cambridge: Harvard University Press, 1993). Such approaches are quite removed from the Bible and its imagery; the dynamic processes of interpretation in which they are engaged, however, do not seem alien to the venturesome ways in which the Bible handles the tradition.

57. Practitioners of feminist and other forms of liberation interpretation do not deny that such interpretation is not disinterested. Their only insistence (which I share) is that those who practice a more traditional, often patriarchal and hegemonic interpretation should also acknowledge that what has long passed for objective scholarship is equally "interested." This common admission by all parties to interpretive conversations gives no special advantage in principle to a liberationist approach, but it does level the playing field, so that all parties are seen to be engaged in advocacy.

reparations. That is, both the powerful and the powerless in Israel understood very well that speech as testimony is not a disinterested enterprise, but is itself a means of claiming power and eventually privilege. Israel understood, even as it continued its generative speech, that boldness in theological utterance was an argument about power as well as about truth.[58]

It would remain to be determined what reparations might mean. I have in mind both a disproportionate honoring of noun-metaphors that critique patriarchal claims, and an acute, self-critical recognition that patriarchal images traditionally exercise a disproportionate influence in text and in traditional interpretations. The disproportion in text and in interpretation needs to be acknowledged (and repented of?), because the disproportion characteristically concerns not only knowledge, but power as well.

Incomparability. The noun-metaphors for Yahweh are an enactment of Israel's testimony of Yahweh as incomparable. Indeed, "Who is like Yahweh"... judge, king, warrior, father! "There is none like Yahweh"... artist, gardener, doctor, mother, shepherd! There is none like Yahweh, who lives inside a rich, open, generative rhetoric, whose character arises from daily life, and who refers back to daily life in governing and sustaining ways.

The student of Old Testament theology must recognize what he or she has in hand. The central Character of the Old Testament, to which Israel bears imaginative testimony, is known in *concrete verbal sentences,* which give accounts of powerful sustenance and radical transformation. Those verbal sentences, moreover, fund *generalizing adjectives* of sovereignty and fidelity, in endless recitals of compassion, faithfulness, steadfast love, righteousness, and justice. And the generalizing adjectives invite *a rich panoply of nouns,* which recognize in (or assign to) Yahweh remarkable authority, but also a kind of hands-on attentiveness to the way life is lived at close range. This field of noun-metaphors, to which we have done little more than make a considered allusion, means that the Subject of the verbs is decisively present in every phase of Israel's life. Yahweh's decisive presence, moreover, is not flat, thin, or predictable. It is, rather, as supple as metaphor can permit. Israel knows no other so alive, decisive, playing, caring, and demanding as the God who lives in and through this collage of nouns. None other!

---

58. Michel Foucault, more than anyone else, has helped us see that discourse is a political activity and that speech (in the interpretive process as well as in the text) is a form of political activity, in which truth takes up all kinds of relationships with power. Thus Foucault's importance for our study is critical and instructive, requiring us to pay attention to our own methodological investments. John E. Grumley, *History and Totality: Radical Historicism from Hegel to Foucault* (London: Routledge, 1989) 184, comments that Foucault provides

a critique of the way in which the human sciences have functioned as instruments of power, social control, discipline, and exclusion. He reveals this hitherto unsuspected story to expose the complicity of the human sciences in the institution of the radically new modern configuration of power/knowledge, to arm us against the human illusions sanctioned by these discourses, to dramatize the frightening completeness of contemporary social control and register this as crisis.

SEVEN

Yahweh Fully Uttered

L IKE EVERY WITNESS who provides testimony, the witness of Israel to Yahweh must proceed slowly, patiently, one detail at a time.[1] Witnesses who seek to slide by with generalized statements are promptly pushed back to the detail. So Israel proceeds, in its articulation of Yahweh, one text at a time. The outcome of such testimony is a mass of detail, a collage of discrete texts. It is not clear how all of the detailed testimonies fit together, or if they can be fitted together sensibly at all, because the details are uttered with no concern for a larger sketch of Yahweh.

When all of the detail of testimony is offered, the profoundly difficult question remains: What does all of this add up to as a presentation of the character of Yahweh? In the face of such utterance of detailed testimony, it remains the hard work of the listener (the court) to imagine or construe or construct a larger portrayal. That is the business of the court and not of the witness. *Mutatis mutandis,* a larger, coherent portrayal of Yahweh, the subject of Israel's testimony, is not the work of the witnesses who stay with the concrete. It is rather the work of those who hear the witnesses—that is, interpreters—to construe or imagine a comprehensive characterization of Yahweh based on the details of Israel's testimony.

This work of fashioning a larger, coherent portrayal of Yahweh is the proper work of an Old Testament theology. Doing Old Testament theology is not finally the same enterprise as commenting on one text at a time. Its work is to construe out of the texts a rendering of God. But at the same time, this work of thematization (not systematization) is the great hazard of an Old Testament theology. Such work of generalization can never take into account all of the data, but must accent or deemphasize, include or exclude, some testimony. Moreover, the decision to include or exclude, to accent or deemphasize, is never innocent. Rather it follows from presupposition, whether it is an inclination toward historical-critical, canonical, liberationist, or some other form of interpretation. We never escape the haunting question about whether thematization, in principle and without reference to any particular substance, violates the very character of the testimony that relishes the detail. *This thematization is our required work and our most profound hazard.*

---

1. To make the witness for Yahweh "text by text" recalls the statement by Anne Lamott, *Bird by Bird: Some Instructions on Writing and Life* (New York: Pantheon Books, 1994). The title of the book answers the question of how to write an ornithological report: "bird by bird." Israel's witness to Yahweh is enacted in parallel fashion.

I deliberately choose the word *thematization* for this aspect of our study. This term claims a great deal, to ask whether we can identify and explicate pervasive tendencies and trajectories in the character of Yahweh as given in this testimony. But I do not intend it to claim too much, for it is a much more modest term than *systematization*. Thematization, unlike systematization, aims only at a rough sketch and not close presentation. It allows for slippage, oddity, incongruity, and variation, and does not propose to arrive at closure. If one succeeds in presenting a persuasive thematization of Yahweh, a further systematization may be undertaken, perhaps by an ecclesial community (systematic theology) or by a critical community (historical or literary criticism). But thematization, as I attempt it here, intends to stop short of such systematizing closure, for it is in the nature of the Subject of the thematization to resist such closure.

The Disjunctive Rendering of Yahweh

My thesis for thematization of Israel's testimony concerning Yahweh is this: Yahweh is a Character and Agent who is evidenced in the life of Israel as an Actor marked by unlimited sovereignty and risky solidarity, in whom this sovereignty and solidarity often converge, but for whom, on occasion, sovereignty and solidarity are shown to be in an unsettled tension or in an acute imbalance. *The substance of Israel's testimony concerning Yahweh, I propose, yields a Character who has a profound disjunction at the core of the Subject's life.* This disjunction, moreover, is the engine that drives Israel's testimony; it is the splendor of Israel's odd faith and the source of the deep vexation that marks Israel's life. The disjunction is a theological datum of substance. It is not a mark of erroneous, primitive religion that later "concepts of God" can leave behind.[2]

The data concerning the disjunctive marking of Yahweh by unlimited sovereignty and risky solidarity may be summarized as follows.

Power and Solidarity

We have, at the outset, considered Israel's two formulas of incomparability: "There is none like you," and "Who is like you?" Israel's testimony, for which the formal assertion is the First Commandment of Exod 20:1, the center of Israel's law, is that there is no one like Yahweh.[3] There is no god who is so powerful, and no god who is so attentive to the weak and needy.

We have seen that the statement of Yahweh's incomparable power—that is, the capacity to assert sovereignty—is the subject of Israel's most sweeping doxologies.

---

2. See Walter Brueggemann, "Texts That Linger, Not Yet Overcome," *TToday* (forthcoming).

3. On the cruciality of the First Commandment for the faith of Israel, see especially Walther Zimmerli, *Old Testament Theology in Outline* (Atlanta: John Knox Press, 1978); Werner H. Schmidt, *The Faith of the Old Testament: A History* (Oxford: Blackwell, 1983); and Schmidt, *Das erste Gebot: Seine Bedeutung für das Alte Testament* (Theologische Existenz Heute 165; Munich: Chr. Kaiser Verlag, 1970).

These hymns articulate Yahweh's mighty power that has been evidenced in Israel's verbal sentences of creation and deliverance. Thus in the great doxology celebrating the Exodus from Egypt, the formula of incomparability (Exod 15:11-12) affirms Yahweh's majesty and awesomeness in doing wonders that defeat the Egyptian gods and Egyptian political power. While the second major unit of the poem (vv. 13-17) alludes to Yahweh's "steadfast love" toward Israel, this is a minor motif in the poem, which is centered in the claim that the incomparable power of Yahweh is greater than the alleged power of Egypt.

Conversely, we have seen that in complaint psalms, the voice of needy, desperate, helpless Israel takes for granted the power of Yahweh to enact transformations (cf. Ps 86:9-10). Indeed the power of Yahweh is commented on almost in passing. The great effort of these prayers is to enlist Yahweh in the immediate crisis of the speaker. The appeal is grounded in the affirmation that Yahweh's incomparability is located in mercy and graciousness in the service of the needy. These prayers assume Yahweh's incomparable power, but that incomparable power is of no consequence for the petitioner unless it is marked by concern for and responsiveness to those who trust in Yahweh's ready solidarity.

If one attends to hymns that celebrate Yahweh's power and complaints that appeal to Yahweh's solidarity, two things become evident in Israel's testimony. First, in the use of the formula of incomparability, Israel never affirms or insists on one of these aspects of Yahweh to the disregard or denial of the other. The formula of Yahweh's incomparability functions pastorally and theologically, because Yahweh is both sovereign and in solidarity. Second, Israel's theological speech sounds very different accents, depending on circumstance and depending on what dimension of Yahweh's person is pertinent to the speaker and the speaker's situation. These formulas, characteristically, hold the two themes together. It is evident that appeal to Yahweh's solidarity must perforce count on Yahweh's power. But the matter is not quite symmetrical. Israel can speak about Yahweh's great power without allusion to Yahweh's solidarity, thus suggesting at least a chance for the two accents to fall apart. In what follows, I will suggest that this temptation to celebrate Yahweh's power to the neglect of Yahweh's solidarity is in substance a temptation to disregard what is most crucial and definitive and peculiar for Israel's life with Yahweh.

Disjunction at the Center

We have considered the way in which Israel's most characteristic adjectives for Yahweh arise out of its verbal sentences of testimony. The adjectival formulations are Israel's first attempt to generalize from its "eyewitness" accounts, to say what Yahweh is really like and who Yahweh is. I have proposed that the stylized assertion of Exod 34:6-7 may be taken as a representative or perhaps even normative expression of Israel's characteristic stock of adjectives for speech about Yahweh.

In the articulation of the character of Yahweh in Exod 34:6-7, we have seen that vv. 6-7a are a wondrous inventory of Yahweh's most positive characteristics, all of which bespeak Yahweh's will to be related to Israel in faithful, generous, and reliable ways. This is a statement of Yahweh's intense resolve to be in solidarity with Israel and to maintain this solidarity in demanding circumstances and at great risk.

We have also seen, however, that in the culmination of the formula in Exod 34:7b, the statement does an abrupt about-face. The second half of the formula seems to break the cadence of the speech by introducing an abrupt infinitive absolute. But there is no hint that this second half of the utterance is an intrusion or an addendum—it belongs fully to Israel's core affirmation about Yahweh, apparently placed in Yahweh's own mouth. I can find no evident way in which the two parts of this formulation can be readily and fully harmonized. The faithful God who forgives (*ns'*) iniquity is the same God who visits (*pqd*) offenders for their iniquity. That is, the very God who is in inordinate solidarity with Israel and who is prepared to stay with Israel in every circumstance, is the God who will act abrasively to maintain sovereignty against any who challenge or disregard that sovereignty.

Either of these statements, concerning generous solidarity or fierce, uncompromising sovereignty, sounds to us like a perfectly anticipated claim of Yahweh. It does not surprise us, moreover, to find either of these statements to be normative for Israel's larger testimony. What startles us is the immediate proximity of one of these statements to the other, with no attempt to work out their relationship or even to give a signal that the juxtaposition is problematic. On almost all occasions, the sovereign power and the gracious solidarity of Yahweh go nicely together. But when they do not, we arrive at Israel's most acute awareness of Yahweh and Israel's oddest theological testimony.

As we have seen, Israel's subsequent uses of this formulation from Exod 34:6-7 tend to take up either one emphasis about the character of Yahweh or the other. Most often the subsequent uses appeal to the first half of the statement, which testifies to Yahweh's caring solidarity with Israel. In such statements, the negative second part of the statement is not even on the horizon of the later witness. On occasion, as in Nah 1:2-3, when Israel wishes to issue a verbal assault against Assyria, the poetry appeals precisely to the second half of the formula, "by no means clear the guilty." Even this formulation includes the phrase "slow to anger," seemingly from the first half of the formula in Exod 34:6-7. That phrase, however, plays no role in Nahum's utterance, or serves only to indicate that Yahweh's "slowness to anger" is now exhausted and does not extend to Assyria. What is left is the harsh sovereignty of Yahweh, who will move massively and destructively against Nineveh. The capacity of Israel to use one part of the formula or the other constitutes no problem for Israel's faith, and it provides for Israel a rich and supple theological resource.

Only once, in Num 14:18, is the recital of Exod 34:6-7 quoted in its entirety. The intent of Moses in the recital is to appeal to Yahweh's faithful solidarity for Israel (that is, to the first half of the formula), for the quote in the mouth of Moses is immediately followed in v. 19 with the imperative petition, "forgive the iniquity of this people...." Thus Moses, by the use of "iniquity" in v. 19, appeals precisely to the phrasing of Exod 34:7a, "forgiving iniquity." Unlike Moses, however, Yahweh will make intentional use of the entire quote from Exod 34:6-7 that Moses has reiterated, attending not only to the first part to which Moses appeals, but also to the second half, over which Moses apparently glides without mention. As a consequence, Yahweh will forgive Israel: "I do forgive, just as you have asked" (v. 20). This assurance, however, is immediately followed by "nevertheless" (*'ûlm*), a disjunctive conjunction matching the conjunction in the middle of Exod 34:7: "Nevertheless... none of those who despised me shall see [the land]" (vv. 21, 23).

This dramatic encounter in Numbers 14 is perhaps an exception to the use made of the paradigmatic characterization of Yahweh. If so, it is a remarkably illuminating exception. In it, Yahweh acts in faithful solidarity, as asked by Moses. But Yahweh also acts in fierce sovereignty, befitting the claim of Exod 34:7b. Except in the case of Caleb, the generation for which Moses intercedes receives nothing of Yahweh's generous solidarity.[4] In this case, Yahweh's fierce sovereignty has won over Yahweh's compassionate solidarity. It is not that sovereignty *always* defeats solidarity. It is rather that Yahweh, as uttered by Israel and confronted by Moses in this text, has as an inclination toward Israel a set of seemingly irreconcilable options. It is these options that give substance to the disjunction in the center of Israel's life and in the center of Yahweh's character, as sketched by Israel the witness.

This disjunction, so fully articulated in Exod 34:6-7, and so oddly enacted in Num 14:18-24, states what is most crucial about Yahweh. And what is most crucial, I submit, is that Yahweh's capacity for solidarity and for sovereignty is the primary reality that Israel finds in the character of Yahweh. This means that Israel's relationship with Yahweh is one of heavily freighted possibility. Yahweh may act in any circumstance in gracious fidelity, and often does. And Yahweh may act in any circumstance in ferocious sovereignty, and sometimes does, sometimes on behalf of Israel and sometimes against Israel. The affirmation of Yahweh's sovereignty is endlessly unsettling and problematic. To be sure, the formulations of Exod 34:7 and Num 14:18 indicate that Yahweh's potential enactment in rage is in response to and correlated with "iniquity." Thus there is something rational and disciplined about the fierce sovereignty. Israel knows, however, in its various utterances about Yahweh, as in Nahum 1–2, that "visiting iniquity" seems sometimes to be undisciplined and well beyond the enactment of sanctions. This second half of the formulation bears witness to something potentially wild, unruly, and dangerous in Yahweh's life.

Our contemporary adjudication of this issue concerning Yahweh is bound to be as problematic as it was in ancient Israel. We have a strong propensity to insist that Yahweh's gracious fidelity has surely, decisively overridden Yahweh's harsh propensity to sovereignty, so that we hope for a God of love. Such an argument is often presented as a certain Christian discernment of God; but such Christian discern-

---

4. On the role of Caleb and Joshua in the Book of Numbers as harbingers of the "new generation" of the faithful, see Dennis T. Olson, *The Death of the Old and the Birth of the New: The Framework of the Book of Numbers and the Pentateuch* (Chico, Calif.: Scholars Press, 1985). In this text, however, the newness is represented only by Caleb, for Joshua is not mentioned.

ment depends, in large part, on a very selective reading of the New Testament. Or perhaps our strong propensity toward a God of love is simply on more general grounds of the tolerance of modernity. But we are given pause about such a claim in the face of twentieth-century barbarism, and we wonder if such brutalities are without moral significance in a world of love, leaving the brutality unanswered and unrequited.

In the midst of a strong propensity to gracious fidelity, however, it is often insisted that we live in a morally reliable, morally symmetrical world in which moral sanctions are inalienably linked to conduct. This insistence, which tends to be held selectively, wants to allow for no slippage for solidarity and fidelity in the face of harsh demand.

In this odd tension between a God of love and stern moral retribution, perhaps we are theologically much like ancient Israel, focusing on the part of the tradition that strikes us, at the moment, as useful. The difference between our current usage and the witness of ancient Israel, I suggest, is that most often we innocently focus on this or that affirmation, as it is pragmatically persuasive, and leave it at that. In contrast, Israel pushed the tension theologically and rhetorically, until it had pushed it into the very life, character, and person of Yahweh. Israel assigned to Yahweh, or found within the person of Yahweh, this profound tension, whereby Yahweh's future life in the world and with Israel is characteristically ominous. At the same time, nonetheless, Yahweh is Israel's last resort of hope. In the end, Israel must stake everything on this unsettled awareness that the God who stands in solidarity and generosity is the God who takes with savage seriousness Yahweh's right to be worshiped, honored, and obeyed. Israel (and perhaps Yahweh) cannot know how this unresolved tension will be enacted in any particular circumstance.

A Certain Kind of Order, a Certain Kind of Power

Chapter 6 explored the ways in which Israel's verbal sentences of testimony eventually issue in stabilizing noun-metaphors, which give some constancy and staying power to Yahweh's character over and through time. We have noted (a) that these nouns are metaphors and so both "are" and "are not," and (b) that a wide range of noun-metaphors yields unsettled incongruities and tensions. For our purposes of thematization, we may suggest that what we have termed metaphors of governance are attempts to speak about Yahweh's sovereign ordering of life, and what we have called metaphors of sustenance are efforts to speak about Yahweh's faithful solidarity.

The metaphors of governance—judge, king, warrior, father—are ways of speaking about Yahweh's capacity to establish a coherent, viable, life-giving, life-permitted order. These ways of speech, which converge and overlap, all bear witness to the power and authority of Yahweh to establish a place for life. The key accent of such testimony is on the *power* of Yahweh, but it is a power that is graciously intended and well used, in which Israel can have glad confidence. Thus,

- the judge "judges the world with righteousness" (Ps 9:8);

- the king is extolled (Ps 145:1) as the one who is just and kind (Ps 145:17);

- the warrior triumphs so that "victory (*t'šû'*) belongs to the Lord" (Prov 21:31);

- the father is "father of orphans and protector of widows" (Ps 68:5; cf. Hos 14:3b).

In each of these statements, to which many others might be added, Yahweh as governor acts powerfully and decisively to establish an ordered, reliable place of life. Clearly this willingness and capacity to act in powerful ways is of paramount importance to Israel (and to the world), for without this ordering capacity there would be no chance for life. The God who works equity, righteousness, victory, and justice is Israel's only line of defense against the powers of chaos and destructiveness that make life wretched and finally impossible.

It is astonishing, and surely worth noting, that these metaphors of governance are not cleanly and one-dimensionally statements of power and order. What the sovereign enacts is *a certain kind of order*. The testimony Israel makes concerning Yahweh is of a powerful governor and orderer, whose policies and actions are impinged on, influenced by, and shaped by the needs and pleas of the subjects whom Yahweh governs. Thus the judge judges equitably and is urged to intervene on behalf of the oppressed (Ps 9:9). The king who is praised for wonders is the one who "upholds all who are falling, and raises up all who are bowed down" (Ps 145:14). The warrior who acts so fiercely is the warrior whose great and ferocious power is precisely mobilized for the slaves who cry out in need (Exod 2:23-25, 15:3). And the father who begets Israel is the one who sides with widows and orphans, those who have no other advocate in a patriarchal society.

Thus Yahweh's extraordinary power, about which Israel is in no doubt, is *a certain kind of power*. It is power used toward Yahweh's subject-partner, power used in the work of redress and rehabilitation of those who lack the requirements of life. The metaphors in and of themselves do not inevitably tilt power and order in such a direction. The rhetoric, especially in the prayers of Israel, however, pushes the nouns of governance in the direction of sustenance and care. The wonder of this portrayal of Yahweh is that Yahweh is not resistant to or unresponsive about this tilt caused by Israel's relentless insistence. This pervasive and characteristic tilt means that Yahweh's sovereign power has a specific content. The sovereignty of Yahweh can indeed be summoned and mobilized by Israel in need. And characteristically, Yahweh is not impervious or unresponsive to need. The righteousness of Yahweh, the capacity to work a good order, is decisively qualified by the fidelity Yahweh has for Yahweh's subject-partners.

Neither is it possible, however, to take as a completely settled matter this qualification of Yahweh's power of governance as trustworthy in fidelity. We have seen that in the adjectival formulation of Exod 34:6-7, just as Yahweh is rhetorically settled in fidelity (vv. 6-7a), a sharp disjunction in v. 7b warns Israel against any temptation to coziness with Yahweh. The very God whose righteousness is marked by fidelity and compassion is surely the God who shows a recurring streak of self-regard that may express itself in vigorous and negative ways. George Mendenhall has proposed that Yahweh's harsh enactments of sovereignty are in defense of Yahweh's legitimate imperium; that is, in defense of Yahweh's will for order and justice.

Thus in Gen 18:16–19:29, Yahweh the judge is ready to act massively and decisively against Sodom and Gomorrah in response to their grave affront:

> How great is the outcry against Sodom and Gomorrah and how very grave their sin! I must go down and see whether they have done altogether according to the outcry that has come to me; and if not, I will know. (18:20-21)

Abraham's role in the narrative is to exercise restraint on Yahweh, to hold Yahweh to a higher standard of justice than Yahweh originally intended (v. 25). The narrative intends that the bargaining between Abraham and Yahweh (18:25-33) asserts a sovereign reasonableness in Yahweh's attitude toward Sodom. That is, the massive judgment of 19:24-25 is appropriate to the massive affront of Sodom. And yet, the two large questions of 18:23-25 hint that Israel wondered about Yahweh's potential for unmitigated rage. The exchange with Abraham leaves a residue of unsettlement and disquiet, a hint that at the edge of Yahweh's judicial work, more than justice is possible.[5] Wonderment about Yahweh's lack of restraint is near the surface, even though it is not finally allowed in the narrative.

The king who "sits in the heavens" in Psalm 2 is primarily concerned with the authorization of David as king in Jerusalem. That is the positive part of the psalm. And yet we cannot fail to notice that in the maintenance of that governance, in Yahweh's response to the nations, "Then he will speak to them in his wrath, and terrify them in his fury..." (v. 5). The presumption is that Yahweh's governance, in heaven and in Zion, is proper and legitimate. Any challenge to that governance or conspiracy against that authority, such as the nations undertake in this psalm, is rebellion that must be quelled. The wrath and fury to be enacted are justified by the claim of Yahweh's sovereignty, which is simply assumed. Inside of that sovereignty, such action is taken as warranted. No case can be made for those who refuse such sovereignty; they may expect to be the target of such enforcement. Note that in this assertion of sovereignty, no case is made for Yahweh's commitment to justice. What counts here is Yahweh's unchallengeable power.

When we ponder the role of Yahweh as warrior, we expect fierceness and violence. Perhaps the most sustained presentation of Yahweh the warrior as freighted with violence is the poetry of Nahum. Yahweh is prepared to do massive, unrestrained violence against Nineveh:

---

5. The density and unresolve of the exchange of Gen 18:25-33 are discussed by Jack R. Lundbom, "Parataxis, Rhetorical Structure, and the Dialogue over Sodom in Genesis 18" (unpublished paper, 1995).

Who can stand before his indignation?
Who can endure the heat of his anger?
His wrath is poured out like fire,
and by him the rocks are broken in pieces.
The Lord is good,
a stronghold in a day of trouble;
he protects those who take refuge in him,
even in a rushing flood.
He will make a full end of his adversaries,
and will pursue his enemies into the darkness. (Nah 1:6-8)

This may indeed be a just response for the way in which the Assyrians have maltreated Israel over a long period. The rhetoric itself, however, suggests a complete lack of restraint in which there is something like delight (Yahweh's delight? Israel's delight?) in anticipation of an orgy of death, blood, and violence (cf. 2:9-10; 3:5-7). The poetry surely reflects the profound resentment of Israel at being too long subjugated by the Assyrians. What interests us, however, is that Israel's resentment is fully taken over, embraced, and acted on by Yahweh.

Concerning Yahweh as father, the pathos-filled poem of Hos 11:1-9 begins in a statement of gentleness (vv. 1-3) and ends in a moving articulation of the pathos-filled love of father Yahweh for darling Ephraim (vv. 8-9). Indeed, with the reference to Admah and Zeboiim in v. 8, it is evident that Yahweh (or Yahweh's witnesses) still has in purview the extreme destruction of Genesis 19. In this poem, Yahweh will not act destructively toward Israel as in that previous occasion with Sodom and Gomorrah. Yet even in this poem, with its wondrous conclusion in forgiveness and graciousness, the father Yahweh is capable of thinking about and yearning for a heavy-handed retaliation against the child Israel:

The sword rages in their cities,
it consumes their oracle-priests,
and devours because of their schemes.
My people are bent on turning away from me.
To the Most High they call,
but he does not raise them up at all. (vv. 6-7)

Responses to the Disjunctive Rendering of Yahweh

In all of these noun-metaphors we can notice, alongside a tender inclination on the part of Yahweh, a dimension of fierceness that tilts toward potential violence. Thus I propose that in the full utterance of Yahweh, the thematization of Yahweh is as the powerful governor and orderer of life who is capable of generous and gracious concern, but this same Yahweh has a potential for extraordinary destructiveness. These texts of destructiveness are endlessly problematic for normative theology.

We may imagine several responses to such texts that would lessen their significance for our theological work:

1. One can insist that these acts of ferociousness on the part of Yahweh are simply acts of sovereignty that take place within Yahweh's well-established sanctions. This is the implication of George Mendenhall's understanding of vengeance. A sovereign power must have a monopoly of force in order to sustain authority. What is done (or spoken) by Yahweh is legitimately in the service of order.

2. Much of this fierceness on the part of Yahweh (though not all of it) is in the service of Israel's special status and privilege under the rule of Yahweh, so that the testimony itself is rather uncritical. Yahweh's fierceness and violence cannot be separated from its positive effect on Israel, and therefore can often be construed as a negative counterpart to Yahweh's intense loyalty to Israel. For example, in the extreme expression of fury from Nahum 1, the counterpoint in the text concerns the well-being of Israel, made possible by the destruction of Assyria.

3. It can be argued that the texts I have cited are rather marginal to the total witness of Israel. They may be taken as random texts and surely not the central texts for a thematized theology.

All of these reservations have some merit. In any case, I have no wish to champion these texts that speak of Yahweh's remarkable savageness, nor to give them undue attention. One must insist, nonetheless, that such texts bear witness to something about Yahweh that Israel knew and did not deny. On the whole these texts assert that Yahweh's enormous power is in the service of a sovereignty marked by both justice and fidelity. But the ferocious rhetoric hinting at Yahweh's delight in rage suggests that not all is contained in Yahweh's graciousness and fidelity, nor even in Yahweh's reasoned sovereignty. There is, in addition to legitimated sovereignty and determined fidelity, an element of Yahweh's power that seems occasionally, in the imaginative testimony of Israel, to spill over into Yahweh's rather self-indulgent self-expression. I do not wish to overstate this element in the rhetoric, but I also do not want to ignore the remarkable assertions in the mouth of Yahweh.

I find this a difficult and close call, and intend only to give full notice to those texts most often submerged in theological exposition.[6] On such occasions, the action or speech of Yahweh seems to have no function other than to permit Yahweh to engage in an unfettered show of self-assertion. Yahweh's governance is a good and essential factor in the well-being of Israel but, in my judgment, Yahweh's governance is not completely rationalized either in relation to Israel or in relation to a commitment to an ordered justice. Yahweh's power is characteristically linked to Yahweh's fidelity... but not always.

---

6. Lawson G. Stone, "Ethical and Apologetic Tendencies in the Redaction of the Book of Joshua," *CBQ* 53 (1991) 25–36, has shrewdly suggested ways in which the textual tradition itself is aware of the problematic element in the violence of conquest and maneuvers to transform that violence into a "gigantic metaphor" for the religious life. That awareness and maneuver, of course, attest to the presence and problem of such violence in the text, which impinges directly on the articulation of Yahweh's character.

The Density of Nouns of Sustenance

The metaphors of sustenance are also more dense than might at first glance appear. The noun-metaphors we have considered in this regard—potter, gardener, shepherd, mother, doctor—stand in their texture and suggestive power some distance away from the metaphors of governance. The metaphors of sustenance seem to imply a more profound engagement with and attentiveness to the object on which the agent (noun-metaphors) works. We may thematize our suggestions about these noun-metaphors in the four following propositions.

Pro Nobis

Each of these nouns speaks of Yahweh, the one who has arisen out of verbal sentences of testimony and been generalized in adjectives, as "for the object" (*pro nobis*). Yahweh becomes engaged on behalf of the object, which is most often Israel. It is integral to the metaphor itself that such relatedness and engagement of a positive kind are intended. Thus:

- Yahweh as potter does a "hands-on" crafting of the object. It has often been noted that the verb *form* (*yṣr*) as it pertains to creation is not by dictum, but by actual engagement with the raw stuff (clay) out of which the object is formed (Gen 2:7, 19, Jer 18:3-6, Isa 45:9).

- Yahweh as gardener is often the subject of the verb *plant*. In Isa 5:1-2 in particular, the gardener-vinedresser is involved with the founding of the garden, and uses care, attentiveness, and extravagance in creating the best possible vineyard.

- Yahweh as shepherd, in the familiar Psalm 23, is subject of a series of verbs bespeaking attentiveness and presence at great risk in order to assure the well-being of the sheep.

- Yahweh as mother is a God who feeds (Num 11:12), who remembers (Isa 49:15), and who comforts (Isa 66:13). It is the purpose of the mother to give beneficent care to the child.

- Yahweh as healer actively intervenes to make a new life possible for Israel, just when all seemed lost. In the initial event of the Exodus (Exod 15:2-6) and subsequently in the Babylonian crisis (Jer 30:17), Yahweh acts to create a future for Israel when Israel otherwise had no prospect of a viable future.

In all of these images, Yahweh is the one whose identity is completely contained in this relation; Yahweh, the one with resources and capacity to act, is given over to the well-being of the object—variously the pot, garden or vineyard, the sheep, the child, the patient.

Yahweh Is Moved by Israel in Exile

These metaphors of sustenance, however, not only witness to Yahweh's activity that gives the object a good life. The images are more radical and intense than simply presenting a strong One moving toward a weak, needy one. These images, in addition to being positively inclined, portray Yahweh as one who can be radically and profoundly impinged on by the situation of the needy object, so that (with the noun-metaphors) Yahweh is moved by the status of the object to do what Yahweh might otherwise not do. This is especially evident in the following:

- The potter who smashes an ill-shaped pot (Jer 19:11) is appealed to, in the same imagery, to move beyond anger to new sympathy, compassion, and attentiveness (Isa 64:8-12). It is clear that the petition of Israel is based on the awareness that Yahweh continues to care about this smashed pot Israel and can be moved to act again, perhaps even against Yahweh's foremost inclination.

- Yahweh as gardener is portrayed, particularly in the promises of the Book of Jeremiah, as one who comes among the shambles of destroyed Israel (Jerusalem) and is resolved to restore. The verbs *plant* and *build*, in this poetry, in fact refer to rebuilding and replanting—restoration after loss (cf. Jer 31:4-6, 23-28).

- Yahweh as shepherd is an image used especially in the promises of the exile. Israel has been "scattered, like a sheep without a shepherd." But the shepherd now will gather the flock (Jer 31:10), and will be moved by the sorry state of the sheep to be attentively engaged on their behalf (Ezek 34:11-16).

- Yahweh as mother is the God who will indeed remember in compassion, when Israel-Jerusalem imagines itself to be completely forgotten (Isa 49:14). In Yahweh's remembering, and nowhere else, is there new possibility.

- Yahweh as healer is one who finds Israel completely bereft of medical care (Jer 8:22), and so concludes that Jerusalem is beyond healing (Jer 30:12-15). Then, because of Yahweh's passionate attentiveness, the doctor moves against the terminal illness and rejects the doctor's own diagnosis:

  > For I will restore health to you,
  > and your wounds I will heal, says the Lord,
  > because they have called you an outcast:
  > "It is Zion; no one cares for her!" (v. 17)

In each of these usages, Yahweh is drawn to the sorry situation of Israel (or Zion) and is thereby moved to intervene. It is the exile of the sixth century B.C.E. that so impinges on Yahweh and moves Yahweh to undertake action that heretofore seemed impossible or not on the horizon of Yahweh. The historical rootage of these texts in exile is of enormous importance for the project of Old Testament theology. The displacement and discontinuity of the exile (in part geographic but more importantly symbolic, emotional, and liturgical) constituted a profound emergency in the faith of Israel. Israel in that moment had its most settled assurances placed in jeopardy, and so was forced to radical questioning and to radical rearticulation of Yahweh.[7] Our theological point in the context of exile is that Yahweh is moved to undertake new actions by the circumstance of Israel; is moved beyond Yahweh's own previous intentionality and, we may believe, beyond Yahweh's self-discernment. The circumstance of Israel and the utterance of Israel act upon Yahweh, making it possible (requiring) that Yahweh commit a new act on behalf of Israel—an act that, previous to Israel's circumstance and utterance, had not been on Yahweh's horizon. Yahweh becomes, by the reality of Israel's insistence, as Yahweh had not yet been.

Relentless Sovereign Intention

The fact that the intensification and increased radicality of these metaphors of sustenance happens in exile, in response to the need, misery, wretchedness, and insistence of Israel, alerts us to a third theme concerning these metaphors. Israel as pot, garden-vineyard, sheep, child, and patient did not end up in that sixth-century circumstance by happenstance. According to its testimony, Israel in all of these figures arrived at wretchedness, either because of the active, destructive intervention of Yahweh or because of the harsh neglect of Yahweh, who was willing to abandon the object of Yahweh's passionate attentiveness. In other words, it is the default of the potter, gardener, shepherd, mother, or doctor that brings trouble on Israel.

This recognition suggests that even these metaphors of sustenance include dimensions of Yahweh's powerful governance, Yahweh's insistence on order of a certain kind. Where that order is not honored or enacted, Yahweh is fully prepared to abandon the object of sustenance. The metaphors of sustenance turn out to have a dimension of demand, reflecting Yahweh's sovereign expectation. On the one hand, Israel's testimony employs metaphors that articulate Yahweh's judgment in the interest of reparations, rehabilitation, and beginning again. See, for example, the plumb line (2 Kgs 21:13; Amos 7:7-9; Isa 28:17), the dirty dish wiped clean (2 Kgs 21:13), the refining fire (Isa 1:21-27). In these cases, the harshness appears to be for the sake of newness. On the other hand, some images seem to bespeak an ending without a new beginning:

- The potter who finds a spoiled pot will smash it (Jer 18:3-6, 19:11).

- The gardener who is disappointed with the produce of the vineyard will "pluck up" and "tear down" (Isa 5:5-7).

- The shepherd may scatter the sheep (Jer 31:10).

---

7. See Ralph Klein, *Israel in Exile: A Theological Interpretation* (OBT; Philadelphia: Fortress Press, 1979); Daniel L. Smith, *The Religion of the Landless: The Social Context of the Babylonian Exile* (Bloomington, Ind.: Meyer-Stone, 1989); and Peter R. Ackroyd, *Exile and Restoration: A Study of Hebrew Thought of the Sixth Century* (OTL; Philadelphia: Westminster Press, 1968).

- The mother is thought to be neglectful and inattentive to the child (Num 11:12, Isa 49:14). In these particular cases, the mother does not act negatively or destructively but may be grossly inattentive, to the great detriment of the child.

- The doctor may finally arrive at a diagnosis that the sick people/city is hopeless and beyond healing (Jer 30:12-13).

Characteristically these uses pertain to the sixth-century crisis of Israel. But they must also be understood, not simply as a historical datum, but as a piece of theological testimony. This is indeed who Yahweh is in the testimony of Israel. Thus in Israel's most preferred nouns-metaphors for Yahweh, the generativity and positive aspects of Yahweh's character and inclination toward Yahweh's object are shaded and given nuance by the One who is judge, king, warrior, and father. Even within more positive roles, Yahweh intends a certain order that must be honored and will not be compromised. When that order is violated, the several roles in which Yahweh is cast are stretched to give expression to a relentless sovereign intention.

Unexpected Radicality

In the turn of these metaphors of sustenance toward governance, it is entirely plausible that Yahweh, marking that turn, is fully justified as the legitimated governor of the processes of forming, planting, guiding, feeding, and healing. That is, the potter, shepherd, gardener, mother, and doctor are modes for the senior member of the relationship, who determines the shape of the transaction. Seen in that way, Yahweh in these several and diverse roles acts in ways that are completely appropriate to Yahweh.

And yet, having said that, one may wonder whether these nouns-metaphors carry at least potential spillover beyond legitimate governance to Yahweh's self-regard, which in seeming excess moves against the object of concern. It is a delicate matter to distinguish between the legitimate governance of Yahweh and excessive self-regard on the part of Yahweh, but the negative force of the images at least requires us to ask about excess that goes beyond legitimate governance. I do not suggest that such excessive self-regard constitutes any theme of Old Testament theology, nor that Israel intends in its testimony to articulate anything like it about Yahweh. Rather the evidence for what may be Yahweh's destructive self-regard comes up almost inadvertently in the testimony, but it becomes available to us precisely because of the suppleness and poignancy of the metaphors. Thus, for example, the potter who attentively works on the clay so that a lovely pot might emerge is capable of breaking the pot in so many pieces that it can never be mended (Jer 19:11). Such an act is not the same as reworking the pot in order to make it right (cf. Jer 18:4). The action suggests a destructive streak in the potter, who intends to vent rage against the clay that refuses to "shape up," presumably out of lack of respect for the potter.

Another example is the gardener lavishing attention on the vineyard (Isa 5:1-2). In the failure of the vineyard to produce grapes as expected by the owner, the owner is completely exasperated. There is finally no additional attempt at care, for the patience and generosity of the owner are exhausted. Enough is enough! In a savage act, the vineyard is trampled and wasted. In Hos 9:10 the imagery of the vinekeeper is somewhat different, and the metaphor is not sustained. That is, the rhetoric moves out of the image, so that we know directly that this is Yahweh dealing with Israel. But even in that context, in the subsequent verses Yahweh, the vinekeeper, acts to terminate Israel, the vine. Yahweh's positive passion is spent. Now Yahweh acts in self-regard against the very object of faithfulness and mercy for whom Yahweh had initiated the act of gardening. Pushed to the edge, the compassionate One has no more compassion. In Jer 51:9 the lack of healing for Babylon is reported not as a refusal to heal by the doctor, but as an inability to heal. Thus extreme situations lie beyond both the doctor's resolve and the doctor's competence.

The metaphors of sustenance, which serve well to articulate Yahweh's caring capacity toward Israel, are enormously elastic. Yahweh may indeed be spoken of through these images, but the images are not permitted to curb or limit Yahweh's wide range of actions and inclinations. Thus one cannot say of this testimony concerning Yahweh that Yahweh's restorative pathos is regularly curbed by an extreme assertion of sovereignty. Nor can one say, conversely, that Yahweh's harsh self-assertion is countered regularly by tender compassion. The interruption of either of these propensities in Yahweh may and often does happen in either direction, so that the noun-metaphors serve, but do not control, Yahweh's self-enactment. Yahweh makes use of the images, exploits them fully, but then breaks beyond them in unexpected radicality. That unexpected radicality is apparently matched only by the rhetorical agility of Israel as witness, on whom the availability of Yahweh's interruptive surprises depends.

In my judgment, this is the true data of Yahweh's character: the capacity of Yahweh (and of Israel's testimony) to surprise us by intervention that may move destructively or rehabilitatively on any given occasion. Thus our thematization of Yahweh must be inherently open and relatively unstable, for we cannot know ahead of time at which extreme Yahweh may be disclosed. Concerning this unsettled dimension of Yahweh, one may say simply that the people who generated the biblical text were indeed venturesome and imaginative, and so we may credit the oddness about Yahweh to rich literary activity. No doubt there is something in this. Or one could say that there is some development in Yahweh from wild destructiveness to compassion as Israel's religion matures, and so we may credit this oddness to the history of religion. No doubt there is something in this as well. But here the issue that concerns us is not exhausted with imaginative literature nor with developmental history, for we intend to be asking about the God given us in the speech of Israel; that is, we have a theological agenda.

The tension, oddness, incongruity, contradiction, and lack of settlement are to be understood, not in terms of literature or history, but as the central data of the character of Yahweh. This suggests that Yahweh, as evidenced in and by Israel, has available as a character a range of inclinations, a repertoire of possible responses, a conundrum of loyalties, commitments, and expectations that are being endlessly adjudicated. While certain tendencies, propensities, and inclinations have some stability, being more or less constant, Israel and Israel's rhetoricians never know beforehand what will eventuate in the life of Yahweh. Thus it is not known whether:

- the judge will sentence or pardon,

- the warrior will fight for or against,

- the king will banish or invite to the table,

- the potter will work attentively or smash,

- the gardener will cultivate and protect or pluck up,

- the shepherd will lead and feed or judge between sheep and sheep,

- the doctor will heal or pronounce the patient terminally ill.

Such a conclusion is not contextless. We do not say these things concerning Yahweh as though every occasion of response were an arbitrary flip of the coin. No, of course not. Yahweh is deeply enmeshed in a tradition of textuality, is committed to what has been previously claimed, and is held accountable for the chance for life together (between Yahweh and Israel). Thus the offer of Yahweh is not sheer capriciousness. But even so, one may ask: Does life with this God not entail anxiety? Even if there is a tendency in a certain reliable direction, there is always a chance of a response in another direction, for Yahweh has a vast repertoire of possible responses. Yes, the faith of Israel is not without anxiety.

This, I suggest, is the severe meaning of the Second Commandment. The One with whom Israel has to deal is not an image, a category, a genre, a concept, or a norm. Rather this is a particular God with a name and a history, who is a free agent and an active character. Israel's faith is finally not trust in something that is transcendent in Yahweh, so as to escape what is contingent. But Israel's life with this God is endlessly dialogical, and it is therefore always open and always capable of newness. Israel is tempted to minimize the risk and curb the danger by boxing Yahweh into its formula. But each time it does so, Yahweh surprises. In times of judgment when sovereign assertion of Yahweh is expected and warranted, we find pathos. In times of terrible need, when Yahweh's delicate generosity may seem appropriate, Yahweh is solemn and demanding. One does not know. Israel does not know. What Israel does know and counts on heavily is that the incomparable Yahweh of these several noun-metaphors will always be "in play" and Israel must always be "in play" with Yahweh, for that is its very life.

A Proximate Resolution in Righteousness

The reader may have detected in this discussion a drift toward *one larger thematization* that seems permitted by the analysis thus far. Here I will suggest that the largest thematization concerning Yahweh, as testified to by Israel, is that *Yahweh is at the same time sovereign and faithful*, severely preoccupied with self-regard and passionately committed to life with the partner. Finally, I shall suggest that these two themes, in considerable tension with each other, have their proximate—but no more than proximate—resolution in Yahweh's *righteousness*.

Yahweh, the God of the First Commandment, is a God who intends to be fully sovereign, who will brook no rival, who practices intense self-regard, and who will not tolerate those who detract from this self-regard. In this aspect of Yahweh's life, Yahweh does indeed practice "common theology"—that is, the way of "being god" that was everywhere available in the ancient Near East.[8] In that propensity, Yahweh imposes an order (moral, political, or otherwise), guarantees the order's system of benefits, and deals with rigorous sanctions toward those who violate the order. To some extent, Yahweh conducts Yahweh's life like any god known in this way.

Israel speaks about Yahweh's uncompromising, unaccommodating sovereignty in three characteristic ways.

The Glory of Yahweh

The glory of Yahweh refers to the claim and aura of power, authority, and sovereignty that must be established in struggle, exercised in authority, and conceded either by willing adherents or by defeated resisters. In many texts Yahweh's glory has a visible, physical appearance of light. But what is seen in the end is Yahweh's rightful claim to governance. That claim is a culmination not only of the legitimacy and appropriateness of Yahweh's authority, but also of the sheer force that can guarantee the claim of legitimacy. The notion of glory thus has within it both a dimension of benign, rightful order, and also a threat where legitimacy is not yet accepted.

At the outset, Yahweh must establish the right to rule by engaging in struggle against other would-be authorities, human and divine. It is entirely plausible that much of the combat, whereby the right to govern is won, is conducted in liturgy. If so, then the right to rule is not a once-for-all achievement, but must be periodically and regularly reasserted.

In the final shaping of Israel's testimony, we may identify three important contexts for combat, out of which Yahweh emerges as the true possessor of glory. First, in the Exodus narrative (in what are judged to be early layers of the tradition), Yahweh is engaged in a struggle with pharaoh on behalf of Israel. But in the

---

8. On the "common theology" of the ancient Near East, see Morton Smith, "The Common Theology of the Ancient Near East," *JBL* 71 (1952) 35–47; and Norman K. Gottwald, *The Tribes of Yahweh: A Sociology of the Religion of Liberated Israel, 1250–1050 B.C.E.* (Maryknoll, N.Y.: Orbis Books, 1979), chaps. 53–54. See my use of it as a heuristic entry into Israel's faith, Walter Brueggemann, "A Shape for Old Testament Theology I: Structure Legitimation," *CBQ* 47 (1985) 28–46.

later (final) form of the materials, Israel's cause is subordinated to Yahweh's self-agenda. In the Exodus combat, conducted in the plague narratives that are contests of power, Yahweh's struggle for control is with Egyptian political power, which is a candidate for glory, and with the Egyptian gods that are also at issue. In the climactic drama of that dispute, Yahweh asserts:

> I will harden Pharaoh's heart, and he will pursue them, so that I will gain glory for myself over Pharaoh and all his army; and the Egyptians shall know that I am the Lord. (Exod 14:4)

> Then I will harden the hearts of the Egyptians so that they will go in after them; and so I will gain glory for myself over Pharaoh and all his army, his chariots, and his chariot drivers. And the Egyptians shall know that I am the Lord, when I have gained glory for myself over Pharaoh, his chariots, and his chariot drivers. (Exod 14:17-18)

Yahweh emerges as more powerful than Egypt, and so is entitled to be honored, worshiped, and obeyed as the true sovereign of the realm.

In a second testimony that matches the Egyptian dispute, Isaiah in exile presents the work of Yahweh as the defeat of Babylonian power, and consequently, the defeat of the Babylonian gods (Isa 46:1-4). Thus the Babylonian gods are mocked and summoned to enter into litigation with Yahweh, in order to establish their claim to be gods (41:21-29). But in both the rhetoric of the liturgy and in the "historical combat" of the empire, Babylonian power is no match for Yahweh. Thus the homecoming of Israel out of the control of Babylon is presented as evidence of Yahweh's glory:

> Then the glory of the Lord shall be revealed,
> and all people shall see it together,
> for the mouth of the Lord has spoken. (Isa 40:5)

The Yahweh who speaks in Isaiah of the exile is a God who is supremely self-confident, who is entitled to all the glory, and who is eager to be recognized as such:

> I am the Lord, that is my name;
> my glory I give to no other,
> nor my praise to idols. (Isa 42:8)

> My glory I will not give to another. (Isa 48:11)

The Exodus from Egypt and the homecoming from Babylon are the two historical narratives whereby Yahweh is known to be the real sovereign power in the earth to whom other powers must submit. From these two narrative recitals, Israel generalizes to assert that Yahweh everywhere and always is the true possessor of glory.

These two historical narratives are matched in yet a third contest for glory, which was presumably a liturgical phenomenon. The very ancient Psalm 29 refers to an apparent contest among the gods. After each candidate for the post of head God has performed, the gods must choose. According to the hypothesis of an enthronement festival, when the vote among the gods is taken, concerning Yahweh, all cry "Glory" (Ps 29:9). That is, all the other gods recognize in (or assign to) Yahweh the rightful claim of glory and all the authority, power, honor, and dignity that go with it. A close parallel to Psalm 29 is Psalm 96, in which all glory is rightly assigned to Yahweh:

> Declare his glory among the nations,
> his marvelous works among all the peoples. (v. 3)

> Ascribe to the Lord, O families of the peoples,
> ascribe to the Lord glory and strength.
> Ascribe to the Lord the glory due his name;
> bring an offering, and come into his courts.
> Worship the Lord in holy splendor;
> tremble before him, all the earth.
> Say among the nations, "The Lord is king!" (vv. 7-10)

The purpose of such narrative recital and liturgical enactment is to make visible and compelling the rightful claim of Yahweh to glory. The temple where Yahweh abides and from which Yahweh enacts glory (=sovereignty) is a place filled with glory. But even in its cultic aspect, we must not spiritualize excessively, for glory has to do with rightful and acknowledged power. The link between historical combat and liturgical presence is evidenced in the processional hymn of Psalm 24, wherein the triumphant Yahweh returns in victory from combat to take up residence in the temple. Yahweh is indeed the "King of glory," having yet again demonstrated the claim that Yahweh holds to power and therefore honor:

> Lift up your heads, O gates!
> and be lifted up, O ancient doors!
> that the King of glory may come in.
> Who is the King of glory?
> The Lord, strong and mighty,
> the Lord, mighty in battle....
> The Lord of hosts,
> he is the King of glory. (Ps 24:7-10)

From this political dimension of glory as the right to wield authority over all rivals, the testimony of Israel takes care to affirm and enhance temple presence as a way in which the presiding power of Yahweh is a constant in Israel. Thus in the final form of the Pentateuch, Moses constructs the tabernacle anticipating the temple as a place for glory of Yahweh. The tabernacle is filled with glory (Exod 24:16-17; 40:34-35; Lev 9:6, 23) as an anticipation of the glory-filled temple of Solomon (1 Kgs 8:11; 2 Chr 7:1-3).

But this cultic presence wherein Yahweh evidences permanent residence is not to be presumed upon. A great deal of the text of Ezekiel asserts that Yahweh's "permanent residence" in the temple is placed in jeopardy by Israel's refusal to conform to Yahweh's rule. Thus in Ezekiel 9–10, the glory of Yahweh simply departs from the temple. This is Ezekiel's most drastic way of asserting that Yahweh has departed Israel, because Yahweh will not stay where Yahweh's awesome sovereignty is mocked. When the glory is gone, Israel is left to its own resources. Israel in that circumstance is sure to fail. Thus glory becomes a way in which the Priestly traditions of Ezekiel witness to the negativity of a people that refuses to submit to the claims of Yahweh's glory. In the end, Ezekiel portrays the return of Yahweh's glory to the temple (Ezekiel 43–44), but it is to a temple now purged and chastened, once again made appropriate for Yahweh.

Israel's testimony concerning Yahweh's glory is given very different nuance in contexts of struggle, wherein Yahweh establishes and sustains authority, and in contexts of cult, wherein glory is a settled constant. The two dimensions of Yahweh's glory, however, should not be contrasted or opposed to each other, for both glory emerging in struggle and glory as a settled constant are ways in which Israel speaks about Yahweh's right to authority and about the way in which the sense of that authority overwhelms Israel. Yahweh, in Yahweh's glory, is a power and a presence like none other, before whom Israel submits in confidence and before whom powers resistant to Yahweh finally submit because they have no choice. The glory of Yahweh is to itself and for itself, and Yahweh, in Yahweh's glory, accommodates to no one and to nothing.

We may notice three aspects of Yahweh's glory that are derivative from this primal assertion of governing presence. First, the glory of Yahweh is a source of ministering assurance and sustenance for Israel. Thus in the manna narrative, it is precisely in the wilderness, seemingly bereft of life-supports, that Yahweh's glory appears (Exod 16:7, 10). The glory is a way of making visible to Israel Yahweh's sovereignty operating even here. As a consequence, life-sustaining bread and quail are wondrously given, out of Yahweh's massive sovereignty. And in Isa 58:8, Yahweh is said to be the protector of Israel:

> Then your light shall break forth like the dawn,
> and your healing shall spring up quickly;
> your vindicator shall go before you,
> the glory of the Lord shall be your rear guard.

The glory of Yahweh is as a bodyguard who stays beside Israel to protect it from every threat. Thus the glory is made available for the sake of Israel. In this case, however, that availability is granted when Israel is obedient to "the fast that I choose" (Isa 58:6).

Second, the glory is a mode of Yahweh's self-presentation to the nations in a posture of power and authority. Thus in Yahweh's mighty action toward Israel in exile, "all flesh shall see it together" (Isa 40:5). The Isaiah tradition culminates with the summoning (drawing) of the nations in deference to Yahweh in Jerusalem:

> They shall bring all your kindred from all the nations as an offering to the Lord, on horses, and in chariots, and in litters, and on mules, and on dromedaries, to my holy mountain Jerusalem, says the Lord, just as the Israelites bring a grain offering in a clean vessel to the house of the Lord. (Isa 66:20)

Third, the arena of Yahweh's glory, Yahweh's evident, visible, inescapable right to rule that both demands and attracts, is larger even than the world of the nations. The same glory of Yahweh locally present in Israel has as its largest theater all of creation: "The heavens are telling the glory of God; and the firmament proclaims his handiwork" (Ps 19:1). Thus Israel in its testimony must utilize the most sweeping doxological language available in order to witness to the largeness and the unrivaled awesomeness of Yahweh's wondrous, sovereign presence. By this reference to creation as a witness to Yahweh's glory, Israel evidences its conviction that Yahweh's glory is to be contrasted with all that is in and of creation. The contrast, however, is not one of antagonism, because all creatures shall gladly cede to Yawheh whatever of glory is found among them. In the great lyrical doxology of Isaiah 35, Israel sings about creation's fruitfulness in the desert, in which "the glory of Lebanon" and "the majesty of Carmel and Sharon" are redeployed, all in deference to Yahweh:

> The glory of Lebanon shall be given to it,
> the majesty of Carmel and Sharon.
> They shall see the glory of the Lord,
> the majesty of our God. (v. 2)

The submission of all creation's glory to Yahweh in vv. 1-2, moreover, is matched by the great doxology in v. 6, in which the blind, the deaf, the lame, and the mute "sing for joy," perhaps joined in v. 7 even by the jackals and the grass. In this lyrical characterization of a revivified wilderness, all of creation sees the glory, the same glory that is on exhibit more serenely in the Jerusalem temple.

In appealing to the overwhelmingness of the glory of Yahweh, the New Testament makes daring moves to situate Jesus in Israel's rhetoric concerning Yahweh's glory. Both Paul (1 Cor 2:8) and John (John 1:14) refer to glory with reference to Jesus. But it is primarily in the trinitarian ascription of praise that glory continues to be spoken of in a way that comprehends Jesus in the claims made for Yahweh. This rhetoric is now fully embedded in the most familiar liturgical formulations of the church, as in the Gloria Patri and the final ascription of praise in conventional forms of the Our Father. These formulations have moved radically in christological and trinitarian directions, but they intend to voice the continuing claims of Israel's witness to Yahweh's unutterable, awe-evoking sovereignty.

The Holiness of Yahweh

A second way in which Israel speaks of Yahweh's sovereign self-regard concerns Yahweh's holiness.[9] The term _holiness_ (which has no analogue in other areas of Israel's life and so is sometimes regarded as the only theological term in Israel that is not derived from other parts of life, and so alone is not metaphorical)[10] refers to the radical otherness of Yahweh, who may not be easily approached, who may not be confused with anyone or anything else, and who lives alone in a prohibitive zone where Israel can enter only guardedly, intentionally, and at great risk. Thus it does not surprise us that Yahweh's holiness is one aspect of Israel's speech about Yahweh's incomparability:

> Who is like you, O Lord, among the gods?
> who is like you, majestic in holiness,
> awesome in splendor, doing wonders? (Exod 15:11)

> Once and for all I have sworn by my holiness;
> I will not lie to David. (Ps 89:35)

As with all such characteristic theological speech by Israel, it is not possible to articulate a clear definition of holiness. The most we can do is to notice the several characteristic uses of the term with reference to Yahweh.

It is evident, first, that holiness as pertains to Yahweh has cultic rootage and concerns the proper use, ordering, and protection of cultic matters.[11] The cult place is the zone of life where Yahweh may reside most intensely, and the place to which Israel must come in order to relate to Yahweh's residing presence. The use of the term _holy_ suggests an almost material, substantive notion of theological danger that must be protected from any contamination by things profane or impure (Ezek 22:26; cf. Hag 2:12-13). Thus much of the priestly instruction in the Old Testament is guidance in the proper maintenance of a sphere of holiness, for such proper maintenance is a technique that makes Yahweh's presence more probable and available. Conversely, failure to honor that special sphere may lead to the withdrawal of the Holy God, who will not stay in a profaned place. Clearly, the withdrawal of the Holy One is an ominous possibility to Israel, for the life of Israel depends on that Presence.

In such a way, we may understand much of the instruction in the Book of Leviticus, which may strike us as punctilious, but which in fact attempts to make Yahweh's holy, life-generating, life-guaranteeing presence available and certain in Israel. This aspect of Israel's relation to Yahweh is cultically elemental, if not primitive. It would, however, be a mistake to dismiss this interpretation of life with the Holy God as silly, as is our propensity in Enlightenment modernity. It

---

9. John G. Gammie, _Holiness in Israel_ (OBT; Minneapolis: Fortress Press, 1989), has provided a convenient survey of the materials on the theme.

10. See Brian Wren, _Which Language Shall I Borrow? God-Talk in Worship: A Male Response to Feminist Theology_ (London: SCM Press, 1989) 95–103.

11. See above pp. 192–93.

may help us to appreciate the sense of the meticulousness that this instruction aimed to produce, if we consider the modern preoccupation and fascination with the cult of health, with its endless regimens and disciplines; or, perhaps more elaborately, if we ponder our seemingly endless fascination with the emerging world of computers, which in "the information age" appear to hold the key to all security, effectiveness, and happiness.[12] The holiness of Yahweh is understood, in texts like Leviticus 11, as the careful management of the mystery of access, which in turn opens the mystery of life. At the center of this preoccupation is Yahweh, who is in Israel the undoubted source of life, but who cannot be lightly or directly or easily apprehended, except with utmost care not to offend or violate. While this preoccupation is concentrated in texts usually disregarded in modern interpretation, the same issues of pollution and impurity are evident in prophetic utterances. Thus, for example, Isa 6:3-5 articulates a vision of Yahweh's holiness that is said to evoke a sense of uncleanness and unworthiness. And in Jer 3:1-3 pollution is said to evoke a death-dealing drought. There is no doubt that this way of speaking of Yahweh is broadly based in the Israel who testifies to Yahweh.

The remarkable aspect of Israel's witness to the holiness of Yahweh is that from this primal-cultic understanding, Israel could extrapolate other aspects of Yahweh's holiness that move beyond characteristic cultic concerns and touch other dimensions of Israel's life. Thus the holiness of Yahweh is drawn into the covenant categories of Israel's faith, so that the Holy One is the related One. Specifically, the Holy One becomes "the Holy One in/of Israel." This fuller formulation should be noted with great care, for it represents an astonishing theological maneuver. It is probable that holiness, understood phenomenologically, remains completely a category of separation. But by linking "Holy One" to the term "of Israel," Israel's testimony asserts that this completely separated One is the characteristically related One. Yahweh's holiness, in this formulation, is in and with and for Israel. The development of the formulation in this way constitutes a radical recharacterization of holiness, to make the category congruent with Yahweh's more elemental propensity. This formula is especially preferred in the Isaiah tradition (Isa 29:19; 30:11-15; 31:1; 41:14, 16, 20; 43:15; 45:11; 47:4; 48:17; 54:5; 55:5). As a consequence of this articulation, the One who might dwell in splendid, guarded isolation is the One who is with Israel, and therefore is or can be mobilized to act on behalf of Israel in order to save and deliver. Thus the formula is drawn toward the active verbs that constitute Israel's most usual mode of testimony.

The best-known use of this formula is in Hos 11:9, which articulates the way in which linkage to Israel pushes Yahweh's holiness in an altogether new direction.[13] Moreover, Israel counts on Yahweh's holiness as a basis on which to pray for help

---

12. The analogy may be carried further negatively by noting that computers are liable to be infected by "viruses." The threat of defilement in the holiness traditions of Israel is not unlike the threat of such infection in a computer.

13. See Walther Eichrodt, "The Holy One in Your Midst: The Theology of Hosea," *Int* 15 (1961) 259–73.

(Ps 22:3). Even in one of its great doxologies, the holiness of Yahweh (Ps 99:5) is sandwiched between reference to justice (v. 4) and Yahweh's response to Israel's concrete prayer (v. 6).

The relatedness that comes to constitute Yahweh's holiness, however, not only concerns readiness to act as Israel's rescuer and advocate. As Yahweh is the Holy One of Sinai (Ps 68:17) and subsequently the Holy One of Jerusalem,[14] the Holy One also commands. The premise of the command of Sinai is that Yahweh is holy, committed to practices of purity and justice. And Israel, who is contingently holy, is to imitate Yahweh and so become holy likewise. Thus, "You shall be holy, for I am holy" (Lev 11:44-45; 19:2; 20:7, 26; 21:8). The demands that follow this formula, moreover, include all manner of concerns, not limited to the cultic. Thus Yahweh's holiness reflects Yahweh's positive concern for Israel. It is equally clear, however, that the holiness of Yahweh continues to concern primarily the demands that go along with Yahweh's special uncompromising character. If Israel will be with Yahweh, Israel must be like Yahweh; that is, with Yahweh on Yahweh's demanding terms.

There is a quality of relatedness in Israel's speech about Yahweh's holiness, and this relatedness is important in some contexts, especially in the tradition of Isaiah; there is nonetheless a solemnness and reservation about the term that borders on the severe. A concern for Yahweh's name—Yahweh's identity and reputation—is articulated. In its praise, when Israel is gladly submissive to Yahweh, Israel celebrates Yahweh's "holy name" (Pss 103:1, 105:3, 111:9, 145:21). In these doxologies, Yahweh's name is holy, recognized on its own terms, with full acknowledgment of Yahweh's peculiar claim and character.

Israel is admonished to be like Yahweh. At the same time, Israel is everywhere and always seen by the nations to be Yahweh's special partner (cf. 1 Sam 6:20). When Israel acts in ways that are congruent with Yahweh's name, then Yahweh's name is made holy; or perhaps we should say, intensified in holiness. Whenever Israel as Yahweh's visible partner acts in ways that are incongruous with Yahweh's holy character, however, Yahweh's name is debased, profaned, and diminished in the eyes of the nations. Israel's actions decisively and substantively effect the quality of Yahweh's holiness. In the end, the notion of Yahweh's holiness suggests that Yahweh cares most about Yahweh's own name, reputation, and character—even more than Yahweh cares for Israel. Yahweh does indeed penultimately care about Israel, and so the Holy One comes to save Israel. Some texts—the more decisive texts, I believe, related to this notion of holiness—make clear that finally Yahweh cares most about Yahweh's own self. Thus ethical, economic, and sexual disorders

---

14. Hartmut Gese, *Essays on Biblical Theology* (Minneapolis: Augsburg Publishing House, 1981) 82–85, has seen that the fierceness of Sinai has been transferred to Zion, as he speaks of the "Zion torah." Jon D. Levenson, *Sinai and Zion: An Entry into the Jewish Bible* (Minneapolis: Winston Press, 1985), however, has shown that for all the claims of Jerusalem, Sinai remains a more ultimate point of reference.

in the community "profane" (*ḥll*) Yahweh's holy name (Amos 2:7), an affront that Yahweh takes with utmost seriousness. Thus,

> My holy name I will make known among my people Israel; and I will not let my holy name be profaned any more; and the nations shall know that I am the Lord, the Holy One in Israel. (Ezek 39:7)

Yahweh will act decisively for Yahweh's own name. There is something stubborn and toughly determined about Yahweh's resolve to recover Yahweh's own name, in light of Israel's debasing of it in the eyes of the nations.

What surprises us is the way in which Yahweh sets out to recover the profaned holy name. We might well expect that Yahweh will deal harshly with Israel in order to show the nations Yahweh's severe character. But no; the opposite occurs. Yahweh has gone too far in being the Holy One in Israel. For that reason, Yahweh cannot at this late date (late in the career of the holy name, whenever the text may be dated) slough off the partner to whom Yahweh has been unreservedly committed. Therefore, Yahweh must act for Israel in order to act for self and for the recovery of Yahweh's holy but now profaned name. Ezek 36:22-32 is an amazing account of the way in which Yahweh's self-regard is now maddeningly enmeshed with the well-being of Israel. As a result, this text must (a) promise Yahweh's good act for Israel, but (b) make it clear that the motivation for such good acts on the part of Yahweh is not love for Israel but Yahweh's self-regard:

- *Introduction concerning self-regard:*

    It is not for your sake, O house of Israel, that I am about to act, but for the sake of my holy name, which you have profaned among the nations to which you came. I will sanctify my great name, which has been profaned among the nations, and which you have profaned among them; and the nations shall know that I am the Lord, says the Lord God, when through you I display my holiness before their eyes. (vv. 22-23)

- *Assurance to Israel:*

    I will take you from the nations, and gather you from all the countries, and bring you into your own land. I will sprinkle clean water upon you, and you shall be clean from all your uncleannesses, and from all your idols I will cleanse you. A new heart I will give you, and a new spirit I will put within you.... (vv. 24-26)

- *Reiteration of self-regard:*

    It is not for your sake that I will act, says the Lord God; let that be known to you. Be ashamed and dismayed for your ways, O house of Israel. (v. 32)

The only way the Holy God can, in this context, enact self-regard is by the rescue and rehabilitation of Israel. The point is echoed in Ezek 39:25-27:

> Now I will restore the fortunes of Jacob, and have mercy on the whole house of Israel; and I will be jealous for my holy name.... when I have brought

them back from the peoples and gathered them from their enemies' lands, and through them have displayed my holiness in the sight of many nations.

These texts accent the self-regard that belongs to Yahweh's indomitable character. The complicating factor for Yahweh, which is at the heart of Israel's testimony about Yahweh, is that Yahweh will not (cannot?) undertake the recovery of the holiness of the name without Israel showing up at least at the edge of the picture. Israel's testimony about Yahweh's holiness intends to be straightforward and uncompromised. In its very utterance, however, Israel notes an aspect of the matter that surprises us, and perhaps surprises Israel, in its very moment of utterance.

There is no doubt, in Israel's testimony, that Yahweh's holiness makes Yahweh completely other, well beyond Israel, not to be presumed upon:

> For thus says the high and lofty one
> who inhabits eternity, whose name is Holy:
> I dwell in the high and holy place.... (Isa 57:15a)

The oddness comes when Israel's characteristic testimony goes on in this verse to say:

> ... and also with those who are contrite and humble in spirit,
> to revive the spirit of the humble,
> and to revive the heart of the contrite. (v. 15b)

There is no ready, easy, or simple resolution of this oddness. Israel's utterance about Yahweh moves back and forth between Yahweh's core of self-regard and the way in which this self-regard has now been irreversibly committed to Israel. It was not possible in Israel to say all of this well at once. And so, on different occasions and in different utterances, Israel says whatever part of the claim of Yahweh's holiness is truthful in the circumstance.

We may take special notice of the characterization of Yahweh as holy when the specific reference is to Yahweh's spirit (*rûaḥ*), thus yielding the phrase "Holy Spirit." It is evident that in the several usages of such phrasing, the witness of the Old Testament does not move in the direction of what became in the Christian formulation the third person of the Trinity. Nonetheless, the witness of the Old Testament does take note of the originary power for life (that is, spirit), which has its sources and locus in the person of Yahweh. As a consequence, Israel speaks about the life-force that Yahweh gives into creation. In Isa 63:10-11 the formula "his holy spirit" (*rûaḥ qdšô*) is used twice. In v. 10 Israel is said to have "grieved his holy spirit," and in v. 11 Yahweh is said to have "put within them his holy spirit"—his power for life. In the penitential Psalm 51, the same language is used: "Do not take your holy spirit from me" (v. 11). The parallel verse uses the verb *create* (*bara'*), suggesting that this reference alludes to the giving of the *rûaḥ* in creation (Gen 1:2). And in Dan 4:8-9, 18, 5:11, the seer is said to have the "spirit of God" (*rûaḥ 'elahin*), though the reference here is to wisdom and likely speaks of "gods" generically, without reference to Yahweh. These several references are attempts to speak about the way in which the power of Yahweh enlivens creation (or a particular creature) in ways that are in the end completely elusive, but undoubted.

The Jealousy of Yahweh

Yahweh is a jealous (*qn'*) God. We add the claim of jealousy to those of glory and holiness in our study of Yahweh's profound self-regard. While the terms *jealous* and *jealousy* may be carefully nuanced, their meaning is the one we commonly connect to the English term *jealous,* for they refer to Yahweh's strong emotional response to any affront against Yahweh's prerogative, privilege, ascendancy, or sovereignty. Thus the terms assume Yahweh's singular preoccupation with self, and the expectation that Yahweh will be fully honored and readily obeyed in every circumstance. Added to the claim of sovereignty is the powerful emotional dimension that may be variously rendered as "passion" or "fury." Thus Yahweh in jealousy is not the cool administrator of an ordered realm, but is engaged with strong feelings about all that is due Yahweh, which is in every case a great deal. Moreover, Yahweh on occasion is prepared to act directly on the basis of those strong feelings.

In the context of the Sinai command, Yahweh is said to be a jealous God, one who will be obeyed and who will brook no rival (Exod 20:5, 34:14; Deut 4:24, 5:9). This claim means that any departure of Israel from singular obedience to Yahweh evokes harsh, destructive response from Yahweh (cf. Deut 32:16, 21; 1 Kgs 14:22; Ps 78:58):

> You cannot serve the Lord, for he is a holy God. He is a jealous God; he will not forgive your transgressions or your sins. If you forsake the Lord and serve foreign gods, then he will turn and do you harm, and consume you, after having done you good. (Josh 24:19-20)

> Neither their silver nor their gold
> will be able to save them
> on the day of the Lord's wrath;
> In the fire of his passion (*qn'*)
> the whole earth shall be consumed;
> for a full, a terrible end
> he will make of all the
> inhabitants of the earth. (Zeph 1:18)

Indeed Yahweh's name is Jealous (Exod 34:14)—that is who Yahweh is. In the indignation and emotion that guard Yahweh's peculiar claim to honor, Yahweh is uncompromising. Yahweh acts in fury and rage, sometimes destructively. Yahweh's force in such matters may cause Yahweh to destroy Yahweh's own people (Ps 79:5), refuse to forgive (Deut 29:20), or be restrained only by acts of intervention that assuage the rage (Num 25:11).

This savage propensity belongs to the core claims of Yahweh, and intensifies what is suggested in the notions of glory and holiness. But as we have seen that holiness is transformed by relatedness, so the jealousy of Yahweh can also provide a ground for Yahweh's passionate positive commitment to Israel. Thus Yahweh can be jealous "for Israel" and therefore can be driven by strong feeling to intervene on behalf of Israel with the same passion and rage elsewhere turned against Israel. This positive inclination toward Israel is articulated with as much force as the potentially negative counterpart of destructive fury:

> Therefore wait for me, says the Lord,
> for the day when I arise as a witness.
> For my decision is to gather nations,
> to assemble kingdoms,
> to pour out upon them my indignation,
> all the heat of my anger;
> for in the fire of my passion (*qn'*)
> all the earth shall be consumed. (Zeph 3:8)

> I am speaking in my hot jealousy against the rest of the nations, and against all Edom, who, with wholehearted joy and utter contempt, took my land as their possession, because of its pasture, to plunder it. Therefore prophesy concerning the land of Israel, and say to the mountains and hills, to the watercourses and valleys, Thus says the Lord God: I am speaking in my jealous wrath, because you have suffered the insults of the nations. . . . (Ezek 36:5-6)

> The Lord goes forth like a soldier,
> like a warrior he stirs up his fury (*qn'*);
> he cries out, he shouts aloud,
> he shows himself mighty against his foes. (Isa 42:13)

Yahweh will be "hot" and enlivened for Israel, utterly enraged at the maltreatment Israel experiences at the hands of other nations (cf. Nah 1:2). In like fashion, moreover, Yahweh may be jealous for Yahweh's land as for Yahweh's people (Joel 2:18) and for Zion (Zech 1:14, 8:2).

This aspect of the character of Yahweh admits of no taming or minimalization. It witnesses to Yahweh at the extremes of love and anger. The extremity of Yahweh's passion will be turned against any who affront Yahweh, and Yahweh will act without restraint or discipline. That passion may be turned against Yahweh's own people, if Yahweh's self-regard is sufficiently affronted or Yahweh's claim for sovereignty is excessively disregarded. But the passion and rage may also be turned against Israel's enemies, so that Yahweh's jealousy becomes a force for well-being for Israel. Yahweh characteristically has both options available in any circumstance. What is to be noted, moreover, is that even Yahweh's jealousy for Israel, when it evokes a defense of Israel, is in the service of Yahweh's self-regard. We have already seen how Yahweh's defense of Yahweh's holy name had as a profound by-product the well-being of Israel (cf. Ezek 36:22-32). Now, in the same way, we cite a text from Ezekiel in which Yahweh's jealousy against the nations results in well-being for Israel:

> Now I will restore the fortunes of Jacob, and have mercy on the whole house of Israel; and I will be jealous for my holy name. They shall forget their shame, and all the treachery they have practiced against me, when they live securely in their land with no one to make them afraid, when I have brought them back from the peoples and gathered them from their enemies' lands, and through them have displayed my holiness in the sight of many nations. Then they shall know that I am the Lord their God because I sent them into exile among the nations, and then gathered them into their own land. I will leave none of them behind; and I will never again hide my face from them, when I pour out my spirit upon the house of Israel, says the Lord God. (Ezek 39:25-29)

The action proposed by Yahweh is to make Yahweh's holiness unmistakably clear to the nations. The mode of that self-manifestation is through Israel's homecoming. Indeed, Yahweh has "displayed my holiness" (*nqdšti*) "through them" (*bm*). The gathering from exile, like the Exodus, is a great good for Israel. It is also an overwhelming vehicle for Yahweh's self-exhibit as a God who will not be affronted. Yahweh here does not need to choose between self-regard and engagement on behalf of Israel. Many other texts in which Yahweh is jealous, however, provide no such happy convergence between the two agendas. In these texts, Yahweh will characteristically choose self-regard, even if to do so requires destructiveness toward Israel.

In the New Testament, reference to God's jealousy most congruent with our discussion is in Paul's quotation of Deut 32:21 in Rom 10:19. Paul appeals to this Deuteronomy text in his tortured discussion of the role of the Jewish community in his articulation of the gospel.

The collage of texts concerning the glory, holiness, and jealousy of Yahweh leave one astonished at the largeness and roughness of the claim made for Yahweh, and the power and intensity with which that claim is made. This is a God who will be taken seriously, who will be honored and obeyed, and who will not be mocked. The nations are warned; and Israel is also on notice. Yahweh must be taken in full capacity as sovereign; there is no alternative.

In seeking to consider the rich variety of uses of this theme of Yahweh's self-regard, two matters are decisive for our final thematization concerning Yahweh. First, it is striking that the claims for Yahweh's self-regard rather consistently (though not everywhere) make room for and accommodate Yahweh's commitment to Israel. Thus:

- Yahweh will not give glory to another (Isa 42:8), and yet the glory of Yahweh is Israel's rear guard (Isa 58:8).

- Yahweh is the Holy One before whom none can stand (1 Sam 6:20), and yet Yahweh is the Holy One of Israel.

- Yahweh is jealous against Israel like an angry, affronted husband (Ezek 16:38), and yet it is through the genuine homecoming and gathering of Israel that Yahweh's jealousy is enacted (Ezek 39:25-28).

Second, one has the sense that all of these qualities of Yahweh are pervaded by a hovering danger in which Yahweh's self-regard finally will not be limited, even by the reality of Israel. One never knows whether Yahweh will turn out to be a loose cannon, or whether Yahweh's commitment to Israel will make a difference. One does not know this in any given occasion, until a specific utterance is made. What one does know is that Yahweh's self-regard is massive in its claim, strident in its expectation, and ominous in its potential.

Yahweh's Resilient Relatedness: Covenant and Pathos

The oddness and the enduring power of Yahweh to compel our attention is that the sovereign One who is marked by glory, holiness, and jealousy is the One who has engaged Israel in a relationship of enduring fidelity. This relationship of enduring fidelity seems regularly to qualify, if not subvert, Yahweh's sovereignty and self-regard. Thus the second dimension of our thematization of Yahweh concerns Yahweh's relatedness, which we will deal with under the rubrics of covenant and pathos.

Covenant. The sovereign God, Yahweh, who exhibits glory, holiness, and jealousy, is known among the nations as "the God of Israel." The terms that most frequently characterize this relationship are those we have seen in Exod 34:6-7a: steadfast love, faithfulness, mercy, graciousness, and the additional terms righteousness, justice, and *shalôm*. The label most often assigned to the relationship marked by these terms of fidelity is *covenant*. The notion of covenant in Israel has had a demanding and strenuous passage through twentieth-century scholarship. Largely through the work of George Mendenhall, but also in German scholarship derived from Albrecht Alt, the biblical theology movement in the middle of the twentieth century argued that covenant was an early, formative, and dominant construct of Israel's practice of faith.[15] By the end of the twentieth century, under the influence of such scholars as Lothar Perlitt and Ernest Nicholson, scholarship now tends to return to a developmental hypothesis that takes covenant to be relatively late in Israel and largely confined to circles under the influence of Deuteronomic thought.[16] But these judgments, whether the maximalist position of Mendenhall

---

15. The basic starting point was Albrecht Alt's distinction between apodictic and casuistic law. See George E. Mendenhall, *Law and Covenant in Israel and the Ancient Near East* (Pittsburgh: Biblical Colloquium, 1954); and Klaus Baltzer, *The Covenant Formulary in the Old Testament, Jewish, and Early Christian Writings* (Oxford: Blackwell, 1971).

16. Lothar Perlitt, *Das Bundestheologie im Alten Testament* (WMANT 36; Neukirchen-Vluyn: Neukirchener Verlag, 1969); Ernest W. Nicholson, *God and His People: Covenant and Theology in the Old Testament* (Oxford: Clarendon Press, 1986).

or the minimalist position of Nicholson, are all critical judgments, seeking to sort out the historicity and historicality of covenant.

For our purposes, we can bracket out such critical distinctions to say that *in Israel's testimony* Yahweh's covenant with Israel is pervasive and definitional for Yahweh, if we keep to a broad theological characterization of covenant as an enduring relationship of fidelity and mutual responsibility.[17] Israel's self-presentation of this faith is that its life is rooted in and shaped by this relationship that Yahweh has initiated, to which Israel must respond in trust and obedience.

Here our concern is not to probe all of the dimensions of covenant, but to consider what it entails for Yahweh to be a God bound in covenant. The covenant generated for Yahweh a people who would endlessly seek to obey Yahweh's commands and sing Yahweh's praises, and thus enhance Yahweh's sovereignty. This gain for Yahweh, however, comes at a great inconvenience, if not cost. For covenant requires of Yahweh a practice of faithfulness and steadfast love, an enduring engagement with and involvement for Israel. The succinct formulation of covenant, "I will be your God and you shall be my people" (Jer 11:4, 24:7, 30:22, 31:33, 32:38; Ezek 11:20, 14:11, 36:28, 37:23, 27), means that Yahweh is marked everywhere as the God of Israel. Yahweh must necessarily be seen in public, before the nations, with Israel. How Yahweh treats Israel, and how Israel fares in the world, are taken as data for how powerful or reliable Yahweh is. This is the point on which Moses bases his daring appeal to Yahweh (Num 14:13-19). It is powerfully on Yahweh's mind to terminate the relationship with Israel, which is tantamount to terminating Israel (v. 12). Indeed it is the relentless thought of the prophets of Israel that Yahweh may indeed terminate Israel in an exercise of sovereign self-regard. And there is no doubt that the textual witness regards Yahweh as fully capable of such a decision to terminate.

One poignant image for termination of the covenant is that of divorce, utilized especially in Hosea.[18] The termination of the relationship is expressed in a poem around the image of divorce:

> Now I will uncover her shame
> in the sight of her lovers,
> and no one shall rescue her out of my hand.
> I will put an end to all her mirth,
> her festivals, her new moons, her sabbaths,

---

17. This is the intent and import of the magisterial approach of Walther Eichrodt in his Old Testament theology. It is important to remember that Eichrodt was prior to and not interested in the critical discussion evoked by the programmatic essay of Mendenhall. Eichrodt was much more focused on the legacy of the Calvinist tradition of interpretation.

18. The theme of divorce and remarriage has most often been taken to be a positive image for the willingness of Yahweh to reengage a fickle partner. More recently, a number of feminist interpreters have noted that Yahweh is an abusive partner in this drama, and is not unmitigatedly a generous and compassionate mate. See Renita Weems, *Battered Love: Marriage, Sex, and Violence in the Hebrew Prophets* (OBT; Minneapolis: Fortress Press, 1995); and Gale A. Yee, "Hosea," *The Women's Bible Commentary* (ed. Carol A. Newsom and Sharon H. Ringe; Louisville: Westminster/John Knox, 1992) 195–200.

and all her appointed festivals.
I will lay waste her vines and her fig trees,
of which she said,
"These are my pay,
which my lovers have given me."
I will make them a forest,
and the wild animals shall devour them.
I will punish her for the festival days of the Baals,
when she offered incense to them
and decked herself with her ring and jewelry,
and went after her lovers,
and forgot me, says the Lord. (Hos 2:10-13)

This act of abandonment of the partner by Yahweh is rooted in Yahweh's uncompromising self-regard. Possible abandonment by Yahweh is much on the horizon of Israel, as it ponders the cruciality of this relationship for its future, and as it considers the dysfunction of the relationship. The Torah and prophetic traditions continue to reflect on this relationship as a sine qua non for Israel, but one that is endlessly jeopardized from Israel's side.

Pathos and passion. In the emerging radicality of Israel's rhetoric about the treasured but jeopardized relationship, the theme of covenant is transposed into a practice of pathos. There is no doubt that Yahweh is capable of terminating the covenantal relationship, and no doubt that Yahweh would be justified in doing so. In the great public acts of destruction in 722 and 587 B.C.E., Israel understands that Yahweh has made a move toward such termination. Indeed, Israel's literary-theological reflection in exile ponders this seeming maneuver on Yahweh's part:

Why have you forgotten us completely?
Why have you forsaken us these many days?
Restore us to yourself, O Lord,
that we may be restored;
renew our days as of old—
unless you have utterly rejected us,
and are angry with us beyond measure. (Lam 5:20-22)

Yahweh's self-regard permits—perhaps requires—such termination as a defense of Yahweh's glory, holiness, and jealousy.

The odd and compelling element in Yahweh's character, as given us in Israel's testimony, is that Yahweh does not irreversibly enact this termination. Indeed, what seemed to be complete abandonment was in fact "for a moment":

For a brief moment I abandoned you,
but with great compassion I will gather you.
In overflowing wrath for a moment
I hid my face from you,

but with everlasting love
I will have compassion on you,
   says the Lord, your Redeemer. (Isa 54:7-8)

Israel did survive the momentary abandonment in the exile. Israel survived, not because of its own staying power, but because Yahweh's covenantal engagement was deepened and intensified in pathos, through the reality of the exile. Yahweh did not terminate or abandon Israel in self-regard, as Yahweh had proposed to do. The poets of Israel dare to imagine that Yahweh did not terminate because Yahweh *could not* terminate. That is, Yahweh could not bring Yahweh's own self to do what Yahweh was fully entitled to do.

The reason for Yahweh's refusal to execute a termination is not to be found in Israel, nor in the "peer pressure" of the nations or of the other gods. The reason is rather that Yahweh found, according to the testimony of Israel, new measures and depths of positive passion for Israel that were not available to Yahweh until this awesome moment of staying or leaving, of loving or destroying. The term *passion* here has a twofold intention.[19] The term of course refers to strong feeling, the kind we have noticed in jealousy. But it also refers to a propensity to suffer with and suffer for, to be in solidarity with Israel in its suffering, and by such solidarity to sustain a relationship that rightfully could be terminated. That is, publicly, boldly, at the moment of ominous deciding, Yahweh refused to act in self-regard, because Yahweh found in Yahweh's own internal life a depth of devotion to the well-being of Israel that was not, until that moment of crisis, available to Yahweh.

It is not surprising that such a presentation of the character of Yahweh requires Israel's most daring and imaginative voices (in the poetry of Hosea, Jeremiah, and late Isaiah). It is not surprising, moreover, that the rhetoric required to narrate such a new emergent in Yahweh's own life requires the metaphors of relationship between husband and wife and between parent and child, for no other images carry such intensity, both positive and negative.[20]

Thus, after the rage of rejection in Hos 2:10-13, the yearning husband speaks:

Therefore, I will allure her,
and bring her into the wilderness,
and speak tenderly to her. . . .

And I will take you for my wife forever; I will take you for my wife in righteousness and in justice, in steadfast love, and in mercy. I will take you for my wife in faithfulness; and you shall know the Lord. (Hos 2:14, 19-20)

---

19. The term that bespeaks pathos has been fully exposited by Abraham Heschel, *The Prophets* (New York: Harper and Row, 1962), in relation to the prophetic articulation of Yahweh.

20. While such metaphors seem irreplaceable as means whereby the intimate connectedness is voiced, we are now increasingly aware of the problems of sexism and abusive patriarchy that are inherent in the imagery.

And after the offended, affronted parent speaks dismissively (Hos 11:4-7), the tone of the poem changes and now the bereft parent speaks, resolved to love in new measure:

> How can I give you up, Ephraim?
> How can I hand you over, O Israel?
> How can I make you like Admah?
> How can I treat you like Zeboiim?
> My heart recoils within me;
> my compassion grows warm and tender.
> I will not execute my fierce anger;
> I will not again destroy Ephraim;
> For I am God and no mortal,
> the Holy One in your midst,
> and I will not come in wrath. (Hos 11:8-9)

In the tradition of Jeremiah, the indignant, humiliated husband appeals to the prohibitive command of Moses (Deut 24:1). But then the yearning husband, who is the wounder but finds himself also wounded in the transaction, speaks:

> Return, faithless Israel, says the Lord,
> I will not look on you in anger,
> for I am merciful, says the Lord. . . . (Jer 3:12)

> Return, O faithless children,
> I will heal your faithlessness. (Jer 3:22a)

The harsh diagnostician speaks of terminal illness (Jer 30:12-13). But then, before the poem is finished, the healer speaks:

> For I will restore health to you,
> and your wounds I will heal, says the Lord,
> because they have called you an outcast:
> "It is Zion; no one cares for her!" (Jer 30:17)

Yahweh speaks a positive word because the angry healer could not tolerate the ridicule of the nations addressed to beloved Israel.

In what may be the most poignant utterance of Yahweh in all of these texts, a parent speaks with uncommon, devoted passion:

> Is Ephraim my dear son?
> Is he the child I delight in?
> As often as I speak against him,
> I still remember him.
> Therefore I am deeply moved for him;
> I will surely have mercy on him, says the Lord. (Jer 31:20)[21]

---

21. On this text, see Kazo Kitamori, *Theology of the Pain of God* (Richmond: John Knox, 1965) 151–67 and passim.

This beloved child is treasured and remembered, even when harshly spoken against in rejection. Yahweh is "deeply moved." Yahweh's innards (*m'h*) are stirred. Yahweh is upset, as in Hos 11:8, and therefore Yahweh "will surely have mercy." The term *mercy* is an infinitive absolute. The verbal form reflects a deep and intense resolve that is against all expectation. Yahweh will cast aside all reasonable objection and act on this powerful sense of yearning and caring that runs directly against the self-regard of this God who has been profoundly affronted. The judge-king speaks now as mother-father, who in this moment acknowledges that the relationship counts for more than self-regard, and that sovereignty is decisively qualified by pathos. It is pathos that preserves the covenant in the face of affronted sovereignty.

This emergence of Yahweh's spousal-parental pathos is echoed in the late Isaiah tradition:

> Can a woman forget her nursing child,
> or show no compassion for the child of her womb?
> Even these may forget,
> Yet I will not forget you.
> See, I have inscribed you on the palms of my hands;
> your walls are continually before me. (Isa 49:15-16)

> As a mother comforts her child,
> so I will comfort you;
> You shall be comforted in Jerusalem. (Isa 66:13)

In his harshness, Ezekiel cannot permit Yahweh the same embrace of pathos. In the witness of Ezekiel, Yahweh remains deeply affronted by Israel and continues to take the affront with great seriousness (16:42-43, 23:45-49). What astonishes us in this witness, in the end, is that even the testimony of Ezekiel finds a way to reverse Yahweh's rejection of Israel. In this testimony, the forgiveness Israel must receive is grounded, not in any compromise of Yahweh's self-regard, but precisely in Yahweh's escalated self-regard:

> As a pleasing odor I will accept you, when I bring you out of the countries where you have been scattered; and I will manifest my holiness among you in the sight of the nations. You shall know that I am the Lord, when I bring you into the land of Israel, the country that I swore to give to your ancestors. There you shall remember your ways and all the deeds by which you have polluted yourselves; and you shall loathe yourselves for all the evils that you have committed. And you shall know that I am the Lord, when I deal with you for my name's sake, not according to your evil ways or corrupt deeds, O house of Israel, says the Lord God. (Ezek 20:41-44; cf. 36:22-32, 39:25-29)

The way in which these witnesses are able to locate in Yahweh a break for relatedness against all self-regard is astonishing. One can say, of course, that such a rhetorical maneuver was a pastoral requirement in the exile, in order to provide a basis for continuing Judaism. No doubt there is such a pragmatic element in this theological testimony. But beyond pastoral pragmatism, these texts constitute serious theological rhetoric. These witnesses mean to declare that an upheaval has occurred in Yahweh's life and character that impinges on Yahweh's sense of self-regard. We are not told whether this upheaval is irreversible nor how deep it is. What we are told is that, according to these witnesses, Yahweh had ample grounds on which to withdraw from the relationship with Israel in justified self-regard, yet Yahweh did not do so.

This move on Yahweh's part, welcomed by Israel but not required by Yahweh, is the ground for any future of Judaism as a theological entity. The matter is of crucial importance for Judaism and for its derivative ecclesial partners (specifically Christianity). Here, however, our concern is to recognize that this fresh emergence is of crucial importance *to Yahweh,* and not simply to the faith communities who respond to Yahweh. The decision to be in a covenant, and the further decision to let this covenant emerge toward pathos, are to be understood as elements in the theological matter of constancy about Yahweh's character. The shaping of Yahweh can be understood as the development of religious insight, or as daring rhetoric. Here, given our theological responsibility to the text, we can say that these texts permit us to watch while Yahweh redecides, in the midst of a crisis, how to be Yahweh and who to be as Yahweh.

Move toward incarnation. The move from covenantal fidelity to costly pathos is a primary articulation of Yahweh in the Old Testament. The emergence of pathos is not everything to be said here about Yahweh, but it is a major and quite intentional affirmation. At least in one dimension, the Old Testament ends with Yahweh profoundly defined by pathos for Israel. It is possible, in the horizon of Christian interpretation in the New Testament, to say that around the person of Jesus, Christian witnesses discerned that the pathos of Yahweh moved the next step to incarnation; that is, God came to be personally and fully engaged in the center of the life of the world.

Such a notion of the incarnation is of course a major step beyond pathos, a step that the Old Testament does not take. One may suggest, however, that the move toward incarnation, no doubt made in Hellenistic rhetoric, is in some inchoate way already present in Yahweh's radical decision for covenantal solidarity with Israel and more radical decision toward pathos with Israel. The recognition of covenantal solidarity and pathos as elements that produced incarnation is not to make a move toward Christian supersessionism. It is, rather, to recognize that whatever may be claimed for the radicality of God in the New Testament is already present in all its radicality in these Jewish witnesses to the character of Yahweh.

Our proposed thematization of the testimony concerning Yahweh may in the end be excessively problematic. We have found in profound tension the sovereign self-regard of Yahweh and the resolve for covenantal relatedness. We have exposited these themes respectively around the motifs of Yahweh's glory, holiness, and jealousy, and Yahweh's steadfast love and fidelity expressed as covenantal solidarity and pathos (and incarnation). It is my judgment that, in the end, the Old Testament witnesses to a persistent tension that does not admit of resolution. To be sure, some resolution of one sort or another may occur in any given crisis or in any specific text.

These resolutions appear to me to be characteristically provisional and tenuous, likely to be unsettled in the next crisis, undone by the next text. The reason for this unsettlement is not finally—speaking theologically—that Israel speaks with many voices (which it does), or that Israel cannot make up its mind (which it cannot); the unsettling quality belongs definitionally to the character of Yahweh. In my judgment, the texts permit no overall solution, because self-regard and regard for Israel are not, in the end, the same. One might imagine that Yahweh's self-regard is given over completely to Israel's well-being. But Israel's text and Israel's lived experience keep facing the reality that something like Yahweh's self-regard keeps surfacing in demanding ways. This self-regard may emerge as unsurprising moral claim, or it may emerge as a kind of wild capriciousness, as sovereignty without principled loyalty. It is this propensity in Yahweh, Yahweh's determination to be taken seriously on Yahweh's own terms, that precludes any final equation of sovereignty with covenantal love or with pathos.

Summary Observations

Old Testament theology, as I understand it, yearns for a resolution of this profound tension in Yahweh, but it can never claim to have such a resolution fully in hand. The following four observations conclude our exposition of Israel's core testimony concerning Yahweh.

Convergence of Yahweh's Self-Regard and Commitment to Israel

There is no doubt that a resolution of the tension between Yahweh's self-regard and Yahweh's regard for Israel (and for the world) is desirable. And there is no doubt that conventional theological interpretation, particularly in the harmonizing tendencies of ecclesial interpretation, most often manages to articulate such a resolution. That resolution is likely to be found in the notion of Yahweh's righteousness, which is perhaps the largest, most comprehensive category for Old Testament theology as it seeks to follow the theological discourse of the Old Testament witness. Yahweh's righteousness entails governance of the world according to Yahweh's purposes, which are decreed at Sinai and which are assured in the very fabric of creation. The substance of that righteousness is the well-being of the world, so that when Yahweh's righteousness (Yahweh's governance) is fully established in the world, the results are fruitfulness, prosperity, freedom, justice, peace, security, and well-being (*shalôm*). Because Yahweh in righteousness wills good for creation, there is a complete convergence of Yahweh's self-regard and Yahweh's commitment to Israel and to creation. Four texts from different strands of the

304 _____ *Israel's Core Testimony*

Old Testament testimony attest to this convergence, though others could be cited as well.

Psalm 143. In a petition made under acute threat, the psalmist asks for a vindicating judgment from Yahweh:

> Hear my prayer, O Lord;
> give ear to my supplications in your faithfulness;
> answer me in your righteousness....
> Let me hear of your steadfast love in the morning,
> for in you I put my trust....
> For your name's sake, O Lord,
> preserve my life.
> In your righteousness bring me out of trouble.
> In your steadfast love cut off my enemies,
> and destroy all my adversaries,
> for I am your servant. (Ps 143:1, 8, 11-12)

At the beginning and at the end of this prayer, the speaker appeals for Yahweh's righteousness (vv. 1, 11), sure that in righteousness Yahweh will deliver. Moreover, Yahweh's righteousness is matched in v. 1 by "your faithfulness" (*'mûnh*) and in v. 12 by "your steadfast love" (*ḥsd*); in v. 8 appeal is made a second time to Yahweh's steadfast love. This psalm assumes complete convergence between Yahweh's rule and the well-being of the speaker.

This psalm figured very large in Luther's discernment of the principle of grace.[22] Luther noticed that in v. 2 the speaker discounts his own righteousness (works), and so in faith appeals to Yahweh's alternative righteousness. This reading of the psalm served Luther's theological insight well. But even if the psalm is not pressed into Luther's categories of grace/works, it is clear that Yahweh's righteousness is here characterized by graciousness and covenantal fidelity. Indeed, as Luther discerned, this is the petitioner's best hope.

Psalm 115. The same convergence is evident in a second, very different, psalm, which is not a complaint but a polemical doxology:

> Not to us, O Lord, not to us,
> but to your name give glory,
> for the sake of your steadfast love and your faithfulness. (Ps 115:1)

This psalm begins in an affirmation that Yahweh's glory is intimately linked to Yahweh's steadfast love (*ḥsd*) and faithfulness (*'mth*). It is astonishing that in a psalm preoccupied with Yahweh's sovereign power (contrasted with the impotence of the idols), the substance of that power at the outset is marked by complete covenantal fidelity. We readily infer in the psalm, when it is not stated, that the scornfully

---

22. The affirmation of the generous and rehabilitative righteousness of Yahweh is contrasted in Ps 143:2 with the righteousness of the speaker and his ilk, which accomplishes nothing. These contrasting modes of righteousness were readily taken up by Luther as articulations of grace and works.

weak idols are incapable of fidelity. Thus the psalm is a passionate articulation of Yahweh's power. But that acknowledgment of power includes Israel's affirmation that Yahweh's power is in the service of covenantal fidelity.

Deut 10:12-22. A variation on the same convergence is evident in Deut 10:17-19:

> For the Lord your God is God of gods and Lord of lords, the great God, mighty and awesome, who is not partial and takes no bribes, who executes justice for the orphan and the widow, who loves the strangers, providing them food and clothing. You shall love the stranger, for you were strangers in the land of Egypt.

The doxological ascription to Yahweh, stated more positively than in Psalm 115, recognizes and celebrates Yahweh's limitless power and authority, as Yahweh presides over and governs all other gods and lords. This God is indeed "mighty and awesome," fully capable of acting in massive self-regard. But then, characteristically, the doxology changes course in the middle of v. 17 and begins to speak of bribes, widows, orphans, strangers, and the Exodus. From that reference point, appeal is made in v. 20 to something like the First Commandment on exclusive loyalty, a formulation that includes echoes of the *shema* of Deut 6:4-5.

In this doxology, Israel has no doubt that Yahweh's massive power and authority are directed precisely to needy objects of love, so that Israel is enjoined, on that basis, to pity and compassion. Israel has little inclination to celebrate Yahweh's great power, except as that power is enacted for well-being in the world. In this particular articulation, unlike Psalms 143 and 115, the dimension of pathos in this resolution is more evident, because of Yahweh's direct engagement in the Exodus community. The same focus is implicit in the two psalms, even without the concrete historical reference to the Exodus. Yahweh's self-regard as "God of gods and Lord of lords" is completely devoted to the well-being of Yahweh's covenant partner, for whom Yahweh will take great risks in acts of solidarity.

Isa 45:21-25. In Isa 45:21-25 we have a vigorous doxology celebrating Yahweh's righteousness, which has as its negative counterpart the dismissal of rival (Babylonian) gods who have no power. What interests us is that Yahweh's righteousness is referenced in the brief poem four times:

> Declare and present your case;
> let them take counsel together!
> Who told this long ago?
> Who declared it of old?
> Was it not I, the Lord?
> There is no other god besides me,
> a *righteous* God and a Savior;
> there is no one besides me.
> Turn to me and be saved,

all the ends of the earth!
For I am God, and there is no other.
By myself I have sworn,
from my mouth has gone forth in *righteousness*
a word that shall not return:
"To me every knee shall bow,
every tongue shall swear."
Only in the Lord, it shall be said of me,
are *righteousness* and strength;
all who were incensed against him
shall come to him and be ashamed.
In the Lord all the offspring of Israel
shall triumph (*ṣdq*) and glory.

In v. 21 Yahweh as righteous God is unlike the would-be gods who have no power to save. In vv. 22-23 Yahweh in righteousness bids for the worship of "all the ends of the earth," because there is no rival candidate worthy of submission. In v. 24 "only in the Lord" can such righteousness be found, and in v. 25 righteousness spills over into the exaltation of Israel. The poem is about Yahweh's massive authority, capacity, and readiness to do right.

But we notice that in vv. 21-22 the term *save* (*yš'*) is used twice, and in v. 25 it is Israel, the object of Yahweh's rescue, who is celebrated. Yahweh's righteousness is engaged in the work of well-being. Israel has benefited from this gift of Yahweh's righteousness, and the nations are invited to participate in the same. But neither Israel nor the nations can receive such transformative activity unless they are among those who bend the knee and swear with the tongue to the sovereignty of Yahweh.

This convergence of sovereignty and compassion is a staple of Israel's faith. Where this convergence functions well, Israel's testimony renders a coherent picture of a character of constancy and reliability. Paul Hanson has carefully explored the way in which Yahweh's righteousness and compassion intersect in Israel's faith, and he adds a third dimension: worship that attests to Yahweh's "sole and sovereign majesty." Speaking of these two aspects of Yahweh's character, Hanson observes:

First, Yahweh is recognized as righteous, and hence as the source of a norm for life which applied to all people without partiality and which ordered a society dependably and securely. Second, Yahweh was recognized as compassionate, as a God who reaches out to redeem even those excluded from life's benefits and society's protection, a God who in that way provides the example for a community which was to extend its compassion to those otherwise vulnerable to abuse, like the widow and orphan, the indebted and alien.[23]

But then Hanson goes on to say,

---

23. Paul D. Hanson, "War and Peace in the Hebrew Bible," *Int* 38 (1984) 346.

There is overwhelming evidence in Hebrew prophecy that the imbalance between righteousness and compassion was constantly endangered also in Israel.[24]

Hanson's concern is with the community, whereas here we are interested in the character of Yahweh. Concerning that character, however, the convergence or identity of Yahweh's sovereign righteousness and Yahweh's covenantal compassion is constantly endangered, and often, so the witnesses insist, falls apart.

The Tension of Sovereignty and Loyalty

We now take up examples of the crisis in Israel's acknowledgment of Yahweh, when it is evident to Israel that Yahweh is not at the same time sovereign and loyal—when Yahweh's self-regard and Yahweh's regard for Israel and the world are in tension with each other. We consider four sorts of evidence for this tension.

Numbers 14. We have seen that the encounter between Yahweh and Moses in Num 14:11-12 is a pivotal point in the articulation of Yahweh, because in that text Moses prays back to Yahweh the self-disclosure of Yahweh given in Exod 34:6-7. On the basis of that self-disclosure, Moses bids Yahweh to

> forgive the iniquity of this people according to the greatness of your stead-
> fast love, just as you have pardoned this people, from Egypt even until now.
> (Num 14:19)

In response, Yahweh accedes to Moses' petition: "I do forgive, just as you have asked" (v. 20). So far Yahweh's sovereign righteousness and Yahweh's covenantal loyalty converge. But v. 21 adds Yahweh's powerful "nevertheless" (*'ûlm*), and in that conjunction Yahweh's righteous will parts company from Yahweh's steadfast love. Yahweh will forgive, but Yahweh will hold accountable and destroy all of those who have "not listened." This distinction, whereby Yahweh acts in destructiveness, shows that in this case at least, there is a limit to Yahweh's long-suffering fidelity toward Israel, a limit already anticipated in Exod 34:7b.

Now Yahweh acts, not in the interest of Israel, but in Yahweh's self-regard. Yahweh's graciousness is only to the one (Caleb) who has "a different spirit and has followed me wholeheartedly" (v. 24). And the "different spirit" that makes well-being possible consists in complete obedience to the will and command of Yahweh. In this text there is not an ounce of room for steadfast love outside of adherence to Yahweh's commanding authority. There is no spillover of graciousness outside of embrace of Yahweh's righteous will.

Ezek 36:22-32. In Ezek 36:22-32 (cf. 20:41-44, 39:25-29), we have seen that Yahweh will indeed be gracious to Israel and will return Israel from exile to its land. It is clear, however, that Ezekiel's testimony gives no hint of pathos or love or covenantal fidelity in Yahweh's resolve. The ground for Yahweh's saving activity is completely Yahweh's self-regard. Thus:

---

24. Ibid.

I will manifest my holiness . . . (20:41)

I will sanctify my great name . . . (36:23)

I will be jealous for my holy name . . . (39:25)

It may well be that Yahweh will act compassionately, but here compassion is no counterpoint to sovereignty, no substance of righteousness, but only an inescapable by-product of Yahweh's self-regard. In these texts it is clear that viewed per se, Yahweh has no positive regard for Israel and is not moved by its plight. Nor, for that matter, does Yahweh mind saving Israel, for it is no special inconvenience for Yahweh. Yahweh in effect has no interest in Israel, but Israel is a convenient, ready-at-hand vehicle for the assertion and enactment of Yahweh's self-regard. This is no bad thing for Israel—but it is not the same as "steadfast love," and it ought not to be construed as such. Yahweh has long since been linked to Israel and must continue to act on that basis. But the action of Yahweh is fully, without reservation, for the enhancement of Yahweh. This same asymmetry is perhaps evident in the assertion of Yahweh in Exod 14:4 and 17, "I will gain glory for myself over Pharaoh." Yahweh will secure glory over pharaoh by the rescue of Israel.

Two-stage sequence. In a variety of texts, all situated in and reflecting on Israel's exile and anticipated homecoming, this tension is expressed as a two-stage sequence. I suggest that the first, destructive act in the sequence is derived from Yahweh's self-regard; in the second act, as though in a recovery of covenantal intentionality, Yahweh expresses fidelity to and regard for Israel. Three texts may be cited for what seems to be a rather common reading of the crisis:

And just as I have watched over them to pluck up and break down, to overthrow, destroy, and bring evil, so I will watch over them to build and to plant, says the Lord. (Jer 31:28)

The verbs in this statement are thematically important for the testimony of Jeremiah. But what concerns us here is that the stronger, more frequent verbs in the negative—*pluck up, break down, overthrow, destroy, bring evil*—are understood as actions of Yahweh's self-regard. Yahweh will not tolerate disobedience, mockery, or trivialization, and so the testimony of Jeremiah must portray Yahweh as a wounded, betrayed lover who lashes out against Israel in anger. We are not told why a reversal of attitude leads to the two positive verbs, *plant* and *build*. It is plausible to imagine that Yahweh is compelled to this rehabilitative action by fresh measures of pathos and by new intentionality about covenant (see vv. 31-34). In any case, it is clear that the two actions, one negative and one positive, articulate in turn Yahweh's self-regard and Yahweh's regard for Israel. The two together form a coherent picture, but that coherence is of little comfort to those who suffer through Yahweh's harsh enactment of self-regard.

In Isa 47:6 a like expression of a two-stage relationship is voiced, ostensibly to Babylon:

I was angry with my people
I profaned my heritage;
I gave them into your hand,
you showed them no mercy....

The first act consists in Yahweh's handing over Judah to the brutal control of Babylon. The poet dares to have Yahweh say that this happened because "I was angry with my people." The verb *qsp* is a very strong one. The statement suggests that Yahweh was in a rage and acted precipitously. There is nothing in this hand-over to the empire except Yahweh's passionate, perhaps out-of-control self-regard.

In the second stage, Yahweh crushes Babylon and reclaims Judah for Yahweh, because Babylon "showed no mercy." This is a remarkable statement. Of course Babylon did not know that Yahweh intended mercy. And indeed, when Yahweh was "angry with my people," we may believe that in that instant Yahweh also did not intend mercy for Judah. It is as though Yahweh expects Babylon to exercise the very mercy Yahweh was not able or willing to enact (cf. Jer 42:11-12). The second action, homecoming, is an act of covenantal loyalty on Yahweh's part. That loyalty, however, happens only after Yahweh's extreme, destructive act of self-regard.

In Deuteronomy 4, in its present form a reflection on the exile and concerned with the same crisis as in Isaiah 47, we can discern the same two-stage articulation of Yahweh:

For the Lord your God is a devouring fire, a jealous God. (v. 24)

From there [from exile] you will seek the Lord your God, and you will find him if you search after him with all your heart and soul. (v. 29)

Because the Lord your God is a merciful God, he will neither abandon you nor destroy you.... (v. 31)

This remarkable assertion begins with Yahweh as a devouring fire and ends with Yahweh as a God of mercy. Through the course of the text, Yahweh is transposed from a God who is jealous in self-regard to a God who is merciful toward the exiles. The first characteristic of Yahweh produces the exile, the second results in the homecoming of Judah. It is not easy or obvious in the life of Israel to see that the jealous, devouring God is consonant with the practice of mercy. In all of these texts, and others that might be cited, Yahweh moves back and forth between self-regard and regard for Israel, between sovereignty and pathos.

Old Testament theology must recognize that certain texts celebrate the convergence of sovereignty and pathos. Perhaps these texts should be regarded as normative for theological interpretation and allowed to govern other texts. Nonetheless, the witnesses to Yahweh also give powerful evidence that things are not so coherent for Yahweh. Indeed, if Yahweh was to be held close to Israel's lived experience for which exile is paradigmatic, Israel had to reckon with a theological discernment that consists in a profound disjunction that is not only a matter of lived experience but also a crucial theological datum. Thus, in my judgment, serious theological interpretation must reckon not only with evidence of the convergence of Yahweh's sovereignty and Yahweh's covenantal fidelity, but also with the tension between these inclinations, tension that on occasion becomes unbearable and unmanageable for Israel.

Continuity and discontinuity. If we take the exile as the paradigmatic locus in which this tension is visible and in which Israel craved resolution, we may articulate the disjunction in yet one more way. Israel in exile, as it pondered Yahweh, struggled with what scholars call the problem of continuity and discontinuity.[25] That is, does Yahweh continue to honor covenant commitments to Israel and practice steadfast love toward Israel right through the exile? Is there continuity in Yahweh's covenantal commitment to Israel through the crisis? Or is the reality of exile evidence that Yahweh has now, whether in legitimate indignation or in uncontrolled pique, terminated the covenant, only to move subsequently to renew it or make a new covenant? While the terms of the question are clear enough, we should not regard this as a simple intellectual puzzle. It is rather a most disturbing, elemental question about Yahweh: Can Yahweh's self-regard result in the complete exhaustion of Yahweh's vows of solidarity?

There is evidence, of course, that Yahweh continues to love Israel in exile, and that is the preferred theological conclusion. The evidence for this conclusion is to be found in texts that speak of Yahweh's *berith 'olam,* the "everlasting covenant." These texts (Gen 9:16; 17:7, 13, 19; 2 Sam 23:5; Isa 54:10, 55:3; Jer 50:5; Ezek 37:26; Ps 89:28) seem to reflect theological witnesses in Israel that focus on Yahweh's sustained fidelity, witnesses that regard the exile as no major disruption in that commitment.

The more disturbing texts, however, are those suggesting that in Israel's recalcitrance, Yahweh's inclination toward Israel is spent, and that Yahweh's self-regard requires the abandonment of a partner who exploited Yahweh's fidelity too much for too long. Israel considered out loud, perhaps in liturgical context, that Yahweh had abandoned Israel in exile (cf. Lam 5:20-22; Isa 49:14). While the latter question of Isa 49:14 is answered, perhaps also liturgically, in the next verse, we must also note that evidence for radical discontinuity is placed in Yahweh's own mouth:

> For a brief moment I abandoned you
> but with great compassion I will gather you.
> In overflowing wrath for a moment
> I hid my face from you,
> but with everlasting love

---

25. On the problematic of continuity and discontinuity, see Peter R. Ackroyd, "Continuity: A Contribution to the Study of the Old Testament Religious Tradition," *Studies in the Religious Tradition of the Old Testament* (London: SCM Press, 1987) 3–16; and "Continuity and Discontinuity: Rehabilitation and Authentication," ibid., 31–45.

> I will have compassion on you,
>
> says the Lord, your Redeemer. (Isa 54:7-8; cf. Ps 30:5)

To be sure, even these texts bespeak a two-stage sequence, in which the outcome is great compassion. Prior to the compassion, however, there was abandonment. Certainly Yahweh was deeply affronted by Israel's recalcitrance. Perhaps Yahweh was embarrassed (shamed) and acted in self-regard. We are not told why Yahweh in these verses expresses reversal with a powerful affirmation of love and fidelity. This might be as close as Yahweh can come to making an honest apology to spouse-Israel. Surely Yahweh moved, in this moment, to new depths of devotion to Israel. The wondrous assurance at the end of Isa 54:7 and again at the end of v. 8 does not cancel out the stark reality of the admission, "I abandoned you." The verb (*'zb*) is the same as the accusation made against Yahweh in the more familiar Ps 22:1, suggesting that in this more-or-less contextless (and therefore much-used) prayer, Israel had grasped a reality of its life with Yahweh: Yahweh does abandon. Yahweh makes a comeback in fidelity after abandonment, but that does not negate the self-regard that sanctions harshness, a harshness powerfully felt by the displaced generation of exiles.

This abandonment, moreover, is not harshness in the service of any rehabilitation. It is simply a departure from solidarity for the sake of self-regard. To the extent that the witnesses have seen rightly, *this testimony places at the center of Israel's life a massive Holy Problem.* Israel must learn to live with the problematic character of Yahweh. The affirmation of everlasting covenant is pastorally reassuring. In Israel's testimony, however, that assurance was not permitted to silence the terrible awareness to which Israel had come: Yahweh's sovereignty does not everywhere and always converge with fidelity, even though fidelity is finally powerfully affirmed.

Cruciform Claim for God

Beyond the Old Testament, it is fair to say that the New Testament and the Christian tradition have, on the whole, moved beyond this tension to affirm a complete identification of God's power with God's love. One specific ground for such a complete identification is found in the truth of the crucifixion of Jesus, wherein God's own life embraces the abandonment of broken covenant. In this theological claim, Christian theology has extended the hints about God already voiced in the most pathos-driven witnesses of the Old Testament.

This "cruciform" discernment of the character of God, so well articulated by Jürgen Moltmann, lives in an odd tension with trinitarian thinking.[26] Characteristically and certainly popularly, this cruciform claim for God, who completely risks sovereignty in solidarity, is guarded by the notion that the Son risks solidarity while

---

26. See Jürgen Moltmann, *The Crucified God: The Cross of Christ as the Foundation and Criticism of Christian Theology* (1974; Minneapolis: Fortress Press, 1993).

the Father maintains sovereignty. Moltmann has seen that such a "division of labor" will not do, in his rich formula, "The Fatherlessness of the Son is matched by the Sonlessness of the Father."[27] If Moltmann's rendering of the issue is correct, as I take it to be, then Christian theology is pushed into issues that are as difficult for Christians as for these witnesses in the Old Testament. We are left with solidarity that is short of sovereignty... except for Easter. This is a huge exception. The Old Testament witnesses, of course, appeal to no Easter, and that may make all the difference.

In any case, three caveats are crucial as one moves from the Old Testament to christological claims. First, care must be taken that Easter does not issue in a Friday-denying triumphalism, or in an easy victory that does not look full in the face at Friday and its terrible truth. Second, it must be borne in mind that the Friday-Sunday dialectic of reconciliation in Christian faith has its complete anticipation in the Old Testament in the mystery of exile and homecoming. That mystery of exile and homecoming dominates the liturgical rhetoric of complaint and response in every period and in every season of Israel's life.[28] Israel characteristically complains at the trouble given by Yahweh. Yahweh characteristically responds in healing, saving resolution. Third, in the end, from the perspective of the final form of the text, fidelity dominates the vision of Israel. This conclusion is as unambiguous in the faith of Israel as it is in the Easter affirmation of the church. In the Old Testament the God who abandons is the God who brings home to well-being.

In the end, I would not want to conclude that Christian faith has an easy resolution to the tension the Old Testament witnesses voice about Yahweh. I would not want to gloss over the dreadfulness in the Christian claim, both because Friday is ultimately serious, and because confessing Christians must live in the real world of Auschwitz and Hiroshima.[29]

On this matter of convergence between sovereignty and solidarity and the tension between the two, I do not imagine Christians know a lot more or much that is different from what these candid witnesses in ancient Israel knew.[30]

---

27. Ibid., 243. The accent on *perichoresis* precludes any notion that the Son suffered and the Father did not. It is inescapable that the negativity in which Jesus is involved touches every dimension of the life and character of Yahweh.

28. Emil Fackenheim, *To Mend the World: Foundations of Post-Holocaust Thought* (New York: Schocken Books, 1989), has clearly understood the irreversible disruption that twentieth-century events have effected in the life of Yahweh and in the work of theological interpretation. Another view on that disruption is the venturesome articulation of David Blumenthal, *Facing the Abusive God: A Theology of Protest* (Louisville: Westminster/John Knox, 1993).

29. On the depths of suffering and hope modeled in Christian affirmations of crucifixion and resurrection, but shared by all attentive persons, see the comment of George Steiner, *Real Presences: Is There Anything in What We Say?* (London: Faber and Faber, 1989) 231–32. I quote his poignant statement in chap. 12.

30. On the rhetorical and liturgical practice of sovereignty and solidarity, see Patrick D. Miller, *They Cried to the Lord: The Form and Theology of Biblical Prayer* (Minneapolis: Fortress Press, 1994) 55–177 and passim.

Resolution . . . and Yet . . .

There may be resolution of this tension, intellectual, historical, or pastoral . . . and yet . . . ! And yet, in Israel's texts—generated in exile and looking full in the face at the Lord of the exile—no ready convergence of sovereignty and solidarity is available. Israel, at its most buoyant, prefers the convergence to the tension, and in popular traffic the convergence will do. Yet the popular consensus does not eliminate the texts to the contrary, nor does it eliminate the ongoing, lived experience that constitutes evidence in support of the texts to the contrary.

Israel makes its bold, confident claim for Yahweh as sovereign and steadfast. But around the edges it keeps giving other signals of candor, which make us uneasy. Surely there is textual testimony that Israel wishes it had not uttered. And perhaps Yahweh also wishes it had not been uttered. But Israel is candid and, at its best, refuses cover-up or denial. It is our work in Old Testament theology to pay attention to these other textual signals, awkward and unsettling as they are, but which may evidence these witnesses at their best, engaged in truth-telling. It is precisely this "and yet" that moves us beyond any conventional conclusion and opens the way for further exposition. Israel's core testimony is able to affirm, in the splendor of its faith, that Yahweh's "steadfast love endures forever."

Part II

ISRAEL'S
COUNTERTESTIMONY

EIGHT

Cross-Examining Israel's Core Testimony

I T IS THE WORK of a witness to present a coherent narrative account of what happened, or to provide materials out of which a coherent narrative account may be constructed. It is the work of a witness to tell the truth. The witness necessarily purports to tell the truth, and may indeed be telling the truth. The court, moreover, may accept the rendering of reality given by the witness as true. Or the witness may be engaged in deception or in self-deception. The witness may be engaged in a form of truth-telling that appears to be inadequate. It is the work of the court to test the adequacy of the witness's version of reality. This testing is done through the process of cross-examination, whereby the court probes the testimony of the witness in order to inquire into its adequacy, coherence, credibility, and congruence with other evidence. If the testimony is found to be not adequate, or not credible, or not coherent, or not congruent, the court is likely to reject the testimony as an unreliable rendering of reality.

I propose that the process of cross-examination is required of Israel's daring testimony, which attests to "mighty acts" whereby Yahweh transforms the world. Moreover, the process of cross-examination seems to go on in the Old Testament text itself, the text being pervasively disputatious. For Israel, everything depends on the adequacy and reliability of its testimony concerning Yahweh. But clearly, there is within Israel an uneasiness about that marvelously positive testimony. A major point I wish to make at the outset is this: Cross-examination, which may be hostile or supportive, is not something done over against the Old Testament by late and outside detractors. It is remarkable that *the process of cross-examination goes on in the Old Testament itself,* partly in the utterance of Israel and partly in the alleged utterance of non-Israelites. As a consequence, the cross-examination constitutes part of the record of testimony, and it is understood in Israel as a way in which the testimony itself must be undertaken.

Thus, while my extended discussion of cross-examination runs counter to my extended discussion of testimony, it is not a case of either/or. The cross-examination is not intended by Israel to obliterate the core testimony. In the disputatious propensity of Israel, rather, core testimony and cross-examination belong to each other and for each other in an ongoing exchange. Thus there will

317

never be a "final" testimony in Israel that will not be subject to cross-examination. Nor will there ever be a cross-examination to which the consensus testimony does not make a vigorous response. Thus a reader of the Old Testament, I suggest, must accept cross-examination as a crucial part of the way in which Israel makes its presentation of disputatious testimony concerning Yahweh. It does not know any other way to speak. As a result, it is evident that Israel's countertestimony is not an act of unfaith. It is rather a characteristic way in which faith is practiced.

Hiddenness, Ambiguity, Negativity

Israel's faith is a probing, questioning, insisting, disjunctive faith. The questions that Israel raises in its cross-examination are not of a speculative or theoretical nature. They are questions of a concrete, practical kind, arising out of life experience. Such questions cohere with the character of Yahweh as given in the testimony of Israel. Israel's testimony to Yahweh has proposed a God who in majestic sovereignty provides a viable life-order in the world through decisive, transformative interventions, a God who in generous compassion attends to the needs of Yahweh's own. But Israel's lived experience appears to deliver neither viable life-order nor generous compassion—certainly not by highly visible, nameable acts of intervention. In this and the following three chapters, I will consider three different facets of Israel's countertestimony: *hiddenness, ambiguity or instability, and negativity.* While they all appropriately belong to a general rubric of countertestimony, they are not all of the same quality or tone. The three topics are arranged in my discussion to move from the more benign to the more problematic. I regard hiddenness (especially in the wisdom traditions) as countertestimony only because Israel's core testimony regarded Yahweh's "action in the world" as highly visible, evoking terror in the enemy and praise in the beneficiaries of that "action." Israel's wisdom traditions—perhaps more sophisticated or more reflective—do not in general continue such visible directness on Yahweh's part, and so do not make a claim for either direct terror or exultation. What Yahweh does, still not doubted, is now much more embedded in the "natural," ongoing processes of life. Such a view of Yahweh is very different from that of the core testimony, much toned down, much less buoyant in any exaggerated claims for Yahweh.

Such a countertestimony, however, is not nearly as demanding for Israel's faith as what I have termed Yahweh's ambiguity and instability. The latter is a function and product of Israel's narrative account of its life, in which Yahweh, a key character in the account, enjoys all the freedom and lack of definition that properly belong to a lively, interesting, serious narrative character. The "exposé" of Israel's core account of reality in the countertestimony is much more serious than is the affirmation of hiddenness.

Even such instability, however, is not as problematic for the core testimony of Israel as is the negativity of Yahweh's failure to do justice. Thus in the third facet of countertestimony, Israel speaks out loud its sense of reality, which largely contradicts the positive claims it has set out for Yahweh.

Thus in varying ways, with various evidences, Israel gives the courtroom pause as it has "on record" core testimony that turns out not to be as simply compelling as when first asserted. Israel's characteristic candor about its life puts its own core testimony in some jeopardy and leaves the truth of the matter still to be adjudicated.

Israel's Questions to Yahweh

The high claims of the core testimony evoke and require the disputatious questioning that constitutes a major dimension of Israel's life of faith. The questions include the following:

How long? The question is raised when Israel knows that its lived experience is incongruous with Yahweh's intentionality and finds the lived experience unbearable. Israel fully anticipates that the God of its core testimony must and will act decisively to intervene and transform unbearable circumstances. But the intervention and transformation are not on the horizon—hence the question. The question is not a request for information or a timetable. It is a restless insistence that amounts to a reprimand of Yahweh, who has not done for Israel what Israel has legitimately expected:

> My soul also is struck with terror,
> while you, O Lord—how long? (Ps 6:3)

The speaker cannot even finish the sentence. The incongruity is too overwhelming.

> How long, O Lord? Will you forget me forever?
> How long will you hide your face from me?
> How long must I bear pain in my soul,
> and have sorrow in my heart all day long?
> How long shall my enemy be exalted over me? (Ps 13:1-2)

> How long, O Lord, will you look on?
> Rescue me from their ravages,
> my life from the lions! (Ps 35:17)

> How long will you assail a person,
> will you batter your victim, all of you,
> as you would a leaning wall, a tottering fence?
> (Ps 62:3; cf. Pss 74:10, 79:5, 80:4, 89:46, 94:3)

This last verse appears to be a critique of other enemies, which has its foil in appeal to Yahweh, but the same language can as well be addressed to Yahweh. The purpose of the insistent, often angry, certainly impatient question is to mobilize Yahweh to act in the way Yahweh is supposed to act, according to the core testimony of Israel.

Why? This question arises out of circumstance of suffering that is senseless, especially in a faith wherein Yahweh is expected to be attentive and helpful. This question does not ask Yahweh to give reasons or justification for inactivity and neglect. The interrogative form functions, rather, as an accusation against Yahweh, who has failed to be Yahweh's true self:

> Why, O Lord, do you stand far off?
> Why do you hide yourself in times of trouble? (Ps 10:1)

> My God, my God, why have you forsaken me?
> Why are you so far from helping me,
> from the words of my groaning? (Ps 22:1)

> Why must I walk about mournfully
> because of the oppression of the enemy? (Ps 43:2)

> Rouse yourself! Why do you sleep, O Lord?
> Awake, do not cast us off forever!
> Why do you hide your face?
> Why do you forget our affliction and oppression? (Ps 44:23-24; cf. Pss
>   74:1, 11; 88:14)

The accusation is that Yahweh, who promised to be present and in whose very character it is to be present, is noticeably absent. And when Yahweh is absent, bad things happen.

Where? The same issue and the same accusation are voiced with the interrogative *where*. The spatial reference is not asking for information about where Yahweh's attentive love has gone. The point is that Yahweh's fidelity is *not here*, not in this circumstance of trouble, where it is needed and where it has been rightly anticipated:

> My tears have been my food day and night,
> while people say to me continually,
> "Where is your God?" (Ps 42:3)

In this complaint, the question is a quote from "people," but we may surmise that this is a rhetorical device of distancing, when in fact the speaker voices the speaker's own wonderment and dismay. Again, the question is placed on the lips of "the nations":

> Why should the nations say,
> "Where is their God?" (Ps 79:10, repeated in Ps 115:2)

And with reference to the promises of fidelity to the house of David,

> Lord, where is your steadfast love of old,
> which by your faithfulness you swore to David? (Ps 89:49; cf. v. 46)

Is? This interrogative is not much used in the way we are considering, but one important usage is noteworthy. In the early confrontation of rebellion in the wilderness, the people complain for water, and by a wonder are given water. But the complaint is taken as a challenge to the leadership, both of Yahweh and of Moses. Of the confrontation, Moses concluded,

> He called the place Massah and Meribah, because the Israelites quarreled and tested the Lord, saying, "Is the Lord among us or not?" (Exod 17:7)

Injustice, Complaint, and Exile as Negation

The questions arise when Israel faces situations of desperate need, as in the case of *unbearable injustice*. Israel's characteristic assumption is that if Yahweh's power and fidelity are operative, as the core witness asserts, there would be no such desperate need and no unbearable injustice. Yahweh makes all the difference, and when Yahweh is not present and engaged on behalf of Israel, things go awry.[1] The purpose of the questions, then, is to mobilize Yahweh to be Yahweh's best, true self. These questions arise not in an act of unfaith, but out of deep confidence that the God of the core testimony, when active in power and fidelity, can prevent and overcome such intolerable life experiences. The questions arise with such urgency because Israel finds that life without the active force of Yahweh is not good.

The characteristic mode of expression for these questions is the *genre of complaint*. These ways of speaking are found most characteristically in the Psalter, but they are uttered in other contexts of Israel's testimony as well. The genre of complaint (lamentation) is an expression of candor about the reality of life experience that is incongruent with Yahweh; at the same time it is an expression of hopeful insistence that if and when the righteous Yahweh is mobilized, the situation will be promptly righted.[2] The evidence given in the texts tells against the core testimony, but at the same time appeals to the core testimony, asking that this particular circumstance should be drawn into the positive reality there attested. Israel will indeed tell the truth about its life, even if that truth is costly to its testimony. But it does so in the expectation that this truth-telling will effectively summon Yahweh back to power and to solidarity.

The paradigmatic event that evokes the questioning of Yahweh is the *exile* and the destruction of the temple (Ps 74:1, 10-11; 79:5, 10; and 89:46).[3] That event looms in the imagination of Israel as the focal, exemplar case in which Yahweh failed in defense of Yahweh's own dynasty, temple, city, and people. To that extent, Israel's countertestimony is context-driven. That locus for questions of

---

1. For the notion that evil comes when Yahweh is absent or inattentive, see Fredrik Lindström, *Suffering and Sin: Interpretations of Illness in the Individual Complaint Psalms* (Stockholm: Almqvist and Wiksell International, 1994).

2. For the genre of lament and its function, see Claus Westermann, *Praise and Lament in the Psalms* (Edinburgh: T. & T. Clark, 1981); and Erhard Gerstenberger, *Der bittende Mensch: Bittritual und Klagelied des Einzelnen im Alten Testament* (WMANT 51: Neukirchen-Vluyn: Neukirchener Verlag, 1980).

3. On the exile as the matrix of Israel's faith, see pp. 74–78.

cross-examination, however, is not exclusive, but only paradigmatic. That is, Israel found itself in many other situations as well in which the same sense of failure, absence, and abandonment was overwhelming, and which required the same candid questioning of Yahweh. Thus what applies to exile for the community as a whole can also be voiced out of the personal experience of individuals in trouble. In many exile-like circumstances, Israel brought evidence out of its own suffering that Yahweh's character as sovereign and merciful did not ring true.

This convergence of *injustice-complaint-exile* in the speech of Israel, which I take as a fulcrum for Israel's countertestimony, is a characteristic and definitional feature of Israel's faith. When Israel spoke about Yahweh, Israel had often and characteristically to speak about *injustice* through *complaint* in *exile*. To this sharp and energetic questioning, Israel's positive testimony had no ready or compelling response, except to reach back into the core testimony and reiterate those claims. The reiterated testimony is indeed forceful and compelling. For those who lived in unresolved dismay, however, the testimony did not silence or dispose of the countertestimony, which must have lingered in Israel as a form of serious faith.

Sense of Abandonment

These questions ask about two distinct but related issues concerning the Yahweh of the consensus testimony. First and perhaps most crucially, Israel asks and wonders about Yahweh's reliability and fidelity. Israel had a sense of being abandoned. The term *abandoned* (*'zb*) includes the arbitrary male prerogative of divorce in the ancient world. In that world, a woman divorced was indeed abandoned. Thus with reference to the exile, Israel asks:

> Why have you forgotten us completely?
> Why have you forsaken (*'zb*) us these many days? (Lam 5:20)

The operative terms are *forget* and *forsake* (abandon). In Isa 49:14, the two terms of the question have become a conclusion:

> But Zion said, "The Lord has forsaken me,
> my Lord has forgotten me."

To be sure, the question is quickly answered, even refuted, in v. 15:

> Can a woman forget her nursing child,
> or show no compassion for the child of her womb?
> Even these may forget,
> yet I will not forget you.

And yet, in the same body of poetry (thus the same witness), Yahweh concedes the point of abandonment, even though it was "for a moment":

> For a brief moment I abandoned (*'zb*) you....
> In overflowing wrath for a moment I hid my face from you.... (Isa 54:7-8)

The question lingers in Israel. It lingers because Israel is so honest in its testimony and because lived reality does not easily conform to the core testimony of Israel. Old Testament theology must recognize that this question lives at the center of Israel's most convinced testimony. It is a lingering question not only for Israel, but for the world that knows about barbarities and watches Israel (and Israel's God) with yearning, bemused curiosity. Israel's detractors will want the countertestimony to prevail over the consensus testimony. But most serious people, not filled with self-hatred, will want Israel's core testimony to prevail. Israel, in the meantime, promises no easy resolution of the issue, but does agree on behalf of all its attendants to continue to struggle with the issue of Yahweh's fidelity.

Yahweh's Sovereignty Questioned

This convergence of *injustice-complaint-exile* raises a question for Israel concerning Yahweh's sovereign power. Most often Israel, like most other religions, assigns power to its God. Israel tends to focus its questions not on the generic issue of power, but on the distinctive quality of Yahweh's pathos-infused fidelity. On occasion, however, Israel is willing to give Yahweh the benefit of the doubt and affirm Yahweh's fidelity and good intention. But if such a willing faithfulness is granted to Yahweh, equally difficult issues of another kind arise. For if Yahweh is willing and faithful, then perhaps Yahweh lacks power and is not sovereign. Thus in such an extreme case, Yahweh will defiantly say to exilic Israel: "Is my hand shortened, that it cannot redeem? Or have I no power to deliver?" (Isa 50:2). Yahweh's defiance suggests that this is a response to something that was voiced by exilic, doubting Israel, something that was wondered out loud—perhaps that Yahweh had a "short hand." Yahweh had, in the past, a "strong arm and outstretched hand" by which to rescue Israel. But that arm now does not seem strong, and the hand seems to have shriveled to irrelevance. Apparently this was a charge made by Israel in exile. Yahweh vigorously refutes the charge, with the vociferousness of grammatically emphatic construction: "Is my hand indeed shortened?" The answer of Isa 50:2b-3 asserts Yahweh's enormous power. And in Isa 59:1 the same issue is raised with the same wording, but now in a resolving indicative statement that vindicates Yahweh and indicts Israel. Thus the suffering of Israel is brought back into the sensible framework of covenantal sanctions, so that the question of Yahweh's power is muted.

No doubt that resolution was satisfying to many, who were able to return in good faith to the core testimony. We may believe, however, that not all were so readily persuaded, and that these texts are evidence of an ongoing unease in Israel about the claim characteristically made for Yahweh. The hard experience of Israel legitimated such questions. It is not so readily evident, given the vagaries of historical suffering, that one can assert Yahweh's complete sovereignty, as though either to deny the enigmas of lived reality or to justify the problematic of lived experience as morally appropriate.[4] Some detractors of Israel will want the sovereignty of Yahweh exposed and defeated, but many will not. Many who watch and hope with Israel will wish that this great God of covenantal sovereignty will prevail, and so will yearn that Israel's core testimony be finally verified. In light of the troubling evidence, however, Israel will not give an easy answer to the issue of Yahweh's power. Israel promises, by its core testimony and by its cross-examination, to keep the question of Yahweh's power under honest review.

The core testimony of Israel, by appeal to the great transformative verbs of Yahweh and by the derivative adjectives and noun-metaphors of Israel's speech, made a case that Yahweh is competently sovereign and utterly faithful. And on most days that conclusion is adequate. It is a welcome conclusion because it issues in a coherent narrative account of reality. Israel, to be sure, affirms that conclusion of competent sovereignty and reliable fidelity. But Israel lives in the real world and notices what is going on around it. Israel is candid, refusing to deny what it notices. And so issues of competent sovereignty and reliable fidelity will remain in the Old Testament as Israel's belief-ful, candid, unfinished business. We know, moreover, that these two issues are paramount for all those who live in the world, whether they engage in God-talk or not. Thus these two points of cross-examination are not a safe intramural exercise for Israel. They are rather issues with which Israel struggles for the sake of the world.

We may believe, moreover, that these two issues, which endlessly surface in the world and with which Israel is never finished, are also the paramount issues *in Yahweh's life*. It is clear in the Old Testament, as Israel gives evidence, that Yahweh wants to be regarded as fully sovereign. That is what it means to "gain glory" and "to sanctify my holy name." It is equally clear that Yahweh wants to be regarded as wholly reliable, utterly trustworthy. That is what it means for Yahweh to be moved to compassion by Israel's petition. Therefore, the outcome of this disputation, which constitutes a great element in Israel's faith, not only depends on Israel's candid questions; it also depends on Yahweh's readiness to enact sovereignty and to evidence fidelity in concrete ways. Israel fully believes that Yahweh could and would do this, but Israel is not prepared to compromise its impatient insistence in the meantime.

Cross-examination does not proceed frontally or in large, sweeping generalization. It is conducted, rather, by the slow, attentive process of teasing out detail, of noticing hints of incongruity that fly in the face of the main claims; as such hints accumulate, a rereading and reuttering of the primary narrative is required. Thus the cross-examination of Israel's testimony concerning Yahweh, in the end, will require a considerably revised narrative about Yahweh.

---

4. Jon D. Levenson, *Creation and the Persistence of Evil: The Jewish Drama of Divine Omnipotence* (San Francisco: Harper and Row, 1988), has shown the ways in which Yahweh's governance of creation is provisional and precarious.

The Context of Cross-Examination

Before proceeding to the evidence, I pause here to consider the project of cross-examination more specifically. I suggest that cross-examination (and therefore disputatious argument) belongs characteristically to the Old Testament. Thus in doing Old Testament theology, one cannot focus on the "what" of large, substantive theological generalizations without attending to the "how" of disputatiousness, in which the substantive generalizations are regularly cast. I believe that the root cause of such theological disputatiousness arises from and is sustained by the Subject of the conversation, namely Yahweh, who prizes candor and rejects all deceiving denial.[5] I understand that this is something of a circular argument. But if we are to be theological in our understanding, we are bound to say that no other explanation is important, for finally God-talk must be congruent with the God about whom it speaks.

One can begin to grasp the distinctive power of this mode of discourse by contrasting it with the generalizing claims and procedures of the classic Greek tradition. Whereas that tradition of thought and reason understood itself to be responsibly engaged in large, coherent claims, Jewish testimony relishes the disjunction that disrupts the large claim and that attends to the contradiction as the truth of the matter.[6] Here I wish to observe four facets of this Jewish propensity toward disjunction that interrupts large claims and that is informed by the work of cross-examination in Israel's testimony about Yahweh.[7] To be sure, these very different critical, interpretive practices range a great distance from the Old Testament text as such. In each case, however, they refuse to accept the universalizing of dominant Western modes of reason. Their critical awareness of ill-fitting particularity, in each case, is informed by the traditions and epistemological postures modeled by and extrapolated from the Old Testament text.

Countertestimony in Midrash

The practice of disjunctive countertestimony, which I have termed cross-examination, may be seen in midrash, a type of Jewish exegesis that tends to focus on elements in the text that do not accommodate themselves to any smoother or larger rendering. The work of midrash is to focus on the ill-fitting element and to extrapolate surpluses of meaning that lie well beyond the explicit articulation of the text. The work of midrash is to expose what is hidden in the text, which might be an embarrassment to the main claim of the text.

---

5. Perhaps the culminating example of this disputatious quality is in Job 42:7-8, wherein Job is affirmed by Yahweh and is said to have spoken "what is right." It is not unambiguously clear that Yahweh's affirmation of Job pertains to Job's savage protest against Yahweh, but that is the most likely intention of the verses.

6. A case has been made that in the Greek classical tradition this same disputatious propensity is found in the Sophists, the opponents of Platonic "realism." Conversely, the Platonic, classical tradition is the practice of those who seek to quiet the disputation, but on their own high ground. See chap. 3, n. 6.

7. For this discussion I am especially indebted to my student Tod Linafelt.

The irregularity or misfit is in the text itself. Thus Geoffrey Hartman can speak of the "frictionality" in the scriptural text, which distinguishes this text from fiction.[8] Hartman's case in point is the narrative of Genesis 32, Jacob wrestling with the angel. Hartman, like many other interpreters, can see that much that is hidden, obscure, and ominous in the text is hinted at but never made explicit. The work of midrash is to exercise enormous interpretive imagination, so as to give visibility and emphasis to precisely what is nearly invisible or pointedly deemphasized in the text. Thus the work of midrash is continuous with the text itself, but goes far beyond it in exposing the oddity that destabilizes and questions the main flow of the text.

James Kugel has shown how midrash works to express dissonance, which he characterizes as "surface irregularities" in the text.[9] An example Kugel cites is the absence of the *nun* verse in the acrostic sequence of Psalm 145. This absent *nun* became the focus in midrashic commentary, so that the missing *nun*, and not the visible alphabet in the text, comes to be the point of interpretation. This approach to the text is relentlessly atomistic.[10] It is necessarily so, because the outlook of interpretation is for the dissonant detail, which then becomes the leverage point for exhibiting the disjunction in the text.

Midrashic interpretation is not explicitly "doing theology," as the Christian tradition and the discipline of Old Testament theology have understood it. Midrashic commentary is interested in every detail in the text, not simply speech about God. Therefore midrash is not an example, but an analogue for what I am suggesting for Old Testament theology. *Mutatis mutandis,* the cross-examination of Israel's testimony about Yahweh looks to the friction, the dissonance, or the surface irregularity in the articulation of Yahweh. Such an approach assumes that the dissonant articulation of Yahweh is not to be explained away literarily or historically, but is indeed a theological datum. Thus, for example, in Amos 9:8 the speech in the mouth of Yahweh is about radical judgment:

> The eyes of the Lord God are
> upon the sinful kingdom,
> and I will destroy it
> from the face of the earth...

But then comes the elliptical conclusion to the verse:

> —except that I will not utterly
> destroy the house of Jacob, says the Lord.

That odd reversal in the middle of the verse might be explained as a redactional outcome. But if taken as a theological datum, the two elements of the verse together, expressing contradictory intentionalities, may bear witness to Yahweh's

---

8. Geoffrey H. Hartman, "The Struggle for the Text," *Midrash and Literature* (ed. Geoffrey H. Hartman and Sanford Budick; New Haven: Yale University Press) 13.

9. James L. Kugel, "Two Introductions to Midrash," *Midrash and Literature,* 80, 92.

10. Ibid., 95.

unresolve or to Yahweh's inability to exercise sustained self-discipline. Too much should not be made of a single verse such as this one, but an eye must be kept open for the range of such "surface irregularities" in the uttering of Yahweh. This attentiveness to "frictionality" is indeed an invitation and challenge to a Christian interpreter of the text, for the propensity of Christian interpretation is toward a universalizing representation of God, which inevitably must disregard much of the available evidence. The outcome of such an investigation as this will not be a set-tled, "establishment" Yahweh, but one with whom Israel endlessly has to do, with all the risks and surprises entailed in such an ongoing engagement. Thus the clue we may take from midrashic exegesis is related to interpretive horizon, and finally is related to the Subject of Israel's God-talk.

Psychoanalytic Practice and Cross-Examination

It is suggested in many quarters that Sigmund Freud's theory of psychoanalysis is a thoroughly Jewish enterprise and is much informed by midrashic practice.[11] Freud's assumption is that a surface articulation or representation of reality is to be treated with great suspicion and not to be taken at face value. When Freud is understood as a social critic and not simply as a therapist (in any popular sense of the term), it is clear that Freud's interest is in a theory of repression that constitutes a practice of pervasive deception. John Murray Cuddihy has suggested that the repression in which Freud is interested pertains especially to the situation of Jews in Western, bourgeoisie Europe, who were forced by dominant gentile society into deceptive modes of conduct.[12] As a consequence, says Cuddihy, Jewishness was often hid-den but would surface in odd ways. Be that as it may, Freud's understanding of the process of psychoanalysis is that in dreams and in dream interpretation, what is repressed, hidden, denied, and ill-fitting will surface. The process of interpre-tation consists in listening and watching for the incongruity between what is said and what is hidden but signaled. Such disclosure not only acknowledges that some-thing is hidden, but makes emancipation possible in the process of disclosing the hiddenness.

Thus Freud's program, like that of midrash, concerns the friction, dissonance, and surface irregularity in self-presentation that suggests that the surface presenta-tion in and of itself is not all there is to say. I am greatly informed on this matter by Susan Handelman, who has explored Freud's links to midrashic practice. On this point of surface and hiddenness in text and in self, Handelman says:

> The conscious gaps and lacunae, the off-centered and neglected phenomena
> to which psychoanalysis directs its attention, are also extended by Freud to
> a general theory of culture: to the evasions, repressions, and omissions of

---

11. See Susan A. Handelman, *The Slayers of Moses: The Emergence of Rabbinic Interpretation in Modern Literary Theory* (Albany: SUNY Press, 1982).

12. John Murray Cuddihy, *The Ordeal of Civility: Freud, Marx, Levi-Strauss and the Jewish Struggle with Modernity* (New York: Basic Books, 1974).

truth underlying our most exalted achievements. Freud's explanation of anti-Semitism, in his own project of recovering his past, is intimately connected with his analysis of civilization and its discontents.[13]

For the Rabbis, while interpretation was from Sinai, "the Torah is not in heaven" but is decided in the ongoing process of debate on earth. This idea of interpretation is a curious hybrid between the belief in an absolute origin and authority and the belief in man's ability to alter and overcome it—a hybrid in the same way that Freud's theories combined, on the one hand, concepts of absolute origins (complexes, primal crimes, desires, and traumas), determining mechanisms which operated from the earliest period and controlled the formation of character, with, on the other hand, the affirmation of the amendment, alteration, and susceptibility to change of these absolute origins through interpretation and insight.[14]

As concerns the task of cross-examination in Israel's testimony about Yahweh, I suggest that our attention to texts includes watching for the incongruity and disjunction in the articulation of Yahweh, which bespeaks Yahweh's rich, unsettled interior life. I do not suggest a "psychoanalysis of Yahweh," but an attentiveness to the odd working of the text. Thus I have elsewhere considered what we may do theologically with Yahweh's history of violence and absence, which is presented in the text on occasion as undisciplined and out of control.[15] If we take such textual matters as theological data about the Character in the narrative who has continuity and constancy, then we may rightly wonder about the ongoing significance of this remembered violence in Yahweh's life and character. Whatever we may make of this memory, we cannot disregard the texts. That would be like an analyst disregarding negative self-articulation as uninteresting or unimportant. Seen in this way, the troubling dimensions of Yahweh in the text suggest that our usual surface articulations of Yahweh must be open enough to give place to the disjunctive data.

The Holocaust: Unanswerable Disruption

The disjunctive quality of interpretation in midrashic practice and in Freudian theory gives us categories, but ill prepares us, for the interpretive disruption of the Holocaust. In my judgment, an Old Testament theology cannot usefully be organized with reference to the Holocaust. But it is equally clear, in my judgment, that an Old Testament theology cannot proceed without acknowledgment of the profound and unutterable disruption of the interpretive enterprise that is embodied in the Holocaust. It is not necessary to enter the debate about whether the Holocaust is unique, or whether it is yet another extreme case in a history of barbarisms.[16]

13. Handelman, *The Slayers of Moses*, 145.
14. Ibid., 150.
15. See Walter Brueggemann, "Texts That Linger, Not Yet Overcome," *TToday* (forthcoming).
16. See the comprehensive study of Steven T. Katz, *The Holocaust in Historical Context* 1: *The Holocaust and Mass Death before the Modern Age* (New York: Oxford University Press, 1994). See also

It is enough to recognize that in relation to the Holocaust, all of our interpretive categories are exhausted.

If we try to make sense of the Holocaust vis-à-vis the Old Testament, we likely would gravitate to the Book of Job. Richard Rubenstein has made the case, however, that the Book of Job does not contain adequate categories for the depth of the Holocaust, which happened well beyond the horizon of the text.[17] Or we may, with David Blumenthal, hold the God of the Holocaust to the covenantal categories of the Old Testament, and conclude that the God of Israel is "abusive...but not always."[18] Or we may, with Emil Fackenheim, simply acknowledge, Jew and Christian together, that the Holocaust constitutes a radical disruption that is without parallel.[19] In the Holocaust, Jews and Christians are confronted with disjunctive evidence that is a massive and unanswerable challenge to claims about Yahweh's sovereignty and fidelity.

It does not follow, in my judgment, that these claims should therefore be abandoned, or one would not engage in the onerous work of Old Testament theology. It does follow, however, that claims for Yahweh's sovereignty and fidelity must now be made quite provisionally, and in the light of the burning flesh of Auschwitz. Thus it is plausible to suggest that the Holocaust is the quintessential and unparalleled occasion of disjunctive evidence against Yahweh, a "surface irregularity" of unspeakable magnitude. It is the extreme case—in the history of the Jews, in the history of the world, in the history of Yahweh—of evidence to the contrary, evidence that will not go away.

One must avoid trivializing the Holocaust by "taking a lesson" from it. Nonetheless, a crucial learning for Old Testament theology is a sharp measure of suspicion toward, or even resistance to, the triumphalist story of faith that is too easily recited on the basis of the Bible. Any triumph is made thin by this event, and every triumph is made unstable by this reality. This disruption is not unlike the many disruptions that are evident in the tale of Israel. But as Fackenheim has taught us so well, this disruption is so different in degree as to be different in kind. Even with the long practice of disruption that belongs to Jewish interpretation, we are not at all prepared for this one. We do not yet know how to do even disruptive interpretation in light of this break. But whatever we are now able to do is profoundly and irreversibly qualified by this break.

Deconstruction: Reading at the Edge

I suggest that Jacques Derrida's program of *deconstruction* is an important payout in which we can see coming together (a) the affinity for disruption in *midrash*, (b) the

---

Richard L. Rubenstein, *After Auschwitz: Theology and Contemporary Judaism* (2d ed.; Baltimore: Johns Hopkins University Press, 1992).

17. Richard L. Rubenstein, "Job and Auschwitz," *USQR* 25 (Summer 1970) 421–37.

18. This is the phrasing of David Blumenthal, *Facing the Abusing God: A Theology of Protest* (Louisville: Westminster/John Knox, 1993) 247 and passim.

19. Emil L. Fackenheim, *To Mend the World: Foundations of Post-Holocaust Thought* (New York: Schocken Books, 1989).

"slips" of *Freudian* discernment that are clues to emancipatory truth, and (c) the sociopolitical-moral-intellectual disruption that is the *Holocaust*. It is evident that Derrida, a Parisian intellectual, is engaged in a thoroughly Jewish enterprise of reading at the edge.[20]

Derrida's enterprise is exceedingly dense, and I do not claim to have probed it adequately. But enough is evident that we may make the following observations pertaining to our task of cross-examination. First, Derrida's enterprise is to be understood as a critical response to the Enlightenment intellectual history of Western Europe. Most specifically, it is a response to French structuralism, which understood truth to come as a system of closed signs, as an inventory of limited codes. That is, everything was controlled, and everything was known in advance. Against this, Derrida protests in the name of unexpected possibility, which has its intellectual, literary, and political dimensions, but which finally—for the biblical witness—is rooted in the God who can do the impossible.

Beyond the program of structuralism, Derrida is a response to the triumphalist history and culture that is embodied, for example, in Martin Heidegger.[21] This triumphalist history, fashioned by a convergence of classical and triumphalist Christian thinking, was able to construct the absolute narrative of absolute history of the West.[22] It is now evident in many quarters, but paradigmatically in Heidegger, that this seduction of absoluteness was incapable of self-criticism or tentativeness, and in the end produced, among its many finalities, "the final solution." Christian theology is implicated in this triumphalism by appropriating to itself and for itself an absoluteness that would entertain no disruption or destabilization. (In passing, we may notice that the classical dimension of this enterprise is rooted in Plato and his attempt to stop the political discourse that was sponsored by the Sophists. It is not for nothing that some of the heavy intellectuals of the West, rooted in Plato, now turn out to be the voices of intellectual and political absoluteness, all in the interest of long-held privilege.)[23] Thus the absoluteness that Derrida seeks to subvert is an intellectual enterprise, but it has direct and intoler-

---

20. The literature on Jacques Derrida is both immense and difficult. A student of Old Testament theology need not probe all of the depth and difficulty of Derrida, but will usefully notice the ways in which his deconstruction reflects an ancient Jewish commitment to iconoclasm. Reference should also be made to Hélène Cixous and Emmanuel Levinas. One reference that has helped me in this difficult area is John D. Caputo, *Demythologizing Heidegger* (Bloomington: Indiana University Press, 1993).

21. Martin Heidegger serves both as a specific reference point and as a symbol for the universalizing of European culture, against which Jewish particularism stands, characteristically at great risk. Christian supersessionism, as a theological practice and as a preemption of the Hebrew Bible, is surely part of the universalizing for which Heidegger is blatant and notorious.

22. Jane Flax, *Thinking Fragments: Psychoanalysis, Feminism, and Postmodernism in the Contemporary West* (Berkeley: University of California Press, 1990), offers an acute analysis of the construction of the "absolute narrative" of the West and its collapse. She is attentive to the linkage of power assertions and truth-claims.

23. The most obvious example of this ideology in the name of elitist intellectualism is that of Allan Bloom, *The Closing of the American Mind: How Higher Education Has Failed Democracy and Impoverished the Souls of Today's Students* (New York: Simon and Schuster, 1987). Bloom's pleading is of exactly the sort that finds expression in the Platonic resistance to the democratic disputatiousness of the Sophists.

able sociopolitical consequences. Derrida undertakes to destabilize continually this long-established and totalizing hubris.

Second, it is clear that Derrida's intention is not nihilistic, much as the term *deconstruction* might suggest, and much as his detractors would like to insist. Derrida's enterprise, rather, is thoroughly dialectical. It does not claim that a particular act of deconstruction is the last word in the process, as though to subvert the last totalizing ideology or to kill the last tyrant. Each moment of deconstruction is a moment in an ongoing process, which recognizes that there will arise, and must arise, new "constructions," which in turn become problematic.[24]

Third, one may wonder, then, if Derrida's program is an endlessly exhausting enterprise that is bottomless in its negative force. Derrida himself draws a line against such an exhausting, futile enterprise:

> Justice in itself, if such a thing exists, outside or beyond the law, is not deconstructible. No more than deconstruction, if such a thing exists. Deconstruction is justice.[25]

This is a remarkable statement that has been too little noticed. Deconstruction is in the service of justice and is a practice of justice, because it aims to overcome all injustice that arises from the illusion of a perfect system.[26] But, of course, the *act* of justice does not create a permanent *state* of justice. It is only an act, which needs endlessly to be reenacted. Thus at bottom, Derrida locates the point of the deconstructive process in a thoroughly Jewish commitment. If we were able to transpose Derrida into more conventional theological terms, we might conclude that Yahweh and Israel's irrevocable commitment to justice require that all false starts on the part of Yahweh be problematized, critiqued, and subverted. These false starts may occur in overstated self-aggrandizing sovereignty, or in self-indulgent pathos that gives in too much to the beloved. In good deconstructive fashion, Israel refuses to leave Yahweh alone, because Yahweh has not yet got it right. And Israel's cross-examination attends to that work vis-à-vis Yahweh.

This extraordinary convergence of (a) midrash, (b) Freud, (c) Holocaust, and (d) Derrida's deconstruction is all of a piece. These practices constitute the ongoing enterprise of theological Jewishness—Jewishness that cannot dispose of the "God issue," which stands over against every totalizing seduction that always ends in self-deception and brutality. Insofar as Israel's countertestimony participates in the same

---

24. Reference here should be made to Blumenthal, *Facing the Abusing God,* and his utilization of the sailing imagery of tacking. Blumenthal sees the critique and affirmation of God as maneuvers similar to tacking, both of which are necessary to serious biblical faith.

25. Jacques Derrida, "Force of Law: The 'Mythical Foundation of Authority,'" *Cardozo Law Review* 11 (1990) 919–1045. The journal has not been available to me, but I here depend on Caputo, *Demythologizing Heidegger,* 193. It is suggestive to notice that George Steiner, *Real Presences: Is There Anything in What We Say?* (Boston: Faber, 1989) 232, regards hope as the quintessentially nondeconstructible element in life.

26. David Jobling, "Writing the Wrongs of the World: The Deconstruction of the Biblical Text in the Context of Liberation Theologies," *Semeia* 51 (1990) 82–118, has suggested the linkage between deconstruction and liberation hermeneutics.

critical activity as these items, *Israel as witness knows that if Yahweh is not endlessly criticized and subverted, Yahweh will also become an absolute, absolutizing idol,* the very kind about which Moses aimed his protesting, deconstructive work at Sinai. Thus the deconstructive program in all of these dimensions is a characteristically Jewish enterprise of "smashing the idols."

The matter is not so easy for Christian theology. It is not so easy because Christian faith is relentless in the absolute claim it makes for Jesus of Nazareth. It is not so easy because Christian habits of theology have become accustomed to the dominant position in the West, politically and intellectually. Thus much of the deconstructive work to be done is the deconstruction of that in which Christian faith is embodied, or with which it is allied. It is not usual for Christians to engage in theological countertestimony of the claims of their own faith. And yet that is the intention of the "Protestant principle," rooted as it is in covenantal-prophetic-Pauline faith.[27]

Christian faith, however, is not without resource. It does have a key access point to this disjunctive enterprise. Christian faith is centered on Good Friday and on the crucifixion, in which we speak of "the Crucified God."[28] Friday is of course linked to Sunday, and death is tailed by the eruption of new life. But the scar tissue of Friday lingers in the body of Christ, and it protests against every totalizing, triumphalist, and absolutizing ambition. In living in the midst of Friday, Christians reach back as far as the command issued at Sinai against idols.[29] And they reach forward as far as Parisian deconstruction in its Jewishness. The cross-examination will not defeat the testimony... probably. But it will cause the testimony to be issued in a sobered, trembling voice. It may be more than a play on words that the *cross-examination* is matched to the *cross* of Friday. To that cross-examination, so difficult for Christians, so characteristic for serious Jews, we now turn.[30]

---

27. Paul Tillich, *The Protestant Era* (Chicago: University of Chicago Press, 1940), has articulated "the Protestant Principle," which he understands as a radical critical perspective to be practiced with reference to the "catholic substance" of faith.

28. In contemporary theology, the phrase recalls the work of Jürgen Moltmann, *The Crucified God: The Cross of Christ as the Foundation and Criticism of Christian Theology* (1974; Minneapolis: Fortress Press, 1993). Notice the term *criticism* in Moltmann's title. Eberhard Jüngel, *God as the Mystery of the World: On the Foundation of the Crucified One in the Dispute between Theism and Atheism* (Grand Rapids: Eerdmans, 1983) 64–66, shows the way in which "the Death of God" as Nietzsche's modern formulation derives from the hymnody of Luther's "theology of the Cross."

29. On the critique of idolatry as elemental to biblical faith, see Gabriel Vahanian, *Wait without Idols* (ed. Pablo Richard; New York: George Braziller, 1964); and *The Idols of Death and the God of Life* (Maryknoll, N.Y.: Orbis Books, 1983).

30. I had settled on the term *cross-examination* for the present enterprise before I noticed that Emil Fackenheim, *To Mend the World,* 11, had used the term *countertestimony* to refer to the Holocaust: "The holocaust poses the most radical counter-testimony to both Judaism and Christianity." Though it is a very different matter serving very different purposes, it is worth noting that Plato uses the term *elenchos* (cross-examination, refutation) as a strategy for challenging ordinary beliefs. See Terence Irwin, *Plato's Moral Theory: The Early and Middle Dialogues* (Oxford: Clarendon Press, 1979) 34–37 and passim.

NINE

The Hiddenness of Yahweh

I N ITS CROSS-EXAMINATION of its own testimony to Yahweh, Israel gives evidence that the God known to be direct and visible in the life of Israel is, on many occasions, hidden—indirect and not visible. The core testimony of active verbs speaks of Yahweh with the claim that Yahweh was known and seen directly in the ongoing life of Israel. A strong and crucial counterclaim, however, maintains that the God of Israel is hidden: "Truly, you are a God who hides himself, O God of Israel, the Savior" (Isa 45:15).

In pondering its daily life and in grappling with the vagaries of its life in distress, Israel knew that the God of Israel is not everywhere and always visible. But Israel was not prepared to draw the conclusion that where Yahweh was not visible, Yahweh was not present and engaged. Therefore it was essential to make an affirmation, against the core testimony, that Yahweh is present in and attentive to the life of Israel in hidden ways.

The Hidden Rule of Yahweh

The theme of the hiddenness of Yahweh has been an important one in Christian theology, with special attention to Martin Luther; Martin Buber has explored the same issue from the perspective of Judaism.[1] In Israel's primary testimony, as we have seen, Yahweh is known by Israel to be the subject of active verbs of transformation, whereby Yahweh dramatically and identifiably intervenes and intrudes into the life of Israel in order to work Yahweh's righteousness, which is marked by justice, equity, and reliability. Even in the testimony of Israel, these dramatic acts of Yahweh's transformative intervention are actually few and far between. For the most part, Israel must get along without such wonders of radical newness, and

---

1. On Luther's use of the term, see John Dillenberger, *God Hidden and Revealed* (Philadelphia: Muhlenberg Press, 1953). See Martin Buber, *The Eclipse of God: Studies in the Relation between Religion and Philosophy* (London: Victor Gollancz, 1953). See also Douglas John Hall, *Lighten Our Darkness: Toward an Indigenous Theology of the Cross* (Philadelphia: Fortress Press, 1976). For the exegetical grounds for such a notion, see Samuel E. Balentine, *The Hidden God: The Hiding of the Face of God in the Old Testament* (Oxford: Oxford University Press, 1983); and Lothar Perlitt, "Die Verborgenheit Gottes," *Probleme biblische Theologie* (ed. Hans Walter Wolff; Munich: Chr. Kaiser Verlag, 1971) 367–82. Samuel Terrien, *The Elusive Presence: Toward a New Biblical Theology* (New York: Harper and Row, 1978), has made much of the notion of the hiddenness of God.

must live in a mundane, day-to-day world where the biological processes of birth and death, the familial processes of love and hate, and the political processes of rise and fall and war and peace go on apace.

The remarkable fact about Israel's countertestimony is that the disappearance of the active, direct, visible Yahweh in its life did not stop Israel from pondering the character, purpose, and implications of Yahweh. Israel learned, living in the absence of Yahweh's great interventions, to speak of Yahweh in yet another way. This way of speaking assigns very few active verbs of transformation to Yahweh. As a consequence Yahweh is presented in the cross-examination as less revolutionary than Yahweh is testified to be in Israel's primary witness. Rather, as Israel pondered the regularities of its daily life, Yahweh is assigned functions that concern especially governance, order, maintenance, and sustenance. The claims made for Yahweh are not nearly so dramatic as in the core testimony. It is as though Israel has toned down its rhetoric, as though Israel pulls back from having spoken too exuberantly and outrageously about Yahweh. Thus, I propose to consider a greatly revised utterance of Yahweh under the rubric of wisdom.[2] As we shall see, the general theme of wisdom theology has as its component parts creation, order, and providence.

Wisdom Theology

It is not easy or obvious to situate the wisdom traditions, especially the Book of Proverbs, in Israel's God-talk.[3] It is important for a student of Old Testament theology to have some general notion of the struggle in Old Testament scholarship to take into account the wisdom traditions. We may identify two scholarly attitudes toward wisdom in a comprehensive articulation of Old Testament theology.

First and certainly most influentially, Old Testament theology in the twentieth century has treated wisdom as an embarrassing stepchild. Because wisdom in Proverbs did not feature any of the major constructs of twentieth-century scholarship (for example, covenant, credo, mighty deeds), and because it had much in common with other ancient Near Eastern religious documents and assumptions, wisdom has been treated as (almost) non-Israelite and certainly not congruent with what was taken to be Israel's primary accents of faith.[4] This view proceeded on a consensus notion in scholarship of what constituted the core of Israel's faith. The problem of the dismissal of the wisdom material is that the material is present in the Old Testament, and certainly some in Israel took it seriously as theological material. Thus we are not in a position to dismiss what Israel itself did not dismiss in its normative literature.

---

2. See especially Gerhard von Rad, *Wisdom in Israel* (Nashville: Abingdon Press, 1972). The fullest exploration of wisdom theology is offered in the myriad of studies by James L. Crenshaw, now compiled in *Urgent Advice and Probing Questions: Collected Writings on Old Testament Wisdom* (Macon, Ga.: Mercer University Press, 1995).

3. See Lennart Bostrom, *The God of the Sages: The Portrayal of God in the Book of Proverbs* (ConBOT Series 19; Stockholm: Almqvist and Wiksell International, 1990).

4. This was certainly a tendency in the influential paradigm of G. Ernest Wright, but it is most clearly articulated in the work of Horst Dietrich Preuss, "Erwägungen zum theologischen Ort alttestamentlicher Weisheitsliteratur," *EvT* 30 (1970) 393–417.

Second, in response to this scholarly judgment, which he himself had largely fostered, Gerhard von Rad offered a dramatically different assessment of wisdom as theological material.[5] In his *Old Testament Theology* 1, von Rad presented wisdom, along with the Psalms, as response to Israel's credo theology.[6] This proposal has the important merit of including the wisdom material on the theological horizon of Israel, and takes the material seriously. Wisdom material is now recognized as "being there" in the Bible as a theological datum. But the rubric of response does not finally work, because the material as such is not in any recognizable way cognizant of the credo perspective.

Von Rad, in his final book, revised this assessment to argue that wisdom is simply an alternative way of doing theology, one that represents a different context of faith and offers very different intellectual, cultural, and sociological options.[7] Indeed, there is much in this approach that may be adequate. If a student of Old Testament theology proceeds with this model, he or she will in any case recognize that the Old Testament articulates more than one way of doing theology.

I have no particular disagreement with the notion of wisdom as an alternative model of theological speech. But I am here seeking to understand the Old Testament in terms of testimony, so I advance the notion of wisdom as alternative in order to suggest that wisdom is not simply an unrelated, second effort, but is an attempt to speak of Yahweh in all of those contexts of Israel's lived experience wherein the main claims of the core testimony are not persuasive. If Israel could not speak of Yahweh as the one who works radical transformations, then Israel in the mode of active verbs had little to say theologically, and had to leave much of its life beyond the horizon of Yahweh.[8] Therefore, I propose, wisdom theology insists that the primary testimony is not everywhere adequate or effective. The countertestimony of wisdom is that in much of life, if Yahweh is to be spoken of meaningfully, it must be a Yahweh who is not direct and not visible, but who in fact is hidden in the ongoing daily processes of life. On the one hand, such a way of speaking of Yahweh is very modest; it does not claim too much. On the other hand, this is a venturesome attempt at Yahwism, because it dares to make a claim about Yahweh's faithful sovereignty and sovereign fidelity in all of those dimensions of life where the Yahweh of the great verbs is not evident.

---

5. Von Rad's *Wisdom in Israel* was profoundly ground-breaking and continues to be the finest available exposition of sapiential theology in the Old Testament.

6. Gerhard von Rad, *Old Testament Theology* 1: *The Theology of Israel's Historical Traditions* (New York: Harper and Row, 1962) 355–459.

7. The most recent survey and summary of the status of intellectual, cultural, and sociological issues related to wisdom in the Old Testament is *Wisdom in Ancient Israel: Essays in Honour of J. A. Emerton* (ed. John Day et al.; Cambridge: Cambridge University Press, 1995).

8. "Mighty acts" as an interpretive principle left much beyond the horizon of theological notice. Thus, for example, G. Ernest Wright could assert that Israel had "little interest in nature." We are now able to see, in retrospect, that such an exclusion was badly misinformed and enormously costly for the theological work of the church. On this point, see Walter Brueggemann, "The Loss and Recovery of Creation in Old Testament Theology," *TToday* 53 (1996) 177–90.

Yahweh as Hidden Guarantor of Order

In the last several decades, to some extent under the impetus of von Rad, Old Testament scholarship has produced an important corpus of literature on this theological effort, now summarized in comprehensive fashion by Leo Perdue and John Gammie.[9] In the United States, attention should be paid to the work of James Crenshaw and Roland Murphy; in Germany to von Rad and a number of his students, including Erhard Gerstenberger and H. J. Hermisson; in Britain to Norman Whybray; and in Switzerland to the two important books of Hans Heinrich Schmid.[10]

In this theology, about which there is now general agreement among scholars, Yahweh is the hidden guarantor of an order that makes life in the world possible. The operational word is *order,* and Israel marvels at, ponders, sings about, and counts on that good order without which life would not be possible. Notice that methodologically, Israel works backward, as "natural theology" always must, to infer Yahweh from the observations and experiences of daily life.[11] The primary mode of expression for this way of speaking of Yahweh is in the wisdom sayings, which often do not mention Yahweh at all (cf., for example, Prov 10:1, 4, 6). On occasion Yahweh is mentioned as the guarantor of the process of order, as in Prov 10:3 and 11:1. Those sayings that do not refer explicitly to Yahweh are preponderant in Proverbs, and only by inference can we determine that Israel intended in these proverbs to make the same affirmation about the character of Yahweh as the hidden insurer of the reliability of this life process necessary to survival and well-being in the world.

Marvelous ordering of creation. Wisdom reflections on Yahweh are attentive to the life processes that constitute creation.[12] The world is seen to be a marvelous system of regularity in food production, which nourishes and sustains all creatures. The ordering that Yahweh guarantees is not a tight hierarchy, as the term

---

9. John G. Gammie and Leo G. Perdue, eds., *The Sage in Israel and the Ancient Near East* (Winona Lake, Ind.: Eisenbrauns, 1990).

10. Crenshaw, *Urgent Advice and Probing Questions;* Roland E. Murphy, *The Tree of Life: An Exploration of Biblical Wisdom Literature* (New York: Doubleday, 1990); Erhard Gerstenberger, *Wesen und Herkunft des 'apodiktischen Rechts'* (WMANT 20; Neukirchen-Vluyn: Neukirchener Verlag, 1965); H. J. Hermisson, *Studien zur Israelitischer Spruch-Weisheit* (WMANT 28; Neukirchen-Vluyn: Neukirchener Verlag, 1968); Norman Whybray, *The Intellectual Tradition in the Old Testament* (BZAW 135; Berlin: de Gruyter, 1974); Hans Heinrich Schmid, *Wesen und Geschichte der Weisheit; eine Untersuchung zur altorientalischen und israelitischen Weisheitsliteratur* (BZAW 101; Berlin: Alfred Töpelmann, 1966); and Schmid, *Gerechtigkeit als Weltordnung; Hintergrund und Geschichte des alttestamentlichen Gerechtigkeitsbegriffes* (Tübingen: J. C. B. Mohr [Paul Siebeck], 1968).

11. See especially James Barr, *Biblical Faith and Natural Theology: The Gifford Lectures for 1991* (Oxford: Clarendon Press, 1993). There can be no doubt that sapiential rhetoric in Israel voices Yahweh very differently than the offer of core testimony. Following Paul Ricoeur, Mark I. Wallace, "Can God Be Named without Being Known? The Problem of Revelation in Thiemann, Ogden, and Ricoeur," *JAAR* 59 (1991) 281–308, concludes, "[T]he power of sapiential discourse [serves] as a corrective to the totalizing impulses of Christian narrative theology" (p. 300). Such a conclusion indicates why I deal with wisdom as a counter to core testimony, which is characteristically tempted to totalizing.

12. Thus Walther Zimmerli, "The Place and Limit of the Wisdom in the Framework of the Old Testament Theology," *SJT* 17 (1964) 148, could assert, "Wisdom thinks resolutely within the framework of a theology of creation."

order might imply; it is rather a network of cooperative, interrelated parts, whereby nourishment and well-being are given to all in due course. Israel could only marvel at the way in which the seasons, and the consequent life cycles, come in reliable sequence:

> As long as the earth endures,
> seedtime and harvest, cold and heat,
> summer and winter, day and night,
> shall not cease. (Gen 8:22)

It marvels as well at how there is adequate water for all creatures (Ps 104:10-13). The world is reliable in its nourishing and sustaining because of the reliability of Yahweh. Thus the most exultant celebration that Israel can voice of the regularities of the creation as gifted by the Creator are poems that have functioned in the ongoing tradition as table grace:

> These all look to you
> to give them their food in due season;
> when you give to them, they gather it up;
> when you open your hand,
> they are filled with good things. (Ps 104:27-28)

> The eyes of all look to you,
> and you give them their food in due season.
> You open your hand,
> satisfying the desire of every living thing. (Ps 145:15-16)

Creation theology, as here expressed, is a glad affirmation that "the thing works!" The sign that it works is that all of Yahweh's creatures are nourished.

Ethical dimension. Israel does not cringe from assigning to Yahweh the functions of a "fertility God."[13] But Israel also insists that this hidden God has ensured that there is an uncompromising ethical dimension to the life-order over which Yahweh graciously governs. Thus the wisdom witness who marvels also warns and traces out the disciplines, costs, and limits that belong to life in this good order. By the long-term observation of recurring patterns of human behavior, wisdom teachers have sorted out the limits of freedom and the shape of acceptable behavior, beyond which conduct dare not go without bringing hurt to self and to others. These limits are understood to be the restraints that Yahweh has ordered into the vary fabric of creation. The wisdom teachers observed that the ordering of reality given by this hidden God is tough, uncompromising, and unforgiving, and cannot be violated with impunity. Thus wisdom is about the God-given boundaries

---

13. The phrase especially recalls the important book of Walter Harrelson, *From Fertility Cult to Worship* (Garden City, N.Y.: Doubleday, 1969); but see also these works by Claus Westermann, "Creation and History in the Old Testament," *The Gospel and Human Destiny* (ed. Vilmos Vajta; Minneapolis: Augsburg Publishing House, 1971) 11–38; *Creation* (Philadelphia: Fortress Press, 1971); *Elements of Old Testament Theology* (Atlanta: John Knox, 1982) 85–117; and *What Does the Old Testament Say about God?* (London: SPCK, 1979) 39–52.

to behavior, and foolishness is destructive behavior that ignores or oversteps those boundaries. Indeed, such foolishness is, as von Rad observed, "practical atheism," for it proceeds as though the guaranteeing work of Yahweh were not in effect, and as though the individual actor were autonomous and completely unfettered.[14]

Two scholarly constructs are useful in articulating this hidden, hovering governance of Yahweh. First, Hans Heinrich Schmid has shown that the ordering of creation to which wisdom bears witness is marked by Yahweh's righteousness.[15] That is, Yahweh's righteous intention consists not only in dramatic, intrusive acts of right-wising, but also in the guaranteeing norms that protect life from self-destruction. Wisdom consists in coming to terms with the norms of viability that Yahweh has ordained into the very fabric of creation.

Second, already in 1955, Klaus Koch proposed a construct of "deeds-consequences," wherein he argued that the very structure of most sayings in the Book of Proverbs (and elsewhere in the Old Testament) assumed and affirmed that human deeds have automatic and inescapable consequences, so that acts for good or for ill produce their own "spheres of destiny."[16] The critical point in Koch's argument is that in "foolish acts"—acts that violate Yahweh's righteousness—Yahweh does not need to intervene directly in order to punish or reward, as in the covenant blessings and curses of Sinai. Rather, the deed carries within it the seed of its own consequence, punishment or reward, which is not imposed by an outside agent (Yahweh). Thus, for example, a lazy person suffers the consequence of poverty, without the instrusion of any punishing agent; likewise, carelessness in choosing friends will produce a life of dissolution, all on its own. Consequently, "responsible acts"—those that cohere with Yahweh's ordering of creation—will result in good for self and for community. Yahweh is *not at all visible* in this process. But, according to Israel, Yahweh is *nonetheless indispensable* for the process. This is not, in Israel's horizon, a self-propelled system of sanctions, but it is an enactment of Yahweh's sovereign, faithful intentionality.

Thus moral accountability belongs to the very character of life in the world offered by the hidden Yahweh. Ethics is not a belated addendum to a pragmatic process; ethics, rather, is a genuine reckoning with the character of this God, who wills life in terms of responsible relatedness to the whole fabric of creation. Israel's imagination is shaped in this venue by an awareness of givens, limits, and payouts authorized by Yahweh, which create large zones of human choice, freedom, responsibility, and the recognition of the human use of power and authority. In the midst of these "humanistic" affirmations, however, is a sober awareness that autonomy, hubris, and foolishness are intrinsically and inevitably destructive. Yahweh is

---

14. Von Rad, *Wisdom in Israel*, 65.

15. Schmid, *Gerechtigkeit als Weltordnung*.

16. Klaus Koch, "Is There a Doctrine of Retribution in the Old Testament?" *Theodicy in the Old Testament* (ed. James L. Crenshaw; IRT 4; Philadelphia: Fortress Press, 1983) 57–87. See the important critique and refinement of Koch's thesis by Patrick D. Miller, *Sin and Judgment in the Prophets: A Stylistic and Theological Analysis* (Chico, Calif.: Scholars Press, 1982).

hidden in the process, as Israel watched (along with its neighbors) the calculus of costs and benefits enacted. Yahweh has not yielded at all, in preserving for Yahweh's own self the shape of the moral world in which Israel lives.

Aesthetic dimension. The ethical dimension of Yahweh's hidden governance is real and inescapable. The problem is that such a rule as "deed-consequence" can be tightened and exploited into a hard system of social control. No doubt many who rebel against "biblical faith" and against "the biblical God" are in fact restless against oppressive modes of social control done in the name of this hidden, hovering holiness. For that reason, it is important to recognize that along with this dimension of ethical demand in the ordering of this hidden God, there is also an aesthetic dimension that exults in the artistry of God, in the beauty of the created order, culminating in a response of amazement and astonishment. The aesthetic dimension of the God of wisdom and the work of this God of wisdom, which is something of a check against excessive ethical intensity, has been well and eloquently articulated by Samuel Terrien.[17] Here we may mention only a few evidences of this dimension of Yahweh's good, life-giving ordering, evidence that attests to the brilliant artistry and generosity of the hidden Yahweh.

In Gen 1:31, at the conclusion of the sixth day of creation, Yahweh exclaimed, "It was very good." Most probably this is an aesthetic judgment and response to a brilliant act of creation.[18] The sense of beauty or loveliness evokes on Yahweh's part a doxological response to the created order, a sense of satisfaction on the part of the artist, a glad acknowledgment of success. Here and in some other places, a glad affirmation of creation is moved more by awe and delight than by ethical insistence or command. Thus Prov 8:30-31, in speaking of creation, culminates in a statement of "delight" and "rejoicing." We may identify five elements of this aesthetic dimension of Yahweh's created order:

(a) In the building of the tabernacle (which may or may not be a harbinger of the Solomonic temple to come), great attention is given to the beauty of its visible appearance. Moses and his cohorts take care to ensure visible loveliness for the arrangement and furnishings of the tabernacle:

> Then Moses said to the Israelites: See, the Lord has called Bezalel son of Uri son of Hur, of the tribe of Judah; he has filled him with divine spirit, with skill (*ḥkmh*), intelligence, and knowledge in every kind of craft, to devise artistic designs, to work in gold, silver, and bronze, in cutting stones for setting, and in carving wood, in every kind of craft. And he has inspired him to teach, both him and Oholiab son of Ahisamach, of the tribe of Dan. He has filled them with skill to do every kind of work done by an artisan or by a designer or by an embroiderer in blue, purple, and crimson yarns, and in

---

17. Terrien, *The Elusive Presence.*

18. Claus Westermann, *Genesis 1–11* (London: SPCK, 1984) 167. Attention here might usefully be paid to Dorothy L. Sayers, *The Mind of the Maker* (Library of Anglican Spirituality; London: Mowbray, 1994).

fine linen, or by a weaver—by any sort of artisan or skilled designer. (Exod 35:30-35)

It is important to note that the artisans are given "the divine spirit" (*rûaḥ 'elohîm*), and that they have wisdom, meaning skill in their artistic craft. This skill is employed to enhance the presence of God's holiness in the midst of Israel.[19]

(b) Joseph is selected to govern Egypt on behalf of pharaoh because he is a man "discerning and wise" (Gen 41:33, 39). This word usage reflects an awareness that governance is a craft or skill and not simply a manipulation of power. There is indeed something lovely about a well-ordered enterprise. There are hints, as von Rad has noted, that Joseph is portrayed as an embodiment of wisdom virtues.[20] Joseph's capacity for good order in Egypt is to provide food for all those along the food chain.

(c) There is no doubt that in the wisdom teaching of the Book of Proverbs, "wise speech" is not only effective communication. It is also an art of finesse, one that requires skill and sensitivity and that evokes appropriate response for what is well-spoken.[21] Thus wise speech is for the good ordering of the community.

(d) In the remarkable doxological inventory of creatures in Ps 104:1-23, the poem proceeds in some detail, moving from the most comprehensive to the finest detail in observing the wonders of creation, including wild asses, birds, wild goats, coneys, lions, bread and wine. The great creation lyric culminates with the recognition that daily (eucharistic?) provision of bread and wine is a sign of gracious and generous governance.

After this comprehensive listing, the speaker can only break out in self-disregarding exultation:

> O Lord, how manifold are your works!
> In wisdom you have made them all;
> the earth is full of your creatures.
> Yonder is the sea, great and wide,
> creeping things innumerable are there,
> living things both small and great. (Ps 104:24-25)

---

19. Terrien, *The Elusive Presence*, characteristically accents the aesthetic and contemplative dimensions of Old Testament faith, which he likens to the eye, as distinct from the standard ethical-covenantal emphasis, which he links to the ear.

20. Gerhard von Rad, "The Joseph Narrative and Ancient Wisdom," *The Problem of the Hexateuch and Other Essays* (New York: McGraw-Hill, 1966) 292-300. Von Rad's general hypothesis concerning a "Solomonic Enlightenment" is now generally rejected, but his specific insights on the text of Joseph, in my judgment, have merit.

21. James Crenshaw, "Wisdom and Authority: Sapiential Rhetoric and Its Warrants," *Congress Volume, Vienna, 1980* (VTSup 32; Leiden: E. J. Brill, 1981) 10–29, has paid attention to the power of persuasion that is operative in sapiential rhetoric. Because the wise had no official authority, they apparently relied on their capacity to persuade. On the power and intention of such speech, see also von Rad, *Wisdom in Israel*, 124–50.

It is in wisdom that Yahweh has done all this, in the artistry and intentionality that makes a world of symmetry, well-being, and generosity available for human enjoyment.

(e) Finally in this connection, the Song of Solomon is an extreme case of the aesthetic dimension of Yahweh's wisdom. I say extreme case because, as is well known, God is absent in this lyrical poetry. Wisdom is not mentioned here either. Thus it is a far reach to relate this literature to our theme. I do so, however, because I propose that this literature is the fullest articulation in the tradition of Israel of celebrative well-being that affirms in exotic, erotic detail the goodness of life as given by the hidden God. For that reason we may refer this celebration to the God who is hidden in creation as hidden in the literature. Dietrich Bonhoeffer has suggested that the Song of Solomon is an articulation of creation theology, an affirmation of the wholeness, goodness, and joyousness of life ordered by Yahweh.[22]

Blessing intrinsic in life created by Yahweh. The convergence of fertility, ethics, and aesthetics characterizes the order of the hidden God who is present in the creation-wisdom texts. This articulation of the hidden God permits Israel to affirm about Yahweh what the dominant "mighty deeds" testimony did not permit, or at least what scholarly attention did not entertain. The wisdom tradition is able to affirm that blessing, Yahweh's power and will for life, is intrinsic in the life process itself.[23] The blessings intrinsic to creation are not something that Yahweh at a whim withholds from the world. This awareness permits Israel to value the ordinariness of daily life and to treasure it as a gift from Yahweh and as a sign of Yahweh. At the same time, it is profoundly important that Israel in this counter-testimony should be able to hold together, as of a piece, the ethical and aesthetic aspects of Yahweh's purpose for the ordered world.

The propensity of church interpretation is to accent the ethical in a way that drives out the aesthetic and produces a coercive harshness.[24] Conversely, a rebound from the ethical accent to a one-sided embrace of the aesthetic may culminate in a kind of self-indulgence that tends toward Gnosticism. I imagine that in Israel and in ongoing interpretation, we are likely in any moment to tilt in one direction or the other. It is nonetheless important to note that Israel refused to choose, and understood that the ordered life of the world is one of uncompromising accountability and one of celebrative, delighted relish. Thus,

> People go out to their work
> and to their labor until the evening. (Ps 104:23)

---

22. See Dietrich Bonhoeffer, *Letters and Papers from Prison* (New York: Macmillan, 1972) 303. Such a reading of the poetry does not appeal to any allegorical interpretation.

23. See Claus Westermann, *Blessing in the Bible and the Life of the Church* (OBT; Philadelphia: Fortress Press, 1978).

24. This is obviously much more fully the case in Protestantism, and especially in some forms of Calvinism, though Calvin himself knew better.

There is work to do. But the evening brings freedom from labor. We are not told what to do in the evening. Rest from labor may yield a night as characterized in the Song of Solomon:

> Upon my bed at night
> I sought him whom my soul loves;
> I sought him, but found him not;
> I called him, but he gave no answer.
> "I will rise now and go about the city,
> in the streets and in the squares;
> I will seek him whom my soul loves."
> I sought him, but found him not.
> The sentinels found me,
> as they went about in the city,
> "Have you seen him whom my soul loves?"
> Scarcely had I passed them,
> when I found him whom my soul loved.
> I held him, and would not let him go.... (Cant 3:1-4a)

In its countertestimony, Israel does not claim too much, too directly, or too strongly for Yahweh. It is enough that Yahweh makes a life-space that is reliable and generous. One can, in that world, receive gifts that bestow life. One therefore need not be anxious about wherewithal for life (cf. Matt 6:25-33). It is enough to seek God's righteousness. All else "will be given to you as well" because "your heavenly Father knows that you need all these things."

Yahweh's Governance: Personification and Providence

Thus far the wisdom of the hidden God who orders is a rule, an intention, a discernment, a purpose. It is something intended by Yahweh, which may be discerned, embraced, and practiced by attentive human agents... or it may be resisted. Wisdom of this sort is common sense that is responsive to Yahweh's lordly, generous will for life. It has in it dimensions of acumen and calculation, of trust and willing submissiveness. But Israel also devised, in its witness to the hidden God, a second way of speaking. (Whether this second way is later, and is a development from "pragmatic" to "metaphysical," is beside the point for our purposes.)

Wisdom as Agent of Yahweh

Israel's wisdom, in a few important utterances, sought to draw the claims of wisdom so close to the reality of Yahweh as to say that wisdom partakes of Yahweh's own character. Thus in many doxological formulations, wisdom is Yahweh's way of working, as though wisdom were an agent of Yahweh:

It is he who made the earth by his power,
who established the world *by his wisdom,*
and by his understanding stretched out the heavens. (Jer 51:15,
  cf. 10:12)

...who *by understanding* (*btbûnh*) made the heavens...(Ps 136:5, cf.
  Ps 104:24)

The Lord *by wisdom* founded the earth;
by understanding he established the heavens;
by his knowledge the deeps broke open,
and the clouds drop down the dew. (Prov 3:19-20; this opposes
  autonomous wisdom also claimed by the arrogant king, Isa 10:13)

Thus wisdom, the skill and artistry to order according to righteousness, is a capacity of the hidden God. This capacity for wisdom is, in this countertestimony, a quality exclusively of Yahweh. But Israel goes even further in drawing providential ordering into the character of Yahweh. Wisdom becomes a personal, active agent in the world, able, in its own self-consciousness and will, to act in order to effect life and well-being (Prov 1:20, 7:4, 8:1, 9:1). Whether this agent is to be understood as simply a rhetorical device or as a "real" agent does not matter for our purposes. The point is that wisdom is now presented as much more than Yahwistic "common sense." Now wisdom (personified as "she") is a differentiated agent of force for life in the world, who bears the markings of Yahweh's own intentionality.

Wisdom's Intimate Link to Yahweh: Job 28 and Proverbs 8

Finally what concerns us is the way in which, in two texts, wisdom is intimately linked to Yahweh's life and being. In Job 28, wisdom is hidden (vv. 12–22) and only God "understands the way to it" (v. 23). In the end, so this poem concludes, wisdom is seen, declared, established, and searched out (v. 27) by the creator God who makes available wind, waters, rain, and thunderbolt. Wisdom is God's force in the working of creation.

Eventually, in the well-known passage of Prov 8:22-31, wisdom is "created" (*qnh*) "at the beginning of his work...before the beginning of the earth. When there were no depths I was brought forth, when there were no springs abounding with water" (vv. 22–24). Wisdom, according to this remarkable poem, occupies an intermediate place between God and the world of creation.[25] On the one hand, wisdom is a "creature" who is "created" by God. On the other hand, wisdom, the capacity and agency for generating life-giving order, is prior to all creation and all (other) creatures:

---

25. The literature on Proverbs 8 is enormous. A good reference point is the discussion of von Rad, *Wisdom in Israel,* 149–57. See also Roland E. Murphy, "The Personification of Wisdom," in Day et al., *Wisdom in Ancient Israel,* 222–33.

> Before the mountains had been shaped,
> before the hills, I was brought forth (*ḥll*)—
> when he had not yet made earth and fields,
> or the world's first bits of soil.
> When he established the heavens, I was there,
> when he drew a circle on the face of the deep,
> when he made firm the skies above,
> when he established the fountains of the deep,
> when he assigned to the sea its limit,
> so that the waters might not transgress his command,
> when he marked out the foundations of the earth,
> then I was beside him.... (Prov 8:25-30)

"I was brought forth...I was there...I was beside him." This second agent of creation has a permanent place in the work of creation and peculiar intimacy with Yahweh in that work. It is ironic and important that in its characterization of the God so well hidden, Israel, at least in this text, is able to people the hiddenness of Yahweh imaginatively, so that alongside Yahweh stands Yahweh's associate in the wondrous achievement of creation (v. 30).[26] In spite of the hiddenness, Israel is able to say a great deal that breaks beyond all of its previous categories of doxology.

This text in Prov 8:22-31 stands oddly alone in the Old Testament, and how much attention should be paid to it is a great question.[27] The text does not appear to exercise much influence in the Old Testament itself. Nonetheless, it warrants our attention. It is clear that the notion of "the wisdom of God" continued to be prevalent after the Old Testament. It developed in apocryphal literature and it became important in New Testament Christianity.[28] The New Testament trajectories that are most common in the practice of the Western church are those of the Synoptic traditions and the juridical casting of the gospel in the Pauline letters to the Romans and Galatians. These letters focus on the ethical dimension of the gospel, which issues in the categories of sin and grace. This theological tendency is linked to the Old Testament through the covenantal-Deuteronomic-prophetic traditions of Israel's testimony concerning Yahweh.

Johannine and Pauline sapiential themes. Two other tendencies in the New Testament bear upon the hidden character of Yahweh that has wisdom as first creation. A usage of the wisdom tradition seems clear in the Fourth Gospel, which has ethical implications but is primarily concerned with the abiding presence of God in the world. Thus John 1:1-18 may indeed begin with an allusion to Gen

---

26. I use the open-ended reference "Yahweh's associate" to refer to the *'amon* mentioned in v. 30. The meaning of the term is not clear. For a review of the problem and of the possible interpretations, see von Rad, *Wisdom in Israel*, 152; Bostrom, *The God of the Sages*, 55; and William McKane, *Proverbs: A New Approach* (OTL; London: SCM Press, 1970) 356–58.

27. See also Sirach 24, on which see von Rad, *Wisdom in Israel*, 240–62.

28. Apparently the Q source in the New Testament is to be understood as the development of a sapiential inclination in early Christianity. See C. M. Tuckett, "Q (Gospel Source)," *ABD* 5:567–72.

1:1, but insofar as the theme of this great overture is Logos, it is a direct derivation from the sapiential account of Proverbs 8, for it is this wisdom that was "with God...and without [whom] not one thing came into being."[29] It is an advance beyond Proverbs, to be sure, to take the step after "was with God" and say, as does the evangelist, "was God." But it is not a far step, for Proverbs 8 already wants to say, under the aegis of wisdom, that the whole of creation is shot through with the rationality and intentionality of Yahweh, a rationality and intentionality that need not be visible and intrusive because they are inherent in the very character and structure and fabric of creation itself. It is this intrinsic quality of intentionality that God has embedded in the working of creation to which John 1:1-18 bears witness, and to which the church testifies in Jesus of Nazareth. As "wisdom theology" of this sort has not been much credited in Old Testament theology, so in like fashion it has been exceedingly difficult in Western catholic faith to allow for an articulation of the gospel that falls outside of and is not shaped by the Pauline categories of sin and grace. But such an articulation of the gospel can be found in the Fourth Gospel, when that testimony is taken for itself and is not squeezed to be a poor replica of the Synoptics and not gerrymandered to serve the more insistent and better-known categories of Paul.

Even in the Pauline trajectory of New Testament Christianity, the wisdom teaching from Proverbs 8 was not neglected. In the letters of Paul himself, two texts evidence an awareness of this tradition. In Rom 11:33-36, Paul has reached the end of his tortured and unsatisfying argument about Jews and Christians. He is not able to bring his argument to a reasonable conclusion that is logically persuasive, but must break out in a doxology to the hidden, inscrutable intentionality of Yahweh that will work out its purposes well beyond human rationality and articulation:

O the depth of the riches and wisdom and knowledge of God! How unsearchable are his judgments and how inscrutable are his ways!

"For who has known the mind of the Lord?
Or who has been his counselor?"
"Or who has given a gift to him,
    to receive a gift in return?" (Rom 11:33-35)

It is significant that it is the riches, wisdom, and knowledge of God that are evoked, without reference to the expected categories of justification. The world, governed by God's goodness, is larger, more inscrutable, and better intentioned— that is, wiser—than Paul can factor out. And in 1 Cor 1:18-25, Paul becomes

---

29. Formally John 1 would seem to parallel the creation narrative of Genesis 1. In terms of substance, however, the Logos of John 1 seems to be much more parallel to the figure of wisdom in Proverbs 8. This indicates that some tradents of early Christianity proceeded in such terms, not flinching from the hints that now vex those in the church who resist the elaboration of "wisdom" in relation to the character of God. Cf. Hans Weder, "Der Weisheit in menschlicher Gestalt: Weisheitstheologie im Johannesprolog als Paradigma einer biblischen Theologie," *New Directions in Biblical Theology* (ed. Sigfried Pedersen; Leiden: E. J. Brill, 1994) 143–79.

eloquent about the wisdom of God, which takes the form of foolishness, which is known in Jesus "who became for us wisdom from God" (v. 30).

To be sure, the motif is more prominent in the Deutero-Pauline texts that break beyond the juridical categories of Paul in a way that parallels the move of wisdom in the Old Testament beyond the categories of covenant. In Eph 1:8-9 and 3:9-10 the wisdom of God is linked to the mystery of God's purposes "hidden for ages in God who created all things." In Col 2:2-3 the writer again links wisdom and mystery to Christ:

> I want their hearts to be encouraged and united in love, so that they may have all the riches of assured understanding and have the knowledge of God's mystery, that is, Christ himself, in whom are hidden all the treasures of wisdom and knowledge.

It cannot be argued that these theological articulations are a direct appropriation of Proverbs 8. Nonetheless, these lyrical affirmations clearly are rooted in something like Proverbs 8, and they bespeak an indwelling mystery in the world, a mystery from God that has been kept hidden but on which the world depends, and that only belatedly has become visible. This is a christological maneuver well beyond the Old Testament, but it is a move that would not be taken without this textual rootage in Proverbs. A student of biblical faith, moreover, especially one who attends to the theological responsibility of the church, must consider that these categories are indeed neglected, unfamiliar, and mostly inaccessible to the horizon of the church that is oriented to Pauline, juridical categories of theology. This accent on the hidden mystery that makes the world possible is, in the testimonial grid of Israel, an attempt to speak meaningfully about Yahweh when the core testimony with its intense preoccupation with active verbs is no longer persuasive.

It may well be that in the Old Testament (with postexilic influence) and in the New Testament (with Hellenistic resources), the testifying community in a new cultural circumstance was required to speak differently. What is more important for theological purposes is the recognition that this testimony moves markedly against the old direct claims for Yahweh. Nonetheless, this way of speaking concedes nothing of importance about Yahweh. If anything, it dares to expand and intensify the scope and depth of the claim made for Yahweh; even before creation, with this delighting agent, Yahweh assured that the world would be fully permeated with an intentionality for life.

World-valuing theological discourse. It may be suggested that the theological adventuresomeness of Prov 8:22-31, in its originary utterance, served to create theological room inside the house of "covenantal nomism," which at times was surely constrictive. That is, Proverbs 8 imagines and articulates a way of God with the world that is not intrusive and occasional, but that is constant in its nurturing, sustaining propensity. It does indeed do "God-talk" in a different tone, which witnesses to the mystery that can only be expressed as intuitive, playful, suggestive, doxological language, and which therefore necessarily opens the way for speculation about the precise relationship between the world and God. Things of God are less clear and specific than in the old covenantalism focused on sovereignty. Thus it is my judgment that the positive intent of current "sophia theology" is to explore an alternative mode of theological discourse that is world-valuing and that pays primary attention to the blessings of life processes—the birthing, growing maternal gifts of God, on which the world daily depends.[30] The sobriety at the end of Proverbs 8 indicates that these gifts intrinsic to life processes are not apart from the insistent expectations of Yahweh:

> And now, my children, listen to me:
> happy are those who keep my ways.
> Hear instruction and be wise,
> and do not neglect it.
> Happy is the one who listens to me,
> watching daily at my gates,
> waiting beside my doors.
> For whoever finds me finds life
> and obtains favor from the Lord;
> but those who miss me injure themselves;
> all who hate me love death. (Prov 8:32-36)

The sobriety does not tone down the exuberance of the affirmation: that wisdom is, above any other creature, a thing of joy and delight to the creator.

"Sophia Theology" as Threat and as Resonance

While the urging of "sophia theology," in my judgment, is a matter of securing room for faith and a protest against a form of faith that allows no room, what worries the critics of this proposal apparently is that "sophia" is treated as a proper noun with a capital *S*, and so is a goddess distinct from Yahweh. Such a way of speech seems to challenge monotheism, which has been cast characteristically in terms of masculine virility.[31] There is no doubt that the Old Testament has a monotheizing tendency.[32] There is also no doubt, however, that the Old Testament allows for Yahweh to be surrounded by a full court of subsidiary agents and is not embarrassed about living at the edge of a continuing polytheism.[33] Yahweh

---

30. These aspects of blessing in the world have been much appreciated by Claus Westermann, though he has not been interested in the "wisdom connection." On the life-force in the processes of creation, see Harrelson, *From Fertility Cult to Worship;* and on the wisdom (*sophia*) of God as a generative force, see Elizabeth A. Johnson, *She Who Is: The Mystery of God in a Feminist Theological Discourse* (New York: Crossroad, 1992).

31. On Yahweh with reference to metaphors of governance, see above pp. 233–50 and 272–75. These metaphors, showing the virility of God, have been exposited especially by G. Ernest Wright, *The Old Testament and Theology* (New York: Harper and Row, 1969) 70–150.

32. So James A. Sanders, "Adaptable for Life: The Nature and Function of the Canon," *From Sacred Story to Sacred Text: Canon as Paradigm* (Philadelphia: Fortress Press, 1987) 9–39.

33. See Larry W. Hurtado, *One God, One Lord: Early Christian Devotion and Ancient Jewish Monotheism* (London: SCM Press, 1988). Conversely, Norman Whybray, *The Heavenly Counsellor in*

may have many messengers, spirits, angels of all sorts, who effect Yahweh's will in and for creation. Clearly, *ḥokmah-sophia* is, in some texts of Proverbs, a free and independent agent who works at the behest of Yahweh; this agent is cast in feminine language, not only in terms of grammar, but metaphorically as in contrast to "the loose woman."[34]

My inclination, then, is to think that the recent explorations in sophia theology are not incongruent with explorations carried on in the text itself, explorations that seem authorized in continuing the process that is present in the text. The text itself is enormously venturesome in voicing Yahweh in this way, at least as venturesome as some present proposals. I suggest that the negative response to this contemporary exploration (a response that strikes me as disproportionate to the work itself) is in part explained by the fact that those biblical ventures and the texts that exhibit them are unknown and unavailable in the church due to the relentless focus of Western theology, so that the venture sounds more "unbiblical" than it may be. Moreover, I have no doubt that the response in part is to a perceived threat to the political-moral interpretive control that reductionist authority in the Western church has practiced and advocated. While this sense of threat, driven at least in part driven by ignorance of the trajectories and in part by anxiety about loss of control, needs to be honored, such a sense of threat is not the last word on the subject.

Inscrutable Mystery and Ethical Reliability

Israel's countertestimony to Yahweh's hiddenness in the fabric of creation—that Yahweh authorized before creation a feminine subsidiary agent—is indeed a move beyond Deuteronomic covenantalism. Whatever else is to be made of it, this venture in countertestimony makes unmistakably clear that Yahweh must be uttered in many ways. One of the alternative ways of utterance is to speak about a life-authorizing, life-giving, life-sustaining mystery that is completely beyond the horizon of Israel's core testimony. Such an articulation of Yahweh will allow the interpretive community, self-aware and self-critical as it may be, no monopoly on its discernment of Yahweh. Privilege yes, but not monopoly.

The countertestimony of Israel makes a nice and compelling connection between the inscrutable mystery of God's wisdom and the unvarying ethical reliability of deeds-consequences. That is, the work of the inscrutable mystery of God in sustaining the world is to make the world coherent, reliable, and viable. To do that, it is necessary that the "reasonableness" of Yahweh's world should issue in an ethical certitude that human actions, undertaken responsibly or irresponsibly, have cosmic

---

Isaiah XL 13-14: A Study of the Sources of the Theology of Deutero-Isaiah (Cambridge: Cambridge University Press, 1971), has shown that in Isa 40:13-14, any associate for Yahweh is explicitly and vigorously denied.

34. On the issues of the personification and/or hypostasis of wisdom in the Book of Proverbs, see Bostrom, *The God of the Sages*, 51–59. See also Carol A. Newsom, "Women and the Discourse of Patriarchal Wisdom: A Study of Proverbs 1-9," *Gender and Difference in Ancient Israel* (ed. Peggy L. Day; Minneapolis: Fortress Press, 1989) 142–60.

significance. And that is indeed the primary claim of proverbial wisdom: There is a match between acts taken and consequences received.[35] Human agents can count on that match. Over time, the community can arrive at a predictability that is almost scientific in its precision. Thus pride will end in disgrace (Prov 11:2). "Those who are kind (*ḥsd*) reward themselves, but the cruel (*'kzr*) do themselves harm" (Prov 11:17). That is how it works. One can count on it.

The problem with such an ethical horizon is that Yahweh's sovereignty evaporates. Yahweh becomes nothing more than a remote "watchmaker," who has authorized a self-operating moral calculus. There is a lot of truth in such a view, and Israel knew that truth and relied on it in its daily life. In the end, however, such a modest role for Yahweh is a conclusion that Israel would not draw, even in its acknowledgment of Yahweh's indirection and hiddenness. On occasion, then, in texts of which von Rad has made a great deal, the countertestimony of Israel refuses the logic of "deeds-consequences" and reasserts the freedom of Yahweh:[36]

> The plans of the mind belong to mortals,
> but the answer of the tongue is from the Lord.
> All one's ways may be pure in one's own eyes,
> but the Lord weighs the spirit. (Prov 16:1-2)

> The human mind plans the way,
> but the Lord directs the steps. (Prov 16:9)

> House and wealth are inherited from parents,
> but a prudent wife is from the Lord. (Prov 19:14)

> The human mind may devise many plans,
> but it is the purpose of the Lord that will be established. (Prov 19:21)

> All our steps are ordered by the Lord;
> How then can we understand our own ways? (Prov 20:24)

> No wisdom, no understanding, no counsel,
> can avail against the Lord.
> The horse is made ready for the day of battle,
> but the victory belongs to the Lord. (Prov 21:30-31)

In each of these sayings an authoritative human act or decision is set alongside and contradicted by a counter-act or decision on the part of Yahweh. The effect of the contrast is to assert that human acts, even "deeds" that produce "consequences," are penultimate. What is ultimate and decisive are the predisposition and inclination of Yahweh, who may override human intentionality and therefore deny a deed its anticipated consequence—that is, break the moral certainty given by the "deeds-consequences" construct.

---

35. See n. 16 above and the programmatic essay of Klaus Koch cited there. This construct of reality is operative both in the "early" prudential wisdom and in "later" theological wisdom.

36. See von Rad, *Old Testament Theology*, 1:438–41.

This characteristic and reiterated conclusion of sapiential countertestimony has at least three possible interpretations. First, on the face of it, this is an assertion that life in the real world is inscrutable and cannot be controlled or predicted; there is something deeply loose and volatile about life in the world. This is an insight much accented later by Ecclesiastes. Second, von Rad understands this conclusion to be primarily an assertion of the limit of human knowledge.[37] That is, human wisdom cannot comprehend what is unruly in experience. Third, as countertestimony concerning Yahweh, these statements are not only a judgment about human limitation, but also an assertion of Yahweh's sovereign freedom. Yahweh is completely unfettered and without obligation, even to righteous people who live inside the deeds-consequences arrangement. This accent becomes primary in the poem of Job. This inscrutability, remarkably enough, does not lead the countertestimony of Israel to retreat from its Yahwistic claims, but to escalate them, even though the decisiveness of Yahweh remains deeply hidden.

The way in which this ultimate affirmation of Yahweh is articulated, however, is odd. These sayings seem reluctant to grant to Yahweh any active verbs. Of the eight verses from Proverbs noted above, five assign Yahweh no verb at all, but only a preposition. Thus in 16:1, 19:14, and 20:24, what is decisive is "from Yahweh." In 21:30-31, the two prepositions are "against" (*ngd*) and "to" (*l*). In 19:21, moreover, the verb is passive, "will be established" (*taqûm*). Only in two of these passages is a direct, active verb assigned to Yahweh. In 16:9, the verb translated "direct" is *kûn;* this, as we shall see, is a preferred word with which to speak about Yahweh's hidden, long-term providential care. The other verb, in 16:2, rendered "weigh," is *tōkēn*, which may be linked to *kûn*.[38] This word is used in Job 28:25, Isa 40:12, and Ps 75:3, in order to assert Yahweh's majestic power as the orderer and governor of all of creation. But it is not a verb that witnesses to any direct, visible act on Yahweh's part.

Thus all of these sayings, which stand over against the more usual and more conventional assertions of deeds-consequences, assert the final, free governance of Yahweh. But that governance keeps the largeness of Yahweh's rule commensurate with the hidden, indirect way of its working. The positive intent of this countertestimony is the claim that human life is lived in a well-ordered, reliable world in which Yahweh grants nothing outside of Yahweh's governance. But the continuing spin-off of the claim is that this sure sovereign governance cannot be harnessed for any human purpose by thought or action. The countertestimony yields a God fully in control, but scarcely accessible and not at all reliable. From that the wisdom tradition may derive a large zone of human freedom and responsibility (as in Proverbs), or on another reading (like that of Ecclesiastes), a great depth of anxiety, which ends in melancholy pointed toward despair.

---

37. Von Rad, *Wisdom in Israel*, 97–110.
38. See BDB, 1067.

Finally, two texts, both linked to David, exhibit this same conviction about hidden governance. In 2 Samuel 15–18, Absalom rebels against David in an attempt to seize the throne. Absalom, in his rebellion, is given wise counsel by Ahithophel, who has defected from David, and false counsel by Hushai, who intends to subvert the rebellion in the interest of serving David. Absalom accepts the false advice of Hushai, to his own great detriment. In commenting on Absalom's foolish decision of strategy, the narrator says:

> For the Lord had ordained to defeat the good counsel of Ahithophel, so that the Lord might bring ruin on Absalom. (2 Sam 17:14)

The key verb *ṣwh* is conventionally translated in most contexts as "command." The conventional English rendering in this text, as in the NRSV, is "ordained." The verb is used, as von Rad had suggested, to speak about the hiddenness and decisiveness of Yahweh in human events, in this case the protection of David's throne. Our interest is in the gingerly but shrewd way in which the narrative makes the statement.[39] It is clear that Yahweh is presiding over the affairs of David and Absalom, but that governance is not visible. Things simply seem to happen, albeit in David's favor. Israel, now without the visible access to which it was accustomed in its core testimony, must make its Yahwistic claim in a very different way.

In 2 Sam 24:1 (cf. 1 Chr 21:1, where the same verb has been reassigned to a different subject), Yahweh is said to have "incited" (*sûth*) David to a self-destructive act, which Yahweh is then eager to punish. Aside from the wonderment about Yahweh's intention in this act, we focus simply on the verb *incite* (elsewhere "allure, instigate"). We are not told in the text how this instigating act of Yahweh was performed. But surely the verb means to suggest that in hiddenness, subtlety, and indirection, David was led (by desire?) to undertake the act of a census. In any other context, one might read "David decided." But the narrator will not have it so. The narrator will not place even the ambitious David beyond the reach of Yahweh's relentless governance. David decided penultimately; but ultimately and unequivocally, it is Yahweh who directs the steps.

The hidden ordering of Yahweh, to which Israel's countertestimony bears witness, matches Israel's sense of inscrutability about its own life. Israel could observe, in its candor, that there is no complete match between the claims of the core testimony and the experienced vagaries of its daily life. It was not difficult for cross-examination to expose the incongruities, even though much could be cited in the life of Israel that was congruous with the high claims made for Yahweh. Because Israel was not prepared, even in its critical countertestimony, to abandon its assertion of Yahweh's faithful sovereignty and sovereign fidelity, Israel was required to assert Yahweh's hiddenness.

---

39. See von Rad, *Wisdom in Israel*, 103–4 on 2 Sam 17:14.

Affirmation of Yahweh's Providence

The hiddenness that runs through and beneath and beyond what is visible in Israel's life is marked by Yahweh's sovereignty (Yahweh's resolve to have Yahweh's own way) and by Yahweh's fidelity (Yahweh's good, positive, and benign intention for Israel and for the world). This substantive content to Yahweh's hiddenness is commonly understood as an affirmation of Yahweh's providence. It is important to note that I discuss that claim of providence as countertestimony and not as part of Israel's core testimony. I place it here because an affirmation of providence became possible and necessary in Israel only when it was apparent that the direct and visible ways of Yahweh's working were not adequate and credible for much of Israel's life.

Providence is not a biblical word, and we cannot easily point to a semantic field to express this conviction about Yahweh, as we have been able to do with much else assigned to Yahweh. Indeed, it may be telling that we are unable to identify characteristic verbs for this affirmation, because the working of what is called providence is too hidden and inscrutable even to admit of direct verbal articulation. We may nonetheless identify two verbs, oddly used, that attest to the hidden way in which Yahweh's faithful sovereignty and sovereign fidelity look after Yahweh's partner in decisive ways. The first verb, *kûn*, might be rendered "arrange," in the sense of "make arrangements for":

> You visit the earth and water it,
> you greatly enrich it;
> the river of God is full of water;
> you provide (*kûn*) the people with grain,
> for so you have prepared (*kûn*) it. (Ps 65:9)

> Even though he struck the rock so
> that water gushed out,
> and torrents overflowed,
> can he also give bread,
> or provide (*kûn*) meat for his people? (Ps 78:20)

> Who provides (*kûn*) for the raven its prey,
> when its young ones cry to God,
> and wander about for lack of food? (Job 38:41)

In all three of these uses, reference is to Yahweh's feeding work, which sustains life.[40] In Ps 78:20, recalcitrant, doubting Israel, while acknowledging the wonder of water from the rock (cf. Exod 17:1-7), asks whether meat can be "arranged" for Israel in the same way. This text is Israel-specific. In two other texts, the horizon is more expansive and concerns Yahweh as the sustaining Creator of the world. Thus

---

40. Rolf P. Knierim, "The Task of Old Testament Theology," *HBT* 6 (June 1984) 38–40, has suggested the need for a "theology of food." These several texts would readily supply the basis for such an enterprise. More generally on providence, see the marvelous exposition by J. R. Lucas, *Freedom and Grace* (London: SPCK, 1976) 38, 48.

in Psalm 65, Yahweh "visits" (*pqd*), "waters" (*šqb*), and "enriches" (*'šr*) the earth, and "arranges" (*kûn*) grain. In the Job reference, by way of a defiant rhetorical question, Yahweh is said to provide food for the raven. Thus Yahweh makes the necessary arrangements so that all of creation and all creatures will have what they need in order to live.

A second verb, used twice in relation to our theme, is *r'h*, "to see":

> Abraham said, "God himself will provide (*r'h*) the lamb for a burnt offering, my son." (Gen 22:8, cf. v. 14)

> I will send you to Jesse the Bethlehemite, for I have provided (*r'h*) for myself a king among his sons. (1 Sam 16:1)

In both of these cases the action of Yahweh concerns Israel, once with reference to Abraham and Isaac, and once concerning a king. But the verb *see* is an odd one in such cases, in which the context clearly requires *provide*. Karl Barth has suggested that *see* means *provide*, if we take it as "pro-video"—to see beforehand, to pro-vide.[41] Thus in Genesis 22, Yahweh has seen beforehand that a ram would be needed for sacrifice, and in 1 Samuel 16, Yahweh has made advance preparations for a new boy-king. The positive aspect of this usage is that Yahweh takes a very long view and plans well ahead to protect the world (and Israel) from crises with which it could not by itself cope. This tradition of hiddenness thus bears witness to a God who is not bound to the present moment of crisis, but who acts in faithful sovereignty over the very long haul for the well-being of Yahweh's partner. But at the same time that the verbs are positive, they are also quite odd. What does it mean to *arrange* or *to see beforehand*? The verbs are not as direct and concrete as the verbs of the core recital. They acknowledge Yahweh's indirectness in governance, or at least recognize Israel's lack of direct access to the inscrutable ways of Yahweh that are reliable but not evident.

In any case, these texts exemplify the sweeping conviction of Israel that Yahweh's long-term, life-guaranteeing intentionality is at work in the world in decisive ways. The world is under Yahweh's powerful care, and the fidelity of Yahweh assures that all that the world needs will be provided. This is indeed a sweeping theological claim, but we should notice that the good intention of Yahweh, while as large as all creation, is as daily and concrete and material as daily bread (cf. Pss 104:27-28; 145:15-16; Matt 6:11, 25-31). This is no absentee ruler, but one who plans ahead, thinks ahead, works ahead, and acts ahead, so that the world of real possibility is ready and waiting in Yahweh's enormous generosity.

Yahweh as Primal Cause of Good and Bad

The claim of hiddenness, as enunciated in the countertestimony of wisdom and the assertion of providence, features Yahweh's large, benign, generous governance

---

41. Karl Barth, *Church Dogmatics* 3/3, *The Doctrine of Creation* (Edinburgh: T. & T. Clark, 1960) 3, 35.

of all of creation. This claim yields a great sovereignty that proceeds in inscrutable ways over long sweeps of time to work good for the world. Such an affirmation, reassuring as it is, does not usually focus on specific moments in the life of Israel. As a result, as we shall see, this claim of hiddenness generates other problems for the faith of Israel. But for now, we may complete this part of our reflection on Israel's countertestimony about Yahweh's hidden, inscrutable, indirect, invisible ways of governance by considering two other affirmations that occur in various textual utterances.

In a variety of contexts, Yahweh is said to be the single cause of all that happens in the world—all that is good and all that is bad:

> See now that I, even I, am he;
> there is no god beside me.
> I kill and I make alive;
> I wound and I heal;
> and no one can deliver from my hand. (Deut 32:39)

> The Lord kills and brings to life;
> he brings down to Sheol and raises up.
> The Lord makes poor and makes rich;
> he brings low, he also exalts. (1 Sam 2:6-7)

> I form light and create darkness,
> I make weal and create woe;
> I the Lord do all these things. (Isa 45:7; cf. Job 5:18; Isa 14:24-27;
>   Dan 4:35)

These statements make an enormous claim for Yahweh, and they occur in a variety of contexts and genres in order to serve a number of functions. The assertions variously function as a reprimand to human pride and autonomy; as a rebuke to would-be rival gods; and, as in the case of Hannah, as an assurance and consolation before the fact of newness, or as a celebration after the fact.

If the statements are taken in a speculative way, they yield a kind of monism that is endlessly problematic.[42] But of course that is not their intention, for Israel's theological rhetoric is not characteristically intended for speculation, even though it has sometimes been taken so in the history of interpretation. These assertions are not in the service of speculative or metaphysical claims. They are addressed to Israel's embrace of faith in concrete situations, and they are disputatious claims. They oppose these thoughts:

- that gods alternative to Yahweh have reality (Deut 32:39);

- that people are hopelessly fated in their circumstance (1 Sam 2:6-7);

---

42. See the review of the problem by Fredrik Lindström, *God and the Origin of Evil: A Contextual Analysis of Alleged Monistic Evidence in the Old Testament* (Lund: CWK Gleerup, 1983).

- that human autonomy can proceed as it wants (Dan 4:35);

- that counter political power can resist Yahweh (Isa 14:24-27).

These assertions of Yahweh's sovereignty thus make a practical and nontheoretical claim, and they intend a decision in the moment of utterance for this version of reality that has the majestic Yahweh at its center.

The Plan of Yahweh

A second way in which Israel presents its countertestimony that Yahweh is sovereign but hidden is to speak about the "plan of Yahweh." This phrase has been endlessly problematic in theological interpretation, as it has lent itself to all kinds of scholastic notions of a blueprint for determinism. In general, scholars have followed Bertil Albrektson in the conclusion that the Old Testament includes no notion of a plan in such a specific and rigid sense.[43] Nonetheless, Israel does speak of Yahweh's *ḥšb*, which may be variously rendered "plan" or "thought," and which has the connotation of an enduring intentionality. We may cite four texts that are fairly representative of this claim made for Yahweh. The story of Joseph, which features a well-hidden God seldom visible in the narrative, culminates with this affirmation, as Joseph addresses his brothers:

> Even though you intended (*ḥšb*) to do harm to me, God intended (*ḥšb*) it for good, in order to preserve a numerous people, as he is doing today. (Gen 50:20)

As the narrative stands, it is only in retrospect that the narrator (or the character in the narrative) can discern that Yahweh's powerful intentionality has been at work, not only through the vagaries of lived experience, but through the malicious intent of the brothers. In this usage, Yahweh's intention is a counterintention that persists to override and defeat the deathly plan of the brothers. It is important that the affirmation is placed at the end of the narrative, for even Israel cannot know this certitude until it looks back on what has happened.

In two texts the same language is used about Yahweh's intention in, through, and beyond the exile:

> For surely I know the plans (*ḥšb*) I have for you, says the Lord, plans for your welfare (*shalôm*) and not for harm, to give you a future with hope. (Jer 29:11)

> For my thoughts (*ḥšb*) are not your thoughts,
> nor are your ways my ways,
> says the Lord.

---

43. Bertil Albrektson, *History and the Gods: An Essay on the Idea of Historical Events as Divine Manifestations in the Ancient Near East and in Israel* (ConBOT Series 1; Lund: CWK Gleerup, 1967). The study of Albrektson has been rightly valued in scholarship as a way past any scholastic understanding of "plan" attributed to God. Yet, without such rigidity, it is clear that the Isaiah tradition, for example, does acknowledge Yahweh's general intentionality, which cannot be reduced to a rigid blueprint. See Walter Brueggemann, "Planned People/Planned Book?" (forthcoming).

> For as the heavens are higher than the earth,
> so are my ways higher than your ways,
> and my thoughts than your thoughts. (Isa 55:8-9)

In its circumstance of exile, Judah might have concluded that Yahweh had a malicious plan for it. Or it might have judged that plans other than those of Yahweh would prevail, either because Yahweh was inattentive or because Yahweh lacked power. The statement of Jeremiah 29 does not go back to undo all that has happened to Israel heretofore, nor even to comment on the recent suffering of Israel. Rather the "plan" now operative for Judah is forward-looking and concerns Israel's future well-being in the land. The point of the assertion is that Yahweh's large, positive intentionality for Israel is indeed operative, even for the moment in which Israel might despair. Thus the countertestimony that focuses on the hiddenness of Yahweh is nonetheless made in force against circumstance. Yahweh's plan is at work and will prevail, even though everything about the circumstance tells otherwise.

In the quote from Isaiah 55, Yahweh's plan runs counter to "your thoughts, your ways." We are not told what the thoughts and plans of Israel in exile, which are here to be overridden, may have been. They are likely plans and thoughts of despair (cf. Isa 49:14), which may have as their outcome a decision to knuckle under and submit to Babylonian power, thus to abandon Israelite-covenantal-Yahwistic identity.[44] The assertion of Yahweh's intentionality, however, vetoes such an intention on Israel's initiative. This assertion of Yahweh thus functions as a powerful assurance: Israel is not to resign itself in its despair. But the assertion is also a summons to remember its identity as Yahweh's people, and to act in the risky ways that are congruent with Yahweh's intentionality. Specifically this means to cease to accommodate Babylonian power and Babylonian ideology. Thus the very assertion of Yahweh's hidden but sovereign intention, which is a consolation and assurance, is also a summons to dangerous obedience.

The same claim for Yahweh's enduring intention that is voiced concerning the public crisis of exile is available for assurance and consolation in personal faith. In Psalm 40 the speaker voices acute trouble and trusts in Yahweh's mercy, steadfast love, and faithfulness (*rḥm, ḥsd, 'mth*). The psalm concludes:

> As for me, I am poor and needy,
> but the Lord takes thought (*ḥšb*) for me.
> You are my help and my deliverer;
> do not delay, O my God. (v. 17)

Yahweh attends to the poor and needy, and therefore hope exists in a context of deep distress. The speaker waits on the long-term positive resolve and regard of

---

44. See Norman K. Gottwald, "Social Class and Ideology in Isaiah 40–55: An Eagletonian Reading," *The Bible and Liberation: Political and Social Hermeneutics* (ed. Norman K. Gottwald and Richard A. Horsley; rev. ed.; Maryknoll, N.Y.: Orbis Books, 1993) 329–42.

Yahweh, which can, when enacted, override every deathly circumstance. All the term *ḥśv* yields, however, is long-term intention. In the complaint of this psalm, it does not yet yield anything direct or visible, but the speaker has confidence nonetheless.

Summary

It is evident that Israel had to learn to live (and testify) in contexts where the intense engagement of Yahweh, as given in the great transformative verbs of the core testimony, simply was not available. It is profoundly important that this lack of availability did not lead Israel to the retreat from its theological claims about Yahweh or to be silent about Yahweh. It led, instead, to venturesome alternative strategies of testimony. Yahweh was "taken underground" into hiddenness and inscrutability. But for all of that, Yahweh in indirectness and invisibility is no less decisive. Indeed, in its countertestimony, Israel used the occasion of Yahweh's hiddenness to magnify its claims for the generous, creative, and faithful governance of Yahweh. Yahweh is, in the face of hard evidence, said to be a practitioner and guarantor of joyous, life-giving coherence, the cause of all good and evil, the one with durable intentions for well-being in Israel.

This cluster of testimonies and the categories in which they are expressed tend to be alien to the current popular rhetoric of the church. But for all of the neglect of these texts and themes in much of the church, they are viable and freighted alternative categories in which Yahweh may be uttered. Recovery of these texts and categories of utterance and attentiveness to them are an urgent matter, in my judgment, in a cultural circumstance of faith in which the "hotter" theological categories tend to lead either to coercive authoritarianism or, alternatively, to an uncritical response that is expressed either as benign, therapeutic subjectivity or as hostile autonomy. *The countertestimony of Israel is more durable, substantive, and wiser than either authoritarianism or distancing subjectivity might suggest.*

While Israel's answers about Yahweh, in countertestimony as response to the questions of cross-examination, might be less powerful than the core testimony, it is in any case important that Israel entertained the questions, honored them, and exercised great intellectual courage and great faith in making response. While the questions posed as cross-examination are nowhere explicitly answered, we may imagine the answers that arise in the material we have considered:

Where now is your God? Here and everywhere, but in ways one cannot administer.

How long? Until I am ready.

Why have you forsaken? My reasons are my own and will not be given to you.

Is Yahweh among us? Yes, in decisive ways, but not in ways that will suit you.

The questions are honored and taken seriously, but the Yahweh given in the cross-examination is not defeated by the questions or made captive to them. The responses offered in fact displace the questions rather than answer them. Yahweh emerges intact from the ordeal of cross-examination in wisdom literature, but not as given in the core testimony uttered prior to the cross-examination and its demanding circumstance.

TEN

Ambiguity and the Character of Yahweh

I<small>N ITS CORE TESTIMONY</small>, Israel has uttered Yahweh as a God who is straightforward in dealing with Yahweh's partners. In Israel's cross-examination, Yahweh emerges not only hidden as in wisdom theology but also on occasion as devious, ambiguous, irascible, and unstable.[1] This aspect of Israel's countertestimony is much more radical than the benign recognition of Yahweh's hiddenness that we have just considered. The evidence for this is not found in what we would regard as self-conscious theological statements in the Old Testament, such as the ones we have considered in Israel's core testimony. Rather the evidence occurs almost inadvertently, in contexts of extreme emotional investment, or as a by-product in narratives that seem to be concerned with other matters. These voices of witness, nonetheless, constitute a part of Israel's countertestimony, and while these texts are commonly disregarded in more formal theology, they are important data for our understanding of who Yahweh is said by Israel to be.

Because of the ad hoc nature of this evidence, we are reduced to a rather ad hoc approach. I will, however, order the evidence under three rubrics: abusiveness, contradictory conduct, and unreliability. It is evident that this, or other material like it, could be cited and ordered in other ways. The intention of cross-examination is not, however, to provide a coherent picture. Its purpose is only to acknowledge and to take into account that which the core testimony, whether by choice and intentional selection or unwittingly, has not recognized.

Does Yahweh Abuse?

There is some evidence that Yahweh is *abusive* on occasion, *acting in ways not congruent with the claim of the core testimony that Yahweh is "steadfast and faithful."* The parade example of this sense of Yahweh is the extremely passionate statement of Jeremiah:

---

1. See Timothy K. Beal, "The System and the Speaking Subject in the Hebrew Bible: Reading for Divine Abjection," *Biblical Interpretation* 2 (July 1994) 171–89.

> O Lord, you have enticed me,
> and I was enticed;
> you have overpowered me,
> and you have prevailed. (Jer 20:7)

This speech employs a human figure, uttered by a voice that reflects profound disturbance. But as elsewhere in the Bible, we are habituated to regard testimony as revelatory.[2] Insofar as we can recover anything about the person of Jeremiah, he suffered mightily for his loyal obedience to Yahweh. Either he, or the tradition that presents him, makes use of the psalms of complaint in order to accuse and assault Yahweh for what is experienced as abusive behavior on Yahweh's part.[3]

Deception and Enticement

The last in the sequence of Jeremiah's complaints, 20:7-18, is surely the most extreme and most savage, as though the speaker has lost the capacity to reason with or about Yahweh. Our interest centers on v. 7, wherein the poem uses the term *pth*, which in this reference is usually rendered "deceive," though the NRSV renders "entice." It is an extraordinary term to use with reference to Yahweh. When it is rendered "deceive," it suggests that Yahweh has been dishonest, has misrepresented or misled in order to have Yahweh's way. The term, however, is more poignant than this suggests, because elsewhere the word characteristically has sexual overtones. It is used directly to refer to manipulative or violent sexual exploitation (Exod 22:16; Judg 14:15, 16:5; Job 31:9), wherein the proposed sexual partner is either taken by deception or is forcibly seized. Thus we are in a world of sexual abuse and violence, so that the term allows for the nuance of rape.

A second way in which the term *pth* is used is for illicit religious affection—worship of illicit gods, who are treated with a sexual metaphor of promiscuity that violates one's proper loyalty (Deut 11:16; Job 31:27; and perhaps Prov 1:10). This latter usage is a metaphorical construal that may imply that the other gods are whores, but the critique is characteristically leveled not against the gods but against those who wrongly worship them. Thus both literally and metaphorically, the term contains dimensions of illicit sexual usage, each of which is grossly negative.

It is astonishing that in three cases, including the Jeremiah text we have cited, the verb is used for Yahweh with such implications. In 1 Kgs 22:20-22, surely a "primitive" prophetic tale, the reader of the text is imagined into a discussion in "the divine council," a cabinet meeting of Yahweh's heavenly government (see parallels in Job 1–2). The discussion turns on the way in which King Ahab can be "enticed" to a military maneuver that will cause his death. The purpose of the narrative, and the purpose of the discussion in the divine council, is to assert Yahweh's

---

2. On the notion of testimony become revelation, see pp. 121–22.
3. On the use of complaint psalms in the laments of Jeremiah, see the classic study of Walter Baumgartner, *Jeremiah's Poems of Lament* (Sheffield: Almond Press, 1988).

decisive hostility toward Ahab and the dynasty of Omri and to assert Yahweh's hand in the governance of history—even royal history.

What interests us is the conversation in the government of Yahweh, which is as cynical and ignoble as anything the "plumbers" in Richard Nixon's White House might have devised. The strategy is to entice Ahab into foolish policy by a prophet who is credentialed by Yahweh to give bad advice to the king. Two matters interest us. First, the term *pth* occurs three times in the reported exchange:

YAHWEH: Who will entice him?

SPIRIT: I will entice him.

YAHWEH: You are to entice him.

The conversation is unambiguous. What is being planned is a massive deception of the king. Second, Yahweh fully colludes in the manipulative discussion, which aims at a royal death. Indeed, Yahweh is at the head of the conspiracy to cause a wrong death in royal Israel. Yahweh here obviously exercises no covenantal self-restraint, but is determined to have Yahweh's own way no matter what the cost, even if it means deceptive violence.

In another text, the term *pth* is used in what we may take to be a more positive way. The long poem of Hos 2:2-23 is arranged in two symmetrical parts.[4] In the first part (vv. 2-13), Yahweh is the affronted husband who with violent threats will terminate the marital relation with which Yahweh-husband is displeased. In v. 14, the poem does an abrupt about-face, and Yahweh now seeks to restore the relationship. The positive restoration of the relationship culminates (as we have seen) with a reiteration of Yahweh's best adjectives (vv. 19-20).[5] At the pivotal point in the poem, however, Yahweh says:

> Therefore, I will now allure her,
> and bring her into the wilderness,
> and speak tenderly to her. (v. 14)

The term rendered "allure" is the same verb, *pth*. The conventional understanding of this statement is that Yahweh "woos" the estranged wife-Israel, as an act of enormous, forgiving generosity, in order to reaccept the fickle wife-Israel back in covenant. That may be what is intended. We are, however, alerted by feminist hermeneutical considerations to pay careful attention to the terms of the reversal now proposed by Yahweh. We are invited by that awareness to wonder why the term *pth* is used for Yahweh's new initiative. Certainly the love-making implied here includes deceptions of exaggeration and overstatement, so that "speak tenderly" may mean "sweet nothings." Thus Yahweh is at least available for the types of deceptions characteristic of passionate love.

---

4. See David J. A. Clines, "Hosea 2: Structure and Interpretation," *Studia Biblica 1978* (JSOTSup 11; Sheffield: JSOT Press, 1979) 87–104.

5. On the recurring adjectives utilized in testimony to Yahweh, see chap. 5.

Beyond that, however, we are required to wonder if the verb also bespeaks something forcible, coercive, or violent about Yahweh. Is this an erratic husband who kicks out the wife, then compels her to return to a relationship that will, according to past evidence, continue to be abusive? Feminist literature notices the potential or implicit violence present in the husband imagery for Yahweh. Very likely, this is an overstatement of what is in the text. We are nevertheless alerted to wonder what the poet intends us to imagine happens in the hidden places where the relationship is restored. Is wife-Israel willing? Or did she have no alternative?

In any case, we return to the usage of *pth* in Jer 20:7. In this passage, there is nothing of a "primitive" justification for what is said about Yahweh, as there may be in 1 Kgs 22:20-22. Nor is there a possibility that the usage is positive, as in Hos 2:14. Jeremiah certainly did not say "allure" or "woo," but at least "deceive," and perhaps "rape." It is asserted that Jeremiah was forcibly, deceptively, abusively pressed into a relationship for loyalty toward Yahweh (cf. 1:4-10), a relationship in which Yahweh has not been fair, supportive, or constructive. To be sure, subsequent verses of the complaint reverse field to articulate trust (v. 11), petition (v. 12), and finally doxology (v. 13). Jeremiah, in his imbalance and extremity, exposes a sense of Yahweh that is less than honorable. One gets the impression from this lean but powerful utterance that Yahweh is, on occasion, an unprincipled bully who will coerce, manipulate, and exploit in order to have Yahweh's own way. Jeremiah has been a faithful and courageous mouthpiece for Yahweh, but he recognizes that his call was a one-way deal, with little support or affirmation from Yahweh. Jeremiah has been "had," and Yahweh is the one who "had" him. One may wonder if, with this verb, Yahweh has "had" others as well.

Does Yahweh Contradict?

There is evidence that Yahweh is a conundrum of contradictions, as though Yahweh's interior life is so convoluted that at some points it lacks consistency. Terence Fretheim has gathered the evidence to show that Yahweh may have a change of mind and heart.[6] But by contradiction and inconsistency, I mean not an acknowledged change, but *a powerful insistence, assertion, or decision that flies in the face of a previous insistence, assertion, or decision, without any acknowledgment of a reversal.*

I will cite four cases. In the first two, the oddness is contained within the text itself. In the second pair of texts, the oddness may be explained away on critical grounds. But because we take these disparate statements as theological data, we shall not take the escape of critical explanation.

---

6. Terence E. Fretheim, *The Suffering of God: An Old Testament Perspective* (OBT; Philadelphia: Fortress Press, 1984).

Flood Narrative

In the well-known flood story of Gen 6:5–9:17, the narrative begins with a profound awareness on Yahweh's part:[7]

> The Lord saw that the wickedness of humankind was great in the earth, and that every inclination of the thoughts of their hearts was only evil continually. (Gen 6:5)

That awareness leads to regret on Yahweh's part, and then a resolve:

> So the Lord said, "I will blot out from the earth the human beings I have created—people together with animals and creeping things and birds of the air, for I am sorry that I have made them." (Gen 6:7)[8]

The end of the narrative echoes 6:5:

> And when the Lord smelled the pleasing odor [of burnt sacrifices], the Lord said in his heart, "I will never again curse the ground because of humankind, for the inclination of the human heart is evil from youth; nor will I ever again destroy every living creature as I have done." (Gen 8:21)[9]

What interests us is the complete reversal of Yahweh's mood and intention from the beginning to the end of the narrative. The narrative does not linger over the motivation for the change, but the entire narrative depends on the change in Yahweh's inclination. Only two reasons are suggested for the reversal on Yahweh's part. In 8:1, "God remembered Noah," and the reversal begins. Such a statement suggests that until this moment, Yahweh had not remembered Noah. Indeed, Gen 9:14-16 also suggests that Yahweh's memory is not entirely dependable, so that it may be forgetfulness that causes Yahweh's destructive proposal. The second motivation suggested for the reversal is the pleasing smell of the sacrifice (8:21), suggesting that Yahweh's action, positive or negative, turns on an incidental human gesture. Taken as a whole, the narrative suggests that Yahweh has conflicting inclinations toward humanity and toward all creation, and that the tilt toward one inclination or the other may be caused by a minor factor.

Exodus Events

A very different sort of instability concerning Yahweh may be suggested in the initiation of the events of the Exodus (Exod 3:7-10). Yahweh is moved to engagement on behalf of Israel by the cry of the slaves (Exod 2:23-25). If we stay inside

---

7. Bernhard W. Anderson, "The Flood Story in Context: From Analysis to Synthesis," *From Creation to New Creation: Old Testament Perspectives* (OBT; Minneapolis: Fortress Press, 1994) 65–74, has shown that source analysis of the flood narrative is not in the end important. What counts is the pattern and structure of the final form of the text.

8. The judgment and resolve in these verses commonly assigned to J are paralleled in the Priestly statement of vv. 11-13.

9. The new resolve of Yahweh in these verses, commonly assigned to J, is paralleled in the Priestly statement of 9:8-17. The structure is exactly the same in what have been regarded as two distinct sources.

the narrative itself, we are offered no hint that Yahweh had noticed the oppression in Egypt until hearing the slaves' cry. It is the voiced pain of the slave community that evokes a response from Yahweh and moves Yahweh to active intervention. Given that motivation of the voiced pain, however, Yahweh is determined to act in intrusive, decisive ways on behalf of the slave community:

> I have observed the misery of my people who are in Egypt; I have heard their cry on account of their taskmasters. Indeed, I know their sufferings, and I have come down to deliver them from the Egyptians, and to bring them up out of that land to a good and broad land.... The cry of the Israelites has now come to me; I have also seen how the Egyptians oppress them. (Exod 3:7-9)

The series of first-person verbs, indicating Yahweh's resolve, intention, and action, is powerful and impressive: "*I know, I have come down* to deliver and to bring up ... *I have seen.*" Yahweh is filled with self-assertiveness.

Given that, the narrative takes an abrupt and odd turn at v. 10:

> So come, I will send you to Pharaoh to bring my people, the Israelites, out of Egypt.

Yahweh still has one active verb: "I will send." But it is Moses who will go. It is Moses who will run the risks, who will be the "point man" with pharaoh. It is legitimate to say with Austin Farrer, "The Hebrew commonly saw divine events as having creaturely agents."[10] We notice that Yahweh's "mighty acts," as attested in Israel's core testimony, are considerably changed by the centrality of a human agent and actor, in this case Moses. To be sure, Yahweh is fully present in full power, as Yahweh had promised: "I will be with you" (Exod 3:12). Yahweh's commitment and engagement are complete, but now they are mediated. Whereas the great verbs of Exod 3:7-9 bespeak Yahweh's direct intervention, in v. 10 it is "I will send you." Yahweh is engaged, but not without human agency.

On the surface, moreover, Moses is "on his own" before pharaoh. The readers of the text know more. They know Yahweh is with Moses, fully engaged in the confrontation. While the arrangement of hidden God–visible human agent is an effective one in the narrative, it is precisely this arrangement that severely tests Israel's confidence in the enterprise (Exod 4:1-9). If we understand the Exodus narrative as a scenario of human liberation, we can hardly object to this presentation of the matter. For our purposes, the point to be noticed is that Yahweh, in spite of determined intention, undertakes Israel's emancipation much less directly than Yahweh had announced.

To test this rhetorical turn, we may compare Yahweh's conduct with that of David in the narrative of 2 Sam 11:1 and 12:26-31. In reference to that narrative,

---

10. Austin Farrer, *Faith and Speculation: An Essay in Philosophical Theology* (London: Adam and Charles Black, 1967) 62.

David is regularly critiqued in commentary for having stayed behind in time of war, sending Joab in his place:

> In the spring of the year, the time when kings go out to battle, David sent Joab with his officers and all Israel with him; they ravaged the Ammonites, and besieged Rabbah. But David remained at Jerusalem. (2 Sam 11:1)

David is the sender, the instigator of the battle, but David runs no risks. Indeed, he has time for much other "sending" of a destructive kind (see the verb in vv. 3, 4, 6, 12, 14). We should not make too much of this, except to notice that Yahweh's role in the defeat of pharaoh is not unlike David's role in the defeat of Rabbah. Israel might have expected more of Yahweh, given Yahweh's bold self-announcement at the outset.

Commands Concerning Marriage

In our third text, Deut 24:1-4, Moses enunciates a case law that is taken, in the Book of Deuteronomy, to be a command of Yahweh. It concerns the rigorous requirements of marriage and the violation and termination thereof. When a marriage is terminated and the rejected wife is remarried, she cannot return to her first husband, even if they both wish it, because she is "defiled" (*ṭm'*). A return to the first husband would defile (*ṭm'*) the land, would make it an "abomination to Yahweh." This text reflects Yahweh as the enforcer and guarantor of patriarchal ordering of society of a most elemental kind. The command reflects the intimate connection between sexuality and the productivity of the land.[11] We might reject such a linkage of human sexuality and land productivity as exploitative and patriarchal, as well as primitive. What concerns us here, however, is not approval of the commandment, but rather Yahweh's complete commitment to the linkage. Yahweh is profoundly impacted and offended by such a disorder, which is a disorder of all of creation *in nuce*.

In the Book of Jeremiah, the poet appeals to this command from Moses:

> If a man divorces his wife
> and she goes from him
> and becomes another man's wife,
> will he return to her?
> Would not such a land be greatly polluted? (Jer 3:1)

The law of Moses is not only cited;[12] here it is the word of Yahweh. Moreover, after the actual citation, vv. 2-5 are an exposition of the command and the disastrous consequences caused by a fickle spouse. Israel, in her pollution, cannot return

---

11. On the intimate connection between treatment of sexuality and of the land, see Walter Brueggemann, "Land, Fertility, and Justice," *Theology of the Land* (ed. Bernard F. Evans and Gregory D. Cusack; Collegeville, Minn.: Liturgical Press, 1987) 41–68. In this regard, I have been much informed by the writings of Wendell Berry.

12. On this text, see Michael Fishbane, *Biblical Interpretation in Ancient Israel* (Oxford: Clarendon Press, 1985) 114–43.

to Yahweh. Yahweh fully subscribes to the old rule of defilement, and understands that the fickleness of Israel has produced a drought; that is, has prevented the earth from its proper function of fruitfulness. The distortion of covenant distorts creation.

What astounds us is that this exposition of the command of Moses in vv. 2-5, an exposition completely congruent with the original command, is immediately thrown over by Yahweh's pathos-filled utterance in vv. 12-14, 19-23. Yahweh now bids, in passionate, plaintive terms, that wife-Israel should return to her first husband, Yahweh. To be sure, the return entails repentance on the part of Israel. Yahweh's will is not mushy and romantic. But it is a powerful resolve that Israel should return, in direct challenge to the old command of Moses. It is clear that the old command, to which Yahweh has just subscribed, and Yahweh's present yearning for fickle Israel are in profound tension with each other. It is equally clear that Yahweh is willing to overthrow and contradict the old command of Moses, Yahweh's own command, for the sake of the relationship. Yahweh, as it turns out, cares more passionately for the relationship than for the old command.

It is easy enough to explain this change in Yahweh by appealing to developmentalism, to conclude that a later poet was required to speak of mercy that would negate the old law. But since the old law is here quoted with approval, and since the departure from it is in Yahweh's own mouth, we must take this as evidence, in the testimony of Israel, that Yahweh has an intense self-contradiction between norms and yearning. In this case, the yearning wins out. The yearning will not win out in every case. But we may imagine that the same issue is everywhere available to Yahweh and inescapable for Yahweh—as indeed it is wherever wounded love is affronted yet no less intense.

Contradiction Concerning Exclusionary Rules

Finally in this brief mention of seeming contradictions in Yahweh's own inclination, we make reference to the old law of Deut 23:1 and the list of "foreigners" in Deut 23:2-7. This list is concerned to maintain the purity of Israelite worship and Israelite community by rigorously excluding all those who are disqualified. The disqualification has to do with physical or genital flaw, or simply being an outsider to the community. It is a long stretch from this old command to the dispute reflected in Isa 56:3-8. But scholars have noticed the connection between the two passages, if for no other reason than the astonishing contrast between them.[13]

In Isaiah 56 the postexilic community is in dispute concerning who qualifies as a member. Against rigorous exclusivism, seemingly sanctioned by Deut 23:1-7, the oracle of Yahweh in Isa 56:3-8 insists that eunuchs (*srîs*) and "a foreigner" can indeed be admitted to the community by "hold[ing] fast my covenant." That is, the prohibition and the exclusionary rule of Deut 23:1-7 are not here operative. The

---

13. So Herbert Donner, "Jesaja LVI 1-7: Ein Abrogationsfall innerhalb des Kanons—Implikationen und Konsequenzen," *Congress Volume: Salamanca, 1983* (ed. J. A. Emerton; VTSup 36; Leiden: E. J. Brill, 1985) 81–95.

same Yahweh who uttered the old command, we are to believe, issues the present oracular invitation. In this latter case, it appears that Yahweh's open invitation prevails, but it will not always be so. We may believe, in considering these texts, that there is profound tension in Yahweh's life about who is "in" and who is "out." Thus Israel's cross-examination provides evidence that matters are not easily, once-for-all settled for Yahweh; through the life of Israel, Yahweh is beset by competing, conflicting inclinations.

Is Yahweh Unreliable?

Israel's countertestimony includes evidence that Yahweh, who has a resolve about Israel's historical process and a profound intentionality, is to some extent unreliable: that is, *unstable in working out that resolve and intentionality.* The evidence arises from Israel's narrative presentation of Israel's "history." The perspective of the narrative is focused on the outcomes of the human process of the story, and comment on the character of Yahweh is only incidental. That is, the narratives do not intend to be "doing theology," but intend rather to tell a marvelous story of human violence and bravery, love and manipulation. But because this is an Israelite tale, Yahweh is characteristically engaged and in purview. It is of enormous interest and importance to us that Israel's storytellers are, without reflection, justification, or defensiveness—indeed, even without self-awareness—able to render Yahweh as a character of some unreliability. The texts to which I refer all concern the triangle of Samuel, Saul, and David, the "great men" who preoccupied Yahweh's effort and Israel's imagination, and who provided the primary material for Israel's storytellers.

Narratives of Samuel, Saul, David

By focusing on this material, we immediately center on David, the "star" of Israel's narrative, who pushes Israel's storytellers to imaginative extremes.[14] More than this, the text as we have it suggests that Yahweh is inordinately and irrationally committed to David. This uncommon commitment causes Yahweh to act in odd and unreliable ways. That this inordinate commitment can produce odd actions in Yahweh is itself an important theological datum in Israel's cross-examination. It is as though when David enters the stage of Israel's activity, Yahweh's characteristic features of sovereignty and fidelity are strained and challenged. What interests us here is the awareness that the entry of David into the story can skew Yahweh's way of being available to Israel. This skewedness in the direction of David can produce, as a downside, the sense of the tragic in the story of Saul, who never really had a chance in Israel's imagination.[15] Being juxtaposed to David, and given Yahweh's

---

14. See Walter Brueggemann, *David's Truth in Israel's Imagination and Memory* (Philadelphia: Fortress Press, 1985).

15. On the tragic dimensions of the Saul story, see David Gunn, *The Fate of King Saul: An Interpretation of a Biblical Story* (JSOTSup 14; Sheffield: JSOT Press, 1980); and W. Lee Humphreys, *The Tragic Vision and the Hebrew Tradition* (OBT; Philadelphia: Fortress Press, 1985) 23–42. It is never

peculiar attentiveness to David, Saul is the wrong man at the wrong time. But the wrongness is not given as a public, political datum—it eventuates only from Yahweh's peculiar affection for David.

In 1 Sam 16:1-13, Saul is rejected by Yahweh. From Yahweh's perspective Israel has no king. Saul is disqualified, even though he retains the ostensible power of the throne. But Yahweh does not linger about Saul. Having given a verdict on Saul, Yahweh moves on to a fresh initiative: the anointment of the heretofore unidentified David. Two matters only need concern us. First, the pursuit of the boy David is completely hidden from Samuel, the kingmaker, and is a work of Yahweh's majestic purpose. Indeed, Yahweh says at the outset: "I have provided for myself a king" (v. 1). The verb see (r'h; to pre-see, pre-video, provide) suggests Yahweh's hidden, inscrutable governance that destines David to be king.[16] Sure enough, the narrative culminates in the boy who is visited by the spirit of the Lord. The narrative has withheld the name of the boy until the end of the tale. But, we are to believe, Yahweh knows well ahead what is to happen. Thus the tale is an exemplar of Yahweh's hidden, inscrutable, majestic purpose for the historical process of Israel, which is well beyond human discernment, even that of Samuel.

What interests us is that this sweeping, lordly intention is juxtaposed to a rather seamy strategy for securing the new king. Samuel is sent by Yahweh on a dangerous mission, not unlike that of Moses in Exod 3:10. Samuel is rightly frightened at his assignment, because his action in seeking the new king is tantamount to treason against Saul: "If Saul hears of it, he will kill me" (v. 2). Yahweh's response to the frightened Samuel is telling:

> Take a heifer with you, and say, "I have come to sacrifice to the Lord." Invite
> Jesse to the sacrifice, and I will show you what you shall do; and you shall
> anoint for me the one whom I name to you. (vv. 2b-3)

The sacrifice here authorized by Yahweh, which Samuel performs in due course, is a subterfuge intended to draw attention away from the real purpose of the mission, which is to implement a coup against Saul. Yahweh's larger purpose is worth engagement in such a strategy, no doubt because "the end justifies the means." The narrative signals no discomfort at presenting Yahweh in this way. The ruse devised by Yahweh is "no big deal"; except that it constitutes an element of duplicity in the working of Yahweh.

In a second point concerning Saul, in 1 Samuel 8, Samuel is in deep dispute with Israel over the function and nature of public leadership. Israel wants a king, in order to be "like the other nations." Samuel, here the reliable voice of Yahweh, refuses them a king, on the grounds that human kingship is an act of distrust in Yahweh. In this narrative, as in 1 Sam 16:1-13, Samuel has direct and immediate

---

without problem to take what is a literary and artistic rendering, as we have it in the Saul-David narrative, and to treat it as theological substance. The artistic and theological are not necessarily distinct from each other, but they are acts with very different perspectives.

16. See my discussion of providence on the part of the hidden God, pp. 352–53.

access to Yahweh, who engages him in conversation. For our purposes, it is important to note that Yahweh instructs Samuel three times "to listen to the people"—to do what they say, even though both Samuel and Yahweh recognize their proposal as foolish and destructive:

> *Listen to the voice of the people* in all that they say to you; for they have not rejected you, but they have rejected me from being king over them. (v. 7)

> Now then, *listen to their voice;* only—you shall solemnly warn them, and show them the ways of the king who shall reign over them. (v. 9)

> *Listen to their voice* and set a king over them. (v. 22)

In the end, the people prevail. Israel will have a king, because Samuel "listened to the people" at the behest of Yahweh.

In the contrasting narrative of 1 Samuel 15, we are treated to the rejection of Saul as king, the one whom Yahweh and Samuel had not wanted in the first place. What interests us at this point is one element of the narrative. When Saul is roundly condemned by Samuel, Saul can only say in his self-defense:

> I have sinned; for I have transgressed the commandment of the Lord and your words, because I feared the people and obeyed their voice. (v. 24)

The term here, emphatically rendered "obey," is *šm'*, as it was in 8:7, 9, 22. Samuel is given warrant to "obey the people," but Saul is condemned for what is, at least to some extent, the same action. This is one of a number of seeming incongruities in the life of Yahweh. Here as elsewhere, the distinctions Yahweh will make are not trustworthy; they can be justified only because of Yahweh's inordinate (and unfair?) commitment in the historical process.

We may note yet a third interesting tension by returning to the narrative of 1 Samuel 15. In the conclusion of this narrative, Saul is condemned by Samuel for having violated the rule of *ḥerem* against the Amalekites. Samuel, as well as Yahweh, we may believe, is adamant on this point. Two oddities arise in the treatment of Saul, compared to subsequent treatment of David.

In the first of these awkward contrasts, we notice that Saul did violate the demand of the old tradition of Moses in Exod 17:8-16 (cf. Deut 25:17-19). This much is beyond doubt. What is interesting, by way of contrast, is that in 1 Samuel 30, David attacks these same Amalekites and roundly defeats them. David recovers all that the Amalekites had taken from him, and in addition seizes spoil from them:

> Nothing was missing, whether small or great, sons or daughters, spoil or anything that had been taken; David brought back everything. David also captured all the flocks and herds, which were driven ahead of the other cattle; people said, "This is David's spoil." (1 Sam 30:19-20)

Indeed, the narrative is preoccupied with David's generous administration of the spoil (*šll*) of the Amalekites:

But David said, "You shall not do so, my brothers, with what the Lord has given us; he has preserved us and handed over to us the raiding party that attacked us. Who would listen to you in this matter? For the share of the one who goes down into battle shall be the same as the share of the one who stays by the baggage; they shall share alike." From that day forward he made it a statute and an ordinance for Israel; it continues to the present day. (vv. 23-25)

David is presented as bold, generous, and successful.

But we notice that the narrative evidences no interest in or even awareness of a problem of spoil (*šll*) from the Amalekites. There are a variety of historical-critical explanations for this. This is a later "developed narrative," in which the narrator has no interest in the ancient Amalekite rule, nor awareness of the prohibition of spoil in holy war (cf. Deut 20:14). Moreover, the agent Samuel is dead, and he is the last enforcer of the rule. But none of that distracts from the awareness that Yahweh is inconsistent in being intensely preoccupied with this practice in one case (that of Saul) and not at all in the other case (David). David can do anything he wants, because David is linked to Yahweh in modes of acceptance and affirmation heretofore unavailable in Israel and certainly unavailable to Saul.

In 1 Samuel 15 we note another matter. Saul is presented as an honorable, straightforward man. He does not argue with Samuel about the savage indictment pronounced against him. He responds to Samuel:

I have sinned; for I have transgressed the commandment of the Lord and your words, because I feared the people and obeyed their voice. Now therefore, I pray, pardon my sin, and return with me, so that I may worship the Lord. (vv. 24-25)

Saul seeks forgiveness for a confessed sin. He seeks to be forgiven and accepted, precisely so that he may "worship the Lord." But Samuel will have no part of forgiveness. It is as though Samuel (and Yahweh) is in a hurry, prepared to use any theological, political occasion in order to displace Saul with "a neighbor of yours" (15:28; cf. 13:14, 28:17).

The contrast between Saul's fate at the hands of Yahweh and that of David is stunning. After the massive indictment of David by Nathan, after the Uriah-Bathsheba episode, David also responds directly, "I have sinned" (2 Sam 12:13). That is all. David does not, like Saul, appeal for forgiveness. But forgiveness is in any case promptly granted by Nathan: "Now the Lord has put away your sin; you shall not die" (v. 13). A qualifying footnote follows, but it does not pertain to David (v. 14).

The narrative evidences no curiosity about why penitent Saul cannot be forgiven while David can. Of course the narrative is engaged in the larger matter of David's kingship. Nonetheless, these contrasts function as countertestimony concerning the character of Yahweh. They attest that Yahweh is not a consistent God of command

and sanction or, alternatively, of deed and consequence. Conversely, they attest that Yahweh is not a God who consistently forgives. There is slippage about sanctions on occasion, but the slippage always seems to work toward the advantage of David and against Saul. Indeed, we may imagine that "the evil spirit" that came upon Saul (1 Sam 18:10) is not unlike the deceiving agent dispatched by the government of Yahweh against King Ahab in 1 Kings 22. What is clear to us, and to the narrative before us, is that the lived experience of Israel has to come to terms with this inexplicable, inscrutable "tilt" that does not act morally or reasonably or honorably or consistently, and that things work out oddly, even though Israel credits the oddity to Yahweh. It is possible to speak of the hidden intentionality of Yahweh, or even of Yahweh's providential care—in this case, of David. What puzzles us about such a conclusion is that even while the text is pro-David in its outcomes, the witness of Israel presents for us the illicit nature of Yahweh's activity as pertains to Saul. In fact, Saul is treated unfairly by Yahweh, and he is assigned a role in the memory of Israel that shows him to be in a position where he can only lose. Saul will lose partly because David is bold, lucky, attractive, and "destined." Saul will lose because "forces" conspire against him. Israel, moreover, does not hesitate to assign those conspiring forces exactly to Yahweh. Thus:

- Yahweh will deceive in order to advance David (1 Sam 16:1);

- Yahweh will counsel Samuel to listen to the people (8:7, 9, 22), and crush Saul for the same action (1 Sam 15:24);

- Yahweh will eliminate Saul for taking Amalekite spoil (15:18-21), but will disregard David's like action (30:19-20);

- Yahweh will forgive David (2 Sam 12:13), but refuse Saul's confession (1 Sam 15:24).

Yahweh will be arbitrary in David's favor and need justify it to none, certainly not to Saul or to Saul's readers.[17]

What then are we to make of 2 Samuel 24, the narrative of David's census? It is clearly wrong in Israel to conduct a census, for a census can only serve ambitious human control through military draft or taxation:

But afterward, David was stricken to the heart because he had numbered the people. (2 Sam 24:10)

It is clear that David's forgiveness in this case will be costly (vv. 12-13). But what interests us here is the initiation of the whole sorry business of the census:

Again the anger of the Lord was kindled against Israel, and he incited David against them, saying, "Go, count the people of Israel and Judah." (2 Sam 24:1)

---

17. On the tensions in the chapter, especially with reference to Yahweh's changelessness and readiness to change, see Terence E. Fretheim, "Divine Foreknowledge, Divine Constancy, and the Rejection of Saul's Kingship," *CBQ* 47 (1985) 595–602.

We are not told why Yahweh is angry with David, but Yahweh is angry with the very one for whom Yahweh had tilted all the powers of destiny in the earlier account. We are not told how Yahweh "incited" David, but Yahweh did so. That is, Yahweh works a "catch-22" upon David: Yahweh tempts David to an act, so that Yahweh may severely punish him for doing it. This is the one from whom Yahweh will never remove *ḥesed*, as it was removed from Saul (2 Sam 7:15). But here, at least provisionally, Yahweh's *ḥesed* is removed (cf. Ps 89:46-49). There is something capricious, or at least hidden, about Yahweh's action. We have seen that Yahweh's actions in this royal narrative are consistently understood as acts of partiality toward David. But here Yahweh acts, apparently with no provocation, *against* the very one whom Yahweh has championed. At bottom, Israel's countertestimony bespeaks something profoundly unreliable about Yahweh, even toward David, to whom Yahweh has pledged ultimate fidelity.

It is evident in 1 Chronicles 21 that Israel itself was belatedly aware of the oddity of assigning such an arbitrary action to Yahweh. The alternative of the Chronicler, to assign the capricious act to Satan, is not much more satisfactory, because we are to imagine Satan as a member of Yahweh's royal court, who acts in the interest of the court and perhaps at its behest. Thus 1 Chronicles 21 gives us a distancing maneuver in Israel's testimony, but no real resolution.

It is odd, and important, that we can trace Yahweh's unreliability precisely in the narrative of David, wherein Yahweh's reliability is most intense and explicit. This last citation (2 Samuel 24, 1 Chronicles 21) is unlike all the other David references we have cited, for it is the only one that goes against David. Perhaps this narrative functions, in the countertestimony of Israel, against any royal usurpation of Yahweh's governance by aligning itself too closely with David.[18] Whatever else this particular narrative may intend, it shows unmistakably that Yahweh is nobody's hostage, not even David's. Perhaps the deception in the anointing, the acceptance of Samuel's listening to the people (and not Saul's), the acceptance of David's act of despoiling of the Amalekites (and not Saul's), the readiness to forgive David (and not Saul), are all evidences in Israel's countertestimony that Yahweh will make provisional alliances in the historical process; thus Yahweh may cohere for a time with historical persons, movements, or power arrangements, but only for a time. The astonishing countertestimony of 2 Samuel 24 (1 Chronicles 21) confirms that Yahweh's alliances are provisional, and in the end Yahweh's holiness, glory, and jealousy will not be captured anywhere in creation.

It is not clear what Israel intends in this tale of David's cost. What is clear is that Israel told the tale, and told it yet again in altered form. The God who establishes is the one who inexplicably undermines. As a consequence, David belatedly finds out about Yahweh something that Saul learned early and repeatedly.

---

18. On these texts as a counterpoint to the royal claims, see Walter Brueggemann, "2 Samuel 21–24: An Appendix of Deconstruction?" *CBQ* 50 (1988) 383–97.

ELEVEN

Yahweh and Negativity

HERE IS EVIDENCE that the sovereign God of fidelity who orders the world as good, who loves Israel to well-being, who is a "lover of justice," and who is "steadfast and faithful," eventuates with a *large dose of negativity* in Israel's cross-examination.

Covenantal Sanctions

The negativity exhibited toward and about Yahweh is in one sense rooted in the covenant curses that, as negative sanctions, come along with the commands of Sinai. It is known and accepted everywhere in Israel that when Yahweh is disobeyed, affronted, or mocked, Yahweh enacts penalties. That much is reasonable, and the severity of the affront matches the severity of the sanction. If that were all, there would be no cross-examination, or no damaging evidence to emerge from cross-examination.

Countertestimony arises and has force, however, because Israel experiences the negativity of Yahweh in seemingly great disproportion to disobedience, affront, or mocking. Israel therefore speaks a great deal about Yahweh, either to protest against Yahweh's disproportion, or to protest against Yahweh's silence and neglect when Israel is in need. The silence is not as damaging to Yahweh as is the protest for disproportion. In the end, however, the two kinds of witness amount to the same thing: *Yahweh's failure to adhere to covenant.*

The basis for Yahweh's negativity toward Israel is rooted in covenantal sanctions, curses that will be enacted when Israel is disobedient. The most complete catalogs of such curses, to which Israel has ostensibly agreed in its covenant oath at Sinai, are presented in Leviticus 26 and Deuteronomy 28 (see also 1 Kgs 8:33-53 and Amos 4:6-11). The length of the passages suggests that the curses were progressively intensified in the course of Israel's life with Yahweh. From the outset in this tradition it is clear that Yahweh's demand for obedience is taken with utmost seriousness, and disobedience will be dealt with seriously.

The warrants for Yahweh's negative treatment of Israel are given in the curse recitals. The frontal statement of the enactment of those sanctions is given in the lawsuit speeches of the prophets. As Claus Westermann has shown in his classic study, the lawsuit speeches of the prophets seek to justify the "sentences" on the basis of the "indictments" the prophets speak.[1] Thus some case can be made, for example in Amos and Micah, that the indictments grow out of the old commands of Sinai, and that the sentences are compelled by the indictments.[2] The sentences themselves, characteristically, are introduced by "therefore," meaning "as a result," linking them to the indictments:

> *Therefore* the land mourns,
> and all who live in it languish;
> together with the wild animals
> and the birds of the air,
> even the fish of the sea are perishing. (Hos 4:3)

> *Therefore* you shall have no one to cast the line
> by lot in the assembly of the Lord. (Mic 2:5)

> *Therefore* because of you
> Zion shall be plowed as a field;
> Jerusalem shall become a heap of ruins,
> and the mountain of the house a wooded height. (Mic 3:12)

> *Therefore* my people go into exile without knowledge;
> their nobles are dying of hunger,
> and their multitude is parched with thirst. (Isa 5:13)

> *Therefore* they shall now be the first to go into exile,
> and the revelry of the loungers shall pass away. (Amos 6:7)

Yahweh is seen to be severe. But Yahweh is also seen to be fair, in terms of the agreements to which Israel is held.

Psalms of Complaint

The curse recitals are a heavy enough basis from which to bear witness against the core testimony of Yahweh's gracious, transformative acts. But Israel's experience of Yahweh, voiced in its countertestimony, cuts deeper against the core testimony. The principal pattern of speech whereby Israel bears this element of countertestimony is the psalm of complaint.[3] It is important to note that these psalms are indeed voices of complaint or judicial protest, and not lamentations, as they are often called. In

---

1. Claus Westermann, *Basic Forms of Prophetic Speech* (Atlanta: John Knox, 1967).

2. On the possible connections in Micah, see Walter Beyerlin, *Die Kulttraditionen Israels in der Verkündigung des Propheten Micah* (FRLANT 54; Göttingen: Vandenhoeck and Ruprecht, 1959). On the linkages in Amos, see Robert Bach, "Gottesrecht und weltliches Recht in der Verkündigung des Propheten Amos," *Festschrift für Günther Dehn* (ed. W. Schneemelcher; Neukirchen: Verlag der Buchhandlung des Erziehungsvereins, 1957) 23–34; Ernst Würthwein, "Amos-Studien," *ZAW* 62 (1950) 10–52; and H. Graf Reventlow, *Das Amt des Propheten bei Amos* (FRLANT 80; Göttingen: Vandenhoeck and Ruprecht, 1962).

3. The basic studies are those of Claus Westermann and Erhard Gerstenberger cited in chap. 8, n. 2.

the psalms of complaint, Israel seeks aid and positive treatment (comfort) from Yahweh, precisely on the basis of extant covenant agreements to which Yahweh is pledged. Westermann has demonstrated that the voicing of complaint regularly concerns three parties.[4] In addition to Israel, who speaks the protest and petition, there is Yahweh, who is being addressed, and there is often the "enemy," against whom help is sought.

The complaint psalms are committed to the general claim that Yahweh has not been faithful to Yahweh's covenant commitments, either by neglect and inattentiveness, or by direct negative action. The assumption of the complaint psalms is the same tight world of covenant sanctions to which the prophets appeal. *Whereas the prophets hold to the sanctions and consequent indictments in asserting that Israel has betrayed the covenant, the complaint psalms hold to the sanctions accusing Yahweh of not having honored the covenant.* For if Yahweh had honored covenant, it is argued, bad things would not have happened to Israel. Bad things would not have been received from the hand of Yahweh. Or bad things would not have been received at the hand of the enemy if Yahweh had not been negligent.

The world in which Israel petitions to Yahweh is one in which enemies seek to do Israel harm. Israel is helpless against those enemies, and so must count on Yahweh to cope with them on its behalf. When Yahweh does not do so, as Yahweh has pledged to do, the enemies will prevail.[5] Therefore the work of petition is to reengage Yahweh—who has, it is alleged, been negligent—with the threat of the enemies. For when Yahweh is engaged on behalf of Israel, the threat dissipates. We must note, however, that while the petition is positive and hopeful, it tends to have a note of reprimand, indicating that to some extent the threat against Israel has become maximum through Yahweh's neglect. Thus,

> O God, the insolent rise up against me;
> a band of ruffians seeks my life,
> and they do not set you before them.
> But you, O Lord, are a God
> merciful and gracious,
> slow to anger and abounding in
> steadfast love and faithfulness.
> Turn to me and be gracious to me;
> give your strength to your servant;
> save the child of your serving girl. (Ps 86:14-16)

This part of the psalm of complaint is in three elements. First, the enemy is named: insolent men and ruffians. Second, Yahweh's faithful character is affirmed as the premise of the appeal. Third, a petition is made, for it is clear that Yahweh's

---

4. Claus Westermann, "Struktur und Geschichte der Klage im Alten Testament," *Forschung am Alten Testament; gesammelte Studien* (ThB 24; Munich: Chr. Kaiser Verlag, 1964) 266–305.
5. This is fundamental to the argument of Fredrik Lindström, *Suffering and Sin: Interpretations of Illness in the Individual Complaint Psalms* (Stockholm: Almqvist and Wiksell International, 1994).

steadfast love and faithfulness have been inoperative and now need to be mobilized. This petition expresses no doubt that Yahweh is faithful. But if Yahweh's fidelity has been inoperative, as it sometimes is, it does Israel no good, and Israel is intensely vulnerable. Thus the very appeal to Yahweh is an understated accusation against Yahweh, who has not been attentive as Yahweh is sworn to be.

A like sequence is evident in Psalm 35. A great deal of coverage is given to the "malicious witnesses":

> Malicious witnesses rise up;
> they ask me about things I do not know.
> They repay me evil for good;
> my soul is forlorn. . . .
> But at my stumbling they gathered in glee,
> they gathered together against me;
> ruffians whom I did not know
> tore at me without ceasing;
> they impiously mocked more and more,
> gnashing at me with their teeth. (vv. 11-12, 15-16)

The speaker reports to Yahweh how unfair the enemies are, because in the enemies' time of need the speaker has been greatly concerned for them (vv. 13-14). Thus the present situation of abuse is grossly unfair and unmerited. Then, in a third maneuver, the speaker asks:

> How long, O Lord, will you look on?
> Rescue me from their ravages,
> my life from the lions! (v. 17; cf. Pss 5:7-9, 6:2-5, 36:5-12)

The clear implication of the prayer is that the malicious witnesses and ruffians have created such a vexing situation for the speaker because Yahweh has "looked on" (*r'h*) but has done nothing to help.

In these two psalms, and many others like them, the speaker does not indict Yahweh for having done anything negative or destructive toward Israel. But Yahweh has indeed been neglectful, absent, inattentive, and thus not "steadfast and faithful." Yahweh, moreover, is Israel's only line of defense against such threats by the enemy. This countertestimony bears witness to two elements of Yahweh's life with Israel. First, the very premise of the accusatory prayer of petition is that Yahweh is indeed steadfast and faithful. These prayers accept the normative adjectives we have already considered.[6] But second, that steadfast love and faithfulness, in a moment of crisis, are shown not to be fully reliable. Israel manages in these prayers to issue complaint and expectant hope in the same utterance. As Claus Westermann has shown, these complaints characteristically move Yahweh to act and to reengage, so that Yahweh's steadfast love and faithfulness, as Israel anticipated,

---

6. On the normative adjectives, see chap. 5.

do indeed prevail.[7] It is evident, however, that it takes vigorous countertestimony in order for the reality of the core testimony to be reenacted by Yahweh. The effect of the countertestimony is to introduce into Israel's utterance about Yahweh an awareness that Yahweh's steadfast love and faithfulness are not everywhere and always reliable. In the course of its life with Yahweh, Israel comes upon circumstances that are seen to fall outside the governance of that covenantal fidelity. When that happens, Israel must protest in hope and with vigor.

The rhetoric is escalated and the stakes are considerably raised in some psalms of complaint that take a very different tack against Yahweh. In these, *Yahweh is not indicted simply for being disengaged* and thereby leaving Israel to its undefended fate in a world of enemies. In a second wave of countertestimony, Israel speaks against Yahweh, who has been *actively and aggressively opposed to Israel* in ways that do direct damage. Thus,

> You have made my days a few handbreadths,
> and my lifetime is as nothing in your sight. . . .
> for it is you who have done it.
> Remove your stroke from me;
> I am worn down by the blows of your hand.
> You chastise mortals in punishment for sin,
> consuming like a moth what is dear to them;
> surely everyone is a mere breath. (Ps 39:5, 9b-11)

> O God, you have rejected us,
> broken our defenses;
> you have been angry; now restore us!
> You have caused the land to quake;
> you have torn it open;
> repair the cracks in it, for it is tottering.
> You have made your people suffer hard things;
> you have given us wine to drink that made us reel. (Ps 60:1-3)

> You have put me in the depths of the Pit,
> in the regions dark and deep.
> Your wrath lies heavy upon me,
> and you overwhelm me with all your waves. . . .
> Your wrath has swept over me;
> your dread assaults destroy me.
> They surround me like a flood all day long;
> from all sides they close in on me.

---

7. On the theological claim that prayer does impinge on Yahweh and cause Yahweh to do what Yahweh would otherwise not have done, see Harold Fisch, "Psalms: The Limits of Subjectivity," *Poetry with a Purpose: Biblical Poetics and Interpretation* (Bloomington: Indiana University Press, 1988) 104–35; and Perry D. LeFevre, *Understanding Prayers* (Philadelphia: Westminster Press, 1981) 31–34, and his discussion of Barth's marvelous allowance for impingement on God.

> You have caused friend and
> neighbor to shun me;
> my companions are in darkness. (Ps 88:6-7, 16-18)

Israel, in its vigorous testimony against Yahweh, utters the charge that Yahweh has been actively engaged to the detriment of Israel.[8] Indeed, Israel's petition to Yahweh suggests that in the purview of Israel, Yahweh has been doing the very negative things Yahweh is now asked not to do:

> Do not, O Lord, withhold
> your mercy from me.... (Ps 40:11a)

> Do not cast me off in the time of old age;
> do not forsake me when my strength is spent....
> O God, do not be far from me. (Ps 70:9, 12)

The petitions suggest that Israel is at least able to contemplate that Yahweh, the God on whom Israel has staked its life and about whom Israel has recited marvelous adjectives, is capable of negative, destructive acts toward Israel.

The countertheme to this reprimand of Yahweh is the assertion that Israel is innocent and does not warrant such treatment from Yahweh. Of course if Israel is guilty, then the negative treatment by Yahweh is to be expected. In the so-called penitential psalms, this acknowledgment is made (cf. Psalms 32, 38, 51). But in many other psalms, as Fredrik Lindström has effectively shown, Israel is indeed innocent, and the suffering inflicted or allowed by Yahweh is unwarranted and indicates a failure in the covenant on Yahweh's part (cf. Pss 25:21; 26:11).[9]

The greatest affirmation Israel can make in this context is that "I put my trust in you" (Ps 56:3). Israel has risked everything in its reliance on Yahweh. Now circumstance indicates that Yahweh has not responded to Israel's radical trust with a commensurate show of reliability. To be sure, the complaint prayers are "on the way"; they do not draw a final conclusion by Israel or about Yahweh. They still hope, expect, and wait upon Yahweh to act to restore the relationship, so that evidence may yet be given that Yahweh is reliable. But in the moment of utterance, the evidence is all to the contrary. Yahweh is not faithful or reliable, and the dysfunction that has come into Israel's life is indeed Yahweh's failure. Even if an enemy has inflicted the trouble, it is Yahweh's failure to respond in protectiveness that is the decisive theological datum.

We may notice three elements in the transaction of faith constituted by prayers of complaint. *First, Israel is profoundly aware of the incongruity between the core claims of covenantal faith and the lived experience of its life.* Covenantal faith had dared to make the claim that the world is completely coherent under the rule of

---

8. This theme has been vigorously explored by David R. Blumenthal, *Facing the Abusive God: A Theology of Protest* (Louisville: Westminster/John Knox, 1993), with particular reference to the Psalms.

9. Lindström, *Suffering and Sin*.

Yahweh, so that complete obedience leads to *shalôm*. Israel's lived experience, however, makes clear that an obedient life on occasion goes unrewarded or even suffers trouble in ways that should not have happened. It is important for biblical faith that Israel, in its countertestimony, values candor about its lived experience, rather than commitment to its core testimony. That is, Israel refuses to subject its life to any ideology, but resolves to tell the truth, even when that truth-telling is damaging to Yahweh's reputation and character.

Thus in Israel's countertestimony the theme of the suffering of the righteous emerges. In these prayers, Israel is not concerned with the prosperity of the wicked, an issue that will arise elsewhere in the countertestimony. The suffering of the righteous, rather than the prosperity of the wicked, is an enigma in a tightly construed covenantal faith. Israel's experience, and therefore its utterance, thus express profound reservation about tightly construed covenantal faith. Israel proposes either that destructiveness is loose in the world and Yahweh either will not or cannot constrain it; or it goes further, to suggest that Yahweh is indeed the very agent of the destructiveness.

One prize example of this theme of the innocent sufferer is Psalm 69. This psalm states with great rhetorical power and with no timidity the central incongruity of Israel's life with Yahweh. The speaker is utterly devoted to Yahweh:

> It is zeal for your house that has consumed me;
> the insults of those who insult you have fallen on me.
> When I humbled my soul with fasting,
> they insulted me for doing so.
> When I made sackcloth my clothing,
> I became a byword to them.
> I am the subject of gossip for
> those who sit in the gate,
> and the drunkards make songs about me. (vv. 9-11)

The speaker, moreover, fully trusts in Yahweh (vv. 13, 16, 30-33), and for that reason is in profound suffering as a victim of shame, humiliation, and abuse (vv. 19-21). The psalm offers as a resolve to this dilemma a powerful, unqualified statement of hope. But it is only confidence about the future that is voiced. The speaker has no data in the present circumstance that confirm such hope and no sign that Yahweh will act any time soon or in any way of rescue. We may take this psalm as a full articulation of Israel's dilemma. This psalm does not accuse or indict Yahweh—the psalmist voices complete confidence in Yahweh, but it is a confidence that will not flinch from truth-telling. The psalm asserts that something has gone terribly wrong in what was to have been a life and a relationship of well-being.

The theme of righteous suffering has caused this psalm to be utilized in the Christian tradition in telling the story of the passion of Jesus (cf. John 2:17, 15:25;

Matt 27:34, 48; Mark 15:36; Luke 23:36; John 19:29; Acts 1:20).[10] Specifically, v. 21 is quoted in all of the gospel narrative accounts with reference to Jesus. While the usage of the psalm in the New Testament shows how the story of Israel is transposed into the story of Jesus, a christological interpretation should not be permitted to preempt the psalm and its testimony. In the end, the psalm concerns testimony about Yahweh, from which Israel does not flinch.

Second, in the psalm of complaint Israel has momentarily wrested from Yahweh the initiative for the relationship. In the core testimony of Israel, Yahweh has held the initiative, and Yahweh's initiative has prevailed in the prophetic announcements. Here, however, Israel in trouble has learned that silent deference to Yahweh is costly (cf. Ps 39:1-2). As a consequence, Israel breaks the silence, ends the deference, and claims rights over against Yahweh. Now Israel is the lead figure in the courtroom, and Yahweh is in the dock. For the dominant drama of the psalms of complaint, Yahweh is under accusation, and the provisional, implied judgment is that Yahweh is found guilty—if not of aggressive destructiveness, at least of negligence. It is an extraordinary rhetorical development that Israel breaks the silence, challenges Yahweh's preeminence, and makes its own uncompromising insistence over against Yahweh.

What is astonishing, moreover, is that such a recasting of the relationship is not treated in Israel's testimony as a rejection of Yahweh or as disapproved behavior on the part of Israel. Rather this positioning of Israel vis-à-vis Yahweh is regarded as a legitimate and proper way in which to relate to Yahweh. Yahweh is placed on the receiving end of hard sayings, and the utterance of those sayings by Israel is regarded as a legitimate and appropriate form of covenantal faith.

Third, Westermann has averred that the complaints of Israel, without exception, receive a positive response and resolution from Yahweh.[11] Westermann has overstated the case, but on the whole the suggestion is correct. The odd thing is that Israel's rhetorical urging of Yahweh and Israel's occasional assault against Yahweh do move Yahweh to new, rescuing activity. Indeed, Yahweh undertakes actions that would not be undertaken without Israel's shrill, insistent utterance. This mode of prayer is a practice of effective mutuality in which one partner impinges decisively on the other. Such a transaction, in normal usage, is a proper and nearly routine way in which Israel's covenant with Yahweh operates. To that extent, laments and complaints are not *counter*testimony. Westermann has failed to note, however, that a few psalms to the contrary do not work according to the normal patterns of covenantalism. Psalm 88 is an extreme case and a prime example of a summons to Yahweh that receives no answer:

---

10. See Hans-Joachim Kraus, *Theology of the Psalms* (Minneapolis: Augsburg Publishing House, 1986) 177–203, on the use of this and other psalms in the New Testament.

11. Claus Westermann, *The Praise of God in the Psalms* (Richmond: John Knox, 1965) 60 and passim. See the review of the issue by Patrick D. Miller, *They Cried to the Lord: The Form and Theology of Biblical Prayer* (Minneapolis: Fortress Press, 1994) 135–77.

O Lord, God of my salvation,
when, at night, I cry out in your presence,
let my prayer come before you;
incline your ear to my cry....
Every day I call on you, O Lord;
I spread out my hands to you....
But I, O Lord, cry out to you;
in the morning my prayer comes before you. (Ps 88:1-2, 9b, 13)

There is no answer, no mutuality, no resolution. In Psalm 88 the matter is left as an enduring, reverberating witness. Yahweh does not answer, and Israel is not rescued. Yahweh's *hesed* has not been enacted (v. 11). Candor is in operation. Israel's initiative in this act is unmistakable, but that is all. In this text, at least, Israel leaves testimony of radical unresolve, in which the countertestimony is not answered. Yahweh does answer often...but not always. When Yahweh does not answer, Israel is left in its dismay and in its despairing utterance, which it can only sound again and again. Israel has no answer against this reality of its experience. It does not seek to justify. It does not acquit Yahweh nor indict itself. Israel is left with its psalm, always to be uttered one more time, always more shrilly, uttered as an act of profound need, of intense indignation, and of relentless, insistent hope. But Israel will in any case refuse silence. And so the psalm stands as testimony to Yahweh...and against Yahweh.

Yahweh's Capacity for Violence

Israel's countertestimony makes clear that Yahweh is a God capable of violence, and indeed the texture of the Old Testament is deeply marked by violence. In the end, a student of the Old Testament cannot answer for or justify the violence, but must concede that it belongs to the very fabric of this faith. This articulation of the negative brings to the surface three issues of countertestimony.

Enforcement of sovereignty. First, Yahweh is said to work violence that belongs to the enforcement of sovereignty. (See the discussion of metaphors of governance in chapter 6.) Every government must maintain a monopoly of force in its sphere of administration, and Yahweh is no exception. Yahweh's will carries with it deep and uncompromising sanctions, so that violence is implemented, even against Yahweh's own people when disobedience is strong and provocative enough.[12] This is a characteristic insistence of the pre-exilic prophets, an insistence that culminates in the destruction of Jerusalem in 587 B.C.E.

In like manner, the violence of sovereignty is in effect outside of Israel. The other peoples, states, and governments are expected to obey Yahweh's will for justice. When they do not, they are punished. This is one way of casting the Exodus:

---

12. The notion of Yahweh's rule as an act of governance is fundamental to George E. Mendenhall's notion of covenant, wherein he understands vengeance to be an undertaking of a legitimated government. See Mendenhall, "The Vengeance of Yahweh," *The Tenth Generation: The Origins of the Biblical Tradition* (Baltimore: Johns Hopkins University Press, 1973) 69–104.

pharaoh must be deposed, because he is a subject and vassal of Yahweh who has been recalcitrant. The same argument is made against recalcitrant Assyria (Isa 10:5-19, 37:22-29) and against arrogant Babylon (Isaiah 47; Daniel 4). This is the background assumption for the judgment announced by Amos against the nations, who had no awareness of Yahweh's governance over them (Amos 1:3–2:3).

Conquest and settlement of land. Second, Yahweh's violence is especially related to the "conquest" of the land of promise and the "settlement" of Israel in a land that was already occupied by others. Israel knows from the outset that the land has other occupants (Gen 12:6), and Israel devotes thought and attention to rationalizing the problem caused by this prior occupation (Exod 23:23-33; Judg 2:1-5, 20-23; 3:1-6).[13] On the whole, however, the narrative testimony of Yahweh, who gives land to the Israelites, does not at all blink at the violence required against other peoples for the sake of the land. That is a given, which considerably qualifies the core testimony that Yahweh is "good to all, and his compassion is over all that he has made" (Ps 145:9). No, not "all"; good to Israel at the expense of others.

Several responses might be made to this element of violence, none of which I consider an adequate justification. One response is to say that Yahweh is insanely committed to Yahweh's firstborn child and heir, and Yahweh will blindly do what is best for this child, no matter what the cost to anyone else (cf. Exod 4:22; Jer 3:19).[14] This is unqualified passion that will do anything necessary on behalf of the child. If we accept this, we must make a very different rendering of "lover of justice."

Another response would point out that land-by-violence is tied up with Israel's political and ideological claims to the land. This suggests that the witnesses are not telling disinterested truth about Yahweh, and so cannot be fully trusted.

Finally, it is possible (perhaps necessary?) to put a "class reading" on the ethnic commitment of Yahweh, to say that the violence is characteristically against the strong (landed) for the sake of the weak (landless).[15] The interface between an *ethnic* reading and a *class* reading is exceedingly tricky, as Jon Levenson has made clear.[16] In any case, land-by-violence is a primary claim for this God. It turns out to be a costly claim for Israel, who learned that land taken *for* Israel in violence

---

13. On the problematic of this particular violence, see Lawson G. Stone, "Ethical and Apologetic Tendencies in the Redaction of the Book of Joshua," *CBQ* 53 (1991) 25–36.

14. On the analogue of a parent who is "crazy" in loyalty toward a child, see Irie Bronfenbrenner, "Who Needs Parent Education?" *Teachers College Record* 79 (1978) 773–74; and Nel Noddings, *Caring: A Feminine Approach to Ethics and Moral Education* (Berkeley: University of California Press, 1984) 59–78.

15. This is popularly expressed in a liberation hermeneutic as "God's preferential option for the poor." Herbert Schneidau, "Let the Reader Understand," *Semeia* 39 (1987) 141, has averred that God's attentiveness to the "underdog" in the Old Testament is without antecedent in the ancient world, a genuine *novum*.

16. See the strong statement Jon D. Levenson makes against a "class reading" in favor of something like an ethnic reading: "Exodus and Liberation," *The Hebrew Bible, the Old Testament, and Historical Criticism: Jews and Christians in Biblical Studies* (Louisville: Westminster/John Knox, 1993) 127–59.

by Yahweh can also be taken *from* Israel by Yahweh's violence.[17] This testimony, saturated with passion and ideology, permeates Israel's sense of land, perhaps in a way that not only feeds the militarism of the Christian West, but also is evident in contemporary Israel. No doubt much nativism in the United States receives some of its theological justification from this tradition. Of course, without Yahweh's forceful resolve enacted as violence, Israel would have had no core story. It may be, in the long sweep, that the violence of Yahweh can be answered for,[18] but it can hardly be justified.

Yahweh's profound irrationality. A third aspect of Yahweh's violence goes beyond any rationality regarding enforced sovereignty or class struggle. There is a profound irrationality about Yahweh, which Yahweh enacts peculiarly against Israel. It has been noted that the metaphors taken up to voice Yahweh's passionate, intimate commitment to Israel are often marital. Moreover, it is evident that Yahweh is always cast in these images as the authoritarian husband, and that Israel is the easily blamed, readily dismissed, vulnerable wife.[19] Thus the very metaphor that bespeaks intimacy also permits intimate violence, in which Yahweh is the forceful husband who imposes his way and will on a hapless, defenseless wife.

The imagery seems already operative in Hosea and Jeremiah, but it reaches its fullest expression in Ezekiel, wherein Yahweh's mad passion for Israel has turned to the kind of irrational destructiveness that appears to be driven by sexuality embedded in violence, or violence embedded in sexuality. The countertestimony given in Ezekiel, in the long recitals of chapters 16, 20, and 23, turns the litany of "mighty deeds" by Yahweh to one of "mighty affronts" against Yahweh. What is not often noticed is that these texts not only displace mighty deeds with sins, they displace a passionately pro-Israel Yahweh with a side of Yahweh not so often visible, a Yahweh who is out of control with the violent, sexual rage of a husband who assaults his own beloved. Thus,

> Adulterous wife, who receives strangers instead of her husband!...I will judge you as women who commit adultery and shed blood are judged, and bring blood upon you in wrath and jealousy....So I will satisfy my fury on you, and my jealousy shall turn away from you; I will be calm, and will be angry no longer. Because you have not remembered the days of your youth, but have enraged me with all these things; therefore, I have returned your deed upon your head, says the Lord God. (Ezek 16:32, 38, 42-43)

I will direct my indignation against you, in order that they may deal with you in fury. They shall cut off your nose and your ears, and your survivors shall

---

17. The thematic terms of the Jeremiah tradition, "pluck up and tear down," are characteristic expressions for Yahweh's resolve to move in violent ways to take the land from Israel.

18. On violence in the faith of Israel, see Walter Brueggemann, *Revelation and Violence: A Study in Contextualization* (Milwaukee: Marquette University Press, 1986).

19. See Renita Weems, *Battered Love: Marriage, Sex, and Violence in the Hebrew Prophets* (OBT; Minneapolis: Fortress Press, 1995).

fall by the sword. They shall seize your sons and your daughters, and your survivors shall be devoured by fire. They shall also strip you of your clothes and take away your fine jewels. So I will put an end to your lewdness and your whoring brought from the land of Egypt; you shall not long for them, or remember Egypt any more. For thus says the Lord God: I will deliver you into the hands of those whom you hate, into the hands of those from whom you turned in disgust; and they shall deal with you in hatred, and take away all the fruit of your labor, and leave you naked and bare, and the nakedness of your whorings shall be exposed. Your lewdness and your whorings have brought this upon you, because you played the whore with the nations, and polluted yourself with their idols. (Ezek 23:25-30)

Even in the subsequent, coded reflection of exilic Isaiah, Yahweh can admit to an "overflowing wrath for a moment" (Isa 54:8). Yahweh's massive act of destroying Jerusalem appears to be the work of a wronged lover who determines to humiliate, and finally to destroy, the erstwhile object of love. It is noteworthy that in all of these cases the fury is spent, and Yahweh returns to recover the relationship. Irrevocable damage has been done, however, and the testimony lingers.

One might wish that this dimension of Yahweh had not been given us, that it had been expunged from the record. But there it is! But how could it have turned out otherwise? Already in the belated testimony of Moses, Yahweh is said to have embraced Israel with a profound passion:

It was not because you were more numerous than any other people that the Lord set his heart (*ḥšq*) on you and chose you—for you were the fewest of all peoples. It was because the Lord loved you and kept the oath that he swore to your ancestors.... (Deut 7:7-8a)

Yet the Lord set his heart in love (*ḥšq*) on your ancestors alone and chose you, their descendants after them, out of all the peoples, as it is today. (Deut 10:15)

This is no casual, formal, or juridical commitment. This is *a passion that lives in the "loins" of Yahweh*, who will risk everything for Israel and, having risked everything, will expect everything and will be vigilant not to share the beloved with any other. This is no open marriage. The outcome of a passion so intensely initiated has within it the seeds of intolerance, culminating in violence. There is indeed a profound awkwardness in this presentation of Yahweh, but Israel does not flinch in its testimony. The God who has been madly in love becomes insanely jealous, which is Israel's deepest threat and most profound hope.

The God of this countertestimony is clearly not the God of the philosophers. This is one who goes wholly overboard in passion, to Israel's great gain and then to Israel's greatest loss. I have no wish to justify or tone down this violent love, which "always hurts the one it loves." It is worth noting that in the Johannine witness in the New Testament, there are those familiar words, "God so loved the world..."

So loved! How loved? In what way? To what extent? So loved . . . to give all . . . and demand all.

Theodicy in the Old Testament

A second consideration of Yahweh's negativity is "the problem of theodicy."[20] The phrase is unfortunate, because it suggests an issue that is speculative and that admits of rational resolve, but it functions as a convenient reference point. Israel had arrived at what I call a *theodic settlement.* In the calculus of the Deuteronomic tradition and in the deeds-consequences ideology of the sapiential tradition, Israel had a rough consensus on who gets what of power, goods, and access, and on what basis. Every community must reach this sort of settlement if it is to be peaceable and viable, even if the settlement lacks precision and is only proximate. The clearest, most guileless statement of that settlement is in Psalm 1.

The problem is that the settlement left much of life unaccounted for. We may believe that in Israel's life, the theodic settlement rooted in the old covenantal claims became less and less convincing. And when the theodic settlement loses credibility, it is inevitable that a *theodic crisis* ensues. Perhaps every society is endlessly negotiating between old theodic settlement and newly voiced theodic challenges.[21] It may well be that this theodic negotiation is most characteristic and everywhere found in Israel's life, from the daring challenges of Moses to the restless protests of late wisdom. It may be that Israel as a community, because of its character vis-à-vis Yahweh, is destined to be preoccupied in disputatious ways with theodicy. In any case, circumstance provides an acute form of the crisis, precisely around the events of 587 B.C.E. and the consequent exile.

The issue of theodicy in Israel is the acute awareness that the promises of the covenantal sanctions were not kept. If one moves behind formal categories, one finds an acute issue concerning Yahweh: namely, that Yahweh's governance and guarantees were no longer reliable in Israel. The crisis of theodicy is voiced sharply in the tradition of Jeremiah, the same tradition that assaulted Yahweh as a "seducer":

> You will be in the right, O Lord,
> when I lay charges against you;
> but let me put my case to you.
> Why does the way of the guilty prosper?
> Why do all who are treacherous thrive?

---

20. For a review of representative studies of theodicy in the Old Testament, see James L. Crenshaw, ed., *Theodicy in the Old Testament* (Philadelphia: Fortress Press, 1983).

21. Peter L. Berger, *The Sacred Canopy: Elements of a Sociological Theory of Religion* (Garden City, N.Y.: Doubleday, 1967) 53–80 and passim, has suggested that every society has two theodicies. See Leo Perdue, "Cosmology and the Social Order in the Wisdom Tradition," *The Sage in Israel and the Ancient Near East* (ed. John G. Gammie and Leo G. Perdue; Winona Lake, Ind.: Eisenbrauns, 1990) 457–78.

You plant them, and they take root;
they grow and bring forth fruit;
you are near in their mouths
yet far from their hearts.
But you, Lord, know me;
You see me and test me—my heart is with you.
Pull them out like sheep for the slaughter,
and set them apart for the day of slaughter.
How long will the land mourn,
and the grass of every field wither?
For the wickedness of those who live in it
the animals and the birds are swept away,
and because people said,
"He is blind to our ways." (Jer 12:1-4)

Not only do the "guilty prosper" (v. 1); the innocent (here Jeremiah) suffer when they are entitled to prosperity and well-being. The coherence of covenantal faith has collapsed, and with it much of the motivation for Yahwism. As a theological issue, theodicy is simply the powerful awareness that Yahweh is unreliable, cannot be trusted, and does not provide guarantees for the righteousness that Yahweh champions. In this primal challenge to Yahweh, we notice that the accepted premise is that Yahweh is indeed righteous (v. 1). The problem is that the evidence cited is to the contrary. It is the wicked who "bring forth fruit," while Yahweh is "far from their hearts" (v. 2).

Job and the Crisis of Theodicy

It is widely agreed that the Book of Job is Israel's most ambitious countertestimony concerning the crisis of theodicy.[22] The Book of Job has important links to the tradition of Jeremiah (cf. Jer 20:14-18 and Job 3), and Westermann has shown that much of the poem of Job is rooted in the complaint psalms, so that the theological issue posed here in extreme form is the same issue posed by the complaint psalms: Yahweh's reliability.[23]

The issue of theodicy is made explicit in Job 21:7, which echoes Jer 12:1-4: "Why do the wicked live on, reach old age, and grow mighty in power?" In v. 7, the character Job raises the central issue of the Book of Job, which is the central issue of Israel's countertestimony. It is the reverberating question of Israel's abrasive wonderment: "Why?" (*mddû*). It is ostensibly a question about "the wicked," but

---

22. As an assertion of the problem of theodicy, most pointedly in Job 21:7, the Book of Job seems to protest against the theodic settlement of either Deuteronomy or Proverbs or the world that both literatures reflect and advocate.

23. On the forms used in the Book of Job, see Claus Westermann, *The Structure of the Book of Job: A Form-Critical Analysis* (Philadelphia: Fortress Press, 1981). See the appeal to Jer 20:7-20 in Job 3. For the tortured way in which John Calvin struggled with the problematic theology of the Book of Job, see Susan E. Schreiner, *Where Shall Wisdom Be Found? Calvin's Exegesis of Job from Medieval and Modern Perspectives* (Chicago: University of Chicago Press, 1994).

clearly it is posed as a question about Yahweh. Why?...because Yahweh is inattentive, unreliable, and therefore the systems of sanctions that assure moral coherence are nullified. It is a fair question, and for Israel, with the old sanctions ringing in its ears, it is an urgent and inevitable one. It is Israel's ultimate question about Yahweh's power and fidelity. The Book of Job turns on the refusal, unwillingness, or inability of Yahweh to answer. Because the question has been asked and left unanswered, Israel's articulation of Yahweh is forever modified. This question dominates the dialogue of the Book of Job (chapters 3–27) and Job's self-acquittal (chapters 29–31). Job in these chapters shares the premise of the "friend" concerning the system of sanctions guaranteed by Yahweh. Job continues to trust that system of sanctions, but nonetheless his urgent demand for an answer remains unheeded.

Moreover, a second question is asked of Yahweh, alongside Job's pivotal question in 21:7. The second question is posed by "Satan" (or "the adversary"), who is one of "the sons of God" (1:6). Even before proceeding to the question, we notice the remarkable assertion in chapter 1, concerning Yahweh. Yahweh presides over a court of advisors and aides. Yahweh still lives in the peopled world of polytheism, surrounded by conversation partners. If we try to "decode" this dramatic language, we may say that "Satan" and the other "sons of God" bear witness to Yahweh's rich, alive, unsettled interior life. The conversation between Yahweh and the advisors concerns the same question put by Job in 21:7, only now it is asked from God's side. In this exchange in chapter 1, Yahweh values the old order of sanctions and confidently exhibits Job as an exemplar of one who is "blameless and upright." But doubt clouds the celebration of Job in the courts of Yahweh, doubt about the innocence, disinterest, and legitimacy of Job's obedience. Indeed, obedience, in the wonderment of Yahweh's court, is not enough. Genuine obedience must include right motivation as well as right action: "Does Job fear God for nothing (1:9)?"— for naught (*ḥnnm*), gratuitously, without hope of reward? The issue is a subtle but crucial one, and it propels the entire Book of Job. The question posed by Job in 21:7 would seem to answer Satan's question in 1:9. No, Job's obedience is not for naught. But from Yahweh's side, the issue is one of trust and authenticity. Is the relation between Yahweh and Job one of calculation, of a formal, mechanical sort that can be managed from either side? Or is the relation of obedience one of uncomplicated, singular devotion, driven only by affection? For our purpose, what counts most is the delicacy of the question posed for and entertained by Yahweh. Obedience—the kind Moses, the prophets, and the sages had urged—is not enough. If it were enough, Satan's question would not have turned out to be so serious and mesmerizing.

The poem of Job thus begins with two parties to the relationship, Yahweh and Job, now in great wonderment about each other. Job asks: *Is God reliable?* And Job, in his rage, entertains the option that Yahweh is not. Yahweh asks: *Is Job serious?* And the heavenly counsel entertains in wonderment the possibility that Job may not be. The practice of cross-examination in itself is an exercise in suspicion. Here both parties have become suspicious of the other.

The other dramatic element that sets up the action is that Job, who asks the question in 21:7, does not know about the conversation around 1:9. Yahweh is summoned to a conversation with Job, to which Job is apparently entitled. But Yahweh is also engaged in another conversation, one that concerns Yahweh's own life, about which Job knows nothing and to which Job has no access. This second conversation has not been much disclosed or emphasized heretofore in Israel's witness. But we have known, from the earliest mention of Yahweh's glory, holiness, and jealousy, that Yahweh has Yahweh's own life to live. That life may alter the possible answers to Job's question, but Job knows nothing of that.

The main body of the Book of Job concerns the exchange of Job with friends (chapters 3–27, 32–37) and Job's self-defense (chapters 29–31). All parties to this exchange with the friends (if it is indeed an exchange) assume the reliability of the old system of covenantal sanctions. Yet Job has overriding data against that claim of reliability, and he refuses to deny that data. Indeed, it is the courage and adamancy of Job that both require the drama and make it possible. Concerning this long exchange, we may note three matters concerning Yahweh.

Harsh verbal assault on Yahweh. First, Yahweh, the God who has pledged moral symmetry and who seems to have reneged on that pledge, is subject to harsh verbal assault. In these chapters, we reach the extreme expression of Israel's countertestimony about Yahweh, who is now shown to be unreliable and who in fact reneged on the claims of fidelity that stand at the center of Israel's core testimony.

Perhaps the most abrasive assault aimed at Yahweh is Job's statement in 9:15-22:

> Though I am innocent, I cannot answer him;
> I must appeal for mercy to my accuser.
> If I summon him and he answered me,
> I do not believe that he would listen to my voice.
> For he crushes me with a tempest,
> and multiplies my wounds without cause;
> he will not let me get my breath,
> but fills me with bitterness.
> If it is a contest of strength, he is the strong one!
> If it is a matter of justice, who can summon him?
> Though I am innocent, my own
> mouth would condemn me;
> though I am blameless, he
> would prove me perverse.
> I am blameless; I do not know myself;
> I loathe my life.
> It is all one; therefore I say,
> he destroys both the blameless and the wicked.

Job does not doubt Yahweh's power, but the evidence is massive that Yahweh is unjust. Indeed, in v. 20, "he would prove me perverse" ('*qš*). That is, Yahweh is a false witness who will give evidence in court that will convict Job, even against the truth of the matter. Everything in this relationship has depended on reliable testimony, and now, so Israel (through Job) asserts, Yahweh violates Yahweh's own command about false witness. The outcome of this is the further conclusion that Yahweh is unreliable and morally indifferent: "[H]e destroys both the blameless and the wicked" (v. 22). The assumption on which Israel and Job have premised their life evaporates. The countertestimony against Yahweh is unambiguous, unrestrained, and without qualification.

Yahweh left unnamed. We note a second element in these "dialogues": In these poems Yahweh is characteristically called by many other names, evidencing the poet's finesse and enormous erudition about ancient Near Eastern religion, but almost never "Yahweh" before the speech in the whirlwind.[24] No doubt this is a self-conscious literary strategy. But perhaps the entire discussion that never names Yahweh is beside the point. Perhaps the participants in this exchange and the poets who voice the witness have got it all wrong, because they never engage Yahweh per se. Perhaps the entire discussion is without contact to the God of Israel's core testimony.

Yahweh's refusal to answer. The third point is that Yahweh refuses to answer, refuses to be drawn into this conversation, and refuses to refute the charges or defend Yahweh's honor. Perhaps Yahweh does not engage because Yahweh has been issued a faulty summons, without being properly addressed by name. More likely, Yahweh has no interest in this calculating argument. The question posed in 1:9 concerns authenticity and genuineness of affection, and this is apparently beside the point in the current exchange. Yahweh remains inscrutably remote from the polemics.

The odd hiddenness of Yahweh is not much modified in the wisdom poem in chapter 28. Yahweh remains hidden and inscrutable. We have already seen in Prov 16:1-2, 9, 19:14, 20:24, and 21:30-31 that Yahweh's governing wisdom is not fully accessible to human penetration. Thus the remoteness of Yahweh is not treated in Job 28 as silence, but as majestic mystery. In the face of the mystery, this reflection on wisdom and its links to Yahweh end in what is characteristically available in Israel:

And he said to humankind,
"Truly, the fear of the Lord, that is wisdom;
and to depart from evil is understanding." (v. 28)

---

24. Andre Neher, *The Exile of the Word: From the Silence of the Bible to the Silence of Auschwitz* (Philadelphia: Jewish Publication Society of America, 1981), has called attention to the several dimensions of silence in the Book of Job.

The urging of v. 28 stands a long distance from the lyric of vv. 1-17. But the distance is the distance between God in God's remoteness and Yahweh who is present in the common wisdom of daily life. And Israel must settle for that urging.

It is important that in v. 28 the name of Yahweh is finally uttered, as though in this verse the sage inches back toward Israel's core testimony. Indeed, the counsel given here is to return to the central advice of the simple wisdom of Prov 3:7-8:

> Do not be wise in our own eyes;
> fear the Lord, and turn away from evil.
> It will be a healing for your flesh
> and a refreshment for your body.

But such a resolution is hardly satisfying. No real disclosure occurs here, no real acknowledgment, no actual meeting. One has the impression that this is penultimate urging that does not solve anything, except to put the hard issues in abeyance. Indeed, if v. 28 were adequate, neither Satan's question in 1:9 nor Job's question in 21:7 would have been asked.

The God of the whirlwind. Only late, in 38:1–42:6, in the awesomeness of the storm, does Yahweh finally speak. After the long hiatus of chapters 3–37, Yahweh is once again called by the right name (as in 28:28). This is indeed the God of Israel, the subject of Israel's core testimony, who speaks. The God of Israel does, in the end, answer, and the answer takes Job seriously. It is not, however, a user-friendly answer, and it concedes nothing to Job. Yahweh is willing to be available to Job. But Yahweh is lordly, haughty, condescending, dismissive, reprimanding, refusing to entertain Job's profound question, refusing to answer the probe of 21:7, and refusing to enter into any discussion about justice, sanctions, moral reliability, or covenantal symmetry. While scholars explore what appears to be the subtlety of these responses of Yahweh, it is evident that the ground of Yahweh's response is in power, the power of the Creator God who is genuinely originary, who can found the earth, bound the sea, summon rain and snow, order the cosmic lights, and keep the food chain functioning.[25] The lyrical, self-congratulatory assertions of Yahweh about the wonder of Behemoth (40:15-24) and Leviathan (41:1-34) open the assertion of power to the claim of artistry.[26] But the whole statement is one of overwhelmingness, not engagement.

These doxological verses strain for words to articulate the massiveness and awesomeness of this God, for whom Rudolf Otto employed the notion of *Tremendum*, and before Otto we may appeal to Immanuel Kant's "Sublime."[27] The response

---

25. Carol Newsom, "The Moral Sense of Nature: Ethics in the Light of God's Speech to Job," *Princeton Seminary Bulletin* 15 (1994) 9–27, has freshly probed the speeches of Yahweh.

26. If the speeches of Yahweh are to be understood as articulation of creation theology, then the mention of Leviathan here may well be related to the mention in Ps 104:26.

27. Immanuel Kant, *The Critique of Judgment* (trans. Jones Creed Meredith; Oxford: Clarendon Press, 1952) 90–203. In his well-known work, Rudolf Otto, *The Idea of the Holy: An Enquiry into the Non-rational Factor in the Idea of the Divine and Its Relation to the Rational* (New York: Oxford University Press, 1950) 63, transposes Kant's notion of the sublime into the holy:

of Yahweh—Yahweh's countertestimony against Job, which intends to nullify Job's countertestimony—moves the character of Yahweh to a new scale of grandeur. This is no longer a God who has reneged on a moral calculus. The friends are right, as far as they go, but this is a God in whose presence the issues of moral calculus of Job and his friends appear unworthy and trivial. This is indeed "God beyond God," who denies to Job (and to Israel) the comfort of moral symmetry.[28] Job (and Israel) now are required to live in a world where *nothing is settled or sure or reliable except the overwhelmingness of God.* Israel is dazzled in a way that endlessly mesmerizes, threatens, and destabilizes. And we are led to imagine that the God over whom Job and his friends have debated is, in the end, precisely one of the images prohibited by the terrible God of Sinai. The God of the whirlwind refuses the domestication to which Israel was intensely tempted.

Job's final enigmatic response to the God of the storm in 42:1-6 appears to be a concession, but scholars suspect that the response is not so straightforward as that.[29] In any case, the reliability question of 21:7 and the assault of 9:20-22 have evaporated. It is not that they have been answered by Yahweh or withdrawn by Job, but now, in light of this massive entry of Yahweh into the conversation, nobody is any longer interested in the question: not Job, not Satan, not Yahweh. The friends who held most firmly to the domesticated calculus are now explicitly rejected (42:7).

Problematic epilogue. The epilogue of 42:7-17 is as problematic as is the final response of Job in 42:1-6. Certainly it will not do any longer to regard the prose conclusion as a late addendum to soften the poetic ending. These prose verses belong integrally to the countertestimony of the poem, but their intention is far from clear. The friends are dismissed because they had settled for an ideological conclusion, without taking into account the problematic of lived experience. Such a posture evokes Yahweh's wrath, for Yahweh does not want ideology to crush experience. And that leaves only two parties for the conclusion: Yahweh and Job, face to face. Job, in contrast to the friends, has spoken what is "right" (42:7-8). This affirmation of Job may refer to his concession in 42:1-6, but those verses are less than clear. If 42:1-6 are "right," then Job is celebrated for entering into and accepting the awesomeness of Yahweh, leaving behind the penultimate issue of moral symmetry. But because v. 6 is so enigmatic, we cannot be sure.

While the element of "dread" is gradually overborne, the connection of "the sublime" and the "holy" becomes firmly established as a legitimate schematization and is carried on into the highest forms of religious consciousness—a proof that there exists a hidden kinship between the numinous and the sublime which is something more than a merely accidental analogy, and to which Kant's *Critique of Judgment* bears distant witness.

Tod Linafelt, "The Undecidability of *barak* in the Prologue to Job and Beyond," *Biblical Interpretation* 4 (1994) 154–72, suggests an interface between Kant's "sublime" and the God of the whirlwind speeches. Otto's explication of the holy explicitly owes much to Kant's categories.

28. See Paul Tillich, *The Courage to Be* (London: Nisbet and Co., 1952) 147–80 and passim.
29. See Jack Miles, *God: A Biography* (New York: Knopf, 1995) 425 n. 324, for a fine comment on this text; more generally on irony in Job, see Edwin M. Good, *In Turns of Tempest: A Reading of Job, with a Translation* (Stanford: Stanford University Press, 1990).

Perhaps what is "right" is *Job's refusal to concede,* and therefore what is celebrated is his entire defiant argument that culminates in 42:6. That is, what Yahweh intends as "right" is that Job (Israel, humankind) should make a legitimate case and rightful claim in the face of holiness, without timidity or cowardice or compromise. Such a conclusion may celebrate not the rightness of Israel's ancient theodic settlement rooted in Sinai (or the sages), but the courage of the human agent to carry the human question of justice into the danger zone of God's holiness.[30]

To be sure, as the poem suggests, there is a terrible mismatch between human justice and Yahweh's sovereign holiness. In such a confrontation, moreover, human justice can never win, for it always borders on the trivial in the presence of this awesome Creator God who overrides all the categories in which Israel characteristically trusts. Thus humankind must carry the issue of justice with courage, even while Israel knows that the issue will not win the day with Yahweh. There is something of Yahweh beyond moral calculus, which will not submit. Nonetheless the moral reliability of the world must be championed, even in the face of such ominous defeat. Even the holiness of God, enigmatic and inscrutable as the way of God is in the world, does not permit abandonment of the primal human agenda of justice. Job (and Israel) have a right to speak always of justice—indeed, have an obligation to speak of justice in the face of the holiness of God.

Why, finally, is everything restored to Job except his children?[31] Perhaps the answer is that neither Job nor Yahweh can sustain such extreme engagement for very long. This extreme engagement is the truth of the matter, but both parties will live for another day with each other. Thus Job's pain is a most serious ground for probe. But it is only a probe, not a sustainable, new level of interaction with Yahweh. This extreme moment of engagement is like a stunning artistic performance...and then one must leave the auditorium and go back to real life. Or it is like a breathtaking moment in therapy when everything becomes clear...and then one must return to "reality." Or it is like the intensity of sexual interaction...and then one must do the dishes. After the moment of pure disclosure comes a return to normalcy. Job must return to his moral passion (we imagine), and be "blameless and upright." And Yahweh will certainly return to the generous fidelity that belongs definitionally to Yahweh. Both parties revert to characteristic behavior. Yahweh is a "restorer of fortunes" (42:10), and Job is the obedient keeper of the Torah. In this world to which Yahweh and Job both seem to return, the view of the friends is adequate.

But neither Yahweh nor Job will ever be the same after this intense encounter, any more than one is the same after stunning artistry or breathtaking therapy or sexual intensity. Both parties have seen beyond what had ever been seen before.

---

30. This accent in Job is urged by Ernst Bloch, *Atheism in Christianity: The Religion of the Exodus and the Kingdom* (New York: Herder and Herder, 1972) 106–22, and is taken up effectively by Gustavo Gutiérrez, *On Job: God-Talk and the Suffering of the Innocent* (Maryknoll, N.Y.: Orbis Books, 1987).

31. On the irreversible loss of the children, see Emil Fackenheim, "New Hearts and the Old Covenant: On Some Possibilities of a Fraternal Jewish-Christian Reading of the Jewish Bible Today," *The Divine Helmsman: Studies on God's Control of Human Events* (ed. James L. Crenshaw and Samuel Sandmel; New York: KTAV, 1980) 191–205.

Now they must live with that blinding awareness, which remains, even if it cools. It is remarkable that at the end, Yahweh does not return to the heavenly court and does not again engage Satan. Yahweh's rightful place is not in the speculations of heaven, but in the realities of the earth. Yahweh is not a member of a mythical cast, but a partner to the bold and the obedient in the earth. Yahweh's continuing engagement is with Job, who is Yahweh's partner in abrasive candor, and who turns out to be Yahweh's proper counterpoint. Job does not yet know why the wicked prosper, and he no longer cares. Yahweh does not yet know if Job serves Yahweh for naught, but Yahweh knows enough. Yahweh is no easy, gentle partner, but then neither is Job. Their transaction includes a measure of honesty and respect that enlivens and ennobles the life they both now are to live. Neither has had the opening question clarified, but they have come to terms with each other. The drama does not bring a settlement that is altogether what either wished. But they make do in their honesty, neither giving in excessively to the other.

Ecclesiastes: The Far Edge of Negativity

The shrill and incessant voicing of negativity about Yahweh takes its toll. Over time, at least in some quarters, confidence in Israel's core testimony seems to erode. Surely in other quarters confidence in that core testimony continued unabated or even intensified, but that is not our concern here. At the very edge of the Old Testament, culturally and epistemologically, the Book of Ecclesiastes gives us the residue and outcome of that shrill and incessant voicing of negativity. The poem of Job is the most strident articulation of that negativity in Israel's countertestimony, but it is done with a passion, for the stakes are high. We have the impression that everyone involved cares intensely—Job and his friends, Yahweh and Satan, the writers of the text, and we the readers.

By the time we arrive at the far edge of negativity in Ecclesiastes, we have the parallel impression of countertestimony: a hostile witness, going through the paces but not really caring if anyone is persuaded by this utterance of guarded negativity. It is not doubted in this countertestimony that Yahweh is the Creator who presides over all of creation with power of an unchallenged kind. This is creation theology at its most formal and most formidable, perhaps seeded by the speeches of Yahweh in Job 38–41. The world does indeed belong to Yahweh. In Ecclesiastes three affirmations are made of Yahweh as Creator, which are congruent with the claims made in the core testimony of Israel. First, God does govern long term:

I know that whatever God does endures forever; nothing can be added to it, nor anything taken from it; God has done this, so that all should stand in awe before him. That which is, already has been; that which is to be, already is; and God seeks out what has gone by. (3:14-15)

Never be rash with your mouth, nor let your heart be quick to utter a word before God, for God is in heaven, and you upon earth; therefore let your words be few. (5:2)

...the dust returns to the earth as it was, and breath returns to God who gave it. (12:7)

God will outlast all creatureliness and will preserve all that is, was, and will be. God is the all-comprehending and all-sufficient.

Second, the God who governs is the one who judges, who pays attention to conduct in the world, and who gives people what they have coming to them. Ecclesiastes includes a heavy dose of the kind of theology-morality championed by the friends of Job:

For to the one who pleases him God gives wisdom and knowledge and joy; but to the sinner he gives the work of gathering and heaping, only to give to one who pleases God. (2:26)

I said in my heart, God will judge the righteous and the wicked, for he has appointed a time for every matter, and for every work. (3:17)

Do not let your mouth lead you into sin, and do not say before the messenger that it was a mistake; why should God be angry at your words, and destroy the work of your hands? (5:6; cf. 7:26; 8:13-14; 11; 12:14)

There is a reckoning and an accountability that cannot be escaped. Moral coherence indeed exists, and conduct counts. The tone of these utterances suggests that this is not a claim made with moral passion, but simply a commonsense assessment of how to manage.

Third, God gives. Indeed, there is nothing except what God gives:

There is nothing better for mortals than to eat and drink, and find enjoyment in their toil. This also, I saw, is from the hand of God; for apart from him who can eat or who can have enjoyment? (2:24)

This is what I have seen to be good: it is fitting to eat and drink and find enjoyment in all the toil with which one toils under the sun the few days of the life God gives us; for this is our lot. Likewise all to whom God gives wealth and possessions and whom he enables to enjoy them, and to accept their lot and find enjoyment in their toil—this is the gift of God. For they will scarcely brood over the days of their lives, because God keeps them occupied with the joy of their hearts. (5:18-20; cf. 6:2, 8:15, 9:7)

God's gifts, however, strike one here as an act of remoteness rather than of generosity. For in fact what God gives is a perplexing, less than satisfying "unhappy business" (1:13). There are gifts for enjoyment (3:12), but they are given along with that which is a vanity. Even what is given of wealth, possession, and honor (6:2) is in fact a vanity, "a grievous ill" (6:2). This witness is no atheist; he does not want to deny God or God's gifts. That much, if taken alone, is unexceptional in Israel's account of Yahweh.

This testimony cannot be taken apart from its context and the tone in which it is cast. For all of these rather stereotypical affirmations about Yahweh, the whole of life at best is mystifying and enigmatic. At most, it is a bewilderment, a tribulation, and vanity. The good that God does by governing, judging, and giving is situated in a context of massive frustration, for none of it is coherent, reliable, or sense-making. Ecclesiastes, as a witness to negativity, pushes past these convictions, which are no doubt serious and positively intended affirmations, to assert the inscrutability of Yahweh. Thus, "God is in heaven, and you upon earth" (5:2). God is remote, transcendent, out of reach. Human utterance had best be kept lean, for human persons are in no position even to address God in any way that matters. Here it is as though the witness has been convinced by the speeches of the whirlwind (Job 38–41). God is beyond challenge or correction; "who can make straight what he has made crooked?" (7:13). The bewilderment is because humankind must live in a world whose sense cannot be deciphered:

> ...then I saw all the work of God, that no one can find out what is happening under the sun. However much they may toil in seeking, they will not find it out; even though those who are wise claim to know, they cannot find it out. (8:17)

The utterance is like a mantra of resignation: "no one can find out" ... "will not find it out" ... "cannot find it out." God makes everything, but no one knows the work of God (11:5). It is all hidden in a meaningless cycle of living and breathing and dying...all is vanity (12:8).

The problem is not simply the enigmatic quality of human life at the behest of a remote God. More than that, God is completely indifferent to differentiations in the world. No evidence is given here that anything on earth matters at all to the way in which Yahweh deals with the world. In his rage, Job had already said: "It is all one; therefore I say, he destroys both the blameless and the wicked" (Job 9:22).[32] This theme seems a fair conclusion in the poem of Job (perhaps overcome in the epilogue, though nothing is conceded). In any case, this theme is rearticulated in the countertestimony of Ecclesiastes:

> For the fate of humans and the fate of animals is the same; as one dies, so dies the other. They all have the same breath, and humans have no advantage over the animals; for all is vanity. All go to one place; all are from the dust, and all turn to the dust again. Who knows whether the human spirit goes upward and the spirit of animals goes downward to the earth? (3:19-21)

The accent, to be sure, is somewhat different here from that of Job. Job had indicated that there is no distinction between the guilty and the innocent among human persons, and here there is no distinction between animals and human

---

32. The point is made differently, with less acrimony, in Ps 49:12, 20, where it is a reiterated refrain: "Mortals cannot abide in their pomp; they are like the animals that perish."

persons. Because animals are not morally accountable, the outcome of these two assertions is the same: Nothing of conduct, not even passionate obedience, counts for God. One may be as stupid or as unresponsive as an animal, and it does not matter at all.

The affirmation of Eccl 9:1-3 is much closer to the claim of Job 9:22:

> All this I laid to heart, examining it all, how the righteous and the wise and their deeds are in the hand of God; whether it is love or hate one does not know. Everything that confronts them is vanity, since the same fate comes to all, to the righteous and the wicked, to the good and to the evil, to the clean and the unclean, to those who sacrifice and to those who do not sacrifice. As are the good, so are the sinners; those who swear are like those who shun an oath. (9:1-3)

Everything on earth's side of creation is finally irrelevant.

The question of the unity of this testimony in Ecclesiastes is a difficult one. Multiple opinions are expressed here, some in contradiction to others. It may be that different voices have judged and said different things. It is as plausible, however, to conclude that it is precisely the contradictions that constitute the substance of this countertestimony. The contradiction is between the normative claims of faith, here repeated as if by rote, and the acute frustration of experience. It is the same contradiction that was the substance of the poem of Job. It is the contradiction between meaningful, valued obedience and responsibility in the world, and the profound awareness of moral indifference writ large, so that in fact nothing really matters. Nothing really matters to God, and therefore the speaker likewise is prepared to quit contesting against the vanity of it all. The core testimony of God's good sovereignty is in jeopardy in this failed sense of resignation, but the testimony is too contradictory and convoluted even to permit that final judgment.

So what shall Israel do when the "command-obey" structure of covenantal sanctions has collapsed? Indeed, what shall humankind do in a world where God is remote, inscrutable, inaccessible, seemingly indifferent? The answer is to enjoy life while one can:

> Go, eat your bread with enjoyment, and drink your wine with a merry heart;
> for God has long ago approved what you do. (Eccl 9:7)

The approval of God sounds pro forma. The affirmation sounds more than a little cynical. But it is an attempt, I suggest, to salvage human significance and well-being in a world that has become theologically incoherent and nearly unbearable. It is, nonetheless, sound advice: Do not be devoured by vexation and anxiety; love your life. By itself, this may be a recipe for self-indulgence in a world where God is morally indifferent. Indeed, this indirect testimony to Yahweh sounds not unlike the "wrong speech" about Yahweh "who will not do good and will not do ill" (Zeph 1:12; Jer 5:12).[33]

---

33. On idolatry as "wrong speech" about Yahweh, see pp. 136–37.

A major exception, however, occurs at the end, as this witness surprises us:

The end of the matter; all has been heard. Fear God, and keep his commandments; for that is the whole duty of everyone. (Eccl 12:13)

For all the tone of resignation and of living at the edge of despair that might sanction self-indulgence, this counterwitness is not outside the circle of the wisdom teachers who endlessly negotiate between experience and communal affirmation. This witness is able and willing, in the end ("The end of the matter..."; *sôph dabar*), to return to the cadences of the old wisdom. Erhard Gerstenberger has suggested that Prov 3:7 functions as a motto for wisdom instruction: "Do not be wise in our own eyes; fear the Lord, and turn away from evil."[34] This counsel is an adequate guidance for responsible life in the world of Yahweh's order. And in any case, "fear of Yahweh" is indeed the beginning of wisdom (Prov 1:7). Acknowledgment of Yahweh is the point of orientation for a well-lived life.[35]

In the poem concerning the hiddenness and inscrutability of wisdom in Job 28, after an extraordinary lyrical doxology in praise of wisdom in all its depth and wonder, the poem concludes with an echo of the old wisdom, an echo of words very like Prov 3:7: "Truly, the fear of the Lord, that is wisdom; and to depart from evil is understanding" (v. 28). Now, at the end of this daring and unsettling statement in Ecclesiastes, a like statement in 12:13 concludes the address by the preacher. The statement is not the same as those of Prov 3:7 or Job 28:28. First, this statement refuses the name "Yahweh" and settles for "God." This is the characteristic way in which Ecclesiastes refers to Yahweh, congruent with the main body of the poem of Job, a distancing procedure that keeps far from the old core testimony. Second, Prov 3:7 and Job 28:28 only enjoin wisdom. Here the witness appeals to the commandments, although to unspecified ones. The reference must be taken to refer to the entire Torah tradition, without differentiation. In the end, the propensity of this witness toward cynicism and resignation is deconstructed by a recognition that in the universe of discourse where this voice lives, the commandments are intransigent and unaccommodating in their claim. We may wonder if the witness compromises and concedes too much in the end, by accommodating the tradition of obedience. Or we may follow critical opinion to say that the evidence of the witness has been tampered with, so that this verse is a belated, correcting addendum. But so the witness now stands. The negativity would stand more impressively without this last concession, of course, but that is not Israel's way. Israel's way is to voice all of its enraged candor, but always to bear in mind the One who must be addressed, and then obeyed.

Yahweh was silent for long stretches in the poem of Job, speaking only near the end, in an eruption. In Ecclesiastes there is no eruption from Yahweh, who is

---

34. Erhard Gerstenberger, *Wesen und Herkunft des 'apodiktischen Rechts'* (Neukirchen-Vluyn: Neukirchener Verlag, 1965) 49.

35. On the liturgic work of orientation, see Walter Brueggemann, *The Message of the Psalms: A Theological Commentary* (Minneapolis: Augsburg, 1984) 25–49.

hardly permitted in the testimony. There is only silence on Yahweh's part, perhaps to match the resignation and the cold concession of the witness. In the end, this witness will say of obedience, this is "the all of humankind" (*zeh kol-'dm*). The "all" is obedience to command. That is not much. The negativity seems to conclude with an awareness that the God who commanded at Sinai still commands and still enacts sanctions. But now the commands stand bare and contextless, without the "mighty deeds" and their powerful verbs. Now the speaker aims to get by, no longer with the energy to master life, a main characteristic of the old wisdom.[36]

Strident Protest in Psalm 88

The silence finally can lead to less energetic, almost phlegmatic obedience; or it can on occasion still evoke strident protest. Thus we take our final consideration of the voicing of negativity from Psalm 88, a very different kind of "limit expression." Ecclesiastes has lost any passion or impetus to cry out to Yahweh. Perhaps that should be our final word on negativity, for with Ecclesiastes we reach, in one sense, the end of the Old Testament. But such melancholy is unrepresentative of Israel's faith and even of Israel's way of negativity. Therefore high-energy protest seems a more appropriate conclusion than low-energy, calculating submissiveness.

Psalm 88 expresses an incessant crying out to Yahweh in need (vv. 1-2, 9b, 13). The cry, remarkably enough, does not even utter a petition. It is all complaint, voiced as accusation against Yahweh. The speaker refers to deep trouble: "Sheol," "the Pit," "no help," "among the dead," "slain," "remembered no more," "cut off," "dark and deep" (vv. 3-6). More than that, it is Yahweh who has done this to the speaker:

> Your wrath...
> you overwhelm...
> you have caused...
> you have made...(vv. 7-8)
>
> your wrath...
> your dread...
> you have caused...(vv. 16-18)

The accusation turns to threat against Yahweh in the rhetorical questions of vv. 10-12. If Yahweh allows the death of the speaker, Yahweh will lose a witness to Yahweh's *ḥesed*. There will be no speech on earth, among the living, of Yahweh's steadfast love or faithfulness or wonders or saving help. *The loss of the speaker will cause Yahweh to lose the speech on which Yahweh's reality in the world depends.*

But there is no answer to this plea. That's negativity! The very silence and remoteness of God, which Ecclesiastes takes as a matter of course, is here a cause for rage and indignation. Here Israel seeks to show that the losses sustained through the silence of Yahweh are not only to the Israelite who speaks. There will be

---

36. See Gerhard von Rad, *Wisdom in Israel* (Nashville: Abingdon Press, 1972) 232.

losses as well *for Yahweh*, who will no longer be praised (v. 10). Ecclesiastes, in its resignation and coping resolve, is a more modern response to the absence and the silence of God, but Psalm 88 is more characteristically Jewish. Ecclesiastes' countertestimony has a terminus, but Psalm 88 has no end. The cry of the psalm will continue.[37] We can imagine that Israel—this Israelite, some Israelites—will continue to sound this shrill psalm. They will not sound it forever. They will only sound it until "my prayer comes before you." That, however, may be a very long time. In this version of countertestimony, however, Israel will not quit in resignation. Israel will not match the silence of God with its own submitting silence. Israel, rather, will keep on speaking its petition until it moves Yahweh into speech and action. That is how Yahweh was moved to enact Yahweh's powerful verbs in the first place (Exod 2:23-25). Israel, in this version of countertestimony, does not propose to stop now...or ever.

---

37. Notice the title of the important book by Patrick D. Miller, *They Cried to the Lord: The Form and Theology of Biblical Prayer* (Minneapolis: Fortress Press, 1994). Miller has understood, perhaps following Gerstenberger on the cruciality of the petition, that "cry" is the core theme of the Psalter. But then, given Exod 2:23-25, it is perhaps the core theme of Israel's life in the world. In his autobiography, Elie Wiesel, *All Rivers Run to the Sea: Memoirs* (New York: Knopf, 1995) 275, reports one exchange in rabbinic teaching:

"So long as he cries, he can hope his father will hear him. If he stops, he is lost...."
"Believe me, I have never ceased to cry out...."
"May the Lord be praised...Then there is hope."

TWELVE

Maintaining the Tension

W E COME NOW to the end of our extended discussion of Israel's testimony to Yahweh. I have suggested that the core testimony of Israel lives in profound tension with the countertestimony of Israel. The core testimony, rooted in the great transformative verbs, ends in an affirmation of Yahweh's faithful sovereignty and Yahweh's sovereign fidelity. The countertestimony, rooted in Israel's lived experience of absence and silence, ends in an articulation of Yahweh's hiddenness, ambiguity, and negativity.

The tension between the core testimony and the countertestimony is acute and ongoing. It is my judgment that this tension between the two belongs to the very character and substance of Old Testament faith, a tension that precludes and resists resolution. The conventional attitude of ecclesial communities, Christian more than Jewish, is to opt for the core testimony of faithful sovereignty and sovereign fidelity and to eliminate or disregard the countertestimony of hiddenness, ambiguity, and negativity from the horizon of faith. Such a process yields a coherent faith, but it requires mumbling through many aspects of lived experience that evoked the countertestimony in the first place. By contrast, the inclination of "outsiders"— those who find the core testimony too insistent or normative or authoritarian, those too wounded by life (wounds readily credited to God), and the urbane modernists who are "the cultured despisers of religion"[1]—is to scuttle the testimony and to conclude that the testimony has been decisively and irreversibly defeated.

To choose either mode of testimony to the disregard of the other is in my judgment not only to cheat the testimonial corpus, but to misunderstand the dialectical, resilient, disputatious quality that is definitional for this faith. Thus David Blumenthal's metaphor of "tacking" between various courses is about right in my judgment.[2] Lived faith in this tradition consists in the capacity to move back and forth between these two postures of faith, one concerned to submit to Yahweh,

---

1. The phrase is from Friedrich Schleiermacher, *On Religion: Speeches to Its Cultural Despisers* (Cambridge: Cambridge University Press, 1988).

2. David Blumenthal, *Facing the Abusive God: A Theology of Protest* (Louisville: Westminster/John Knox, 1993) 47–54, proposes that one element in the tacking of Israel's faith, along with submissive trust, is the disputatious quality of protest; on this see Elie Wiesel concerning the dialectic of protest and submissiveness. On Wiesel's presentation of the dialectic, see Robert McAfee Brown, *Elie Wiesel, Messenger to All Humanity* (Notre Dame, Ind.: University of Notre Dame Press, 1983) 154.

culminating in *self-abandoning praise,* the other concerned to assert self in the face of God, culminating in *self-regarding complaint* that takes a posture of autonomy.

Right faith, taking all this testimony into account, recognizes that in different contexts, each of us will be required and permitted to align ourselves with one sort of testimony or the other, which will be adequate in the context. As we do so, however, it will be important to remember that at that very moment of adequacy, others, in other circumstances, in this same universe of discourse will be speaking very differently, heeding different witnesses, with the same sense of adequacy.

In stating this dialectic, which therefore requires both centrist and marginated interpreters, I have tried to stay within the bounds of the Old Testament itself and to heed its unmistakably Jewish propensity.[3] At the same time, I live my life and practice my faith as a Christian. Thus I have pondered the fact that in the face of this unresolved and unresolvable dialectic, the Christian tradition of interpretation and theology has tended toward closure in the direction of the core testimony. The Christian tradition knows full well that "in the world you have tribulation" (John 16:33, RSV). In the same verse it is able to say in an Easter context, however, "be of good cheer, I have overcome the world." And in that high claim made through Jesus, the countertestimony of Israel seems to be silenced.

I think not, however. The Christian tradition, with its propensity for christological closure in the events of Good Friday and Easter, continues the same dialectic, *mutatis mutandis.* Thus Friday is the day of countertestimony in the Christian tradition, centered in Jesus' recital of Psalm 22, but also including the taunts addressed to Jesus by those around the cross (Matt 27:39-44). Clearly Easter is taken to be substantiation of the core testimony concerning Yahweh's faithful sovereignty and sovereign fidelity. There is a sense that Sunday resolves Friday, that the core testimony resolves the countertestimony—except that liturgically, *both claims linger.* Jürgen Moltmann has seen that crucifixion and resurrection in Christian theological interpretation are not, together, a once-for-all sequenced event. They are together, rather, a "dialectic of reconciliation," in which both sides of the dialectic are still urgent.[4] Thus a feel-good, triumphalist, or therapeutic gospel may permit Sunday to obliterate Friday. But in our honest reading of the New Testament, and in our honest liturgic reckoning, the Friday of negativity persists to make its claim.

In any case, the lived reality of the world, with its barbarism and alienation, indicates unambiguously that Easter has not singularly settled all. Thus in its eucharistic confession when the church, rooted in Israel's testimony, must "proclaim the mystery of faith," it not only asserts: "Christ has died, Christ has risen." It must also add: "Christ will come again." It ends with an acknowledgment of waiting, albeit full of belief; confident waiting, but nonetheless waiting.

---

3. See my general comments on centrist and marginated practitioners of Old Testament theology, pp. 89–102. Given the disputatious quality of Israel's faith, I suggest that centrist interpreters (of whom I am one) must always expect to be instructed and illuminated by their marginated counterparts.

4. Jürgen Moltmann, *Theology of Hope: On the Ground and the Implication of Christian Eschatology* (1967; Minneapolis: Fortress Press, 1993); *The Crucified God: The Cross of Christ as the Foundation and Criticism of Christian Theology* (1974; Minneapolis: Fortress Press, 1993).

Is that waiting not in close proximity to the waiting of Psalm 88, which does not doubt, in its persistence and shrillness and stubbornness, that there will be a hearing and an answer? Thus Christians, for all the claim of the core testimony of Easter, still wait for resolution very sure, but sure only in hope. Thus I submit that in the end, if we keep our Christian confession close to the text and to lived reality, all the communities propelled by this testimony wait together. All wait in the conviction that the core testimony of faithful sovereignty and sovereign fidelity will defeat hiddenness, ambiguity, and negativity. It is a waiting done in profound hope, but it is nevertheless a waiting. George Steiner has eloquently expressed the common, dread-filled, resilient waiting that Jews and Christians must do together on behalf of all humanity:

> There is one particular day in Western history about which neither historical record nor myth nor Scripture make report. It is a Saturday. And it has become the longest of days. We know of that Good Friday which Christianity holds to have been that of the Cross. But the non-Christian, the atheist, knows of it as well. That is to say that he knows of the injustice, of the interminable suffering, of the waste, of the brute enigma of ending, which so largely make up not only the historical dimension of the human condition, but the everyday fabric of our personal lives. We know, ineluctably, of the pain, of the failure of love, of the solitude which are our history and private fate. We also know about Sunday. To the Christian, that day signifies an intimation, both assured and precarious, both evident and beyond comprehension, of resurrection, of a justice and love that have conquered death. If we are non-Christians or non-believers, we know of that Sunday in precisely analogous terms. We conceive of it as the day of liberation from inhumanity and servitude. We look to resolutions, be they therapeutic or political, be they social or messianic. The lineaments of that Sunday carry the name of hope (there is no word less deconstructible).
>
> But ours is a long day's journey of the Saturday. Between suffering, aloneness, unutterable waste on the one hand and the dream of liberation, of rebirth the other. In the face of the torture of a child, of the death of love which is Friday, even the greatest art and poetry are almost helpless. In the Utopia of the Sunday, the aesthetic will, presumably, no longer have logic or necessity. The apprehensions and figurations in the play of metaphysical imagining, in the poem and the music, which tell of pain and of hope, of the flesh which is said to taste of ash and of the spirit which is said to have the savour of fire, are always Sabbatarian. They have risen out of an immensity of waiting which is that of man. Without them, how could we be patient?[5]

This waiting where the Old Testament ends is not, as some supersessionist Christian interpretation suggests, because Old Testament faith is flawed, inadequate, or

---

5. George Steiner, *Real Presences: Is There Anything in What We Say?* (London: Faber and Faber, 1989) 231–32.

incomplete. The waiting is inescapable because of the unresolved condition of life in the world, an unresolve shared by Christians with Jews and with all others.

The unresolve is as profound in the New Testament as in the Old.[6] The Old ends with the waiting of Elijah "before the great and terrible day of the Lord comes" (Mal 4:5). The New ends with a prayer, "Come, Lord Jesus!" (Rev 22:20). And even in the Jewish Bible with its different ordering, the end is "Let us go up" (2 Chr 36:22). All wait not doubting, but having nothing in hand except this rich, complex, disturbing testimony.[7]

---

6. Concerning the shared, common waiting of Jews and Christians, Elie Wiesel, *All Rivers Run to the Sea: Memoirs* (New York: Knopf, 1995) 354–55, reports an anecdote of Martin Buber, who told a group of priests:

"What is the difference between Jews and Christians? We all await the Messiah. You believe He has already come and gone, while we do not. I therefore propose that we await Him together. And when He appears, we can ask Him: Were you here before?" Then he paused and added: "And I hope that at that moment I will be close enough to whisper in his ear, 'For the love of heaven, don't answer.'"

7. I complete the first draft of this section of my study on Good Friday. It is an apt day for the comments I have made. Likely I could not have made them were it not that time in the church year.

Part III

ISRAEL'S UNSOLICITED TESTIMONY

THIRTEEN

Israel's Unsolicited Testimony

I N THIS SECTION we take up the governing metaphor of courtroom testimony again, this time in order to speak about Israel's unsolicited testimony. First we will consider the meaning of the phrase "unsolicited testimony" inside the metaphor of the courtroom, and then consider the character and purpose of Israel's unsolicited testimony.

Possible Motives for Unsolicited Testimony

In much courtroom procedure, witnesses are carefully monitored and prepared by attorneys, so that the testimony they give should contribute to the case the attorneys seek to construct. In order to build such a case, the attorneys must have certain things said in court, and so they prompt the witness to be sure those things are said. But equal care must be taken in order to preclude other statements that, for the cause of the case being constructed, must not be uttered by the witness. Thus the witness is regularly instructed to "just answer the questions." That is, answer only what is asked; do not volunteer any testimony beyond circumspect answers to the questions. Extra testimony, unsolicited by the attorney, may be harmful to the case.

And yet, often a witness will proceed to give extra, unsolicited testimony, even though warned against it by the judge or attorney. The witness may ignore such warnings, in seeming reckless indifference to the damage that may be done. Why would a witness offer unsolicited testimony against the strong urging of the court? It may be that the witness is simply loquacious and an exhibitionist who enjoys the opportunity to be at the center of attention, and so extends testimonial time with extra talk. But there may also be good and positive reasons why a witness would proceed with unsolicited testimony. The witness may simply want to help and is concerned to give the fullest evidence possible. And it may well be that the witness is peculiarly insightful and discerns connections between matters that no one else in the court has yet noticed. The witness may reason that certain matters are intimately and intrinsically connected to each other, so that one cannot possibly understand "this" unless one is also informed about "that," which decisively impinges upon and affects "this." Therefore the witness will proceed to make connections that are enormously illuminating to the matter before the court, even if neither the judge nor the attorneys could anticipate the connection.

It is evident that *in the Old Testament, Israel gives a good deal of "unsolicited testimony."* I have, at the outset, limited our subject matter to theo-logy (*theos-logos*): speech about God, the single, proper subject of "theology." I have asked at the outset, "How does Israel speak about God?"[1] An extended answer to that question has been given under the rubrics of "core testimony" and "countertestimony." By posing this question and answering it this way, I have intended to instruct and limit the witness, Israel. "The court" has made clear that its only interest is in how Israel speaks about God, and has sought to limit Israel's testimony to that single question. Israel has been enormously forthcoming about that question.

Any careful consideration of Israel's testimony about God indicates that Israel is indeed an unrestrained witness who will not stop with testimony about Yahweh. Without taking an extra breath, without a pause, in the very same utterance, Israel continues to talk about many other matters beyond what has been asked. It is these other matters that constitute Israel's unsolicited testimony.

Thus we must reflect upon Israel's unsolicited testimony, which goes well beyond the scope of our proper investigation. We may wonder why Israel insists on this additional commentary, and we may suggest the same three possible explanations for extra testimony suggested above. First, Israel may give the unsolicited testimony of Israel because Israel enjoys the attention it attracts in being a witness and is not shy about self-presentation. There is a quality of delight in Old Testament utterance, so that much is stated extravagantly, inordinately, hyperbolically. In its witness, Israel delights to make a bold presentation in front of the watching nations, for it is to "the nations" that Israel often bears witness about Yahweh (see Ps 96:10).

A second motivation for unsolicited testimony is that Israel wants to be helpful, to be sure that the court has the full picture. So Israel fills in the details around Yahweh and sketches in the other characters in the narrative construal of Yahweh, so that the court can see Yahweh in context rather than in a dramatic vacuum.

Third, it may be that Israel as a witness is peculiarly insightful in its utterance of Yahweh. Israel discerns connections concerning Yahweh that no one else in the court has noticed. Israel has come to the conclusion that certain relationships are intimately and intrinsically pertinent to the character of Yahweh. Moreover, Yahweh cannot possibly be discerned rightly and fully unless one also knows about the partners who decisively impinge upon and affect Yahweh. Therefore Israel proceeds to "make connections" that are enormously illuminating concerning Yahweh, connections that none, prior to Israel's testimony, had rightly and fully discerned.

Yahweh's Partners

For these parties "connected" to Yahweh intimately and intrinsically, I use the term *partner*.[2]

---

1. On this question as an organizing theme for this study, see pp. 117–20.

2. Much scholarship now proposes that Yahweh, prior to the monotheistic imposition of the canonical process, had a sexual partner. See Judith M. Hadley, "Wisdom and the Goddess," *Wisdom*

I intend this to be a neutral term, leaving open the dynamic of the relationship. What is important now is the recognition that Yahweh, as given in Israel's testimony, never comes "alone" but is always Yahweh-in-relation. Thus Rolf Knierim rightly asserts: "The Old Testament, strictly speaking, does not speak about Yahweh. It speaks about the relationship between Yahweh or God and reality."[3] Israel has seen that Yahweh will never be rightly discerned unless it is clear that any faithful utterance about Yahweh must at the same time be an utterance about Yahweh's partner.

It is important at the outset to be clear about the character of the relationship between Yahweh and these partners. In our early consideration of the grammar of Israel's testimony, we observed that characteristically Yahweh is embedded in complete sentences. In these sentences, Yahweh is the active subject of powerful, transformative verbs. Thus for example: "Yahweh creates," "Yahweh saves," "Yahweh commands," "Yahweh leads." We noted in passing that Yahweh's partners are the direct objects of Yahweh's active, transformative verbs. That is, Yahweh's partners are the objects of Yahweh's activity: acted-upon recipients of what Yahweh chooses to enact. Such a mode of grammar, which is characteristic in Israel's testimony to Yahweh, retains for Yahweh all the active force and initiative in the transaction.

But we have just said that these partners decisively impinge upon and affect Yahweh. Such an awareness means that Yahweh's partners, while they paradigmatically are the object in the relationship, cannot be securely slotted in that single role as recipient. Israel's testimony to Yahweh includes a recognition that the delicacy and vitality of the interaction between Yahweh and Yahweh's partners cannot be contained in such a simple grammatical construct. The partners in turn break out

---

in Ancient Israel: Essays in Honour of J. A. Emerton (ed. John Day et al.; Cambridge: Cambridge University Press, 1995) 234–43, for a sober review of the data. While the evidence is mixed and we cannot be sure, it is clear that Old Testament theology as such is not concerned with traces of such a prior relationship. See the thoughtful conclusion drawn by Patrick D. Miller, "The Absence of the Goddess in Israelite Religion," *HAR* 10 (1986) 239–48.

Writing of Yahweh's dealings with uncredentialed persons in the Old Testament, Frederick E. Greenspahn, *When Brothers Dwell Together: The Preeminence of Younger Siblings in the Hebrew Bible* (Oxford: Oxford University Press, 1994) 160, writes: "God works with these figures because He can and He must. He created them and He chose them. As things turned out, neither God nor Israel is as perfect as they should be. Perhaps that is why they make such good partners."

Writing more generically about human placement in the world, John Carmody, "Noetic Differentiations: Religious Implications," *Voegelin and the Theologians: Ten Studies in Interpretation* (ed. John Kirby and William M. Thompson; Toronto Studies in Theology 10; Toronto: Edwin Mellen Press, 1983) 141–42, says:

> The truth of the cosmos is that we are partnered to nature, society, and divinity—that the "world" is a living whole of participation. Because of the fundament our materiality gives us in nature, and because of nature's over-againstness or quasi-independence of our awareness, there is no dissolving the cosmos, no living as though we are not participants or ecological with the rest of creation. For that reason, the truth of differentiated noesis cannot simply replace the truth of the cosmological myth. For all their momentousness, the Israelite prophets and the Hellenistic philosophers "merely" declare in discrete, unfolded form what their mythopoeic brothers and sisters experienced and expressed compactly.

3. Rolf P. Knierim, "The Task of Old Testament Theology," *HBT* 6 (June 1984) 36.

of the role of object and, on occasion, become an active subject and agent face-to-face with Yahweh, and so impact Yahweh in ways that cause Yahweh to be different from the way Yahweh was prior to the contact.[4]

These relationships evidence a dimension of mutuality that speaks insistently against any notion that Yahweh is transcendent beyond Israel. This quality of relationship (conventionally referred to as "covenant") is what makes Yahweh a most peculiar God and makes the Old Testament endlessly interesting, generative, and unsettling. Indeed, the "turn back" that Yahweh's partners are able to effect on Yahweh suggests that Yahweh's person and character are indeed fully available in the relationship, that nothing about Yahweh is held back or kept immune from this relationship. This does not mean that in this fully available relationship, where Yahweh is accessible for being impacted, Yahweh is "like any other." Indeed not. And so the Old Testament continues to ponder and puzzle over the character of Yahweh, who is fully available to Yahweh's partners, but in such ways that it is always the Yahweh of the transformative verbs who is available.

Linkage of Freedom and Passion

It is exceedingly difficult to articulate this double claim of partnership, the claim of full availability and the equally important claim of Yahweh's oddness. The reason for the difficulty is that our conventionally Aristotelian logic and rhetoric is ill-suited for utterance concerning a character who is genuinely transactional. As a thesis formulation that will guide our exposition of Israel's unsolicited testimony, I propose the following: *Yahweh is committed to Yahweh's partners in freedom and in passion.* It is this odd linkage of freedom and passion that constitutes the space for Israel's unsolicited testimony.

Yahweh is *committed to the partner in freedom.* This assertion means that Yahweh's connection to the partner is undertaken as sovereign, unfettered choice on Yahweh's part. Yahweh makes a commitment of care, fidelity, and obligation to the partner that Yahweh did not need to make. In the end, Israel can give no reason for this act of Yahweh's freedom. It is simply a given that is available in Israel's discernment of its life in the world. In freedom, Yahweh surely retains sovereignty over the relationship, evidenced in the continuing control of the decisive verbs.

Because this commitment of fidelity to the partner is undertaken in sovereign freedom, it follows that Yahweh can indeed withdraw from the relationship and cancel the commitment. Indeed, Yahweh will do what Yahweh pleases. Moreover,

---

4. Roy Schafer, *Retelling a Life: Narrative and Dialogue in Psychoanalysis* (New York: Basic Books, 1992) 94–95, offers a helpful comment on the sexual relationship between two partners who must at various times be alternately "agent" and "milieu" for the partner:

> A whole person allows the reversibility in a relatively conflict-free fashion. He or she refrains from insisting on being only agent or object.... The reversibility is itself a form of action.... A whole person is neither threatened by reversibility nor incapable of enjoying either position in a relationship.

Mutatis mutandis, I suggest that in the partnership between Yahweh and Israel, both partners are, on occasion, agent and milieu for the other.

it is evident in Yahweh's relationship to Israel, as Israel moves amid prophetic rage and anguish toward 587 B.C.E., that Yahweh can terminate the relationship. In the utterances of Jeremiah and Ezekiel, in particular, such a termination seems evident. And in like manner, the beginning of the flood narrative (Gen 6:5-13) evidences that while God "loves the world" (creation), Yahweh can in indignant freedom terminate the relationship. Israel's testimony does not flinch from crediting Yahweh with the capacity to slough off such commitments.

But our second affirmation is that Yahweh is *committed to the partner in passion.* The term *passion,* as Jürgen Moltmann has most recently and helpfully shown, has a double meaning.[5] It refers, first of all, to powerful and strong feeling. Yahweh does commit to the partner with powerful and strong feelings of concern, care, and affection. Yahweh becomes "involved" with the partner in compelling ways, in ways that the scholastic attributes usually assigned to God (omnipotence, omnipresence, omniscience) do not allow. But the term *passion* means, secondly, the capacity and readiness to suffer with and to suffer for, to stay with a partner in trouble, vexation, and danger. We have seen that Yahweh's characteristic adjectives of fidelity lead to a practice of covenantal engagement that issues in Yahweh's pathos, that moves against Yahweh's sovereign indignation.[6] And so it is, on occasion, that Yahweh surprisingly does not exercise sovereign freedom to terminate a dysfunctional relationship, even when Yahweh clearly has the right to do so. Yahweh, on occasion, stays with the partner, seemingly because Yahweh is so engaged in the relationship that Yahweh is unable or unwilling to terminate it.

This extraordinary dialectic of freedom and passion in the character of Yahweh prevents Israel's unsolicited testimony about Yahweh's partners from being flat, one-dimensional, and readily exhausted. If Yahweh were only committed in sovereign freedom, the partner would long ago have been disposed of. If Yahweh were committed only in suffering love, the partner would be completely safe in the relationship. But as long ago as Exod 34:6-7 we have seen an unresolve in the character of Yahweh, which now reemerges in our consideration of Yahweh's partners.[7] The most characteristic thing to be said about Yahweh's partners is that the partners exist in the first place because of Yahweh's sovereign freedom, and that the partners continue to exist because of Yahweh's faithful passion. These inclinations of Yahweh, however, are not flatly resolved. Therefore, the life of the partner is one that requires a good bit of testimony, in order that Yahweh should be fully articulated in these relationships.

For the purposes of our exposition of Israel's unsolicited testimony, I propose to deal with Yahweh's partners under four headings: Israel, individual human persons, the nations, and creation. It may be that other topics could be devised, but these, if

---

5. Jürgen Moltmann, *The Crucified God: The Cross of Christ as the Foundation and Criticism of Christian Theology* (1974; Minneapolis: Fortress Press, 1993).

6. On the dialectic of Yahweh's sovereignty and pathos, see pp. 267–313.

7. Concerning Exod 34:6-7 as foundational for my argument, see pp. 215–18 and 269–70.

not exhaustive, will at least be representative of Israel's unsolicited testimony. For these four headings, I shall begin with Israel's general claim:

- Yahweh is committed to Israel in freedom and passion.

- Yahweh is committed to human persons in freedom and passion.

- Yahweh is committed to the nations in freedom and passion.

- Yahweh is committed to creation in freedom and passion.

Because these four statements are roughly symmetrical, moreover, the claims made for any of these partners may, *mutatis mutandis,* be extended to the other three partners.

FOURTEEN

Israel as Yahweh's Partner

W E HAVE ALREADY SEEN that Israel is indeed the special object of Yahweh's most characteristic verbs: Yahweh *saved* Israel, Yahweh *promised* to Israel, Yahweh *led* Israel, Yahweh *commanded* Israel. Yahweh is committed to Israel in freedom and passion.

In Israel's unsolicited testimony, Israel becomes the key partner to Yahweh and the subject of the testimony. In these ancient texts and in its ongoing life in the world, Israel is indeed an oddity and a mystery,[1] because Israel is a theological phenomenon that has concrete sociopolitical embodiment and is expected to live differently in a world of power. This odd combination of the theological and political realms is definitional for Israel, and therefore Israel is an unassimilable entity in the world. Whatever else may be said of Israel, in the end Israel in these texts must regard itself Yahwistically. That is, in some impenetrable way, Israel's existence is referred to and derived from Yahweh. Israel will not be discerned in these texts without reference to Yahweh. But it is equally odd and noteworthy that Yahweh will not be discerned in these texts without reference to Israel.[2]

We may organize our reflection on this primal partner of Yahweh under rubrics that are in a general way historical, except that the canonically construed "history" of Israel is theologically paradigmatic.[3]

---

1. Martin Buber and Abraham Heschel have written most eloquently about the inscrutable theological quality of Israel. See Martin Buber, *Israel and the World: Essays in a Time of Crisis* (New York: Schocken Books, 1948); *On Zion: The History of an Idea* (New York: Schocken Books, 1973); and *On Judaism* (ed. Nahum N. Glatzer; New York: Schocken Books, 1967); Abraham J. Heschel, *God in Search of Man: A Philosophy of Judaism* (New York: Farrar, Straus & Cudahy, 1955); and *Between God and Man: An Interpretation of Judaism* (New York: Harper and Row, 1959). To be sure, important writing in the subject has been done since the period of Buber's and Heschel's generative work, especially by Emil Fackenheim and Richard L. Rubenstein. Nonetheless, for the interface of Judaism and Christian theology, Buber's and Heschel's works seem to me of paramount and continuing importance.

2. That is, in the primary claims of the Old Testament, Yahweh is never without Israel, and Israel is never without Yahweh. Cf. Rudolf Smend, *Die Bundesformel* (ThStud 68; Zürich: EVZ-Verlag, 1963).

3. Erich Voegelin, *Israel and Revelation: Order and History* 1 (Baton Rouge: Louisiana State University Press, 1956), has discussed these matters very generally as the interplay of "pragmatic" and "paradigmatic," though by "paradigmatic" he apparently means theological-ideational.

413

Yahweh's Originary Love for Israel

Israel's existence is rooted in Yahweh's inescapable, originary commitment to Israel. According to its unsolicited testimony, there was a time when Israel did not exist. Israel came to exist because of the decisive, initiatory action of Yahweh. It may well be that there were ethnic or sociological antecedents for Israel, but as a community, as a sociotheological entity, Israel came to exist in the world of the Near East because of the sovereign, free action of Yahweh.

This action of Yahweh—this inexplicable, irreversible commitment of Yahweh—is rendered in two distinct narratives: the stories of the ancestors (Genesis 12–36) and the Exodus-Sinai narrative revolving around Moses (Exodus 1–24).[4] In these two very different narratives, Yahweh in sovereign power speaks, and by speech evokes Israel into existence. In Gen 12:1-3 Yahweh addresses barren Sarah and failed Abraham, and issues a summons, command, and promise. In Exod 3:7-10 Yahweh addresses bondaged Israel and issues a promise that is subsequently matched by command (cf. Exod 20:1-17).

These two dissimilar versions of initiation no doubt reflect very different circles of tradition. They are, nonetheless, agreed on the main points. The people that became Israel are without hope, possibility, or future. The sorry situation of these people, barren and bondaged, is dramatically transformed by the sovereign utterance of Yahweh. No ground or rationale is given for the utterance of Yahweh, but because the utterance is on the lips of the Holy One, the utterance must be accepted, embraced, and obeyed by Israel.[5]

Thus from the outset there is something odd, enigmatic, and inexplicable about Israel's origin and continued existence. James Robinson is correct when he writes: "For the wonder that Israel is, rather than not being at all, is the basic experience of Israel in all its history."[6] It is important to remember that as Israel pondered and spoke about its existence, it offered no explanation for its existence. What appear to be explanations are in fact articulations of wonder, awe, astonishment, and gratitude, all addressed back to Yahweh.

Israel characteristically uses three verbs, love ('ahab), choose (bḥr), and set one's heart (ḥšq), to express its awareness that its existence as a people in the world is rooted only in Yahweh's commitment.

The first verb is love ('ahab).[7] Yahweh is the one who loves Israel, who loves what was not-yet-Israel, and who by the full commitment of Yahweh's self causes

---

4. On the relation of the two clusters of material to each other, see R. W. L. Moberly, *The Old Testament of the Old Testament: Patriarchal Narratives and Mosaic Yahwism* (OBT; Minneapolis: Fortress Press, 1992).

5. Except that in Exod 2:23-25 (and characteristically) it is the initiatory cry of need and distress by Israel that evokes and mobilizes Yahweh's transformative activity. In this sense the classic notion of divine initiative needs to be kept under criticism.

6. James M. Robinson, "The Historicity of Biblical Language," *The Old Testament and Christian Faith* (ed. Bernhard W. Anderson; London: SCM Press, 1964) 156.

7. On this term in its political-covenantal dimension, see William L. Moran, "The Ancient Near Eastern Background of the Love of God in Deuteronomy," *CBQ* 25 (1963) 77–87.

Israel to be. We may identify three clusters of uses of the term in this context of Yahweh's generative inclination toward Israel. Deuteronomy is the theological tradition that ponders in most sustained fashion Israel's election by Yahweh:

> It was because the Lord loved you and kept the oath that he swore to your ancestors, that the Lord has brought you out with a mighty hand, and redeemed you from the house of slavery, from the hand of Pharaoh king of Egypt. (Deut 7:8, cf. v. 13)

> ...the Lord your God turned the curse into a blessing for you, because the Lord your God *loved* you. (Deut 23:5)

This testimony is impressed not only with the sheer grace of Yahweh's love for Israel, but by the recognition that this love of Yahweh has singled out Israel, who is treated as no other is treated.

Second, the prophet Hosea, ostensibly out of personal experience, articulates Yahweh's love for Israel like no other love:

> The Lord said to me again, "Go, love a woman who has a lover and is an adulteress, just as the Lord *loves* the people of Israel, though they turn to other gods and love raisin cakes." (Hos 3:1)

> When Israel was a child, I *loved* him, and out of Egypt I called my son. (Hos 11:1)

The first of these texts voices the undeserving status of Israel in relation to Yahweh's love. The second uses the verb with reference to the initiatory event of the Exodus rescue.

Third, in the midst of the crisis of the exile, when Israel has ample ground to imagine that Yahweh's love for Israel is spent, the verb reemerges among the poets of the exile:

> I have *loved* you with an everlasting love; therefore I have continued my faithfulness to you. (Jer 31:3)

> I give Egypt as your ransom,
> Ethiopia and Seba in exchange for you.
> Because you are precious in my sight,
> and honored, and I *love* you,
> I give people in return for you,
> nations in exchange for your life. (Isa 43:3-4; cf. 48:14; Hos 14:4)

These latter statements attest to the durability and resilience of Yahweh's love for Israel, and therefore Israel's capacity to continue in life and in faith, in extreme circumstance.

A second verb, *choose* (*bḥr*), is regularly cited to speak more frontally of election, whereby Israel is given a special role and relation as having received a nomination or appointment by decree of the sovereign. This term *chosenness* has been treated in scholarship as peculiarly problematic in a perspective that yearns for universal religion.[8] In such a context, peculiar chosenness is an embarrassment and a scandal—"the scandal of particularity." It is to be noted, however, that the specificity of Israel's chosenness evokes no embarrassment or need for explanation in Israel's own self-understanding. Israel accepts and relishes its specialness. Again it is Deuteronomy that most fully attends to this verb and to its importance for Israel's self-presentation:

> For you are a people holy to the Lord your God; the Lord your God has *chosen* you out of all the peoples on earth to be his people, his treasured possession. (Deut 7:6-7; repeated in 14:2)

> And because he loved your ancestors, he *chose* their descendants after them. (Deut 4:37)

> ...yet the Lord set his heart in love on your ancestors alone and *chose* you, their descendants after them, out of all the peoples, as it is today. (Deut 10:15)

The latter two uses refer in particular to the ancestors, linking the communities of Genesis and Exodus.

The same term is used in a retrospect by Ezekiel:

> On the day when I chose Israel, I swore to the offspring of the house of Jacob—making myself known to them in the land of Egypt—I swore to them, saying, I am the Lord your God. (Ezek 20:5)

The term resurfaces in exile, in order to assert Yahweh's continuing valuing of Israel in a peculiar way:

> But now hear, O Jacob my servant,
> Israel, whom I have *chosen!* (Isa 44:1)

The third term, *set one's heart* (*ḥšq*), is used only twice, again in Deuteronomy, in texts I have just cited:

> It was not because you were more numerous than any other people that the Lord *set his heart* on you and chose you—for you were the fewest of all peoples. (Deut 7:7)

> ...yet the Lord *set his heart* in love on your ancestors alone and chose you.... (Deut 10:15)

---

8. For the classic study that keeps election in a general, liberal framework, reflective of the so-called biblical theology movement, see H. H. Rowley, *The Biblical Doctrine of Election* (London: Lutterworth Press, 1950).

The first of these texts concerns the community of Moses; the second, the ancestral community. But what is most important is that the verb *ḥšq* has strong, passionate emotional overtones (cf. Gen 34:8; Deut 21:11). The term bespeaks a lover who is powerfully in pursuit of the partner, perhaps in lustful ways. Thus Yahweh's commitment to Israel is not simply a formal, political designation, but it is a personal commitment that has a dimension of affection and in which Yahweh is emotionally extended for the sake of Israel.

At the risk of modest repetition, we may notice that two texts use all three verbs, *love* (*'ahab*), *choose* (*bḥr*), *set one's heart* (*ḥšq*), in extraordinarily powerful assertions:

> For you are a people holy to the Lord your God; the Lord your God has *chosen* you out of all the peoples on earth to be his people, his treasured possession. It was not because you were more numerous than any other people that the Lord *set his heart* on you and *chose* you—for you were the fewest of all peoples. It was because the Lord *loved* you and kept the oath that he swore to your ancestors.... (Deut 7:6-8)

> ...yet the Lord *set his heart* in *love* on your ancestors alone and *chose* you, their descendants after them, out of all the peoples, as it is today. (Deut 10:15)

These two texts serve different functions. The first is to assert a powerful "either/or" against other inhabitants of the land. The second is to contrast the particularity of Israel over against the universal governance of Yahweh. Both state Yahweh's peculiar commitment to Israel, and Israel's peculiar identity vis-à-vis Yahweh. In both cases, the peculiar commitment of Yahweh and the peculiar identity of Israel are offered as grounds from which appeal is made for serious, radical, concrete obedience.

Israel's Covenantal Obligation

The surfacing of the theme of obedience in these texts about inexplicable love moves us to a second aspect of Yahweh's inexplicable originary commitment to Israel. The initiatory act of love, rescue, and designation is made by a sovereign who in this act of love does not cease to be sovereign. Therefore this relationship, marked by awe and gratitude for its inexplicable generosity, brings with it the expectations and requirements of the sovereign who initiates it. The common rubric for this sovereign expectation is covenant. Yahweh designates Israel as Yahweh's covenant partner, so that Israel is, from the outset, obligated to respond to and meet Yahweh's expectations. As covenant partner of Yahweh, Israel is a people defined by obedience.

A great deal of scholarly energy has been spent on the matter of covenant, and a student of Old Testament theology needs to know a bit about that scholarly discussion.[9] In the older critical scholarship from the last century, it was assumed that the covenant did not become a working construct in Israel until the emergence of ethical monotheism in the eighth and seventh centuries B.C.E., under the aegis of the Deuteronomic tradition. Then in the middle of the twentieth century, under the impetus of George Mendenhall and Klaus Baltzer, it was argued that covenant was an early and constitutive notion in Israel.[10] Most recently, led by Lothar Perlitt, E. Kutsch, and Ernest Nicholson, scholars have returned to the older critical position.[11] Be that as it may, Israel's theological self-presentation is not constrained by such critical judgments, but presents itself from the outset as Yahweh's covenant people.[12]

If we take Israel's self-presentation (witness) as the proper subject for interpretation, scholars still have made important distinctions concerning Yahweh's covenant with Israel. Thus it can be argued that the covenant Yahweh made with Abraham (and so with the Genesis ancestors) is one of divine initiative that is unconditional, and the covenant made with Israel at Sinai is one of human obligation.[13] Or the matter may be expressed thus: the covenant may be unilaterally established by Yahweh (with the verb *establish*, *qûm*) or it may be bilaterally agreed to (with the verb *cut*, *krt*).

---

9. Good summary statements of recent scholarship may be found in Delbert Hillers, *Covenant: The History of a Biblical Idea* (Baltimore: Johns Hopkins University Press, 1969); Dennis J. McCarthy, *Covenant: A Summary of Current Opinions* (Oxford: Blackwell, 1972); Norbert Lohfink, *The Covenant Never Revoked: Biblical Reflections on Christian-Jewish Dialogue* (New York: Paulist Press, 1991); and especially Ernest W. Nicholson, *God and His People: Covenant and Theology in the Old Testament* (Oxford: Clarendon Press, 1986).

10. George W. Mendenhall, *Law and Covenant in Israel and in the Ancient Near East* (Pittsburgh: Biblical Colloquium, 1955); Klaus Baltzer, *The Covenant Formulary in the Old Testament, Jewish, and Early Christian Writings* (Oxford: Blackwell, 1971). See also Dennis J. McCarthy, *Treaty and Covenant: A Study in Forms in the Ancient Oriental Documents and in the Old Testament* (Rome: Pontifical Biblical Institute, 1978).

11. Lothar Perlitt, *Bundestheologie im Alten Testament* (WMANT 36; Neukirchen-Vluyn: Neukirchener Verlag, 1969); E. Kutsch, "Gesetz und Gnade. Probleme des alttestamentlicher Bundesbegriff," *ZAW* 79 (1976) 18–35; and Nicholson, *God and His People*.

12. The classic formulation is that of Walther Eichrodt, *Theology of the Old Testament* (2 vols.; OTL; Philadelphia: Westminster Press, 1961–67). James Barr, "Some Semantic Notes on the Covenant," *Beiträge zur Alttestamentlichen Theologie: Festschrift für Walther Zimmerli* (ed. Herbert Donner et al.; Göttingen: Vandenhoeck and Ruprecht, 1977) 37–38, is surely correct in his judgment that the reality of covenant must be recognized as present in the assumed world of Israel, even if the actual word *berith* is a later usage. Speaking of Perlitt's negative conclusion concerning covenant, Barr writes:

> Yet with all the will in the world it is a little hard to believe that the covenant of Yahweh with Israel became significant only so late. The sort of analysis that is roughly adumbrated in this article, especially through its implying the existence of syntactical and linguistic, rather than ideological and theological, restrictions on the use of the term *berith*, might possibly suggest other explanations of why this term is not found in certain types of sources. A current of tradition that used *berith* in one kind of linguistic context might use other terminology in another without this being evidence of a basic theological conflict.

13. Moshe Weinfeld, "The Covenant of Grant in the Old Testament and in the Ancient Near East," *JAOS* 90 (1970) 184–203, has provided the most compelling notion of unconditional covenant in terms of "land grant." On the dialectic, see David Noel Freedman, "Divine Commitment and Human Obligation," *Int* 18 (1964) 419–31. Jon D. Levenson, *Sinai and Zion: An Entry into the Jewish Bible* (Minneapolis: Winston Press, 1985), refuses any suggestion of tension or contrast and subsumes the royal (unconditional) covenant under the Mosaic (Torah-based) covenant.

Conditional and Unconditional: A Misleading Distinction

Different accents are made in different texts out of different traditions and in response to different circumstances. On the whole, however, in my judgment, it is futile and misleading to sort out unconditional and conditional aspects of Yahweh's covenant with Israel. The futility and misleading quality of such an enterprise can be stated on two quite different grounds. First, even in the covenant with the ancestors of Genesis, the covenant includes an imperative dimension (Gen 12:1, 17:1).[14] Israel, as Yahweh's covenant partner, is expected to order its life in ways that are appropriate to this relationship. It is unthinkable that the God who is holy, glorious, and jealous, who is the Creator of heaven and earth, will extend self in commitment without such an expectation. Second, if this relationship is indeed one of passionate commitment, as it surely is, it is undoubtedly the case (by way of analogy) that every serious, intense, primary relationship has within it dimensions of conditionality and unconditionality that play in different ways in different circumstances.

The attempt to factor out conditional and unconditional aspects of the covenant is an attempt to dissect and analyze the inscrutable mystery of an intimate, intense relation that, by definition, defies all such disclosure. Yahweh is all for Israel, and that includes both Yahweh's self-giving and Yahweh's intense self-regard.

A student of Old Testament theology must ponder this issue with some care. It is my judgment that the attempt by scholars to identify the conditional and the unconditional in this relationship is rooted in Paul's effort to distinguish the gospel of Jesus Christ from its Jewish counterparts, whereby Paul claimed for Christian faith the "gospel beforehand" in Abraham (Gal 3:8) and assigned to his Jewish opponents "Moses and the law." That same false distinction then showed up in the Pelagian controversy in the history of Christian doctrine; now, in a "therapeutic society," it issues variously in "cheap grace" and "works righteousness."

All such distinctions betray the character of this covenant, which is at the same time utterly giving and utterly demanding. Thus I suggest that E. P. Sanders's term *covenantal nomism* is about right, because it subsumes law (*nomos*) under the rubric of covenant.[15] By inference, I suggest that grace must also be subsumed under covenant. Covenant is the larger, working category through which this witness understands its life with Yahweh, which entails a full relationship of self-giving and self-regarding in which embrace of commandment (in obedience) and embrace of love (in trust) are of a piece. To forgo the umbrella notion of covenant

---

14. In the earlier discussion of covenant, Genesis 15 played a peculiarly important part. See Ronald Clements, *Abraham and David: Genesis 15 and Its Meaning for Israelite Tradition* (SBT 5, 2d series; London: SCM Press, 1967). Since that time, however, critical assumptions have shifted drastically so that Genesis 15 is not regarded as an early tradition. See Rolf Rendtorff, "Genesis 15 im Rahmen der theologischen Bearbeitung der Vatergeschichte," *Werden und Wirken des Alten Testaments: Festschrift für Claus Westermann* (Neukirchen-Vluyn: Neukirchener Verlag, 1980) 74–81; and John Ha, *Genesis 15: A Theological Compendium of Pentateuchal History* (BZAW 181; Berlin: Walter de Gruyter, 1989).

15. E. P. Sanders, *Paul and Palestinian Judaism: A Comparison of Patterns of Religion* (Philadelphia: Fortress Press, 1977) 75 and passim.

and to sort out cleanly "grace" and "law" is a distortion of the way in which the Old Testament speaks about this relationship. Such a false distinction may serve on the one hand to remove grace from the expectant, insistent relationship of covenant, or it may serve to reduce covenant simply to law. Either maneuver is a distortion of the testimony of Israel.

Such a distinction does incredible mischief to Jewish-Christian relationships, and comparable mischief in self-discernment about persons in community. (That is, grace and law as twin aspects of covenant become competing issues of entitlement and responsibilities, when in fact both belong inescapably to a workable covenantal community.) Of course Israel was to respond in love to the self-giving love of Yahweh. As in any serious relationship of love, the appropriate response to love is to resonate with the will, purpose, desire, hope, and intention of the one who loves. It is for that reason that the traditions of Deuteronomy, without apology or qualification, understand that Israel's proper response to Yahweh's inexplicable love is obedience, to do the purpose of the One whose love has made life in the world possible.

Thus the evocative, summoning, forming power of Yahweh, which gives life to Israel, puts Israel under profound and unqualified obligation to Yahweh. When we try to give substance to that obligation, it is clear that the testimony of Israel is diverse and variegated. Israel's obligation to Yahweh is to be fully responsive to, complementary to, and in full accord with the character of Yahweh, so that the way in which obligation is understood is commensurate with the way in which Yahweh is construed. *In sum, the obligation of Israel to Yahweh is to love Yahweh.* Thus, the "First Commandment":[16]

> You shall love the Lord your God with all your heart, and with all your soul, and with all your might. (Deut 6:5)

> The Lord your God you shall follow, him alone you shall fear, his commandments you shall keep, his voice you shall obey, him you shall serve, and to him you shall hold fast. (Deut 13:4)

Love is a dense term. Clearly it is a covenant word that means to acknowledge sovereignty and to keep one's oath of loyalty, on which the covenant is based. But such a political dimension to the term does not rule out an affective dimension, in light of the term *set one's heart* (*ḥšq*), which we have already considered. Thus at the core of Israel's obligation to Yahweh is the desire to please Yahweh and to be with Yahweh (Pss 27:4, 73:25). This dimension of desire and joy is what, in the best construal, keeps Israel's obligation to Yahweh from being a burden. At its best this obligation is not a burden, but is simply living out Israel's true

---

16. On the cruciality of the First Commandment for Old Testament theology, see Norbert Lohfink, *Das Hauptgebot: Eine Untersuchung literarischer Einleitungsfragen zu Dtn 5–11* (AnBib 20; Rome: Pontifical Biblical Institute, 1963); Werner H. Schmidt, *The Faith of the Old Testament: A History* (Oxford: Blackwell, 1983); Walther Zimmerli, *The Old Testament and the World* (London: SPCK, 1976); and Zimmerli, *Old Testament Theology in Outline* (Atlanta: John Knox, 1978).

character and identity, for Israel lives by and for and from Yahweh's freedom and passion. This same dimension of desire has permitted the reading of the erotic love poems of the Song of Solomon as a reflection of the affective commitment between Yahweh and Israel.[17] Thus we may focus the obligation of Israel around a yearning devotion for Yahweh; but with that focus we must recognize that the enactment of that obligation takes many different forms, depending on time, place, circumstance, and perspective.

In the exploration of this obligation, I will first thematize the material around the topics of *hearing* and *seeing,* and then I will draw two extended conclusions. It is recognized that in the Deuteronomic-covenantal-prophetic traditions, Israel's obligation is to listen as the sovereign Yahweh, through many interpreters, issues commands: "Hear, O Israel: The Lord is our God, the Lord alone" (Deut 6:4). Thus one aspect of Israel's obligation is *to hear* and to respond by doing (cf. Exod 24:3, 7).[18] Less recognized is a second perspective on obligation, stemming from the tradition of tabernacle-temple-Priestly tradition: that Israel is *to see,* to look on the splendor and beauty of Yahweh. These two accents, one in the tradition of Deuteronomy and the other in the Priestly traditions, eventuates in a hermeneutical program of proclamation and manifestation, which in turn may be understood in Christian tradition as word and sacrament.[19]

The Obligation to Listen and to Do Justice

Israel is to "listen" to the command of Yahweh and to respond in obedience. While the commands in the tradition concerning listening are many and varied, we may say in sum that *Israel's obligation is to do justice.* Israel is a community put in the world, so the testimony suggests, for the sake of justice. The justice commanded by Yahweh, moreover, is not the retributive justice of "deeds-consequences" wherein rewards and punishments are meted out to persons and the community according to conduct. Rather, Israel understands itself, in its unsolicited witness, as a community of persons bound in membership to each other, so that each person-as-member is to be treated well enough to be sustained as a full member of the community. In its articulation of justice as its principal obligation, Israel is acutely alert to sociopolitical differentiations and is aware that the strong and the weak,

---

17. This theological assumption has dominated much of the history of interpretation of the love poems. The classic example is the long series of sermons by Bernard of Clairvaux. See *On the Song of Songs* (trans. Kilian Walsh and Irene Edmunds; Kalamazoo, Mich.: Cistercian Publications, 1971–80). Continuing the exegetical trajectory of Bernard, see C. E. Hocking, *Rise Up My Love* (Precious Seeds, 1988). More generally see Wilfred Cantwell Smith, *What Is Scripture? A Comparative Approach* (Minneapolis: Fortress Press, 1993) 21–44. See the deconstructive interpretation of David J. A. Clines, "Why Is There a Song of Songs, and What Does It Do to You If You Read It?" *Interested Parties: The Ideology of Writers and Readers of the Hebrew Bible* (JSOTSup 205; Sheffield: Sheffield Academic Press, 1995) 94–121.

18. Rabbinic interpreters noted that "do" has priority in the text over "hear."

19. On the dialectic of manifestation and proclamation in Christian theology and liturgy, see David Tracy, *The Analogical Imagination: Christian Theology and the Culture of Pluralism* (New York: Crossroad, 1984) 371–404. Tracy follows the categories of Paul Ricoeur. The themes of manifestation and proclamation, in the actual practice of ministry, become ministry of "word and sacrament."

the rich and the poor, live differently and need to be attended to in different ways. It is not belated ideology to recognize that Israel's covenantal-prophetic sense of Yahweh's justice does indeed have a preferential inclination for the poor and the marginated. This preferential option that is mandated to Israel is rooted in Yahweh's own practice and inclination, so that in the practice of justice Israel is indeed to imitate Yahweh.[20] Thus, in Deut 10:17-18, Yahweh is one who "loves strangers":

> For the Lord your God is God of gods and Lord of lords, the great God, mighty and awesome, who is not partial and takes no bribe, who executes justice for the orphan and the widow, and who loves the strangers, providing them food and clothing.

As an immediate consequence, Israel is enjoined to do the same:

> You shall also love the stranger, for you were strangers in the land of Egypt. (v. 19)

This act toward strangers is understood as a way to "fear Yahweh," for the next verse makes the connection:

> You shall fear the Lord your God; him alone you shall worship; to him you shall hold fast, and by his name you shall swear. (v. 20)

In the hearing tradition of Israel, there are many and differentiated commands: some are conservative in order to maintain social equilibrium, and some are downright reactionary to protect status quo advantage. Without denying any of this, it is evident that Israel's most characteristic and theologically intentional practice is to attend to the needs of those too weak to protect themselves. In the tradition of Deuteronomy, these too weak are characteristically "widows, orphans, and resident aliens" (cf. Deut 14:29; 16:11, 14; 24:19-21; 26:12-15; Isa 1:17; Jer 7:6; 22:3; Zech 7:10).

It is clear that in these most radical injunctions, understood as Israel's covenantal obligations, the wealth and social resources of Israel are understood not in privatistic or acquisitive ways, but as common resources that are to be managed and deployed for the enhancement of the community by the enhancement of its weakest and most disadvantaged members. This linkage between Yahwistic obligation and commitment to the well-being of the marginated, while especially featured in the covenantal traditions, is also present on the horizon of the wisdom teachers:

> Those who oppress the poor insult their Maker,
> but those who are kind to the needy honor him. (Prov 14:31)

---

20. It is difficult to avoid something like "God's preferential option for the poor" in these texts. On the theme, see Gustavo Gutiérrez, *A Theology of Liberation: History, Politics, and Salvation* (Maryknoll, N.Y.: Orbis Books, 1988). On the theme of justice, see José Miranda, *Marx and the Bible: A Critique of the Philosophy of Oppression* (Maryknoll, N.Y.: Orbis Books, 1977) 109–99; Miranda shows that justice in this tradition is not maudlin or romantic in its implementation, but concerns the reality of economic and political life in community.

> Those who mock the poor insult their Maker;
> those who are glad at calamity will not go unpunished. (Prov 17:5)

This specific and radical command to do justice is to characterize the whole life of Israel. Such a command, understood as a poignant reflection of Yahweh's own way in the world (as evidenced in the Exodus), clearly is intrusive in and critical of a life of self-protection, self-sufficiency, and self-indulgence. This mandate marks Israel as a community that practices an intense openness to the neighbor, and it balances that openness by a keen sense of self-criticism about sociopolitical-economic advantage. That is, the function of these commandments is not to protect acquired advantage, but to call that advantage into question when it does not benefit the community.

The command to justice is understood as marking the polity of the community of Israel. That is, justice is not charity, nor is it romantic do-goodism. It is rather a mandate to order public policy, public practice, and public institutions for the common good and in resistance to the kind of greedy initiative that damages the community. The public quality of this command is evident, on the one hand, in the primitive narrative of Achan, who withheld for private purposes the goods of the community, and so did immense damage to the community:

> Israel has sinned; they have transgressed my covenant that I imposed on them. They have taken some of the devoted things; they have stolen, they have acted deceitfully, and they have put them among their own belongings. . . . And Achan answered Joshua, "It is true; I am the one who sinned against the Lord God of Israel. This is what I did: when I saw among the spoil a beautiful mantle from Shinar, and two hundred shekels of silver, and a bar of gold weighing fifty shekels, then I coveted them and took them. They now lie hidden in the ground inside my tent, with the silver underneath." (Josh 7:11, 20-21)

This same public quality of the command to justice, on the other hand, is evident in the doxological mandate to the Davidic king:

> Give the king your justice, O God,
> and your righteousness to a king's son.
> May he judge your people with righteousness,
> and your poor with justice. . . .
> May he defend the cause of the poor of the people,
> give deliverance to the needy,
> and crush the oppressor. (Ps 72:1-2, 4)[21]

---

21. On possible ideological aspects of Psalm 72, a poem ostensibly about justice, see David Jobling, "Deconstruction and the Political Analysis of Biblical Texts: A Jamesonian Reading of Psalm 72," *Semeia* 59 (1992) 95–127.

The public good requires that active social power must be mobilized to enhance the entire community and to resist personal aggrandizement of some at the expense of others.

Unambiguously, Israel believes that the violation of this mandate from Yahweh, which is congruent with Yahweh's own way in the world, will be inordinately destructive. Thus the prophets observe the cost of private coveting, as for example by the king and the powerful around him. The same term *covet* (*ḥmd*) that was used in the indictment of Achan is employed by the prophet Micah:

> Alas for those who devise wickedness
> and evil deeds on their beds!
> When the morning dawns, they perform it,
> because it is in their power.
> They covet fields, and seize them;
> houses, and take them away;
> they oppress householder and house,
> people and their inheritance. (Mic 2:1-2; cf. Isa 5:8-10)[22]

In the denunciation of kingship, the kingship enjoined to justice in Psalm 72, Ezekiel sees the ruin caused when established social power enhances itself at the expense of the defenseless:

> You eat the fat, you clothe yourselves with the wool, you slaughter the fatlings; but you do not feed the sheep. You have not strengthened the weak, you have not healed the sick, you have not bound up the injured, you have not brought back the strayed, you have not sought the lost, but with force and harshness you have ruled them. So they were scattered, because there was no shepherd.... (Ezek 34:3-5)

In this powerful tradition of obligation, Israel is understood as a community that is to be preoccupied with the well-being of the neighbor, and it is to be prepared to exercise public power for the sake of the neighbor, even when that exercise of public power works against established interests.

To be sure, many other commands are less daring, less demanding, and less "noble." But *if we are to identify what is most characteristic and most distinctive in the life and vocation of this partner of Yahweh, it is the remarkable equation of love of God with love of neighbor,* which is enacted through the exercise of distributive justice of social goods, social power, and social access to those without leverage; for those without social leverage are entitled to such treatment simply by the fact of their membership in the community. While the case has sometimes been overstated, there is ample ground for the recognition that Israel, as a community under obligation, is indeed a community of social revolution in the world.[23] Israel's insistence

---

22. On this text in Micah, see Marvin Chaney, "You Shall Not Covet Your Neighbor's House," *Pacific Theological Review* 15:2 (Winter 1982) 3–13.

23. This has been seen most clearly by Norman K. Gottwald, *The Tribes of Yahweh: A Sociology of the Religion of Liberated Israel, 1250–1050 B.C.E.* (Maryknoll, N.Y.: Orbis Books, 1979).

on this command to justice, moreover, roots this concrete social insistence precisely in the character of Yahweh, who loves the widow and orphan (cf. Hos 14:3).

The Invitation to See

A second tradition of obligation that articulates the requirement made of Israel as Yahweh's partner is not so well known or so much valued in Western Protestantism. This is the tradition of seeing, which focuses on the cultic presence of Yahweh, and wherein *Israel is invited to gaze on a vision of Yahweh's presence, holiness, and beauty.*[24] This tradition has not received nearly as much attention in scholarly interpretation, and perhaps it is not as characteristic or pervasive in Israel's unsolicited testimony about itself. Nevertheless it occupies a good bit of textual space.

It is extraordinary that in the midst of the Sinai encounter, where Israel hears the commands and pledges loyalty to them (Exod 24:3, 7), in the same context of allegiance to command, Israel gives testimony of a very different kind of obligation, an obligation to "see God" and to be fully in the presence of Yahweh. In a text commonly assigned to the Priestly tradition, it is affirmed of Moses, Aaron, Nadab, Abihu, and seventy elders that in the ascent to the mountain "they saw (*ra'ah*) the God of Israel . . . they beheld (*ḥzh*) God, and they ate and drank" (Exod 24:10, 11). It is clear that we are in a very different environment of testimony from that of the Deuteronomists who insist that, "You heard the sound of words but saw no form; there was only a voice" (Deut 4:12).

The assertion of Exod 24:9-11 does not tell us what the leadership of Israel saw. But there is no doubt that this testimony means to say that one of the characteristic markings of +Israel is to be in Yahweh's presence, to see God, to commune with Yahweh directly, face to face. This encounter at the mountain, moreover, is not instrumental, not for the sake of something else. It is a moment of wondrous abiding in the Presence.

This testimony about this singular encounter at Sinai makes clear that it is a one-time encounter, to which only the leadership is invited. It is nonetheless clear that this encounter obligates Israel not only to do justice for the neighbor, but also to be in the presence of God, to see God, to submit to the unutterable over-whelmingness that is the very character of God. It belongs to the life and character of Israel to be with and to be before this One to whom Israel is responding part-ner. Israelite traditions, which are rooted in the Sinai encounter, attest to the ways in which this awesome moment of presence is made continually available in Is-rael's cultic practice. It is clear in the development of this tradition of obligation that Israel has a keen aesthetic sensibility, suggesting that Yahweh to whom Is-rael responds is not only righteous but also beautiful. The encounter is conducted in an environment of beauty, which makes the communion possible and which is reflective of Yahweh's own character.

---

24. Samuel Terrien, *The Elusive Presence: Toward a New Biblical Theology* (New York: Harper and Row, 1978), has gone furthest in contemporary scholarship in giving attention to "the tradition of seeing" in the structure and shape of Old Testament theology.

Beauty in the tabernacle tradition. It is clear, first, that the tabernacle tradition (Exodus 25–31; 35–40) is preoccupied with beauty. Thus the required offering for the construction of the tabernacle includes

> gold, silver, and bronze, blue, purple, crimson yarns and fine linen, goats' hair, tanned rams' skins, fine leather, acacia wood, oil for the lamps, spices for the anointing and for the fragrant incense, onyx stones and gems to be set in the ephod and for the breastpiece. (Exod 25:3-7)

The skilled artisans work in a variety of materials to construct an adequate and acceptable place of presence:

> ... he has filled him with divine spirit, with skill, intelligence, and knowledge in every kind of craft, to devise artistic designs, to work in gold, silver, and bronze, in cutting stones for setting, and in carving wood, in every kind of craft.... to do every kind of work done by an artisan or by a designer or by an embroiderer in blue, purple, and crimson yarns, and in fine linen, or by a weaver—by any sort of artisan or skilled designer. (Exod 35:31-33, 35)

The culmination of this elaborate preparation is the coming of "the glory of the Lord," which takes up residence in the tabernacle (Exod 40:34-38). The tabernacle is made into a suitable and appropriate place for Yahweh's visible presence by the practice of a beauty commensurate with Yahweh's character. It is possible to host the holiness of Yahweh, and in this tradition the purpose of life is communion with Yahweh, a genuine, real, and palpable presence.[25] Such hosting, moreover, is done only with great care, costly investment, and scrupulous attention to detail.

Aesthetic dimensions of the temple tradition. The tabernacle traditions are either an anticipation or reflection of the temple traditions.[26] The tradition of Solomon's temple reflects royal self-indulgence, which replicates other, non-Israelite royal self-indulgence. Nonetheless, the temple of Solomon is presented in Israel's testimony as a thing of beauty (Ps 48:2) befitting of Yahweh, which becomes a place for Yahweh's appropriate habitat in the midst of Israel. First Kings 6:14-38 makes clear that nothing is spared in order to create for Yahweh a place of beauty. In due course, the glory of Yahweh is seen and known to be present in the temple (1 Kgs 8:11).[27]

---

25. Tracy, *The Analogical Imagination,* has explored this facet of Christian faith under the twin rubrics of "prophetic" and "mystical," which correspond roughly to "proclamation" and "manifestation." The theme of cultic presence that understands God in sacramental terms (i.e., via mystical manifestation) is clearly reflected in these texts, but is largely neglected in Protestant critical scholarship. That neglect seems to have its counterpart in the characteristic preference of Pauline to Johannine New Testament Christianity.

26. When taken canonically, there is no doubt that the tabernacle is presented as an anticipation of the temple of Solomon. By contrast, critical scholarship has generally taken the tabernacle to be a subsequent reflection of the actual temple.

27. On the presence of Yahweh in the temple, see Tryggve N. D. Mettinger, *The Dethronement of Sabaoth: Studies in the Shem and Kabod Theologies* (Lund: CWK Gleerup, 1982) 19–37; and Ben C. Ollenburger, *Zion, City of the Great King: A Theological Symbol of the Jerusalem Cult* (JSOTSup 41; Sheffield: Sheffield Academic Press, 1987).

In the reconstruction of the temple after the exile, it is evident that similar care was taken for proportion and symmetry (Ezek 40:1–42:20).[28] The tradition of Ezekiel is more interested in symmetry and proportion than in the extravagance of the furnishings, but it is unmistakable that an aesthetic sensibility is at work, by which it is again possible for the glory of Yahweh to be in the midst of Israel (cf. Ezek 43:5). The temple tradition, both in Solomon's temple and in the Second Temple, assures that Yahweh's presence is palpably available to Israel.

There is no doubt, moreover, that the liturgical experience in the temple has a powerful aesthetic dimension, for the God of Israel is known to be present in an environment of physical, visible loveliness. Thus Israel is summoned to worship Yahweh in a holy place of unspeakable splendor (Pss 29:2, 96:9; 1 Chr 16:29; 2 Chr 20:21). The old, familiar translation of the recurring phrase in these texts is "the beauty of holiness." The NRSV prefers to render "holy splendor," thus accenting awe, which precludes any ease or artistic coziness. What interests us in this recurring formula, rendered either way, is that the visibly powerful sense of presence in the shrine has a mark of holiness to it, which variously reflects symmetry, proportion, order, extravagance, awe, and overwhelmingness. This is a sense of the "surplus" of Yahweh, situated at the center of Israel's life, which is experienced as visual and which from its central and dominant position resituates and recharacterizes everything in Israel's mundane world in relation to this center of occupying holiness.

Beauty and holiness. Thus we can make a connection between beauty and holiness, which draws us closer to the obligation at the root of this tradition of presence. We have already seen that Yahweh is holy, and we have seen that Yahweh is "the Holy One in Israel."[29] This marking of Yahweh bespeaks Yahweh's transcendence, separateness, distance, awe, and sovereignty. But what interests us now is that Israel in obedience is commensurate with Yahweh. Israel is also to be holy as Yahweh is holy. That is, Israel's holiness is derivative from, responsive to, and commensurate with the holiness of Yahweh (Lev 11:44-45, 19:2, 20:26).

The tradition of obligation, as understood in the Priestly tradition, like the justice tradition in Deuteronomy, is rich and diverse. It cannot be easily summarized. The specific texts that explicitly enjoin holiness in Israel warn against defilement (*ṭm'*) through eating (Lev 11:44-45), and against mixing the clean (*ṭhr*) and the unclean (*ṭm'*) (20:25).[30] The most extensive reference is in Lev 19:2-4:

Speak to all the congregation of the people of Israel and say to them: You shall be holy, for I the Lord your God am holy. You shall each revere your

---

28. See Jon D. Levenson, *Theology of the Program of Restoration of Ezekiel 40–48* (HSM 10; Missoula, Mont.: Scholars Press, 1976).

29. On the "holy one in Israel," see pp. 288–93.

30. On the sociotheological significance of this perspective in the faith of Israel, see Fernando Belo, *A Materialist Reading of the Gospel of Mark* (Maryknoll, N.Y.: Orbis Books, 1981). See the critical discussion of Israel Knohl, *The Sanctuary of Silence: The Priestly Torah and the Holiness School* (Minneapolis: Fortress Press, 1995).

mother and father, and you shall keep my sabbaths: I am the Lord your God. Do not turn to idols or make cast images for yourselves: I am the Lord your God.

This invitation to holiness concerns the commands to honor (*yr'*) mother and father, to keep Sabbath, and to shun idols and images. One may suggest that reference to three of the commands of the Decalogue permits an extrapolation to the entire ten. That is, to be holy as Yahweh is holy means to devote every aspect of life to the will and purpose of Yahweh. More specifically, however, with reference to the context of the "Holiness Code" (the name scholars have given to this section of Leviticus), Israel's obligation to holiness means to practice the disciplines of purity and cleanness of a cultic kind, which makes admission to the presence of Yahweh possible.[31] That is, *Israel is to order its life so that it is qualified for communion with Yahweh, even as it is to practice justice for the sake of the community.* In this tradition of obligation, the purpose of Israel's life is to host the holiness of Yahweh. We have already seen that Yahweh's holiness is indeed demanding, and there is no frivolous or careless access to that holiness.

If we understand holiness as the practice of disciplines that make entry into the presence of the Holy God possible, then we are not surprised to recognize that in a few texts, the goal and fruition of life is to see God as did the elders at Mount Sinai. In three texts, individuals in Israel give testimony about the visual experience of Yahweh:

> For the Lord is righteous;
> he loves righteous deeds;
> the upright shall behold (*ḥzh*) his face. (Ps 11:7)

> As for me, I shall behold (*ḥzh*) your face in righteousness;
> when I awake I shall be satisfied,
> beholding your likeness. (Ps 17:15)

> So I have looked (*ḥzh*) upon you in the sanctuary,
> beholding (*ra'ah*) your power and glory. (Ps 63:2)

In all three texts, the same verb is used as in Exod 24:11. And in the first two texts, the condition of such access to Yahweh is righteousness.

It does not surprise us that in these texts, as in Exod 24:11, the tradition that celebrates "seeing God" refuses to say in any way what this seeing entails, or what was seen. This profound reticence is yet another way in which Israel guards against any iconic temptation. We do not know if the rhetoric of seeing is to be taken as

---

31. On the "Holiness Code," in addition to Knohl, *The Sanctuary of Silence*, see John G. Gammie, *Holiness in Israel* (OBT; Minneapolis: Fortress Press, 1989) 9–44; and Dale Patrick, *Old Testament Law* (London: SCM Press, 1986) 145–88.

a metaphor for a nonvisual communion.[32] What we do know is that the practice of worship in the sanctuary and the disciplines of holiness make possible this enunciation of the fullness of the life of faith concerning communion with Yahweh.

Tension between Hearing and Seeing

It is clear that hearing the commands of justice and seeing the "face" of Yahweh live in profound tension with each other. This tension is no doubt deep in Israel, as bespeak the powerful advocacies of the Deuteronomic and Priestly traditions. One may imagine vigorous debate among the witnesses, of the same kind that characteristically occurs in the ecclesial communities of this text. *It is clear that the two accents of these twin traditions of obligation cannot be harmonized.* Nor finally are we permitted to say that one is more decisive or more ultimate than the other. It is important that the canonical form of Israel's unsolicited testimony refuses to choose between the two. In different contexts and in different circumstances, one or the other of these traditions may become crucial. It is likely a good rule of thumb, in the ecclesial communities of the text, to attend always to the tradition that is more problematic and demanding. The two traditions together are complementary of the twin affirmations we have seen earlier: that the sovereign faithfulness of Yahweh is for the world (thus justice), but that Yahweh's faithful sovereignty concerns Yahweh's own life (thus holiness).

The obedience of Israel as Yahweh's partner concerns the demanding practice of neighborliness and the rigorous discipline of presence with God. It is not possible to bring these two accents any closer together, but we may reference the notion of *integrity* (*tam*) as a way of linking these modes of obligation. This term means to be whole, complete, coherent, innocent, unimpaired, sound. It may be adequate to speak, in terms of this word, as "willing one thing"—that is, to live a life that is undivided, to be altogether unified in loyalty and intention.[33] Without minimizing the distinctions or tensions between the two traditions of obedience, I suggest that the Israelite with integrity is the one who fully practices neighborliness and who lives with passion the disciplines of holiness.

This term is used in the singular command to Abraham in the making of the covenant: "I am God almighty; walk before me, and be blameless (*tamim*)" (Gen 17:1). This same quality is recognized in Job, who is the paradigmatic person utterly devoted to the will of Yahweh:

---

32. That is, one cannot determine from the statement of the text whether the words intend a direct, "primitive" experience or a mediated presence through the cultic apparatus. This is a distinction not considered in the text, as it is never considered by the actual practitioners of a cult. Notice how carefully John Calvin, *Commentary on the Book of Psalms* (Grand Rapids: Baker Book House, 1979), 1:253, resists any cultic claim in the words: "*To behold God's face*, is nothing else than to have a sense of his fatherly favour, with which he not only causes us to rejoice by removing our sorrows, but also transports us even to heaven."

33. I make reference to the phrase of Søren Kierkegaard, *Purity of Heart Is to Will One Thing: Spiritual Preparation for the Office of Confession* (New York: Harper and Brothers, 1948).

> ...a blameless (*tam*) and upright (*yšr*) man who fears God and turns away from evil. (Job 1:8, cf. 2:9)

Indeed, the drama of the Book of Job turns on Job's integrity, which Job will not renounce:

> Far be it from me to say that you are right; until I die I will not put away my integrity (*tam*) from me. (Job 27:5)

The well-known self-defense of Job in chapter 31, moreover, provides particulars for the life of integrity that the model Israelite lives. It is evident that the tradition of justice provides the primary content of this catalog of integrity.[34] But it is equally clear that the tradition of holiness is on the horizon, as in vv. 26-27, which concern false worship. Thus Job is offered as the model for faith and life, a faith that is without qualification committed in every aspect of life to obedience to Yahweh.

This same preoccupation and possibility is elsewhere attested in Israelite piety. In two psalms of complaint, the ground for an appeal to Yahweh is precisely the claim of *tam*:

> May integrity (*tm*) and uprightness (*yšr*) preserve me,
> for I wait for you. (Ps 25:21)

> Vindicate me, O Lord,
> for I have walked in my integrity (*tam*),
> and I have trusted (*bṭḥ*) in the Lord without wavering....
> But as for me, I walk in my integrity (*tam*);
> redeem me, and be gracious to me.
> My foot stands on level ground;
> in the great congregation I will bless the Lord. (Ps 26:1, 11-12)

The work of Israel is indeed to "trust" (*bṭḥ*) in Yahweh "without wavering." Israel affirms that in its role as Yahweh's partner, every aspect of life, personal and public, cultic and economic, is a sphere in which complete devotion to Yahweh is proper to Israel's existence in the world.

Israel's Role in the World

Beyond this twofold tradition of obedience as justice and holiness, we may notice that in some traditions, Israel's obligation to Yahweh reaches well beyond justice in the community and holiness in the sanctuary. Indeed, *Israel is said to have as part of its vocation and destiny a role in the well-being of the world.* Three text traditions attest to this larger responsibility of Israel, a responsibility that pushes Israel

---

34. On Job 31, see Georg Fohrer, "The Righteous Man in Job 31," *Essays in Old Testament Ethics (J. Philip Hyatt, in Memoriam)* (ed. James L. Crenshaw and John T. Willis; New York: KTAV, 1974) 1–22.

beyond its own confessional recital to the larger vista of creation. That is, Israel has theological significance for the proper ordering and for the well-being of all of creation.

First, in the précis to the Sinai encounter, Yahweh asserts through Moses to Israel: "Indeed, the whole earth is mine, but you shall be for me a priestly kingdom and a holy nation" (Exod 19:5-6). Thus an astonishing vocation is assigned to Israel. And it is even more astonishing in the context of Sinai, fresh from Egypt, and in a tradition that is preoccupied with Israel, and without the nations even on the horizon of Israel. Israel is to be a "priestly kingdom" (or "kingdom of priests") and a holy nation.[35] This peculiar phrasing is exposited nowhere in Israel's testimony. But if Israel is to be a priestly kingdom (or a kingdom of priests), we may wonder, priestly for whom or to whom? On the one hand, the answer is to Yahweh, offering up sacrifices to Yahweh.

But on the other hand, perhaps this nation is offered as priest for other nations, as mediator and intercessor for the well-being of the other nations of the world. The other nations also inhabit Yahweh's territory, for "the whole earth is mine." The phrasing is only a tease that is left unexplored. But even in this tradition in which Israel thinks mostly about itself, we see on the horizon that Israel has an agenda other than its own well-being: the life of the world. The priestly function is to make well-being and healing in the world possible.[36] And finally it is to make communion between Yahweh and the world possible.

This remarkable role of Israel is only hinted at in the meeting of Sinai. It is made much more explicit in the Genesis tradition, which has a quite different horizon. The Abraham-Sarah tale begins abruptly, after the quick account of the way in which creation has become a world of trouble, vexation, and curse (Genesis 3–11). Through the tales of Genesis 3–11, Yahweh has no effective antidote for the recalcitrance of the world; the world refuses to be Yahweh's faithful creation. As the text is now arranged, Hans Walter Wolff has suggested, the call to the family of Abraham and Sarah is positioned as a response of Yahweh to the recalcitrance of the world.[37] While the summons of Yahweh to Abraham includes assurances and blessings that become definitional for the life of Israel, it is remarkable that the nations of Genesis 1–11 are very much on the horizon of the text: "[I]n you all the families of the earth shall be blessed" (Gen 12:3).

The call of Israel is juxtaposed to the crisis of the world, a crisis that arises because the nations have not accepted their role in a world where Yahweh is sovereign. One reason for Israel's existence is that creation is under curse for

---

35. On the peculiar character and role of Israel according to this text, see Martin Buber, *The Kingship of God* (3d ed.; London: Allen and Unwin, 1967).

36. The function recalls the rabbinic phrase taken up by Emil Fackenheim, *To Mend the World: Foundations of Post-Holocaust Thought* (New York: Schocken Books, 1989). More specifically, see Richard D. Nelson, *Raising Up a Faithful Priest: Community and Priesthood in Biblical Theology* (Louisville: Westminster/John Knox, 1993) 39–53 and passim.

37. Hans Walter Wolff, "The Kerygma of the Yahwist," *Int* 20 (1966) 131–58.

disobedience, and Yahweh insistently wills that the world should be brought to blessing. Israel's life is for the well-being of the world.[38]

Hans Walter Wolff has shown how this theme of "blessing to the nations" runs as a leitmotif throughout the ancestral narrative (cf. Gen 18:18, 22:18, 26:4, 28:14).[39] The way in which Israel's life and faith evoke the well-being of the nations is not made explicit, though Wolff suggests a variety of inferences permitted by the text. It is noteworthy that the formula of Gen 12:3 is not reiterated in the Joseph narrative. Concerning that silence in the Joseph narrative, it can be suggested that Joseph, the son of the ancestors, works a mighty blessing for Egypt (Gen 41:25-36). But the blessing for Egypt is commensurate with the reduction of Israel to bondage (cf. Gen 47:13-26).

Two texts are especially poignant in relation to the theme of Israel as a blessing-bearer for the nations. The narrative culminates so that the old man Jacob, carrier of the blessing, at long last is ushered into the regal presence of the pharaoh, who is here emblematic of the nations. It is clear that Jacob is the suppliant and pharaoh the one with resources to dispense. Nonetheless, the narrative deftly and laconically inverts their relationship, so that Jacob blesses pharaoh:

> Then Joseph brought in his father Jacob, and presented him before Pharaoh, and Jacob blessed Pharaoh.... Then Jacob blessed Pharaoh, and went out from the presence of Pharaoh. (Gen 47:7, 10)

Pharaoh is the recipient of the generative power of life that Israel possesses, a power for life uttered by Jacob and enacted by Joseph.

This dramatic inversion of roles is made even more extreme in Exod 12:29-32, Moses' last meeting with pharaoh. In this midnight episode, it is clear that conventional power arrangements between master and slave have been completely inverted and no longer pertain. Even pharaoh now knows this. Pharaoh, who has defied, dismissed, and attempted to dupe Moses, is now without resource and must petition Moses for a blessing. Pharaoh, still lord of his realm, issues a series of frantic imperatives:

> Rise up, go away from my people, both you and the Israelites! Go, worship the Lord, as you said. Take your flocks and your herds, as you said, and be gone. (Exod 12:31-32)

Finally, desperately, at the last moment, pharaoh adds to Moses:

> And bring a blessing on me too! (Exod 12:32)

The blessing actually given in response to the petition is not reported as it was in Genesis 47; perhaps no blessing is given. Nonetheless, the well-being of pharaoh

---

38. See Gerhard von Rad, "The Form-Critical Problem of the Hexateuch," *The Problem of the Hexateuch and Other Essays* (New York: McGraw-Hill, 1966) 66.

39. Wolff, "The Kerygma of the Yahwist."

and of mighty Egypt is now at the behest of Israel, who carries, even as a slave community, the power of blessing on which the superpower depends.

Isaiah 40–55 provides a third cluster of texts in which Israel's obligation to Yahweh is presented as a responsibility for the nations. In Isaiah of the exile, the horizon of Israel's testimony is expansive and takes in the whole human world as the scope of Yahweh's sovereignty and concern. More specifically, two texts situate Israel among the nations:

> I have given you as a covenant to the people,
> a light to the nations,
> to open the eyes that are blind,
> to bring out the prisoner from the dungeon,
> from the prison those who sit in darkness. (Isa 42:6)

> It is too light a thing that you should be my servant
> to raise up the tribes of Jacob
> and to restore the survivors of Israel;
> I will give you as a light to the nations,
> that my salvation may reach to the end of the earth. (Isa 49:6)

The two phrases, "covenant to the people" (42:6) and "light to the nations" (42:6, 49:6), have most often been taken to mean that Israel has a mandate to bring the news of Yahweh's rule to the gentile world of nations, so that the gentile world may also be rescued and saved. On this reading, the well-being of the non-Jewish nations is entrusted to the life and work of Israel (cf. Luke 2:32).

Harry Orlinsky and Norman Snaith have issued a powerful dissent to this rather common view.[40] It is their judgment, in a careful reading of the text, that the mission here spoken of is to Jews scattered in the known world, who are to be gathered from exile and brought home. On this reading, the poetic phrasing has a horizon no more inclusive than all members of the Jewish community. It is Orlinsky and Snaith's judgment that the notion that Jews have a mission to Gentiles is not in the purview of the text.

Perhaps Orlinsky and Snaith are right, and therefore too much emphasis should not be placed on this phrasing when considering the obligation of Israel to the nations. I mention these texts here for two reasons, with full recognition of the force of the argument of these two scholars. First, Isa 49:6 is notoriously difficult, even for their dissenting interpretation. Indeed, Orlinsky concedes that such a reading as he rejects is possible in v. 6 if it is taken without v. 7.[41] He believes that v. 7 vitiates such a reading. It needs to be recognized, however, that while v. 6 is indeed problematic on a conventional reading, it is also difficult on the dissenting reading. Second, the conventional reading is a powerful and attractive one that continues to

---

40. Harry M. Orlinsky and Norman H. Snaith, *Studies on the Second Part of the Book of Isaiah* (VTSup 14; Leiden: E. J. Brill, 1967).

41. Harry M. Orlinsky, "The So-Called 'Servant of the Lord' and 'Suffering Servant' in Second Isaiah," ibid., 103.

exercise great power. It may well be, as Orlinsky suggests, that such a reading is a Christian imposition on the text, but it is not necessarily so. Thus I conclude that these texts in Isaiah of the exile, and their seemingly expansive phrasing, need to be noted in the context of Exod 19:6 and Gen 12:3. Israel does not understand itself, in light of Yahweh's governance of the world, as living in a vacuum or in isolation. Its obligation to Yahweh is to take seriously all that Yahweh has given it, in its context of the nations. Yahweh has summoned Israel in love to be Yahweh's peculiar partner. And Israel is under intense obligation to respond in obedience to Yahweh's sovereign love, an obligation to be holy as Yahweh is holy (Lev 19:2-4), to love the stranger as Yahweh loves the stranger (Deut 10:19). Response to Yahweh's sovereign goodness is Israel's proper life in the world.

Israel Recalcitrant and Scattered

The third facet of Israel's life with Yahweh, as attested in its unsolicited testimony, is that Israel did not respond to Yahweh's goodness adequately nor to Yahweh's command faithfully, and thereby Israel jeopardized its existence in the world. Israel came into existence by the sovereign freedom of Yahweh, and by that same sovereign freedom Israel would perish. Thus the third dimension (or "season") of Israel's life with Yahweh is as *a recalcitrant partner* who stands under judgment and threat for its very life.

The indictment of Israel is principally given in two modes of testimony. First, the studied narrative account of Israel's "history" in Joshua-Judges-Samuel-Kings portrays Israel as a community that has failed in its obligation to Yahweh, a failure that is pervasive in the entire account.[42] This indictment of Israel culminates in 2 Kgs 17:7-41 and is echoed in Psalm 106, a recital of Israel's life with Yahweh thematized as one of sin and rebellion. Second, the prophets of the monarchal period characteristically address Israel (and Judah) with a lawsuit speech form that evidences disobedience and that anticipates harsh punishment for Israel from the hand of Yahweh.[43]

Yahweh's majestic governance over this recalcitrant partner, which had at the outset been marked by generosity, now comes as judgment. The judgment is in fact the complete nullification of Israel, so that Israel ceases to be. The historical mode of nullification is exile. Israel is "scattered" (*pûṣ*), a new term in Israel's Yah-

---

42. It is possible to see all of the Deuteronomic history, Joshua through Kings, as a lawsuit that indicts Israel and points to the exile as the legitimate judgment pronounced on the basis of the indictment. This perspective on the Deuteronomists was suggested by the early work of Gerhard von Rad, *Studies in Deuteronomy* (SBT 9; London: SCM Press, 1953) 74–91. This view is strengthened if we regard Deuteronomy 32 as a model from which the larger history is composed. G. Ernest Wright, "The Law-Suit of God: A Form-Critical Study of Deuteronomy 32," *Israel's Prophetic Heritage* (ed. Bernhard W. Anderson and Walter Harrelson; London: SCM Press, 1962) 26–67, has shown that Deuteronomy 32 is an early poem that is shaped as a lawsuit, and so it is possible to see this linkage between the poem and the history.

43. On the lawsuit in the prophets, see Claus Westermann, *Basic Forms of Prophetic Speech* (London: Lutterworth Press, 1967).

wistic vocabulary, of which Yahweh is characteristically the active subject. Israel is scattered to the winds, away from its promised place, and away from its resources for identity. Exile is indeed the complete defeat, loss, and forfeiture of life with Yahweh. The exile is to be understood as an actual geopolitical event in the life of this community. There were indeed displaced persons and refugee communities.[44] It is possible to give a geopolitical explanation for the exile: the displacement of the Jews from their homeland was an effect of Babylonian expansionism under Nebuchadnezzar.

But the exile is not exhausted in its geopolitical dimension. In the end, the exile is a theological datum concerning Israel's life with Yahweh.[45] While one may quibble about how extensive the deportation was and what percentage of Israelites were removed from the land, such issues do not matter with a theological datum. For now, in its relation to Yahweh, Israel is nullified, and the displacement seemed destined to last in perpetuity. In sovereign righteousness, Yahweh acts in self-regard and is capable of sloughing off this partner who refuses partnership. Thus it belongs to the fundamental marking of Israel that as a people summoned in love by Yahweh and addressed by Yahweh's command, Israel is a community scattered by none other than Yahweh, the God of sovereign fidelity and faithful sovereignty, to the null point.[46] Israel's unsolicited testimony about itself can imagine the complete negation of Israel. Israel has no guarantee of life in the world beyond the inclination of Yahweh, and that inclination has now been exhausted. Israel must, in perpetuity, ponder its scatteredness, out beyond the well-being intended by Yahweh.

In that situation of nullity, Israel is compelled to new ways in its practice and life of faith. We may mention five new practices that are active acknowledgments of nullification at the hands of Yahweh.

Practice of Faith in Exile

Israel must intentionally and honestly face its true situation, refuse denial, and resist pretense. Exile is and will be a reality. This is now Israel's place to be, and Israel must learn to practice its life of faith in exile:

> Build houses and live in them; plant gardens and eat what they produce. Take wives and have sons and daughters; take wives for your sons, and give your daughters in marriage, that they may bear sons and daughters; multiply there, and do not decrease. But seek the welfare of the city where I have sent you into exile, and pray to the Lord on its behalf, for in its welfare you will find your welfare. (Jer 29:5-7)

---

44. See Daniel L. Smith, *The Religion of the Landless: The Social Context of the Babylonian Exile* (Bloomington, Ind.: Meyer-Stone, 1989).

45. Jacob Neusner, *Understanding Seeking Faith: Essays on the Case of Judaism* (Atlanta: Scholars Press, 1986), 1:137–41, has nicely articulated the way in which exile becomes the paradigmatic, definitive mark of Jews, even for those not in exile.

46. On the exile as the "null point," see Walther Zimmerli, *I Am Yahweh* (ed. Walter Brueggemann; Atlanta: John Knox, 1982) 111–33.

Repentance

Israel now undertakes repentance.[47] The tradition of Deuteronomy urges that even in exile, Israel is required and permitted to forgo its self-serving autonomy and remember its life with Yahweh:

> When your people Israel, having sinned against you, are defeated before an enemy but turn again to you, confess your name, pray and plead with you in this house, then hear in heaven, forgive the sin of your people Israel, and bring them again to the land that you gave to their ancestors. (1 Kgs 8:33-34)

This theology of repentance is an extraordinary development in Israel's self-discernment. One might have concluded, after Jeremiah and Ezekiel, that Israel had reached a point of no return with Yahweh. But now Israel is permitted a chance:

> From there [from exile] you will seek the Lord your God, and you will find him if you search after him with all your heart and soul. In your distress, when all these things [sufferings of displacement] have happened to you in time to come, you will return to the Lord your God and heed him. (Deut 4:29-30)[48]

Thus repentance in itself is an act of hope. A return to Yahweh, and to land and to well-being, is possible. Any such return, however, will be on the terms of the sovereign God who waits to be merciful (Deut 4:31). The repentance entails the very issues that were the causes of Israel's condemnation: remembrance, holiness, and justice.

The Practice of Grief

In the meantime, Israel is not to grow silent about its deserved plight. Israel in exile is a community that grieves and protests. Indeed, in exile the ancient social practice of lament and complaint becomes a crucial theological activity for Israel.[49] The practice of grief is an exercise in truth-telling. It is, as evidenced in Psalm 137 and Lamentations, an exercise in massive sadness that acknowledges, with no denial or deception, where and how Israel is. But the grief is not resignation, for in the end, Israel is incapable of resignation. Resignation would be to give up finally on Yahweh and on Yahweh's commitment to Israel. This Israel will not do, even if Yahweh gives hints of such abandonment.[50] This grief of Israel in exile spills over

---

47. See Hans Walter Wolff, "The Kerygma of the Deuteronomist," *The Vitality of Old Testament Traditions*, Walter Brueggemann and Hans Walter Wolff (Atlanta: John Knox, 1982) 83–100.

48. See ibid., 91–93, on Deut 4:29-30, 30:1-10, and 1 Kgs 8:33-53.

49. See Gary A. Anderson, *A Time to Mourn, a Time to Dance: The Expression of Grief and Joy in Israelite Religion* (University Park: Pennsylvania State University Press, 1991); and Alan Mintz, *Ḥurban: Response to Catastrophe in Hebrew Literature* (New York: Columbia University Press, 1984).

50. Erhard Gerstenberger, "Der klagende Mensch: Anmerkungen zu den Klagegattungen in Israel," *Probleme biblischer Theologie* (ed. Hans Walter Wolff; Munich: Chr. Kaiser Verlag, 1971) 64–72, has shown that Israel's lament is in fact an act of resilient and determined hope.

into protest. We have seen that Israel's countertestimony concerning Yahweh has its natural habitat in exile.[51] For all of its acknowledgment of its own failure, Israel is not willing to let Yahweh off the hook. As a result, in some of its exilic utterances Israel moves stridently past its own failure to focus on Yahweh, to protest Yahweh's abandoning propensity and to invoke Yahweh's new attentiveness to Israel.

Thus in Psalm 74, which expresses grief for the loss of the temple, Israel begins in protest and accusation:

O God, why do you cast us off forever?
Why does your anger smoke against the sheep of your pasture? (v. 1)

Then Israel issues a series of insistent demands to Yahweh, who let all this destruction happen:

Remember your congregation,
which you acquired long ago,
which you redeemed to be the tribe of your heritage.
Remember Mount Zion, where you came to dwell.
Direct your steps to the perpetual ruins. . . .
Remember this, O Lord, how the enemy scoffs,
and an impious people reviles your name. . . .
Rise up, O God, plead your cause;
remember how the impious scoff at you all day long.
Do not forget the clamor of your foes,
the uproar of your adversaries
that goes up continually. (vv. 2-3, 18, 22-23)

Israel's plight is related to Yahweh's own honor and reputation.

Even in the unrelieved sadness of Lamentations, the final phrasing of the poetry begins in a doxology that reminds Yahweh of Yahweh's proper sovereignty (5:19), asks an accusatory question (5:20), makes a strong petition (5:21), and ends in a wistful wonderment: ". . . unless you have utterly rejected us, and are angry with us beyond measure" (5:22).[52] Clearly the next move in Israel's life with Yahweh is up to Yahweh.

In this utterance of protest and grief that acknowledges present trouble, Israel refuses to accept present trouble as final destiny. Even in this circumstance, Israel assumes Yahweh's sovereignty, Yahweh's capacity to override exile. Israel makes appeal to Yahweh's fidelity, which now, in exile, moves to pathos. Israel believes that the sovereign God can be evoked and moved by petition. Thus, while Israel's judgment is a function of Yahweh's sovereignty, Israel's grief and protest are a complement to Yahweh's faithfulness and pathos. The grief and protest permit Yahweh to move beyond sovereign anger and rage to rehabilitation and restoration. It is

---

51. On lament in exile as testimony to Yahweh, see pp. 74–78, 321–22, and 374–81.
52. On the translation of this problematic verse, see Delbert Hillers, *Lamentations: A New Translation with Introduction and Commentary* (rev. ed.; AB 7A; New York: Doubleday, 1992) 160–61.

evident, moreover, in the ongoing life of the exile of Israel, that grief as candor and protest as hopeful insistence are effective. For Yahweh is indeed moved toward Israel in new, caring ways.

Presence in Absence

In the meantime, with Israel in exile, far from home and from Jerusalem and temple, we may imagine that along with a theology of repentance (which was essentially a demanding imperative in Deuteronomic texts), there was a priestly theology of presence that was affirmative and indicative. That is, the priestly disciplines and liturgies, testimonies that received normative form in exile, were devices to help order an acutely disordered community and to assure Israel a mode of Yahweh's presence in a venue of acute absence.[53] Thus while the tabernacle may be in anticipation of the temple, it is also a movable temple, a mode of presence not only imagined prior to the temple of Solomon, but available after the temple of Solomon. It is a mark of the inventiveness and courage of Israel in exile that it refused to settle for flat, angry, one-dimensional absence, and continued to address itself in the direction of Yahweh in Yahweh's hiddenness. Thus in exile Israel is a people celebrating and practicing presence in absence.

Resilient Hope for Regathering

What most strikes one about Israel in its scatteredness is its resilient refusal to accept the exile as the culmination of its destiny. Thus the great promissory oracles of Israel in exile, in Jeremiah, Ezekiel, and Isaiah, are surely oracles addressed to the exiles.[54] But they are also oracles and articulations of hope that arise out of exile. Thus one of the characteristics of Israel in its scatteredness is the insistent hope for a gathering. The oracles in exile, heard in the mouth of Yahweh, insist that the scattered may soon be gathered:

> Hear the word of the Lord, O nations,
> and declare it in the coastland far away;
> say, "He who scattered Israel will gather him,
> and will keep him as a shepherd a flock." (Jer 31:10)

> For you shall go out in joy,
> and be led back in peace;
> the mountains and the hills before you
> shall burst into song,
> and all the trees of the field shall clap their hands.

---

53. In the exile, Israel as a displaced community had need of a God who was mobile and not rooted in the temple in Jerusalem. Mettinger, *The Dethronement of Sabaoth*, has reviewed the strategies of the Deuteronomic and Priestly traditions in rearticulating Yahweh as a mobile God available to the displaced community.

54. On the crucial innovation of these traditions, see Gerhard von Rad, *Old Testament Theology* (San Francisco: Harper and Row, 1965), 2:163–77 and passim; and Walter Brueggemann, *Hopeful Imagination: Prophetic Voices in Exile* (Minneapolis: Fortress Press, 1986).

Instead of the thorn shall come up the cypress;
and it shall be to the Lord for a memorial,
for an everlasting sign that shall not be cut off. (Isa 55:12-13)

"I am going to open your graves, and bring you up
from your graves, O my people; and I will bring you
back to the land of Israel. And you shall know that I
am the Lord, when I open your graves, and bring you up from
your graves, O my people. I will put my spirit within
you, and you shall live, and I will place you on your own
soil; then you shall know that I, the Lord, have spoken and
will act," says the Lord. (Ezek 37:12-14)

Hope belongs characteristically to Israel, and its most acute practice occurs in exile. If we fully credit the articulations of judgment in the texts contemplating exile, we may believe that Yahweh's intention is to end things with Israel, who is like a pot that "can never be mended" (Jer 19:11). It is not credible, in my opinion, that the sovereign judgment of Yahweh was a strategic ploy to be followed predictably by pathos-filled love. The judgment is not for instruction or chastening or improvement. It is simply judgment of a sovereign who will not be mocked.

If this assessment of Yahweh's decisive negativity toward Israel is correct, then one may draw a startling conclusion about Israel in exile. As a scattered community, terminated by Yahweh, Israel refused to accept the scattering as its final destiny. Israel believed and insisted, in sadness and in protest but also in anticipation, that the God who scattered would also gather. If this is correct, then we may say that *Israel hoped beyond the hope or intention even of Yahweh, who had no such hope or intention for Israel.* That is, Israel's courage and shrillness, its defiance of its present circumstances, talked Yahweh into something Yahweh had not yet entertained or imagined or intended. In its countertestimony of argument with Yahweh, Israel moved Yahweh to a new place of gracious intentionality toward Israel. Israel did so partly by appealing to its own need, partly by appealing to Yahweh's sovereign fidelity, and partly by shaming Yahweh as Moses had done long ago. In its earlier history, Yahweh had taken all the initiatives with and for Israel in creating, covenanting, and judging. But now Israel in exile, in its abandonment and desperation, takes the initiative and evokes a turn in Yahweh, creating a future for Israel where none had seemed possible.

The Book of Job, as difficult as it is, provides a clue to the strange eventuation in the case of Israel. If the Book of Job is taken as belated countertestimony of Israel, then we may imagine that in 42:7-17 we are given hints of how faith is practiced in extremis. Job in protest speaks what is "right" (42:7-8). In response Yahweh restores everything (except Job's children). Yahweh "restored the fortunes" (42:10).[55]

---

55. On this crucial formula, see the classic study of Ernst L. Dietrich, שוב שבות *Die endzeitliche Wiederherstellung bei der Propheten* (BZAW 40; Geissen: Töpelmann, 1925); and John M. Bracke, "Šûb šebût: A Reappraisal," *ZAW* 97 (1985) 233–44.

Job is not Israel, to be sure, but the script of Job lives out of the imagination of Israel. Job 42:7-17, a small postscript to the drama of the poem, holds the future of regathered Israel. That, I suggest, is how scattered Israel is in exile. What comes after, in the Old Testament, is a small postscript. But that postscript is the future of gathered Israel, the rootage of Judaism. The gathering takes place by the active engagement of Yahweh's sovereign fidelity. But that awesome sovereign fidelity is surely triggered, in this paradigmatic case, by Israel who repents, who practices exilic presence, and who also grieves in honesty, protests in vigor, and hopes in insistence.

Yahweh's Fresh Turn toward Israel

Israel's consignment to exile (and death and termination?) by Yahweh is a principal theological datum in articulating Israel's theological self-articulation. Given the assertion that such judgment stems from Yahweh's uncompromising covenantal expectation, Israel offers a variety of proximate explanations of this disastrous turn in its life: its own guilt, the inordinate fury of Yahweh that is incommensurate with the affront of Israel, and the hubristic self-assertion of Babylon as a rival of Yahweh. In the end, Israel's more-or-less settled verdict on the matter of exile is a complex articulation of all of these factors. In any case, the drastic rejection of Israel by Yahweh is a decisive and irreversible reality in Israel's self-discernment. What Israel has been given by Yahweh is now matched by what Israel has suffered at the hands of Yahweh.

Our theme now, however, is Yahweh's reach toward Israel beyond the scattering. It is an equally certain theological datum in Israel's self-understanding that *at the depth of the exile, at the bottom of Yahweh's rage toward and rejection of Israel, Yahweh does an about-face and reconstitutes a viable relationship with Israel,* restoring Israel to full and valued partnership. The turn in Yahweh's inclination toward Israel is an extraordinary wonderment in Israel's unsolicited testimony. In this turn Israel ponders the central mystery of its own existence, and its core wonderment and amazement about Yahweh.

As we have seen, Israel does not have a single, clear understanding of what produced the harsh judgment of Yahweh. In like manner, Israel does not know what produced this decisive, positive turn in Yahweh toward Israel. It is a hidden moment in Yahweh's life. In Israel's testimony it is variously suggested that Israel has repented, that Israel's vigorous protest has moved Yahweh back to fidelity, that the nations punishing Israel at Yahweh's behest have overstepped their mandate, thus evoking Yahweh's counter-action of rescue. On this question, special attention should be paid to Isa 40:2, where it is affirmed of Israel "that her penalty is paid." There has been a severe and appropriate punishment of Israel (exile), but it is not a limitless punishment. The debt to Yahweh has been satisfied, so that Yahweh can now move positively toward Israel. Or it may be that the hurt of exile reached deep into Yahweh's pathos, touching and mobilizing unrecognized measures of love and unknown, unacknowledged depths of compassion that heretofore have been completely unavailable to Israel, and perhaps to Yahweh. What is clear is that Israel's life after exile, and Israel's status as Yahweh's partner after rejection, are made possible only by Yahweh's inexplicable turn toward Israel. Israel imagines that the new relationship it is to have as Yahweh's partner is in full continuity with the past relationship, yet completely different, now rooted in Yahweh's self-investment in Israel in quite fresh ways. That is, whatever turn has occurred is a turn on the part of Yahweh.[56]

Israel is dazzled by this decisive turn in Yahweh, and treasures it much more than it understands it—perhaps treasures it more than it can speak adequately about it. The three great exilic prophets make an effort to speak about this dramatic reversal, on which everything for Israel's future depends. Jeremiah employs the image of terminal illness as a way to speak about terminal judgment:

> For thus says the Lord:
> Your hurt is incurable,
> your wound is grievous.
> There is no one to uphold your cause,
> no medicine for your wound,
> no healing for you. (Jer 30:12-13)

Then, abruptly, without comment, Yahweh reverses course in mid-poem:

> Therefore all who devour you shall be devoured,
> and all your foes, everyone of them, shall go into captivity;
> those who plunder you shall be plundered,
> and all who prey on you I will make a prey.
> For I will restore health to you,
> and your wounds I will heal, says the Lord,
> because they have called you an outcast:
> "It is Zion; no one cares for her!" (vv. 16-17)[57]

In Ezekiel, Yahweh speaks of harsh judgment under the image of sexual infidelity, which must be punished:

> You must bear the penalty of your lewdness and your abominations, says the Lord. Yes, thus says the Lord God: I will deal with you as you have done, you who have despised the oath, breaking the covenant.... (Ezek 16:58-59)

But then Ezekiel moves abruptly and without explanation or justification to "yet":

---

56. See Walter Brueggemann, *Genesis* (Interpretation; Atlanta: John Knox, 1982) 75–88, for the suggestion that in the flood narrative of Genesis 6–9, nothing has changed except the inclination of Yahweh. The restoration of the earth after the flood is possible not because humanity has changed, but because Yahweh has a new inclination driven by pathos.

57. See Walter Brueggemann, "'The Uncared For' Now Cared For (Jer 30:12-17): A Methodological Consideration," *JBL* 104 (1985) 419–28.

...yet I will remember my covenant with you in the days of your youth, and
I will establish with you an everlasting covenant. (v. 60)

And in Isaiah of the exile, Yahweh continues the metaphor of affronted marital
love, but without the pornographic propensity of Ezekiel:

> For a brief moment I abandoned you....
> In overflowing wrath for a moment
> I hid my face from you.... (Isa 54:7a, 8a)

In both of these verses, however, the rejection is promptly countered by reembrace:

> ...but with great compassion I will gather you....
> but with everlasting love I will have compassion on you.... (Isa
> 54:7b, 8b)[58]

In Isa 54:7-8, and certainly in Jeremiah 30 and Ezekiel 16, the abrupt rhetorical turn most often is explained away by a kind of criticism that fragments the
poems and so nullifies the artistic tension of the utterance. If, however, we refuse
to dissolve the poems in order to make them credible to our reason or to our theology, we are left in each case with an amazing utterance, the propulsion of which
is kept hidden in Yahweh's own life. In each case there is a condemning utterance
of Yahweh. But in each case that judgment is directly countered by an utterance
of reversal that generates a new possibility for Israel in history, a possibility solely
dependent on the utterance and the utterer.

Israel's unsolicited testimony about its own life with Yahweh is completely based
in these utterances. It may be the case that the "return from exile" is also experienced as a historical-political inversion of fortunes, as Persian hegemony displaced
Babylonian expansionism.[59] As a theological datum, however, everything depends
on the generation of a future of well-being that is rooted in nothing other than in
Yahweh's inexplicable good intention and recommitment to Israel.

Israel Regathered in Obedience

The new, anticipated possibility for Israel as a community given new life as Yahweh's partner is rooted only in Yahweh's inclination toward Israel. As in every other
aspect of its life with Yahweh, Israel must use a variety of terms to express its new
lease on life granted by Yahweh. We may mention four such usages, each of which
bespeaks renewed Israel as the object of Yahweh's powerful verbs.

---

58. On the cruciality of this statement for Israel's exilic problem of continuity, see Walter Brueggemann, "A Shattered Transcendence? Exile and Restoration," *Biblical Theology: Problems and Perspectives*
(ed. Steven J. Kraftchick et al.; Nashville: Abingdon Press, 1995) 169–82.

59. It is altogether plausible, on the basis of the evidence we have, that Persian imperial policy did
indeed effect a reversal of the policy of deportation. In light of that change, however, it is not evident
that there was an immediate (i.e., in 539 B.C.E.), wholesale return of Jews from Babylon.

Gather. The most prominent is the verb *gather* (*qbṣ*):

> See, I am going to bring them from the land of the north, and gather them from the farthest parts of the earth, among them the blind and the lame, those with child and those in labor, together; a great company, they shall return here. (Jer 31:8)

> I will take you from the nations, and gather you from all the countries, and bring you into your own land. (Ezek 36:24)

> Do not fear, for I am with you; I will bring your offspring from the east, and from the west I will gather you; I will say to the north, "Give them up," and to the south, "Do not withhold; bring my sons from far away and my daughters from the end of the earth...."(Isa 43:5-6; cf. Isa 54:7; Jer 23:3, 29:14, 31:10; Ezek 37:21; Zeph. 3:20)

The term is the antithesis of *scatter* (*pûṣ*) and appeals to a positive metaphor.[60] The image is of the flock of the good shepherd that had been scattered in vulnerability, now to be gathered by the attentive shepherd into well-being.

Love. Yahweh's rehabilitation of Israel is an act of "love" (*'ahab*), thus echoing the claims placed early in the tradition by Deuteronomy:[61]

> I have loved you with an everlasting love; therefore I have continued my faithfulness to you. (Jer 31:3)

> Assemble, all of you, and hear!
> Who among them has declared these things?
> The Lord loves him;
> he will perform his purpose on Babylon,
> and his arm shall be against the Chaldeans. (Isa 48:14)

Heal. A third verb is *heal,* thus echoing Exod 15:26, in which Yahweh promises to heal Israel of the "diseases of Egypt":[62]

> For I will restore health to you,
> and your wounds I will heal, says the Lord. (Jer 30:17)

Forgive. Yahweh finally overcomes the judgment of Israel by an act of free forgiveness:

> I will forgive their iniquity,
> and remember their sin no more. (Jer 31:34)

> ...let the wicked forsake their way,
> and the unrighteous their thoughts;

---

60. See the discussion of *scatter* (*pûṣ*), p. 434.
61. See the discussion of *love* (*'ahab*), pp. 414–15.
62. See the discussion of Yahweh under the metaphor of healer (doctor), pp. 252–54.

let them return to the Lord, that he may
have mercy on them,
and to our God, for he will abundantly pardon. (Isa 55:7; cf. Jer 33:8,
36:3; and Ezek 16:63, though here with a different verb, *kpr*)

All of these verbs, and Yahweh's actions to which they testify, mean that Israel is freed from all that had failed. Israel is now completely unburdened by its past, including the past of the exile (cf. Isa 40:2). This God, as the old tradition of Exod 34:6-7a had asserted, is one who "keep[s] steadfast love for the thousandth generation, forgiving iniquity and transgression and sin..." (v. 7a). This is the God known in Israel as the one who forgives, heals, redeems, crowns, and satisfies (Ps 103:3-5):

He will not always accuse,
nor will he keep his anger forever.
He does not deal with us according to our sins,
nor repay us according to our iniquities.
For as the heavens are high above the earth,
so great is his steadfast love
toward those who fear him;
as far as the east is from the west,
so far he removes our transgressions from us.
As a father has compassion for his children,
so the Lord has compassion for those who fear him.
For he knows how we were made;
he remembers that we are dust. (Ps 103:9-14)

Reshaping Life in Obedience and Hope

It remained for Israel to map out and reconstruct its new life granted by Yahweh in forgiveness. This remapping and reconstruction becomes the ongoing work of Judaism. It is clear that the work of Judaism is always postexile and is always in the horizon of Yahweh's gathering, healing, forgiving, loving propensity. How Israel is to shape its life in response to that miracle of a future is a matter always yet to be renegotiated in light of all the negotiations already enacted.

Scholars such as Otto Plöger and Paul Hanson have surely been correct, from a critical perspective, in recognizing and thematizing the recurring tensions in Israel's self-articulation.[63] Plöger has done so under the rubric of "theocracy and eschatology," and Hanson has utilized the terms "visionary" and "pragmatist." In utilizing such critical constructs for theological purposes, we may make use of their work, and yet move beyond such thematization in two ways. First, such labels as those employed in a critical way are inherently reductionist, for the theological

---

63. Otto Plöger, *Theocracy and Eschatology* (Richmond: John Knox, 1968); Paul D. Hanson, *The Dawn of Apocalyptic: The Historical and Sociological Roots of Jewish Apocalyptic Eschatology* (Philadelphia: Fortress Press, 1979).

self-presentation of Judaism set out to be neither pragmatic nor visionary, but to be Yahweh's partner in a real world. Second, while there are surely tensions of the kind that can be identified critically, Israel in its theological self-articulation insisted always on taking seriously both sides of the tension, and finally refused to opt for either side as a full and faithful resolution of its way with Yahweh. This is evident in the canonizing process, which in the end is an accommodation of accents in tension in the community of faith.[64] Our constructs of Israel as the rehabilitated partner of Yahweh are informed by these critical judgments, but must be articulated in a very different way.

It is clear that emerging Judaism is enormously variegated.[65] Here we will consider Israel's postexilic self-discernment under the rubrics of obedience and hope.[66] No doubt Israel, in its new circumstance as a marginated political community, understood itself to be primarily a community of obedience.[67] Like all such obedience, it is likely that the obedience here urged and practiced contained a prudential element: if disobedience caused exile, "let's not do it again." Granting that, as theological testimony we are bound to conclude that Israel's fresh resolve to obedience is a serious one, undertaken in good faith. Israel now is living only by forgiveness, living "on borrowed time," and so is markedly moved toward Yahweh by gratitude.

Israel then is a community of Torah piety.[68] We may particularly appeal to two sources for this characterization of restored Judaism. First, the great psalms of Torah (Psalms 1, 19, 119) surely reflect a community whose horizon is indeed defined by the Torah, which here presumably means the whole tradition and memory that gave identity to Israel and that shaped and specified obedience. Israel as a community of obedience resolved to "meditate day and night" on Yahweh's Torah (Ps 1:2). One may take that as an obsession of exhibitionist legalism, as is often the case in Christian stereotypes of Jews. Or one may understand this commitment to Torah as an acceptance of the reality of Yahweh as the horizon, limit, and center of communal imagination. What is clear is that this piety, an intentional life with Yahweh, was driven neither by guilt nor by fear and coercion.

This acceptance of Yahweh as the horizon of life is a matter of joy, comfort, and well-being (Ps 119:1-2, 50, 52, 97). Such an orientation of life sounds outrageous and endlessly self-deceptive if measured by the norm of modernist autonomy. But of course modern autonomy is no adequate norm for what Israel is doing and what Israel is becoming. Israel is now a vulnerable, outsider community, endlessly

---

64. On the canonizing process in the midst of theopolitical tensions, see Rainer Albertz, *A History of Israelite Religion in the Old Testament Period* 2: *From the Exile to the Maccabees* (Louisville: Westminster/John Knox, 1994).

65. On pluralism as a defining mark of Judaism in this period, see ibid.; and Michael E. Stone and David Satron, *Emerging Judaism: Studies in the Fourth and Third Centuries B.C.E.* (Minneapolis: Fortress Press, 1989).

66. The tension between obedience and hope as theological reference points trades upon critical judgments, such as those made by Hanson and Plöger; see n. 63 above.

67. See Jacob Neusner, *From Politics to Piety: The Emergence of Pharisaic Judaism* (Englewood Cliffs, N.J.: Prentice-Hall, 1973).

68. See James L. Mays, "The Place of the Torah-Psalms in the Psalter," *JBL* 106 (1987) 3–12.

at risk, without serious social power. Therefore commitment to this relationship with Yahweh and to the norms of that relationship provided a source of reassuring constancy.

The second source of comment on Israel as a community of obedience is the reform instituted by Ezra and Nehemiah.[69] Commonly regarded as the moment of the reconstitution of postexilic Judaism, the reform led by Ezra is one of great rigor and vigor, whereby Israel publicly pledged, as at Sinai, to be a people of the Torah (Neh 8:9). The accent of the reordering of Israel's life is on the distinctiveness of Israel, which entailed a "separation" (*bdl*) of Israel from the other peoples, and a fresh resolve about tithes, sabbaths, and marriage (Nehemiah 10–13). It also involved a fresh resolve about justice in the community (Nehemiah 5).

In a Christian discernment of the Old Testament and of emerging Judaism, what most needs to be resisted is the conventional Christian stereotype of legalism. In any serious commitment to obedience, to be sure, zeal may spill over into legalism. But in any attempt to set as antithesis "Christian grace" and "Jewish law," Israel's sense of itself will be distorted and caricatured. Israel, in these interpretive maneuvers and acts of self-discernment led by Ezra, is with considerable daring seeking to order its life in a way that is commensurate with the God who creates, saves, and commands.

The second mark of reconstituted Israel is that Israel is a community of hope. In its reconstituted form, Israel continued to believe that Yahweh had futures yet to work, futures of which the Israelite community would be a primary beneficiary. Thus it is telling and poignant that in Psalm 119, the quintessential psalm of Torah obedience, Israel can speak passionately of its hope along with its resolve to obey: "I hope for your salvation, O Lord, and I fulfill your commandments" (v. 166; cf. vv. 43, 49, 74, 81, 114, 147).

Three dimensions of hope. The hope of Israel is in three dimensions. First, there continued to be alive in Israel hope for a politically serious, Davidic (messianic) recovery, of which Zech 9:9-10 is a well-known witness. Second, Israel's vigorous hope moved beyond political realism in a transcendent direction, issuing in apocalyptic-visionary expectation of world scope. The most comprehensive of these hopes may be the enigmatic "Ancient of Days" in Dan 7:9. Third, in a less differentiated way, Israel continued to hope that, in Yahweh's own time and way, the world would be brought right by Yahweh (cf. Isa 65:17-25). This latter sort of hope is not messianic (=Davidic), but neither is it apocalyptic.

It is possible to comment on and arrange these several promises in a variety of patterns and grids, as scholars have done. For our purposes, it is enough to see that for reconstituted Israel it is a sure datum that the future is not in hock to the present and will not be extrapolated from it. The future, moreover, is not to

---

69. On the difficult critical questions concerning this movement of reform, see especially Hugh G. Williamson, *Ezra, Nehemiah* (WBC 16; Waco, Tex.: Word Books, 1985) xxxvi–lii; and Geo Widengren, "The Persian Period," *Israelite and Judean History* (ed. John H. Hayes and J. Maxwell Miller; Philadelphia: Westminster Press, 1977) 489–538.

be determined by Israel's obedience; the future, as it has been since Israel's most daring core testimony, is in the hands of the One who is sovereignly faithful and faithfully sovereign.

It is enormously important for fully receiving Israel's self-construal that the profound resolve to obedience and the energetic articulation of hope in Yahweh's future possibilities are kept side by side in Israel's self-presentation. This dual accent is surely definitional to Israel's self-discernment, rooted in the confession of the God who saves and commands. The God who commands continues to command, and Israel must obey in the present. And the God who saves is resolved to save in the largest scale of all creation. The obedience of Israel makes possible, on the ground, a community of holiness in a creation tempted to contaminate, and a community of justice in a creation tempted to brutality. Obedience gives sharpness and urgency to Israel's existence. But it is the promises of Yahweh, in which Israel hopes, which keep this community from turning in on itself, either in despair or in self-congratulation. Israel as a holy people refuses to give up on the commandments of Yahweh as the anchor of its significance in the world. Israel as a holy people refuses to doubt the promises, which assert that the future is dependent on nothing in this world, not even on Israel's obedience, but only on Yahweh's good intention, which is more reliable than the world itself.

Israel's Narrative Life in Four Texts

These themes thus form one coherent construal of Israel's unsolicited testimony about its life as Yahweh's primary partner:

(a) loved to existence,

(b) commanded to obedience,

(c) scattered to exile,

(d) recipients of Yahweh's hidden turn, and

(e) gathered to obedience and hope.

To some extent, this sequence of themes is an articulation of Israel's normative, historical-canonical recital. Indeed, Israel cannot "tell itself" except through this normative sequence. But we must be clear that while Israel's theological self-articulation is never remote from its "historical" memory, we are here concerned with these themes as theological data. Thus we see the themes not only in sequence. We also see them whole, as an interrelated network of self-discernment in which Israel is linked to Yahweh's characteristic propensities. That is, these themes, taken theologically, are not simply once-for-all occurrences. They are how it characteristically is with Yahweh, and therefore how it characteristically is with Israel. At the center of this testimony is this disastrous fissure in Israel's life, matched by a profound turn in Yahweh, on which everything depends.

The construal of Israel as Yahweh's partner that we offer here is pieced together from many utterances of Israel; these utterances could be pieced together somewhat differently. Having recognized that, we may also notice some larger renditions of Israel's way with Yahweh that follow more or less this network of assertions, albeit with important variations.

We may mention four such renditions:

(1) Deut 32:1-43[70]

vv. 1-6	introduction
vv. 7-14	appeal to the mighty acts of Yahweh
vv. 15-18	indictment
vv. 19-29	sentence
vv. 30-38	assurance
vv. 39-42	confirmation of the poet's words of hope
v. 43	praise

(2) Hos 2:2-23[71]

vv. 2-13	indictment and sentence
vv. 14-15	invitation
vv. 16-20	renewed covenant
vv. 21-23	restored creation

(3) Ezek 16:1-63

vv. 1-14	Yahweh's initiatory goodness
vv. 15-52	indictment and sentence
vv. 53-63	forgiveness and restoration

(4) Ps 106:1-48

vv. 1-5	introduction
vv. 6-12	rebellion and rescue
vv. 13-39	rebellion
vv. 40-43	judgment
vv. 44-46	rescue
v. 47	petition
v. 48	doxology

These four extended narratives of Israel, drawn from quite different traditions, evidence the same general pattern of sovereignty and fidelity, disobedience and judgment, rescue and rehabilitation. What may interest us is that the climactic point in these several narratives varies a great deal and on the whole is uncertain. Indeed, the climactic point must be uncertain when Israel speaks in its own circumstance of unresolve. It is evident, in each of these model cases, that Israel testifies

---

70. On this text, see what has become the decisive discussion in English: Wright, "The Law-Suit of God."

71. On this chapter and its symmetrical shape, see David J. A. Clines, "Hosea 2: Structure and Interpretation," *Studia biblica 1978* (JSOTSup 11; Sheffield: University of Sheffield, 1979) 83–103.

to assert that its entire life is in relation to Yahweh. No other factor pertains to Israel in this theological self-discernment. This is a "God-toward" people, a fact that issues in its most determined certainty and in its most unsettling risk.

Israel and, Belatedly, the Church

As an addendum to our discussion of Israel's unsolicited testimony about itself, we may pause briefly once again to reflect on the relation of the church to Israel in making its communal, ecclesial claim as the people of God. Here we consider only one reference in the New Testament, in which Paul clearly makes a supersessionist claim by referring to the church as "the Israel of God."

> For neither circumcision nor uncircumcision is anything; but a new creation is everything! As for those who will follow this rule—peace be upon them, and mercy, and upon the Israel of God. (Gal 6:15-16)

In this text, Paul completes his argument against legalism. He takes up the contrast between pragmatic concerns (circumcision) and visionary concerns (new creation). Here he opts for the visionary as the mark of "the Israel of God." Paul must argue here against those who are flatly pragmatic. Elsewhere, however, Paul can be as pragmatic in the maintenance of the community as any pragmatic framer of Judaism (cf. 1 Cor 6:12, 10:23).[72] While Paul can overstate in one direction in order to make his case against "the Judaizers," it is clear that in the long run and in the whole picture, Paul cannot escape the tensions that beset the reformation of Israel after the exile.

If Christians are to think with theological seriousness about the church as the partner of the sovereign, faithful God, then it seems clear that the same thematics pertain to that relationship as pertain to Israel as Yahweh's partner: the same assurances, the same demands, the same costs, and the same surprises. It strikes me that for all the polemics that sustain supersessionism, the truth is that these two communities, because they face the same God, share the same reassuring, demanding life. It is perhaps with such realization that Franz Rosenzweig could dare to imagine that were both communities honest, they would recognize that they live parallel histories, with the same hopes to hope and the same obediences to obey.[73]

---

72. On the social reality from which these texts cannot be separated, see Wayne A. Meeks, *The First Urban Christians: The Social World of the Apostle Paul* (New Haven: Yale University Press, 1983).

73. I refer especially to Franz Rosenzweig, *The Star of Redemption* (London: Routledge and Kegan Paul, 1970). See also Eugen Rosenstock-Huessy, ed., *Judaism Despite Christianity: The "Letters on Christianity and Judaism" between Eugen Rosenstock-Huessy and Franz Rosenzweig* (Tuscaloosa: University of Alabama Press, 1969).

FIFTEEN

The Human Person
as Yahweh's Partner

THE OLD TESTAMENT yields a peculiar and important notion of humanness. Scholarship, moreover, has used great energy in articulating what used to be called "an Old Testament understanding of man."[1] In contrast to the several ideologies of modernity, moreover, much that the Old Testament has to say about human personhood is strikingly odd. There is a reason for the oddness of Israel's unsolicited testimony about humanness, a reason that has not been noticed and appreciated often enough. The oddity, I suggest, stems from the fact that *the Old Testament has no interest in articulating an autonomous or universal notion of humanness.* Indeed, such a notion is, for the most part, not even on the horizon of Old Testament witnesses.

The Old Testament has no interest in such a notion, because its articulation of what it means to be human is characteristically situated in its own Yahwistic, covenantal, interactionist mode of reality, so that humanness is always Yahwistic humanness or, we may say, Jewish humanness. The Old Testament, for the most part, is unable and unwilling, as well as uninterested, to think outside the categories and boundaries of its own sense of Yahweh and Yahweh's partner. As a consequence, the primary categories of articulation that we have found elsewhere—sovereignty, fidelity, covenant, and obedience—pertain for this topic as well. Thus Emmanuel Levinas is correct when he writes in his own mystical, lyrical way of the human person:

> But his soul, which Genesis 2:7 calls divine breath, remains near the Throne of God, around which are gathered all the souls of Israel, i.e., (we must accept this terminology!) all the souls of the authentically human humanity, which is conceived in Haim of Volozhen as being subsumed beneath the category of Israel.... Hence, there is a privileged relationship between the human soul, the soul of Israel, and God. There is a connaturality between

---

1. Without much variation or nuance, Walther Eichrodt, *Man in the Old Testament* (SBT 4; London: SCM Press, 1951), resolves human identity into a mandate of obedience, without any countertheme to balance or qualify obedience. In this regard, Eichrodt's reading seems to reflect a rather one-dimensional Calvinism.

man and the manifold entirety of the creature on the one hand, and a special intimacy between man and Elohim on the other.[2]

Levinas goes on to speak of "man's" commitment to the Torah as decisive for the well-being of the world.[3]

Such an odd linkage between the human and Israel does not mean that the Old Testament yields nothing beyond Jewishness. Nor does it mean that Jewish persons are superior human beings. It means, rather, that in the Old Testament human persons are understood as situated in the same transactional processes with the holiness of Yahweh as is Israel, so that in a very general way the character and destiny of human persons replicates and reiterates the character and destiny of Israel. This transactional process causes a "biblical understanding" of human persons to stand at a critical distance and as a critical protest against all modern notions of humanness that move in the direction of autonomy.[4] This means that when the Old Testament speaks of the human person, its primary and inescapable tendency is to think first of the Israelite human person, from which all others are extrapolated.

Covenantal Notions of Personhood

Given this general linkage of the "human soul" and the "soul of Israel" (to use the terms of Levinas), we may at the outset issue two disclaimers in order to focus on the covenantal-transactional character of human persons that is so crucial for Israel's testimony. In issuing such disclaimers, I intend to put my exposition completely on the side of a relational, dynamic notion of personhood, and thus to reject all essentialist notions of human personhood, even though the latter have dominated much of theological discussion.

First, a great deal of scholarly energy has gone into expositing the Old Testament phrase "image of God."[5] Five primary emphases concerning this notion should be on our horizon:

---

2. Emmanuel Levinas, *In the Time of the Nations* (London: Athlone Press, 1994) 124.
3. My point here is not to underscore the use of masculine terminology by Levinas, but rather to note his insistence that human persons, even non-Israelites, are within the scope of the Torah.
4. Concerning the destructive alternative of human autonomy, see Abraham Heschel, *Who Is Man?* (Stanford, Calif.: Stanford University Press, 1966). On the general theme of autonomy, see John S. Macken, *The Autonomy Theme in the "Church Dogmatics": Karl Barth and His Critics* (Cambridge: Cambridge University Press, 1990). Macken shows how Barth moves away from Kant's "turn to the subject." See also Daniel H. Frank, ed., *Autonomy and Judaism: The Individual and the Community in Jewish Philosophical Thought* (Albany: SUNY Press, 1992).
5. The literature is enormous on the notion of "image of God" as a theological theme. Among the more important recent exegetical studies are the following: James Barr, "The Image of God in the Book of Genesis—a Study of Terminology," *BJRL* 51 (1968–69) 11–26; Phyllis Bird, "Male and Female He Created Them: Genesis 1:27 on the Context of the Priestly Account of Creation," *HTR* 74 (1981) 129–59; Kari E. Borresen, ed., *The Image of God* (Minneapolis: Fortress Press, 1995); Ulrich Mauser, "Image of God and Incarnation," *Int* 24 (1970) 336–56; Gerhard von Rad, *Genesis* (OTL; Philadelphia: Westminster Press, 1972) 57–61; Ellen M. Ross, "Human Persons as Images of the Divine," *The Pleasure of Her Text: Feminist Readings of Biblical and Historical Texts* (ed. Alice Bach; Philadelphia: Trinity Press, 1990) 97–116; John F. A. Sawyer, "The Meaning of בְּצֶלֶם אֱלֹהִים ('In the Image of God') in Genesis I–XI," *JTS* 25 (1974) 418–26; and Krister Stendahl, "Selfhood in the Image of God," *Selves, People, and Persons: What Does It Mean to Be a Self?* (ed. Leroy S. Rouner; Notre Dame, Ind.: University

(1) The human person in the image of God is characteristically "male and female" (Gen 1:27), so that the communal, intersexual character of human personhood is affirmed.[6]

(2) The human person in the image of God appears to be royal, that is, the human person is charged with "dominion" over the earth (Gen 1:28).

(3) The human person in the image of God, like the image of a sovereign on a coin, is a representative and regent who represents the sovereign in the midst of all other subjects where the sovereign is not directly and personally present. Thus the human person is entrusted with "dominion" (Gen 1:28, Ps 8:5-8).

(4) The human person as image is an alternative to all other images of God in this aniconic tradition, so that the human person most fully provides clues to the character of God as "person" and "personal." This claim has important positive force as well as negative, aniconic intention.

(5) Reference to the image of God in Gen 5:1 and 9:6 affirms that the "primal sin" of the first couple ("The Fall") does not deny to all subsequent humanity the character of the image of God.

No doubt these are all crucial theological ingredients in a responsible articulation of humanness, and they have rightly played a major role in much theological articulation. Having said that, my disclaimer about this theme is based on the awareness that *the notion of humanity in "the image of God" plays no primary role in Old Testament articulations of humanity;* it does not constitute a major theological datum for Israel's reflection on the topic. I do not mean that a student of Old Testament theology should not be informed by this ongoing discussion, but that the discussion is evoked by subsequent theological categories, especially Pauline, and is largely imposed on the Old Testament. For that reason I have concluded that the theme falls beyond the scope of Israel's intention concerning the subject.

My second disclaimer is perhaps as seemingly irresponsible as the first. Great scholarly energy has been given to Old Testament evidence about the physiology of human personhood, which revolves characteristically around the categories of *spirit* (*rûaḥ*), *flesh* (*basar*), *living being* (*nephesh*), and *heart* (*lēb*).[7] Again, we have good discussions of this subject, and a student of Old Testament theology must attend to these matters. This matter of physiology has yielded four important insights that have occupied the center of continued study:

---

of Notre Dame Press, 1992) 141–48. The most comprehensive and most helpful discussion known to me is that of Claus Westermann, *Genesis 1–11: A Continental Commentary* (1984; Minneapolis: Fortress Press, 1994) 142–61.

6. The bibliography on this issue is enormous. Among the more influential and helpful is Phyllis Trible, *God and the Rhetoric of Sexuality* (OBT; Philadelphia: Fortress Press, 1978) 1–30 and passim.

7. Concerning human physiology, see the still useful discussion of Aubrey R. Johnson, *The Vitality of the Individual in the Thought of Ancient Israel* (Cardiff: University of Wales Press, 1949); Hans Walter Wolff, *Anthropology of the Old Testament* (London: SCM Press, 1974) 7–79; and Werner H. Schmidt, "Anthropologische Begriffe im Alten Testament," *EvT* 24 (1964) 374–88.

(1) The human person is formed of earth and is breathed upon by God, in order to become a "living being" (*nephesh*) (Gen 2:7, cf. Ps 103:14). This means that the human person is, at origin and endlessly, dependent on the attentive giving of Yahweh in order to have life (cf. Ps 104:29-30). This dependence raises the acute problematic of mortality, which is not in itself related to sin.[8]

(2) The human person has vitality as a living, empowered agent and creature only in relation to the God who faithfully gives breath. Thus the human person is to be understood in relational and not essentialist ways.

(3) The articulation of "breathed on dust" in order to become a "living being" precludes any dualism. It is unfortunate that "living being" (*nephesh*) is commonly rendered "soul," which in classical thought has made a contrast to the "body," a distinction precluded in Israel's way of speaking. Thus the human person is a dependent, vitality-given unity, for which the term *psychosomatic entity* might be appropriate, if that phrasing did not itself reflect a legacy of dualism.

(4) Derivative from this physiology, though no direct part of it, is the sense that human persons are not isolated individuals, but are members of a community of those authorized by the life-giving breath of Yahweh, and so have humanity only in that membership.

Again, it is evident that this physiology, in the service of Israel's interactionist model of reality, stands in important tension with various modern notions of humanness. This physiology becomes important in the Christian tradition when consideration of incarnation and resurrection is undertaken. But because I am here concerned with human beings as partners of Yahweh, I shall insist that this physiology, which largely participates in the standard articulation of its ancient social environment, is to be understood as a way of speaking about the human person in order to say *theologically* what was important for Israel to say. That is, we must know about how Israel speaks in terms of breath, flesh, soul, and heart; but it is not this in itself that is pivotal for Israel's unsolicited testimony.

I have no itch to dismiss either the notion of image or the ancient physiology reflected in the text. But I do not want to be sidetracked from what seems to me the central concern of Israel regarding humanity: namely, that the human person is *a person in relation to Yahweh*, who lives in an intense mutuality with Yahweh. This mutuality invites a "matchup" between the character of Yahweh and the character of human personhood, but that matchup does not compromise the decisive incommensurability between Yahweh and human persons. All of that—concerning relationship, mutuality, matchup, and incommensurability—is articulated in the

---

8. On this question, James Barr, *The Garden of Eden and the Hope of Immortality: The Reid-Tucker Lectures for 1990* (Minneapolis: Fortress Press, 1993), has suggested a radical and significant alternative to the long-established consensus position of Oscar Cullmann.

supple notion of *covenant*, for it is affirmed in Gen 9:8-17 that there is an "everlasting covenant" between God and "every living creature" (*nephesh ḥyyh*), of "all flesh" (*basar*) in the earth. Among those with whom Yahweh has an everlasting covenant are human persons, whose covenant with Yahweh is evidently different from that of other, nonhuman creatures, though that point is not accented here.[9] Thus human persons are covenant partners with Yahweh. This is not the same as Israel's covenant with Yahweh but, as we shall see, Israel does permit its sense of its own covenant with Yahweh to spill over in a generalizing way to this more inclusive relationship of interaction and mutuality.

Human Persons Commensurate to Yahweh's Sovereignty and Mercy

We may first of all articulate the character of human-person-in-relation by focusing on three aspects of humanness that are matchups to three central claims made for Yahweh.

Sovereignty and Obedience

First, Yahweh as Creator of humankind and of each human person is sovereign in that relationship. Human persons are creatures who are dependent on and created for obedience.[10] Even before any concrete content is applied to the commands of Yahweh and the obedience of human persons, the category of sovereignty and obedience is a crucial and definitional mark of humans. The One who makes human life possible is holy, glorious, and jealous. Consequently, the force, possibility, and significance of human life are not lodged in an autonomous agent who has been either given full freedom or abandoned, but are lodged in and with the One who makes human life possible by the constant, reliable giving of breath. The human person is not, and cannot be, sufficient to self, but lives by coming to terms with the will and purpose of the One who gives and commands life.

When we ask about the content of that sovereignty to which the appropriate response is obedience, the Old Testament is not especially forthcoming. We may reference the "commands of creation" in Gen 1:26 that authorize "dominion" and the command and prohibition of Gen 2:15-17.[11] Along with these texts, moreover,

---

9. We are only beginning to notice and appreciate the accent on nonhuman creatures in the creation theology of the Old Testament, largely because of a new ecological awareness. On the animals as God's creatures belonging on the horizon of human responsibility, see especially the work of Douglas John Hall, *The Stewardship of Life in the Kingdom of Death* (Grand Rapids: Eerdmans, 1988); *The Steward: A Biblical Symbol Come of Age* (Grand Rapids: Eerdmans, 1990); and *Imaging God: Dominion as Stewardship* (Grand Rapids: Eerdmans, 1986).

10. So Eichrodt without much nuance or suppleness; see n. 1 above.

11. For an impressive review of the matter of human "dominion" in the modern world and its roots in the Bible, see Cameron Wybrow, *The Bible, Baconism, and Mastery over Nature: The Old Testament and Its Modern Misreading* (American University Studies, series 7, vol. 112; New York: Peter Lang, 1991). Wybrow in a most helpful way takes issue with the well-known thesis of Lynn White that the Bible provides the basis for an exploitative relation to the earth.

it is customary to cite the prohibition of murder and the protection of human life in Gen 9:1-6. To focus on these several commands, however, is to give, in my judgment, undue emphasis to the early chapters in Genesis.

It is more characteristic in Israel to imagine that human persons are in a rough way held accountable for the claims and expectations of the Torah, even though it is not assumed that all human persons or human communities were present at Sinai. Levinas demonstrates the way in which Israel may situate the human person under the commands of the Torah:

> Man, by acts in agreement with the Torah, *nourishes* the association of God with the world; or, by his transgression, he exhausts the powers of that di-vine association. The growth of the holiness, the elevation and the being of the worlds depend on man, as does their return to nothingness.... it is man...which ensures being, elevation and holiness...depending upon whether man is or is not in accordance with the will of God as written in the Torah.[12]

Israel is imprecise about the ways in which this responsibility for creation is to be understood, and Israel does not reflect critically on the matter of "natural revela-tion."[13] It is simply affirmed and assumed that the Torah and its commands pertain to all of creation and thus to human persons.

We may cite three texts in support of this notion that all human persons are summoned to obedience to Yahweh's commands. In two psalms that celebrate creation, Psalms 104 and 145, the rhetoric has in purview all of creation and all human persons, with no reference to covenant or to Torah. And yet, both psalms end with a sober warning:

> Let sinners be consumed from the earth,
> and let the wicked be no more. (Ps 104:35)

> The Lord watches over all who love him,
> but all the wicked he will destroy. (Ps 145:20)

No content is given in either case to "the wicked," but it is clear that the wicked are those who live their lives in resistance to the will and purposes of the Creator, and who damage creation.

In Job 31, moreover, we are provided with a concrete ethical inventory, surely reflective of Israel's best Torah thinking.[14] Here speaks no Israelite, but a human person who is accountable and obedient. There is no doubt that in such ar-ticulations as these, Israel's unsolicited testimony trades upon the substance of

---

12. Levinas, *In the Time of the Nations*, 124–25.

13. See James Barr, *Biblical Faith and Natural Theology: The Gifford Lectures for 1991* (Oxford: Clarendon Press, 1993).

14. On this pivotal chapter in the Old Testament, see Georg Fohrer, "The Righteous Man in Job 31," *Essays in Old Testament Ethics (J. Philip Hyatt, in Memoriam)* (ed. James L. Crenshaw and John T. Willis; New York: KTAV, 1974).

Torah commandments. There is also no doubt that all human creatures are held accountable for the maintenance of healthy life in the world. Human persons are commanded, by virtue of their very creatureliness, to live lives for the sake of the well-being of the world.[15] There can be no pre-commandment or non-commandment human person. Being birthed into Yahweh's creation brings the human person under the rule of the Sovereign who creates.

Human Freedom in the World

Second, we have seen that Yahweh's sovereignty is in tension with Yahweh's fidelity, which is intense and deep, which issues in pathos, and which on occasion profoundly qualifies what appears to be Yahweh's determined sovereignty. As the human person is "matched" to Yahweh and as human obedience "matches" Yahweh's sovereignty, so the human person is authorized to come to terms with Yahweh's fidelity, which runs to pathos.

The assurance given to all human persons is that,

> As long as the earth endures,
> seedtime and harvest, cold and heat,
> summer and winter, day and night,
> shall not cease. (Gen 8:22)

There is a generous reliability to the order of the world, on which human beings can count. The world is ordered by Yahweh so that it provides what all human creatures must have to live (cf. Pss 104:27-28, 145:15-16). Thus human creatures live in a world that leaves them elementally free of anxiety, because of the goodness, reliability, and generosity of Yahweh.[16] But more than this, Yahweh is

> good to all,
> and his compassion is over all that he has made....
> The Lord is faithful in all his words,
> and gracious in all his deeds. (Ps 145:9, 13b)

Yahweh is not hostile toward humankind and does not work in enmity, but is positively inclined to sustain, heal, and forgive. Human persons are, by the very inclination of Yahweh, provided a sure life-space in which to exercise freedom, power, responsibility, and authority, in order to use, enjoy, and govern all of creation.

---

15. Hans Heinrich Schmid has most helpfully exposited the Old Testament notion of an ordering of creation to which human persons must submit and for the maintenance of which they are responsible. His crucial statement in English is "Creation, Righteousness, and Salvation: 'Creation Theology' as the Broad Horizon of Biblical Theology," *Creation in the Old Testament* (ed. Bernhard W. Anderson; Philadelphia: Fortress Press, 1984) 102–17. This article is reflective of his two basic studies, which have not been translated into English: *Wesen und Geschichte der Weisheit: Eine Untersuchung zur altorientalischen und israelitischen Weisheitsliteratur* (BZAW 101: Berlin: A. A. Töpelmann, 1966); and *Gerechtigkeit als Weltordnung: Hintergrund und Geschichte des alttestamentlichen Gerechtigkeits Begriffes* (BHT; Tübingen: J. C. B. Mohr [Paul Siebeck], 1968).

16. Matt 6:25-31 is completely congruent with this accent on Yahweh the Creator who is faithful to human persons; cf. Pss 104:27-28 and 145:15-16.

> ... what are human beings that you are mindful of them,
> mortals that you care for them?
> Yet you have made them a little lower than God,
> and crowned them with glory and honor.
> You have given them dominion over the works of your hands;
> you have put all things under their feet,
> all sheep and oxen,
> and also the beasts of the field,
> the birds of the air, and the fish of the sea,
> whatever passes along the paths of the seas. (Ps 8:4-8)

Yahweh's profound commitment to fidelity and compassion generates life-space for wondrous human freedom in the world, freedom to eat and drink and exult in a world of goodness.[17]

But the fidelity of Yahweh inclined toward pathos gives far more than this to human creatures. Because Yahweh is genuinely interactive, on occasion human persons are emboldened to take the initiative with Yahweh, to insist on their right over against Yahweh, to address Yahweh in a voice of advocacy and insistence. For this claim, Job finally is the model. Job is all of humanity gathered and mobilized against Yahweh, insistent on rights and entitlements that belong to responsible human creatures who have full membership in Yahweh's creation.

It is characteristically Jewish to go even further than this in the exaltation of human creatures, not only in the presence of God, but over against God. Again, I defer to Emmanuel Levinas. In his discussion of God's kenosis, Levinas offers two points. First, "everything depends upon man":

> Man is answerable for the universe! Man is answerable for others. His faithfulness or unfaithfulness to the Torah is not just a way of winning or losing his salvation; the being, elevation and light of the worlds are dependent upon it. Only indirectly, by virtue of the salvation or downfall of the worlds does his own identity depend on it. As if through that responsibility, which constitutes man's very identity, one of us were similar to *Elohim*.[18]

The dominion of human beings over creation, expressed in Genesis 1-2 and especially in Psalm 8, yields to human creatures great power and freedom. That same permit means that human persons have standing ground over against God, which yields something like final answerability for the world (but not autonomy), and which can plead to Yahweh's face (like Job) for a better outcome of the relationship.

Levinas goes one step further in his second topic, "God needs Man's Prayer."[19] Levinas is able to imagine that the relationship between Yahweh and human beings is one of genuine mutuality. Whereas Yahweh in sovereignty holds the initiative

---

17. These themes are at the center of the Christian anthropology proposed by Wolfhart Pannenberg, *Anthropology in Theological Perspective* (Edinburgh: T. & T. Clark, 1985).

18. Levinas, *In the Time of the Nations*, 125.

19. Ibid., 127-32.

over human beings, so in pathos (Levinas's "kenosis") Yahweh acknowledges the initiative of human beings and awaits the agency of human initiative. We have already seen in the psalms of complaint that Israel at prayer is able to cajole, threaten, and coerce Yahweh in ways that assume human initiative.[20] Levinas cites Prov 15:8 as a prize example of prayer that is a need of God: "The sacrifice of the wicked is an abomination to the Lord, but the prayer of the upright is his delight."[21] The human person, in this tradition, is assigned an extraordinary role of authority and entitlement, not only in the service of God, but even over against God. There is indeed a second side to the covenantal, transactional quality of this relationship, which tilts the God-human encounter toward human initiative.

Dialectic of Assertion and Abandonment

Third, it will be evident that I have set up in dialectical fashion a profound tension in this relationship, a tension that is, I believe, reflective of the text and derivative from Israel's own disputatious relationship with Yahweh. As humankind deals with Yahweh's *sovereignty*, obedience is the proper order of the day. As humankind deals with Yahweh's *fidelity moving toward pathos*, humankind is authorized to freedom and initiative.

There is a profound tension in this relationship, for dealing with Yahweh's sovereignty and fidelity does not permit compartmentalization. I fear that in practice we incline to compartmentalization, being excessively scrupulous in some areas of command (such as money or sexuality) and completely autonomous in other spheres of life (such as money or sexuality).[22] In this relationship, however, as in any serious, demanding, intimate relationship, matters are more troubled and complex than such a sorting out might indicate. The human person, like Israel, is invited, expected, and insistently urged to engage in a genuine interaction that is variously self-asserting and self-abandoning, yielding and initiative-taking. As this tradition of testimony does not envision human persons who are arrogantly autonomous, so it does not envision human beings who are endlessly and fearfully deferential to Yahweh.

It will be noticed that Levinas and Abraham Heschel, to whom I have made an important appeal, work out of a Jewish ethical and mystical tradition and do not cite many biblical texts for their perspective, because their argument is more broadly traditional and theological than it is biblical. I have cited them, nevertheless, because this particular Jewish tradition of interpretation voices a countertheme to the predominant Christian inclination to accent in a singular way the tradition

---

20. See my discussion of Israel's countertestimony in this regard, pp. 374–81.

21. Abraham Heschel, in a reference now lost to me, writes, "Man is also necessary to God, to the unfolding of his plans in the world. Man is needed; he is a need of God."

22. The practical outcome of this compartmentalization in the contemporary church is that so-called conservatives tend to take careful account of the most rigorous claims of the Bible concerning sexuality, and are indifferent to what the Bible says about economics. *Mutatis mutandis*, so-called liberals relish what the Bible says in demanding ways about economics, but tread lightly around what the Bible says about sexuality.

of sovereignty and deferential obedience. It may well be that the tradition of sovereignty and obedience is the predominant one in the biblical text, but it is not the only one. By itself, it is not the reason that the biblical tradition has continued to be compelling, authoritative, and endlessly pertinent to ongoing reflection about the character of humanity.

We have seen, since Exod 34:6-7, that Yahweh has at Yahweh's core an unsettled interiority of fidelity and sovereignty.[23] Now we are able to say that with humankind, as with Israel, this unsettled interiority in Yahweh has as its counterpoint in the partner an unsettled practice of deference and autonomy, each of which is endlessly qualified by the other. What full humanness requires and expects in this tradition, moreover, is the *courage to assert* and the *confidence to yield.* Either posture by itself betrays both the tradition and the One with whom human beings are summoned to partner. Moreover, either propensity by itself distorts the partnership and makes a caricature of the character of Yahweh, who in incommensurability will be obeyed, but who in mutuality invites challenge. The high classical tradition of Christian interpretation has not paid sufficient attention to this latter aspect of Yahweh's fidelity, which issues in pathos and vulnerability to the human partner. Consequently and inevitably, that classical Christian tradition has not reflected sufficiently on the ways in which humankind is invited to assertion in the face of Yahweh. As a result of that neglect, the dominant Christian tradition has not fully appreciated the way in which *the dialectic of assertion and abandonment in the human person is a counterpart to the unsettled interiority of Yahweh's sovereignty and fidelity.* It seems to me that the classical Christian tradition must relearn this aspect of the interaction of God and human persons from its Jewish counterpart. This is the enduring imperative of ecumenism, to recover from others what one's own interpretive focus has made unavailable.

Characteristic Markings of Covenantal Humanness

Thus far we have suggested in broad outline that the human person, as presented in Israel's unsolicited testimony, is commensurate with Yahweh:

- Yahweh is sovereign...the human person is summoned to obedience and deference.

- Yahweh is faithful...the human person is invited to freedom and initiative.

- Yahweh is covenantal in the enactment of sovereignty that claims and fidelity that authorizes...human persons are understood as Yahweh's transactional partners who are endlessly engaged in obedience and freedom, in glad yielding to Yahweh's sovereignty and in venturesome freedom from Yahweh's fidelity.

---

23. See my discussion of this pivotal passage, pp. 215–18 and 269–70.

We now consider in more detail *the specificities of this covenantal-transactional creature* who yields in obedience and who asserts in freedom. The Old Testament provides few texts that explicitly and intentionally address the questions we are considering. Rather the evidence is provided "on the run" and in an ad hoc fashion. The text sketches out human persons in the actual practice of their humanness before Yahweh. Methodologically I am informed by the work of Alfons Deissler, who provides a sketch of human practice through the text of Psalm 22.[24] Deissler does not derive any essentialist attributes of humanness from the text, but observes the subject of the psalm "doing humanness" in a concrete situation. We shall pay attention to the accent points in Deissler's exposition of Psalm 22, but shall add to it other aspects of transactional humanness that fall beyond the scope of the psalm he studied. I shall summarize the practice of covenantal humanness vis-à-vis Yahweh in eight topics, organized into three groups.

Three Disciplines of Humanness

In this first group of topics, I will consider the human person as one who listens (obeys), discerns, and trusts. These three disciplines of humanness together provide a foundation for a life of buoyant freedom, free of fear and cynicism, a life rooted in complete commitment to Yahweh, full adherence to Yahweh's sovereignty, and full confidence in Yahweh's reliable ordering of reality.

Listening (obeying). The human person, as Yahweh's creature, is one who *listens* as Yahweh addresses in sovereignty.[25] As Yahweh speaks sovereign command, a key element of humanness is obedience, responding to the address of command that is heard. We have already noted that the command of Yahweh concerns both the practice of justice in imitation of Yahweh (Deut 10:17-19) and the practice of holiness in imitation of Yahweh (Lev 19:2-4). This notion of humanness is parallel to and derived from the notion of Israel as Yahweh's covenant partner. That is, all human persons do, after Israel, what Israel does as Yahweh's partner. We may notice the parallel by comparing two texts:

- concerning Israel:

  So now, O Israel, what does the Lord your God require of you? (Deut 10:12)

- concerning human persons:

  He has told you, O mortal (*'adam*), what is good; and what does the Lord require of you...? (Mic 6:8)

---

24. Alfons Deissler, "'Mein Gott, Warum hast du mich verlassen'...(Ps 22.2)," *Ich will euer Gott werden* (Stuttgarten Bibel-Studien 100; Stuttgart: Verlag Katholisches Bibelwerk, 1981) 99–121.

25. Thus the *shema'* of Deut 6:4 is at the center of an Old Testament understanding of human personhood. It is important, however, to remember that *shema'* in the first instant means "hear" before it means "obey." Paul Ricoeur, in one of his early writings, observes that to listen is to concede that one is not self-made and autonomous. Listening—responding in obedience to another—is recognition that one is derivative and inherently connected to one who has the right to address.

The question is put first to Israel and then to "mortals." It belongs to the character of the human creature, according to Israel's unsolicited testimony, that humanness means to hear and obey the elemental, world-defining, world-sustaining, world-ordering will of Yahweh for justice and holiness.

The practice of holiness concerns the disciplined awareness that life is to be ordered with the profound acknowledgment that the core of reality lies outside self and is not given over to human control. Thus the priestly instruction elaborately hedges the mystery of holiness away from human control.

The practice of justice, in concrete ways, is the enactment of Yahweh's *ṣedāqāh*, whereby the cosmos can be ordered for life, and whereby the human community can be kept viable and generative.[26] In the doing of justice, the role of humanness is not simply the keeping of rules, but consists in the venturesome enactment of positive good, whereby human solidarity is maintained and enhanced. The exercise of obedience is the wise use of responsible social power as given in the key warrants of the creation texts (cf. Gen 1:18, 2:15; Ps 8:6-8).

Human persons are authorized to "have dominion" over all of creation, but that dominion, given the verbs of Gen 2:15, is to "till" (*'bd*) and "keep" (*šmr*) the earth. The verbs suggest not exploitative, self-aggrandizing use of the earth, but gentle care for and enhancement of the earth and all its creatures. In this regard the mandate of obedience issues in stewardship, the wise care for the world and its creatures, who are entrusted to human administration.[27]

Old Testament testimony, however, does not linger over such theological generalities, but always gets down to cases. And when the Old Testament witness gets down to cases, the practice of justice, which is a core human vocation, concerns not nonhuman creatures primarily, but the enhancement of the human community by mobilizing social power, especially the power and resources of the strong for the well-being of the whole community. While many texts might be cited, we shall select four.

First, the mandate for power for justice is voiced negatively in Ezek 34:3-4, which has as its positive counterpoint vv. 14-16:

> You have not strengthened the weak, you have not healed the sick, you have not bound up the injured, you have not brought back the strayed, you have not sought the lost.... I will feed them with good pasture, and the mountain heights of Israel shall be their pasture; there they shall lie down in good grazing land, and they shall feed on rich pasture on the mountains of Israel. I myself will be the shepherd of my sheep, and I will make them lie down, says the Lord God. I will seek the lost, and I will bring back the strayed, and I will bind up the injured, and I will strengthen the weak, but the fat and the strong I will destroy. I will feed them with justice. (Ezek 34:4, 14-16)

26. Hans Heinrich Schmid, *Gerechtigkeit als Weltordnung*, has shown that justice is not only Sinai-focused in the Old Testament. *Ṣedāqāh* belongs to the very structure and fabric of creation and must not be violated; see Prov 8:10-21.

27. See reference to the work of Hall, n. 9 above.

In this text, echoed in Matt 25:31-46, Yahweh undertakes the rehabilitative work that properly belongs to obedience among the powerful.

Second, in a dispute over proper obedience, the practice of rehabilitative justice is championed, as over against the pseudo-practice of holiness:

> Is not this the fast that I choose:
> to loose the bonds of injustice,
> to undo the thongs of the yoke,
> to let the oppressed go free,
> and to break every yoke?
> Is it not to share your bread with the hungry,
> and to bring the homeless poor into your house;
> when you see the naked, to cover them,
> and not to hide yourself from your own kin? (Isa 58:6-7)

The true desire of Yahweh is for neighborliness of a radical kind. That desire of Yahweh certainly applies to Israelites; but surely that desire can be extrapolated, so that it is a demand made of every human person, in the interest of a viable human community.

Third, Job 31 offers a rich and comprehensive inventory of human obligation:

> If I have walked with falsehood,
> and my foot has hurried to deceit—
> let me be weighed in a just balance,
> and let God know my integrity!—
> if my step has turned aside from the way,
> and my heart has followed my eyes,
> and if any spot has clung to my hands; . . .
> If my heart has been enticed by a woman,
> and I have lain in wait at my neighbor's door; . . .
> If I have rejected the cause of my male or female slaves,
> when they brought a complaint against me; . . .
> If I have withheld anything that the poor desired,
> or have caused the eyes of the widow to fail,
> or have eaten my morsel alone,
> and the orphan has not eaten from it—
> for from my youth I reared the orphan like a father,
> and from my mother's womb I guided the widow—
> if I have seen anyone perish for lack of clothing,
> or a poor person without covering,
> whose loins have not blessed me,
> and who was not warmed with the fleece of my sheep;
> if I have raised my hand against the orphan,
> because I saw I had supporters at the gate; . . .

> If I have made gold my trust,
> or called fine gold my confidence;
> if I have rejoiced because my wealth was great,
> or because my hand had gotten much;
> if I have looked at the sun when it shone,
> or the moon moving in splendor,
> and my heart has been secretly enticed,
> and my mouth has kissed my hand; ...
> If I have rejoiced at the ruin of those who hated me,
> or have exulted when evil overtook them—
> I have not let my mouth sin
> by asking for their lives with a curse—
> if those of my tent ever said,
> "O that we might be sated with his flesh!"—
> the stranger has not lodged in the street;
> I have opened my doors to the traveler—
> if I have concealed my transgressions as others do,
> by hiding my iniquity in my bosom, ...
> If my land has cried out against me,
> and its furrows have wept together;
> if I have eaten its yield without payment,
> and caused the death of its owners ...
> (Job 31:5-7, 9, 13, 16-21, 24-27, 29-33, 38-39)

I have here quoted only the "if-clauses," which are followed in each case by a curse, thus negatively asserting innocence.

What interests us, however, is not the dramatic structure of the chapter nor the function of its assertion in the mouth of Job, but the substance of responsibility and obligation articulated in the process of Job's acquittal. It is clear that obedience and responsibility touch every sphere and zone of human existence: sexuality, economics, religion, and personal integrity. In the last verses, moreover, obligation includes care of the earth. It is equally clear that the main body of this text concerns responsibility to take positive, rehabilitative action toward the weak, the poor, and the vulnerable. The resources of the strong are held in trust for the community. Job's protestations of innocence, moreover, are precisely that he has devoted his great resources to the community and has not used them only for himself. Job stands as a powerful contrast to the rejected, condemned rulers of Ezekiel 34, who used their great resources only for themselves.

Fourth, Psalm 112 offers a portrayal of "the blessed person" who delights in the commandments of Yahweh. Such a one is diligent, generous, and acts in justice:

> It is well with those who deal
> generously and lend,
> who conduct their affairs with justice. ...

> They have distributed freely,
> they have given to the poor;
> their righteousness endures forever.... (Ps 112:5, 9)

The conduct of such a person matches the propensity of Yahweh in the matching Psalm 111.

Thus elementally, human obedience means to care for the community, to practice rehabilitative hospitality, to engage in responsible stewardship, and quite concretely,

- to share your bread with the hungry,

- to bring the homeless poor into your house,

- to cover the naked.

In our contemporary context, it may be wondered, and even debated, whether this is the work of "the private sector," or if this is thought to be societal policy. The short answer is that the Old Testament, in its unsolicited testimony, makes no distinction between private and public responsibility. The assertion of Isaiah 58 does indeed sound like individual initiative. The same is true, at first glance, in Psalm 112 and Job 31. In both of these latter cases, however, we have the characterization of a wealthy, powerful, influential person in a feudal society who stands at the top of the economic stratification of society, and therefore action by such a powerful person is tantamount to public policy. And clearly Ezekiel 34 is concerned with the use of the government apparatus to take rehabilitative initiatives toward the marginalized. Human agents, in ancient society as in contemporary society, are embedded in social institutions. These social institutions are vehicles for obedience and for the implementation of justice in the community, which is a human obligation to the command and will of Yahweh.

The four texts that I have cited, to which many others could be added, make clear that the large claims of obedience to Yahweh come down concretely to neighborly needs of a daily kind. The disciplines of hearing and responding in obedience constitute a powerful rejection of autonomy that predictably issues in destructive coveting, and that sets individual gain over against the community and its needs. The obedient human agent is a creature deeply embedded in and with and for the community.

Wisdom and discernment. Because obedience issues in the responsible use of power for the sake of community in the service of Yahweh's will for justice, being human means to be "wise and discerning" (*ḥkm wnbôn*). In the first instant, it is a considerable leap from obedience to wisdom. But on closer reflection, it is clear that true wisdom is to adhere to the commands (Prov 10:8), and that the keeping of commands entails *the practice of wisdom* (Deut 1:13-15, 4:6). Viewed theologically, rhetoric about commands and about wisdom are intimately linked in the Old Testament. Both concern attentiveness to the mysterious, God-given coherence of reality that is not simply at the disposal of human aggressiveness. In the idyllic presentation at the beginning of his reign, Solomon asks for a "hearing heart" (1 Kgs 3:9) and is given a "wise and discerning" (*ḥkm wnbôn*) heart (v. 12). In the end, the wise are to celebrate Yahweh's fidelity, justice, and righteousness (Jer 9:23-24).

An Old Testament articulation of humanness does not flinch from celebrating shrewdness and insight of a tough-minded kind.[28] But the discernment to which human persons are enjoined is not simply technical knowledge. It is, rather, a sense of how things are put together and how things work in God's inscrutable deployment of creation. It is the delicate recognition that reality is an intricate network of limits and possibilities, of givens and choices that must be respected, well-managed, and carefully guarded, in order to enhance the well-being willed by and granted by Yahweh for the whole earth. In addition to Solomon, who is presented as a model of one who can enhance his realm,[29] we may cite as a model figure Joseph, who like Solomon is said to be "discerning and wise" (Gen 41:33). As a consequence of this special gift from God, Joseph is able to mobilize the resources of the earth and the power of the Egyptian empire for the sake of "bread for the world."[30]

Leaders in Israel are regularly expected to be "wise and understanding." In Deut 4:6, however, the matter is widened and democratized in order to make such discerning wisdom an attribute of all Israel. Insofar as this quality of discernment is sapiential, one may even extrapolate more generally beyond Israel. Such discernment is a God-given capacity of human creatures. Thus Israel's wise leaders embody this general human quality, perhaps in special measure.

This accent on discernment is not commonly made in Old Testament theology when speaking of human personhood, for in recent time focus has been on commandments and obedience. I include this emphasis and place it immediately after obedience for two reasons. First, a recovery of the wisdom-creation traditions of the Old Testament makes clear that human persons vis-à-vis Yahweh are to be understood, not simply in terms of the Moses traditions that are so intensely Israelite, but also in terms of the creation traditions that proceed from a larger horizon. It is well known that the wisdom testimony of Proverbs, for example, sketches out a picture of responsible, Yahwistic humanness without any intense ap-

---

28. It is a complete misunderstanding to reduce the God-human relation in the Old Testament to the practice of a flat, one-dimensional, uncritical obedience. See Dorothee Sölle, *Beyond Mere Obedience: Reflections on a Christian Ethic for the Future* (Minneapolis: Augsburg, 1970); and Stanley Milgram, *Obedience to Authority: An Experimental View* (London: Tavistock, 1974).

29. I use the term *model* because a great deal of scholarship now regards the historical evidence for Solomon as a wisdom figure as minimal if not nonexistent. Nonetheless, as a model for subsequent tradition, Solomon is a powerful force. See Walter Brueggemann, "The Social Significance of Solomon as a Patron of Wisdom," *The Sage in Israel and the Ancient Near East* (ed. John G. Gammie and Leo G. Perdue; Winona Lake, Ind.: Eisenbrauns, 1990) 117–32.

30. On the role of Joseph as an ambivalent figure of Israelite faith while in the service of the empire, see W. Lee Humphreys, "A Life-Style for Diaspora: A Study of the Tales of Esther and Daniel," *JBL* 92 (1973) 211–23.

peal to the commandments.[31] Humanness in this tradition means to pay attention to the generous mystery that drives reality, and to know how, in respectful and constructive ways, to channel that generous mystery toward the well-being of the earth and of the human community.

The second reason I cite this facet of humanness immediately after obedience is that I believe it is a ground from which to resist two acute distortions of humanness in contemporary society. On the one hand, the wisdom traditions make clear that obedience is not simply slavish, fearful conformity to rules and laws. Thus wisdom is a guard against legalism. Obedience, according to the traditions of wisdom, entails the imaginative capacity to take positive initiatives for the enhancement of creation. "Fear of Yahweh is the beginning of wisdom." With that beginning as the reference point, wisdom is also the practice of vast learning and insight. On the other hand, wisdom and discernment are an antidote to unbridled technical knowledge in a "can-do" society that seems bent on damaging the earth for immediate private gain. Wisdom, the ability and willingness to see reality whole as God's generous, fragile gift, is a check on technical capacity and technical reason that refuse every restraint of value. Wisdom is an invitation to be present in the world in ways that resist both abdicating obedience and unrestrained technical freedom, by putting the inscrutable insistences and generosities of Yahweh at the core of the decision-making process.[32]

Primal trust. The juxtaposition of obedience and discernment, which together give a warrant for accountability and venturesome initiative, leads to a third element, *trust*.[33] This notion of trust is very close to a phrase made popular by Erik Erikson, "basic trust."[34] By this phrase, Erikson refers to the most elemental confidence that a baby begins to have in its mother—trusting that the mother is reliably concerned and attentive even when not visibly present. From such a concrete confidence in the mother, says Erikson, the baby begins to accept a basic confidence toward the reliability of the world and all creatures. This trust is the primal alternative to a profound anxiety, which regards the world as untrustworthy, like a neglectful mother.

To be fully human, so Israel testifies, is to have a profound, unshakable, elemental trust in Yahweh as reliable, present, strong, concerned, engaged for; and, like Erikson's child, to live and act on the basis of that confidence, even when Yahweh

---

31. Proverbs is a sustained reflection on the cruciality of human discernment in the practice of human freedom, human responsibility, and human power. Reference should be made to Gerhard von Rad, *Wisdom in Israel* (Nashville: Abingdon Press, 1972), as well as the work of James L. Crenshaw and Roland E. Murphy (see chap. 9, nn. 2, 10, 21, 25).

32. See my own foray into this subject matter in Walter Brueggemann, *In Man We Trust: The Neglected Side of Biblical Faith* (Louisville: Westminster/John Knox, 1986). This study was early in the scholarly recovery of wisdom, and would now need to be stated somewhat differently.

33. On trust as a theme in the discernment of humanness, see Deissler, "Mein Gott," 111–13; Hugo Goeke, "Die Anthropologie der individuellen Klagelieder," *Bibel und Leben* 14 (1973) 14–15; and Horst Seebass, "Über den Beitrag des Alten Testaments zu einer theologische Anthropologie," *KD* 22 (1976) 52.

34. Erik H. Erikson, *Identity and the Life Cycle* (New York: Norton, 1980) 57–67.

is not visible and circumstance attests to the contrary. One way of speaking of this basic trust is the term *'emeth* (and its variant, *'amen*), which Gerhard von Rad has nicely explicated as a full reliability on Yahweh in adverse circumstance (especially when under assault in war).[35] Thus Abraham is to "believe" (*'amen*) the promise of Yahweh against the data (Gen 15:6), and Judah is to "stand firm in faith" when under threat (Isa 7:9). This term, however, is directly the practice of Israel vis-à-vis Yahweh; that is, it is intensely focused on the communal practice of Israel.

We may also consider the notion of humanness as marked by confidence of a broader kind. Thus we look to a second term that is not so focally concerned with Israel: *bṭḥ*, to trust and have confidence in Yahweh and in Yahweh's good governance of the world. This term for undoubting human confidence in Yahweh is no less Yahwistic in substance, but it is used in contexts other than in the community of Israel per se. It is found especially in individual songs of complaint. In such songs, the speaker is characteristically in very difficult circumstance. Even in such circumstance, however, the speaker expresses complete confidence in Yahweh, confidence that not only sustains the speaker, but also intends to motivate Yahweh to act in positive ways, so as not to disappoint the trust of the speaker. That is, Yahweh must act so that such confidence is not, in the end, misplaced or betrayed. Thus:

> O my God, in you I put my *trust;*
> do not let me be put to shame;
> do not let my enemies exult over me.
> Do not let those who wait for you be put to shame;
> let them be ashamed who are wantonly treacherous. (Ps 25:2-3)

> Vindicate me, O Lord,
> for I have walked in my integrity,
> and I have *trusted* in the Lord
> without wavering.
> Prove me, O lord, and try me;
> test my heart and mind.
> For your steadfast love is before my eyes,
> and I walk in faithfulness to you. (Ps 26:1-3)[36]

> The Lord is my strength and my shield;
> in him my heart *trusts;*
> so I am helped, and my heart exults,
> and with my song I give thanks to him. (Ps 28:7)

---

35. Gerhard von Rad, *Holy War in Ancient Israel* (Grand Rapids: Eerdmans, 1991) 101–14, has situated Israel's notion of faith in the context of holy war, i.e., the readiness to trust Yahweh when Israel is helpless and has no resources to face the threat in which it finds itself. Von Rad, moreover, proposed that faith from such a context of threat is then transposed in the prophetic tradition of Isaiah so that it becomes a more sophisticated theological motif, but does not lose the concrete reference of its origin. On the usage in Isaiah, see Gerhard von Rad, *Old Testament Theology* (London: Oliver and Boyd, 1965), 2:174.

36. Notice that while *bṭḥ* is used in v. 1, *'emeth* is used in v. 3.

Many are the torments of the wicked,
but steadfast love surrounds those who *trust* in the Lord.
(Ps 32:10; cf. 31:14; 55:23; 56:4, 11)

It is noteworthy that trust, in many of these cases, is the alternative to fear, which we might render as elemental anxiety:

In God, whose word I praise,
in God I trust; I am not afraid;
what can flesh do to me? . . .
in God I trust; I am not afraid.
What can a mere mortal do to me? (Ps 56:4, 11)

Surely God is my salvation;
I will trust, and will not be afraid,
for the Lord God is my strength and my might;
he has become my salvation. (Isa 12:2)

Human persons, as Erikson saw well, are finally confronted with the options of trust or fear. The celebrated human person, in Israel's horizon, is embedded deeply in trust. This trust is not vague and amorphous; it focuses on Yahweh as an active agent who sustains and intervenes.[37] From that personal and intimate focus, however, Israel is able to generalize, so that one may come to trust the world over which Yahweh presides as a safe and reliable place in which to live.

Thus the same term, as a noun, may be rendered "security," referring to the milieu of safety available where Yahweh's rule is willingly accepted and where Yahweh's blessings are consequently offered and received. In such contexts, there is no cause for anxiety:

I will give you your rains in their season, and the land shall yield its produce, and the trees of the fields shall yield their fruit. Your threshing shall overtake the vintage, and the vintage shall overtake the sowing; you shall eat your bread to the full, and live *securely* in your land. (Lev 26:4-5)

I will make with them a covenant of peace and banish wild animals from the land, so that they may live in the wild and sleep in the woods *securely*. . . . They shall no more be plunder for the nations, nor shall the animals of the land devour them; they shall live in *safety*, and no one shall make them afraid. (Ezek 34:25, 28)

. . . but those who listen to me will be *secure* and will live at ease, without dread of disaster. (Prov 1:33)

---

37. This is the counterpoint to Israel's core testimony about Yahweh who sustains and intervenes. The functioning human person, as envisioned by Israel, is one who trusts in Yahweh's faithful sustenance and intervention and on that basis lives freely. The focus is evident in Isaiah 36–37, for the Assyrians did not reckon with Yahweh as a decisive and particular force in the common history of Judah. They do not know, moreover, about Israel's readiness to act on the basis of trust in Yahweh.

In all three of these traditions—cultic blessing (Lev 26:4-5), prophetic promise (Ezek 34:25, 28), and sapiential assurance (Prov 1:33)—Israel knows about the prospect of finding Yahweh's world to be a viable place in which to live free of anxiety. Such confidence is especially linked to the full functioning of creation. But it is also a more intimate confidence that Yahweh is fully and adequately reliable, in the face of any threat, in any circumstance, including both external assault and the pressures of guilt and death.

In two other texts this practice of trust in Yahweh is fully exhibited, even though the terms *'emeth* and *bth* are not utilized. The first of these, Psalm 131, is an example of trust in the midst of the routinization of daily life. This is a psalm of utter and complete confidence in Yahweh. The speaker is willing to dismiss any thinkable anxiety and to be completely at ease in confidence:

> O Lord, my heart is not lifted up,
> my eyes are not raised too high;
> I do not occupy myself with things
> too great and too marvelous for me.
> But I have calmed and quieted my soul,
> like a weaned child with its mother;
> my soul is like the weaned child that is with me. (Ps 131:1-2)

From this intimacy, moreover, Israel is able to generalize:

> O Israel, hope in the Lord
> from this time on and forevermore. (v. 3)

A second text, Dan 3:16-18, exhibits the same confidence in a quite different context. Shadrach, Meshach, and Abednego demonstrate confidence in the face of an immediate and fierce threat:

> O Nebuchadnezzar, we have no need to present a defense to you in this matter. If our God whom we serve is able to deliver us from the furnace of blazing fire and out of your hand, O king, let him deliver us. But if not, be it known to you, O king, that we will not serve your gods and we will not worship the golden statue that you have set up. (Dan 3:16-18)

These three trusting Jews are fully confident of Yahweh's rescue, but even failing that, they remain utterly confident. It is no wonder that "Nebuchadnezzar was...filled with rage" (v. 19), for such confidence puts these trusters in Yahweh completely beyond the reach of the king's brutalizing intimidation. This confidence, which to the world is an absurdity, has made it possible for martyrs (witnesses) of faith not to yield in the face of severe testing.

These three aspects of humanness—obeying, discerning, and trusting—are of a piece, even though they are characteristically evidenced in different circles of tradition. These three markings (or disciplines or practices) of humanness articulate the sine qua non of what it means to be human in the purview of Israel's testimony. Humanness requires:

- listening and responding to the summons of the sovereign,

- discernment in wisdom in response to the hidden generosity of God in God's world,

- trusting completely, without reservation, in the reliability of Yahweh and Yahweh's world.

These practices provide positive linkage to Yahweh, from whom life comes, and permit buoyancy for an effective life in the world. These three markings portray humanness at peace, in equilibrium, fully authorized for and entrusted with the fullness of life. These characteristic practices of humanness are commensurate with Israel's core testimony about Yahweh. They are appropriate disciplines when the sovereignty and fidelity of Yahweh can be credibly asserted and gladly accepted.

Life in Crisis

A second grouping of markings of humanness, in which I follow Deissler, concerns life with Yahweh when human existence is troubled, disturbed, and at risk; when obedience, discernment, and trust have either failed or are shown to be inadequate. In such a time of dismay, the human person vis-à-vis Yahweh must take initiatives to right the trouble, which is not the proper condition of humanness in Yahweh's world.

This second grouping of practices and disciplines emerges when the human person is left in "the Pit" (cf. Pss 28:1, 30:3, 40:2, 88:6). A common image in the life of human prayer, "the Pit" refers to any diminishment or impairment of human well-being. Thus it may refer to sickness, imprisonment, social isolation and rejection, or, in extremity, physical death. It comprehends the whole gamut of troubles that beset human beings. In its realism, Israel knows that the disciplines of equilibrium—obedience, discernment, and trust—are not first of all appropriate to such human crises. Thus the human person, according to Israelite testimony, undertakes raw and insistent disciplines in the pit, practices that are constitutive of humanness and commensurate with Israel's countertestimony concerning Yahweh. These activities correspond to the evidence and conviction of Yahweh's hiddenness, unreliability, and negativity.

Complaint. First, the human person in great trouble is a *complaining* person."[38] The complaining person is one who treats his or her troubles as serious and legitimate and not to be accepted as normal. The complaining person refuses silence and resignation, but rather issues a vigorous and shrill protest grounded in the covenantal right to be granted well-being and to be taken seriously. Here we may refer to

---

38. See Deissler, "Mein Gott," 109–11; and Erhard Gerstenberger, "Der klagende Mensch: Anmerkungen zu den Klagegattungen in Israel," *Probleme biblischer Theologie* (ed. Hans Walter Wolff; Munich: Chr. Kaiser Verlag, 1971).

any of the complaint psalms, for which Psalm 13 is a convenient model, and to the witness of complaint psalms even outside of Israel.[39] The complaint psalm is expressed variously in a mood of vexation, insistence, anger, rage, indignation, doubt, and hope, but never indifference or resignation.[40]

The complaint is sometimes focused directly on Yahweh, who has been absent, silent, indifferent, and neglectful, and who is therefore indirectly responsible for the present plight of the speaker. In such contexts it is assumed that a third party (the enemy) has been the perpetrator of the trouble, but has been able to do so only by Yahweh's default. Thus Fredrik Lindström has written about the void created by Yahweh's inattentiveness, which permits the power of death to seize the initiative and to cause trouble.[41] But on occasion, Yahweh is said in these prayers to be not only negligent and guilty by default, but more directly and aggressively involved as the perpetrator of the trouble.

What is important about this feature of humanness is that Israel understands, in its courageous disputatiousness, that the human agent has rights, and that these rights require voiced protest and insistence; thus the person shuns every temptation of docile, deferential silence. Israel is clear, moreover, that such angry and insistent protests addressed to Yahweh are not acts of unfaith, as they are often thought to be in quietistic Christian piety, but are a vigorous act of freedom and responsibility.[42] The human person must insist on his or her own well-being, even with shrillness; therefore, when appropriate, the person must call Yahweh to accountability. Thus humans in trouble are mandated by the character of Yahweh to take the initiative toward Yahweh. The purpose of the complaint is to summon Yahweh to the trouble, to motivate Yahweh to accept the responsibility that is properly the burden of Yahweh in this relationship of fidelity and mutuality, and so to effect decisive change in circumstance.

Petition. The voicing of shrill protest and insistence is not merely catharsis. It issues in *petition*, in imperatives addressed to Yahweh with urgency.[43] Petition follows complaint closely and regularly; in petition the needy person addresses

---

39. The basic study is that of Claus Westermann, *Praise and Lament in the Psalms* (Edinburgh: T. & T. Clark, 1981). Geo Widengren, *The Akkadian and Hebrew Psalms of Lamentation as Religious Documents: A Comparative Study* (Uppsala: Almqvist and Wiksell, 1937), has shown that Israel's complaints draw on a vast background of such religious practice. The most recent comprehensive study of this genre and practice of faith is Patrick D. Miller, *They Cried to the Lord: The Form and Theology of Biblical Prayer* (Minneapolis: Fortress Press, 1994).

40. Erhard Gerstenberger, "Jeremiah's Complaints: Observations on Jer 15:10-21," *JBL* 82 (1963) 405 n. 50, has helpfully distinguished between "complaint" (*Anklage*) and "lament" (*Klage*): "A lament bemoans a tragedy that cannot be reversed, while a complaint entreats God for help in the midst of tribulation." Israel characteristically engages in complaint, not lament.

41. Fredrik Lindström, *Suffering and Sin: Interpretations of Illness in the Individual Complaint Psalms* (Stockholm: Almqvist and Wiksell International, 1994).

42. Claus Westermann, "The Role of the Lament in the Theology of the Old Testament," *Int* 28 (1974) 25 and passim, has nicely contrasted the characteristic practice of Christian piety (which is in a mood of submissiveness and docility) with Jewish piety (which characteristically does not shrink from protest of a most vigorous kind).

43. See Miller, *They Cried to the Lord,* 86–114; and Deissler, "Mein Gott," 113–15.

Yahweh in an imperative. The imperative is not trivial or routine. It consists in a command to Yahweh about life-and-death issues:

> Consider and answer me, O Lord my God!
> Give light to my eyes.... (Ps 13:3)

> Do not be far from me,
> for trouble is near
> and there is no one to help....
> But you, O Lord, do not be far away!
> O my help, come quickly to my aid!
> Deliver my soul from the sword,
> my life from the power of the dog!
> Save me from the mouth of the lion! (Ps 22:11, 19-20)

> To you, O Lord, I call;
> my rock, do not refuse to hear me,
> for if you are silent to me,
> I shall be like those who go down to the Pit.
> Hear the voice of my supplication,
> as I cry to you for help,
> as I lift up my hands
> toward your most holy sanctuary. (Ps 28:1-2)

The speaker of imperatives to Yahweh, authorized by deep trouble, must find voice to express pain in speech. Everything depends on this maneuver. This is an act of profound self-assertion and self-regard, which is the key act of initiative in getting something done to assuage the trouble. This act of imperative is not done in a mood of resignation or of deference; it is an act of insistent hope. The speaker knows in profound ways that the present trouble is not how life is supposed to be, is not as Yahweh intends it. Moreover, the speaker proceeds on the sure conviction that circumstance can be transformed and will be righted... if Yahweh can be mobilized.

Everything depends on mobilizing the undoubted power of Yahweh, and so the petition is regularly attended by motivations aimed at urging Yahweh to a much-needed action.[44] The imperative addressed to Yahweh is characteristically followed

---

44. On motivations, see Miller, *They Cried to the Lord*, 114–26. The motivations offered for Yahweh's actions in time of need are of various kinds, some of which are not congruent with "innocent" Christian piety. That is, in addition to confessions of sin and statements of need and trust, Israel also seeks to motivate Yahweh to act by appealing to Yahweh's honor, vanity, and risk of shame (e.g., Num 14:13-16). I take it that the willingness of Israel to appeal to such risky motivations is a measure of the urgency of the petition. It is not possible or necessary to tone down such motivations to conform to a kind of "pure faith," for the Old Testament is not engaged in "pure faith," and no amount of Christian romanticism can make it so. Israel is engaged in faith that must live honestly in the midst of an unfair and threatening world.

and reinforced by motivational clauses that give God reason to act. Thus the imperative is not a command, but it is an act of persuasion, "to make a persuasive case to God that divine help is the thing to do."[45]

This act of self-insistence, which is enacted in hope, assumes and articulates a right ordering of the human person vis-à-vis Yahweh. The human agent legitimately takes initiative and makes an assertion, an urgent and insistent request that Yahweh do for the speaker what the speaker cannot do for himself/herself. That is, Yahweh retains the power in the relationship, the power to act in transformative ways. But that transformative power, of which Yahweh is indisputably capable, depends on the triggering power of the human agent, for none but the needful human person can make the utterance that will move Yahweh. From Israel's perspective, this utterance of petition, which characteristically (but not always) results in Yahweh's rescuing activity, indicates in a compelling way that life is indeed relational and transactional. Israel's understanding of complaint and petition rules out any resignation. It also rules out the notion that this action by the troubled person is simply cathartic or, as Gerald Sheppard opines, is a political stratagem to be overheard by powerful people.[46] It may be that, but it is not merely that. Israel's unsolicited testimony about human persons is that they are indeed partnered to Yahweh, who is able to transform, but who must be moved to such action in concrete ways.

Thanksgiving. According to Israel, the utterance of complaint and petition issues characteristically in rehabilitative action on Yahweh's part. This action entails Yahweh's verbs, which we have already considered extensively in Israel's core testimony.[47] On the enactment of Yahweh's transformation, the complaint and petition of the human person issues in *thanksgiving*, which we have seen is a cultic act of sacrifice, and which on occasion may take the form of generous activity toward the community.[48] It belongs to humanness to give thanks, to receive and acknowledge Yahweh's rehabilitative action, and to give visible, public expression of that

---

45. Patrick D. Miller, "Prayer as Persuasion: The Rhetoric and Intention of Prayer," *WW* 13 (Fall 1993) 362. Miller nicely summarizes the range of motivations that seek to persuade God to be present and to act in transformative ways. These include appeal to Yahweh's faithfulness, Yahweh's reputation, Israel's protestation of innocence, and Israel's readiness to praise Yahweh. Israel's prayers are permeated with such speech, indicating the urgency of persuasion and defining the dynamic between the two partners in the exchange.

46. Gerald T. Sheppard, "Theology and the Book of Psalms," *Int* 46 (1992) 143–55; and "Enemies and the Politics of Prayer in the Book of Psalms," *The Bible and the Politics of Exegesis: Essays in Honor of Norman K. Gottwald on His Sixty-Fifth Birthday* (ed. David Jobling et al.; Cleveland: Pilgrim Press, 1991) 61–82. While there may be an element of politics in the complaint, as Sheppard suggests, it also must be insisted that the prayers are indeed prayers addressed to God, anticipating an active response. On the theological seriousness of the psalms as prayers, see Harold Fisch, *Poetry with a Purpose: Biblical Poetics and Interpretation* (Bloomington: Indiana University Press, 1990) 104–35.

47. The response of Yahweh to the complaints of Israel is perhaps to be understood in terms of salvation oracles. On that genre and practice, see the basic study of Joachim Begrich, "Das priesterliche Orakel," *ZAW* 52 (1934) 81–92; the critical assessment of the theory by Edgar W. Conrad, *Fear Not Warrior: A Study of 'al tira' Pericopes in the Hebrew Scriptures* (BJS 15; Chico, Calif.: Scholars Press, 1985); and Miller, *They Cried to the Lord*, 135–77.

48. See my comments on thanks-offering, in which I have proposed that this is the most elemental act of worship and faith in Israel, pp. 126–30; and see Miller, *They Cried to the Lord*, 179–204.

acknowledgment in the congregation.[49] The completion of the process of coming "out of the Pit" is the glad, visible recognition that the trouble has been overcome by Yahweh; connection has been reestablished, in which the human person is properly the recipient of Yahweh's goodness and not the primary agent. By this culmination of complaint and petition in thanksgiving, the human agent is restored and resituated to life in the midst of Yahweh's generous equilibrium.

This sequence of complaint-petition-thanksgiving, which is the characteristic plot line of Israel's complaint psalms, is a primary datum for Israel's discernment of human personhood. It should be noted that both the courage to speak petition and the buoyancy of thanksgiving are linked to assertions of confidence and trust in Yahweh. That is, Israel has grounds in memory as well as in hope to participate in this drama with Yahweh, fully prepared, even in complaint, to count heavily and finally on Yahweh. As is characteristic in Israel, this central plot line of humanness was not worked out in theory, but emerged concretely in practice in response to the sort of contradictions that beset human existence. At the same time, that plot line is intensely Yahwistic and interrelational. This "drama of restoration" is not a thought process of an autonomous human individual; it is a genuine transaction in which this vigorous Other is indeed present and available to the process.[50]

Parallels in contemporary psychology. Contemporary psychology in its central modes—rooted in Freud and evolving into a variety of transactional theories and practices—is parallel to this plot line and (I believe) derivative. To be sure, in a secularized form, personality theories do not retain Yahweh at the center of the process, but characteristically have substituted the human therapist for the role of Yahweh. Because Freud lived in a positivistic climate and early psychoanalytic theory was determined to be "scientific," the theological dimension of the process was mostly lost. It is welcome and surely important that with the general exhaustion of such positivism, a rapprochement with religion is under way among those who practice therapy of an interpersonal kind.[51] Indeed I suggest that in the derivatives

---

49. See Deissler, "Mein Gott," 115–16.

50. The several works by Gerstenberger cited earlier suggest the actual social practice and context of the drama. It is to be insisted, following Fisch, that the complaint of Israel and the ensuing drama are not merely cathartic (though they are that), but the process is genuinely relational and transactional. Israel proceeds in the deep conviction that Yahweh is indeed engaged in the process. Thus it will not do to interpret these prayers according to modern notions of autonomy, which is as close as Elisabeth Kübler-Ross, *On Death and Dying* (London: Tavistock, 1970), can come to a parallel. The real claim of prayer is affirmed in the comment by Karl Barth, *Prayer: According to the Catechisms of the Reformation* (Philadelphia: Westminster Press, 1952) 23:

> Prayer is not only *directed* to God (one is not talking to one's self), but it *reaches* God. God hears. God answers. God allows prayer to affect and move him.

In *Church Dogmatics* 3/3, *The Doctrine of Creation* (Edinburgh: T. & T. Clark, 1960) 285, Barth writes:

> His sovereignty is so great that it embraces both the possibility, and as it is exercised, the actuality that the creation can actively be present and cooperate in His overruling.

My references to Barth are taken from Perry D. LeFevre, *Understandings of Prayer* (Philadelphia: Westminster Press, 1981) 34.

51. See James W. Jones, *Contemporary Psychoanalysis and Religion: Transference and Transcendence* (New Haven: Yale University Press, 1993); W. W. Meissner, *Life and Faith* (Washington: Georgetown University Press, 1987); and Mary Lou Randour, *Exploring Sacred Landscapes: Religious and Spiritual*

from object relations theory, the cruciality of an initial sense of omnipotence is precisely the sense given, claimed, and voiced in this process of complaint, petition, and thanksgiving.[52]

Moreover, the loss of this standard practice of complaint and petition from theological perspective, which has entailed the loss of self-assertion over against Yahweh and the forfeiture of countertestimony about Yahweh, is precisely what has produced "false selves," both in an excessively pietistic church that champions deference and in an excessively moralistic, brutalizing society that prizes conformity

---

Experience in Psychotherapy (New York: Columbia University Press, 1993). More generally on the development of complex human interiority, see Charles Taylor, *Sources of the Self: The Making of Modern Identity* (Cambridge: Harvard University Press, 1989); William S. Schmidt, *The Development of the Notion of Self: Understanding the Complexity of Human Interiority* (Lewiston, N.Y.: Edwin Mellen, 1994); and S. E. Hormuth, *The Ecology of the Self* (Cambridge: Cambridge University Press, 1990).

52. The classic theory is that of D. W. Winnicott, *The Maturational Processes and the Facilitating Environment: Studies in the Theory of Emotional Development* (New York: International Universities Press, 1965). Winnicott's important concepts that bear upon our theme concern an elemental omnipotence and the emergence of "false self" where omnipotence is not practiced. It is my judgment that complaint addressed to Yahweh can be understood as Israel's moment of "omnipotence." Further, it is my judgment that because Christian practice has denied people this dimension of piety, the church inclines to produce "false selves" who cannot be honest before God and so must "fake it" with God. As a derivative study, see Walter Brueggemann, "The Costly Loss of Lament," *JSOT* 36 (1986) 57–71.

I do not believe that biblical faith ever has an enduring alliance with any theory of personality. Nonetheless in the present range of available personality theories, I believe that object relations theory now articulates the formation and maintenance of humanness in ways that are peculiarly congruent with Israel's covenantal, transactional notion of self. See Michael St. Clair, *Object Relations and Self Psychology* (Monterey, Calif.: Brooks/Cole, 1986).

Moving away from Freud's notion of self as a conundrum of internal conflicts, object relations theory has proposed that the formation of self is situated in an ongoing relation with a real person (i.e., a real object, not a figment of imagination, hence the term "object relations"), most often the mother or someone who performs mothering functions. A key insight of this theory is that in its youngest days and weeks, the infant must experience omnipotence vis-à-vis its mother—must have the sense that the mother exists solely for the child, who is then able to exult fully and celebrate a sense of self with his or her own needs and wants. Such an experience of omnipotence requires the mother's total attention to the child, and permits the beginning of the formation of a strong sense of self.

Alternately, if the mother cannot cede self fully to the child, the child quickly learns to fake it, to please and manipulate the mother in order to satisfy the child's wants. Such a faking procedure produces a "false self," who is never able to be honest but must always pretend, and so develops a capacity for (unrecognized) duplicity between genuine want and need and what is permitted with the mother. Thus everything about emotional health depends on the mother as a strong agent who willingly becomes "useful" to the child for the sake of the child. Other important theorists pertinent to this discussion (in addition to Winnicott) are Otto Kernberg, Heinz Kohut, and W. Ronald Fairbairn.

Of course, it is a long move from a "good enough" mother to the self in relation to a "good enough" Yahweh. It occurs to me, nonetheless, that complaint and petition whereby the speaker can be fully honest before Yahweh and expect Yahweh to accept the self so expressed requires a strong sense of self on the part of the petitioner; it also requires, with equal urgency, a God who can cede initiative and authority in the transaction to the petitioner who speaks imperatives to Yahweh and so enjoys an instant of omnipotence. Thus in Israel's practice such prayer belongs to a healthy self. Such a transaction is not to be understood as mere psychology, but theologically depends on a God who is sovereign (like a "good enough" mother), but who in the instant of prayer invites and welcomes omnipotence in the voice of the petitioner.

In my judgment this matter of omnipotence before Yahweh in prayer relates to healthy believers before Yahweh. If one must always please God (like always pleasing mother), one learns to fake it and so become a "false self" vis-à-vis Yahweh. I suggest that in its characteristically flat articulation of God as omnipotent, the church has unwittingly done much to nourish believers to be false selves. The predictable consequence, now so evident, is church persons who are inordinately moralistic in an insistence that others should please God in the same undifferentiated way they have learned to do.

and the stifling of rage. Quietistic piety and conformity moralism together have encouraged docility and deference that generate phoniness at the most elemental levels of human existence. Israel's sense of healthy humanness is profoundly transactional, with the two parties in turn exercising initiative. Israel, moreover, understood that the drama of rehabilitation, including the sequence of complaint, petition, and thanks, requires the Holy One, over against whom the human person in extremis must take shrill and vigorous initiative.

Praise and Hope

In tracing the practices and disciplines of humanness according to Israel's testimony, we may finally refer to two practices that properly are placed, understood, and enacted at the culmination of the drama of rehabilitation: praise and hope. Of course, the entire drama of rehabilitation is shot through with praise and hope. The entire drama is rooted in hope, or it would never be undertaken in the first place.[53] Praise occurs throughout the drama as motivation for Yahweh. Nonetheless, praise and hope in their full utterance belong to a life that is fully and well restored by the action of Yahweh, who has been moved to action by the shrill voicing of need.

Lyrical affirmation of Yahweh. We have already seen that the drama of rehabilitation culminates in thanks, and from thanks we are able to say that *praise* belongs definitionally to human personhood. That is, healthy humanness requires a lyrical ceding of self to the holiness of God.[54] As Claus Westermann has suggested, whereas thanks is particular and concrete, praise is that generalizing affirmation of Yahweh that moves beyond "services rendered" and gifts received, to a lyrical expression of amazement, astonishment, and gratitude toward the Holy One who lies beyond everything the human person can generate.[55]

Thus the drama of restoration has a marking of praise to it:

> In God, whose word I praise,
> in the Lord, whose word I praise,

---

53. In addition to Gerstenberger, "Der klagende Mensch," see the definitive work of Jürgen Moltmann, *Theology of Hope: On the Ground and Implication of a Christian Eschatology* (1967; Minneapolis: Fortress Press, 1993). Moltmann has shown that hope is not one theme among many in Christian theology, but is the foundation for everything. For Old Testament theology, it is important that Moltmann depends on the Old Testament scholarship of Albrecht Alt and Gerhard von Rad in making this judgment.

54. On praise as the "ceding of self," see Walter Brueggemann, "Praise and the Psalms: A Politics of Glad Abandonment," *The Psalms and the Life of Faith* (ed. Patrick D. Miller; Minneapolis: Fortress Press, 1995) 112–32; and "The Daily Voice of Faith: The Covenanted Self," *Sewanee Theological Review* 37 (Easter 1994) 123–43.

55. The relationship between praise and thanksgiving is a delicate and tricky one. In a most influential way, Claus Westermann, *Praise and Lament in the Psalms*, 25–30, has tended to collapse the two into one. Nonetheless, he regards praise as much more important and dynamic, for he understands thanks as being more calculating and quid pro quo. Against Westermann, Harvey H. Guthrie, *Theology as Thanksgiving: From Israel's Psalms to the Church's Eucharist* (New York: Seabury Press, 1981) 12–30, inclines to regard thanksgiving as more elemental than praise, and therefore as more at the core of a practice of faith. While the tension between the positions of Westermann and Guthrie is not easily resolved, the question that concerns them both is of enormous importance.

in God I trust; I am not afraid.
What can a mere mortal do to me? (Ps 56:10-11)

Awake, my soul!
Awake, O harp and lyre!
I will awake the dawn.
I will give thanks to you, O Lord,
among the peoples;
I will sing praise to you among the nations.
For your steadfast love is as high as the heavens;
your faithfulness extends to the clouds. (Ps 57:8-10)

But I will sing of your might;
I will sing aloud of your steadfast love in the morning.
For you have been a fortress for me,
and a refuge in the day of my distress. (Ps 59:16-17)

These doxologies break out in exuberance at the end of the process of trouble resolved. The speaker sings in hyperbolic language, because the impossible has happened and well-being has been restored by the sovereign fidelity of Yahweh, even where circumstance seemed to dictate that well-being was impossible. To the person in the Pit, the trouble seems to last in perpetuity. But when Yahweh is mobilized, all things become possible.

Praise in Israel's presentation of humanness is not limited to resolutions at the end of complaint. The texts of praise take on a life of their own, providing for Israel a corpus of hymnody marked by exuberance, hyperbole, and lack of restraint. Indeed, the lack of restraint in praise matches the lack of restraint evident in the complaints. Both modes of speech addressed to Yahweh are in extremes of need and of joy:

Make a joyful noise to the Lord,
all the earth.
Worship the Lord with gladness;
come into his presence with singing. (Ps 100:1-2)

Praise the Lord, all you nations!
Extol him, all you peoples!
For great is his steadfast love toward us,
and the faithfulness of the Lord endures forever.
Praise the Lord! (Psalm 117)

Praise the Lord!
Praise the Lord, O my soul!
I will praise the Lord as long as I live;
I will sing praises to my God all my life long. (Ps 146:1-2)

> Praise the Lord!
> Praise God in his sanctuary;
> praise him in his mighty firmament!
> Praise him for his mighty deeds;
> praise him according to his surpassing greatness!
> Praise him with trumpet sound; praise him with lute and harp!
> Praise him with tambourine and dance;
> praise him with strings and pipe!
> Praise him with clanging cymbals;
> praise him with loud clashing cymbals!
> Let everything that breathes praise the Lord!
> Praise the Lord! (Psalm 150)

Praise is a key marking of Israel's discernment of humanness.[56] To be human means to be willing and able to praise. We have seen that the drama of rehabilitation consists in complaint, petition, and then thanks, as an act of shrill self-assertion. Now we see the countermove in Israel: praise as a glad act of self-abandonment, the active gesture of accepting that life is ceded beyond self, that well-being is rooted in an Other, and that without any claim for self, the human agent is glad to defer to and rely fully on Yahweh, who can only be expressed in lyrical language. Such self-abandoning praise consists in the glad relinquishment that is an unembarrassed cultic act, but the relinquishment is not simply one of a cultic moment. We may believe that Israel's practice of praise included relinquishment of all resistant emotions and of all acquisitive self-securing propensities; in this practice of praise the human person lives best and well and most freely when all of the self and all of the claims of the self are given over in full, unreserved surrender to Yahweh.[57]

We must note well that such an act of self-abandonment to Yahweh is dialectically related to an act of self-assertion against Yahweh. Because these two markings, expressed as complaint and as hymn, are genuinely dialectical, one may not give priority to either. In trying to understand how this peculiar Yahwistic dialectic actually functions, however, I suggest that practically and provisionally, priority in the dialectic belongs to the complaining activity of self-regard. I make

---

56. On the theological significance of praise, see Daniel W. Hardy and David F. Ford, *Praising and Knowing God* (Philadelphia: Westminster Press, 1985). Hardy and Ford (pp. 20, 142) speak of praise as the "jazz factor" of the Christian life. The image is a suggestive one, for it bespeaks the fact that life rooted in biblical faith, Jewish or Christian, in generous surrender (a) has a regular cadence to it, (b) pushes forward into newness, and (c) allows for newness and radical variation amid the reliable cadences. My own experience of the cruciality of praise is highlighted by a presentation of what I thought was a Calvinist accent on praise as the foundation of Christian life. In response, the great Roman Catholic bishop Rembert G. Weakland observed to me that my comments concerning praise were completely Benedictine in orientation. Aside from certain code words, traditions as distinct as Benedictine and Calvinist recognize this foundation for faithful living.

57. Relinquishment here is to be understood first of all as liturgical, symbolic, and emotional. But such a practice has an inevitable and unavoidable counterpart in socioeconomic and political relinquishment; on this see Marie Augusta Neal, *A Socio-theology of Letting Go: The Role of a First World Church Facing Third World Peoples* (New York: Paulist Press, 1977).

this suggestion because (a) in object relations theory this primal experience of omnipotence is pivotal for a self that is adequate to practice covenant; (b) one must have a self in order to yield a self;[58] and (c) Western Christian piety has given this facet of Yahwistic humanness short shrift. I suggest this as a practical matter, but do not want to detract from the more important recognition that, seen as a whole, the two maneuvers of Yahwistic humanness are indeed genuinely dialectical.

Four dimensions of hope. The final markings of humanness to which we point is that the human person is one who *hopes*.[59] It seems to me logical to place this discipline of humanness at the end of the rehabilitative drama along with praise. But Jürgen Moltmann has taught our generation that hope is not something that belongs only at the far edge of biblical faith, but in fact it pervades it.[60] Thus hope, in its effect, is close to what I have called "trust" (*bth*), a complete and pervasive confidence in Yahweh in every phase of life. Moreover, Erhard Gerstenberger has made clear that the entire process of complaint and petition is only undertaken in Israel because the speaker in the Pit has complete confidence that Yahweh presides over every trouble and fully intends a good resolve, and has the power and will to enact that good resolve.[61] Thus, functionally, humanness is pervasively hope-filled, not in the sense of a buoyant, unreflective optimism, but in the conviction that individual human destiny is powerfully presided over by this One who wills good and who works that good:

> Lead me in your truth, and teach me,
> for you are the God of my salvation;
> for you I wait all day long. . . .
> May integrity and uprightness preserve me,
> for I *wait* for you. (Ps 25:5, 21)

> And now, O Lord, what do I wait for?
> My hope is in you. (Ps 39:7)

> For you, O Lord, are my hope,
> my trust, O Lord, from my youth. (Ps 71:5; cf. 69:3, 6; 130:5; 146:5)

It is important that in these utterances, which characteristically come in the midst of complaints, Israel does not hope for something, but hopes in God. That is, Yahweh is not *instrumental* to the hope of Israel, but Yahweh is in fact the very *substance* of that hope. Therefore we may conclude that Israel hopes, in trouble as in well-being, that Yahweh shall be all in all. The act of hope is focused on

---

58. Thus I mean to suggest that self-denial is fraudulent and pathological unless one has arrived at a self that can be willingly ceded and surrendered. Without such a self to give, self-denial is likely simply a refusal to live one's life.

59. See Seebass, "Über den Beitrag des Alten Testaments," 47–53.

60. See n. 53 above on Moltmann's appeal to the Old Testament in his systematic formulation.

61. See Erhard Gerstenberger, *Der bittende Mensch: Bittritual und Klagelied des Einzelnen im Alten Testament* (WMANT 51; Neukirchen-Vluyn: Neukirchener Verlag, 1980); and "Der klagende Mensch." More broadly, see Walther Zimmerli, *Man and His Hope in the Old Testament* (SBT 20, 2d series; London: SCM Press, 1971).

restoration and rehabilitation, but beyond that, this hope is lacking in concreteness. We may imagine that because Israel's life is intensely covenantal, human hope finally concerns communion and well-being with Yahweh. But because Israel's faith is intensely material in its intent, human hope is also for the material gifts of life, enough to make life peaceable, safe, joyous, and fruitful.

We may identify four dimensions of hope in Israel's purview of the human person:

(1) The future of the hoping human person is largely unspecified in Israel's testimony and enormously open. Much may happen that is good, because the future is a gift of Yahweh. One prospect of the hoping human person is that such a person may come to full "knowledge of Yahweh." The large royal vision of Isa 11:1-9 is focused, first of all, on the coming king of righteousness and justice. But from that image, the poem offers a vision of restored creation that culminates in this way:

> They will not hurt or destroy
> on all my holy mountain;
> for all the earth will be full of the knowledge of the Lord
> as the waters cover the sea. (v. 9)

"Knowledge of Yahweh" is given peculiarly to Israel, but here it is anticipated that all creatures shall come to such knowledge. Indeed, the wisdom materials in the Book of Proverbs variously speak of "the fear of the Lord" as "the beginning of knowledge" (1:7), "fear of the Lord" and ... the "knowledge of God" (2:5). The usages suggest that these phrases are synonymous. It is anticipated that human persons may come to "know Yahweh."

The phrase itself is not transparent in its meaning. It may refer to political-theological sovereignty of Yahweh, expressed as obedience.[62] It may in some contexts mean cognitive knowledge of Israel's historical traditions.[63] But it may also mean personal engagement and intimacy with Yahweh; not knowledge about, but engagement with. In the wisdom traditions, the phrase clearly refers to an awed, discerning sense of responsible, liberated, caring life in Yahweh's world. In any case, the phrase is a promise and expectation that the hoping human person may be, in the end, fully immersed in the wondrous mystery that is Yahweh—the overcoming of every distance between Yahweh and Yahweh's cared-for human creature.

(2) In the "tradition of presence," that is, the Priestly tradition, it is anticipated that human persons may come to live in the very presence of Yahweh, so that the hoped-for goal of human existence is indeed communion with God, or in Martin

---

62. On this aspect of the notion of "knowledge of Yahweh," see Herbert B. Huffmon, "The Treaty Background of Hebrew *yāda'*," *BASOR* 181 (1966) 31–37; and Herbert B. Huffmon and Simon B. Parker, "A Further Note on the Treaty Background of Hebrew *yāda'*," *BASOR* 184 (1966) 36–38.

63. This is the accent made by Hans Walter Wolff, "Wissen um Gott bei Hosea als Urform von Theologie," *EvT* 12 (1952/53) 533–54. See also Dwight R. Daniels, *Hosea and Salvation: The Early Traditions of Israel in the Prophecy of Hosea* (BZAW 191; Berlin: de Gruyter, 1990) 111–16.

Buber's terms, "meeting."[64] To be sure, the cultic apparatus is distinctly Israelite, and access to communion, as mediated in worship in these traditions, is for highly disciplined Israelites. But because the overlap of Israelite and human person is crucial to our exposition, the hope is that the absence, abrasion, and distance that occur between God and human persons are provisionally overcome in cultic worship, and are finally overcome in the full restoration of creation, wherein the human person may appear in the presence of Yahweh naked, defenseless, unashamed, and unafraid. The hope is that the fractured quality of that relationship narrated in Genesis 3 may be overcome, as hinted at in Isa 55:13 and 65:23.

We may also pay attention to the drama of the text of Psalm 73.[65] This psalm moves according to the three dimensions of the human tale we have suggested, from well-being (v. 1) through alienation (vv. 2-16), to refocus on Yahweh (v. 17), and finally to new life (vv. 18-28). Our interest here is in the affirmation of v. 25: "Whom have I in heaven but you? And there is nothing on earth that I desire other than you." Yahweh is the "delight" (*ḥpṣ*) of this life—Yahweh alone, not the gifts of Yahweh.

It may be that this poem pertains singularly to Israelites. A great deal turns on the reading of v. 1.[66] The Hebrew text has "God is good to Israel." But a variant reading in the Greek (which is much preferred) suggests "to the upright," that is, to any responsible person, such as the kind of person envisioned in the Book of Proverbs. If such a reading is entertained, then Yahweh is the "true desire" of all human persons who hope Yahwistically.

This accent on communion is of enormous importance, not only because of the large attention given to "hosting the holy" in the Priestly tradition, and not only because of the powerful sacramental commitments of the ecclesial community. The promise of presence and of communion is important because it tells powerfully against the commoditization of contemporary culture, as expressed in market ideology and as it invades the ecclesial community as well. If the promise concerns only God's gifts, then God becomes only instrumental to human hope, and the hoper lives in a world of commodities, which in the end give neither joy nor safety. Thus it is affirmed that Yahweh is the true heart's desire of human persons, the true joy of human life,[67] and the sure possibility of life lived in hope. This hope is voiced in the familiar conclusion of Psalm 23:

---

64. Martin Buber, *Meetings* (La Salle, Ill.: Open Court, 1973), suggests ways in which human transactions are themselves occasions for "presence."

65. On this psalm and its distinct testimony, see Martin Buber, *Right and Wrong* (London: SCM Press, 1952) 34–52; J. Clinton McCann, "Psalm 73: A Microcosm of Old Testament Theology," *The Listening Heart* (ed. Kenneth Hoglund; JSOT Sup 58; Sheffield: JSOT Press, 1987) 247–57; and Walter Brueggemann, *The Psalms and the Life of Faith*, 203–10.

66. On the textual problem in v. 1, see Ernst Würthwein, "Erwägungen zu Psalm 73," *Wort und Existenz: Studien zum Alten Testament* (Göttingen: Vandenhoeck and Ruprecht, 1970) 163–71. More generally see Walter Brueggemann and Patrick D. Miller, "Psalm 73 as a Canonical Marker," *JSOT* (forthcoming).

67. The notion of desire as a core aspect of the life of faith was especially appreciated by Augustine, who distinguished it in subtle ways from lust. For a thoughtful discussion of the problem in Augustine, see Margaret R. Miles, *Desire and Delight: A New Reading of Augustine's Confessions* (New

> Surely goodness and mercy shall follow me
> all the days of my life,
> and I shall dwell in the house of the Lord
> my whole life long. (v. 6)

(3) Having said that, Old Testament hope for the human person never flies off into spiritualizing fantasy. Alongside the promise of *presence and communion* in the Priestly traditions (and in much of the Psalter), and alongside the promise of *knowledge of God* in the sapiential and prophetic traditions, the Deuteronomic-prophetic traditions, on the whole, affirm that the promise to humanity is *a material world* in which justice will prevail, there will be bread for all, and the human community will "dwell securely." This theological tradition of hope concerns the restoration of fertility, the yielding of the produce of the earth, so that there is enough for all (cf. Amos 9:13-15; Hos 2:21-23; Isa 11:6-9, 65:17-25).

Psalm 85:10-11, in a lyrical act of imagination, anticipates the time when heaven and earth will be in full harmony:

> Steadfast love and faithfulness will meet;
> righteousness and peace will kiss each other.
> Faithfulness will spring up from the ground,
> and righteousness will look down from the sky.

The use of the familiar covenantal vocabulary of steadfast love, faithfulness, righteousness, and peace, however, does not remain focused simply on the relationship, but turns promptly to matters of produce, blessing, and fertility:

> The Lord will give what is good,
> and our land will yield its increase. (v. 12)

The practice of justice bespeaks the full restoration of the generosity of creation.

In the Christian tradition, this materiality of human hope is familiarly expressed in the Lord's Prayer. The prayer is one of reconciliation. But the reconciliation among neighbors is in the context of bread enough for the day:

> Give us this day our daily bread.
> And forgive us our debts,
> as we also have forgiven our debtors. (Matt 6:11-12)

Human hope that awaits God's generosity and extravagance is an act of expectation that flies in the face of every ideology of scarcity. Much human conflict is rooted in the conviction, born of greed and enacted in acquisitiveness, that there is not enough and one must seize what one can. Israel's sense of human hope is grounded in Yahweh's faithful intention of abundance, which liberates humans

---

York: Crossroad, 1992). In this context, also recall Johann Sebastian Bach's great "Jesu, Joy of Man's Desiring."

from the driving grip of scarcity in order that they begin to act, in hope, out of a conviction of abundance.[68] This material abundance as an alternative to scarcity is a parallel to communion as an alternative to commodity. In both anticipations of communion and abundance, Israel's sense of the human future is derived from and legitimated by Yahweh, who is accessible and generous, with self and with the blessings of creation.

(4) The core narrative of human life and human destiny is "into the Pit" of trouble and "out of the Pit" by the power of Yahweh. This in-out model of humanness is no doubt informed by Israel's own narrative of "out of bondage" and "into the land of promise," as articulated in Israel's most elemental recitals of faith. It is a model that permeates Israel's sense of life and Israel's articulation of Yahweh and is evidenced in the structure and drama of the complaint psalms.

Only at the edge of the Old Testament, however, is this model of "out of the Pit" related to human destiny beyond the span of lived historical, physical existence. Only late and rarely does Israel extend its lyric of hope beyond death to life resumed after death. It is beyond doubt that the materials for this affirmation are long available in Israel's sense of the drama of human life. On the one hand, all Israel's speech about "the Pit" is already imagistically aimed at the extremity of death.[69] On the other hand, Israel's own historical experience of exile prepares for this extreme affirmation (cf. Ezek 37:1-14). Nonetheless, it is only late, apparently, that Israel has either the courage or the need to push its horizon yet further, to speak about life that endures death; or, more properly, life that resumes in the midst of the reality of death.

While Mitchell Dahood has suggested many references to resurrection in the Psalter, it is more commonly agreed by interpreters of the Old Testament that only twice does the Old Testament explicitly refer to resurrection:[70]

---

68. Claus Westermann, *Elements of Old Testament Theology* (Atlanta: John Knox, 1978) 106–7, has shrewdly seen that Josh 5:12 stands at the end of the wilderness period of Israel, which began with the giving of free bread in Exodus 16. Thus Exodus 16 and Joshua 5 bracket the time in Israel's normative narrative when the abundance of Yahweh was driven out by the scarcity of coveting. It is not accidental, I assume, that the narrative of coveting in Joshua 7–8 follows so quickly after Israel arrives in the promised land. There is something odd and insidious about the fact that *having* makes persons more greedy. Thus the reception of gift from Yahweh makes for a circumstance of scarcity, precisely when gifts should locate persons and communities amid God's abundance. This odd turn of matters is well documented in statistics about affluence and the corresponding loss of generosity.

69. It is characteristic of Israel's way of speaking that the word *death* is fluid and never precise in its meaning. In the psalms of complaint, when used as a synonym for *pit*, the term *death* seems close to mythological connotations in which death is not far removed from Mot, the Canaanite god of death. But the term also refers to physical expiration. Sometimes, moreover, the term can mean either or both at the same time. It is crucial for Israel not to be too precise. See Walter Brueggemann, "Death, Theology of," *IDBSup* (Nashville: Abingdon Press, 1976) 219–22; and *Praying the Psalms* (Winona, Minn.: St. Mary's Press, 1982) 39–48.

70. See Mitchell Dahood, *Psalms I: 1–50, Introduction, Translation, and Notes* (AB 16; Garden City, N.Y.: Doubleday, 1965) 91, 252–53, 33; Nicholas J. Tromp, *Primitive Conceptions of Death and the Nether World in the Old Testament* (Rome: Pontifical Biblical Institute, 1969); and Robert Martin-Achard, *From Death to Life: A Study of the Development of the Doctrine of the Resurrection in the Old Testament* (Edinburgh: Oliver and Boyd, 1960). It is entirely cogent that Isa 52:13–53:12 may be cited as a third text where such a claim is to be recognized.

> Your dead shall live, their corpses shall rise.
> O dwellers in the dust,
> awake and sing for joy!
> For your dew is a radiant dew,
> and the earth will give birth to those long dead. (Isa 26:19)

Many of those who sleep in the dust of the earth shall awake, some to everlasting life, and some to shame and everlasting contempt. (Dan 12:2)

The first of these verses concerns the faithful who are in distress with grief.

The language of Isa 26:19, the rhetoric of birth, refers to the resumption of the processes of fruitfulness, the recovery of the function and future of creation.[71] The reference in Dan 12:2 is from a context of persecution. Here resurrection is for all, not only the just, in order that Yahweh's ethical distinctions in the earth will not be lost or defeated, but can be implemented and sustained, even if their triumph is beyond the scope of lived experience. That is, the future of life in the face of death is due to the uncompromising moral agenda of Yahweh.

In these texts Israel's testimony breaks finally even the boundary of death, in order to extend the aegis of Yahweh's sovereignty and fidelity to all imaginable reality. The rhetoric does indeed move into new scope. The theological claim made here, however, is not a new one for Israel; Israel had long asserted Yahweh's full sovereignty. Now, however, the extent of that fullness is made exhaustive. No realm of life, not even that which seems to limit Yahweh (that is, death), can limit the claims of the God of Israel.

Too much should not be made of these two texts, nor should too much be made of the absence of more texts like them. The affirmation that Yahweh will bring human life right is so deep and so wide in Israelite conviction that the lack of "resurrection texts," in my judgment, does not evidence a lack of intellectual or theological courage to make a claim of this sort. Rather Israel's full trust in Yahweh's will and power to right the world is such that an explicit statement is not particularly required in this faith. In its canonical testimony, Israel seldom engages in speculation about such matters. But Israel is unflinching in its theological assertion about the good destiny of human creatures who fight through the drama of rehabilitation and rest themselves in the new life Yahweh gives.

In the end, the future of humanity—which we have variously addressed under the topics of full knowledge of Yahweh, full communion with Yahweh, and full enjoyment of an abundant earth—now comes to full confidence in Yahweh at death. This confidence is only inchoately imagined in Israel's testimony. Much about the human future is hidden, unknown, and full of risk for Israel, and therefore unarticulated by Israel. That future, for hoping human creatures, however, is not one of

---

71. Gary A. Anderson, *A Time to Mourn, a Time to Dance: The Expression of Grief and Joy in Israelite Religion* (University Park: Pennsylvania State University Press, 1991), has shown how joy is related to creation, procreation, and the power for life that is concretely enacted in the community through birth and reproduction.

threat but of peaceable confidence. That peaceable confidence is not grounded in evidence about the future, whether philosophical and logical or empirical and technological, but in the faithful sovereignty of Yahweh already known in Israel's core testimony. How that faithful sovereignty will be fully enacted in ages to come is not known, and Israel manifests no great speculative curiosity on the subject. The One who has been fully obeyed is the One who can be fully trusted with whatever shape the future holds.

The several seasons of this drama of human life with Yahweh—gift (obedience, discernment, trust), loss (complaint, petition, thanks), and renewal (praise, hope)—provide no clear scheme. I propose only to piece the fragmentary evidence together in this particular way provisionally; I do not want to reduce the elusive evidence too tightly. Enough emerges of a pattern in such an undertaking, however, to suggest what life in relation to the sovereign, faithful One can mean, in terms of glad obedience, trustful freedom, and venturesome relatednesss. Every aspect of this portrayal of humanness depends on seeing the human creature in relation to this God, a relationship that is a strange, resilient offer of mutuality and incommensurability.

Covenantal Existence as Alternative Humanness

Because the struggle for humanness is crucial in the world of "late capitalism," and because much theological conflict is now extrapolated into a conflict over humanness, we may pause to consider the ways in which this construct of human personhood, which eschews all essentialism and which stakes humanness on relatedness, contrasts with the predominant temptations of our self-destructive culture. I will not exposit these contrasting features, but suggest an outline that evidences the resources available in the Old Testament for an alternative, subverting notion of humanness.

1. The human person in well-being and equilibrium:
   (a) obedience   vs. *autonomy* that denies accountable relatedness
   (b) discernment   vs. *technique* that denies a fabric of order
   (c) human trust   vs. *anxiety*

2. The human person in extremis:
   (d) complaint   vs. *docility*
   (e) petition   vs. *resignation*
   (f) thanksgiving vs. *self-sufficiency*

3. The human person delivered from "the Pit" and living on "borrowed time":
   (g) praise   vs. *satiation*
   (h) hope   vs. *despair*

I understand that such contrasts are much too simplistic; they run the risk of creating easy opponents for Israel's advocacy. My concern, however, is not for competing theories of personality, but for actual human practices in a commodity-driven society that is fundamentally alienated through an ideology of consumer individualism. The point of this exercise in contrasts is to insist that in Israel's un-solicited testimony, (a) there is indeed a serious alternative to common practice in our society, (b) but this alternative depends on active reference and engagement with Yahweh, (c) in an incommensurate but mutual interaction that costs much and requires great risks, costs and risks commensurate with a possible reliving of human life.

Given the practices of contemporary society, especially in its religious activity, this sketch of the human person as a partner to Yahweh yields important resources for pastoral care. It is no secret that the so-called pastoral care movement could make little use of scholastic theology or its subjective-liberal alternative early in this century, and so there was an eager and mostly uncritical embrace of psychological categories in the emergence of self-conscious pastoral care.[72] Now it is to be celebrated that present thinking and practice in pastoral care are reengaging with theological categories, not to reject psychological learnings, but to treat such learnings with a greater critical alertness, informed by a theological grounding.

The model of humanness that I have sketched here, which I take to be faithful to Israel's unsolicited testimony, provides a model of human health and wholeness that is a stunning alternative to the notions of humanness offered in what I now term *commodity militarism*. When the contrasting models are made clear, it is evident that pastoral care, which I have elsewhere called a work of transformation,[73] is indeed the work of conversion, in order to embed one's self in this alternative relationship and in the testimony that sustains this alternative relationship.

The work of conversion is slow, gentle, detailed, and ad hoc. But the model gives clarity for the work of day-to-day summons, nurture, and authorization. It is the claim of Israel's testimony that this Yahwistic relationship is indispensable for full humanness. This testimony asserts that no other humanness can finally be full and joyous, because it is not able to tell the truth of humanness, truth focused in Yahweh and in relation to Yahweh.[74]

---

72. Thomas C. Oden, *Care of Souls in the Classic Tradition* (Philadelphia: Fortress Press, 1984), has traced the way in which the vocabulary of pastoral care shifted from theological references to psychological references in the twentieth century.

73. Walter Brueggemann, "The Transformative Agenda of the Pastoral Office," *Interpretation and Obedience: From Faithful Reading to Faithful Living* (Minneapolis: Fortress Press, 1991) 161–83.

74. While I present this alternative mode of humanness with as much passion as I can, I would not, in a final, formal sense, urge that it is better. I would insist only that it is different from commodity theories of personality. When the difference has been made clear, one has no objective means to adjudicate or choose. It is the fuzzy confusion of models that I believe has been most costly in recent ecclesial and pastoral practice.

Covenantal Humanness in Two Texts

We may conclude our reflection on human personhood by considering in some detail two texts that peculiarly illuminate our theme.

Psalm 103

The speakers in this great hymn are Israelite, and its assumptions of humanness are Israelite. And yet the addressees of Psalm 103, the ones invited to join the praise, are not particularly identified as Israelites. On the one hand, the address is intimate and personal, "my soul" (vv. 1-2, 22b). On the other hand, the addressees include all of Yahweh's creatures in heaven and on earth:

> Bless the Lord, O you his angels,
> you mighty ones who do his bidding,
> obedient to his spoken word.
> Bless the Lord, all his hosts,
> his ministers that do his will.
> Bless the Lord, all his works,
> in all places of his dominion. (vv. 20-22a)

Thus the psalm is cosmic and universal in scope, but comes down to the particular realities of the individual person who speaks. The speaker is portrayed as, and summoned to be, a human being engaged in praise. But in neither the universal nor the intimate address is an appeal made to concrete Israel.

What interests us in this psalm is that after the hymn enumerates Yahweh's characteristic actions toward humanity that serve well-being (vv. 3-5), the psalm takes up the two major predicaments that place all human persons in extremis, namely guilt and mortality. I take up this psalm because, writ large, guilt and mortality constitute the fissure in human life, the place wherein the old equilibriums fail, where the human agent is required to take venturesome action in order to engage Yahweh in a drama of rehabilitation. Indeed, in that moment of the fissure, so Israel suggests, everything about the future depends on the readiness of human agents to take venturesome action toward Yahweh.

Concerning the problem of guilt, Psalm 103 asserts:

> He will not always accuse,
> nor will he keep his anger forever.
> He does not deal with us according to our sins,
> nor repay us according to our iniquities.
> For as the heavens are high above the earth,
> so great is his steadfast love
> toward those who fear him;
> as far as the east is from the west,
> so far he removes our transgressions from us.
> As a father has compassion for his children,

so the Lord has compassion for those who fear him.
For he knows how we were made;
he remembers that we are dust. (vv. 9-14)

The speaker does not wallow in a guilty conscience and does not appeal to anything like original sin. The speaker simply knows that sin is a reality that disrupts life, so that the human agent is alienated from the Holy One and is helpless in the face of that alienation. Having introduced the topic of guilt for transgression, the psalm speaks no more of the reality of the human creature, except as recipient of Yahweh's actions. The reality of human sin requires Israel to bear witness to Yahweh. Yahweh is here said to have real anger at sin (v. 9), but an anger that has limits. The overriding reality of Yahweh, as concerns human guilt, is that Yahweh is marked by steadfast love (vv. 8, 11), and compassion (vv. 8, 13). Yahweh overrides the power and significance of sin and, with the gentleness of a father, embraces the fragility of human life (vv. 13-14). To be sure, the object of this inclination on Yahweh's part is not just any human agent, but one who actively and seriously embraces Yahweh as partner—that is, who "fears him" (vv. 11, 13). The human extremity of guilt is overridden by a God who in mutuality has compassion, but who is completely incommensurate in overriding and vetoing this human reality.

The second great human crisis, mortality, is treated in parallel fashion in the psalm:

As for mortals, their days are like grass;
they flourish like a flower of the field;
for the wind passes over it, and it is gone,
and its place knows it no more.
But the steadfast love of the Lord is from
everlasting to everlasting
on those who fear him,
and his righteousness to children's children,
to those who keep his covenant
and remember to do his commandments. (vv. 15-18)

At the center of these verses is yet another affirmation of Yahweh's *ḥesed* (v. 17). Again, to be sure, that offer of fidelity is given to the ones who fear, obey, and keep covenant.

In both cases, which mark all human persons, the theological datum that counts is not anything about human persons, but a statement about the partner to human persons who overcomes the risk and the danger of both guilt and mortality. Notice that in this articulation, there is almost no explanation or speculation about why this reality of Yahweh is the way it is. Everything depends on this relation to the One who is utterly reliable. This utterly reliable One is the primary truth about human personhood.

The Book of Job

The second text we mention in our concluding comment on human personhood is the Book of Job. While the Book of Job is certainly, in its canonical presentation, an Israelite document that pertains to Israelite faith, it intends clearly to ponder the human predicament. Many scholars now agree that the three parts of the book, the prose introduction (chapters 1–2), the poetry in the center (3:1–42:6), and the prose conclusion (42:7-17), are to be seen as a dramatic, artistic whole.[75] This may be the fullest, most self-conscious reflection on humanness in the Old Testament.

The three parts of the book, as it stands canonically, may provide a grid for the drama of human life with Yahweh, a drama that begins in blessed equilibrium (chapters 1–2), moves into and through a disputatious encounter (3:1–42:6), and then culminates in restoration and affirmation (42:7-17). This sequence nicely reflects the sequence of orientation/disorientation/new orientation that I have suggested for the Psalms some time ago, a sequence that focuses on the middle term of disorientation.[76] It may also be suggested that the whole drama of the Book of Job correlates roughly with the grid of humanness I have suggested above:

- blessed equilibrium: obedience, discernment, trust

- disruption: complaint, petition, thanksgiving

- restoration: praise, hope

I suggest three matters of interest for our topic:

Open drama with Yahweh as key character. Neither the more explicitly Yahwistic prose at the beginning and end, nor the implicitly Yahwistic center, is permitted to override the other element. It is traditional in popular thought to let the "patient" Job silence the impatient one, whereas in critical scholarship the protesting Job is valued at the expense of the deferential one. But in this full drama of humanness, each element is in place properly and crucial to the whole. If we move beyond literary and form-critical distinctions, we may say that theologically Job moves to a "second naiveté," in which he denies nothing, but in the acknowledgment of his trouble, he continues in a transaction with Yahweh that is not fully resolved or free of pain but is the crucial condition of his life.[77] This human life, as modeled by Job, never arrives at a stasis; it is a dramatic process that stays always open. But the open, dramatic process fully credits Yahweh as a key character,

---

75. Recent scholarship, such as the commentaries of Norman Habel, *The Book of Job: A Commentary* (OTL; Philadelphia: Westminster Press, 1985); David J. A. Clines, *Job 1–20* (WBC; Waco, Tex.: Word Books, 1989); and J. Gerald Janzen, *Job* (Interpretation; Atlanta: John Knox, 1985), have attempted to see the book whole and to see its various parts as elements of a larger artistic intentionality. This represents an important departure from the older critical analysis that dissected the book.

76. Walter Brueggemann, "Psalms and the Life of Faith: A Suggested Typology of Function," *The Psalms and the Life of Faith*, 3–32.

77. On the term from Paul Ricoeur, "second naiveté," see Mark I. Wallace, *The Second Naiveté: Barth, Ricoeur, and the New Yale Theology* (StABH 6; Macon, Ga.: Mercer University Press, 1990). On the Book of Job in relation to models for faith and life, see Walter Brueggemann, "The Third World of Evangelical Imagination," *Interpretation and Obedience*, 9–27. Job's interaction with God is "not fully resolved or free of pain," and can never be, because Job's children remain lost (cf. 1:18-19, 42:13-16).

in presence and in absence, who is the overriding and shaping reality of Job's existence. Full and faithful human life requires continuing engagement in this open drama with this character, Yahweh.[78]

The marginal Satan. The role of Satan is marginal to the drama of the book, but Satan is there, as the serpent is in Genesis 3. Not a great deal is made of Satan in the Book of Job. I suggest, however, that the character of Satan constitutes (at least in Israel's testimony) the statement that the issues of human life are both more inscrutable and more ominous than simple moralism, either covenantal or sapiential, will allow. There is something large and external at work in the world that is antagonistic to human life.[79]

In any case, what matters for the practice of humanness here is that Yahweh governs and finally overrules and dispenses with this ominous force. Whatever it is that militates against viable human life is, so the text allows, subject to the will and purpose of Yahweh. Job therefore not only has no knowledge about Satan, he also has no occasion to spend his energy on this character. He need deal only with Yahweh, with whom his destiny is deeply embedded.

Job as counterpoint to Abraham. We may finally consider Job as counterpoint to Israel's model person of faith, Abraham. It would be possible, with Ernst Bloch, to juxtapose Job and Moses;[80] or, as Ezek 14:14, 20 does, to situate Job with Noah and Daniel. I take Abraham as his counterpart, however, because Abraham is the supreme person of faith, who lives completely inside Israel's narrative construal of reality.[81] Abraham evidences in Genesis 22 his unqualified faith in Yahweh, and in 17:1 is summoned to integrity ("blameless," *tamim*). Like Abraham, Job is "blameless," a man of unqualified faith (Job 1:21). The two are alike. And yet they are very different, for Job is a mature man who will not submit blindly. Indeed, Job is such a model human that we are not fully at ease in situating him in Israel's covenantal narrative of faith. Thus he stands a little distance from the simple picture of Abraham. And yet, as Jon Levenson has seen, following the rabbis, Abraham in Genesis 18 also turns out to be seen standing over against Yahweh and willing to carry on a risky dispute with Yahweh, precisely as a man of faith.[82]

Thus the disputatious Job is a man of faith; and Abraham, the man of faith, is capable of intense dispute with Yahweh. I submit that popular interpretation has cast both figures too simplistically. A closer study evidences that both persons of faith are able to submit in obedience. And both, on occasion and when appropriate, enact faith as counterinsistence in the face of Yahweh. Abraham, it turns out, is not only a good Israelite but a profoundly human person. Job, it is clear, is in the end

---

78. The character Job could be tested with the eight markings for humanness I have noted, p. 485.

79. Paul Ricoeur, *The Symbolism of Evil* (Boston: Beacon Press, 1969) 252–60.

80. Ernst Bloch, *Atheism in Christianity: The Religion of the Exodus and the Kingdom* (New York: Herder and Herder, 1972) 84–122.

81. See particularly the rendering of Abraham as "the knight of faith" by Søren Kierkegaard, *Fear and Trembling, Repetition* (Princeton, N.J.: Princeton University Press, 1983) 9–23.

82. Jon D. Levenson, *Creation and the Persistence of Evil: The Jewish Drama of Divine Omnipotence* (San Francisco: Harper and Row, 1988) 149–56.

not only a man but a man of faith. Both live fully toward Yahweh. But without any awkwardness, both know what to do in extremis.

There is no doubt that Yahweh relates to human creatures as free and sovereign. They are created out of Yahweh's great generosity, and perhaps out of Yahweh's yearning. They are situated in the midst of Yahweh's sovereignty and commanded to live on Yahweh's terms. When those terms are violated, trouble comes. The world of human persons in their life with Yahweh is a fairly tight moral system. The amazing thing is that in the midst of the sanctions that Yahweh pronounces, in the face of guilt and in the face of mortality, in the face of both situations in which the human person is helpless, Yahweh is attentive. Full of steadfast love and compassion, Yahweh is like a father who pities, like a mother who attends. Yahweh is indeed for human persons, for them while they are in the Pit, willing and powering them to newness. It is the central conviction of Israel that human persons in the Pit may turn to this One who is powerfully sovereign and find that sovereign One passionately attentive. That is the hope of humanity and in the end its joy.

SIXTEEN

The Nations as Yahweh's Partner

THERE IS NO DOUBT that in Israel's unsolicited testimony, Israel itself is presented as Yahweh's preferred and privileged partner. Israel is endlessly fascinated and perplexed by its own role vis-à-vis Yahweh's sovereignty and fidelity. We have seen, moreover, that as a second partner to Yahweh, the human person is characterized in this testimony only by derivation and extrapolation from the character of Israel, so that human persons are and do, by reiteration and replication, what Israel is and does. Like Israel, human persons are formed in love and summoned to obedience. Like Israel, human persons face judgment as a result of disobedience, come to trouble, and must take initiatives out of that trouble. Like Israel, human persons are beyond trouble opened for a new life of obedience, praise, and hope. The second partner lives always in reflection from the first partner, Israel.

When we come to a third partner who is linked to Yahweh by Yahweh's freedom and passion and who stands as the direct object in Yahweh's characteristic sentences with transformative verbs, the same linkage to Israel pertains. Israel did not live its life or practice its faith in a sociopolitical vacuum. From beginning to end, Israel lived among the nations who, in varying ways, decisively impinge upon Israel's life. On the one hand, Israel had to work out its relation to the nations, which was not obvious in light of Israel's peculiar theological identity. On the other hand, Israel had to articulate how the nations were related to Yahweh, a relation that in part was mediated through Israel but in part stood independent of Israel. The tension between "through Israel" and "independent of Israel," as we shall see, is a complicated matter, and one that admitted of no obvious or simple articulation. It is true that the Old Testament is pervasively preoccupied with Israel; and therefore it comes as a surprise to notice the richness of the material in which this unsolicited testimony is willing and able to open its horizon beyond Israel, to the larger scope of Yahweh's freedom and passion.

The Large Horizon of Yahweh's Governance

We may begin our study of this partner of Yahweh by reflecting on a pivotal and characteristic affirmation of the Jerusalem liturgy, a liturgy in which Israel bears witness to the nations concerning Yahweh: "Say among the nations, 'The Lord is king!'" (Ps 96:10). The purpose of the liturgy, reflected in Psalm 96, is *to assert and to enact Yahweh's legitimate governance* over the nations and the peoples of the world (v. 10), and over the "gods of the peoples" (v. 5). This liturgical exclamation asserts the primary claim of this unsolicited testimony: that Yahweh holds sovereign authority over all the nations and that all the nations must come to accept that rule, which is characterized by equity (v. 10), righteousness, and truth (v. 13). This assertion, critically, is a rejection of any loyalty other nations may give to any other gods and a rejection of any imagined autonomy on the part of any political power. Positively, the assertion promptly brings the nations under the demands and sanctions of Yahweh's will for justice.

The rhetoric of Ps 96:10 is so familiar to us that we may miss its sweeping and remarkable character. In a quick liturgical utterance, the temple-dynastic establishment in Jerusalem sweeps away all other claims to legitimacy and subsumes all other worldly powers under their theological governance.

The locus of this assertion is the Jerusalem temple, which means that the Yahwistic claim is shadowed by the interest of the Davidic-Solomonic establishment. That is, the Yahwistic claim, surely theological in intent, is never completely free of socioeconomic-political-military interest. Israel, as a witness, is not above giving testimony that serves its own interest and reputation. Thus our theme of "nations" never completely escapes this ideological dimension, although, as we shall see, the testimony includes significant, self-conscious critical moves against that ideological interest.

Recognition of the ideological element in the assertion of Ps 96:10 in itself does not dispose of nor delegitimate the theological claim that is here made. Simply because we recognize such an interest does not mean that the claim of Yahweh's sovereignty is reduced to and equated with Israelite interest, for this is, nonetheless, a God who is committed to justice and holiness that are not coterminous with Israel's political interest. In the process of working out this quandary, moreover, Israel makes important moves beyond its own self-interest.

The nations are subjects of Yahweh's sovereignty, to whom Yahweh relates in freedom and passion. The liturgic declaration of Ps 96:10, said in v. 2 to be "gospel" (*bsr*), receives a fuller narrative articulation in Gen 9:8–11:30. These different elements of narrative and genealogy, pieced together from different sorts of materials in different traditions, bear witness to the claim of Yahweh's postflood governance of the nations. The genealogies of the nations are contemplations of the juxtaposition of universalism (or, better stated, internationalism) and particularism of Israel that pervades this material.[1] We may, in this horizon-giving material, identify the following motifs.

---

1. On the structure and function of the genealogies, see Marshall D. Johnson, *The Purpose of Biblical Genealogies with Special Reference to the Settings of the Genealogies of Jesus* (Cambridge: Cambridge University Press, 1969); and Robert R. Wilson, *Genealogy and History in the Biblical World* (New Haven: Yale University Press, 1977).

Motifs in Genesis Genealogy

First, Yahweh makes an "everlasting covenant" with Noah and Noah's descendants, with "every animal of the earth," with the whole of creation. Yahweh's sovereignty over creation is cast in the language of fidelity and promise (Gen 9:8-17). The entire world of creation is in covenant with Yahweh.[2]

Second, Noah and his sons are the progenitors of all creation, so that the Noachic covenant applies to all of the nations. This assertion begins in the re-iteration of the promise spoken over creation (Gen 1:28), now reasserted to the family of Noah (Gen 9:1, 7). The human community is placed under the power of Yahweh's generous blessing.[3] It is intended that all descendant nations shall be fruitful and productive beneficiaries of Yahweh's will for life, as evidenced in the blessing-laden character of creation.

Third, all of humanity is derived from this family. Thus the horizon is focused on Noah and his sons (9:1, 18-28). The sons are transformed, in the next extrapolation, to nations (Gen 10:1-32). Of these, the family of Shem becomes the focal point, so that the family of humanity is drawn inexorably toward Israel (Gen 11:10-29). By this route, all nations are bound together, all live under the life-giving covenant of Yahweh, and all are recipients of Yahweh's blessing for life.

Fourth, the nations are restless with their status as subjects of Yahweh and recipients of Yahweh's gifts (Gen 11:1-9). They crave autonomy (v. 4). As a consequence of their rejection of the status as covenanted, blessed, promised subjects of Yahweh, the nations who were authorized by Yahweh now are "scattered" (*pûs*), and the coherence and unity of humanity irreversibly violated (v. 8).[4] The nations are made to receive "scattering," exposed displacement, just as Israel's worst negation is the scattering from which it is always being gathered.[5] In the process of this recalcitrance, the blessed state of the family of humanity has been transformed into a circumstance of vexation, alienation, and jeopardy. As the tracing of humanity in the family of Noah becomes ever more specific, the jeopardy of the human community culminates in Gen 11:30: "Now Sarai was barren..." Until this point, we do not identify Sarai and Abram as a special family of blessing. Here we know them only as the quintessential family of failure, in which the primal promise of fruitfulness, already uttered over creation, has been nullified in barrenness.

From a critical perspective, this portrayal of humanity in Genesis 9–11 is enormously difficult. But as a theological datum, the arrangement of texts announces

---

2. On the cruciality of the Noah covenant for the scope of biblical theology, see Patrick D. Miller, "Creation and Covenant," *Biblical Theology: Problems and Perspectives* (ed. Steven J. Kraftchick et al.; Nashville: Abingdon Press, 1995) 155–68.

3. The important exception in this pericope is vv. 25-27 and the curse of Canaan.

4. To take "scattering" as a curse is a consensus position. See Bernhard W. Anderson, "The Tower of Babel: Unity and Diversity in God's Creation," *From Creation to New Creation* (OBT; Minneapolis: Fortress Press, 1994) 165–78, for an alternative interpretation that suggests that the scattering is also a positive good.

5. The same verb is used for Israel and for the nations. On the term in relation to Israel, see p. 434.

the major themes that concern the nations as Yahweh's partner. The themes are fully resonant with the liturgical proclamation of Ps 96:10:

- Yahweh is king, and so the nations are under promise.
- Yahweh is king, and so the nations bear a blessing.
- Yahweh is king, and so the nations live in covenant under command.
- Yahweh is king, and so the recalcitrant nations are scattered.

The story of the nations, up until Gen 11:29, is in fact deeply unresolved, as indeed it is in the world. This skillful rendering of the nations affirms both the glad sovereignty of Yahweh over the nations and the problematic character of the relationship that gives life to the nations, but on terms that the nations characteristically refuse. Israel's unsolicited testimony leaves for more concrete probe the questions whether the scattered nations have a future, and whether Yahweh's free sovereign will, as it has for Israel, can move to a restorative passion. This overview, given at the outset of Israel's testimony, poses the questions. The answers can only be given concretely, in particular cases.

The Nations vis-à-vis Israel

The nations are a proper subject of Yahweh's attention. According to the juxtaposition of Genesis 9–11 and Gen 12:1-3, moreover, the nations are with Yahweh and under Yahweh's sovereignty, even before the existence of Israel. But Israel's portrayal of the matter is, in the first instant, always aimed at keeping the nations in the purview of Israel. Thus our first exploration of nations as partner of Yahweh will consider *the destiny of the nations as a partner, when the nations must make their way in a testimony that is Israel-driven,* testimony that interprets everything as though its primary point of concern is Israel. That is, "nations as partner" is first of all a function of the scandal of Israel's particularity, Israel's self-preoccupation, and Israel's self-serving ideology that shows up as testimony. The nations must make their way, according to this unsolicited testimony, in a world of Israel's preferential status with Yahweh.

Enthronement Psalms in Israel's Ideology

We may consider Psalm 2 as an entry point into this more-or-less Israel-ideology reading of the nations.[6] We have taken Psalm 96, one of the "enthronement psalms," as our starting point for our topic. These psalms of enthronement (Psalms 47, 93, 96–99) concern the kingship and governance of Yahweh, and Israel is not explicitly on the horizon of Psalm 96 (but see 97:8, 99:6-7). But the enthronement

---

6. For a reading of this psalm that focuses on its apparent ideology, see David J. A. Clines, "Psalm 2 and the MLF (Moabite Liberation Front)," *Interested Parties: The Ideology of Writers and Readers of the Hebrew Bible* (JSOTSup 205; Sheffield: Sheffield Academic Press, 1995) 244–75.

psalms that exalt Yahweh are, in the Psalter, a close fit to the "royal psalms" that are preoccupied with the royal house, and so they draw Yahweh's sovereignty into the Israelite-Davidic hegemony.[7] Psalm 2, as a case in point, is placed at the outset of the Psalter, along with Psalm 1, in order to establish Davidic hegemony in the liturgical imagination of Israel, along with Torah obedience, as a pivotal theological accent in Israelite piety.[8] Psalm 2 vigorously asserts Yahweh's governance and rejects the attempt of the nations to cast off Yahweh's rule (as in Gen 11:1-9):

> Why do the nations conspire,
> and the peoples plot in vain?
> The kings of the earth set themselves,
> and the rulers take counsel together,
> against the Lord and his anointed, saying,
> "Let us burst their bonds asunder,
> and cast their cords from us."
> He who sits in the heavens laughs;
> the Lord has them in derision.
> Then he will speak to them in his wrath,
> and terrify them in his fury.... (Ps 2:2-5)

In this lordly utterance, it is clear in v. 2 ("and his anointed") and in vv. 6-7 that Yahweh's governance of the nations is in and through David and the Jerusalem monarchy. David is at the same time both an embodiment of Israelite privilege in the world and a concrete political means whereby Yahweh rules in the earth. The twin themes of Yahweh's governance and David's priority nicely join our topic of the nations to the claim of Israel, a claim that resists the notion that the nations are in fact a full partner of Yahweh.

Violent Destruction of Nations

In this linkage of nations and Israel, there is a deep claim at the core of Israel's ideological self-understanding that Yahweh intends to displace and destroy the "seven nations" in order to make room for Israel in "the land of promise."[9] Thus one aspect of "nations as partner" is a violent insistence that the nations do not count when Yahweh gives gifts to Israel.[10] This way of thinking is found in the

---

7. On the royal psalms, see the older but reliable brief study of Keith R. Crim, *The Royal Psalms* (Richmond: John Knox, 1962); and Hans-Joachim Kraus, *The Theology of the Psalms* (1986; Minneapolis: Fortress Press, 1992) 107–23.

8. On the relation of Psalms 1 and 2, see Patrick D. Miller, *Interpreting the Psalms* (Philadelphia: Fortress Press, 1986) 87–93; Miller, "The Beginning of the Psalter," *The Shape and Shaping of the Psalter* (ed. J. Clinton McCann; JSOTSup 159; Sheffield: Sheffield Academic Press, 1993) 83–92; and the discussions by David M. Howard, Jr., and Gerald H. Nelson in the latter volume.

9. The "seven nations" is an ideological cipher referring to those who resist or impede the intention of Yahweh for Israel, who must therefore be destroyed. It is not possible to identify the seven nations nor a time when there may have been seven such nations together.

10. Jon D. Levenson, "Is There a Counterpart in the Hebrew Bible to New Testament Anti-Semitism," *Journal of Ecumenical Studies* 22 (1985) 242–60, makes the compelling suggestion that just

most militant assertions of Israel's preferentiality, found, not surprisingly, in the traditions of Deuteronomy:

> When the Lord your God brings you into the land that you are about to enter and occupy, and he clears away many nations before you—the Hittites, the Girgashites, the Amorites, the Canaanites, the Perizzites, the Hivites, and the Jebusites, seven nations mightier and more numerous than you— and when the Lord your God gives them over to you and you defeat them, then you must utterly destroy them. Make no covenant with them and show them no mercy. Do not intermarry with them, giving your daughters to their sons or taking their daughters for your sons, for that would turn away your children from following me, to serve other gods. (Deut 7:1-4a)

> When the Lord your God has cut off before you the nations whom you are about to enter to dispossess them, when you have dispossessed them and live in their land, take care that you are not snared into imitating them, after they have been destroyed before you; do not inquire concerning their gods, saying, "How did these nations worship their gods? I also want to do the same." (Deut 12:29-30; cf. Deut 4:38, 7:22, 8:20, 11:23)

This is an exceedingly harsh presentation of the nations in the interest of Israel. We may term this presentation ideological, because it is likely that "the seven nations" are a theological construct without any historical base, and because in this case the sovereignty of Yahweh is drawn most blatantly and directly into the service of Israel's political agenda. The "seven nations" are presented as rival claimants to the land, and so their destruction serves negatively to establish the legitimacy of Israel's claim to the land.[11]

This capacity and willingness to slot the seven nations under the rubric of extermination is linked to a larger agenda about the land, and it places at the center of our topic an explicit endorsement of violence, which of necessity is finally situated in Yahweh's own will and purpose. These nations are on the horizon of the narrative only because they are an impediment to Israel, an impediment of which Yahweh will, so the testimony asserts, dispose. This extreme ingredient in our general topic comes to its most strident expression in the notion of *ḥerem*, the authorization to destroy the nations as "devotion" to Yahweh, and in the odd, troubling fixation of the tradition on the Amalekites as the quintessential and paradigmatic enemy of Israel (cf. Exod 17:8-16; Deut 25:17-19; 1 Sam 15:18-21).[12]

---

as Christians rapaciously superseded Jews in their use of the Hebrew Bible, so in the Old Testament the Israelites practice the same kind of negation of the nations who preceded them in the land.

11. This antithesis is true on any of the available theories of Israel's "conquest." The precise meaning of the phrase varies with the different theories of conquest.

12. On the meaning and function of the notion of *ḥerem* in ancient Israel, see Susan Niditch, *War in the Hebrew Bible: A Study in the Ethics of Violence* (New York: Oxford University Press, 1993) 28–77. It is especially worth noting that in 1 Samuel 15 Saul is fully expected, in the terms of the narrative, to implement *ḥerem* against the Amalekites, but in 1 Samuel 30 David does not execute it, nor is the

Blessing to the Nations

This vigorous negation of "the seven nations" is found especially in the Moses-Joshua traditions and in the Deuteronomic materials that are aggressively exclusivistic (cf. Deut 23:2-8).[13] The remarkable countertheme to this harshness, still with Israel as the focus, is the program of the ancestral narrative of Genesis 12–36, wherein Israel is the one who blesses the cursed nations (cf. 12:3, 18:18, 22:18, 26:4, 28:13).[14] Hans Walter Wolff and a host of scholars after him have seen that the summons and mandate to Abraham (and Sarah) in Gen 12:1-3 is situated as the antidote to the sorry state of the nations in Genesis 3–11.[15] Thus the nations are under curse (cf. Gen 3:14-19, 4:11-12, 9:25), and now Israel is presented as the agent and instrument of Yahweh in the world, to bring a blessing to the world of curse. As we have indicated, this series of texts is as close as Israel comes to a "theology of mission," whereby Israel has a vocation of transformation vis-à-vis the nations.[16]

The narrative of Genesis 12–36 (and by extension Genesis 37–50) still focuses on the special status of Israel. But here, in contrast to the Moses-Joshua-Deuteronomy traditions, the nations are prominently on the horizon, regarded as legitimate and treated positively. Thus the "rejected brothers," Ishmael (25:9) and Esau (35:29), are allowed dignity and space within the narrative. The Genesis narratives, while they compromise nothing of the specialness of Israel, stand outside the orbit of Mosaic ideology and contain nothing of aggressive exclusivism.[17] The "vocation of transformation" is still presented as a thoroughly Israelite reality, but

practice on the horizon of that narrator. On this distinction in the expectations of Saul and of David, see above pp. 369–70.

13. Notice should be taken of Isa 56:3-8, with its inclusive statement that oddly abrogates the Torah provision of Deut 23:2-8. See Herbert Donner, "Jesaja LVI 1-7: Ein Abrogationsfalls innerhalb des Kanons—Implikationen und Konsequenzen," *Congress Volume: Salamanca, 1983* (ed. J. A. Emerton; VTSup 36; Leiden: E. J. Brill, 1985) 81–95.

14. The role of Israel as one who blesses the nations comes under the rubric of the promises of Yahweh, on which see pp. 168–69. Claus Westermann, "The Way of Promise in the Old Testament," *The Old Testament and Christian Faith* (ed. Bernhard W. Anderson; New York: Harper and Row, 1964) 200–224, has explored the way in which the themes of blessing and promise are linked in the Genesis texts.

15. Hans Walter Wolff, "The Kerygma of the Yahwist," *Int* 20 (1966) 131–58. See also Gerhard von Rad, "The Form-Critical Problem of the Hexateuch," *The Problem of the Hexateuch and Other Essays* (New York: McGraw-Hill, 1966) 65 and passim; and Claus Westermann, *Genesis 12–36: A Commentary* (Minneapolis: Augsburg Publishing House, 1986) 146 and passim.

16. On a theology of mission toward the nations, concerning Exod 19:5-6, the blessing theme in Genesis, and Isa 42:6-7, 49:6-9, see pp. 430–34. In a close study of the form and grammatical structure of Gen 12:1-3, Patrick D. Miller, "Syntax and Theology in Genesis xii 3a," *VT* 34 (1984) 472–75, has demonstrated that the ultimate purpose of Abraham's departure at the behest of Yahweh is so that the nations may be blessed. Miller has shown, moreover, that the statement on curse is not symmetrical to the statement of blessing and is not a part of the purpose of the journey.

17. There is no doubt that Genesis provides an alternative to a dominant harsh ideology. It is of immense importance, however, that this more generous alternative is evident not only in Genesis, but also in Deuteronomy, i.e., in the heart of the harsh ideology. It is recognized that Edom is derived from "Esau your brother," in both narrative (Deut 2:1-8) and in command (Deut 23:7-8). Moab and Ammon, kinsmen of Israel by Lot, are also given more generous treatment (Deut 2:8-25), though not without negativity (Deut 23:3-6). In any case, it is clear that even in Deuteronomy, something other than a flat, violent dismissal of the nations is on the horizon of Israel.

now Israel's vocation is regularly in the presence of other peoples, and most often to their benefit—the nations characteristically profit from Israel's presence among them. In these narratives the linkage of Israel to the nations, unlike that of the traditions derivative from Moses, is positive, affirmative, and intentional.

Thus both of these traditions, ancestral and Mosaic-covenantal, treat the nations as incidental to the life and destiny of Israel and not for their own sake, but they do so very differently. These two clusters of texts set the outer limits of the nations vis-à-vis Israel: on the one hand as an impediment to be eliminated, according to Yahweh's will; on the other hand to be blessed and enhanced, according to Yahweh's mandate.

Nations Join in Praise and Obedience

Both of these traditions concerning ways in which Israel is to relate to the nations continue to be available in ongoing Israel, for either constructive ("blessing") or destructive ("blot out") use. Without for an instant minimizing the cruciality of the negative tradition of the legitimated destruction of the nations, there is also evidence that as Israel kept the nations on its horizon, Israel could imagine that the nations could share willingly in the service of Yahweh, becoming a part of Yahweh's community of praise and obedience. This account of the expansiveness of Israel's generosity toward non-Israelites shows it as a generosity rooted in its discernment of the expansiveness of Yahweh. It must be said, however, that this emphasis on praise and obedience stays within the orbit and categories of Israel's own life with Yahweh. Thus there is an ideological, self-serving hint that the nations are permitted linkage to Yahweh, but only on Israel's terms.

And yet, Israel's ideological self-service is not great in this emphasis, because without respect to Israel as such, praise and obedience are indeed the ways in which Yahweh's sovereignty will be approached. In praise and obedience, the nations are to do what Israel does vis-à-vis Yahweh. But they are to do it as themselves, and not as Israel nor as an adjunct to Israel.

The nations are summoned to praise Yahweh, in an act of lyrical self-abandonment, so that the sovereignty of Yahweh is acknowledged and gladly accepted. In Ps 86:9-10 it is anticipated that the nations will join in praise of Yahweh:

> All the nations you have made shall come
> and bow down before you, O Lord,
> and shall glorify your name.
> For you are great and do wondrous things;
> you alone are God.

This anticipation is in the context of an assertion of Yahweh's incomparability, which all nations must recognize soon or late. The basis of that recognition is that Yahweh does "wondrous things" (*npl'ôth*) which will draw the nations, like Israel, to glad praise. In Psalm 117, the anticipation is transposed into a summons:

> Praise the Lord, all you nations!
> Extol him, all you peoples!
> For great is his steadfast love toward us,
> and the faithfulness of the Lord endures forever.
> Praise the Lord!

The nations are invited (and expected) to join Israel in praise. The ground for such praise is not unlike that of Ps 86:9-10, only now the "wondrous things" are made a bit more specific. They are actions marked by Yahweh's most characteristic adjectives, steadfast love and faithfulness. In making this summons to the nations, doxological Israel makes a bold connection. We may believe that Yahweh's acts of "steadfast love and faithfulness" are characteristically and quintessentially taken as actions toward Israel.

In Israel's perception, however, these characteristic actions of Yahweh are so compelling and so overwhelming that the nations will want to join Israel in praise, on the basis of actions done for Israel. This is made especially clear in Psalm 126, where the confession of the nations concerning Yahweh (v. 2) is symmetrical to Israel's own confession of Yahweh, but it is given *prior* to Israel's confession. The nations are drawn to what they see of Yahweh in the life of Israel. We may allow that the actions of steadfast love and faithfulness done toward Israel are taken as paradigmatic of the same actions Yahweh performs for the other nations, but that is not expressed in this summons. Indeed, if such an extrapolation is granted, then we are observing a move well beyond Israel's self-satisfied ideological claim.

In a third text of praise-by-the-nations, Psalm 67, our theme receives its fullest exposition. Verse 1 contains phrasing quite parallel to the familiar blessing of Num 6:24-26, a conventional blessing pronounced over Israel. Verse 1, moreover, is dominated by the direct object "us," clearly indicating Israel. The verse invites rich blessings upon "us." But the blessings, graciousness, and presence of v. 1 are instrumental, serving only as an introduction to v. 2. The point of blessing to Israel is in order that Yahweh's "way" and "saving power" (ys') will be known among the nations. Israel offers to be a case study, so that the nations may know of Yahweh (v. 2) and may join in "thanks" (ydh) (v. 3, rendered twice in NRSV as "praise"). In v. 4, the language is not unlike Psalm 96, concerning Yahweh's governance of all the earth, and v. 5 reiterates v. 3. In vv. 6-7, yet another step is taken away from the specificity of Israel, now surely in the rhetoric of creation, blessing, and fruitfulness. Thus the psalm moves from Israel (v. 1), to the nations (vv. 2-5), to all creation (v. 6).

In v. 7 two readings are possible, depending on the identity of "us." If the "us" of v. 7 refers again to Israel as in v. 1, then the two lines of v. 7 again make the odd but crucial connection between Israel (line 1) and "all the ends of the earth" (line 2). It may be, however, that the "us" of v. 7 is not the same as in v. 1, but now has been expanded and redefined to refer to all of creation—"all the ends of the earth." Thus v. 7, the clue to the connections the doxology makes, either links "us"

(Israel) to the praise of the earth, or it shows the "us" of Israel now completely moving beyond Israel to the larger sphere of Yahweh's glad sovereignty. Either way, the psalm envisions a whole earth and all its peoples now gladly affirming Yahweh's sovereignty and gratefully receiving from Yahweh all the blessings of a rightly governed creation.

The obedience of the nations is not as clear as is the praise. But we may refer especially to Isa 2:2-5 (cf. Mic 4:1-4). In this anticipatory text, the unsolicited testimony of Israel envisions a time when all nations will come in procession to Jerusalem, there to be inducted into Yahweh's way, to be judged by Yahweh, and to make decisions that lead to peace. The text is a bold and daring act of imagination. On the one hand, the focus of the process is toward Jerusalem, the place of Yahweh's residence. Of course the Jerusalem focus is never without some claim for the cruciality of Israel, and more specifically for the large claims of the Davidic house. To that extent, the vision is powerfully Israelite, and not without specific ideological intent.

On the other hand, it is important to note that in this oracle, nothing is made of the Davidic connection. The focus is on the Torah that is situated in Jerusalem, to which the nations come for instruction:

> Many peoples shall come and say,
> "Come, let us go up to the mountain of the Lord,
> to the house of the God of Jacob;
> that he may teach us his ways
> and that we may walk in his paths."
> For out of Zion shall go forth instruction,
> and the word of the Lord from Jerusalem. (Isa 2:3)

The verbs of v. 3 are *teach* (*yrh*) and *walk*, and the important nouns are *tôrah* (derived from the verb *yrh*, rendered as "instruction" in the NRSV), and *word of Yahweh*. Jerusalem is the place where the concrete clues to well-being are given, which come as the requirements of Yahweh for a viable life. The oracle operates on the claim that the nations, short of the Jerusalem Torah, do not have the knowledge about peace and justice that is necessary, and so must come here to receive necessary guidance.[18]

Two matters are important in this vision. First, the nations come gladly, willingly, and expectantly. They are not coerced or compelled by the political force of the Davidic house, but have come in recognition that this is the only place where the way to peace and justice is available. Second, in the process of coming gladly, it is affirmed that the nations, like Israel, are subject to the Torah of Yahweh. That is, the Torah is as pertinent to the nations as it is to Israel. This makes clear that the nations must deal with Yahweh's sovereignty, but it also makes clear that the

---

18. On the Torah situated in Jerusalem, see Hartmut Gese, *Essays on Biblical Theology* (Minneapolis: Augsburg Publishing House, 1981) 82 and passim.

Torah, while seated in Jerusalem, is no exclusive Israelite property. It belongs to the nations as much as to Israel.[19]

Yahweh and the Superpowers

We may now suggest that the nations, in their dealings with Yahweh, are not always presented as having to deal with Israel at the same time. It is thinkable in Israel's unsolicited testimony, though not often articulated, that Yahweh's sovereignty extended *directly* to the nations, without mediating reference to Israel either as the vehicle of blessing to the nations or as the agent of destruction, or even as the locus of Torah. To be sure, these testimonies do not break completely out of Israelite categories, and one would not expect them to. But there is a marginal awareness in Israel's testimony that the relation of the nations to Yahweh is, on occasion, direct and not dependent on or derivative from Israel's status and condition. This applies particularly to the oracles against the nations, a standard genre of prophetic speech that is present in most of the prophetic collections (cf. Isaiah 13–23; Jeremiah 46–51; Ezekiel 25–32; Amos 1–2; Zephaniah 2).[20]

Oracles against the Nations

These oracles occupy a distinct place in the prophetic literature and seem to be an enactment of the proclamation of Ps 96:10, that is, a way in which Yahweh exercises kingship in the world. Yahweh has "become king" over the nations and will exercise that sovereignty.

To be sure, difficult historical questions are related to these oracles, but theologically they are not difficult to situate in our exposition. Their assumption is that Yahweh has created the nations (see the verb in Ps 86:9), has given them life, authorized them to be, and placed in their midst the possibility of life and blessing. This general assumption is everywhere the beginning point in these oracles. The oracle itself, however, characteristically takes the form of a judgment speech. In these oracles, the nations have violated the mandate and command of Yahweh to which they are subject, and so they must be punished or even nullified. This characteristic presentation of the nations is an enterprise of enormous boldness and imagination. Klaus Koch uses the term *metahistory* for the claim made that Yahweh can call the nations to accountability because there is in the historical process

---

19. This generosity with the Torah, i.e., making it available to the nations, is in deep tension with Deut 4:7-8, where Torah is prized as the distinctive property of Israel. In Zech 8:20-23, see a different perspective on the nations vis-à-vis Israel. There the nations are required and expected to recognize "that God is with you" (i.e., Israel).

20. On the oracles against the nations, see Norman K. Gottwald, *All the Nations of the Earth: Israelite Prophecy and International Relations in the Ancient Near East* (New York: Harper and Row, 1964); and Paul R. Raabe, "Why Prophetic Oracles against the Nations?" *Fortunate the Eyes That See: Essays in Honor of David Noel Freedman* (ed. Astrid B. Beck et al.; Grand Rapids: Eerdmans, 1995) 236–57.

a reality that overrides historical realities.[21] Because of Yahweh's massive, overriding sovereignty, these oracles assert that the nations are subject to a governance, a requirement, and an expectation, no matter how secure and self-sufficient they seem to be or think they are. This governance, moreover, cannot be overcome, disregarded, or evaded.

The violation of the governance of Yahweh may be that Yahweh is mocked by arrogance (Isa 37:17, 23) or that Israel is abused (Isa 47:6). What astonishes us and warrants our attention is that on occasion the affront against Yahweh is not a direct mocking of Yahweh or an abuse of Israel, but abuse of a third people that has nothing to do with Israel but, as it turns out, has everything to do with Yahweh:[22]

> For three transgressions of the Ammonites,
> and for four, I will not revoke the punishment;
> because they ripped open pregnant women in Gilead
> in order to enlarge their territory....
> For three transgressions of Moab,
> and for four, I will not revoke the punishment;
> because he burned to lime the bones of the king of Edom. (Amos
>   1:13, 2:1)

This rhetoric permits Israel to enunciate the claim that under the aegis of Yahweh's sovereignty, there is a kind of international law or code of human standards that seems to anticipate the Helsinki Accords of 1975 in a rough way, a code that requires every nation to act in civility and humaneness toward others.[23] Any affront of this standard is taken to be an act of autonomy, arrogance, and self-sufficiency, which flies in the face of Yahweh's governance.[24] Thus Yahweh is the guarantor, not only of Israel, but of the nations in their treatment of each other.

The sanctions these oracles express consist in punishment for the offending party at the hand of Yahweh, most often termination. This theological claim is a remarkable one. Clearly Israel, in its intellectual milieu, did not attend to secondary causes. But we must not, in my judgment, imagine this to be a simpleminded supernaturalism.[25] The theology of these oracles is not simply an abstract defense of Yahweh's sovereignty, nor is it merely an ideological protection of Israel. It is, along with a defense of Yahweh and a protection of Israel, a notice that more is at

21. Klaus Koch, *The Prophets* 1: *The Assyrian Period* (Minneapolis: Fortress Press, 1983) 70–76; *The Prophets* 2: *The Babylonian and Persian Periods* (Minneapolis: Fortress Press, 1984) 71, 171, and passim.

22. On motivations for the oracles against the nations, see Graham I. Davies, "The Destiny of the Nations in the Book of Isaiah," *The Book of Isaiah: Le Livre d'Isaïe* (ed. Jacques Vermeylen; BETL 81; Leuven: Leuven University Press, 1989) 93–120.

23. Walter Harrelson, *The Ten Commandments and Human Rights* (OBT; Philadelphia: Fortress Press, 1980) 173–201, links the Helsinki Accords to the Decalogue.

24. On this theme, see Donald W. Gowan, *When Man Becomes God: Humanism and Hubris in the Old Testament* (Pittsburgh: Pickwick Press, 1975).

25. John Barton, *Amos's Oracles against the Nations: A Study of Amos 1:3–2:5* (Cambridge: Cambridge University Press, 1980), has shown that the reasons for condemnation of the nations are not narrowly Yahwistic, but pertain "to a human convention held to be obviously universal...a common ethos" (2, 45).

work in international processes than brute power. There are limits to brute power, and the curb on such brutalizing, arrogant power is the indefatigable resolve of Yahweh, which regularly defeats the greatest powers, who thought they were situated for success to perpetuity. Israel had no way (and no desire) to speak about this limit on public-military power, except by reference to Yahweh's sovereignty, which concerned uncompromising demand and irresistible sanction. The demand and the sanction serve, theologically, to enhance Yahweh, but they also serve as a nonnegotiable line of defense against barbarism. Israel's unsolicited testimony asserts that there is at work in the world a defense of human rights that is beyond the challenge or resistance of even the most powerful state. That is what it means to "judge the world in righteousness, equity, and truth" (cf. Pss 96:10, 13; 67:4; Isa 2:4).

The upshot of these oracles against the nations, organized around indictment (derived from command) and sanctions (which implement curse), is that the nations characteristically are under threat from Yahweh because they refuse to be Yahweh's obedient subjects and vassals. For the most part, the oracles against the nations are simple lawsuits of indictment and sentence, beyond which there is no future for recalcitrant nations. This is the great preponderance of testimony.

While Israel's unsolicited testimony has in purview the nations close at hand (as in the "seven" of Deuteronomy and those in Amos 1–2), great attention in the Old Testament is given to those nations that are the dominant superpowers: Egypt, Assyria, Babylon, and Persia.[26] Everything for Israel depends on the relation of these powers to Yahweh, because Israel is almost always in the position of the client of one of the superpowers, and always in a position to be made a victim of aggressive, expansionist colonialism. For that reason we shall consider the destiny of each superpower on the horizon, in their sequence, according to the imaginative utterance of Israel.

Egypt: Abuser and Oppressor

Egypt is the first superpower Israel faces, one that endlessly occupies Israel's imagination, even as it endlessly occupied Israel's geopolitics. When the narrative of Israel's life begins, Egypt is already there, established, prosperous, enjoying a monopoly of food (Gen 12:10). Egypt is the place where Israel fled in famine and was fed (Gen 41:53 and the entire Joseph narrative), and Egypt is the land that receives the special blessing of father Jacob (Gen 47:7-10).

All of that is a backdrop that articulates the goodness and generosity of Yahweh in making Egypt a place of fruitfulness and blessing, but that is not the primary presentation of Egypt in Israel's unsolicited testimony. Egypt may be blessed by Yahweh, but it is characteristically a place of abuse and oppression. In the end, in

---

26. It should be noted that in the list of superpowers that are under criticism in these oracles, the several Hellenic powers are not, for the most part, dealt with. In the later texts they are treated, as in the Book of Daniel, under the cipher of Nebuchadnezzar, or in rhetoric that is not explicit but that moves toward transhistorical, apocalyptic imagery. This, however, represents no less an intense theological concern with these powers, but only a general move of Judaism toward apocalyptic rhetoric.

Israel's rhetoric of demonization, Egypt is the very embodiment of primordial evil (cf. Ps 87:4), which brings death and destruction in its wake (Exod 1:22). Egypt embodies the antithesis of Yahweh's good intention for Israel and the terminal point of Yahweh's attentive care for Israel.[27]

As a consequence of its role as abuser and oppressor, Egypt stands completely under the lawsuit speech of Israel, which is characteristic of the prophetic oracles against the nations. The indictment of Egypt is of course that Egypt abused Israel, but much more than that, Egypt is the recalcitrant vassal of Yahweh who refuses to obey Yahweh and who thereby disrupts Yahweh's good creation.[28] Thus Terence Fretheim can write, "Pharaoh's anti-life measures against God's creation have unleashed chaotic powers that threaten the very creation that God intended."[29] Egypt under pharaoh is the great disrupter of creation, whose actions evoke a punishing chaos from which all suffer.[30]

The lawsuit against Egypt, a paradigmatic complaint against a paradigmatic enemy, is given in two prominent places. In the narrative of Exodus 1–15, pharaoh refuses to obey Yahweh's command, "Let my people go" (*šlḥ*), so that pharaoh is visited by punishment culminating in broad-scale death (Exod 12:29-32). The second, most extensive articulation of the lawsuit against Egypt, a recalcitrant vassal of Yahweh, is in Ezekiel 29–32. This indictment of Egypt is staggering, both in its sheer quantity and in its hyperbolic fierceness. This is the enemy par excellence, on whom Yahweh (Israel) heaps scorn and rage. The pivotal indictment that warrants such venom is not primarily concerned with Israel, but consists in defiance of Yahweh:

> I am against you,
> Pharaoh king of Egypt,
> the great dragon sprawling
> in the midst of its channels,
> saying, "My Nile is my own;
> I made it for myself." (Ezek 29:3)

It is Yahweh who gave Egypt life by providing the Nile. But, in the recalcitrant imagination attributed to pharaoh, the gift of Yahweh is converted into a royal property. It is, moreover, this inversion, this fundamental rejection of the truth of Yahweh, that gives pharaoh occasion to transform the gift of the Nile into a

---

27. Thus in Jeremiah 43–44, a return to Egypt is portrayed as the end of the *Heilsgeschichte* that began in the emancipation of Israel from Egypt. With the return to Egypt, Israel has now come full circle from bondage to freedom with Yahweh and back to bondage. See Richard E. Friedman, "From Egypt to Egypt: Dtr[1] and Dtr[2]," *Traditions in Transformation: Turning Points in Biblical Faith* (ed. Baruch Halpern and Jon D. Levenson; Winona Lake, Ind.: Eisenbrauns, 1981) 167–92.

28. On the presentation of Egypt as a transhistorical force that disrupts creation, see Terence E. Fretheim, "The Plagues as Ecological Signs of Historical Disaster," *JBL* 110 (1991) 385–96; and, more generally, Fretheim, *Exodus* (Interpretation; Louisville: John Knox, 1991).

29. Fretheim, "The Plagues as Ecological Signs," 393.

30. I say "all," but of course the Exodus narrative poignantly notes that Israel is an exception. See Exod 9:4, 6, 26; 11:7.

canal of death (Exod 1:22, 7:14-25; cf. Isa 19:5-10). That is the whole of the matter . . . except that in Ezek 32:31-32, at the end of the most enormous lawsuit speech against Egypt, a curious note is added. The conventional rendering of the key term is "be consoled" (*nḥm*):

> When Pharaoh sees them, he will be consoled (*nḥm*) for all his hordes—Pharaoh and all his army killed by the sword, says the Lord God. For he spread terror in the land of the living; therefore he shall be laid to rest among the uncircumcised, with those who are slain by the sword—Pharaoh and all his multitude, says the Lord God.

On this reading, it is anticipated that when pharaoh sees the death of many other enemies, he will be consoled. The calculus of such a response is problematic. Recently, however, Ellen Davis has offered a different reading of the verb: that "Pharaoh will repent" of all the devastation he has wrought.[31] On this reading (as of now a minority one), pharaoh will at long last, at the eleventh hour, repent and become a willing vassal of Yahweh. If this reading can be accepted (and I find it persuasive), the brutal, sad tale of Egypt unexpectedly portrays even Egypt coming, at the last moment, out of the fissure of devastating punishment to new life with Yahweh. Such a reading is a resilient insistence in Israel that Yahweh's will cannot finally be thwarted. In any case, Egypt is a cipher for massive resistance to Yahweh, one of two such ciphers in the Old Testament, Babylon being the other.[32] (The final end of Egypt is here held in abeyance; we will return to Isa 19:23-25.)

Assyria: Arrogance and Autonomy

The second, utterly recalcitrant international power, a suitable twin for Egypt (cf. Hos 7:11), is Assyria.[33] Assyria occupies much of Israel's political attention and theological imagination in the monarchal period. While Assyria is politically and experientially as important as Egypt, it does not take on as full a theological existence in the rhetoric of Israel as does Egypt. Nonetheless it occupies a parallel position, and what is said of Egypt readily applies as well to Assyria. Assyria stands under the same lawsuit of Yahweh as does Egypt, and for the same reasons.

We may focus our attention on three texts concerning Assyria. Isa 10:5-19 provides a complete "philosophy of history" concerning Assyria and all such superpowers. The indictment and sentence of Assyria take place in a sequence of two conventional parts. First, Assyria is a usable instrument of Yahweh in international politics:

---

31. Ellen Davis, "'And Pharaoh Will Change His Mind . . .' (Ezek 32:31)," paper read at Society of Biblical Literature, 1993.

32. Jürgen Kegler, "Zu Komposition und Theologie der Plagenzahlungen," *Die Hebraische Bibel und ihre zweifache Nachgeschichte: Festschrift für Rolf Rendtorff* (ed. Erhard Blum et al.; Neukirchen-Vluyn: Neukirchener Verlag, 1990) 55–74, has suggested that in the later strata of the plague cycle of the Exodus narrative, "Egypt" is to be understood as a coded reference to Babylon.

33. In the geopolitical horizon of the Old Testament, Assyria is the inevitable counterpart to Egypt. Sometimes Assyria is specifically intended when it is named, at other times it appears to be a cipher for whatever northern superpower threatens Israel.

> Ah, Assyria, the rod of my anger—
> the club in their hands is my fury!...
> Shall the ax vaunt itself over the one who wields it,
> or the saw magnify itself against the one who handles it? (Isa 10:5, 15)

Yahweh is willing and able to use such a tool, and Assyria, we are led to believe, willingly accepts its role as an obedient vassal in the service of Yahweh. Assyria conforms to Yahweh's intention to "take spoil and seize plunder" against "a godless nation," Israel (Isa 10:6). This Assyria does willingly. We may set aside the issue of whether this is genuine obedience or simply a convenient warrant for brutal acquisitiveness. Such a distinction does not delay the poet.

Second, Assyria, in arrogant boasting and haughty pride (v. 12), oversteps the mandate of Yahweh, begins to act autonomously (v. 13), and sets out to destroy this "godless nation" (v. 6). This is clearly an act of disobedience against Yahweh, for Yahweh does not intend the destruction of Israel, even when angry with Israel. The indictment of Assyria thus concerns its autonomy, which is not congruent with Yahweh's intent. To be sure, this is all poetry, and Israel refuses to speak differently about these ominous matters.

What astonishes us is that Assyria is indicted for not limiting its destructiveness, as though Assyria is supposed to know Yahweh's intention of limited assault against Judah without being told. Assyria should have known that Yahweh's anger toward Israel is not unlimited and endless! This great, ruthless empire, preoccupied with its own designs, should have curbed its military capacity in recognition of Yahweh's core commitment to Israel, a commitment around which ancient Near Eastern politics are said to revolve.

And so this recalcitrant vassal, which violated its mandate from Yahweh, is subject to massive, destructive punishment, according to the will of Yahweh:

> The glory of his forest and his fruitful land
> the Lord will destroy, both soul and body,
> and it will be as when an invalid wastes away.
> The remnant of the trees of his forest will be so few
> that a child can write them down. (Isa 10:18-19)

Assyria will be terminated; no power can stand against Yahweh's will.

The second text that works the same themes with reference to Assyria is Isaiah 36–37 (2 Kings 18–19).[34] The rhetorical pattern is here somewhat more dramatic than in Isaiah 10, but the issues are much the same. In this encounter, now situated later in the life of Judah when Hezekiah, the obedient king, governs Jerusalem, Assyria is not said to be on a mission from Yahweh (as in chapter 10) but is simply enacting its own territorial expansionism. Assyria here is not at all doing Yahweh's

---

34. On these texts, see Brevard S. Childs, *Isaiah and the Assyrian Crisis* (SBT 3, 2d series; London: SCM Press, 1967); and Christopher Seitz, *Zion's Final Destiny: The Development of the Book of Isaiah: A Reassessment of Isaiah 36–39* (Minneapolis: Fortress Press, 1991).

will, even though the voice of Assyria in this text speaks in theological accents. Indeed, Assyria here is seen to be directly opposing the intentions of Yahweh. Because the threat to Judah is cast in theological categories, the affront of Assyria is all the greater. Assyria, in its arrogance, both claims a mandate from Yahweh (Isa 36:10, perhaps referring back to chapter 10) and completely misunderstands Yahweh by refusing to recognize Yahweh's incomparability, comparing Yahweh to other, impotent gods (Isa 36:18-20). In this text, the great affront of Assyria is that it mocks Yahweh: it refuses to take Yahweh seriously, to acknowledge Yahweh's incomparability, and to accept Yahweh's sovereignty.

The judgment on Assyria, in this text, is pronounced by the prophet in Isa 37:26-29. The rhetoric is structured as a lawsuit:

• Indictment:

> Because you have raged against me
> and your arrogance has come to my ears,

• Sentence:

> I will put my hook in your nose
> and my bit in your mouth;
> I will turn you back on the way
> by which you came. (Isa 37:29)

The great empire has been able to have military success, only by the decree of Yahweh:

> Have you not heard
> that I determined it long ago?
> I planned from days of old
> what now I bring to pass,
> that you should make fortified cities
> crash into heaps of ruins,
> while their inhabitants, shorn of strength,
> are dismayed and confounded;
> they have become like plants of the field
> and like tender grass,
> like grass on the housetops,
> blighted before it is grown. (Isa 37:26-27)

This assertion parallels the mandate of Isa 10:5 but makes it more extensive. Arrogance and autonomy bring to a failed end what might have been a Yahweh-ordered success. There are limits to brutality and self-aggrandizement. Thus again, as in Isa 10:5-19, Assyria is mandated, violates the mandate, and is severely and irreversibly punished.

The third text concerning Assyria, which need only be mentioned here, is the poem of Nahum against the capital city of Nineveh. Not much attention is given in the poem to an indictment of Nineveh, though the poet can voice the warrant for the destruction now celebrated:

> From you one has gone out
> who plots evil against the Lord,
> who counsels wickedness. . . .
> Because of the countless debaucheries of the prostitute,
> gracefully alluring, mistress of sorcery,
> who enslaves nations through her debaucheries,
> and peoples through her sorcery . . . (1:11, 3:4)

Mostly, however, the poem of Nahum is unrestrained rage that anticipates the destruction of Nineveh at the hand of Yahweh. While the substance of this poem is profoundly emotional, with severe hatred as its substance, the poem is kept within the orbit of Yahweh. The Israelites profoundly resent Assyria and Nineveh. Their testimony makes the claim that their deep antipathy toward Nineveh is rooted in Yahweh's own profound antipathy toward the Assyrians (on which see Ps 139:21). The rage of Israel at barbarism is the rage of an oppressed people, too long exploited.

The rhetoric, however, claims more than simple rage. It claims that emotive aversion to brutality is located in the heart of Yahweh, so that political abuse becomes, in the end, theological reality. I write this during the celebration of the fiftieth anniversary of V-E day, with its accompanying ecclesial discussion of whether to pray for the forgiveness of Adolf Hitler. Assyria is like Hitler for Judah, perhaps eventually to be prayed for in Israel, but not soon, not yet in the poem of Nahum. Thus Assyrian imperialism is contained Yahwistically in the categories of mandate-violation of mandate-sanctions. The empire cannot outflank Yahweh, who wills compassion in the political process.

Assyria, in the Old Testament, comes to a condemned, hopeless end . . . except for Isa 19:23-25, to which we shall return. Perhaps we may find an adumbration of the oracle of Isa 19:23-25 in the narrative of Jonah. To be sure, this narrative does not concern itself with Assyria, but this is precisely the sort of unsolicited testimony that helps us most to understand Yahweh's partners. According to this narrative, Assyria (Nineveh) does repent, does submit to Yahweh, and so is the recipient of Yahweh's steadfast love (Jonah 3:5-10). The ground for steadfast love—even for Nineveh—is found in a quotation of the primal assertion of Exod 34:6-7a. The story line of Jonah indicates that such an outcome for the hated and feared empire is contrary to the wish-world of Israelite ideology. Where Yahweh is not simply reduced to an agent of that ideology, such an outcome is possible.

Babylon and Nebuchadnezzar

The third superpower with which Israel had to deal is Babylon, regularly linked to the person of Nebuchadnezzar. The contours of the relationship between Yahweh and Babylon are the ones by now familiar to us: mandate, defiant autonomy, punishment.

The positive mandate given Babylon by Yahweh, on the horizon of Israel's testimony, is especially championed by the tradition of Jeremiah, refracted through the convictions of Deuteronomic circles.[35] Because those circles of political interpreters are ready to comply with Babylonian policy, it does not surprise us that the tradition of Jeremiah understands Babylon (and Nebuchadnezzar), in their onslaught against Jerusalem, to be doing Yahweh's bidding (as did Assyria in Isa 10:5). Thus Yahweh, in this testimony, refers to Nebuchadnezzar as "my servant" (Jer 25:9, 27:6). Nebuchadnezzar, moreover, is expected to show mercy toward Judah congruent with Yahweh's own propensity:[36]

> Do not be afraid to serve the Chaldeans. Stay in the land and serve the king of Babylon, and it shall go well with you.... Do not be afraid of the king of Babylon, as you have been; do not be afraid of him, says the Lord, for I am with you, to save you and to rescue you from his hand. I will grant you mercy, and he will have mercy on you and restore you to your native soil. (Jer 40:9, 42:11-12)

As a tool of Yahweh's measured punishment of Judah, Nebuchadnezzar's role against Judah, it is anticipated, will also be measured and limited. Thus Yahweh and Nebuchadnezzar are allied, with an agreed-upon policy that is severe but not without limit and restraint.

The actual working out of Babylonian policy, however, reflects no such restraint, no mercy congruent with the intended mercy of Yahweh. Predictably the erstwhile ally of Yahweh is indicted by Yahweh as a recalcitrant vassal and an arrogant violator of Yahweh's sovereign intention for Judah, as for Babylon. Thus the Book of Jeremiah, so long supportive of Babylonian policy as reflective of Yahweh's intention, culminates in a savage, extended oracle against Babylon (chapters 50–51).[37] There is, in Judah, gleeful anticipation of Babylon's fall:

> Declare among the nations and proclaim,
> set up a banner and proclaim,
> do not conceal it, say:
> Babylon is taken,
> Bel is put to shame,
> Merodach is dismayed.
> Her images are put to shame,
> her idols are dismayed. (Jer 50:2)

---

35. On the ideological struggle with Babylonian policy in the Book of Jeremiah, see Christopher R. Seitz, *Theology in Conflict: Reactions to the Exile in the Book of Jeremiah* (BZAW 176; Berlin: de Gruyter, 1986).

36. See Walter Brueggemann, "At the Mercy of Babylon: A Subversive Rereading of the Empire," *JBL* 110 (1991) 3–22.

37. On this text, see Alice Ogden Bellis, *The Structure and Composition of Jeremiah 50:2–51:58* (New York: Edwin Mellen, 1994).

Moreover, the nation from the north (50:3) that will take Babylon will be cruel and will show "no mercy" (50:42), just as Babylon had shown no mercy on Judah (Jer 6:23). Superpowers like Babylon have a Yahwistic warrant in geopolitics, according to this witness, but a Yahwistic restraint applies to them, beyond which they cannot go in brutalizing autonomy.

Thus after the mandate of Yawheh to Nebuchadnezzar, the recurrent theme in Israel's testimony concerning Babylon is indictment and sentence: the destruction of the superpower as the implementation of Yahweh's sovereign will for world history. Two texts from the tradition of Isaiah bear on this theme. In Isaiah 13–14, Babylon is invested with primordial, promethean power and significance, in which Babylon stands as a bold, mythic alternative and contrast to Yahweh. The ambition of autonomous Babylon is transparent:

> You said in your heart,
> "I will ascend to heaven;
> I will raise my throne
> above the stars of God;
> I will sit on the mount of assembly
> on the heights of Zaphon;
> I will ascend to the tops of the clouds,
> I will make myself like the Most High." (Isa 14:13-14)

But the one who anticipates "ascending to heaven" will in fact be brought low:

> But you are brought down to Sheol,
> to the depths of the Pit. (v. 15)

Such pretensions to power and ambition are workable in a world of raw power and unashamed might. The testimony of Israel, however, counters such a representation of reality with an insistence that raw power and unashamed might are never unchecked, but are always and everywhere subject to the will and restraint of Yahweh. Because of Yahweh's metahistory, the mighty must surely fall.

The tradition of Isaiah had already waxed eloquent about the exalted being humbled, the high being made low. The initial poetry on the theme concerns Israel:

> The haughtiness of people shall be humbled,
> and the pride of everyone shall be brought low;
> and the Lord alone will be exalted on that day. (Isa 2:17)

Now, however, the issues concern the superpower Babylon. Yahweh will cause a reversal with the superpower, as Yahweh has caused it with beloved Israel. In the tradition of Isaiah, Babylon is the quintessential embodiment of pride and autonomy that must surely fail.

This sequence of Yahweh's action toward Babylon (which parallels Isa 10:5-19 concerning Assyria) is succinctly expressed in Isa 47:6-9:

- Mandate from Yahweh:
  I was angry with my people,
  I profaned my heritage;
  I gave them into your hand, ...

- Failure of the mandate and consequent indictment:
  ... you showed them no mercy;
  on the aged you made your yoke exceedingly heavy.
  You said, "I shall be mistress forever,"
  so that you did not lay these things to heart
  or remember their end.

- Sentence:
  ... both these things shall come upon you
  in a moment, in one day;
  the loss of children and widowhood
  shall come upon you in full measure,
  in spite of your many sorceries
  and the great power of your enchantments. ...
  But evil shall come upon you,
  which you cannot charm away;
  disaster shall fall upon you,
  which you will not be able to ward off,
  and ruin shall come on you suddenly,
  of which you know nothing. (Isa 47:6-7, 9, 11)

As in Isa 10:6 with Assyria, Babylon did not stay within its mandate from Yahweh. Babylon failed to show the mercy required (cf. Jer 40:9, 42:11-12). As a consequence, Babylon, a power willed to proximate power by Yahweh, forfeits power by overstepping Yahwistic restraint. The pivotal notion is mercy. Of course, no mention of showing mercy had been made to Babylon (as no mention had been made to Assyria in Isaiah 10). Indeed this invading people is initially summoned for "no mercy" (Jer 6:23). But, according to Israel's testimony, Nebuchadnezzar should have known. He was, after all, dealing with Yahweh and with Yahweh's beloved people. Yahweh was angry (*qsph*), to be sure, but anger is not Yahweh's final intention. Nebuchadnezzar was not told; but he should have known. For not knowing, the "glory and grandeur" that was Babylon must end.

That much is conventional in Israel's testimony about this third superpower, but the testimony of Israel cannot finish so simply with Babylon, as it tended to do with Egypt and Assyria. In the Book of Daniel, oddly enough, Nebuchadnezzar resurfaces, now surely as a dehistoricized cipher for world power in general and for the abusive belated Hellenistic rulers in particular. What is odd about this articulation of Nebuchadnezzar is that Yahweh's relation to Nebuchadnezzar, as given here, is not flat and predictable, but remarkably nuanced and differentiated.

We may pay particular attention to two extended narratives. First in Daniel 3, Israel bears testimony that the king who was nullified for his autonomy is transformed into a worshiper of Yahweh. This narrative does not move through the conventional sequence of mandate-indictment-judgment; the narrative shows the rehabilitation of the king, from one crazed with self-importance, into an acceptable, willing subject of Yahweh. The story moves in three clear dramatic scenes:

(a) At the outset, Nebuchadnezzar is a shameless, autonomous ruler:

> You are commanded, O peoples, nations, and languages, that when you hear the sound of the horn, pipe, lyre, trigon, harp, drum, and entire musical ensemble, you are to fall down and worship the golden statue that King Nebuchadnezzar has set up. Whoever does not fall down and worship shall immediately be thrown into a furnace of blazing fire. (Dan 3:4-6)

(b) Nebuchadnezzar must deal with the three representative Jews, Shadrach, Meshach, and Abednego, and is foiled by them as a result of their intense faith (vv. 8-27).

(c) Out of that bewildering encounter, Nebuchadnezzar is completely converted, and issues as a decree a doxology to their God:

> Blessed be the God of Shadrach, Meshach, and Abednego, who has sent his angel and delivered his servants who trusted in him. They disobeyed the king's command and yielded up their bodies rather than serve and worship any god except their own God. Therefore I make a decree: Any people, nation, or language that utters blasphemy against the God of Shadrach, Meshach, and Abednego shall be torn limb from limb, and their houses laid in ruins; for there is no other god who is able to deliver in this way. (vv. 28-29)

The importance and the astonishing character of this narrative is that it breaks the simple pattern of judgment against the nation, and allows for the reconstitution of a superpower obedient to the God of Israel. According to this testimony, Yahweh is not, in principle, opposed to superpowers, but only to those that disregard the mandate of heaven and arrogate to themselves ultimate power and authority. It is deeply ironic that for this remarkable assertion of Yahweh's relation to worldly power, the testimony of Israel focuses on Nebuchadnezzar, the one who presided over the pivotal dismantling of Israel.

In Daniel 4 the same sequence of transactions between Yahweh and Nebuchadnezzar is narrated, this time with richer rhetorical flourish.[38] At the outset, Nebuchadnezzar sings praise to the Most High God:

> How great are his signs,
> how mighty his wonders!

_____

38. See Walter Brueggemann, *Finally Comes the Poet: Daring Speech for Proclamation* (Philadelphia: Fortress Press, 1989) 111-42.

> His kingdom is an everlasting kingdom,
> and his sovereignty is from generation to generation. (v. 3)

The subsequent narrative tells how this extraordinary doxological commitment has come to be on the lips of the Babylonian king. The narrative is a complicated one, featuring a dream and its interpretation (vv. 4-27), and then the implementation of the dream (vv. 28-37). The story line is, as we have seen in chapter 3:

(a) Nebuchadnezzar is sure in his self-congratulations (4:29-31).

(b) Nebuchadnezzar is profoundly debilitated, as the dream had anticipated (vv. 31-33).

(c) His reason returns (v. 34a), issuing in doxology to "the Most High," and in the restoration and enhancement of his rule (vv. 34b-37).

Thus the story of Nebuchadnezzar is no longer one of mandate-disobedience-punishment; now it is autonomy-demise-restoration.

In this narrative of the "humiliation and exaltation" of Nebuchadnezzar, we may notice two decisive utterances by Daniel, who in this narrative enacts the claims of Israel's faith. First, Daniel repeatedly affirms that: "the Most High is sovereign over the kingdom of mortals; he gives it to whom he will and sets over it the lowliest of human beings" (4:17, cf. vv. 25, 32). Yahweh, not Nebuchadnezzar, is sovereign and is the one who establishes proximate sovereignty in the earth. All worldly power is provisional, derivative, and penultimate, and may be given and taken away by the authority of Yahweh. Indeed, Yahweh is completely free in actions concerning world power, and need conform to no worldly expectation:

> All the inhabitants of the earth are accounted as nothing,
> and he does what he wills with the host of heaven
> and the inhabitants of the earth.
> There is no one who can stay his hand
> or say to him, "What are you doing?" (v. 35)

The Israelite answer to this rhetorical question, from beginning to end, is:

> ...no one...can stay his hand
> or say to him, "What are you doing?"

Second, Daniel urges the king, still in his crazed autonomy, to practice "mercy to the oppressed" (v. 27). This is the mercy that Jeremiah (40:9, 42:10-12) anticipated from Babylon, and that in Isa 47:6 is noticed as absent in Babylonian policy. It is characteristically Jewish to assert that world power is entrusted with mercy, even as Yahweh's own governance is endlessly rearticulated in mercy. This counsel of Daniel is, at the end, reiterated in Nebuchadnezzar's own mouth:

> Now I, Nebuchadnezzar, praise and extol and honor
> the King of heaven;
> for all his works are truth,
> and all his ways are justice;
> and he is able to bring low
> those who walk in pride. (v. 37)

Nebuchadnezzar has caught on! The one who rules the nations rules in truth and in justice (cf. Ps 96:10, 13), and even the model superpower now accepts this inescapable reality. The rehabilitation of Nebuchadnezzar, in this astonishing redefinition of world power, is fully authorized by Yahweh, when the king of Babylon conforms to the reality of Yahweh's own nonnegotiable intention.

Persia: Positive, Responsive Partner

The fourth and final superpower with whom Israel had to deal is Persia. Persian policy and influence were profound on the shaping of Judaism. Our knowledge of this relationship is only now being seriously addressed as a major issue in Old Testament interpretation. It is clear, moreover, that the rhetoric and imagination of the Old Testament are not evoked by Persia in the way that the previous superpowers had done. Thus, even though the Persian empire is crucial for the shaping of Judaism, it does not figure so largely in matters that concern theological interpretation.

We may therefore confine ourselves to two sorts of statements concerning Yahweh's relation to Persia. First, as with Assyria (Isa 10:5) and Babylon (Jer 25:6, 27:6), Persia is understood in Israelite testimony to be a world power designated by Yahweh to overthrow its predecessor, in this case Babylon, and thereby to permit a Jewish homecoming from exile. In Jer 51:41-42, "a people coming from the north" surely is Persia, who is to be "cruel and without mercy" toward Babylon. Persia now is assigned the role, in Yahwistic purview, previously assigned to Babylon. The accent in Israel's unsolicited testimony, however, is not on Persian treatment of Babylon, but on the role to be played by Persia as the rescuer of Israel.

The two central and most remarkable texts are in Isaiah of the exile:

> Thus says the Lord, your Redeemer,
> who formed you in the womb:
> I am the Lord, who made all things,
> who alone stretched out the heavens,
> who by myself spread out the earth;
> who frustrates the omens of liars,
> and makes fools of diviners;
> who turns back the wise, and makes their knowledge foolish;
> who confirms the word of his servant,
> and fulfills the prediction of his messengers; who says of Jerusalem, "It
> shall be inhabited,"

and of the cities of Judah, "They shall be rebuilt,
and I will raise up their ruins";
who says to the deep, "Be dry—
I will dry up your rivers";
who says of Cyrus, "He is my shepherd,
and he shall carry out all my purpose";
and who says of Jerusalem, "It shall be rebuilt,"
and of the temple, "Your foundation shall be laid." (Isa 44:24-28)

Thus says the Lord to his anointed, to Cyrus,
whose right hand I have grasped
to subdue nations before him
and strip kings of their robes,
to open doors before him—
and the gates shall not be closed:
I will go before you
and level the mountains,
I will break in pieces the doors of bronze
and cut through the bars of iron,
I will give you the treasures of darkness
and riches hidden in secret places,
so that you may know that it is I, the Lord,
the God of Israel, who calls you by your name.
For the sake of my servant Jacob,
and Israel my chosen,
I call you by your name,
I surname you, though you do not know me.
I am the Lord, and there is no other;
beside me there is no god.
I arm you, though you do not know me,
so that they may know, from the rising of the sun
and from the west, that there is no one besides me;
I am the Lord, and there is no other.
I form light and create darkness,
I make weal and create woe;
I the Lord do all these things. (Isa 45:1-7)

It is necessary to consider these more extended texts because of the references to Cyrus, the first and for Israel the most decisive of the Persian kings and the one who destroyed the kingdom of Babylon. In the first of these texts, Yahweh's dictum authorizing Cyrus (44:28) occurs in a sequence of sovereign utterances of Yahweh that concern, most broadly, creation and, most explicitly, the rebuilding of Jerusalem. That is, the rebuilding of Jerusalem is rhetorically on a par with creation. Cyrus, moreover, is "my shepherd" (v. 28), a term regularly reserved in Israel for

Davidic kings. Thus Cyrus is positioned in terms of Israel's creation theology and in line with royal theology.

The second oracle is more astonishing on two counts. First, Cyrus is "his messiah" (v. 1; the Hebrew word can be rendered "anointed"). The rhetoric reassigns a Davidic title to Cyrus, who now becomes the carrier of Israel's most urgent hopes. Israel's theological horizon now reaches well beyond itself, into the gentile world, in order to locate the continuing working of Yahweh's saving intention. Second, this oracle is directly addressed to Cyrus by Yahweh, "though you do not know me" (v. 4), "so that you may know..." (v. 3). The address to Cyrus may be fictive and strategic for Israel's hope in exile. Nonetheless, Yahweh is willing, according to this rhetoric, to engage this foreign ruler, as with the Assyrians and Babylonians before him, to do a work that enhances Israel.

Thus concerning Persia as partner of Yahweh, Israel employs remarkable theological rhetoric in order to define Persia (and Cyrus) as Yahweh's agent in the world of international power. As we have it in the testimony, moreover, Persia does effectively implement the restorative policies of Yahweh. It is true, at least to some extent, that Persian imperial policy was more respectful of local traditions (including local Jewish traditions) than were the Assyrians or Babylonians.[39] And it is beyond doubt that this articulation of Persia is done through the testimony of those most sympathetic to and dependent on Persian beneficence to the Jewish community. In any case, this testimony portrays Persia as a patron of a recovering Jewish cult in Jerusalem, as is evident in the testimony given by Haggai and Zechariah and in the reform movement of Ezra and Nehemiah, financed by Persia (cf. Ezra 1:2-4, 6:3-5, 2 Chr 36:23).

The political-theological claim made for the Persians is telling:

> So the elders of the Jews built and prospered, through the prophesying of the prophet Haggai and Zechariah son of Iddo. They finished building by command of the God of Israel and by decree of Cyrus, Darius, and King Artaxerxes of Persia.... (Ezra 6:14)

The cruciality of Persian support for the reconstructive work of Yahwism is indicated by the fact that in much of this literature, time is reckoned by Persian royal chronology, a concession not granted by Israel to any other superpower.

We may finally mention that Dan 6:1-28 presents testimony in which (a) Daniel is protected by God, and (b) the Persians are deferential to Daniel and to the God of Daniel. In the end, Darius issues a doxological decree:

> For he is the living God,
> enduring forever.
> His kingdom shall never be destroyed,
> and his dominion has no end.

---

39. On Persian policy as a reversal of Babylonian policy, see Daniel L. Smith, *The Religion of the Landless: The Social Context of the Babylonian Exile* (Bloomington, Ind.: Meyer-Stone, 1989).

> He delivers and rescues,
> he works signs and wonders in heaven and on earth;
> for he has saved Daniel
> from the power of the lions. (Dan 6:26-27)

Darius the Persian is able to enter fully into praise of the God of Israel. Compared to the complicated and vexed story of Yahweh with the Egyptians, the Assyrians, and the Babylonians, the story of Yahweh with the Persians lacks drama. On the horizon of this testimony, the Persians are not recalcitrant vassals of Yahweh, need not be broken by Yahweh, and so need no Yahwistic recovery. In this modeling of nations as partners, Persia is the exemplar of a positive, responsive partner.[40]

The Possibility of Legitimate Power in the World of Yahweh

We are now in a position to summarize and schematize the data concerning Yahweh's relationship to these four superpowers. Our attempt to do this, of course, depends on piecing together bits of testimony that do not easily or intentionally form a pattern. Without suggesting that the articulation of these several partnerships is everywhere the same, we may roughly suggest the tendency in Israel's testimony as shown in the chart on the following page.

Even if things are not perfectly symmetrical, this presentation of Yahweh and Yahweh's partners constitutes a remarkable sketch. We may make the following observations on these data.

Yahweh's mandate. Yahweh intends that there should be world powers, and that these world powers should indeed govern, but govern within the bounds of Yahweh's mandate. The mandate variously consists in special consideration for Israel and occasionally the more generic practice of human civility. Thus Egyptian prosperity is verified by Jacob's blessing (Gen 47:7-10), Assyria is mandated to be a devastating power (Isa 10:5-6, 37:26-27), Babylon is given a mandate by Yahweh (Jer 25:9, 27:6; Isa 47:6a) and is crowned with well-being (Dan 4:19-22). Persia is given a mandate unlike that of Assyria and Babylon, for now the purpose of the mandate from Yahweh is the rehabilitation of Jerusalem. The Old Testament witness is explicit in voicing Yahweh's powerful, positive interest in the public process.

Temptation to absolutize power. The seduction to autonomy, which is assigned in this testimony to the first three of these superpowers, is the temptation to absolutize power that appears to be absolute but is not. Clearly such absolutizing is impossible in a world where Yahweh's sovereignty is said to be beyond challenge.

---

40. On the large panorama of the nations in the Book of Daniel, see Martin Noth, "The Understanding of History in Old Testament Apocalyptic," *The Laws in the Pentateuch and Other Essays* (London: Oliver and Boyd, 1966) 194–214.

Taxonomy of Yahweh's Relationship to Four Superpowers

	Mandate	*Autonomous Rebellion*	*Dismantling*	*Rehabilitation*
Egypt	Gen 47:7-10 (all of Exodus 5–15)	Exod 5:2 Ezek 29:3 (all of Ezekiel 29–32)	Exod 15:4-10 Isa 19:23-25[41]	Ezek 32:31?
Assyria	Isa 10:5-6 Isa 37:26-27	Isa 10:7-14 Isa 37:29a	Isa 10:15-19 Isa 37:29b	Isa 19:23-25 Jonah
Babylon	Jer 25:9, 27:6 Isa 47:6a Dan 4:19-22	Isa 47:6b-8 Isa 14:13-14 Dan 3:4-6 4:29-30	Isa 47:9, 11 Isa 14:15 Dan 3:23-27, 31-33	Dan 4:34-37
Persia	Isa 44:24-28 45:1-7			

Decisive break in power. In the case of the first three superpowers we have considered, there is a decisive break in their power. In world history great kingdoms rise and fall. What is noteworthy in this testimony, and not everywhere self-evident, is that no explanation for the fall of great powers is credited except the governance of Yahweh. Yahweh's sovereignty is partly raw, unchallengeable authority, partly devotion to Israel, and partly intolerance of arrogant injustice. What is important for our purposes is the recognition that this fissure in the life of a great power is completely parallel to the fissure of exile in the life of Israel. Where Yahweh is not obeyed, a decisive break occurs in every individual life and in the life of every community or state. No power can live defiantly in the face of Yahweh's sovereignty.

Hope for recovery. The notion of the recovery of lost power is characteristically an act of hope, not accomplished yet in reportable history. This act of hope, in the largest horizon of world history, is closely parallel to the hope of Israel that is mostly detained and not yet actualized. The hope for Egypt, based on an available reading of Ezek 32:31, is modest indeed, pending one text to which we have yet to come. The hope for Assyria, pending the same text, has broken beyond concrete history and lives in the world of Israel's imaginative rhetoric. The tale of Jonah probably has an agenda quite other than the destiny of Assyria (Nineveh) and is most often interpreted with other accents. That tale does suggest, nonetheless, that even hated Nineveh (Assyria), upon repentance (see Ezek 32:31 on Egypt), is a possible focus of Yahweh's steadfast love. The references to Babylon in the Book of Daniel are especially important on this score, and suggest that Nebuchadnezzar

---

41. It is evident that this rehabilitation is not in hand but is anticipated.

has sanity restored, and his governance as well, when he learns that "the Most High is sovereign over the kingdom of mortals, and gives it to whom he will." This is a hard lesson for the powerful, but it must be learned, according to the witness of Israel. This tale of Nebuchadnezzar, moreover, provides a positive case in that the lesson is indeed learned, to the great advantage of the superpower. Power finally need not be defiant of Yahweh.

Parallels to Yahweh's relation to humans. Finally, the pattern of blessing–breakpoint–restoration is quite like the sequence of ways in which Yahweh relates to Israel, and *mutatis mutandis*, the ways in which Yahweh relates to human persons.

Two Texts of Radical Hope

We come now to two remarkable texts that I have deferred until now. Both concern Yahweh's intention for the nations as it is given us in Israel's testimony. These texts in turn enunciate hope for Israel's "little neighbors," and then for the great superpowers.

Our first text of radical hope for the nations is in Amos 9:7:[42]

> Are you not like the Ethiopians to me,
> O people of Israel? says the Lord.
> Did I not bring Israel up from the land of Egypt,
> and the Philistines from Caphtor
> and the Arameans from Kir?

This odd verse, not closely linked to its immediate context, is apparently uttered in a context of Israel's celebrative self-preoccupation. It is addressed to an Israel that is utterly convinced of its core testimony concerning Yahweh and, derivatively, convinced of its own peculiar role as Yahweh's exclusive partner and as the peculiar object of Yahweh's transformative verbs.

The utterance of this verse in the Amos collection does nothing to undermine or question the positive claim that Yahweh is a God who saves, rescues, and liberates, or that Yahweh has enacted those verbs for Israel. Yahweh's great verbs are affirmed in this prophetic testimony. What is challenged is Israel's attempt to monopolize the verbs, to imagine that as Yahweh is the only Subject of the verbs, so Israel is the only possible object. The Exodus of Israel is fully affirmed: "Did I not bring Israel up from the land of Egypt?"

The stunning departure from self-congratulation is that this testimony makes the same verbs of Yahweh available for other peoples, including Israel's most serious enemies, the Philistines and the Arameans. Indeed, if the Ethiopians are understood as blacks, and so referenced by race, racist bias is here rejected as well as ethnocentrism. What happens in this striking assertion is that *Israel's monopoly on Yahweh is broken.* This does not deny that Israel is a recipient of Yahweh's powerful,

---

42. On this text, see Walter Brueggemann, "'Exodus' in the Plural (Amos 9:7)" (forthcoming in a Westminster John Festschrift).

positive intervention, but it does deny any exclusive claim or any notion that Israel is the singular center of Yahweh's attention. That surely is the force and intention of this utterance.

In our context, however, we may also notice two other claims, perhaps not so intentional, but present nonetheless. First, it is asserted that Israel's closest neighbors, most despised and most feared, are the objects of Yahweh's great verbs and Yahweh's transformative attentiveness. The way in which Israel is treated by Yahweh in the Exodus is the way in which every people may expect to be treated by Yahweh. Second, it is asserted that Yahweh is characteristically and everywhere the subject of the verb "bring up" (*'lh*). Yahweh, who is known in Israel's core testimony by the great verbs, is everywhere the same God as the one known in the core testimony. And because this Exodus God avowedly performs rescues indiscriminately, even among Israel's enemies, all of world history is reconfigured as an arena for Yahweh's great, positive, transformative verbs. All sorts of communities may expect to be the object of those verbs.

Our second concluding text concerns the superpowers. Isaiah 19:23-25 is commonly regarded as late in Israel's imagination, and it surely lives at the edge of Israel's horizon concerning the nations. Nonetheless, it is a piece of Israel's testimony concerning the future of the nations under the sovereignty of Yahweh. The utterance has in purview the whole of the Fertile Crescent. The geopolitical arrangement of the Fertile Crescent is always Egypt in the south and Israel in the vulnerable middle. In this case it is Assyria in the north, though over time the key player in the north changes, even if policies remain much the same. The dynamic of this "map of the world" makes clear that the two superpowers, north and south, Egypt and Assyria, are perpetual enemies, and that Israel is in the middle with two exposed frontiers.[43]

This poetic scenario of Isaiah 19 envisions, "on that day," an end to this perpetual hostility. "On that day," when Yahweh's intention is fulfilled, there will be a free flow of traffic (and no doubt commerce) between these powers, without barriers, customs, tariffs, or hostility. Moreover, there will be common worship, all submitting to a God larger than their own state ideology. The ultimate promise for the nations as partners of Yahweh is the complete end of hostility and the rule of a shared *shalōm*.

In Isa 19:24-25, the vision grows more radical—not only peace and traffic and trade, not only shared worship, but now a positive relationship to Yahweh for all three parties:

> On that day Israel will be the third with Egypt and Assyria, a blessing in the midst of the earth, whom the Lord of hosts has blessed, saying, "Blessed be Egypt my people, and Assyria the work of my hands, and Israel my heritage."

---

43. Nothing has changed geopolitically, even in the present state of Israel. Israel is positioned, even now, so that it must pursue defense and peace on two fronts to the north and to the south. In contemporary political reality, moreover, the northern front is characteristically less stable and more problematic.

This utterance takes up three special names for Israel that are rooted in its peculiar and privileged relationship to Yahweh: "my people," "the work of my hands," and "my heritage." These three names, all heretofore assigned exclusively to Israel, are now distributed across the Fertile Crescent, assigned to people who have been a great threat to Israel and a great vexation to Yahweh. In this daring utterance we witness the process by which other peoples are redesignated to be Yahweh's chosen peoples so that, taken paradigmatically, all peoples become Yahweh's chosen peoples.

In the end, Israel retains one phrase of privilege, "my heritage" (cf. Deut 32:9; Jer 10:16). Thus Israel has lost two of its pet names. The loss must be like the loss when an older child begins to notice that pet names are being reused, now for a new member of the family. This redistribution of names of affection bespeaks a loss of privilege for Israel, as did the assertion of Amos 9:7. It is unmistakable that these two references constitute countertestimony, counter to the unqualified sense of privilege Israel claims for itself vis-à-vis Yahweh in its core testimony. This recognition of countertestimony reminds me, contrary to much of chapter 8 above, that countertestimony is not always negative, but may be healthy and emancipatory, whenever the core testimony becomes ideologically self-serving and self-indulgent. Except that the loss of privilege permits the redefinition of the entire Near East as a safer, more hospitable place. Israel is now permitted to assume a normal role among the nations, without a privilege that always endangers, even as it enhances. This revisioned Near East leaves all of these states not only renamed by a Yahwistic name, but also blessed. The old acrimonies, hostilities, and defiances, in an instant of utterance, become decisively inappropriate and unnecessary. For now the entire geopolitical horizon is brought under the governance of Yahweh's fruitfulness.

It is remarkable that the utterance pertains to the two most despised and perhaps cruelest enemies of Israel. This is the real move beyond the fissure in the life of the nations, taken not in response to their repentance (though I do not discount the significance of Ezek 32:31 and Jonah for the larger drama of the nations), but as a free, unqualified, inexplicable promise of Yahweh. The promise is an invitation to Israel to move beyond itself and its self-serving ideology, to reposition itself in the family of beloved nations, and to reimagine Yahweh, beyond any self-serving, privileged claim, into the largest possible horizon, as the one who intends well-being for all the nations, including the ones formerly defiant and condemned.

Yahweh's Freedom with the Nations

Yahweh does indeed deal with the nations according to Yahweh's own freedom and passion. Yahweh's *freedom* is evident in two dimensions of the grid I have sketched concerning the history and destiny of the nations. First, Yahweh in freedom has the power and capacity to recruit nations for Yahweh's own purposes, even if those purposes are not the intention of the nations, or even if those purposes run against the expectation of Israel. Thus nations are pressed into Yahweh's service, both to punish Israel (Assyria, Babylon), and also to save Israel (Persia). That is, a large intentionality operates in the geopolitical process that runs well beyond and perhaps counter to what the agents of the process themselves imagine. And while it may have been repulsive to have Nebuchadnezzar termed "my servant" (Jer 25:9, 27:6) in the process of nullifying Judah, it was no less abhorrent to have Cyrus termed "his messiah" (Isa 45:1) in support of Judah (cf. Isa 45:9-13). Yahweh's governing capacity is not derivative from or contingent on the intention of the nations, but operates in complete and commanding freedom.

Second, Yahweh's freedom is evident in Yahweh's capacity, according to Israel's unsolicited testimony, to terminate nations, even great superpowers. Thus we would not have imagined, of any of the great superpowers of the time, that they would abruptly drop out of the geopolitical process. Of course, this nullification of power can be explained in a variety of geopolitical terms. But Israel's testimony resolutely intends to offer a peculiar version of reality, which serves to subvert every version of reality that relies finally on sociopolitical or military explanations. In the end, the nations figure in the testimony of Israel as functions and instruments for Yahweh's work in the process of the nations. It is an act of sanity, Israel proposes, when Nebuchadnezzar finally comes to his senses and is able to reimagine and resituate his own proximate power in relation to that of Yahweh:

When that period was over, I, Nebuchadnezzar, lifted my eyes
to heaven, and my reason returned to me.

I blessed the Most High,
and praised and honored the one who lives forever.
For his sovereignty is an everlasting sovereignty,
and his kingdom endures from generation to generation.
All the inhabitants of the earth are accounted as nothing,
and he does what he wills with the host of heaven
and the inhabitants of the earth.
There is no one who can stay his hand
or say to him, "What are you doing?" (Dan 4:34-35; cf. Jer 49:19)

It is much less explicit that Yahweh's governance of the nations is marked as much by *passion* as it is by freedom. Here we move in the realm of inference, but we must at least ponder the rehabilitative utterances of Yahweh concerning the nations, which we have noticed in Amos 9:7, Isa 19:23-25, Isa 56:3, 6-7, and Jonah. In each of these, Yahweh makes a positive move toward the nations, for which there seems to be no evident motivation. The texts do not explicitly indicate any positive passion on Yahweh's part toward the nations.[44] Knowing what we know about Yahweh's passion toward Israel, however, we may at least wonder if there are not inchoate hints in these texts that "God so loved the world"—the world of the nations.

---

44. The Book of Jonah is an important exception to both of these statements: (a) There is an evident motivation in Nineveh's repentance, and (b) there is an allusion to Yahweh's passion in 4:2, with reference to Yahweh's steadfast love and compassion.

Thus in Amos 9:7, we are told of multiple exoduses worked by Yahweh. We are not told that the Philistines or the Arameans groaned and cried out, as did Israel in Exod 2:23, but we may entertain the notion that something like that happened. Indeed the remarkable promise made to Egypt in Isa 19:23-25 is preceded by an equally remarkable assertion concerning Egypt in vv. 20-21:

> ...when they cry to the Lord because of oppressors, he will send them a savior, and will defend and deliver them. The Lord will make himself known to the Egyptians; and the Egyptians will know the Lord on that day, and will worship with sacrifice and burnt offering, and they will make vows to the Lord and perform them.

Since Exod 11:6, 12:23, Egypt has had to "cry out." Here Yahweh hears and answers. Such a usage is of course remote from the Exodus narrative. The connection, however, indicates how all of Israel's memory is available and usable in the ongoing work of testimony. But we do know that when Yahweh utters such a promise over Israel, it is because Yahweh is moved, either by old commitments or by present troubles.

We may wonder, moreover, if the same motivations operate here with the nations. In the formula for the inclusion of foreigners in Isa 56:3-6, Herbert Donner has seen that the text directly challenges the Torah provision of Deut 23:2-8.[45] We do not know why. But the culminating assertion of Isa 56:7 suggests that Yahweh has finally an inclusive propensity:

> ...these I will bring to my holy mountain,
> and make them joyful in my house of prayer;
> their burnt offerings and their sacrifices
> will be accepted on my altar;
> for my house shall be called a house of prayer
> for all peoples.

Positive assertion on the part of Yahweh nullifies the old exclusion of Israel's enemies. Yahweh, belatedly, appears here to accept Israel's ancient enemies as legitimate candidates for membership in the covenant. In the narrative of Jonah, moreover, a dramatic act of repentance on the part of Nineveh authorizes and evokes Yahweh's positive and forgiving response (3:5-10). The protest of Jonah, however, suggests that even the repentance of Nineveh would not have been sufficient cause for forgiveness and acceptance, unless Yahweh were already "a gracious God" (4:2). That is, with the most recalcitrant of nation-partners, Yahweh acts in a characteristic rehabilitative way, moving beyond the harshness of rejecting sovereignty, in order to reembrace the established enemy.

In all of these cases, the move beyond judgment and nullification toward new national possibility is rooted in Yahweh's freedom, freedom to restore an enemy.

---

45. Donner, "Jesaja LVI 1-7: Ein Abrogationsfalls innerhalb des Kanons," 81–95.

But more is at work in these instances than unfettered freedom. There is also, it appears to me, a predilection toward forgiveness, restoration, and rehabilitation, propelled by an old and enduring positive concern and not undercut even by resistance and rebellion. I do not want to overstate this point, but these odd and intriguing verses are indeed present in Israel's testimony. These texts suggest that, at the edge of Israel's notice, and therefore at the edge of Yahweh's propensity, free sovereignty is given a cast that has the marking of enduring, responsive commitment.

Yahweh in Geopolitical Scope

It is not usual for the nations to figure so prominently in an Old Testament theology, as I have taken time and space to do here. That decision on my part warrants an explanatory comment. I judge "the nations" as partner to Yahweh's sovereignty and pathos to be important for our consideration for two reasons. First, *attention to the texts corrects the easy impression that the Old Testament is singularly preoccupied with Yahweh's powerful commitment to Israel.* To a great extent it is true that Israel is the singular topic of Yahweh's sovereignty and freedom in this testimony. To that extent, Israel's testimony is an interpretive comment about itself. But this claim of centrality for Israel needs to be sharply qualified. Israel does not live in a sociopolitical vacuum. Israel is always in the presence of more powerful nations that impinge on Israel's life and destiny in uninvited ways. Moreover, Yahweh has a rich field of engagement with the nations. Some of that engagement is conditioned by the centrality of Israel in this articulation of world history, but much of it is not. According to this testimony, Yahweh's concern with the nations is not shaped or determined simply by the needs and propensities of Israel. Yahweh has Yahweh's own life to live, and it will not be monopolized by Israel. This recognition requires something of a rearticulation both of Israel who is not alone the partner of Yahweh, and of Yahweh who is not exclusively committed to Israel.

The second reason I have taken so much time and energy on this topic is a contemporary interpretive concern. Over the long haul of the Enlightenment, Western Christianity has been progressively privatized in terms of individuals, families, and domestic communities. By and large, out of bewilderment and embarrassment, the ecclesial communities have forgotten how to speak about national and international matters, except in times of war to mobilize God for "the war effort." The inevitable outcome of this privatization is to relinquish geopolitics to practical, technical analysis, as in Joseph Stalin's cynical question, "How many divisions has the Pope?" That is, *if the theological dimension drops out of international purview, and with it any credible, critical moral dimension, then the world becomes one in which might makes right.* To some extent, that is what has happened among us, because Yahwistic rhetoric in this arena of life strikes any modern person as mindless supernaturalism.

Two matters suggest to me that, in terms of theological intentionality, the coming turn of the millennium is a circumstance in which we may courageously reconsider the forfeiture of Yahwistic rhetoric. First, the studies of Paul Kennedy,

The Rise and Fall of the Great Powers, and (to a lesser extent) of Douglas Johnston and Cynthia Sampson, *Religion: The Missing Dimension of Statecraft,* invite such reconsideration.[46] Kennedy's book makes the remarkable argument that military power, if cut off from the realities of territory, population, and natural and economic resources, brings devastation to a nation-state. Kennedy's book is a cold, social scientific analysis, and Kennedy apparently would resist any move to introduce a moral dimension into his calculus. It occurs to me, however, that Kennedy's analysis, given in very different categories, is not far removed from prophetic analysis. It is the characteristic urging of Israel's prophets that arrogant nations, which overreach in imagined self-sufficiency, operate autonomously at their own peril. Yahweh, in this rhetoric, is a critical principle of restraint, which arrests both self-aggrandizement and brutality in the service of self-aggrandizement.

The book by Johnston and Sampson is much less satisfying, because it is concerned with what appear to me calculated dimensions of religious rhetoric that appeal to prudence more than to any more profound critical principle. Nonetheless, their consideration of the general theme suggests that any discernment of power that eliminates moral issues is inadequate. This is not simply a matter of rhetoric, but it is a substantive question about whether any restraints and sanctions are operative in the geopolitical process. Given our long-term Enlightenment silence on the question, it is at this juncture worth recognizing that Israel had no doubt on this interpretive issue.

The second reason for reconsidering the forfeiture of Yahwistic rhetoric concerns the immediate context of interpretation at the end of the twentieth century. No interpreter can fail to notice the extraordinary demise of the Soviet Union, the remarkable, relatively nonviolent end of apartheid in South Africa, and the apparent opening of ideological intransigence in Northern Ireland and in contemporary Israel vis-à-vis the Palestinians. Interpretation now takes place in a context of the astounding reordering of power in the world. The issues are enormously complex, of course, and no doubt many factors, some visible and some hidden, have been at work in these turns of power. I do not propose any theological naiveté about a theo-moral dimension to these matters.

One may, nonetheless, after the manner of Israel's unsolicited testimony, entertain the thought that the resilient intention of Yahweh for justice in the world is at work. That resolve for justice, which negatively limits raw power and which positively emboldens advocates of justice, can indeed be delayed by terror, intimidation, and brutality. At the turn of the century, we may reraise the question in light of undoubted delay: Can that impetus for justice that Israel finds rooted in Yahweh's own resolve be fully stopped? Perhaps one may suggest that theological rhetoric, even as it can be recruited for repressive purposes, also was, in these most recent cases, near the heart of the turn of power. That is, God-talk is not mere strategic

46. Paul M. Kennedy, *The Rise and Fall of the Great Powers: Economic Change and Military Conflict from 1500 to 2000* (New York: Random House, 1987); Douglas Johnston and Cynthia Sampson, *Religion: The Missing Dimension of Statecraft* (Oxford: Oxford University Press, 1994).

rhetoric, though it may be that. It is also an utterance of a substantive claim that a crucial force is embedded in geopolitics that is beyond conventional manipulation.

Having said that about our contemporary circumstance of interpretation, I offer two addenda. First, surely the Holocaust places an awesome question mark over any claim of a moral dimension in world history. Continued reflection on that unutterable event continues to revolve precisely around that issue. And at least the analysis of Zygmunt Bauman, *Modernity and Holocaust,* understands even Holocaust as an extreme articulation of uncriticized, unchecked moral autonomy.[47]

Second, most readers of this exposition of Old Testament theology will be citizens of the United States, "the last superpower," which has survived and prospered until the very "End of History."[48] I intend that my analysis of Yahweh and the nations should finally settle in the presence of the United States, which has no viable competitor for power, and which is in an economic, military position to imagine, like Egypt, that it produces its own Nile. The good news is that there is a residue of moral awareness in the ethos of the United States. The threat to that good news is that economic ideology and military self-justification tend easily and eagerly to override that residue of awareness. In such a situation one may wonder: Have we arrived at last at a nation-state that is finally immune to this witness of metapolitics, so that we come to a point in which Israel's witness is seen to be outmoded or self-deceived rhetoric? Or is the United States, like every superpower before it, on notice? Liberal autonomy is certainly the primary alternative in the modern world to this ancient insistence on covenantalism. Israel makes its testimony in a courtroom of competing testimonies. I imagine that this ancient witness would judge liberal autonomy to be nothing new, but one often and anciently utilized in the service of self-deceiving self-sufficiency.

---

47. Zygmunt Bauman, *Modernity and Holocaust* (Cambridge, England: Polity Press, 1991). See also Richard Rubenstein, *After Auschwitz: History, Theology, and Contemporary Judaism* (2d ed.; Baltimore: Johns Hopkins University Press, 1992).

48. On this insensitive and arrogant claim for the United States, see Francis Fukuyama, *The End of History and the Last Man* (New York: Free Press, 1992).

SEVENTEEN

Creation as Yahweh's Partner

I NOW CONSIDER the most expansive horizon of Israel's testimony concerning the transactional quality of Yahweh's life. Yahweh takes creation—the whole known, visible world—to be Yahweh's partner. This is of course a commonplace of theology, because Genesis 1–2 is perhaps the most familiar text in our culture. But the character of the relationship between Creator and creation is not so obvious as familiarity with the theme might suggest. The transactional quality of this relationship is what must concern us, but it has been covered over and made invisible, both by the reductionism of church theology and by the confusion of creation with the categories of "natural science."[1] As we have seen with Israel's unsolicited testimony about the human person as Yahweh's partner and the nations as Yahweh's partner, in this case as well it seems clear that Israel's own lived experience and sense of itself vis-à-vis Yahweh matter greatly in determining how Israel bears witness to creation. As with the other partners, creation as Yahweh's partner is read through Israel's sense of itself.

A World Blessed and Fruitful

Creation, the network of living organisms that provides a viable context and "home" for the human community, is an outcome of Yahweh's generous, sovereign freedom.[2] No reason is given for Yahweh's unutterable act of forming an earth that is viable for life. I have already considered the ways in which Israel speaks about Yahweh's creating activity.[3] Here I focus on the outcome of that generous

---

1. Reductionism in church theology in a conservative, fundamentalist way has been especially noted by Mark A. Noll, *The Scandal of the Evangelical Mind* (Grand Rapids: Eerdmans, 1994). While his analysis pertains to the reductionism of the right, the same may be said of the left in church theology; on which see Stephen Sykes, "Authority in the Church of England," *Unashamed Anglicanism* (Nashville: Abingdon Press, 1995) 163–77. On pp. 195–97, Sykes comments on "authoritarian liberalism." Moreover, Jon Levenson, *Creation and the Persistence of Evil: The Jewish Drama of Divine Omnipotence* (San Francisco: Harper and Row, 1988), has noted a like reductionism in Jewish theology, with reference to Yehezkel Kaufmann. On creationism and its confusion of categories, see Langdon B. Gilkey, *Creationism on Trial: Evolution and God at Little Rock* (Minneapolis: Winston Press, 1985).

2. I speak of "human home" because that seems to be how the issue is articulated in Israel's testimony. It is self-evident that creation is a home for all creatures, including nonhuman creatures. See Ps 104:14-23 and, negatively, Eccl 3:18-20.

3. See pp. 145–64.

activity. I have also heretofore concluded, along with a consensus of Old Testament scholarship, that Israel's horizon of creation is not *ex nihilo*.[4] That is, Yahweh did not create the world where there was nothing. Rather Yahweh so ordered the "preexistent material substratum," which was wild, disordered, destructive, and chaotic, to make possible an ordered, reliable place of peaceableness and viability.[5] This act of ordering is an act of sovereignty on the largest scale, whereby Yahweh's good intention for life imposes a will on destructive, recalcitrant forces and energies. The outcome, according to Israel's testimony, is a place of fruitfulness, abundance, productivity, extravagance—all terms summed up in the word *blessing*. Thus in Gen 1:28, at the center of that first great chapter, Yahweh asserts, in a mood of authorization:

> God blessed them, and God said to them, "Be fruitful and multiply, and fill the earth and subdue it; and have dominion over the fish of the sea and over the birds of the air and over every living thing that moves upon the earth."

It is Yahweh's will for this newly ordered world that it should be fruitful, invested with "the power of fertility."[6] Yahweh has authorized in the world the inscrutable force of generosity, so that the earth can sustain all its members, and so that the earth has within itself the capacity for sustenance, nurture, and regeneration. This capacity for generosity is no human monopoly; it is assured that every genus and species of creation can "bring forth," according to its kind.

The evident wonder and inexplicable gift of blessing evokes in Israel awed doxology, which is the appropriate response to the miracle of creation that enacts Yahweh's will for life:

> The heavens are telling the glory of God;
> and the firmament proclaims his handiwork.
> Day to day pours forth speech,
> and night to night declares knowledge.
> There is no speech, nor are there words;
> their voice is not heard;
> yet their voice goes out through all the earth,
> and their words to the ends of the world. (Ps 19:1-4)[7]

---

4. On the issue of creation *ex nihilo*, see p. 158.

5. See Levenson, *Creation and the Persistence of Evil*, 5.

6. See Claus Westermann, *Creation* (London: SPCK, 1974) 49, and Walter Harrelson, *From Fertility Cult to Worship: A Reassessment for the Modern Church of the Worship of Ancient Israel* (Garden City, N.Y.: Doubleday, 1969).

7. This text is often cited as a basis of natural theology, whereby creation itself "reveals" Yahweh. See James Barr, *Biblical Faith and Natural Theology: The Gifford Lectures for 1991* (Oxford: Clarendon Press, 1993) 85–89; and Rolf P. Knierim, *The Task of Old Testament Theology: Substance, Method, and Cases* (Grand Rapids: Eerdmans, 1995) 322–50. It is to be noted, nonetheless, that the utterance of the psalm is on the lips of Israel. Without Israel's awed doxology, the testimony of "nature" is not direct or explicit. I will not say it is mute, but in any practical way, this witness depends on Israel.

> The earth is the Lord's and all that is in it,
> the world, and those who live in it;
> he has founded it on the seas,
> and established it on the rivers. (Ps 24:1-2)

Psalm 104 provides the fullest and most extensive Israelite witness to creation, as a dynamic operation of life-giving blessing:

> You cause the grass to grow for the cattle,
> and plants for people to use,
> to bring forth food for the earth,
> and wine to gladden the human heart,
> oil to make the face shine,
> and bread to strengthen the human heart.
> The trees of the Lord are watered abundantly,
> the cedars of Lebanon that he planted.
> In them the birds build their nests;
> the stork has its home in the fir trees.
> The high mountains are for the wild goats;
> the rocks are a refuge for the coneys.
> You have made the moon to mark the seasons;
> the sun knows its time for setting.
> You make the darkness, and it is night,
> when all the animals of the forest come creeping out.
> The young lions roar for their prey,
> seeking their food from God.
> When the sun rises, they withdraw
> and lie down in their dens.
> People go out to their work
> and to their labor until the evening. (Ps 104:14-23)

All creation, including human creatures but not especially human creatures, are looked after, cared for, sustained, and protected by the generous guarantees that the Creator has embedded in the creation. Israel is dazzled.

This emphasis on generativity, which is expressed in largest scope, is also made intimate and concrete in Israel's horizon, because the sure sign and embodiment of the generosity of creation is the birth of a baby, which assures well-being of the family into the next generation. This is evident in the ancestral narratives of Genesis 12–36, but it is made even more concrete in psalms that voice the joys of a secured home:

> Sons are indeed a heritage from the Lord,
> the fruit of the womb a reward.
> Like arrows in the hand of a warrior
> are the sons of one's youth.

Happy is the man who has
his quiver full of them.
He shall not be put to shame
when he speaks with his enemies in the gate. (Ps 127:3-5)

Happy is everyone who fears the Lord,
who walks in his ways.
You shall eat the fruit of the labor of your hands;
you shall be happy, and it shall
go well with you.
Your wife will be like a fruitful vine
within your house;
your children will be like olive shoots
around your table.
Thus shall the man be blessed
who fears the Lord.
The Lord bless you from Zion.
May you see the prosperity of Jerusalem
all the days of your life.
May you see your children's children.
Peace be upon Israel! (Psalm 128)

This latter psalm envisions in general the productivity of the world, which supplies daily needs, and then it more specifically alludes to the birth of children. The casting of these psalms is intensely patriarchal—sons are most prized in Psalm 127 (with no mention of daughters), and the role of the wife in 128:3 is to create blessedness for the man.[8]

Even the patriarchal casting, however, does not detract from the awareness that the birth of a baby, the inscrutable gift of newness into the routineness of daily human life, in peasant hut and among the urban elite, is the most specific evidence of the wonder, generosity, and generativity of creation as intended by Yahweh. In Ps 128:5-6, moreover, this intimate gift of a child in the family is generalized into a gift of prosperity for all of Israel.

Wisdom, Righteousness, and Worship

Concerning this context of blessing that Yahweh guarantees for all creatures, Israel's unsolicited testimony treats three themes that we may regard as addenda to this exuberant reception and celebration of blessing. First, creation requires of human persons, the ones given dominion, that they practice *wisdom*.[9] Westermann concludes: "But the Old Testament knows a wisdom . . . that grows out of

---

8. The same patriarchal utilization of women is articulated in royal garb in Ps 45:12b-17.
9. See the review of the theme of dominion by Cameron Wybrow, *The Bible, Baconism, and Mastery over Nature* (New York: Peter Lang, 1991). See also Norbert Lohfink, "'Subdue the Earth?' (Genesis 1:28)," *Theology of the Pentateuch: Themes of the Priestly Narrative and Deuteronomy* (Minneapolis: Fortress Press, 1994) 1–17.

God's power to bless, and therefore, even though it is secular wisdom, has a direct relationship to God's activity and work."[10]

Wisdom is the critical, reflective, discerning reception of Yahweh's gift of generosity. That gift is not for self-indulgence, exploitation, acquisitiveness, or satiation. It is for careful husbanding, so that resources should be used for the protection, enhancement, and nurture of all creatures. Wisdom is the careful, constant, reflective attention to the shapes and interconnections that keep the world generative. Where those shapes and interconnections are honored, there the whole world prospers, and all creatures come to joy and abundance. Where those shapes and interconnections are violated or disregarded, trouble, conflict, and destructiveness are sure. There is wisdom in the very fabric of creation. Human wisdom consists in resonance with the "wisdom of things," which is already situated in creation before human agents act on it.

Second, this ordering of creation, with which human wisdom may resonate, has *an ethical dimension* to it, which H. H. Schmid terms righteousness.[11] The world, as Yahweh's creation, is not ordered so that some may set themselves over against the whole to their own advantage. The world, as Yahweh's creation, requires daily, endless attention to the gifts of creation, for their abuse and exploitation can harm and impede the generosity that makes life possible. Creation, moreover, has within it sanctions to bring death on those who neglect the enhancement of generosity.[12]

Third, while creation as generosity is not an Israelite property, Israel's testimony holds that *public worship is a context within which the generosity of creation can be received and enhanced.*[13] Thus the power of blessing is alive and loose within the world. At the same time, in such a well-known text as Num 6:24-26, the power for blessing is situated or intensified in the holy place and in the utterance of designated and professional "blessers":

> The Lord bless you and keep you;
> The Lord make his face to shine
> upon you, and be gracious to you;
> The Lord lift up his countenance
> upon you, and give you peace.[14]

---

10. Claus Westermann, *Blessing in the Church and the Life of the Church* (OBT; Philadelphia: Fortress Press, 1978) 39.

11. H. H. Schmid, *Gerechtigkeit als Weltordnung: Hintergrund und Geschichte des alttestamentlichen Gerechtigkeitsbegriffs* (BHT; Tübingen: J. C. B. Mohr [Paul Siebeck], 1968); and Knierim, *The Task of Old Testament Theology*, 86–122.

12. See the definitive discussion on "deed-consequence" by Klaus Koch, "Is There a Doctrine of Retribution in the Old Testament?" *Theodicy in the Old Testament* (ed. James L. Crenshaw; Philadelphia: Fortress Press, 1983) 57–87. Koch's categories are important for the argument developed by Schmid; see n. 11 above.

13. On the centrality of creation in the worship of Israel, see Bernhard W. Anderson, *Creation versus Chaos: The Reinterpretation of Mythical Symbolism in the Bible* (Philadelphia: Fortress Press, 1987) 78–109; and Harrelson, *From Fertility Cult to Worship*, 81–152.

14. On this text, see Patrick D. Miller, "The Blessing of God: An Interpretation of Numbers 6:22-27," *Int* 29 (1975) 240–50; and Michael Fishbane, *Biblical Interpretation in Ancient Israel* (Oxford: Clarendon Press, 1985) 329–34.

Now it may well be that this cultic articulation of the power of blessing is simply to be understood as the sociological monopoly of God-given power of blessing by the priests. Except that in Israel, this cultic concentration of blessing in legitimate utterance was found to mobilize and mediate the gifts of generosity that are present in all of creation.[15]

Creation as Counter-Experience in Worship

One other peculiar practice in Israel's worship life bears on our theme. It is evident in Gen 1:1–2:4a that creation and its gift of blessing are understood to be accomplished through (a) utterance, (b) separation of day from night and the waters from the waters, and (c) in the culminating practice of Sabbath.

It is widely held that creation became a crucial claim of Israel's faith in exile, when Gen 1:1–2:4a is commonly dated. This setting for creation faith suggests that affirmation of creation as an ordered, reliable arena of generosity is a treasured counter to the disordered experience of chaos in exile. If this critical judgment is accepted, creation then is an "enactment," done in worship, in order to resist the negation of the world of exile. As a consequence, creation is not to be understood as a theory or as an intellectual, speculative notion, but as a concrete life-or-death discipline and practice, whereby the peculiar claims of Yahweh were mediated in and to Israel.

This assumption has led a series of scholars to notice that the Priestly construct of the tabernacle in Exodus 25–31 has an odd and seemingly intentional parallel to the creation liturgy of Gen 1:1–2:4a.[16] That is, the instructions for the making of the tabernacle, given by Yahweh to Moses, consist in seven speeches, matching the seven days of creation, and culminating, like Gen 2:1-4a, in the provision for the Sabbath (Exod 31:12-17).[17] Moreover, the assertion that the tabernacle is finally "finished" (Exod 39:32, 40:33) corresponds to the "finish" of creation in Gen 2:4.[18]

This parallelism suggests that while creation may be an experience of the world, in a context where the world is experienced as not good, orderly, or generative, Israel has recourse to the counter-experience of creation in worship. Such an exercise, we may suspect, permitted Israelites who gave themselves fully over to the

---

15. Westermann, *Blessing in the Church*, 103–20, has commented on the distinction between blessing that is present in all of creation and blessing as it is mediated institutionally. Sigmund Mowinckel has urged the cult as a generative, constitutive force for blessing. See, derivatively, Walter Brueggemann, *Israel's Praise: Doxology against Idolatry and Ideology* (Philadelphia: Fortress Press, 1988) 1–28.

16. See Peter J. Kearney, "The P Redaction of Exod 25–40," *ZAW* 89 (1977) 375–87; and Joseph Blenkinsopp, *Prophecy and Canon: A Contribution to the Study of Jewish Origins* (Notre Dame, Ind.: University of Notre Dame Press, 1977) 54–69.

17. The seven speech units are Exod 25:1–30:10; 30:11-16; 30:17-21; 30:22-33; 30:34-38; 31:1-11; and 31:12-17.

18. In addition to the uses of the term *finish* in Gen 2:4 and Exod 39:32 and 40:33, see Josh 19:49-51. Thus, as Blenkinsopp observes, the uses assert the intentional parallel of *creation, tabernacle,* and *land distribution.*

drama and claims of the creation liturgy to live responsible, caring, secure, generative, and (above all) sane lives, in circumstances that severely discouraged such resolved living. Thus creation, in such a context, has concrete and immediate pastoral implication.

Creation in Jeopardy

The world of blessing under the settled rule of Yahweh is a major affirmation of Israel's testimony. This affirmation would suggest that trust in the world and its generosity is a settled given in Israel's faith and in Israel's experience. We have come by now to expect, however, that any such settled theological claim in Israel is sure to be unsettled, both by experience, which Israel refused to deny, and by texts, which testify to that experience.

So it is with Israel's sense of creation. Israel bears witness to the awareness that there is alive in the world a force that is counter to the world of Yahweh, a force that seeks to negate and nullify the world as a secure place of blessing. There is no doubt that Israel took over this mythic-poetic articulation from its cultural environment and antecedents, but one cannot for that reason discount it. This awareness of a counter-creation force was articulated in prebiblical texts because life includes this dimension of experience. We may believe, moreover, that Israel rearticulated this claim in its own texts, not because Israel was a careless borrower of texts from its environment, but because these articulations are seen to be a faithful witness to a dimension of reality that Israel is not able or willing to deny.

Israel bears witness, as did its antecedents, to an enduring force of chaos in its life. This chaos may go by many different names—Tiamat, Leviathan, Rahab, Yam, Mot—which we may summarize under the names of Death or Nihil. In a variety of texts, this rhetoric in Israel points to a recognition that something is at work in the world seeking to make impossible the life of blessing willed by Yahweh. Israel, moreover, finds itself helpless in the face of this powerful force. Israel has no resources of its own with which to cope or respond to this threat. In turn we shall consider two ways in which Israel situated this undoubted experience in its theological rhetoric.

Dualism-in-Creation

First, it is possible to conclude, with some Israelite texts, that this power of the Nihil is still loose in the world and still actively opposes Yahweh. That is, in the sovereign act of creation, whereby Yahweh orders chaos, Yahweh provisionally defeated the power of Nihil but did not destroy or eliminate the threat of chaos. As a result, this power of Nihil from time to time gathers its force and conducts forays into creation to work havoc, for it has not yet come under the rule of Yahweh. Thus is posed a primordial dualism in which Yahweh has the upper hand but is not fully in control, and so from time to time creation is threatened.

The clearest exposition of this dualism-in-creation is in Jon Levenson's book *Creation and the Persistence of Evil.*[19] It is Levenson's formidable argument that evil does indeed continue with vitality, and therefore Yahweh's sovereignty over creation is fragile and under threat.[20] Levenson opposes the scholastic claim of Yehezkel Kaufmann and asserts that "the defeated enemy" (chaos) still survives, and therefore creation rhetoric is juxtaposed to threat.[21]

The two texts that provide the core of Levenson's case are in Psalm 74 and Isaiah 51:

> Yet God my King is from of old,
> working salvation in the earth.
> You divided the sea by your might;
> you broke the heads of the
> dragons in the waters.
> You crushed the heads of Leviathan;
> you gave him as food for the
> creatures of the wilderness.
> You cut openings for springs and torrents;
> you dried up ever-flowing streams.
> Yours is the day, yours also the night;
> you established the luminaries and the sun.
> You have fixed all the foundations of the earth;
> you made summer and winter. (Ps 74:12-17)

> Awake, awake, put on strength,
> O arm of the Lord!
> Awake, as in the days of old, the generations of long ago!
> Was it not you who cut Rahab in pieces,
> who pierced the dragon?
> Was it not you who dried up the sea,
> the waters of the great deep;
> who made the depths of the sea a way
> for the redeemed to cross over? (Isa 51:9-10)

Both of these texts mention the chaos-monster. In both texts, moreover, this poetic language is drawn close to Israel's lived reality. In Psalm 74 it is the reality of the destroyed temple in Jerusalem; in Isaiah 51 it is the exile. These lived realities cause Israel to recall the ancient threat of chaos, surely with the surmise that Yahweh's absolute sovereignty is in jeopardy.[22]

This sort of dualism works against much settled theology of an ecclesial kind. In Levenson's case, he resists the Jewish theological claims of Kaufmann. But we

---

19. In the discussion that follows, I am informed by the exposition of Levenson.
20. Levenson, *Creation and the Persistence of Evil,* 47.
21. Ibid., 232.
22. Ibid., 26, 233.

should also note that in Christian theology, perhaps especially in high Calvinism with its remarkable assertions of Yahweh's sovereignty, the same temptation to an absolute claim for Yahweh is made. Against such a settled notion, Karl Barth says of the threat of *Das Nichtige* (nothingness):

> There is opposition and resistance to God's world-dominion. There is in world-occurrence an element, indeed an entire sinister system of elements which is not comprehended by God's providence in the sense thus far described.... This opposition and resistance, this stubborn element and alien factor, may be provisionally defined as nothingness.[23]

Levenson, in the face of the data of the texts, makes two theological claims. First, it is promised in Israel that soon or late (likely late), Yahweh will prevail over the threats (see, for example, Isa 25:6-8). Second, creation requires for its durability the special act and special solicitude of God.[24] It is Israel's claim that Yahweh enacts this special solicitude on a regular and reliable basis. The precariousness is that Yahweh can never be at ease, for given any relaxation of Yahweh's attentiveness, the power of the Nihil will immediately surge into the unattended space.

This notion of an effective, powerful adversary to Yahweh the Creator pervades the mythological world of the Old Testament.[25] Some residue of this thinking is evident in the serpent in Genesis 3 and the emergence of Satan in Job 1–2 and 1 Chronicles 21.[26] It is possible, as Paul Ricoeur suggests, to see these powers of negativity as unresolved elements in the character of Yahweh, which are split off as "agents." In any case, this line of thinking poses important questions for Old Testament theology. Such thinking, rooted in texts that are unambiguous, flies in the face of more settled ecclesial thinking. There is a temptation to gloss over and ignore such texts and to treat them only in terms of the history of religion, beyond which Israel's more mature faith has moved.

It is my estimate, informed as I am especially by Levenson, but also by Bernhard Anderson, Karl Barth, and Terence Fretheim, that to disregard these texts and their theological counterclaim is impossible on the basis of the texts; moreover, such disregard loses important theological-pastoral resources. Here I refer to two studies, one concerning public power and the other concerning personal misery.

Fretheim on pharaoh as mythic force. Terence Fretheim has done a careful and bold rereading of Exodus 1–15 and the distinctive role played by pharaoh in the narrative.[27] Pharaoh, in this narrative, is presented as a *historical* character. In

23. Karl Barth, "God and Nothingness," *Church Dogmatics* 3/3, *The Doctrine of Creation* (Edinburgh: T. & T. Clark, 1960) 289. To be sure, Barth will not finally leave nothingness beyond God's providential sovereignty, as Levenson does. Nonetheless, Barth recognizes the depth and seriousness of this recalcitrance toward God.

24. Levenson, *Creation and the Persistence of Evil*, 12.

25. See Anderson, *Creation versus Chaos*, 144–70; and Barth, *Church Dogmatics* 3/1, *The Doctrine of Creation* (Edinburgh: T. & T. Clark, 1958) 107 and 352ff.

26. On the serpent as the adumbration of Satan, see Paul Ricoeur, *The Symbolism of Evil* (Boston: Beacon Press, 1969) 255–60.

27. See chap. 16, n. 28 above.

his study of the Exodus plagues, however, Fretheim suggests that pharaoh's oppressive policies are a deep disruption of creation. That is, the plagues are not natural acts that concern Israel; they are "hypernatural" occurrences, whereby pharaoh is presented as a *mythic* force that disrupts the generativity of creation and draws Yahweh's retaliatory punishment. On the basis of this narrative, Fretheim makes possible an awareness that historical agents do indeed take on mythic proportion in their enactment of the Nihil. This is an important interpretive maneuver at the end of the twentieth century, a period of human history visited by unthinkable devastation, wrought by human agents in their mythic capacity—for example, Auschwitz, Hiroshima, Dresden, and the Soviet Gulags. Such an interpretive stance permits one to look candidly into the face of evil, without offering any too-easy Yahwistic antidote.

Lindström on personal crises. Fredrik Lindström has done a detailed study of the psalms of complaint.[28] It is his judgment that these psalms operate with a profound dualism. That is, trouble has come upon the speaker when (and only when) Yahweh is negligent, so that the power of the Nihil occupies neglected territory. These psalms, on Lindström's reading, give almost no attention to sin and guilt, but are pleas that a neglectful Yahweh should again pay attention, for the power of the Nihil cannot withstand the solicitous attention of Yahweh. Moreover, the psalms are cult-centered, believing that the cult is where Yahweh must come to reassert a generative sovereignty.

It is especially important that Lindström did his study at the behest of a pastor friend dealing with people living with AIDS. It is Lindström's intent to show that the power of the Nihil is not to be reduced to or explained by sin and guilt. Rather, the onslaught of negation is due to the power of death still on the loose in creation, which may at any time cause havoc. Lindström's analysis makes clear that this notion of dualism is not a speculative, intellectual exercise, but a serious pastoral resource. It is not, moreover, a diminishment of Yahweh. To the contrary, it is an assertion of how urgently indispensable Yahweh is to a viable life in the world. Yahweh is the guarantor of blessing; but where that power of blessing is not concretely enacted and guaranteed, the undoing of creation takes place.

Yahweh Conquers the Forces of Evil

A second way of speaking about this negation in Israel's unsolicited testimony is to recognize that there is indeed such negation in the world, but instead of a primordial dualism in which negation operates independently of and against Yahweh, some texts see the power of negation as a force now conquered by Yahweh, in the service of Yahweh, and operative only at the behest of Yahweh. This view has the merit of precluding a primordial dualism, and it avoids situating some power of reality beyond the sphere of Yahweh's sovereignty. But this gain is traded off for

---

28. Fredrik Lindström, *Suffering and Sin: Interpretations of Illness in the Individual Complaint Psalms* (Stockholm: Almqvist and Wiksell International, 1994).

the assignment of severe negation to Yahweh's own sovereign capacity, in which Yahweh does evil as well as good (cf. Deut 32:39; Isa 45:7).

The hymnic tradition of Israel, surely aware of the old and pervasive mythos of primordial combat, exuberantly announces that Yahweh has defeated and dispelled the forces of evil. Among the more important assertions of that singular, unchallengeable sovereignty of Yahweh are statements that Yahweh is indeed the Creator of all the "hosts," the powers of heaven and their work at Yahweh's command:

> To whom then will you compare me,
> or who is my equal? says the Holy One.
> Lift up your eyes on high and see:
> Who created these?
> He who brings out their host and numbers them,
> calling them all by name;
> because he is great in strength,
> mighty in power,
> not one is missing. (Isa 40:25-26)

The whirlwind speeches in Job, moreover, claim control of creatures by Yahweh who were erstwhile monsters, but who are now obedient, treasured creatures in whom Yahweh revels (Job 40:15-24, 41:1-34). Yahweh is said also to control the floodwaters of the cosmos (Job 38:8-11, 25-33). The most idyllic statement is in Ps 104:25-26, which assumes Yahweh's complete mastery of threatening forces:

> Yonder is the sea, great and wide,
> creeping things innumerable are there,
> living things both small and great.
> There go the ships, and Leviathan that you formed to sport in it.[29]

In this view, which competes with dualism and likely predominates in Israel's testimony, there are no causes of the destabilization of creation except the will of Yahweh, who in freedom and sovereignty can indeed destabilize the world, when Yahweh's sovereignty is excessively mocked and sufficiently provoked.

Of course, the classic case of such radical destabilization of the world at the behest of Yahweh is the flood narrative of Gen 6:5–7:24. There is no doubt that Yahweh has caused the floodwaters, and there is no doubt that it was disobedience (corruption and violence, 6:11-13) that evoked Yahweh to act:

> And all flesh died that moved on the earth, birds, domestic animals, wild animals, all swarming creatures that swarm on the earth, and all human beings; everything on dry land in whose nostrils was the breath of life died. He blotted out every living thing that was on the face of the ground, human beings

---

29. Levenson, *Creation and the Persistence of Evil*, 17, refers to Leviathan in this passage as God's "rubber duckey."

and animals and creeping things and birds of the air; they were blotted out from the earth. (Gen 7:21-23)

This is indeed the complete undoing of creation at the behest of the Creator (cf. Isa 54:9-10).

More tersely, the narrative of the destruction of Sodom is a parallel story. In sovereign freedom Yahweh undertakes the radical punishment of the city, by unleashing all the ominous forces of creation:

Then the Lord rained on Sodom and Gomorrah sulfur and fire from the Lord out of heaven; and he overthrew those cities and all the Plain, and all the inhabitants of the cities, and what grew on the ground. (Gen 19:24-25)

The destruction of Sodom continues to play upon the imagination of Israel (cf. Isa 1:9-10, 3:9; Jer 23:14, 49:18, 50:40; Ezek 16:46-51; and Hos 11:8-9).

The situation, moreover, is not different in the plague narrative, in which Yahweh unleashes the forces of thunder, hail, and fire against pharaoh, a recalcitrant vassal:

Then Moses stretched out his staff toward heaven, and the Lord sent thunder and hail, and fire came down on the earth. And the Lord rained hail on the land of Egypt; there was hail with fire flashing continually in the midst of it, such heavy hail as had never fallen in all the land of Egypt since it became a nation. The hail struck down everything that was in the open field throughout all the land of Egypt, both human and animal; the hail also struck down all the plants of the field, and shattered every tree in the field. (Exod 9:23-25)

Indeed, Fretheim observes that at the end of the plague cycle (acts of sovereignty, evoked by disobedience), Yahweh's final assault on pharaoh is a return of the earth to the "heavy darkness" of the first day:[30]

The the Lord said to Moses, "Stretch out your hand toward heaven so that there may be darkness over the land of Egypt, a darkness that can be felt." So Moses stretched out his hand toward heaven, and there was a dense darkness in all the land of Egypt for three days. People could not see one another and for three days they could not move from where they were.... (Exod 10:21-23a; cf. 12:29-30)

The unleashing of these forces in the three paradigmatic accounts of flood, Sodom, and Egypt pertains to the powers that are believed, in the divine speeches in the Book of Job, to be the gifts of creation held only by the Creator. Yahweh has retained these awe-evoking powers for Yahweh's own self. Thus while Yahweh can unloose the forces of blessing (or fecundity) into the world, Yahweh can also unloose the forces of curse and death—and will do so, in an extreme case, when

---

30. See the comment of Fretheim, "The Plagues as Ecological Signs," 391–92.

Yahweh's sovereignty is mocked. From our perspective, this is almost a grotesque articulation of Yahweh's relationship to the world. This view of Yahweh's potentially destructive capacity, however, is evidently a staple of Israel's sense of the world, for which Israel exhibits neither wonderment nor embarrassment.

Indeed, this capacity of Yahweh is stylized in the standard recital of covenant curses that provide sanctions for the commandments.[31] Thus Yahweh, according to this testimony, warns Israel at the outset:

> I in turn will do this to you: I will bring terror on you; consumption and fever that waste the eyes and cause life to pine away. You shall sow your seed in vain, for your enemies shall eat it.... If in spite of these punishments you have not turned back to me, but continue hostile to me, then I too will continue hostile to you: I myself will strike you sevenfold for your sins. I will bring the sword against you, executing vengeance for the covenant; and if you withdraw within your cities, I will send pestilence among you, and you shall be delivered into enemy hands.... I in turn will punish you myself sevenfold for your sins. (Lev 26:16, 23-25, 28)

Yahweh promises disease, pestilence, drought, wild animals, sword, famine, and finally desolation. The threat includes "historical-military" assault, but it also includes the complete disruption of the processes of food production that depend on the fruitful function of creation. Israel makes no distinction between "historical" and "natural" threats; both are of a piece, and both do damage to Israel's environment. The food-producing, life-sustaining infrastructure of creation will be terminated, because Yahweh will be obeyed. When Yahweh is not obeyed, all of creation is placed in profound jeopardy. There are limits to Yahweh's toleration of Israel's recalcitrance in this curse recital, just as there were limits for the world (Genesis 6–7) and for Sodom (Genesis 19).

The implementation of such curses is evident in the lawsuit speeches of the prophets. Zephaniah, in a harsh articulation, imagines the termination of creation:

> I will utterly sweep away everything
> from the face of the earth, says the Lord.
> I will sweep away humans and animals;
> I will sweep away the birds of the air
> and the fish of the sea. (Zeph 1:2-3)

Jeremiah envisions a great drought that will undo the earth (Jer 14:4-6). Most especially, Amos provides a catalog of curses, in a highly stylized form that seems to echo the old curse tradition:[32]

---

31. On these curses, see Delbert R. Hillers, *Treaty-Curses and the Old Testament Prophets* (Rome: Pontifical Biblical Institute, 1964); and C. F. Fensham, "Maledictions and Benedictions in Ancient Near-Eastern Vassal-Treaties and the Old Testament," *ZAW* 74 (1962) 1–19.

32. See H. Graf Reventlow, *Das Amt des Propheten bei Amos* (FRLANT 80; Göttingen: Vandenhoeck and Ruprecht, 1962) 75–90.

I gave you cleanness of teeth in all your cities,
and lack of bread in all your places,
yet you did not return to me, says the Lord.
And I also withheld the rain from you
when you were still three months to the harvest;
I would send rain on one city,
and send no rain on another city;
one field would be rained upon,
and the field on which it did not rain withered;
so two or three towns wandered to one town
to drink water, and were not satisfied;
yet you did not return to me, says the Lord.
I struck you with blight and mildew;
I laid waste your gardens and your vineyards;
the locust devoured your fig tress and your olive trees;
yet you did not return to me, says the Lord.
I sent among you a pestilence after the manner of Egypt;
I killed your young men with the sword;
I carried away your horses;
and I made the stench of your camp go up into your nostrils;
yet you did not return to me, says the Lord.
I overthrew some of you,
as when God overthrew Sodom and Gomorrah,
and you were like a brand
snatched from the fire;
yet you did not return to me, says the Lord. (Amos 4:6-11)

It may well be that the affront to Yahweh concerns only the people Israel in any one particular context, or perhaps only one of the other peoples, as in the case of Egypt. But when the punishment is administered, it is characteristically undifferentiated. It strikes at "the whole earth."[33]

This entire sequence of texts bespeaks Yahweh's terrible and ready capacity to enact curses upon the earth, which disrupt the system of blessing and fertility and make the world unlivable. Just as Israel's doxologies celebrate the world when it is under the blessing of Yahweh, so the various narratives and poems of judgment witness to the capacity of Yahweh to place the whole earth under the power of curse, which produces only death.

In its most stylized articulations, as in Leviticus 26 and Amos 4, the curses are the direct and enraged enactment of Yahweh. But there is also a second form of curse, in which creation by itself turns deathly (without the disruptive agency of Yahweh) in response to recalcitrance, abuse, disobedience, and oppression. That is, the uncompromising requirements of creation are self-actualizing in

---

33. Having said "the whole earth," we shall promptly note the crucial exception. See chap. 16, n. 30.

their sanctions. This is expressed, for example, in Hos 4:1-3, which we may take as paradigmatic for the awareness that creation can be nullified when the affront against Yahweh's will for creation becomes intense enough:[34]

> There is no faithfulness or loyalty,
> and no knowledge of God in the land.
> Swearing, lying, and murder,
> and stealing and adultery break out;
> bloodshed follows bloodshed.
> Therefore the land mourns,
> and all who live in it languish;
> together with the wild animals
> and the birds of the air,
> even the fish of the sea are perishing. (Hos 4:1-3)

To be sure, Yahweh is present in the process of dismantling, but there is no direct action from Yahweh. The scope of the indictment is "the land," but as the term *'eres* is used in vv. 1, 2, and 3, it seems to move from the "land of Israel" to "the earth"—the whole of creation. In any case, the assertion of the poem is that as a consequence of the violations of vv. 1-2, without any stated intervention on the part of Yahweh, creation is undone through drought. The disappearance of "wild animals...birds of the air...fish of the sea" bespeaks the collapse of the entire life-producing structure of the earth. Local disobedience, here disobedience to the Decalogue, will evoke Yahweh's enormous power of anti-creation.

In the canonical shape of Israel's witness, all of this threat of Yahweh, Yahweh's capacity to turn the processes of blessing into the dead end of curse, comes to focus in the exile. The exile of Israel concerns not just geographical displacement, but the cessation of life possibilities, the withdrawal of fruitfulness. The fullest, most drastic articulation of Yahweh's deathly judgment on Jerusalem as "the end of creation" is given in Jer 4:23-26:

> I looked on the earth, and lo,
> it was waste and void;
> and to the heavens, and they had no light.
> I looked on the mountains, and lo,
> they were quaking;
> and all the hills moved to and fro.
> I looked, and lo, there was no one at all,
> and all the birds of the air had fled.
> I looked, and lo, the fruitful land was a desert,

---

34. On this text, see Walter Brueggemann, "The Uninflected *Therefore* of Hosea 4:1-3," *Reading from this Place* 1: *Social Location and Biblical Interpretation in the United States* (ed. Fernando F. Segovia and Mary Ann Tolbert; Minneapolis: Fortress Press, 1995) 231–49.

and all its cities were laid in ruins
before the Lord, before his fierce anger.

This poem, in a stylized and intentional catalog, walks through all the elements of creation. It begins in earth and heavens and culminates with "fruitful land and cities." All are gone! Everything is systematically dismantled. The nullification is complete and intentional. Reality has returned to *tohû wabohû*, the pre-creation state of Gen 1:2—that is, the disordered, formless mass of "preexistent material substratum,"[35] before Yahweh had uttered a sovereign word or committed a forming action in order to turn this mass into a fruitful place of blessing and joyous life. All of this undoing and nullification has happened because of Yahweh's "fierce anger." What Yahweh has formed in generosity as a place of blessing can, in Yahweh's indignation, revert to a place of curse. The world that Yahweh created in freedom can be terminated, nullified, and abandoned in like freedom.

This massive, ruthless portrayal of the story of creation as Yahweh's partner has two qualifications that Israel never finally resolves or fully integrates into its high claim for Yahweh. On the one hand, the complete sovereignty of Yahweh, as Levenson has shown, never completely drives out what seems to be the autonomous force of chaos. On the other hand, the freedom assigned to Yahweh as Creator, in Israel's rhetoric, is never free from moral condition, in which Israel has brought negation upon itself; thus the act of negation is not completely a free act of Yahweh, but is at the same time an act required and mandated by covenant sanctions. Yahweh's sovereign freedom, according to Israel's testimony, must endlessly contend with these two qualifications.

The World beyond Nullification

The astonishing feature of this statement of Yahweh's freedom and sovereignty (though less astonishing in light of what we have seen about Israel as partner, the human person as partner, and the nations as partner) is that *Israel's witness does not leave the account of creation as Yahweh's partner as a tale of termination, negation, and nullification.* Perhaps one cannot speak of Yahweh's passion or pathos-filled love for creation, for there is no hint of such emotional commitment to the creation on the part of Yahweh. It is evident, nonetheless, that something is at work in Yahweh's interior, something to which Israel boldly bears witness, that works against, disrupts, and mitigates Yahweh's free exercise of wrathful sovereignty. Something moves against destructiveness, either to qualify it or to begin again postdestruction. There is, in any case, more to Yahweh's relation to creation than a one-dimensional response of indignant sovereignty.

I will divide my consideration of this mitigating factor in the life of Yahweh into two parts. First I shall consider the qualification given in the texts of termination;

---

35. The phrase is from Levenson, *Creation and the Persistence of Evil,* 5.

second I will consider three other texts that suggest not only a limit on the rage of Yahweh, but a quite new intention of blessing on Yahweh's part.

Qualification in Texts of Termination

Several mitigating factors in the texts of destruction evidence that Yahweh is unable or unwilling to "go the whole way" with the termination of creation.

Flood. In the flood narrative of Gen 6:5–7:24, we have seen Yahweh's resolve to "blot out" humanity (Gen 6:7) and the narrative report of fulfillment:

> He blotted out every living thing that was on the face of the ground, human beings and animals and creeping things and birds of the air; they were blotted out from the earth. (Gen 7:23)

But of course, the resolve of Gen 6:7 is already modestly countered in the verse that follows:

> But Noah found favor in the sight of the Lord. (6:8)

The theme of the exception of Noah is reiterated in 7:23b:

> Only Noah was left, and those that were with him in the ark.

And yet a third time, Noah is a mitigating factor:

> But God remembered Noah and all the wild animals and all the domestic animals that were with him in the ark. And God made a wind blow over the earth, and the waters subsided. (8:1)

Bernhard Anderson has shown that architecturally, Gen 8:1 is the pivotal point of the narrative, after which the waters recede, the threat of the flood ends, and the earth is made safe again.[36] Noah is not said to be loved by Yahweh; but it is said, "Noah found favor in the sight of the Lord." In 6:9, moreover, Noah is said to be "righteous," but the governing statement in what is usually thought to be the older text is "found favor" (*ḥnn*), thus making contact with Yahweh's graciousness (same word in Exod 34:6). The narrative asserts that, along with Yahweh's indignant sovereignty, there is "favor," and Yahweh "remembered Noah." The narrator does not say that Yahweh remembered Noah's righteousness, but simply remembered Noah, the one who was situated in Yahweh's "favor." We are led to believe, subsequently, that it is this odd and unexplored relation to Noah, perhaps in righteousness, perhaps in graciousness, that leads to the restoration of blessing in a cursed earth (Gen 8:22) and eventually to a promise of "everlasting covenant," in which Yahweh pledges:

> I establish my covenant with you, that never again shall all flesh be cut off by the waters of a flood, and never again shall there be a flood to destroy the earth. (9:11)

---

36. Bernhard W. Anderson, "From Analyses to Syntheses: The Interpretation of Genesis 1–11," *JBL* 97 (1978) 31–39.

Not much is made of Noah in the subsequent testimony of Israel (cf. Ezek 14:14, 20; 2 Pet 2:5). Noah is in any case the occasion for Yahweh's reversal of field, the reason whereby Yahweh may relove and reembrace the world as a system of blessing.[37]

Sodom. In the Sodom story, the countertheme is even more minimal, but it is there. The story turns on the effort to save Lot (Gen 19:17) and the loss of Lot's wife (19:26). What interests us, however, is in 19:29:

> ...God remembered Abraham, and sent Lot out of the midst of the overthrow, when he overthrew the cities in which Lot had settled.

This terse statement is parallel to that of Gen 8:1, and it performs the same function. Yahweh has no compelling memory of Lot, but Yahweh remembers Abraham, already identified in this story as an intimate of Yahweh and as a carrier of the blessing (Gen 18:17-19). Abraham is the one on whom Yahweh has staked everything positive, so that Abraham becomes the wedge whereby the power of blessing is reasserted into the creation under curse.

Plagues against Egypt. The curses (plagues) enacted against Egypt and pharaoh are massive and uncompromising, but they are qualified by a cubit:

> Only in the land of Goshen, where the Israelites were, there was no hail. (Exod 9:26)

> ...but all the Israelites had light where they lived. (Exod 10:23)

> But not a dog shall growl at any of the Israelites—not at people, not at animals—so that you may know that the Lord makes a distinction between Egypt and Israel. (Exod 11:7)

Perhaps these exceptions are to be understood simply as comments on the "chosenness" of Israel, and there is that motif in the story. But read from the perspective of the future of creation, Israel, in this narrative, is the means whereby the history of blessing for the world is kept alive in a world under curse.

Chaos but not "full end." In the wholesale judgment of Jer 4:23-26, everything reverts to originary chaos. The prose comment on the poetry reinforces the devastation: "For thus says the Lord: The whole land shall be a desolation..." (Jer 4:27a). But then this is added: "...yet I will not make a full end" (4:27b). This last phrase has suffered at the hands of many commentators, who deem it a later addition. But there it is! Why? Was it added because the traditionists could not tolerate the nullification of the world in such a massive way, and so they toned it down? Perhaps. But in theological exposition, we are entitled to the thought that Yahweh could not tolerate the termination of the world. Yahweh has too much at stake in

---

37. See Isa 54:9-10, where the same narrative is turned to be an assurance specifically to Israel. On the text, see Walter Brueggemann, "A Shattered Transcendence? Exile and Restoration," *Biblical Theology: Problems and Perspectives* (ed. Steven J. Kraftchick et al.; Nashville: Abingdon Press, 1995) 169–82.

the creation. The "grace" (*ḥn*) extended to Noah, to Abraham (Lot), to Israel and Moses continues to mean something. Yahweh is, perhaps at great cost, resolved to maintain creation as a system of blessing, and so will not give in, even to Yahweh's own propensity to enraged destruction. Israel ponders this terrible interiority in Yahweh, and Israel dares give it voice. Yahweh is deeply torn about the future of the world. Dare we suggest that it is this quality of tornness in Yahweh's own life that, according to Israel's unsolicited testimony, constitutes the hope of creation?

Renewed Creation out of Hopelessness

I also mention three texts that articulate the way in which Yahweh acts in astonishingly new ways for the sake of creation, when all seemed hopelessly to have come to an end.

Hos 2:2-23. This text concerns Israel in the first instant, as Yahweh's rejected partner, and not creation. I cite it in this context, however, because in the horizon of this poem, Israel's past and future are intimately linked to the presence and/or absence of blessing in creation. The poem is arranged in two parts, which we may treat as Israel "under curse" (vv. 2-13) and Israel "under blessing" (vv. 14-23). In the first part Yahweh had given to Israel the abundance of creation:

> She did not know that it was I who gave her
> the grain, the wine, and the oil,
> and who lavished upon her silver
> and gold that they used for Baal. (v. 8)

But now, in rage, Yahweh will withdraw the blessings of creation, so that Israel's life is no longer viable:

> Therefore I will take back
> my grain in its time,
> and my wine in its season;
> and I will take away my wool and my flax,
> which were to cover her nakedness....
> I will lay waste her vines and her fig trees....
> I will make them a forest,
> and the wild animals shall devour them. (vv. 9, 12)

The guarantees and gifts of creation are in Yahweh's sovereign grasp, to give and to withdraw.

In the second part of the poem Yahweh is moved by passion to allure Israel back to a relationship. Among the acts of allurement is a covenant with the elements of creation, the ones lost in 2:3:

> I will make for you a covenant on that day with the wild animals, the birds
> of the air, and the creeping things of the ground.... (2:18)

The result of that restoration of relationship is the resumption of the processes of fruitfulness in creation:

> On that day I will answer, says the Lord,
> I will answer the heavens
> and they shall answer the earth;
> and the earth shall answer the grain, the wine, and the oil, and they
>   shall answer Jezreel;
> and I will sow him for myself in the land.
> And I will have pity on Lo-ruhamah,
> and I will say to Lo-ammi,
> "You are my people";
> and he shall say, "You are my God." (vv. 21-23)

In the future to be given by Yahweh, it is no longer possible to keep distinct the future of Israel and the future of creation, for Israel is deeply situated in the minuses and pluses of creation.

This poem is of interest for our theme on several counts. (a) The statement of the poem, when considered as a statement about creation, concerns Yahweh's capacity to nullify creation. (b) The poem has as its primary subject Israel, so that creation is not a mechanistic system, but is fully embedded with the practice of human covenanting. (c) The well-being or failure of creation depends on the practice of fidelity, not least the fidelity of Yahweh. It is likely that this poem, and others like it, have been read too singularly with reference to Israel, when the poem can also be seen as concerning the way in which Yahweh's unsettled interior inclination also impinges on the well-being or nullification of creation.

Isa 45:18-19. Isaiah of the exile intends to counteract and overcome the several nullifications of the exile. Among these is the rhetoric of Israel that links exile to the nullification of creation, as we have seen it most vividly in Jer 4:23-26. I take Jer 4:23-26 to be a hyperbolic way in which Israel speaks about its exilic situation as a crisis of world proportion. In order now to overcome that hyperbolic rhetoric, Israel must counter it in equally hyperbolic positive speech. Thus in Isa 45:18-19 the poet speaks twice of chaos (*tohû*): "[H]e did not create it a chaos.... 'Seek me in chaos,'" in order to present the contrast of a well-created order over which Yahweh the Creator presides. Appeal to the reality of chaos is made a foil for the positive affirmation of Yahweh, now available on the far side of exile. Thus chaos language is peculiarly appropriate for Israel's exile. Speech of new creation or re-creation or restored creation functions for Israel's emergence from the nullity of exile.

Isa 62:3-5. In the extravagant poetry of Isaiah 60–62, the poet strains to voice the new possibility of Israel after exile. In the midst of that exaggerated rhetoric of possibility, these verses concern the restoration of the fecundity of creation:

> You shall be a crown of beauty in
> the hand of the Lord,

and a royal diadem in the hand of your God.
You shall no more be termed Forsaken,
and your land shall no more be termed Desolate,
but you shall be called My Delight Is in Her,
and your land Married;
for the Lord delights in you,
and your land shall be married.
For as a young man marries a young woman,
so shall your builder marry you,
and as the bridegroom rejoices over the bride,
so shall your God rejoice over you. (Isa 62:3-5)

The specific language of fertility interests us because of the power of its contrasts. Thus the "forsaken" and "desolate" one is now "My Delight Is in Her" and "Married." The last term is explicated in vv. 4b-5, appealing to the joy of the newly married. It is crucial that the term *married* (*b'ûlah*) appeals to the oldest traditions known to Israel concerning fertility. This language (cf. Hos 2:16) intends to speak about the restoration of the processes of blessing in creation, whereby Israel is to flourish. Gary Anderson has shown how the recovery of sexual capacity is emblematic in Israel of the full restoration of joy and volition.[38] Thus the God who presided over the devastation of creation is the God who now has the power and the will to cause creation, for the benefit of Israel, to function fully. All the causes and motivations for the nullification of exile are now forgiven and forgotten (cf. Isa 54:7-8). The world begins again!

The most extreme statement of this capacity for the recovery of creation is Isa 65:17-25, perhaps the most sweeping resolve of Yahweh in all of Israel's testimony:

For I am about to create new heavens and a new earth;
the former things shall not be remembered
or come to mind.
But be glad and rejoice forever in what I am creating;
for I am about to create Jerusalem as a joy,
and its people as a delight.
I will rejoice in Jerusalem,
and delight in my people;
no more shall the sound of weeping be heard in it,
or the cry of distress.
No more shall there be in it
an infant that lives but a few days,
or an old person who does not live out a lifetime;
for one who dies at a hundred years will be considered a youth,

---

38. Gary A. Anderson, *A Time to Mourn, a Time to Dance: The Expression of Grief and Joy in Israelite Religion* (University Park: Pennsylvania State University Press, 1991) 82–97 and passim.

and one who falls short of a hundred will be considered accursed.
They shall build houses and inhabit them;
they shall plant vineyards and eat their fruit.
They shall not build and another inhabit;
they shall not plant and another eat;
for like the days of a tree shall the days of my people be,
and my chosen shall long enjoy the work of their hands.
They shall not labor in vain,
or bear children for calamity;
for they shall be offspring blessed by the Lord—
and their descendants as well.
Before they call I will answer,
while they are yet speaking I will hear.
The wolf and the lamb shall feed together,
the lion shall eat straw like the ox;
but the serpent—its food shall be dust!
They shall not hurt or destroy
on all my holy mountain, says the Lord.

This remarkably rich rhetoric suggests that the new creation that comes now, after the resurgence of chaos, warrants a fuller exposition than I can provide here. We may simply and briefly note some aspects of this extravagant promise. First, the poem is a declaration in the mouth of Yahweh, who publicly and pointedly claims authority to replicate the initial creation, only now more grandly and more wondrously. This promised action of Yahweh is clearly designed to overcome all that is amiss, whether what is amiss has been caused by Yahweh's anger, by Israel's disobedience, or by other untamed forces of death. Second, the newness of creation here vouchsafed touches every aspect and phase of life. All elements of existence are to come under the positive, life-yielding aegis of Yahweh. Third, the promise in v. 23 may refer to the disability pronounced in Gen 3:16. That is, whatever is amiss in creation will now be restored and made whole, even the most deeply embedded distortions in Yahweh's world. Fourth, the culminating verse (on which see also Isa 11:6-9) indicates that the new creation now promised concerns not only Israel, not only the entire human community, but all of creation, so that hostilities at every level and in every dimension of creation will be overcome. "All will be well and all will be well."[39]

Creation at Yahweh's Behest

Thus creation is seen, as we piece together the testimony, in three seasons:

1. The *season of blessing*, activating Yahweh's free sovereignty, devoted to the well-being and productivity of the world. Yahweh has the power and the inclination to form a world of life-generating proportion.

---

39. The phrase is from Julian of Norwich, *Showings* (New York: Paulist Press, 1978).

2. A *radical fissure* in the life of the world may come about, according to Israel's rhetoric, most often understood as an act of Yahweh's angry, sovereign freedom. Creation is not necessary to Yahweh, and Yahweh will tolerate no creation that is not ordered according to Yahweh's intention for life. The world can be lost!

3. In the face of devastating nullification, experienced by Israel in the fissure of its exile, and experienced by human persons in the fissures of "the Pit," it is characteristic of Yahweh to work *a radical newness.* Israel's testimony is restrained on Yahweh's motivation for this remarkable act of new creation. In Isa 65:17-25, no reason is given; there is only a declaration of lordly intention. In Isa 45:18-19, it is perhaps suggested that creation is in the very character of Yahweh. It is not in Yahweh's character to be a God who settles for chaos. It is in Yahweh's most elemental resolve to enact blessing and order and well-being.

In Isa 62:3-5, where creation language is in the service of Israel's fruitful future, we are closer to receiving a reason for this fresh way of resolve. Yahweh had kept silent (*ḥšh*) and been dormant (*šqṭ*) (v. 1). We are not told why. Perhaps Yahweh was punishing Israel by such withdrawn, neglectful silence. Or perhaps Yahweh was so provoked by Israel as to be sulky and ready provisionally to abandon Israel to the cursed situation it had chosen for itself. For whatever reason, Yahweh now resolves to speak "for Zion's sake" (Isa 62:1). Yahweh announces the resurgence of blessing for the sake of Jerusalem. The same language is more fully utilized, for the same reason, in Isa 42:14:

> For a long time I have held my peace,
> I have kept still and restrained myself;
> now I will cry out like a woman in labor,
> I will gasp and pant.

Again we are not told the reason for the silence, but we are told the character of the new speech as Yahweh breaks the silence too long kept. Yahweh speaks in Isaiah 42 about the restoration of Israel and in Isaiah 62 about the restoration of blessing for Israel. Yahweh breaks the chaos-permitting silence "like a woman in labor." This is a birthing surge of energy that wills to be generative. Perhaps it is action out of affection for Israel, like a mother for a child, an irrepressible, indomitable will for the well-being of the child (cf. Isa 49:14-15). Perhaps it is generative energy within the bones and body of Yahweh. In either case, what now is asserted is new energy that refuses to leave things nullified and in a state of exile/chaos/death.

The recovery of Isa 42:14ff. is historical and concerns the recovery of Israel. But the rhetoric also concerns action in the reordering of all of creation:

> I will lay waste mountains and hills,
> and dry up all their herbage;
> I will turn the rivers into islands,
> and dry up the pools.
> I will lead the blind

by a road they do not know,
by paths they have not known
I will guide them.
I will turn the darkness before them into light,
the rough places into level ground.
These are the things I will do,
and I will not forsake them. (Isa 42:15-16)

This is a powerful, irresistible, transformative resolve, to be undertaken with a high level of emotional intensity. It is a burst of generativity that is going to change everything and create a newness. This is a God who will not forsake:

... I will not forsake them. (Isa 42:16)

You shall no more be termed Forsaken. ... (Isa 62:4)

In this resolve to new creation, Yahweh promises to overcome all forsakenness and abandonment known in Israel and in the world. When creation is abandoned by Yahweh, it readily reverts to chaos. Here it is in Yahweh's resolve, and in Yahweh's very character, not to abandon, but to embrace. The very future of the world, so Israel attests, depends on this resolve of Yahweh. It is a resolve that is powerful. More than that, it is a resolve that wells up precisely in *tohû wabohû* and permits the reality of the world to begin again, in blessedness.

EIGHTEEN

The Drama of Partnership with Yahweh

MANY OTHER THINGS, of course, can be said usefully on these four subjects—Israel, human persons, the nations, and creation. I suggest, nonetheless, that the discussion in the preceding four chapters considers the major aspects of the four subjects in relationship to Yahweh. Indeed, even in relationship to Yahweh, the materials can be construed and pieced together somewhat differently from the way I have done it. It is my judgment, however, that if one begins with (a) the incommensurability of Yahweh's sovereign freedom, (b) mutuality rooted in Yahweh's generous pathos-inclined fidelity, and (c) the unsettled, always to-be-negotiated tension of incommensurate sovereignty and mutual fidelity, something like the above picture is sure to emerge. As a concluding statement on these four partners of Yahweh, I will first consider a recurring pattern in the four partners, then a reflection on Yahweh as given us in this unsolicited testimony, and finally a reflection on the significance of this witness amid the dominant ideologies of our interpretive venue.

Recurring Pattern in the Partners

It is a temptation and a bane of Old Testament theology to try to thematize or schematize data excessively, and I have no wish to impose a pattern on the material. Because of the character of Yahweh, however, I suggest that for each of these partners, the data permit *a dramatic movement:*

Dramatic Movement for Yahweh's Partners

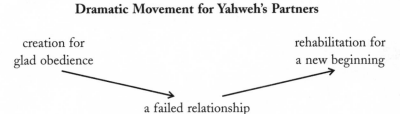

creation for
glad obedience

rehabilitation for
a new beginning

a failed relationship

I suggest this pattern only as a rough perspective, which has to be adjusted for each partner; indeed, it needs to be given different nuance in each text. Nonetheless, this drama of brokenness and restoration is the primary ingredient of life with Yahweh.

The Pattern with Israel

Israel's life with Yahweh is presented in this testimony as:

(a) created in love for glad obedience;

(b) scattered into exile;

(c) restored through Yahweh's pathos-filled love for obedience and hope.

If we trace this movement historically, we can see that it roughly correlates with the movement of: (a) early traditions, (b) the prophetic traditions, and (c) the emergence of Judaism.[1] Since we are here concerned with theology of Israel with reference to Yahweh, we more appropriately focus on the verbal sentences with Yahweh as subject, and not simply on "historical eventualities." Thus Israel's life is told as a drama of a people chosen and formed; judged and scattered; gathered, loved, forgiven, and remembered.

The Pattern with Human Persons

I have already observed that human persons, in Israel's unsolicited testimony, are in some way a replication of Israel's own life. Therefore the parallel to Israel does not surprise us. Thus human life, vis-à-vis Yahweh, is presented as:

(a) created for obedience, discernment, and trust;

(b) authorized in the Pit for complaint, petition, and thanksgiving;

(c) raised to new life for praise and hope.

It is of particular importance that in tracing human life into the Pit and out of the Pit, we observe that this sequence seems parallel to the creation-sin-redemption pattern of Christian theology—except that it is very different. It is possible to transpose this sequence, which we have found in Israel's testimony, into a doctrinal pattern of "creation-fall-redemption." But that is not at all what happens in Israel's testimony. Israel is not consistent in its judgment about how human persons end in the Pit. It never occurs to Israel to reduce entry into the Pit to guilt or anything like "the fall." Israel's way of thinking is much more in medias res, without great explanatory curiosity.

In a second way, Israel's mode of speaking is important. We have noticed that reference to resurrection is very slight in the Old Testament. In the purview of this

---

1. Notice that (a) early traditions and (b) the prophetic traditions parallel Gerhard von Rad's scheme for Old Testament theology. It is important, given Christian supersessionist tendencies, that von Rad's scheme did not allow for emerging Judaism as a distinct component of Old Testament theology, not simply as an important aspect of the history of religion, but as a theological rehabilitation after exile.

testimony, it is likely that it is unnecessary and unhelpful to distinguish between the many rescues that occur in life with Yahweh and the "Big One" of life after death. All placements in the Pit are face to face with the power of death, and physical death is only an extreme case, different in degree but not in kind from all the other threats to human life. It is characteristically enough in Israel to assert that "the Pit" is a reality, and that when Yahweh can be mobilized, the grip and threat of the Pit can be overcome.[2] The truth of human personhood vis-à-vis Yahweh is that the human person is not helplessly and hopelessly consigned to the Pit, because the power of Yahweh can break the grip of the Pit. It was not necessary in Israel, nor especially useful, to move beyond such metaphorical language, because everyone understood what was being said, especially "Death," who imagined that he controlled the Pit (cf. Hos 13:14).

In one other important way this presentation differs from that of classical Christian theology. The person in the Pit is not to be passive and docile, awaiting the initiative of Yahweh. The whole pattern of the psalms of complaint suggests that in the Pit, the human person can and must initiate the process of rescue by shrill protest and insistent hope. It is not possible or appropriate, in the horizon of Israel, to worry about works and grace in such a transaction, because the mutuality of covenanting requires that both parties should be mightily engaged in the demanding, hopeful act of rescue.

The Pattern with the Nations

The situation is not different with the nations as partners of Yahweh, as we have seen, both with Israel's near neighbors and with the great imperial superpowers. Thus the nations:

(a) are summoned as Yahweh's vassals and instruments in the geopolitical process;

(b) are punished to nullification in their recalcitrance and arrogant autonomy;

(c) are promised new life with reason restored, as they come to terms with Yahweh's generous but uncompromising governance.

On this subject Israel speaks with great inventiveness and daring, willing and able to construe the international history of the world in ways congruent with its own life with Yahweh.

The Pattern with Creation

Again, the fundamental experience of Israel is writ large in the theme of creation. Creation is:

---

2. The imagery of "the Pit" is used typologically in a Kings College Chapel (Cambridge) window, which juxtaposes Joseph missing from the pit (Gen 37:29) with the scene of the empty tomb of Jesus in the gospel narrative.

(a) formed and founded in Yahweh's generosity as a world of blessing, given within the framework of Yahweh's governance;

(b) relinquished to the power of chaos and curse when human agents, charged with the well-being of creation, renege on their caretaking responsibility;

(c) imagined in newness, according to Yahweh's indomitable resolve.

It seems clear that Israel thinks and speaks from its own experience outward. For that reason, however, we do not conclude that Israel "cheated" in articulating creation. In the canonical formation of this testimony, it is Yahweh's sovereign fidelity with creation that provides the arena for the life of all the partners, including Israel. Thus we may say that the life of each of these partners is ordered into a drama of brokenness and restoration as shown in the accompanying diagram.

Drama of Brokenness and Restoration for Each of the Partners

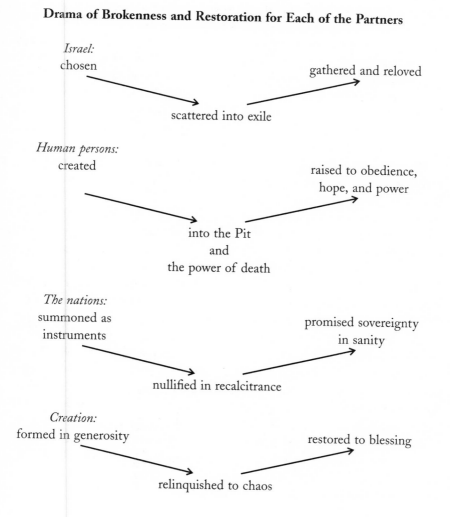

Israel:
chosen — scattered into exile — gathered and reloved

Human persons:
created — into the Pit and the power of death — raised to obedience, hope, and power

The nations:
summoned as instruments — nullified in recalcitrance — promised sovereignty in sanity

Creation:
formed in generosity — relinquished to chaos — restored to blessing

The unsolicited testimony of Israel yields a drama with profound risk and enormous dynamic, in which none of Yahweh's partners have any continuing power of their own. In the end, they are summoned outside themselves, in order to rely on this One whom Israel confesses to be uncompromising in sovereignty, but moved to always new measures of fidelity.

Israel's Articulation of Yahweh

My purpose in examining this testimony, in the context of our theological focus, is not primarily to learn something about the partners, though that in itself is a gain. My purpose, rather, is to learn more of Israel's articulation of Yahweh. I have said, at the outset of my exposition of this unsolicited testimony, that Israel as a witness had perhaps understood that *speech about these partners is necessary to a proper understanding of Yahweh*, because Yahweh is always Yahweh-in-relation.[3] Thus the drama of brokenness and restoration, which we have suggested for each of the partners, is a telling affirmation of Yahweh as articulated in Israel.

Self-giving engagement. Yahweh, in authorizing the life of each of these partners, is discerned by Israel as an agent of incomparable power, but one whose incomparable power is not simply for the celebration and enhancement of Yahweh's self, but for the generation of a partner. Yahweh, by the act of self-giving engagement, evokes partners who can be the objects of Yahweh's sovereignty and fidelity. Before the partner exists, Yahweh is for the partner in generous ways, creating an arena of blessing.

Rejection of autonomy. Yahweh, however, is seen to be uncompromising in the midst of that generosity. None of the partners is finally permitted autonomy. It may be that the partners' character is such that they are not qualified to be autonomous. But the reason given for the rejection of autonomy is characteristically not located in the partner, but in Yahweh. Yahweh's self-regard is massive, savage, and seemingly insatiable. That self-regard sets boundaries to Yahweh's initiatory generosity. Israel does not vex about the oddity of Yahweh's readiness to nullify Yahweh's own beloved partners. But neither does Israel flinch from acknowledging that Yahweh is a jealous God who is capable of irrational destructiveness.

Life-denying fissure. Yahweh can be addressed in the life-denying fissure of exile-death-impotence-chaos, to which Yahweh's partners seem inevitably to come. This affirmation may be one of the distinctive surprises of Yahweh as given in Israel's testimony. To the extent that the fissure is an outcome of Yahweh's rejecting rage, or to the extent that it is a result of Yahweh's loss of power in the face of the counterpower of death, we might expect that a loss to nullity is irreversible. Thus, "when you're dead, you're dead," "when you're in exile, you're in exile."

Yahweh mobilized by cries from the Pit. This unsolicited testimony of Israel, however, moves beyond irreversibility in two stunning affirmations. First, Yahweh

---

3. See my programmatic comments on this claim at the beginning of Part 4, pp. 567–68.

is inclined toward and attentive to those in the nullity. Yahweh can be reached, summoned, and remobilized for the sake of life. Beyond Yahweh's harsh sovereignty, Yahweh has a soft underside to which appeal can be made. Israel (and we) are regularly astonished that working in tension with Yahweh's self-regard is Yahweh's readiness to be engaged with and exposed for the sake of the partner.

Second, the mobilization of Yahweh in the season of nullity characteristically requires an act of initiative on the part of the abandoned partner. This is classically articulated in the complaints of Israel, subsequently retold in songs of thanksgiving:

> To you, O Lord, I cried,
> and to the Lord I made supplication:
> "What profit is there in my death,
> if I go down to the Pit?
> Will the dust praise you?
> Will it tell of your faithfulness?
> Hear, O Lord, and be gracious to me!
> O Lord, be my helper!" (Ps 30:8-10)

> I waited patiently for the Lord;
> he inclined to me and heard my cry.
> He drew me up from the desolate pit,
> out of the miry bog,
> and set my feet upon a rock,
> making my steps secure.
> He put a new song in my mouth,
> a song of praise to our God.
> Many will see and fear,
> and put their trust in the Lord. (Ps 40:1-3)

> Then they cried to the Lord in their trouble, and he delivered them
> from their distress.... (Ps 107:6; cf. vv. 13, 19, 28)

This capacity to mobilize Yahweh to new activity by cries in the Pit is also evident in Israel's inadvertent triggering of the Exodus by its shrill cry of need and anguish:

> The Israelites groaned under their slavery, and cried out. Out of slavery their
> cry for help rose up to God. God heard their groaning, and God remembered
> his covenant with Abraham, Isaac, and Jacob. God looked upon the Israelites,
> and God took notice of them. (Exod 2:23-25)

The cry may not always be a prerequisite for rescue; Yahweh may also take initiative. The cry is prominent enough, however, to undermine any theological conclusion about deferential waiting for Yahweh's initiative. Thus even in Psalm 40, where the speaker "waits patiently," the waiting is in the context of having cried out. Israel is not at all deferential, and does not imagine that human persons in such situations will be deferential. It is in this context that Israel issues its countertestimony against Yahweh, in order to mobilize the Yahweh of the core testimony to act characteristically one more time. Thus the God who by incommensurate sovereignty can rescue from nullity is addressed and reached, precisely by play on Yahweh's available mutuality. Yahweh is seen by Israel to be Yahweh's variegated self, precisely in the fissure. Indeed, Israel's faith is formed, generated, and articulated, precisely with reference to the fissure, which turns out to be the true place of life for Yahweh's partner and the place wherein Yahweh's true character is not only disclosed, but perhaps fully formed.[4] The reality of nullity causes a profound renegotiation of Yahweh's sovereignty vis-à-vis Yahweh's pathos-filled fidelity.

The miracle of radical newness. Yahweh, who is addressed and reached in the nullity, is known in Israel to be a God willing and able to enact a radical newness for each of Yahweh's partners, a newness that the partners cannot work for themselves. This newness is deeply shaped by Yahweh's initial acts of sovereign generosity, but it runs well beyond the imagination of those in the nullity. Because this inexplicable, unanticipated newness is the same for all of these partners, it is with good reason that H. H. Schmid has concluded that *creatio ex nihilo*, justification by faith, and resurrection of the dead are synonymous phrases.[5] These phrases are not isolated dogmatic themes. They are, rather, ways in which Yahweh's characteristic propensities of generosity are made visible in different contexts with different partners.

Materials for a Metanarrative

This drama of brokenness and restoration is the primary outcome of the transactions between Yahweh and Yahweh's partners. The work of Old Testament theology, it seems to me, is an articulation of a metanarrative that is a strong contrast to the metanarratives currently available in our society (and in the church, to the extent that the church also partakes of the dominant narratives of society).

I am profoundly ill at ease with the use of the term *metanarrative*, by which I mean simply a more-or-less coherent perspective on reality. I am ill at ease, first, because I am impressed with the plurality, diversity, and fragmented quality of the Old Testament text, and I have no wish to engage in reductionism. Second, I am ill at ease with the term because I take seriously, along with my deconstructionist friends and colleagues, Jean-François Lyotard's suspicion of metanarrative, with its hegemonic potential.[6] For all of that, however, I am impressed with the

---

4. On the exile as the matrix of Israel's faith, see pp. 74–78.

5. H. H. Schmid, "Rechtfertigung als Schöpfungsgeschehen: Notizen zur alttestamentlichen Vorgeschichte eines neutestamentlichen Themas," *Rechtfertigung: Festschrift für Ernst Käsemann* (ed. Johannes Friedrich et al.; Göttingen: Vandenhoeck and Ruprecht, 1976) 403–14.

6. Jean-François Lyotard, *The Postmodern Condition: A Report on Knowledge* (Minneapolis: University of Minnesota Press, 1984).

odd—Yahwistically odd and Jewishly odd—offer of a perspective in these texts that clearly is in profound tension with the regnant metanarratives of our society. I will settle for the judgment that the Old Testament is not a metanarrative but offers the materials out of which a metanarrative is to be construed. I will settle for that, so long as it is recognized that any metanarrative construed out of these materials must include certain claims and awarenesses that cannot be compromised.

I will exposit those nonnegotiable awarenesses in relation to Enlightenment liberalism and in relation to the standard claims of classical Christianity.[7] Vis-à-vis the claims of Enlightenment liberalism, Israel's Yahwistic account of brokenness and restoration may yield several enormously important insistences.

Limitless Generosity at Root of Reality

At the root of reality is a *limitless generosity* that intends an extravagant abundance. This claim is exposited in Israel's creation texts, sapiential traditions, and hymnic exuberances. This insistence flies in the face of the theory of scarcity on which the modern world is built. An *ideology of scarcity* produces a competitiveness that issues in brutality, justifies policies of wars and aggression, authorizes an acute individualism, and provides endless anxiety about money, sexuality, physical fitness, beauty, work achievements, and finally mortality.[8] It seems to me that, in the end, all of these anxieties are rooted in an ideology that resists a notion of limitless generosity and extravagant abundance.

It is a hard question how literally and how seriously to take Israel's lyrical claims, which Israel itself often did not take seriously. Do these claims mean simply that all humankind should be nice and share, and we will all get along? Do they mean that as we trust abundance, we will learn a kind of joy that does not need so much? Or might they mean, in a venturesome antimodernity, that the genuine practice of trust causes the earth to produce more, so that justice evokes the blessings of the earth? That is the claim of the blessing theology of Lev 26:3-13 and Deut 28:1-14. From the perspective of our several Enlightenment metanarratives, such a claim is outrageous and absurd. But the outrage may at bottom signify nothing more than the totalizing power of the ideology of scarcity. One must depart the narrative of scarcity in order to host this lyrical affirmation of generosity and abundance, a departure to which Israel was summoned each time it engaged in worship and reflection.[9]

---

7. Enlightenment liberalism is now variously expressed and practiced in the church, both as "conservatism" and as "liberalism," for both parties to current quarrels tend to move from the presuppositions of such liberalism. These competing theological postures tend to correlate with the categories of "propositional" theology and "expressive-experiential" hermeneutics, suggested by George Lindbeck, *The Nature of Doctrine: Religion and Theology in a Postliberal Age* (Philadelphia: Westminster Press, 1984).

8. M. Douglas Meeks, *God the Economist: The Doctrine of God and Political Economy* (Minneapolis: Fortress Press, 1989), has shrewdly and compellingly analyzed the function of the myth of scarcity.

9. The departure from the narrative of scarcity (on which see Isa 55:12-13) is liturgical and symbolic, but finally is economic and political. See Marie Augusta Neal, *A Socio-theology of Letting Go: The Role of a First World Church Facing Third World Peoples* (New York: Paulist Press, 1977).

Fissure at Center of Reality

At the center of reality is a deep, radical, painful, costly *fissure*, that will, soon or late, break every self-arranged pattern of well-being. This claim is exposited in the texts of the Deuteronomic tradition, the prophetic lawsuits, the complaint psalms, and the theology of the Book of Job. In the Old Testament, no creaturely arrangement survives Yahweh's governance unscathed—not mighty Babylon, not the temple of Yahweh's presence in Jerusalem, not the beloved Davidic king to whom Yahweh has made unconditional promises. The chosen people are forced into exile, people suffer and die, nations and empires fall, and floods come upon the earth. It cannot be helped, and it cannot be avoided.

We have seen, moreover, that Israel's struggle to bear true witness about this reality is complicated and unresolved. Much of the nullity besetting the partners of Yahweh comes as a consequence of sin and defiance, as punishment of the sovereign, but there is more. The partner who suffers is often perpetrator, but also sometimes victim. Sometimes the partner is victim of Yahweh's negligence, whereby the hosts of the Nihil run rampant in the earth; sometimes the partner is victim of Yahweh's mean-spirited irascibility... sometimes.

In any case, as perpetrator or as victim or as both, the partner of Yahweh must make claim against Yahweh. It is in this context that Israel voices its countertestimony. Israel seizes the initiative against Yahweh, protests Yahweh's hiddenness, unreliability, and negativity. Sometimes—not always—these protests lead to restoration and rehabilitation by the resolve of Yahweh.

This insistence on the reality of brokenness flies in the face of the Enlightenment practice of *denial*. Enlightenment rationality, in its popular, uncriticized form, teaches that with enough reason and resources, brokenness can be avoided. And so Enlightenment rationality, in its frenzied commercial advertising, hucksters the goods of denial and avoidance: denial of headaches and perspiration and loneliness, impotence and poverty and shame, embarrassment and, finally, death.[10] In such ideology there are no genuinely broken people. When brokenness intrudes into such an assembly of denial, as surely it must, it comes as failure, stupidity, incompetence, and guilt. The church, so wrapped in the narrative of denial, tends to collude in this. When denial is transposed into guilt—into personal failure—the system of denial remains intact and uncriticized, in the way Job's friends defended "the system."

The outcome for the isolated failure is that there can be no healing, for there has not been enough candor to permit it. In the end, such denial is not only a denial of certain specifics—it is the rejection of the entire drama of brokenness and healing, the denial that there is an incommensurate Power and Agent who comes in pathos

---

10. This rationality has been well exposited by Jacques Ellul, *The Technological Society* (London: Jonathan Cape, 1965). Ellul, *Propaganda: The Formation of Men's Attitudes* (New York: Vintage Books, 1973), has also explored the power of advertising to promote and sustain the unexamined values of that rationality. As advertising is largely a practice of denial supported and sustained by technology, see the ominous analysis of Ernst Becker, *The Denial of Death* (New York: Free Press, 1973).

into the brokenness, and who by coming there makes the brokenness a place of possibility.

The denial precludes participation in the *candor* that assaults the system and that makes newness possible. Israel, of course, knew about the practice of denial. Israel knew how to imagine its own immunity from threat and risk:

> As for me, I said in my prosperity,
> "I shall never be moved." (Ps 30:6)

In its honest embrace of Yahweh, however, Israel did not freeze in its denial, but moved on in a way that made newness a possibility:

> You have turned my mourning into dancing;
> you have taken off my sackcloth
> and clothed me with joy,
> so that my soul may praise you
> and not be silent.
> O Lord my God, I will give
> thanks to you forever. (Ps 30:11-12)

Israelite Hope versus Enlightenment Despair

At the culmination of Israel's portrayal of reality is a certitude and a vision of newness, a full restoration to well-being that runs beyond any old well-being. This culmination in well-being, assured by the resolve of Yahweh, is articulated in the conclusion of most psalms of complaint and in prophetic promises that eventuate in messianic and apocalyptic expectations. Israel's speech witnesses to *profound hope*, based in the promise-maker and promise-keeper for whom all things are possible.

Israel refuses to accept that any context of nullity—exile, death, chaos—is a permanent conclusion to reality. Israel, in such circumstance, articulated hope rooted, not in any discernible signs in the circumstance, but in the character of Yahweh (based on old experience), who was not a prisoner of circumstance but was able to override circumstance in order to implement promises. This hope is not incidental in Israel's life; it is a bedrock, identity-giving conviction, nurtured in nullity, that Yahweh's good intentions have not and will not be defeated. As a consequence, complainers anticipate well-being and praise. Israel awaits homecoming, the dead look to new life, creation expects reordering.

All of this requires confidence in an agent outside the system of defeat. Enlightenment liberalism, which sets the liberated, self-sufficient human agent at the center of reality, can entertain or credit no such agent outside the system. Without such an agent who exists in and through Israel's core testimony, there are no new gifts to be given and no new possibilities to be received. Thus, put simply, the alternative to Israelite hope is *Enlightenment despair.* In such a metanarrative, when human capacity is exhausted, all is exhausted. Ultimate trust is placed in human capacity, human ingenuity, and human technology. It is self-evident that such a trust cannot deliver, and so ends in despair, for self-sufficiency is only a whisker away from despair. Such a reading of reality engenders fear and hate, self-hate, and brutality. But Israel, inside its peculiar testimony, refuses such a reading.

I state the contrast as boldly and sweepingly as I know how. The drama of brokenness and restoration, which has Yahweh as its key agent, features *generosity*, *candor* in brokenness, and resilient *hope*, the markings of a viable life. The primary alternative now available to us features *scarcity*, *denial*, and *despair*, surely the ingredients of nihilism.

To be sure, for all its venturesome witness, Israel did not always choose cleanly. Israel accommodated and compromised. It practiced scarcity as much as it trusted generosity. It engaged occasionally in denial, for all its embrace of brokenness. It lived close to despair, for all its resources of hope. The amazing thing, in my judgment, is not that Israel compromised; it is that Israel kept its testimony as sustained as it did amid the pressures and demands of its circumstance. It kept its testimony enough of a coherent assertion that it was able to say, in the voice of Yahweh, to itself, to its own children, and to any others who would listen:

> See, I have set before you today life and prosperity, death and adversity. If you obey the commandments of the Lord your God that I am commanding you today, by loving the Lord your God, walking in his ways, and observing his commandments, decrees, and ordinances, then you shall live and become numerous, and the Lord your God will bless you in the land that you are entering to possess. But if your heart turns away and you do not hear, but are led astray to bow down to other gods and serve them, I declare to you today that you shall perish; you shall not live long in the land that you are crossing the Jordan to enter and possess. I call heaven and earth to witness against you today that I have set before you life and death, blessings and curses. Choose life so that you and your descendants may live, loving the Lord your God, obeying him, and holding fast to him; for that means life to you and length of days, so that you may live in the land that the Lord swore to give to your ancestors, to Abraham, to Isaac, and to Jacob. (Deut 30:15-20)

This Deuteronomic assertion, derivative from the vision of Moses, proved durable enough for Israel that in its season of rehabilitation, Ezra could still affirm:

> Nevertheless, in your great mercies you did not make an end of them or forsake them, for you are a gracious and merciful God. (Neh 9:31)

The choosing between construals of reality is something Israel always had to do again. And the choosing is not yet finished.

Classical Christianity's Tilt toward Closure

A second vision of reality against which the Old Testament may play is the articulation of classical Christianity. Here I will deal much more briefly with the interface and the tension between construals, for on the whole, classical Christianity shares claims with Israel's testimony against Enlightenment liberalism. That is, classical Christianity, like ancient Israel, affirms *generosity* over scarcity, *brokenness* in the face of denial, and *hope* instead of despair. I want to assert only one point that is sharply at issue between these narrative offers. I have repeatedly stressed that Israel deals with an incommensurate God who is endlessly at risk in mutuality. That is, Yahweh is seen by Israel to be genuinely dialectical, always on one end of a disputatious transaction that may effect change in Yahweh as well as in Yahweh's partners. We have seen this profound unresolve already in Exod 34:6-7. We have seen it regularly in the noun-metaphors used for Yahweh. Most largely, we have seen this dialectical quality in the juxtaposition of what I have called core testimony and countertestimony. Israel's transactions with Yahweh are indeed characteristically open and unsettled.

It appears to me, granting the enormous difference made by a christological center in Christian faith, that the real issue that concerns us in Old Testament theology is this: Classical Christianity is tilted in a transcendental direction, which gives closure to Yahweh and to Yahweh's relationships with the partners. There may be many reasons for such a closure; perhaps not least is the need of a derivative tradition (Christianity) to substantiate its claim against the precursive tradition (Judaism). For whatever reason, this tendency to transcendental closure compromises the genuinely dialectical quality of Jewish testimony. That compromise, moreover, is of crucial importance for what is possible and what is precluded in our discernment of God, world, and self.[11]

I do not imagine that Christianity in its classical forms will yield much, soon, on this score. But there are hints that as Christianity in the West is increasingly disestablished, and so may distance itself from its Hellenistic-Constantinian propensity, it may move in the direction of its Jewish dimension of genuine unsettlement between Yahweh and Yahweh's partners. There is no doubt that this drama of brokenness and restoration is shared by Judaism and Christianity. In Judaism, it is a drama of:

exile and homecoming,

death and resurrection,

Pit and rescue, and

chaos and creation.

---

11. Edward T. Oakes, *Pattern of Redemption: The Theology of Hans Urs von Balthasar* (New York: Continuum, 1994), especially 72–78, 277–99, has suggested that in contemporary Roman Catholic theology, Urs von Balthasar, for all his deep conservatism, indicates an openness to the possibility that this dialectic may indeed be present in the very character of God. Oakes suggests that Urs von Balthasar is more receptive to this than is Karl Rahner, for all the apparent openness of the latter.

To that set of categories of discernment, Christianity adds (decisively for its identity) crucifixion and resurrection. That of course is a specific move the Old Testament (and Judaism) do not make. The differential on this point is very great.

What strikes me more, however, is that these traditions are, in the main, agreed. That agreement is the basis for a genuine alternative to the nihilism of the modern world, a nihilism contained in the elimination of this incommensurate, mutual One in the interest of autonomy and self-sufficiency. This testimony of Israel, echoed by Christianity, not only gives different answers—it insists on different questions, wherein the answers offered are perforce thin and tenuous, but not for that reason unuttered. The intramural quarrels in the church, and the ancient alienations between Christians and Jews, are unconscionable, in my judgment, when this lean, resilient tradition stands as a fragile alternative to the embrace of the Nihil.

Part IV

ISRAEL'S EMBODIED
TESTIMONY

NINETEEN

Mediating the Presence of Yahweh

I T IS NOW NECESSARY to step away somewhat from our governing metaphor of testimony, inside of which we have attempted to stay until now. We have sought to pay attention to the internal dynamic and to the intentionality of that witness, without raising any of the usual critical questions that preoccupy scholars. We have proceeded in this way because, insofar as it is possible, we have tried to pay attention solely to Israel's utterance of Yahweh, and consideration of that subject does not require consideration of many of the usual historical questions.

By paying attention solely to that utterance, we have seen that, everywhere in Israel's testimony about Yahweh, the God to which Israel bears witness is Yahweh-in-relation. For that reason we have given extensive attention to Yahweh's partners, for Yahweh is characteristically, in freedom and passion,

in relation to Israel,

in relation to human persons,

in relation to the nations, and

in relation to creation.

That much seems unarguable.

Moreover, we have seen that this in-relatedness is pervasively unsettled and unsettling. The relationships remain unsettled and unsettling because of the character of Yahweh, who is at the same time nonnegotiably sovereign (incommensurate) and endlessly faithful (engaged in mutuality). Israel can find no way in its testimony to resolve the jaggedness of a relationship marked by both incommensurability and mutuality. It is for that theological reason—a reason rooted in Yahweh's own character without respect to sociohistorical, cultural factors—that the relatedness of Yahweh is so problematic. For after Israel has given witness to the relatedness of Yahweh, one who hears the testimony still wonders: What in fact is the nature of this relationship?

Michelangelo's painting of creation on the Sistine Chapel ceiling offers something of an illuminating commentary on this problematic. In the painting, God appears to have flung out the first human creatures into creation. In their initial moment of existence as God's creatures, the first humans are juxtaposed to God.

Both God and the humans have their hands and arms extended to one another. One senses that it is appropriate that Creator and creature should be connected. Their fingertips come close to each other . . . but they do not touch. In that moment of not touching, Michelangelo has articulated the strange otherness of the Creator God, with whom the creature has no direct contact.

In Israel, however, unlike the Sistine Chapel, they do make contact! While the incommensurability of Yahweh would seem to require that they do not, Yahweh, in mutuality, moves out of incommensurability (kenosis) for the sake of contact;[1] but it is contact that does not compromise Yahweh's sovereign incommensurability. This difficult problem and its several resolutions in ancient Israel constitute the subject of our present discussion. It is daring of Israel to insist on relatedness with Yahweh. But to be specific about that relatedness requires that along with the daring of Israel's utterance, we pay attention, as best we can, to the practices that give the testimony *concrete embodiment*. It is clear that Israel's work, in matching practice to rhetoric, was to articulate and accept modes of mediation, whereby the fullness of Yahweh's sovereign, faithful self was genuinely available to Israel. While admitting that this issue is endlessly problematic, we see that Israel was not lacking in ways whereby Yahweh's presence, power, and purposes were available to it.

The Unmediated Presence of Yahweh

Before considering the mediated forms of Yahweh's presence that mark the life and practice of Israel, we must inquire about the immediacy of Yahweh's presence—that is, the ways in which Yahweh is available directly in Israel without any mediating agents.

I will treat the subject of immediacy in two parts: public and personal. In doing so, I suggest that in fact Israel has no particular, primary interest in this question, but says what it says on the subject only as a means of getting to some other more important point.

Public Immediacy in Theophany

The public presentation of Yahweh's immediacy is characteristically expressed in theophany, a genre of testimony that describes Yahweh's massive intrusion into life in a way that exhibits Yahweh's awesome, ferocious power. Jörg Jeremias has shown that a theophany in Israel, in general, is characterized as an intrusive presence coming from a specific place, an intrusion that is disruptive and cataclysmic in nature and that leaves in its wake a decisively changed situation.[2] Jeremias's study is concerned primarily with the literary genre. The examples he considers include:

---

1. I. A. Dorner, *Divine Immutability: A Critical Reconsideration* (Minneapolis: Fortress Press, 1994), has provided a classic statement of the way in which kenosis undermines incommensurability (which in his rhetoric is treated under the rubric of "immutability").

2. Jörg Jeremias, *Theophanie; Die Geschichte einer alttestamentlichen Gattung* (WMANT 10; Neukirchen-Vluyn: Neukirchener Verlag, 1965). See also J. Kenneth Kuntz, *The Self-Revelation of God* (Philadelphia: Westminster Press, 1967).

Judg 5:4ff., Deut 33:2, Hab 3:3, Ps 68:8ff., Mic 1:3ff., Amos 1:2, Ps 46:7, and Isa 19:1. When we move beyond genre analysis to consider theophany as a way in which Yahweh relates to Yahweh's partners, it is clear that theophany is an enactment of sovereignty and that it is completely originary. It has no antecedent and is not extrapolated from anything else, but is decisively generative of that which follows from it. It is impossible to provide a theological critique of theophany, and we must say that it is a primary theological datum itself—that is, a premise of all that follows. In the mode of theophany, Yahweh relates as Yahweh chooses, without condition, reservation, qualification, or explanation. Israel is on the receiving end of holy intrusion, left to characterize in human speech, as best it can, what is unutterable in the sublimity of Yahweh.

Theophany at Sinai. When we come to think theologically about Yahweh as given in theophany, our focus is most obviously drawn to the theophany of Sinai. In Exod 19:9-25, and its peculiar culmination in Exod 24:9-18, Israel as a community gathers around Moses and, as the community that lives in the core traditions, has its definitive and decisive encounter with Yahweh. Jeremias, in addition to noting the complex critical issues in this textual unit, observes that no "upheaval of nature" is mentioned in this report of theophany.[3] But there is indeed an awesome, disruptive coming of the Holy One. We may identify the central elements in this theophany, which we take as originary for Israel as a community of faith:

(a) Exod 19:9-25. With appropriate cultic preparation (which already suggests mediation), Yahweh looms in the life of Israel as a dangerous, holy presence.

(b) Exod 20:1-17. The Decalogue is uttered directly from the mouth of Yahweh, so that fundamental Torah requirements are lodged in Israel's originary experience—beyond explanation, criticism, or management.

(c) Exod 20:18-21. The confrontation just reported evokes great fear in Israel, fear that requires a mediator, so that Israel moves promptly from immediacy to mediation.

(d) Exod 24:9-11. The leadership of Israel gazes upon Yahweh, though there is no reported transaction. This is a purely visual experience.

(e) Exod 24:12-14. The reality of Yahweh's sovereignty is coded into Written Torah.

(f) Exod 24:15-18. The confrontation is stylized in "glory," into which Moses enters.[4]

This is an extraordinary narrative report that defies decoding. There is no doubt, according to the testimony of Israel, that at Sinai an immediacy of meeting occurred that evoked fear (20:18) and invited communion (24:9-11). The encounter that engendered both fear and communion is direct and immediate.

Prompt move to mediation. The witness of Israel cannot stay long in such directness and immediacy, but promptly moves out of this mode of relatedness to

---

3. Jeremias, *Theophanie*, 106.
4. See pp. 671–72 on "glory" in cultic mediation.

one that is mediated and indirect. These mediated modes of presence take the form of (a) glory (which remains to be developed in the following Priestly narrative); (b) the role of Moses; and (c) the role of the coded, materially given Torah (which eventuates in Deuteronomic accents). I do not think it possible (or preferable) to minimize the definitional power of this theophany. Israel attests that it was indeed an awesome, physical presence of Yahweh.

Without minimizing this theophany in its directness and immediacy, however, it is equally clear that the theophany, in Israel's testimony, takes on an instrumental function. It operates in the completed text to verify and legitimate the modes of mediation on which Israel crucially relies: the person of Moses, the cultic glory, and the Written Torah. In the sacramental parlance of the church, the Sinai theophany is "the words of institution." Thus theophany promptly moves, in the witness of Israel, to mediated, stylized, regularized forms of transaction. Israel could not do, in its testimony, without an account of originary confrontation as a trigger to all that follows. But Israel moves with dispatch beyond such accents to the practice of mediated faith. (This is parallel to resurrection, which is a theophany in the early church. The church could not do without narratives of direct resurrection encounter; but it moves in its life of obedience and praise to more regularized forms.)

Personal Encounters

In addition to the great public ways of direct relationship in theophany, it is evident in Israel's testimony that Yahweh on occasion deals directly with individual persons. Much of this evidence is unreflective and almost incidental. Among such evidences, Israel partakes of something like mythic presentations of intimacy with God (as in Gen 3:8). Human persons meet God in dreams and sleep, and God visits individual persons by invasions of the spirit (1 Sam 10:9-13; 19:18-24). In these sorts of references, Israel exhibits no special curiosity and no self-consciousness. We may conclude that such accounts are reflective of the modes of mediation assumed in the religious environment in which Israel participated. In general, these sorts of encounters tend to have no enduring significance for Israel; that is, Israel does not often refer back to them. Beyond such incidental references, we may mention three personal encounters that surely are more significant for Israel's sense of its relatedness to Yahweh.

Abraham. First, Yahweh's way with Abraham is direct and immediate, a means whereby the power and summons of promise are irreversibly embedded in the life of Israel. Yahweh's relatedness to Abraham includes direct speech (Gen 12:1-3, 15:1-6, 22:1-2). Moreover, Abraham is decisively impinged upon by Yahweh in his sleep (Gen 15:12-16). But it is especially in Genesis 18 that Abraham has direct interaction with Yahweh. This includes (a) conversation in which Yahweh is unrecognized (vv. 1-15); (b) Yahweh's extraordinary acknowledgment of intimacy with Abraham, from whom Yahweh will hide nothing (vv. 17-19, cf. Isa 41:8); and

(c) the remarkable bargaining session between the two (vv. 22-32).[5] It is clear in this last episode that all distance between the two partners is overcome, so that the promise to Abraham becomes a central datum for the way in which Yahweh will continue to be related to Israel.

Moses. It is with Moses that Yahweh has the most direct and significant contact. This includes the initial contact at the burning bush (Exod 3:1-6; and derivatively 3:7–4:17). In this encounter, we notice that (a) Yahweh holds complete initiative for the exchange; (b) Moses participates in the encounter as a lively, legitimate partner (not unlike Abraham in Gen 18:22-32); and (c) the upshot of the encounter is a vocation assigned to Moses for the sake of Israel. That is, the personal encounter is not for its own sake—it is for the sake of the community, as was the case with Abraham. In addition to his familiarly assigned role as mediator (Exod 20:18-21), Moses is established as one who has a personal connection with Yahweh, to the great benefit of Israel. This twofold connection with Yahweh, as intimate friend and as designated mediator, is exhibited and exploited in the subsequent narrative. Thus in Exod 32:11-14 Moses is able to intervene effectively on behalf of Israel. In 33:7-11 Yahweh is said to speak "to Moses face to face, as one speaks to a friend" (v. 11). In 33:11–34:10 and in Num 11:10-17, Moses acts in the face of Yahweh with great freedom and courage, for the sake of Israel.

Elijah. In 1 Kgs 19:5-18 Elijah is presented as recipient of a theophany.[6] It seems likely that Elijah is here understood as something of a replica of Moses. In any case, part of the encounter is in sleep (v. 5), and the outcome of the whole is vigorous, risky intervention in the life of Israel and of its neighbors (vv. 15-18).

Clearly a great deal more can be said about these exemplar cases, and about other cases as well, especially in the prophets. This evidence, however, is enough for the purposes of our investigation of the immediacy of Yahweh in relation to Israel. These personal encounters suggest three observations that pertain to the larger issue of immediacy and mediation.

Originary theological data. These narrative accounts, which are originary and inscrutable, are pivotally important for the life and self-presentation of Israel. Yahweh does indeed enter into such direct encounters with identifiable individual persons, who subsequently give shape and identity to Israel. If these encounters are not reduced to psychological explanations, they must be left as originary theological data, as the authorizing beginning point for Israel's faith.

Rare, freighted occurrences. These personal encounters, as given us in narrative accounts, are rare and pertain, characteristically, to specially designated persons. No general immediacy or directness is offered to Israelites. When these encounters occur, they are indeed freighted, dangerous, and special. Israel's sense of Yahweh's relatedness is that Yahweh is only guardedly and rarely available to individual persons.

---

5. Note should be taken of the "scribal correction" in v. 22. If the text is read without the "correction," Abraham's standing vis-à-vis Yahweh is even more prominent and authoritative.

6. Jeremias, *Theophanie*, 112–15.

Communal import. These characteristic encounters, rare and crucial as they are, issue regularly in matters of communal import. While the "experience" of Yahweh is valued, what matters in the narrative testimony of Israel is a vocation of obedience that is given, undertaken at great risk, and with weighty implications for the community:

> Take your son, your only son Isaac, whom you love, and go to the land of Moriah, and offer him there as a burnt offering on one of the mountains that I shall show you. (Gen 22:2)

> So come, I will send you to Pharaoh to bring my people, the Israelites, out of Egypt. (Exod 3:10)

> Go, return on your way to the wilderness of Damascus; when you arrive, you shall anoint Hazael as king over Aram. Also you shall anoint Jehu son of Nimshi as king over Israel; and you shall anoint Elisha son of Shaphat of Abel-meholah as prophet in your place. (1 Kgs 19:15-16)

These encounters with individual persons are characteristically not ends in themselves, but concern Yahweh's larger purposes. Individual persons are recruited for great risks.

The testimony of Israel concerning these direct meetings is indeed religious testimony, and so it tells of religious encounters. Whatever is "religious" in the Old Testament—a subject about which Israel is not terribly forthcoming—is characteristically reconstrued in the testimony of Israel, submitted to the oddness of Yahweh for which religion may be a vehicle. Israel did not shun or resist the resources of its religious environment, but participated in them fully. The religious resources available to Israel, however, are characteristically reread in the witness to Yahweh.

Mediations of Yahweh's Presence

Because Yahweh is such an irascible God, meeting with and relating to Yahweh is never easy, obvious, or predictable. Insofar as such meeting is dangerous (cf. Exod 20:18-21), or insofar as the meeting aims at the community and not just individual persons, the data given us show that the meetings are regularly stylized and routinized, to make possible the ongoing relatedness of Yahweh to the community. Thus the data about immediate relatedness are important, but they are also minimal. So we must consider the ways in which Yahweh is mediated in relation to Israel.[7]

---

7. There is something endlessly inexplicable and inscrutable about mediation. Thus David Tracy, *The Analogical Imagination: Christian Theology and the Culture of Pluralism* (New York: Crossroad, 1981) 377, 385, can speak of "mediated immediacy." Martin Noth, "The Re-presentation of the Old Testament in Proclamation," *Essays on Old Testament Hermeneutics* (ed. Claus Westermann; Richmond: John Knox, 1963) 85, can speak of the tension between "mediateness" and "immediateness." See Robert R. Wilson, *Prophecy and Society in Ancient Israel* (Philadelphia: Fortress Press, 1980) 157–66, especially his citation of Hans-Joachim Kraus (n. 43) and James Muilenburg (n. 44).

Mediations toward Israel

When we come to speak about mediations, we are, so far as the Old Testament is concerned, focused on mediations of Yahweh *toward Israel*. This is an exceedingly important recognition that to some extent makes our task a bit more manageable. This recognition of a limit pertains in two ways. First, of the four partners of Yahweh we have discussed, we are concerned here only with Israel. This means, negatively, that we will not take up the question of how Yahweh relates to human persons, the nations, and creation—even as the Old Testament is not greatly interested in this question. We have seen, moreover, that in a general way, how Yahweh is understood in relation to these other partners is inferred by and derivative from Yahweh's ways of relating to Israel.[8] Thus, if we are able to be clear on that relationship between Yahweh and Israel, we shall have gone far in preparing for a more general statement of Yahweh's relatedness in a variety of arenas, each of which is quite particular. Second, because mediations in the Old Testament are toward Israel, we are permitted (and required) to focus on the modes of mediation that belong to Israel as a community with a historical identity and a more or less discernible social practice. That is, we are not concerned with theoretical mediations, but rather with real mediations whereby Israel understood (and so testified) itself as being seriously, palpably related to Yahweh.

The Text Itself as Mediator

Old Testament study in general and Old Testament theology in particular are in the first instant preoccupied with and limited to a text, to a practice of codified rhetoric. Thus at the first level, we may say that the only mediation of Yahweh from ancient Israel to which we have any access is the rhetorical operation of the text, which is variously an exercise of persuasion and testimony. While the text is what we have in hand, it is also evident that the text, in its stylized "final form," is removed from the concrete practice of the ancient community.

It is clear, from our exposition, as from elsewhere, that the rhetoric of the text is indeed a lively mode of mediation in which the community gathered around the text has found itself connected to Yahweh. James Kugel has observed how "the scroll" took on remarkable properties in the life of Judaism.[9] Moreover, in every contemporary "battle for the Bible" among Christians (and especially among Protestants), the text itself is understood as a mediation, which connects the listening, reading community to the central character of the text.

We are able to draw two conclusions when we consider the text itself as mediator. First, in rhetoric as mediation, in the utterance that bespeaks this connectedness everything is possible, everything is imaginable, and everything is

---

8. See pp. 499–500, where I have suggested the paradigmatic quality of Yahweh's relation to Israel for all of Yahweh's other relationships.

9. James L. Kugel, "The Rise of Scripture," *Early Biblical Interpretation*, James L. Kugel and Rowan A. Greer (Philadelphia: Westminster Press, 1986) 20 and passim. Kugel articulates the dynamic of the scroll as "the flying scroll."

utterable. Acts can be committed, miracles can be performed that in any other arena would be problematic. Second, the rhetoric of the text as mediation of Yahweh is enormously elusive, for the speech of the Bible conceals Yahweh even while it discloses Yahweh.[10] Thus to say that the Bible mediates God is not to say that the Bible "hands God over" to the reading community as possession or as prisoner. The reading community has been wont, on occasion, to imagine that it possessed or imprisoned the God of the Bible. Such a self-deception takes a Protestant form in bibliolatry and a Catholic form in magisterial infallibility. Such self-deceptions, however, are acts of serious disregard of the text in its daring specificity. The daring, maddeningly deconstructive temper of the text keeps its central character elusive and refuses to make Yahweh available in ways that violate Yahweh's odd character. Thus the function of the text as a mode of mediation confronts the reading community with all of the problematic that belongs to Yahweh's own unsettlement as a God who is both mutual and incommensurate.

Yahweh Generated in Communal Practice

In any case, *the rhetorical mediation of Yahweh in the Bible is not a disembodied, ideational operation.* In making this important point, I am greatly indebted to Gary Anderson.[11] It is Anderson's argument, informed by Clifford Geertz's notion of "thick description" and George Lindbeck's proposal for theological authority as "cultural-linguistic," that religious ideas are embedded in religious experience and practice, and that religious reality is constituted and generated by actual, sustained, concrete, communal practice.[12] Thus, I propose, Yahweh is generated and constituted, so far as the claims of Israel are concerned, in actual practices that mediate. The Bible is the product generated by a community, and the source that generates and nurtures the community as it practices Yahweh-in-relation. Thus the question of mediation is not a question of right theology (as in orthodoxy), a great and pervasive theological temptation, but it is a question of characteristic social practice that generates, constitutes, and mediates Yahweh in the midst of life.

For a long time, Old Testament scholarship has talked about Yahweh as "the God who acts in history," meaning in great transformative public events. Then, two-thirds of the way through the twentieth century, Old Testament scholarship largely ceased to talk this way, in its acute epistemological embarrassment. I am emboldened by Anderson's categories to suggest that we may recover the phrase "God's acts in history," if by the phrase we may mean that God acts in, emerges from, and is seen to be available in the regular disciplined, concrete enterprise that keeps Yahweh palpably on the horizon of Israel.

---

10. On the theme, see Samuel Terrien, *The Elusive Presence: Toward a New Biblical Theology* (New York: Harper and Row, 1978).

11. Gary A. Anderson, *A Time to Mourn, a Time to Dance: The Expression of Grief and Joy in Israelite Religion* (University Park: Pennsylvania State University Press, 1991).

12. Anderson's reference is to Clifford Geertz, "Religion as a Cultural System," *The Interpretation of Cultures* (New York: Basic Books, 1973) 87–125; and George A. Lindbeck, *The Nature of Doctrine: Religion and Theology in a Postliberal Age* (Philadelphia: Westminster Press, 1984).

Mediation in Daily Practice

In the following discussion I shall review five prominent mediations in the Old Testament—Torah, kingship, prophecy, cult, and wisdom—which consistently and with great discipline and reliability were practiced in ancient Israel.[13] These practices generated, constituted, mediated, and made Yahweh available in Israel. Some may protest that such an understanding of Yahweh, in the midst of these mediations, compromises Yahweh's reality as a metaphysical being who stands outside Israel's practice. We have in this exposition, however, long since refused to make a claim for Yahweh metaphysically, but have insisted that Yahweh lives in and through these testimonies of Israel, about whose truth, in the face of competing truths, decisions must be made.

More practically, I take up these practices of mediation as the arenas in which the rhetorical articulation of Yahweh, accompanied by whatever dramatic gestures were appropriate and commensurate, were undertaken.[14] Thus I entertain the judgment that Yahweh, as known, trusted, obeyed, and feared in Israel, is "there" in Israel only because of these sustained mediations that incessantly focus on Yahweh's oddity. Without these sustained mediations, Yahweh, who is so odd and irascible, so wondrous and awesome, would disappear from the life of Israel and from the life of the world. I take this notion to be an extension of Paul's declaration in Rom 10:14-15:

> But how are they to call on one in whom they have not believed? And how are they to believe in one of whom they have never heard? And how are they to hear without someone to proclaim him? And how are they to proclaim him unless they are sent?

The reality of Yahweh depends on the compelling case made regularly by the witnesses. And the witnesses make their case in utterance and gestures of mediation.

This emphasis on the practical, concrete mediations of Yahweh in the actual life of the community provides a tilt to this exposition of Old Testament theology, toward which I have been moving since settling on the governing metaphor of testimony. Thus my thesis is that Yahweh is given to Israel in practice (a practice made credible by the originary events that stand at the beginning of the process of these mediations). This judgment leads to two derivative observations. First, this is an important reminder that Old Testament theology is not simply an intellectual exercise. Wherever this testimony has been taken seriously, in ancient time or in

---

13. On the latter three, the most helpful and recent assessment is by Joseph Blenkinsopp, *Sage, Priest, Prophet: Religious and Intellectual Leadership in Ancient Israel* (Louisville: Westminster/John Knox, 1995). Blenkinsopp considers these figures in terms of social roles, precisely the approach useful for the question of their social embodiment.

14. I speak here consistently of both the rhetorical (speech) and the dramatic (gesture), even though we have no direct access to gesture. It is clear that gesture, as well as speech, was present in these mediations. In subsequent Christian theology, speech and gesture are transposed into "Word and Sacrament."

any time since then, it has been taken seriously in practice. Second, this judgment is an affirmation to ecclesial communities, Jewish and Christian, that the day-to-day disciplines and practices of the community are indeed theological activities, for such activities are the modes and arenas in which the utterances and gestures of Yahweh can be nurtured. These activities are received as reliable disclosures of the partner in relationship.[15] These practices, in ancient times and since, are thus not overly splashy or innovative or noteworthy. They are as slow, steady, and mundane as life itself. It is this history of day-to-dayness, conducted with some intentionality and courage, in which Yahweh is seen to be related to Israel, in ways of demanding, promissory sovereignty and forgiving, restorative fidelity.

The conclusion at which we arrive is that *available, visible daily practice, constituted and undertaken humanly, implements the defining linkages between Yahweh and Israel.* If we return to the painting of Michelangelo, it is clear that in the normal run of things, Yahweh in heaven and Israel on earth do not touch. Yahweh-in-relation, however, is not Yahweh-in-relation unless there is real connection—unless they do touch. Everything in Israel's testimony about Yahweh depends on this contact being not only possible but effective, known, and trusted in Israel.

Israel's practical resolution of this problem of effecting the impossible contact is undertaken, it is asserted, at the behest and under the authority of Yahweh. Effecting the impossible contact is done, because these five modes of mediation (and others that might also be added) are given and taken and accepted and enacted in Israel as effective signs from God's side. By effective sign, I mean that they decisively enact the thing (Yahweh's presence and purpose) to which they point.[16] Thus, "this" signifies "that." Prophetic activity by human persons signifies word. Priestly acts signify presence. Royal acts signify Yahweh's political governance. Wisdom sayings signify the discernible order of creation given by God.

Said another way, these modes of mediation have a sacramental force. As my childhood eucharistic liturgy affirmed, "We have to do here not merely with these signs, but with the realities which these signs represent."[17] And the "reality" that these "signs represent" is the reality of Yahweh, who in incommensurability and mutuality deals with Israel. It is not possible to say why or how such signs are efficacious. Read sociologically, this community generates significance and socializes its members into that significance. Read theologically, these are acts of generosity by Yahweh, who not only intends to be related, but who provides the reliable means of such relatedness.

It has been my wont to say that Yahweh's "natural habitat" is the text of the Old Testament, and there is no Yahweh outside this text. Now I intend to push

---

15. On the cruciality of such gestures for the maintenance and survival of an intentional community, see Jacob Neusner, *The Enchantments of Judaism: Rites of Transformation from Birth to Death* (Atlanta: Scholars Press, 1991).

16. I.e., they are "performative" actions and utterances.

17. This formula of the Evangelical and Reformed Church was devised in an ecumenical climate in order to allow not only for Lutheran and Calvinist understandings of the Eucharist, but also Zwinglian. Given the battles fought over the Eucharist, the formula is as shrewd as it is delicate.

behind that textual-rhetorical claim, to say that Yahweh's habitat is *in these practices*. Where Israel engages in these practices, Yahweh is connected to Israel. Where these practices flag, Yahweh wanes. Where these practices cease, Yahweh floats off as a treasured historical memory or as a remote metaphysical claim. But Old Testament theology does not deal with the waning or the ceasing, but with the practice that gives Yahweh life in Israel, and that gives Israel life in Yahweh.

TWENTY

The Torah as Mediator

THE TORAH occupies the primary place of authority, significance, and influence in the mediation of Yahweh's purpose, presence, and power to Israel.
In the context of Old Testament theology, Christians have much to unlearn and
relearn about the Torah. In the interpretive trajectory from Paul, by way of Augustine and Luther, the Torah has been grossly reduced to "law," understood in a
regime of legalism.[1] As I shall seek to articulate, Torah has within it more that is
dynamic, open, and elusive than is conveyed in the usual Western, gentile notion
of Jewish law.

Torah evolved out of a series of ad hoc proclamations, oracular utterances, and
commandments, into a more holistic literature and practice that retained some
properties of those initial utterances, but also took on a life of its own. It is not our
responsibility or proper task here to trace the difficult and obscure route of the development of the Torah. It is enough, as a baseline, to insist that whatever remains
of those specific utterances in the present completed Torah, they are now to be read
as part of a larger whole, which impinges upon and reshapes concrete utterance.[2]

Moses as Giver of Torah

Moses is the historical agent in Israel who is foundationally linked to the authority,
reception, and ongoing practice of the Torah. While there are difficult historical-
critical issues related to the person of Moses, in the canonical articulation of Israel's
memory and faith the cruciality and centrality of Moses are clear and unambiguous. Moses, confronted and summoned by Yahweh in an originary meeting (Exod
3:1–4:17),[3] is the one privileged and burdened at Mount Sinai to stand face-to-
face with Yahweh in the inscrutability of the mountain, there to receive the tablets
of Torah, the materials that are linked as the disclosure of Yahweh's intention at

---

1. See Krister Stendahl, "The Apostle Paul and the Introspective Conscience of the West," *Paul
among Jews and Gentiles and Other Essays* (Philadelphia: Fortress Press, 1976) 78–96.
2. Max Kadushin, *Worship and Ethics: A Study in Rabbinic Judaism* (New York: Bloch Publishing
Company, 1963), and *The Rabbinic Mind* (New York: Bloch Publishing Company, 1972), has shown
how Torah is to be understood in rabbinic Judaism as organismic, so that all parts signify and pertain
to the whole.
3. See pp. 568–69 on this narrative and its originary authority for Israel.

Sinai. It is impossible to overstate or overaccent the pivotal role of Moses. In Israel's imaginative articulation of its past, there was a time and a place when Moses received the Torah from Yahweh. There was, moreover, a time and a place when Moses proclaimed Torah to listening Israel. Moses is not a concept, an idea, a theory, or a cipher. Moses is a concrete agent of reception and proclamation, whereby Yahweh's intention and presence were mediated effectively in, to, and for Israel.[4] Torah-addressed Israel is indeed Moses-addressed Israel, so that it is the historical, nameable person of Moses who convenes and constitutes Israel as the peculiar partner of Yahweh. Of this Mosaic Torah mediation of Yahweh to Israel, we may make six observations.

Moses' uncompromising authority. This Torah is the authoritative rendering of this relationship between Yahweh and Israel, a relationship that would tolerate no deviation. It is Moses who is fully accepted by Yahweh and fully affirmed by Israel (Exod 20:19). We may believe that the person of Moses was accepted by both parties as the single founder of Yahwism, and that strenuous, authoritarian means were employed to counter alternatives and challenges to Moses' role, as in the cases of Aaron (Exodus 32), Aaron and Miriam (Numbers 12), and Korah, Dathan, and Abiram (Numbers 16). We are permitted no romanticism about the theological authority of Moses, for it carried with it the political leverage to subdue all competitors. We may locate in the person and office of Moses a zeal for leadership that smacks of authoritarianism and that is a harbinger of the authoritarianism that pervades Israel's testimony that is now marked as patriarchalism. This same intolerance of rivals eventuates, in the Christian tradition, in various claims of infallibility and in the sanctions of the Inquisition, and eagerly identifies as "heresy" whatever deviates from the interpretive hegemony of the moment. There is something forcefully uncompromising in the authority of Moses, justified by the claim that any challenge to Mosaic authority places in jeopardy the possibility of Israel.

Transactional quality. The Torah as given us in Mosaic teaching and testimony is pervasively covenantal and transactional. That is, Moses is the sponsor and articulator par excellence of the covenant that binds Yahweh and Israel into an exclusive mutuality, so that each is marked by a profound and defining commitment to the other, throughout the vicissitudes of every circumstance.[5] In this transactive practice, Yahweh is seen to be a God always in relation, and Israel is marked as belonging inalienably in this relation to Yahweh.

This transactional quality of the life of Israel and the life of Yahweh is wondrously exhibited in two extended texts, though others might be cited. First, in Exod 3:1–4:17, the initial summons to Moses (3:10) introduces a series of five

---

4. Thomas B. Dozeman, *God on the Mountain: A Study of Redaction, Theology, and Canon in Exodus 19–24* (Atlanta: Scholars Press, 1989), has carefully chronicled the relative role of Moses and other functionaries in the Sinai narrative, according to different strands of the tradition.

5. On the "covenant formula" of mutual fidelity, see Rudolf Smend, *Die Bundesformel* (ThStud 68; Zürich: EVZ Verlag, 1963). More generally on the covenant's theological significance in the Old Testament, see Ernest W. Nicholson, *God and His People: Covenant and Theology in the Old Testament* (Oxford: Clarendon Press, 1986).

exchanges between Moses and Yahweh, presented as protest and response. From the outset, Mosaic Yahwism is marked by a capacity for vigorous protest, and an equally powerful capacity for response by Yahweh that overrides the protest.[6] Second, Exod 32:1–34:28 offers an extended narrative in which Israel is placed in extreme jeopardy by its departure from the intolerant requirement of Yahweh.[7] Israel and Yahweh are "talked through" the jeopardy by the courage and insistence of Moses, who impinges upon Yahweh and evokes Yahweh's at-risk fidelity. It is evident, in both of these transactions, that Moses' relationship with Yahweh is lively and disputatious and will have endless seasons of risk, alienation, and restoration. All of this belongs as much to the person of Moses as it does to the character of Yahweh.

Conditional summons to obedience. The constituting of Torah-Israel is, from the outset, marked by a summons to obedience that has a conditional quality to it. Yahweh's first utterance to Moses at Sinai culminates in a radical call to obedience:

> Now therefore, if you obey my voice and keep my covenant, you shall be my treasured possession out of all the peoples. (Exod 19:5)

Israel responds appropriately, even before the commands are enunciated:

> Everything that the Lord has spoken we will do. (Exod 19:8)

Two features are noteworthy in Yahweh's summons at Sinai. First, the whole is governed by an "if." This relationship is marked by the conditionality that marks any such primal relationship.[8] Israel is Israel through obedience. Second, the verb *obey* (*šmʿ*) is expressed as an absolute infinitive, giving it additional force and intensity. That verb is reinforced, however, by *keep* (*šmr*), which is not an absolute infinitive. Israel is to be addressed and is prepared to accept a relationship of command and obedience. Yahweh is Israel's normative way in the world.

Monotheism. The mediation of Yahweh by Moses in the Torah of Sinai is monotheistic. James Sanders's notion of "monotheizing tendency" may be pertinent, but so far as the utterance of Moses is concerned, this is not a tendency but a premise of all that follows.[9] The relationship will be singular and exclusive. There will be no other gods, no images, no idols, no alternatives, no rivals, no competitors. Israel is allowed no "wiggle room" in this relationship. Yahweh, the single voice of authority, mediated through the voice of Moses, the single authorized mediator, will speak, and Israel will answer. The horizon of this testimony

---

6. On this aspect of the work of Moses vis-à-vis Yahweh, it is important to notice the way in which Ernst Bloch, *Atheism in Christianity: The Religion of the Exodus and the Kingdom* (New York: Herder and Herder, 1972) 84–122, has juxtaposed Moses and Job as indispensable elements in serious faith.

7. On this narrative, see the careful discussion of R. W. L. Moberly, *At the Mountain of God: Story and Theology in Exodus 32–34* (JSOTSup 22; Sheffield: JSOT Press, 1983).

8. On the delicate and dialectical matter of conditionality of covenant, see pp. 417–21.

9. James A. Sanders, "Adaptable for Life: The Nature and Function of Canon," *Magnalia Dei, the Mighty Acts of God: Essays on the Bible and Archaeology in Memory of G. Ernest Wright* (ed. Frank M. Cross et al.; Garden City, N.Y.: Doubleday, 1976) 531–60.

includes none of the categories that surface in a history-of-religions approach: no henotheism, no practical monotheism, no residue of polytheism, no developmentalism. It is all Yahweh and only Yahweh. This singularity comes to be expressed, as we have seen, in the jealousy of Yahweh, a jealousy like that of a scorned husband (Ezek 16:38-43).[10]

Singular commitment to Israel. The counterpart of Yahweh's singular (monotheistic) claim is that Yahweh has no other partner, but is solely and singularly committed to Israel. As there is one God, so there is one people, and this people is marked not only by the peculiar presence of Yahweh, but by the peculiar gift of Torah, which gives identity to Israel:

> For what other great nation has a god so near to it as the Lord our God is whenever we call to him? And what other great nation has statutes and ordinances as just as this entire law that I am setting before you today? (Deut 4:7-8)

Thus the theological claim enunciated for Yahweh serves to enhance the legitimated authority of Moses and, in turn, serves to fix and celebrate Israel as Yahweh's singular partner, a community with an odd identity and vocation in the world:

> ... but you shall be for me a priestly kingdom and a holy nation. (Exod 19:6)

This twinning of "only Yahweh" and "only Israel" is articulated as a single claim in a much later prayer of David:

> Therefore you are great, O Lord God; for there is no one like you, and there is no God besides you, according to all that we have heard with our ears. Who is like your people, like Israel? Is there another nation on earth whose God went to redeem it as a people, and to make a name for himself, doing great and awesome things for them, by driving out before his people nations and their gods? And you established your people Israel for yourself to be your people forever; and you, O Lord, became their God. (2 Sam 7:22-24)

The Torah centers in the incomparability of Yahweh, which mediates the incomparability of Israel.[11]

Command and instruction. As Gunnar Östborn has made clear, the notion of Torah, in its Mosaic regimen, partakes both of command and of instruction or guidance.[12] The dimension of command, most celebrated in Christian understandings, is straightforward and explicit. As articulated by and articulated to Moses, the tradition of command intends to bring Israel's life under the governance of Yahweh. Israel's life is to be a practice of bringing every phase of its existence under the rule of Yahweh, thereby rejecting the authority and claim of any other god or any other loyalty. This dimension of Torah is uncompromising and completely

---

10. On the jealousy of Yahweh, see pp. 293–96.
11. See pp. 139–42, 206–9, and 266 concerning the incomparability of Yahweh.
12. Gunnar Östborn, *Tōra in the Old Testament: A Semantic Study* (Lund: Hakan Ohlsson, 1945).

unaccommodating. Because Yahweh is sovereign, there is no latitude or slippage or negotiability. Moses mediates to Israel, directly from Yahweh's own utterance, the ways in which it is possible to belong to Yahweh and to be Yahweh's acknowledged, treasured people in the world.

A second aspect of Torah has most often been unnoticed in a Christian tradition, which has been determined to reduce Torah to "law." This second aspect, which is equally constitutive for Israel, is that Torah means also guidance, instruction, and nurture—a process of exploration and imagination that cannot be flatly subsumed under obedience. This aspect of Torah is evident in the term *Torah* itself, for the verb *yarah* means to direct or point, to give direction. More important, it is also evident in the text. If Torah as command is a summons to the ways in which to belong to Yahweh, then Torah as guidance, instruction, and nurture teaches how to engage in practices that make it possible to be Israel in an inhospitable world. Whereas Torah as command is focused on the ethical dimension of existence, Torah as instruction, guidance, and nurture is preoccupied with the aesthetic and artistic, a realm that comes to be expressed as the mystical and sacramental. That is, *Torah is as much concerned with the inscrutable mystery of presence as it is with the nonnegotiability of neighborly obedience.*

Specifically, this sacramental dimension to Torah, largely ignored in critical scholarship or interpreted without regard to its sacramental quality, is found in those texts most often attributed to P, which include provision for the tabernacle (Exodus 25–31, 35–40), for the Priestly sacrifices (Leviticus 1–8), for the ritual of Day of Atonement (Leviticus 16), and for the disciplines of holiness (Leviticus 17–26). It is important to note that the provisions for tabernacle and sacrifice are not actions commanded of Israel; they are directions to Moses. In these commands from Yahweh to Moses, Moses does not receive commands to be transmitted to Israel.[13] They are provisions that Moses himself, at the outset of Israel's life with Yahweh, is to perform and establish. That is, in these traditions of Sinai, Moses is the founder of institutional practices, and these specific instructions are the originary "words of institution," uttered and treasured as the guarantee that makes these "vehicles of presence" legitimate, reliable, and authoritative.

These instructions offer a set of practices in which Israel is to live. They are freighted with sacramental significance, and in the practice of them Israel engages in an "alternative world" of "legitimated imagination," in which it becomes Israel in the presence of Yahweh.[14] Thus Moses is authorized, for example, to take materials of acacia wood and bronze, in various modes and arrangements, and to transform them into an altar (Exod 27:1-8). In that act, Israel is given a reliable vehicle for presence; acacia wood becomes a vehicle for presence. Or again, Moses is authorized to identify an unblemished bull, and to use its bodily parts as a burnt offering

---

13. Gerhard von Rad, *Studies in Deuteronomy* (SBT 9; London: SCM Press, 1953) 25–36, had seen this distinction on form-critical grounds.

14. See Jacob Neusner, *The Enchantments of Judaism: Rites of Transformation from Birth to Death* (Atlanta: Scholars Press, 1991), on the generative power of imaginative acts for an alternative world.

to Yahweh, which becomes a mode of communion with Yahweh (Lev 1:3-9). A bull is a vehicle for communion. We are not told why or how this becomes effica-cious; as is the case with all such sacramental acts, no explanation is finally needed or given. The authorization is both command to Moses and promise to Israel, and Israel becomes the practitioner of what is given and commanded through Moses. In the process, Israel takes up the means of communion that are inscrutable in power and significance, in which Yahweh's life is present in Israel. Moses, the giver of Torah from Mount Sinai, provides both the commands of Yahweh that Israel is capable of obeying (Deut 30:11-14), and the provisions of Yahweh, wherein Israel may host the holy and enjoy God's presence. All of this is given in Moses' Torah. And Israel is invited to be the Israel that Mosaic mediation authorizes it to be.

The Interpretive Dynamic of Torah

It is clear that the Torah mediated by Moses at Mount Sinai is not fixed, closed, and settled at the termination of Moses' work. The Torah as mediation includes an open-ended dynamic and an ongoing vitality that goes beyond Moses, albeit with the enduring authority of Moses. We are led to believe that some form of periodic assemblies or convocations were held in Israel, wherein the community gathered to hear again the summons, promises, and demands of the Torah, and to swear again its resolve to live under the demands and inside the imagination that constituted this Torah:

> You stand assembled today, all of you, before the Lord your God—the lead-ers of your tribes, your elders, and your officials, all the men of Israel, your children, your women, and the aliens who are in your camp, both those who cut your wood and those who draw your water—to enter into the covenant of the Lord your God, sworn by an oath, which the Lord your God is mak-ing with you today; in order that he may establish you today as his people and that he may be your God, as he promised you and as he swore to your ancestors, to Abraham, to Isaac, and to Jacob. (Deut 29:10-13)

> Then Moses and all the elders of Israel charged all the people as follows: Keep the entire commandment that I am commanding you today.... Then Moses and the levitical priests spoke to all Israel, saying: Keep silent and hear, O Israel! This very day you have become the people of the Lord your God. Therefore obey the Lord your God, observing his commandments and his statutes that I am commanding you today. (Deut 27:1, 9-10)

> Moses commanded them: "Every seventh year, in the scheduled year of re-mission, during the festival of booths, when all Israel comes to appear before the Lord your God at the place that he will choose, you shall read this law before all Israel in their hearing. Assemble the people—men, women, and children, as well as the aliens residing in your towns—so that they may hear

and learn to fear the Lord your God and to observe diligently all the words of this law, and so that their children, who have not known it, may hear and learn to fear the Lord your God, as long as you live in the land that you are crossing over the Jordan to possess." (Deut 31:10-13)

The concrete practice of Torah consists not simply in having a scroll from Moses as a fixed, settled law. Rather the practice of Torah consists in regular, stated, public meetings in which Israel, as an identifiable, self-conscious community under promise and discipline, is constituted and reconstituted. This meeting is presented in the text as a replication of Sinai, whereby Israel was constituted in speaking and hearing, only now the reconstitution is performed in different times and places and circumstances, and with different lead characters (cf. Deut 5:3). The purpose of such meetings (we may believe that such meetings eventuated in the synagogue and house of study, and derivatively in the Christian tradition in the "ministry of word and sacrament") was to rehear promises and demands and to repledge fidelity to this mediated covenant partner. The purpose of this Torah-centered meeting was to permit the assembly to become Israel once again.

Post-Mosaic Leadership: The Levites

When Israel sought to continue the Mosaic function, without which it would not be this covenant people, it had to identify and authorize post-Moses leaders. This practice is historically obscure. But because I am here interested in concrete practice as evidenced in Israel's testimony, I will venture a historical guess. Scholars have proposed that the Levites are the leading candidate for such a Mosaic function. (If it was not the Levites, some such agent seems indispensable for the "practice of Torah," whereby Israel is regularly reconstituted.) The evidence for the Levites as the continuation of the Mosaic function of Torah proclamation is pieced together from texts that only hint and never assert. We may cite two principal texts that suggest this scholarly proposal. In Exod 32:25-29 the Levites are ordained as those most militantly faithful to the uncompromising Yahwism of Moses. In Deut 33:8-11, moreover, the Levites are entrusted with "your law" (Torah):

> And of Levi he said:
> Give to Levi your Thummim,
> and your Urim to your loyal one,
> whom you tested at Massah,
> with whom you contended at the waters of Meribah;
> who said of his father and mother,
> "I regard them not";
> he ignored his kin,
> and he did not acknowledge his children.
> For they observed your word,
> and kept your covenant.
> They teach Jacob your ordinances,

and Israel your law;
they place incense before you,
and whole burnt offerings on your altar.
Bless, O Lord, his substance,
and accept the work of his hands;
crush the loins of his adversaries,
of those that hate him, so that
they do not rise again.

While the historical data are far from clear, the Levites are a formidable candidate for this role in Israel. In scholarly hypothesis the prominence of the Levites is firmly based in the study of Max Weber, who avers:

> The Levites were the only permanent champions of Yahweh belief and by virtue of their socially important function felt themselves as men knowing what offenses would bring misfortunes and how to make good again....
>
> To the Levitical priests the task of teaching the Torah to the people, which they claimed as their rightful responsibility, served the same purpose of keeping the community free of sin in order to ward off Yahweh's wrath.[15]

Frank M. Cross has offered a speculative reconstruction of the history of priesthood, assigning a major role to the Levites.[16] And Norman Gottwald regards the Levites as a "revolutionary cadre" who provided intellectual funding for the social revolution that was Israel:

> The Levitical priesthood, the bearers of Yahwism, form an intellectual and organizational cadre of leadership which cuts across and penetrates the several autonomous social segments, binding them together for actions based on common sentiment.... Positively, there was the overwhelming, demonstrated, military and cultic-ideological appeal of the Levites in convincing the coalition that Yahweh, who had defeated Egypt on its home ground, could defend an enlarged anti-imperial and anti-feudal order in Canaan.[17]

While Gottwald's historical reconstruction is much criticized, it has the merit of linking the practice of Torah to the actual, concrete life of Israel in the world, making clear that Torah practice is a lived enterprise, and not an intellectual, remote ethical proposal.

Deuteronomy: Sinai Interpreted

Whatever may be said of the Levites historically, consideration of the Book of Deuteronomy is crucial to Torah as mediation, for it is the tradition of Deuteronomy that has the most fully developed, self-conscious notion of Torah. The

---

15. Max Weber, *Ancient Judaism* (Glencoe, Ill.: Free Press, 1952) 220, 240–41; cf. 263.

16. Frank Moore Cross, *Canaanite Myth and Hebrew Epic* (Cambridge: Harvard University Press, 1973) 195–215.

17. Norman K. Gottwald, *The Tribes of Yahweh: A Sociology of the Religion of Liberated Israel, 1250– 1050 B.C.E.* (Maryknoll, N.Y.: Orbis Books, 1979) 490, 496, cf. 688.

dominant hypothesis concerning Deuteronomy is that the Levites are the responsible agents who continue the Torah work of Moses.[18] Indeed, one of the purposes of Deuteronomy is to model to Israel how to continue to be faithfully and passionately the people of the Torah of Moses when Moses is no longer present to mediate and instruct. Given the resilience of the tradition of Deuteronomy, it is clear that Moses in person is no longer required by Israel. Without dwelling on the historical reliability of that claim, it is clear that Deuteronomy occupies a pivotal place in Torah practice in Israel. The specific substance of the Book of Deuteronomy as proclaimed Torah (Gerhard von Rad's "preached law") was to enunciate the peculiarity of Israel and to urge Israel to practice a distinctive ethic that had Yahwistic justice at its center.[19] That is, Deuteronomy is an interpretive practice that seeks to rearticulate the claims of Sinai in a new circumstance. Whatever agents speak in Deuteronomy, they intend to "respeak" Moses for a new time and place.

The presentation of the Book of Deuteronomy situates its utterance in the plains of Moab, far from Sinai, and focusing on the problems and possibilities in the land of promise (Deut 1:1-5). On the one hand Deuteronomy claims the authority of Moses. On the other hand, it is not situated at Sinai. Thus what is presented as Torah is removed from Sinai, as an ongoing enterprise. Torah can be given in places other than Sinai, as long as it carries the authority of Moses. At the outset, the Book of Deuteronomy is said to be an exposition of the Torah:

> Beyond the Jordan in the land of Moab, Moses undertook to expound this law as follows.... (Deut 1:5)[20]

In 5:3, as an introduction to the reiteration of the Decalogue, Moses asserts:

> Not with our ancestors did the Lord make this covenant, but with us, who are all of us here alive today.

That is, Deuteronomy is not *Sinai repeated*. It is *Sinai interpreted*, extrapolated and exposited in order to keep the claims of Sinai-Mosaic Yahwism pertinent to a new time, place, and circumstance. In the actual practice of the text of Deuteronomy, the post-Moses Torah practitioners are authorized to introduce wholly new subjects into the Torah, as a way to bring wholly new spheres of life into the horizon of Yahwism.

Thus the Book of Deuteronomy not only introduces *new material* into the Torah. It also introduces, exemplifies, and authorizes new *interpretive practices,*

---

18. The point is urged, especially by Gerhard von Rad. See the assessment of the role of the Levites by Nicholson, *God and His People.*

19. Von Rad, *Studies in Deuteronomy,* 16, understood the peculiar rhetoric of Deuteronomy as "preached law." While the intention of this material is clearly justice, it is justice within an uncriticized, unacknowledged patriarchal horizon.

20. The term *expound* is *b'r.* On the term, see Moshe Weinfeld, *Deuteronomy 1–11: A New Translation with Introduction and Commentary* (AB 5; New York: Doubleday, 1991) 128–29; more generally on the passage, see Zecharia Kallai, "Where Did Moses Speak (Deuteronomy I 1–5)?" *VT* 45 (1995) 188–97.

whereby Torah is shown to be no settled corpus of teaching, but a process of interpretation that continues lively in its authority and pertinent in its practice. It is precisely the Book (and practice) of Deuteronomy that prevents the Mosaic Torah of Sinai from being closed off, fixed, and settled. The dynamic process of the Book of Deuteronomy precludes any strict constructionism about the Torah, any notion that the text can mean only what its original speaker said and intended, for the Decalogue is now shown to be enormously open for continuing processing.[21]

Israel's Series of Great Mediators

The Book and tradition of Deuteronomy, perhaps sponsored and voiced by the Levites, provides a major influence and force in making Torah crucial and definitional for the identity of Israel. We may identify a series of great mediators who perform the function, according to Israel's narrative testimony, of keeping Israel in the context of Torah.[22] To be sure, these mediators are presented in texts decisively shaped by Deuteronomic circles, so that we are not able to sort out what is "history." But in terms of the cultural-linguistic density of Israel's self-understanding, these great pivotal leaders are crucial.

Joshua (who is placed at Sinai with Moses in Exod 24:13) is Moses' successor who is to continue the practice of Torah mediation in the land after Moses' death. Thus in a great convocation, Joshua binds Israel to Torah:

So Joshua made a covenant with the people that day, and made statutes and ordinances for them at Shechem. (Josh 24:25)

Moreover, Joshua is, so the tradition has it, empowered precisely for Torah, for the great work of bringing Israel to its promise:

Only be strong and very courageous, being careful to act in accordance with all the law that my servant Moses commanded you; do not turn from it to the right hand or to the left, so that you may be successful wherever you go. This book of the law shall not depart out of your mouth; you shall meditate on it day and night, so that you may be careful to act in accordance with all that is written in it. For then you shall make your way prosperous, and then you shall be successful. (Josh 1:7-8)

Samuel, in like manner, in something like Deuteronomic language, summons Israel to radical Torah obedience:

If you will fear the Lord and serve him and heed his voice and not rebel against the commandment of the Lord, and if both you and the king who

21. See Walter Brueggemann, *Finally Comes the Poet: Daring Speech for Proclamation* (Minneapolis: Fortress Press, 1989) 79–110; and "The Commandments and Liberated, Liberating Bonding," *Interpretation and Obedience* (Minneapolis: Fortress Press, 1991) 145–58.

22. See Hans-Joachim Kraus, *Die prophetische Verkündigung des Rechts in Israel* (Zollikon: EVZ Verlag, 1957); and James Muilenburg, "The 'Office' of the Prophet in Ancient Israel," *The Bible in Modern Scholarship* (ed. J. P. Hyatt; New York: Abingdon Press, 1965) 74–97.

reigns over you will follow the Lord your God, it will be well; but if you will not heed the voice of the Lord, but rebel against the commandment of the Lord, then the hand of the Lord will be against you and your king. (1 Sam 12:14-15)

Josiah. There is, moreover, no doubt that according to the account of the Deuteronomists, Josiah the king is the quintessential proclaimer of Torah, who seeks to reorder and reconstitute Israel on the bases of the Torah:

> Then the king commanded the priest Hilkiah, Ahikam son of Shaphan, Achbor son of Micaiah, Shaphan the secretary, and the king's servant Asa-iah, saying, "Go inquire of the Lord for me, for the people, and for all Judah concerning the words of this book that has been found; for great is the wrath of the Lord that is kindled against us, because our ancestors did not obey the words of the book, to do according to all that is written concerning us." (2 Kgs 22:12-13)[23]

In these several articulations, obedience to Torah is made the single criterion of the life or death, weal or woe, of Israel. The tradition of Deuteronomy takes up the insistences of Moses and Sinai and makes them more sweeping, more intense, and more decisive. The good news is that in the ongoing interpretive processes of Torah, Israel knows the substance of obedience:

> No, the word is very near to you; it is in your mouth and in your heart for you to observe. (Deut 30:14)

The bad news is that the Torah requirements are uncompromising. Disobedience will cause Israel to be "swept away" (1 Sam 12:25).

The great prophets. In addition to the Levites and these occasional mediators, the great prophets of Israel form a third group of practitioners of Torah mediation. The phenomenon of prophecy is rich and varied and largely ad hoc. The prophets derive from many traditions. In the canonical form of Israel's testimony, however, this disparate material has been largely ordered around themes of judgment and hope, which appear to be derived from Torah claims of blessing and curse.[24] The sequence of prophets as canonically constructed shows that the prophets, with their intense Yahwism, summon Israel and interpret to Israel on its way to disaster. In the perspective of the Deuteronomic Torah, it is precisely disobedience to Torah that results in the catastrophe of 587 B.C.E., which plunges Israel into the fissure of exile. In canonical form, the prophets are informed by Torah and give accent to its invitation to life and its warning about death.[25]

---

23. We take into account the report of the Deuteronomist without making any judgment about the facticity of such matters. That the text is artistically formed is clear from the analysis of Lyle Eslinger, "Josiah and the Torah Book: A Comparison of 2 Kgs 22:1–23:28 and 2 Chr 34:1–35:19," *HAR* 10 (1986) 37–62.

24. See my discussion of the prophets in relation to Israel's "forms of life," chap. 22.

25. This is the evident claim and intention of the canonical arrangement of the literature. That the relation is other than this has been a major premise of conventional historical criticism. See W. Zim-

More specifically we may mention two prophets who seem closest to the Torah traditions of Deuteronomy. Hans Walter Wolff has proposed that Hosea's "spiritual home"—that is, the tradition that nurtured his faith—is in the circle of the Levites and so very close to the traditions of Deuteronomy.[26] Moreover, Karl Gross has shown that in important ways Hosea's traditions impacted Jeremiah.[27] We cannot be at all confident about direct historical influence. What we can say is that the prophetic traditions of Hosea and Jeremiah, as we now have them, articulate and mediate Yahweh's will and purpose in categories very close to those of Deuteronomy, which in the Old Testament offers itself as the normative and definitive trajectory of Torah out of Sinai. Like the putative Levites and the great mediators given us in the traditions of Deuteronomy, these prophets understand Israel's life and destiny in terms of Torah categories. Von Rad has written: "Jeremiah stands and acts upon the Exodus-Sinai tradition, and in this gives his preaching a very broad foundation."[28] These two prophets seem, in a pivotal way, to cite the Decalogue (Hos 4:2, Jer 7:9). And if, in the latter case, this is to be regarded as an imposition of the Deuteronomist (as well it might be), this only attests to the enormous power and influence of this interpretive tradition and process, in its claim to be the authentic, continuing voice of Moses in Israel.

This powerful tradition of covenantal obedience—rooted in Moses, voiced by the Levites, the circles of Deuteronomy, the great mediators, and the prophets under the influence of this trajectory—produced the "Yahweh alone party" that is definitional for Israel in the Old Testament.[29] While this claim, as it was variously enunciated, may on occasion be regarded as uncompromising and heavily ideological, it is also this tradition, above all, that provided Israel and emerging Judaism with the resources for survival and coherence in a highly contested and inhospitable situation.

Canonical Process: Compromise between Deuteronomic and Priestly Traditions

We must not singularly accent the ethical dimension of the Torah, as Christians are wont to do, to the neglect of the sacramental quality of the Torah. Over time, the substance and function of the Torah came to be much more comprehensive than "command," even though it never lost its intense ethical import. In the crisis of the seventh and sixth centuries, out of which Judaism emerged, the Torah, which may have been specific priestly instruction, or which may have been primarily codification of the commandments, became a full and comprehensive literature with

merli, *The Law and the Prophets: A Study of the Meaning of the Old Testament* (New York: Harper Torchbooks, 1963).

26. See Hans Walter Wolff, "Hoseas Geistige Heimat," *TLZ* 81 (1956) 83–94.

27. Karl Gross, "Hoseas Einfluss auf Jeremias Anschuungen," *NKZ* 42 (1931) 241–56, 327–43.

28. Gerhard von Rad, *Old Testament Theology* (San Francisco: Harper and Row, 1965), 2:217.

29. See Morton Smith, *Palestinian Parties and Politics That Shaped the Old Testament* (New York: Columbia University Press, 1971).

a large and profound canonical authority. While the process by which the canonical process occurred is lost to us, somewhere around the time of the exile or just after, perhaps at the behest of the Persians, the Torah took the form of the completed Pentateuch, the first five books of the canon.[30] While the Deuteronomists may have been peculiarly engaged in the canonizing process, the completed Pentateuch includes not only Deuteronomic traditions, but also many materials formed and transmitted in the very different Priestly circles. Thus the completed Torah is a compromise between these two powerful interpretive traditions, which could not be easily harmonized.[31] The canonical process, moreover, did not eventuate in a triumph for either interpretive tradition, so that the first canon of Scripture has compromise written all over it.

This compromise, which holds together and in tension Israel's principal interpretive traditions, assures a central focus on Mosaic authority and the foundational revelation of Sinai. Other, belated materials now included as Torah prevent the "commandments of Moses" from providing a Torah that is flatly command. Specifically, the completed Torah includes a great lyrical narrative of the world (Genesis 1–11), treasured family memories (Genesis 12–36, 37–50), and the narrative of Moses (on Exodus and wilderness). These narratives provide a context for the disclosures of Sinai. The large blocks of Priestly materials in Exodus, Leviticus, and Numbers are not commands as we know them in Deuteronomy, but are provisions and disciplines that make the presence of Yahweh possible in Israel and provide the means for mediated communion. Because the Torah in Exodus, Leviticus, and Numbers is literature and not cultic activity, we may entertain the possibility that the very pondering of these texts was itself a mediated access point to the reality of Yahweh. Thus the completed Torah, I suggest, is not simply a set of commands that determined the conditions of Israel's existence; it is also *a rich, dense field of imagination in which Israel is free to receive its life, playfully, as the people of God.* That is, the text becomes a sacramental vehicle for Israel, an offer that was increasingly important as Israel lived in a hostile, inhospitable environment. What Israel could not discern in the world of events was given in the artistic world of Israel's sacramental texts.

Beyond its ethical dimension, then, it is important to recognize that Torah is the material out of which Israel continues to receive its peculiar identity, as it continues to retain its odd, Yahwistic character as given in these materials. Thus the study of Torah is not simply to find out God's will. Study of Torah is as well an experience of being immersed in the oddity of Israel, which is commensurate with the oddity of Yahweh.[32]

---

30. See Norman Whybray, *The Making of the Pentateuch: A Methodological Study* (JSOTSup 53; Sheffield: Sheffield Academic Press, 1987).

31. So Rainer Albertz, *A History of Israelite Religion in the Old Testament Period 2: From the Exile to the Maccabees* (OTL; Louisville: Westminster/John Knox, 1994) 468, 481, and passim.

32. James A. Sanders, "Torah and Christ," *Int* 29 (1975) 372–90, has helpfully articulated the parallel understandings of Torah and Christ in Jewish and Christian forms of faith. Thus Sanders suggests that Christ, like the Torah, is not only law but also communion.

The Holistic Function of Torah: Four Practices

Four practices of Torah provide evidence of this larger, holistic function of Torah, which is both ethical and sacramental.

Reading and hearing with interpretation. The great moment of "the founding of Judaism" by Ezra revolves around the reading of the Torah (Neh 8:1-12):

> And Ezra opened the book in the sight of all the people, for he was standing above all the people; and when he opened it, all the people stood up. Then Ezra blessed the Lord, the great God, and all the people answered, "Amen, Amen," lifting up their hands. Then they bowed their heads and worshiped the Lord with their faces to the ground.... Levites... helped the people to understand the law, while the people remained in their places. So they read from the book, from the law of God, with interpretation. They gave the sense, so that the people understood the reading. (Neh 8:5-8)

Israel is constituted by the reading and hearing of the Torah "with interpretation." Most scholars believe this reading was of the entire Pentateuch, or at least the Priestly portions of it. The response of listening Israel (Neh 8:9-12) does not bespeak simply law, but an affirmation in the reading that confirmed the legitimacy and identity of this people. Ezra assured the community in the imaginative field of Torah, whereby Israel was reconstituted.

The Psalter and enhanced Jewish identity. Recent study of the Psalter has suggested that its canonical form is arranged to impose a "Torah piety" on the entire Psalter.[33] That is, the various Psalms in many different genres surely arise from many sources and in many contexts. The completed form of the Psalter, however, shows that the formation of the canonical arrangement provides clues about how to read the Psalter, including the intent that some psalms should be read in a way different from their original purpose.

Specifically, since the Psalter is a product of late, postexile Judaism, the temple Psalms must be transposed to serve a Torah-oriented community. This is accomplished especially by the location of the Torah psalms (Psalms 1, 19, 119) at pivotal points and in juxtaposition to royal Psalms that come belatedly to express messianic hope.[34] Thus in Psalm 1, concerning the righteous, "their delight is in the law of the Lord, and on his law they meditate day and night" (Ps 1:2). There is no doubt that the Torah "meditated" upon has an ethical component. But it seems most plausible that what righteous Israel did was to settle its meditation, receptively and imaginatively, on all that is given in the Torah tradition, which includes but is much more than commandment. And in Ps 19:7-10, this material, certainly focused on the ethical, is found to be generative, constitutive, transformative in its power in Israel. Indeed, the Torah "revives the soul" (Ps 19:7), the same restorative work

---

33. See James L. Mays, "The Place of Torah-Psalms in the Psalter," *JBL* 106 (1987) 3–12.

34. Thus Mays, ibid., observes the patterned juxtaposition of Psalms 1 and 2, 18 and 19, 118 and 119.

assigned to Yahweh in Ps 23:2. Thus we may believe that in pondering the Torah, Jews are revivified in their peculiar identity. They receive back their true selves in their true community, in covenant with their true God. No wonder the Israelite who pondered this Torah could exclaim: "Oh, how I love your law! It is my meditation all day long" (Ps 119:97). No wonder a Torah-receptive Jew could come to powerful hope (cf. Ps 119:74, 81, 114, 116, 147, 166). The Torah-pondering Jew intended obedience, but it is obedience in a context of confirmed, affirmed, assured, enhanced identity. There is nothing in this piety of abrasion, resistance, or burden.

Torah and wisdom teaching. Wisdom teaching in ancient Israel moved in circles very different from those of the Mosaic Torah, but scholarship has probably been too rigid in compartmentalizing matters. It is probable, as evidenced in Jer 8:8, that the "wise" were understood to be articulating instruction, guidance, and nurture that were not unlike Torah. Distinctions between Torah and wisdom can be made, but we should not insist on those distinctions too heavily.

In any case, it is commonly thought that Torah did not become formally connected to or equated with wisdom teaching until the end of the Old Testament period. Thus Sirach 24, where wisdom speaks in its own voice and says of itself:

> All this is the book of the covenant of the Most High God,
> the law that Moses commanded us
> as an inheritance for the congregations of Jacob.
> It overflows, like the Pishon, with wisdom,
> and like the Tigris at the time of the first fruits.
> It runs over, like the Euphrates, with understanding,
> and like the Jordan at harvest time.
> It pours forth instruction like the Nile,
> like the Gihon at the time of vintage.
> The first man did not know wisdom fully,
> nor will the last one fathom her.
> For her thoughts are more abundant than the sea,
> and her counsel deeper than the great abyss. (Sir 24:23-29)

Only late, in this sweeping doxological articulation, is the eloquence and expansiveness of wisdom equated with Torah. In the process, which we may believe was not abrupt but occurred over a long period as sages became crucial authorities in the community, wisdom is regarded as authoritative and normative, and not merely happenstance. In the process of this emerging equation, however, something decisive happens to Torah as well as to wisdom. Torah is no longer simply the revelation of Sinai; Torah is now drawn more centrally into the large, wondrous realm of all of creation. The Torah is, for that, no less Israelite, but now it comprehends all the gifts and offers of life from Yahweh, which are everywhere signaled in the life of the world and in the experience of Judaism in a gentile world.[35] Torah

---

35. The Torah is open to what has come to be called natural theology, on which see James Barr, *Biblical Faith and Natural Theology: The Gifford Lectures for 1991* (Oxford: Clarendon Press, 1993).

becomes, in this later venturesome development, a Yahweh-oriented pondering of and engagement with the life that is everywhere available in Yahweh's world. Thus in Sirach 24, wisdom is food that nourishes (vv. 19-22) and water that sustains (vv. 25-31). That is, Torah is the very gift of life from Yahweh that permeates the world. And Israel, in its Mosaic stance, are the people who are first of all invited to "choose life."

Zion: Internationalization and eschatologization. There is evidence that the Torah came to be thought of as situated in Zion, and so was associated with the dynastic-temple establishment. Hartmut Gese has explored most fully the odd transference and redefinition of Torah, as it was relocated.[36] This should not surprise us, because with the establishment of the Solomonic temple, Jerusalem became the focal center of Israel's theological reflection and a magnet that drew all of Israel's theological and cultic instruments to its ambience.[37] Gese can speak of "Zion Torah," which reminds us of the enormous vitality of Torah, even when it is drawn into a new and inhospitable matrix. Such a notion as Zion Torah precludes any fundamentalist commitment to Sinai, for Israel itself regarded Torah as a mobile force, which stayed processively alive and responsive to Israel's changing circumstances.

Among the texts Gese cites is Ps 46:10:

> Be still, and know that I am God!
> I am exalted among the nations,
> I am exalted in the earth.

Gese suggests that "know that I am God" is an embrace of Torah in Zion, for knowledge of God means an intimate embrace of who Yahweh is and what Yahweh commands. In Isaiah 25, Gese proposes, Zion is portrayed as the mountain and place of mystery, protection, and encounter, in the same way that Sinai had functioned in the traditions of Moses and Elijah.[38] But it is above all Psalm 50 that makes clear that the covenantal expectations, summons, sanctions, and promises are now located in Zion:

> Out of Zion, the perfection of beauty,
> God shines forth.
> Our God comes and does not keep silence,
> before him is a devouring fire,
> and a mighty tempest all around him.
> He calls to the heavens above
> and to the earth, that he may judge his people;
> "Gather to me my faithful ones,
> who made a covenant with me by sacrifice!"

---

36. Hartmut Gese, *Essays on Biblical Theology* (Minneapolis: Augsburg Publishing House, 1981) 79-85.

37. On the cruciality of Jerusalem as a magnet for cultic traditions and practices, see pp. 654-62.

38. See Gese, *Essays on Biblical Theology*, 83, on the "covering" in Isa 25:7.

The heavens declare his righteousness,
for God himself is judge. (Ps 50:2-5; cf. Ps 81:9-10, which Gese does
not cite)

Zion, given the political force with which it is invested, has the capacity to expand the claims of Torah as could not happen at Sinai. This expansion of the claims of Torah happened in two ways. First, Zion, unlike Sinai, places Israel (and the God of Israel) on the horizon of the nations.[39] From Zion, the Torah takes on international scope, and it can be imagined that all nations are subject to Yahweh's Torah. This is the great vision of Torah for the nations:

Many peoples shall come and say,
"Come, let us go up to the mountain of the Lord,
to the house of the God of Jacob;
that he may teach us his ways
and that we may walk in his paths."
For out of Zion shall go forth instruction,
and the word of the Lord from Jerusalem.
He shall judge between the nations,
and shall arbitrate for many peoples;
they shall beat their swords into plowshares,
and their spears into pruning hooks;
nation shall not lift up sword against nation,
neither shall they learn war any more. (Isa 2:3-4; cf. Mic 4:1-4; Zech
8:20-23; Isa 42:4)

This poetry envisions a great international procession to Zion, not as the seat of David, but as the locus of Yahweh's Torah. The nations must come here, and willingly do so, to embrace the ways of international peace and to unlearn the ways of war.[40] The intention of Yahweh, as embodied in the Torah, is the clue and guidance to world peace.

The second expansion of Torah at Zion suggested by Gese is that the Torah is taken to be not only present demand and instruction, but also a promise for the future. It has been "eschatologized" as a way in which Israel can be different and confident concerning the future. Thus, in the oracle of a "new covenant" it is promised:

But this is the covenant that I will make with the house of Israel after those days, says the Lord: I will put my law within them, and I will write it on their hearts; and I will be their God, and they shall be my people. (Jer 31:33; cf. Prov 6:20-22, which seems to anticipate Deut 6:7-8 on the same theme)

---

39. See Kadushin, *Worship and Ethics*, 29.
40. Norman K. Gottwald, *All the Kingdoms of the Earth: Israelite Prophecy and International Relations in the Ancient Near East* (New York: Harper and Row, 1964) 202–3, has suggested that as war is "learned," so here it is unlearned and peace is learned in its place.

In Ezekiel 36, moreover, it is anticipated that Israel will be given, in time to come, a new capacity and disposition to practice the Torah already entrusted to it:

> A new heart I will give you, and a new spirit I will put within you; and I will remove from your body the heart of stone and give you a heart of flesh. I will put my spirit within you, and make you follow my statutes and be careful to observe my ordinances. (Ezek 36:26-27)

These two expansions of Torah, internationalization and eschatologization, together offer the Torah as a vision and possibility for a peaceable, well-ordered world, within which Israel can practice joyous community as Yahweh's blessed people. Thus the Torah is enormously supple, providing a field of imagination in which Israel is permitted to focus all its energy and loyalty on Yahweh and to receive its full life in the world from Yahweh.

The Dynamic Practice of Torah

It is evident that Torah as a concrete interpretive practice in Israel is enormously dynamic and supple, and it has the capacity to impinge on every aspect of Israel's imaginative life. Christians who seek to understand what is intended in Torah will have to move beyond conventional, polemical caricatures of legalism, in order to ponder an interpretive practice that is (a) intransigently normative and yet enormously open to adaptation; and (b) has an uncompromising sovereign at its center, but with a capacity to attend in delicate ways to the detail of daily existence. This elasticity, moreover, invites and requires endless, ongoing interpretive work, never reaching closure, but always being responsive in ways that preclude final settlement.

This elasticity, in Jewish tradition, is articulated in the claim that along with Written Torah there is Oral Torah, a live and still developing practice of interpretive utterance. The Oral Torah is given to Moses at Sinai, but it is not known or available until it is uttered subsequently by an authoritative proclaimer of Torah, eventually in the rabbinic tradition. For purposes of understanding the Old Testament, a Christian expositor does not have to delve deeply into the Oral Torah but at a minimum must recognize that ongoing Jewish interpretation is not closely bound to the letter. Interpretive openings and resources permit the Written Torah to be reread afresh in endlessly imaginative ways.

Interpretation in the Christian Tradition

To Christians who are schooled in the usual charges of legalism toward Jewishness, such a notion is odd indeed. It may be useful to recognize the several devices present in the Christian tradition that render the same interpretive possibility. In the polemics of the Council of Trent, it was concluded that Scripture and tradition are "two sources" of revelation. In that polemical situation in the sixteenth century, Reformation Christians felt a deep obligation to resist this "compromise" of *sola scriptura*. And yet, any serious practical reflection indicates that all serious interpretive communities, including churches of the Reformation, have a tradition of interpretation that both permits and precludes some readings; that is, a tradition of covert as well as overt understandings and assumptions that are not available to outsiders.

In a different mode, the Catholic tradition affirmed beyond "plain reading" a "fuller sense" (*Sensus Plenior*) of the text, so that the text had meanings beyond those intended by the human "author," fuller meanings that continued to be revelatory and authoritative, under the guidance of the spirit.[41] More recently, without the scholastic categories of *Sensus Plenior*, what came to be called "The New Hermeneutic" understood and justified many imaginative rereadings of the text in a heavily theoretical way.[42] With less theoretical complexity, David Tracy has well understood that a "classic" is a text to which the community returns again and again, for "more" and "other."[43] Tracy's notion of classic has been much criticized because it is foundational. It is clear, however, that rereading classics in any community of interpretation tends to follow the "rules of grammar" operative in that community.[44]

If these several notions of "two sources," *Sensus Plenior*, and "New Hermeneutic" are too mystifying, we may point simply to the core practice of Protestantism, in which texts take on new vitality in the moment of preaching, which is an interpretive act of theological importance.[45] Indeed such a notion of preaching is not far removed from the liberated, liberating move of Deuteronomy to relocate Torah from Sinai to "the Plains of Moab," and subsequently the relocation of Torah to Zion. All of these openings in the interpretive process serve to transform "there" to "here," and "then" to "now."[46] The Old Testament itself understood Torah in this processive way.

Distortions of Legalism and Self-Indulgence

At the same time, there is no doubt that Torah, as an interpretive practice that situated the sovereign God in the midst of Israel's daily life, is subject to distortion. Like the Christian community in its effort at fidelity, Israel in the Old Testament struggles with the twin distortions of legalism and self-indulgence in its valuing of

---

41. The classic statement is by Raymond E. Brown, *The Sensus Plenior of Sacred Scripture: A Dissertation* (Baltimore: Pontifical Theological Faculty of St. Mary's University, 1955).

42. See James M. Robinson and John B. Cobb, Jr., eds., *The New Hermeneutic* (NFT 2; New York: Harper and Row, 1964).

43. David Tracy, *The Analogical Imagination: Christian Theology and the Culture of Pluralism* (New York: Crossroad, 1981).

44. On such rules of grammar, see George A. Lindbeck, *The Nature of Doctrine: Religion and Theology in a Postliberal Age* (Philadelphia: Westminster Press, 1984) 94–95 and passim.

45. See Karl Barth, *Church Dogmatics* 1/1 (Edinburgh: T. & T. Clark, 1936) 117–18, and the entire section on testimony and the oral enterprise.

46. The Old Testament program for this process has been termed *Vergegenwärtigung*, on which see Martin Noth, "The Re-presentation of the Old Testament Proclamation," *Old Testament Hermeneutics* (ed. Claus Westermann; Richmond: John Knox, 1963) 76–88. In very different categories, see Garrett Green, *Imagining God: Theology and the Religious Imagination* (San Francisco: Harper and Row, 1989).

Torah. It is plausible that the most characteristic case of legalism in the Old Testament concerns Job's friends. I say "plausible," because the friends characteristically argue on the basis of "purity" and "wisdom," without explicit reference to Torah. But their argument is saturated with the categories of "righteous" and "wicked" and thoughts of rewards and punishment, so that the Torah in a rigorous form is not far from their horizon. Israel, with its ethical intensity, could at times become destructively rigid on a point of commandment and ethical requirement. Indeed that ethical intensity is intrinsic to the work assigned to Moses in the Sinai traditions. Moreover, such rigidity is characteristically a mix of honest moral passion and unacknowledged social control.

What is to be recognized is that such a legalism, when it occurs, is a departure from the centrist understanding and function of the Torah. This does not at all detract from the ethical seriousness and intensity of Israel at its best, but Israel's ethical intensity was not driven by self-hatred or self-destructiveness. And indeed, the testimony of Ezekiel has Yahweh say, in a context of enormous ethical intensity:

> Therefore I will judge you, O house of Israel, all of you according to your ways, says the Lord God. Repent and turn from all your transgressions; otherwise iniquity will be your ruin. Cast away from you all the transgressions that you have committed against me, and get yourselves a new heart and a new spirit! Why will you die, O house of Israel? For I have no pleasure in the death of anyone, says the Lord God. Turn, then, and live. (Ezek 18:30-32)

A second distortion of Torah is less recognized among Christian interpreters: that Torah interpretation tends to make the truth of Torah slack and accommodating. Jeremiah delivers a wholesale critique of Israel's leadership, including those who interpret Torah (in this case, the wise):

> How can you say, "We are wise,
> and the law of the Lord is with us,"
> when, in fact, the false pen of the scribes
> has made it into a lie? (Jer 8:8)

The Torah is distorted, made false, by relaxing its rigor:

> They have treated the wound of my people carelessly,
> saying "Peace, peace,"
> when there is no peace.
> They acted shamefully,
> they committed abomination;
> yet they were not ashamed,
> they did not know how to blush. (Jer 8:11-12a)

This refusal to bear honest witness to Yahweh's claims on Israel, moreover, has dire consequences, for mendacity about the Torah is intolerable:

> Therefore I will give their wives to others
> and their fields to conquerors,
> because from the least to the greatest
> everyone is greedy for unjust gain;
> from prophet to priest
> everyone deals falsely....
> Therefore they shall fall among those who fall;
> at the time when I punish them,
> they shall be overthrown,
> says the Lord. (Jer 8:10, 12b)

It is ironic that Christians tend to worry excessively about Jewish legalism, when perhaps the great temptation for Jewish ethical reflection, as it is for Christian ethical reflection, is compromise in order to make matters less burdensome. But Torah is not the imposition of an arbitrary God, Israel insists. It is, rather, a discernment of the reality of things. Therefore, misrepresentation of the reality of things by the compromising of Torah cannot, in any circumstance, be genuinely helpful, even if it is more attractive than reality.

Practice of Torah as Worship

Torah is indeed intentional ethical practice, and so it is command. But it is also, as Östborn has shown, instruction, guidance, and nurture, whereby Israel is invited to probe, in the most intimate and caring ways, what it means to be related to and derived from this inscrutable God. That is, practice of Torah is not only study; it is also worship. It is being in the presence of the One who lives in, with, and under this authoritative text, and who is present in the ongoing work of imagination from this text.[47]

We may intensify this claim in two ways. First, the practice of Torah, which includes study and reflection as well as intentional living, is a way of being Jewish. That is, Torah is the field of possibility in which Jewishness is fully embraced, so that one comes to one's true identity. Second, as one comes through the practice of Torah to one's full identity, this means embrace of the Torah and obedience to it are a form of communion with the God whose Torah this is. In this way, any dualism between study and worship is indeed overcome in this tradition. Thus the tendency to divide worship and study, obedience and interpretation, communion and submission, is banished in the joy of the Torah.

---

47. See S. Dean McBride, "The Yoke of the Kingdom: An Exposition of Deuteronomy 6:4-5," *Int* 27 (1973) 273–306; and Patrick D. Miller, *Deuteronomy* (Interpretation; Louisville: John Knox, 1990) 53–57. McBride and Miller propose that the Torah is a surrogate for Yahweh, so that Yahweh is present in the Torah and is said to be "near" Israel (cf. Deut 4:7-8, 30:11-14). The ark of the covenant, which contains the tablets of the Torah, is a vehicle for Yahweh's presence and nearness.

It may seem to some that I have carried Torah in a Jewish direction that ill serves Christian readers. I have proceeded in this fashion, first, because it is important for Christian readers of the Old Testament to overcome stereotypes about legalism. Second, the practice of Torah as a practice of obedience and imagination that issues in communion is a way of thinking not only about Torah; for Christians it is a way of understanding Christ, who is both the one who commands and the one who offers self in intimacy.

The freedom of the Torah is a freedom in obedience.[48] This freedom is not autonomy, for autonomy is in any case an illusion. It is freedom of living with and for and in the presence of the One whose power is seen in creation, whose passion is evident in Exodus, and whose requirements are known in Sinai. Israel, as it "meditated day and night on Torah," understood well how Yahweh related to Yahweh's partners. The relationship is one of love:

> You shall love the Lord your God with all your heart, and with all your soul, and with all your might. (Deut 6:5)

> You shall not take vengeance or bear a grudge against any of your people, but you shall love your neighbor as yourself; I am the Lord. (Lev 19:18)

Israel well understood the linkage between these two commandments to love:

> Those who say, "I love God," and hate their brothers or sisters, are liars; for those who do not love a brother or sister whom they have seen, cannot love God whom they have not seen. The commandment we have from him is this: those who love God must love their brothers and sisters also. (1 John 4:20-21)

---

48. On the dialectic of freedom and obedience in Torah faith, see Walter Brueggemann, "Duty as Delight and Desire," *Journal for Preachers* 28:1 (1994) 2–14.

TWENTY-ONE

The King as Mediator

T HE TORAH as the most comprehensive mode of mediation between Yahweh and Israel pertains to every sphere of life. Indeed it makes none of the distinctions between various spheres of life—personal and public, civil and cultic—that we might make. All of life constitutes an undifferentiated arena in which Israel practices glad, imaginative obedience to Yahweh. Kingship, as a belatedly emerging mode of mediation in Israel, unlike Torah, pertains especially to public political life in which Israel thought, as best it could, about order, power, and justice.[1]

In its largest claim, all public, political questions of power were settled in Israel with the affirmation that "Yahweh is king."[2] As an alternative to pretentious, oppressive political authority, represented early in Israel's imagination by pharaoh, Israel proposes to order its public life under the direct rule of Yahweh, in a sort of theocracy, "the kingdom of Yahweh" (cf. Exod 19:6). While it may be disputed how early the notion of "Yahweh as king" is evident in Israel, such a notion dominates Israel's rhetoric (cf. Judg 8:22-23; Isa 6:1, 33:17-22; Zeph 3:15; Zech 14:16-17; plus the several enthronement psalms).

But Israel had to live in the real world of political possibility and political threat. Because the origins of Israel's life as a historical entity are exceedingly obscure, we cannot say with any certainty what made the "kingship of Yahweh" a viable political formulation, or what subsequently made it problematic. The most likely scenario, the one offered us in Israel's own testimony, is that Israel began, either in Egypt or in Canaan, as an alternative to established power. Its own political needs and possibilities were modest indeed, and so no great established authority was required. Moreover, if Israel emerged as an escape from and alternative to absolutist, oppressive political authority, it is plausible that Israel not only did not need such a power arrangement, but that it was actively resistant to any such apparatus. Israel's self-presentation is pervaded by a suspicion about public power that on occasion takes active revolutionary form.

As Israel tells its tale of public life, however, the maintenance of such pure power as Yahweh's *direct* governance could hardly be sustained. As a consequence,

---

1. See Lester L. Grabbe, *Priests, Prophets, Diviners, and Sages: A Socio-historical Study of Religious Specialists in Ancient Israel* (Valley Forge, Pa.: Trinity Press International, 1995) 20–40; and Rodney R. Hutton, *Charisma and Authority in Israelite Society* (Minneapolis: Fortress Press, 1994) 71–104.

2. Concerning Yahweh under the rubric of king, see pp. 238–41.

we are able to spot, very early in Israel's testimony, an inclination toward permanent human political power (kingship). Israel's resistance to and suspicion of established political power early conflicted with the needs, requirements, and hopes of Israel's public existence. This conflict between theological conviction and practical necessity entailed what must have been a long and profound ideological-interpretive struggle in Israel, to determine the character of the community and its appropriate forms of leadership.

The Practical Requirements of Kingship

It is clear that the requirement of monarchy arose from practical sociopolitical, economic realities. The impetus is not ideological or theological, but concerns, as political issues always do, military security and economic prosperity. We may identify three dimensions of this particular requirement.

Imitation of other nations. The reason given for monarchy (presented in a polemic against monarchy) is that Israel wanted to imitate the other nations:

> ...appoint for us, then, a king to govern us, like other nations.... No! but we are determined to have a king over us, so that we also may be like other nations, and that our king may govern us and go out before us and fight our battles. (1 Sam 8:5, 19-20)

That is, Israel had neighbors whose political life was seen to be more substantive. Israel, moreover, could recognize that sustained forms of political power give coherence and sustained policy, which contribute to security and prosperity.[3]

Response to military threat. The conventional view offered in the text is that some in Israel wanted monarchy in response to a concrete danger, the acute military threat of the Philistines. The military dimension of kingship is explicit in the urging of 1 Sam 8:20.

Protection of advantage. Norman Gottwald has proposed, more subtly, that the impetus for monarchy came from those who had monopolized wealth and who wanted a strong central government in order to protect and legitimate their considerable economic and political advantage.[4]

On this latter reading, the need for monarchy came from an *internal struggle* for advantage in the community, while appeal to the Philistine threat was offered as an *external cover* for the pursuit of internal advantage. (This is not the last time that the "Philistine threat" has been used as a warrant for internal political manipulation.) This ground for monarchy suggests why the question of human kingship became an intense internal ideological dispute in Israel. Advocacy for monarchy

---

3. See Isaac Mendelssohn, "Samuel's Denunciation of Kingship in Light of the Akkadian Documents from Ugarit," *BASOR* 143 (October 1956) 17–22.

4. Norman K. Gottwald, "The Participation of Free Agrarians in the Introduction of Monarchy to Ancient Israel: An Application of H. A. Landsberger's Framework for the Analysis of Peasant Movements," *Semeia* 37 (1986) 77–106.

was not community-wide, but represented the voice of one interest group and advocacy of one ideology in the community, one that was resisted by others. Any or all of these three understandings make clear that the emergence of monarchy came for reasons "on the ground."

Interpretive Problems with Monarchy

This felt requirement created important interpretive problems for the establishment of human kingship, which inevitably was perceived by some as a challenge to or overthrow of Yahweh's kingship (thus 1 Sam 8:7-8). The textual evidence suggests that this theological dispute, as we might expect, divided along practical lines. The ones who were able to harmonize the two kingships, divine and human, wanted monarchy and found it easy to legitimate; those who preferred (and benefited from?) the old arrangements of power focused on what they regarded as an untenable challenge to well-established claims for Yahweh. Thus, kingship as mediation was wrought out of felt practical necessity and settled upon through acute interpretive dispute.

The pro-king opinion obviously prevailed, and the testimony of Israel is shot through with allusion to royal-Davidic-messianic claims that are regarded as fully legitimated. It is odd, indeed, that the testimony about the actual dispute is preserved in assertions that clearly oppose the monarchy. Thus in Judges 8, the political success of Gideon as a military rescuer of Israel leads to political adventurism, which is resolved in deference to the kingship of Yahweh:

> Gideon said to them, "I will not rule over you, and my son will not rule over you; the Lord will rule over you." (Judg 8:23; notice that in vv. 24-27, Gideon does not so well resist the temptation to economic advantage made possible by his success.)

The principal dispute concerning the legitimacy of monarchy is given us in 1 Samuel 8, a distinctly anti-monarchial rendering.[5] A proposal for kingship is voiced by elders who have found the old system of judges dysfunctional and corrupt (vv. 1-5). This pivotal chapter is told, however, from the perspective of resistance to monarchy, in which Samuel (the leader of the old power establishment), Yahweh, and the narrator all agree that monarchy is unacceptable and is in fact an act of rejection of Yahweh (v. 7). This interpretation is in agreement with Judg 8:22-23: human monarchy detracts from Yahweh's rightful governance.

In the end, perhaps in the face of irresistible leverage from its advocates, the narrative of this chapter concedes monarchy. Samuel and Yahweh agree to accept it, most reluctantly. Monarchy is not, however, granted before this old-guard theocratic tradition issues its famous and massive warning against monarchy:

---

5. On this text, see Dennis J. McCarthy, "The Inauguration of Monarchy in Israel (A Form-Critical Study of 1 Samuel 8–12)," *Int* 17 (1973) 401-12.

These will be the ways of the king who will reign over you: he will take your sons and appoint them to his chariots and to be his horsemen, and to run before his chariots; and he will appoint for himself commanders of thousands and commanders of fifties, and some to plow his ground and to reap his harvest, and to make his implements of war and the equipment of his chariots. He will take your daughters to be perfumers and cooks and bakers. He will take the best of your fields and vineyards and olive orchards and give them to his courtiers. He will take one-tenth of your grain and your vineyards and give it to his officers and his courtiers. He will take your male and female slaves, and the best of your cattle and donkeys, and put them to his work. He will take one-tenth of your flocks and you shall be his slaves. And in that day you will cry out because of your king whom you have chosen for yourselves; but the Lord will not answer you in that day. (1 Sam 8:11-18)

This interpretive tradition, suspicious of concentrations of power, anticipates that the centralized government is in principle exploitative, usurpatious, and self-serving. We may say that this recognition is fundamental to a biblical critique of power. But it is evident that this is only one voice in the testimony, a powerful, authoritative voice, but one that did not prevail. In the end, monarchy was established. As the testimony presents it, by the time of the crowning of David, the question of monarchy had evaporated, and the "liberals" had won. After David, the issue was not, "Shall we have a king?" but "Who shall be king?" (1 Kgs 1:27).

In the end, Israel opts irreversibly for monarchy as its central expression of power.[6] Sigmund Mowinckel, in his magisterial study of kingship, is able to draw the conclusion:

Accordingly there is for the thought of Israel and the Old Testament no conflict between the kingly rule of Yahweh and that of the Messiah, just as, ideally, there is no conflict between Yahweh's kingly rule and that of His son, the anointed, earthly king. . . . Nowhere are his [the human king's] status and power so emphasized that they threaten the exclusive dominion of Yahweh or the monotheism of the Old Testament.[7]

"The Two Kings"

Mowinckel's reassuring and unqualified judgment about kingship may be a correct one, but it is in some ways a deception. The deception is that Mowinckel's line of reasoning concerns only the theological-theoretical matters. In that regard, a settlement of the competing claims of "the two kings" could be worked out. But

---

6. The notion of "irreversible" must be qualified, for after 587 B.C.E. Israel did indeed revert to non-monarchial ways of life. In the ideology of monarchial Israel, however, including the horizon of the prophets, the move to monarchy with rare exceptions was viewed as irreversible.

7. Sigmund Mowinckel, *He That Cometh* (Oxford: Blackwell, 1956) 171–72.

human monarchy in Israel is never simply a matter of theological-theoretical interpretation. Human monarchy in Israel, as anywhere, concerns the distribution of power, goods (land), and access. If Yahweh be understood as the critical principle of egalitarian distribution (as was to some extent true in the Sinai traditions), then human monarchy stands under suspicion because it became in Israel, as elsewhere, an engine for preference, privilege, monopoly, and self-indulgence. In its material practice, then, the monarchy was often seen to be inimical to the purposes of Yahweh.[8]

The equanimous conclusion of Mowinckel can be reached only by intense interpretive work, which must have gone on in Israel. That interpretive work consists in adjudication between two ideological locations of human kingship in the governance of Yahweh. On the one hand, the settlement of the Davidic king in the rule of Yahweh is accomplished by the articulation of a "royal ideology," that is, a theory of governance that was situated in Jerusalem and that asserted, in high liturgical fashion, that Yahweh had made an irreversible commitment to the Davidic house, so that the Davidic dynasty became in principle (and not by historical accident) a nonnegotiable fixture in Israel's life.[9] It is likely that this interpretive achievement was in part borrowed from Israel's political-religious environment.

Cruciality of the Davidic Kingship

In the witness of Israel, this theological claim for the cruciality of Davidic kingship is offered in two important places. It is most powerfully voiced in the narrative and oracle of 2 Samuel 7, commonly regarded as the interpretive pivot of messianism in Israel. In this text, Yahweh, through Nathan's oracle, promises to David (and his son) Yahweh's abiding fidelity:

> When your days are fulfilled and you lie down with your ancestors, I will raise up your offspring after you, who shall come forth from your body, and I will establish his kingdom. He shall build a house for my name, and I will establish the throne of his kingdom forever. I will be a father to him, and he shall be a son to me. When he commits iniquity, I will punish him with a rod such as mortals use, with blows inflicted by human beings. But I will not take my steadfast love from him, as I took it from Saul, whom I put away from before you. Your house and your kingdom shall be made sure forever before me; your throne shall be established forever. (2 Sam 7:12-16)

---

8. Only Hos 8:4, among the prophets, opposes monarchy in principle.

9. The standard works on this scholarly issue are Henri Frankfort, *The Intellectual Adventure of Ancient Man: An Essay on Speculative Thought in the Ancient Near East* (Chicago: University of Chicago Press, 1972); Ivan Engnell, *Studies in Divine Kingship in the Ancient Near East* (Oxford: Blackwell, 1967); S. H. Hooke, *Myth and Ritual: Essays in the Myth and Ritual of the Hebrews in Relation to the Culture Patterns of the Ancient East* (London: Oxford University Press, 1933); and Hooke, *Myth, Ritual, and Kingship: Essays on the Theory and Practice of Kingship in the Ancient Near East* (Oxford: Clarendon Press, 1958). It was Frank Moore Cross, *Canaanite Myth and Hebrew Epic* (Cambridge: Harvard University Press, 1973), who first took these studies seriously in U.S. scholarship.

This is an extraordinary declaration, a genuine *novum* in Israel's faith. In one sweeping assurance, the conditional "if" of the Mosaic Torah (Exod 19:5-6) is overridden, and David is made a vehicle and carrier of Yahweh's unqualified grace in Israel. This statement may be regarded as the beginning point for graciousness without qualification as a datum of Israel's life and for the assertion of messianism wherein this particular human agent (and his family) is made constitutive for Yahweh's way with Israel. The assurance of this oracle is reiterated in the first part of Psalm 89:

> Forever I will keep my steadfast love for him,
> and my covenant with him will stand firm.
> I will establish his line forever,
> and his throne as long as the heavens endure.
> If his children forsake my law
> and do not walk according to my ordinances,
> if they violate my statutes
> and do not keep my commandments,
> then I will punish their transgression with the rod
> and their iniquity with scourges;
> but I will not remove from him my steadfast love,
> or be false to my faithfulness.
> I will not violate my covenant,
> or alter the word that went forth from my lips.
> Once and for all I have sworn by my holiness;
> I will not lie to David.
> His line shall continue forever,
> and his throne endure before me like the sun.
> It shall be established forever like the moon,
> an enduring witness in the skies. (Ps 89:28-37)

These assertions, celebrated liturgically, established the monarchy not as a historical institution, but as a part of the way in which Yahweh would relate to Israel. David and his dynasty are indeed a mode of mediation, carriers in Israel of unconditional fidelity.

This high interpretive claim is enunciated secondly in a series of royal psalms, of which the most prominent are Psalms 2 and 110.[10] The texts that emerged from royal liturgies in Jerusalem reiterate the claim of the oracle of 2 Samuel 7.[11] In Psalm 2, we hear uttered what is likely an enthronement formula:

> I will tell of the decree of the Lord:
> He said to me, "You are my son;

---

10. On kingship in the Psalms, see Hans-Joachim Kraus, *Theology of the Psalms* (1986; Minneapolis: Fortress Press, 1992) 107–23.

11. See the venturesome piecing together of these texts into a liturgical coherence by Aubrey R. Johnson, *Sacral Kingship in Ancient Israel* (Cardiff: University of Wales Press, 1955).

> today I have begotten you.
> Ask of me, and I will make the nations your heritage,
> and the ends of the earth your possession.
> You shall break them with a rod of iron,
> and dash them in pieces like a potter's vessel." (Ps 2:7-9)

The oracle assures Yahweh's protective commitment to the monarchy. In Psalm 110, "The Lord" assures "my lord" (David):

> "Sit at my right hand
> until I make your enemies your footstool." (Ps 110:1)

The dynasty in Jerusalem is to function with military success (vv. 2-7), but also with sacerdotal efficaciousness (v. 4) that will assure the success and well-being of the people (v. 3).

No doubt this interpretation of David and his dynasty is informed by powerful political interests, not only of the family, but of that segment of society (urban elite) who benefited from a centralized government. The claim of the dynasty reflects undeniable material—that is, socioeconomic—interests. In this regard, David is, as the creed later on is to say of Jesus, "truly human." At the same time, we notice that in the coronation decree of Ps 2:7, Yahweh calls him "my son." Surely this is an exalted political title. The notion of king as "son of God" does not concern any ontological claim or metaphysical status, but is a powerful political claim of peculiar legitimacy.[12] But this interpretive trajectory is not precise in its formulations. What is claimed is that in the Davidic king, Yahweh has made a new and unconditional commitment to protect and prosper Israel.

The ideological dimension of this claim is that in order to receive such peace and prosperity, the well-being, prosperity, and authority of the king must be beyond criticism, celebrated in exuberant allegiance. This interpretive claim for what the king signifies radically alters the way in which Yahweh is understood to be in the midst of Israel.

Efforts to Subsume Royal Claims under Torah

A second, quite different interpretive effort in Israel, however, seeks to accommodate this new institutional development. This second effort lives in important tension with the first. The "old guard" believed (or claimed to believe, in its own self-interest) that Torah obedience is an adequate source of peace and prosperity, and that kingship would impede, not serve, these ends. In resistance to the interpretation of kingship as unconditionally guaranteed, this second interpretive effort worked vigilantly to subsume royal claims under the requirements of Torah.

What this notion of kingship does is to curb royal power and authority, and to insist that kingship, like everything else in Israel, is subject to the Torah. The king, in the end, is only one more Israelite, subject like all others to obedience, which

---

12. Perhaps an important exception is Ps 45:6, which appears to address the king as "elohim."

is the primal source of all well-being in the world. That is, insistence on Torah serves to deabsolutize the claims of kingship. The foremost text that articulates this deabsolutizing insistence is Deut 17:14-20, the primary text in the Pentateuch concerning monarchy. Negatively, the rapacious power of monarchy, anticipated in 1 Sam 8:11-18, is severely limited in this theory of kingship:

> Even so, he must not acquire many horses for himself, or return the people to Egypt in order to acquire more horses, since the Lord has said to you, "You must never return that way again." And he must not acquire many wives for himself, or else his heart will turn away; also silver and gold he must not acquire in great quantity for himself. (Deut 17:16-17)

Positively, the primary activity of the king is to study Torah, to submit to the demands and conditions of the Mosaic covenant (Deut 17:18-20).

This intensely Deuteronomistic insistence, which lives in tension with high royal claims, is reiterated in the initial authorization of Solomon as David's successor. Solomon asks for endowments to be a wise king:

> Give your servant therefore an understanding mind to govern your people, able to discern between good and evil; for who can govern this your great people? (1 Kgs 3:9)

Because Solomon petitioned Yahweh wisely, he is given all the luxuries of kingship:

> Because you have asked this, and have not asked for yourself long life or riches, or for the life of your enemies, but have asked for yourself understanding to discern what is right, I now do according to your word. Indeed I give you a wise and discerning mind; no one like you has been before you and no one like you shall arise after you. I give you also what you have not asked, both riches and honor all your life; no other king shall compare with you. (1 Kgs 3:11-13)

All these other things—riches and honor—are added (cf. Matt 6:33). But they are not first in the process; they are not first asked or first given. Before the text ends, the "if" of Moses is reinforced:

> If you walk in my ways, keeping my statutes and commandments, as your father David walked, then I will lengthen your life. (1 Kgs 3:14)

Thus the tradition that curbs royal aggrandizement here resituates monarchy in the context of Torah, and it refuses to entertain the notion of an institution that can supersede or transcend Torah obedience. This Torah-insisting "if" occurs in a variety of royal texts, all no doubt derivative from the Deuteronomic tradition of Torah.

(a) In 2 Samuel 11, David conducts himself as though he is an autonomous potentate who is above the law. The narrative laconically asserts: "But the thing that David had done displeased the Lord..." (v. 27b).[13] This understatement is intensified in chapter 12 by the Torah-based indictment of Nathan:

> Why have you despised the word of the Lord, to do what is evil in his sight? You have struck down Uriah the Hittite with the sword, and have taken his wife to be your wife, and have killed him with the sword of the Ammonites. Now therefore the sword shall never depart from your house, for you have despised me, and have taken the wife of Uriah the Hittite to be your wife. (2 Sam 12:9-10)

David, in all his glory, is not free beyond the old, covenantal restraints of the Torah. The subsequent narrative continues to regard this incident as crucial in David's life (cf. 1 Kgs 15:5).

(b) It is not different with Solomon. Just after the grand and glorious establishment of the temple, the crusty, killjoy narrative introduces the tight symmetry of Torah obedience as the condition of royal prosperity:

> As for you, if you will walk before me, as David your father walked, with integrity of heart and uprightness, doing according to all that I have commanded you, and keeping my statutes and my ordinances, then I will establish your royal throne over Israel forever, as I promised your father David, saying, "There shall not fail you a successor on the throne of Israel." If you turn aside from following me, you or your children, and do not keep my commandments and my statutes that I have set before you, but go and serve other gods and worship them, then I will cut Israel off from the land that I have given them; and the house that I have consecrated for my name I will cast out of my sight; and Israel will become a proverb and taunt among all the peoples. (1 Kgs 9:4-8)

In the end, Solomon is devastatingly critiqued as a king who proceeded autonomously:

> Then the Lord was angry with Solomon, because his heart had turned away from the Lord, the God of Israel, who had appeared to him twice, and had commanded him concerning this matter, that he should not follow other gods; but he did not observe what the Lord commanded. Therefore the Lord

---

13. I have here quoted the NRSV. The rendering is unfortunate, because it dissolves the tension that is surely intended with v. 25. The NRSV translates the two texts:

Do not let this matter trouble you.... (v. 25)

But the thing that David had done displeased the Lord.... (v. 27)

The Hebrew of the two verses is parallel and might better be rendered:

Do not let this thing be evil in your eyes.... (v. 25)

But the thing David had done was evil in the eyes of Yahweh.... (v. 27)

said to Solomon, "Since this has been your mind and you have not kept my covenant and my statutes that I have commanded you, I will surely tear the kingdom from you and give it to your servant." (1 Kgs 11:9-11)

(c) In the farewell address of Samuel, Samuel employs rhetoric that makes the king, like every Israelite, completely subject to the Torah:

> If you will fear the Lord and serve him and heed his voice and not rebel against the commandment of the Lord, and if *both you and the king* who reigns over you will follow the Lord your God, it will be well; but if you will not heed the voice of the Lord, but rebel against the commandment of the Lord, then the hand of the Lord will be against *you and your king.* . . . Only fear the Lord, and serve him faithfully with all your heart; for consider what great things he has done for you. But if you still do wickedly, you shall be swept away, *both you and your king.* (1 Sam 12:14-15, 24-25)

The haunting formula "you and your king" is a vigorous reminder that in this purview, the king is nobody special. The king lives under the same demand as all of Yahweh's people.

(d) The oracle of Ps 132:11-12 is closely parallel to Psalm 89:

> The Lord swore to David a sure oath
> from which he will not turn back:
> "One of the sons of your body
> I will set on your throne.
> If your sons keep my covenant
> and my decrees that I shall teach them,
> their sons also, forevermore,
> shall sit on your throne."

A comparison of this text with Ps 89:30-37, however, indicates a drastic difference. The "if" of Ps 89:30-31 is important, but it is penultimate to the "but" of v. 33. The statement is structured like that of 2 Sam 7:14-15, which makes unconditional the final utterance. In Psalm 132, there is nothing after the "if" of v. 12. Thus Psalm 132 retreats from the absolutizing claim of 2 Samuel 7 and Psalm 89 in the direction of obedience.

The settlement of the relation between Yahweh and the king may in the end be as irenic as Mowinckel's verdict suggests. But such a settlement is not easily arrived at, if indeed it is achieved at all. Pervasively, in Israel's witness, the conditionality of Torah and the unconditionality of royal ideology live in deep tension.[14] In my judgment, this tension itself is the datum that concerns us in understanding

---

14. Jon D. Levenson, *Sinai and Zion: An Entry into the Jewish Bible* (Minneapolis: Winston Press, 1985), has nicely articulated the tension, refusing any either/or accommodation. See his discussion of Genesis 18 and 22 as two sides of the tension: "The Dialectic of Covenantal Theonomy," *Creation and the Persistence of Evil: The Jewish Drama of Divine Omnipotence* (San Francisco: Harper and Row, 1988) 140–56.

this mode of mediation theologically. It is a tension that must persist, because the "truly divine" now is committed to the "truly human," which means that the promise of Yahweh to Israel is embedded in a concrete, material practice. Therefore, in the concrete material practice, high theological claims and specific, experienced demands and costs live intimately together. What emerges is that the "high and holy one" has devolved power and authority into human, historical, political, material form. Put more succinctly, the purposes of Yahweh have now been entrusted to a human agent. Yahweh's work is to be done by David's family. Yahweh's kingdom takes the form of the house of David. And when cast as human agent in human form, what is from Yahweh's side a singular intention becomes complicated both by high aggrandizing ideology and by uncurbed self-service. But Israel cannot pick and choose. When it receives kingship, it gets with it all the singular intention, high aggrandizing ideology, and uncurbed self-service. That is how Yahweh's presence is mediated, in this form, in the world.

This odd, unsorted mix presents two temptations. On the one hand, it is possible, as the church tends to do in its christological inclination, to take the high lyrical claims of oracle and royal psalm and "supersede" the narratives of sordidness, so that kingship takes on a somewhat docetic flavor. On the other hand, given an opening for cynicism, one can focus on the self-serving propensity of the monarchy and dismiss the entire dynastic business as an invention of the urban elites, removed from the God of Israel. The witness of Israel, however, refused to choose either of these temptations to the neglect of the other accent. And so Israel's testimony reiterates and trusts in the high claims made for the king, but does nothing to deny the reality of self-service that distorts monarchy as a mediator of Yahweh.[15]

If we move past that problematic, we are left with the larger problem of Torah and kingship. Here Christians have made the characteristic maneuver of appropriating for Christology the highest claims of kingship (witness the use of Psalms 2, 110) and assigning to Judaism the demands of the Torah.[16] Such a split of resources, however, is an untenable conclusion. It distorts both the way in which Jewish interpretation kept Torah and messiah in fruitful tension, and it overlooks the way in which this same tension continues to swirl around Jesus. Indeed, one can suggest that Jesus' own commitment to Torah faith is more intense than the high Christology of church interpretation can tolerate.

Our study thus far suggests that in the emergence of this mode of mediation, Israel dealt with real-life issues, which in turn required difficult and sustained interpretive negotiation. Kingship emerges as a mode of Yahweh's relatedness. Kingship is Israel's odd assertion that Yahweh's way toward Israel is visible in human agency, a human agency that is deeply subject to the conditionality of the historical process.

---

15. In this regard, the decision of the Chronicler to pass over negative narratives in silence appears to be something of a cover-up congruent with the entire perspective of the Chronicler.

16. See Kraus, *Theology of the Psalms,* 177–203, on the royal psalms in the New Testament.

Without denying the "warts" of David (as in 2 Samuel 11–12), Solomon (as in 1 Kings 11), and their ilk, kingship in Israel emerged, in Jerusalem interpretation, as a great gift from God. The king's intimacy and congruity with Yahweh indicate that the actual performance of Yahweh's way in the world is a human possibility. Thus, despite great ambiguity and compromise, it is expected and celebrated that the king will bring the world right for Israel.

Kingship and Torah

Thus kingship as mediator is to be understood (a) as congruent with the kingship of Yahweh; and (b) as somehow situated between the high royal ideology and the reservation and qualification of the Torah traditions springing from the Mosaic covenant. These difficult requirements were reached in the text only raggedly, with many hints that the settlement was not easy or complete or everywhere accepted. Nonetheless, we are able to say that these requirements for kingship as mediator were satisfied with the predominant claim that Davidic kingship had the establishment and maintenance of justice as its primary obligation to Yahweh and to Israelite society. This justice, moreover, is distributive justice, congruent with Israel's fundamental covenantal vision, intending the sharing of goods, power, and access with every member of the community, including the poor, powerless, and marginated. The clearest articulation of this notion of mediation is in the royal Psalm 72:

> Give the king your justice, O God,
> and your righteousness to a king's son.
> May he judge your people with righteousness,
> and your poor with justice.
> May the mountains yield prosperity for the people,
> and the hills, in righteousness.
> May he defend the cause of the poor of the people,
> give deliverance to the needy,
> and crush the oppressor. . . .
> For he delivers the needy when they call,
> the poor and those who have no helper.
> He has pity on the weak and the needy,
> and saves the lives of the needy.
> From oppression and violence he redeems their life;
> and precious is their blood in his sight. (vv. 1-4, 12-14; cf. Psalm 101)

These remarkable mandates to the king, undoubtedly articulated in royal liturgies, have as their countertheme the prosperity and well-being of the king, expressed in the most hyperbolic language of the court:

> May he live while the sun endures,
> and as long as the moon,

> throughout all generations.
> May he be like rain that falls on the mown grass,
> like showers that water the earth.
> In his days may righteousness flourish
> and peace abound, until the moon is no more.
> May he have dominion from sea to sea,
> and from the River to the ends of the earth.
> May his foes bow down before him,
> and his enemies lick the dust.
> May the kings of Tarshish and of the isles
> render him tribute,
> may the kings of Sheba and Seba bring gifts.
> May all kings fall down before him,
> all nations give him service. (vv. 5-11; cf. vv. 15-17)

It is evident that this ideology links the royal practice of justice to the proper functioning of fertility, so that the king is, in the end, responsible for the full functioning of creation.[17] This full functioning of creation, moreover, is dependent on the serious practice of social justice.

"Justice" is an old ideological assignment of kings, made long before Israel, and one may therefore conclude that such speech is only liturgical, ideological cant. David Jobling, moreover, has argued that Psalm 72 is quite subtle but intentional ideology to benefit the elite class that practices the psalm in liturgy.[18] Such reservations and qualifications are no doubt in order. It is nonetheless important that royal ideology in the Old Testament is set down in the middle of Mosaic commitments. Therefore it is evident that some, at least, took the rhetoric of justice seriously and expected public power not merely to recite slogans, but to engage in such practices. While the actual work of kings may be endlessly ambivalent about justice and self-indulgence, kingship as presented in Yahwistic formulation takes the king as an agent of justice and righteousness. That is, the king is to do what Yahweh as king proposes to do. The visionary insistence of kingship is that faithful kingship mediates Yahweh's sovereignty precisely in the performance of the transformation of public power in the interest of communal well-being.

This insistence on the intensely Yahwistic character of monarchy (that is, as committed to justice) is voiced in various ways in the prophets, who appeal to the covenantal traditions (see, for example, Mic 3:9-12), and it is championed especially in the traditions of Deuteronomy. Specifically, the Deuteronomist presents Josiah as the model king who fully practiced the Torah commands:

---

17. See, for example, 1 Kgs 18:5-6 on the royal management of the drought.
18. David Jobling, "Deconstruction and the Political Analysis of Biblical Texts: A Jamesonian Reading of Psalm 72," *Semeia* 59 (1992) 95–127.

> He did what was right in the sight of the Lord, and walked in all the ways of his father David; he did not turn aside to the right or to the left. (2 Kgs 22:2)[19]

Josiah is presented as fully responsive to the requirements of Torah (22:11). The account given in 2 Kings 22–23 portrays Josiah primarily as a cultic reformer who purged foreign elements from the practice of Israel's worship. It is probable that Josiah's "reform" was intended primarily as an act of political independence. Yet it is plausible to conclude that such accommodations in cult that he resisted had slackened intense Yahwism and led to a lessening of the passion for justice. Conversely, the purging of foreign accoutrements in worship is likely to be linked to the recovery of an ethic of public justice.

Because the historical reality and the ideological inclination of the Deuteronomist are not easy to sort out, we cannot go beyond this probable, intended linkage. In any case, we notice that in Jeremiah's assessment of Israel's later kings, the prophetic, poetic verdict on Josiah is remarkable:

> Did not your father eat and drink
> and do justice and righteousness?
> Then it was well with him.
> He judged the cause of the poor and needy;
> then it was well.
> Is not this to know me? says the Lord. (Jer 22:15-16)

This is a remarkable assertion, apparently concerning Josiah, father of Jehoiakim. Josiah is said to have practiced justice and righteousness (the very terms of Ps 72:1), and prospered as a consequence. But it is v. 16 that is most astonishing. In this utterance the prophet equates judging the cause of the poor and needy with "knowing" Yahweh. Note well these lines do not say that judging the poor and needy is the cause and knowing Yahweh the consequence; nor, conversely, that judging the poor and needy is the consequence and knowing Yahweh the cause.[20] Rather, the two are equated. Judging the cause of the poor and needy *is the substance* of knowledge of Yahweh (cf. Hos 6:6). And so, when the king engages in these practices in the administration of public power, knowledge of Yahweh is indeed mediated in the community of Israel.

This same visionary expectation of the king as mediation of Yahweh's rule is evidenced in two well-known oracles in Isaiah that perhaps are related to royal coronations. In Isa 9:2-7 anticipation of a great Davidic military victory (vv. 4-5) culminates in a characterization of Davidic government now to be practiced in the well-established and secure monarchy:

---

19. This portrayal of Josiah reflects the ideology of the Deuteronomists, so that Josiah becomes a model and cipher for "how it should have been," if indeed it does not factually present Josiah.

20. On the text, see José Miranda, *Marx and the Bible: A Critique of the Philosophy of Oppression* (Maryknoll, N.Y.: Orbis Books, 1974).

> His authority shall grow continually,
> and there shall be endless peace
> for the throne of David and his kingdom.
> He will establish and uphold it with justice
> and with righteousness
> from this time onward and forevermore.
> The zeal of the Lord of hosts will do this. (Isa 9:7)

The same tag words, "justice and righteousness," are utilized, which charge the king with radical administration of public power in the interests of the whole community (cf. 1 Kgs 10:9 for the same word pair). Yahweh is present, through the Davidic king, wherever such practices of public power are undertaken.

The same visionary mandate is expressed in a prose section of Jeremiah, surely reflective of covenantal, Deuteronomic commitment, in which the "if" of Mosaic conditionality is prominent:

> Hear the word of the Lord, O King of Judah sitting on the throne of David—you and your servants, and your people who enter these gates. Thus says the Lord: Act with justice and righteousness, and deliver from the hand of the oppressor anyone who has been robbed. And do no wrong or violence to the alien, the orphan, and the widow, or shed innocently blood in this place. For if you will indeed obey this word, then through the gates of this house shall enter kings who sit on the throne of David, riding in chariots and on horses, they, and their servants, and their people. But if you will not heed these words, I swear by myself, says the Lord, that this house shall become a desolation. (Jer 22:2-5)

Here the mandate is made even more specific, concerning economic justice and the cruciality of care for the alien, orphan, and widow. This tradition affirms that through this human agency, Yahweh's sovereign will for well-being in the world, with concrete socioeconomic, political dimensions, can be implemented and established.

Kingship and Exile

One defining mark of Israel's life is that the royal system was not finally effective in sustaining Israel. For at the center of Israel's self-awareness is the debacle of 587 B.C.E., when king, temple, and city all failed. Because of this devastating core reality, which Israel could not and would not deny, it does not surprise us that some in Israel will attribute the destruction of 587 to the failure of the monarchy to do its duty in terms of justice and righteousness.

Two texts make this linkage explicit. Again, the tradition of Jeremiah, which is relentlessly negative about kingship, links kingship and exile:

Woe to the shepherds who destroy and scatter the sheep of my pasture! says the Lord. Therefore thus says the Lord, the God of Israel, concerning the shepherds who shepherd my people: It is you who have scattered my flock, and have driven them away, and you have not attended to them. (Jer 23:1-2)

It is the kings who have "scattered," that is, caused exile. A fuller assertion of the same connection is given in Ezekiel 34:

You eat the fat, you clothe yourselves with the wool, you slaughter the fatlings; but you do not feed the sheep. You have not strengthened the weak, you have not healed the sick, you have not bound up the injured, you have not brought back the strayed, you have not sought the lost, but with force and harshness you have ruled over them. So they were scattered, because there was no shepherd; and scattered, they became food for all the wild animals. My sheep were scattered, they wandered over all the mountains and on every high hill; my sheep were scattered over all the face of the earth, with no one to search or seek for them. (vv. 3-6)

The indictment against the monarchy is severe, with the repeated sounding of the word "scatter." Indeed, in the long chapter on kings in Jeremiah, the poem ends with anticipation of the termination of the monarchy (Jer 22:28-30).

The linkage made in this testimony between royal failure and public demise is so clear and so familiar to us that we might miss the enormous theo-ethical claim made for kingship. The claim made is that power—political, economic, military— cannot survive or give prosperity or security, unless public power is administered according to the requirement of justice, justice being understood as attention to the well-being of all members of the community. In an alternative theory of public power, alive in the ancient world as in the contemporary world, power can sustain itself willy-nilly, even if it practices endless self-aggrandizement and brutalizing self-indulgence. Moreover, those who come to power are, characteristically, convinced (a little at a time) that their own well-being is the key factor in the maintenance of general well-being, prosperity, and security.

The debacle of 587 could be explained in ways other than this criterion of covenantal justice. It is nonetheless astonishing that some in Israel continued to hold to this primal explanation of what evoked the crisis. Those who so argued insisted that when Davidic kings depart from Yahweh's sovereign will for justice, public power is inevitably jeopardized, and, in the end, cannot be sustained.

In any case, the demise of 587 brought the claims and the fortunes of Davidic monarchy very low. The monarchy, according to any practical judgment, had failed. And with that failure, expression is given to wonderment about Yahweh's unconditional oath to David given in 2 Samuel 7:

But now you have spurned and rejected him;
you are full of wrath against your anointed.
You have renounced the covenant with your servant;

you have defiled his crown in the dust.
You have broken through all his walls;
You have laid his strongholds in ruins.
All who pass by plunder him;
he has become the scorn of his neighbors.
You have exalted the right hand of his foes;
you have made all his enemies rejoice.
Moreover, you have turned back the edge of his sword,
and you have not supported him in battle.
You have removed the scepter from his hand,
and hurled his throne to the ground.
You have cut short the days of his youth;
you have covered him with shame....
Lord, where is your steadfast love of old,
which by your faithfulness you swore to David?
Remember, O Lord, how your servant is taunted;
how I bear in my bosom the insults of the peoples,
with which your enemies taunt, O Lord,
with which they taunted the footsteps of your anointed. (Ps 89:38-
45, 49-51)

Psalm 89 had been an exemplar of high Davidic claim (vv. 19-37). But now, in the same psalm, the institution of monarchy has failed, and with it the ideology with which it was invested.

Kingship and Hope

The amazing power of monarchy as mediator, and of the vision carried by it, is evident in the fact that the historical fissure, which was inescapable for Israel's interpreters, did not terminate the ideological power of the institution. Sigmund Mowinckel has argued that as historical developments continued to foil and defeat the practical claims of kingship, so Israel managed, in its liturgical life, to continue the promissory dimension of Yahweh's commitment to David.[21] The dynastic promise, rooted in 2 Samuel 7 and explicated in Psalm 89, was turned to the future, so that Israel expected the good, faithful, effective king to come, even though all present and known incumbents had failed. Out of concrete political practice arose an expectation of the coming of messiah: a historical agent to be anointed, commissioned, and empowered out of the Davidic house to do the Davidic thing in time to come, to establish Yahweh's justice and righteousness in the earth.

Interpreters are at a loss to know why this promise, now removed from political reality and carried only in Israel's liturgical, visionary, ideological hopes, continued

---

21. Sigmund Mowinckel, *Psalmenstudien 2: Das Thronbesteigungsfest Jahwas und der Ursprung der Eschatologie* (Oslo: Jacob Dybwad, 1922); and derivatively, *He That Cometh*.

to have shaping power for the life and imagination of Israel; but unarguably it did. Israel continued to hope for the king who would make visible in the earth Yahweh's governance. The hope is much attested in Israel after exile. Perhaps best known and most used is the attestation of Isaiah's expectation from the "stump of Jesse":

> He shall not judge by what his eyes see,
> or decide by what his ears hear;
> but with righteousness he shall judge the poor,
> and decide with equity for the meek of the earth;
> he shall strike the earth with the rod of his mouth,
> and with the breath of his lips he shall kill the wicked.
> Righteousness shall be the belt around his waist,
> and faithfulness the belt around his loins. (Isa 11:3b-5)

The king to come who effects social rehabilitative well-being (consequently?) causes the rehabilitation of the earth:

> The wolf shall live with the lamb,
> the leopard shall lie down with the kid,
> the calf and the lion and the fatling together,
> and a little child shall lead them.
> The cow and the bear shall graze,
> their young shall lie down together;
> and the lion shall eat straw like the ox.
> The nursing child shall play over the hole of the asp,
> and the weaned child shall put its hand on the adder's den.
> They will not hurt or destroy
> on all my holy mountain;
> for the earth will be full of the knowledge of the Lord
> as the waters cover the sea. (Isa 11:6-9)

Jeremiah, who has no great brief for the monarchy, follows the stricture of 23:1-2 with a promise of "shepherds who will shepherd them" (v. 4), and then with an expectation of Davidic "justice and righteousness":

> The days are surely coming, says the Lord, when I will raise up for David a righteous Branch, and he shall reign as king and deal wisely, and shall execute justice and righteousness in the land. In his days Judah will be saved and Israel will live in safety. And this is the name by which he will be called: "The Lord is our righteousness." (Jer 23:5-7; cf. 33:14-16)

Ezekiel, who had massively dismissed kingship in 34:1-16, now awaits David:[22]

---

22. It is possible that vv. 23-24 are an addition to the text, under pressure from advocates of restored monarchy. Jon Levenson, *Theology of the Program of Restoration of Ezekiel 40–48* (HSM 10; Missoula, Mont.: Scholars Press, 1976) 87–91, regards the verses as belonging to the original articulation and so intrinsic to the new reality anticipated in this tradition.

> I will set up over them one shepherd, my servant David, and he shall feed them: he shall feed them and be their shepherd. And I, the Lord, will be their God, and my servant David shall be prince among them; I, the Lord, have spoken. (34:23-24)[23]

Moreover, that Davidic hope, of a quite political kind, continued with power after the exile:

> On that day, says the Lord of hosts, I will take you, O Zerubbabel my servant, son of Shealtiel, says the Lord, and make you like a signet ring; for I have chosen you, says the Lord of hosts. (Hag 2:23)

> Rejoice greatly, O daughter Zion!
> Shout aloud, O daughter Jerusalem!
> Lo, your king comes to you;
> triumphant and victorious is he,
> humble and riding on a donkey,
> on a colt, the foal of a donkey.
> He will cut off the chariot from Ephraim
> and the war horse from Jerusalem;
> and the battle bow shall be cut off,
> and he shall command peace to the nations;
> his dominion shall be from sea to sea,
> and from the River to the ends of the earth. (Zech 9:9-10)[24]

This mode of mediation of Yahweh continued in Judaism with enormous power. Four aspects of this hope are pertinent for its continuation as a hoped-for mediation of Yahweh to Israel and to the world:

(a) The possibility of such a human agent is completely dependent on the fidelity of Yahweh to Yahweh's own promise. In the end, the hope for messiah is hope based on Yahweh's capacity to be fully faithful to Yahweh's own promise.

(b) The messiah is a human agent. "Son of God" (as in Ps 2:7) is a royal, liturgical title, reflecting no ontological linkage to Yahweh. Thus messianism is a hope for human work in the world. This mode of mediation is both an affirmation of human agents who are to "have dominion," and of the materiality of Yahweh's intention.[25] Yahweh intends something for the earth.

(c) The messiah is expected to exercise political power and leverage of a public kind, in order to transform and rehabilitate the public community. Thus messian-

---

23. On "the prince" (*nasi '*), see ibid., 37–107.

24. The Davidic shape of anticipation in the prophetic corpus is difficult to date, and therefore to assess. See, for example, Amos 9:11-12, Hos 3:5, and Mic 5:2-5. Of these texts, the Micah text has the most widely accepted claim to being genuine in its location. But different judgments must be made with reference to each specific text.

25. See Brevard S. Childs, *Biblical Theology in Crisis* (Philadelphia: Westminster Press, 1970) 151–63, on Psalm 8, as he interprets "dominion" in a royal and then christological direction.

ism, in Old Testament testimony, is charged with justice and righteousness, with the restoration of viable communal practices in the real world.

(d) The practice of human power for communal restoration is entrusted to the descendants of this particular human family, the heirs of David. This is indeed "the scandal of particularity" as an uncompromising claim. But of course that is how royal power and royal authority work. It is worth noting that as the Davidic line comes to its historical end in the sixth century B.C.E., Cyrus the Persian is termed "his anointed" (Isa 45:1). Peter Ackroyd has ventured the thought that in Isaiah of the exile, Davidic claims are reassigned to the Persian.[26] More plausibly, Otto Eissfeldt leads a number of scholars in suggesting that in Isa 55:3 the Davidic mandate has been "democratized" in order to include all of Israel.[27] In the case of either of these reassignments of the claim of David, the particularity of the family of Jesse is still a powerful and resilient claim that provides energy and identity for continuing Israel.

Messianism with Reference to Jesus

In passing we should notice two particular texts and titles that in Christian interpretation have often been linked to messianic claims. First, the poetry of Isa 52:13–53:12 has eventuated in the figure of the "Suffering Servant," which comes to play a powerful role in Christian interpretation when it is fused with royal claims.[28] It is fair to say, however, that the notion of a king as "suffering servant" plays no role in Old Testament witness as such. Attempts have been made to identify the "ritual humiliation" of the king and to read the escape of David from Jerusalem, under the threat of Absalom, as a ritual enactment of death and restoration (2 Samuel 15–19).[29] Such efforts have not been found convincing, and in any case exercise no discernible influence in Old Testament testimony.

Second, the reference to "son of man" in Dan 7:13 has been linked in Christian tradition to Jesus' presentation of himself as Son of man and so has been fused to the notion of messiah.[30] This reference to "son of man," while important in subsequent apocryphal and Christian texts, plays no role in the Old Testament itself. The reference in Daniel is late and marginal in the Old Testament, and it too constitutes no discernible influence in Old Testament theology.

---

26. Peter Ackroyd in a paper presented at the Society for Old Testament Study, 1987.

27. See Otto Eissfeldt, "The Promises of Grace to David in Isaiah 55:1-5," *Israel's Prophetic Heritage* (ed. Bernhard W. Anderson and Walter Harrelson; London: SCM Press, 1962) 196–207.

28. For one older, standard review of the problem, see Morna D. Hooker, *Jesus and the Servant: The Influence of the Servant Concept of Deutero-Isaiah in the New Testament* (London: SPCK, 1959). More recently see Adela Yarbro Collins, "The Suffering Servant: Isaiah Chapter 53 as a Christian Text," *Hebrew Bible or Old Testament? Studying the Bible in Judaism and Christianity* (ed. Roger Brooks and John Collins; Notre Dame, Ind.: University of Notre Dame Press, 1990) 201–6.

29. Concerning the ritual humiliation of the king, see generally Johnson, *Sacral Kingship*, 103–4; and John H. Eaton, *Kingship and the Psalms* (SBT 32, 2d series; London: SCM Press, 1976) 109–11, 142–46.

30. Mowinckel, *He That Cometh*, 346–450, offers a full review of the data. See also Morna D. Hooker, *The Son of Man in Mark: A Study of the Background of the Term "Son of Man" and Its Use in St. Mark's Gospel* (London: SPCK, 1967).

An Old Testament theology in the end cannot avoid a comment on the utilization of the theme of messianism with reference to Jesus and to the emerging Christology of the church. There is no doubt that the notion of king as mediator thrust itself into the future as promised, anticipated messiah (that is, an anointed human agent) who will do Yahweh's work of justice and righteousness in the earth. All the heirs of this text (Jewish, Christian, Islamic) have this promissory possibility available to them, but the possibility is kept open only by Yahweh's large promise. The community that treasured this text after the exile knew to expect, but it did not know with any precision *what* to expect.

The first century B.C.E. and the first century C.E., the time of Jesus, was a time of enormous need and commensurate anticipation in Jewish life. As the earliest Christians confronted the overwhelming reality of the person of Jesus, it was inevitable (and not inappropriate?) that linkages would be made between this powerful and pervasive expectation and this transformative personal presence. What else could hoping, anticipating Jews do? Thus we are able to say of this reception of Jesus as messiah:

(a) The interpretive connections between messianic hope and Jesus were made in powerful and imaginative ways. The New Testament is permeated with the determination to show Jesus as the fulfillment of the promise.

(b) Much in the life of Jesus portrays Jesus as enacting the mandate of the expected messiah, though it is not easy to adjudicate what in New Testament testimony is stylized to establish this fit.

(c) There is evidence that Jesus is remembered as resisting the Davidic designation, or finding it awkwardly suited to his work and destiny (see Mark 12:35-37).

In any case, the claim of Jesus as messiah was made and was found by many to be compelling. The linkage, however, is all necessarily made on the fulfillment end of the bridge of promise and fulfillment. How could it be otherwise? Thus it is my judgment that the promise of a messiah is available and open-ended in the witness of Israel. It is Christian interpretive work to claim the promise for Jesus. It is, moreover, Christian work to claim the promise exclusively—to eliminate all other claimants to this role, which may have many occupants, and to attach it singularly and exclusively to Jesus.[31] Old Testament theology, it seems to me, may acknowledge the linkage made to Jesus but may at the same time wonder about the exclusiveness of the claim, since it is in the nature of the Old Testament witness to allow for other historically designated agents to do Yahweh's work of justice and righteousness in the earth.

Finally, we may notice that the New Testament dared to employ the phrase "Son of God" concerning Jesus. We have suggested that in Ps 2:7 and 2 Sam

---

31. Jon D. Levenson, *The Death and Resurrection of the Beloved Son: The Transformation of Child Sacrifice in Judaism and Christianity* (New Haven: Yale University Press, 1993), has exhibited in powerful ways the Jewish utilization of the theme of the father giving the son and has considered the interpretive preemption of the theme by Christian tradition.

7:14 the title is a royal, political term. Elsewhere in the interpretive process of the Christian community, somewhere between the New Testament itself and the high ecumenical councils of the Catholic tradition, that political title has been transformed into a biological, metaphysical linkage, eventuating in the formula of homoousios. I state the matter in this way, because it is not clear to me to what extent the title is already used in this way in the New Testament itself, though it is clear that it has received this content by the time of the creeds. This development in Christian theology is in any case beyond the scope of Old Testament theology. It is important to note both: (a) that the turn of the royal, political title into an ontological claim goes well beyond the usage of the Old Testament itself;[32] and (b) it is an interpretive development that is not incongruous with the hyperbolic trajectory from which it is derived.

But then, that is the nature of this material from the Old Testament: It invites such daring reuse. The Christian community has taken up the invitation given by the text, but it cannot monopolize the text nor its invitation to imaginative reuse. I suggest that the Christian appropriation of the promise, authoritative as it claims to be, stands alongside other uses, none of which can defeat or deny the other uses. Every interpretive community that appeals to this powerful vision shares in Israel's conviction, to which it testifies through thick and thin, that Yahweh will indeed designate particular human agents to do the work of justice and righteousness in the earth. That designation of human agent by Yahweh, with fullness of power and fidelity, may indeed be understood as a designation so massive and energetic that, in an extreme form, it is articulated as an ontological linkage. That is what happened in the classic, extreme articulation of the Christian claim for Jesus.

---

32. Almost alone among scholars, Engnell, *Studies in Divine Kingship*, has affirmed the claim that the Near Eastern practice moved toward an ontological affirmation concerning the king in relation to the gods.

TWENTY-TWO

The Prophet as Mediator

THE GENERAL PHENOMENON of prophecy in Israel is enormously diverse in its many manifestations.[1] Any generalization about prophecy is likely to fail to comprehend the data, and yet our interpretive task of necessity entails an attempt at generalization. Prophecy as a mode of mediation begins in the inexplicable appearance of individual persons who claim to speak Yahweh's revelatory word, and who are accepted by some as being indeed carriers of such a revelatory word. Prophecy culminates as this cadre of individual persons and their remembered, transmitted words (and actions) are stylized into a fixed body of literature and achieve canonical status. Stated in brief, prophecy as mediation refers both to *individual persons* and to a *literary corpus*.

Odd Originary Speakers

The emergence of individual persons who speak with an authority beyond their own is indeed an odd, inexplicable, originary happening in Israel. Their remembered utterances of these prophets provide enough hints so that scholars can piece together some semblance of historically placed persons. Thus we imagine that we can identify the various traditions from which they emerge and the characteristic styles, images, and issues that they addressed.[2] At the same time, we must recognize that our reliable data about them, beyond consensus hypothesis, are very lean. What we can be sure of is that there were indeed specific, uncredentialed individuals who made "out of the ordinary" utterances,[3] and who were understood as having a peculiarly intimate connection with Yahweh, which made them effec-

---

1. See Lester L. Grabbe, *Priests, Prophets, Diviners, and Sages: A Socio-historical Study of Religious Specialists in Ancient Israel* (Valley Forge, Pa.: Trinity Press International, 1995) 66–118; and Rodney R. Hutton, *Charisma and Authority in Israelite Society* (Minneapolis: Fortress Press, 1994) 105–37.

2. Gerhard von Rad, *Old Testament Theology* 2 (San Francisco: Harper and Row, 1965), has given primary attention to the placement of the prophets in traditions and as practitioners of continuing traditions. A somewhat different approach has been taken by Hans Walter Wolff in a series of arguments in which he situates (a) Hosea among the Levites, (b) Amos among the wise, and (c) Micah among rural peasants. On the "social role" of the prophets, see David L. Petersen, *The Roles of the Prophets* (JSOTSup 17; Sheffield: JSOT Press, 1981).

3. John Barton, *Oracles of God: Perceptions of Ancient Prophecy in Israel after the Exile* (London: Darton, Longman, and Todd, 1986) 102.

tive channels of communication between Yahweh and Israel.[4] In their function as channels, they were heard to deliver Yahweh's own utterance to Israel, and as intercessors they were effective in speaking Israel's urgent petitions to Yahweh. Because they are channels of communication, theological interest focuses much more on their utterances than on their personalities. Of these several individuals, we may make the following general observations.

Yahweh's Summons

The prophets speak because they are compelled by an inexplicable force that is taken to be the summons of Yahweh. There are hints that these several individuals are recipients of odd, psychic experiences, being visited by the "supernatural" in odd ways such as dream, vision, and trance.[5] John Barton goes so far as to use the term "mystic."[6] But whatever explanation might be suggested, they are, as Barton observes, "non-establishment figures who will not be silenced."[7] In that regard, they exemplify a kind of openness in Israelite society, suggesting that administrative order was not so tight or so effective as to preclude an outbreak of unadministered opinion. In their appearance, Yahweh is taken to be directly and palpably present in Israel.

Tradition and Personal Experience

These originary individuals are odd and cannot be explained by any antecedent. In that regard the older notion of "lonely geniuses" has an element of truth in it.[8] These individuals, however, did not live in a sociopolitical vacuum, but seem to emerge from, be influenced by, and reflect different theological traditions and their accompanying social perspectives.[9] This does not mean that they explicitly or intentionally mouth such traditions and perspectives. Rather they have learned over time to perceive and experience the world through a particular prism of memory and interpretation. Thus, as we have suggested, Hosea and Jeremiah appear to be nurtured in the traditions of Levitical-Deuteronomic covenantalism.[10] It has been

---

4. See especially Thomas W. Overholt, *Channels of Prophecy: The Social Dynamics of Prophetic Activity* (Minneapolis: Fortress Press, 1989); more broadly, see Joseph Blenkinsopp, *Sage, Priest, Prophet: Religious and Intellectual Leadership in Ancient Israel* (Louisville: Westminster/John Knox, 1995) 115–65. Unfortunately Blenkinsopp considers only pre-exilic prophecy, thus still operating on Julius Wellhausen's general categories. Blenkinsopp's historical approach is nicely complemented by that of Barton, *Oracles of God.*

5. Johannes Lindblom, *Prophecy in Ancient Israel* (Oxford: Blackwell, 1963), has provided the classic study. See also Robert R. Wilson, *Prophecy and Society in Ancient Israel* (Philadelphia: Fortress Press, 1980).

6. Barton, *Oracles of God,* 261.

7. Ibid., 112.

8. Ibid., 272.

9. Wilson, *Prophecy and Society,* has accented social location and interest, as he has utilized the categories of "central" and "peripheral" in order to identify social location and interest.

10. On the location of Hosea and Jeremiah in the traditions of Israel, see the studies of Wolff and Gross cited in chap. 20, nn. 26, 27.

suggested that Amos reflects international wisdom thought.[11] Isaiah surely reflects the royal ideology of the Zion establishment, and Ezekiel, Haggai, and Zechariah give evidence of nurture in priestly environs. The institutional setting of Micah is less clear, but he appears to reflect the passions and resentments of a peasant community.[12] One cannot be precise about such matters, nor excessively confident. The nurturing traditions need to be kept in purview, nonetheless, because in this ancient society, communities and their members had long, poignant memories, and because these several traditions/memories were often in conflict in their particulars, each contending for the role of final interpretive authority.

The prophets require for their understanding acknowledgment of both particular communal practice (immersion in and influence of a tradition and perspective) and inexplicable originary personal experience, which moves the uncredentialed to claim abrupt authority and to run enormous risk in asserting that authority. How one balances or adjudicates tradition and personal experience likely reflects the mood and assumptions of one's interpretive culture. In the nineteenth century, accent was on personal experience, an accent retained in much popular, homiletic interpretation. In the twentieth century, under the influence of Gerhard von Rad and reflected in sociological and anthropological studies, greater attention is given to placement in community.[13] Both factors are undoubtedly present and important, but neither one nor both of them together can adequately explain or justify the emergence of these speakers.

Responding to Crisis, Evoking Crisis

These uncredentialed, authoritative speakers do not utter universal truths, but speak concretely to a particular time, place, and circumstance.[14] They characteristically perceive their time and place as a circumstance of crisis, a context in which dangers are great and life-or-death decisions must be made. Or perhaps it is better to say that the appearance and utterance of the prophets *evokes* a crisis circumstance where none had been perceived previously. That is, the prophets not only respond to crisis, but by their abrupt utterance, they generate crisis.

---

11. Hans Walter Wolff, *Amos the Prophet: The Man and His Background* (Philadelphia: Fortress Press, 1973); Samuel Terrien, "Amos and Wisdom," *Israel's Prophetic Heritage* (ed. Bernhard W. Anderson and Walter Harrelson; London: SCM Press, 1962) 108–15.

12. Hans Walter Wolff, "Micah the Moreshite—The Prophet and His Background," *Israelite Wisdom: Theological and Literary Essays in Honor of Samuel Terrien* (ed. John G. Gammie et al.; Missoula, Mont.: Scholars Press, 1978) 77–84. See also George V. Pixley, "Micah—A Revolutionary," *The Bible and the Politics of Exegesis* (ed. David Jobling et al.; Cleveland: Pilgrim Press, 1991) 53–60; and Itumeleng J. Mosala, "A Materialist Reading of Micah," *The Bible and Liberation: Political and Social Hermeneutics* (ed. Norman K. Gottwald and Richard A. Horsley; Maryknoll, N.Y.: Orbis Books, 1993) 264–95.

13. In his study of the prophets, Gerhard von Rad worked primarily with textual traditions and did not take up sociological, archaeological data, as for example is done in the work of Wilson, who pays attention to the material dimensions of social location.

14. On these particularities, see Klaus Koch, *The Prophets 1: The Assyrian Age* (Philadelphia: Fortress Press, 1983); *The Prophets 2: The Babylonian and Persian Periods* (Philadelphia: Fortress Press, 1984); and Joseph Blenkinsopp, *A History of Prophecy in Israel: From the Settlement in the Land to the Hellenistic Period* (London: SPCK, 1984).

Specifically, the emergence of prophetic mediation in Israel characteristically happened in the presence of and in response to royal power. In the pre-exilic period the prophets are regularly in encounter with kings, who are perceived as being entrusted with great responsibilities for Yahweh,[15] and who have characteristically failed in their implementation. Elijah (1 Kgs 18:1, 17; 21:17) and Micaiah (1 Kgs 22:8) are juxtaposed to Ahab in the ninth century. Isaiah in the eighth century deals in turn with Ahaz (Isa 7:3-17) and Hezekiah (Isa 37:1-7). Amos has his "close encounter" with Amaziah, priest of Jeroboam (Amos 7:10-17), and Jeremiah must deal with Zedekiah (Jeremiah 37–38). The situation is different in the exilic and postexilic periods, when there is no king in Israel. But *mutatis mutandis*, these prophets also must deal with dominant modes of power and dominant definitions of reality.

The Power of Poetic Imagination

While the prophets are characteristically immersed in public crises, they are not primarily political agents in any direct sense and rarely urge specific policy. Nor are they, against popular liberal opinion, social activists. They are most characteristically "utterers," and until later developments alter their way of functioning, they speak most often with all of the elusiveness and imaginative power of poetry. Their utterances are not self-evident in their relevance, but they speak in images and metaphors that aim to disrupt, destabilize, and invite to alternative perceptions of reality. In my own work, I have paid particular attention to the power of imagination in the work of the prophets, by which I have meant the capacity to construe, picture, and image reality outside of the dominant portrayals of reality that have been taken as givens.[16]

The poetic idiom and the elusive quality of imagination together constitute a strategy among the prophets for taking the listening community outside of administered ideology, which is most often identified with royal policy and royal imagination. The prophets speak in outrageous and extreme figures because they intend to disrupt the "safe" construals of reality, which are sponsored and advocated by dominant opinion makers. In their utterance of "limit expressions"— that is, utterances that carry Israel to the edge of imagination—the prophets characteristically exhibit acute sensitivity in two regards.[17]

Acute awareness of distress. First, the prophets are acutely aware of the distress, pain, and dysfunction that are present in the community that they understand to be freighted with coming disaster. Thus, Amos can utter a funeral lament as he envisions Israel in its death:

---

15. On the responsibilities of kings as perceived in Yahwistic perspective, see chap. 21.
16. Walter Brueggemann, *The Prophetic Imagination* (Philadelphia: Fortress Press, 1978); and *Hopeful Imagination: Prophetic Voices in Exile* (Philadelphia: Fortress Press, 1986).
17. On "limit expressions," which are linked to "limit experiences," see Paul Ricoeur, "Biblical Hermeneutics," *Semeia* 4 (1975) 75–106.

Fallen, no more to rise,
is maiden Israel;
forsaken on her land,
with no one to raise her up. (Amos 5:2)

Zephaniah can envision disaster sure to come:

That day will be a day of wrath,
a day of distress and anguish,
a day of ruin and devastation,
a day of darkness and gloom,
a day of clouds and thick darkness,
a day of trumpet blast and battle cry
against the fortified cities
and against the lofty battlements. (Zeph 1:15-16)

Jeremiah dares to portray Jerusalem as a vulnerable woman being violently assaulted:

For I heard a cry as of a woman in labor,
anguish as of one bringing forth her first child,
the cry of daughter Zion gasping for breath,
stretching out her hands,
"Woe is me! I am fainting before killers!" (Jer 4:31)

Except for these odd utterers, it is fair to assume that the freighted politics of death practiced by the monarchy were largely unacknowledged in conventional circles and, where recognized, were vigorously denied by those who presided over and benefited from the status quo.

Images of new possibility. Second, as these poets found fresh and attention-getting ways of imagining Israel into the fissure of death that it chose to deny and disregard, so there were poets who, in extraordinary acts of courage, spoke about possible futures that invited Israel beyond its several fissures, when dominant Israel had arrived at despair.[18] Thus in a startling use of imagery, Ezekiel imagines exiled Israel in a valley of dry bones that will be enlivened and rehabilitated by the wind of Yahweh:

Mortal, these bones are the whole house of Israel. They say, "Our bones are dried up, and our hope is lost; we are cut off completely." Therefore prophesy, and say to them, Thus says the Lord God: I am going to open your graves, and bring you up from your graves, O my people; and I will bring you back to the land of Israel. (Ezek 37:11-12)

---

18. Von Rad, *Old Testament Theology*, 2:263–77, has fully appreciated the hopeful imagination of the prophets in the sixth-century exile. Such acts of hope, which functioned subversively, were not confined to exile, however.

Zechariah, in what must have been a context of hopelessness, imagines the resumption of buoyant royal ritual:

> Rejoice greatly, O daughter Zion!
> Shout aloud, O daughter Jerusalem!
> Lo, your king comes to you;
> triumphant and victorious is he,
> humble and riding on a donkey,
> on a colt, the foal of a donkey. (Zech 9:9)

Micah, having contemplated the defeat of coveting Israel (2:1-5), imagines a new royal possibility of peasant stock who will prevail even over Assyria:

> But you, O Bethlehem of Ephrathah,
> who are one of the little clans of Judah,
> from you shall come forth for me
> one who is to rule in Israel,
> whose origin is from of old,
> from ancient days....
> And he shall stand and feed his flock in the strength of the Lord,
> in the majesty of the name of the Lord his God.
> And they shall live secure, for now he shall be great
> to the ends of the earth;
> and he shall be the one of peace. (Mic 5:2, 4-5)

In both the images of deathliness and in the metaphors of new possibility, those eloquent tongues were able to utter beyond the commonplaces of their contemporaries and to invite their listeners to step outside the dominant commonplaces to entertain an alternative scenario of their life with Yahweh.

Yahweh's own utterance. Perhaps the prophets are simply gifted and skilled practitioners of rhetoric. And that is enough. On many occasions, however, they claimed that their odd rhetoric, perhaps rooted in tradition but certainly not informed by what their contemporaries were able to discern, is entrusted to them by Yahweh. Thus skilled poetry that refuses to conform to dominant perceptions is equated, in the prophet's own claim and by some of their listeners, as Yahweh's own utterance. This vivid, disruptive poetry is taken as revelatory, by which Israel has "revealed" to it a dimension of reality that was otherwise not available. This mode of mediation suggests a convergence or equation of uncredentialed human utterance and Yahweh's own utterance that debunks and dispels the social reality that Israel had constructed for itself by removing Yahweh from its center. Yahweh, however, will not be removed from Israel's center! One of the ways in which Yahweh returns to and remains at Israel's center is by the utterance of these odd, abrasive, mostly unwelcome voices.

Authoritative Utterance

The testimony of Israel provides no clear answer to the question of the authority and reliability of this mode of mediation.[19] In principle, the prophets are uncredentialed. But because their utterances characteristically speak against dominant culture, either the buoyancy of dominant culture or its despair, it is inevitable that they are challenged and that they must seek to give some justification for their utterance. That is, revelation (as given in the prophets, but perhaps all revelation) is profoundly unwelcome, for it invades a life well-ordered without serious reference to Yahweh. We have only hints and traces concerning this justification of authority, but the following aspects may be noted.

The Divine Council

The dominant rubric for authority is "the divine council."[20] It was of crucial importance that the prophet was not uttering his own word out of his own imagination. It is asserted that the word uttered by the prophet is actually the word of Yahweh. As an imaginative means of articulating prophetic authority, appeal is often made in the prophets to "the divine council." This phrase refers to a poetic scenario (likely taken literally) that has Yahweh in heaven presiding over a government consisting in Yahweh and Yahweh's advisors and messengers, who make decisions about the disposition of matters on earth.[21] This imagery has the effect of asserting that there is an agency of God's government that is completely beyond the reach of any human agent or authority, which makes decisions that are definitive in the earth. The practical effect of such a claim is to deny to earthly power (kings) any practical control over their own realm, because the real decisions have been made elsewhere.

The most detailed and poignant presentation of this divine council is given in 1 Kgs 22:19-23, reported in the testimony of Micaiah the prophet. In this scenario, Micaiah can say:

> I saw the Lord sitting on his throne, with all the host of heaven standing beside him to the right and to the left of him. And the Lord said, "Who will entice Ahab, so that he may go up and fall at Ramoth-gilead?" Then one said one thing, and another said another, until a spirit came forward and

---

19. The criteria for "true prophecy" are notoriously elusive. For representative discussions, see James L. Crenshaw, *Prophetic Conflict: Its Effect upon Israelite Religion* (BZAW 124; Berlin: Alfred Töpelmann, 1971); and James A. Sanders, "Canonical Hermeneutics: True and False Prophecy," *From Sacred Story to Sacred Text: Canon as Paradigm* (Philadelphia: Fortress Press, 1987) 87–105. Grabbe, *Priests, Prophets, Diviners, Sages*, 113–18, recognizes that the crucial distinctions made among the prophets are of a theological kind, not accessible to social-scientific investigation.

20. See the thorough study of the theme by E. Theodore Mullen, *The Divine Council in Canaanite and Early Hebrew Literature* (Chico, Calif.: Scholars Press, 1980); and Patrick D. Miller, "Cosmology and World Order in the Old Testament: The Divine Council as Cosmic-Political Symbol," *HBT* 9 (December 1987) 53–78.

21. As Jon Levenson, *Creation and the Persistence of Evil: The Jewish Drama of Divine Omnipotence* (San Francisco: Harper and Row, 1988), has argued, there is an openness toward polytheism in this image. Yahweh governs with the consent of other gods.

stood before the Lord, saying, "I will entice him." "How?" the Lord asked him. He replied, "I will go out and be a lying spirit in the mouth of all his prophets." Then the Lord said, "You are to entice him, and you shall succeed; go out and do it." So you see, the Lord has put a lying spirit in the mouth of all these your prophets; the Lord has decreed disaster for you. (1 Kgs 22:19-23)

The vision reported by Micaiah is that Yahweh, in consultation with the heavenly government, plots in a most ignoble way to overthrow the rule of Ahab. Two things are evident, in addition to the awareness that Yahweh can act in such a cunning and unprincipled way. First, it is suggested that the real decisions affecting the government in Samaria (and by implication all governments) are made remotely, out of reach of the king. The real governance of earth is in the lordly, cunning hands of Yahweh. Second, the prophet is privy to the actions of the council, either as observer, participant, or envoy.

The prophet Jeremiah appeals to his own access to the divine council in establishing authentic prophetic authority. Prophets who have access to the council speak a word that is from the government of God; those not in the council speak their own word, and so have no real claim to authority. Thus "divine council" is a stratagem for linking Yahweh and the human enterprise, Yahweh and the prophetic assertion. Jeremiah indicts his opponents, whom he dismisses as false, because they have not been in the divine council, and they make up the things they attribute to Yahweh:

> For who has stood in the council of the Lord
> so as to see and to hear his word?
> Who has given heed to his word
> so as to proclaim it? . . .
> I did not send the prophets,
> yet they ran;
> I did not speak to them,
> yet they prophesied.
> But if they had stood in my council,
> then they would have proclaimed my words to my people,
> and they would have turned them from their evil way,
> and from the evil of their doings. (Jer 23:18, 21-22)

The positive inference to be drawn is that Jeremiah, unlike his opponents, has been in the divine council, and so speaks a genuine word of Yahweh.[22]

The Messenger Formula

In this imagery, the prophet is identified as a messenger who speaks a word other than his own. The prophet carries to earth (to the king) the policy decisions of the

---

22. See Crenshaw, *Prophetic Conflict*, 60.

heavenly government, so that earthly agents may appropriately implement the decisions. The ones on earth who receive such messages through the prophets (kings) are not invited to share in the decision-making process, but are only to receive and accept decisions already made.

The formula by which a prophet asserts that the message is not his own is expressed in what scholars have termed a messenger formula, which may appear variously as "hear the word of the Lord," "thus says the Lord," or "said the Lord."[23]

These formulas occur in varying wordings throughout the prophetic corpus. The formula may be part of the primary prophetic utterance, or it may be an editorial framing device. Either way, it is a claim that here, in this moment of utterance, specific persons in Israel in specific times and places have mediated to them and through them a verdict or a disclosure that arises beyond human generativity.

The Prophetic Call

In addition to appeal to the divine council and utilization of the messenger formula, a third way in which the prophets seek to establish transhistorical authority for themselves is by articulation of a prophetic call. In such a narrative, the prophet purports to narrate the direct encounter with Yahweh whereby the prophet was pressed into service as a messenger for Yahweh. Norman Habel has explored the rather stylized accounts of the prophets and has shown that whatever may have been "experienced" by the prophetic persons, the narrative accounts contain recurrent elements.[24] Some of the calls include resistance to Yahweh's initiative, as in the cases of Moses (Exod 3:1–4:17), Gideon (Judg 6:11-24), and Jeremiah (Jer 1:4-10). Others, such as Isa 6:1-8, report a willingness to be recruited into Yahweh's service. The call narrative characteristically intends to assert that Yahweh holds the initiative for any particular prophetic activity or utterance, and that prophets on occasion are compelled to speak, even against their will. While it is impossible to assess initiative, willingness, or resistance as an experienced reality, the stylized pattern of the call has suggested that the narrative already moves the claim of experience into a traditional, institutionalized form.

Challenges to Claims of Authority

In any case, it is evident that appeal to divine council, utilization of the messenger formula, and narratives of call are all attempts to authorize prophetic utterance when authority cannot be claimed in any proximate human, institutional form. We are unable to determine the extent to which such maneuvers are intrinsic to the experience of the prophetic person, and the extent to which this is a traditional

---

23. On the messenger formula, see the review by W. Eugene March, "Prophecy," *Old Testament and Criticism* (ed. John H. Hayes; San Antonio: Trinity University Press, 1974) 149–53, with particular attention to the work of Ludwig Koehler and Joachim Begrich.

24. Norman Habel, "The Form and Significance of the Call Narratives," *ZAW* 36 (1965) 297–323. See also Robert P. Carroll, *From Chaos to Covenant: Uses of Prophecy in the Book of Jeremiah* (London: SCM Press, 1981) 31–58.

imposition on what might have been a free, spontaneous, and undomesticated encounter.[25] John Barton suggests that such marks of prophetic authority may be no more than "a ploy to command a hearing."[26] If they are ploys, we do not know whether the ploy is from the prophet or from the subsequent traditioning process.

What is clear is that prophetic mediation makes a claim of authority that is impossible to verify. That is, all of these claims and uses are reports of a quite personal, subjective experience. No objective evidence can be given that one has been in the divine council. No objective support can be given to a messenger formula. No verification of a call experience is possible. These are all formulations that seek to confirm a hidden experience of transcendence.

It is not surprising, then, that the high claims of the prophet to be an authentic mediator of Yahweh are not always accepted, but are often dismissed or challenged by those who resist the utterance and who wish to remain undisturbed within certain beneficial construals of reality. In Hos 9:7 the prophet is dismissed as a "fool" or a "madman" (*mšugʿ*). In Amos 7:12, Amos is rejected as a "prophet for hire." The issue of true and false prophets is explored especially in the tradition of Jeremiah. The false prophets are dismissed as primarily "feel-good" messengers who could not possibly be from Yahweh (6:14, 8:11). In Jeremiah 27–28, Jeremiah is in profound conflict with Hananiah, who is said to be false (see also Ezekiel 13).[27]

Scholars are agreed that there are no objective criteria for such an issue. In the end the canonizing process has accepted certain prophets as genuine, even though these prophets were not readily accepted in the context of their utterance. We must not imagine, moreover, that a decision in such a canonizing process is necessarily an innocent or neutral one. Undoubtedly the process of determining who speaks a true word of Yahweh is decisively controlled by larger, albeit not disinterested, notions of what constitutes genuine Yahwism in any particular moment of crisis. The canonizing process, which produced and authenticated the voices now accepted by Israel as "true prophets," is surely itself an ideological struggle, both to define Yahwism and to determine who would define it.[28]

There is a sort of congruity to the entire corpus of the prophets. Nonetheless it is far from clear how (a) the free, originary utterances of the prophetic figures, and (b) the stylized patterns that result in canon are related to each other. We can go no further than to conclude that in the process of imaginative-utterance-become-authoritative-corpus, Israel accepted that an unfettered disclosure of Yahweh's way in Israel is made available. To say that the prophets refused to be silenced is to

---

25. The stylized form of prophetic calls is perhaps not unlike the "calls to ministry" that are regularly recited before church commissions of seminarians. Each such tale is peculiar to the person, but there is a remarkable reiteration of common themes.

26. Barton, *Oracles of God*, 272.

27. On this particular confrontation, see Henri Mottu, "Jeremiah vs. Hananiah: Ideology and Truth in Old Testament Prophecy," *The Bible and Liberation*, 313–28.

28. See Christopher R. Seitz, *Theology in Conflict: Reactions to the Exile in the Book of Jeremiah* (BZAW 176; Berlin: Walter de Gruyter, 1989), on the larger disputes behind the personal conflict, disputes that are reflected in the Book of Jeremiah.

say, in context, that Yahweh will not be crowded out of the interpretive process in Israel. That high theological claim is carried in the prophetic process by these passionate poets who will not be silenced.

Prophetic Words Unheeded

The prophets provide only tenuous, highly subjective grounds for their disturbing utterances. Because what they say is often disputatious, and because their ground of authority is not self-evident, it is not surprising that the prophets effect no great successes. Amos, we are told, is banished (Amos 7:12). Isaiah, according to late tradition, had his life ended brutally.[29] Jeremiah, in the end, is carried off to Egypt against his will (Jer 43:1-7). The prophets characteristically speak a word grounded, they say, in Yahweh's own disclosure, which is against dominant authority. It is for this reason that Isaiah's "call" culminates in 6:9-10 with the assurance that the prophetic word will not be heeded:

> "Keep listening, but do not comprehend;
> keep looking, but do not understand."
> Make the mind of this people dull,
> and stop their ears,
> and shut their eyes,
> so that they may not look with their eyes,
> and listen with their ears,
> and comprehend with their minds,
> and turn and be healed.

The power structure of Israel was able, characteristically, to silence the prophets and to prevent serious impact from "the word." The personal fate of the prophets was perhaps not unlike the characteristic experience of poets who are silenced by totalitarian regimes, for no totalitarian regime can tolerate the generative, subversive, counterword of the poet.

Thus the characteristic fate of the prophets, articulated in stylized form, is to be killed:[30]

> Nevertheless they were disobedient and rebelled against you and cast your law behind their backs and killed your prophets, who had warned them in order to turn them back to you, and they committed great blasphemies. (Neh 9:26)

> Therefore also the Wisdom of God said, "I will send them prophets and apostles, some of whom they will kill and persecute," so that this generation

---

29. The late tradition that Isaiah came to a violent end by being sawed in two is based in Heb 11:37, which may refer to the tradition of the ascension of Isaiah. In any case, the tradition seems to be beyond the scope of normal historical assessment and surely cannot be credited.

30. On this theme, see Odil H. Steck, *Israel und das gewaltsame Geschick der Propheten: Untersuchungen zur Überlieferung des deuteronomistischen Geschichtsbildes im Alten Testament, Spätjudentum und Urchristentum* (WMANT 23; Neukirchen-Vluyn: Neukirchener Verlag, 1967).

may be charged with the blood of all the prophets shed since the foundation of the world.... (Luke 11:49-50)

Jerusalem, Jerusalem, the city that kills the prophets and stones those who are sent to it! (Luke 13:34; cf. Luke 6:22; Matt 23:31)[31]

To be sure, this is highly stylized commentary, but the general picture does not surprise us. As an originary historical phenomenon, prophecy lives at the margin of Israel's life. And yet...some remembered, and preserved, and treasured the prophets' words. The odd power of these utterances, now become canon, is that they linger and resound in the ongoing life of Israel and in its derivative communities. In the end, prophecy as mediation is not a personal-historical enterprise, but a rhetorical-canonical one. To that dimension of the topic we now turn.

The Canonizing Process

There is no doubt that a great deal has happened to prophetic utterance by the time it is available to us as Scripture. In the canonizing process the prophetic enterprise has been drastically transformed. If, however, we accept that the work of prophecy is to enable Israel to reconstrue and reimagine its life in relation to Yahweh in the face of other interpretive options, then we may say that the completed canonical form of the prophets continues to provide material and impetus for the reimagining and reconstrual of life with Yahweh.[32] Concerning the canonizing process, which both reconfigured prophecy and actualized it more fully as itself, we may pursue three avenues of reflection.

Mosaic Influence

We have seen that Moses is Israel's mediator par excellence. Therefore it is to be expected that prophecy is drawn into close relation to Moses in the canonizing process. The prophets, in their individual idiosyncrasies, may have had nothing in common with Moses; indeed, it may well be that much of the Mosaic tradition as we have it postdates the prophets. In the present form of the Old Testament, nonetheless, the priority and dominating position of Moses is unmistakable and unchallenged. We have seen that Deut 17:14-20 is the single important Torah provision for kingship that brings kingship under the aegis of Mosaic expectation. Now in parallel fashion, we are able to see that Deut 18:15-22 is the single most important Torah provision concerning the prophets.[33] The crucial point in this Torah provision is that Yahweh will generate prophets "like me," that is, like Moses,

---

31. Ibid., 105–9 and passim.
32. On this process, see Johanna W. H. van Wijk-Bos, *Reimagining God: The Case for Scriptural Diversity* (Louisville: Westminster/John Knox, 1995).
33. On the cruciality of this passage, see Wilson, *Prophecy and Society*, 157–66. For its context in the Book of Deuteronomy, see Norbert Lohfink, "Distribution of the Functions of Power," *Great Themes from the Old Testament* (Edinburgh: T. & T. Clark, 1982) 55–75.

each of whom will do in his time and place what Moses has done paradigmatically for Israel.

In the tradition of Deuteronomy, the vexing question of how to determine true and false prophets is much on the horizon. In this text, the criterion for a true prophet is clear:

> If a prophet speaks in the name of the Lord but the thing does not take place or prove true, it is a word that the Lord has not spoken. The prophet has spoken it presumptuously; do not be frightened by it. (18:22)

That is, a true prophet will be known by the fruition of the prophetic utterance. Such a criterion is of course most problematic, for some prophetic words are taken in the canon to be true, even if not implemented in detail. An alternative criterion for true prophecy is given in Deut 13:1-6:

> If prophets or those who divine by dreams appear among you and promise you omens or portents, and the omens or the portents declared by them take place, and they say, "Let us follow other gods" (whom you have not known) "and let us serve them," you must not heed the words of those prophets or those who divine by dreams; for the Lord your God is testing you, to know whether you indeed love the Lord your God with all your heart and soul. The Lord your God you shall follow, him alone you shall fear, his commandments you shall keep, his voice you shall obey, him you shall serve, and to him you shall hold fast. But those prophets or those who divine by dreams shall be put to death for having spoken treason against the Lord your God...to turn you from the way in which the Lord your God commanded you to walk. So you shall purge the evil from your midst.

This statement is remarkable because it dismisses the criterion of chapter 18. Even if the word of the prophet comes to pass, this is not proof of legitimacy. What counts now is theological substance. The first commandment of "only Yahweh" is the test of a true prophet. This is a much more helpful criterion theologically, but it leaves open difficult questions of interpretation.

In any case, in the purview of the tradition of Deuteronomy, there is assumed in Israel a sequence of prophets (not a regular succession), each of which in a particular time and place replicated the constitutive word of Moses. This sequence is roughly established by the Deuteronomistic history that identifies a procession of prophets in the midst of the royal chronology, and in a different way in the prophetic canon of three "major prophets" and "the twelve." Both the Deuteronomic narrative and the canonical grouping attest to the claim that this mode of mediation is recurrent in Israel. Each time a prophet emerges in this sequence, moreover, the utterance of the counterword of the prophet is once again problematic and disruptive. That is, Israel did not accept prophets any more easily because they had some sustained practice with prophecy.

This sequence, now somewhat tamed into a Mosaic frame of reference, asserts that each such prophet does what Moses did, that is, enables Israel in a particular time and place to be fully and intentionally the covenant people of Yahweh. (This is a canonical judgment, not under the discipline of facticity.) This means, positively, that Israel must reckon with Yahweh's sovereign intention for its life. It requires, negatively, that Israel must forgo and repent of all of its proximate loyalties, which in the end are idolatrous and which will only lead to death. The rich, wild, and imaginative utterances of the prophets as odd characters are channeled into Mosaic categories. The extent to which this channeling is a domestication or distortion is worth considering. But the channeling in most cases seems to have been done by placement, arrangement, and editorial addition, not by modification or censoring. One must also weigh the gains of such channeling of the canonizing process that made possible the preservation and transmission of the utterances, in order to make old acts of mediation continually available as potentially fresh acts of mediation.

Three Typical Genres

Form-critical analysis of the prophetic utterances is relatively stable and conclusive.[34] While the prophets, in their various ways of inventiveness, spoke in what we regard as many different genres, three genres most typify prophetic utterance in mediating Yahweh as sovereign and faithful.

Lawsuit speech. Claus Westermann has shown that the prophets of the eighth and seventh centuries especially appealed to the lawsuit speech with endless variations. Such speech sought to establish the failure of Israel to keep covenant with Yahweh and to anticipate the disaster to come as just punishment for failure to be faithful to Yahweh.[35] To be sure, in some of the lawsuits, only a person, or a leadership class, or the dynasty is under threat, not the entire community. And some prophetic oracles pertained to the northern kingdom of Israel and were only belatedly redirected toward the southern Jerusalem establishment. It is equally clear, moreover, that after the fall of Jerusalem, the same patterns of rhetoric could be used against other nations and other gods as had previously been addressed against Israel.

Given all of these nuances and imaginative extrapolations, it is nonetheless the case that the lawsuit speech served well the purposes of militant Yahwism, which asserted that acknowledgment of Yahweh's sovereign purpose is the single condition for well-being in the world; and conversely, failure to acknowledge that sovereignty could only lead to trouble, which eventually becomes stylized as "sword, famine, and pestilence" (Jer 21:9, 24:10, 29:17; Ezek 6:11; 2 Chr 20:9). Among the clearest examples of the genre, from which there are endless derivations, are Hos 4:1-3, Amos 4:1-3, Mic 3:9-12, Isa 3:13-17, 5:1-7 (as a love song), and Jer 2:4-13. We may note particularly the exemplary usage of Mic 3:9-12:

34. See March, "Prophecy," 141–77.
35. Claus Westermann, *Basic Forms of Prophetic Speech* (London: Lutterworth Press, 1967).

> Hear this, you rulers of the house of Jacob
> and chiefs of the house of Israel,
> who abhor justice
> and pervert all equity,
> who build Zion with blood
> and Jerusalem with wrong!
> Its rulers give judgment for a bribe,
> its priests teach for a price,
> its prophets give oracles for money;
> yet they lean upon the Lord and say,
> "Surely the Lord is with us!
> No harm shall come upon us."
> Therefore because of you
> Zion shall be plowed as a field;
> Jerusalem shall become a heap of ruins,
> and the mountain of the house a wooded height.

The oracle is addressed against the leadership for its exploitative practices of injustice and for its complacent attitude toward Yahweh, who is assumed to be indulgent toward Jerusalem. The threat of v. 12 is that the city of Jerusalem will be reduced to ruins and abandoned. In canonical usage, this utterance from the eighth century is taken up again in the seventh century as a way of rescuing the prophet Jeremiah. Micah's utterance is cited as a precedent whereby prophets are allowed to speak in the name of Yahweh what is otherwise treasonable (Jer 26:17-19).

The lawsuit form asserts the abrasion and alienation that are at work between Yahweh and Israel, which arise from Israel's recalcitrant way of life and issue in vexation and suffering for recalcitrant Israel at the hands of Yahweh. Thus the lawsuit form, expressed with great rhetorical intensity, asserts that everything is at stake for Israel in this relationship. The poets are remarkably skillful in driving from the horizon any other explanation for the trouble or well-being of Israel.

Appeal for repentance. Often the speech of judgment ends in a death sentence that is final and nonnegotiable. In such harsh instances, that is the end of the matter. On occasion, however, the prophetic rhetorical strategy is not to announce disaster as a foregone conclusion, but to warn Israel that it is late in a dysfunctional relationship, but not too late. In such rhetoric, it is accepted that Israel has not yet reached a point of no return with Yahweh. Israel can turn and repent, reembrace Yahweh, and so avert disaster.[36] This appeal is no less solemn and severe than the lawsuit utterance, but it leaves Israel a chance to alter its course and reengage Yahweh in dutiful obedience. This utterance offers hope to Israel, but it is hope that requires Israel to make a drastic change in its conduct.

Among these appeals for repentance are the following:

---

36. On repentance as a theme in late pre-exilic prophecy, see Thomas M. Raitt, *A Theology of Exile: Judgment/Deliverance in Jeremiah and Ezekiel* (Philadelphia: Fortress Press, 1977).

Sow for yourselves righteousness;
reap steadfast love;
break up your fallow ground;
for it is time to seek the Lord,
that he may come and rain
righteousness upon you. (Hos 10:12)

But as for you, return to your God,
hold fast to love and justice,
and wait continually for your God. (Hos 12:6)

Wash yourselves; make yourselves clean;
remove the evil of your doings
from before my eyes;
cease to do evil,
learn to do good;
seek justice,
rescue the oppressed,
defend the orphan,
plead for the widow. (Isa 1:16-17; cf. Amos 5:4-6, 14-15)

It is disputed among scholars, however, whether this form of speech is a primary one for the prophets, or whether it is quite marginal to the material and, indeed, whether these occurrences are mostly late adjustments under the influence of the Deuteronomic propensity to reformism (on which see 2 Kgs 17:13, Zech 1:4). Jochen Vollmer has argued most directly that this sort of utterance belongs definitionally to prophetic speech, whereas Hans Walter Wolff holds to the judgment that the prophets are primarily announcers of doom.[37] A. Vanlier Hunter, in a subtle argument, suggests that in some of the prophetic collections, appeals for repentance (which are undeniably present in the text) are in fact earlier appeals that have failed and been rejected, so that the present function of the form is as a strategic introduction to judgment that is now certain and without hope of recall.[38] My own judgment is that the varying evidences cannot be forced into any single explanation. The rhetorical capacity of these utterances is as rich and varied as circumstances required, given the vitality of covenantal possibility and covenantal requirement.

Oracles of promise. The third characteristic utterance of this mediation of Yahweh in prophetic speech is the oracle of promise, introduced characteristically by the formula "in that day," or "behold the days are coming." In this speech form, which occurs in almost all of the prophetic collections, prophetic utterance breaks

---

37. Jochen Vollmer, *Geschichtliche Rückblicke und Motive in der Prophetie des Amos, Hosea, und Jesaja* (BZAW 119; Berlin: Walter de Gruyter, 1971); Hans Walter Wolff, "Das Thema 'Umkehr' in der alttestamentlichen Prophetie," *ZTK* 48 (1951) 129–48.

38. A. Vanlier Hunter, *Seek the Lord! A Study of the Meaning and Function of the Exhortations in Amos, Hosea, Isaiah, Micah, and Zephaniah* (Baltimore: St. Mary's University, 1982).

completely beyond the limits of the conditional covenant of Moses in order to assert the unconditionally positive resolve of Yahweh. It may well be that this positive conviction about Yahweh's resolve to work a good future for Israel is rooted in the unconditionality of the Davidic promise, but in fact the content of the promises is not closely tied to the Davidic possibilities. Thus whereas Isaiah can anticipate a new Davidic king (Isa 11:1-9; cf. Amos 9:11-12), Jeremiah can anticipate a new covenant of forgiveness that is Mosaic in its terms (Jer 31:31-34), and Ezekiel can anticipate a homecoming for Judah that seems to speak in quite fresh and underived categories (Ezek 37:1-14).

It is widely recognized, and has been well considered by von Rad, that the promises tend to cluster most notably in Jeremiah (especially chapters 30–33), Ezekiel 33–48, and Isaiah of the exile.[39] The exile, moreover, is the sphere in which the most sweeping and profound promises are generated and uttered. Such promises are also found in earlier prophets, although considerable scholarly opinion has judged that such oracles, on the whole, likely are editorial additions from the exilic period. However one may decide these issues, it is clear that the promises characteristically articulate Yahweh's intention to work a radical newness in Israel's life, which can in no way be derived from present circumstance.[40] (The extreme case of apocalyptic anticipation is utterly underived.) Moreover, the specific anticipations in these promises derive much of their substance from Israel's old core memory, so that Yahweh will do again what Yahweh had done in time past: new creation, new covenant, new kingship, new exodus, new land distribution.[41] The substance of the promises is derived from old memories, but the power to generate the newly promised reality is rooted not in what is old, but in what is fresh and alive about Yahweh.

It may be, if we heed the historical-critical judgment that promises arise in and as an antidote to exile, that the promises are to be understood as pastoral responses to the desperation and helplessness of an exilic condition. This seems to me completely plausible. It will not do, however, to take that pastoral impetus as an adequate ground of the promises, if they are to be taken with theological seriousness. Theologically, the promises claim to mediate a word other than the word of the prophet. Not only are these uttered promises, but they are, so the prophets claim, the uttered promises of Yahweh. The promises voice to Israel Yahweh's sovereign resolve to govern history for Israel's well-being in and through and beyond the fissure of exile. In these utterances, so the prophets insist, Israel is given access

---

39. Von Rad, *Old Testament Theology*, 2:188–262.

40. Israel is resilient and intransigent on this point. Jürgen Moltmann, *Theology of Hope: On the Ground and the Implications of Christian Eschatology* (1967; Minneapolis: Fortress Press, 1993), has shown how this stubborn insistence of Israel is foundational for biblical faith.

41. Paul D. Hanson, "Israelite Religion in the Early Postexilic Period," *Ancient Israelite Religion: Essays in Honor of Frank Moore Cross* (ed. Patrick D. Miller et al.; Philadelphia: Fortress Press, 1987) 485–508, has demonstrated the ways in which exilic hope is a transposed rearticulation of Israel's old memories. Von Rad's foundational appeal to Isa 43:18-19 in reference to prophetic hope is surely a clue for much derivative scholarship on the theme.

to Yahweh's intention to begin again, as much as the lawsuit oracles state Yahweh's unfettered capacity to terminate what is not congruent with Yahweh's governance.

Leitmotifs of Judgment and Hope

These three modes of speech—lawsuit, appeal for repentance, and promise—provide the materials out of which Israel can reimagine its life in Yahwistic categories. If we regard the appeal for repentance as something of an addendum to the speech of judgment, it is clear that the leitmotifs of the prophets are judgment and hope. Indeed, Ronald Clements has suggested that in canonical form, prophetic speech has been administered in an editorial process around these two themes.[42] In this somewhat reductive process, which is already evidenced in the text itself, it is clear that oracles of judgment and oracles of hope correlate completely with the core themes of Mosaic faith, which we have seen at root in the testimony of Exod 34:6-7.[43]

In Israel's narrative sketch of its life with Yahweh, lawsuit judgment and promissory hope come in sequence, divided by the fissure of exile. Thus hope can come only after judgment. Understood theologically, however, judgment and hope are not to be understood sequentially, but as expressions of twin aspects of Yahweh, who is present to Israel in faithful sovereignty and in sovereign fidelity. Promise does not cancel lawsuit, but surely opens for Israel yet another season in its life with Yahweh. It is for that reason that the (editorial) interweaving of lawsuit and promise into a single literary corpus, in any particular prophetic collection, is precisely a theological interweaving, articulating aspects of Yahweh's way with Israel.

Monarchic and Exilic/Postexilic Periods

The twin genres of lawsuit and promise may in a generalized way be correlated with the two great seasons of Israel's life with Yahweh (that is, after the foundational narrative of the Mosaic period): the monarchic period and the exilic/postexilic period. Very different needs, crises, and possibilities arose for Israel vis-à-vis Yahweh in these two periods.

Monarchic period. In the monarchic period, from the ideological foundation of David and Solomon until the disaster of 587 B.C.E., Israel-Judah enjoyed considerable worldly success. In those times when it did not enjoy such success but was a pawn in larger geopolitical games, it continued to imagine and claim for itself a special privilege in the world, a special entitlement that would sooner or later come to fruition. This conviction, remotely rooted in Mosaic memories but more directly driven by royal and temple ideology, invited pride and self-indulgence and an illusion about Israel's place in the world. These seductions all converged to make

---

42. Ronald E. Clements, "Patterns in the Prophetic Canon," *Canon and Authority: Essays in Old Testament Religion and Theology* (ed. George W. Coats and Burke O. Long; Philadelphia: Fortress Press, 1977) 42–55. The same insight recurs in Brevard Childs's treatment of the prophets in "the final form of the text."

43. On the cruciality of this text for Old Testament theology, see pp. 215–18.

Yahweh a patron God who was understood to have, as a primary function and inclination, the guarantee of Israel in the world. That is, the purposes of Yahweh were melded into the economic and political pretensions of monarchic Israel.

In that context of self-assured pride, which could be expressed in every aspect of policy and practice, the reality of Yahweh tended to be distorted away from Yahweh's own purposes in the world. The prophets of the ninth, eighth, and seventh centuries, in various ways, reasserted the sovereign reality of Yahweh, which is not an addendum to Israelite self-delusion. The prophets, in a collage of specific utterances around a rich diversity of images and metaphors, bear a common witness to the claim that Yahweh will order all of public history according to Yahweh's will for justice, righteousness, and equity, without special privilege for Israel. Thus the prophets characteristically resist the exceptionalism of election faith. Before Yahweh's large sovereignty, Israel stands summoned as every other people. In the following terse utterances, Amos appeals to and then nullifies Israel's specialness:

> You only have I known
> of all the families of the earth;
> therefore I will punish you
> for all your iniquities. (Amos 3:2)

> Are you not like the Ethiopians to me,
> O people of Israel? says the Lord.
> Did I not bring Israel up from the land of Egypt,
> and the Philistines from Caphtor
> and the Arameans from Kir? (Amos 9:7)

Jeremiah, nearer the fissure in time, addresses the claims of temple and monarchy. In Jeremiah 7 the prophet debunks temple claims (v. 4) and insists that obedience to Torah is the condition of security (vv. 5-7). In like manner, by making a contrast of "wicked" Jehoiakim and Torah-driven Josiah, Jeremiah debunks kingship as a source of well-being:

> Woe to him who builds his house by unrighteousness,
> and his upper rooms by injustice;
> who makes his neighbors work for nothing,
> and does not give them their wages;
> who says, "I will build myself a spacious house
> with large upper rooms,"
> and who cuts out windows for it,
> paneling it with cedar, and painting it with vermilion.
> Are you a king
> because you compete in cedar?
> Did not your father eat and drink
> and do justice and righteousness?
> Then it was well with him. . . .

But your eyes and heart
are only on your dishonest gain,
for shedding innocent blood,
and for practicing oppression and violence. (Jer 22:13-15, 17)

In this way of asserting the singular, uncompromised, undomesticated rule of Yahweh, contained by neither king nor temple nor any other human vehicle for self-securing, the prophets take from Israel every means and possibility of well-being outside of the claims of Torah.

Exile and postexile. In and after exile, however, everything is changed. Now Israel has no strong means of self-securing. All of that has now been nullified. If pride is the temptation of the monarchic period, then despair is the primary seduction in the exile. Israel can imagine that the triumphant government and victorious gods of Babylon (or even of Persia) are to prevail and should be served. The negative counterpoint to the exaggerated claims of the empire, inevitably, is the loss of confidence in Yahweh, wonderment whether Yahweh has lost power (cf. Isa 50:2, 59:1), speculation that Yahweh is fickle and has forgotten (Isa 49:14). Despair in Israel is the growing sense that there is no reliable Yahweh to whom to appeal, and therefore one must be governed by circumstance and accommodate oneself to the managers of that circumstance. As lawsuit was the preferred means of rhetoric among the prophets to counter autonomous pride, so promise is the chosen utterance of the prophets to counter immobilizing despair. In the alternative utterance of promise, the prophet enunciates Yahweh's resolve to work a newness in a context where no newness seems possible.

Based on the broad categories of judgment and hope, I suggest a rough pattern to the rhetoric whereby the prophets mediated Yahweh to Israel:

Genre	*Circumstance*	*Yahwistic Assertion*
lawsuit	pride of monarchy	Yahweh will govern recalcitrant Israel
promise	despair of exile	Yahweh will override circumstance in generosity

In this schema, which is proximately reflected in the shape of the canonical form of the several prophetic books, Israel has greatly thematized the specific utterances of specific prophets. I would insist, however, that the canonizing process has not in substance distorted the primal utterance of the prophets, but has remained faithful to it and has found a stylized way to preserve utterance as an enduring mediation of Yahweh.

Yahwistic Metahistory

In this interpretive process from utterance to canon, Israel has presented to it a Yahwistic metahistory. It is characteristic of Israel that its prophets would not speak in large, universal claims. Rather, as Paul Ricoeur states:

> The prophet . . . does not "think" in the Hellenic sense of the word; he cries out, he threatens, he orders, he groans, he exults. His "oracle" . . . possesses the breadth and the depth of the primordial word that constitutes the dialogical situation at the heart of which sin breaks forth.[44]

Nonetheless, there is a large coherence to the prophet's utterance, which asserts that in the midst of the vagaries, pretensions, and illusions of the public process, Yahweh stands at the center of Israel's life and at the center of all creation. The vagaries, pretensions, and illusions may consist in taking oneself too seriously, as was the case of Israel in the monarchic period. Those same pretensions and illusions in the exilic and postexilic periods consisted in taking others too seriously. And when either one's own operation or the realities of others is taken with ultimate seriousness, yielding respectively pride or despair, so the prophets assert, reality is distorted in ways that lead to death. The metahistory voiced in these odd utterances consists in the claim that Israel's life, in its prosperity, is at most a penultimate assurance subject to the righteous intention of Yahweh.[45] In like fashion, the successful life of other nations and empires that seem assured to perpetuity is at the most a penultimate claim, subject to the faithful resolve of Yahweh to make all things new.

The prophets who make these utterances likely had no such large picture in which their specific utterances would be placed. The canonical process is perhaps an editorial reflection on these ad hoc utterances, which can be seen whole only at the end. We may identify three texts that, in the midst of exile, can see the issue whole, voicing both Yahweh's sovereign judgment and Yahweh's gracious rescue:

> For thus says the Lord: Only when Babylon's seventy years are completed will I visit you, and I will fulfill to you my promise and bring you back to this place. For surely I know the plans I have for you, says the Lord, plans for your welfare and not for harm, to give you a future with hope. Then when you call upon me and come and pray to me, I will hear you. When you search for me, you will find me; if you seek me with all your heart, I will let you find me, says the Lord, and I will restore your fortunes and gather you from all the nations and all the places where I have driven you, says the Lord, and I will bring you back to the place from which I sent you into exile. (Jer 29:10-14)

> The days are surely coming, says the Lord, when I will sow the house of Israel and the house of Judah with the seed of humans and the seed of animals. And just as I have watched over them to pluck up and break down, to overthrow, destroy, and bring evil, so I will watch over them to build and to plant, says the Lord. (Jer 31:27-28)

---

44. Paul Ricoeur, *The Symbolism of Evil* (Boston: Beacon Press, 1969) 53.

45. On the notion of "metahistory," see Koch, *The Prophets*, 1:144–56, 165–66, and passim; and 2:71–80, 171–75, and passim.

> For a brief moment I abandoned you,
> but with great compassion I will gather you.
> In overflowing wrath for a moment
> I hid my face from you,
> but with everlasting love I will
> have compassion on you,
> says the Lord, your Redeemer. (Isa 54:7-8)

In every season of its life, in power and in despair, in security and in exile, Israel must come to terms with Yahweh.

Seen in this way, the prophets, give or take important oddities, are "like Moses" (Deut 18:15). They are passionate in their claim for Yahweh, and they intend to summon and energize Israel to be Israel, the one sworn to, derived from, and trusting in Yahweh. Israel always has reason, so it imagines, to fall away from Yahweh and to cease to be Israel. It can fall away in pride and conclude:

> My power and the might of my own hand have gotten me this wealth. (Deut 8:17)

Or it can fall away in despair and conclude,

> I am one who has seen affliction
> under the rod of God's wrath;
> he has driven and brought me
> into darkness without any light;
> against me alone he turns his hand,
> again and again, all day long....
> He has made my teeth grind on gravel,
> and made me cower in ashes;
> my soul is bereft of peace;
> I have forgotten what happiness is;
> so I say, "Gone is my glory,
> and all that I had hoped for from the Lord." (Lam 3:1-3, 16-18)

Indeed, we may believe that without the irascible work of the prophets who endlessly assault, summon, remind, and assure Israel, Israel might have ceased to be Israel.

Ethics and Eschatology

If I may attempt yet one more step toward thematization, I suggest that the prophets are advocates of a Yahwistic *ethic* (along with the Deuteronomist), and practitioners of a Yahwistic *eschatology* (which eventuates in apocalyptic).[46] These

---

46. I use the terms "ethics and eschatology" after the fashion of John Barton, *Oracles of God*, chaps. 5–7.

terms, ethics and eschatology, are of course formal and alien to Israel's way of speaking. Nonetheless they provide a focus for the following comments.

Mosaic Practice of Justice

There can be little doubt that the prophets who mediate Yahweh to Israel understand Yahweh in terms of a powerful ethical shaping of reality. Indeed, the Mosaic revolution, as remembered in the Pentateuch, proposes a neighborly alternative to pharaoh, which includes important checks on rapacious exploitation. To be sure, the Mosaic tradition reflects disturbing practices that are gender-based and class-biased. Without denying any of that, there is also no doubt that the Mosaic revolution, as remembered in Israel, has at its center the practice of justice; that is, provision for neighborly mutuality and respect.

Insofar as the prophets are "like Moses" (which is very far indeed in canonical construal), the prophets continue this ethical accent.[47] Thus already in the Davidic narrative, in the face of abusive royal power, Nathan appeals to provision of the commandment that David transgressed (2 Sam 12:9-10). And while Ahijah addressed Solomon concerning false gods (1 Kgs 11:33), the next chapter suggests that the concern about the fact that "his heart was not true to the Lord his God" (1 Kgs 11:4) was a concern over abusive governmental policy related to taxes and forced labor (1 Kgs 12:6-15). The familiar narrative of Naboth's vineyard is concerned with unjust royal land policies that permitted the crown to appropriate property which, according to old tribal practice, was inalienable. The affront is intensified, moreover, when the royal prerogative entailed murder as well (1 Kgs 21:1-14).

To be sure, all of these narratives are now situated in the Deuteronomic narrative. But the accent seems not to be different in the later prophets who continually make justice and righteousness the key to well-being (cf. Amos 5:7, 24; 6:12; Hos 6:6; Mic 6:8; Isa 5:7; Jer 5:20-29; 7:5-7; 22:3, 13-17; Hab 2:9-14). Even in the much later prophetic texts, these accents are reiterated:

> If a man is righteous and does what is lawful and right—if he does not eat upon the mountains or lift up his eyes to the idols of the house of Israel, does not defile his neighbor's wife or approach a woman during her menstrual period, does not oppress anyone, but restores to the debtor his pledge, commits no robbery, gives his bread to the hungry and covers the naked with a garment, does not take advance or accrued interest, withholds his hand from iniquity, executes true justice between contending parties, follows my statutes, and is careful to observe my ordinances, acting faithfully—such a one is righteous; he shall surely live, says the Lord God. (Ezek 18:5-9)

---

47. Wilson, *Prophecy and Society*, 157–66, has considered the claim that the prophets are "like Moses." On the ethical focus of the prophets, see Barton, *Oracles of God*, 154–78.

Render true judgments, show kindness and mercy to one another; do not oppress the widow, the orphan, the alien, or the poor; and do not devise evil in your heart against one another. (Zech 7:9-10)

> Maintain justice, and do what is right,
> for soon my salvation will come,
> and my deliverance be revealed. (Isa 56:1)

I have cited the most obvious and most familiar verses. But these verses are obvious and familiar for a reason. They form the core of the prophetic threat (against those who fail to obey) and the prophetic possibility (of a coming new order).

It remains, concerning this prophetic emphasis, to make clear its uncompromising urgency. I take the core of this prophetic accent to be that all members of the community, rich and poor, urban and rural, wise and foolish, powerful and marginated, are bound to each other in a common historical and social enterprise. Every member, by virtue of membership in the community, has entitlement that cannot be abrogated. Thus "widow, orphan, alien" are ciphers for those most vulnerable and powerless and marginated in a patriarchal society, who are without legal recourse or economic leverage. They are entitled and must be given their share.

The negative counterpart to this affirmation is that there are no escape hatches or exceptional treatments for the wise, the rich, the powerful, or the well-connected. Their destiny is linked to the destiny of the whole community. Thus the Mosaic ethic, as practiced by prophetic mediation, is a broadly based covenantal communitarianism, in which justice and righteousness assure that individual good is a subset of communal well-being.

In every season of prophetic utterance, but especially the prophets situated in the decline of the monarchy in the eighth and seventh centuries, this claim that community membership has on each of its members, especially on the rich and powerful, is made a nonnegotiable condition of a viable future. There can be no viable future of well-being for the Jerusalem establishment, except on the condition of the well-being of the entire community. This conviction is characteristically stated in the negative, as in the prophetic lawsuit speech. It is not, however, difficult to transpose the threat into a possibility. When the strong and powerful mobilize their resources and energy for the weak and vulnerable, peace and prosperity are generated for all. The prophets state these matters with Yahwistic specificity. The argument being made, however, is that this future, conditioned by justice, is not an arbitrary imposition of an angry God, but is a conditionality found in the very fabric of creation. It is indeed how life works, no matter how much the strong and the powerful engage in the illusion of their own exceptionality. In the final form of the prophetic text, the failure of the Jerusalem establishment is offered as a sad but not-to-be-denied confirmation of this assertion of conditionality.

Prophetic mediation of Yahweh, rooted deep in covenantalism, strikes a profound blow against all individualism that assumes that private gifts from Yahweh can be had at the expense of the community. The community to which Yahweh attends is grounded in nothing less than Yahweh's summons to membership, a summons that cannot be evaded. For this reason the prophets stand against kings who characteristically imagined they were exceptional. For this reason, moreover, prophetic faith in its largest sweep stands intransigently opposed to the Cartesian and Lockean ideology of modern individualism, which issues in barbarism in the presence of opulence. Such ill-conceived exceptionalism will, the prophets insist, bring an end to the historical process. In the purview of the Old Testament, royal history ended, as the prophets anticipated, in 587 B.C.E. In our own time, we are surely witnessing on a far more menacing scale the inevitable outcome of opulence-cum-barbarism, rooted as it is in an ideology of individualism that views the neighbor as impediment. Prophetic ethics greatly illuminates the shutdown of historical possibility.

Daring Tilt toward Eschatology

It is not likely that the prophets would have reached canonical form and continued to be generative if their only accent had been ethics and the ominous consequences of a misspent ethic. Alongside this intense preoccupation with the burden and demand of the present, the prophets characteristically anticipate Yahweh's future; that is, they think eschatologically, and mediate to Israel an imagined possibility willed by Yahweh. This daring tilt toward the future might perhaps be understood phenomenologically in terms of visions and trances—extrabodily experience and perception. Given our theological focus, however, we are bound to say that openness to the future is rooted in a conviction of Yahweh's indefatigable resolve to bring creation, and all in it, to Yahweh's sovereign intention for creation. The prophets are not fortune-tellers or predictors, working with esoteric means or data.[48] They are, rather, those who attend to Yahweh's resolve, which will not be defeated, even by the "end of history" that comes with failed ethics. Eschatology is simply Yahweh's capacity to move in and through and beyond the end of history, to reinitiate the life-giving processes of history.

This prophetic eschatology is articulated in oracles of promise, in which these mediators move beyond the tight constructs of blessing and curse, deed and consequence, reward and punishment, and banish the Mosaic "if" from the horizon of possibility. The oracles of promise are originary utterances without antecedent, certainly not rooted in or derived from the data or circumstance at hand, but rooted in Yahweh's circumstance-defying capacity to work newness.

The actual utterance of promise and new possibility, which will not be held in check by ethical failure, takes many forms. It takes as many different forms and

---

48. Mantic wisdom, which is tilted toward Gnosticism, does occur in the Old Testament. See B. A. Mastin, "Wisdom and Daniel," *Wisdom in Ancient Israel: Essays in Honour of J. A. Emerton* (ed. John Day et al.; Cambridge: Cambridge University Press, 1995) 161–69; more broadly, see Grabbe, *Priests, Prophets, Diviners, Sages,* 119–51. I judge, however, that mantic wisdom is quite marginal to the theological claims of the Old Testament.

images as specific circumstance requires, and as many nuances as are possible, given the several circles of tradition in which particular prophets are located.

Thus Isaiah's promissory utterances, for example, revolve around the artifacts of the Jerusalem establishment, to which Yahweh will remain faithful. The promises of Isa 9:2-7 and 11:1-9 are Davidic in substance, so that Yahweh's future, as anticipated in this tradition, is a royally shaped future, in which "a proper king" will do the work of monarchy in order to bring the world right. And in Isa 2:2-4 and 4:2-6, the future is temple shaped, so that God will make use of the temple as a gathering place of instruction, protection, and well-being.

Jeremiah, nurtured in the traditions of the Mosaic covenant, anticipates a Torah-centered future in a quite different way (Jer 31:31-34). The motivations for this complete renovation of Israel, however, are not found simply in stubborn fidelity on the part of Yahweh, but in wounded love and pathos (31:20) and in profound grief over loss (31:15), which cause Yahweh to move beyond indignation in profound caring. While Isaiah of the exile attends to the dominant images of the Isaiah tradition, moreover, one can also see that metaphors of marriage, family, and the production of wistfulness, pathos, and love are operative in Isaiah of exile, as in the mother-love of Isa 49:14-15 and the marital restoration of Isa 54:4-8.

The traditions that inform Ezekiel are of another kind, rooted in the temple and its severe holiness. Therefore, access to the future is not driven by pathos or even by fidelity, but by stark holiness that attends to Yahweh's honor. That honor, however, has as its inalienable counterpart the well-being of Israel, without whom Yahweh is not honored. Thus in Ezek 36:22-32 and 39:25-29, Yahweh's holiness eventuates in the restoration of Israel, and subsequently, the restoration of the temple (Ezekiel 40–48).

These remarkable variations, reflecting great flexibility and imaginative energy, all agree on the main point that Yahweh will claim a future for the good of Israel and, derivatively, for the good of the world. As Yahweh refuses to be governed by circumstance, so the prophets urge Israel to refuse to succumb to circumstance, even when the circumstance is generated by Israel's ethical failure.

This refusal to let circumstance determine the future and to make Yahweh a hostage is nicely and familiarly expressed in Hab 3:17-19, which in turn acknowledges the power of circumstance and then appeals to Yahweh beyond circumstance:

> Though the fig tree does not blossom,
> and no fruit is on the vines;
> though the produce of the olive fails
> and the fields yield no food;
> though the flock is cut off from the fold
> and there is no herd in the stalls,
> yet I will rejoice in the Lord;
> I will exult in the God of my salvation.

> God, the Lord, is my strength;
> he makes my feet like the feet of a deer,
> and makes me tread upon the heights.

The anticipation of the prophets, rooted in Yahweh's powerful resolve, can attend at the same time to the largest sweep of history and to the most intimate detail of Israel's life, for nothing of Israel is omitted from Yahweh's assured possibility.

Two promissory statements leave the prophetic enterprise open to Yahweh's newness. In Joel 2:28-29, the oracle promises that Yahweh's spirit—Yahweh's life-giving, chaos-ordering, exile-resisting, death-overcoming force—will be alive and loosed in the world:

> Then afterward
> I will pour out my spirit on all flesh;
> your sons and your daughters shall prophesy,
> your old men shall dream dreams,
> and your young men shall see visions.
> Even on the male and female slaves,
> in those days, I will pour out my spirit.

And in Mal 4:5-6, the prophetic canon concludes with reference to Elijah, remembered prophet and harbinger of Yahweh's newness:

> Lo, I will send you the prophet Elijah before the great and terrible day of the Lord comes. He will turn the hearts of parents to their children and the hearts of children to their parents, so that I will not come and strike the land with a curse.

We are not told how a remembered figure becomes an anticipated agent. Elijah, as prelude to "the great and terrible day," will effect transformation that will fend off Yahweh's harshness. These two texts from Joel and Malachi reflect openness in prophetic mediation.

It is evident that the New Testament, in seeking to bear testimony to Jesus, finds these texts (and others like them) a ground for seeing the promised newness of Yahweh in the present tense. Thus Luke, at the beginning of his tale of Jesus, reiterates Malachi:

> With the spirit and power of Elijah he will go before him, to turn the hearts of parents to their children, and the disobedient to the wisdom of the righteous, to make ready a people prepared for the Lord. (Luke 1:17)

In his second volume Luke appeals to Joel (Acts 2:17-21). These uses of the prophetic texts do not establish that this moment fulfills the Old Testament prophets. They attest, rather, that prophetic promises continue to be generative and revelatory, for the shape of Yahweh's promised newness is always yet again to be discerned and received.

The themes of ethics and eschatology serve well to summarize prophetic mediation of Yahweh, yet we must take care that we do not engage in excessive reduction. In the end, the prophets, even as presented in a more stylized canonical form, are not ethical teachers or eschatological speakers. They are simply vehicles of un-domesticated utterance, who utter what the present order regards as outrageous, obscene, treasured, crazy—and sometimes true. These utterances bear upon the ethical present and the promised future, but their burden is of another kind. They mediate Yahweh, make Yahweh palpably available, as threat and as possibility. They demand a hearing. In their memorable utterances, the prophets leave images and metaphors so ringing in the ears of Israel that life is never again thinkable or livable without reference to the "Wild One" who lives at the center of Israel's life, who in sovereign severity will dispense with Israel and who with impervious resolve will begin again. No wonder the anemic, self-serving, cowardly center wanted regularly to eliminate such utterance that mediated disruption, on which Israel in every time depends, and from which it receives always again its life.

TWENTY-THREE

The Cult as Mediator

T HE PLACE AND ACTIVITY of public worship, the cult, overseen by authorized priests, plays an enormously important role in the faith and life of the Old Testament community.[1] The cult, moreover, claims a large portion of Old Testament texts. Thus an Old Testament theology must reckon with the fact that the community which generates testimony about Yahweh is, in principle and in practice, a community of worship. Much of Israel's sense of who Yahweh is arises from and is generated by worship of a regularized, stylized kind, and not by history (meaning ad hoc unique events), as much Old Testament scholarship in the twentieth century has contended. The textual traditions concerning Israel's worship are rich and diverse. They are agreed, however, in their primary claim that the cult, in its many forms and expressions, mediates Yahweh's "real presence." In worship, Israel is dealing with the person, character, will, purpose, and presence of Yahweh. While this presence is *mediated* by ritual and sacramental practice, it is the *real presence* of Yahweh that is mediated. Thus these texts about worship seek to articulate and make available real presence. More than that, the concrete practice of these rituals and sacraments shaped Israel as a community related intensely and definitionally to Yahweh.

---

1. See especially Joseph Blenkinsopp, *Sage, Priest, Prophet: Religious and Intellectual Leadership in Ancient Israel* (Louisville: Westminster/John Knox, 1995) 66–114. Blenkinsopp rightly focuses historical considerations on the later priesthood. See also Lester L. Grabbe, *Priests, Prophets, Diviners, and Sages: A Socio-historical Study of Religious Specialists in Ancient Israel* (Valley Forge, Pa.: Trinity Press International, 1995) 41–65; and Rodney R. Hutton, *Charisma and Authority in Israelite Society* (Minneapolis: Fortress Press, 1994) 138–71. Among the more helpful discussions of cult in ancient Israel, its history and several functions, see Gary A. Anderson, *Sacrifices and Offerings in Ancient Israel: Studies in Their Social and Political Implications* (HSS 41; Atlanta: Scholars Press, 1987); David P. Wright, *The Disposal of Impurity: Elimination Rites in the Bible and in Hittite and Mesopotamian Literature* (SBLDS 101; Atlanta: Scholars Press, 1987); Richard D. Nelson, *Raising Up a Faithful Priest: Community and Priesthood in Biblical Theology* (Louisville: Westminster/John Knox, 1993); Israel Knohl, *The Sanctuary of Silence: The Priestly Torah and the Holiness School* (Minneapolis: Fortress Press, 1995); Baruch Levine, *In the Presence of the Lord* (Leiden: E. J. Brill, 1974); and Jacob Milgrom, *Leviticus 1–16* (AB 3; New York: Doubleday, 1991).

Problematics Created by Stereotypes, Critical and Theological

It is now conventional and popular to speak of this mode of cultic presence as *shekinah*, a term taken up programmatically by Elizabeth Johnson and much used in feminist thought.[2] It is important to note that the term is talmudic and does not occur in the Old Testament. For that reason too much must not be made of the term as such. Nonetheless, it is useful to notice that the feminine noun *shekinah* is derived from the verb *škn*, used in the Old Testament to characterize Yahweh's way of being present in Israel. The verb *škn*, rendered "abide" or "dwell," refers to being actually present in an abiding way, but not necessarily permanently. Thus it is a useful term to hold together Yahweh's readiness to be available to Israel in designated times and places, while at the same time acknowledging Yahweh's freedom from and sovereignty over the place and time wherein Yahweh is agreed to be present.[3] This double accent on commitment and freedom, which we have seen pervasively concerning Yahweh, is what makes the articulation of cultic presence so difficult and so delicate in Israel's practice and textual testimony.

Christian Supersessionism and Aversion to Cult

At the outset, we must note two related kinds of problems that arise in expositing this material. First, we may notice interpretive propensities that have dominated Old Testament interpretation while remaining largely hidden and unacknowledged. This problem, which is not easily overcome, stems from the fact that Christians (mostly Protestants) have dominated what has come to be called Old Testament theology. Christians have harbored a deep assumption that the disclosure of Jesus has "superseded" Old Testament practice, with particular reference to cultic texts and practices. So the "Christian revelation" has regarded the worship traditions of the Old Testament as obsolete, except as they are understood as "types" of Jesus. This attitude is especially evident in Hebrews 7–10, wherein Jesus is said to be "unlike the other high priests" (7:27).[4] This general Christian attitude toward the Old Testament is intensified by classical Protestantism, which has had a profound aversion to cult, regarding cultic activity as primitive, magical, and manipulative, thus valuing from the Old Testament only the prophetic-ethical traditions. This Protestant attitude of dismissiveness is especially evident in the notorious topic of Ludwig Koehler under which he discusses cult: "Man's Expedient for His Own Redemption."[5] The Christian inclination to supersessionism in

---

2. Elizabeth A. Johnson, *She Who Is: The Mystery of God in a Feminist Theological Discourse* (New York: Crossroad, 1992).

3. See Moody Smith, "Shekinah," *IDB* (Nashville: Abingdon Press, 1962), 4:319. See especially John 1:14. On the medieval Jewish mystical use of the term, see Gershom Scholem, *Major Trends in Jewish Mysticism* (New York: Schocken Books, 1941) 229–33. It is only at this much later stage that the term comes to designate an explicitly feminine aspect of the deity.

4. See the helpful discussion of Nelson, *Raising Up a Faithful Priest*, 141–54.

5. Ludwig Koehler, *Old Testament Theology* (London: Lutterworth Press, 1957) 181–98. In explicating this judgment, Koehler writes:

general and the Protestant aversion to cult in particular are not the same, but they reinforce each other.

History-of-Religions and Wellhausian Approaches

These interpretive propensities that discounted texts concerning Israel's worship have as their counterpart two assumptions that have dominated critical scholarship, assumptions that are not the same as the hermeneutical inclinations I have just mentioned, but are surely related to them. The first of these critical assumptions arises from a history-of-religions approach. A study of other religious communities in the environment of ancient Israel, particularly Ugaritic materials, indicates that Israel in the Old Testament took over and used much of the practice and terminology of the cultic practices of their non-Israelite neighbors.[6] Thus it is not difficult to conclude that practices which strike an interpreter as primitive are in fact borrowed, and therefore "not really Israelite." The common strategy is to recognize that Israel borrowed a great deal, but to insist that what is valued is radically transformed in the borrowing and used in different ways. What was borrowed and left untransformed is taken to be inferior and not seriously Israelite. These comparative data, of which we have ample amounts, thus are still open to weighted interpretation, as the interpreter picks and chooses what to value or devalue, what to take with theological seriousness and what to dismiss as pagan and unworthy.

The second critical assumption is even more pervasive in Old Testament scholarship, so pervasive that I am not sure how to treat it. This is the common construct of the history of Israel's religion, commonly linked to the name of Julius Wellhausen, which concluded that the Priestly material of the Pentateuch—that is, the large body of cultic material in Exodus, Leviticus, and Numbers—represents a very late period in Israel's religious practice.[7] It is now clear that this judgment is informed by the interpretive propensities I have mentioned, Christian super-

---

There is no suggestion anywhere in the Old Testament that sacrifice or any other part of the cult was instituted by God. It is begun and continued and accomplished by man; it is works, not grace; an act of self-help, not a piece of God's salvation. Indeed, the cult is a bit of ethnic life. Israel took it from the heathen. (181)

Nelson, *Raising Up a Faithful Priest*, 101–5, cites similar judgments from the same period by Walther Eichrodt and Otto Procksch. In a mark of how scholarship has changed, Nelson writes: "The ritual system, along with the rest of the Torah, had been revealed by a gracious God to meet human need" (199). And that from a Lutheran scholar!

6. Thus Koehler, *Old Testament Theology*, 181. On the appropriation of sacrifice from the religious environment of Israel, see René Daussaud, *Les Origines Cananéenes du sacrifice Israélite* (Paris: Ernest Leroux, 1921); more generally on the temple, see G. Ernest Wright, *Biblical Archaeology* (Philadelphia: Westminster Press, 1962) 121–46. The problem is that Israel seems to have taken over much else as well, much that Christians (and especially Protestant Christians) value; e.g., prophecy.

7. Important exceptions to this scholarly consensus on dating, which may yet carry the day, are Jacob Milgrom, "On the Parameters, Date, and Provenance of P," *Leviticus 1–16*, 13–35; Menahem Haran, *Temples and Temple-Service in Ancient Israel: An Inquiry into the Character of Cult Phenomena and the Historical Setting of the Priestly School* (Oxford: Clarendon Press, 1978) 146–48, and passim; Haran, "Behind the Scenes of History: Determining the Date of the Priestly Sources," *JBL* 100 (1981) 321–33; and Israel Knohl, *The Sanctuary of Silence: The Priestly Torah and the Holiness School* (Minneapolis: Fortress Press, 1995).

sessionism and Protestant cultic aversion, so that the material is treated not only as late, but also as legalistic, punctilious, and religiously inferior.

These two factors, which are closely interrelated interpretive propensities and critical assumptions, have conspired to sideline the worship materials of the Old Testament in deference to the prophets and the Psalms, so that Israel as a worshiping community has not been much appreciated in Old Testament theology. If, however, we follow Gary Anderson, relying on Clifford Geertz's "thick description" and George Lindbeck's "cultural-linguistic approach," then we must take careful account of the practices of worship in Israel—or, better, careful account of the texts wherein Israel testifies to its practices of worship.[8] For it is in worship, and not in contextless, cerebral activity, that Israel worked out its peculiar identity and sustained its odd life in the world. Worship life, over time, takes on an internal logic of its own in the community of practice, an internal logic not accessible to outsiders and about which the community does not trouble to speak very clearly or precisely. That is, at least to some extent, Israel did not "talk about" its worship, but it worshiped. Out of its actual worship, we have textual traces and residues. Our purpose here is not to reiterate, yet one more time, the "history of the cult," or to determine "what happened." It is rather to see, if we can, what was mediated of Yahweh through these cultic activities or through these texts that point to and remember cultic acts.[9]

I must confess, at the outset, that I have been nurtured, as a Protestant Christian, with the limiting, dismissive perspective noted above. I am, moreover, nurtured in that way as an Old Testament scholar, for critical scholarship has been little interested in the actual theological intention of Israel's worship. Therefore, I propose a model for considering this material theologically, but I do so with considerable diffidence, recognizing that we are only at the beginning of a reappropriation of the serious worship of Israel as an important theological datum. Israel understood, as the Western disestablished church is only now having to learn again, that *there must be important and intentional lines of defense and maintenance if a peculiar identity is to endure,* and worship is the most likely place in which such an identity is to be guarded and maintained.[10] Without such intentional worship, a community of an odd identity will first be co-opted and domesticated, and then it will evaporate. I understand the worship materials of the Old Testament to be precisely practices, proposals, and acts of imagination whereby Israel sought to maintain its oddity as the people of Yahweh. My comments will focus first on the temple in

---

8. See above, chap. 19, nn. 11, 12 on the cruciality of Anderson's insistence for my discussion.

9. The bibliography on cult in ancient Israel is extensive, but much of it is reiterative of a certain perspective. For a reliable summary of the data, see the older book by H. H. Rowley, *Worship in Ancient Israel: Its Forms and Meaning* (London: SPCK, 1976); see also the theologically more sensitive discussion of Hans-Joachim Kraus, *Worship in Israel: A Cultic History of the Old Testament* (Oxford: Blackwell, 1966).

10. Jacob Neusner, *The Enchantments of Judaism: Rites of Transformation from Birth to Death* (Atlanta: Scholars Press, 1991), has made the point unmistakably that worship is a primary and privileged place for generative imagination.

Jerusalem, and then I will consider the ways in which that temple continued to be focal for a community scattered beyond access to it.

Zion: The Jerusalem Offer of Presence

The Jerusalem temple, built by Solomon and destroyed in 587 B.C.E., dominated Israel's liturgical imagination through the high period of Israel's monarchic power.[11] The Jerusalem temple served as a *magnet* that drew into itself, comprehended, and appropriated all of the antecedent liturgical traditions of Israel. Thus the ark, the tent, and whatever continued of value in Israel's more heterodox worship traditions came to be in the temple. Indeed, we have seen that even the Mosaic Torah, so clearly rooted in Sinai, is in Israel's liturgic imagination transferred to and appropriated by the Jerusalem temple.[12]

The Jerusalem temple is also the *engine* that continued to power and structure Israel's liturgical imagination long after the temple itself ceased to be available. Even in exile, the grip of the Jerusalem temple gave Israel energy and generativity in its ongoing work of the maintenance of an adequate symbol system. I do not deny that there were non-Jerusalem liturgical operations in emerging Judaism; yet for purposes of Old Testament theology, the proper focus must be on the Jerusalem temple: for itself, as a magnet for antecedents, and as an engine for subsequent work in maintaining a displaced community.

The Jerusalem temple, in providing for Israel's liturgical imagination, managed through David's daring and Solomon's masterful administration to combine Israel's most treasured covenantal traditions with an openness to and appropriation of much larger, apparently non-Israelite, perhaps Canaanite theological traditions. This combination is commonly thought to be reflected in David's appointment of two priests, Ahimelech, son of Abiathar and Zadok, who respectively represent these traditions (2 Sam 8:17). I do not wish to minimize the importance of the Mosaic traditions that were lodged in Zion, but it seems plausible that the more powerful religious traditions of Jerusalem were the expansive creation traditions— perhaps Canaanite, perhaps already in Jerusalem before David, perhaps mediated by Zadok the priest—which give Zion its grip on Israel's worship.[13]

---

11. In my discussion I have not dealt separately with the Second Temple. For purposes of theological interpretation, the Second Temple, *mutatis mutandis*, takes up the claims of the first temple, with perhaps two important adjustments: (a) Its lively anticipation is much more intense than in the first temple, in which eschatology tends to be "realized"; and (b) Second Temple Judaism moved away from generative liturgy of a dramatic kind toward study (thus the rise of the synagogue). Even the temple was impinged upon by the scribal inclinations that became powerful in the later period of biblical Judaism.

12. See my appeal to Hartmut Gese on this claim, pp. 593–95.

13. H. H. Rowley, "Zadok and Nehushtan," *JBL* 58 (1939) 113–41; and "Melchizedek and Zadok (Gen 14 and Ps 110)," *Festschrift Alfred Bertholet zum 80 Geburtstag* (ed. Walter Baumgartner et al.; Tübingen: J. C. B. Mohr [Paul Siebeck], 1950) 461–72. Rowley has in particular championed a proposed linkage between Zadok and the pre-David Jebusite cult. Such a hypothesis illuminates a great deal, but it is not necessary to the general recognition that Israel stands in important continuity with its Canaanite environment.

Ben Ollenburger has carefully reviewed this material, and my discussion is much informed by his study.[14] The evidence for a theological-liturgical tradition in Zion is evident especially in the "Songs of Zion" (Psalms 46, 48, 76, 84, 87, 122) and the enthronement psalms (Psalms 47, 93, 96–99). It is clear from these Psalms that worship in Jerusalem had a life of its own, in its own categories, and without close reference to the traditions of Moses.[15] This tradition independent of Moses seems to reflect the older notion of a sacred mountain that was the residence of God. It may well be that Zion appropriated older traditions of a mountain in the north:

> Great is the Lord and greatly to be praised
> in the city of our God.
> His holy mountain, beautiful in elevation,
> is the joy of all the earth,
> Mount Zion, in the far north,
> the city of the great King.
> Within its citadels God
> has shown himself a sure defense. (Ps 48:1-3)

Two things are clear in this liturgical affirmation. First, Yahweh, the God of Zion, is really there; this is a place of divine residence. Second, Yahweh is there as king.[16]

The notion of Yahweh as king apparently was central for the Jerusalem temple. Scholarship has been dominated by the hypothesis of Sigmund Mowinckel, who proposed that an annual festival was held in the temple, a drama in which Yahweh was each year newly crowned king of creation.[17] This (hypothetical) festival correlated with the seasons of the year, so that the renewal of Yahweh's kingship matched (caused?) the coming of the rains and the fertility season. The hypothesis has exercised great influence among scholars and has been much disputed. Ollenburger has carefully reviewed the evidence and has given his support to the hypothesis.[18] My own judgment, in agreement with that of Ollenburger, is that the hypothesis has considerable merit, but that it is not necessary to assume such a festival in order to comment on the theological import of what is affirmed in the Psalms.

In one way or another, it is evident that the Jerusalem liturgy celebrated the kingship of Yahweh. There was in the Jerusalem temple, presumably in some

---

14. Ben C. Ollenburger, *Zion, City of the Great King: A Theological Symbol of the Jerusalem Cult* (JSOTSup 41; Sheffield: Sheffield Academic Press, 1987).

15. See ibid. for reference to the "Mount of the north" in the research of Otto Eissfeldt; also see Richard Clifford, *The Cosmic Mountain in Canaan and the Old Testament* (HSM 4; Cambridge: Harvard University Press, 1972), and the work of Otto Eissfeldt cited by Ollenburger.

16. On Yahweh as king, see pp. 238–41.

17. Sigmund Mowinckel, *Psalmenstudien 2: Das Thronbesteigungsfest Jahwas und der Ursprung der Eschatologie* (Amsterdam: P. Schippers, 1961).

18. Ollenburger, *Zion*, 33. See Walter Brueggemann, *Israel's Praise: Doxology against Idolatry and Ideology* (Philadelphia: Fortress Press, 1988), on the generative, constitutive power of cult, which is among Mowinckel's primary points. It is important to recognize the resistances of Protestant scholarship (e.g., Ludwig Koehler) in its refusal to countenance anything in worship like "representation," which is thought to smack of "Catholic sacramentalism."

regularized way, great joy in the awareness that Yahweh is a sovereign who has established governing control, who has enunciated policies of justice and well-being (*shalôm*), and who will be "in residence" and available for those who come there. Worship in the Jerusalem temple is something like a royal drama, and entry into "the place of Yahweh" is something like a royal audience with a monarch who in generosity and mercy can enact well-being for his adherents.

The kingship of Yahweh, seen and known palpably in the actual mediation of liturgy, had the effect of imposing a life-giving order on every aspect of Israel's life and on the life of the world.

Enduring Battle between Creation and Chaos

The kingship of Yahweh resolved the enduring battle between the life-giving creation order and the restless, surging destructiveness of chaos. Jon Levenson has shown that surging chaos is known in Israel to be still on the loose and as yet untamed by Yahweh.[19] Israel's dominant metaphor for this threat of chaos, which is both cosmic and intensely existential, is "the mighty waters" that surge out of control so that the life of Israel and the life of the world are under threat. In the liturgy of Yahweh's kingship, worship is the drama wherein the waters are driven back, defeated, and contained. Thus in Ps 24:2:

> For he has founded it on the seas,
> and established it on the rivers.

And in Ps 29:10, after an awesome display of Yahweh's power in a storm, Yahweh's serene throne is established:

> The Lord sits enthroned over the flood;
> the Lord sits enthroned as king forever.

Yahweh places Yahweh's throne *on the flood*. That is, the waters are so tamed and obedient to Yahweh in this moment that what was threatening chaos becomes an adequate locus for the power of Yahweh. In Psalm 46 the restless threat of chaos is characterized:

> Therefore we will not fear,
> though the earth should change,
> though the mountains shake in the heart of the sea;
> though its waters roar and foam,
> though the mountains tremble with its tumult....
> The nations are in an uproar, the kingdoms totter;
> he utters his voice, the earth melts. (Ps 46:2-3, 6)

In the face of such dangers and threats that jeopardize creation, Yahweh speaks and immediately all the threats of chaos subside:

---

19. Jon D. Levenson, *Creation and the Persistence of Evil: The Jewish Drama of Divine Omnipotence* (San Francisco: Harper and Row, 1988).

Be still, and know that I am God!
I am exalted among the nations,
I am exalted in the earth. (Ps 46:10)

The imperative, "Be still," is not a pious, devotional act of contemplation. It is, rather, a forceful, sovereign decree, a lordly command to chaos, which chaos promptly obeys (cf. Mark 4:39).

We may imagine that the drama of "creation versus chaos" was something like liturgic drama, though we cannot reconstruct any such drama.[20] In any event, the exercise whereby Yahweh governs chaos is liturgical. The drama fully contained in the temple, however, was a liturgical invitation for the participants to depart the temple, confident that what happened there intensely was true everywhere, beyond the confines of the temple. In the encounter with the power and authority of Yahweh, chaos has retreated and the world has been made safe.[21]

Yahweh's Kingship and Davidic Monarchy

As the cosmos is protected from jeopardy by the power of the creator, so the kingship of Yahweh in the temple has important implications for the political order in Jerusalem. The Davidic monarchy and the Zion theology of Yahweh's kingship are intimately connected. Ollenburger is at some pains to insist that the two traditions of king and temple are quite distinct. That may be so in terms of the fundamental tradition of the temple. There is no doubt, however, that the kingship of Yahweh in Zion functions as a guarantor for the political claims of the Davidic dynasty. It is in the nature of a temple in that ancient world to have that function.

As Ollenburger notes, the king, in going into battle, voices petitions to receive help and assurance from Zion:[22]

May he send you help from the sanctuary,
and give you support from Zion....
Now I know that the Lord will help his anointed;
he will answer him from his holy heaven
with mighty victories by his right hand.
Some take pride in chariots, and some in horses,
but our pride is in the name of the Lord our God.
They will collapse and fall,
but we shall rise and stand upright. (Ps 20:2, 6-8)

Notice that the appeal is to God in "the sanctuary" and "from his holy heaven." This ambiguity is present in these traditions, which we will consider later. But it is

---

20. On the phrase, see Bernhard W. Anderson, *Creation versus Chaos: The Reinterpretation of Mythical Symbolism in the Bible* (Philadelphia: Fortress Press, 1987).

21. On the claim of Yahweh's kingship over chaos as it pertains to the particularity of Israel's exile, see the enthronement formula in Isa 40:9-11, 52:7, and Walter Brueggemann, "Kingship and Chaos: A Study in Tenth Century Theology," *CBQ* 33 (1971) 317-32, and "Weariness, Exile, and Chaos (A Motif in Royal Theology)," *CBQ* 34 (1972) 19-38.

22. Ollenburger, *Zion*, 90-92.

first of all asserted that help comes from Zion. In the introductory Psalm 2, surely placed at the head of the Psalter to make the Davidic point, the God who attends to Zion is also the one who articulates and authorizes the Davidic king:

"I have set my king on Zion, my holy hill."
I will tell of the decree of the Lord:
He said to me, "You are my son;
today I have begotten you.
Ask of me, and I will make the nations your heritage,
and the ends of the earth your possession." (Ps 2:6-8)

The God who decrees order for creation and defeats chaos is the same God who may provide protection for king and state and assure that the political order will not be disrupted by enemies, who are a concrete assertion of the power of chaos in political form.

No doubt the king in Zion is a guarantee of the Davidic king (thus Ps 89:19-37). And no doubt the monarchic establishment made good ideological use of the presence of the Divine King in the temple, as though the human monarch were simply an extension of Yahweh's kingship. But, as we have seen in Ezekiel 34, the kingship of Yahweh also deabsolutizes the kingship of David and makes the king not an ultimate authority, but a penultimate agent of Yahweh's authority, which the king finally cannot usurp. This delicate relationship means that the authority of the king is provisional and is subject to the larger intention of Yahweh for justice, righteousness, truth, and equity. Thus, the enthronement psalms suggest that the temple provided for and enacted a large vision of Yahweh's powerful, good intention, which works as an *assurance* to the political order of Israel, but also as a *critical principle* with respect to monarchy.[23]

Kingship of Yahweh in the Temple as Consolation and Assurance

It is, in my judgment, indisputable that the temple was easily enlisted for reasons of state. Given what we know about the construction and maintenance of temples by kings, and given the nice phrase of Amos 7:13, "the king's chapel" (KJV), we may imagine that the temple was an important place for the king and his entourage. In any case, in practice the temple seems to have been organized on an exclusivist principle, with gradations of holiness and varying zones of admission to holiness; like all such differentiations, these likely benefited some at the expense of others. In principle, however, the temple did not purport to be exclusivist. It intended to be the residence of "the king" of all those in the realm (cf. Isa 56:7, on the

---

23. Ibid., 158, articulates the critical principle of Yahweh's kingship in Zion, but on p. 159 acknowledges ideological usage of that kingship which violates the critical principle of Zionism. This critical principle of Yahweh's kingship, which deabsolutizes every other claim, is surely operative with reference to the nations. See Ps 96:10 and the oracles against the nations in the several prophetic collections.

Second Temple).[24] This principle, we may believe, was compelling enough to fuel the imagination of all Israelites who appealed to the God resident in the temple.

I suggest that as the kingship of Yahweh assured creation against chaos and political well-being against political threat, so the kingship of Yahweh in the temple was also an important source of consolation and assurance to individual worshipers, as evidenced in personal psalms. We do not know who used these psalms; their use may have been limited to a small, privileged constituency. In principle, however, they invite broad, egalitarian use, and so I cite the personal psalms as evidence that the king in Zion was a source of well-being for individual worshipers.

Ollenburger suggests that the poor had special trust in Yahweh who was in Zion (compare Pss 9:11, 40:17, 86:1-2).[25] Zion, moreover, is a refuge, even as Yahweh is a refuge (Ps 46:1, 7, 11). Thus there is lyrical identification of Yahweh and the city of Yahweh, which is evidently a visibly powerful fortress. As the temple is fortress, so Yahweh is taken to be fortress for those who have no other defense.

Gerhard von Rad goes much further and into more detail than does Ollenburger. He states as his premise that Yahweh's "word of life" is in the cult:

> The word of life was certainly not just an elemental truth, nor yet primarily a matter of dogma, but arose from an actual decision in a concrete situation, and there can be no question but that it was communicated to Israel through the cultus.[26]

When von Rad cites psalms in which "the word of life" is either received or interpreted, the temple connection is unmistakable:

> One thing I asked of the Lord,
> that will I seek after:
> to live in the house of the Lord
> all the days of my life,
> to behold the beauty of the Lord,
> and to inquire in his temple. (Ps 27:4)

> Surely goodness and mercy
> shall follow me
> all the days of my life,
> and I shall dwell in the house of the Lord
> my whole life long. (Ps 23:6)

---

24. Thus even if the temple is for the entire community, evidently not everyone had equal access, for access is privileged entry to power. The same social reality pertains to any place where power is in strong supply, as the U.S. White House or Buckingham Palace. Such places are "for all"—but not really.

25. Ollenburger, *Zion*, 68. On this he follows John Gray, *The Biblical Doctrine of the Reign of God* (Edinburgh: T. & T. Clark, 1979).

26. Gerhard von Rad, "'Righteousness' and 'Life' in the Cultic Language of the Psalms," *The Problem of the Hexateuch and Other Essays* (New York: McGraw-Hill, 1966) 253. In a very different mode, Gary A. Anderson, *A Time to Mourn, a Time to Dance: The Expression of Grief and Joy in Israelite Religion* (University Park: Pennsylvania State University Press, 1991), proposes that physical, communal activity is indeed generative of social reality.

> Happy are those whom you
> choose and bring near
> to live in your courts.
> We shall be satisfied with
> the goodness of your house,
> your holy temple. (Ps 65:4; cf. 36:7-9, 63:2-5, 84:4)[27]

It is clear that the temple is a safe place, because to be there is to be in the presence of and under the protection of the king.

Life versus Death in the Sanctuary

Following Christoph Barth, von Rad indicates that *the sanctuary is the place where life and death are fought through.*[28] This insight is made the focus of Fredrik Lindström's fine study of the psalms of individual complaint.[29] Lindström shows that the needful person who petitions in these psalms is not suffering because of guilt. Lindström proposes a dualism, so that the speaker has fallen into trouble because Yahweh has been absent or neglectful. Where Yahweh is absent or neglectful, the power of death occupies the open space and besets the petitioner. Thus the petition of these psalms is that Yahweh should actively return to the sanctuary and drive out the threat of death. The dualism is a cosmic one, but the focus of the conflict between Yahweh and the power of death is in the temple.

Lindström refers in some detail to Psalms 3, 57, 61, and 63.[30] In these psalms, Lindström observes that the speaker: (a) is under profound threat, (b) trusts Yahweh profoundly and anticipates joyous well-being, and (c) refers to Yahweh's locus in the temple. On this last point, see for example:

> I cry aloud to the Lord,
> and he answers me from his holy hill. (Ps 3:4)

> Let me abide in your tent forever,
> find refuge under the shelter of your wings. (Ps 61:4)

> So I have looked upon you in the sanctuary,
> beholding your power and glory. (Ps 63:2)

Lindström proposes that such phrases as "refuge," "strong tower," and "shelter of your wings" allude to the temple.

---

27. Von Rad, "'Righteousness' and 'Life,'" 256–66, has seen that these prayers reflect on the notion of a "portion" from Yahweh (cf. Pss 16:5-11, 73:23-28, and 142:5). The "portion," before it became a spiritualized notion, seemed to refer to priestly enjoyment of temple space, as an alternative to land as portion.

28. Ibid., 255–59; and Christoph Barth, *Die Errettung vom Tode in den individuellen Klage- und Dankliedern des Alten Testaments* (Zollikon: Evangelischer Verlag, 1947) 44–51.

29. Fredrik Lindström, *Suffering and Sin: Interpretation of Illness in the Individual Complaint Psalms* (Stockholm: Almqvist and Wiksell International, 1994).

30. Ibid., 390–413.

Von Rad raised the question whether these petitions and hopes are to be "taken literally or not."[31] To be sure, the language is characteristically elusive. Christoph Barth inclines to take the need and the deliverance literally. Von Rad suggests a mysticism that spiritualizes.[32] Lindström resists von Rad's mysticism and speaks of: "an affliction which can only be annulled by the meeting with YHWH's *ḥsd*, which has been made visible in the worship service, but which embraces all of life."[33]

Drama of the Temple: As Large as Life

It is likely that we do not know enough to sort out matters into such refined categories as these scholars have used. In any case, liturgic language functions in a suggestive, impressionistic way that cannot be fully slotted and categorized. No doubt Lindström is correct to say that what happens in the cult is linked to what happens in life, but it is not an either/or issue between "real life" and the mystical. It is enough to see that the entire "drama of rehabilitation" is conducted in or toward the temple, whereby Yahweh's powerful, faithful presence is known to be intense enough to defeat all that diminishes life.[34]

Rainer Albertz and Erhard Gerstenberger have proposed a much more intimate ritual of rehabilitation that may take place in the family or clan.[35] But even if that proposal is accepted (and I find it persuasive), it is not possible to drive a wedge between *Grosskult* and *Kleinkult*. There can be little doubt that what was practiced locally was authorized and legitimated by the categories and practices of the larger sanctuary liturgy.

Thus we may propose, with particular reference to the Psalms, that the Jerusalem temple was the locus of dramatic activity whereby all of life—cosmic, political, personal—was brought under the rule of Yahweh. In coming under the rule of Yahweh, moreover, all of life was made whole and safe. It is important to emphasize the full dramatic enactment, which seems evident, even if we cannot be precise about the actions undertaken. The liturgy was a series of actions whereby Israel bodily received from Yahweh the assurance of an ordered life. This enterprise of the dramatization of life under Yahweh is not done simply by thin verbalization, but seems filled with action as well as speech, action in which something is "done," something sacramental. Moreover, if we consider the full gamut of petition, complaint, thanksgiving, and praise, this activity was one of candor, without need to deny or cover up failures from the side of Yahweh. I imagine that the drama of the temple was as large, daring, and candid as life itself. It is no wonder that temple worship was undertaken with eagerness and joy.

---

31. Von Rad, "'Righteousness' and 'Life,'" 255.
32. Ibid., 259.
33. Lindström, *Suffering and Sin*, 411.
34. See my discussion of the "drama of rehabilitation," pp. 460–85, 552–56.
35. Erhard S. Gerstenberger, *Der bittende Mensch: Bittritual und Klagelied des Einzelnen im Alten Testament* (WMANT 51; Neukirchen-Vluyn: Neukirchener Verlag, 1980); Rainer Albertz, *Persönliche Frömmigkeit und Offizielle Religion: Religionsinterner Pluralismus in Israel und Babylon* (Calwer Theologische Monographiehren 9; Stuttgart: Calwer Verlag, 1978).

The temple is indeed the place where Israel entered into Yahweh's full zone of *shalôm*. In practice, it seems self-evident that the covenantal, mythic, and ideological factors were always in important tension. At its best, the activity of the temple no doubt served the fullness of Yahwism. Thus von Rad writes: "Yahweh created in the sacrificial cult too an institution which opened up for Israel a constant way of living intercourse with him."[36] Kraus, following von Rad, concludes: "The purpose is to relate all of life to *berith* [covenant], to establish *berith*."[37]

Because worshipers are not single-minded, this singular Yahwism was no doubt regularly compromised. And because life does not imitate art, and worship is not magic, the drama of the liturgy did not always "work." But it must have made an enormous difference to keep one's life, one's state, and one's cosmos fully and animatedly situated in this drama with Yahweh. Mediated here are resources that fend off the powers of death. These resources are the gladly given gifts of Yahweh. Indeed, the resources of cult are the means of Yahweh's self-giving to Israel.

Mosaic Authorization of Presence

As Israel testifies about its life with Yahweh, it had an important existence before the founding of the Jerusalem temple (on which see 2 Samuel 24). In that earlier period of it life, so Israel testifies, Yahweh gave the large gift of cultic mediation.[38] Here I refer to the Priestly materials of Exodus 25–31, 35–40, the Book of Leviticus, and Numbers 1–10. There are, to be sure, important critical questions about this material. It is conventional to date this material to the exile or thereafter, though Menahem Haran, Jacob Milgrom, and Israel Knohl urge an earlier dating. Even if it is dated late, the material surely reflects older practices. In this canonical placement of the material, however, it is prior to the founding of the temple and has in that regard important theological-canonical functions: (a) It roots the entire sacrificial practice of Israel in the authority of Moses, the most elemental giver of "institutional words" in Israel; (b) the material is made to predate the temple, making Yahweh's intention for a place of presence prior to Solomon's construction, thus preempting any royal authority over the place; and (c) it provides a mobile shrine, thus looking past the fixed locale of the Jerusalem temple, in anticipation of the subsequent need of exiles, who required a God who could move with them.

For our purposes, it is unhelpful to cling too closely to the historical-critical dating of this material. At this point we make an important break with the conventional consensus about the history of Israelite religion; not in challenging that preferred historical construction, but in moving beyond it to raise canonical questions. The historical-critical issues are difficult, in part because of the complex and

---

36. Kraus, *Worship in Israel*, 123, quotes von Rad without citation. See von Rad, *Old Testament Theology*, 1:260.

37. Kraus, *Worship in Israel*, 122–23.

38. This assertion is, among other things, directly opposed to the sort of verdict rendered by Koehler, on which see n. 5 above.

obscure problems both of literature and history, and critical conclusions can at best receive only speculative answers. But more important, it is clear that in these texts we are dealing with foundational authorization that lies before and behind and out of reach of any historical practice.

Theologically, these texts are words of institution, which for the faithful lie beyond the reach of critical examination. Our purpose, then, is to see, as best we can, what is understood as being mediated in these provisions. The short answer is that Yahweh's own self is being mediated, made graciously accessible and available to Israel in these cultic arrangements. The One being mediated is the One we have sought to render under the rubrics of core testimony and countertestimony. In these texts, Israel is dealing with the God who is sovereignly glorious, holy, and jealous, but who intends relatedness that puts Yahweh's own life at risk in the midst of Israel.[39] The cult is concerned with nothing less than and nothing other than such presence, and therefore we may well understand the extreme care taken with these arrangements, so extreme that the provisions may strike us as excessively punctilious. Already at Sinai, in authorizing this cultus, Yahweh had promised through Moses, "And have them make me a sanctuary (*miqdoš*), so that I may dwell (*škn*) among them" (Exod 25:8). What may strike us as punctilious in this material is in the service of "Real Presence." God's own life will be in the very midst of Israel. Here I will comment on five aspects of the foundational cult, which is authorized by Yahweh and intended to make Presence possible.

Great Care in Constructing Tabernacle

Moses' project in this material is to construct, at the command of Yahweh, a tabernacle made of expensive materials, constructed with Israel's best artistic skill, and filled with carefully appointed furniture necessary to appropriate cultic activity. All of this is evident in the instructions at Sinai (Exodus 25–31). But what interests us here is the term *tabernacle* (*mškn*), derived from the verb *škn*. The entire project is undertaken in order that Yahweh may "abide" in reality and in freedom, in the very midst of Israel.[40] Yahweh is an awesome, demanding agent whose presence is not casual, trivial, incidental, or ad hoc. Therefore no effort and no resource is to be spared. The promise of presence is more exaggeratedly stated in a provisional conclusion: "I will dwell (*škn*) among the Israelites, and I will be their God" (Exod 29:45). It may well be that the two parts of this sentence are only incidentally juxtaposed, but perhaps not. The statement suggests that being "their God" is equivalent to being available and accessible, and this is the only important evidence given here of being "their God." Presence is everything.

---

39. See pp. 283–302 above on the testimony of Israel concerning Yahweh as glorious, holy, and jealous, but related. Thus the "forms of life" in cult *do* what Israel's testimony *says*.

40. The term *abide*, used in this way, is a crucial theme in the Fourth Gospel. See Moody Smith in n. 3 above, on "Shekinah," and finally the hope articulated in Rev 21:3-4. On the term in Old Testament traditions concerning presence, see Tryggve N. D. Mettinger, *The Dethronement of Sabaoth: Studies in the Shem and Kabod Theologies* (Lund: CWK Gleerup, 1982) 90–97.

The care of these provisions for presence may strike one with "low church" tendencies as odd and extravagant, if not scandalous. Perhaps this extreme care can be understood if we think about the anticipated visit of an important political leader. Because the Priestly tradition has royal images in purview, we may even think of the visit of a royal person. For such a visit, elaborate preparations may be made, commensurate with the dignity and importance of the visitor. Everything must be freshly decorated, lawns trimmed, flowers rented, lounges secured, for nothing unseemly or amiss must be permitted to distract from "the royal presence." Such a view of a royal visitor may offend one with extreme democratic tendencies. By analogy, such preparations for Yahweh's Presence may equally offend religious sensitivities that imagine easy intimacy with the holy. But both democratic inclination and cuddly communion are beyond the horizon of this Mosaic enterprise. The One to be hosted here as holy is awesome, terrifying, and sovereign, who will not come on a regular and "abiding" basis unless preparation is commensurate with Yahweh's personhood.

It is odd that this extended provision for the tabernacle (and its priesthood) concludes in Exod 31:12-17 with provision for the Sabbath, which has nothing to do with tabernacle or any kind of holy space. This provision for Sabbath seems to be an intrusion in Yahweh's directions to Moses, which may reflect an emerging accent on Sabbath as a mark of Israel as these texts are being framed. Or the Sabbath provision may be to fill out the "seven speeches" that precede it, in order to match the seven days of creation.[41] It may also suggest that when Holy Presence is properly hosted, all is restful in earth as in heaven. If that is so, then we may suggest that the worship intended here is a counterworld to Israel's lived experience, which is dangerous and disordered. The counterworld offered in the tabernacle holds out the gift of a well-ordered, joy-filled, peace-generating creation. (See Ezekiel 40–48 for an even more "ordered" notion of cultic space.) No wonder Israel took such care to "get it right"!

Role of the Priests

It is the cult itself that mediates the Presence. For this priests are required. The priests are a subset of the cult, the necessary legitimators, enactors, and guarantors of rightly hosted holiness. My impression is that the priests themselves do not mediate, but they supervise and attest the visual, material, physical acts of worship that do the mediation.

It is clear that in this founding document, the preparation and ordination of the priests who will preside over the tabernacle is a crucially important enterprise (Exodus 28–29, Leviticus 8–10). The priests, properly garbed in extravagant vest-

---

41. On the links between Priestly provisions for cult and creation, see Joseph Blenkinsopp, *Prophecy and Canon: A Contribution to the Study of Jewish Origins* (Notre Dame, Ind.: University of Notre Dame Press, 1977) 54–69; Peter J. Kearney, "The P Redaction of Ex. 25–40," *ZAW* 89 (1977) 375–87; and Robert B. Coote and David R. Ord, *In the Beginning: Creation and the Priestly History* (Minneapolis: Fortress Press, 1991).

ments, are to be properly inducted into this awesome service, but only after they have been fully and properly "made holy." With the particular ordaining activity of Exod 29:20, the priest seems to be *fully* priest, right down to the toes! It is apparent that the priests themselves are to be an embodiment, enactment, and representative of the purity and holiness of Yahweh's self. This view of priesthood is indeed not simply functional, but organic. The priests in their bodily presence bespeak the availability of Yahweh's self.

Julius Wellhausen's dominant hypothesis is that this priestly model of presence represents a late, degenerate, hierarchal development in Judaism.[42] Perhaps so. It seems more plausible, however, if we are ever to break free from Wellhausen's evolutionary construct, to suggest that the priestly enterprise, congruent with the dignity and solemnity of royal models of reality, likely represents a religious sensibility that is present and powerful in Israel everywhere, in every time. It may well be that such priesthood displaced kingship and established enormous sacerdotal clout after the end of the monarchy. On liturgic and theological grounds, however, we must pay attention to the practice of order, symmetry, coherence, and dignity— all of which bespeak a certain beauty. This order is to be treasured when contrasted with the disordered, alienating, threatening life of Israel in the world. While the temptation to a dualism that divides "life" from "worship" is real, it is important to see that worship models and enacts an alternative world of sanity that prevents Israel from succumbing to the seductive insanities of a world raging against the holiness of Yahweh the Creator. The priesthood is to protect and guarantee the maintenance of this alternative world, wherein Israel could "see" God, and so see itself differently in the world.

The Mercy Seat

A particular aspect of the tabernacle merits comment. Exod 25:1-9, the introduction to these provisions, concerns the tabernacle. In v. 17 the text abruptly speaks of the *kapporeth*, which in the NRSV is rendered "mercy seat":

> Then you shall make *a mercy seat* of pure gold; two cubits and a half shall be its length, and a cubit and a half its width. You shall make two cherubim of gold; you shall make them of hammered work, at the two ends of *the mercy seat*. Make one cherub at the one end, and one cherub at the other; of one piece with *the mercy seat* you shall make the cherubim at its two ends. The cherubim shall spread out their wings above, overshadowing *the mercy seat* with their wings. They shall face one to another; the faces of the cherubim shall be turned toward *the mercy seat*. You shall put *the mercy seat* on the top of the ark; and in the ark you shall put the covenant that I shall give you. There I will meet with you, and from above *the mercy seat*, from between the

---

42. This judgment, best framed by Wellhausen, is a commonplace of older historical criticism that exhibited passions (and biases) that were not only anti-Jewish but in fact also anti-Catholic, insofar as cult in principle is taken to be an inferior form of faith.

two cherubim that are on the ark of the covenant, I will deliver to you all my commands for the Israelites. (Exod 25:17-22)[43]

As with other cultic objects, nothing is said about function in this text of authorization. We may first attend to the word *kapporeth* itself. *Kapporeth* derives from the verb *kipper*, which means "to cover." Here it refers to the "covering" of sin, guilt, and offense that alienate Israel from Yahweh. Moses is to construct, within the tabernacle, a vehicle whereby Israel's sin is regularly and effectively overcome, both to make Yahweh's presence possible in Israel and to make communion between Yahweh and Israel possible. Other than the instruction to construct such a vehicle, the primary use of the term is in Leviticus 16, concerning "the Day of Atonement" (*yôm kippur*), when the priest "makes atonement" (*kipper*) for "all the assembly of Israel" (v. 17).

The astonishing claim of these texts, and of the vehicle to which they witness, is that *Yahweh has granted to Israel a reliable, authorized device whereby Israel can be restored to full relationship with Yahweh.* It is the same claim that the early church makes for Jesus, that Jesus is God's new "sacrifice of atonement" (Rom 3:25), whereby alienation is overcome. The New Testament is adamant about supersession of this vehicle of Moses at Sinai. Even the claim made for Jesus, however, becomes nonsensical unless Christians, like Jews, fully marvel at the graciousness of Yahweh in authorizing such a cultic apparatus and at the bold responsiveness of Israel in constructing it.

The "mercy seat," the particular place of Yahweh's readiness to reenter relationship with Israel, is a gift from God that decisively contrasts the alienated world "out there" and the reconciling possibility "in here." This cultic offer is indeed an alternative world of life that contradicts and contrasts with the deathliness where Yahweh's graciousness is as yet under harsh challenge and heavy resistance.

Sacrificial Practices

While the mercy seat in the tabernacle, utilized in the remarkable festival of atonement, is at the center of Israel's liturgic imagination, it is clear in Leviticus 1–7 that Yahweh, through Moses at Sinai, has provided more regular devices and avenues for Israel's life with Yahweh. It is usual to speak of "the sacrificial system" of Israel with the phrase having a pejorative connotation, suggesting a manipulative claim of *ex opere operato*. If we wish simply to dismiss such serious religious intentions as are reflected in these texts, we may view the whole matter negatively. And that has been done often enough in Christian exposition.

In my judgment, we do better to pay attention to the particulars of the sacrifices authorized through Moses. These sacrifices constitute practices whereby Israel can interact with Yahweh. That relationship, like any such relationship, may exist

---

43. The translation of *kapporeth* is manifestly difficult. Thus the LXX rendered *hilastērion* (on which see Rom 3:25), the Vulgate *propiatorium*, and Luther, famously, *Gnadenstuhl.* The several renderings reflect the awareness that translation here concerns not only linguistic probity, but exceedingly freighted theological issues.

in a condition of well-being and authentic mutuality, or it may be in a condition of alienation and hostility. The excessive accent in some Christian traditions, especially classical Christian liturgical traditions dominated by a sense of sin, tends to assume that worship always begins in alienation and hostility that require pardon at the outset. But Israel's sketch of available sacrifices indicates otherwise.

The action appropriate to a working relationship of well-being and authentic mutuality, when all is well between Yahweh and Israel, is expressed in three kinds of offerings: "burnt offerings" (Leviticus 1; 6:8-13); "grain offerings" (Leviticus 2; 6:14-23); and "offerings of well-being" (*šlmim*) (Leviticus 3; 7:11-26).[44] These are acts whereby Israel brings offerings and sacrifices as gestures of commitment, loyalty, and gratitude. In bringing them, Israel engages in what was regarded as well-being and mutuality in the presence of Yahweh. Such activity in such a particular, well-ordered place is what makes Israel most truly "at home." Israel in this activity in this place can, without embarrassment or deception, give itself over completely to this relationship.

The actions appropriate to this relationship, when marked by Israel's failure and consequent alienation and hostility, are "sin offerings" (Lev 4:1–5:13, 6:24-30), and "guilt offerings" (Lev 5:14-19, 7:1-10). These are gestures of repentance, regret, acknowledgment, and resolve to return to a viable relationship with Yahweh. Israel took sin and alienation seriously, but Israel was not morbid about them or preoccupied with them. Because of Yahweh's gracious provision of these practices, sin and guilt can be handled, dealt with, and overcome. We may observe three aspects of these practices of reconciliation.

Reparations. First, the gestures of sacrifice must be accompanied by or preceded by reparations (cf. Lev 6:1-6).[45] An affront against the neighbor cannot be overcome by a ritual act toward Yahweh, unless a substantive gesture is also made toward the affronted neighbor. No cheap grace! I deliberately use the term *reparations*, as it is currently used in social policy matters. Whereas reparations in Lev 6:1-6 concern face-to-face neighborliness and not large issues of public policy, the same awareness pertains, as issues now surface in a more complex urban society. The gestures of sin offering and guilt offering are not efficacious in and of themselves, unless a serious social restoration takes place at the same time.

Penitential psalms. Second, it is plausible that the penitential psalms (Psalms 6, 32, 38, 51, 130) are to be understood in relation to these conciliatory actions. This point cannot be established as a certainty, but it is likely that the sacrifice provides the social, institutional setting for such acts of penitence. These psalms suggest that forgiveness entails not only a material offering, but also a voiced acknowledgment

---

44. This particular rendering in NRSV of "offerings of well-being" seems to me especially felicitous in light of the root word *shalôm*.

45. Jacob Milgrom, "The Priestly Doctrine of Repentance," *Studies in Cultic Theology and Terminology* (SJLA 36; Leiden: E. J. Brill, 1983) 58, explicitly refers to Matt 5:23-24 as a closely linked text.

of failure that precludes any denial.[46] Word and act go together. Such a linkage would illuminate the odd juxtaposition of Ps 51:17, which spiritualizes sacrifice, and Ps 51:19, which treats sacrifice in a way congruent with the Mosaic program.

Effective restoration of relationship. Third, the enactment of such sacrifice (together, we may assume, with reparations and voiced repentance) is effective. Thus the priest is ready to say, without reservation, "You shall be forgiven" (Lev 5:13, 18). These acts are devices whereby a crucial relationship is restored. Protestant traditions, more conscious of sin than of grace, tend to regard liturgic restoration as not nearly as serious as an affront committed in "the real world." In such a purview, while the ritual may be performed, the power of sin lingers. This text, however, suggests otherwise; the reason is that Yahweh is gracious.

The sacrificial system, thus, is in the service of this relationship to which Yahweh is devoted. The relationship of Yahweh and Israel is not an intellectual-cognitive one, nor is it solely ethical. It is concretely material and dramatic, and it must be embodied, not as instrumental to something else, but as the thing itself. Moses at Sinai authorizes such embodiment and provides ways for the dramatic performance of the relationship. It is a thing done.

Accent on the Visual

What strikes one repeatedly in this exposition of tabernacle, priesthood, mercy seat, and sacrificial system is the visual, material quality of everything that is authorized and proposed. Thus at the outset, Yahweh commands Moses: "In accordance with . . . the pattern (*tabnith*) of the tabernacle and all its furniture, so you shall make it" (Exod 25:9). Moses and the workmen have available a model for their work. Moreover, the construction of the tabernacle requires exotic materials (Exod 25:3-7, 35:5-9) and intense artistic skill (Exod 35:30–36:7). The tabernacle and all of the vehicles for presence are designed to appeal to the senses, and especially to visual sensibility.

This is matched by a recognition that the tabernacle evokes a sense of dramatic participation, so that the active verbs of making and doing, bringing and offering require Israelites to be actively, physically engaged in the practice of presence. I suggest that the visual power of the sanctuary is to be all-containing and all-consuming, so that any reservation of disbelief is overwhelmed, and the participant is able to give self wholly and fully and without qualification to this relationship. The active verbs make clear that participants in this ritual of relationship cannot be passive observers, but must expend energy before the assembly as an act of loyalty and acknowledgment.

This accent on the visual perhaps is the basis from which the pious in the Psalter imagine that they can "see God" (Pss 11:7, 17:15, 36:9, 63:2). It may be that this rhetoric refers to a mystical, transcendent experience. It seems more likely to me

---

46. Ps 32:3-5 is especially aware of the temptation to denial. For that reason, material offering is not in itself adequate, but must be accompanied by voiced acknowledgment.

that what is intended is that the "vision of God" is mediated through the furnishings of presence, so that what is seen is the furniture from which the religious affirmation is extrapolated.[47] In any case, such analytical distinctions are irrelevant for the participants, for the "vision of God" is surely cultic and more, so that in this act of presence Israel has to do not only with signs but with the realities that these signs represent. The furnishings of the tabernacle are clearly not the thing itself, but they are the context in which the One who is Lord of the tabernacle agrees to be present.

It is clear that from Sinai on, Israel anticipates a life with Yahweh that is rich, full, and all-encompassing. It may be that this anticipation of presence is to be understood as the anticipation of Solomon's temple (cf. 1 Kgs 6:14-36). But the anticipation to which Moses is invited is more than an anticipation (canonically) or retrospect (critically) of the Jerusalem temple. It is a theological statement promising Yahweh's readiness to be with Israel in every circumstance. This "being with" is not merely ethical, cognitive, or intellectual, as a thin, Protestant theology of the word might have it, but it is holistic and involves the full engagement of the whole person in the gathered community.

Worship that is visual, active, dramatic, and all-comprehending was a thing of joy for Israel, not a burden. In the temple-monarchy period, such worship may have had intense and uncritical ideological substance, in order to enhance the Jerusalem political establishment. Given the precarious character of the Israelite community, however, in both monarchy and in exilic/postexilic settings, this enterprise of cult should not be dismissed as crass ideology. Israel was always at risk for its Yahwistic commitment and self-understanding, always tempted to compromise, always seduced to alternatives, always ready to doubt its own testimony. I suggest that the rich, artistic dimension of this Mosaic-Aaronide apparatus was designed, canonically and narratively, to provide space and resources whereby Israel could shamelessly enact its oddity, an intensely Yahwistic oddity.[48]

In the environs of tabernacle and mercy seat, in its practice of sacrifice and offerings, Israel does not have to give account of itself or justify its existence or activity. It can in this moment be wholly itself before Yahweh, without denying either its well-being or its failure, its agony or its ecstasy. This worship is theater and play, an act of nonproductive imagination whereby practice generates reality. It is for this reason that the priestly system seems to hang in the air, unconnected and unreasonable. That is precisely its intention and its function, whereby Israel can be, for a time, distanced from the pressures of concrete context, given over only to Yahweh. And if this text is late and post-temple, as much critical opinion holds, then

---

47. For this reason an iconic dimension in temple worship is important; see Mettinger, *The Dethronement of Sabaoth*, 19–37; and *No Graven Image: Israelite Aniconism in Its Ancient Near Eastern Context* (ConBOT 42; Stockholm: Almqvist and Wiksell International, 1995).

48. On the Aaronide contribution to the fullness of cult, see Aelred Cody, *A History of Old Testament Priesthood* (AnBib 35; Rome: Pontifical Biblical Institute, 1969), especially 156–74; Haran, *Temples and Temple-Service*, 84–111; and Nelson, *Raising Up a Faithful Priest*, 1–15.

the text itself, without temple, stands as an invitation to imagination of a completely alternative existence, on grounds that expect nothing from its environment and concede nothing to that environment.

In so doing, of course, Israel ran the risk of withdrawal into irrelevance. That risk, I suggest, could be undertaken in order to combat the greater risk of compromise and of forfeiting its Yahwistic oddness. For this priestly sensibility, an imagined alternative life with Yahweh has a quality of reality, more real than anything "out there." This is why the authorization for this enterprise of worship did not occur amid the artistry of the temple or in the postexilic reconstruction, determined as it was. The authorization occurred *on the mountain*, prior to Israel's "historical existence," where such authorization has privilege and priority not granted amid historical pressures. As we shall see subsequently, there are temptations in such a transcendental reserve. Both prophets and kings sought to respond to those temptations, in which this flight of daring, faithful imagination became, all too easily, a chance for self-indulgence.

Twin Jerusalem Trajectories

As the Mosaic pattern anticipated what became the Solomonic temple, so belated cultic traditions remembered the Solomonic temple and continued to draw strength and sustenance from it. The temple itself, in the period of high monarchic well-being and security, could go far toward concretizing the Real Presence in the practice of the sanctuary. In such unabashed well-being as the monarchy seemed to assure, uncritical thought could affirm in innocence, "Yahweh is really here." As a foil for his study of exilic notions of presence, Tryggve Mettinger has summarized the evidence for the notion that the temple of Solomon practiced and claimed an unqualified presence for Yahweh. This is evident, for example, in the dedicatory anthem of 1 Kgs 8:12-13:

> The Lord has said that he would dwell in thick darkness.
> I have built you an exalted house,
> a place for you to dwell in forever.[49]

Moreover, Mettinger proposes that it is the visual presentation of carved cherubim that yields the formula of presence, "[He] who is enthroned on the cherubim" (1 Sam 4:4; 2 Sam 6:2 [1 Chr 13:6]; 2 Kgs 19:15 [Isa 37:16]; Pss 80:2; 99:1).[50] The actual initiation of this claim in the temple is in 1 Kgs 6:23-28:

> In the inner sanctuary he made two cherubim of olivewood, each ten cubits high. Five cubits was the length of one wing of the cherub, and five cubits the length of the other wing of the cherub; it was ten cubits from the tip

---

49. See Mettinger, *The Dethronement of Sabaoth*, 29–32, and his comment on Ps 11:4, Jer 25:30, Joel 4:16, and Amos 1:2.

50. Ibid., 23–24.

of one wing to the tip of the other. The other cherub also measured ten cubits; both cherubim had the same measure and the same form. The height of one cherub was ten cubits, and so was that of the other cherub. He put the cherubim in the innermost part of the house; the wings of the cherubim were spread out so that a wing of one was touching the one wall, and a wing of the other cherub was touching the other wall; their other wings toward the center of the house were touching wing to wing. He also overlaid the cherubim with gold.

What interests us beyond the artistry, however, is the theology of Real Presence that is attached to the artistic work. The temple of Solomon did indeed mediate the Real Presence of Yahweh in quite palpable form.

The destruction of the temple in 587 b.c.e. created an enormous crisis, both because the temple and its liturgy were abandoned and because displaced persons no longer had access to whatever it was that continued in Jerusalem.[51] Jerusalem continued to be looked to, remembered, and cherished (cf. Ps 137:5-6). The liturgic power of Jerusalem in an exilic situation, however, had to be radically reformulated to meet new needs. A way had to be found to affirm that the Yahweh known to be available in the temple was available elsewhere and had freedom from the temple so as not to be a victim of its destruction. Scholarship now concludes that Israel found two ways to formulate "presence" that could no longer be flatly in Jerusalem.[52] Both of these efforts, by the Priestly tradition and the Deuteronomists, continue to appeal to the high temple tradition of presence, but they do so in a way that permitted interpretive, liturgical maneuverability.[53]

Priestly Theology of Glory

The Priestly adjustment to new circumstance was to articulate a "theology of glory."[54] "Glory" is way of speaking about Yahweh's powerful, sovereign, transcendent presence, without making a claim that is flat, one-dimensional, or crassly material. This theology shows up in the Priestly materials that we have already considered as Mosaic "anticipation." Moses' work of construction of the tabernacle—a mobile temple—is completed when the tabernacle is found to be an adequate place for the glory of Yahweh:

---

51. Some worship apparently did continue on the site of the destroyed temple; see Jer 41:5.

52. Given this neat polarity, it is not easy to place the Chronicler in relation to the Deuteronomic and Priestly traditions, though he seems to have most in common with the Deuteronomist. I have not taken up the Chronicler, because his work follows in general the more readily discerned practices of these two traditions.

53. Gerhard von Rad, *Studies in Deuteronomy* (SBT 9; London: SCM Press, 1953) 37–44, had already determined these categories, which have guided subsequent scholarship. He expanded his discussion of them in *Old Testament Theology*, 1:69–84. See also Mettinger, *The Dethronement of Sabaoth*, 38–134.

54. See my discussion of glory as an attribute of Yahweh, pp. 283–87. It is not necessary to link this notion of cultic glory to the negative connotations that Luther assigned to a "theology of glory," for it has been qualified and mitigated in the tradition in important ways. It has, however, been treated in the same negative way by some zealously Protestant scholars, e.g., Ludwig Koehler.

Then the cloud covered the tent of meeting, and the glory of the Lord filled the tabernacle. Moses was not able to enter the tent of meeting because the cloud settled upon it, and the glory of the Lord filled the tabernacle. (Exod 40:34-35)

The same theology of glory is structurally crucial to the Book of Ezekiel, a companion piece to Priestly theology.[55] In Ezekiel 8–10 the temple of Jerusalem is characterized as a place of affrontive blasphemy and idolatry where Yahweh, in holiness, cannot possibly remain. As a result, in Ezek 10:15-22 the "glory of Yahweh" leaves the temple, to fly off to be in the midst of the Babylonian exiles. This strategy in the tradition of Ezekiel seems both to assert the Yahwistic abandonment of failed Jerusalem and to articulate Yahweh as mobile and willing to be in exile with the exiles. After due purgation of the temple, we are told in Ezek 43:1-5 that the glory of Yahweh returned to the temple. By this narrative in two parts, the progress of Yahweh's glory out of Jerusalem and back to Jerusalem is characterized. The tradition of Ezekiel values the temple, but also breaks the one-to-one linkage between Yahweh and temple that had been featured in high temple theology. The glory of Yahweh, Yahweh's sovereign presence, may settle in the temple, but it is more than and other than the temple, and may indeed be seen and available elsewhere than in the temple (cf. Exod 16:7, 10).

Deuteronomic Theology of Name

In parallel fashion, the Deuteronomic tradition develops a theology of presence, "name theology," which adjusts to the temple crisis.[56] It is the wont of the Deuteronomic tradition, like the Priestly tradition, to assign great value to the temple but to hedge the totalizing linkage of temple and Yahweh that was in vogue in better times. It makes this interpretive move by asserting that Yahweh's "name" (which in some sense is Yahweh's self) is there, but Yahweh's full self is elsewhere, in heaven, beyond the ideological arrangements of Israel.

Already in the pageant of temple dedication, immediately after the high claim of the anthem of 1 Kgs 8:12-13, Deuteronomic theologians put us on notice that temple ideology claims too much:

But will God indeed dwell on the earth? Even heaven and the highest heaven cannot contain you, much less this house that I have built! Regard your servant's prayer and his plea, O Lord my God, heeding the cry and the prayer that your servant prays to you today; that your eyes may be open night and day toward this house, this place of which you said, "My name shall be there," that you may heed the prayer that your servant prays toward this place.

---

55. See Mettinger, *The Dethronement of Sabaoth*, 97–111; and Jon Levenson, *Theology of the Program of Restoration of Ezekiel 40–48* (HSM 10; Missoula, Mont.: Scholars Press, 1976).

56. See von Rad, *Studies in Deuteronomy*, 37–44; Mettinger, *The Dethronement of Sabaoth*, 38–79; S. Dean McBride, "The Deuteronomic Name Theology," Ph.D. diss., Harvard University, 1969; and Patrick D. Miller, *Deuteronomy* (Interpretation; Louisville: John Knox, 1990) 129–33.

Hear the plea of your servant and of your people Israel when they pray toward this place; O hear in heaven your dwelling place; heed and forgive.
(1 Kgs 8:27-30)

Thus, (a) Yahweh's name is in the temple, (b) Yahweh is in heaven, but (c) Yahweh in heaven attends constantly to the temple. Therefore prayers addressed to the
temple are heard in heaven and answered. Even with this qualification, the temple
is still a crucial and indispensable mode of mediation.

It is enough, for our purposes, that the Priestly theology of glory and the
Deuteronomic theology of name are imaginative and, we may believe, successful
strategies of presence, which serve both to meet the needs of non-Jerusalem Jewish
exiles and to extricate Yahweh from a failed temple system.

Tension between Priestly and Deuteronomic Strategies

We may make two other observations concerning these two strategies of presence
for exiles. First, these two strategies, Priestly and Deuteronomic, are in important tension with each other. The Priestly trajectory is what one might call "high
church," and leads in a visual, artistic direction that is open to and ready to receive many cultural expressions. The Deuteronomic trajectory, by contrast, is "low
church," depending primarily on utterances, and issues in a "theology of the word"
as is evident in "sermons" in the Deuteronomic history, and it tends in a separatist
direction.

While any reader of the Old Testament may prefer one of these exilic theologies
of presence to the other, it is important that *the canonizing process retained both,
assigned both to Moses, and refused to choose between them.*[57] The compromise is a
recognition that, in the end, "presence" is problematic, and any single settlement
is likely to be partial and need an (ecumenical) correction. Mediation through cult
thus requires continual and renewed adjudication. In order that a student of Old
Testament theology may continue to extrapolate out of this polarity, I suggest three
pairs of notions that derive from these traditions:

Priestly theology:	*Deuteronomic theology:*
a hermeneutics of retrieval	a hermeneutics of suspicion[58]
manifestation	proclamation[59]
sacrament	word

---

57. See Rainer Albertz, *A History of Israelite Religion in the Old Testament Period 2: From the Exiles
to the Maccabees* (Louisville: Westminster/John Knox, 1994) 387–99 and passim.

58. The categories are from Paul Ricoeur, *Freud and Philosophy: An Essay on Interpretation* (New
Haven: Yale University Press, 1970), and other works of his, and have been taken up especially by
David Tracy, *The Analogical Imagination: Christian Theology and the Culture of Pluralism* (New York:
Crossroad, 1981) 190 n. 21, 373, and passim.

59. On this pair of terms, see Tracy, *The Analogical Imagination*, 376–404, in which he follows
Ricoeur.

It is clear that non-ecumenical or pre-ecumenical Christianity has not done well at maintaining the fruitful and essential tension that is a key insistence of Israel's canon.

Relationship of Person and Place

Second, the linkage of Yahweh to the temple and the problematic of an adequate formulation of that relationship are somewhat parallel to the problematic of an adequate Christian articulation of the relation of Jesus to Yahweh. That is, in the Christian doctrine of the Trinity it is crucial to articulate both the "oneness" of Jesus with "the Father," and the differentiation between the two. Only the maintenance of both affirmations makes possible the claim of catholic Christianity concerning salvation in Jesus.

Mutatis mutandis, it was exceedingly important in Israel's testimony to articulate with some precision the relationship between Yahweh and the temple in Jerusalem. The mythic claims that were present in the Jerusalem temple, surely rooted in non-Mosaic, pre-Mosaic religion, articulated a "high" notion of presence, in which the place of the temple seems almost to be identified with the personal presence of Yahweh; that is, to be in the place assured personal communion. This high claim, no doubt energized by the ideological needs of the monarchy, made the salvific gift of Yahweh palpably present and provided enough religious certitude for the claims of the establishment. This palpable presence is expressed through use of the verb *yšb*, which claims much more than the verb *škn*, in terms of permanent residence (cf. 1 Kgs 8:12-13), and in the claim to "behold God," who sits "enthroned above the cherubim." Yahweh is really there in full splendor!

Yet there was a danger in full identification of person with place, for in such an enormously reassuring articulation, the peculiar freedom, fidelity, and sovereignty of Yahweh tended to disappear into the sacerdotal woodwork. It is clear, moreover, that Israel is fully aware of this problematic, so clearly voiced in 1 Kgs 8:27-30, immediately after the high claim of 1 Kgs 8:12-13. There are two reasons why Yahweh must not be completely identified with the temple.

The first reason is that the destruction of the temple in 587 B.C.E. could not be understood in Israel as implying the corollary destruction of Yahweh. Yahweh, moreover, must continue to be present to exiles, who had no access to Jerusalem and who required a God more practically available in the Diaspora. But the fundamental reason for the ultimate refusal of such an identification of person and place is not pastoral and practical, but theological. It pertains to the very character of Yahweh, as given elsewhere and pervasively in Israel's testimony, a matter voiced by Nathan in his resistance to David's intention to build a temple:

> Are you the one to build me a house to live in? I have not lived in a house since the day I brought up the people of Israel from Egypt to this day, but I have been moving about in a tent and a tabernacle. Wherever I have moved about among all the people of Israel, did I ever speak a word with any of the

tribal leaders of Israel, whom I commanded to shepherd my people Israel, saying, "Why have you not built me a house of cedar?" (2 Sam 7:5-7)

Yahweh is a roving, moving, free God who will not be hemmed in or domesticated by a temple, even if the temple traditions on occasion tried to contain Yahweh. Indeed the cultus offers nothing that is essential to Yahweh, who has no need to await Israel's attention:

> I will not accept a bull from your house,
> or goats from your folds.
> For every wild animal of the forest is mine,
> the cattle on a thousand hills.
> I know all the birds of the air,
> and all that moves in the field is mine.
> If I were hungry, I would not tell you,
> for the world and all that is in it is mine.
> Do I eat the flesh of bulls,
> or drink the blood of goats?
> Offer to God a sacrifice of thanksgiving,
> and pay your vows to the Most High.
> Call on me in the day of trouble;
> I will deliver you, and you shall glorify me. (Ps 50:9-15)

The relationship between Yahweh and Israel, when Yahweh's awesome holiness is voiced, is such that Yahweh is self-sufficient and Israel is needful and can call on Yahweh "in the day of trouble." The sovereign character of Yahweh refuses any relaxation of this dynamic or any temptation to invert the relationship. This reality of Yahweh places a severe check on cultic claims that are overstated or practiced uncritically.

So Israel's sacerdotal traditions must continue to trouble over and adjudicate the delicacy of the matter of cultic presence. Yahweh must be in the temple, if Israel is to find wholeness and assurance there. Yahweh must not be bound to the temple, if Yahweh's true holiness is to be fully recognized. The array of different testimonies on this point of "Real Presence" indicates that in different circumstances Israel experienced, practiced, and articulated Real Presence in many ways. Presence too closely claimed for the temple belittles Yahweh's true character, but presence too leanly affirmed leaves Israel excessively exposed. Therefore no single, simple articulation of presence will suffice. The canonical testimony of Israel provides ample evidence for both a "catholic" sacramentalism and a "protestant" protest against a controlled, controlling sacramentalism.

Presence as Gift and Problem

The claim for Yahweh as Real Presence in the temple was endlessly problematic for Israel. On the one hand, Yahweh may exercise freedom and be absent from the temple. This crisis is exhibited in the psalms of complaint, wherein Israel experiences Yahweh's absence and muteness. On the other hand, the sovereign freedom of Yahweh can be collapsed into the routinization of the temple, so that Yahweh's true character is forfeited in the taken-for-granted sacramental practices of the temple. This is an acute problem for Israel, for Israel did not want to deny that the temple was the place of Yahweh's intense presence from which Israel might properly expect succor. At the same time, however, exploitation and domestication of Yahweh evoked in Israel reform and protest that sought to reorder the cult in ways congruent with Yahweh's intention, as it is given in Israel's testimony.

Royal Reform of Temple

The reform of the temple was a proper responsibility of kings in Jerusalem, who were the overseers (as well as beneficiaries) of the temple. Indeed, it was an important act of piety for the king to attend to the temple.[60] The account of the royal history of Israel in the Chronicles features, as its centerpiece, the commitment of David as the progenitor of the temple (1 Chr 21:18–26:32; 28:1–29:22) and Solomon as its great builder and benefactor (2 Chronicles 2–7).

The royal histories given us by both the Deuteronomist and the Chronicler report royal efforts at temple reform, but we cannot be sure about the historical reliability of the reports. What we can be sure of is that Israel's theological testimony regarded temple reform as crucial for authentic Yahwism and held kings accountable for that reform. The narratives report modest or compromised reforms on the part of Asa (1 Kgs 15:11-15), Jehoshaphat (1 Kgs 22:43, 46), Azariah (2 Kgs 15:3-4), and Jotham (2 Kgs 15:34-35; 2 Chr 27:2).

It is, however, principally in the reigns of Hezekiah (2 Kgs 18:3-4, 20:3; 2 Chronicles 29–31) and Josiah (2 Kgs 23:4-25; 2 Chr 34:29–35:19) that reform appears to have been extensive and serious. Reform under these latter two kings may have had a powerful political motivation as an assertion of independence from Assyrian control, but that is not how the matter is reported in the narrative testimonies. In the case of the two principal royal reformers, the negative concern is to remove from the temple those signs and symbols that violate exclusive loyalty to Yahweh (cf. 2 Kgs 18:4-5). The positive work of reform is to institute or reinstate practices that articulate and enact singular loyalty to Yahweh, with particular reference to the Passover. It is no longer clear, at our distance, why some symbols and actions were taken to be for or against true Yahwism, but there is no doubt that the internal logic of reform was unambiguous.

The second important achievement of these royal reforms is that they appear to have generated important testimonial literature. That literature may have been ideologically motivated in the royal interest and perhaps at some point functioned as

---

60. On the linkage of king and temple in centrist ideology, see John M. Lundquist, "What Is a Temple? A Preliminary Typology," *The Quest for the Kingdom of God: Studies in Honor of George E. Mendenhall* (ed. H. B. Huffmon et al.; Winona Lake, Ind.: Eisenbrauns, 1983) 205–19.

royal propaganda. As the literature became canon, it stands nonetheless as enduring testimony in Israel and to Israel that "right worship" is crucial to Israel. Thus in both the Deuteronomic history and in the Chronicler, Hezekiah and Josiah receive important coverage (2 Kings 18–20; 22:1–23:30; 2 Chronicles 29–32; 34–35). Moreover, it is widely assumed that some form of the Book of Deuteronomy is linked to Josiah's reform. Menahem Haran, moreover, has proposed that some form of the Priestly material is linked to the reform of Hezekiah, but such an early dating of the material is against the current scholarly consensus.[61] In any case, attentiveness to right worship, to the faithful management of public symbols, is a primary royal responsibility.

It is clear that the royal reforms, perhaps undertaken with mixed motives, were only marginally successful. Indeed, it may be that "royal reform" is something of an oxymoron, for the reforming kings also depend on the maintenance of the sacramental system to legitimate their power. Therefore, we turn from the royal reforms to the much harsher prophetic polemics against the cult.

Prophetic Polemics against Cult

It is everywhere evident that the prophets who come to dominate the canon articulate a broad and shrill polemic against the sanctuary. Among the more familiar and obvious texts voicing such a polemic are the following:

> What to me is the multitude of your sacrifices?
> says the Lord;
> I have had enough of burnt offerings of rams
> and the fat of fed beasts;
> I do not delight in the blood of bulls,
> or of lambs, or of goats.
> When you come to appear before me,
> who asked this from your hand?
> Trample my courts no more;
> bringing offerings is futile;
> incense is an abomination to me.
> New moon and sabbath and calling of convocation—
> I cannot endure solemn assemblies with iniquity.
> Your new moons and your appointed festivals
> my soul hates;
> they have become a burden to me,
> I am weary of bearing them.
> When you stretch out your hands,
> I will hide my eyes from you;
> even though you make many prayers,

---

61. Haran, "The Centralizations of the Cult," *Temples and Temple-Service,* 132–48.

I will not listen;
your hands are full of blood. (Isa 1:11-15)

Come to Bethel—and transgress;
to Gilgal—and multiply transgression;
bring your sacrifices every morning,
your tithes every three days;
bring a thank offering of leavened bread,
and proclaim freewill offerings,
publish them;
for so you love to do, O people of Israel!
says the Lord God. (Amos 4:4-5; cf. Hos 6:6; Jer 7:4, 8-11; Mic 6:6-8;
    Isa 58:2-4)

In the critique of the prophets, the cult has become a place of self-indulgence and satiation. Yahweh has become a function of a religious enterprise that is manipulative and self-satisfying, but that has completely forfeited any reference to the sovereign God of the core testimony. Whereas the cult was authorized to be a vehicle for the unlikely practice of communion with Yahweh, it has now become a place where the reality of Yahweh, in Yahweh's true character, is almost completely disregarded and forfeited.

A great deal of scholarly energy has gone into the question of whether these prophetic utterances oppose cult in principle, or oppose cult only where it is abusive and denies the reality of Yahweh.[62] That scholarly conversation in the past was conducted in a context of extreme Protestant polemics against liturgical practice; this is not the way the question of criticism of cult might now be put. In our present understandings, it is commonly judged that the prophets are concerned with the gross abuses in the cult and would not have entertained the notion of abolishing the cult.

What seems to be important in these prophetic polemics is that the cult should be a witness to and embodiment of the practice of communion with Yahweh, in Yahweh's true character as sovereign and merciful. It is no longer credible to juxtapose in an easy way "ethics" and "cult," as a simpler Protestant critique might have done, for it is evident in the contemporary world, as in the ancient world, that *a regularized, stylized practice of symbolization is indispensable for the sustenance of intentional ethical practice.* Beyond its instrumental use as a necessary support for ethical intentionality, moreover, the cult is a place in which Israel may indeed be in the presence of the Holy One.

There is no evidence that the prophets opposed public worship itself, when that worship is focused on the oddness of the true God of Israel. It is evident that in Israel's worship, which we may take as "rightly construed" according to Israel's own

---

62. The most extreme statement of dismissal, already cited, is that of Ludwig Koehler. See Amos 5:25, Jer 7:22, for hints that some in Israel regarded sacrifice, in principle, as an aberration in Israel.

testimony, Israel engaged the great memories of its core testimony, in which the God of Israel's most elemental testimony is taken with definitional seriousness in the present. That core testimony includes both Yahweh as the One who intrudes into Israel's public experience in dramatic ways, and Yahweh as the One who sanctions and maintains Israel's life-giving home of creation.[63] It is most plausible that the prophetic polemic is an insistence that Israel's worship should, in every season, be engaged with this God.

---

63. Both Walter Harrelson, *From Fertility Cult to Worship* (Garden City, N.Y.: Doubleday, 1969) 81–99, and Anderson, *Creation versus Chaos*, 78–109, include creation and its "practice" as accepted and crucial aspects of Israel's worship.

TWENTY-FOUR

The Sage as Mediator

PERHAPS THE MOST important matter to notice about "the sage" as a mediator of Yahweh is that the sage is included at all along with Torah, king, prophet, and cult.[1] This inclusion represents an important departure from the primary categories of dominant twentieth-century Old Testament theology, a departure made possible especially by the scholarship of the 1960s and 1970s, which moved beyond the singular focus on historical deeds as the data of Israel's Yahwism.[2] That scholarship, especially led by Gerhard von Rad, Roland Murphy, James Crenshaw, and Norman Whybray, suggested a mode of theological reflection and articulation in ancient Israel that was parallel or alternative to that of historical deeds.[3]

A Scholarly Consensus

The outcome of this research can now be regarded as something of a consensus among scholars, summarized in six points:

(a) Wisdom theology is theology reflecting on creation, its requirements, orders, and gifts.[4]

---

1. "Sage" is increasingly used as an umbrella term for wisdom teachers and scribes. Cf., e.g., Leo G. Perdue and John G. Gammie, eds., *The Sage in Israel and the Ancient Near East* (Winona Lake, Ind.: Eisenbrauns, 1990); and Joseph Blenkinsopp, *Sage, Priest, Prophet: Religious and Intellectual Leadership in Ancient Israel* (Louisville: Westminster/John Knox, 1995) 9–65. I suppose part of the reason for the usage is to avoid the gender-specific term "wise man." See also Rodney R. Hutton, *Charisma and Authority in Israelite Society* (Minneapolis: Fortress Press, 1994) 172–205; and Lester L. Grabbe, *Priests, Prophets, Diviners, and Sages: A Socio-historical Study of Religious Specialists in Ancient Israel* (Valley Forge, Pa.: Trinity Press International, 1995) 152–80.

2. On this crucial shift in scholarship, influenced especially by Claus Westermann, see Westermann, "Creation and History in the Old Testament," *The Gospel and Human Destiny* (ed. Vilmos Vajta; Minneapolis: Augsburg Publishing House, 1971) 11–38, in response to Gerhard von Rad; and Frank M. Cross, *Canaanite Myth and Hebrew Epic: Essays in the History of the Religion of Israel* (Cambridge: Harvard University Press, 1973), in response to G. Ernest Wright. See also Leo G. Perdue, *The Collapse of History: Reconstructing Old Testament Theology* (OBT; Minneapolis: Fortress Press, 1994) 113–50; and Walter Brueggemann, "A Shifting Paradigm: From 'Mighty Deeds' to 'Horizon,'" *The Papers of the Henry Luce III Fellows in Theology* (ed. Gary Gilbert; Atlanta: Scholars Press, 1996) 7–47; and "The Loss and Recovery of Creation in Old Testament Theology" *TToday* 53 (1996) 177–90. See chap. 9, n. 10 for this literature.

3. Most recently, see a compendium of the important work of James L. Crenshaw, *Urgent Advice and Probing Questions: Collected Writings on Old Testament Wisdom* (Macon, Ga.: Mercer University Press, 1995).

4. The programmatic statement is that of Walther Zimmerli, "Wisdom thinks resolutely within the framework of a theology of creation," in "The Place and Limit of the Wisdom Framework of the

(b) The data for such theology is lived experience that is not, for the most part, overridden by imposed interpretive categories or constructs. Thus wisdom teachers stay close to the enigmatic quality of experience.

(c) Experience is understood and seen to have a reliability, regularity, and coherence, so that one may make generalizing observations that can be sustained across a richness of concrete experience.

(d) The reliability, regularity, and coherence of lived experience has an unaccommodating ethical dimension, so that certain kinds of conduct produce beneficial outcomes and other kinds of conduct have negative consequences. The linkage of deed and consequence is intrinsic to the shape of created reality and cannot be violated.[5]

(e) The valuing of lived experience as a coherence of ethical requirement and ethical assurance is seen to be something like "natural theology"; that is, it is theology that discloses to serious discernment something of the hidden character and underpinnings of all of reality.[6] Thus the wisdom teachers do not rely for insight on prophetic utterance or decrees from Sinai that explicitly claim to be revelatory, but believe that what is given as "true" arises in lived experience rightly (wisely) discerned.

(f) As "natural theology," this deposit of sustained reflection is indeed revelatory: it reveals and discloses the God who creates, orders, and sustains reality. Thus "natural theology" as revelation does indeed mediate Yahweh, who is seen to be the generous, demanding guarantor of a viable life-order that can be trusted and counted on, but which cannot be lightly violated. The wisdom teachers, for the most part, do not speak directly about God, but make inferences and invite inferences about God from experience discerned theologically.

Our purpose here, however, is not to explicate wisdom theology, but to consider the embodiments of wisdom in regularized social, institutional practice.[7] Here we are largely in an area of speculation, because firm evidence is very thin.[8] We necessarily proceed by inference and must be cautious in not claiming too much. Thus my comments here can at most reflect the general, provisional consensus of scholarship. What is most important for us, as we consider sages as mediators, is that there were indeed actual agents of wisdom who "talked the talk" of this theology, who had regular, socially accepted occasions for such utterance, and who were ac-

---

Old Testament Theology," *SJT* 17 (1964) 148. See, more generally, Perdue and Gammie, *The Sage in Israel*; Perdue, *The Collapse of History*; and John Day et al., eds., *Wisdom in Ancient Israel: Essays in Honour of J. A. Emerton* (Cambridge: Cambridge University Press, 1995).

5. The classic statement is that of Klaus Koch, "Gibt es ein Vergeltsdogma im Alten Testaments?" *ZTK* 52 (1955) 1–42. See an English translation in *Theodicy in the Old Testament* (ed. James L. Crenshaw; Philadelphia: Fortress Press, 1983) 57–87.

6. See especially James Barr, *Biblical Faith and Natural Theology: The Gifford Lectures for 1991* (Oxford: Clarendon Press, 1993).

7. See my discussion of wisdom theology as an element of countertestimony, pp. 334–35, under the rubric of "The Hidden Rule of Yahweh."

8. See especially the caution expressed by Stuart Weeks, *Early Israelite Wisdom* (Oxford: Clarendon Press, 1994).

cepted as authoritative in such utterance, albeit an authoritativeness congruent with the style utilized and the epistemology advocated. There were those who made Yahweh available through utterance as the reliable, generous, demanding orderer of a viable life-world.

Contexts and Social Locations for Wisdom

It has become conventional among scholars to suggest three plausible arenas in which the sages worked in a sustained way to assure that Israel lived in a world of Yahwism and not some other world. The first widely accepted social circle for this mediation is the clan or family.[9]

Role of the Family

This accent in sapiential instruction is especially emphasized by Erhard Gerstenberger and is reflected in "family sayings" that turn up frequently in the wisdom books of the Old Testament, especially in Proverbs.[10] The wisdom teacher speaks as a parent to a child, thus "listen, my son." Carole Fontaine has rightly urged that mothers as well as fathers functioned in this way. The family or clan is, among other things, a decisive socializing agent, which constructs a world of limit and choice, of symbol and imagination, in which the child may safely live. Much of the socialization is done through direct imperative, but some of it is done, especially in a folk society, by oft-repeated sayings that make linkages that become accepted givens. The givens of this mediation, which provide for the child a plausibility structure, concern both the buoyancy of Yahweh's creation and the severe limitations against destructive behavior.

Gerstenberger has gone so far as to suggest that it is from the expectations and prohibitions of the clan leader that Israel receives the imperative form "thou shalt not," subsequently sounding at Sinai from the mouth of Yahweh. Such an imperative is first issued to a child in the family unit, warning the child by unquestioned authority about dangers of unacceptable behavior. Gerstenberger cites as a principal example the prohibitions embraced by the Rechabites, a highly disciplined religious group who followed the disciplines of "our ancestor":[11]

> We will drink no wine, for our ancestor Jonadab son of Rechab commanded us, "You shall never drink wine, neither you nor your children; nor shall you ever build a house, or sow seed; nor shall you plant a vineyard, or even own one; but you shall live in tents all your days, that you may live many days in the land where you reside." We have obeyed the charge of our ancestor

---

9. See Erhard Gerstenberger, *Wesen und Herkunft des apodiktischen Rechts* (WMANT 20; Neukirchen-Vluyn: Neukirchener Verlag, 1965). But notice as well the caution of Carole R. Fontaine, "The Sage in Family and Tribe," *The Sage in Israel*, 155–64.

10. The accent on the clan in general as a crucial unit for Israel's faith is urged by Erhard Gerstenberger and Rainer Albertz; see chap. 23, n. 35.

11. Gerstenberger, *Wesen und Herkunft*, 110–17.

Jonadab son of Rechab in all that he commanded us, to drink no wine all our days, ourselves, our wives, our sons, or our daughters, and not to build houses to live in. We have no vineyard or field or seed; but we have lived in tents, and have obeyed and done all that our ancestor Jonadab commanded us. (Jer 35:6-10)

Thus it is possible to accept the proposal that the family, as a socializer at a very practical level, inculcates a Yahwistic horizon into the family.

This work of parental authority, instruction, and nurture, surely to be understood here as a multigenerational matter in an extended family, is not unlike what has in old-fashioned religious terminology been phrased "the nurture and admonition of the Lord." In such family socialization, the "nurture and admonition" is likely to be a mixed matter of high Yahwistic faith, with a large measure of common sense and some elements of family values, hopes, fears, and biases.[12] All of these together constitute a way in which the family proceeds with intentionality to keep its life-world intact, functioning, and authoritative into the next generation.

One of the terms that expresses this enterprise of nurture, admonition, and socialization is *mûsar*.[13] We may notice in this regard two sayings that reflect a commitment to such nurture, admonition, and socialization:

Those who spare the rod hate their children,
but those who love them are diligent to discipline (*mûsar*) them.
(Prov 13:24)

Folly is bound up in the heart of a boy,
but the rod of discipline (*mûsar*) drives it far away. (Prov 22:15,
cf. 23:13)

The "rod of discipline" (*mûsar*) here is not be to be understood as an instrument of abuse. It is, rather, an instrument of guidance and protection, as the term *rod* is used in Ps 23:4 with reference to the guidance and protection a shepherd gives to sheep. Israel does not flinch from nurture of a certain kind, which it accepted as a primary responsibility. That nurture, in the mode of wisdom, however, is not characteristically direct and coercive; it is inviting and playful, as much so as the "family sayings" that make connections but draw no direct imperatives or conclusions. Such nurture and admonition induct the young person into the life-world of the family, to piece together in imaginative ways this life-world from the elements given by the parental generation.

---

12. The phrase "nurture and admonition" recalls to me the baptismal formula of my nurturing church. While the "nurture and admonition" intended in that social location was intentional and authoritative, it contained almost none of the mean-spirited coercion and tone of shrillness current in the yearning for "family values." We are led by the text to conclude that the same lack of such coercive shrillness is characteristically the case in ancient Israel.

13. On the term, see Hans-Joachim Kraus, "Geschichte also Erziehung," *Probleme Biblischer Theologie* (ed. Hans-Walter Wolff; Munich: Chr. Kaiser Verlag, 1971) 167–68. See James L. Crenshaw, "Education in Ancient Israel," *JBL* 104 (1985) 601–15.

The Role of the School

A second arena for sapiential mediation is the school.[14] The evidence for schools in ancient Israel is not unambiguous and is largely inferential. Nonetheless, it is cogent, given the practical and ideological needs of the royal-urban establishment, to suppose that wisdom prospered under royal patronage, perhaps under Solomon, more likely in the time of Hezekiah. Such schools, as we here assume (as do many scholars), were surely for the privileged class, which was educated for vocations in the state and in the economy. As Israel moved out of a tribal, segmented society and its public life became more complex, specialized, and stratified, possession of skills of speech and the capacity to manipulate symbols must have been highly prized. It does not surprise us if such nurture and instruction included reference to courtly manner, skill in speech, and the prudential practices that might advance one in the purview of the powerful. Indeed, the management of power must have been important.[15] What is of more interest to us is that such nurture in schools was never fully secular, and surely contained an important ingredient of the Yahwism noted above.[16] Thus the hidden coherence of the world as the creation of Yahweh is an important check on political power reduced to technical manipulation.

The Royal Court

The third context in which wisdom was, in all probability, practiced as a way of keeping Yahweh available to Israel was in the royal court.[17] Kings in Israel had advisors and counselors who were able to bring larger perspective to policy issues that needed to be decided. Hushai and Ahithophel in the court of David are clear examples, and the narratives of Joseph and Daniel attest to Israel's awareness of this royal function, even if these cases concern foreign courts.[18] Norman Whybray has suggested that there was an intellectual tradition of learned, skilled persons in ancient Israel who operated in a variety of ways throughout society, in order to shape learning and also to impinge upon public policy formation and implementation.

---

14. See Andre Lemaire, "The Sage in School and in Temple," *The Sage in Israel*, 165–81, and his full documentation. Note especially the work by H. J. Hermisson, which Lemaire cites in n. 6. See G. I. Davies, "Were There Schools in Ancient Israel?" *Wisdom in Ancient Israel: Essays in Honour of J. A. Emerton*, 199–211.

15. See E. W. Heaton, *Solomon's New Men: The Emergence of Ancient Israel as a National State* (London: Thames and Hudson, 1974); and *The School Tradition of the Old Testament: The Bampton Lectures for 1994* (Oxford: Oxford University Press, 1994). George Mendenhall (see n. 21 below) also sees the wise as political players. He views them, however, much more negatively.

16. This is against the assumptions of William McKane in his important commentary, *Proverbs: A New Approach* (OTL; London: SCM Press, 1970), but it represents what is surely a scholarly consensus.

17. See Walter Brueggemann, "The Social Significance of Solomon as a Patron of Wisdom," *The Sage in Israel*, 117–32; and R. N. Whybray, "The Sage in the Israelite Royal Court," *The Sage in Israel*, 133–39.

18. The case of Hushai and Ahithophel is the classic example in the Old Testament, on which see William McKane, "Old Wisdom and the Case of Ahithophel," *Prophets and Wise Men* (SBT 44; Naperville, Ill.: Alec R. Allenson, 1965) 13–62. On the wise of Israel in foreign courts, see W. Lee Humphreys, "A Life-Style for Diaspora: A Study of the Tales of Esther and Daniel," *JBL* 92 (1973) 211–23; and Daniel L. Smith, *The Religion of the Landless: The Social Context of the Babylonian Exile* (Bloomington, Ind.: Meyer Stone, 1989). Both Humphreys and Smith consider not primarily historical questions, but strategies for historical circumstance as undertaken in literary form.

This tradition of publicly oriented wisdom included many persons acknowledged to be wise. According to Whybray, however, they do not constitute any special class in society.[19] Insofar as they continued to speak, think, and interpret the world according to the Yahwistic creation theology noted above, they may be reckoned as mediators of Yahweh.

"Practical Theologians"

These practitioners of wisdom—in family, school, royal court, and public life—may be regarded as "practical theologians" in two senses. First, they are practical in the ordinary meaning of utilizing great common sense. They saw how things worked and how things are inalienably related to each other. Second, they are engaged in "actual practice"; that is, they are constantly facing new experience that must not only be integrated into the deposit of learning, but must be permitted to revise the deposit of learning in light of new data. This means that their word of nurture and instruction is very much "on the run." Thus it is important to recognize that Yahweh is mediated to Israel, not only in stated, visible, credentialed, institutional operations that are most evident in Israel's testimony, but also in ad hoc ways, wherein categories of creation theology yield a great deal of insight and freedom for interpretation of Yahweh. Indeed, practical theology is theology "on the run," perhaps increasingly important in a society where credentials and recognized institutional modes of mediation claim less and less attention.

Available Distortions

Because wisdom teaching as nurture, instruction, and interpretation is ad hoc, on the run, and engaged in the daily responsibility of coping with life, it is to be expected that wisdom theology cannot be coherent and controlled in any predictable way. This means, in turn, that wisdom teaching is easily distorted, even as we have seen that the other modes of mediation of Yahweh are also open to perversion. Here we may suggest three sorts of distortion that are evident in the text.

Settled Traditionalism

Insofar as wisdom reflection is teaching designed to socialize and inculcate the young into a settled community, it is possible for wisdom instruction to settle into a kind of traditionalism that simply reiterates and repeats, without critical reflection or without attention to new, demanding experience. Such a settled traditionalism, neither wisdom teaching nor Yahwism at its best, may result from a lazy refusal to think anew. More likely, such an inclination reflects reactionary social commitments that want to resist change, even if emergent experience seems to demand it.

We may cite a prominent example in which an old, oft-repeated proverb is challenged as no longer valid:

---

19. See Norman Whybray, *The Intellectual Tradition in the Old Testament* (BZAW 135; Berlin: de Gruyter, 1974).

> What do you mean by repeating this proverb concerning the land of Israel, "The parents have eaten sour grapes, and the children's teeth are set on edge"? As I live, says the Lord God, this proverb shall no more be used by you in Israel. Know that all lives are mine: the life of the parent as well as the life of the child is mine: it is only the person who sins that shall die. (Ezek 18:2-4; cf. Jer 31:29-30)

The proverb sounds like a traditional tribal saying, asserting the solidarity of the community over generations, affirming that decisions made by one generation continue to have important impact on the next generations. The critique of the proverb in Jeremiah and Ezekiel, however, indicates that the exile has undermined the truth of the long-trusted proverb. These exilic prophets want to assert that the new generation in exile has freedom for new actions and is not fated to live in paralysis generated by decisions previously made. In order to establish that the present moment is an arena for new action and new possibility, the old proverb must be defeated; long-trusted proverbial wisdom must be overthrown.

I suspect that the crisis of such long-trusted proverbial wisdom, which is never innocent of social interest and social advantage, is characteristic of any society that is in rapid change and in which old assumptions are exposed and placed in jeopardy by new experience. Indeed, one may suggest that the acute quarrels now alive in the Western church, under assault from unprecedented secularism, are quarrels about experience and old folk wisdom that have a proximate relation to biblical faith, but in large part are long-accepted prudential wisdom. The quarrel, at least to some extent, is not about truth; it is about keeping intact a known, manageable social world.

To some extent, the world of the sages is a world of settled assertion. To some extent, however, it is at the same time a world of ongoing dispute, because "time makes ancient good uncouth." Surely there were in Israel in the exilic period continuing and vigorous proponents of the old proverb quoted in Jer 31:29 and Ezek 18:2, who remained to be convinced that the exile was a time and place of radically new possibility. The dispute of wisdom with traditionalism admits of no settlement "from on high," but only provisional settlements "from below," in experience.

Legalism

Closely linked to traditionalism is legalism, in which old linkages between deed and consequence became frozen into absolutist principle. The clearest expression of this is found in Job's friends, an artistic portrayal of what must have been a powerful opinion of pious wisdom. In this portrayal, the friends, pastorally inclined sages, are intransigent in their pious absolutism, which is inhospitable to Job's experience.[20] The friends are surely traditionalists, who in the face of protest and pain refuse to take into account any new learning from new experience.

---

20. See Rainer Albertz, "The Sage and Pious Wisdom in the Book of Job: The Friends' Perspective," *The Sage in Israel*, 243–61.

To be sure, the prose epilogue to the Book of Job is not disinterested (cf. 42:7-8). Nonetheless, the verdict rendered is startling: that the friends have evoked Yahweh's wrath, "for you have not spoken of me what is right" (42:8). Wisdom teaching is an ongoing, developing process. Therefore, to halt the process by refusing to consider new experience is not "right," for it misrepresents Yahweh and Yahweh's reality in the world. It is one thing to acknowledge that the initial deposit of wisdom has arisen from experience. It is quite another thing, with the deposit of experience firmly in hand, to acknowledge new truth—new revelation carried in new experience. Job's friends could not.

Opportunism of Professional Sages

The public, professional sage faced a temptation very different from the ethical responsibility of tribal wisdom. These sages, according to hypothesis, moved in arenas of enormous power. Here the temptation is more likely a kind of opportunism, which meant tailoring advice and counsel to one's own interest, or to the interest of one's more powerful employers. In a polemical statement, George Mendenhall has observed that the sages in ancient Israel embodied a highly skilled, highly privileged class that functioned in terms of public policy and that was closely linked to the educational system, "by which the children of the elite class of society were trained in the necessary skills that enabled them to compete in the ancient pecking order determined by the ancient states and empires."[21] In this role of specialized expertise and privileged connection, the wise might be principled advisors who "speak truth to power." But often, suggests Mendenhall, the wise were committed to the "big three of the wisdom tradition: power, wealth, and wisdom itself."[22] Mendenhall appeals especially to Jer 9:23-24 as a prime example of the values embraced by calculating wisdom, and the alternative values urged by the prophet, values that were on the horizon of wisdom tradition, but easily jettisoned in concrete cases.

To refer to such advisors who compromised principle for advance as "wise" is, in the end, ironic. But it is this irony, attached to the adjudication of power that is endlessly ambiguous, that rightly and consistently characterizes the role of such "wise." This matrix for the wise readily calls to mind the remarkable analysis of U.S. foreign policy by Walter Isaacson and Evan Thomas, *Wise Men: Six Friends and the World They Made.*[23] The study is an analysis of six U.S. foreign policy experts—Dean Acheson, Charles Bohler, Averell Harriman, George F. Kennan, Robert Lovette, and John J. McCloy, Jr.—privileged specialists who dominated and shaped U.S. foreign policy during the Cold War. The study is of interest to us—given the shrewd title of the book—because of the military-industrial and class

21. George E. Mendenhall, "The Shady Side of Wisdom: The Date and Purpose of Genesis 3," *A Light unto My Path: Old Testament Studies in Honor of Jacob M. Myers* (ed. Howard W. Bream et al.; Philadelphia: Temple University Press, 1974) 321.
22. Ibid., 330.
23. Walter Isaacson and Evan Thomas, *Wise Men: Six Friends and the World They Made* (London: Faber, 1986).

interests that came to be equated with the national interest, an equation that ultimately produced the cul-de-sac of the Vietnam war. In the end, these "wise men" were deluded by their expertise, and their common careers culminated in "A March of Folly."[24] Writing separately of McCloy, Kai Bird observes that these "experts" could not sort out their own interests from the interest of the nation.[25] Something of the same self-deception was available in the ancient world, where the wise were recruited into the service of power. Given the character of Yahweh, such delusions of human power eventuated in a mediation of Yahweh that became, on such occasions, a gross distortion.

Mediation in the Ordinariness of Life

Wisdom teaching could, in various contexts, fall into patterns of traditionalism, legalism, opportunism, and, as exemplified in Ecclesiastes, perhaps into cynicism or fatalism. For all of that, however, the wise were engaged in odd and regularly present-tense acts of mediation of Yahweh to Israel. Indeed, we have seen that every mode of mediation is subject to some abuse and distortion; but abuse and distortion do not cancel out the positive potential of wisdom teaching, as they do not cancel out any of the other mediations we have noted.

Wisdom teachers as a mode of mediation for Yahweh are peculiarly important because, unlike the other modes of mediation we have mentioned, the wisdom teachers live very close to concrete, daily reality and give to Israel a sense that Yahweh is present in, with, and under daily, lived experience. It is well known that wisdom teachers shunned the standard "historical" claims of Yahwism and did not traffic in sacerdotal traditions. They were secularists in ancient Israel, but their secular ways of discernment and speech continued to reflect on lived reality as the carrier of Yahweh in the world.[26] Thus the Book of Proverbs is a sustained reflection on life as Yahweh's ordered, coherent, ethically reliable and ethically insistent creation. The poem of Job, moreover, continues to focus on experience and refuses to transcend experience for safer interpretive categories.

Because the sages focus on the raggedness and unresolved quality of experience (which they try to tame by their rhetoric), their way of speaking about Yahweh concerns the conditions of equilibrium and the endless threat of disequilibrium.

24. For the phrase, see Barbara W. Tuchman, *The March of Folly: From Troy to Vietnam* (London: Joseph, 1984).

25. Kai Bird, *The Chairman: John J. McCloy, the Making of the American Establishment* (New York: Simon and Schuster, 1992) 663, concludes:

> As men possessing a measure of *gravitas*, McCloy and the other Establishment figures always claimed they could rise above the private interests they represented and discern the larger public good. Ultimately, this claim is not sustainable.

See also Robert S. McNamara and Brian Vandemark, *In Retrospect: The Tragedy and Lessons of Vietnam* (New York: Random House, 1995). McNamara was a "whiz kid" whose technical capacity for knowledge lacked rootage and critical reference. Even in the book it is not clear that he has been able to move beyond such a rationality of technical control.

26. This "secular" dimension is only relatively so. It might be more precise to say "worldly."

Leo Perdue has succinctly observed how wisdom is an endless adjudication of order and conflict, a dialectic that I have elsewhere termed theodic settlement and theodic crisis.[27] As concerns the character of Yahweh, the primary inclination is to portray Yahweh as the reliable guarantor of order.[28] But Yahweh is also drawn into the conflict and is seen to be a party to the disaster. In both accents, Yahweh is given in this mediation as intimately linked to lived reality, so that an experience of the world is indeed an experience of Yahweh.[29] Thus in the end, wisdom is the profound valuing of lived experience as a theological datum from which attention must not be distracted.

Derivative Trajectories of Wisdom

Wisdom teaching is situated in the real life of the community of faith and insists on reflecting on life with reference to Yahweh. It is also true, however, that in the emergence of Judaism, wisdom teaching was radically transposed with the new shaping of Israel's faith. This "afterlife" of wisdom in Judaism—that is, after the dominant forms of faith in the Old Testament—lives only at the edge of the Old Testament and largely emerges beyond the scope of the Old Testament. Nonetheless, a student of Old Testament theology must attend to these matters, because we are able to see them adumbrated in the Old Testament itself. We may identify three aspects of the new, transposed shape of wisdom teaching, as it becomes an increasingly important force in emerging Judaism.

Convergence of Torah and Wisdom

At the end of the Old Testament period, wisdom teaching came to be identified with the Torah. A recognition of this convergence is commonly assigned to Ben Sirach in the second century B.C.E., but the development itself is gradual and long-term. We might imagine that because of the cruciality of the Torah for Israel and for emerging Judaism, wisdom would surrender its character to Torah. But a case can also be made that the impact worked in the other direction, so that Torah became increasingly a sapiential enterprise.

Most broadly we can say that as scribes became increasingly authoritative teachers, the convergence of Torah and wisdom eventuated in the interpretive practices of rabbinic Judaism. By this I refer particularly to the ongoing, open-ended, never-completed process of continual reflection upon and interpretation of old traditions in light of new experience. Michael Fishbane has recognized in this development "a profound shift of religious sensibility: a deepening of religious experience *in and*

---

27. Leo G. Perdue, "Cosmology and the Social Order in the Wisdom Tradition," *The Sage in Israel*, 457–78. See Walter Brueggemann, "Theodicy in a Social Dimension," *JSOT* 33 (1985) 3–25.

28. See Lennart Bostrom, *The God of the Sages: The Portrayal of God in the Book of Proverbs* (Stockholm: Almqvist and Wiksell International, 1990).

29. Gerhard von Rad, *Wisdom in Israel* (Nashville: Abingdon Press, 1972) 74–96, 144–66.

through the Torah study."[30] Judaism now took as its "experience of God" not direct encounter, as had been proclaimed earlier, but encounter with the textual tradition. Thus Fishbane concludes: "*En route* 'from scribalism to rabbinism,' exegesis thus makes the decisive claim that it is the very means of redemption. . . . through Torah one inherits God."[31]

Judaism becomes an interpretive process, and truth—truth about God and world—is continually mediated through the disputatious challenge of different interpretations of the tradition in which God is present. As the older sages disputed in interpreting *experience*, now the dispute is characteristically in interpreting *tradition*, for in that conflictual process the shape of faith and eventually the shape of Yahweh is at issue.

This matter of sages establishing rabbinic modes of teaching is important for Christian readers of the Old Testament in at least two regards. First, it is in the matrix of disputatious rabbinic interpretation that the Christian movement emerges. One can detect, for example, that in Jesus' dispute with the Pharisees and Herodians (Mark 12:13), Sadducees (Mark 12:18), and scribes (Mark 12:28), Jesus himself is presented as a full participant in the interpretive disputes that constitute Judaism.[32] In this regard the early Christian movement is present in Judaism as one of the possible Judaisms available. In like manner, the reference to "Gamaliel, a teacher of the law" (Acts 5:34) and the linkage proposed between Paul and Gamaliel (Acts 22:3) suggest that Paul and his disputatious way with the Torah show him also engaged in the sort of disputes that constituted Judaism, so that the scribal traditions, derived from the ancient sages, show Christianity coming to its peculiar identity in the same way in which rabbinic authority did so, through disputed interpretations of the tradition.

Second, a great deal of mischief has been done in Christianity through a misuse of Paul's dictum, "the letter kills, but the Spirit gives life" (2 Cor 3:6).[33] This simple formulation helps cast Jews as punctilious literalists, while Christians are emancipated from all such attentiveness to the textual tradition. Both in principle and in practice, however, nothing could be further from reality. If it is anything, the Christian movement is an ongoing interpretive reflection on the tradition that has identifiable shape and intransigent angularity. This is self-evident in the Reformation traditions of the church, which are committed to *sola scriptura*.[34]

---

30. Michael Fishbane, "From Scribalism to Rabbinism: Perspectives on the Emergence of Classical Judaism," *The Sage in Israel*, 447.

31. Ibid., 451, 456.

32. On a thematic approach to the issue, see Fernando Belo, *A Materialist Reading of the Gospel of Mark* (Maryknoll, N.Y.: Orbis Books, 1981). For the rabbinic cast of much of the formative articulation of early Christianity, see W. D. Davies, *Christian Origins and Judaism* (London: Darton, Longman, and Todd, 1962); and *Paul and Rabbinic Judaism: Some Rabbinic Elements in Pauline Theology* (London: SPCK, 1970).

33. On the density of this statement in 2 Cor 3:6, see Richard B. Hays, *Echoes of Scripture in the Letters of Paul* (New Haven: Yale University Press, 1993) 122–53.

34. The point is accented by Gerhard Ebeling, "The Significance of the Critical Historical Method for Church and Theology in Protestantism," *Word and Faith* (London: SCM Press, 1963) 17–61.

It is, *mutatis mutandis,* the same in Roman Catholicism, where two issues must be faced. First is the question of magisterial authority to interpret the tradition, a question also present in Protestant traditions, but less formally and less institutionally. Second, there is the unending question about the openness of the tradition and the finality of formulation. The advantaged interpreters—those who possess hegemonic interpretive authority—prefer "the faith . . . once for all delivered to the saints" (Jude 3; RSV). Close examination, however, indicates a remarkable suppleness in the textual tradition and a large capacity to accommodate, even among those who prize fixity.

Thus the formulation of Paul in 2 Cor 3:6 has had two unfortunate consequences in its subsequent use. It has provided a ground from which to polemicize against and caricature Judaism. It has beguiled the church, so that the actual interpretive power in the life of the church is mostly unacknowledged, and if unacknowledged, then surely uncriticized. The convergence of Torah and wisdom has prescribed for the Jewish and Christian enterprises, these two "peoples of the book," the inescapable, definitive, and unending work of exegesis, and the inevitable interface of tradition and experience. This crucial and identity-giving work of interpretation means that the work is never finished, that the work is necessarily conflictual, and that interpretation remains as unsettled as life itself. Wisdom teachers may encounter Yahweh with a tone of finality. It is known among such interpreters, however, that the work must all be done again, tomorrow.

Wisdom and the Canonization Process

Because the scribes became teachers and interpreters, and because in Judaism the traditions of worship became the traditions of study, it does not surprise us that the wisdom traditions of interpretation are operative in the canonical enterprise of Israel. Canonically, it is conventional to situate wisdom in the third section of the Old Testament, among the writings. Gerald Sheppard, however, in a close study of Sirach and Baruch, has shown that the later texts have a remarkable capacity to reuse older materials, including Torah materials, recasting them in sapiential modes.[35] As a consequence, the influence of wisdom is not confined to the later part of the canon, but seems to claim older materials for its perspective, thus sapientializing older canonical materials. This enterprise is important, because what

---

35. Gerald T. Sheppard, *Wisdom as a Hermeneutical Construct: A Study in the Sapientializing of the Old Testament* (BZAW 151; Berlin: Walter de Gruyter, 1980). More generally see Ronald E. Clements, *Wisdom in Theology* (Grand Rapids: Eerdmans, 1992) 151–79. Clements, *Wisdom for a Changing World: Wisdom in Old Testament Theology* (Berkeley: Bibal Press, 1990) 35, comments, "Wisdom reinvented and reinvigorated the ideas and language of the cultus to suit the needs of scattered communities of Jews living in exile. . . ." See also Donn F. Morgan, *Between Text and Community: The "Writings" in Canonical Interpretation* (Minneapolis: Fortress Press, 1990); and most recently, Clements, "Wisdom and Old Testament Theology," *Wisdom in Ancient Israel,* 269–86.

the sapiential reinterpretation of ancient tradition accomplishes is an authoritative literature that is not turned in on a defensive religious community, but is turned outward in order to provide a perspective for the reinterpretation of all experience. A sapientialization of canonical traditions, including Torah traditions, means that Judaism speaks a wisdom to the world. It is a wisdom that is at the same time relentlessly Yahwistic, intensely ethical, and uncompromising in insisting on the world as Yahweh's creation. It is telling that Sheppard concludes his study with a comment on Eccl 12:13-14, which he regards as a sapiential addendum in the process of canonization:

> Fear God, and keep his commandments; for that is the whole duty of every-one. For God will bring every deed into judgment, including every secret thing, whether good or evil.

Sheppard comments about the belated traditions of Sirach and Baruch: "They recognized how fully the biblical description of righteousness had been both deep-ened and complicated by the call to 'fear God and obey his commandments.'"[36] Sheppard comments on the epilogue to Qoheleth:

> The epilogue provides a rare glimpse into a comprehensive, canon conscious formulation concerning the theological function of biblical wisdom. When the assumed ideological coherency of the wisdom books is clarified in such a manner, the complementarity between the canonical function of the bib-lical wisdom books and the function of certain inner-biblical sapientizing redaction becomes all the more obvious and compelling.[37]

Emergence of Apocalyptic

With singular influence, Gerhard von Rad has proposed that apocalyptic is a late development of wisdom teaching: "The apocalyptist is a wise man."[38] A primary point of von Rad's much-noted proposal is that apocalyptic texts urge that the times are fixed and the outcomes for world history are all prepared in a way that reflects the wisdom teachers in their notion of "proper times" (Eccl 3:1-8). Thus von Rad concludes:

> One can recognize God's total sovereignty over history by its precise deter-mination, and its division into periods helps the observer to recognize his own place in history, namely at the end of the world's first age, and imme-diately before the dawn of the new.... Of absolutely central significance for the apocalyptics is the looking to an end to the present course of events, to a

---

36. Sheppard, *Wisdom as a Hermeneutical Construct*, 160.
37. Ibid., 128–29.
38. Von Rad, *Wisdom in Israel*, 277. See his discussion of apocalyptic in ibid., 263–83; *Old Testament Theology* (2 vols.; San Francisco: Harper and Row, 1962, 1965), 1:407–8, 2:301–8.

judgment and the dawning of a time of salvation, that is, its thoroughgoing eschatological orientation.[39]

Von Rad's linkage between wisdom and apocalyptic has been much challenged, for many scholars prefer to connect apocalyptic to prophecy.[40]

In my judgment, the question of the antecedent of apocalyptic, in either wisdom or prophecy, cannot be answered. Apocalyptic, as it emerges late in the Old Testament, is a synthesis of many traditions that were not neatly compartmentalized, and it is more than the sum of all these, a genuine *novum*. What we may retain of von Rad's insight, without committing to his entire proposal, is that wisdom understands that Yahweh has a resolute will and a hidden purpose that cannot be defeated in the workings of historical vagaries. That is, Yahweh's hidden purpose, intrinsic to the processes of creation (*logos; sophia*) cannot and will not be defeated. Apocalyptic is the categoric assertion of Yahweh's wise and resolute sovereignty and wisdom. In its appeal to the sovereign creator, wisdom teaching provides material for the fashioning of an apocalyptic articulation of faith.

Insofar as Christianity is the child of apocalyptic, we may consider as a sapiential-apocalyptic statement Paul's theology of the cross:[41] "For God's foolishness is wiser than human wisdom, and God's weakness is stronger than human strength" (1 Cor 1:25). God's weakness defies human strength. God's foolishness defies human wisdom. The strength and wisdom of the world, when opposed to God, are of no consequence. This assertion, profoundly radicalized in Paul's theology of the cross, is congruent with the most elemental teaching of wisdom in family and school. God will be God! It is profound stupidity to think or live otherwise. The teachers, early and late, warned those in Israel not to be fools, for fools are bent on death:

> For whoever finds me finds life
> and obtains favor from the Lord;
> but those who miss me injure themselves;
> all who hate me love death. (Prov 8:35-36)

> But God said to him, "You fool! This very night your life is being demanded of you. And the things you have prepared, whose will they be?" So it is with those who store up treasures for themselves but are not rich toward God. (Luke 12:20-21)[42]

---

39. Von Rad, *Wisdom in Israel*, 274, 278.

40. See Paul D. Hanson, *The Dawn of Apocalyptic: The Historical and Sociological Roots of Jewish Apocalyptic Eschatology* (Philadelphia: Fortress Press, 1979); and especially Peter von der Osten-Sacken, *Die Apokalyptik in ihren Verhaltnis zu Prophetie und Weisheit* (Theologische Existenz Heute; Munich: Chr. Kaiser Verlag, 1969).

41. Ernst Käsemann, "On the Subject of Primitive Christian Apocalyptic," *New Testament Questions Today* (London: SCM Press, 1969) 137.

42. It is reasonable to suggest that this parable has behind it an awareness of the narrative of 1 Samuel 25, which has as a lead character a man named "fool" (*nabal*).

These three developments of wisdom—convergence with Torah, impingement on the processes of canonization, and emergence of apocalyptic—all lie at the edge of the Old Testament. They are not central themes or concerns of Old Testament theology. They do, however, attest to the enduring vitality and influence of the sapiential tradition in the life and faith of Israel.

TWENTY-FIVE

Modes of Mediation and Life with Yahweh

E ACH OF THE ABOVE named modes of mediation of Yahweh in Israel is quite distinct. Moreover, each of these modes, insofar as we can determine, has a rich history and takes on a plurality of forms and expressions over time. Therefore any summation is bound to be somewhat reductionist. Nonetheless, I shall suggest five general conclusions.

Yahweh's Gifts to Israel

Each of these modes of mediation is, according to Israel's testimony, *instituted as Yahweh's gift to Israel*. These modes are not human devices, whereby Yahweh may be mobilized, manipulated, or coerced into a particular agenda.[1]

1. The Torah manifestly is given by Yahweh to Moses at Sinai. The Sinai meeting is Israel's most extreme attempt to situate Yahweh's self-disclosure to Israel beyond human invention and administration. The laws of Sinai are the commands of Yahweh, and are in no way positive or royal law. Judaism, moreover, has safeguarded the continuing dynamic of the Torah by way of the Oral Torah, also given to Moses at Sinai.

2. Kingship is authorized by Yahweh, so that the king in Israel is the human, anointed agent to do Yahweh's will in the earth. To be sure, in the Deuteronomic tradition (Deut 17:14-20, 1 Sam 8:22), Yahweh's gift of kingship is given reluctantly and with explicit covenantal restrictions. In the Jerusalem cultus, by contrast, the monarchy is celebrated, seemingly with no such reservation concerning Yahweh's intention.

3. Prophets are authorized by Moses to be "like me," for Yahweh "will raise up from you a prophet" (Deut 18:15-22). Moreover, the individual prophetic figures attest to the impingement of Yahweh upon their lives, to recruit them to carry a message other than their own.

---

1. This conclusion is not in agreement with Ludwig Koehler (see p. 651 above and its note 5). It would be difficult indeed to know what kind of assertion would satisfy Koehler that provisions for worship in Israel are indeed of Yahweh, if the statements in Israel's text do not suffice.

4. The cultus and its several supervising priesthoods are authorized directly by Yahweh at Sinai.

5. The matter of the sages is not as simple and direct as in the other cases. It is conventional among scholars to say that wisdom teachers are simply those who are seen to be gifted in discernment. Perhaps consistent with the epistemology of the sages, such giftedness arises in the processes of experience, and certainly not through any recognizable, institutional way. Thus in any case, this mode of mediation is understood as having a different sort of authorization and legitimation.

We may note three uses, however, in which it is acknowledged that wisdom is given by Yahweh. All three instances are royal, and surely are rather exceptional, so that we must not generalize from them. But they are worth noting, for from these we may perhaps extrapolate more generally about wisdom as a gift from Yahweh.

(a) Pharaoh recognizes Joseph's special acumen and makes a theological acknowledgment of its source: "Since God has shown you all this, there is no one so discerning and wise as you" (Gen 41:39).

(b) Solomon, by tradition the wise king, prays for "a listening heart" (1 Kgs 3:9), and it is granted:

> I now do according to your word. Indeed I give you a wise and discerning mind; no one like you has been before you and no one like you shall arise after you. I give you also what you have not asked, both riches and honor all your life; no other king shall compare with you. (1 Kgs 3:12-13)

(c) Daniel, who regularly moves in the dangerous environs of the Babylonian court, is recognized as especially endowed by Yahweh:

> Then Daniel went to his home and informed his companions, Hananiah, Mishael, and Azariah, and told them to seek mercy from the God of heaven concerning this mystery, so that Daniel and his companions with the rest of the wise men of Babylon might not perish. Then the mystery was revealed to Daniel in a vision of the night, and Daniel blessed the God of heaven. (Dan 2:17-19)

In the poem that follows (vv. 20-23), the verb *give* (*yhb*) is used twice with Yahweh as the subject and wisdom as the topic, and the verbs *reveal* (*gl'*) and *know* (*yd'*) indicate that Daniel's wisdom is from God (see also Dan 4:9; 5:11, 14). These cases perhaps are so extraordinary that they are different in kind from the sages of the family, school, or court. Yet these uses attest to the awareness that true discernment is not simply human cleverness or common sense, but it is a special endowment or empowerment from Yahweh. And so it must have been in every social context in Israel.

The claim that these mediations are willed and authorized by Yahweh is important, because they evidence that Yahweh wills to be related to Israel and, derivatively, to all of Yahweh's partners. Understood as Yahwistically instituted practices, these concrete modes of mediation attest that the connection with Yahweh is from Yahweh's side, at Yahweh's behest.

Real-Life Circumstances

These several modes of mediation are *situated in the midst of real-life circumstances,* designed and intended to address real issues and to position Israel on the "Yahwistic side" in disputed issues of the day.

1. The Torah is intended to guard Israel against idolatry; that is, against the wrong discernment and practice of God, the disregard of God's holiness, and the distortion of Israel's odd identity rooted in Yahweh's holiness. Idolatry, however, is not a vacuous religious idea. In practice idolatry (hatred of the true God) comes down to oppression (hatred of the neighbor). Thus the Torah binds Israel singularly to Yahweh in the two practices of love of God and love of neighbor. Without Torah, Israel would disappear, and life would be handed over, without protest, to the brutalizing, oppressive ways of life known elsewhere, rooted in the worship of wrongly discerned gods.

2. Kingship in Israel is authorized for the practice of Torah (cf. Deut 17:14-20), which is to assure in Israel a covenantal mode of communal existence. When kingship is marked by Yahweh's purposes, self-aggrandizement and acquisitiveness are curbed (Deut 17:16-17), and Yahweh's justice and righteousness may become concrete social practice (Ps 72:1-4, 12-14). Where kings depart from their true Yahwistic vocation, however, the monarchy may use power exploitatively and abusively (cf. Jer 22:13-14; Ezek 34:1-6). The existence and effectiveness of kingship, extrapolated into messianism, concerns the right deployment of public power for all members of the community.

3. Prophets arise in Israel when covenantal modes of existence are endangered. It is the work of the prophets to insist that all of Israel's life is to be lived in relation to and in response to Yahweh's will and purposes, and to enunciate the consequences of a life lived without regard to this defining relationship. Thus prophets are to invite a "turning" in Israel (cf. Ezek 3:16-21, 33:7-9), a turn from pride to trust, a turn from despair to hope, or a turn from abusiveness to covenantal neighborliness. Without that prophetic invitation and warning, Israel has no chance of turning, but will surely die (cf. Ezek 18:30-32).

4. The cult in Israel is devised as a place wherein Israel is assured of Yahweh's presence, where Israel may receive forgiveness and reconciliation and enjoy a life of genuine communion with Yahweh. In this place Israel may voice its needs, assert its grievances, and utter its doxologies. In this authorized place, Israel can without restraint and with appropriate extravagance luxuriate in being Yahweh's people. But without cult, communion becomes impossible for the community. Israel would then be destined to live a life of alienation, with sins unforgiven, needs unarticulated, and praises unuttered. Without a locus for these characteristic expressions

of loyalty, Israel would cease to be connected to Yahweh, and would in turn cease to be Israel.

5. The wisdom teachers, scribes, and sages serve to make available to Israel a sense of buoyant, delicate order and sustaining coherence that belongs to the fabric of Yahweh's creation. That order and coherence may be grandly affirmed, but it is the wisdom teachers who pay attention to the giftedness, graciousness, and demanding quality of life, in concrete experience. Without this constant articulation and reflection, the discerned fabric of Yahweh's creation might disappear from view, and life could devolve to a practice of discrete, technical operations, which would diminish the joy, significance, and well-being of shared human life.

The concrete purpose of these mediations, then, is to make available the peculiar qualities of life with Yahweh, and to protect against the distortions of that life:

	Gift	*Negatives negated*
Torah:	Identity rooted in holiness	Idolatry toward oppression
King:	Justice and righteousness	Exploitation and abuse
Prophet:	Covenantal turning	Death
Cult:	Genuine communion	Alienation
Wisdom:	Buoyant order and sustaining coherence	Life as technique

These somewhat reductionist tabulations suggest that these mediations are life-and-death matters for Israel. These mediations are not "good ideas" or simple pieties. They make a decisive difference to the possibility of Israel, for Israel is a real people in the world, and it must practice the means Yahweh has given for the sustenance and maintenance of its oddity in the world.

Human Enterprises Subject to Perversion

Although these modes of mediation are authorized and legitimated by Yahweh, they are, in actual practice, *concrete human enterprises*. And because they are human enterprises that depend on human courage, passion, and fidelity, they are *subject to profound perversion*.

1. Torah can indeed take on an ideological intensity, so that it jeopardizes the character of Israel in its legalistic insistence. It is plausible that the extreme measures of Ezra's reform approach this danger. Job's friends—surely a theatrical caricature—move in the direction of legalism that requires the ideological denial of lived experience.

2. We have ample evidence of kingship that eventuates in disaster because of self-aggrandizement and the failure to attend to proper public trust. According to prophetic indictment, moreover, when kings renege on their Yahwistic mandate, they bring immense suffering on themselves and the whole realm.

3. Prophecy, according to Israel's testimony, becomes fraudulent when prophets do not speak Yahweh's true word, but speak some other word (Jer 23:21). Particularly in the polemics of Jeremiah and Ezekiel, this self-invented word is characterized as an ideological defense of the status quo. It is a word that heals too lightly (Jer 6:14, 8:11), that softens and compromises the sovereign requirements of Yahweh. Such prophets who "see false visions and utter lying divinations" (Ezek 13:9) delude with phony promises of peace and prosperity (Ezek 13:10). That is, such distorting prophets promise the gift of Yahweh without the requirements of Yahweh, and thereby evoke a people "great and rich...fat and sleek" (Jer 5:27).

4. The perversion of cult, which we know from prophetic polemic (cf. Isa 1:11-15; Amos 4:4-5), is that cult may become an end in itself and a practice of manipulative self-indulgence (Isa 58:1-4). In such practice, worship no longer attends to Yahweh. Such a cult deceives and promises what it cannot deliver, intimate communion with Yahweh. It substitutes self-referenced manipulation for trustful submissiveness.

5. Wisdom is the practice of discernment, whereby life is taken as evidence of the demand and gift of Yahweh. But wisdom can be distorted, so that it becomes a calculation of interest and advantage, and Yahweh disappears as a critical principle. Wisdom is distorted when it manages to make credible the practice of foolishness, the mistaken sense that one is autonomous and the measure of one's own life (cf. Psalms 10, 14). Instead of wisdom as a norm of Yahweh's purposes, one becomes wise in one's own eyes; that is, self-referential (cf. Prov 12:15, 21:2; Isa 5:21). Two extreme cases of such self-deluding autonomy, perhaps both directly influenced by false confidence in Israel's sense of autonomy, occur in Deut 8:17 and in David's easy acceptance of prudential killing (2 Sam 11:25-27).

Thus distortion may result in

(a) Torah as ideological intensity, taking the form of legalism;

(b) kingship as justifiable self-aggrandizement;

(c) prophecy as easy peace without Yahweh as a critical reference;

(d) cult as self-indulgence;

(e) wisdom as self-deluding autonomy.

In these several potential perversions, which may be willful and systemic but may also arise through neglect and lack of intentionality, Israel's life with Yahweh is jeopardized. What puts the life of Israel at risk is not wrong ideas but wrong practice, practices that fail to mediate Yahweh in ways that energize and summon Israel to its true character.

Yahweh Made Available

Each of these modes of mediation *makes Yahweh available* to Israel. That is their purpose. The way in which Yahweh is mediated in each mode is specific to the character of the mode of mediation itself.

1. Torah gives to Israel the Holy One of Israel, the One we have long ago seen in Exod 34:6-7, a sovereign who will not be mocked, yet is gracious and merciful, yearning for Israel.

2. Kingship gives to Israel Yahweh who is a "lover of justice" (Ps 99:4; Isa 61:8).

3. Prophecy gives to Israel a God who watches over Israel, a God who promises:

And just as I have watched over them to pluck up and break down, to over-throw, destroy, and bring evil, so I will watch over them to build and to plant.... (Jer 31:28)

It is especially prophecy that takes Israel into the fissure of death, and moves Israel out of that fissure to newness.

4. Cult gives to Israel Yahweh who fully participates in Israel's drama of restoration:

... who forgives all your iniquity,
who heals all your diseases,
who redeems your life from the Pit,
who crowns you with steadfast love and mercy,
who satisfies you with good as long as you live ... (Ps 103:3-5)

In the cult Yahweh meets Israel in its well-being and attends in restorative ways to Israel in trouble.

5. Wisdom gives to Israel Yahweh who has formed the world as a joyous, reliable home:

The Lord by wisdom founded the earth;
by understanding he established the heavens;
by his knowledge the deeps broke open,
and the clouds drop down the dew. (Prov 3:19-20)

In articulating such a summary, I am aware that I have reached a high level of thematization and consequently a high level of reductionism. Indeed, at this level of thematization and reductionism, the functions I suggest for each of the modes of mediation may be interchangeable, so that all of these modes perform all these offerings. I dare summarize any single point for any particular mode of mediation only because I have taken some trouble to exposit the detailed material that precedes and anticipates such a summary. That is, I do not want my summation taken apart from my more detailed exposition.

What I most want to insist on in this connection is that in these actual, concrete social enactments, it is Yahweh, in all of Yahweh's density, who is mediated.

Indeed, I would go further to say that if it were not for these forms of mediation, Yahweh, as known in Israel's testimony, would not be available to Israel. When the mediations are distorted, the Yahweh given in the mediation is to that extent distorted. Yahweh is not some universal idea floating around above Israel. Yahweh is a concrete practice in the embodied life of Israel. For that reason everything depends on faithful, sustained, intentional mediation.

Embodied Communal Practice

These mediations are *concrete, communal practices* conducted by human agents. Thus I return to Gary Anderson's insistence on practice. Israel is practiced into Yahweh, and consequently into its life as Israel. I wish to exposit this notion of embodied practice in two ways. First, these mediations take place in meetings that are stylized and communally recognizable over time. This is most evident in three of these modes. Torah as practice consists in a great assembly, or subsequently in synagogue study. Kingship is largely pageant, in which the practices of legitimate power are made visible and kept under public scrutiny. And cult is obviously performance in an agreed-upon calendar in a holy place. In a less prominent way, the messenger formula and the meeting of prophet and audience suggest that such confrontation was frequent enough so that recurring patterns of exchange were recognized. I have taken some pains, moreover, to exhibit the likely institutional setting of wisdom, even if those institutional settings are as modest and intimate as mother and child, when both parties assume their agreed-upon roles for wisdom instruction. I should insist that these mediations have institutional force; the participants in these interactions are aware of and willing to accept their several roles, in which the mediating agent is credentialed and the listening audience more or less entertains what is given, perhaps willingly, perhaps reluctantly or even resistantly.

The institutional character of mediation means that Israel is not happenstance or accidental. It is an enduring presence in history over time. It therefore requires and necessitates agreed-upon disciplines, without which this force in history would cease to exist.

Mediation as Institutional Discourse

I make the transition from my first point of institutional practice to a drama of speech and gesture by reference to an observation of Wesley Kort. Following Michel Foucault, Kort observes: "Institutions are embodied or established discourse.... The more powerful and significant an institution becomes, the more difficult it may be to articulate the discourse it embodies."[2] I wish now to focus

---

2. Wesley Kort, *Bound to Differ: The Dynamics of Theological Discourses* (University Park: Pennsylvania State University Press, 1992) 19. Kort's comment is worth connecting to my title for Part IV, "Israel's Embodied Testimony." In the end, the faith and testimony of Israel must come down to the

on mediation as "institutional discourse" or "established discourse."[3] As we consider these five modes of mediation, and as we ask what happened in these socially structured meetings where Yahweh is made available, the answer is *speech and gesture*.[4] Israel remained Israel over time because of its disciplined readiness to come together periodically to reimagine being Israel.[5]

It is clear that Torah, kingship, and cult concerned regularized meetings, though kingship surely had ad hoc crisis (such as wars) in addition to festivals. The Torah meetings were indeed specific:

> Three times a year all your males shall appear before the Lord your God at the place that he will choose: at the festival of unleavened bread, at the festival of weeks, and at the festival of booths. They shall not appear before the Lord empty-handed.... (Deut 16:16; cf. Exod 23:14-15)

In addition, the confrontations of prophet and of sage were surely more ad hoc. Nonetheless, all are more or less stylized. What happens in each of these modes is *speech and gesture:*

(a) Torah is spoken interpretation (Neh 5:5-8);

(b) kingship is largely liturgical celebration and affirmation;

(c) prophecy is utterance and acted speech;[6]

(d) cult is more nearly action, but actions are assertions;

(e) wisdom teaching is interpretive speech.[7]

The character of these mediations as occasions for speech and gesture is perhaps a straightforward and simple observation, but it is not often enough noticed. Israel as a community has access to Yahweh, because it is a community that regularly, in disciplined ways (and also in ad hoc ways), comes to be addressed, to listen, to respond, to enact a world out loud, construed with Yahweh at its center.

Authorized speech matters decisively for this community. Where authorized speech is not conducted, Yahweh is not readily available. Where speech and act are distorted, Yahweh is distorted. When Israel refuses to listen or to look, Israel

---

practice of an actual community, if they matter at all. It will not do to regard Old Testament faith as a series of "good ideas," or "ideas" of any kind.

3. See ibid., 18.

4. Samuel Terrien, *The Elusive Presence: Toward a New Biblical Theology* (New York: Harper and Row, 1978), has gone furthest in restoring the eye to a legitimate place in Israel's faith, which is dominated by the ear. On the phenomenological priority of hearing, either as a valid priority or as an interpretive bias, see Erwin W. Strauss, "Aethesiology and Hallucinations," *Existence: A New Dimension in Psychiatry and Psychology* (ed. Rollo May et al.; New York: Basic Books, 1958) 139–69.

5. See Jacob Neusner, *The Enchantments of Judaism: Rites of Transformation from Birth to Death* (Atlanta: Scholars Press, 1991) 211–16.

6. On the acted element in the prophets, reference may still be made to Georg Fohrer, "Die Gattung der Berichte über symbolische Handlungen der Propheten," *ZAW* 64 (1952) 101–20.

7. That is, it is aimed at listeners, and so must be persuasive. See James L. Crenshaw, "Wisdom and Authority: Sapiential Rhetoric and Its Warrants," *Congress Volume, Vienna, 1980* (VTSup 32; Leiden: E. J. Brill, 1981) 10–29.

is diminished and Yahweh disappears. Thus Israel's self-discernment is endlessly at risk in this interpretive, institutional, lyrical, testimonial activity.

This quality of mediation seems important in our present circumstance of interpretation for two reasons. First, this insight about the practice of speech and gesture has enormous implications for contemporary ecclesial practice. The community of faith generated by these texts is extremely fragile and vulnerable. On the one hand, this quality and character of mediation requires a community under disciplines of ready attentiveness. On the other hand, this community requires authorized, recognized agents of speech and gesture, who apply care, attentiveness, and intention to utterance and gesture that make Yahweh available with embodied, institutional force. Thus practice is urgent, especially now in the disestablished church of the West. For a very long time, under Constantinian aegis, it could be assumed that Yahweh was an established figure, always there. Disestablished communities, however, have long known that Yahweh is not "always there," but is there in, with, and under the disciplined enactments of utterance and gesture.

Second, this character of mediation as concrete speech and gesture, it seems to me, is particularly urgent in a technological context beset by "the humiliation of the word."[8] The media industry and its well-funded, vacuous appeal have nearly emptied speech of testimonial power. It is my judgment, moreover, that historical criticism of a positivistic kind in Scripture study has conspired with such vacuousness, because the informed interpreter—the educated critic—is permitted to talk about everything except the theological Actor in the text and the claims made by that theological agent. I do not know if the necessary courage and imagination are now available in order to sustain the extravagant, costly, counterrational utterance that will mediate Yahweh in concrete ways. That, it appears it me, is the issue this community has faced since its inception.[9] It is now a peculiarly acute challenge.

Performative Speech

I conclude this exposition with the suggestion of Dale Patrick and Allen Scult, who have recognized that serious substantive rhetoric, of the kind about which we have been reflecting, is indeed performative speech.[10] That is, much of Old Testament rhetoric, performed in disciplined meeting, is performative speech in which the utterance does what it says. What is "performed" in these utterances and gestures is Israel as a community that has seen and heard and answered. What is performed in these utterances and gestures is the world of gift and demand in Yahweh's creation. Indeed, what is performed in these utterances and gestures is Yahweh, sovereign and faithful, incommensurate and mutual.

---

8. See my citations to Jacques Ellul and Neil Postman in chap. 27, nn. 11–13.

9. On the intergenerational problem indicated in Deut 6:4-5, see Michael Fishbane, "Deuteronomy 6:20-25: Teaching and Transmission," *Text and Texture: Close Readings of Selected Biblical Texts* (New York: Schocken Books, 1979) 79–83.

10. Dale Patrick and Allen Scult, *Rhetoric and Biblical Interpretation* (JSOTSup 82; Sheffield: Almond Press, 1990).

A good place to finish our exposition of this theme is the sweeping question of Paul:

> But how are they to call on one in whom they have not believed? And how are they to believe in one of whom they have never heard? And how are they to hear without someone to proclaim him? And how are they to proclaim him unless they are sent? (Rom 10:14-15)

How indeed! I transpose Paul's question: How is Israel to "have" Yahweh unless Yahweh is adequately and faithfully mediated? I imagine that there is in Israel (and in Israel's implied courtroom) a stunned, gasping silence when Israel completes its testimony, when its credentialed speakers and enactors finish their mediation. There is so much to decide about this testimony, so much that this version of reality subverts, so much to be embraced...perhaps so much to be relinquished. That peculiar deciding, subverting, embracing, and relinquishing happens wherever and whenever Israel's testimony is faithfully embodied.

Part V

PROSPECTS FOR THEOLOGICAL INTERPRETATION

TWENTY-SIX

Interpretation in a Pluralistic Context

I T REMAINS TO CONSIDER what may come next in Old Testament theology, to anticipate where theological interpretation of the Old Testament may next turn and what shapes it may take. I cannot prognosticate with any certainty, or with much confidence, but I offer some comments that are complementary to the retrospect that I offered in chapters 1 and 2.

Disestablishment: From Hegemonic Interpretation to Pluralism

The great fact of the emerging context of theological interpretation of the Old Testament is *the disestablishment of our usual modes of interpretation and the parallel disestablishment of the institutional vehicles of such interpretation.* That is, disestablishment concerns both epistemological and sociopolitical factors, for as Karl Marx understood most clearly, knowledge and power are intimately connected ("the ideas of the dominant class become the dominant ideas"). This disestablishment is an exceedingly important matter for Old Testament theology, even though the establishment assumptions of long-established scholarship were not particularly noticed, critiqued, or valued; for to be established entails not noticing that one is established, and not entertaining the thought that it could be otherwise.

The establishment assumptions that have long dominated Old Testament theological interpretation have been of two kinds. On the one hand, Old Testament theology, as a Christian enterprise, could assume that it was dealing with the normative socio-religious-moral convictions of the West. It could therefore readily entertain a direct flow to the New Testament, because the dominant West was a Christian West. It could, moreover, assume that it studied the text that was generally taken as the normative text of the West, which carried with it more or less normative interpretations.[1]

On the other hand, Old Testament theology, in its centrist forms, has been largely an academic matter, shaped in German universities, slightly altered in the

---

1. On this function and character of the biblical text, see Northrop Frye, *The Great Code: The Bible and Literature* (London: Routledge and Kegan Paul, 1982).

great graduate schools of the United States, and taught in United States theological seminaries by those educated in the university tradition. This academic shaping assured that Old Testament theology—in its epistemological assumptions, which are still very powerful—from the eighteenth century on would be an Enlightenment enterprise, in which the Cartesian skeptic and the Kantian knower would prevail over the text. These epistemological assumptions, by the nineteenth century, were committed to (a) historicism that could determine "what happened," for there could be no meaning beyond "what happened"; (b) evolutionism, so that religious development occurred in a straight line of unilateral progress from the primitive to the sophisticated; and (c) a rationalism that felt a need to explain away much of the contradiction that violated "reasonableness" or that made claims beyond a naturalistic, scientifically available world.

Established modes of scholarship consisted in a rather uneasy but widely shared settlement that theological claims of an idealistic and triumphal kind could be sustained in the midst of critical scrutiny, a compromise that is perhaps inevitable in a modern world where Enlightenment modes of knowledge had declared war on theological tradition, but where the Bible as the subject of scholarship would not fully yield to such modes of knowledge, nor would the institutions of interpretation fully yield to a purely skeptical approach, the university no more than the church.[2]

My purpose here is not to attack or malign this phase of scholarship, for as far as Old Testament interpretation was concerned, there was nothing sinister about this enterprise.[3] Rather it is my judgment that Old Testament interpretation, and theological interpretation more generally, cannot escape the epistemological and political context in which it operates, and our forebears could do so no more than we can. It is relatively easy to critique that enterprise.[4] But that is not my purpose, for everything we are now able to do is dependent on that era of study. My purpose is rather to recognize that it was, like all serious interpretation, intensely context-bound, in this case bound to the context of positivistic historicism.[5]

---

2. We may cite G. Ernest Wright as a model figure in the United States who embraced and practiced this uneasy, widely shared settlement with great effectiveness. He was a vigorous critical historian, yet managed to turn his research toward theological affirmation. On this uneasy settlement in U.S. scholarship, see Leo G. Perdue, *The Collapse of History: Reconstructing Old Testament Theology* (OBT; Minneapolis: Fortress Press, 1994) 19–44.

3. More recently, criticism that kept a check on more programmatic skepticism has given way, in some quarters, to criticism that is militantly and admittedly skeptical. Thus in his recent study, David Penchansky, *The Politics of Biblical Theology: A Postmodern Reading* (StABH 10; Macon, Ga.: Mercer University Press, 1995) 5, can speak of younger scholars who have "hatred" toward the older perspectives that operated with theological assumptions. The source and power of this hatred are yet to be explored, but they likely have to do with a great deal beyond academic, critical questions.

4. See the generous but critical assessment of Perdue, *The Collapse of History*, and the more aggressive dismissal of that enterprise by Penchansky, *The Politics of Biblical Theology*. The difference between the perspectives of Perdue and Penchansky in tone and outlook is worth noting. In my judgment, Perdue takes into account the context of that older scholarship, a matter that seems to interest Penchansky very little.

5. See Perdue, *The Collapse of History*, 3–68.

This alliance between triumphalist Christendom and critical positivism produced a pattern of hegemonic interpretation.[6] How could it do otherwise? It is this hegemonic pattern of interpretation that now needs to be noticed, and that now is in enormous jeopardy. The hegemony assumed Christian-normative truth as taught by the church, hedged about and kept intellectually respectable by criticism that was also hegemonic—that is, a centrist project built on consensus assumptions. This hegemonic practice meant that, give or take some adjustments, there was a central, consensus practice, and the fact that it was undertaken almost exclusively by white, Western males is both a cause and a consequence of its dominance. Moreover, there was a monopoly of interpretation: only a few did it with any visible influence or effect, and everyone knew who they were. This social establishment, like every social establishment, maintained itself by limiting access and membership through the alliance of church authority and academic criteria. I imagine that this hegemonic enterprise was sustained as long as it was because the world it produced "worked," and dissidents could be easily contained or silenced. One begins to notice the "masters of suspicion" in the period of positivistic historicism, but only now have dissidence and variation become so deep and so broad as to challenge the hegemony in serious and effective ways.[7]

The disestablishment of a triumphalist church in the West can hardly be contested. In the place of a consensus authority, we have within the church an amazing pluralism that is matched outside the church by vigorous, competing religious claims and by a profound secularization of culture. It is especially evident that the Enlightenment establishment with which the church in its dominance had allied itself is equally disestablished.[8] As a consequence, even within the university, confidence in positivistic rationality is much challenged, in the sciences as in the humanities. What goes under the general term of *postmodern* signifies the breakup of any broad consensus about what we know or how we know what we know. This means, in my judgment, that no interpretive institution, ecclesial or academic, can any longer sustain a hegemonic mode of interpretation, so that our capacity for a magisterial or even a broadly based consensus about a pattern of interpretation

---

6. Jon Levenson, *The Hebrew Bible, the Old Testament, and Historical Criticism: Jews and Christians in Biblical Studies* (Louisville: Westminster/John Knox, 1993), especially chaps. 4–5, makes a vigorous critique of both Christian appropriation of the Hebrew Bible and the numbing effect of positivistic criticism.

7. The notion of "masters of suspicion" is provided by Paul Ricoeur, *Freud and Philosophy: An Essay in Interpretation* (New Haven: Yale University Press, 1970) 32–36 and passim, as he makes reference to Freud, Marx, and Nietzsche.

8. It was perhaps the events surrounding the Watergate scandal and the Vietnam War that lethally damaged the legitimacy of Enlightenment institutions. Anyone who remembers the Vietnam War with any critical sensitivity will recall the arrogance of Henry Kissinger and McGeorge Bundy, major university figures, in claiming their monopoly of knowledge about the war. See David Halberstam, *The Best and the Brightest* (New York: Fawcett Books, 1992), and see the belated, sad acknowledgments of Robert S. McNamara and Brian Vandemark, *In Retrospect: The Tragedy and Lessons of Vietnam* (New York: Random House, 1995). The crisis of confidence around these events can hardly be overestimated in its importance for the new U.S. context in which biblical interpretation must now be done.

will be hard to come by. In fact, interpretation is no longer safely in the hands of certified, authorized interpreters, but we are faced with a remarkable pluralism.

Thus I propose a *contextual shift from hegemonic interpretation* (still reflected in the mid-twentieth century by Walther Eichrodt and Gerhard von Rad and more recently by Brevard Childs) *toward a pluralistic interpretive context* (reflected in the texts themselves, in biblical interpreters, and in the culture at large).

Plurality of Testimonies in the Text

We are now able to recognize, against any hypothesis of a unilateral development of Israel's religion or Israel's "God-talk," that the texts themselves witness to a plurality of testimonies concerning God and Israel's life with God.[9] This pluralism is perhaps most clear when one considers the rich array of literary-theological responses to the crisis of the exile. No one response was adequate and no one articulation of Yahweh in exile was sufficient.[10] It is, moreover, clear that the several testimonies to Yahweh, in any particular moment of Israel's life, were often in profound dispute with one another, disagreeing from the ground up about the "truth" of Yahweh. The several stances of testimony in the Book of Job are evidence of such dispute. In similar fashion, Christopher Seitz has shown how interpretive conflict gives shape to the Book of Jeremiah.[11]

In the end, it is clear that "the final form of the text," in its canonizing process, did not feature a complete hegemonic victory for any interpretive trajectory. As Rainer Albertz has shown, the canonizing process is one of accommodation and compromise.[12] The decision to hold the Priestly and Deuteronomic traditions in tension, accepting and acknowledging both as truth, is a striking evidence of pluralism. Old Testament theology must live with that pluralistic practice of dispute and compromise, so that the texts cannot be arranged in any single or unilateral pattern. It is the process of dispute and compromise itself that constitutes Israel's mode of theological testimony. (Gerhard von Rad saw this pluralism clearly, but he did not point to the constitutive process of dispute and compromise reflected in the pluralism as definitional for Israel's faith.)

Dispute and Accommodation in Interpretation

Our new emerging context of theological interpretation evidences that the pluralism of dispute and accommodation found within the text is matched by a pluralism of dispute and accommodation within the ongoing interpretive enterprise. I have

---

9. See especially Rainer Albertz, *A History of Israelite Religion in the Old Testament Period* 1: *From the Beginnings to the End of the Monarchy* and 2: *From the Exile to the Maccabees* (OTL; Louisville: Westminster/John Knox, 1994).

10. In addition to Albertz, *A History of Israelite Religion in the Old Testament Period* 2, see also Ralph W. Klein, *Israel in Exile: A Theological Interpretation* (OBT; Philadelphia: Fortress Press, 1979). The fact of the inadequacy of any single articulation of faith is especially clear in the canonical juxtaposition of the Priestly and Deuteronomic traditions.

11. Christopher R. Seitz, *Theology in Conflict: Reactions to the Exile in the Book of Jeremiah* (BZAW 176; Berlin: Walter de Gruyter, 1989).

12. Albertz, *A History of Israelite Religion in the Old Testament Period,* 2:468, 481, and passim.

already given attention to the stance of what I have called centrist interpreters and marginated interpreters. Such categories may be too simplistic and reductionist, but the point will be clear.

With the proliferation of interpretive methods, and with interpretive voices speaking as never before from a wide range of socio-ecclesial-political-economic contexts, Old Testament theology is now an active process of dispute that does from time to time end in some compromises, accommodations, or acknowledged settlements, albeit provisional ones. Because different interpretations in different contexts—driven by different hopes, fears, and hurts—ask different questions from the ground up, it is clear that there will be no widely accepted "canon within the canon," which is itself a function of hegemonic interpretation. As a consequence, we are now able to see that every interpretation is context-driven and interest-driven to some large extent.[13]

This recognition, now almost a commonplace, is a recent recognition that was not available to previous interpretation. In established, hegemonic interpretation it was possible to imagine (perhaps innocently) that the questions asked of the texts and the methods of interpretive response were obvious, given, and intrinsic to the text. No more so! The ecclesial-academic enterprise of interpretation, like the testimonial process of Israel itself, is a pluralistic one of dispute and accommodation. What is important to recognize is that in such a disputatious interpretive undertaking, every interpretive gesture is a provisional one that must be adjudicated yet again. Thus it helps very little to claim high moral ground or high critical ground, or orthodoxy or solemnity of voice or indignation against ideology, because these stances tend to be acknowledged only in privileged contexts.

The theological offer of any particular interpretive voice in any particular interpretive context must make its way in a disputatious process with no evident rules of engagement beyond the readiness to be serious in the dispute.[14] To be sure, there are some elemental agreements in the interpretive process (as there were in the testimonial processes of ancient Israel) that permit the exchange to continue. But these elemental agreements are almost always inchoate. As soon as they are expli-

---

13. Penchansky, *The Politics of Biblical Theology*, has made this clear in a succinct fashion. What he has not made clear is the interest driving postmodern perspectives. I suspect that such perspectives, in rage and resentment against theological authoritarianism, constitute an unwitting lust for Cartesian autonomy. In my judgment that uncritical embrace of autonomy is as costly as the alternative of authoritarianism.

It remains to be seen whether a mode of interpretation is possible that stays clear of both authoritarianism and autonomy. Carl E. Braaten and Robert W. Jenson, eds., *Reclaiming the Bible for the Church* (Grand Rapids: Eerdmans, 1995), seem to me correct on their warnings against autonomous interpretation. But their shrill insistence on "canonical interpretation" sounds profoundly authoritarian to my ears.

14. By a disputatious process, I do not mean, as postmodern adherents often seem to suggest, each one doing his or her "own thing." If the matter at issue is serious, then it must be disputed. On a serious matter, no advocate is content simply to let another opinion stand side-by-side unchallenged. The pluralistic, disputatious process requires, in my judgment, a resolve to stay engaged and an ability to listen as well as speak.

cated, they take on the shading of more concrete advocacy, which reinvigorates the dispute whereby Israel always arrives afresh at Yahweh.

Postmodern Accounts of Reality

With the demise of Western Christendom and the parallel demise of the old epistemological consensus, it is evident that, beyond the Old Testament and beyond the world of Old Testament interpretation, other very different and very serious accounts of reality are alive in the world. Old Testament theology (or biblical theology or Christian theology) can no longer imagine that it is enunciating a consensus view of reality. This new intellectual situation, widely dubbed "postmodern," has been explicated by Jean-François Lyotard as a situation in which there is no confidence in metanarratives.[15] In that frame of reference, the Old Testament articulates a metanarrative that, because of its central character Yahweh, is sharply distinguishable from all other metanarratives.[16] In that important regard, moreover, there is a kinship among the various modes of Old Testament theological interpretation.

In my judgment, however, we should not too readily accept Lyotard's verdict about a loss of confidence in metanarratives. I prefer to think that our situation is one of conflict and competition between deeply held metanarratives, which are seldom enunciated and only evidenced in bits and pieces. For example, the metanarrative of ancient Israel is rarely explicated fully in current usage, but rather is presented in bits and pieces in lectionary readings and in scholarly preoccupation with minutiae in the text. In the same way, the dominant metanarrative of military consumerism is seldom articulated in toto, but is exhibited in fragments such as television commercials. As lectionary readings of the Bible appeal to the larger, hidden metanarrative of ancient Israel, so television commercials appeal to the largely (and deliberately?) hidden metanarrative of consumer exploitation.

The important point for our consideration is that the metanarrative of the Old Testament (or of the Bible or of the church) no longer enjoys any hegemonic privilege. It must enter into a pluralistic context of interpretation, in order to see what of dispute and accommodation is possible.

These three pluralisms, which displace three long-established hegemonies, seem to me not in question. I am not advocating these displacements, but only insisting that they are powerfully operative and that they constitute the context in which Old Testament theology must now be conducted and will be conducted into the

---

15. Jean-François Lyotard, *The Postmodern Condition: A Report on Knowledge* (Minneapolis: University of Minnesota Press, 1984).

16. I am not sure whether I should speak of the Old Testament as providing a metanarrative, or as providing the materials out of which a metanarrative might be constructed. I am inclined to the latter. And yet, over against any other metanarrative, all of the metanarratives likely to be constructed out of the materials of the Old Testament are apt to have a striking family resemblance. I prefer to leave the matter open, as it does not affect my argument here. I shall speak simply of metanarrative for purposes of convenience, but with an acknowledgment of my uncertainty, which I do not prejudice by my shorthand usage.

foreseeable future. The loss of hegemony on the part of Western Christendom and on the part of Enlightenment rationality are, in my judgment, irresistible. One need not spend time wishing otherwise. The important point, for the future of Old Testament theology, is how we may assess the shift from a hegemonic to a pluralistic environment.

It is tempting—certainly for this white, Western male—to view the new pluralism as a loss and threat, and to wish for a more ordered circumstance of unacknowledged privilege. In my judgment, however, such a temptation should be resisted. It may well be that our pluralistic context of dispute and accommodation is one of liberation for those who assent to the testimony of the Bible. For in such a context, interpretive work does not have to bear the weight of the entire socioeconomic-political-moral-military establishment. It is possible that the testimony of Israel is to be seen, even in our own time, not as the dominant metanarrative that must give order and coherence across the full horizon of social reality, but as *a subversive protest* and as *an alternative act of vision* that invites criticism and transformation.

Old Testament Theology in Relation to Pluralism

Given this new context in which political and epistemological claims to hegemony seem to be inappropriate, the larger question occurs: Will Old Testament theology be possible at all in time to come? The immediate answer is yes, because people like me will go on doing it and will not be stopped. But we must consider the question more carefully and in relation to the three pluralisms we have identified.

The Metaphor of Testimony

In the work offered here, I have attempted to fashion an approach that honors precisely the variegated nature of the texts themselves. The hallmark of this approach is the governing metaphor of *testimony*. It is not for me to decide whether this attempt has proved successful. I wish nonetheless to make some observations concerning the present work, which I believe are important to any future work in Old Testament theology.

I have proposed that Old Testament theology focus on Israel's speech about God. The positive warrant for this proposal is that what we have in the Old Testament is speech, nothing else.[17] My approach assumes that speech is constitutive of reality, that words count, that the practitioners of Yahweh are indeed *homo rhetori-*

---

17. In the Old Testament, of course, speech has become writing. I do not minimize the importance of the difference between speech and writing, on which see Walter J. Ong, *Orality and Literacy: The Technologizing of the Word* (London: Methuen, 1982); and Werner H. Kelber, *The Oral and the Written Gospel: The Hermeneutics of Speaking and Writing in the Synoptic Tradition, Mark, Paul, and Q* (Philadelphia: Fortress Press, 1983). The distinction, however, is not important for the point being made here. Thus I refer to "speech" in order to comprehend the entire process of speech-becoming-text.

cus.[18] Yahweh lives in, with, and under this speech, and in the end depends on Israel's testimony for an access point in the world. This is, of course, a sweeping statement, one that I shall perhaps regret before I am finished.

But the point of settling on speech is that I wish to distinguish Old Testament theology from two temptations that characteristically vex Old Testament interpretation. On the one hand, the Old Testament in the modern world is endlessly vexed by and tempted to historicity; that is, to "what happened."[19] Even Gerhard von Rad, for all his daring, could not escape the modernist trap of history. It is my judgment that Enlightenment modes of history have almost nothing to do with Israel's sense of Yahweh. What "happened" (whatever it may mean) depends on testimony and tradition that will not submit to any other warrant.[20] On the other hand, Old Testament theology is endlessly seduced by the ancient Hellenistic lust for Being, for establishing ontological reference behind the text.[21] Thus, for example, Brevard Childs reaches for "the Real." Perhaps such thinking is inevitable, given our Hellenistic, philosophical inheritance. The truth of the matter, as far as Israel is concerned, is that if one believes the testimony, one is near to reality. And if not, one is not near reality, for the Real is indeed uttered.

Such a construal will not satisfy modernist historicism nor the philosophically minded. It is my impression that to satisfy either of these requires one to give up the venturesome, risky way in which Israel affirms its faith and the equally venturesome and risky way Yahweh lives in the world. It may well be that I have not given correct nuance to these matters because I lack knowledge in the appropriate adjunct disciplines. I have no doubt, nonetheless, that Old Testament theology in the future must do its work in reliance on the lean evidence of utterance.

---

18. On "rhetorical man," see Richard A. Lanham, *The Motives of Eloquence: Literary Rhetoric in the Renaissance* (New Haven: Yale University Press, 1976) 1–8 and passim.

19. See Yosef Hayim Yerushalmi, *Zakhor: Jewish History and Jewish Memory* (Seattle: University of Washington Press, 1982), on the crucial distinction between history (as scientifically understood) and memory; and Perdue, *The Collapse of History*, on the problems of positivistic history.

20. The cul-de-sac of "history" as a governing mode of serious theology was made evident by Van Austin Harvey, *The Historian and the Believer: The Morality of Historical Knowledge and Christian Belief* (London: SCM Press, 1967), even though he drew conclusions very different from those I imply here. It is important, for example, that in 1 Corinthians 15 Paul speaks of faith being "futile" (v. 17) if the resurrection has not happened. But his grounding is in explicit testimony (vv. 5-8) and in no other mode of certainty or evidence. Certitude arises in the process of testimony, and not in "objective" recovery of data.

21. It is my judgment that as far as Israel is concerned, "being" is established in and through speech and not behind it. It is not my intention to be anti-ontological. It is rather to insist that whatever might be claimed for ontology in the purview of Israel's speech can be claimed only in and through testimonial utterance. That is, once the testimony of Israel is accepted as true—once one believes what it claims—one has ontology, one has the reality of Yahweh.

But to have the reality of God apart from the testimony of Israel is sure to yield some God other than the Yahweh of Israel. My impression is that the cruciality of speech to reality here is not unlike the claim of the Sophists in ancient Greece; cf. chap. 3, n. 6. This is against the Platonic tradition that claims to shun rhetoric for "being," but in fact only makes that claim as a way to practice very conservative politics, and to preclude challenge that can only be made by rhetoric. I am resistant to the claim of "the real" for the God of the Bible apart from testimonial rhetoric, because such a claim seems to me predictably to issue in and serve conservative if not reactionary politics. See the polemical analysis of the issue by José Miranda, *Being and the Messiah: The Message of St. John* (Maryknoll, N.Y.: Orbis Books, 1973).

The metaphor of testimony is particularly suited to the disputatious quality of Old Testament interpretation. In any serious courtroom trial, testimony is challenged by other, competing testimony. In any serious trial, no unchallenged testimony can expect to carry the day easily. Thus I want to insist, against any unilateral rendering of Yahweh's life, or against any systematic portrayal of Yahweh, that Yahweh in the horizon and utterance of Israel is inescapably disputatious and disjunctive.

Testimony for Yahweh is deeply in dispute with other available metanarratives in the contemporary world, as it was in deep dispute with ancient imperial systems and ancient religious alternatives. Following Fernando Belo, one can see Yahweh as the force of a tradition of order and purity (allied with sociologies of equilibrium) and as the force of a tradition of debt cancellation (allied with sociologies of conflict and revolution).[22] Sufficient texts are given concerning Yahweh to sustain each of these perspectives.

In using the rubrics of "core testimony" and "countertestimony," I have pointed to the undeniable fact that in Israel's own testimony in the text, the "good claims" made for Yahweh as sustainer and transformer are offset and undermined by evidence to the contrary. On many occasions in its canonized testimony, Israel asserts that the sustainer is not always reliable and the transformer is sometimes ineffective. In many texts, but in exemplar fashion in Exod 34:6-7, we have seen that, if the text is to be taken as "witnesses to the real," the ground of dispute is not to be found simply in modern, undisciplined pluralism or in Israel's ancient disputatiousness, but in the very character of Yahweh.[23]

I have insisted that this disputatious quality is definitional for Israel and for Yahweh. The dispute cannot be settled ultimately but only provisionally. In that regard, I believe Old Testament theology is a lively option at the moment of the breakup of the Christian hegemony in the West, for the faith of Israel and the God of Israel precisely refuse the kind of settlement that makes hegemony possible.

The metaphor of testimony is not only verbal, but is embodied as a form of life. In my consideration of the communal, structural, institutional ways in which Israel conducted its testimony, we are speaking of an embodied community that seeks to live out its testimony and therefore the practice of Yahweh. It seems clear on many counts that the old Cartesian dualism that permits faith to be a reasoned, intellectual activity has failed. Indeed Yahweh, in Yahweh's contradictory self-presentations, is a failure by such norms in any case. The Western hegemonic church, with its sorry record on economics and sexuality, has a long tradition of body-denying in its faith. To be sure, there have been and continue to be vigor-

---

22. Fernando Belo, *A Materialist Reading of the Gospel of Mark* (Maryknoll, N.Y.: Orbis Books, 1981). See also Walter Brueggemann, "Trajectories in Old Testament Literature and the Sociology of Ancient Israel," *JBL* 98 (1979) 161–85.

23. On the openness and risk intrinsic to this text, see James L. Crenshaw, "Who Knows What YHWH Will Do? The Character of God in the Book of Joel," *Fortunate the Eyes That See: Essays in Honor of David Noel Freedman* (ed. Astrid B. Beck et al.; Grand Rapids: Eerdmans, 1995) 185–96.

ous protests against such dualism, but they have not prevailed. And Old Testament theology, in its "idealism," has too often colluded with such denying dualism.[24]

Thus I have insisted that Yahwism in ancient Israel is a matter of communal praxis.[25] We may expect, with emerging pluralism and collapsed hegemony, that the serious, intentional, disciplined practice of Yahweh may take many forms, some local and some larger, some ecclesial and some extraecclesial. Old Testament theology will perhaps on occasion be concrete and bodily enough to authorize such practices in the face of dominant metanarratives that resist such radical embodiment.

Thus, whether I have the nuances correct or not, I anticipate that Old Testament theology, in its attempts to honor the plurality of the text, will have to reckon with

- the cruciality of speech as the mode of Yahweh's actuality,
- the disputatious quality of truth, and
- the lived, bodied form of testimonial communities.

These marks, I propose, are congruent with our interpretive situation in the West and present an important contrast to the old, hegemonic forms of Old Testament theology.

Old Testament Theology: Impossible or Unwelcome?

A powerful contemporary opinion holds that Old Testament theology is both an impossibility and an aberration in the wider enterprise of biblical studies. The notion that Old Testament theology is *impossible* stems from the above awareness that the Old Testament itself is profoundly pluralistic, and any notion of Old Testament theology is thought, by definition, to be reductionist, thus riding roughshod over the rich diversity of the text. The notion in Old Testament scholarship that Old Testament theology is *an unwelcome and ignoble project in principle* stems from a very different but related notion. Whereas the notion of impossibility derives from the sense that theological interpretation is inherently reductionist by classifying matters into a neat system, the notion of theological interpretation as an unwelcome aberration, in my view, stems from the sense that theological interpretation is inherently authoritarian, reflective of experiences or impressions of an ecclesial interpretive authority that was coercive in its requirements. Indeed, a long history exists of wounding theological interpretation that is both reductionist and coercive.

Back in the days of a unified historical criticism, scholarship in general seemed to tolerate a gap between critical conclusions and theological assumptions, a gap

---

24. For a careful critique of such idealistic perspectives in Old Testament scholarship, see Norman K. Gottwald, *The Tribes of Yahweh: A Sociology of the Religion of Liberated Israel, 1250–1050 B.C.E.* (Maryknoll, N.Y.: Orbis Books, 1979) 592–607. On the materiality of biblical faith, see the venturesome extrapolation of Sallie McFague, *The Body of God: An Ecological Theology* (Minneapolis: Fortress Press, 1993).

25. On Old Testament faith as praxis, see Gottwald, *The Tribes of Yahweh*, 700–709 and passim.

hidden by slippery language (especially about "history") and seldom exposed. Thus one had the odd result of rigorous critical scholarship that ostensibly yielded a most innocent theological interpretation. It is a curious, and in my view unfortunate, mark of current scholarship that many scholars have moved beyond historical criticism in its older modes, but have moved into the kinds of rhetorical and literary studies that are skeptical if not resistant to theological interpretation. These recent studies often are marked with insightful observations of an artistic and aesthetic kind about the strategies of the text, so that attention is given to everything except the "testimony" *to Yahweh* that is offered in the text.[26]

It is my impression that such resistance to theological claim about the character of Yahweh as the God to whom Israel bears witness is not rooted in anything about the testimony as such. It is rooted, rather, in old wounds of reductionism and coercion, wounds that are kept hidden or are denied in the name of scientific distancing. My impression, further, is that this aversion to theological interpretation occurs especially among Roman Catholic scholars who have suffered at the hands of an imposing, insistent magisterium, and among scholars with a Protestant upbringing in which coercive social control was confused with the God given in the testimony of Israel.

I have no negative judgment to make about scholarship that stays clear of theological interpretation because of past oppressive experiences at the hands of ecclesial interpretive communities, though I think one would be better served if such scholars shared that shaping personal reality in their work. The greater problem, it appears to me, is that such scholars tend to regard Enlightenment rationality with a kind of naive innocence, as though that perspective were not as ideology-laden, and ultimately as reductionist and coercive, as any ecclesial interpretation could ever be.[27]

It is my hope that I have modeled a responsible way of doing Old Testament theological interpretation that is a genuine alternative to these stereotypical modes that so deeply offend and so profoundly wound. It is my expectation that Old Testament theological interpretation that is viable in our new interpretive situation need not and dare not be reductionist. That is why I have focused on disputatious testimony that refuses closure. In parallel fashion, Old Testament theological interpretation, in my judgment, need not and dare not be coercive, because it does not aim at a consensus conclusion. It aims, rather, at an ongoing, contested conversation about the character of Yahweh.

It is a great problem for Old Testament scholars who, for reasons of their own, are resistant to what they regard as theological interpretation, to imagine that the character of God lives "outside the text," that is, has metaphysical substance. But that objection in principle imposes a dualism of text/nontext that passionate testi-

---

26. See the protest of Jack Miles, *God: A Biography* (New York: Knopf, 1995), against Enlightenment positivistic scholarship that can speak of everything except Yahweh.

27. Thus Hans-Georg Gadamer, *Truth and Method* (New York: Seabury Press, 1975) 239–40, can speak of the Enlightenment "prejudice against prejudice itself."

mony never entertains. Thus I am content to have theological interpretation stay inside the text—to refrain from either historical or ontological claim extrinsic to the text—but to take the text seriously as testimony and to let it have its say alongside other testimonies, including the testimony of Enlightenment rationality that, with like force, affirms and precludes. It is my hope that if consideration of Israel's God-talk can be separated from hegemonic administration that has largely monopolized that God-talk, then Old Testament scholars might be free to consider this testimony also outside the hegemonic rationality of the Enlightenment. In my judgment, we are at a moment in Old Testament theology when we might reconsider the categories in which the power of Israel's testimonial utterance might be reconsidered, apart from every heavy-handed enforcer, ecclesial as well as academic, confessional as well as rationalistic.

The Metanarrative of Military Consumerism

Our context within which to consider the viability of Old Testament theology is the wider social context of the West, where another metanarrative is more powerful and compelling. I have already suggested a correction to Lyotard's notion of no confidence in metanarratives, to suggest instead competing metanarratives that exercise enormous power, even if they are kept strangely hidden. Pluralism in the public arena does not mean "anything goes." Such a notion of unmitigated freedom is itself a function of military consumerism. In reality, in any particular circumstance, public or personal, we are not confronted by a myriad of limitless options, but we are met with only a few choices, each of which is situated in a (often unrecognized) metanarrative.[28]

It is my judgment that the dominant metanarrative of Western society, and therefore the primary alternative to Israel's Yahwistic construal of reality, is military consumerism. I shall premise my discussion here on that basis. (In other social settings one might focus on some other primary alternative to Israel's Yahwistic construal of reality.) By "military consumerism" I refer to a construal of the world in which individual persons are reckoned as the primary units of meaning and reference, and individual persons, in unfettered freedom, are authorized (self-authorized) to pursue well-being, security, and happiness as they choose.

This metanarrative has, as its "consumer" component, the conviction that well-being, security, and happiness are the result of getting, having, using, and consuming, activities that may be done without restraint or limit, even at the expense of others. This construal of reality has its "military" component in the conviction that having a disproportion of whatever it takes to enjoy well-being, security, and happiness is appropriate, and that the use of force, coercion, or violence, either to secure or to maintain a disproportion, is completely congruent with this notion of happiness.

---

28. Alasdair MacIntyre, *Whose Justice? Which Rationality?* (Notre Dame, Ind.: University of Notre Dame Press, 1988), and *Three Rival Versions of Moral Enquiry: Encyclopedia, Genealogy, and Tradition* ((Notre Dame, Ind.: University of Notre Dame Press, 1990), suggests that there are three fundamental options.

This construal of reality, moreover, exercises a totalizing effect among us, by its technological availability and by its capacity to control public imagination through the media. This metanarrative is so massive and so compelling that it largely defines the thinkable, imaginable options, holding together, as it does, enormous freedom of a certain kind with a tight conformity that precludes any serious challenge to the current, disproportionate deployment of power, goods, and access.

In these broad strokes, I may have caricatured the dominant metanarrative; that is not my intention. I believe that this is a rough portrayal of our true ideological situation. Many "users" and interpreters of the Old Testament, moreover, find it altogether possible to take bits and pieces of Israel's testimony in the Old Testament and accommodate them to the main claims of the metanarrative of military consumerism, thus removing these bits and pieces from their own habitat in Israel's testimony, and thereby completely distorting them.

It is in this ideological context that we ask our question: Is Old Testament theology possible in the wider social context of the West, where another metanarrative is more powerful and compelling? In other words, can the world be imagined in any sustained way according to Israel's testimony, when the imaginative power of military consumerism is so overwhelming? The answer to that question is not obvious, and surely a positive answer is not easy. If Old Testament theology—that is, Israel's characteristic construal of the world around the character of Yahweh—is to be credible in authorizing an alternative life in the world, then I suggest that an interpretive, interpreting community must attend to the issues that stand between this construal of reality and the claims of military consumerism.

Israel's testimony invites "the court" into a world of *undomesticated holiness,* marked by staggering sovereignty and inexplicable fidelity, but given in ways that are disjunctive and disruptive. Such an offer testifies against the hegemonic vision of military consumerism, which imagines that the world can be secured, explained, mastered, and controlled, and which makes convenient common cause with the domesticated divinity of bourgeois Christianity. Israel invites residence in a world beset by ambiguity and unsettlement, rooted in the life of the central Character.

Israel's testimony invites "the court" into a world of *originary generosity* in which gifts are inexplicably given for "more than all we can ask or imagine" (Eph 3:20). Such an offer testifies against the grudging inclination of military consumerism, which concludes that no gifts are given, that there is no generosity, that everything is quid pro quo, and that one must have self-sufficient resources in order to get more. Israel invites residence in a world saturated by an inexplicable generosity, rooted only in the life of the central Character.

Israel's testimony invites "the court" into a world of *indefatigable possibility,* in which promises are endlessly enacted beyond all visible circumstance, and in which new waves of promise are being uttered that permit passionate hope beyond every explanatory option. Such an offer tells against the closed-down world of military consumerism that imagines there are no more promises to be kept and no more words to be uttered, and so concludes in a self-destructive, world-destructive despair. Israel invites residence in a world overrun with freighted promises that dazzle in their fulfillments, and that sustain in the long, dry season between; promises and possibilities rooted only in the resolve of the central Character.

Israel's testimony invites "the court" into a world of *open-ended interaction,* a covenantal exchange that continually redeploys power between the strong and the weak and that even invites demanding, insistent interventions against Yahweh. Such an offer of a lively covenantal existence testifies against the fixed, fated world of military consumerism, in which the poor only become poorer, the rich become richer, and together the rich and the poor end in a paralysis of pride, despair, and a futile death. Israel invites residence in a world that is genuinely open for giving and receiving, for the full exchange of value in trust and confidence, an openness rooted in the life of the central Character, who can on occasion be on the receiving end and often on the giving end.

Israel's testimony invites "the court" into a world of *genuine neighborliness,* in which members in a community share without fear and practice justice that assures well-being for every member of the community. Such an invitation to community testifies against the harsh, definitional selfishness of military consumerism, in which every neighbor is reduced to a usable commodity, where the process of commoditization eventually empties even the subject of the individual of all human possibility. Israel invites residence in a world of caring and sharing, in which members know that something counts more than the surface offers of well-being, security, and happiness that have no human depth.

In rough outline, Israel's testimony yields a world as deeply opposed to military consumerism as it is to every other alternative metanarrative that lacks the markings of the central Character. It is not a given that a world marked by undomesticated holiness, originary generosity, indefatigable possibility, open-ended interaction, and genuine neighborliness is more compelling than other metanarratives, for the chief alternative among us does make some surface promises that it can keep. Only in the presence of the richer, more dense metanarrative of Yahwism can the inadequacy of the dominant metanarrative be observed. And where the metanarrative of Yahwism is not fully and courageously voiced, the dominant metanarrative appears as the only available one. I believe that this inability or refusal to voice the metanarrative made possible in Israel's testimony has, in no small way, permitted the metanarrative of military consumerism to dominate by default.

It is the task of Old Testament theology, set in the large arena of competing alternatives, to evidence the ways in which a counter metanarrative may have authority. There is nothing inherently or especially reductionist or coercive about this alternative wrought of Israel's testimony. Israel uttered this construal of reality to itself, to its young, and to outsiders, because Israel believed the issues were as serious as life and death. It is possible, here and there in odd and local ways, that this construal of reality takes on authority. That finally is what is at stake in Old Testament theology.

TWENTY-SEVEN

The Constitutive Power
of Israel's Testimony

I N MY DISCUSSION, I have staked a great deal on the claim that the testimony of Israel is fundamentally constituted by *concrete utterance*, which is generative of social reality. This is an enormous claim; I believe, however, it is of interest not only for the exposition I have offered. It is equally important, in my judgment, for the future of Old Testament theology more generally, as disestablishment leaves biblical interpretation without many of its accustomed institutional, sociopolitical supports. I suggest that concrete utterance is more elemental to Israel's embrace and explication of Yahweh than are the two accustomed claims of history and ontology.

Concerning history, I suggest that the question of what "happened" is now hopelessly intertwined with positivistic historicism, which intends, characteristically, to remove what is awkward or scandalous (and normative) in utterances-become-texts. Utilization of historical research as an instance of theological skepticism seems to me evident in the current rage to date everything in the Old Testament late. Thus: "It is late, therefore it did not really happen, therefore it could hardly be authoritative." Some such inclination appears to be at work in the "Third Quest" of the "Jesus Seminar."[1]

Conversely, in a reaction against such debunking historicism, others are making a positive effort to reach outside the text to get at the "really real"—at the God who is outside and beyond the text, so that the text references beyond itself.[2] This push, it appears to me, is pursued in the conviction that the utterance-become-text

---

1. On the "Jesus Seminar," see the fine forum offered in *TToday* 52 (1995) 1–97, especially Marcus J. Borg, "The Historian, the Christian, and Jesus," 6–16, and Howard Clark Kee, "A Century of Quests for the Culturally Compatible Jesus," 17–28. See also Luke Timothy Johnson, *The Real Jesus* (San Francisco: Harper, 1996).

2. See Brevard S. Childs, *Biblical Theology of the Old and New Testaments: Theological Reflection on the Christian Bible* (Minneapolis: Fortress Press, 1993) 20 and passim; and more recently see Childs, "On Reclaiming the Bible for Christian Theology," *Reclaiming the Bible for the Church* (ed. Carl E. Braaten and Robert W. Jenson; Grand Rapids: Eerdmans, 1995) 1-17. Karl Barth, *Church Dogmatics* 1/1 (Edinburgh: T. & T. Clark, 1975), focuses on the word as testimony in a way congruent with what I am suggesting. But Barth could not finally let word as utterance (proclamation) stand apart from a threefold notion of word (Jesus, Bible, proclamation), which for him in the end is more "being" than speech.

721

itself is not adequate, so that utterance spoken loudly enough and in capital letters becomes metaphysics.

Both of these temptations to want more (or less in the case of dismissive historicism) than the text seem to me hopeless enterprises and surely ones that Old Testament theology must eschew. To be sure, compared to confident historical reconstructionism and to conventional metaphysical claims, utterance-become-text seems a thin basis for life in the world. It is my judgment, however, that in the ancient world of Israel's utterance it was enough for the most yielding of Israelites.[3] Moreover, in our own time and place, I propose that we must consider carefully whether theological interpretation may trust the utterance enough to receive the God given in the text, for finally "history" or "ontology," as starting points for theological interpretation, will appeal to utterance-become-text as its pivot point.[4] I suggest that what we must examine is not how Israel could rely on such a lean resource, but why that utterance now seems to us so untrustworthy and flimsy.

In making this claim I refer to Israel's characteristic utterance, which, over much time and in many circumstances, has a recognizable cadence. I do not refer to any attempt to locate "original" or early utterance, but only reliable, recurring utterance, which is the substance of Old Testament theology. This recognizable, peculiar utterance is such that for one of its adherents, only a few words need be heard to complete the utterance; if some words cannot be heard, they can be filled in by those who know the way this utterance works. The identifiability of this utterance is not unlike hearing one's own language on the street in a location where another language is normally spoken. It takes only a little overhearing to recognize the pattern of speech of one's native tongue and to have its utterance be a welcoming, sense-making moment. Having recognized the familiarity of the utterance, it is then possible as well to recognize and appreciate the variations and deviations from the familiar, which we may assume are enacted with great intentionality. At some important level, faith consists in a willingness to live in the world of this utterance, and to accept as reliable its speech as testimony.

Such speech—spoken regularly, in season and out of season—recruits persons into this community and into its faith (that is, its construal of reality; cf. Deut 6:4-9; Ps 78:5-8) by a *pedagogy of saturation*. This speech is summons, demand, assurance, and invitation to belong to this community of utterance and to the world uttered by this community, including the God at the center of this uttered world. Adherents to Yahweh, in the Old Testament, are those who accept this characteristic testimony as a valid articulation of reality, on which they are prepared to act.

---

3. My impression is that those who "yielded," who found this uttered world compelling, did so not because of some prior religious disposition, but because of desperation wrought by their real-life, sociopolitical situation. That is, the utterance "made sense" of nonsensical situations of deathliness.

4. See Walter Brueggemann, *Biblical Perspectives on Evangelism: Living in a Three-Storied Universe* (Nashville: Abingdon Press, 1993) 94–128.

In the context of this community, which recruits, nurtures, disciplines, and admonishes its members and candidates for membership, these utterances are indeed constitutive of reality. Israel regularly speaks a particular world into availability. Its polemical speech, moreover, intends at the same time to nullify worlds it dismisses as false, unreliable, and deathly.

In making this claim, it is important to recognize that there is, outside speech, no objectively given world that stands as a measuring rod of reality, whereby one can test to see if Israel is "realistic."[5] In its iconoclastic insistence, Israel holds that such worlds that have come to be regarded as given over time are in fact only other spoken worlds, spoken so long, so authoritatively, and so credibly that they appear to be given. Thus Israel's testimony about a world with Yahweh at its center intends to debunk and nullify all other proposed worlds that do not have Yahweh at their center. This testimony undertaken persistently by Israel is not neutral or descriptive, but it is thoroughly and pervasively partisan advocacy. This partisan advocacy, moreover, is generative and constitutive of a new world, when "recruits" sign on to this world of utterance. In signing on, such recruits and members at the same time depart other worlds that are based in other normative utterances (cf. Josh 24:23).

This peculiar world of utterance, with Yahweh at its center, has a quality of constancy to it through time, and it is this constancy that constitutes the material of Old Testament theology. Two features of this constancy are in deep tension. On the one hand, the Yahwistic constancy of Israel's testimony is deeply laden with ideological freight. This is especially evident in the "Yahweh alone" party associated with the Deuteronomic traditions, a stance intolerant of variation or deviation.[6] That "Yahweh alone" party provided a rhetorical world that is not only insistently Yahwistic, but also tends to be deeply patriarchal and capable of sanctioning violence against all deviations from its ideology.

On the other hand, having recognized its ideological heavy-handedness, we must also recognize that Yahwistic constancy has a relentless quality of elusiveness. Thus the Yahweh who is authoritarian also turns out to be the Yahweh who is beyond domestication and imprisonment.[7] This elusive quality seems to be almost inherent in the notion of Israel's testimonial utterance, which is marked by teasing ambiguity, expressed in metaphors that cannot be flattened to precision. In

---

5. I refer to the temptation to foundationalism. While more philosophically inclined theological interpretation may make a case for foundationalism, I do not see any opening for it in core Old Testament claims as such. It is the great force of Old Testament testimony to Yahweh (as well as its great problematic) that utterance of Yahweh is not measured by previous historical or ontological reality.

6. On the "Yahweh alone" party, see Morton Smith, *Palestinian Parties and Politics that Shaped the Old Testament* (New York: Columbia University Press, 1971); and Martin Rose, *Der Ausschliesslichkeitsanspruch Jahwes; Deuteronomische Schultheologie und die Volksfrommigkeit in der Späten Konigszeit* (BWANT 6; Stuttgart: W. Kohlhammer Verlag, 1975).

7. In a study of Micah, my student Timothy K. Beal, "System and Speaking Subject in the Hebrew Bible: Reading for Divine Abjection," *Biblical Interpretation* 2 (1994) 171–89, has shown how the ideological critique of Julia Kristeva in fact misses the intention of the text to allow Yahweh considerable instability, certainly more instability than is welcomed by harsh, ideological critics of the text.

the end this elusive quality is desconstructive of the ideological rigor noted above, so that when Yahweh is portrayed in savage ideology, one can regularly notice hints to the contrary.

This quality of constancy as both *ideology* and *elusiveness* is a rich interpretive invitation. I suppose, in the end, we must make a crucial judgment about whether ideology or elusiveness has the last word.[8] In my own reading, I find that no ideological statement of Yahweh is permitted finally to prevail, always being undermined by elusiveness. But some other readers, perhaps wounded by authoritarian interpretation as I have not been, will find that ideology finally wins out over the elusiveness. Or it may be simply that the issue of ideology and elusiveness is the very marking of constancy that belongs to Yahweh who is endlessly responsive and available and at the same time intransigently sovereign. That unresolved, and perhaps unresolvable, issue is precisely what is so compelling and so maddening about Old Testament theology.

The constancy and generativity of this characteristic utterance of Israel has a profound density to it, which is available only to its committed practitioners. This density means that the Yahwistic testimony of Israel is deeply coded, so that there is always allusion and reference within an utterance that refers to another utterance.[9] The density is not simply moral or cognitive, but it has a practical, material aspect that pertains to the lived, public, institutional life of Israel. As a result, any hearing of these utterances that seeks to keep them separated from their radical socioeconomic counterparts is a mishearing. Thus serious hearing of such utterance entails bodily practice in the disciplines and freedoms arising from the utterance—and the greatest of these is neighbor love.

Israel's elemental reliance on utterance has characteristically had rough going in the world. It is perhaps this odd quality of utterance, nearly ideological, characteristically elusive, that marks Israelite oddity in the world, an oddity that must be resisted if control of the world is to be secured.[10] Here useful appeal may be made to Jacques Ellul's phrase, "The Humiliation of the Word."[11] Already in 1967 in *The Technological Society*, Ellul had considered the dehumanizing power of modern technology.[12] His book advances the analysis by its insistence that manipulated

---

8. Those who regard the text as ideological are likely to tilt toward skepticism, and those who find in the text elusiveness will move in a fideistic direction. But fideism also is open to reductionism as is skepticism. There is no "answer in the back of the book." I insist only that skeptical-as-ideological propensities have no privilege in interpretation. I suspect that polemics between skepticism and fideism are misguided, because the real issue is between ideological reductionism and openness to elusiveness. It is not difficult to align fideism and skepticism together around questions of reductionism and elusiveness.

9. The basic study in intertextuality is by Michael Fishbane, *Biblical Interpretation in Ancient Israel* (Oxford: Clarendon Press, 1985). See above my discussion of an intertextual perspective, pp. 78–80.

10. On the oddity and the overcoming of oddity under the pressure of universalism, see John Murray Cuddihy, *The Ordeal of Civility: Freud, Marx, and Levi-Strauss and the Jewish Struggle with Modernity* (New York: Basic Books, 1974). Cuddihy proposes that "Freudian slips" are a peculiarly Jewish phenomenon when suppressed Jewishness will out. On such a notion, I suggest that the Bible is full of such "slips," some on the lips of Yahweh.

11. Jacques Ellul, *The Humiliation of the Word* (Grand Rapids: Eerdmans, 1988).

12. Jacques Ellul, *The Technological Society* (New York: Alfred A. Knopf, 1965).

image has displaced speech in the modern world, in the service of technological control.[13]

It is not my purpose here to review or assess Ellul's thesis about the word. Rather I suggest that theology in general and Old Testament theology in particular have either participated in "the humiliation of the word," or at least have been seduced by it, so that there has been a deep yearning for something more (or something other) than the utterance itself, either historical or ontological. My argument is an insistence that utterance is all we have—utterance as testimony—and that utterance as testimony is enough, as it was for the community of Israel.

This recognition, that utterance is all we have and is enough, assures that Israel's knowledge of God is endlessly elusive, under challenge, and in dispute. Israel thereby refuses the kind of certitude that either historical positivism or theological positivism can give. Therefore, I propose that serious theological readers of the Old Testament are either adherents to and practitioners of the world rendered in this utterance, or they are candidates and potential recruits into this uttered world. Those who are adherents are endlessly under challenge, for this world must be lived in the presence of other worlds, also given in utterance. It is because the challenge to the adherents is incessant that the utterance of Israel includes countertestimony. In like fashion, candidates and potential recruits for this uttered world have not yet decided about the reliability of this utterance, and do indeed have alternative utterances and alternative worlds—that is, alternative metanarratives—available to them. This utterance of Israel is not a dictator. It will not impose its will. It can only issue its summons and its invitation, and await a decision that is always to be made yet again. When an affirmative decision is made, a real world of ontological substance follows.

---

13. See also Neil Postman, *Amusing Ourselves to Death: Public Discourse in the Age of Show Business* (New York: Penguin Books, 1985); and *Conscientious Objections: Stirring Up Trouble about Language, Technology, and Education* (London: Heinemann, 1988); see also the more fundamental study of Eugen Rosenstock-Huessy, *Speech and Reality* (Norwich, Vt.: Argo Books, 1970), who comments on the "pathology of speech" in modern life.

TWENTY-EIGHT

Some Pervasive Issues

I N THE FORESEEABLE FUTURE, Old Testament theology (a) lives in a pluralistic world without hegemonic privilege; and (b) is utterance-dependent. Having situated our future work in Old Testament theology in this way, which is in profound contrast with the long Enlightenment period of scholarship, I wish to return briefly to the four pervasive issues that I have flagged as elemental and enduring concerns for our continuing work.[1] I here ask about these issues in a world that is pluralistic and utterance-dependent.

Old Testament Theology in Relation to Historical Criticism

No doubt Brevard Childs is correct in his contention that the relationship between Old Testament theology and historical criticism is of crucial importance to any advance in Old Testament theology.[2] Equally, there is no doubt that historical criticism, broadly construed, is crucial for responsible biblical theology, especially Reformed versions of it, as Gerhard Ebeling has insisted.[3] One cannot undo the long and complex history that has held criticism and theological exposition together and in tension. One cannot, moreover, wish as a contemporary expositor to abandon the intellectual restraints and resources of one's time and place. Thus I take it as a truism that Old Testament theological interpretation must be seriously engaged with criticism, and any serious student of Old Testament theology cannot retreat into a "safe" fideism because he or she fears the results of critical inquiry.

But Ebeling's insistence, in my judgment, does not touch the real issues that must now be addressed. Ebeling is concerned to insist that Christian faith has real historical roots in what "has happened," and he uses the term *historical* in that way. In fact, however, the term *historical* with reference to "what happened" is not at

---

1. On these four pervasive questions, see pp. 102–14.
2. Brevard S. Childs, "Critical Reflections on James Barr's Understanding of the Literal and the Allegorical," *JSOT* 46 (1990) 3–9, and again in "On Reclaiming the Bible for Christian Theology," *Reclaiming the Bible for the Church* (ed. Carl E. Braaten and Robert W. Jenson; Grand Rapids: Eerdmans, 1995) 1–17.
3. Gerhard Ebeling, "The Significance of the Critical Historical Method for Church and Theology in Protestantism," *Word and Faith* (London: SCM Press, 1963) 17–61. See Childs, *Biblical Theology of the Old and New Testaments: Theological Reflection on the Christian Bible* (Minneapolis: Fortress Press, 1993) 6–9, for his comment on the accent of Ebeling.

all the way that the word has come to be used in "historical criticism" in much Old Testament scholarship. While agreeing with Ebeling's general point, I insist that what is appropriate as criticism in relation to Old Testament theology is to be measured by two criteria: (a) an approach that is congruent with the material of the text itself; and (b) an approach that is congruent with the intellectual environment in which exposition is to be done.

The conclusion to which I am drawn is that the enormous apparatus of high historical criticism that reached its zenith in the nineteenth century and continued its dominance well into the twentieth century is not, in the first instant, of primary relevance to theological exposition at the end of the twentieth century. By such a conclusion, I do not intend any appeal to an anti-intellectual fideism; I appeal rather to criticism that is congruent in the two ways suggested. In drawing this conclusion, I only reflect what in practice has turned out to be the case for a great number of responsible scholars at the present moment, namely, that scholars have moved well beyond the critical categories that have come to represent historical criticism.[4]

In my judgment, historical criticism (by which I shall refer to the entire Enlightenment enterprise that came to be associated with Julius Wellhausen and that now seems to reappear as neo-Wellhausianism) was committed to a Cartesian program that was hostile (in effect if not in intention) to the main theological claims of the text. That is, historical criticism did not confine itself to consideration of the specific historical locus of texts (which seems to be Ebeling's concern), but operated with naturalistic assumptions, so that everything could and must be explained, without reference to any theological claim. The outcome is a "history of religion" that not only resists theological metanarrative, but resists any notion of Yahweh as an agent in Israel's life.

I fully recognize that to claim "Yahweh as agent" is enormously problematic.[5] It is problematic, however, only when interpretation is conducted according to the assumptions of Enlightenment rationality that, in principle, resist every theological claim. In its avoidance of fideism, criticism slipped over into skepticism so that, in the words of Jack Miles, everything could be talked about except Yahweh. It is evident that such skeptical criticism is indispensable when one focuses on uncritical fundamentalism of "the first naïveté."[6] That work, on the grounds of Enlighten-

---

4. Concerning the "new criticisms," reference should be made especially to sociological, literary, rhetorical, and canonical criticism. Of these, the sociological is still most closely linked to the older historical criticism. Brevard Childs insists that canonical criticism is not just one more method, but is in fact a theological perspective. See the review of current "options" in Steven L. McKenzie and Stephen R. Haynes, *To Each Its Own Meaning: An Introduction to Biblical Criticisms and Their Application* (Louisville: Westminster/John Knox, 1993).

5. To refer to "Yahweh as agent" reintroduces the whole vexed issue of a "God who acts." For a review of the issue, see Thomas F. Tracy, *God, Action, and Embodiment* (Grand Rapids: Eerdmans, 1984).

6. The phrase is from Paul Ricoeur. See Mark I. Wallace, *The Second Naïveté: Barth, Ricoeur, and the New Yale Theology* (Macon, Ga.: Mercer University Press, 1990).

ment rationality, has been done well and continues to be done well in most U.S. theological schools.

The problem is that such Enlightenment positivism no longer pertains in any critical discipline. The emergence of hermeneutical reflection is now a major dimension of any critical undertaking, and Ebeling himself defines criticism in this way: "Everything depends on the critical historical method being freed from this mistaken curtailment to a mere technical tool and being understood in such a way as to include in itself the whole of the hermeneutic process."[7] Thus what is required in a new, antipositivistic intellectual climate is a criticism that is not thinly positivistic, but that is open to the density of social and rhetorical processes that generate social reality beyond our "realism."[8]

I suggest that in a new settlement still to be worked out between criticism and interpretation, three considerations are pertinent:

1. Serious energy needs to be given to discern what of the older historical criticism is to be retained and how it is to be used. There is much in the history of the literature and perhaps in the history of religion that still needs to be valued, even though almost every old "consensus" opinion is now under heavy assault. The challenge in retaining learning from the older historical criticism is to do so without a hidden commitment to the theological skepticism that seemed endlessly to accompany that criticism, but was not a necessary part of a critical perspective. There may be a place for skepticism, but it should be explicit along with its grounds, and not surreptitiously taken along with critical judgment.

2. There is much in emerging methods—sociological (including the new archaeology) and rhetorical—that can be valued, because these methods allow both for the density of social processes coded in the text and for the generative, constitutive power of the textual utterance. These methods in general, in my judgment, meet the expectation of Ebeling's notion of criticism, but they do in principle commit to skeptical rationality.

3. Since the complete domination of scholarship by historical criticism in the nineteenth century, it has been assumed, almost without question, that criticism is the lead figure, taking the initiative in the scholarly process, and that theological interpretation must follow along in the categories established by criticism. Certainly in a period of high positivism, this shape to the relationship is inevitable.

With the emergence of a hermeneutical dimension in criticism that has moved beyond sheer positivism, this widely assumed relationship might be reexamined and reordered.[9] For example, an accent on the disputatious quality in Israel's theological rhetoric might lead to a criticism of documents that resists Enlightenment

---

7. Ebeling, "The Significance of the Critical Historical Method," 50.

8. Reference might be made here to Richard R. Niebuhr, *Resurrection and Historical Reason: A Study of Theological Method* (New York: Charles Scribner's Sons, 1957), and W. B. Gallie, "The Historical Understanding," *History and Theory* (ed. George H. Nadel; Middletown, Conn.: Wesleyan University Press, 1977) 149–202.

9. Above all, see Hans-Georg Gadamer, *Truth and Method* (New York: Seabury Press, 1975). Note especially his accent on language, 345–491. As Gadamer seeks to refute the *knowledge-claims* of

fragmentation, which seeks to dissolve all of the odd tensions and abrasions in the text. Indeed, having moved beyond positivism into an entertainment of the density of the text, we may observe emerging methods that are willing to allow for a theological dimension that moves in a direction of a "second naiveté."

The real issue in the relationship between interpretation and criticism is to be aware that fideism and skepticism are twin temptations, and that criticism is an effort to be thoughtful in a way that does not permit fideism and that does not require skepticism. In much "scientific" study of the Old Testament, it is generally assumed that skepticism is much more intellectually respectable than is fideism. With the demise of positivism, that unstated but widespread assumption might well be reconsidered. Skepticism, often voiced as hostility to theological claim, is in fact not a given element in responsible intellectual inquiry.[10] What passes for uncommitted objectivity in Old Testament study, moreover, is often a thinly veiled personal hostility to religious authority, which is displaced on the interpretive task as though such hostility is an intellectual virtue. No doubt an oppressive fideism and a hostile skepticism endlessly evoke and feed each other. We may now be at a moment when totalizing fideism is exposed as inadequate and when skeptical positivism is seen to be equally inadequate, when a genuinely thoughtful criticism can engage the density and depth of the text, which is available neither to fideism nor to skepticism.

Old Testament Theology in Relation to the New Testament and to Church Theology

Old Testament theology has been characteristically a Christian enterprise, for it is a Christian, as distinct from a Jewish, propensity to think in large, systematic theological categories.[11] And because the recurring categories of Old Testament theology have been determined and practiced by Christian interpreters, it is not surprising that Old Testament theology has been conducted on the assumption that the Old Testament is integrally and exclusively aimed at the New Testament. Because interpretation has been conducted on this assumption, moreover, it is altogether understandable that Old Testament theology should have become a major contributor to supersessionism, whereby Jewish religious claims are overridden in the triumph of Christian claims. This way of thinking is evident in the notorious

---

positivism, so Martin Buber in his dialogic articulation of reality seeks to overturn the *being-claims* of Cartesianism.

10. See the powerful critique of liberal skepticism as it has occupied the center of academic activity in the United States: George Marsden, *The Soul of the American University: From Protestant Establishment to Established Non-Belief* (Oxford: Oxford University Press, 1994). For a very different posture toward the issue, see Martin E. Marty, "Committing the Study of Religion in Public," *JAAR* 57 (1989) 1–22.

11. See Jon D. Levenson, "Why Jews Are Not Interested in Biblical Theology," *The Hebrew Bible, the Old Testament, and Historical Criticism: Jews and Christians in Biblical Studies* (Louisville: Westminster/John Knox, 1993) 33–61; and Childs, *Biblical Theology of the Old and New Testaments,* 25–26, on "Jewish theology."

statement of Rudolf Bultmann that the Old Testament is "a history of failure," and most recently in the assertion of Brevard Childs that the two Testaments "bear witnesses to Jesus Christ."[12] Such a way of presenting the Old Testament proceeds as if the community of Judaism was only an interim community, which existed until the New Testament and then withered into nonexistence and insignificance.[13]

It should be evident to the reader by now that I do not subscribe to such a view, but understand the relation of the Old to the New Testament in a very different way. Since the church rejected the views of Marcion in the second century c.e., it has been impossible in Christian theology to dissolve the Old Testament into the New. The church, in a programmatic decision, held on to the Old Testament as Scripture because the Old Testament affirmed something definitional for Christianity that was not elsewhere affirmed and that Christians dared not lose.

Over time, various attempts have been made to identity the relationship between the Old Testament and the New Testament in Christian theology, especially under the rubrics of promise-fulfillment, law-gospel, salvation history, and topology.[14] Each of these rubrics offers something of importance. It is equally clear, however, that none of these rubrics nor all of them together catch what is decisive in the Old Testament for the New Testament and for Christian faith. It is not easy or obvious to identify what must be retained from the Old Testament for the truth of Christianity. But surely in some sense it is the "scandal of particularity," by which the Creator of heaven and earth has sojourned with the Israelite community and has self-disclosed in the odd and concrete ways of Jewishness.[15] The Jewish markings of elusiveness, materiality, and concreteness that belong to the very character of Yahweh are what Marcionite Christianity always wants to scuttle. It is the purpose of Christian Old Testament theology, I judge, to pay particular attention to these aspects of Old Testament testimony, which are most problematic for Hellenized, Enlightenment Christianity.

---

12. Rudolf Bultmann, "The Significance of the Old Testament for the Christian Faith," *The Old Testament and Christian Faith* (ed. Bernhard W. Anderson; London: SCM Press, 1964) 8–35; Childs, *Biblical Theology of the Old and New Testaments,* 78 and passim. For two Jewish perspectives, see Levenson, "Why Jews Are Not Interested in Biblical Theology," and M. H. Goshen-Gottstein, "Tanakh Theology: The Religion of the Old Testament and the Place of Jewish Biblical Theology," *Ancient Israelite Religion: Essays in Honor of Frank Moore Cross* (ed. Patrick D. Miller, Jr., et al.; Philadelphia: Fortress Press, 1989) 617–44.

13. The Old Testament, for the most part, disappears as Childs seeks to do "biblical theology" under the aegis of christological claims. Rolf Rendtorff, *Canon and Theology* (OBT; Minneapolis: Fortress Press, 1993), has most seriously suggested a recognition of Jewish reality in considering the task of Old Testament theology. Reference will usefully be made to the title of Rendtorff's recent *Festschrift, Die Hebräische Bibel und ihre zweifache Nachgeschichte* (ed. Erhard Blum et al.; Neukirchen-Vluyn: Neukirchener Verlag, 1990).

14. For an older but helpful review of the issues, see A. H. J. Gunneweg, *Understanding the Old Testament* (OTL; London: SCM Press, 1978).

15. Paul M. Van Buren, *Discerning the Way: A Theology of the Jewish-Christian Reality* 1: *Discerning the Way* (San Francisco: Harper and Row, 1987), has well articulated the large theological commonality of Jews and Christians.

Maneuvers toward the New Testament

It has been usual to do a two-stage theological interpretation of the Old Testament, first to interpret the Old Testament "on its own terms," and then second and quite distinctly to interpret with reference to the New Testament. This procedure is evident in Brevard Childs's *Biblical Theology of the Old and New Testaments*, whereby in the second major part of the book, the Old Testament is enveloped in New Testament claims and nearly disappears.[16] Given the exclusive claims of the New Testament in its christological focus, this is perhaps the best that can be done. Any serious Old Testament interpretation, however, must be uneasy with such a procedure, precisely because it is so clear that the Old Testament does not obviously, cleanly, or directly point to Jesus or to the New Testament.

As a Christian interpreter, I think we would do better to acknowledge the independent status of the Old Testament text, and then to move toward the New Testament in something like the following maneuvers:

1. One must recognize that the Old Testament is powerfully polyphonic in its testimony, both in its substantive claims and in its characteristically elusive modes of articulation. Nothing about the theological claims of the Old Testament is obvious or one-dimensional. They remain remarkably open.

2. The polyphonic openness of the Old Testament, in substance and in modes of articulation, insists on interpretation. It is in the nature of the text to require, in each new circumstance of reading, an interpretive act that draws the text close to the circumstance and horizon of the interpretive community. The elusive quality of the text, moreover, invites interpretation that is free, expansive, and enormously imaginative. Thus I insist that expansive, imaginative interpretation is not an illicit abuse of the text. It is rather activity permitted and insisted on by the text.[17] This is an awareness about the text that has been vigorously resisted by positivistic historical criticism. Moreover, by identifying this quality in the text, I intend to deny the long-standing distinction between "meant" and "means," as though there is a recoverable "meant" prior to all interpretive, imaginative "means."[18] From the outset, from the ground up, the reader is engaged in giving shape to the elusiveness of the text. Historical criticism is, in fact, only one such procedure in shaping the elusive, polyphonic text in ways congruent with its circumstance, which happens to be a circumstance of positivistic rationality.

3. With the recognition that the text is polyphonic and elusive and insists on imaginative construal, it is then credible and appropriate to say that the early

---

16. Childs, *Biblical Theology of the Old and New Testaments*, first part on pp. 95-207, second part on pp. 349-716. In Childs's presentation it is not clear how the two expositions are to be related to each other, so the problem is simply deferred.

17. Such expansive interpretation is evident in the biblical text itself, as Michael Fishbane, *Biblical Interpretation in Ancient Israel* (Oxford: Clarendon Press, 1985), has shown. See, for example, Jer 3:1 as a theological redeployment of Deut 24:1-4.

18. On the distinction, see the well-known statement by Krister Stendahl, "Biblical Theology, Contemporary," *IDB* (1962), 1:418-32; see also the critical response to Stendahl by Ben C. Ollenburger, "What Krister Stendahl 'Meant'—A Normative Critique of 'Descriptive Biblical Theology,'" *HBT* 8 (June 1986) 61-98.

church, mesmerized by the person of Jesus, found it inescapable that it would draw this elusive, polyphonic text to its own circumstance, close to its experience, its memory, and its continuing sense of the transformative presence of Jesus. Thus as a confessing Christian, I believe that the imaginative construal of the Old Testament toward Jesus is a credible act and one that I fully affirm.

For purposes of Old Testament theology, however, it is important, theologically as well as historically, to insist that the connections between the two Testaments are made, as surely they must be, from the side of the New Testament and not from the side of the Old Testament. Thus it is completely appropriate to say in an act of bold, imaginative construal, as the New Testament frequently does, "The scriptures were fulfilled." Such an affirmation can be made only from the side of the fulfillment, not from the side of the Old Testament.

4. This recognition has important implications for limiting the task of Old Testament theology. It is suggested in some quarters that a Christian interpreter can only write a "biblical theology," meaning a theology of both testaments, for the Old Testament is not available except in the presence of the New. Brevard Childs has presented a formidable example of such an enterprise. But if the Old Testament text is as polyphonic and elusive as I take it to be, then such a procedure is inherently reductionist, because it reduces the polyphonic, elusive testimony of the Old Testament to one single, exclusivist construal, namely the New Testament-christological construal, thereby violating the quality of generative openness that marks the Old Testament text. Thus my resistance to a closed model of Old Testament-New Testament is not only a practical one because I do not know enough to do it; it is also a resistance in principle.

Against such an exclusivistic linkage, I propose an alternative: that the task of Old Testament theology, as a Christian enterprise, is to articulate, explicate, mobilize, and make accessible and available the testimony of the Old Testament in all of its polyphonic, elusive, imaginative power and to offer it to the church for its continuing work of construal toward Jesus. That is, Old Testament theology, in my judgment, must prepare the material and fully respect the interpretive connections made in the New Testament and the subsequent church; but it must not make those connections, precisely because the connections are not to be found in the testimony of ancient Israel, but in the subsequent work of imaginative construal that lies beyond the text of the Old Testament. This is more than a division of labor. It is an awareness both of the *limit* of the text itself, and of the *generative power* of the text to evoke and authorize interpretations that lie beyond the scope or intention of the textual testimony as such.

The Christian imaginative construal of the Old Testament moves well beyond anything to be found in the Old Testament. The Old Testament vulnerably and willingly tolerates such use, for which it seems to present itself. The most obvious transpositions made from the ground of the Old Testament in characteristic Christian imagination include:

- transposition of "messiah" to "the messiah";
- identification of the church as "the Israel of God";
- eucharistic preemption of covenant for "the new covenant";
- adversarial challenges to "the law" by an antithesis of law-grace;
- "enfleshment" of the word or spirit or wisdom in the person of Jesus.

The Old Testament text evidently permits these interpretations (but does not require them), or they would not have arisen. Old Testament theology, as a Christian enterprise, it seems to me, must resist both (a) the untenable claim that such mutations in meaning are at all *intended* by or hinted at in the Old Testament; and (b) the historical-critical, rationalistic notion that the Old Testament *precludes* such interpretive moves, for such a notion of preclusion fails to recognize the polyphonic, elusive, generative intentionality of the text.

A recognition of a permitted, but not required, imaginative construal might deliver us Christians from a two-stage interpretive process in which the second stage seems to violate the first, or from an antithesis between historical-critical and confessional-theological modes of interpretation. Better simply to recognize that these materials are deliberately evocative, and what they evoke in an interpretive practice always draws the ancient testimony into contemporaneity. The text refuses to stay past. For the church, such contemporaneity is characteristically concerned with Jesus as a historical agent, or Jesus as an undoubted and enduring power, presence, and authority in the church.

Old Testament Theology in Relation to Jewish Tradition and the Jewish Community

This theme is the counterpart to the point just expressed. That is, I have insisted that a Christian theological construal of the Old Testament is legitimate but cannot be exclusivist, as if the Old Testament pointed directly and singularly to the New Testament. Here I insist that if the church has no interpretive monopoly on the Old Testament, then it must recognize the legitimacy of other interpretive communities, of whom the primary and principal one is the Jewish community.

Old Testament theology, as a Christian enterprise, takes place in the full awareness that Judaism continues, through the centuries and generations of Christian history, to be a functioning, vibrant community of faith that has not shriveled, according to Christian dismissiveness. That community of Judaism is not consumed in Jewish legalism, according to Christian stereotype. It is not eradicated by the brutal history of Christian-sanctioned anti-Semitism. It is not, moreover, to be equated with simplistic forms of political Zionism.

I think it impossible to overstate the significance of religious Judaism for contemporary Old Testament theology, because Judaism makes unmistakably clear that this text, albeit construed in the modes of rabbinic, talmudic teaching, continues to nourish and summon a serious community of faith other than the church and alongside the church. There is no doubt, moreover, that the wonder of God's power and the majesty of God's mercy are evident in this community. This concrete, visible reality might cause Christians to lower our voices in the proclamation of exclusiveness, for it makes abundantly evident that Christian faith has no exclusive lock on the attention of the God of the Bible. Beyond voice-lowering, this recognition of Judaism might suggest that serious theological-liturgic engagement with actual Jewish communities of practice is an appropriate dimension of the practice of faithful interpretation, even with the awareness of how exceedingly difficult such engagement is.

Theological interpretation of the text is not a contextless, cerebral undertaking. It is conducted by real people who are concretely located in the historical process. That is, Old Testament theology, at the beginning of the twenty-first century, is not just an activity preoccupied with an ancient text, though it is indeed that. It is preoccupied with an ancient text in a particular circumstance. I have indicated that it was legitimate in the first century (and has been so ever since) for Christian interpretation to draw the Old Testament text to its circumstance, namely to its life with Jesus. It was legitimate, I affirm as a confessing Christian, because the text permits such evocative construal of its polyvalent quality. *Mutatis mutandis,* for us as Christians at the outset of the twenty-first century, it is legitimate and necessary to draw the Old Testament text closely to our circumstance, which is what every interpretive community inescapably does, wittingly or unwittingly.[19]

If we are to interpret the Old Testament in our circumstance, it is clear that Jewish faith and an actual Jewish community must be on the horizon of Christians. More specifically, Old Testament theology as a Christian enterprise must be done in light (or darkness!) of the Holocaust and the unthinkable brutality wrought against the Jewish community in a society with Christian roots.[20] I do not flinch from the acknowledgment that our particular post-Holocaust situation of interpretation imposes on us important interpretive requirements, even if attentiveness to Jewishness were not integral to the text itself.[21]

Christian interpretation of the Old Testament and its characteristic supersessionism stand a long distance removed from the Holocaust. Yet the thinking behind and around supersessionism, of which Christian Old Testament theology

---

19. This is what historical criticism did in the nineteenth century in the name of objectivity, as it embraced developmentalism in the context of great cultural developmentalist undertakings.

20. On the cruciality of the Holocaust for the future of both Jewish and Christian theology, see especially Emil Fackenheim, *To Mend the World: Foundations of Post-Holocaust Thought* (2d ed.; New York: Schocken Books, 1989); and *The Jewish Bible after the Holocaust: A Rereading* (Bloomington: Indiana University Press, 1990).

21. The Holocaust is unique, even when we recognize that it serves paradigmatically to call attention to other programmatic abuses of the vulnerable. Thus my comments on the issue of Jewishness in Old Testament theology are intrinsically connected to my comments on justice in Old Testament theology. The Holocaust is the quintessential betrayal of justice, which is why it continues to evoke such a rich and troubled theological response.

has been one aspect, is indeed linked to the Holocaust. Therefore Christian Old Testament theology, at the end of the twentieth century, must make important and generous adjustments in our conventional and uncritical exclusivist claims on the Old Testament. That is, what is theologically required *by the text* as such is positively reinforced *by historical circumstance* and its enduring demands.

If Christian appropriation of the Old Testament toward Jesus is an act of claiming the elusive tradition toward a Jesus-circumstance, we can recognize that other imaginative appropriations of this elusive tradition are equally legitimate and appropriate. We have yet to decide how christological exclusiveness is to be articulated so that it is not an ideological ground for the dismissal of a co-community of interpretation.[22] Thus our most passionate affirmation of Jesus as the "clue" to all of reality must allow for other "clues" found herein by other serious communities of interpretation. And of course this applies to none other so directly as it does to Judaism.

Thus Christians are able to say of the Old Testament, "It is ours," but must also say, "It is not ours alone." This means to recognize that Jewish imaginative construals of the Old Testament text are, in Christian purview, a legitimate theological activity. More than that, Jewish imaginative construal of the text is a legitimate theological activity to which Christians must pay attention. I have no doubt that Christian supersessionism, enforced as it is by the classical modes of Hellenistic thought, has made it nearly impossible for Christians to attend to the riches of Judaism. Once we recognize that theological construal and imagination other than our own is legitimate, however, we may take it into serious account. I do not imagine that attention to this primal alternative construal of the text will lead to an abrupt overthrow of distinctive Christian claims. But I also do not imagine that such attention would leave Christian claims untouched, certainly not untouched in their fearful, destructive aspects, but perhaps also not untouched in good-faith exclusivism, rooted in a text that remains as elusive as its Subject and that relentlessly resists closure.

Old Testament Theology and the Problem of Justice

Whatever one may think of Israel's historical antecedents and Yahwism's religious antecedents (and there were plenty of both), it is clear that in something like "the Mosaic revolution" Yahweh burst into world history as a theological *novum*. This Mosaic revolution has political, economic, moral, and ethnic connotations, but its main force, I suggest, is to establish justice as the core focus of Yahweh's life in the world and Israel's life with Yahweh.

The Mosaic revolution, which is the principal focus of the Pentateuch (and which in turn is the principal reference point of Israel's subsequent tradition), has

---

22. Among Christian theologians, Jürgen Moltmann, *The Way of Jesus Christ: Christology in Messianic Dimensions* (1990; Minneapolis: Fortress Press, 1993), has given particular care precisely to this issue.

two points of accent: as event and as institution. The event that forms the center of Israel's liturgic imagination is the Exodus. The Exodus, as it has been stylized in Israel's liturgic texts, is for the glorification of Yahweh (cf. Exod 14:4, 17). But that glorification of Yahweh was possible only through the emancipation of the Hebrew slaves from the oppressiveness of Egyptian bondage (Exod 14:14, 25; see also Ezek 36:22-32; 39:25-29). From the outset, Yahweh is known to be a God committed to the establishment of concrete, sociopolitical justice in a world of massive power organized against justice.

In that event, as given us in Israel's core testimony, Yahweh's profound resolve toward the reordering of social power is voiced in the initial imperative addressed to Pharaoh: "Let my people go" (Exod 5:1). Behind that resolve, which is then relentlessly implemented in the plague narrative, is the voiced suffering of the slaves (Exod 2:23) that becomes the driving power of Yahweh's alternative history (Exod 2:23-25, 3:7-10). It is voiced suffering that sets in motion Yahweh's uncompromising resolve for the transformation of earthly power arrangements.

The second accent of the Mosaic revolution is the Sinai proclamation of Yahweh's commandments, which seeks to give stable, institutional form to the social possibilities engendered in the Exodus. Thus the commandments appeal to Yahweh's iconoclastic inclination (Exod 20:4-7) and from that inclination enunciate an alternative social possibility in the world.

It is fair to say that given its subsequent exposition through time, the Exodus event and the Sinai structure do indeed witness to Yahweh's preferential option for the poor, weak, and marginated.[23] Or said another way, Yahweh is here known to be a resilient and relentless advocate of and agent for justice, which entails the complete reordering of power arrangements in the earth.

In the context of Israel's completed testimony, it is difficult to overstate the pivotal importance for the rest of Israel's testimony of the Mosaic revolution and the commitment of Yahweh (and of Israel) to justice. If we consider in turn the prophetic, psalmic, sapiential, and apocalyptic texts, it seems evident that Israel, everywhere and without exhaustion, is preoccupied with the agenda of justice that is rooted in the character and resolve of Yahweh. This justice rooted in Yahweh, moreover, is to be enacted and implemented concretely in human practice.

It is important that we recognize with some precision the quality and intention of Mosaic, Yahwistic justice, for it is easily misunderstood, given the easy and careless use of the term *justice*. The intention of Mosaic justice is to redistribute social goods and social power; thus it is distributive justice.[24] This justice recognizes that social goods and social power are unequally and destructively distributed in Israel's

---

23. The Exodus event and the Sinai structure are of course particularly and peculiarly Jewish. They are, at the same time, paradigmatic for every marginated human community. See Jon Levenson, "Exodus and Liberation," *The Hebrew Bible, the Old Testament, and Historical Criticism*, 127–59; and Walter Brueggemann, "Pharaoh as Vassal: A Study of a Political Metaphor," *CBQ* 57 (1995) 27–51.

24. The most articulate presentation of distributive justice in the Old Testament known to me is by José Miranda, *Marx and the Bible: A Critique of the Philosophy of Oppression* (Maryknoll, N.Y.: Orbis Books, 1974) 77-108 and passim. See also Rolf P. Knierim, *The Task of Old Testament Theology* (Grand

world (and derivatively in any social context), and that the well-being of the community requires that social goods and power to some extent be given up by those who have too much, for the sake of those who have not enough.

This enormously radical principle is constitutive for revolutionary Israel and for Yahweh, as is evidenced in various traditions.[25] We may cite three specific cases that witness to this distributive intention.

1. In Exodus (3:21-22, 11:2, and 12:35-36) the Israelites are urged by Moses to take "jewelry of silver and gold" from the Egyptians when they depart slavery. This remembered action perhaps is nothing more than the resentful seizure of the "have-nots" from the "haves," but that it occupies so prominent a place in the narrative texts suggests that it constitutes something of a principle of redeployment. Moreover, David Daube has proposed that this act is related to the "law of release" in Deut 15:1-11, wherein the released bond-servant is entitled to economic viability.[26]

2. The narrative of manna, a sign of Yahweh's protective generosity toward Israel, is a model of alternative management of food supplies. As the manna is given and gathered, it is reported: "... those who gathered much had nothing over, and those who gathered little had no shortage; they gathered as much as each of them needed" (Exod 16:18; cf. 2 Cor 8:15). This statement is no doubt intended as a model for how a community should mobilize its resources for the benefit of all.

3. The legal corpus of Deuteronomy is preoccupied with "widows, orphans, and aliens," those who lack resources and who lack social leverage to secure resources.[27] The Mosaic revolution, broadly construed, intends that the powerful are under obligation to practice distributive justice.

The reason we should pay careful attention to the substance of distributive justice is that the term *justice*, which in many texts of Israel requires reparations, more conventionally in our society means retributive justice: giving to persons what is their just desert on the basis of performance; that is, a system of rewards and punishments, not informed by the communal obligation or the generosity of the community. No doubt the practice of retributive justice has a presence in the Old Testament, as it does in the religious environment of the ancient world.[28] There

---

Rapids: Eerdmans, 1995) 86–122, and Moshe Weinfeld, *Social Justice in Ancient Israel and in the Ancient Near East* (Minneapolis: Fortress Press, 1995).

25. Norman Gottwald has been vigorously criticized for his use of the term *egalitarian* with reference to the Sinai revolution. More recently, he has articulated his sense of the revolutionary dimension of Mosaism by the use of the term *communitarian*; *The Hebrew Bible in Its Social World and Ours* (Atlanta: Scholars Press, 1993) xxv–xxvii.

26. David Daube, *The Exodus Pattern in the Bible* (London: Faber and Faber, 1963) 55–61. On this text, see also Jeffries M. Hamilton, *Social Justice and Deuteronomy: The Case of Deuteronomy 15* (SBLDS; Atlanta: Scholars Press, 1992).

27. Moshe Weinfeld, "Humanism," *Deuteronomy and the Deuteronomic School* (Oxford: Clarendon Press, 1972) 282–97, refers to this agenda in the Book of Deuteronomy as "humanistic."

28. See Exod 21:23, Deut 19:21. More generally, the Book of Proverbs inclines in this direction. See Norman Whybray, *Wealth and Poverty in the Book of Proverbs* (JSOTSup 99; Sheffield: Sheffield Academic Press, 1990); and J. David Pleins, "Poverty in the Social World of the Wise," *JSOT* 37 (1987) 61–78.

is no doubt, moreover, that the term *justice*, as used in the contemporary world, usually refers to retributive justice, as in the widespread zeal for "law and order."

Both *distributive* justice and *retributive* justice can find warrant in the text of Israel. It seems unambiguous, however, that in Israel's core texts related to the Mosaic revolution, Yahwism is a practice of *distributive* justice. If that is the case, interpreters of the Old Testament must always be precise in their articulation, or they are sure to be misheard in terms of a justice that is less costly and less demanding on those with a disproportion of power and goods.[29]

It is important not to romanticize the commitment of Yahwism to distributive justice, even though it stands at the core of Israel's testimony about Yahweh. In the Old Testament, not everyone everywhere is an enthusiast for distributive justice. Distributive justice, if taken seriously (as in the practice of Jubilee), is inherently destabilizing of the status quo, for redistribution means to place established interests in jeopardy. Thus it does not surprise us that the benefactors of the status quo—those who are advantaged by present political, economic, and legal arrangements—believe that the maintenance of "order"—that is, the present order—is a primary function of Yahweh. It is likely that this social interest is reflected in the sapiential traditions of Proverbs that seem to urge generosity, but not structural change or serious redistribution.[30] And it seems plausible to understand the familiar strictures of the early prophets against self-indulgence to be in dispute with royal traditions, which seem to justify accumulations of surplus value. Israelite society, like every society, was deeply vexed in the ongoing tension between "haves" and "have-nots" who become, respectively, advocates (in the name of Yahweh) of social equilibrium and social transformation.

A study of Old Testament theology must recognize, with social realism, that both advocates of distributive justice and of order are present and vocal in the community, and both claim the support of Yahweh in their theological testimony. At the minimum, it is important to recognize and explicate this tension. In my judgment, however, one may go further to insist that while both sorts of advocates bear testimony to Yahweh, there can be little doubt that the adherents of distributive justice occupy the central space in the theological testimony of Israel, so that in canonical Yahwism, distributive justice is indeed a primary urging.

Having acknowledged that both justice and order are present as theological claims in the text, we may suggest that in rough outline, there is a general commitment in Israel's testimony to justice as a primary agenda of Yahweh. This is a somewhat reductionist or thematized judgment on my part. It is important to make it, however, in order to observe that when Israelite tradition is placed in juxtaposition to the great classical traditions of Hellenistic philosophy, justice is clearly a Jewish, Yahwistic preoccupation, whereas the Greeks endlessly focus on

---

29. See Miranda, *Marx and the Bible,* on Jer 22:15-16 for a most radical statement on the matter.

30. See Robert Gordis, "The Social Background of Wisdom Literature," *Poets, Prophets, and Sages: Essays in Biblical Interpretation* (Bloomington: Indiana University Press, 1971) 160–97.

order.[31] Indeed, nothing in the Greek tradition approximates a Yahwistic passion for distributive justice, which anticipates that the present social order stands under criticism and in jeopardy, in the interest of a promised and coming just order that benefits all members of the community. Thus appeals to order in the royal, sapiential texts of Israel must not be overstated, for when contrasted with the Greeks, the Israelite tradition is as odd as it is insistent on this point.

Thus there is something revolutionary, transformative, and subversive about Israel's testimony.[32] No doubt, as Norman Gottwald has indicated, much of this tendency is sociologically driven.[33] But as Gottwald also recognizes, the sociological has a theological counterpoint, and Israel does not flinch, in the end, from locating the base of its passion for revolutionary justice in the character of Yahweh.[34]

Having said that justice for Israel is rooted in the very character of Yahweh, we may go on to notice a peculiar note in Israel's candor about Yahweh. In its narratives and hymns celebrating Yahweh's justice, Yahweh is said to be a "lover of justice" (cf. Ps 99:4; Isa 61:8).[35] That much is not in dispute, and Israel counts heavily on it. But Israel is realistic and candid about its life situation. It knows very well that life is not as just as it might be if Yahweh's passionate, sovereign will for justice were enacted. It is this realism and candor that evoke in Israel what has come to be called theodicy.

We must, however, be quite clear on what this theme entails in Israel. In the philosophical tradition of theodicy since Gottfried Wilhelm Leibniz, theodicy has been understood as an explanatory enterprise: to "justify the ways of God to man." In Israel, however, what is called theodicy is not explanation but protest.[36] Acknowledging that the world is unjust, Israel has no interest in justifying an unjust world in making excuses for Yahweh, or in protecting Yahweh from criticism for failure to right the world. Rather, Israel characteristically presents itself, in "theodic" texts, as the great advocate and champion of justice, on which Yahweh has reneged. Thus in the most obvious texts of Jer 12:1-3 and Job 21:7, Israel voices its vexation toward Yahweh. In the psalms of complaint and in the larger poem of Job, moreover, Yahweh is under assault for not in fact practicing the justice to which Yahweh is ostensibly committed by covenant oath.[37]

---

31. Northrop Frye, *The Critical Path: An Essay on the Social Context of Literary Criticism* (Bloomington: Indiana University Press, 1971) 334–55, comments on the contrast between a general "myth of concern" and a more concrete "myth of freedom" that has its roots in the Bible.

32. On the revolutionary generativity of Israel's testimony, see Michael Walzer, *Exodus and Revolution* (New York: Basic Books, 1986).

33. Gottwald, *The Tribes of Yahweh: A Sociology of the Religion of Liberated Israel, 1250-1050 B.C.E.* (London: SCM Press, 1980) 608–18.

34. Ibid., 618–21. See James L. Mays, "Justice: Perspectives from the Prophetic Tradition," *Int* 37 (1983) 5–17.

35. On the peculiar piety of the poor, see Norbert Lohfink, *Lobgesange der Armen: Studien zum Magnifikat, den Hodajot von Qumran und einigen späten Psalmen* (Stuttgart: Verlag Katholisches Bibelwerk, 1990).

36. On theodicy, see the collection of essays in James L. Crenshaw, ed., *Theodicy in the Old Testament* (IRT 4; Philadelphia: Fortress Press, 1983).

37. Most radically Job 9:15-22.

In its deepest vexation, then, Israel makes a distinction between Yahweh and the reality of justice. While we might expect that Yahweh is ultimate and justice penultimate, in some of Israel's most desperate utterances, matters are inverted. Justice is held up as ultimate, and Yahweh as an agent of justice is critiqued for failure of justice. That is, Israel is aware that there is more to Yahweh than justice: there is holiness and downright capricious irascibility. Sometimes Israel is awed and deferential before this staggering ultimacy of Yahweh. In its texts of protest, however, Israel has no time for or interest in Yahweh's wild, unresponsive quality. In those texts, Israel would seem to value justice more than Yahweh. This is not because Israel is legalistic, or because Israel prefers a set of principles to a live agent. On the contrary, it is because Israel is irreducibly committed to material, concrete well-being, and not even Yahweh's own character will talk Israel out of its passion for well-being in the earth. Thus Yahweh in heaven must "get with the program" of *shalôm* on earth!

This curious inversion is oddly and wondrously voiced by Jacques Derrida. Derrida is known primarily as the progenitor of deconstruction, a program in which nothing is finally absolute enough to escape critique. It is clear, however, that Derrida's deconstruction is indeed a form of Jewish iconoclasm.[38] It is for that reason that Derrida, in the face of his passion for deconstruction, can finally write of "the indeconstructability of justice."[39] This is not only a mouthful (and especially a mouthful for Derrida), it is a characteristically Jewish mouthful. In this phrasing, Derrida is appealing back to the center of the Mosaic revolution, to what is finally and normatively the case with Yahweh. There are, to be sure, many compromises of this claim in the interest of established social interest in the testimony of the Old Testament. At the same time, there is no doubt that none of these compromises or uneasinesses touches the main claim made about Yahweh and about the future of the earth.[40] In the tradition of Job (and of Derrida), I suggest, Yahweh is held to justice, and if Yahweh cannot subscribe to this earthly passion, then the claims of heaven must be deconstructed.

Theological interpreters of the Old Testament at the end of the twentieth century must, in my judgment, pay primal attention to this irreducible claim of justice, which is, in the most abrasive parts of the testimony, a demanding summons even to Yahweh. This passion for justice stands as a revolutionary, subversive challenge to Jews and to Christians, and to every alternative metanarrative. Specifically, I suggest, at the end of the twentieth century Israel's testimony about Yahweh stands

---

38. See my discussion of the links between deconstruction and Jewish iconoclasm, pp. 329–32.

39. Jacques Derrida, "Force of Law: The 'Mythical Foundation of Authority,'" *Cardozo Law Review* 11 (1990) 919–1045. I have not had access to the article by Derrida, but refer to it from the citation of John D. Caputo, *Demythologizing Heidegger* (Bloomington: Indiana University Press, 1993) 193.

40. I refer to the readiness of Israel's testimony to proceed in an uncritical way on patriarchal assumptions. I have no wish to deny that the text is pervasively committed to such assumptions. Rather than to dismiss the text on these grounds, however, I count on Israel's characteristic propensity to mount a serious, shrill protest and summons to Yahweh (and to Yahweh's text) to new accountability.

as a profound challenge to the dominant metanarrative of technological, military consumerism. The claim that capitalist ideology has irrevocably defeated every rival, a claim brazenly articulated by Francis Fukuyama, is the context in which Old Testament theology must now be undertaken.[41]

The apparent defeat of Marxist ideology and the incredible concentration of power in the market economies of the United States and Japan indicate a drastic reordering of social relationships in the twenty-first century. I have termed the driving power of this new economic wealth "technological, military consumerism." I would not quibble about the phrasing, but I mean by this phrase that: (a) consumerism is the conviction that the unit of social meaning is the detached individual whose self and identity consist in consumption; (b) such unbridled consumption requires a disproportion of wealth and advantage, which must be defended by military means (for example, immigration policy); and (c) this defense of advantage is readily and simply justified by a one-dimensional technological mind-set that in principle brackets out of consideration all human questions. There can be little doubt of the pragmatic power of this ideology, however it be named or stylized in specifics.

This ideology is indeed totalizing, so that every aspect of the life of every one of us is impinged on and to some extent constrained by it. It is evident that this totalizing ideology has enormous power. It is equally evident, I take it, that this ideology is in the end deathly, so that it robs us of our humanness as it robs, at the same time, our environment of creation of a chance for life. I have no desire to exaggerate the case in theatrical terms, though it seems to me well-nigh impossible to overstate the case.

While the above comments may seem odd in an Old Testament theology, I have not strayed from my topic. Israel's testimony, with its uncompromising and irreducible commitment to justice, stands as the primary alternative to the deathly ideology of technological, military consumerism. In a variety of ways, in an endless variety of textual utterances, Israel's testimony is to the effect that Yahweh's passion for justice, passion for the well-being of the human community, and passion for the *shalôm* of the earth will refuse to come to terms with the power of death, no matter its particular public form or its ideological garb.[42]

It is possible to transpose the testimony of Israel about Yahweh, so that the issue with alternative metanarratives is never joined, or so that Yahweh is made to be so anemic that there can be no conflict. The transposition of this testimony into an innocuous text can take place in many ways, such as the distancing effect of critical study that recognizes everything except the main claims, or scholastic theology that

---

41. Francis Fukuyama, *The End of History and the Last Man* (New York: Free Press, 1992).
42. On the aggressive power of death as it threatens the life-world offered by Yahweh, see Jon Levenson, *Creation and the Persistence of Evil: The Jewish Drama of Divine Omnipotence* (San Francisco: Harper and Row, 1988); and Fredrik Lindström, *Suffering and Sin: Interpretations of Illness in the Individual Complaint Psalms* (Stockholm: Almqvist and Wiksell International, 1994).

turns elusive testimony into closed system, or what I call "horizontal liberalism," in which the agency of Yahweh evaporates into social ideology.

If Old Testament theology is worth doing in time to come, it will be required to focus on primary theological claims. The focus on these main claims will not be a mere interesting theological exploration, but a life-and-death struggle for the future of the world. After all, Israel's articulation of this testimony was not innocuous. It sought to convince "the court" that this construal of reality was true, over against false alternatives. That work of convincing is not finished. As in any court where capital punishment is the option,[43] true testimony becomes a life-and-death matter.

---

43. I use the term *capital punishment* in order to refer not only literally to its practice, but also metaphorically to the "execution" of the entire creation.

TWENTY-NINE

Moving toward True Speech

O LD TESTAMENT THEOLOGY in the future, I have proposed, will be reflection on Israel's disclosing speech that is in a pluralistic context and therefore
inescapably disputatious. It is my sense that a community of interpretation that
engages in a serious undertaking of Old Testament theology will itself be a community that attends to disclosing speech in a pluralistic context that is inescapably
disputatious. I mean by this that Old Testament theology is not simply a detached
analysis of an ancient practice of speech, but it is *an engagement with* those speech
practices, in order to adjudicate what is and what is not "true speech," that is,
speech about the truth.

It follows that an engagement that is such a dispute about true speech both
evokes and requires a certain kind of community—a community with an intentional speech practice of its own. There must be a place and a group of people,
over time and through time and in time, who engage in such a practice. Therefore
a community intent on Old Testament theology must have a certain form of life
to it, a life that is prepared to acknowledge the rootedness, richness, and density
of the practice it undertakes.

By insisting that Old Testament theology requires a certain form of life, I am,
in the end, accepting that Old Testament theology is an enterprise that belongs
properly to an ecclesial community, a community that is unembarrassed about commitment that, in the parlance of "objective rationality," may be categorized as bias
or ideology. (I do not intend to make any assumption that such an ecclesial community must be in official, traditional, recognized, institutional forms, but only
that it should be intent on dangerous life in the presence of the God attested in
this testimony.)

I suggest that we acknowledge, more forthrightly than has been the case, *a division of labor between the academic and ecclesial interpreting communities.* The academy,
for historical reasons of self-understanding, is in the modern world committed to
a rationality that precludes the density of commitment and passion that I believe
necessarily pertains to serious Old Testament theology.[1] By such a statement I do

---

1. There are, to be sure, important exceptions to this statement; e.g., the great group of German
expositors who grew out of the Confessing Church and who produced the poignant commentaries
in the Biblischer Kommentar series. I am speaking of the characteristic epistemological situation of

743

not concede that the academy is "objective" or "neutral" or "scientific," for its commitments are as visible and demanding and exclusionary as those of any ecclesial community. They are, however, very different, and therefore in its practice of its rationality it is likely that the academy will never move seriously beyond "history of religion." For myself, I believe that is an acceptable, legitimate, and needed undertaking.

The other side of the matter is to recognize that such an undertaking, given its epistemological stance, is never likely to engage the serious theological claims of the text with an intensity commensurate to the intensity of the claims in the text. Such full engagement would require a community of interpretation that is as unrestrained (neither held in discipline nor blinded and disabled, depending on one's view) as is the academy, but is free to host the truth of the testimony given here. Such a division of labor requires, in my judgment, that both enterprises, academic and ecclesial, are recognized as legitimate, that both are engaged in something important and indispensable to full understanding, and that both communities must pay attention to the work of the other. That is, Old Testament theology, as it may be conducted in ecclesial communities, is not in principle a second-rate or secondhand enterprise, but it can be a serious intellectual and moral undertaking that is not enthralled to a Cartesian attempt to think without body. It is my view that the academic community (of which I am gladly a part), except for the most extreme and most irresponsible cases, can respect and take seriously such ecclesial exposition, when it is well done and when it is congruent with the actual practice of the community. To refuse to learn from such ecclesial scholarship because it is not "scientific" enough strikes me as irresponsible and obscurantist.

Such ecclesial theological interpretation, however, must be responsibly done, making use of the best learning available and engaging in practice commensurate with its interpretation. That is, in the end, theological interpretation that engages the theological claims of the text must host the testimony in all its oddness, and must be engaged in the practice of the core testimony and countertestimony, in practice and in obedience, in protest and complaint, with its whole life. The phrase "engaged in practice" means for me not only hearing the text, but living intentionally in response to its proposed world. Here I briefly reiterate two sorts of arguments I have already made, this time with an eye on practical implementation in contemporary life.

---

the academy in the United States. See the discussion of Robert A. Segal, *Explaining and Interpreting Religion: Essays on the Issues* (Toronto Studies in Religion 16; New York: Peter Lang, 1992). Segal's appeal to the distinction between explanation and interpretation is telling about his assumptions. Notice that on p. 122, he speaks of the "fear" "religionists" have of social scientific explanations of religion. This seems to me a peculiarly self-serving judgment.

Four Enduring Issues

Ecclesial communities of interpretation that attend in serious ways to this text may focus intentionally on what I have identified as four enduring issues intrinsic to Old Testament theology:[2]

1. Attendance to a form of *criticism* of the text that is congruent with our intellectual circumstance of pluralism, which reckons with the density and elusiveness of the text.

2. Self-conscious mobilization of the Old Testament text *toward the New Testament,* but with full awareness that the text so construed is open, polyphonic, elusive, and imaginative, beyond any single rendering, including that of the church.

3. Attendance to the *Jewish community* as co-reader, co-hearer, and co-practitioner of this text, whereby the community that Christians have long demonized becomes a heeded truth-teller.

4 Awareness that at the core of this construed world is a claim of *distributive justice* that is concrete, material, revolutionary, subversive, and uncompromising.

Form of Life for Community of Interpretation

Concrete practice as a "form of life" may be guided and informed by what I have marked as the "form of life" this testimony necessarily has taken in the practice of ancient Israel.[3] Thus an ecclesial community of interpretation may:

1. Dwell in the tradition of *Torah,* accepting the narratives and the commands of purity and of debt cancellation as the principal sources of funding for obedient imagination.

2. Engage, after the manner of *royal agency,* in the practice of power for well-being, a practice of power that is always a temptation and always under criticism.

3. Host the disruptive *prophetic voices,* which concern the costs and pains of the historical process, and the possibilities that well up in the midst of the costs and pains.

4. Practice, after the manner of *the Priestly traditions,* the presence of Yahweh, which embraces the sacramental freightedness of all of life.

5. In an embrace of the *traditions of wisdom,* know the dailiness of life in all of its contested, buoyant density.

Such a community, when it proceeds with intentionality, draws the text and its testimony close to its own life. But it also moves its own life under the assurances and demands of a text that continues in its odd, inscrutable, nonnegotiable otherness.

---

2. For my discussion of these four issues, see pp. 102–14 and chap. 28.
3. For my discussion of the five elements of Israel's "form of life" to which I have alluded, see chaps. 20–24.

The Idiom of Israel's Faith

I am helped by a recent phrase of Christopher Bollas, who, in his reflection on personality theory, has transposed Freud's id as the most elemental dimension of self into "idiom."[4] Bollas suggests that health, well-being, and maturity depend on identifying, embracing, and practicing the peculiar, distinctive idiom of life with which one is born. *Mutatis mutandis*, I suggest that responsible Old Testament theology in an ecclesial community of interpretation is interpretation done in an idiom that is congruent with the life setting of the community, but that is drawn from, informed by, and authorized by the idiom of the testimony of the text. For all its variation through time and in different circumstances, there is a recognizable idiom to Israel's testimony, especially as some texts take great liberties with it.[5] That idiom is the one we have identified in the core testimony, made fuller and richer by the countertestimony that is evoked in response against the core testimony and its power. The combination of core testimony and countertestimony constitutes the idiom of Israel's faith. It is, then, this idiom that may be practiced in an ecclesial community of interpretation.

In contemporary ecclesial communities of theological interpretation, that ancient idiom is recoverable when the community accepts that its own cadences and dialect are derivative from that idiom. That is, such a community of interpretation moves past the Cartesian dilemma—now aware of the great suspicions of Freud and Marx, fully present to the great ruptures of Auschwitz and Hiroshima—to a buoyant "second naiveté," in the end convinced that no cadence of speech, no dialect of communication, no idiom of self-discernment is as powerful, as compelling, as liberating, or as transformative as this one, whereby one may speak and live unencumbered in a world of threat.[6]

In the end, my appeal to ecclesial communities, and especially to their leaders and pastors, is that there be a serious reengagement with this idiom, which is the *Muttersprach* of the church (as of the synagogue).[7] It is my impression that the church in the West has been sorely tempted to speak in everyone's idiom except its own. Liberals, embarrassed by the otherness of the biblical idiom, have kept

---

4. Christopher Bollas, *Being a Character: Psychoanalysis and Self Experience* (London: Routledge, 1993) 17, 64–65, 70–71. Bollas considers the psychic process as one of deconstructing and then constructing a new "form of existence."

5. The extreme cases are the Song of Solomon and Ecclesiastes. The canonizing and interpretive processes no doubt have drawn these texts into the orbit of Israel's more characteristic testimony, so that in canonical location and form one may perhaps hear echoes of standard Israelite cadences. Admittedly this requires some stretch of hearing, but that is what Israel characteristically undertakes, though the push to consensus must not be overstated.

6. On the rupture of the Holocaust as it bears on theological work, see the citations for Emil Fackenheim in chap. 28, n. 20; and Richard L. Rubenstein, *After Auschwitz: History, Theology, and Contemporary Judaism* (2d ed.; Baltimore: Johns Hopkins University Press, 1992). On the second naiveté, see above chap. 2, n. 81.

7. Reference might usefully be made to John Murray Cuddihy, *The Ordeal of Civility: Freud, Marx, Levi-Strauss and the Jewish Struggle with Modernity* (New York: Basic Books, 1974), for it is modernity that has required Jews to squelch their *Muttersprach*. See Cynthia Ozick, "Toward a New Yiddish," *Art and Ardor: Essays* (New York: Alfred A. Knopf, 1983) 151–77.

control of matters through rationalistic speech that in the end affirms that "God has no hands but ours," issuing in burdensome self-congratulations. Conservatives, fearful of speech that is undomesticated, have insisted on flattening biblical testimony into the settled categories of scholasticism that freezes truth.[8] In both sorts of speech, the incommensurate, mutual One disappears. Neither liberal rationalism nor scholastic conservatism will yield any energy or freedom for serious, sustained obedience or for buoyant elemental trust. Old Testament theology is, in an ecclesial setting, an activity for the recovery of an idiom of speech and of life that is congruent with the stuff of Israel's faith. Where that idiom is engaged and practiced, openings may appear in the shut-down world of contemporaneity, openings for core testimony revisited and for countertestimony reuttered.

Acknowledgment of Yahweh Requires Reordering of Everything Else

I conclude this exposition with two references to the cruciality of testimony in the life and identity of Israel, the people of this text. The testimony of Israel concerning Yahweh is always of two kinds, one to reorder *the internal life* of the community in ways faithful to Yahweh, the other to invite *the world out beyond* this community to reorder its life with reference to Yahweh. Both enterprises are preoccupied with the recognition that the acknowledgment of Yahweh at the center of life (the life of Israel or the life of the world) requires a reordering of everything else. Both texts I will cite advocate a particular construal of reality but are finally aware that alternative, competing construals of reality are available and might be chosen. The recognition of a viable alternative to the world of Yahweh adds to the sense of urgency in the text.

The first text, in Joshua 24, is of peculiar importance in recent scholarship. In this text Joshua, successor to Moses, gathers together the traditions of the Torah (vv. 2-13) and invites the assembly to make a decision for or against the God of this recital—and consequently, for or against the alternative gods "beyond the River and in Egypt" (vv. 14-15).[9] The meeting at Shechem is one of serious, even dangerous adjudication, in order to decide the truth of competing gods, based on competing testimonies. At the outset the assembly is prepared to serve Yahweh, to attest to the truth and reliability of the Yahweh-story (vv. 16-18). Joshua, however, as a loyal adherent to rigorous Mosaism, does not make an embrace of Yahweh an easy one, for Yahweh is a harsh, demanding, uncompromising God:

---

8. It will be evident that in my own practice of a cultural-linguistic perspective, my opposition is to perspectives and approaches that George A. Lindbeck, *The Nature of Doctrine: Religion and Theology in a Postliberal Age* (London: SPCK, 1984), has termed, respectively, "expressive-experiential" and "propositional."

9. On this text and its praxis, see Walter Brueggemann, *Biblical Perspectives on Evangelism: Living in a Three Storied Universe* (Nashville: Abingdon Press, 1993) 48–70.

You cannot serve the Lord, for he is a holy God. He is a jealous God; he will not forgive your transgressions or your sins. If you forsake the Lord and serve foreign gods, then he will turn and do you harm, and consume you, after having done you good. (vv. 19-20)

The community is not deterred by Joshua's warning and persists in its resolve to embrace Yahweh. (v. 21)

Having tested their resolve, Joshua responds with a harsh and onerous warning:

"You are witnesses against yourselves that you have chosen the Lord, to serve him." And they said, "We are witnesses." (v. 22)

I cite this exchange as evidence that Israel's role as witness is a heavy one. Israel takes a solemn oath and substantiates it in a most solemn way. Israel has been warned and is fully informed about the rigors of a life with Yahweh. Israel's first testimony is that it has engaged with Yahweh willingly, knowingly, and without reservation. This act of testimony, moreover, requires a purging of all competing loyalties and a resolve for obedience (v. 23). Testimony is not easy talk; it is rather an elemental decision to reorder the life of the community with an entirely different set of risks and possibilities. This community, set in motion that day at Shechem by Joshua, continues wherever this decision for loyalty is undertaken. Israel's decision for loyalty to Yahweh is in the presence and awareness of alternative loyalties, here vigorously and intentionally rejected.

The second text I cite is Isa 43:8-13. This text is as disputatious as the one in Joshua 24, only in a different arena. The text in Joshua 24 concerned the internal ordering of Israel's life vis-à-vis competing religious alternatives. In Isaiah 43 the scope of concern is larger, for now the contested issue concerns Yahweh versus the gods of Babylon and a decision about the truth of world governance. This text in Isaiah 43 is articulated in a mode of advocacy, and it has been rightly recognized by Claus Westermann as a "trial speech."[10]

The subject of the disputation concerns "the true God," whether Yahweh or the gods of the empire. The argument about "true God," however, turns on the effectiveness of competing witnesses. Claus Westermann comments:

The figure he uses, that of a legal process, is intended to suggest that the present hour in history is the time for the final decision of the claim of divinity as between the God of Israel on one side and *all* the gods of all the nations on the other.... In this legal process, the evidence under consideration consists of objective facts, which both sides must accept. If therefore the gods do bring such evidence, then the other side, too—that is, Yahweh and Israel—are bound to listen to it and allow that it is true. What a daring thing to say! Everything staked on one throw!... This, however, requires

---

10. Claus Westermann, *Isaiah 40–66: A Commentary* (OTL; Philadelphia: Westminster Press, 1969) 120–26. On p. 119, Westermann speaks of "trial speech."

witnesses to testify to it, that is, those who confess the divinity of the god in question.[11]

The oracle of Isa 43:8-9 begins with a taunting invitation by Yahweh to the witnesses for the alternative gods, witnesses who are taken to be blind, deaf, and ineffectual.[12] That is, the allegedly pitiful quality of the gods is, in this imaginative scenario, expressed in terms of the disability of the witnesses:

> Bring forth the people who are blind, yet have eyes,
> who are deaf, yet have ears!
> Let all the nations gather together,
> and let the peoples assemble.
> Who among them declared this,
> and foretold to us the former things? (Isa 43:8-9)

The poem abruptly changes course with "You" at the beginning of v. 10, now addressing Israel. In the address to Israel, two matters are skillfully interwoven. One is a repeated insistence on Yahweh as the only God, who created and formed and saved, besides whom there is no other god, no alien god. Second is a reiterated statement, "You are my witnesses," who are to attest to these singular, lyrical claims:

> You are my witnesses, says the Lord,
> and my servant whom I have chosen,
> so that you may know and believe me
> and understand that I am he.
> Before me no god was formed,
> nor shall there be any after me.
> I, I am the Lord,
> and besides me there is no savior.
> I declared and saved and proclaimed,
> when there was no strange god among you;
> and you are my witnesses, says the Lord.
> I am God, and also henceforth I am He;
> there is no one who can deliver from my hand;
> I work and who can hinder it? (vv. 10-13)

Yahweh has taken the initiative in choosing the witnesses so that they may know and believe in Yahweh; and because they know and believe, they can and must testify.

What concerns us is the intimate connection between the role of the witnesses and the singular theological claims of Yahweh. It is clear that in the drama of the courtroom, the claim of Yahweh depends on the word of the witnesses.

---

11. Ibid., 121–22.

12. With the scholarly consensus, Westermann regards the blind and deaf witnesses as Yahweh's witnesses. Against that view, I take them to be witnesses for the other, dysfunctional gods. The point, however, is not important to my argument.

In Isa 44:8 the same linkage is evident.[13] "There is no other rock," and "you are my witnesses." The poem clearly does not make a metaphysical appeal, but depends on the dramatic effectiveness of the claim enacted and substantiated in court. The cruciality of the witnesses for the future of the world, as the world of Yahweh or as the world of some other god, is inescapable. Indeed, pains are taken to discredit other witnesses (41:24b, 44:9) as a means of discrediting the god-claims they voice. The dramatic, courtroom location of Israel proceeds with a recognition that "what is" (*reality*) effectively derives from "what is said" (*testimony*). Testimony leads reality and makes a decision for a certain kind of reality both possible and inescapable.

The two scenarios of Joshua 24 and Isaiah 43 are, *mutatis mutandis,* paradigmatic in every generation and every circumstance for those who engage in the God-talk modeled here. Which witnesses are believed—concerning Yahweh or the gods "beyond the River and in Egypt"—will determine the internal shape of the community. Which witnesses are believed—concerning Yahweh or the gods of the empire—will determine the shape of the world. Testimony to this particular, peculiar God, voiced in ways that are as odd as the God to which witness is borne, is characteristically offered from a position of vulnerability. This vulnerability, however, is not evidence against its veracity. The testimony is neither reductionist nor coercive. It is given in all its elusiveness and density, and then the witnesses await the decision of the court, while other testimony is given by other witnesses for other gods. The waiting is long and disconcerting, because witnesses to other gods are sometimes most formidable. And the jury only trickles in—here and there, now and then.

---

13. See, negatively, v. 9 on the failed witnesses of the failed gods.

Index of Scriptural References

OLD TESTAMENT

NEW TESTAMENT

Index of Names